KT-560-114

KEY TO WORLD MAP PAGES

— **Large scale maps**
  (> 1:2 500 000)
— **Medium scale maps**
  (1:2 800 000–1:9 000 000)
— **Small scale maps**
  (< 1:10 000 000)

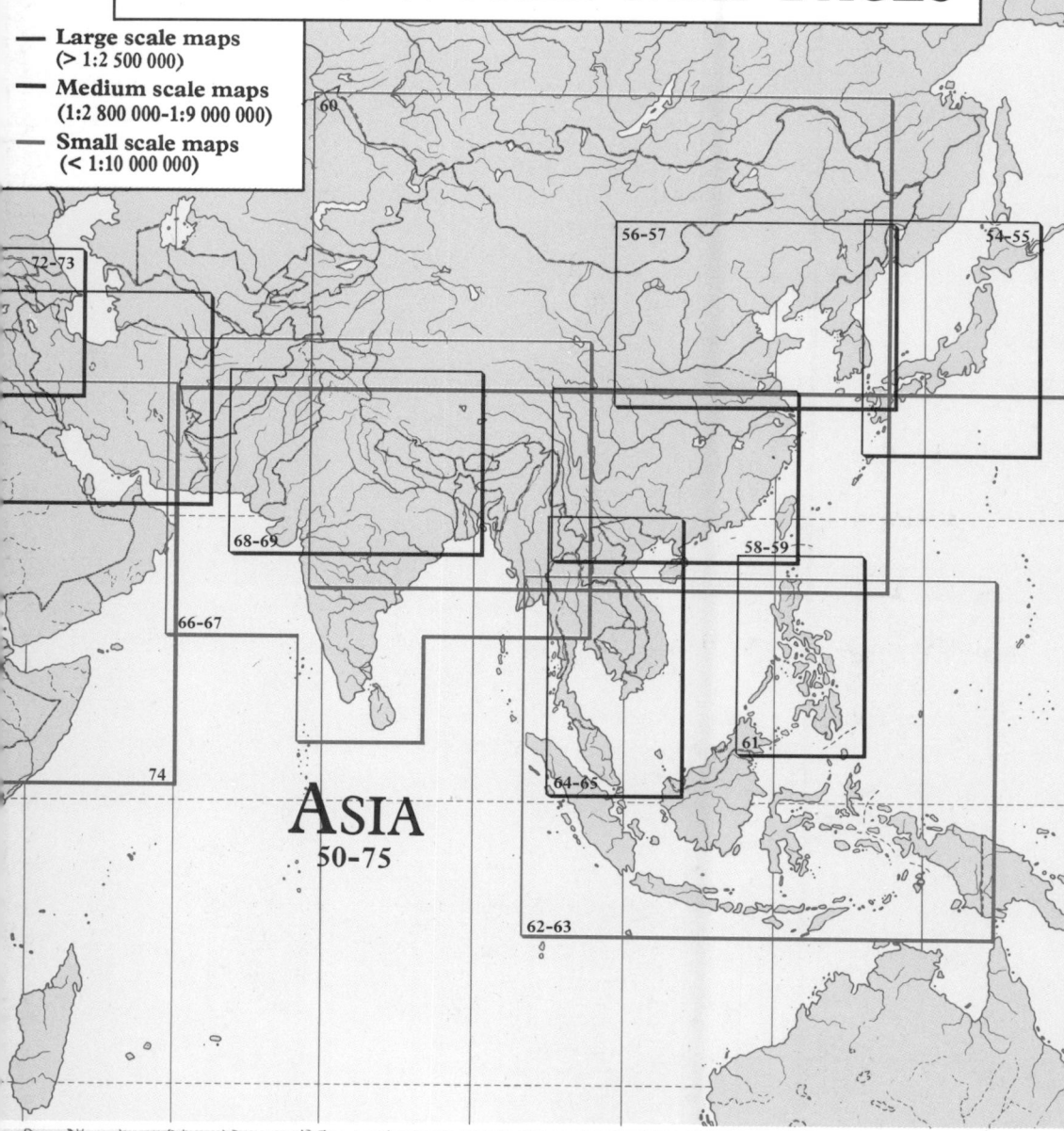

ASIA
50–75

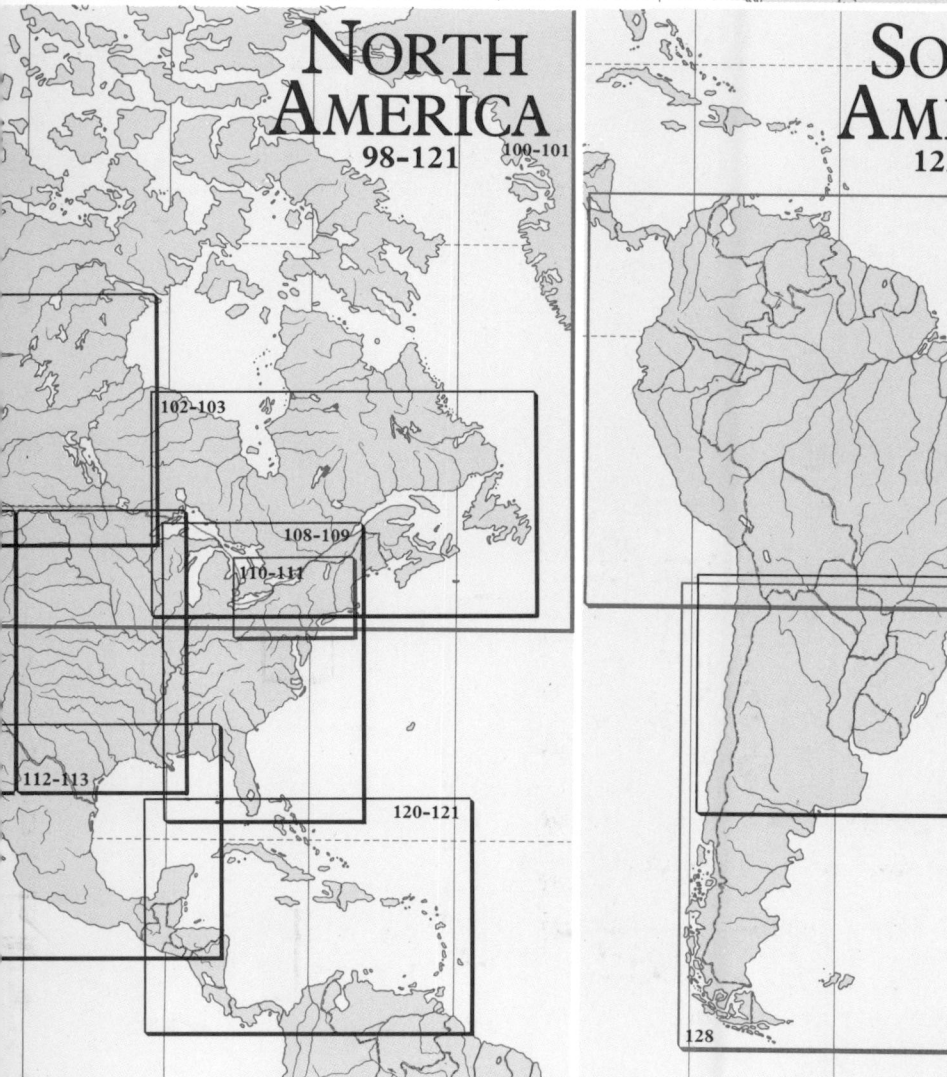

NORTH AMERICA
98–121

SOUTH AMERICA
122–128

COUNTRY INDEX

Country	Page	Country	Page
Afghanistan	66	Kuwait	70–71
Albania	40	Kyrgyzstan	50
Algeria	78		
Angola	84–85	Laos	64
Argentina	126, 128	Latvia	46
Armenia	73	Lebanon	75
Australia	92–95	Lesotho	88–89
Austria	26–27	Liberia	82
Azerbaijan	73	Libya	79
		Lithuania	46
Bahamas	120–121	Luxembourg	17
Bahrain	71		
Bangladesh	67	Macedonia	40
Barbados	121	Madagascar	89
Belarus	46–47	Malawi	87
Belgium	17	Malaysia	62–63
Belize	120	Mali	78, 82–83
Benin	83	Malta	36
Bhutan	67	Mauritania	78, 82
Bolivia	124	Mauritius	77
Bosnia-		Mexico	118–119
Herzegovina	29, 40	Moldova	43
Botswana	88–89	Mongolia	60
Brazil	124–127	Morocco	78
Brunei	78	Mozambique	85, 87
Bulgaria	40–41		
Burkina Faso	82–83	Namibia	88
Burma	67	Nepal	69
Burundi	86	Netherlands	17
		New Zealand	91
Cambodia	64–65	Nicaragua	120
Cameroon	84	Niger	83
Canada	100–101	Nigeria	83
Central African		Northern Ireland	15
Republic	84	Norway	8–9
Chad	79		
Chile	124, 128	Oman	74
China	56–60		
Colombia	124	Pakistan	68
Congo	84	Panama	120
Congo, Dem. Rep.		Papua New Guinea	90
of the	84–85	Paraguay	126–127
Costa Rica	120	Peru	124
Croatia	29, 42	Philippines	61
Cuba	120–121	Poland	44–45
Cyprus	36	Portugal	34–35
Czech Republic	26–27	Puerto Rico	121
Denmark	11	Qatar	71
Djibouti	74		
Dominican		Romania	42–43
Republic	121	Russia	50–51
		Rwanda	86
Ecuador	124		
Egypt	80	Saudi Arabia	74
El Salvador	120	Scotland	14
England	12–13	Senegal	82
Equatorial Guinea	84	Sierra Leone	82
Eritrea	80–81	Singapore	65
Estonia	46	Slovak Republic	27
Ethiopia	74, 81	Slovenia	29
		Somali Republic	74
Fiji	91	South Africa	88–89
Finland	8–9	Spain	32–35, 37
France	18–21	Sri Lanka	66
French Guiana	125	Sudan	79, 81
		Surinam	124–125
Gabon	84	Swaziland	89
Gambia	82	Sweden	8–9
Georgia	73	Switzerland	25
Germany	24–25	Syria	72–73
Ghana	82–83		
Greece	38–41	Taiwan	59
Greenland	4	Tajikistan	50
Guatemala	120	Tanzania	86–87
Guinea	82	Thailand	64–65
Guinea-Bissau	82	Togo	83
Guyana	124	Trinidad and	
		Tobago	121
Haiti	121	Tunisia	78–79
Honduras	120	Turkey	72–73
Hungary	42	Turkmenistan	50
Iceland	8	Uganda	86
India	66–69	Ukraine	47
Indonesia	62–63	United Arab Emirates	71
Iran	70–71	United Kingdom	12–15
Iraq	70–71	USA	106–117
Irish Republic	15	Uruguay	126–127
Israel	75	Uzbekistan	50
Italy	28–31		
Ivory Coast	82	Venezuela	124
		Vietnam	64–65
Jamaica	120		
Japan	54–55	Wales	12–13
Jordan	75		
		Yemen	74
Kazakstan	50	Yugoslavia	40, 42
Kenya	86		
Korea, North	57	Zambia	84–85, 87
Korea, South	57	Zimbabwe	87

PHILIP'S

WORLD ATLAS

PHILIP'S

WORLD ATLAS

THE EARTH IN SPACE
Cartography by Philip's

Text
Keith Lye

Illustrations
Stefan Chabluk

Star Charts
John Cox
Richard Monkhouse

PICTURE ACKNOWLEDGEMENTS
Robert Harding Picture Library /PHOTRI 13, /Bill Ross 41, /Adam Woolfitt 43
Hutchison Library /Melanie Friend 47, /John Hatt 46
Image Bank /Peter Hendrie 20, /Daniel Hummel 34, /Image Makers 8 top,
/Pete Turner 39
Images Colour Library Limited 15
Japan National Tourist Organisation 45
NASA/Galaxy Picture Library 8 bottom left
Panos Pictures /Howard Davies 35
Chris Rayner 19 top
Rex Features /SIPA Press /Scott Andrews 12
Science Photo Library /Martin Bond 14, /CNES, 1992 Distribution Spot
Image 27 top, /Luke Dodd 3, 6, /Earth Satellite Corporation 25 bottom,
/NASA 9 centre right, 9 top, 22, 23, 24, /David Parker 26, /Peter Ryan 27
below, /Jerry Schad 4, /Space Telescope Science Institute /NASA 9 centre left,
9 bottom right, /US Geological Survey 8 centre right
Space Telescope Science Institute /R. Williams /NASA 2
Starland Picture Library /NASA 8 centre left
Still Pictures /Francois Pierrel 28, /Heine Pedersen 31, 40
Tony Stone Images 33, /Glen Allison 38, /James Balog 16, /John Beatty 21,
/Neil Beer 30, /Kristin Finnegan 11, /Jeremy Horner 42, /Gary Norman 36,
/Frank Oberle 25 top, /Dennis Oda 17, /Nigel Press 37, /Donovan Reese 18,
19, /Hugh Sitton 32, /Richard Surman 44, /Michael Townsend 29, /World
Perspectives 10
Telegraph Colour Library /Space Frontiers 9 bottom left

Published in Great Britain in 1998
by George Philip Limited,
an imprint of Reed Consumer Books Limited,
Michelin House, 81 Fulham Road, London SW3 6RB,
and Auckland and Melbourne

This edition produced for Lomond Books, 1998

Copyright © 1998 George Philip Limited

Cartography by Philip's

ISBN 0–540–07632–5

A CIP catalogue record for this book is available from the British Library.

All rights reserved. Apart from any fair dealing for the purpose of private study,
research, criticism or review, as permitted under the Copyright Designs and Patents
Act, 1988, no part of this publication may be reproduced, stored in a retrieval system,
or transmitted in any form or by any means, electronic, electrical, chemical, mechanical,
optical, photocopying, recording, or otherwise, without prior written permission.
All enquiries should be addressed to the Publisher.

Printed in China

Philip's World Maps

The reference maps which form the main body of this atlas have been prepared in accordance with the highest standards of international cartography to provide an accurate and detailed representation of the Earth. The scales and projections used have been carefully chosen to give balanced coverage of the world, while emphasizing the most densely populated and economically significant regions. A hallmark of Philip's mapping is the use of hill shading and relief colouring to create a graphic impression of landforms: this makes the maps exceptionally easy to read. However, knowledge of the key features employed in the construction and presentation of the maps will enable the reader to derive the fullest benefit from the atlas.

MAP SEQUENCE

The atlas covers the Earth continent by continent: first Europe; then its land neighbour Asia (mapped north before south, in a clockwise sequence), then Africa, Australia and Oceania, North America and South America. This is the classic arrangement adopted by most cartographers since the 16th century. For each continent, there are maps at a variety of scales. First, physical relief and political maps of the whole continent; then a series of larger-scale maps

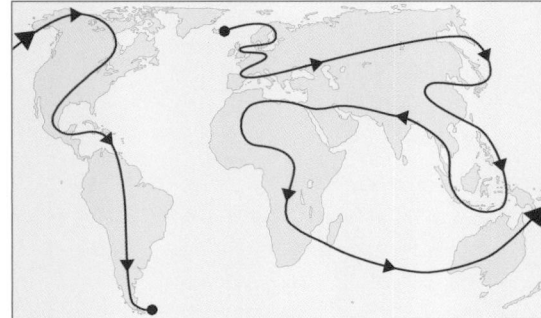

of the regions within the continent, each followed, where required, by still larger-scale maps of the most important or densely populated areas. The governing principle is that by turning the pages of the atlas, the reader moves steadily from north to south through each continent, with each map overlapping its neighbours. A key map showing this sequence, and the area covered by each map, can be found on the endpapers of the atlas.

MAP PRESENTATION

With very few exceptions (e.g. for the Arctic and Antarctic), the maps are drawn with north at the top, regardless of whether they are presented upright or sideways on the page. In the borders will be found the map title; a locator diagram showing the area covered and the page numbers for maps of adjacent areas; the scale; the projection used; the degrees of latitude and longitude; and the letters and figures used in the index for locating place names and geographical features. Physical relief maps also have a height reference panel identifying the colours used for each layer of contouring.

MAP SYMBOLS

Each map contains a vast amount of detail which can only be conveyed clearly and accurately by the use of symbols. Points and circles of varying sizes locate and identify the relative importance of towns and cities; different styles of type are employed for administrative, geographical and regional place names to aid identification. A variety of pictorial symbols denote landscape features such as glaciers, marshes and coral reefs, and man-made structures including roads, railways, airports, canals and dams. International borders are shown by red lines. Where neighbouring countries are in dispute, for example in parts of the Middle East, the maps show the *de facto* boundary between nations, regardless of the legal or historical situation. The symbols are explained on the first page of the World Maps section of the atlas.

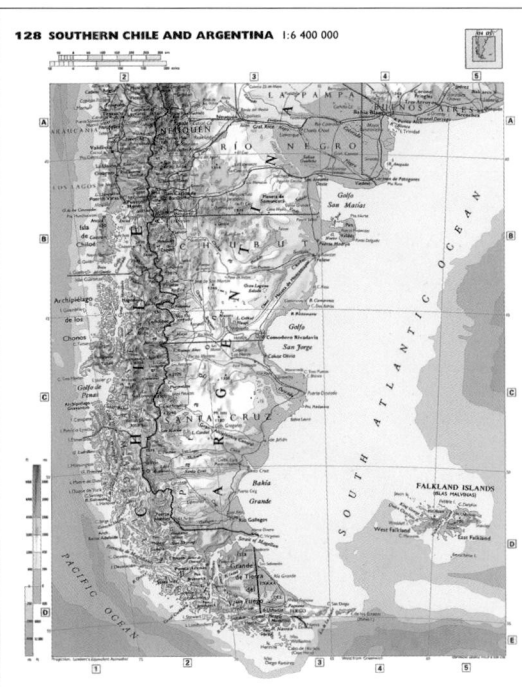

MAP SCALES

1:16 000 000
1 inch = 252 statute miles

The scale of each map is given in the numerical form known as the 'representative fraction'. The first figure is always one, signifying one unit of distance on the map; the second figure, usually in millions, is the number by which the map unit must be multiplied to give the equivalent distance on the Earth's surface. Calculations can easily be made in centimetres and kilometres, by dividing the Earth units figure by 100 000 (i.e. deleting the last five 0s). Thus 1:1 000 000 means 1 cm = 10 km. The calculation for inches and miles is more laborious, but 1 000 000 divided by 63 360 (the number of inches in a mile) shows that 1:1 000 000 means approximately 1 inch = 16 miles. The table below provides distance equivalents for scales down to 1:50 000 000.

LARGE SCALE		
1:1 000 000	1 cm = 10 km	1 inch = 16 miles
1:2 500 000	1 cm = 25 km	1 inch = 39.5 miles
1:5 000 000	1 cm = 50 km	1 inch = 79 miles
1:6 000 000	1 cm = 60 km	1 inch = 95 miles
1:8 000 000	1 cm = 80 km	1 inch = 126 miles
1:10 000 000	1 cm = 100 km	1 inch = 158 miles
1:15 000 000	1 cm = 150 km	1 inch = 237 miles
1:20 000 000	1 cm = 200 km	1 inch = 316 miles
1:50 000 000	1 cm = 500 km	1 inch = 790 miles
SMALL SCALE		

MEASURING DISTANCES

Although each map is accompanied by a scale bar, distances cannot always be measured with confidence because of the distortions involved in portraying the curved surface of the Earth on a flat page. As a general rule, the larger the map scale (i.e. the lower the number of Earth units in the representative fraction), the more accurate and reliable will be the distance measured. On small-scale maps such as those of the world and of entire continents, measurement may only

be accurate along the 'standard parallels', or central axes, and should not be attempted without considering the map projection.

MAP PROJECTIONS

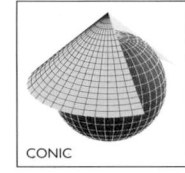  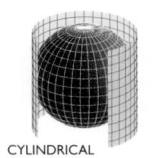

Unlike a globe, no flat map can give a true scale representation of the world in terms of area, shape and position of every region. Each of the numerous systems that have been devised for projecting the curved surface of the Earth on to a flat page involves the sacrifice of accuracy in one or more of these elements. The variations in shape and position of landmasses such as Alaska, Greenland and Australia, for example, can be quite dramatic when different projections are compared.

For this atlas, the guiding principle has been to select projections that involve the least distortion of size and distance. The projection used for each map is noted in the border. Most fall into one of three categories – conic, cylindrical or azimuthal – whose basic concepts are shown above. Each involves plotting the forms of the Earth's surface on a grid of latitude and longitude lines, which may be shown as parallels, curves or radiating spokes.

LATITUDE AND LONGITUDE

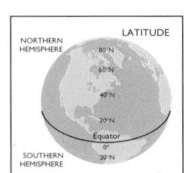 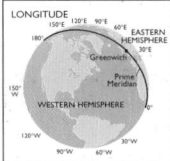 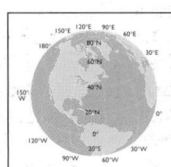

Accurate positioning of individual points on the Earth's surface is made possible by reference to the geometrical system of latitude and longitude. Latitude *parallels* are drawn west–east around the Earth and numbered by degrees north and south of the Equator, which is designated 0° of latitude. Longitude *meridians* are drawn north–south and numbered by degrees east and west of the *prime meridian*, 0° of longitude, which passes through Greenwich in England. By referring to these co-ordinates and their subdivisions of minutes (1/60th of a degree) and seconds (1/60th of a minute), any place on Earth can be located to within a few hundred yards. Latitude and longitude are indicated by blue lines on the maps; they are straight or curved according to the projection employed. Reference to these lines is the easiest way of determining the relative positions of places on different maps, and for plotting compass directions.

NAME FORMS

For ease of reference, both English and local name forms appear in the atlas. Oceans, seas and countries are shown in English throughout the atlas; country names may be abbreviated to their commonly accepted form (e.g. Germany, not The Federal Republic of Germany). Conventional English forms are also used for place names on the smaller-scale maps of the continents. However, local name forms are used on all large-scale and regional maps, with the English form given in brackets only for important cities – the large-scale map of Russia and Central Asia thus shows Moskva (Moscow). For countries which do not use a Roman script, place names have been transcribed according to the systems adopted by the British and US Geographic Names Authorities. For China, the Pin Yin system has been used, with some more widely known forms appearing in brackets, as with Beijing (Peking). Both English and local names appear in the index, the English form being cross-referenced to the local form.

Contents

World Statistics

Countries   x

Cities   xi

Climate   xii

Physical Dimensions   xiv

Regions in the News   xvi

The Earth In Space

The Universe   2–3

Star Charts and Constellations   4–7

The Solar System   8–9

The Earth: Time and Motion   10–11

The Earth From Space   12–13

The Dynamic Earth   14–15

Earthquakes and Volcanoes   16–17

Forces of Nature   18–19

Oceans and Ice   20–21

The Earth's Atmosphere   22–23

Climate and Weather   24–25

Water and Land Use   26–27

The Natural World   28–29

The Human World   30–31

Languages and Religions   32–33

International Organizations   34–35

Agriculture   36–37

Energy and Minerals   38–39

World Economies   40–41

Trade and Commerce   42–43

Travel and Communications   44–45

The World Today   46–47

Glossary of Terms   48

World Maps

Map Symbols   1

The World: Political
1:71 100 000   **2–3**

Arctic Ocean
1:31 100 000   4

Antarctica
1:31 100 000   5

Europe

Europe: Physical
1:17 800 000   **6**

Europe: Political
1:17 800 000   **7**

Scandinavia
1:4 400 000

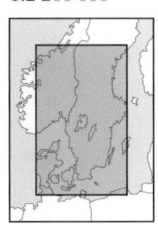

8–9

Denmark and Southern Sweden
1:2 200 000

10–11

England and Wales
1:1 800 000

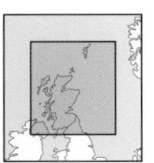

12–13

Scotland
1:1 800 000

14

Ireland
1:1 800 000

15

British Isles
1:4 400 000

16

Netherlands, Belgium and Luxembourg
1:2 200 000

17

Northern France
1:2 200 000

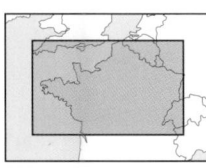

18–19

Southern France
1:2 200 000

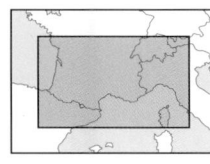

20–21

Middle Europe
1:4 400 000

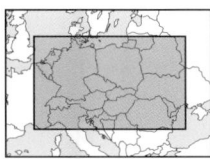

22–23

Germany and Switzerland
1:2 200 000

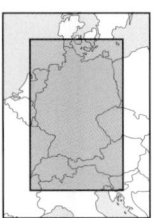
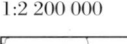

24–25

**Austria, Czech Republic
and Slovak Republic**
1:2 200 000

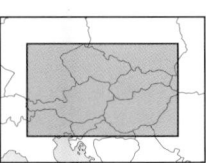

26–27

Northern Italy, Slovenia and Croatia
1:2 200 000

28–29

Southern Italy
1:2 200 000

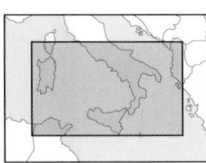

30–31

Eastern Spain
1:2 200 000

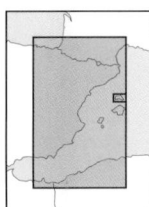

32–33

Western Spain and Portugal
1:2 200 000

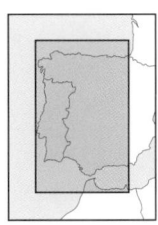

34–35

Malta, Crete, Corfu, Rhodes and Cyprus
1:900 000 / 1:1 200 000

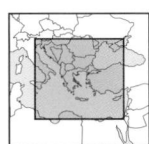

36

Balearics, Canaries and Madeira
1:900 000 / 1:1 800 000

37

Southern Greece
1:2 200 000

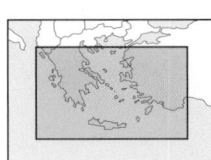

38–39

Northern Greece, Bulgaria and Albania
1:2 200 000

40–41

Hungary, Romania and the Lower Danube
1:2 200 000

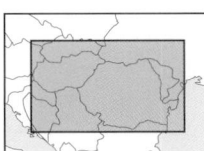

42–43

Poland and the Southern Baltic
1:2 200 000

44–45

Baltic States, Belarus and Ukraine
1:4 400 000

46–47

Volga Basin and the Caucasus
1:4 400 000

48–49

Asia

Russia and Central Asia
1:17 800 000

50–51

Asia: Physical
1:44 400 000   **52**

Asia: Political
1:44 400 000   **53**

Japan
1:4 400 000

54–55

Northern China and Korea
1:5 300 000

56–57

Southern China
1:5 300 000

58–59

China
1:17 800 000

60

Philippines
1:6 700 000

61

Indonesia and the Philippines
1:11 100 000

62–63

Mainland South-east Asia
1:5 300 000

64–65

South Asia
1:8 900 000

66–67

The Indo-Gangetic Plain
1:5 300 000

68–69

The Middle East
1:6 200 000

70–71

Turkey and Transcaucasia
1:4 400 000

72–73

Arabia and the Horn of Africa
1:13 300 000

74

The Near East
1:2 200 000

75

Africa

Africa: Physical
1:37 300 000   **76**

Africa: Political
1: 37 300 000   **77**

North Africa
1:13 300 000

78–79

The Nile Valley and the Nile Delta
1:7 100 000 / 1:3 600 000

80–81

West Africa
1:7 100 000

82–83

Central and Southern Africa
1:13 300 000

84–85

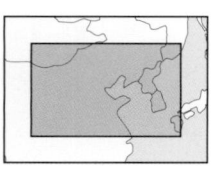
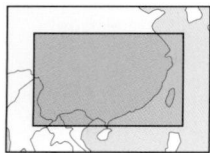
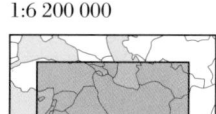
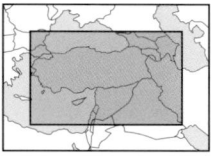
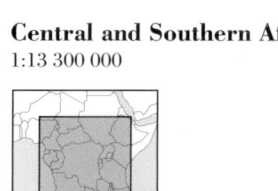

East Africa
1:7 100 000

86–87

Southern Africa
1:7 100 000

88–89

Australia and Oceania

**Australia and Oceania:
Physical and Political**
1:44 400 000   90

New Zealand
1:5 300 000

91

Western Australia
1:7 100 000

92–93

Eastern Australia
1:7 100 000

94–95

Pacific Ocean
1:48 000 000   96–97

North America

North America: Physical
1:31 100 000   98

North America: Political
1:31 100 000   99

Canada and Alaska
1:13 300 000 / 1:26 700 000

100–101

Eastern Canada
1:6 200 000

102–103

Western Canada
1:6 200 000

104–105

United States and Hawaii
1:10 700 000 / 1:8 900 000

106–107

Eastern United States
1:5 300 000

108–109

North-eastern United States
1:2 200 000

110–111

Middle United States
1:5 300 000

112–113

Western United States
1:5 300 000

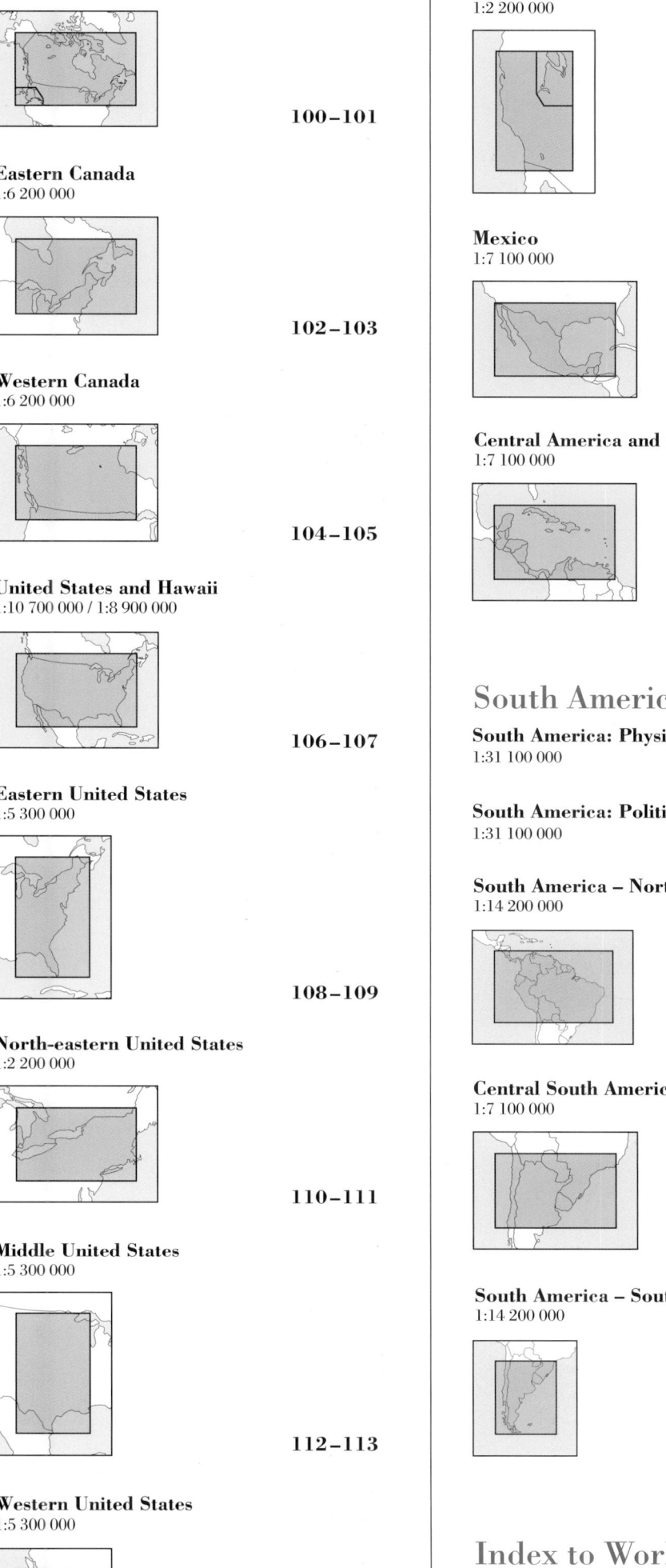

114–115

**Central and Southern California
and Washington**
1:2 200 000

116–117

Mexico
1:7 100 000

118–119

Central America and the West Indies
1:7 100 000

120–121

South America

South America: Physical
1:31 100 000   122

South America: Political
1:31 100 000   123

South America – North
1:14 200 000

124–125

Central South America
1:7 100 000

126–127

South America – South
1:14 200 000

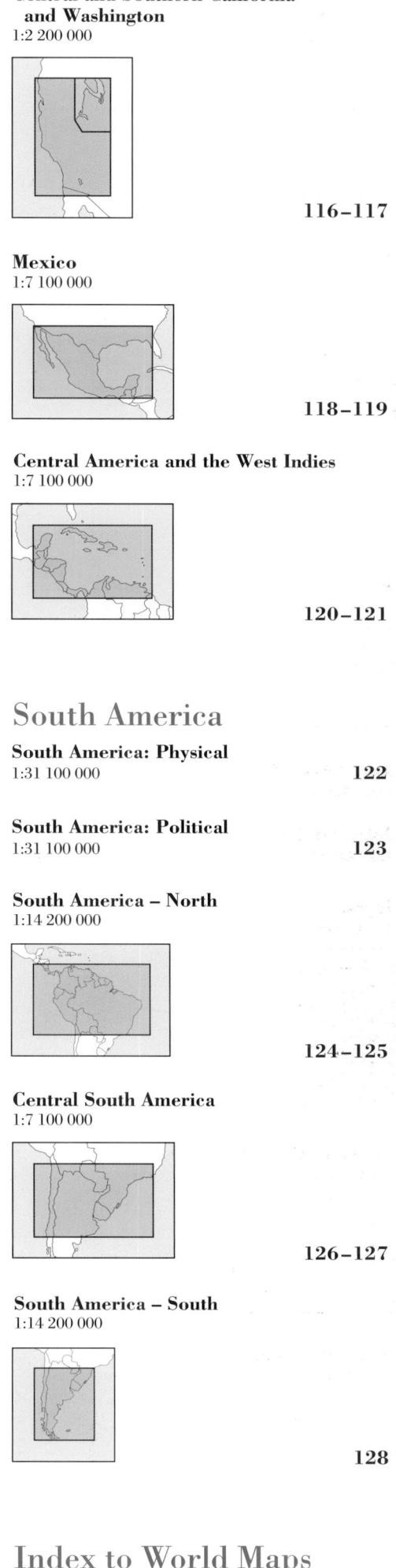

128

Index to World Maps

129–224

World Statistics: Countries

This alphabetical list includes all the countries and territories of the world. If a territory is not completely independent, then the country it is associated with is named. The area figures give the total area of land, inland water and ice. Units for areas and populations are thousands. The population figures are 1997 estimates. The annual income is the Gross National Product per capita in US dollars. The figures are the latest available, usually 1995.

Country/Territory	Area km^2 Thousands	Area $miles^2$ Thousands	Population Thousands	Capital	Annual Income US $
Afghanistan	652	252	23,000	Kabul	300
Albania	28.8	11.1	3,600	Tirana	670
Algeria	2,382	920	29,300	Algiers	1,600
American Samoa (US)	0.20	0.08	62	Pago Pago	2,600
Andorra	0.45	0.17	75	Andorra-la-Vella	14,000
Angola	1,247	481	11,200	Luanda	410
Anguilla (UK)	0.1	0.04	10	The Valley	6,800
Antigua & Barbuda	0.44	0.17	66	St John's	6,390
Argentina	2,767	1,068	35,400	Buenos Aires	8,030
Armenia	29.8	11.5	3,800	Yerevan	730
Aruba (Netherlands)	0.19	0.07	70	Oranjestad	17,500
Australia	7,687	2,968	18,400	Canberra	18,720
Austria	83.9	32.4	8,200	Vienna	26,890
Azerbaijan	86.6	33.4	7,700	Baku	480
Azores (Portugal)	2.2	0.87	238	Ponta Delgada	–
Bahamas	13.9	5.4	280	Nassau	11,940
Bahrain	0.68	0.26	605	Manama	7,840
Bangladesh	144	56	124,000	Dhaka	240
Barbados	0.43	0.17	265	Bridgetown	6,560
Belarus	207.6	80.1	10,500	Minsk	2,070
Belgium	30.5	11.8	10,200	Brussels	24,710
Belize	23	8.9	228	Belmopan	2,630
Benin	113	43	5,800	Porto-Novo	370
Bermuda (UK)	0.05	0.02	65	Hamilton	27,000
Bhutan	47	18.1	1,790	Thimphu	420
Bolivia	1,099	424	7,700	La Paz/Sucre	800
Bosnia-Herzegovina	51	20	3,600	Sarajevo	2,600
Botswana	582	225	1,500	Gaborone	3,020
Brazil	8,512	3,286	159,500	Brasília	3,640
Brunei	5.8	2.2	300	Bandar Seri Begawan	14,500
Bulgaria	111	43	8,600	Sofia	1,330
Burkina Faso	274	106	10,900	Ouagadougou	230
Burma (= Myanmar)	677	261	47,500	Rangoon	1,000
Burundi	27.8	10.7	6,300	Bujumbura	160
Cambodia	181	70	10,500	Phnom Penh	270
Cameroon	475	184	13,800	Yaoundé	650
Canada	9,976	3,852	30,200	Ottawa	19,380
Canary Is. (Spain)	7.3	2.8	1,494	Las Palmas/Santa Cruz	–
Cape Verde Is.	4	1.6	410	Praia	960
Cayman Is. (UK)	0.26	0.10	35	George Town	20,000
Central African Republic	623	241	3,400	Bangui	340
Chad	1,284	496	6,800	Ndjaména	180
Chile	757	292	14,700	Santiago	4,160
China	9,597	3,705	1,210,000	Beijing	620
Colombia	1,139	440	35,900	Bogotá	1,910
Comoros	2.2	0.86	630	Moroni	470
Congo	342	132	2,700	Brazzaville	680
Congo (= Zaïre)	2,345	905	47,200	Kinshasa	120
Cook Is. (NZ)	0.24	0.09	20	Avarua	900
Costa Rica	51.1	19.7	3,500	San José	2,610
Croatia	56.5	21.8	4,900	Zagreb	3,250
Cuba	111	43	11,300	Havana	1,250
Cyprus	9.3	3.6	800	Nicosia	11,500
Czech Republic	78.9	30.4	10,500	Prague	3,870
Denmark	43.1	16.6	5,400	Copenhagen	29,890
Djibouti	23.2	9	650	Djibouti	1,000
Dominica	0.75	0.29	78	Roseau	2,990
Dominican Republic	48.7	18.8	8,200	Santo Domingo	1,460
Ecuador	284	109	11,800	Quito	1,390
Egypt	1,001	387	63,000	Cairo	790
El Salvador	21	8.1	6,000	San Salvador	1,610
Equatorial Guinea	28.1	10.8	420	Malabo	380
Eritrea	94	36	3,500	Asmara	500
Estonia	44.7	17.3	1,500	Tallinn	2,860
Ethiopia	1,128	436	58,500	Addis Ababa	100
Faroe Is. (Denmark)	1.4	0.54	45	Tórshavn	23,660
Fiji	18.3	7.1	800	Suva	2,440
Finland	338	131	5,200	Helsinki	20,580
France	552	213	58,800	Paris	24,990
French Guiana (France)	90	34.7	155	Cayenne	6,500
French Polynesia (France)	4	1.5	226	Papeete	7,500
Gabon	268	103	1,200	Libreville	3,490
Gambia, The	11.3	4.4	1,200	Banjul	320
Georgia	69.7	26.9	5,500	Tbilisi	440
Germany	357	138	82,300	Berlin/Bonn	27,510
Ghana	239	92	18,100	Accra	390
Gibraltar (UK)	0.007	0.003	28	Gibraltar Town	5,000
Greece	132	51	10,600	Athens	8,210
Greenland (Denmark)	2,176	840	57	Nuuk (Godthåb)	9,000
Grenada	0.34	0.13	99	St George's	2,980
Guadeloupe (France)	1.7	0.66	440	Basse-Terre	9,500
Guam (US)	0.55	0.21	161	Agana	6,000
Guatemala	109	42	11,300	Guatemala City	1,340
Guinea	246	95	7,500	Conakry	550
Guinea-Bissau	36.1	13.9	1,200	Bissau	250
Guyana	215	83	820	Georgetown	590
Haiti	27.8	10.7	7,400	Port-au-Prince	250
Honduras	112	43	6,300	Tegucigalpa	600
Hong Kong (China)	1.1	0.40	6,500	–	22,990
Hungary	93	35.9	10,200	Budapest	4,120
Iceland	103	40	275	Reykjavik	24,950
India	3,288	1,269	980,000	New Delhi	340
Indonesia	1,905	735	203,500	Jakarta	980
Iran	1,648	636	69,500	Tehran	4,800
Iraq	438	169	22,500	Baghdad	1,800
Ireland	70.3	27.1	3,600	Dublin	14,710
Israel	27	10.3	5,900	Jerusalem	15,920
Italy	301	116	57,800	Rome	19,020
Ivory Coast	322	125	15,100	Yamoussoukro	660
Jamaica	11	4.2	2,600	Kingston	1,510
Japan	378	146	125,900	Tokyo	39,640
Jordan	89.2	34.4	5,600	Amman	1,510
Kazakstan	2,717	1,049	17,000	Aqmola	1,330
Kenya	580	224	31,900	Nairobi	280
Kiribati	0.72	0.28	85	Tarawa	710
Korea, North	121	47	24,500	Pyŏngyang	1,000
Korea, South	99	38.2	46,100	Seoul	9,700
Kuwait	17.8	6.9	2,050	Kuwait City	17,390
Kyrgyzstan	198.5	76.6	4,700	Bishkek	700
Laos	237	91	5,200	Vientiane	350
Latvia	65	25	2,500	Riga	2,270
Lebanon	10.4	4	3,200	Beirut	2,660
Lesotho	30.4	11.7	2,100	Maseru	770
Liberia	111	43	3,000	Monrovia	850
Libya	1,760	679	5,500	Tripoli	7,000
Liechtenstein	0.16	0.06	32	Vaduz	33,500
Lithuania	65.2	25.2	3,700	Vilnius	1,900
Luxembourg	2.6	1	400	Luxembourg	41,210
Macau (Portugal)	0.02	0.006	450	Macau	7,500
Macedonia	25.7	9.9	2,200	Skopje	860
Madagascar	587	227	15,500	Antananarivo	230
Madeira (Portugal)	0.81	0.31	253	Funchal	–
Malawi	118	46	10,300	Lilongwe	170
Malaysia	330	127	20,900	Kuala Lumpur	3,890
Maldives	0.30	0.12	275	Malé	990
Mali	1,240	479	11,000	Bamako	250
Malta	0.32	0.12	400	Valletta	11,000
Marshall Is.	0.18	0.07	60	Dalap-Uliga-Darrit	1,500
Martinique (France)	1.1	0.42	405	Fort-de-France	10,000
Mauritania	1,030	412	2,400	Nouakchott	460
Mauritius	2.0	0.72	1,200	Port Louis	3,380
Mayotte (France)	0.37	0.14	105	Mamoundzou	1,430
Mexico	1,958	756	97,400	Mexico City	3,320
Micronesia, Fed. States of	0.70	0.27	127	Palikir	1,560
Moldova	33.7	13	4,500	Chişinău	920
Monaco	0.002	0.0001	33	Monaco	16,000
Mongolia	1,567	605	2,500	Ulan Bator	310
Montserrat (UK)	0.10	0.04	12	Plymouth	4,500
Morocco	447	172	28,100	Rabat	1,110
Mozambique	802	309	19,100	Maputo	80
Namibia	825	318	1,700	Windhoek	2,000
Nauru	0.02	0.008	12	Yaren District	10,000
Nepal	141	54	22,100	Katmandu	200
Netherlands	41.5	16	15,900	Amsterdam/The Hague	24,000
Netherlands Antilles (Neths)	0.99	0.38	210	Willemstad	10,500
New Caledonia (France)	18.6	7.2	192	Nouméa	16,000
New Zealand	269	104	3,700	Wellington	14,340
Nicaragua	130	50	4,600	Managua	380
Niger	1,267	489	9,700	Niamey	220
Nigeria	924	357	118,000	Abuja	260
Northern Mariana Is. (US)	0.48	0.18	50	Saipan	11,500
Norway	324	125	4,400	Oslo	31,250
Oman	212	82	2,400	Muscat	4,820
Pakistan	796	307	136,000	Islamabad	460
Palau	0.46	0.18	17	Koror	2,260
Panama	77.1	29.8	2,700	Panama City	2,750
Papua New Guinea	463	179	4,400	Port Moresby	1,160
Paraguay	407	157	5,200	Asunción	1,690
Peru	1,285	496	24,500	Lima	2,310
Philippines	300	116	73,500	Manila	1,050
Poland	313	121	38,800	Warsaw	2,790
Portugal	92.4	35.7	10,100	Lisbon	9,740
Puerto Rico (US)	9	3.5	3,800	San Juan	7,500
Qatar	11	4.2	620	Doha	11,600
Réunion (France)	2.5	0.97	680	Saint-Denis	4,500
Romania	238	92	22,600	Bucharest	1,480
Russia	17,075	6,592	147,800	Moscow	2,240
Rwanda	26.3	10.2	7,000	Kigali	180
St Kitts & Nevis	0.36	0.14	42	Basseterre	4,470
St Lucia	0.62	0.24	150	Castries	3,370
St Vincent & Grenadines	0.39	0.15	114	Kingstown	2,280
San Marino	0.06	0.02	26	San Marino	20,000
São Tomé & Príncipe	0.96	0.37	135	São Tomé	350
Saudi Arabia	2,150	830	19,100	Riyadh	7,040
Senegal	197	76	8,900	Dakar	600
Seychelles	0.46	0.18	78	Victoria	6,370
Sierra Leone	71.7	27.7	4,600	Freetown	180
Singapore	0.62	0.24	3,200	Singapore	26,730
Slovak Republic	49	18.9	5,400	Bratislava	2,950
Slovenia	20.3	7.8	2,000	Ljubljana	8,200
Solomon Is.	28.9	11.2	410	Honiara	910
Somalia	638	246	9,900	Mogadishu	500
South Africa	1,220	471	42,300	C. Town/Pretoria/Bloem.	3,160
Spain	505	195	39,300	Madrid	13,580
Sri Lanka	65.6	25.3	18,700	Colombo	700
Sudan	2,506	967	31,000	Khartoum	750
Surinam	163	63	500	Paramaribo	880
Swaziland	17.4	6.7	1,000	Mbabane	1,170
Sweden	450	174	8,900	Stockholm	23,750
Switzerland	41.3	15.9	7,100	Bern	40,630
Syria	185	71	15,300	Damascus	1,120
Taiwan	36	13.9	21,700	Taipei	12,000
Tajikistan	143.1	55.2	6,000	Dushanbe	340
Tanzania	945	365	31,200	Dodoma	120
Thailand	513	198	60,800	Bangkok	2,740
Togo	56.8	21.9	4,500	Lomé	310
Tonga	0.75	0.29	107	Nuku'alofa	1,610
Trinidad & Tobago	5.1	2	1,300	Port of Spain	3,770
Tunisia	164	63	9,200	Tunis	1,820
Turkey	779	301	63,500	Ankara	2,780
Turkmenistan	488.1	188.5	4,800	Ashkhabad	920
Turks & Caicos Is. (UK)	0.43	0.17	15	Cockburn Town	5,000
Tuvalu	0.03	0.01	10	Fongafale	600
Uganda	236	91	20,800	Kampala	240
Ukraine	603.7	233.1	51,500	Kiev	1,630
United Arab Emirates	83.6	32.3	2,400	Abu Dhabi	17,400
United Kingdom	243.3	94	58,600	London	18,700
United States of America	9,373	3,619	268,000	Washington, DC	26,980
Uruguay	177	68	3,300	Montevideo	5,170
Uzbekistan	447.4	172.7	23,800	Tashkent	970
Vanuatu	12.2	4.7	175	Port-Vila	1,200
Venezuela	912	352	22,500	Caracas	3,020
Vietnam	332	127	77,100	Hanoi	240
Virgin Is. (UK)	0.15	0.06	13	Road Town	–
Virgin Is. (US)	0.34	0.13	105	Charlotte Amalie	12,000
Wallis & Futuna Is. (France)	0.20	0.08	15	Mata-Utu	–
Western Sahara	266	103	280	El Aaiún	980
Western Samoa	2.8	1.1	175	Apia	1,120
Yemen	528	204	16,500	Sana	260
Yugoslavia	102.3	39.5	10,500	Belgrade	1,400
Zambia	753	291	9,500	Lusaka	400
Zimbabwe	391	151	12,100	Harare	540

At the time of going to press, the government of Kazakstan planned to rename the capital Aqmola to Astana.

World Statistics: Cities

This list shows the principal cities with more than 500,000 inhabitants (for China and India only cities with more than 1 million inhabitants are included). The figures are taken from the most recent census or population estimate available, and as far as possible are the population of the metropolitan area, e.g. greater New York, Mexico or Paris. All the figures are in thousands. Local name forms have been used for the smaller cities (e.g. Kraków).

AFGHANISTAN
Kabul 1,565
ALGERIA
Algiers 1,722
Oran 664
ANGOLA
Luanda 2,250
ARGENTINA
Buenos Aires 10,990
Córdoba 1,198
Rosario 1,096
Mendoza 775
La Plata 640
San Miguel de Tucumán 622
Mar del Plata 520
ARMENIA
Yerevan 1,226
AUSTRALIA
Sydney 3,713
Melbourne 3,189
Brisbane 1,422
Perth 1,221
Adelaide 1,071
AUSTRIA
Vienna 1,560
AZERBAIJAN
Baku 1,081
BANGLADESH
Dhaka 7,832
Chittagong 2,041
Khulna 877
Rajshahi 517
BELARUS
Minsk 1,700
Homyel 512
BELGIUM
Brussels 952
BENIN
Cotonou 537
BOLIVIA
La Paz 1,126
Santa Cruz 767
BOSNIA-HERZEGOVINA
Sarajevo 526
BRAZIL
São Paulo 16,417
Rio de Janeiro 9,888
Salvador 2,056
Belo Horizonte 2,049
Fortaleza 1,758
Brasília 1,596
Curitiba 1,290
Recife 1,290
Nova Iguaçu 1,286
Pôrto Alegre 1,263
Belém 1,246
Manaus 1,011
Goiânia 921
Campinas 846
Guarulhos 781
São Gonçalo 748
São Luís 696
Duque de Caxias 665
Maceió 628
Santo André 614
Natal 607
Teresina 598
São Bernado de Campo 565
Osasco 563
Campo Grande 526
BULGARIA
Sofia 1,117
BURKINA FASO
Ouagadougou 690
BURMA (MYANMAR)
Rangoon 2,513
Mandalay 533
CAMBODIA
Phnom Penh 920
CAMEROON
Douala 884
Yaoundé 750
CANADA
Toronto 4,264
Montréal 3,327
Vancouver 1,832
Ottawa-Hull 1,010
Edmonton 863
Calgary 822
Québec 672
Winnipeg 667
Hamilton 624
CENTRAL AFRICAN REP.
Bangui 706
CHAD
Ndjaména 530
CHILE
Santiago 5,077
CHINA
Shanghai 15,082
Beijing 12,362
Tianjin 10,687
Hong Kong (SAR)[1] 6,205
Chongqing 3,870
Shenyang 3,762
Wuhan 3,520

Guangzhou 3,114
Harbin 2,505
Nanjing 2,211
Xi'an 2,115
Chengdu 1,933
Dalian 1,855
Changchun 1,810
Jinan 1,660
Taiyuan 1,642
Qingdao 1,584
Fuzhou, Fujian 1,380
Zibo 1,346
Zhengzhou 1,324
Lanzhou 1,296
Anshan 1,252
Fushun 1,246
Kunming 1,242
Changsha 1,198
Hangzhou 1,185
Nanchang 1,169
Shijiazhuang 1,159
Guiyang 1,131
Ürümqi 1,130
Jilin 1,118
Hefei 1,110
Tangshan 1,110
Baotou 1,033
COLOMBIA
Bogotá 5,026
Cali 1,719
Medellín 1,621
Barranquilla 1,064
Cartagena 746
CONGO
Brazzaville 938
Pointe-Noire 576
CONGO (ZAIRE)
Kinshasa 3,804
Lubumbashi 739
Mbuji-Mayi 613
Kolwezi 544
COSTA RICA
San José 1,186
CROATIA
Zagreb 931
CUBA
Havana 2,143
CZECH REPUBLIC
Prague 1,217
DENMARK
Copenhagen 1,353
DOMINICAN REPUBLIC
Santo Domingo 2,135
Santiago 691
ECUADOR
Guayaquil 1,925
Quito 1,444
EGYPT
Cairo 9,656
Alexandria 3,380
El Gîza 2,144
Shubra el Kheima 834
EL SALVADOR
San Salvador 1,522
ETHIOPIA
Addis Ababa 2,316
FINLAND
Helsinki 525
FRANCE
Paris 9,469
Lyon 1,262
Marseille 1,087
Lille 959
Bordeaux 696
Toulouse 650
Nice 516
GEORGIA
Tbilisi 1,279
GERMANY
Berlin 3,472
Hamburg 1,706
Munich 1,245
Cologne 964
Frankfurt 652
Essen 618
Dortmund 601
Stuttgart 588
Düsseldorf 573
Bremen 549
Duisburg 536
Hanover 526
GHANA
Accra 1,781
Kumasi 540
GREECE
Athens 3,097
GUATEMALA
Guatemala 1,814
GUINEA
Conakry 1,508
HAITI
Port-au-Prince 1,402
HONDURAS
Tegucigalpa 739
HUNGARY
Budapest 1,909

INDIA
Bombay (Mumbai) 15,093
Calcutta 11,673
Delhi 9,882
Madras (Chennai) 5,361
Hyderabad 4,280
Bangalore 4,087
Ahmadabad 3,298
Pune 2,485
Kanpur 2,111
Nagpur 1,661
Lucknow 1,642
Surat 1,517
Jaipur 1,514
Coimbatore 1,136
Vadodara 1,115
Indore 1,104
Patna 1,099
Madurai 1,094
Bhopal 1,064
Vishakhapatnam 1,052
Varanasi 1,026
Ludhiana 1,012
INDONESIA
Jakarta 11,500
Surabaya 2,701
Bandung 2,368
Medan 1,910
Semarang 1,366
Palembang 1,352
Ujung Pandang 1,092
Bandar Lampung 832
Malang 763
IRAN
Tehran 6,750
Mashhad 1,964
Esfahan 1,221
Tabriz 1,166
Shiraz 1,043
Ahvaz 828
Qom 780
Bakhtaran 666
Karaj 588
IRAQ
Baghdad 3,841
Diyala 961
As Sulaymaniyah 952
Arbil 770
Al Mawsil 644
Kadhimain 521
IRELAND
Dublin 1,024
ISRAEL
Tel Aviv 1,880
Jerusalem 562
ITALY
Rome 2,688
Milan 1,334
Naples 1,062
Turin 946
Palermo 695
Genoa 660
IVORY COAST
Abidjan 2,500
JAMAICA
Kingston 644
JAPAN
Tokyo-Yokohama 26,836
Osaka 10,601
Nagoya 2,159
Sapporo 1,732
Kobe 1,509
Kyoto 1,452
Fukuoka 1,269
Kawasaki 1,200
Hiroshima 1,102
Kitakyushu 1,020
Sendai 951
Chiba 851
Sakai 806
Kumamoto 640
Okayama 605
Hamamatsu 561
Sagamihara 560
Funabashi 540
Kagoshima 540
Higashiosaka 515
JORDAN
Amman 1,300
Az-Zarqā 609
KAZAKSTAN
Almaty 1,151
Qaraghandy 613
KENYA
Nairobi 2,000
Mombasa 600
KOREA, NORTH
Pyöngyang 2,639
Hamhung 775
Chöngjin 754
Chinnampo 691
Sinüiju 500
KOREA, SOUTH
Seoul 11,641
Pusan 3,814
Taegu 2,449

Inchon 2,308
Taejön 1,272
Kwangju 1,258
Ulsan 967
Söngnam 869
Puch'on 779
Suwön 756
Chönju 563
KYRGYZSTAN
Bishkek 584
LATVIA
Riga 840
LEBANON
Beirut 1,500
Tripoli 500
LIBYA
Tripoli 960
LITHUANIA
Vilnius 576
MACEDONIA
Skopje 541
MADAGASCAR
Antananarivo 1,053
MALAYSIA
Kuala Lumpur 1,145
MALI
Bamako 746
MAURITANIA
Nouakchott 600
MEXICO
Mexico City 15,643
Guadalajara 2,847
Monterrey 2,522
Puebla 1,055
León 872
Ciudad Juárez 798
Tijuana 743
Culiacán Rosales 602
Mexicali 602
Acapulco de Juárez 592
Mérida 557
Chihuahua 530
San Luis Potosí 526
Aguascalientés 506
MOLDOVA
Chişinău 700
MONGOLIA
Ulan Bator 619
MOROCCO
Casablanca 2,943
Rabat-Salé 1,220
Marrakesh 602
Fès 564
MOZAMBIQUE
Maputo 2,000
NEPAL
Katmandu 535
NETHERLANDS
Amsterdam 1,100
Rotterdam 1,074
The Hague 695
Utrecht 546
NEW ZEALAND
Auckland 929
NICARAGUA
Managua 974
NIGERIA
Lagos 10,287
Ibadan 1,365
Ogbomosho 712
Kano 657
NORWAY
Oslo 714
PAKISTAN
Karachi 9,863
Lahore 5,085
Faisalabad 1,875
Peshawar 1,676
Gujranwala 1,663
Rawalpindi 1,290
Multan 1,257
Hyderabad 1,107
PARAGUAY
Asunción 945
PERU
Lima-Callao 6,601
Callao 638
Arequipa 620
Trujillo 509
PHILIPPINES
Manila 9,280
Quezon City 1,677
Davao 961
Cebu 688
Caloocan 643
POLAND
Warsaw 1,638
Lódz 826
Kraków 745
Wroclaw 643
Poznań 582
PORTUGAL
Lisbon 2,561
Oporto 1,174
ROMANIA
Bucharest 2,061

RUSSIA
Moscow 9,233
Petersburg 4,883
Nizhniy Novgorod 1,425
Novosibirsk 1,418
Yekaterinburg 1,347
Samara 1,223
Omsk 1,161
Chelyabinsk 1,125
Kazan 1,092
Ufa 1,092
Perm 1,086
Rostov 1,023
Volgograd 1,000
Krasnoyarsk 914
Voronezh 905
Saratov 899
Togliatti 689
Simbirsk 670
Izhevsk 653
Krasnodar 638
Vladivostok 637
Irkutsk 632
Yaroslavl 631
Khabarovsk 609
Barnaul 596
Novokuznetsk 593
Orenburg 558
Penza 551
Tyumen 550
Tula 535
Ryazan 526
Naberezhnyye-Chelny 524
Kemerovo 513
Astrakhan 512
SAUDI ARABIA
Riyadh 2,000
Jedda 1,400
Mecca 618
Medina 500
SENEGAL
Dakar 1,729
SIERRA LEONE
Freetown 505
SINGAPORE
Singapore 2,874
SOMALIA
Mogadishu 1,000
SOUTH AFRICA
Cape Town 2,350
East Rand 1,379
Johannesburg 1,196
Durban 1,137
Pretoria 1,080
West Rand 870
Port Elizabeth 853
Vanderbijlpark-Vereeniging 774
Soweto 597
Sasolburg 540
SPAIN
Madrid 3,041
Barcelona 1,631
Valencia 764
Sevilla 714
Zaragoza 607
Málaga 531
SRI LANKA
Colombo 1,863
SUDAN
Khartoum 561
Omdurman 526
SWEDEN
Stockholm 1,553
Göteburg 788
SWITZERLAND
Zürich 915
SYRIA
Damascus 2,230
Aleppo 1,640
Homs 644
TAIWAN
Taipei 2,653
Kaohsiung 1,405
Taichung 817
Tainan 700
Panchiao 544
TAJIKISTAN
Dushanbe 602
TANZANIA
Dar-es-Salaam 1,361
THAILAND
Bangkok 5,876
TOGO
Lomé 590
TUNISIA
Tunis 1,827
TURKEY
Istanbul 7,490
Ankara 3,028
Izmir 2,333
Adana 1,472
Bursa 1,317
Konya 1,040
Gaziantep 930
Icel 908
Antalya 734

Diyarbakir 677
Kocaeli 661
Urfa 649
Kayseri 648
Manisa 641
Hatay 561
Samsun 557
Eskisehir 508
Balikesir 501
UGANDA
Kampala 773
UKRAINE
Kiev 2,630
Kharkiv 1,555
Dnipropetrovsk 1,147
Donetsk 1,088
Odesa 1,046
Zaporizhzhya 887
Lviv 802
Kryvyy Rih 720
Mariupol 510
Mykolayiv 508
UNITED KINGDOM
London 8,089
Birmingham 2,373
Manchester 2,353
Liverpool 852
Glasgow 832
Leeds 529
Newcastle 525
UNITED STATES
New York 16,329
Los Angeles 12,410
Chicago 7,668
Philadelphia 4,949
Washington, DC 4,466
Detroit 4,307
Houston 3,653
Atlanta 3,331
Boston 3,240
Dallas 2,898
Minneapolis-St Paul 2,688
San Diego 2,632
St Louis 2,536
Phoenix 2,473
Baltimore 2,458
Pittsburgh 2,402
Cleveland 2,222
San Francisco 2,182
Seattle 2,180
Tampa 2,157
Miami 2,025
Denver 1,796
Portland (Or.) 1,676
Kansas City (Mo.) 1,647
Cincinnati 1,581
San Jose 1,557
Norfolk 1,529
Indianapolis 1,462
Milwaukee 1,456
Sacramento 1,441
San Antonio 1,437
Columbus (Oh.) 1,423
New Orleans 1,309
Charlotte 1,260
Buffalo 1,189
Salt Lake City 1,178
Hartford 1,151
Oklahoma 1,007
Jacksonville 665
Omaha 663
Memphis 614
El Paso 579
Austin 514
Nashville 505
URUGUAY
Montevideo 1,326
UZBEKISTAN
Tashkent 2,106
VENEZUELA
Caracas 2,784
Maracaibo 1,364
Valencia 1,032
Maracay 800
Barquisimeto 745
Ciudad Guayana 524
VIETNAM
Ho Chi Minh City 4,322
Hanoi 3,056
Haiphong 783
YEMEN
Sana 972
YUGOSLAVIA
Belgrade 1,137
ZAMBIA
Lusaka 982
ZIMBABWE
Harare 1,189
Bulawayo 622

[1] SAR = Special Administrative Region of China

World Statistics: Climate

Rainfall and temperature figures are provided for more than 70 cities around the world. As climate is affected by altitude, the height of each city is shown in metres beneath its name. For each location, the top row of figures shows the total rainfall or snow in millimetres, and the bottom row the average temperature in degrees Celsius; the average annual temperature and total annual rainfall are at the end of the rows. The map opposite shows the city locations.

CITY	JAN.	FEB.	MAR.	APR.	MAY	JUNE	JULY	AUG.	SEPT.	OCT.	NOV.	DEC.	YEAR
EUROPE													
Athens, Greece	62	37	37	23	23	14	6	7	15	51	56	71	402
107 m	10	10	12	16	20	25	28	28	24	20	15	11	18
Berlin, Germany	46	40	33	42	49	65	73	69	48	49	46	43	603
55 m	−1	0	4	9	14	17	19	18	15	9	5	1	9
Istanbul, Turkey	109	92	72	46	38	34	34	30	58	81	103	119	816
14 m	5	6	7	11	16	20	23	23	20	16	12	8	14
Lisbon, Portugal	111	76	109	54	44	16	3	4	33	62	93	103	708
77 m	11	12	14	16	17	20	22	23	21	18	14	12	17
London, UK	54	40	37	37	46	45	57	59	49	57	64	48	593
5 m	4	5	7	9	12	16	18	17	15	11	8	5	11
Málaga, Spain	61	51	62	46	26	5	1	3	29	64	64	62	474
33 m	12	13	16	17	19	29	25	26	23	20	16	13	18
Moscow, Russia	39	38	36	37	53	58	88	71	58	45	47	54	624
156 m	−13	−10	−4	6	13	16	18	17	12	6	−1	−7	4
Odesa, Ukraine	57	62	30	21	34	34	42	37	37	13	35	71	473
64 m	−3	−1	2	9	15	20	22	22	18	12	9	1	10
Paris, France	56	46	35	42	57	54	59	64	55	50	51	50	619
75 m	3	4	8	11	15	18	20	19	17	12	7	4	12
Rome, Italy	71	62	57	51	46	37	15	21	63	99	129	93	744
17 m	8	9	11	14	18	22	25	25	22	17	13	10	16
Shannon, Ireland	94	67	56	53	61	57	77	79	86	86	96	117	929
2 m	5	5	7	9	12	14	16	16	14	11	8	6	10
Stockholm, Sweden	43	30	25	31	34	45	61	76	60	48	53	48	554
44 m	−3	−3	−1	5	10	15	18	17	12	7	3	0	7
ASIA													
Bahrain	8	18	13	8	<3	0	0	0	0	0	18	18	81
5 m	17	18	21	25	29	32	33	34	31	28	24	19	26
Bangkok, Thailand	8	20	36	58	198	160	160	175	305	206	66	5	1,397
2 m	26	28	29	30	29	29	28	28	28	28	26	25	28
Beirut, Lebanon	191	158	94	53	18	3	<3	<3	5	51	132	185	892
34 m	14	14	16	18	22	24	27	28	26	24	19	16	21
Bombay (Mumbai), India	3	3	3	<3	18	485	617	340	264	64	13	3	1,809
11 m	24	24	26	28	30	29	27	27	27	28	27	26	27
Calcutta, India	10	31	36	43	140	297	325	328	252	114	20	5	1,600
6 m	20	22	27	30	30	30	29	29	29	28	23	19	26
Colombo, Sri Lanka	89	69	147	231	371	224	135	109	160	348	315	147	2,365
7 m	26	26	27	28	28	27	27	27	27	26	26	26	27
Harbin, China	6	5	10	23	43	94	112	104	46	33	8	5	488
160 m	−18	−15	−5	6	13	19	22	21	14	4	−6	−16	3

CITY	JAN.	FEB.	MAR.	APR.	MAY	JUNE	JULY	AUG.	SEPT.	OCT.	NOV.	DEC.	YEAR
ASIA (continued)													
Ho Chi Minh, Vietnam	15	3	13	43	221	330	315	269	335	269	114	56	1,984
9 m	26	27	29	30	29	28	28	28	27	27	27	26	28
Hong Kong, China	33	46	74	137	292	394	381	361	257	114	43	31	2,162
33 m	16	15	18	22	26	28	28	28	27	25	21	18	23
Jakarta, Indonesia	300	300	211	147	114	97	64	43	66	112	142	203	1,798
8 m	26	26	27	27	27	27	27	27	27	27	27	26	27
Kabul, Afghanistan	31	36	94	102	20	5	3	3	<3	15	20	10	338
1,815 m	−3	−1	6	13	18	22	25	24	20	14	7	3	12
Karachi, Pakistan	13	10	8	3	3	18	81	41	13	<3	3	5	196
4 m	19	20	24	28	30	31	30	29	28	28	24	20	26
Kazalinsk, Kazakhstan	10	10	13	13	15	5	5	8	8	10	13	15	125
63 m	−12	−11	−3	6	18	23	25	23	16	8	−1	−7	7
New Delhi, India	23	18	13	8	13	74	180	172	117	10	3	10	640
218 m	14	17	23	28	33	34	31	30	29	26	20	15	25
Omsk, Russia	15	8	8	13	31	51	51	51	28	25	18	20	318
85 m	−22	−19	−12	−1	10	16	18	16	10	1	−11	−18	−1
Shanghai, China	48	58	84	94	94	180	147	142	130	71	51	36	1,135
7 m	4	5	9	14	20	24	28	28	23	19	12	7	16
Singapore	252	173	193	188	173	173	170	196	178	208	254	257	2,413
10 m	26	27	28	28	28	28	28	27	27	27	27	27	27
Tehran, Iran	46	38	46	36	13	3	3	3	3	8	20	31	246
1,220 m	2	5	9	16	21	26	30	29	25	18	12	6	17
Tokyo, Japan	48	74	107	135	147	165	142	152	234	208	97	56	1,565
6 m	3	4	7	13	17	21	25	26	23	17	11	6	14
Ulan Bator, Mongolia	<3	<3	3	5	10	28	76	51	23	5	5	3	208
1,325 m	−26	−21	−13	−1	6	14	16	14	8	−1	−13	−22	−3
Verkhoyansk, Russia	5	5	3	5	8	23	28	25	13	8	8	5	134
100 m	−50	−45	−32	−15	0	12	14	9	2	−15	−38	−48	−17
AFRICA													
Addis Ababa, Ethiopia	<3	3	25	135	213	201	206	239	102	28	<3	0	1,151
2,450 m	19	20	20	19	18	18	19	21	22	21	20	20	20
Antananarivo, Madag.	300	279	178	53	18	8	8	10	18	61	135	287	1,356
1,372 m	21	21	21	19	18	15	14	15	17	19	21	21	19
Cairo, Egypt	5	5	5	3	3	<3	0	0	<3	<3	3	5	28
116 m	13	15	18	21	25	28	28	28	26	24	20	15	22
Cape Town, S. Africa	15	8	18	48	79	84	89	66	43	31	18	10	508
17 m	21	21	20	17	14	13	12	13	14	16	18	19	17
Jo'burg, S. Africa	114	109	89	38	25	8	8	8	23	56	107	125	709
1,665 m	20	20	18	16	13	10	11	13	16	18	19	20	16

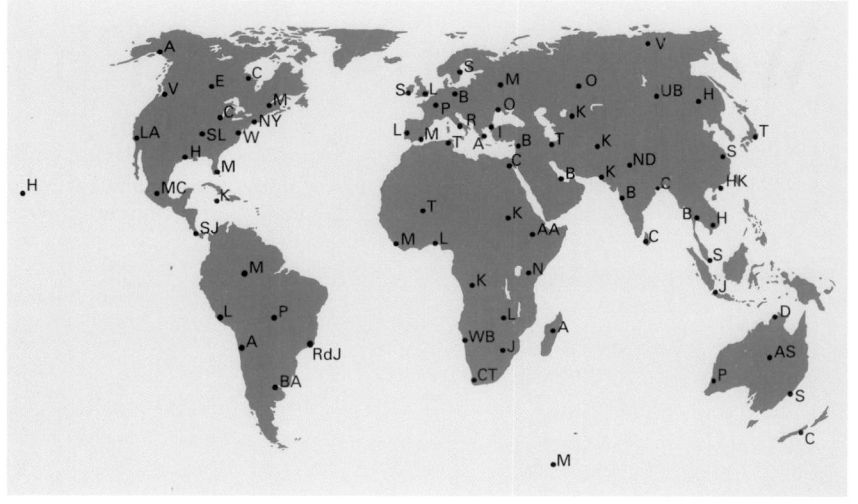

AFRICA (continued)

CITY	JAN.	FEB.	MAR.	APR.	MAY	JUNE	JULY	AUG.	SEPT.	OCT.	NOV.	DEC.	YEAR
Khartoum, Sudan	<3	<3	<3	<3	3	8	53	71	18	5	<3	0	158
390 m	24	25	28	31	33	34	32	31	32	32	28	25	29
Kinshasa, Congo (Z.)	135	145	196	196	158	8	3	3	31	119	221	142	1,354
325 m	26	26	27	27	26	24	23	24	25	26	26	26	25
Lagos, Nigeria	28	46	102	150	269	460	279	64	140	206	69	25	1,836
3 m	27	28	29	28	28	26	26	25	26	26	28	28	27
Lusaka, Zambia	231	191	142	18	3	<3	<3	0	<3	10	91	150	836
1,277 m	21	22	21	21	19	16	16	18	22	24	23	22	21
Monrovia, Liberia	31	56	97	216	516	973	996	373	744	772	236	130	5,138
23 m	26	26	27	27	26	25	24	25	25	25	26	26	26
Nairobi, Kenya	38	64	125	211	158	46	15	23	31	53	109	86	958
820 m	19	19	19	19	18	16	16	16	18	19	18	18	18
Timbuktu, Mali	<3	<3	3	<3	5	23	79	81	38	3	<3	<3	231
301 m	22	24	28	32	34	35	32	30	32	31	28	23	29
Tunis, Tunisia	64	51	41	36	18	8	3	8	33	51	48	61	419
66 m	10	11	13	16	19	23	26	27	25	20	16	11	18
Walvis Bay, Namibia	<3	5	8	3	3	<3	<3	3	<3	<3	<3	<3	23
7 m	19	19	19	18	17	16	15	14	14	15	17	18	18

AUSTRALIA, NEW ZEALAND AND ANTARCTICA

CITY	JAN.	FEB.	MAR.	APR.	MAY	JUNE	JULY	AUG.	SEPT.	OCT.	NOV.	DEC.	YEAR
Alice Springs, Aust.	43	33	28	10	15	13	8	8	8	18	31	38	252
579 m	29	28	25	20	15	12	12	14	18	23	26	28	21
Christchurch, N.Z.	56	43	48	48	66	66	69	48	46	43	48	56	638
10 m	16	16	14	12	9	6	6	7	9	12	14	16	11
Darwin, Australia	386	312	254	97	15	3	<3	3	13	51	119	239	1,491
30 m	29	29	29	29	28	26	25	26	28	29	30	29	28
Mawson, Antarctica	11	30	20	10	44	180	4	40	3	20	0	0	362
14 m	0	-5	-10	-14	-15	-16	-18	-18	-19	-13	-5	-1	-11
Perth, Australia	8	10	20	43	130	180	170	149	86	56	20	13	881
60 m	23	23	22	19	16	14	13	13	15	16	19	22	18
Sydney, Australia	89	102	127	135	127	117	117	76	73	71	73	73	1,181
42 m	22	22	21	18	15	13	12	13	15	18	19	21	17

NORTH AMERICA

CITY	JAN.	FEB.	MAR.	APR.	MAY	JUNE	JULY	AUG.	SEPT.	OCT.	NOV.	DEC.	YEAR
Anchorage, USA	20	18	15	10	13	18	41	66	66	56	25	23	371
40 m	-11	-8	-5	2	7	12	14	13	9	2	-5	-11	2
Chicago, USA	51	51	66	71	86	89	84	81	79	66	61	51	836
251 m	-4	-3	2	9	14	20	23	22	19	12	5	-1	10
Churchill, Canada	15	13	18	23	32	44	46	58	51	43	39	21	402
13 m	-28	-26	-20	-10	-2	6	12	11	5	-2	-12	-22	-7
Edmonton, Canada	25	19	19	22	43	77	89	78	39	17	16	25	466
676 m	-15	-10	-5	4	11	15	17	16	11	6	-4	-10	3
Honolulu, USA	104	66	79	48	25	18	23	28	36	48	64	104	643
12 m	23	18	19	20	22	24	25	26	26	24	22	19	22
Houston, USA	89	76	84	91	119	117	99	99	104	94	89	109	1,171
12 m	12	13	17	21	24	27	28	29	26	22	16	12	21

NORTH AMERICA (continued)

CITY	JAN.	FEB.	MAR.	APR.	MAY	JUNE	JULY	AUG.	SEPT.	OCT.	NOV.	DEC.	YEAR
Kingston, Jamaica	23	15	23	31	102	89	38	91	99	180	74	36	800
34 m	25	25	25	26	26	28	28	28	27	27	26	26	26
Los Angeles, USA	79	76	71	25	10	3	<3	<3	5	15	31	66	381
95 m	13	14	14	16	17	19	21	22	21	18	16	14	17
Mexico City, Mexico	13	5	10	20	53	119	170	152	130	51	18	8	747
2,309 m	12	13	16	18	19	19	17	18	18	16	14	13	16
Miami, USA	71	53	64	81	173	178	155	160	203	234	71	51	1,516
8 m	20	20	22	23	25	27	28	28	27	25	22	21	24
Montréal, Canada	72	65	74	74	66	82	90	92	88	76	81	87	946
57 m	-10	-9	-3	-6	13	18	21	20	15	9	2	-7	6
New York City, USA	94	97	91	81	81	84	107	109	86	89	76	91	1,092
96 m	-1	-1	3	10	16	20	23	23	21	15	7	2	11
St Louis, USA	58	64	89	97	114	114	89	86	81	74	71	64	1,001
173 m	0	1	7	13	19	24	26	26	22	15	8	2	14
San José, Costa Rica	15	5	20	46	229	241	211	241	305	300	145	41	1,798
1,146 m	19	19	21	21	22	21	21	21	21	20	20	19	20
Vancouver, Canada	154	115	101	60	52	45	32	41	67	114	150	182	1,113
14 m	3	5	6	9	12	15	17	17	14	10	6	4	10
Washington, DC, USA	86	76	91	84	94	99	112	109	94	74	66	79	1,064
22 m	1	2	7	12	18	23	25	24	20	14	8	3	13

SOUTH AMERICA

CITY	JAN.	FEB.	MAR.	APR.	MAY	JUNE	JULY	AUG.	SEPT.	OCT.	NOV.	DEC.	YEAR
Antofagasta, Chile	0	0	0	<3	<3	3	5	3	<3	3	<3	0	13
94 m	21	21	20	18	16	15	14	14	15	16	18	19	17
Buenos Aires, Arg.	79	71	109	89	76	61	56	61	79	86	84	99	950
27 m	23	23	21	17	13	9	10	11	13	15	19	22	16
Lima, Peru	3	<3	<3	<3	5	5	8	8	8	3	3	<3	41
120 m	23	24	24	22	19	17	16	17	18	19	21	20	
Manaus, Brazil	249	231	262	221	170	84	58	38	46	107	142	203	1,811
44 m	28	28	28	27	28	28	28	28	29	29	29	28	28
Paraná, Brazil	287	236	239	102	13	<3	3	5	28	127	231	310	1,582
260 m	23	23	23	23	23	21	21	22	24	24	24	23	23
Rio de Janeiro, Brazil	125	122	130	107	79	53	41	43	66	79	104	137	1,082
61 m	26	26	25	24	22	21	21	21	21	21	22	23	23

World Statistics: Physical Dimensions

Each topic list is divided into continents and within a continent the items are listed in order of size. The order of the continents is as in the atlas, Europe through to South America. The lists down to this mark > are complete; below they are selective. The world top ten are shown in square brackets; in the case of mountains this has not been done because the world top 30 are all in Asia. The figures are rounded as appropriate.

WORLD, CONTINENTS, OCEANS

THE WORLD	km²	miles²	%
The World	509,450,000	196,672,000	
Land	149,450,000	57,688,000	29.3
Water	360,000,000	138,984,000	70.7
Asia	44,500,000	17,177,000	29.8
Africa	30,302,000	11,697,000	20.3
North America	24,241,000	9,357,000	16.2
South America	17,793,000	6,868,000	11.9
Antarctica	14,100,000	5,443,000	9.4
Europe	9,957,000	3,843,000	6.7
Australia & Oceania	8,557,000	3,303,000	5.7
Pacific Ocean	179,679,000	69,356,000	49.9
Atlantic Ocean	92,373,000	35,657,000	25.7
Indian Ocean	73,917,000	28,532,000	20.5
Arctic Ocean	14,090,000	5,439,000	3.9

SEAS

	km²	miles²
South China Sea	2,974,600	1,148,500
Bering Sea	2,268,000	875,000
Sea of Okhotsk	1,528,000	590,000
East China & Yellow	1,249,000	482,000
Sea of Japan	1,008,000	389,000
Gulf of California	162,000	62,500
Bass Strait	75,000	29,000

ATLANTIC	km²	miles²
Caribbean Sea	2,766,000	1,068,000
Mediterranean Sea	2,516,000	971,000
Gulf of Mexico	1,543,000	596,000
Hudson Bay	1,232,000	476,000
North Sea	575,000	223,000
Black Sea	462,000	178,000
Baltic Sea	422,170	163,000
Gulf of St Lawrence	238,000	92,000

INDIAN	km²	miles²
Red Sea	438,000	169,000
The Gulf	239,000	92,000

MOUNTAINS

EUROPE		m	ft
Mont Blanc	France/Italy	4,807	15,771
Monte Rosa	Italy/Switzerland	4,634	15,203
Dom	Switzerland	4,545	14,911
Liskamm	Switzerland	4,527	14,852
Weisshorn	Switzerland	4,505	14,780
Taschorn	Switzerland	4,490	14,730
Matterhorn/Cervino	Italy/Switz.	4,478	14,691
Mont Maudit	France/Italy	4,465	14,649
Dent Blanche	Switzerland	4,356	14,291
Nadelhorn	Switzerland	4,327	14,196
> Grandes Jorasses	France/Italy	4,208	13,806
Jungfrau	Switzerland	4,158	13,642
Barre des Ecrins	France	4,103	13,461
Gran Paradiso	Italy	4,061	13,323
Piz Bernina	Italy/Switzerland	4,049	13,284
Eiger	Switzerland	3,970	13,025
Monte Viso	Italy	3,841	12,602
Grossglockner	Austria	3,797	12,457
Wildspitze	Austria	3,772	12,382
Monte Disgrazia	Italy	3,678	12,066
Mulhacén	Spain	3,478	11,411
Pico de Aneto	Spain	3,404	11,168
Marmolada	Italy	3,342	10,964
Etna	Italy	3,340	10,958
Zugspitze	Germany	2,962	9,718
Musala	Bulgaria	2,925	9,596
Olympus	Greece	2,917	9,570
Triglav	Slovenia	2,863	9,393
Monte Cinto	France (Corsica)	2,710	8,891
Gerlachovka	Slovak Republic	2,655	8,711
Galdhöpiggen	Norway	2,468	8,100
Hvannadalshnúkur	Iceland	2,119	6,952
Kebnekaise	Sweden	2,117	6,946
Ben Nevis	UK	1,343	4,406

ASIA		m	ft
Everest	China/Nepal	8,848	29,029
K2 (Godwin Austen)	China/Kashmir	8,611	28,251
Kanchenjunga	India/Nepal	8,598	28,208
Lhotse	China/Nepal	8,516	27,939
Makalu	China/Nepal	8,481	27,824
Cho Oyu	China/Nepal	8,201	26,906
Dhaulagiri	Nepal	8,172	26,811
Manaslu	Nepal	8,156	26,758
Nanga Parbat	Kashmir	8,126	26,660
Annapurna	Nepal	8,078	26,502
Gasherbrum	China/Kashmir	8,068	26,469
Broad Peak	China/Kashmir	8,051	26,414
Xixabangma	China	8,012	26,286
Kangbachen	India/Nepal	7,902	25,925
Jannu	India/Nepal	7,902	25,925
Gayachung Kang	Nepal	7,897	25,909
Himalchuli	Nepal	7,893	25,896
Disteghil Sar	Kashmir	7,885	25,869
Nuptse	Nepal	7,879	25,849
Khunyang Chhish	Kashmir	7,852	25,761
Masherbrum	Kashmir	7,821	25,659
Nanda Devi	India	7,817	25,646
Rakaposhi	Kashmir	7,788	25,551
Batura	Kashmir	7,785	25,541
Namche Barwa	China	7,756	25,446
Kamet	India	7,756	25,446
Soltoro Kangri	Kashmir	7,742	25,400
Gurla Mandhata	China	7,728	25,354
Trivor	Pakistan	7,720	25,328
> Kongur Shan	China	7,719	25,324
Tirich Mir	Pakistan	7,690	25,229
K'ula Shan	Bhutan/China	7,543	24,747
Pik Kommunizma	Tajikistan	7,495	24,590
Elbrus	Russia	5,642	18,510
Demavend	Iran	5,604	18,386
Ararat	Turkey	5,165	16,945
Gunong Kinabalu	Malaysia (Borneo)	4,101	13,455
Yu Shan	Taiwan	3,997	13,113
Fuji-San	Japan	3,776	12,388

AFRICA		m	ft
Kilimanjaro	Tanzania	5,895	19,340
Mt Kenya	Kenya	5,199	17,057
Ruwenzori (Margherita)	Uganda/Congo (Z.)	5,109	16,762
Ras Dashan	Ethiopia	4,620	15,157
Meru	Tanzania	4,565	14,977
Karisimbi	Rwanda/Congo (Z.)	4,507	14,787
Mt Elgon	Kenya/Uganda	4,321	14,176
Batu	Ethiopia	4,307	14,130
Guna	Ethiopia	4,231	13,882
Toubkal	Morocco	4,165	13,665
Irhil Mgoun	Morocco	4,071	13,356
Mt Cameroon	Cameroon	4,070	13,353
Amba Ferit	Ethiopia	3,875	13,042
Pico del Teide	Spain (Tenerife)	3,718	12,198
Thabana Ntlenyana	Lesotho	3,482	11,424
Emi Koussi	Chad	3,415	11,204
> Mt aux Sources	Lesotho/S. Africa	3,282	10,768
Mt Piton	Réunion	3,069	10,069

OCEANIA		m	ft
Puncak Jaya	Indonesia	5,029	16,499
Puncak Trikora	Indonesia	4,750	15,584
Puncak Mandala	Indonesia	4,702	15,427
> Mt Wilhelm	Papua NG	4,508	14,790
Mauna Kea	USA (Hawaii)	4,205	13,796
Mauna Loa	USA (Hawaii)	4,170	13,681
Mt Cook (Aoraki)	New Zealand	3,753	12,313
Mt Balbi	Solomon Is.	2,439	8,002
Orohena	Tahiti	2,241	7,352
Mt Kosciuszko	Australia	2,237	7,339

NORTH AMERICA		m	ft
Mt McKinley (Denali)	USA (Alaska)	6,194	20,321
Mt Logan	Canada	5,959	19,551
Citlaltepetl	Mexico	5,700	18,701
Mt St Elias	USA/Canada	5,489	18,008
Popocatepetl	Mexico	5,452	17,887

NORTH AMERICA (continued)		m	ft
Mt Foraker	USA (Alaska)	5,304	17,401
Ixtaccihuatl	Mexico	5,286	17,342
Lucania	Canada	5,227	17,149
Mt Steele	Canada	5,073	16,644
Mt Bona	USA (Alaska)	5,005	16,420
Mt Blackburn	USA (Alaska)	4,996	16,391
Mt Sanford	USA (Alaska)	4,940	16,207
Mt Wood	Canada	4,848	15,905
Nevado de Toluca	Mexico	4,670	15,321
Mt Fairweather	USA (Alaska)	4,663	15,298
Mt Hunter	USA (Alaska)	4,442	15,573
Mt Whitney	USA	4,418	14,495
Mt Elbert	USA	4,399	14,432
Mt Harvard	USA	4,395	14,419
Mt Rainier	USA	4,392	14,409
> Blanca Peak	USA	4,372	14,344
Longs Peak	USA	4,345	14,255
Tajumulco	Guatemala	4,220	13,845
Grand Teton	USA	4,197	13,770
Mt Waddington	Canada	3,994	13,104
Mt Robson	Canada	3,954	12,972
Chirripó Grande	Costa Rica	3,837	12,589
Pico Duarte	Dominican Rep.	3,175	10,417

SOUTH AMERICA		m	ft
Aconcagua	Argentina	6,960	22,834
Bonete	Argentina	6,872	22,546
Ojos del Salado	Argentina/Chile	6,863	22,516
Pissis	Argentina	6,779	22,241
Mercedario	Argentina/Chile	6,770	22,211
Huascaran	Peru	6,768	22,204
Llullaillaco	Argentina/Chile	6,723	22,057
Nudo de Cachi	Argentina	6,720	22,047
Yerupaja	Peru	6,632	21,758
N. de Tres Cruces	Argentina/Chile	6,620	21,719
Incahuasi	Argentina/Chile	6,601	21,654
Cerro Galan	Argentina	6,600	21,654
Tupungato	Argentina/Chile	6,570	21,555
> Sajama	Bolivia	6,542	21,463
Illimani	Bolivia	6,485	21,276
Coropuna	Peru	6,425	21,079
Ausangate	Peru	6,384	20,945
Cerro del Toro	Argentina	6,380	20,932
Siula Grande	Peru	6,356	20,853
Chimborazo	Ecuador	6,267	20,561
Alpamayo	Peru	5,947	19,511
Cotapaxi	Ecuador	5,896	19,344
Pico Colon	Colombia	5,800	19,029
Pico Bolivar	Venezuela	5,007	16,427

ANTARCTICA	m	ft
Vinson Massif	4,897	16,066
Mt Kirkpatrick	4,528	14,855
Mt Markham	4,349	14,268

OCEAN DEPTHS

ATLANTIC OCEAN	m	ft	
Puerto Rico (Milwaukee) Deep	9,220	30,249	[7]
Cayman Trench	7,680	25,197	[10]
Gulf of Mexico	5,203	17,070	
Mediterranean Sea	5,121	16,801	
Black Sea	2,211	7,254	
North Sea	660	2,165	
Baltic Sea	463	1,519	
Hudson Bay	258	846	

INDIAN OCEAN	m	ft
Java Trench	7,450	24,442
Red Sea	2,635	8,454
Persian Gulf	73	239

PACIFIC OCEAN	m	ft	
Mariana Trench	11,022	36,161	[1]
Tonga Trench	10,882	35,702	[2]
Japan Trench	10,554	34,626	[3]
Kuril Trench	10,542	34,587	[4]
Mindanao Trench	10,497	34,439	[5]
Kermadec Trench	10,047	32,962	[6]

PACIFIC OCEAN (continued)		m	ft	
Peru–Chile Trench		8,050	26,410	[8]
Aleutian Trench		7,822	25,662	[9]

ARCTIC OCEAN		m	ft
Molloy Deep		5,608	18,399

LAND LOWS

		m	ft
Caspian Sea	Europe	−28	−92
Dead Sea	Asia	−403	−1,322
Lake Asale	Africa	−116	−381
Lake Eyre North	Oceania	−16	−52
Death Valley	N. America	−86	−282
Valdés Peninsula	S. America	−40	−131

RIVERS

EUROPE		km	miles	
Volga	Caspian Sea	3,700	2,300	
Danube	Black Sea	2,850	1,770	
Ural	Caspian Sea	2,535	1,575	
Dnepr (Dnipro)	Black Sea	2,285	1,420	
Kama	Volga	2,030	1,260	
Don	Black Sea	1,990	1,240	
Petchora	Arctic Ocean	1,790	1,110	
Oka	Volga	1,480	920	
Belaya	Kama	1,420	880	
Dnister (Dniester)	Black Sea	1,400	870	
Vyatka	Kama	1,370	850	
Rhine	North Sea	1,320	820	
N. Dvina	Arctic Ocean	1,290	800	
Desna	Dnepr (Dnipro)	1,190	740	
Elbe	North Sea	1,145	710	
Wisla	Baltic Sea	1,090	675	
Loire	Atlantic Ocean	1,020	635	

ASIA		km	miles	
Yangtze	Pacific Ocean	6,380	3,960	[3]
Yenisey–Angara	Arctic Ocean	5,550	3,445	[5]
Huang He	Pacific Ocean	5,464	3,395	[6]
Ob–Irtysh	Arctic Ocean	5,410	3,360	[7]
Mekong	Pacific Ocean	4,500	2,795	[9]
Amur	Pacific Ocean	4,400	2,730	[10]
Lena	Arctic Ocean	4,400	2,730	
Irtysh	Ob	4,250	2,640	
Yenisey	Arctic Ocean	4,090	2,540	
Ob	Arctic Ocean	3,680	2,285	
Indus	Indian Ocean	3,100	1,925	
Brahmaputra	Indian Ocean	2,900	1,800	
Syrdarya	Aral Sea	2,860	1,775	
Salween	Indian Ocean	2,800	1,740	
Euphrates	Indian Ocean	2,700	1,675	
Vilyuy	Lena	2,650	1,645	
Kolyma	Arctic Ocean	2,600	1,615	
Amudarya	Aral Sea	2,540	1,575	
Ural	Caspian Sea	2,535	1,575	
Ganges	Indian Ocean	2,510	1,560	
Si Kiang	Pacific Ocean	2,100	1,305	
Irrawaddy	Indian Ocean	2,010	1,250	
Tarim–Yarkand	Lop Nor	2,000	1,240	
Tigris	Indian Ocean	1,900	1,180	

AFRICA		km	miles	
Nile	Mediterranean	6,670	4,140	[1]
Congo	Atlantic Ocean	4,670	2,900	[8]
Niger	Atlantic Ocean	4,180	2,595	
Zambezi	Indian Ocean	3,540	2,200	
Oubangi/Uele	Congo (Zaïre)	2,250	1,400	
Kasai	Congo (Zaïre)	1,950	1,210	
Shaballe	Indian Ocean	1,930	1,200	
Orange	Atlantic Ocean	1,860	1,155	
Cubango	Okavango Swamps	1,800	1,120	
Limpopo	Indian Ocean	1,600	995	
Senegal	Atlantic Ocean	1,600	995	
Volta	Atlantic Ocean	1,500	930	

AUSTRALIA		km	miles
Murray–Darling	Indian Ocean	3,750	2,330
Darling	Murray	3,070	1,905
Murray	Indian Ocean	2,575	1,600
Murrumbidgee	Murray	1,690	1,050

NORTH AMERICA		km	miles	
Mississippi–Missouri	Gulf of Mexico	6,020	3,740	[4]
Mackenzie	Arctic Ocean	4,240	2,630	
Mississippi	Gulf of Mexico	3,780	2,350	
Missouri	Mississippi	3,780	2,350	
Yukon	Pacific Ocean	3,185	1,980	
Rio Grande	Gulf of Mexico	3,030	1,880	

NORTH AMERICA (continued)		km	miles	
Arkansas	Mississippi	2,340	1,450	
Colorado	Pacific Ocean	2,330	1,445	
Red	Mississippi	2,040	1,270	
Columbia	Pacific Ocean	1,950	1,210	
Saskatchewan	Lake Winnipeg	1,940	1,205	
Snake	Columbia	1,670	1,040	
Churchill	Hudson Bay	1,600	990	
Ohio	Mississippi	1,580	980	
Brazos	Gulf of Mexico	1,400	870	
St Lawrence	Atlantic Ocean	1,170	730	

SOUTH AMERICA		km	miles	
Amazon	Atlantic Ocean	6,450	4,010	[2]
Paraná–Plate	Atlantic Ocean	4,500	2,800	
Purus	Amazon	3,350	2,080	
Madeira	Amazon	3,200	1,990	
São Francisco	Atlantic Ocean	2,900	1,800	
Paraná	Plate	2,800	1,740	
Tocantins	Atlantic Ocean	2,750	1,710	
Paraguay	Paraná	2,550	1,580	
Orinoco	Atlantic Ocean	2,500	1,550	
Pilcomayo	Paraná	2,500	1,550	
Araguaia	Tocantins	2,250	1,400	
Juruá	Amazon	2,000	1,240	
Xingu	Amazon	1,980	1,230	
Ucayali	Amazon	1,900	1,180	
Marañón	Amazon	1,600	990	
Uruguay	Plate	1,600	990	

LAKES

EUROPE		km²	miles²
Lake Ladoga	Russia	17,700	6,800
Lake Onega	Russia	9,700	3,700
Saimaa system	Finland	8,000	3,100
Vänern	Sweden	5,500	2,100
Rybinskoye Res.	Russia	4,700	1,800

ASIA		km²	miles²	
Caspian Sea	Asia	371,800	143,550	[1]
Aral Sea	Kazakstan/Uzbekistan	33,640	13,000	[6]
Lake Baykal	Russia	30,500	11,780	[9]
Tonlé Sap	Cambodia	20,000	7,700	
Lake Balqash	Kazakstan	18,500	7,100	
Lake Dongting	China	12,000	4,600	
Lake Ysyk	Kyrgyzstan	6,200	2,400	
Lake Orumiyeh	Iran	5,900	2,300	
Lake Koko	China	5,700	2,200	
Lake Poyang	China	5,000	1,900	
Lake Khanka	China/Russia	4,400	1,700	
Lake Van	Turkey	3,500	1,400	

AFRICA		km²	miles²	
Lake Victoria	E. Africa	68,000	26,000	[3]
Lake Tanganyika	C. Africa	33,000	13,000	[7]
Lake Malawi/Nyasa	E. Africa	29,600	11,430	[10]
Lake Chad	C. Africa	25,000	9,700	
Lake Turkana	Ethiopia/Kenya	8,500	3,300	
Lake Volta	Ghana	8,500	3,300	
Lake Bangweulu	Zambia	8,000	3,100	
Lake Rukwa	Tanzania	7,000	2,700	
Lake Mai-Ndombe	Congo (Zaïre)	6,500	2,500	
Lake Kariba	Zambia/Zimbabwe	5,300	2,000	
Lake Albert	Uganda/Congo (Z.)	5,300	2,000	
Lake Nasser	Egypt/Sudan	5,200	2,000	
Lake Mweru	Zambia/Congo (Z.)	4,900	1,900	
Lake Cabora Bassa	Mozambique	4,500	1,700	
Lake Kyoga	Uganda	4,400	1,700	
Lake Tana	Ethiopia	3,630	1,400	

AUSTRALIA		km²	miles²
Lake Eyre	Australia	8,900	3,400
Lake Torrens	Australia	5,800	2,200
Lake Gairdner	Australia	4,800	1,900

NORTH AMERICA		km²	miles²	
Lake Superior	Canada/USA	82,350	31,800	[2]
Lake Huron	Canada/USA	59,600	23,010	[4]
Lake Michigan	USA	58,000	22,400	[5]
Great Bear Lake	Canada	31,800	12,280	[8]
Great Slave Lake	Canada	28,500	11,000	
Lake Erie	Canada/USA	25,700	9,900	
Lake Winnipeg	Canada	24,400	9,400	
Lake Ontario	Canada/USA	19,500	7,500	
Lake Nicaragua	Nicaragua	8,200	3,200	
Lake Athabasca	Canada	8,100	3,100	
Smallwood Reservoir	Canada	6,530	2,520	
Reindeer Lake	Canada	6,400	2,500	
Lake Winnipegosis	Canada	5,400	2,100	
Nettilling Lake	Canada	5,500	2,100	

SOUTH AMERICA		km²	miles²
Lake Titicaca	Bolivia/Peru	8,300	3,200
Lake Poopo	Peru	2,800	1,100

ISLANDS

EUROPE		km²	miles²	
Great Britain	UK	229,880	88,700	[8]
Iceland	Atlantic Ocean	103,000	39,800	
Ireland	Ireland/UK	84,400	32,600	
Novaya Zemlya (N.)	Russia	48,200	18,600	
W. Spitzbergen	Norway	39,000	15,100	
Novaya Zemlya (S.)	Russia	33,200	12,800	
Sicily	Italy	25,500	9,800	
Sardinia	Italy	24,000	9,300	
N.E. Spitzbergen	Norway	15,000	5,600	
Corsica	France	8,700	3,400	
Crete	Greece	8,350	3,200	
Zealand	Denmark	6,850	2,600	

ASIA		km²	miles²	
Borneo	S. E. Asia	744,360	287,400	[3]
Sumatra	Indonesia	473,600	182,860	[6]
Honshu	Japan	230,500	88,980	[7]
Sulawesi (Celebes)	Indonesia	189,000	73,000	
Java	Indonesia	126,700	48,900	
Luzon	Philippines	104,700	40,400	
Mindanao	Philippines	101,500	39,200	
Hokkaido	Japan	78,400	30,300	
Sakhalin	Russia	74,060	28,600	
Sri Lanka	Indian Ocean	65,600	25,300	
Taiwan	Pacific Ocean	36,000	13,900	
Kyushu	Japan	35,700	13,800	
Hainan	China	34,000	13,100	
Timor	Indonesia	33,600	13,000	
Shikoku	Japan	18,800	7,300	
Halmahera	Indonesia	18,000	6,900	
Ceram	Indonesia	17,150	6,600	
Sumbawa	Indonesia	15,450	6,000	
Flores	Indonesia	15,200	5,900	
Samar	Philippines	13,100	5,100	
Negros	Philippines	12,700	4,900	
Bangka	Indonesia	12,000	4,600	
Palawan	Philippines	12,000	4,600	
Panay	Philippines	11,500	4,400	
Sumba	Indonesia	11,100	4,300	
Mindoro	Philippines	9,750	3,800	

AFRICA		km²	miles²	
Madagascar	Indian Ocean	587,040	226,660	[4]
Socotra	Indian Ocean	3,600	1,400	
Réunion	Indian Ocean	2,500	965	
Tenerife	Atlantic Ocean	2,350	900	
Mauritius	Indian Ocean	1,865	720	

OCEANIA		km²	miles²	
New Guinea	Indon./Papua NG	821,030	317,000	[2]
New Zealand (S.)	Pacific Ocean	150,500	58,100	
New Zealand (N.)	Pacific Ocean	114,700	44,300	
Tasmania	Australia	67,800	26,200	
New Britain	Papua NG	37,800	14,600	
New Caledonia	Pacific Ocean	19,100	7,400	
Viti Levu	Fiji	10,500	4,100	
Hawaii	Pacific Ocean	10,450	4,000	
Bougainville	Papua NG	9,600	3,700	
Guadalcanal	Solomon Is.	6,500	2,500	
Vanua Levu	Fiji	5,550	2,100	
New Ireland	Papua NG	3,200	1,200	

NORTH AMERICA		km²	miles²	
Greenland	Atlantic Ocean	2,175,600	839,800	[1]
Baffin Is.	Canada	508,000	196,100	[5]
Victoria Is.	Canada	212,200	81,900	[9]
Ellesmere Is.	Canada	212,000	81,800	[10]
Cuba	Caribbean Sea	110,860	42,800	
Newfoundland	Canada	110,680	42,700	
Hispaniola	Dom. Rep./Haiti	76,200	29,400	
Banks Is.	Canada	67,000	25,900	
Devon Is.	Canada	54,500	21,000	
Melville Is.	Canada	42,400	16,400	
Vancouver Is.	Canada	32,150	12,400	
Somerset Is.	Canada	24,300	9,400	
Jamaica	Caribbean Sea	11,400	4,400	
Puerto Rico	Atlantic Ocean	8,900	3,400	
Cape Breton Is.	Canada	4,000	1,500	

SOUTH AMERICA		km²	miles²
Tierra del Fuego	Argentina/Chile	47,000	18,100
Falkland Is. (East)	Atlantic Ocean	6,800	2,600
South Georgia	Atlantic Ocean	4,200	1,600
Galapagos (Isabela)	Pacific Ocean	2,250	870

Regions in the News

FORMER YUGOSLAVIA

THE CAUCASUS

TAIWAN

THE NEAR EAST

CENTRAL EAST AFRICA

SOUTH CHINA SEA

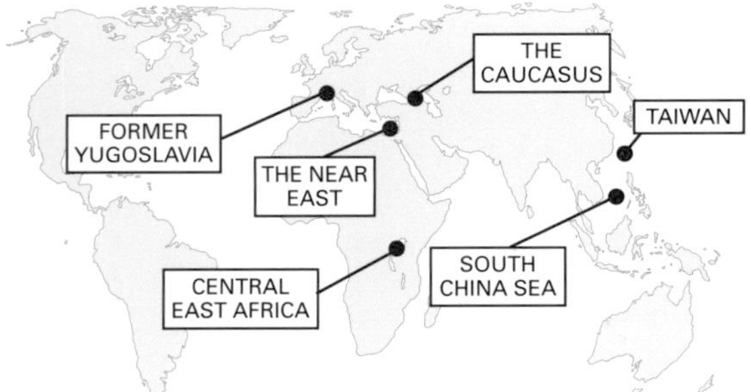

Maps show the situation in June 1998

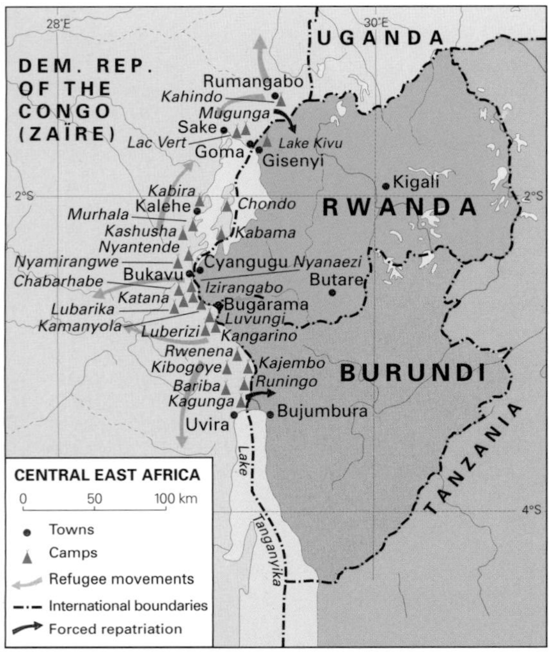

THE BREAK-UP OF YUGOSLAVIA

The former country of Yugoslavia comprised six republics. In 1991 Slovenia and Croatia declared independence. Bosnia-Herzegovina followed in 1992 and Macedonia in 1993. Yugoslavia now comprises the remaining two republics, Serbia and Montenegro.

YUGOSLAVIA
Population: 10,881,000 (Serb 62.6%, Albanian 16.5%, Montenegrin 5%, Hungarian 3.3%, Muslim 3.2%)

Serbia Population: 6,060,000 (Serb 87.7%, excluding the provinces of Kosovo and Vojvodina)
Kosovo Population: 1,989,050 (Albanian 81.6%, Serb 9.9%)
Vojvodina Population: 2,131,900 (Serb 56.8%, Hungarian 16.9%)
Montenegro Population: 700,050 (Montenegrin 61.9%, Muslim 14.6%, Albanian 7%)

CROATIA
Population: 4,850,000 (Croat 78.1%, Serb 12.2%)

SLOVENIA
Population: 2,000,000 (Slovene 88%)

MACEDONIA (F. Y. R. O. M.)
Population: 2,150,000 (Macedonian 64%, Albanian 21.7%, Turkish 5%)

BOSNIA-HERZEGOVINA
Population: 3,600,000 (Muslim 49%, Serb 31.2%, Croat 17.2%)

FORMER YUGOSLAVIA

0   50   100   150   200 km

- –·– International boundaries
- –··– Republic boundaries
- – – Province boundaries
- ■ Capital cities
- — Dayton Peace Agreement Boundary
- Muslim–Croat Federation
- Bosnian Serb Republic

CENTRAL EAST AFRICA

0   50   100 km

- • Towns
- ▲ Camps
- → Refugee movements
- –·– International boundaries
- → Forced repatriation

THE NEAR EAST

0   25   50 km

- —— 1949 Armistice Line
- – – 1974 Cease-fire Lines
- *Efrata* ● Main Jewish settlements in the West Bank and Gaza Strip
- *Halhul* ■ Main Palestinian Arab towns in the West Bank and Gaza Strip

ISRAEL
Population: 5,900,000 (inc. East Jerusalem and Jewish settlers in the areas under Israeli administration. (Jewish 82%, Arab Muslim 13.8%)

West Bank
Population: 1,122,900 (Palestinian Arabs 97% [of whom Arab Muslim 85%, Jewish 7%, Christian 8%])

Gaza Strip
Population: 748,400 (Arab 98%)

JORDAN
Population: 5,600,000 (Arab 99% [of whom about 50% are Palestinian Arab])

LEBANON
Population: 3,200,000 (Arab 93% [of whom 83% are Lebanese Arab and 10% Palestinian Arab])

COUNTRIES AND REPUBLICS OF THE CAUCASUS REGION

RUSSIA
North Ossetia (Alania)
Population: 695,000 (Ossetian 53%, Russian 29%, Chechen 5.2%)
Chechenia Population: 1,308,000 (Chechen and Ingush 70.7%, Russian 23.1%, Armenian 1.2%)
Ingushetia (Split from Chechenia in June 1993) Population: 250,000

GEORGIA
Population: 5,450,000 (Georgian 70.1%, Armenian 8.1%, Russian 6.3%, Azerbaijani 5.7%, Ossetian 3%, Greek 2%, Abkhazian 2%)
Abkhazia Population: 537,500 (Georgian 45.7%, Abkhazian 17.8%, Armenian 14.6%, Russian 14.3%)
Ajaria Population: 382,000 (Georgian 82.8%, Russian 7.7%, Armenian 4%)

ARMENIA
Population: 3,800,000 (Armenian 93%, Azerbaijani 3%)
Nagorno-Karabakh Population: 192,400 (Armenian 76.9%, Azerbaijani 21.5%)

AZERBAIJAN
Population: 7,650,000 (Azerbaijani 83%, Russian 6%, Armenian 6%)
Naxçivan Population: 300,400 (Azerbaijani 95.9%)

THE CAUCASUS

0   100   200 km

- –·– International boundaries
- –··– Republic boundaries

Abkhazia, Ajaria and South Ossetia seek independence from Georgia. Chechenia has been trying to break away from Russia since 1991, but Russia has resisted with military force. Hostility also continues between Armenia and Azerbaijan over the enclave of Nagorno-Karabakh.

TAIWAN

0   50   100   150   200 km

- Territory of People's Republic of China
- Territory of Republic of China (Taiwan)

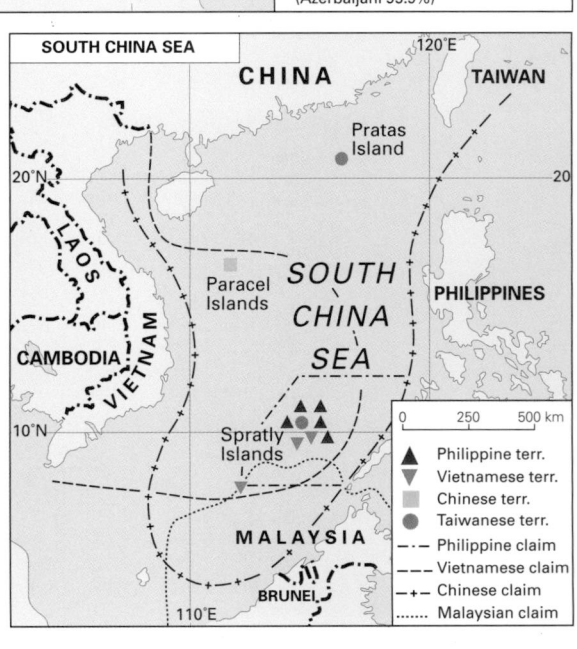

SOUTH CHINA SEA

0   250   500 km

- ▲ Philippine terr.
- ▼ Vietnamese terr.
- ■ Chinese terr.
- ● Taiwanese terr.
- –·– Philippine claim
- – – Vietnamese claim
- –+– Chinese claim
- ···· Malaysian claim

The Earth in Space

The Universe 2
Star Charts and Constellations 4
The Solar System 8
The Earth: Time and Motion 10
The Earth from Space 12
The Dynamic Earth 14
Earthquakes and Volcanoes 16
Forces of Nature 18
Oceans and Ice 20
The Earth's Atmosphere 22
Climate and Weather 24
Water and Land Use 26
The Natural World 28
The Human World 30
Languages and Religions 32
International Organizations 34
Agriculture 36
Energy and Minerals 38
World Economies 40
Trade and Commerce 42
Travel and Communications 44
The World Today 46
Glossary of Terms 48

The Universe

The depths of the Universe
This photograph shows some of the 1,500 or more galaxies that were recorded in the montage of photographs taken by the Hubble Space Telescope in 1995.

THE NEAREST STARS

The 20 nearest stars, excluding the Sun, with their distance from the Earth in light-years*.

Proxima Centauri	4.2
Alpha Centauri A	4.3
Alpha Centauri B	4.3
Barnard's Star	6.0
Wolf 359	7.8
Lalande 21185	8.3
Sirius A	8.7
Sirius B	8.7
UV Ceti A	8.7
UV Ceti B	8.7
Ross 154	9.4
Ross 248	10.3
Epsilon Eridani	10.7
Ross 128	10.9
61 Cygni A	11.1
61 Cygni B	11.1
Epsilon Indi	11.2
Groombridge 34 A	11.2
Groombridge 34 B	11.2
L789-6	11.2

* A light-year equals approximately 9,500 billion km [5,900 billion miles].

Just before Christmas 1995, the Hubble Space Telescope, which is in orbit about 580 km [360 miles] above the Earth, focused on a tiny area in distant space. Over a ten-day period, photographs taken by the telescope revealed unknown galaxies billions of times fainter than the human eye can see.

Because the light from these distant objects has taken so long to reach us, the photographs transmitted from the telescope and released to the media were the deepest look into space that astronomers have ever seen. The features they revealed were in existence when the Universe was less than a billion years old.

The Hubble Space Telescope is operated by the Space Telescope Science Institute in America and was launched in April 1990. The photographs it took of the Hubble Deep Field have been described by NASA as the biggest advance in astronomy since the work of the Italian scientist Galileo in the early 17th century. US scientists have graphically described the astonishing photographs received from the Telescope as 'postcards from the edge of space and time'.

THE BIG BANG

According to the latest theories, the Universe was created, and 'time' began, about 15,000 million (or 15 billion) years ago, though other estimates range from 8 to 24 billion years. Following a colossal explosion, called the 'Big Bang', the Universe expanded in the first millionth of a

The End of the Universe
The diagram shows two theories concerning the fate of the Universe. One theory, top, suggests that the Universe will expand indefinitely, moving into an immense dark graveyard. Another theory, bottom, suggests that the galaxies will fall back until everything is again concentrated in one point in a so-called 'Big Crunch'. This might then be followed by a new 'Big Bang'.

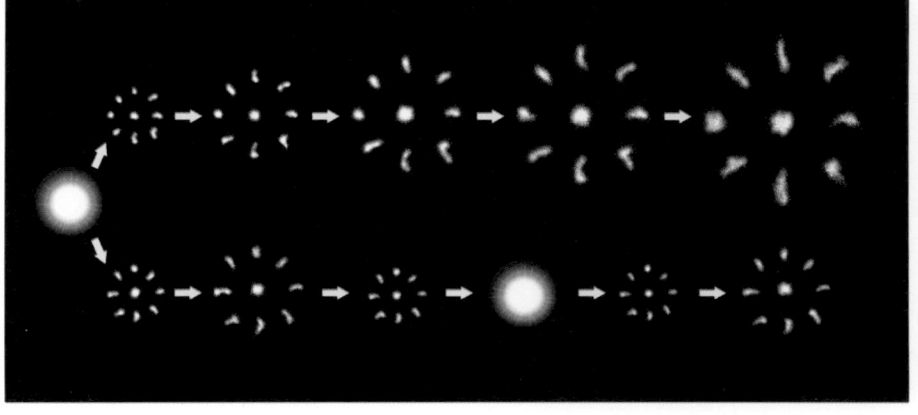

second of its existence from a dimensionless point of infinite mass and density into a fireball, about 30 billion km [19 billion miles] across. The Universe has been expanding ever since, as demonstrated in the 1920s by Edwin Hubble, the American astronomer after whom the Hubble Space Telescope was named.

The temperature at the end of the first second was perhaps 10 billion degrees – far too hot for composite atomic nuclei to exist. As a result, the fireball consisted mainly of radiation mixed with microscopic particles of matter. Almost a million years passed before the Universe was cool enough for atoms to form.

A few billion years later, atoms in regions where matter was relatively dense began, under the influence of gravity, to move together to form proto-galaxies – masses of gas separated by empty space. The proto-galaxies were dark, because the Universe had cooled. But a few billion years later, stars began to form within the proto-galaxies as particles were drawn together. The internal pressure produced as matter condensed created the high temperatures required to cause nuclear fusion. Stars were born and later destroyed. Each generation of stars fed on the debris of extinct ones. Each generation produced larger atoms, increasing the number of different chemical elements.

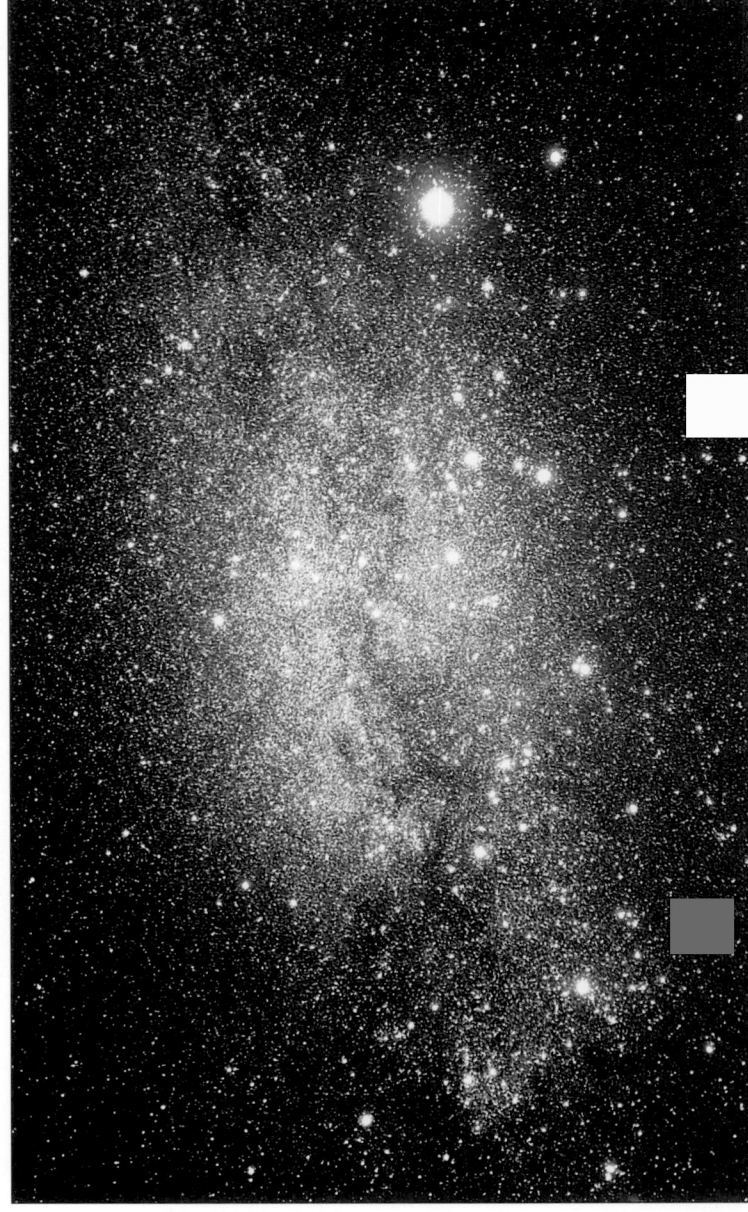

The Home Galaxy
This schematic plan shows that our Solar System is located in one of the spiral arms of the Milky Way galaxy, a little less than 30,000 light-years from its centre. The centre of the Milky Way galaxy is not visible from Earth. Instead, it is masked by light-absorbing clouds of interstellar dust.

Solar System

THE GALAXIES
At least a billion galaxies are scattered through the Universe, though the discoveries made by the Hubble Space Telescope suggest that there may be far more than once thought, and some estimates are as high as 100 billion. The largest galaxies contain trillions of stars, while small ones contain less than a billion.

Galaxies tend to occur in groups or clusters, while some clusters appear to be grouped in vast superclusters. Our Local Cluster includes the spiral Milky Way galaxy, whose diameter is about 100,000 light-years; one light-year, the distance that light travels in one year, measures about 9,500 billion km [5,900 billion miles]. The Milky Way is a huge galaxy, shaped like a disk with a bulge at the centre. It is larger, brighter and more massive than many other known galaxies. It contains about 100 billion stars which rotate around the centre of the galaxy in the same direction as the Sun does.

One medium-sized star in the Milky Way galaxy is the Sun. After its formation, about 5 billion years ago, there was enough leftover matter around it to create the planets, asteroids,

The Milky Way
This section of the Milky Way is dominated by Sirius, the Dog Star, top centre, in the constellation of Canis Major. Sirius is the brightest star in the sky.

moons and other bodies that together form our Solar System. The Solar System rotates around the centre of the Milky Way galaxy approximately every 225 million years.

Recent discoveries suggest that other stars similar to our Sun have planets orbiting around them, while evidence from the Hubble Space Telescope suggests that the raw materials from which planets are formed is common in dusty disks around many stars. This provokes one of the most intriguing of all the questions that has ever faced humanity. If there are other planets in the Universe, then do living organisms exist elsewhere?

Before the time of Galileo, people thought that the Earth lay at the centre of the Universe. But we now know that our Solar System and even the Milky Way galaxy are tiny specks in the Universe as a whole. Perhaps our planet is also not unique in being the only one to support intelligent life.

Star Charts and Constellations

THE BRIGHTEST STARS

The 15 brightest stars visible from northern Europe. Magnitudes are given to the nearest tenth.

Sirius	−1.5
Arcturus	0.0
Vega	0.0
Capella	0.1
Rigel	0.1
Procyon	0.4
Betelgeuse	0.4
Altair	0.8
Aldebaran	0.8
Antares	1.0
Spica	1.0
Pollux	1.1
Fomalhaut	1.2
Deneb	1.2
Regulus	1.3

The Plough

The Plough, or Big Dipper, above glowing yellow clouds lit by city lights. It is part of a larger group called Ursa Major one of the best-known constellations of the northern hemisphere. The two bright stars to the lower right of the photograph (Merak and Dubhe) are known as the Pointers because they show the way to the Pole Star.

On a clear night, under the best conditions and far away from the glare of city lights, a person in northern Europe can look up and see about 2,500 stars. In a town, however, light pollution can reduce visibility to 200 stars or less. Over the whole celestial sphere it is possible to see about 8,500 stars with the naked eye and it is only when you look through a telescope that you begin to realize that the number of stars is countless.

SMALL AND LARGE STARS

Stars come in several sizes. Some, called neutron stars, are compact, with the same mass as the Sun but with diameters of only about 20 km [12 miles]. Larger than neutron stars are the small white dwarfs. Our Sun is a medium-sized star, but many visible stars in the night sky are giants with diameters between 10 and 100 times that of the Sun, or supergiants with diameters over 100 times that of the Sun.

Two bright stars in the constellation Orion are Betelgeuse (also known as Alpha Orionis) and Rigel (or Beta Orionis). Betelgeuse is an orange-red supergiant, whose diameter is about

400 times that of the Sun. Rigel is also a supergiant. Its diameter is about 50 times that of the Sun, but its luminosity is estimated to be over 100,000 times that of the Sun.

The stars we see in the night sky all belong to our home galaxy, the Milky Way. This name is also used for the faint, silvery band that arches across the sky. This band, a slice through our

THE CONSTELLATIONS

The constellations and their English names. Constellations visible from both hemispheres are listed.

Andromeda	Andromeda	Delphinus	Dolphin	Perseus	Perseus
Antlia	Air Pump	Dorado	Swordfish	Phoenix	Phoenix
Apus	Bird of Paradise	Draco	Dragon	Pictor	Easel
Aquarius	Water Carrier	Equuleus	Little Horse	Pisces	Fishes
Aquila	Eagle	Eridanus	River Eridanus	Piscis Austrinus	Southern Fish
Ara	Altar	Fornax	Furnace	Puppis	Ship's Stern
Aries	Ram	Gemini	Twins	Pyxis	Mariner's Compass
Auriga	Charioteer	Grus	Crane	Reticulum	Net
Boötes	Herdsman	Hercules	Hercules	Sagitta	Arrow
Caelum	Chisel	Horologium	Clock	Sagittarius	Archer
Camelopardalis	Giraffe	Hydra	Water Snake	Scorpius	Scorpion
Cancer	Crab	Hydrus	Sea Serpent	Sculptor	Sculptor
Canes Venatici	Hunting Dogs	Indus	Indian	Scutum	Shield
Canis Major	Great Dog	Lacerta	Lizard	Serpens*	Serpent
Canis Minor	Little Dog	Leo	Lion	Sextans	Sextant
Capricornus	Sea Goat	Leo Minor	Little Lion	Taurus	Bull
Carina	Ship's Keel	Lepus	Hare	Telescopium	Telescope
Cassiopeia	Cassiopeia	Libra	Scales	Triangulum	Triangle
Centaurus	Centaur	Lupus	Wolf	Triangulum Australe	
Cepheus	Cepheus	Lynx	Lynx		Southern Triangle
Cetus	Whale	Lyra	Lyre	Tucana	Toucan
Chamaeleon	Chameleon	Mensa	Table	Ursa Major	Great Bear
Circinus	Compasses	Microscopium	Microscope	Ursa Minor	Little Bear
Columba	Dove	Monoceros	Unicorn	Vela	Ship's Sails
Coma Berenices	Berenice's Hair	Musca	Fly	Virgo	Virgin
Corona Australis	Southern Crown	Norma	Level	Volans	Flying Fish
Corona Borealis	Northern Crown	Octans	Octant	Vulpecula	Fox
Corvus	Crow	Ophiuchus	Serpent Bearer		
Crater	Cup	Orion	Hunter	** In two halves: Serpens Caput, the*	
Crux	Southern Cross	Pavo	Peacock	*head, and Serpens Cauda, the tail.*	
Cygnus	Swan	Pegasus	Winged Horse		

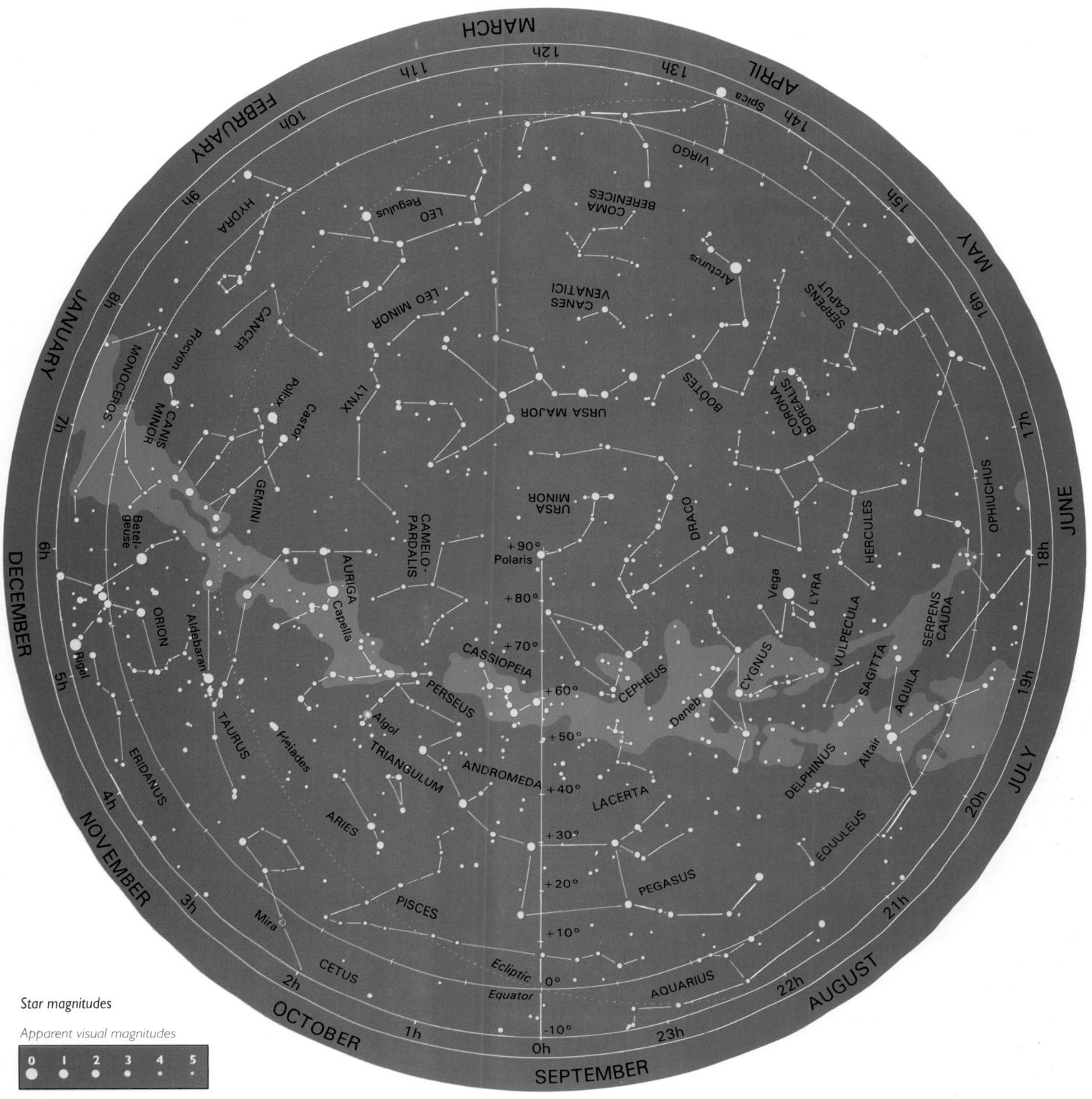

Star magnitudes

Apparent visual magnitudes

0	1	2	3	4	5

The Milky Way is shown in light blue on the above chart.

Star chart of the northern hemisphere

When you look into the sky, the stars seem to be on the inside of a huge dome. This gives astronomers a way of mapping them. This chart shows the sky as it would appear from the North Pole. To use the star chart above, an observer in the northern hemisphere should face south and turn the chart so that the current month appears at the bottom. The chart will then show the constellations on view at approximately 11pm Greenwich Mean Time. The map should be rotated clockwise 15° for each hour before 11pm and anticlockwise for each hour after 11pm.

galaxy, contains an enormous number of stars. The nucleus of the Milky Way galaxy cannot be seen from Earth. Lying in the direction of the constellation Sagittarius in the southern hemisphere, it is masked by clouds of dust.

THE BRIGHTNESS OF STARS

Astronomers use a scale of magnitudes to measure the brightness of stars. The brightest visible to the naked eye were originally known as first-magnitude stars, ones not so bright were second-magnitude, down to the faintest visible, which were rated as sixth-magnitude. The brighter the star, the lower the magnitude. With the advent of telescopes and the development of accurate instruments for measuring brightnesses, the magnitude scale has been refined and extended.

Very bright bodies such as Sirius, Venus and the Sun have negative magnitudes. The nearest star is Proxima Centauri, part of a multiple star system, which is 4.2 light-years away. Proxima Centauri is very faint and has a magnitude of 11.3. Alpha Centauri A, one of the two brighter members of the system, is the nearest visible star to Earth. It has a magnitude of 1.7.

These magnitudes are what are called appar-ent magnitudes – measures of the brightnesses of the stars as they appear to us. These are the mag-nitudes shown on the charts on these pages. But the stars are at very different distances. The star Deneb, in the constellation Cygnus, for example, is over 1,200 light-years away. So astronomers also use absolute magnitudes – measures of how bright the stars really are. A star's absolute magnitude is the apparent magnitude it would have if it could be placed 32.6 light-years away. So Deneb, with an apparent magnitude of 1.2, has an absolute magnitude of –7.2.

The brightest star in the night sky is Sirius, the Dog Star, with a magnitude of –1.5. This medium-sized star is 8.64 light-years distant but it gives out about 20 times as much light as the Sun. After the Sun and the Moon, the brightest objects in the sky are the planets Venus, Mars and Jupiter. For example, Venus has a mag-nitude of up to –4. The planets have no light of their own however, and shine only because they reflect the Sun's rays. But whilst stars have fixed positions, the planets shift nightly in relation to the constellations, following a path called

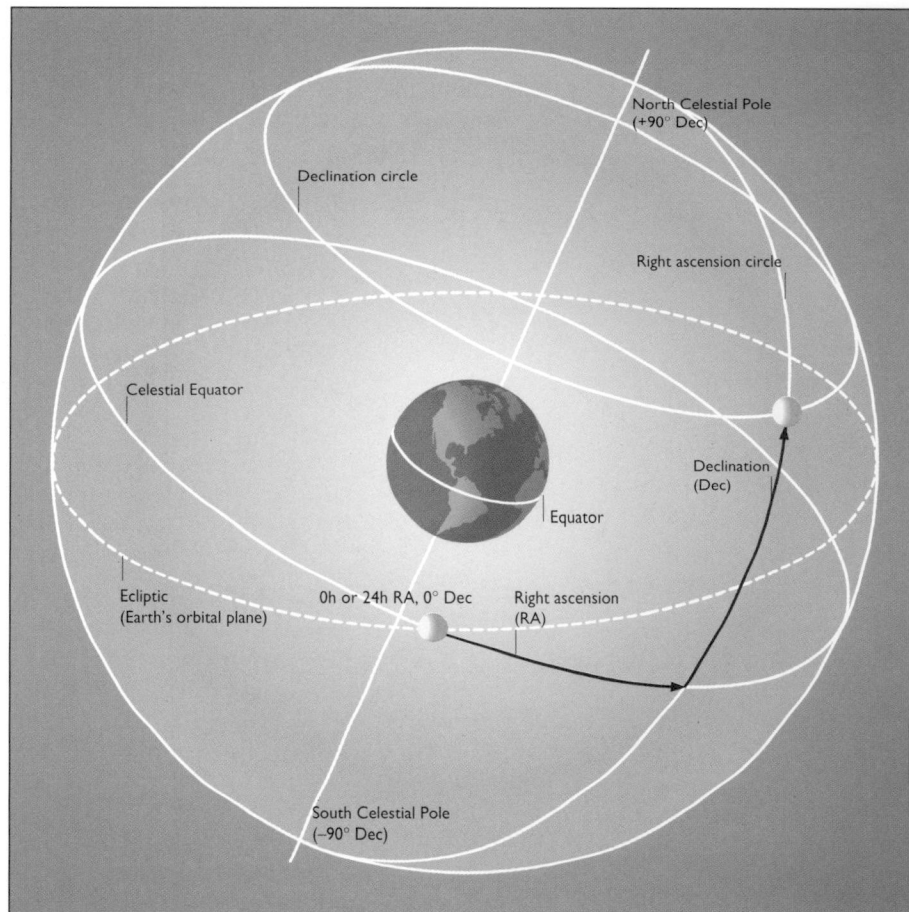

Celestial sphere

The diagram shows the imaginary surface on which astronomical positions are measured. The celestial sphere appears to rotate about the celestial poles, as though an extension of the Earth's own axis. The Earth's axis points towards the celestial poles.

The Southern Cross

The Southern Cross, or Crux, in the southern hemisphere, was classified as a constellation in the 17th century. It is as familiar to Australians and New Zealanders as the Plough is to people in the northern hemisphere. The vertical axis of the Southern Cross points towards the South Celestial Pole.

the Ecliptic (shown on the star charts). As they follow their orbits around the Sun, their dis-tances from the Earth vary, and therefore so also do their magnitudes.

While atlas maps record the details of the Earth's surface, star charts are a guide to the heavens. An observer at the Equator can see the entire sky at some time during the year, but an observer at the poles can see only the stars in a single hemisphere. As a result, star charts of both hemispheres are produced. The northern hemisphere chart is centred on the North Celes-tial Pole, while the southern hemisphere chart is centred on the South Celestial Pole.

In the northern hemisphere, the North Pole is marked by the star Polaris, or North Star. Polaris lies within a degree of the point where an extension of the Earth's axis meets the sky. Polaris appears to be stationary and navigators throughout history have used it as a guide. Unfortunately, the South Pole has no convenient reference point.

Star charts of the two hemispheres are bounded by the Celestial Equator, an imaginary line in the sky directly above the terrestrial Equator. Astronomical co-ordinates, which give the loca-tion of stars, are normally stated in terms of right ascension (the equivalent of longitude) and dec-lination (the equivalent of latitude). Because the stars appear to rotate around the Earth every 24 hours, right ascension is measured eastwards in hours and minutes. Declination is measured in degrees north or south of the Celestial Equator.

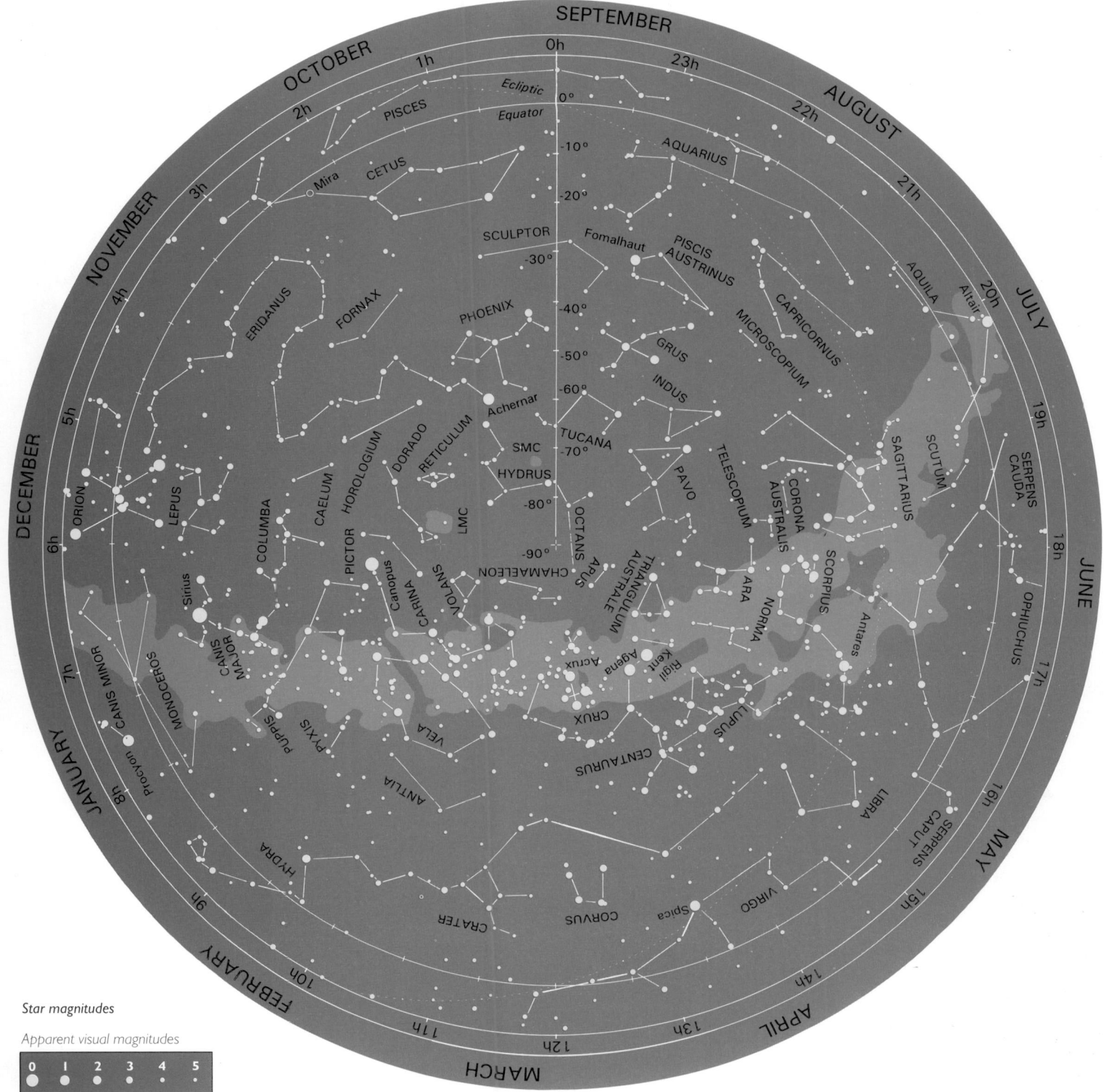

Star magnitudes

Apparent visual magnitudes

| 0 | 1 | 2 | 3 | 4 | 5 |

The Milky Way is shown in light blue on the above chart.

Star chart of the southern hemisphere

Many constellations in the southern hemisphere were named not by the ancients but by later astronomers. Some, including Antila (Air Pump) and Microscopium (Microscope), have modern names. The Large and Small Magellanic Clouds (LMC, SMC) are small 'satellite' galaxies of the Milky Way. To use the chart, an observer in the southern hemisphere should face north and turn the chart so that the current month appears at the bottom. The map will then show the constellations on view at approximately 11pm Greenwich Mean Time. The chart should be rotated clockwise 15° for each hour before 11pm and anticlockwise for each hour after 11pm.

CONSTELLATIONS

Every star is identifiable as a member of a constellation. The night sky contains 88 constellations, many of which were named by the ancient Greeks, Romans and other early peoples after animals and mythological characters, such as Orion and Perseus. More recently, astronomers invented names for constellations seen in the southern hemisphere, in areas not visible around the Mediterranean Sea.

Some groups of easily recognizable stars form parts of a constellation. For example, seven stars form the shape of the Plough or Big Dipper within the constellation Ursa Major. Such groups are called asterisms.

The stars in constellations lie in the same direction in space, but normally at vastly differ-ent distances. Hence, there is no real connection between them. The positions of stars seem fixed, but in fact the shapes of the constellations are changing slowly over very long periods of time. This is because the stars have their own 'proper motions', which because of the huge distances involved are imperceptible to the naked eye.

The Solar System

Although the origins of the Solar System are still a matter of debate, many scientists believe that it was formed from a cloud of gas and dust, the debris from some long-lost, exploded star. Around 5 billion years ago, material was drawn towards the hub of the rotating disk of gas and dust, where it was compressed to thermonuclear fusion temperatures. A new star, the Sun, was born, containing 99.8% of the mass of the Solar System. The remaining material was later drawn together to form the planets and the other bodies in the Solar System. Spacecraft, manned and unmanned, have greatly increased our knowledge of the Solar System since the start of the Space Age in 1957, when the Soviet Union launched the satellite Sputnik I.

THE PLANETS

Mercury is the closest planet to the Sun and

the fastest moving. Space probes have revealed that its surface is covered by craters, and looks much like our Moon. Mercury is a hostile place, with no significant atmosphere and temperatures ranging between 400°C [750°F] by day and −170°C [−275°F] by night. It seems unlikely that anyone will ever want to visit this planet.

Venus is much the same size as Earth. But it is the hottest of the planets, with temperatures reaching 475°C [885°F], even at night. The reason for this scorching heat is the atmosphere, which consists mainly of carbon dioxide, a gas that traps heat thus creating a greenhouse effect. The density of the atmosphere is about 90 times that of Earth and dense clouds permanently mask the surface. Active volcanic regions discharging sulphur dioxide may account for the haze of sulphuric acid droplets in the upper atmosphere.

From planet Earth, Venus is brighter than any other star or planet and is easy to spot. It is often the first object to be seen in the evening sky and the last to be seen in the morning sky. It can even be seen in daylight.

Earth, seen from space, looks blue (because of the oceans which cover more than 70% of the planet) and white (a result of clouds in the atmosphere). The atmosphere and water make Earth the only planet known to support life. The Earth's hard outer layers, including the crust and the top of the mantle, are divided into rigid plates. Forces inside the Earth move the plates, modifying the landscape and causing earthquakes and volcanic activity. Weathering and erosion also change the surface.

Mars has many features in common with Earth, including an atmosphere with clouds and polar caps that partly melt in summer. Scientists once considered that it was the most likely planet on which other life might exist, but the two Viking space probes that went there in the 1970s found only a barren rocky surface with no trace of water. But Mars did have flowing water at one time and there are many dry channels – but these are not the fictitious 'canals'. There are also giant, dormant volcanoes.

PLANETARY DATA

Planet	Mean distance from Sun (million km)	Mass (Earth=1)	Period of orbit (Earth yrs)	Period of rotation (Earth days)	Equatorial diameter (km)	Average density (water=1)	Surface gravity (Earth=1)	Number of known satellites
Sun	–	333,000	–	25.38	1,392,000	1.41	28	–
Mercury	57.9	0.055	0.2406	58.67	4,878	5.43	0.38	0
Venus	108.2	0.815	0.6152	243.0	12,100	5.24	0.90	0
Earth	149.6	1.0	1.00	1.00	12,756	5.52	1.00	1
Mars	227.9	0.107	1.88	1.028	6,794	3.93	0.38	2
Jupiter	778.3	317.8	11.86	0.411	142,800	1.33	2.69	18
Saturn	1,426.8	95.2	29.46	0.427	120,000	0.69	1.19	20
Uranus	2,869.4	14.5	84.01	0.748	52,400	1.25	0.93	15
Neptune	4,496.3	17.1	164.8	0.710	48,400	1.64	0.98	8
Pluto	5,900.1	0.002	2447.7	6.39	2,445	1.40	0.05	1

Asteroids are small, rocky bodies. Most of them orbit the Sun between Mars and Jupiter, but some small ones can approach the Earth. The largest is Ceres, 913 km [567 miles] in diameter. There may be around a million asteroids bigger than 1 km [0.6 miles].

Jupiter, the giant planet, lies beyond Mars and the asteroid belt. Its mass is almost three times as much as all the other planets combined and, because of its size, it shines more brightly than any other planet apart from Venus and, occasionally, Mars. The four largest moons of Jupiter were discovered by Galileo. Jupiter is made up mostly of hydrogen and helium, covered by a layer of clouds. Its Great Red Spot is a high-pressure storm. Jupiter made headline news when it was struck by fragments of Comet Shoemaker–Levy 9 in July 1994. This was the greatest collision ever seen by scientists between a planet and another heavenly body. The fragments of the comet that crashed into Jupiter created huge fireballs that caused scars on the planet that remained visible for months after the event.

Saturn is structurally similar to Jupiter but it is best known for its rings. The rings measure about 270,000 km [170,000 miles] across, yet they are no more than a few hundred metres thick. Seen from Earth, the rings seem divided

into three main bands of varying brightness, but photographs sent back by the *Voyager* space probes in 1980 and 1981 showed that they are broken up into thousands of thin ringlets composed of ice particles ranging in size from a snowball to an iceberg. The origin of the rings is still a matter of debate.

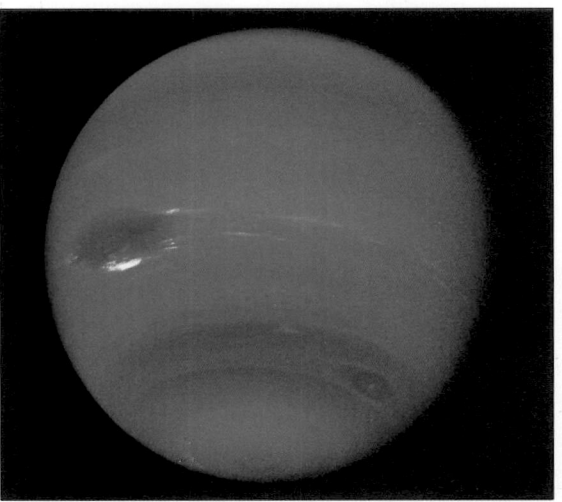

Uranus was discovered in 1781 by William Herschel who first thought it was a comet. It is broadly similar to Jupiter and Saturn in composition, though its distance from the Sun makes its surface even colder. Uranus is circled by thin rings which were discovered in 1977. Unlike the rings of Saturn, the rings of Uranus are black, which explains why they cannot be seen from Earth.

Neptune, named after the mythological sea god, was discovered in 1846 as the result of mathematical predictions made by astronomers to explain irregularities in the orbit of Uranus, its near twin. Little was known about this distant

body until *Voyager 2* came close to it in 1989. Neptune has thin rings, like those of Uranus. Among its blue-green clouds is a prominent dark spot, which rotates anticlockwise every 18 hours or so.

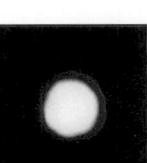

Pluto is the smallest planet in the Solar System, even smaller than our Moon. The American astronomer Clyde Tombaugh discovered Pluto in 1930. Its orbit is odd and it sometimes comes closer to the Sun than Neptune. The nature of Pluto, a gloomy planet appropriately named after the Greek and Roman god of the underworld, is uncertain. At Pluto's distance and beyond are many small, asteroid-like bodies the first of which was found in 1992.

Comets are small icy bodies that orbit the Sun in highly elliptical orbits. When a comet swings in towards the Sun some of its ice evaporates, and the comet brightens and may become visible from Earth. The best known is Halley's Comet, which takes 76 years to orbit the Sun.

The Earth: Time and Motion

The Earth is constantly moving through space like a huge, self-sufficient spaceship. First, with the rest of the Solar System, it moves around the centre of the Milky Way galaxy. Second, it rotates around the Sun at a speed of more than 100,000 km/h [more than 60,000 mph], covering a distance of nearly 1,000 million km [600 million miles] in a little over 365 days. The Earth also spins on its axis, an imaginary line joining the North and South Poles, via the centre of the Earth, completing one turn in a day. The Earth's movements around the Sun determine our calendar, though accurate observations of

The Earth from the Moon
In 1969, Neil Armstrong and Edwin 'Buzz' Aldrin Junior were the first people to set foot on the Moon. This superb view of the Earth was taken by the crew of Apollo 11.

the stars made by astronomers help to keep our clocks in step with the rotation of the Earth around the Sun.

THE CHANGING YEAR

The Earth takes 365 days, 6 hours, 9 minutes and 9.54 seconds to complete one orbit around the Sun. We have a calendar year of 365 days, so allowance has to be made for the extra time over and above the 365 days. This is allowed for by introducing leap years of 366 days. Leap years are generally those, such as 1992 and 1996, which are divisible by four. Century years, however, are not leap years unless they are divisible by 400. Hence, 1700, 1800 and 1900 were not leap years, but the year 2000 will be one. Leap years help to make the calendar conform with the solar year.

Because the Earth's axis is tilted by 23½°, the middle latitudes enjoy four distinct seasons. On 21 March, the vernal or spring equinox in the northern hemisphere, the Sun is directly overhead at the Equator and everywhere on Earth has about 12 hours of daylight and 12 hours of darkness. But as the Earth continues on its journey around the Sun, the northern hemisphere tilts more and more towards the Sun. Finally, on 21 June, the Sun is overhead at the Tropic of Cancer (latitude 23½° North). This is

The Seasons
The 23½° tilt of the Earth's axis remains constant as the Earth orbits around the Sun. As a result, first the northern and then the southern hemispheres lean towards the Sun. Annual variations in the amount of sunlight received in turn by each hemisphere are responsible for the four seasons experienced in the middle latitudes.

Tides
The daily rises and falls of the ocean's waters are caused by the gravitational pull of the Moon and the Sun. The effect is greatest on the hemisphere facing the Moon, causing a 'tidal bulge'. The diagram below shows that the Sun, Moon and Earth are in line when the spring tides occur. This causes the greatest tidal ranges. On the other hand, the neap tides occur when the pull of the Moon and the Sun are opposed. Neap tides, when tidal ranges are at their lowest, occur near the Moon's first and third quarters.

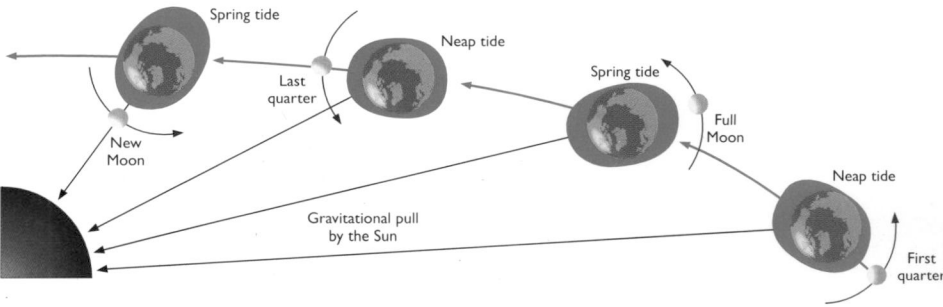

SUN DATA

DIAMETER	1.392×10^6 km
VOLUME	1.412×10^{18} km³
VOLUME (EARTH = 1)	1.303×10^6
MASS	1.989×10^{30} kg
MASS (EARTH = 1)	3.329×10^6
MEAN DENSITY (WATER = 1)	1.409
ROTATION PERIOD	
AT EQUATOR	24.25 days
AT POLES	about 35 days
SURFACE GRAVITY	
(EARTH = 1)	27.9
MAGNITUDE	
APPARENT	−26.9
ABSOLUTE	+4.71
TEMPERATURE	
AT SURFACE	5,400°C [5,700 K]
AT CORE	14×10^{16} K

MOON DATA

DIAMETER	3,476 km
MASS (EARTH = 1)	0.0123
DENSITY (WATER = 1)	3.34
MEAN DISTANCE FROM EARTH	384,402 km
MAXIMUM DISTANCE (APOGEE)	406,740 km
MINIMUM DISTANCE (PERIGEE)	356,410 km
SIDERIAL ROTATION AND REVOLUTION PERIOD	27.322 days
SYNODIC MONTH (NEW MOON TO NEW MOON)	29.531 days
SURFACE GRAVITY (EARTH = 1)	0.165
MAXIMUM SURFACE TEMPERATURE	+130°C [403 K]
MINIMUM SURFACE TEMPERATURE	−158°C [115 K]

Phases of the Moon

The Moon rotates more slowly than the Earth, making one complete turn on its axis in just over 27 days. This corresponds to its period of revolution around the Earth and, hence, the same hemisphere always faces us. The interval between one full Moon and the next (and also between new Moons) is about 29½ days, or one lunar month. The apparent changes in the appearance of the Moon are caused by its changing position in relation to Earth. Like the planets, the Moon produces no light of its own. It shines by reflecting the Sun's rays, varying from a slim crescent to a full circle and back again.

the summer solstice in the northern hemisphere.

The overhead Sun then moves south again until on 23 September, the autumn equinox in the northern hemisphere, the Sun is again overhead at the Equator. The overhead Sun then moves south until, on around 22 December, it is overhead at the Tropic of Capricorn. This is the winter solstice in the northern hemisphere, and the summer solstice in the southern, where the seasons are reversed.

At the poles, there are two seasons. During half of the year, one of the poles leans towards the Sun and has continuous sunlight. For the other six months, the pole leans away from the Sun and is in continuous darkness.

Regions around the Equator do not have marked seasons. Because the Sun is high in the sky throughout the year, it is always hot or warm. When people talk of seasons in the tropics, they are usually referring to other factors, such as rainy and dry periods.

DAY, NIGHT AND TIDES

As the Earth rotates on its axis every 24 hours, first one side of the planet and then the other faces the Sun and enjoys daylight, while the opposite side is in darkness.

The length of daylight varies throughout the year. The longest day in the northern hemisphere falls on the summer solstice, 21 June, while the longest day in the southern hemisphere is on 22 December. At 40° latitude, the length of daylight on the longest day is 14 hours, 30 minutes. At 60° latitude, daylight on that day lasts 18 hours, 30 minutes. On the shortest day, 22 December in the northern hemisphere and 21 June in the southern, daylight hours at 40° latitude total 9 hours and 9 minutes. At latitude 60°, daylight lasts only 5 hours, 30 minutes in the 24-hour period.

Tides are caused by the gravitational pull of the Moon and, to a lesser extent, the Sun on the waters in the world's oceans. Tides occur twice every 24 hours, 50 minutes – one complete orbit

Total eclipse of the Sun

A total eclipse is caused when the Moon passes between the Sun and the Earth. With the Sun's bright disk completely obscured, the Sun's corona, or outer atmosphere, can be viewed.

of the Moon around the Earth.

The highest tides, the spring tides, occur when the Earth, Moon and Sun are in a straight line, so that the gravitational pulls of the Moon and Sun are combined. The lowest, or neap, tides occur when the Moon, Earth and Sun form a right angle. The gravitational pull of the Moon is then opposed by the gravitational pull of the Sun. The greatest tidal ranges occur in the Bay of Fundy in North America. The greatest mean spring range is 14.5 m [47.5 ft].

The speed at which the Earth is spinning on its axis is gradually slowing down, because of the movement of tides. As a result, experts have calculated that, in about about 200 million years, the day will be 25 hours long.

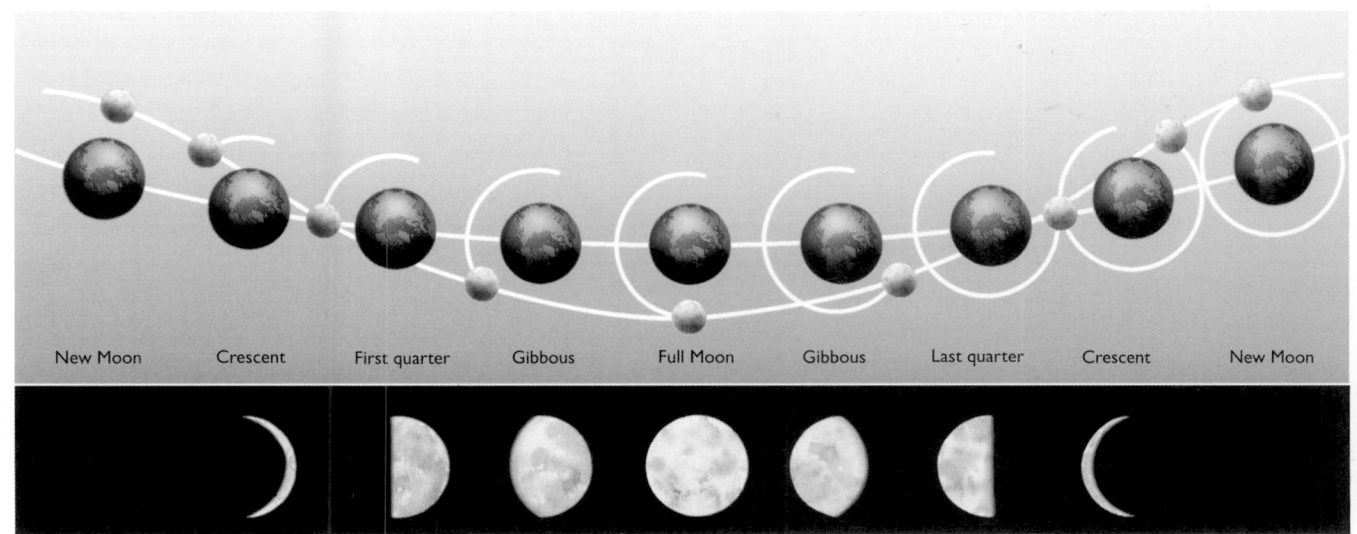

| New Moon | Crescent | First quarter | Gibbous | Full Moon | Gibbous | Last quarter | Crescent | New Moon |

The Earth from Space

Any last doubts about whether the Earth was round or flat were finally resolved by the appearance of the first photographs of our planet taken at the start of the Space Age. Satellite images also confirmed that map- and globe-makers had correctly worked out the shapes of the continents and the oceans.

More importantly, images of our beautiful, blue, white and brown planet from space impressed on many people that the Earth and its resources are finite. They made people realize that if we allow our planet to be damaged by such factors as overpopulation, pollution and irresponsible over-use of resources, then its future and the survival of all the living things upon it may be threatened.

VIEWS FROM ABOVE

The first aerial photographs were taken from balloons in the mid-19th century and their importance in military reconnaissance was recognized as early as the 1860s during the American Civil War.

Launch of the Space Shuttle Atlantis
Space Shuttles transport astronauts and equipment into orbit around the Earth. The American Space Shuttle Atlantis, *shown below, launched the Magellan probe, which undertook a radar mapping programme of the surface of Venus in the early 1990s.*

Since the end of World War II, photographs taken by aircraft have been widely used in map-making. The use of air photographs has greatly speeded up the laborious process of mapping land details and they have enabled cartographers to produce maps of the most remote parts of the world.

Aerial photographs have also proved useful because they reveal features that are not visible at ground level. For example, circles that appear on many air photographs do not correspond to visible features on the ground. Many of these mysterious shapes have turned out to be the sites of ancient settlements previously unknown to archaeologists.

IMAGES FROM SPACE

Space probes equipped with cameras and a variety of remote sensing instruments have sent back images of distant planets and moons. From these images, detailed maps have been produced, rapidly expanding our knowledge of the Solar System.

Photographs from space are also proving invaluable in the study of the Earth. One of the best known uses of space imagery is the study of the atmosphere. Polar-orbiting weather satellites that circle the Earth, together with geostationary satellites, whose motion is synchronized with the Earth's rotation, now regularly transmit images showing the changing patterns of weather systems from above. Forecasters use these images to track the development and the paths taken by hurricanes, enabling them to issue storm warnings to endangered areas, saving lives and reducing damage to property.

Remote sensing devices are now monitoring changes in temperatures over the land and sea, while photographs indicate the melting of ice sheets. Such evidence is vital in the study of global warming. Other devices reveal polluted areas, patterns of vegetation growth, and areas suffering deforestation.

In recent years, remote sensing devices have been used to monitor the damage being done to the ozone layer in the stratosphere, which prevents most of the Sun's harmful ultraviolet radiation from reaching the surface. The discovery of 'ozone holes', where the protective layer of ozone is being thinned by chlorofluorocarbons (CFCs), chemicals used in the manufacture of such things as air conditioners and refrigerators, has enabled governments to take concerted action to save our planet from imminent danger.

EARTH DATA

MAXIMUM DISTANCE FROM SUN (APHELION)
152,007,016 km

MINIMUM DISTANCE FROM SUN (PERIHELION)
147,000,830 km

LENGTH OF YEAR — SOLAR TROPICAL (EQUINOX TO EQUINOX)
365.24 days

LENGTH OF YEAR — SIDEREAL (FIXED STAR TO FIXED STAR)
365.26 days

LENGTH OF DAY — MEAN SOLAR DAY
24 hours, 03 minutes, 56 seconds

LENGTH OF DAY — MEAN SIDEREAL DAY
23·hours, 56 minutes, 4 seconds

SUPERFICIAL AREA
510,000,000 km^2

LAND SURFACE
149,000,000 km^2 (29.3%)

WATER SURFACE
361,000,000 km^2 (70.7%)

EQUATORIAL CIRCUMFERENCE
40,077 km

POLAR CIRCUMFERENCE
40,009 km

EQUATORIAL DIAMETER
12,756.8 km

POLAR DIAMETER
12,713.8 km

EQUATORIAL RADIUS
6,378.4 km

POLAR RADIUS
6,356.9 km

VOLUME OF THE EARTH
1,083,230 × 10^6 km^3

MASS OF THE EARTH
5.9 × 10^{21} tonnes

Satellite image of San Francisco Bay

Unmanned scientific satellites called ERTS (Earth Resources Technology Satellites), or Landsats, were designed to collect information about the Earth's resources. The satellites transmitted images of the land using different wavelengths of light in order to identify, in false colours, such subtle features as areas that contain minerals or areas covered with growing crops, that are not identifiable on simple photographs using the visible range of the spectrum. They were also equipped to monitor conditions in the atmosphere and oceans, and also to detect pollution levels. This Landsat image of San Francisco Bay covers an area of great interest to geologists because it lies in an earthquake zone in the path of the San Andreas fault.

The Dynamic Earth

The Earth was formed about 4.6 billion years ago from the ring of gas and dust left over after the formation of the Sun. As the Earth took shape, lighter elements, such as silicon, rose to the surface, while heavy elements, notably iron, sank towards the centre.

Gradually, the outer layers cooled to form a hard crust. The crust enclosed the dense mantle which, in turn, surrounded the even denser liquid outer and solid inner core. Around the Earth was an atmosphere, which contained abundant water

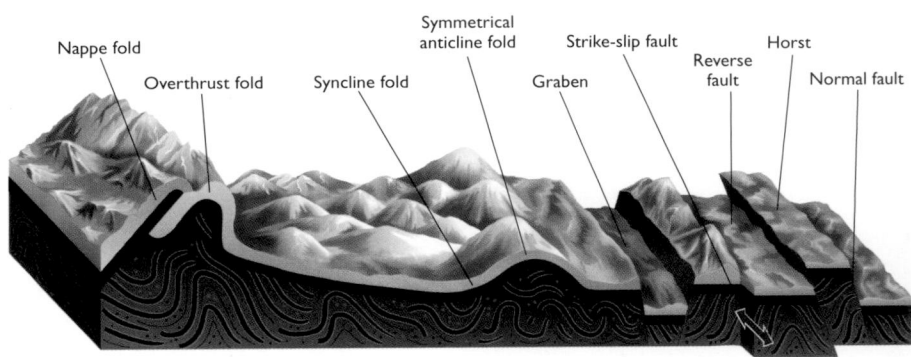

Lulworth Cove, southern England
When undisturbed by earth movements, sedimentary rock strata are generally horizontal. But lateral pressure has squeezed the Jurassic strata at Lulworth Cove into complex folds.

vapour. When the surface cooled, rainwater began to fill hollows, forming the first lakes and seas. Since that time, our planet has been subject to constant change – the result of powerful internal and external forces that still operate today.

THE HISTORY OF THE EARTH

From their study of rocks, geologists have pieced together the history of our planet and the life forms that evolved upon it. They have dated the oldest known crystals, composed of the mineral zircon, at 4.2 billion years. But the oldest rocks are younger, less than 4 billion years old. This is because older rocks have been weathered away by natural processes.

The oldest rocks that contain fossils, which are evidence of once-living organisms, are around 3.5 billion years old. But fossils are rare in rocks formed in the first 4 billion years of Earth history. This vast expanse of time is called the Precambrian. This is because it precedes the Cambrian period, at the start of which, about 590 million years ago, life was abundant in the seas.

The Cambrian is the first period in the Paleozoic (or ancient life) era. The Paleozoic era is followed by the Mesozoic (middle life) era, which witnessed the spectacular rise and fall of the dinosaurs, and the Cenozoic (recent life) era, which was dominated by the evolution of mammals. Each of the eras is divided into periods, and the periods in the Cenozoic era, covering the last 65 million years, are further divided into epochs.

THE EARTH'S CHANGING FACE

While life was gradually evolving, the face of the Earth was constantly changing. By piecing together evidence of rock structures and fossils, geologists have demonstrated that around 250 million years ago, all the world's land areas were grouped together in one huge landmass called Pangaea. Around 180 million years ago, the supercontinent Pangaea, began to break up. New oceans opened up as the continents began to move towards their present positions.

Evidence of how continents drift came from studies of the ocean floor in the 1950s and 1960s. Scientists discovered that the oceans are young features. By contrast with the continents, no part of the ocean floor is more than 200 million years old. The floors of oceans older than 200 million years have completely vanished.

Studies of long undersea ranges, called ocean ridges, revealed that the youngest rocks occur along their centres, which are the edges of huge plates – rigid blocks of the Earth's lithosphere, which is made up of the crust and the solid upper layer of the mantle. The Earth's lithosphere is split into six large and several smaller

Mountain building
Lateral pressure, which occurs when plates collide, squeezes and compresses rocks into folds. Simple symmetrical upfolds are called anticlines, while downfolds are synclines. As the pressure builds up, strata become asymmetrical and they may be tilted over to form recumbent folds. The rocks often crack under the intense pressure and the folds are sheared away and pushed forward over other rocks. These features are called overthrust folds or nappes. Plate movements also create faults along which rocks move upwards, downwards and sideways. The diagram shows a downfaulted graben, or rift valley, and an uplifted horst, or block mountain.

The Himalayas seen from Nepal
The Himalayas are a young fold mountain range formed by a collision between two plates. The earthquakes felt in the region testify that the plate movements are still continuing.

plates. The ocean ridges are 'constructive' plate margins, because new crustal rock is being formed there from magma that wells up from the mantle as the plates gradually move apart. By contrast, the deep ocean trenches are 'destructive' plate edges. Here, two plates are pushing against each other and one plate is descending beneath the other into the mantle where it is melted and destroyed. Geologists call these areas subduction zones.

A third type of plate edge is called a transform fault. Here two plates are moving alongside each other. The best known of these plate edges is the San Andreas fault in California, which separates the Pacific plate from the North American plate.

Slow-moving currents in the partly molten asthenosphere, which underlies the solid lithosphere, are responsible for moving the plates, a process called plate tectonics.

MOUNTAIN BUILDING

The study of plate tectonics has helped geologists to understand the mechanisms that are responsible for the creation of mountains. Many of the world's greatest ranges were created by the collision of two plates and the bending of the intervening strata into huge loops, or folds. For example, the Himalayas began to rise around 50 million years ago, when a plate supporting India collided with the huge Eurasian plate. Rocks on the floor of the intervening and long-vanished Tethys Sea were squeezed up to form the Himalayan Mountain Range.

Plate movements also create tension that cracks rocks, producing long faults along which rocks move upwards, downwards or sideways. Block mountains are formed when blocks of rock are pushed upwards along faults. Steep-sided rift valleys are formed when blocks of land sink down between faults. For example, the basin and range region of the south-western United States has both block mountains and down-faulted basins, such as Death Valley.

Geological time scale
The geological time scale was first constructed by a study of the stratigraphic, or relative, ages of layers of rock. But the absolute ages of rock strata could not be fixed until the discovery of radioactivity in the early 20th century. Some names of periods, such as Cambrian (Latin for Wales), come from places where the rocks were first studied. Others, such as Carboniferous, refer to the nature of the rocks formed during the period. For example, coal seams (containing carbon) were formed from decayed plant matter during the Carboniferous period.

Pre-Cambrian	Lower	Paleozoic (Primary)		Upper			Mesozoic (Secondary)			Cenozoic (Tertiary, Quaternary)	Era
Pre-Cambrian	Cambrian	Ordovician	Silurian	Devonian	Carboniferous	Permian	Triassic	Jurassic	Cretaceous	Paleocene Eocene Oligocene Miocene Pliocene Quaternary	System
			CALEDONIAN FOLDING		HERCYNIAN FOLDING					LARAMIDE FOLDING ALPINE FOLDING	Orogeny
600	550	500	450	400	350	300 250	200	150	100	50	

Millions of years before present

Earthquakes and Volcanoes

On 4 February 1998, the remote province of Takhar in northern Afghanistan was struck by a devastating earthquake which razed 30 villages to the ground. More than 4,200 people died, and 15,000 more were made homeless. Relief efforts were hampered by strong aftershocks, difficult terrain, poor weather and continuing civil war.

THE RESTLESS EARTH

Earthquakes can occur anywhere, whenever rocks move along faults. But the most severe and most numerous earthquakes occur near the edges of the plates that make up the Earth's lithosphere. Japan, for example, lies in a

San Andreas Fault, United States
Geologists call the San Andreas fault in south-western California a transform, or strike-slip, fault. Sudden movements along it cause earthquakes. In 1906, shifts of about 4.5 metres [15 ft] occurred near San Francisco, causing a massive earthquake.

particularly unstable region above subduction zones, where plates are descending into the Earth's mantle. It lies in a zone encircling the Pacific Ocean, called the 'Pacific ring of fire'.

Plates do not move smoothly. Their edges are jagged and for most of the time they are locked together. However, pressure gradually builds up until the rocks break and the plates lurch forwards, setting off vibrations ranging from tremors that are recorded only by sensitive instruments to terrifying earthquakes. The greater the pressure released, the more destructive the earthquake.

Earthquakes are also common along the ocean trenches where plates are moving apart, but they mostly occur so far from land that they do little damage. Far more destructive are the earthquakes that occur where plates are moving alongside each other. For example, the earthquakes that periodically rock south-western California are caused by movements along the San Andreas Fault.

The spot where an earthquake originates is called the focus, while the point on the Earth's surface directly above the focus is called the epicentre. Two kinds of waves, P-waves or compressional waves and S-waves or shear waves, travel from the focus to the surface where they make the ground shake. P-waves travel faster than S-waves and the time difference between their arrival at recording stations enables scientists to calculate the distance from a station to the epicentre.

Earthquakes are measured on the Richter scale, which indicates the magnitude of the shock. The most destructive earthquakes are shallow-focus, that is, the focus is within 60 km [37 miles] of the surface. A magnitude of 7.0 is a major earthquake, but earthquakes with a somewhat lower magnitude can cause tremendous damage if their epicentres are on or close to densely populated areas.

NOTABLE EARTHQUAKES
(since 1900)

Year	Location	Mag.
1906	San Francisco, USA	8.3
1906	Valparaiso, Chile	8.6
1908	Messina, Italy	7.5
1915	Avezzano, Italy	7.5
1920	Gansu, China	8.6
1923	Yokohama, Japan	8.3
1927	Nan Shan, China	8.3
1932	Gansu, China	7.6
1934	Bihar, India/Nepal	8.4
1935	Quetta, India[†]	7.5
1939	Chillan, Chile	8.3
1939	Erzincan, Turkey	7.9
1964	Anchorage, Alaska	8.4
1968	N. E. Iran	7.4
1970	N. Peru	7.7
1976	Guatemala	7.5
1976	Tangshan, China	8.2
1978	Tabas, Iran	7.7
1980	El Asnam, Algeria	7.3
1980	S. Italy	7.2
1985	Mexico City, Mexico	8.1
1988	N. W. Armenia	6.8
1990	N. Iran	7.7
1993	Maharashtra, India	6.4
1994	Los Angeles, USA	6.4
1995	Kobe, Japan	7.2
1995	Sakhalin Is., Russia	7.5
1996	Yunnan, China	7.0
1997	N. E. Iran	7.1
1998	N. Afghanistan	6.1

[†] *now Pakistan*

Earthquakes in subduction zones
Along subduction zones, one plate is descending beneath another. The plates are locked together until the rocks break and the descending plate lurches forwards. From the point where the plate moves – the origin – seismic waves spread through the lithosphere, making the ground shake. The earthquake in Mexico City in 1985 occurred in this way.

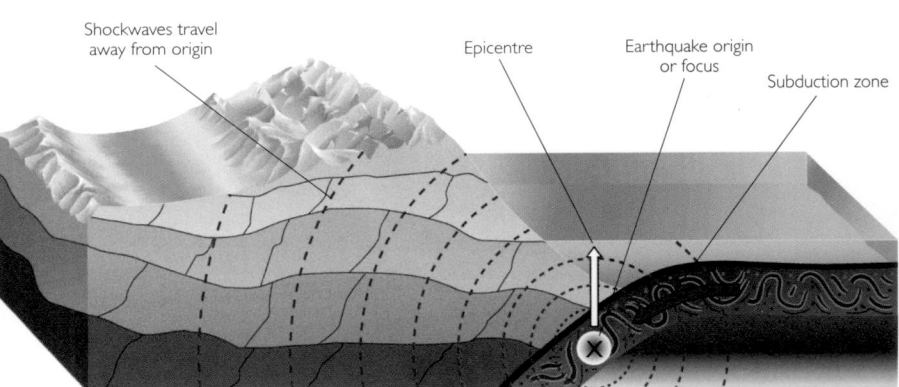

Shockwaves travel away from origin

Epicentre

Earthquake origin or focus

Subduction zone

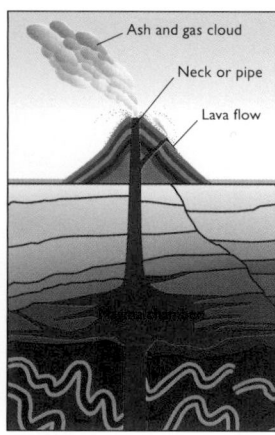

Cross-section of a volcano
Volcanoes are vents in the ground, through which magma reaches the surface. The term volcano is also used for the mountains formed from volcanic rocks. Beneath volcanoes are pockets of magma derived from the semi-molten asthenosphere in the mantle. The magma rises under pressure through the overlying rocks until it reaches the surface. There it emerges through vents as pyroclasts, ranging in size from large lumps of magma, called volcanic bombs, to fine volcanic ash and dust. In quiet eruptions, streams of liquid lava run down the side of the mountain. Side vents sometimes appear on the flanks of existing volcanoes.

Scientists have been working for years to find effective ways of forecasting earthquakes but with very limited success. Following the Kobe earthquake in 1995, many experts argued that they would be better employed developing techniques of reducing the damage caused by earthquakes, rather than pursuing an apparently vain attempt to predict them.

VOLCANIC ERUPTIONS

Most active volcanoes also occur on or near plate edges. Many undersea volcanoes along the ocean ridges are formed from magma that wells up from the asthenosphere to fill the gaps created as the plates, on the opposite sides of the ridges, move apart. Some of these volcanoes reach the surface to form islands. Iceland is a country which straddles the Mid-Atlantic Ocean Ridge. It is gradually becoming wider as magma rises to the surface through faults and vents. Other volcanoes lie alongside subduction zones. The magma that fuels them comes from the melted edges of the descending plates.

A few volcanoes lie far from plate edges. For example, Mauna Loa and Kilauea on Hawaii are situated near the centre of the huge Pacific plate. The molten magma that reaches the surface is created by a source of heat, called a 'hot spot', in the Earth's mantle.

Magma is molten rock at temperatures of about 1,100°C to 1,200°C [2,012°F to 2,192°F]. It contains gases and superheated steam. The chemical composition of magma varies. Viscous magma is rich in silica and superheated steam, while runny magma contains less silica and steam. The chemical composition of the magma affects the nature of volcanic eruptions.

Explosive volcanoes contain thick, viscous magma. When they erupt, they usually hurl clouds of ash (shattered fragments of cooled magma) into the air. By contrast, quiet volcanoes emit long streams of runny magma, or lava. However, many volcanoes are intermediate in type, sometimes erupting explosively and sometimes emitting streams of fluid lava. Explosive and intermediate volcanoes usually have a conical shape, while quiet volcanoes are flattened, resembling upturned saucers. They are often called shield volcanoes.

One dangerous type of eruption is called a *nuée ardente*, or 'glowing cloud'. It occurs when a cloud of intensely hot volcanic gases and dust particles and superheated steam are exploded from a volcano. They move rapidly downhill, burning everything in their path and choking animals and people. The blast that creates the *nuée ardente* may release the pressure inside the volcano, resulting in a tremendous explosion that hurls tall columns of ash into the air.

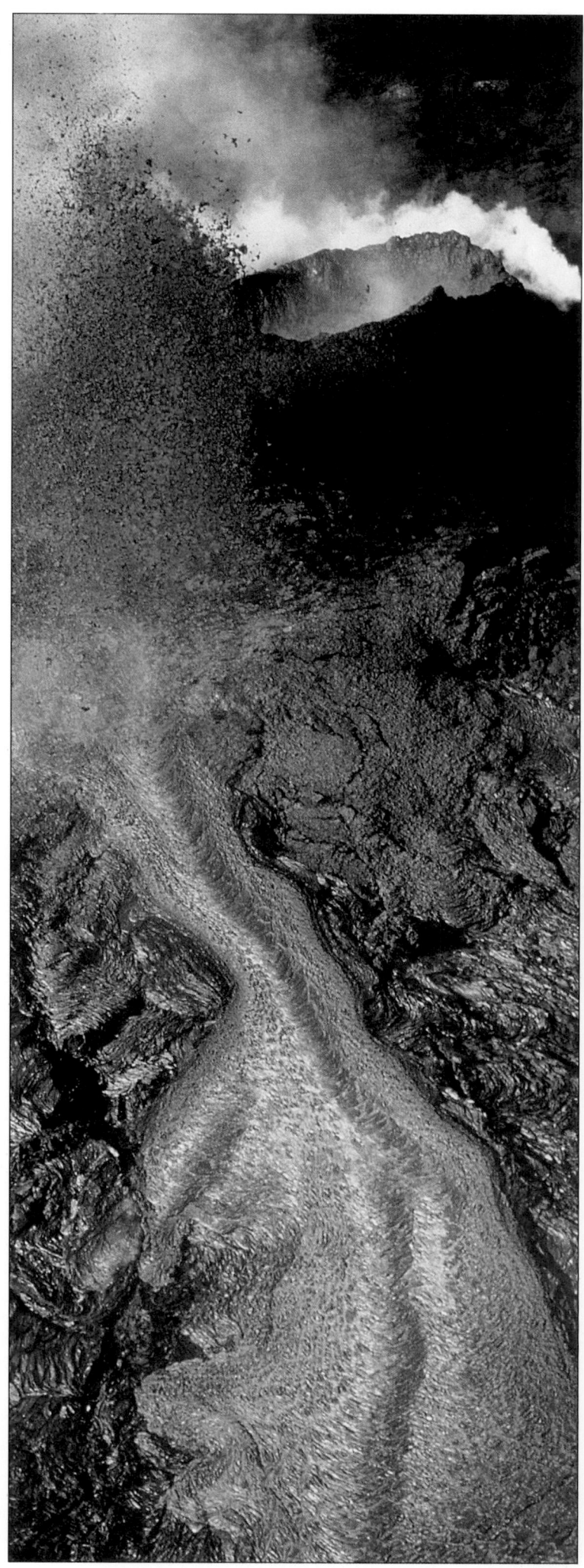

Kilauea Volcano, Hawaii
The volcanic Hawaiian islands in the North Pacific Ocean were formed as the Pacific plate moved over a 'hot spot' in the Earth's mantle. Kilauea on Hawaii emits blazing streams of liquid lava.

Forces of Nature

When the volcano Mount Pinatubo erupted in the Philippines in 1991, large areas around the mountain were covered by ash. Later, rainwater mixed with the loose ash on sloping land, created lahars, or mudflows, which swept down river valleys burying many areas. Such incidents are not only reminders of the great forces that operate inside our planet but also of those natural forces operating on the surface, which can have dramatic effects on the land.

The chief forces acting on the surface of the Earth are weathering, running water, ice and winds. The forces of erosion seem to act slowly. One estimate suggests that an average of only 3.5 cm [1.4 in] of land is removed by natural processes every 1,000 years. This may not sound much, but over millions of years, it can reduce mountains to almost flat surfaces.

WEATHERING

Weathering occurs in all parts of the world, but the most effective type of weathering in any area depends on the climate and the nature of the rocks. For example, in cold mountain areas,

Grand Canyon, Arizona, at dusk
The Grand Canyon in the United States is one of the world's natural wonders. Eroded by the Colorado River and its tributaries, it is up to 1.6 km [1 mile] deep and 29 km [18 miles] wide.

RATES OF EROSION

	SLOW ← WEATHERING RATE → FAST		
Mineral solubility	low (e.g. quartz)	moderate (e.g. feldspar)	high (e.g. calcite)
Rainfall	low	moderate	heavy
Temperature	cold	temperate	hot
Vegetation	sparse	moderate	lush
Soil cover	bare rock	thin to moderate soil	thick soil

Weathering is the breakdown and decay of rocks in situ. It may be mechanical (physical), chemical or biological.

when water freezes in cracks in rocks, the ice occupies 9% more space than the water. This exerts a force which, when repeated over and over again, can split boulders apart. By contrast, in hot deserts, intense heating by day and cooling by night causes the outer layers of rocks to expand and contract until they break up and peel away like layers of an onion. These are examples of what is called mechanical weathering.

Other kinds of weathering include chemical reactions usually involving water. Rainwater containing carbon dioxide dissolved from the air or the soil is a weak acid which reacts with limestone, wearing out pits, tunnels and networks of caves in layers of limestone rock. Water also combines with some minerals, such as the feldspars in granite, to create kaolin, a white

Rates of erosion
The chart shows that the rates at which weathering takes place depend on the chemistry and hardness of rocks, climatic factors, especially rainfall and temperature, the vegetation and the nature of the soil cover in any area. The effects of weathering are increased by human action, particularly the removal of vegetation and the exposure of soils to the rain and wind.

clay. These are examples of chemical weathering which constantly wears away rock.

RUNNING WATER, ICE AND WIND

In moist regions, rivers are effective in shaping the land. They transport material worn away by weathering and erode the land. They wear out V-shaped valleys in upland regions, while vigorous meanders widen their middle courses. The work of rivers is at its most spectacular when earth movements lift up flat areas and rejuvenate the rivers, giving them a new erosive power capable of wearing out such features as the Grand Canyon. Rivers also have a constructive role. Some of the world's most fertile regions are deltas and flood plains composed of sediments

Glaciers

During Ice Ages, ice spreads over large areas and the effect of glacial erosion on landscapes is enormous. However, during warm periods, the world's ice sheets and glaciers retreat. The chart shows that in recent years, the volumes of many glaciers around the world have been decreasing, possibly as a result of global warming.

ANNUAL FLUCTUATIONS FOR SELECTED GLACIERS

Glacier name and location	Changes in the annual mass balance†		Cumulative total
	1970–1	1990–1	1970–90
Alfotbreen, Norway	+940	+790	+12,110
Wolverine, USA	+770	−410	+2,320
Storglaciaren, Sweden	−190	+170	−120
Djankuat, Russia	−230	−310	−1,890
Grasubreen, Norway	+470	−520	−2,530
Ürümqi, China	+102	−706	−3,828
Golubin, Kyrgyzstan	−90	−722	−7,105
Hintereisferner, Austria	−600	−1,325	−9,081
Gries, Switzerland	−970	−1,480	−10,600
Careser, Italy	−650	−1,730	−11,610
Abramov, Tajikistan	−890	−420	−13,700
Sarennes, France	−1,100	−1,360	−15,020
Place, Canada	−343	−990	−15,175

† The annual mass balance is defined as the difference between glacier accumulation and ablation (melting) averaged over the whole glacier. Balances are expressed as water equivalent in millimetres. A plus indicates an increase in the depth or length of the glacier; a minus indicates a reduction.

Juneau Glacier, Alaska

Like huge conveyor belts, glaciers transport weathered debris from mountain regions. Rocks frozen in the ice give the glaciers teeth, enabling them to wear out typical glaciated land features.

periodically dumped there by such rivers as the Ganges, Mississippi and Nile.

Running water in the form of sea waves and currents shapes coastlines, wearing out caves, natural arches, and stacks. The sea also transports and deposits worn material to form such features as spits and bars.

Glaciers in cold mountain regions flow downhill, gradually deepening valleys and shaping dramatic landscapes. They erode steep-sided U-shaped valleys, into which rivers often plunge in large waterfalls. Other features include cirques, armchair-shaped basins bounded by knife-edged ridges called *arêtes*. When several glacial cirques erode to form radial *arêtes*, pyramidal peaks like the Matterhorn are created. Deposits of moraine, rock material dumped by the glacier, are further evidence that ice once covered large areas. The work of glaciers, like other agents of erosion, varies with the climate. In recent years, global warming has been making glaciers retreat in many areas, while several of the ice shelves in Antarctica have been breaking up.

Many land features in deserts were formed by running water at a time when the climate was much rainier than it is today. Water erosion also occurs when flash floods are caused by rare thunderstorms. But the chief agent of erosion in dry areas is wind-blown sand, which can strip the paint from cars, and undercut boulders to create mushroom-shaped rocks.

Oceans and Ice

Since the 1970s, oceanographers have found numerous hot vents on the ocean ridges. Called black smokers, the vents emit dark, mineral-rich water reaching 350°C [662°F]. Around the vents are chimney-like structures formed from minerals deposited from the hot water. The discovery of black smokers did not surprise scientists who already knew that the ridges were plate edges, where new crustal rock was being formed as molten magma welled up to the surface. But what was astonishing was that the hot water contained vast numbers of bacteria, which provided the base of a food chain that included many strange creatures, such as giant worms, eyeless shrimps and white clams. Many species were unknown to science.

Little was known about the dark world beneath the waves until about 50 years ago. But through the use of modern technology such as echo-sounders, magnetometers, research ships equipped with huge drills, submersibles that can carry scientists down to the ocean floor, and satellites, the secrets of the oceans have been gradually revealed.

The study of the ocean floor led to the discovery that the oceans are geologically young features – no more than 200 million years old. It also revealed evidence as to how oceans form and continents drift because of the action of plate tectonics.

THE BLUE PLANET

Water covers almost 71% of the Earth, which makes it look blue when viewed from space. Although the oceans are interconnected, geographers divide them into four main areas: the Pacific, Atlantic, Indian and Arctic oceans. The average depth of the oceans is 3,370 m [12,238 ft], but they are divided into several zones.

Around most continents are gently sloping continental shelves, which are flooded parts of the continents. The shelves end at the continental slope, at a depth of about 200 m [656 ft]. This slope leads steeply down to the abyss. The deepest parts of the oceans are the trenches, which reach a maximum depth of 11,033 m [36,198 ft] in the Mariana Trench in the western Pacific.

Most marine life is found in the top 200 m [656 ft], where there is sufficient sunlight for plants, called phytoplankton, to grow. Below this zone, life becomes more and more scarce, though no part of the ocean, even at the bottom of the deepest trenches, is completely without living things.

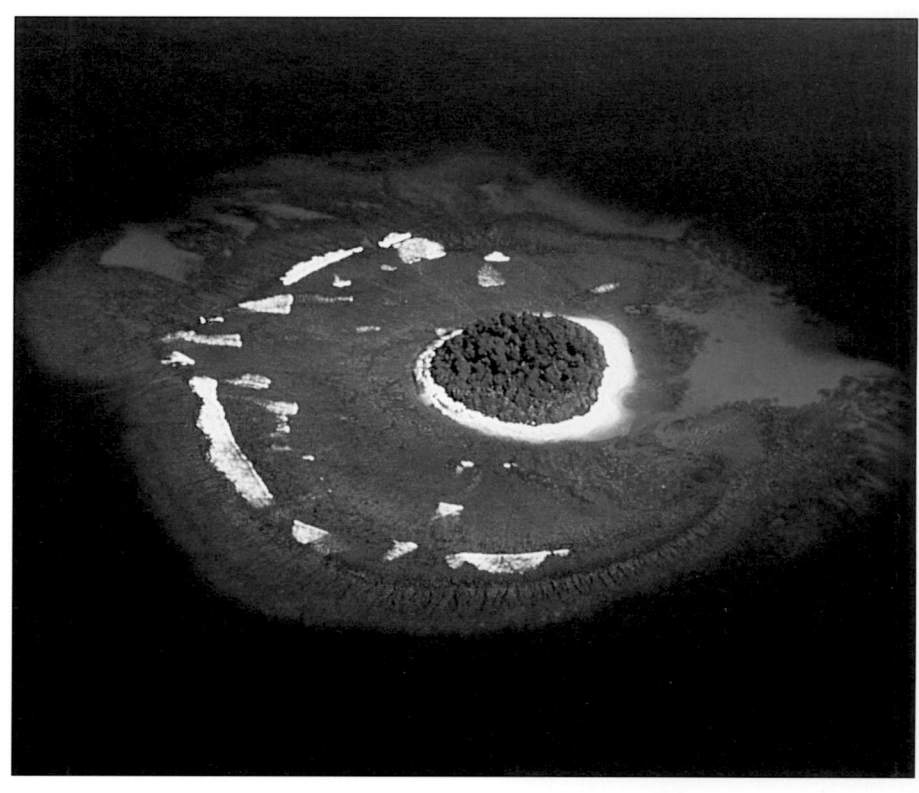

Vava'u Island, Tonga
This small coral atoll in northern Tonga consists of a central island covered by rainforest. Low coral reefs washed by the waves surround a shallow central lagoon.

Continental islands, such as the British Isles, are high parts of the continental shelves. For example, until about 7,500 years ago, when the ice sheets formed during the Ice Ages were melting, raising the sea level and filling the North Sea and the Strait of Dover, Britain was linked to mainland Europe.

By contrast, oceanic islands, such as the Hawaiian chain in the North Pacific Ocean, rise from the ocean floor. All oceanic islands are of volcanic origin, although many of them in warm parts of the oceans have sunk and are capped by layers of coral to form ring- or horseshoe-shaped atolls and coral reefs.

OCEAN WATER

The oceans contain about 97% of the world's water. Seawater contains more than 70 dissolved elements, but chloride and sodium make up 85% of the total. Sodium chloride is common salt and it makes seawater salty. The salinity of the oceans is mostly between 3.3–3.7%. Ocean water fed by icebergs or large rivers is less saline than shallow seas in the tropics, where the evaporation rate is high. Seawater is a source of salt but the water is useless for agriculture or drinking unless it is desalinated. However, land

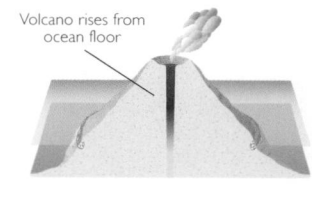

Volcano rises from ocean floor

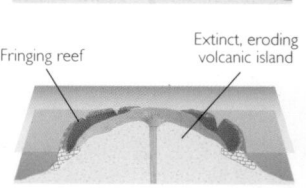

Fringing reef

Extinct, eroding volcanic island

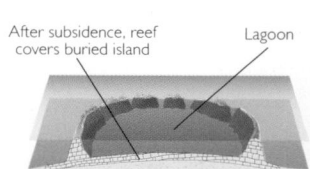

After subsidence, reef covers buried island

Lagoon

Development of an atoll
Some of the volcanoes that rise from the ocean floor reach the surface to form islands. Some of these islands subside and become submerged. As an island sinks, coral starts to grow around the rim of the volcano, building up layer upon layer of limestone deposits to form fringing reefs. Sometimes coral grows on the tip of a central cone to form an island in the middle of the atoll.

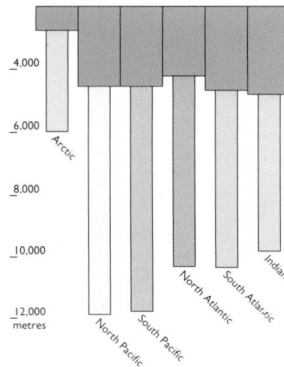

The ocean depths
The diagram shows the average depths (in dark blue) and the greatest depths in the four oceans. The North Pacific Ocean contains the world's deepest trenches, including the Mariana Trench, where the deepest manned descent was made by the bathyscaphe Trieste in 1960. It reached a depth of 10,916 metres [35,813 ft].

Relative sizes of the world's oceans:
PACIFIC 49%   ATLANTIC 26%
INDIAN 21%   ARCTIC 4%
Some geographers distinguish a fifth ocean, the Southern or Antarctic Ocean, but most authorities regard these waters as the southern extension of the Pacific, Atlantic and Indian oceans.

areas get a regular supply of fresh water through the hydrological cycle (see page 26).

The density of seawater depends on its salinity and temperature. Temperatures vary from –2°C [28°F], the freezing point of seawater at the poles, to around 30°C [86°F] in parts of the tropics. Density differences help to maintain the circulation of the world's oceans, especially deep-sea currents. But the main cause of currents within 350 m [1,148 ft] of the surface is the wind. Because of the Earth's rotation, currents are deflected, creating huge circular motions of surface water – clockwise in the northern hemisphere and anticlockwise in the southern hemisphere.

Ocean currents transport heat from the tropics to the polar regions and thus form part of the heat engine that drives the Earth's climates. Ocean currents have an especially marked effect on coastal climates, such as north-western Europe. In the mid-1990s, scientists warned that global warming may be weakening currents, including the warm Gulf Stream which is responsible for the mild winters experienced in north-western Europe.

ICE SHEETS, ICE CAPS AND GLACIERS
Global warming is also a threat to the world's ice sheets, ice caps and glaciers that together account for about 2% of the world's water. There are two ice sheets in the world, the largest

covers most of Antarctica. With the ice reaching maximum depths of 4,800 m [15,748 ft], the Antarctic ice sheet contains about 70% of the world's fresh water, with a total volume about nine times greater than the Greenland ice sheet. Smaller bodies of ice include ice caps in northern Canada, Iceland and Scandinavia. Also throughout the world in high ranges are many valley glaciers, which help to shape dramatic mountain scenery.

Only about 11,000 years ago, during the final phase of the Pleistocene Ice Age, ice covered much of the northern hemisphere. The Ice Age, which began about 1.8 million years ago, was not a continuous period of cold. Instead, it consisted of glacial periods when the ice advanced and warmer interglacial periods when temperatures rose and the ice retreated.

Some scientists believe that we are now living in an inter-glacial period, and that glacial conditions will recur at some time in the future. Others fear the opposite, that global warming, caused mainly by pollution, may melt the world's ice, raising sea levels by up to 55 m [180 ft]. Many fertile and densely populated coastal plains, islands and great cities would vanish from the map.

Weddell Sea, Antarctica
Antarctica contains two huge bays, occupied by the Ross and Weddell seas. Ice shelves extend from the ice sheet across parts of these seas. Pack ice covers the open sea in winter.

The Earth's Atmosphere

Since the discovery in 1985 of a thinning of the ozone layer, creating a so-called 'ozone hole', over Antarctica, many governments have worked to reduce the emissions of ozone-eating substances, notably the chlorofluorocarbons (CFCs) used in aerosols, refrigeration, air conditioning and dry cleaning.

Following forecasts that the ozone layer would rapidly repair itself as a result of controls on these emissions, scientists were surprised in early 1996 when a marked thinning of the ozone layer occurred over the Arctic, northern Europe, Russia and Canada. The damage, which was recorded as far south as southern Britain, was due to pollution combined with intense cold in the stratosphere. It was another sharp reminder of the dangers humanity faces when it interferes with and harms the environment.

The ozone layer in the stratosphere blocks out most of the dangerous ultraviolet B radiation in the Sun's rays. This radiation causes skin cancer and cataracts, as well as harming plants on the land and plankton in the oceans. The ozone layer is only one way in which the atmosphere protects life on Earth. The atmosphere also provides the air we breathe and the carbon dioxide required by plants. It is also a shield against meteors and it acts as a blanket to prevent heat radiated from the Earth escaping into space.

LAYERS OF AIR

The atmosphere is divided into four main layers. The troposphere at the bottom contains about 85% of the atmosphere's total mass, where most weather conditions occur. The troposphere is about 15 km [9 miles] thick over the Equator and 8 km [5 miles] thick at the poles. Temperatures decrease with height by approximately 1°C [2°F] for every 100 m [328 ft]. At the top of the troposphere is a level called the tropopause where temperatures are stable at around –55°C [–67°F]. Above the tropopause is the stratosphere, which contains the ozone layer. Here, at about 50 km [31 miles] above the Earth's surface, temperatures rise to about 0°C [32°F].

The ionosphere extends from the stratopause to about 600 km [373 miles] above the surface. Here temperatures fall up to about 80 km

CIRCULATION OF AIR

	HIGH PRESSURE
	LOW PRESSURE
	WARM AIR
	COLD AIR
	SURFACE WINDS
	CLOUDS

The circulation of the atmosphere can be divided into three rotating but interconnected air systems, or cells. The Hadley cell (figure 1 on the above diagram) is in the tropics; the Ferrel cell (2) lies between the subtropics and the mid-latitudes, and the Polar cell (3) is in the high latitudes.

Moonrise seen from orbit
This photograph taken by an orbiting Shuttle shows the crescent of the Moon. Silhouetted at the horizon is a dense cloud layer. The reddish-brown band is the tropopause, which separates the blue-white stratosphere from the yellow troposphere.

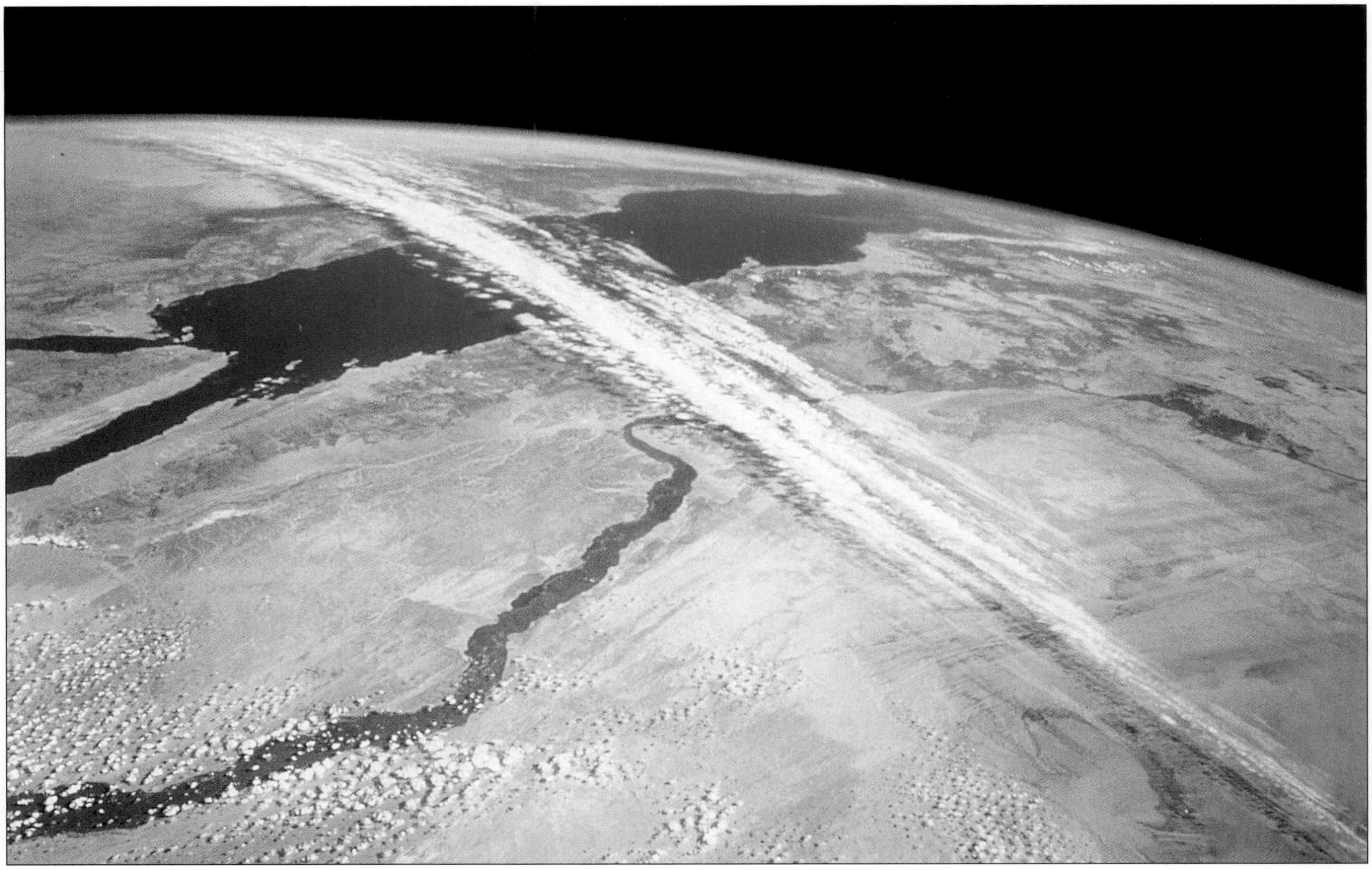

Jetstream from space
Jetstreams are strong winds that normally blow near the tropopause.
Cirrus clouds mark the route of the jet stream in this photograph,
which shows the Red Sea, North Africa and the Nile valley, which
appears as a dark band crossing the desert.

[50 miles], but then rise. The aurorae, which occur in the ionosphere when charged particles from the Sun interact with the Earth's magnetic field, are strongest near the poles. In the exosphere, the outermost layer, the atmosphere merges into space.

CIRCULATION OF THE ATMOSPHERE

The heating of the Earth is most intense around the Equator where the Sun is high in the sky. Here warm, moist air rises in strong currents, creating a zone of low air pressure: the doldrums. The rising air eventually cools and spreads out north and south until it sinks back

to the ground around latitudes 30° North and 30° South. This forms two zones of high air pressure called the horse latitudes.

From the horse latitudes, trade winds blow back across the surface towards the Equator, while westerly winds blow towards the poles. The warm westerlies finally meet the polar easterlies (cold dense air flowing from the poles). The line along which the warm and cold air streams meet is called the polar front. Depressions (or cyclones) are low air pressure frontal systems that form along the polar front.

COMPOSITION OF THE ATMOSPHERE

The air in the troposphere is made up mainly of nitrogen (78%) and oxygen (21%). Argon makes up more than 0.9% and there are also minute amounts of carbon dioxide, helium, hydrogen, krypton, methane, ozone and xenon. The atmosphere also contains water vapour, the gaseous form of water, which, when it condenses around minute specks of dust and salt, forms tiny water droplets or ice crystals. Large masses of water droplets or ice crystals form clouds.

Classification of clouds

Clouds are classified broadly into cumuliform, or 'heap' clouds, and stratiform, or 'layer' clouds. Both types occur at all levels. The highest clouds, composed of ice crystals, are cirrus, cirrostratus and cirrocumulus. Medium-height clouds include altostratus, a grey cloud that often indicates the approach of a depression, and altocumulus, a thicker and fluffier version of cirrocumulus. Low clouds include stratus, which forms dull, overcast skies; nimbostratus, a dark grey layer cloud which brings almost continuous rain and snow; cumulus, a brilliant white heap cloud; and stratocumulus, a layer cloud arranged in globular masses or rolls. Cumulonimbus, a cloud associated with thunderstorms, lightning and heavy rain, often extends from low to medium altitudes. It has a flat base, a fluffy outline and often an anvil-shaped top.

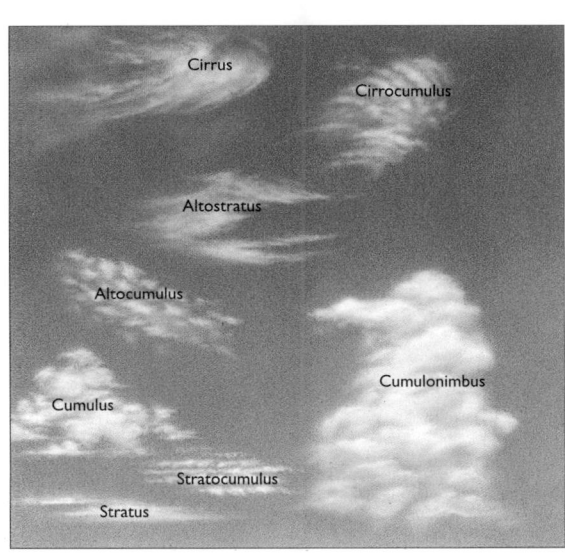

Climate and Weather

In April 1989, a tornado destroyed the town of Shaturia in Bangladesh, killing 1,300 people. In April 1991, at least 139,000 people died when a tropical cyclone (known also as a hurricane, a typhoon or a willy-willy) struck Bangladesh. In June and July 1993, record floods in the North American Midwest did enormous damage. And in May 1998, a series of mudslides caused by unusually heavy and prolonged rainfall killed over 100 people in the southern Italian region of Campania.

Every year, exceptional weather conditions cause disasters around the world. Modern forecasting techniques now give people warning of advancing storms, but the toll of human deaths continues as people are powerless in the face of the awesome forces of nature.

Weather is the day-to-day condition of the atmosphere. In some places, the weather is nomally stable, but in other areas, especially the middle latitudes, it is highly variable, changing from hour to hour with the passing of a depression. By contrast, climate is the average, or usual weather of a place, based on data obtained over a long period.

Hurricane Elena, 1995
Hurricanes form over warm oceans north and south of the Equator. Their movements are tracked by satellites, enabling forecasters to issue storm warnings as they approach land. In North America, forecasters identify them with boys' and girls' names.

CLIMATIC FACTORS

Climate depends basically on the unequal heating of the Sun between the Equator and the poles. But ocean currents and terrain also affect climate. For example, despite their northerly positions, Norway's ports remain ice-free in winter. This is because of the warming effect of the North Atlantic Drift, an extension of the Gulf Stream which flows across the Atlantic Ocean from the Gulf of Mexico.

By contrast, the cold Benguela current which flows up the coast of south-western Africa cools the coast and causes arid conditions. This is because the cold onshore winds are warmed as they pass over the land. The warm air can hold more water vapour than cold air, giving the winds a drying effect.

The terrain affects climate in several ways. Because temperatures fall with altitude, highlands are cooler than lowlands in the same

CLIMATIC REGIONS

Tropical rainy climates
All mean monthly temperatures above 18°C [64°F].

■ RAINFOREST CLIMATE

■ MONSOON CLIMATE

SAVANNA CLIMATE

Dry climates
Low rainfall combined with a wide range of temperatures.

STEPPE CLIMATE

■ DESERT CLIMATE

Warm temperate rainy climates
The mean temperature is below 18°C [64°F] but above −3°C [26°F] and that of the warmest month is over 10°C [50°F].

DRY WINTER CLIMATE

■ DRY SUMMER CLIMATE

■ CLIMATE WITH NO DRY SEASON

Cold temperate rainy climates
The mean temperature of the coldest month is below 3°C [37°F] but the warmest month is over 10°C [50°F].

■ DRY WINTER CLIMATE

CLIMATE WITH NO DRY SEASON

Polar climates
The temperature of the warmest month is below 10°C [50°F], giving permanently frozen subsoil.

TUNDRA CLIMATE

■ POLAR CLIMATE

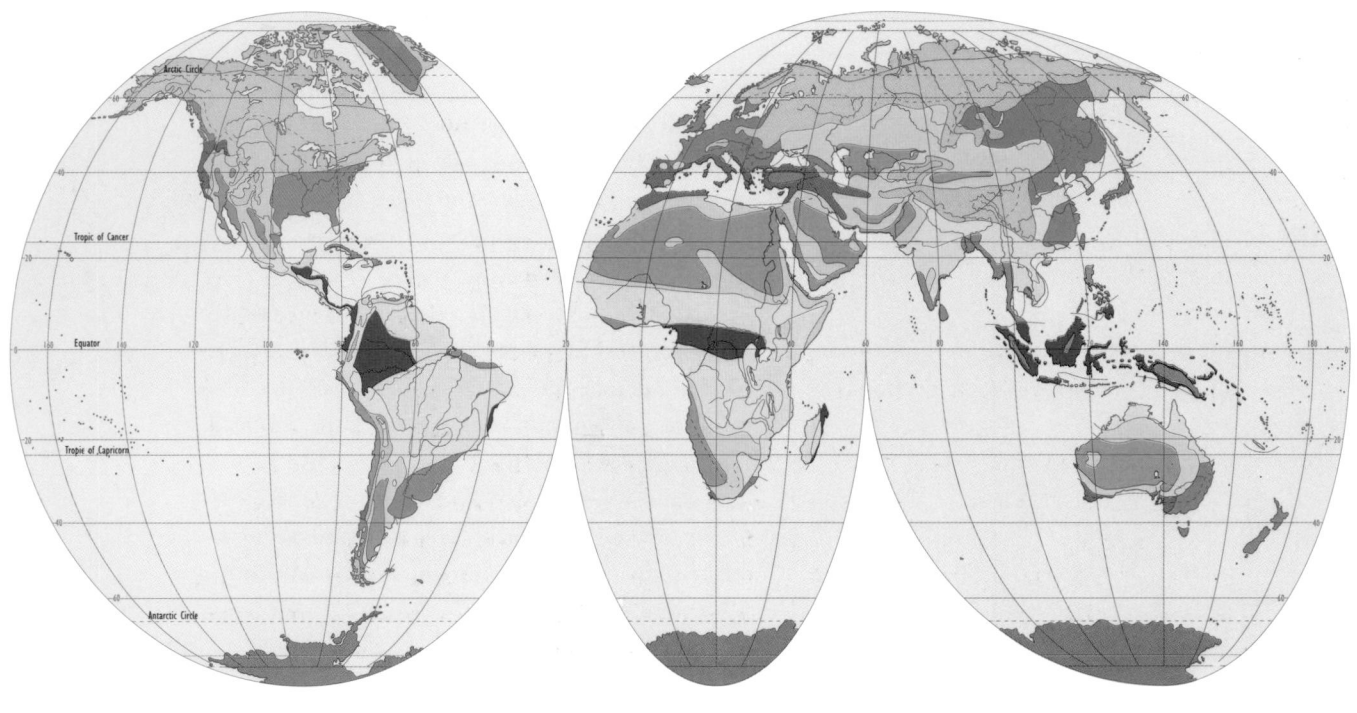

Floods in St Louis, United States

The satellite image, right, shows the extent of the floods at St Louis at the confluence of the Mississippi and the Missouri rivers in June and July 1993. The floods occurred when very heavy rainfall raised river levels by up to 14 m [46 ft]. The floods reached their greatest extent between Minneapolis in the north and a point approximately 150 km [93 miles] south of St Louis. In places, the width of the Mississippi increased to nearly 11 km [7 miles], while the Missouri reached widths of 32 km [20 miles]. In all, more than 28,000 sq km [10,800 sq miles] were inundated and hundreds of towns and cities were flooded. Damage to crops was estimated at $8 billion. The USA was hit again by flooding in early 1997, when heavy rainfall in North Dakota and Minnesota caused the Red River to flood. The flooding had a catastrophic effect on the city of Grand Forks, which was inundated for months.

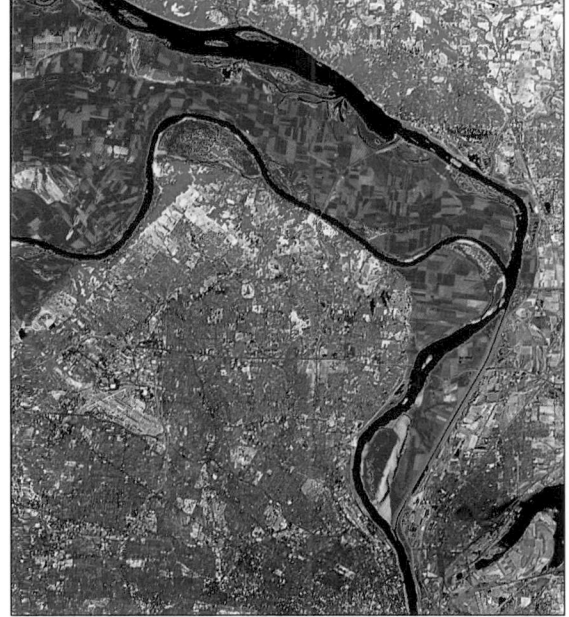

Flood damage in the United States

In June and July 1993, the Mississippi River basin suffered record floods. The photograph shows a sunken church in Illinois. The flooding along the Mississippi, Missouri and other rivers caused great damage, amounting to about $12 billion. At least 48 people died in the floods.

CLIMATIC REGIONS

The two major factors that affect climate are temperature and precipitation, including rain and snow. In addition, seasonal variations and other climatic features are also taken into account. Climatic classifications vary because of the weighting given to various features. Yet most classifications are based on five main climatic types: tropical rainy climates; dry climates; warm temperate rainy climates; cold temperate rainy climates; and very cold polar climates. Some classifications also allow for the effect of altitude. The main climatic regions are subdivided according to seasonal variations and also to the kind of vegetation associated with the climatic conditions. Thus, the rainforest climate, with rain throughout the year, differs from monsoon and savanna climates, which have marked dry seasons. Similarly, parched desert climates differ from steppe climates which have enough moisture for grasses to grow.

latitude. Terrain also affects rainfall. When moist onshore winds pass over mountain ranges, they are chilled as they are forced to rise and the water vapour they contain condenses to form clouds which bring rain and snow. After the winds have crossed the mountains, the air descends and is warmed. These warm, dry winds create rain shadow (arid) regions on the lee side of the mountains.

Water and Land Use

All life on land depends on fresh water. Yet about 80 countries now face acute water shortages. The world demand for fresh water is increasing by about 2.3% a year and this demand will double every 21 years. About a billion people, mainly in developing countries, do not have access to clean drinking water and around 10 million die every year from drinking dirty water. This problem is made worse in many countries by the pollution of rivers and lakes.

In 1995, a World Bank report suggested that wars will be fought over water in the 21st century. Relations between several countries are already soured by disputes over water resources. Egypt fears that Sudan and Ethiopia will appropriate the waters of the Nile, while Syria and Iraq are concerned that Turkish dams will hold back the waters of the Euphrates.

However, experts stress that while individual countries face water crises, there is no global crisis. The chief global problems are the uneven distribution of water and its inefficient and wasteful use.

THE WORLD'S WATER SUPPLY

Of the world's total water supply, 99.4% is in the oceans or frozen in bodies of ice. Most of the rest circulates through the rocks beneath our feet as ground water. Water in rivers and lakes, in the soil and in the atmosphere together make up only 0.013% of the world's water.

The freshwater supply on land is dependent on the hydrological, or water cycle which is driven by the Sun's heat. Water is evaporated from the oceans and carried into the air as invisible water vapour. Although this vapour averages less than 2% of the total mass of the atmosphere, it is the chief component from the standpoint of weather.

When air rises, water vapour condenses into visible water droplets or ice crystals, which eventually fall to earth as rain, snow, sleet, hail or frost. Some of the precipitation that reaches the ground returns directly to the atmosphere through evaporation or transpiration via plants. Much of the rest of the water flows into the rocks to become ground water or across the surface into rivers and, eventually, back to the oceans, so completing the hydrological cycle.

WATER AND AGRICULTURE

Only about a third of the world's land area is used for growing crops, while another third

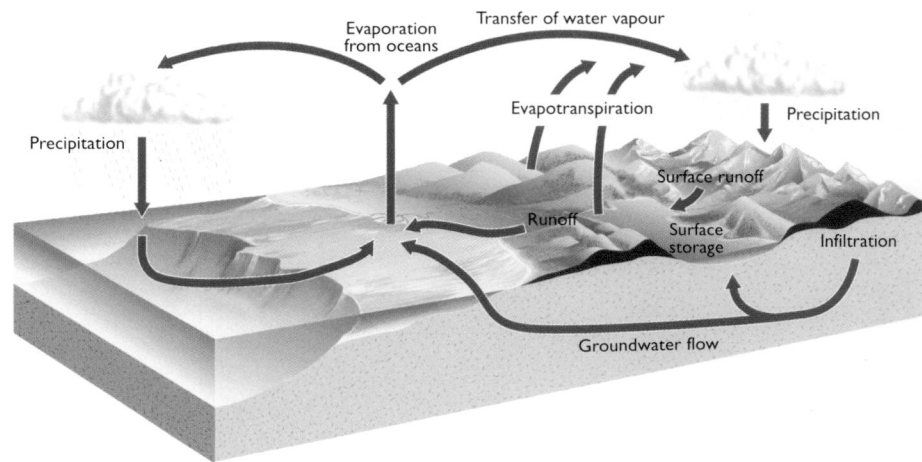

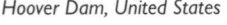

Hoover Dam, United States

The Hoover Dam in Arizona controls the Colorado River's flood waters. Its reservoir supplies domestic and irrigation water to the south-west, while a hydroelectric plant produces electricity.

The hydrological cycle

The hydrological cycle is responsible for the continuous circulation of water around the planet. Water vapour contains and transports latent heat, or latent energy. When the water vapour condenses back into water (and falls as rain, hail or snow), the heat is released. When condensation takes place on cold nights, the cooling effect associated with nightfall is offset by the liberation of latent heat.

WATER DISTRIBUTION

The distribution of planetary water, by percentage.

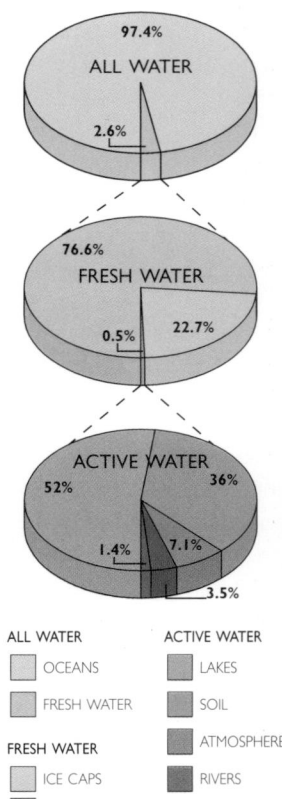

97.4%
ALL WATER
2.6%

76.6%
FRESH WATER
0.5%   22.7%

ACTIVE WATER
52%   36%
1.4%   7.1%
3.5%

ALL WATER
☐ OCEANS
☐ FRESH WATER

ACTIVE WATER
☐ LAKES
☐ SOIL

FRESH WATER
☐ ICE CAPS
☐ GROUND WATER
☐ ACTIVE WATER

☐ ATMOSPHERE
☐ RIVERS
☐ LIVING THINGS

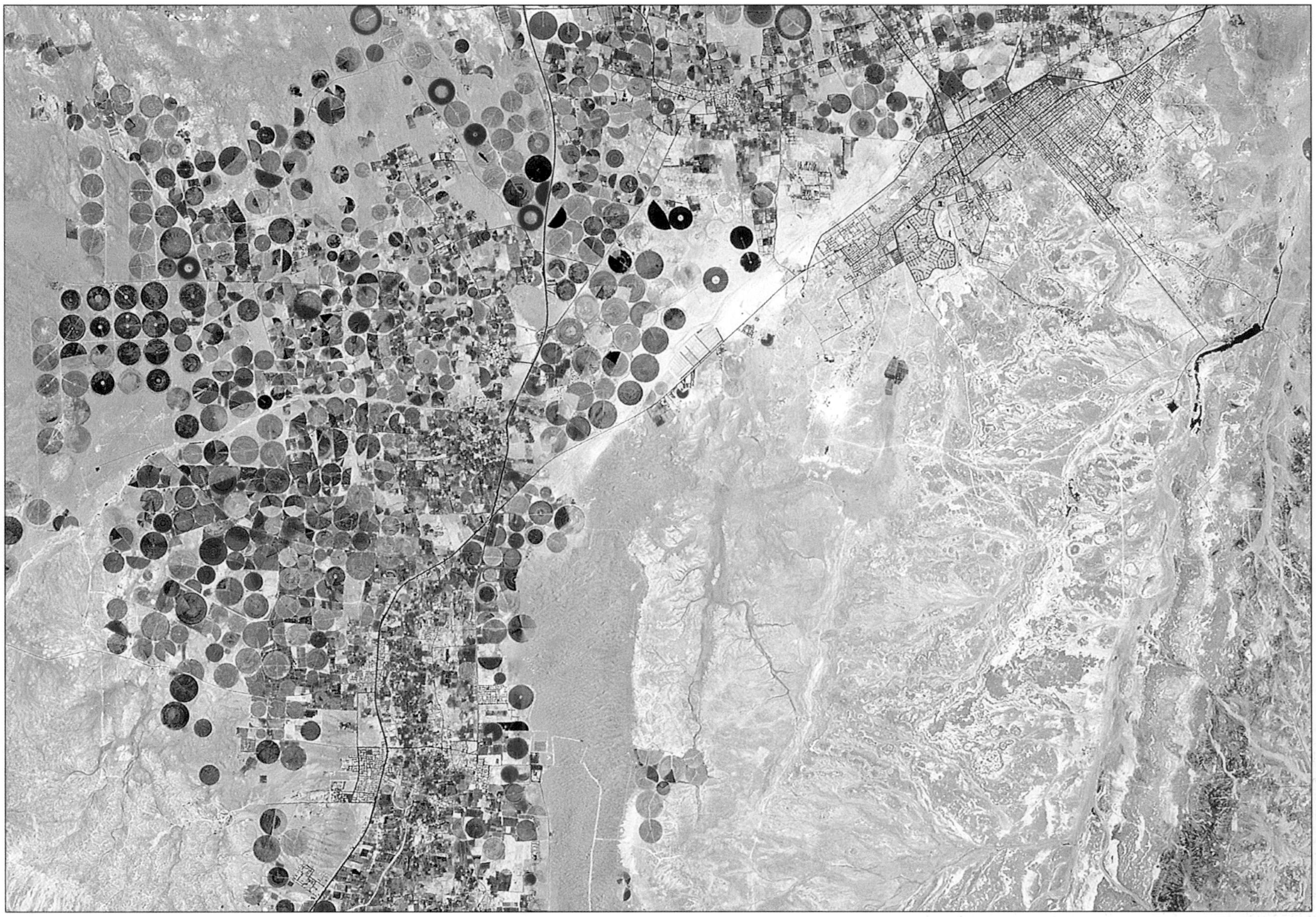

Irrigation in Saudi Arabia
Saudi Arabia is a desert country which gets its water from oases, which tap ground water supplies, and desalination plants. The sale of oil has enabled the arid countries of south-western Asia to develop their agriculture. In the above satellite image, vegetation appears brown and red.

Irrigation boom
The photograph shows a pivotal irrigation boom used to sprinkle water over a wheat field in Saudi Arabia. Irrigation in hot countries often takes place at night so that water loss through evaporation is reduced. Irrigation techniques vary from place to place. In monsoon areas with abundant water, the fields are often flooded, or the water is led to the crops along straight furrows. Sprinkler irrigation has become important since the 1940s. In other types of irrigation, the water is led through pipes which are on or under the ground. Underground pipes supply water directly to the plant roots and, as a result, water loss through evaporation is minimized.

consists of meadows and pasture. The rest of the world is unsuitable for farming, being too dry, too cold, too mountainous, or covered by dense forests. Although the demand for food increases every year, problems arise when attempts are made to increase the existing area of farmland. For example, the soils and climates of tropical forest and semi-arid regions of Africa and South America are not ideal for farming. Attempts to work such areas usually end in failure. To increase the world's food supply, scientists now concentrate on making existing farmland more productive rather than farming marginal land.

To grow crops, farmers need fertile, workable land, an equable climate, including a frost-free growing period, and an adequate supply of fresh water. In some areas, the water falls directly as rain. But many other regions depend on irrigation.

Irrigation involves water conservation through the building of dams which hold back storage reservoirs. In some areas, irrigation water comes from underground aquifers, layers of permeable and porous rocks through which ground water percolates. But in many cases, the water in the aquifers has been there for thousands of years, having accumulated at a time when the rainfall

was much greater than it is today. As a result, these aquifers are not being renewed and will, one day, dry up.

Other sources of irrigation water are desalination plants, which remove salt from seawater and pump it to farms. This is a highly expensive process and is employed in areas where water supplies are extremely low, such as the island of Malta, or in the oil-rich desert countries around the Gulf, which can afford to build huge desalination plants.

LAND USE BY CONTINENT

	Forest	Permanent pasture	Permanent crops	Arable	Non-productive
North America	32.2%	17.3%	0.3%	12.6%	37.6%
South America	51.8%	26.7%	1.5%	6.6%	13.4%
Europe	33.4%	17.5%	3.0%	26.8%	19.3%
Africa	23.2%	26.6%	0.6%	5.6%	44.0%
Asia	20.2%	25.0%	1.2%	16.0%	37.8%
Oceania	23.5%	52.2%	0.1%	5.7%	18.5%

The Natural World

In 1995, a United Nations Environment Programme report stated that 11% of all mammal species, 18% of birds and 5% of fish are now threatened with extinction. Furthermore, it predicted that half of all bird and mammal species will become extinct within 300 years, or sooner if current trends continue. This will greatly reduce the biodiversity of our planet, causing the disappearance of unique combinations of genes that could be vital in improving food yields on farms or in the production of drugs to combat diseases.

Extinctions of species have occurred throughout Earth history, but today the extinction rate is estimated to be about 10,000 times the natural average. Some scientists have even compared it with the mass extinction that wiped out the dinosaurs 65 million years ago. However, the main cause of today's high extinction rate is not some natural disaster, such as the impact of an asteroid a few kilometres across, but it is the result of human actions, most notably the destruction of natural habitats for farming and other purposes. In some densely populated areas, such as Western Europe, the natural

Rainforest in Rwanda

Rainforests are the most threatened of the world's biomes. Effective conservation policies must demonstrate to poor local people that they can benefit from the survival of the forests.

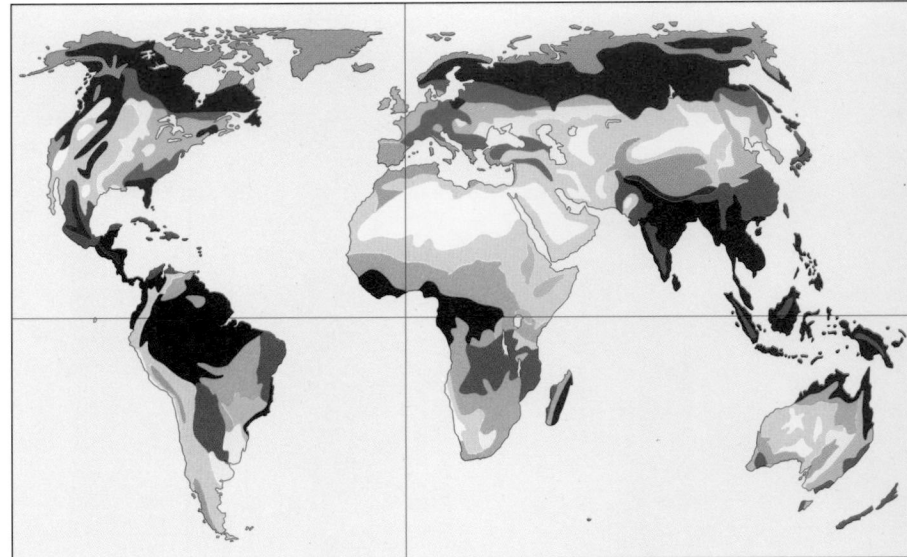

habitats were destroyed long ago. Today, the greatest damage is occurring in tropical rainforests, which contain more than half of the world's known species.

Modern technology has enabled people to live comfortably almost anywhere on Earth. But most plants and many animals are adapted to particular climatic conditions, and they live in association with and dependent on each other. Plant and animal communities that cover large areas are called biomes.

THE WORLD'S BIOMES

The world's biomes are defined mainly by climate and vegetation. They range from the tundra, in polar regions and high mountain regions, to the lush equatorial rainforests.

The Arctic tundra covers large areas in the polar regions of the northern hemisphere. Snow covers the land for more than half of the year and the subsoil, called permafrost, is permanently frozen. Comparatively few species can survive in this harsh, treeless environment. The main plants are hardy mosses, lichens, grasses, sedges and low shrubs. However, in summer, the tundra plays an important part in world animal geography, when its growing plants and swarms of insects provide food for migrating animals and birds that arrive from the south.

The tundra of the northern hemisphere merges in the south into a vast region of needleleaf evergreen forest, called the boreal forest or taiga. Such trees as fir, larch, pine and spruce are adapted to survive the long, bitterly cold winters of this region, but the number of plant and animal species is again small. South of the boreal forests is a zone of mixed needleleaf evergreens and broadleaf deciduous trees, which

NATURAL VEGETATION

- TUNDRA & MOUNTAIN VEGETATION
- NEEDLELEAF EVERGREEN FOREST
- MIXED NEEDLELEAF EVERGREEN & BROADLEAF DECIDUOUS TREES
- BROADLEAF DECIDUOUS WOODLAND
- MID-LATITUDE GRASSLAND
- EVERGREEN BROADLEAF & DECIDUOUS TREES & SHRUBS
- SEMI-DESERT SCRUB
- DESERT
- TROPICAL GRASSLAND (SAVANNA)
- TROPICAL BROADLEAF RAINFOREST & MONSOON FOREST
- SUBTROPICAL BROADLEAF & NEEDLELEAF FOREST

The map shows the world's main biomes. The classification is based on the natural 'climax' vegetation of regions a result of the climate and the terrain. But human activities have greatly modified this basic division. For example, the original deciduous forests of Western Europe and the eastern United States have largely disappeared. In recent times, human development of some semi-arid areas has turned former dry grasslands into barren desert.

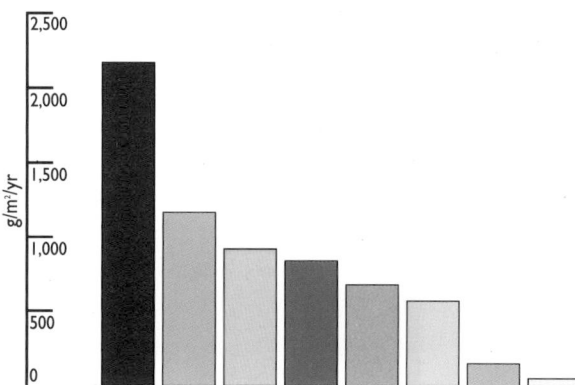

Tundra in subarctic Alaska

The Denali National Park, Alaska, contains magnificent mountain scenery and tundra vegetation which flourishes during the brief summer. The park is open between 1 June and 15 September.

shed their leaves in winter. In warmer areas, this mixed forest merges into broadleaf deciduous forest, where the number and diversity of plant species is much greater.

Deciduous forests are adapted to temperate, humid regions. Evergreen broadleaf and deciduous trees grow in Mediterranean regions, with their hot, dry summers. But much of the original deciduous forest has been cut down and has given way to scrub and heathland. Grasslands occupy large areas in the middle latitudes, where the rainfall is insufficient to support forest growth. The moister grasslands are often called prairies, while drier areas are called steppe.

The tropics also contain vast dry areas of semi-desert scrub which merges into desert, as well as large areas of savanna, which is grassland with scattered trees. Savanna regions, with their marked dry season, support a wide range of mammals.

Tropical and subtropical regions contain three types of forest biomes. The tropical rainforest, the world's richest biome measured by its plant and animal species, experiences rain and high temperatures throughout the year. Similar forests occur in monsoon regions, which have a season of very heavy rainfall. They, too, are rich in plant species, though less so than the tropical rainforest. A third type of forest is the subtropical broadleaf and needleleaf forest, found in such places as south-eastern China, south-central Africa and eastern Brazil.

NET PRIMARY PRODUCTION OF EIGHT MAJOR BIOMES

- TROPICAL RAINFORESTS
- DECIDUOUS FORESTS
- TROPICAL GRASSLANDS
- CONIFEROUS FORESTS
- MEDITERRANEAN
- TEMPERATE GRASSLANDS
- TUNDRA
- DESERTS

The net primary production of eight major biomes is expressed in grams of dry organic matter per square metre per year. The tropical rainforests produce the greatest amount of organic material. The tundra and deserts produce the least.

2,500

2,000

1,500

g/m²/yr

1,000

500

0

The Human World

Every minute, the world's population increases by between 160 and 170. While forecasts of future growth are difficult to make, most demographers are in agreement that the world's population is likely to increase from around 5.8 billion in 1997 to 10 billion by 2050, reaching a peak of around 11 billion by 2075. It is then expected to level out or even decline a little towards the year 2100. The fastest rates of increase will take place in the developing countries of Africa, Asia and Latin America – the places least able to afford the costs incurred by such a rapidly expanding population.

Average world population growth rates have declined from about 2% a year in the early 1960s to 1.3% in 1997. This was partly due to a decline in fertility rates – that is, the number of births to the number of women of child-bearing age – especially in developed countries where, as income has risen, the average size of families has fallen.

Declining fertility rates were also evident in many developing countries. Even Africa shows signs of such change, though its population is expected to triple before it begins to fall. Population growth is also dependent on death rates, which are affected by such factors as famine, disease and the quality of medical care.

THE POPULATION EXPLOSION

The world's population has grown steadily throughout most of human history, though certain events triggered periods of population growth. The invention of agriculture around 10,000 years ago, led to great changes in human society. Before then, most people had obtained food by hunting animals and gathering plants. Average life expectancies were probably no more than 20 years and life was hard. However, when farmers began to produce food surpluses, people began to live settled lives. This major milestone in human history led to the development of the first cities and the emergence of the early civilizations.

From an estimated 8 million in 8000 BC, the world population rose to about 300 million by AD 1000. Between 1000 and 1750, the rate of world population increase was around 0.1% per year, but another period of major economic and social change – the Industrial Revolution – began in the late 18th century. The Industrial Revolution led to improvements in farm technology and increases in food production. The world population began to increase quickly as industrialization spread across Europe and into North America. By 1850, it had reached 1.2 billion. The 2 billion mark was passed in the 1920s, and then the population rapidly doubled to 4 billion by the 1970s.

POPULATION FEATURES

Population growth affects the structure of societies. In developing countries with high annual rates of population increase, the large majority of the people are young and soon to become parents themselves. For example, in Kenya, which had until recently an annual rate of population growth of around 4%, just over half

Elevated view of Ki Lung Street, Hong Kong
Urban areas of Hong Kong, a Special Administrative Region on the southern coast of China, contain busy streets overlooked by crowded apartments. They reflect the early days of urbanization in China.

LARGEST CITIES

Within 10 years, for the first time ever, the majority of the world's population will live in urban areas. Almost all the urban growth will be in developing countries. Below is a list of cities with their estimated populations in the year 2015, in millions.

1	Tokyo	28.7
2	Bombay (Mumbai)	27.4
3	Lagos	24.1
4	Shanghai	23.2
5	Jakarta	21.5
6	São Paulo	21.0
7	Karachi	20.6
8	Beijing	19.6
9	Dhaka	19.2
10	Mexico City	19.1
11	Calcutta	17.6
12	Delhi	17.5
13	New York City	17.4
14	Tianjin	17.1
15	Metro Manila	14.9
16	Cairo	14.7
17	Los Angeles	14.5
18	Seoul	13.1
19	Buenos Aires	12.5
20	Istanbul	12.1

These city populations are based on figures for urban agglomerations rather than actual city limits.

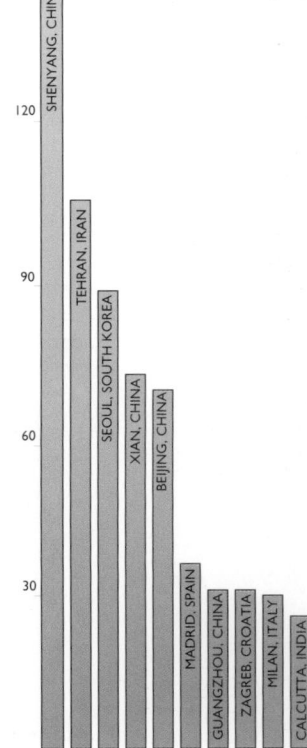

Urban air pollution
This diagram of the world's most polluted cities indicates the number of days per year when sulphur dioxide levels exceed the WHO threshhold of 150 micrograms per cubic metre.

Hong Kong's business district
By contrast with the picturesque old streets of Hong Kong, the business district of Hong Kong City, on the northern shore of Hong Kong Island, is a cluster of modern high-rise buildings. The glittering skyscrapers reflect the success of this tiny region, which has one of the strongest economies in Asia.

of the population is under 15 years of age. On the other hand, the populations of developed countries, with low population growth rates, have a fairly even spread across age groups.

Such differences are reflected in average life expectancies at birth. In rich countries, such as Australia and the United States, the average life expectancy is 77 years (74 years for men and 80 for women; women live longer, on average, than their male counterparts). As a result, an increasing proportion of the people are elderly and retired, contributing little to the economy. The reverse applies in many of the poorer countries, where average life expectancies are below 60 years. In more than a dozen countries in Africa, the average life expectancy is less than 50.

Paralleling the population explosion has been a rapid growth in the number and size of cities and towns, which contained nearly half of the world's people by the 1990s. This proportion is expected to rise to nearly two-thirds by 2025.

Urbanization occurred first in areas undergoing the industrialization of their economies, but today it is also a feature of the developing world. In developing countries, people are leaving impoverished rural areas hoping to gain access to the education, health and other services available in cities. But many cities are unable to provide the housing and other facilities necessitated by rapid population growth. As a result, slums grow up around the cities. Pollution, crime and disease become features of everyday life.

The population explosion poses another probem for the entire world. No one knows how many people the world can support or how consumer demand will damage the fragile environments on our planet. The British economist Thomas Malthus argued in the late 18th century that overpopulation would lead to famine and war. But an increase in farm technology in the 19th and 20th centuries, combined with a green revolution, in which scientists developed high-yield crop varieties, has greatly increased food production since Malthus' time.

However, some modern scientists argue that overpopulation may become a problem in the 21st century. They argue that food shortages leading to disastrous famines will result unless population growth can be halted. Such people argue in favour of birth control programmes. China, the only country with more than a billion people, has introduced a one-child family policy. Their action has slowed the growth of China's huge population, though rising living standards seem to be the most effective brakes on rapid population growth.

POPULATION CHANGE 1990–2000
The predicted population change for the years 1990–2000.

- OVER 40% POPULATION GAIN
- 30–40% POPULATION GAIN
- 20–30% POPULATION GAIN
- 10–20% POPULATION GAIN
- 0–10% POPULATION GAIN
- NO CHANGE OR LOSS

TOP 5 COUNTRIES

Kuwait	+75.0%
Namibia	+62.5%
Afghanistan	+60.1%
Mali	+55.5%
Tanzania	+54.6%

BOTTOM 5 COUNTRIES

Belgium	–0.1%
Hungary	–0.2%
Grenada	–2.4%
Germany	–3.2%
Tonga	–3.2%

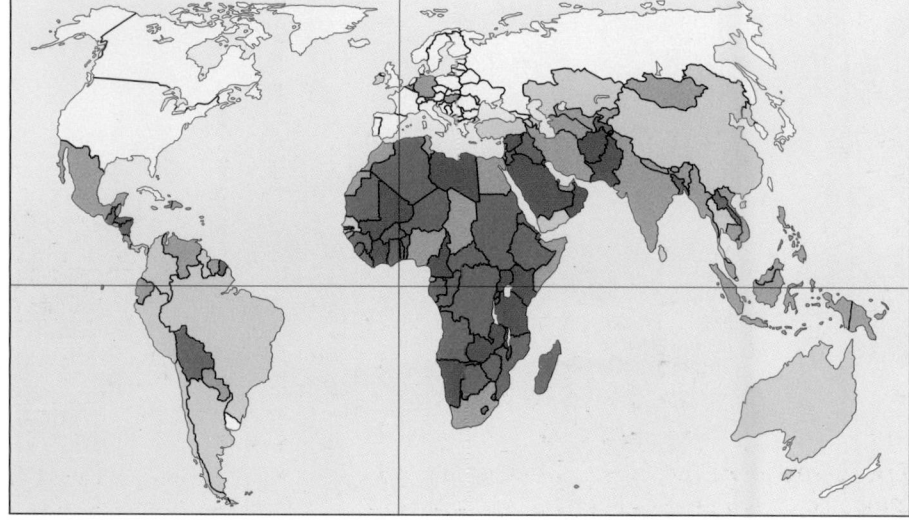

Languages and Religions

In 1995, 90-year-old Edna Guerro died in northern California. She was the last person able to speak Northern Pomo, one of about 50 Native American languages spoken in the state. Her death marked the extinction of one of the world's languages.

This event is not an isolated incident. Language experts regularly report the disappearance of languages and some of them predict that between 20 to 50% of the world's languages will no longer exist by the end of the next century. Improved transport and communications are partly to blame, because they bring people from various cultures into closer and closer contact. Many children no longer speak the language of their parents, preferring instead to learn the language used at their schools. The pressures on

children to speak dominant rather than minority languages are often great. In the first part of the 20th century, Native American children were punished if they spoke their native language.

The disappearance of a language represents the extinction of a way of thinking, a unique expression of the experiences and knowledge of a group of people. Language and religion together give people an identity and a sense of belonging. However, there are others who argue that the disappearance of minority languages is a step towards international understanding and economic efficiency.

THE WORLD'S LANGUAGES
Definitions of what is a language or a dialect vary and, hence, estimates of the number of languages spoken around the world range from about 3,000 to 6,000. But whatever the figure, it is clear that the number of languages far exceeds the number of countries.

RELIGIOUS ADHERENTS	
The number of adherents to the world's major religions, in millions.	
Christian	1,667
Roman Catholic	952
Protestant	337
Orthodox	162
Anglican	70
Other Christian	148
Muslim	881
Sunni	841
Shia	40
Hindu	663
Buddhist	312
Chinese Folk	172
Tribal	92
Jewish	18
Sikhs	17

Buddhist monks in Katmandu, Nepal
Hinduism is Nepal's official religion, but the Nepalese observe the festivals of both Hinduism and Buddhism. They also regard Buddhist shrines and Hindu temples as equally sacred.

Countries with only one language tend to be small. For example, in Liechtenstein, everyone speaks German. By contrast, more than 860 languages have been identified in Papua New Guinea, whose population is only about 4.3 million people. Hence, many of its languages are spoken by only small groups of people. In fact, scientists have estimated that about a third of the world's languages are now spoken by less than 1,000 people. By contrast, more than half of the world's population speak just seven languages.

The world's languages are grouped into families. The Indo-European family consists of languages spoken between Europe and the Indian subcontinent. The growth of European empires over the last 300 years led several Indo-European languages, most notably English, French, Portuguese and Spanish, to spread throughout much of North and South America, Africa, Australia and New Zealand.

English has become the official language in many countries which together contain more than a quarter of the world's population. It is now a major international language, surpassing in importance Mandarin Chinese, a member of the Sino-Tibetan family, which is the world's leading first language. Without a knowledge of English, businessmen face many problems when conducting international trade, especially with the United States or other English-speaking countries. But proposals that English, French, Russian or some other language should become a world language seem unlikely to be acceptable to a majority of the world's peoples.

WORLD RELIGIONS

Religion is another fundamental aspect of human culture. It has inspired much of the world's finest architecture, literature, music and painting. It has also helped to shape human cultures since prehistoric times and is responsible for the codes of ethics by which most people live.

The world's major religions were all founded in Asia. Judaism, one of the first faiths to teach that there is only one god, is one of the world's oldest. Founded in south-western Asia, it influenced the more recent Christianity and Islam, two other monotheistic religions which

The Church of San Giovanni, Dolomites, Italy
Christianity has done much to shape Western civilization. Christian churches were built as places of worship, but many of them are among the finest achievements of world architecture.

now have the greatest number of followers. Hinduism, the third leading faith in terms of the numbers of followers, originated in the Indian subcontinent and most Hindus are now found in India. Another major religion, Buddhism, was founded in the subcontinent partly as a reaction to certain aspects of Hinduism. But unlike Hinduism, it has spread from India throughout much of eastern Asia.

Religion and language are powerful creative forces. They are also essential features of nationalism, which gives people a sense of belonging and pride. But nationalism is often also a cause of rivalry and tension. Cultural differences have led to racial hatred, the persecution of minorities, and to war between national groups.

MOTHER TONGUES
Native speakers of the major languages, in millions (1990).

- MANDARIN CHINESE 834M
- ENGLISH 443M
- HINDI 352M
- SPANISH 341M
- RUSSIAN 293M
- ARABIC 197M
- BENGALI 184M
- PORTUGUESE 173M
- MALAY 142M
- JAPANESE 125M

OFFICIAL LANGUAGES: % OF WORLD POPULATION

English	27.0%
Chinese	19.0%
Hindi	13.5%
Spanish	5.4%
Russian	5.2%
French	4.2%
Arabic	3.3%
Portuguese	3.0%
Malay	3.0%
Bengali	2.9%
Japanese	2.3%

Polyglot nations
The graph, right, shows countries of the world with more than 200 languages. Although it has only about 4.3 million people, Papua New Guinea holds the record for the number of languages spoken.

Brazil (210)
Congo (Z.) (220)
Australia (230)
Mexico (240)
Cameroon (275)
India (410)
Nigeria (470)
Indonesia (701)
Papua New Guinea (862)

International Organizations

Twelve days before the surrender of Germany and four months before the final end of World War II, representatives of 50 nations met in San Francisco to create a plan to set up a peace-keeping organization, the United Nations. Since its birth on 24 October 1945, its membership has grown from 51 to 185.

Its first 50 years have been marked by failures as well as successes. While it has helped to prevent some disputes from flaring up into full-scale wars, the Blue Berets, as the UN troops are called, have been forced, because of their policy of neutrality, to stand by when atrocities are committed by rival warring groups.

THE WORK OF THE UN

The United Nations has six main organs. They include the General Assembly, where member states meet to discuss issues concerned with peace, security and development. The Security Council, containing 15 members, is concerned with maintaining world peace. The Secretariat, under the Secretary-General, helps the other organs to do their jobs effectively, while the Economic and Social Council works with specialized agencies to implement policies concerned with such matters as development, education and health. The International Court of Justice, or World Court, helps to settle disputes between member nations. The sixth organ of the UN, the Trusteeship Council, was designed to bring 11 UN trust territories to independence. Its task has now been completed.

The specialized agencies do much important

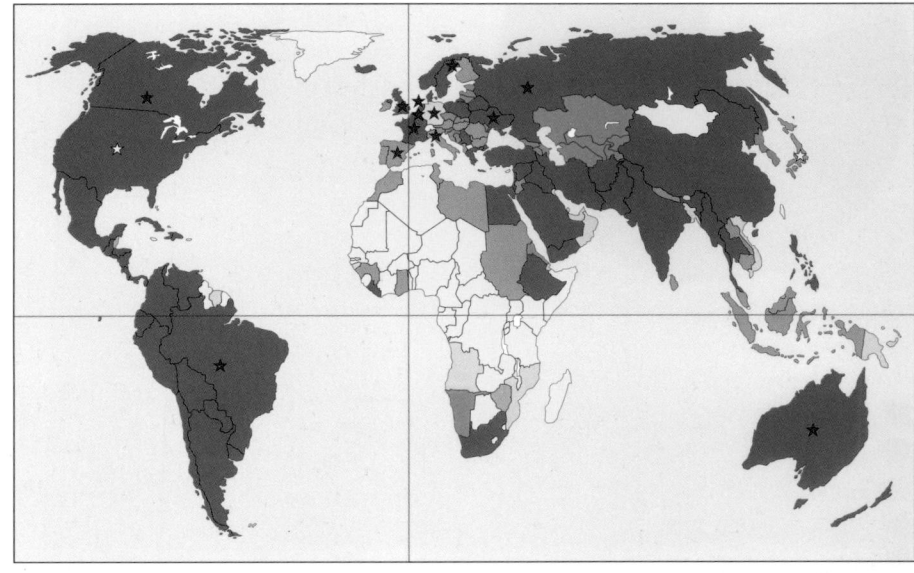

work. For example, UNICEF (United Nations International Children's Fund) has provided health care and aid for children in many parts of the world. The ILO (International Labour Organization) has improved working conditions in many areas, while the FAO (Food and Agricultural Organization) has worked to improve the production and distribution of food. Among the other agencies are organizations to help refugees, to further human rights and to control the environment. The latest agency, set up in 1995, is the WTO (World Trade Organization), which took over the work of GATT (General Agreement on Tariffs and Trade).

OTHER ORGANIZATIONS

In a world in which nations have become increasingly interdependent, many other organizations have been set up to deal with a variety of problems. Some, such as NATO (the North Atlantic Treaty Organization), are defence alliances. In the early 1990s, the end of the Cold War suggested that NATO's role might be finished, but the civil war in the former Yugoslavia showed that it still has a role in maintaining peace and security.

Other organizations encourage social and economic co-operation in various regions. Some are NGOs (non-governmental organizations), such as the Red Cross and its Muslim equivalent, the Red Crescent. Other NGOs raise funds to provide aid to countries facing major crises, such as famine.

Some major international organizations aim at economic co-operation and the removal of trade barriers. The best known of these organizations is the European Union, which has 15 members. Its

Food aid to Bosnia-Herzegovina

International organizations supply aid to people living in areas suffering from war or famine. In Bosnia-Herzegovina, the UN Protection Force supervised the movements of food aid.

MEMBERS OF THE UN
Year of joining.

■ 1940s
■ 1950s
□ 1960s
□ 1970s
■ 1980s
■ 1990s
□ NON–MEMBERS
★ 1% – 10% CONTRIBUTION TO FUNDING
☆ OVER 10% CONTRIBUTION TO FUNDING

INTERNATIONAL AID AND GNP
Aid provided as a percentage of GNP, with total aid in brackets (1995).

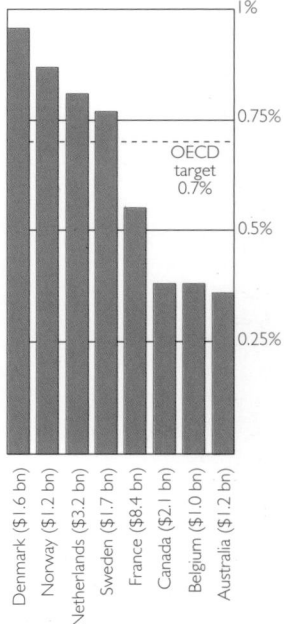

UNHCR-funded jetty, Sri Lanka
In 1994, the UN High Commission for Refugees was responsible for 23 million people. Sometimes, it has to provide transport facilities, such as this jetty, to get aid to the refugees.

economic success has led some people to support the idea of setting up a federal Europe. Others oppose such developments, they fear that a 'United States of Europe' would lead to a loss of national identity among the member states.

Other groupings include ASEAN (the Association of South-east Asian Nations) which aims at reducing trade barriers between its members (Brunei, Burma, Indonesia, Laos, Malaysia, the Philippines, Singapore, Thailand and Vietnam). APEC (the Asia-Pacific Co-operation Group)

was founded in 1989 with the aim of creating a free trade zone between the countries of eastern Asia, North America, Australia and New Zealand by 2020. Meanwhile, Canada, Mexico and the United States have formed NAFTA (the North American Free Trade Agreement), while other economic groupings link most of the countries in Latin America. Another grouping with a more limited but important objective is OPEC (the Organization of Oil-Exporting Countries). OPEC works to unify policies concerning trade in oil on the world markets.

Some organizations exist to discuss matters of common interest between groups of nations. The Commonwealth of Nations, for example, initially developed from links created by the British Empire. In North and South America, the OAS (Organization of American States) aims at increasing understanding in the Western hemisphere. The OAU (Organization of African Unity) has a similar role in Africa, while the Arab League represents the Arab nations of North Africa and the Middle East.

COUNTRIES OF THE EUROPEAN UNION

	Total land area (sq km)	Total population (1997)	GNP per capita, US$ (1995)	Unemployment rate, % (1994)	Year of accession to the EU	Seats in EU parliament (1998)
Austria	83,850	8,200,000	26,890	4.3%	1995	21
Belgium	30,510	10,225,000	24,710	9.7%	1958	25
Denmark	43,070	5,350,000	29,890	10.7%	1973	16
Finland	338,130	5,180,000	20,580	18.4%	1995	16
France	551,500	58,800,000	24,990	12.2%	1958	87
Germany	356,910	82,300,000	27,510	8.6%	1958	99
Greece	131,990	10,600,000	8,210	9.4%	1981	25
Ireland	70,280	3,625,000	14,710	15.2%	1973	15
Italy	301,270	57,750,000	19,020	11.4%	1958	87
Luxembourg	2,590	425,000	41,210	3.4%	1958	6
Netherlands	41,526	15,900,000	24,000	7.6%	1958	31
Portugal	92,390	10,100,000	9,740	6.7%	1986	25
Spain	504,780	39,300,000	13,580	24.4%	1986	64
Sweden	449,960	8,850,000	23,750	7.4%	1995	22
United Kingdom	243,368	58,600,000	18,700	9.7%	1973	87

Agriculture

In 1995, the world production of grains was lower than average – the result mainly of a wet spring in the United States, and bad weather combined with economic turmoil in the former Soviet Union. Downward trends in world food production in the 1990s reopened an old debate – whether food production will be able to keep pace with a rapidly rising world population in the 21st century.

Some experts argue that the lower than expected production figures in the 1990s herald a period of relative scarcity and high prices of food, which will be felt most in the poorer developing countries. Others are more optimistic. They point to the successes of the 'green revolution' which, through the use of new crop varieties produced by scientists, irrigation and the extensive use of fertilizers and pesticides,

Rice harvest, Bali, Indonesia
More than half of the world's people eat rice as their basic food. Rice grows well in tropical and subtropical regions, such as in Indonesia, India and south-eastern China.

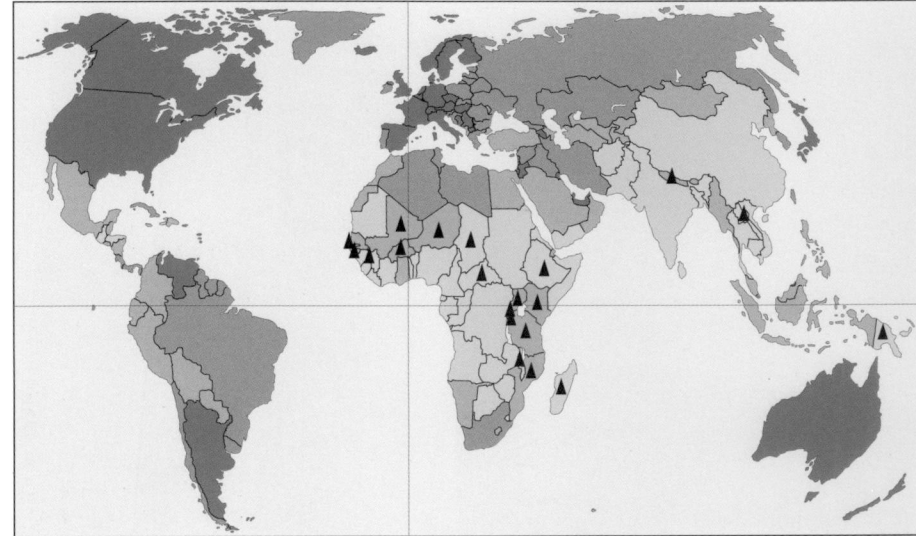

has revolutionized food production since the 1950s and 1960s.

The green revolution has led to a great expansion in the production of many crops, including such basic foods as rice, maize and wheat. In India, its effects have been spectacular. Between 1955 and 1995, grain production trebled, giving the country sufficient food reserves to prevent famine in years when droughts or floods reduce the harvest. While once India had to import food, it is now self-sufficient.

FOOD PRODUCTION

Agriculture, which supplies most of our food, together with materials to make clothes and other products, is the world's most important economic activity. But its relative importance has declined in comparison with manufacturing and service industries. As a result, the end of the 20th century marked the first time for 10,000 years when the vast majority of the people no longer had to depend for their living on growing crops and herding animals.

However, agriculture remains the dominant economic activity in many developing countries in Africa and Asia. For example, in the late 1990s, 90% or more of the people of Bhutan, Burundi, Nepal and Rwanda depended on farming for their living.

Many people in developing countries eke out the barest of livings by nomadic herding or shifting cultivation, combined with hunting, fishing and gathering plant foods. A large proportion of farmers live at subsistence level, producing little more than they require to provide the basic needs of their families.

The world's largest food producer and exporter is the United States, although agriculture employs

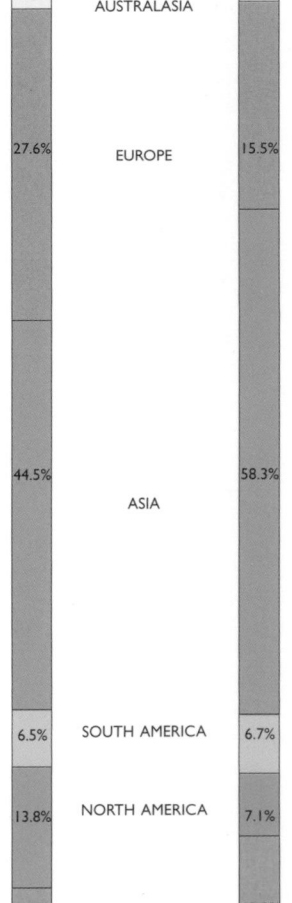

IMPORTANCE OF AGRICULTURE
Percentage of the population dependent on agriculture (1994).
- OVER 75% DEPENDENT
- 50–75% DEPENDENT
- 25–50% DEPENDENT
- 10–25% DEPENDENT
- UNDER 10% DEPENDENT
▲ Over 75% of the total workforce employed in agriculture, forestry and fishing in 1995

A comparison of world food production and population by continent.

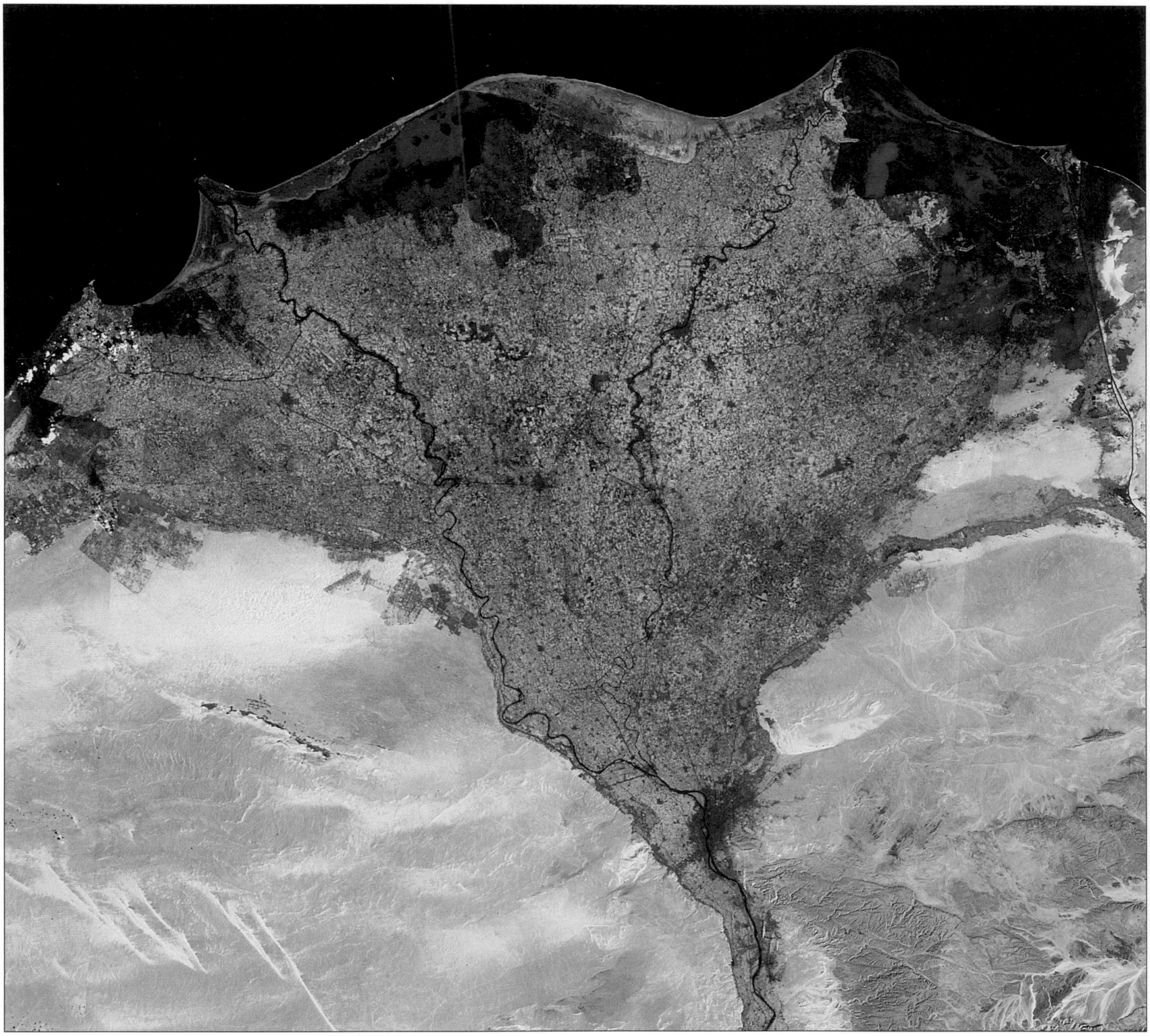

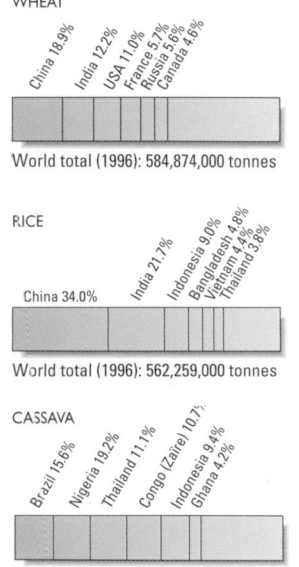

Landsat image of the Nile delta, Egypt
Most Egyptians live in the Nile valley and on its delta. Because much of the silt carried by the Nile now ends up on the floor of Lake Nasser, upstream of the Aswan Dam, the delta is now retreating and seawater is seeping inland. This eventuality was not foreseen when the Aswan High Dam was built in the 1960s.

WHEAT

China 18.9% India 12.2% USA 11.0% France 5.7% Russia 5.6% Canada 4.6%

World total (1996): 584,874,000 tonnes

RICE

China 34.0% India 21.7% Indonesia 9.0% Bangladesh 4.8% Vietnam 4.1% Thailand 3.6%

World total (1996): 562,259,000 tonnes

CASSAVA

Brazil 15.6% Nigeria 19.2% Thailand 11.1% Congo (Zaire) 10.7% Indonesia 9.4% Ghana 4.2%

World total (1996): 162,942,000 tonnes

less than 3% of its total workforce. The high production of the United States is explained by its use of scientific methods and mechanization, which are features of agriculture throughout the developed world.

INTENSIVE OR ORGANIC FARMING
By the late 20th century, some people were beginning to question the dependence of farmers on chemical fertilizers and pesticides. Many people became concerned that the widespread use of chemicals was seriously polluting and damaging the environment.

Others objected to the intensive farming of animals to raise production and lower prices. For example, the suggestion in Britain in 1996 that BSE, or 'mad cow disease', might be passed on to people causing CJD (Creuzfeldt-Jakob Disease) caused widespread alarm.

Such problems have led some farmers to return to organic farming, which is based on animal-welfare principles and the banning of chemical fertilizers and pesticides. The costs of organic foods are certainly higher than those produced by intensive farming, but an increasing number of consumers in the Western world are beginning to demand organic products from their retailers.

Energy and Minerals

In March 1996, floods in Ukraine carried radioactive waste dumped near Chernobyl hundreds of kilometres downstream. This was the latest chapter in the disaster caused by the explosion at the Chernobyl nuclear power station in 1986, the worst nuclear accident in history. Nuclear power now provides about 17% of the world's electricity and experts once thought that it would eventually supply much of the world's energy supply. But concern about safety and worries about the high costs involved make this seem unlikely. Several developed countries have already abandoned their nuclear programmes.

FOSSIL FUELS

Huge amounts of energy are needed for heating, generating electricity and for transport. In the early years of the Industrial Revolution, coal

Wind farms in California, United States
Wind farms using giant turbines can produce electricity at a lower cost than conventional power stations. But in many areas, winds are too light or too strong for wind farms to be effective.

formed from organic matter buried beneath the Earth's surface, was the leading source of energy. It remains important as a raw material in the manufacture of drugs and other products and also as a fuel, despite the fact that burning coal causes air pollution and gives off carbon dioxide, an important greenhouse gas.

However, oil and natural gas, which came into wide use in the 20th century, are cheaper to produce and easier to handle than coal, while, kilogram for kilogram, they give out more heat. Oil is especially important in moving transport, supplying about 97% of the fuel required.

In 1995, proven reserves of oil were sufficient to supply the world, at current rates of production, for 43 years, while supplies of natural gas stood at about 66 years. Coal reserves are more abundant and known reserves would last 200 years at present rates of use. Although these figures must be regarded with caution, because they do not allow for future discoveries, it is clear that fossil fuel reserves will one day run out.

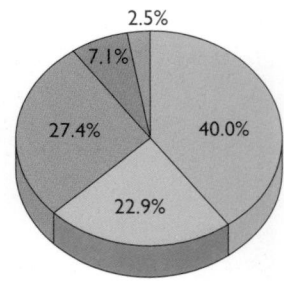

2.5%
7.1%
27.4%
40.0%
22.9%

WORLD ENERGY CONSUMPTION

- OIL
- GAS
- COAL
- NUCLEAR
- HYDRO

The diagram shows the proportion of world energy consumption in 1993 by type. Total energy consumption was 7,804 million tonnes of oil equivalent. Such fuels as wood, peat and animal wastes, together with renewable forms of energy, such as wind and geothermal power, are not included, although they are important in some areas.

SELECTED MINERAL PRODUCTION STATISTICS (1995)

Bauxite		Diamonds	
Australia	38%	Australia	38%
Guinea	13%	Congo (Zaïre)	18%
Jamaica	10%	Botswana	16%
Brazil	9%	Russia	12%
China	6%	South Africa	8%

Gold		Iron ore	
South Africa	23%	China	15%
USA	14%	Brazil	12%
Australia	11%	Australia	9%
Canada	7%	Russia	4%
Russia	6%	India	4%

Potash		Zinc	
Canada	37%	China	12%
Germany	13%	Canada	8%
Belarus	11%	Japan	8%
Russia	11%	USA	7%
USA	6%	Germany	5%

MINERAL DISTRIBUTION

Location of the principal mines and deposits.

IRON & FERRO-ALLOYS
- ● IRON
- ◖ CHROME
- ▲ MANGANESE
- ■ NICKEL

PRECIOUS METALS
- ▽ GOLD
- ◠ SILVER

PRECIOUS STONES
- ◆ DIAMONDS

LIGHT METALS
- ● BAUXITE

BASE METALS
- ■ COPPER
- ▲ LEAD
- ▽ MERCURY
- ▽ TIN
- ◆ ZINC

Potash mines in Utah, United States

Potash is a mineral used mainly to make fertilizers. Much of it comes from mines where deposits formed when ancient seas dried up are exploited. Potash is also extracted from salt lakes.

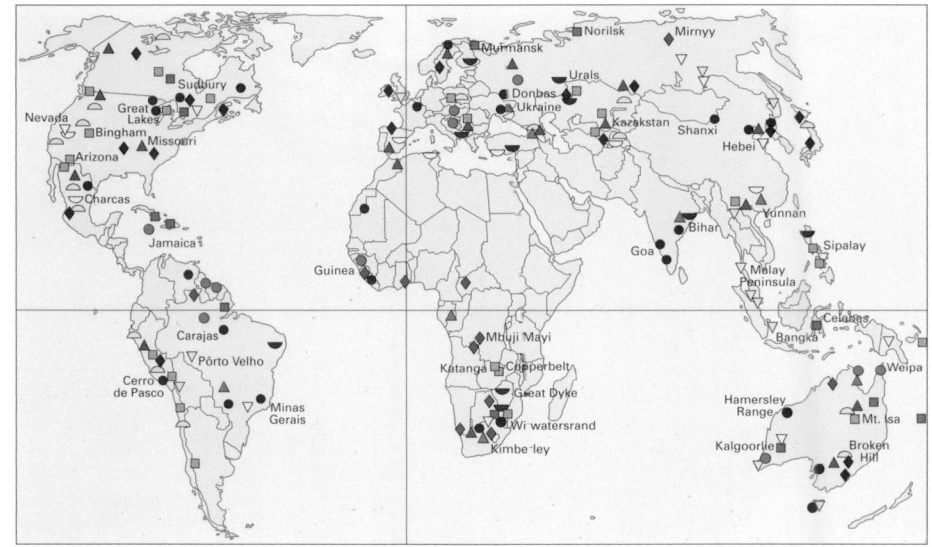

ALTERNATIVE ENERGY

Other sources of energy are therefore required. Besides nuclear energy, the main alternative to fossil fuels is water power. The costs of building dams and hydroelectric power stations is high, though hydroelectric production is comparatively cheap and it does not cause pollution. But the creation of reservoirs uproots people and, in tropical rainforests, it destroys natural habitats. Hydroelectricity is also suitable only in areas with plenty of rivers and steep slopes, such as Norway, while it is unsuitable in flat areas, such as the Netherlands.

In Brazil, alcohol made from sugar has been used to fuel cars. Initially, this government-backed policy met with great success, but it has proved to be extremely expensive. Battery-run, electric cars have also been developed in the United States, but they appear to have limited use, because of the problems involved in regular and time-consuming recharging.

Other forms of energy, which are renewable and cleaner than fossil fuels, are winds, sea waves, the rise and fall of tides, and geothermal power. These forms of energy are already used to some extent. However, their contribution in global terms seems likely to remain small in the immediate future.

MINERALS FOR INDUSTRY

In addition to energy, manufacturing industries need raw materials, including minerals, and these natural resources, like fossil fuels, are being used in such huge quantities that some experts have predicted shortages of some of them before long.

Manufacturers depend on supplies of about 80 minerals. Some, such as bauxite (aluminium ore) and iron, are abundant, but others are scarce or are found only in deposits that are uneconomical to mine. Many experts advocate a policy of recycling scrap metal, including aluminium, chromium, copper, lead, nickel and zinc. This practice would reduce pollution and conserve the energy required for extracting and refining mineral ores.

World Economies

In 1995, Tanzania had a per capita GNP (Gross National Product) of US$120, as compared with Switzerland, whose per capita GNP stood at $40,630. These figures indicate the vast gap between the economies and standards of living of the two countries.

The GNP includes the GDP (Gross Domestic Product), which consists of the total output of goods and services in a country in a given year, plus net exports – that is, the value of goods and services sold abroad less the value of foreign goods and services used in the country in the same year. The GNP divided by the population gives a country's GNP per capita. In low-income developing countries, agriculture makes a high contribution to the GNP. For example, in Tanzania, 56% of the GDP in 1995 came from

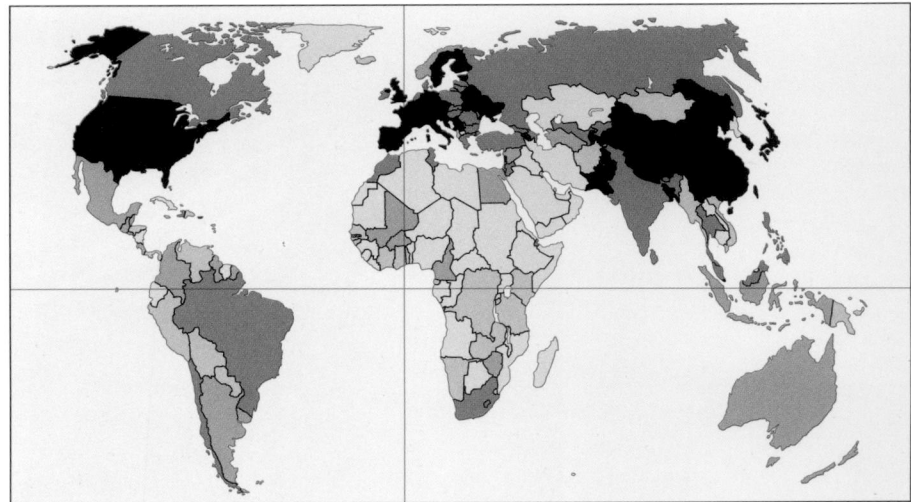

Microchip production, Taiwan

Despite its lack of resources, Taiwan is one of eastern Asia's 'tiger' economies. Its high-tech industies have helped it to achieve fast economic growth and to compete on the world market.

agriculture. On the other hand, manufacturing was small-scale and contributed only 5% of the GDP. By comparison, in high-income economies, the percentage contribution of manufacturing far exceeds that of agriculture.

INDUSTRIALIZATION

The Industrial Revolution began in Britain in the late 18th century. Before that time, most people worked on farms. But with the Industrial Revolution came factories, using machines that could manufacture goods much faster and more cheaply than those made by cottage industries which already existed.

The Industrial Revolution soon spread to several countries in mainland Europe and the United States and, by the late 19th century, it had reached Canada, Japan and Russia. At first, industrial development was based on such areas as coalfields or ironfields. But in the 20th century, the use of oil, which is easy to transport along pipelines, made it possible for industries to be set up anywhere.

Some nations, such as Switzerland, became industrialized even though they lacked natural resources. They depended instead on the specialized skills of their workers. This same pattern applies today. Some countries with rich natural resources, such as Mexico (with a per capita GNP in 1995 of $3,320), lag far behind Japan ($39,640) and South Korea ($9,700), which lack resources and have to import many of the materials they need for their manufacturing industries.

SERVICE INDUSTRIES

Experts often refer to high-income countries as industrial economies. But manufacturing employs only one in six workers in the United

INDUSTRY AND TRADE

Manufactured goods (including machinery and transport) as a percentage of total exports.

■	OVER 75%
■	50–75%
■	25–50%
■	10–25%
□	UNDER 10%

Eastern Asia, including Japan (98.3%), Taiwan (92.7%) and Hong Kong (93.0%), contains countries whose exports are most dominated by manufactures. But some countries in Europe, such as Slovenia (92.5%), are also heavily dependent on manufacturing.

GROSS NATIONAL PRODUCT PER CAPITA US$ (1995)

1	Luxembourg	41,210
2	Switzerland	40,630
3	Japan	39,640
4	Norway	31,250
5	Denmark	29,890
6	Germany	27,510
7	USA	26,980
8	Austria	26,890
9	Singapore	26,730
10	France	24,990
11	Iceland	24,950
12	Belgium	24,710
13	Netherlands	24,000
14	Sweden	23,750
15	Hong Kong	22,990
16	Finland	20,580
17	Canada	19,380
18	Italy	19,020
19	Australia	18,720
20	UK	18,700

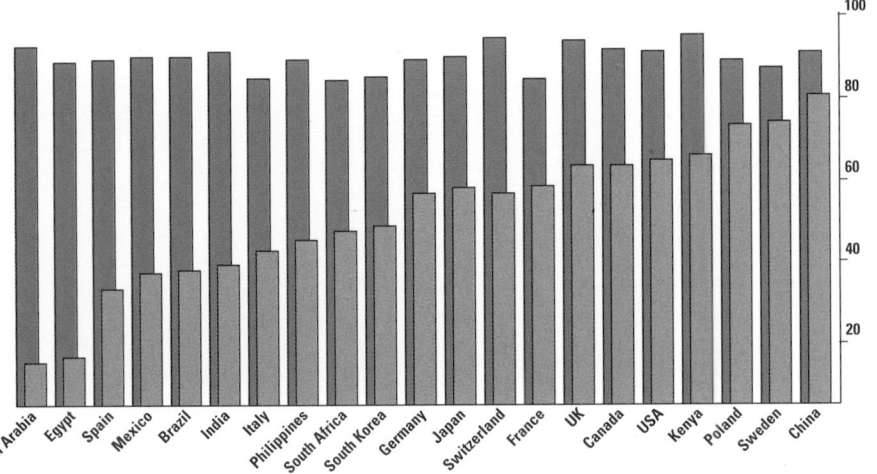

New cars awaiting transportation, Los Angeles, United States
Cars are the most important single manufactured item in world trade, followed by vehicle parts and engines. The world's leading car producers are Japan, the United States, Germany and France.

States, one in five in Britain, and one in three in Germany and Japan.

In most developed economies, the percentage of manufacturing jobs has fallen in recent years, while jobs in service industries have risen. For example, in Britain, the proportion of jobs in manufacturing fell from 37% in 1970 to 21% in 1995, while jobs in the service sector rose from just under 50% to 66%. While change in Britain was especially rapid, similar changes were taking place in most industrial economies. By 1995, service industries accounted for well over half the jobs in the generally prosperous countries that made up the OECD (Organization for Economic Co-operation and Development). Instead of being called the 'industrial' economies, these countries might be better named the 'service' economies.

Service industries offer a wide range of jobs and many of them require high educational qualifications. These include finance, insurance and high-tech industries, such as computer programming, entertainment and telecommunications. Service industries also include marketing and advertising, which are essential if the cars and television sets made by manufacturers are to be sold. Another valuable service industry is tourism; in some countries, such as the Gambia, it is the major foreign exchange earner. Trade in services now plays an important part in world economics. The share of services in world trade rose from 17% in 1980 to 22% in 1992.

THE WORKFORCE
Percentage of men and women between 15 and 64 years old in employment, selected countries (latest available year).

■ MEN
■ WOMEN

Trade and Commerce

The establishment of the WTO (World Trade Organization) on 1 January 1995 was the latest step in the long history of world trade. The WTO was set up by the eighth round of negotiations, popularly called the 'Uruguay round', conducted by the General Agreement on Tariffs and Trade (GATT). This treaty was signed by representatives of 125 governments in April 1994 after many difficulties.

GATT was first established in 1948. Its initial aim was to produce a charter to create a body called the International Trade Organization. This body never came into being. Instead, GATT, acting as an *ad hoc* agency, pioneered a series of agreements aimed at liberalizing world trade by reducing tariffs on imports and other obstacles to free trade.

GATT's objectives were based on the belief that international trade creates wealth. Trade occurs because the world's resources are not distributed evenly between countries, and, in theory, free trade means that every country should concentrate on what it can do best and purchase from others goods and services that they can supply more cheaply. In practice, however, free trade may cause unemployment when imported goods are cheaper than those produced within the country.

Trade is sometimes an important factor in world politics, especially when trade sanctions are applied against countries whose actions incur the disapproval of the international community. For example, in the 1990s, worldwide trade sanctions were imposed on Serbia because of its involvement in the civil war in Bosnia-Herzegovina.

CHANGING TRADE PATTERNS

The early 16th century, when Europeans began to divide the world into huge empires, opened up a new era in international trade. By the 19th century, the colonial powers, who were among the first industrial powers, promoted trade with their colonies, from which they obtained unprocessed raw materials, such as food, natural fibres, minerals and timber. In return, they shipped clothes, shoes and other cheap items to the colonies.

From the late 19th century until the early 1950s, primary products dominated world trade, with oil becoming the leading item in the later part of this period. Many developing countries still depend heavily on the export of one or two primary products, such as coffee or iron ore, but overall the proportion of primary products in world trade has fallen since the 1950s. Today the most important elements in world trade are

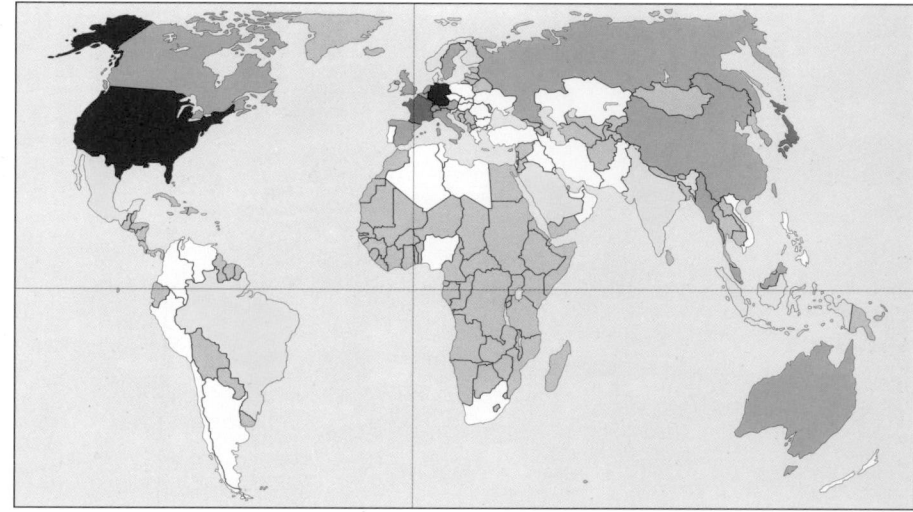

New York City Stock Exchange, United States

Stock exchanges, where stocks and shares are sold and bought, are important in channelling savings and investments to companies and governments. The world's largest stock exchange is in Tokyo, Japan.

WORLD TRADE

Percentage share of total world exports by value (1995).

- OVER 10% OF WORLD TRADE
- 5–10% OF WORLD TRADE
- 1–5% OF WORLD TRADE
- 0.5–1% OF WORLD TRADE
- 0.1–0.5% OF WORLD TRADE
- UNDER 0.1% OF WORLD TRADE

The world's leading trading nations, according to the combined value of their exports and imports, are the United States, Germany, Japan, France and the United Kingdom.

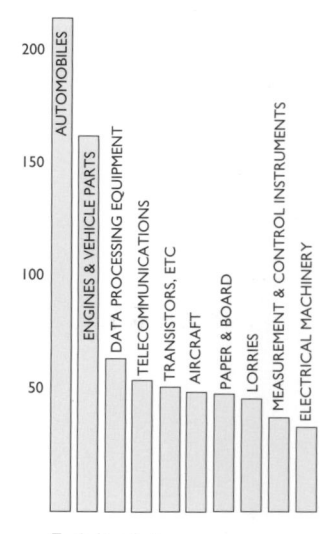

Traded products

Top ten manufactures traded by value in billions of US$ (latest available year).

Rotterdam, Netherlands
World trade depends on transport. Rotterdam, the world's largest port, serves not only the Netherlands, but also industrial areas in parts of Germany, France and Switzerland.

DEPENDENCE ON TRADE

Value of exports as a percentage of GNP (1995).

- OVER 50% GNP FROM EXPORTS
- 40–50% GNP FROM EXPORTS
- 30–40% GNP FROM EXPORTS
- 20–30% GNP FROM EXPORTS
- 10–20% GNP FROM EXPORTS
- UNDER 10% GNP FROM EXPORTS
- MOST DEPENDENT ON INDUSTRIAL EXPORTS (OVER 75% OF TOTAL)
- MOST DEPENDENT ON FUEL EXPORTS (OVER 75% OF TOTAL)
- MOST DEPENDENT ON METAL & MINERAL EXPORTS (OVER 75% OF TOTAL)

manufactures and semi-manufactures, exchanged mainly between the industrialized nations.

THE WORLD'S MARKETS

Private companies conduct most of world trade, but government policies affect it. Governments which believe that certain industries are strategic, or essential for the country's future, may impose tariffs on imports, or import quotas to limit the volume of imports, if they are thought to be undercutting the domestic industries.

For example, the United States has argued that Japan has greater access to its markets than the United States has to Japan's. This might have led the United States to resort to protectionism, but instead the United States remains committed to free trade.

Other problems in international trade occur when governments give subsidies to its producers, who can then export products at low prices. Another difficulty, called 'dumping', occurs when products are sold at below the market price in order to gain a market share. One of the aims of the newly-created WTO is the phasing out of government subsidies for agricultural products, though the world's poorest countries will be exempt from many of the WTO's most severe regulations.

Governments are also concerned about the volume of imports and exports and most countries keep records of international transactions. When the total value of goods and services imported exceeds the value of goods and services exported, then the country has a deficit in its balance of payments. Large deficits can weaken a country's economy.

Travel and Communications

In the 1990s, millions of people became linked into an 'information superhighway' called the Internet. Equipped with a personal computer, an electricity supply, a telephone and a modem, people are able to communicate with others all over the world. People can now send messages by e-mail (electronic mail), they can engage in electronic discussions, contacting people with similar interests, and engage in 'chat lines', which are the latest equivalent of telephone conferences.

These new developments are likely to affect the working lives of people everywhere, enabling them to work at home whilst having many of the facilities that are available in an office. The Internet is part of an ongoing and astonishingly rapid evolution in the fields of communications and transport.

TRANSPORT

Around 200 years ago, most people never travelled far from their birthplace, but today we are much more mobile. Cars and buses now provide convenient forms of transport for many millions of people, huge ships transport massive cargoes around the world, and jet airliners, some travelling faster than the speed of sound, can transport high-value goods as well as holiday-makers to almost any part of the world.

Land transport of freight has developed greatly

Jodrell Bank Observatory, Cheshire, England
The world's first giant radio telescope began operations at Jodrell Bank in 1957. Radio telescopes can explore the Universe as far as 16 billion light-years away.

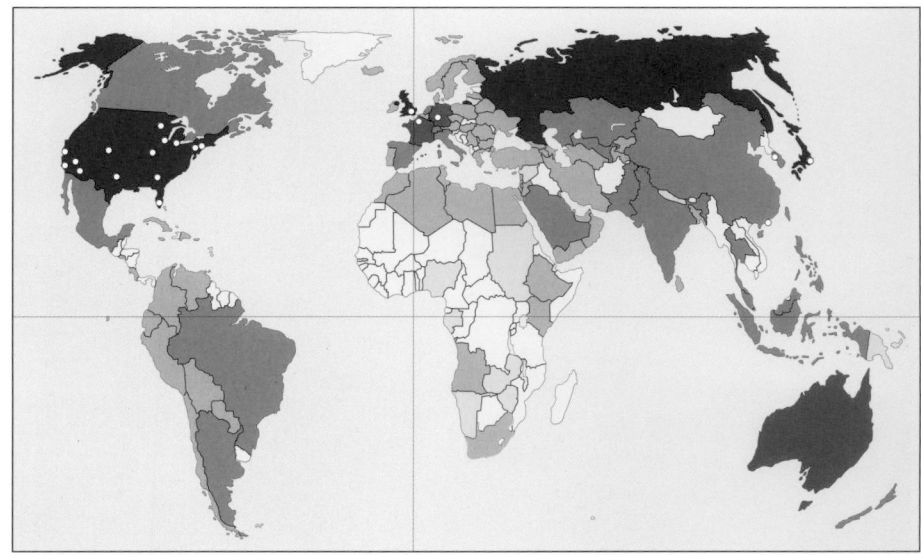

since the start of the Industrial Revolution. Canals, which became important in the 18th century, could not compete with rail transport in the 19th century. Rail transport remains important, but, in the 20th century, it has suffered from competition with road transport (especially in the United Kingdom), which is cheaper and has the advantage of carrying materials and goods from door to door.

Road transport causes pollution and the burning of fuels creates greenhouse gases that contribute to global warming. Yet privately owned cars are now the leading form of passenger traffic in developed nations, especially for journeys of less than about 400 km [250 miles]. Car owners do not have to suffer the inconvenience of waiting for public transport, such as buses, though they often have to endure traffic jams at peak travel times.

Ocean passenger traffic is now modest, but ships carry the bulk of international trade. Huge oil tankers and bulk grain carriers now ply the oceans with their cargoes, while container ships

AIR TRAVEL – PASSENGER KILOMETRES* FLOWN *(1994)*.

- OVER 100,000 MILLION
- 50,000–100,000 MILLION
- 10,000–50,000 MILLION
- 1,000–10,000 MILLION
- 500–1,000 MILLION
- UNDER 500 MILLION

o MAJOR AIRPORTS (HANDLING OVER 25 MILLION PASSENGERS IN 1995)

* Passenger kilometres are the number of passengers (both international and domestic) multiplied by the distance flown by each passenger from the airport of origin.

SELECTED NEWSPAPER CIRCULATION FIGURES (1995)

France			**Russia**	
Le Monde	357,362		*Pravda*	1,373,795
Le Figaro	350,000		*Ivestia*	700,000
Germany			**Spain**	
Bild	4,500,000		*El Pais*	407,629
Süddeutsche Zeitung	402,866			
			United Kingdom	
Italy			*The Sun*	4,061,253
Corriera Della Sella	676,904		*Daily Mirror*	2,525,000
La Republica	655,321		*Daily Express*	1,270,642
La Stampa	436,047		*The Times*	672,802
			The Guardian	402,214
Japan				
Yomiuri Shimbun	(a.m. edition)	9,800,000	**United States**	
	(p.m. edition)	4,400,000	*New York Times*	1,724,705
Manichi Shimbun	(a.m. edition)	3,200,000	*Chicago Tribune*	1,110,552
	(p.m. edition)	1,900,000	*Houston Chronicle*	605,343

Kansai International Airport, Japan
The new airport, opened in September 1994, is built on an artificial island in Osaka Bay. The island holds the world's biggest airport terminal at nearly 2 km [1.2 miles] long.

carry mixed cargoes. Containers are boxes built to international standards that contain cargo. Containers are easy to handle, and so they reduce shipping costs, speed up deliveries and cut losses caused by breakages. Most large ports now have the facilities to handle containers.

Air transport is suitable for carrying goods that are expensive, light and compact, or perishable. However, because of the high costs of air freight, it is most suitable for carrying passengers along long-distance routes around the world. Through air travel, international tourism, with people sometimes flying considerable distances, has become a major and rapidly expanding industry.

COMMUNICATIONS

After humans first began to communicate by using the spoken word, the next great stage in the development of communications was the invention of writing around 5,500 years ago.

The invention of movable type in the mid 15th century led to the mass production of books and, in the early 17th century, the first newspapers. Newspapers now play an important part in the mass communication of information, although today radio and, even more important, television have led to a decline in the circulation of newspapers in many parts of the world.

The most recent developments have occurred in the field of electronics. Artificial communications satellites now circle the planet, relaying radio, television, telegraph and telephone signals. This enables people to watch events on the far side of the globe as they are happening. Electronic equipment is also used in many other ways, such as in navigation systems used in air, sea and space, and also in modern weaponry, as shown vividly in the television coverage of the 1991 Gulf War.

THE AGE OF COMPUTERS

One of the most remarkable applications of electronics is in the field of computers. Computers are now making a huge contribution to communications. They are able to process data at incredibly high speeds and can store vast quantities of information. For example, the work of weather forecasters has been greatly improved now that computers can process the enormous amount of data required for a single weather forecast. They also have many other applications in such fields as business, government, science and medicine.

Through the Internet, computers provide a free interchange of news and views around the world. But the dangers of misuse, such as the exchange of pornographic images, have led to calls for censorship. Censorship, however, is a blunt weapon, which can be used by authoritarian governments to suppress the free exchange of information that the new information super-highway makes possible.

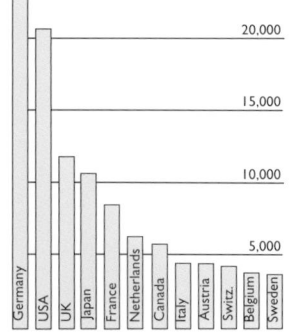

Spending on tourism
Countries spending the most on overseas tourism, US$ million (latest available year).

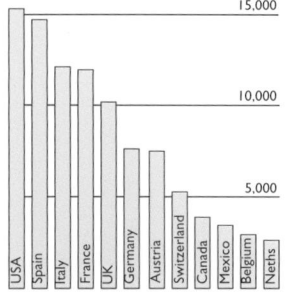

Receipts from tourism
Countries receiving the most from overseas tourism, US$ million (latest available year).

The World Today

The early years of the 20th century witnessed the exploration of Antarctica, the last uncharted continent. Today, less than 100 years later, tourists are able to take cruises to the icy southern continent, while almost no part of the globe is inaccessible to the determined traveller. Improved transport and images from space have made our world seem smaller.

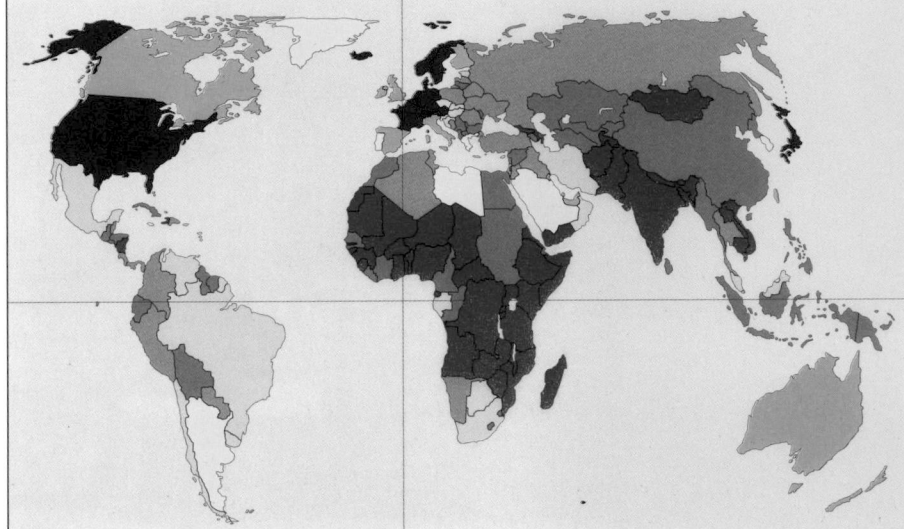

A DIVIDED WORLD

Between the end of World War II in 1945 and the late 1980s, the world was divided, politically and economically, into three main groups: the developed countries or Western democracies, with their free enterprise or mixed economies; the centrally planned or Communist countries; and the developing countries or Third World.

This division became obsolete when the former Soviet Union and its old European allies, together with the 'special economic zones' in eastern China, began the transition from centrally planned to free enterprise economies. This left the world divided into two broad camps: the prosperous developed countries and the poorer developing countries. The simplest way of distinguishing between the groups is with reference to their per capita Gross National Products (per capita GNPs).

The World Bank divides the developing countries into three main groups. At the bottom are the low-income economies, which include China, India and most of sub-Saharan Africa. This group contains about 56% of the world's population but

its average per capita GNP in 1994 was only US$390. The other two groups are the lower-middle-income economies with an average GNP per capita of $1,650, and the upper-middle-income economies, with an average GNP per capita of $4,640. By contrast, the high-income economies, also called the developed countries, contain less than 15% of the world's population but have the high (and rising) average GNP per capita of $24,170.

ECONOMIC AND SOCIAL CONTRASTS

Economic differences are coupled with other factors, such as rates of population growth. For example, in 1980–93, the low-income economies had a high rate of population growth of 2% per year, while the populations of the middle-income economies were increasing by 1.7%. By contrast, the populations of countries in the high-income category were increasing by only 0.6%.

Stark contrasts exist worldwide in the quality

GROSS NATIONAL PRODUCT PER CAPITA

The value of total production divided by the population (1995).

- OVER 400% OF WORLD AVERAGE
- 200–400% OF WORLD AVERAGE
- 100–200% OF WORLD AVERAGE

[WORLD AVERAGE WEALTH PER PERSON US$5,714]

- 50–100% OF WORLD AVERAGE
- 25–50% OF WORLD AVERAGE
- 10–25% OF WORLD AVERAGE
- UNDER 10% OF WORLD AVERAGE

RICHEST COUNTRIES

Luxembourg	$41,210
Switzerland	$40,630
Japan	$39,640
Norway	$31,250

POOREST COUNTRIES

Mozambique	$80
Ethiopia	$100
Congo (Zaïre)	$120
Tanzania	$120

Porters carrying luggage for tourists, Selous Park, Tanzania

Improved and cheaper transport has led to a boom in tourism in many developing countries. Tourism provides jobs and foreign exchange, though it can undermine local cultures.

![Birth control poster, China]

Birth control poster, China
China is the only country with more than a billion people. Central to its economic development policies is population control. Posters exhort the advantages of one-child families.

of life. Generally, the people in Western Europe and North America are better fed, healthier and have more cars and better homes than the people in low- and middle-income economies.

The average life expectancy at birth in low-income economies in 1993 was 62 years, 15 years less than in the high-income economies. Illiteracy in countries in the low-income category is high, at 42% in 1992, while for women, who get fewer opportunities, the percentage of those who could not read and write stood at 54%. By contrast, illiteracy is relatively rare in the high-income economies.

FUTURE DEVELOPMENT

In the last 50 years, despite all the aid supplied to developing countries, much of the world still suffers from poverty and economic backwardness. Some countries are even poorer now than they were a generation ago while others have become substantially richer.

The most remarkable success has been achieved in eastern Asia. Japan and the 'tiger economies' of Hong Kong, Indonesia, Malaysia, Singapore, South Korea, Thailand and Taiwan had an average annual economic growth rate of 5.5% between 1965 and 1993, while their share in the exports of manufactured goods more than doubled in the same period. In 1997, however,

an Asian market crash temporarily halted this dramatic economic expansion.

Reasons advanced to explain the success of the eastern Asian countries include low wage scales, strong family structures, low state expenditure on welfare and large investment in education for both sexes. Some of the arguments are contradictory. For example, while some argue that the success of Hong Kong is due to free enterprise, the governments of Japan and South Korea have intervened substantially in the development of their economies.

Eastern Asia's economic growth has been exceptional and probably cannot be regarded as a model for the developing world. But several factors suggest that poor countries may find progress easier in the 21st century. For example, technology is now more readily transferable between countries, while improved transport and communications make it easier for countries to take part in the world economy. But industrial development and rising living standards could lead to an increase in global pollution. Hence, any strategy for global economic expansion must also take account of environmental factors.

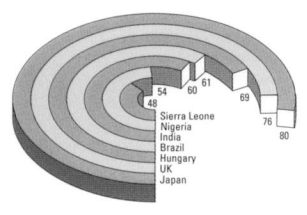

Years of life expectancy at birth, selected countries (1997).
The chart shows the contrasting range of average life expectancies at birth for a range of countries, including both low-income and high-income economies. Generally, improved health services are raising life expectancies. On average, women live longer than men, even in the poorer developing countries.

Glossary

Abyss The lowest part of the oceans, at the foot of the continental slope, which forms the true edge of the continents.

Apparent magnitude The magnitude of a star as seen from Earth; it depends on the absolute magnitude (the apparent magnitude if the star was observed from a standard distance of 32.6 light-years) and the distance of the star from the Earth.

Aquifer A layer of rock which contains water and allows water to percolate through it. It may be porous, as in sandstone, or fissured, as in limestone.

Atmosphere The layer of air which surrounds the Earth, which includes gases, such as nitrogen and oxygen, and water vapour.

Biome A major type of plant and animal community, such as tundra, taiga (boreal forest) or tropical rainforest.

Comet A body in the Solar System consisting of a nucleus and a tail. It is composed of ice particles, gases and dust.

Declination How far north or south a star is above the Celestial Equator, an imaginary line in the sky directly above the Equator. It is measured in degrees.

Delta An area of land at the mouths of some rivers which is made up of sediment deposited there by the river. It gets its name from the triangular Greek letter delta (Δ), though some deltas are not triangular.

Demographers People who study human populations, such as their numbers and distribution.

Developed country A country with a balanced economy, including a major manufacturing sector.

Developing country A poor country in which agriculture (often at subsistence level) is usually the mainstay of the economy.

Element A basic chemical substance which cannot be broken down into other substances by chemical means.

Equinox Two days during the year when the Sun is overhead at the Equator and everywhere on Earth has 12 hours of darkness. The equinoxes occur on or around 21 March and 23 September.

Erosion The processes by which natural forces, including weathering, running water, ice and winds, constantly modify the land.

Fault A crack or fracture in the Earth's crust along along which the rocks have moved so that the rocks on either side are displaced.

Fold Bends in rock strata caused by enormous lateral pressure.

Fossil fuel Any non-renewable fuel formed from once-living plant or animal matter, including peat and coal, oil and natural gas.

Glacier A body of ice which flows down a valley. It is composed of compacted snow.

Ice Age A period in history when global temperatures fell and ice covered large areas that are now ice-free.

Ice sheet A huge body of ice covering a large area. The world's two ice sheets cover Antarctica and Greenland. Small ice sheets are called ice caps.

Internet A global network of interconnected computer networks. Until the late 1980s the Internet was used only by governments and universities. By the mid-1990s, millions of home computers were connected.

Lithosphere The hard outer layer of the Earth, consisting of the crust and the hard upper layer of the mantle.

Monsoon A seasonal wind, especially in southern Asia, where the prevailing north-easterly trade winds in winter are replaced in summer by moist south-westerly winds which bring heavy rain.

Moraine Eroded rock ranging from clay to large boulders, that is transported and deposited by glaciers and other bodies of ice.

Neutron star A star made up almost entirely of atomic particles called neutrons.

Nuclear fision The process in stars by which hydrogen nuclei change into helium nuclei, creating energy which escapes in the form of light.

Ozone layer A layer of the gas ozone in the stratosphere that blocks out most of the Sun's harmful ultraviolet radiation.

Population growth A change in human population caused by natural increase (the difference between births and deaths) and migration.

Primary products Raw materials, such as crops, minerals or timber, that have not been processed.

Pyroclasts Fragments of magma thrown out by explosions during volcanic activity.

Porous rock A rock, such as sandstone, that contains pores through which water can percolate.

Right ascension A measure in hours of the position of a star east of the place where the Sun crosses the Celestial Equator on 21 March. One hour represents 15 degrees.

Solstice Two days during the year when the overhead Sun reaches either its northernmost point (the Tropic of Cancer) or its southernmost point (the Tropic of Capricorn).

Special economic zones Areas in eastern China where the government has encouraged foreign investment and where economic growth has been exceptionally rapid.

'Tiger' economies The name given to the developing economies of rapidly industrializing countries of eastern Asia, including Indonesia, Malaysia, South Korea, Singapore, Thailand and Taiwan.

Tornado A small, but violent whirlwind which occurs over land areas.

Trade wind A prevailing wind that blows from the high-pressure horse latitudes towards the low-pressure doldrums around the Equator.

Tropical cyclone A large storm which forms over warm seas north and south of the Equator. It may cause great damage to coastal areas, but it dies out quickly when it reaches land. Other names for this kind of storm are hurricane (in North America), typhoon (in Asia) and willy-willy (in Australia).

WORLD MAPS

MAP SYMBOLS

SETTLEMENTS

⬭ PARIS   ▣ Berne   ◉ Livorno   ◉ Brugge   ◉ Algeciras   ○ Fréjus   ○ Oberammergau   ○ Third

Settlement symbols and type styles vary according to the scale of each map and indicate the importance of towns on the map rather than specific population figures

∴ Ruins or Archæological Sites   ˅ Wells in Desert

--- ADMINISTRATION ---

——— International Boundaries

– – – Internat;onal Boundaries (Undefined or Disputed)

········ Internal Boundaries

⬭ National Parks

Country Names

NICARAGUA

Administrative Area Names

KENT

CALABRIA

Internat onal boundaries show the *de facto* situation where there are rival claims to territory

--- COMMUNICATIONS ---

——— Principal Roads

〜 Other Roads

-·-·- Trails and Seasonal Roads

⤸ Passes

✿ Airfields

〜 Principal Railways

---- Railways Under Construction

〜 Other Railways

⌐--⌐ Railway Tunnels

|||||||| Principal Canals

--- PHYSICAL FEATURES ---

〜 Perennial Streams

······ Intermittent Streams

⬭ Perennial Lakes

⬭ Intermittent Lakes

Swamps and Marshes

Permanent Ice and Glaciers

▲ 8848 Elevations in metres

▾ 8050 Sea Depths in metres

1134 Height of Lake Surface Above Sea Level in metres

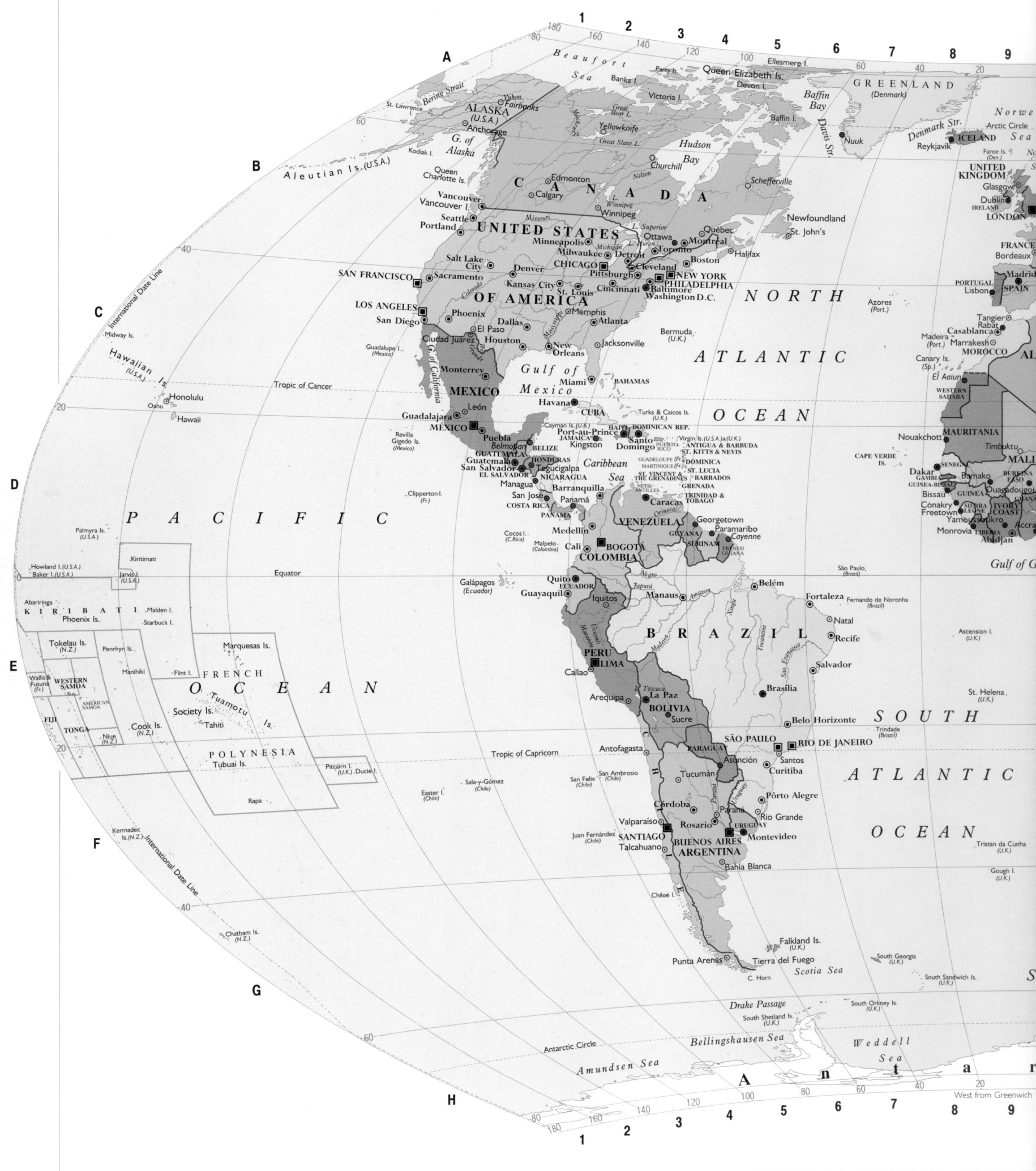

A

Beaufort Sea
Banks I.
Parry Is.
Queen Elizabeth Is.
Ellesmere I.
Devon I.
GREENLAND
(Denmark)
Norwe

St. Lawrence I.
Bering Strait
Yukon
Fairbanks
ALASKA
(U.S.A.)
Anchorage
Yellowknife
Great Bear L.
Victoria I.
Baffin
Bay
Baffin I.
Davis Str.
Nuuk
Denmark Str.
ICELAND
Arctic Circle
Reykjavik
Faroe Is. (Den.)
No

B

Aleutian Is. (U.S.A.)
Kodiak I.
G. of Alaska
Great Slave L.
Hudson
Bay
Churchill
Schefferville
UNITED
KINGDOM
Glasgow
Dublin
IRELAND
LONDON

Queen
Charlotte Is.
Edmonton
Calgary
Winnipeg
Nelson
L. Winnipeg
Newfoundland
St. John's

Vancouver
Vancouver I.
Seattle
Portland
UNITED STATES
Minneapolis
Milwaukee
L. Superior
L. Michigan
L. Huron
Québec
Ottawa
Montreal
Toronto
Boston
Halifax
FRANCE
Bordeaux

International Date Line
Salt Lake
City
Denver
Kansas City
CHICAGO
Detroit
Cleveland
Pittsburgh
NEW YORK
PHILADELPHIA
Baltimore
Washington D.C.
NORTH
PORTUGAL
Lisbon
SPAIN
Madrid

C

SAN FRANCISCO
Sacramento
OF AMERICA
St. Louis
Cincinnati
Missouri
Azores
(Port.)
ATLANTIC
Tangier
Rabat
Casablanca
MOROCCO

LOS ANGELES
San Diego
Phoenix
Dallas
El Paso
Memphis
Atlanta
Jacksonville
Bermuda
(U.K.)
Madeira
(Port.)
Marrakesh
Canary Is.
(Sp.)
El Aaiún
AL

Midway Is.
Ciudad Juárez
Houston
Rio Grande
New
Orleans
OCEAN
WESTERN
SAHARA

*Hawaiian Is.
(U.S.A.)*
Guadalupe I.
(Mexico)
G. of California
Monterrey
Gulf of
Mexico
Miami
BAHAMAS
MAURITANIA
Nouakchott
Timbuktu

Tropic of Cancer
Honolulu
Oahu
Hawaii
MEXICO
Guadalajara
León
Havana
CUBA
Turks & Caicos Is.
(U.K.)
CAPE VERDE
IS.
Dakar
SENEGAL
MALI

Revilla
Gigedo Is.
(Mexico)
MÉXICO
Puebla
Belmopan
BELIZE
Cayman Is. (U.K.)
JAMAICA
HAITI
Port-au-Prince
Kingston
DOMINICAN REP.
Santo
Domingo
PUERTO
RICO
Virgin Is. (U.S.A.)a (U.K.)
ANTIGUA & BARBUDA
ST. KITTS & NEVIS
GUADELOUPE (Fr.)
DOMINICA
MARTINIQUE (Fr.)
ST. LUCIA
BARBADOS
Nouakchott
GAMBIA
BURKINA
FASO
GUINEA-BISSAU
Bamako
Ouagadougou
GUINEA
IVORY
COAST

D

PACIFIC
Palmyra Is.
(U.S.A.)
Clipperton I.
(Fr.)
GUATEMALA
Guatemala
San Salvador
EL SALVADOR
HONDURAS
Tegucigalpa
NICARAGUA
Managua
Caribbean
Sea
ST. VINCENT &
THE GRENADINES
NETH.
ANTILLES
GRENADA
TRINIDAD &
TOBAGO
Bissau
Conakry
Freetown
SIERRA
LEONE
Monrovia
LIBERIA
Yamoussoukro
Abidjan
Accra

Howland I. (U.S.A.)
Baker I. (U.S.A.)
Jarvis I.
(U.S.A.)
Cocos I.
(C.Rica)
San José
COSTA RICA
Panamá
PANAMA
Barranquilla
Caracas
VENEZUELA
Georgetown
GUYANA
Paramaribo
SURINAM
Cayenne
FRENCH
GUIANA
Gulf of G

Equator
Kiritimati
(U.S.A.)
Galápagos
(Ecuador)
Medellín
Mulpelo I.
(Colombia)
Cali
BOGOTÁ
COLOMBIA
Orinoco
Négro
São Paulo
(Brazil)
Belém
Fortaleza
Fernando de Noronha
(Brazil)

Abariringa
KIRIBATI
Malden I.
Phoenix Is.
Starbuck I.
Quito
ECUADOR
Guayaquil
Iquitos
Japurá
Manaus
Amazon
BRAZIL
Xingu
Natal

E

Tokelau Is.
(N.Z.)
Penrhyn I.
Marquesas Is.
PERU
LIMA
Callao
Marañón
Ucayali
Recife
Ascension I.
(U.K.)

Manihiki
Flint I.
FRENCH
Arequipa
L. Titicaca
La Paz
BOLIVIA
Sucre
Brasília
St. Helena
(U.K.)

Wallis &
Futuna
(Fr.)
WESTERN
SAMOA
AMERICAN
SAMOA
Society Is.
Tahiti
Tuamotu
OCEAN
Belo Horizonte
SOUTH

FIJI
TONGA
Niue
(N.Z.)
Cook Is.
(N.Z.)
POLYNESIA
Tubuai Is.
Tropic of Capricorn
Antofagasta
SÃO PAULO
PARAGUAY
Asunción
RIO DE JANEIRO
Santos
Curitiba
ATLANTIC

Pitcairn I.
(U.K.) Ducie I.
Easter I.
(Chile)
Sala-y-Gómez
(Chile)
San Félix
(Chile)
San Ambrosio
(Chile)
Tucumán
Paraná
Pôrto Alegre
Rio Grande

Rapa
Paraná
Valparaíso
Córdoba
Rosario
URUGUAY
Montevideo
Trindade
(Brazil)
OCEAN
Tristan da Cunha
(U.K.)

F

Kermadec
Is. (N.Z.)
International Date Line
Juan Fernández
(Chile)
SANTIAGO
Talcahuano
BUENOS AIRES
ARGENTINA
Bahía Blanca
Gough I.
(U.K.)

Chatham Is.
(N.Z.)
Chiloé I.

Falkland Is.
(U.K.)
South Georgia
(U.K.)

G

Punta Arenas
Tierra del Fuego
C. Horn
Scotia Sea
South Sandwich Is.
(U.K.)
S

Drake Passage
South Orkney Is.
(U.K.)

Bellingshausen Sea
South Shetland Is.
(U.K.)
Weddell
Sea

Antarctic Circle
Amundsen Sea
A n t a r

H

West from Greenwich

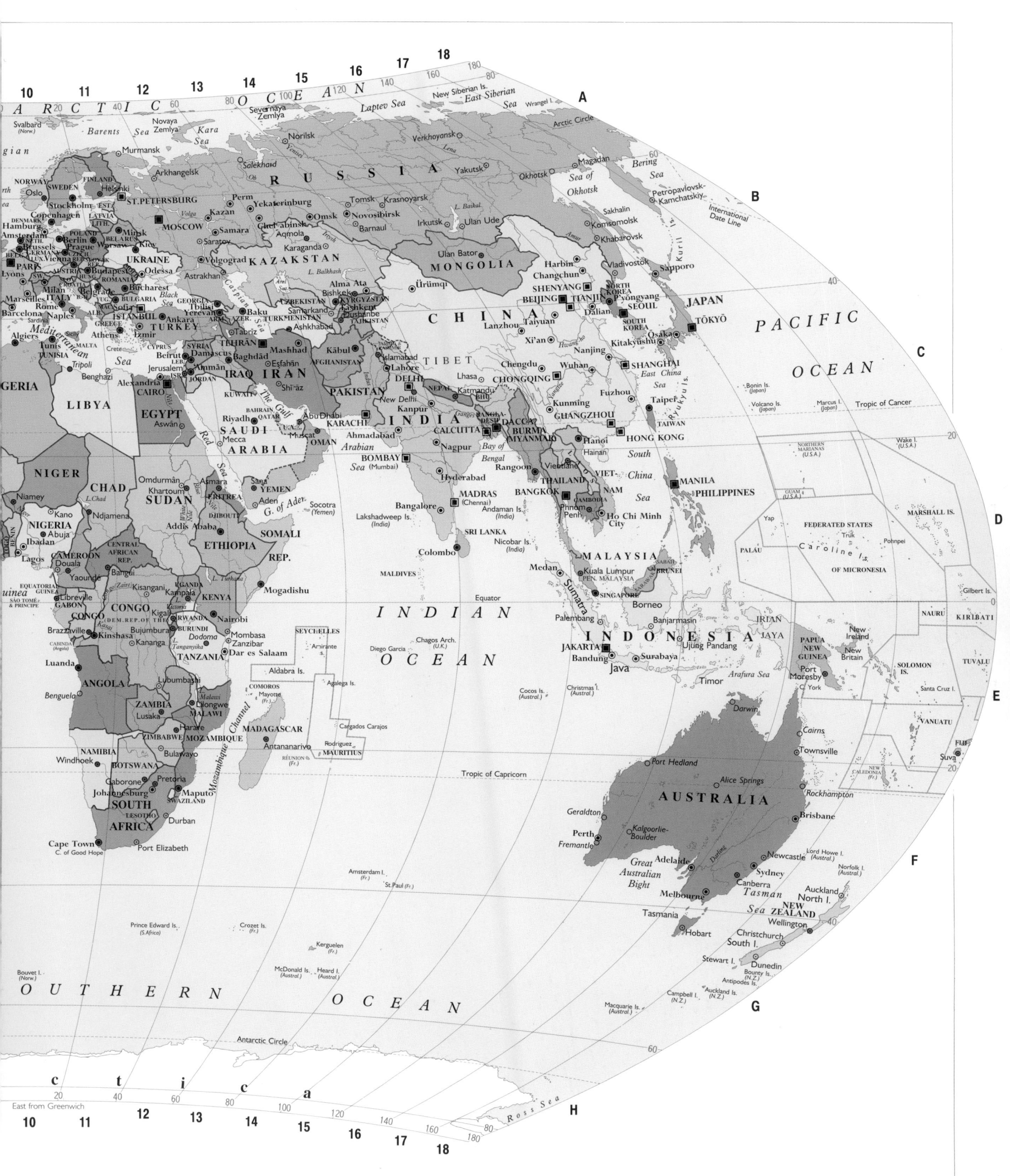

Hanoi ● Capital Cities

CARTOGRAPHY BY PHILIP'S. COPYRIGHT REED INTERNATIONAL BOOKS LTD.

100 0 200 400 600 800 1000 1200 1400 km
100 0 200 400 600 800 1000 miles

| 18 | 17 | 16 | 15 |

140

PACIFIC OCEAN

Aleutian Islands (U.S.A.)
Dutch Harbor
Unimak I.
Bristol Bay
Kodiak I.
Pribilof Is. (U.S.A.)
St. Matthew (U.S.A.)
Nunivak
St. Lawrence I. (U.S.A.)

Bering Sea

Near Is. (U.S.A.)
Komandorskiye Ostrova
Petropavlovsk Kamchatskiy
Gora Klyuchevskaya 4850
Poluostrov Kamchatka
Ostrov Karaginskiy
Mys Olyutorski

JAPAN
Hokkaidō
Kurilskiye Ostrova (Russia)
La Perouse Str.
Sakhalin (Russia)
Sakhalinskiy Zaliv
Vanino

Sea of Okhotsk

Nikolayevsk
Ulbanskiy Zaliv
Udskaya Guba
Amur
Khabarovsk

G. of Alaska
Seward
Prince William Sd.
Cook Inlet
Anchorage Mt. McKinley 6194
Cordova
Mt. St. Elias 5489
Skagway Mt. Logan 6050
Fairbanks
ALASKA
Whitehorse
Prince Rupert
Kuskokwim
Yukon
Nome
Kotzebue Sd.
Norton Sd.
Prince of Wales
Bering Str.

Anadyrskiy Zaliv
Mys Navarin
Anadyr
Kys Dezhneva
Chukotskoye Nagorye
Penzhino
Gizhiginskaya Guba
Penzhinskaya G.
Tauiskaya Guba
Okhotsk
Omolon

Penzhino
Kolymskoye Nagorye
Stanovoy Khrebet
Aldan
Yakutsk

ROCKY MOUNTAINS
Dawson Creek
Fort St. John
Liard
Fort Nelson
Fort Simpson
Mackenzie
Great Bear Lake
Fort Good Hope
Tulita
Fort McPherson
Herschel I.
Mackenzie Bay
Prudhoe Bay
Pt. Barrow
C. Halkett
Harrison Bay
Pt. Hope
C. Lisburne
Prolio Longa
Chukchi Sea

Ostrov Vrangelya (Russia)
Chaunskaya G.
Nizhne Kolymsk
Kolyma
Srednekolymsk
Russkoye Ustie
Indigirka
Zashiversk
Verkhoyansk
Yana
Kazachye
Zhigansk
Lena
Vilyuy
Olekma

NORTH AMERICA

Fort Vermilion
Peace
Athabasca
Athabasca Lake
Great Slave Lake
Yellowknife
Coppermine
Kugluktuk
C. Bathurst
C. Kellett
Banks I.
C. Prince Alfred
Prince Patrick I.
Victoria Island
Melville I.
Parry Is.
Borden I.
Ellef Ringnes I.
Sverdrup Is.
North Magnetic Pole 1990
Axel Heiberg I.
Nansen Sd.

Beaufort Sea
Canada Basin
3767
3327
4007
Alpha Cordillera
3546
Makarov Basin
Mendeleyev Ridge
Lomonosov Ridge
NORTH POLE
3700
2104
4100
4418
Fram Basin
Nansen Cordillera
4484
3741

ARCTIC OCEAN

7822
60
Novosibirskiye Ostrova
O. Bennetta (Russia)
Lyakhovskiye Ostrova
Kotelnyy
Tiksi
Bulun
Olenek

Laptev Sea
3849
Ostrova Petra
Nordvik
Poluostrov Taymyr
Ozero Taymyr
Khatanga
Anabar
Nordik
Pyasina
Norilsk
Dudinka
Igarka
Yenisey

SIBERIA
Stanovoy Khrebet
Verkhoyanskiy Khrebet
Cherskogo
Gory Putorana
Nizhnyaya Tunguska
Podkamennaya Tunguska

Hudson Bay
Chesterfield Inlet
Southampton I.
Coats I.
Mansel I.
Roes Welcome Sd.
Melville Pen.
Foxe Basin
Prince Charles I.
Foxe Chan.
Boothia Pen.
Somerset
Prince of Wales I.
King William I.
M'Clintock Chan.
Viscount Melville Sd.
Bathurst I.
Prince Albert Pen.
Wollaston Pen.
Dolphin & Union Str.
Coronation G.
Amundsen G.
McClure Str.
M'Clure Str.
Prince Regent Inlet
Gulf of Boothia
Barrow Str.
Lancaster Sound
Devon I.
Eureka
2399
Ellesmere I. (Canada)
Alert
C. Columbia
Lincoln Sea
Robeson Chan.
Kane Basin
Smith Sund
Qaanaaq
Uummannaq
Kong Christian X.s Land
Knud Rasmussen Land
Peary Land
K. Morris Jesup
Independence Fjord
Kong Frederik VIII.s Land

McKinley Sea

Severnaya Zemlya
Oktyabrskoy Revolyutsii
O. Uedineniya
O. Vise
O. Ushakova
O. Graham Bell
Z. Vilcheka
O. Belyy
Zemlya Frantsa Iosifa (Russia)
Z. Aleksandry (Russia)
Zemlya Georga
Kara Sea
Poluostrov Yamal
Baydaratskaya Guba
Novyy Port
Nadym
Urengoy
Ob
Salekhard
Berezovo
Vorkuta
Surgut
Tobolsk

Baffin Island
Baffin Bay
Igloolik
C. Dyer
Cumberland Sd.
Resolution I.
C. Chidley
Hudson Str.
Ungava Bay
Labrador
Hamilton Inlet
Davis Str.
Upernavik
Qeqertarsuaq
Uummannaq
Qeqertarsuaq
GREENLAND (Denmark)
KALAALLIT NUNAAT
Kong Frederik IX.s Land
Nuuk
Paamiut
Mt. Forel 3360
Kong Christian IX.s Land
Gunnbjørn Fjeld 3700
Ittoqqortoormiit
Ammassalik
Qaqortoq
Alluitsup Paa
Kap Farvel (Nunap Isua)
Kong Frederik VI.s Kyst
Kong Oscar Fjord
Kong Franz Joseph Fd.
Kap Brewster
Denmark Str.
Iceland Plateau
Horn
Breiðafjörður
Fontur
Reykjavík ICELAND
Öræfajökull 2119

Nordkapp
Vestspitsbergen
Svalbard (Norway)
Longyearbyen
Edgeøya
Nordaustlandet
Novaya Zemlya

Greenland Sea
Jan Mayen (Norway)

Barents Sea
Bjørnøya
O. Kolguyev
Mys Kanin Nos
Pechora
Uralskie Gory
Narodnaya 1894
Mezen
Arkhangelsk
Sev. Dvina
Onega
Onezhskoye Ozero

YEKATERINBURG
PERM
UFA
SAMARA

Norwegian Sea
3800

Nordkapp
Hammerfest
Tromsø
Lofoten
Vardø
Varangerfjorden
Murmansk
Kolskiy Poluostrov
Beloye More

RUSSIA
Ladozhskoye Ozero
ST. PETERBURG
Chudskoye Ozero
Volga
Saratov
VOLGOGRAD

Arctic Circle

Trondheim
Bergen
Oslo
NORWAY
SWEDEN
STOCKHOLM
Gulf of Bothnia
FINLAND
Helsinki
G. of Finland
Tallinn
EST.
Riga
LAT.
LITH.
Vilnius
BELARUS
Kaliningrad
Baltic Sea

Føroyar (Den.)
Shetland Is. (U.K.)
Orkney Is. (U.K.)
Hebrides (U.K.)
Rockall (U.K.)
Mid-Atlantic Ridge
4755

ATLANTIC OCEAN

North Sea
SCOTLAND
Edinburgh
UNITED KINGDOM
Belfast
Dublin
IRELAND
ENGLAND
LONDON
C. Clear

KØBENHAVN
DENMARK
HAMBURG
BERLIN
GERMANY
AMSTERDAM
NETH.
Elbe
Wisła
POLAND
WARSZAWA
PRAHA
Odra

MOSKVA
KYYIV
UKRAINE
ROSTOV
Black Sea
ODESA

| 20 | 7 | West from Greenwich | 0 | East from Greenwich | 8 | 20 | 9 |

Legend:
- Maximum extent of sea ice
- Summer extent of sea ice
- Ice caps and permanent ice shelf

ft m
12 000 4000
6000 2000
4500 1500
1200 400
600 200
0 0
500 1500
1000 3000
2000 6000
3000 9000
4000 12 000
5000 15 000
m ft

Projection : Zenithal Equidistant

CARTOGRAPHY BY PHILIP'S. COPYRIGHT REED INTERNATIONAL BOOKS LTD

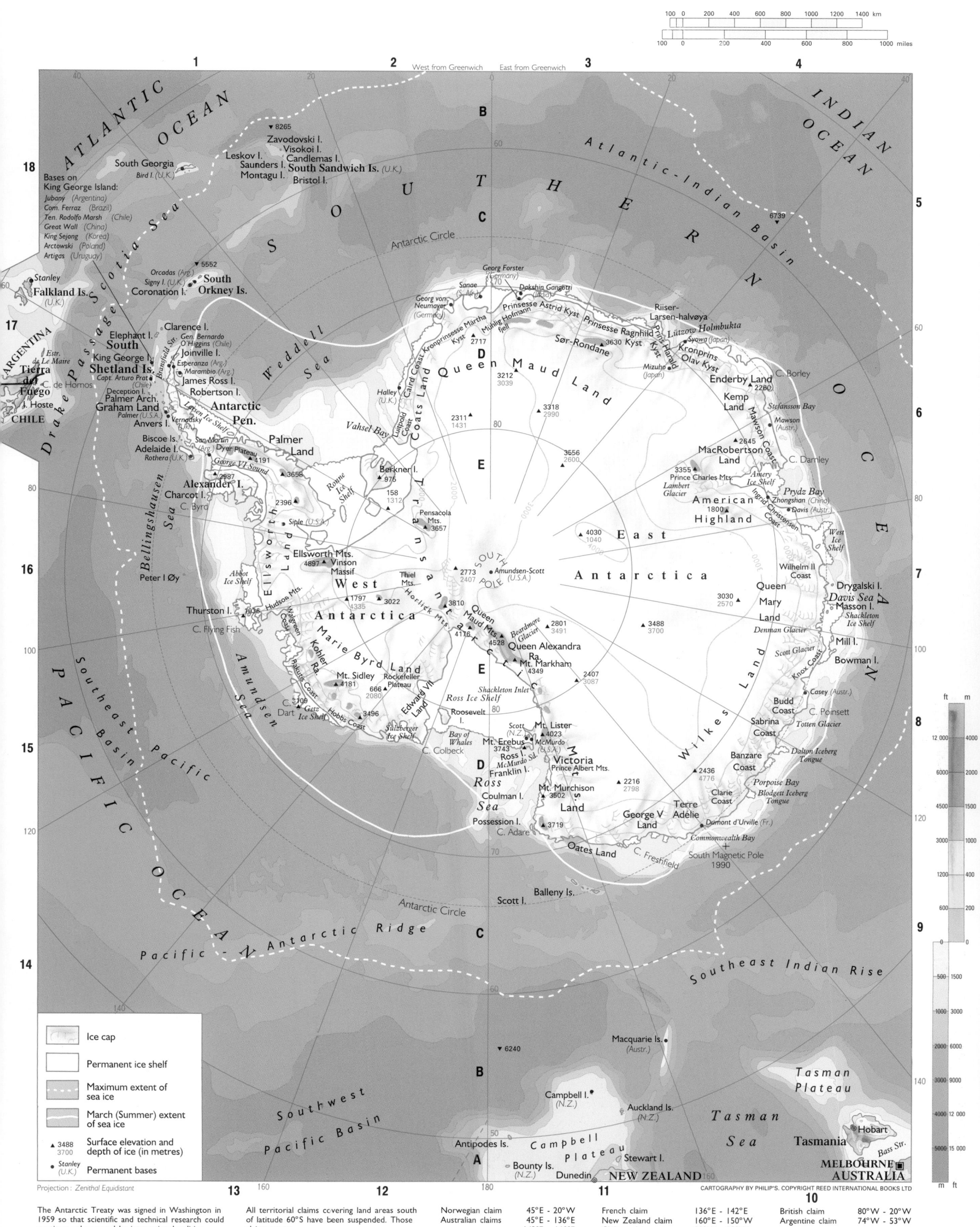

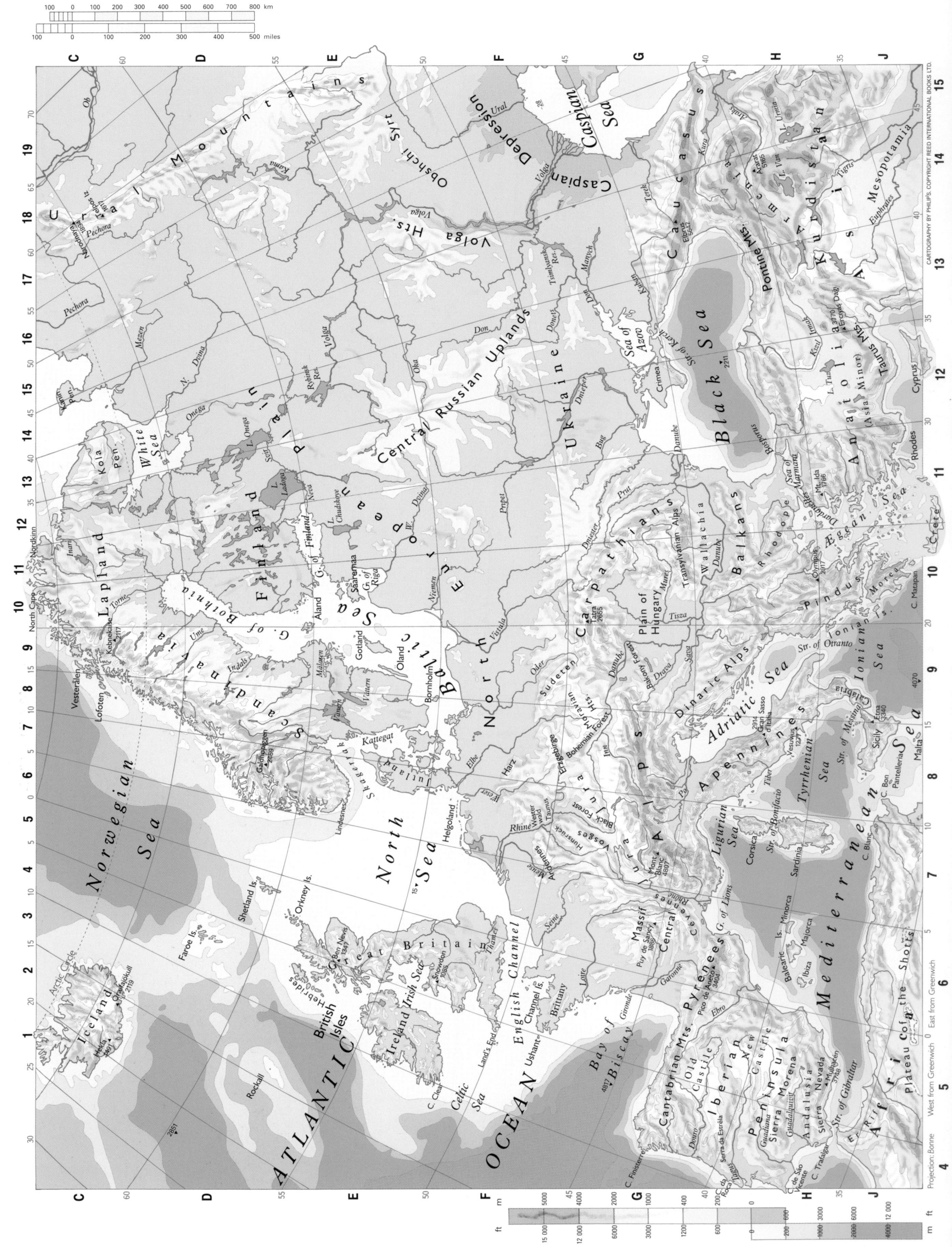

CARTOGRAPHY BY PHILIP'S COPYRIGHT REED INTERNATIONAL BOOKS LTD.

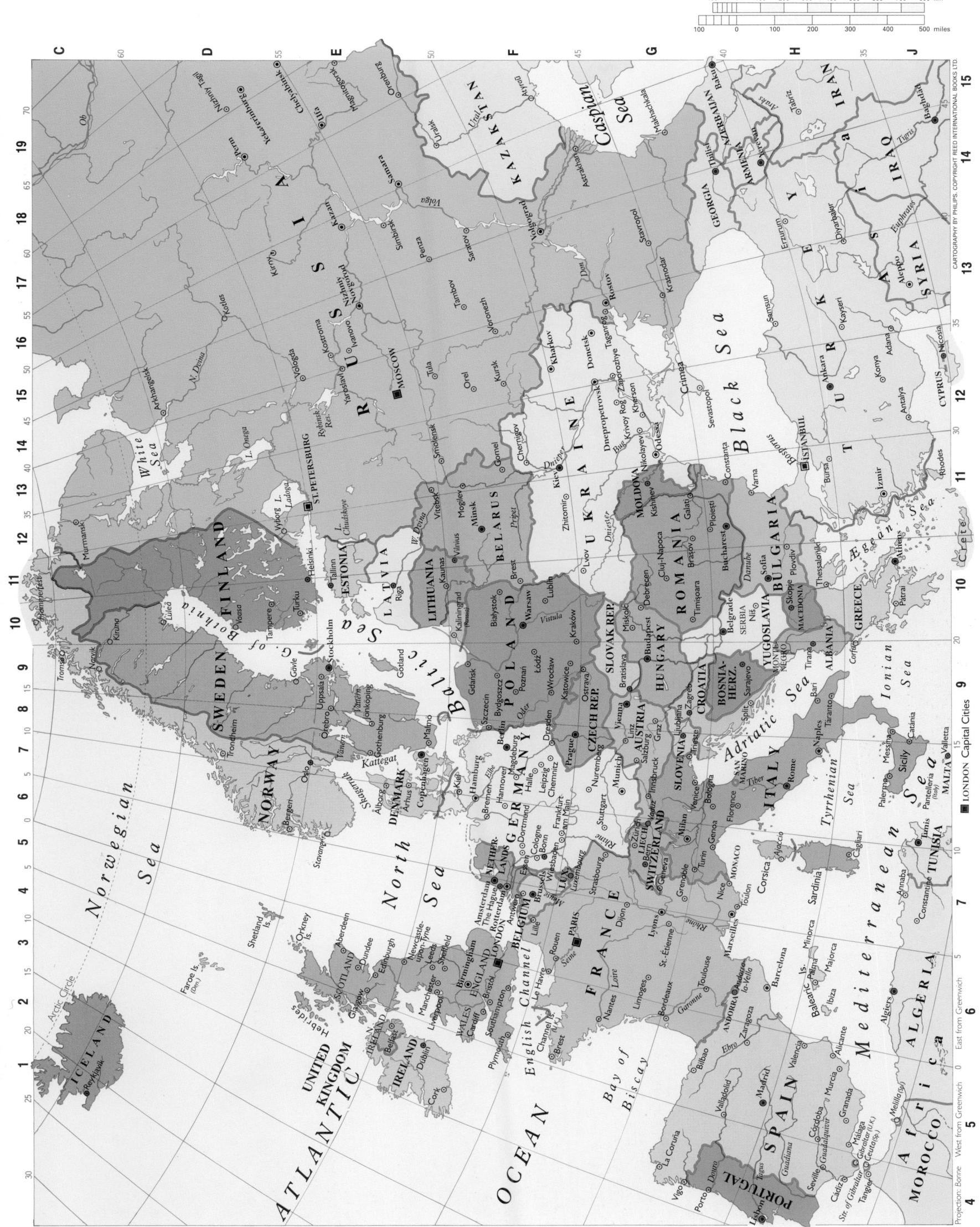

CARTOGRAPHY BY PHILIP'S. COPYRIGHT REED INTERNATIONAL BOOKS LTD.

SCANDINAVIA 1:4 400 000

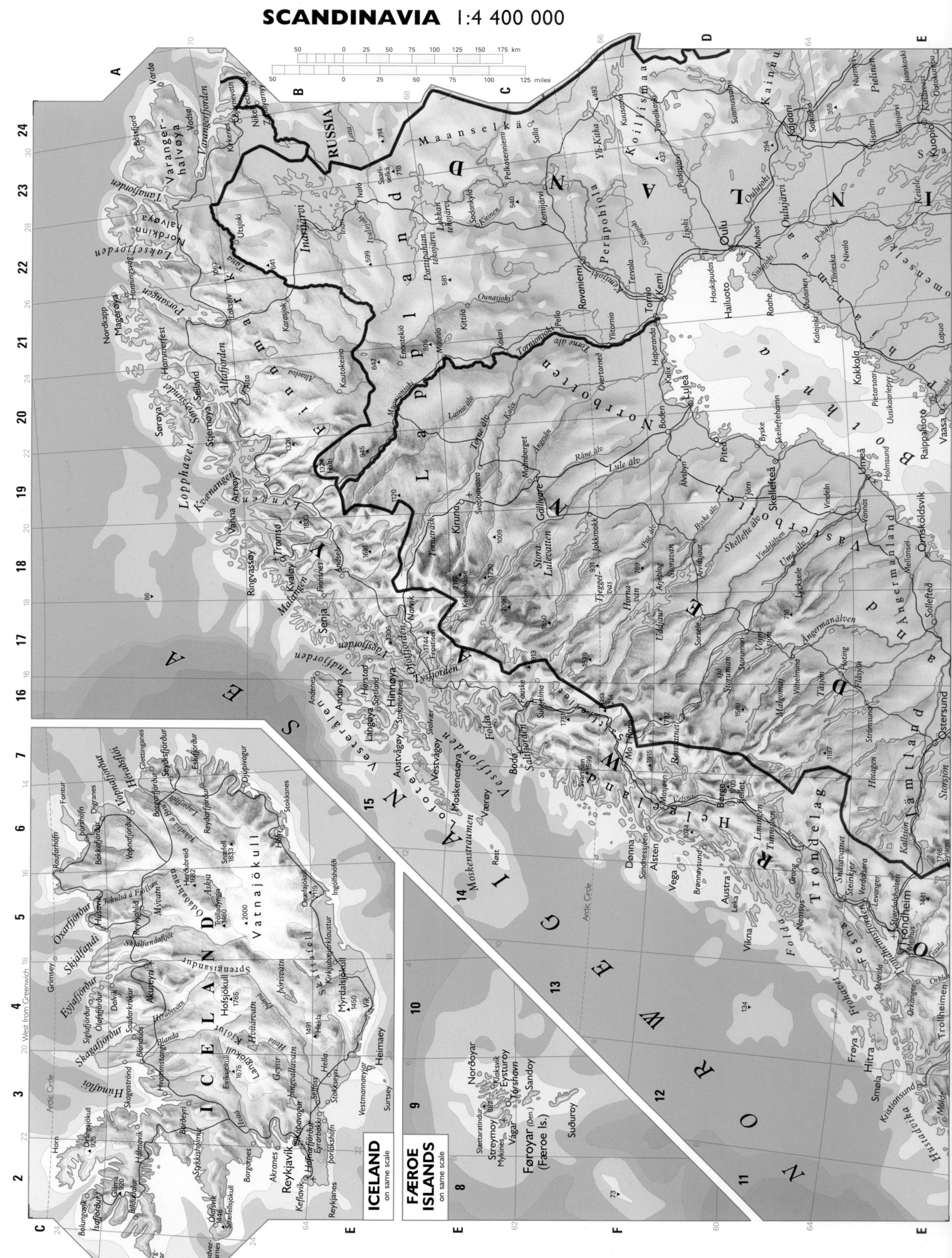

ICELAND
on same scale

FÆROE
ISLANDS
on same scale

COPYRIGHT GEORGE PHILIP LTD.

Suomen selkä

FINLAND

Uleåborg

Varkaus
Savonlinna
Mikkeli
Leppävirta
Äänekoski
Jyväskylä
Saarijärvi
Keuruu
Mänttä
Ilmajoki
Kurikka
Seinäjoki
Alavus
Kankaanpää
Kaskinen
Kristiinankaupunki
Parkano
Jalasjärvi
Lappeenranta
Kouvola
Anjalankoski
Kuusankoski
Lahti
Riihimäki
Heinola
Imatra
Kotka
Kymijoki
Hämeenlinna
Janakkala
Hyvinkää
Kerava
Järvenpää
Vantaa
Espoo
Helsinki (Helsingfors)
Porvoo
Tampere
Nokia
Valkeakoski
Forssa
Toijala
Salo
Turku (Åbo)
Raisio
Uusikaupunki
Rauma
Pori
Hanko
Tammisaari
Kirkkonummi
Parainen
Naantali

Gulf of Finland
Gulf of Bothnia

ESTONIA
Tallinn
Narva
Gdov
Ozero Chudskoye
Ostrov Bolshoy Tyuters
Sillamäe
Jõhvi
Kohtla-Järve
Rakvere
Tapa
Paide
Kunda
Tartu
Põlva
Võru
318 Munamägi
Viljandi
Rapla
Kehra
Kärdla
Hiiumaa (Dago)
Vormsi
Muhu
Saaremaa (Ösel)
Kuressaare
Orissaare
Kardla
Haapsalu
Pärnu
Kihnu
Ruhnu saar 54
Kolkas rags
Gulf of Riga

Võrts Järv
Valga
Valmiera
Sigulda
Cēsis
Limbaži
Ainaži
Roja
Talsi
Tukums
Jūrmala
Riga
Ogre
Jelgava
Bauska
Aizkraukle
Dobele
Mažeikiai
Saldus
Kuldīga
Aizpute
Priekule
Venstpils
Pāvilosta
Liepāja
Palanga
Klaipėda
Neringa
Nida

LATVIA
Daugava
Daugavpils
Balvi
Alūksne
Gulbene
Madona
Lubānas Ezers
311 Ēgli
Preili
Rēzekne
Rokiškis
Biržai
Panevėžys
Radviliškis
Šiauliai
Telšiai
Plungė
Skuodas
Kretinga
Raseiniai
Šakiai
Jurbarkas
Neman
Šilutė
Taurage
Sovetsk
Zalty

LITHUANIA
Daugavpils
288
Zarasai
Utena
Ukmergė
Jonava
Kėdainiai
Kaunas
Marijampolė
Vilkaviškis
Alytus
Prienai
Druskininkai
Vilnius
Ashmyny
Lida
Lyntupy
Vidzy
Braslaw
Polesk
Zelenogradsk
Gvardeysk
Bagrationovsk
Kaliningrad (Russia)
Chernyakhovsk
309
Gusev
Nesterov
Ketrzyn
Bartoszyce
Braniewo
Gdynia
Gdańsk

BALTIC SEA

STOCKHOLM
Uppsala
Norrtälje
Märsta
Sigtuna
Enköping
Västerås
Eskilstuna
Strängnäs
Södertälje
Nyköping
Trosa
Oxelösund
Katrineholm
Flen
Nynäshamn

Åland (Ahvenanmaa)
Ålands hav
Mariehamn
Maarianhamina

Gotska Sandön
Fårö
245
Gotland
Visby
Slite
Roma
Hemse
Burgsvik
Hoburgen

Sundsvall
Härnösand
Kramfors
Sollefteå
Hudiksvall
Söderhamn
Ljusne
Bollnäs
Gävle
Sandviken
Hofors
Falun
Borlänge
Avesta
Hedemora
Ludvika
Mora
Rättvik
Leksand

SVEALAND
Dalarna
Värmland
Västmanland
Uppland
Södermanland

GÖTALAND
Örebro
Lindesberg
Kumla
Karlskoga
Askersund
Motala
Linköping
Norrköping
Finspång
Mjölby
Hällefors
Hallsberg
Vänern
Karlstad
Kristinehamn
Säffle
Arvika
Filipstad
Mariestad
Lidköping
Skövde
Tidaholm
Falköping
Skara
Ulricehamn
Borås
Alingsås
Trollhättan
Vänersborg
Uddevalla
Lysekil
Bohuslän
Dalsland
Åmål
Mellerud
Orust
Tjörn
Göteborg (Gothenburg)
Kungsbacka
Varberg
Falkenberg
Halmstad
Laholm
Halland
Bolmen
Gislaved
Värnamo
Ljungby
Vetlanda
Nässjö
Jönköping
Vättern
Eksjö
Tranås
Vimmerby
Västervik
Oskarshamn
Högsby
Nybro
Kalmar
Öland
Borgholm
Mönsterås
Hultsfred
Växjö
Alvesta
Åsnen
Älmhult
Osby
Hässleholm
Kristianstad
Simrishamn
Karlshamn
Karlskrona
Ronneby
Sölvesborg
Blekinge
Småland
Ystad
Trelleborg
Skanör med Falsterbo
Malmö
Lund
Landskrona
Helsingborg
Ängelholm
Båstad

Bornholm
Rønne
Nexø

Skagerrak
Kattegat

NORWAY
Ålesund
Molde
Kristiansund
Dovrefjell
Oppdal
Romsdal
Åndalsnes
Sunndalsøra
Rondane
Gudbrandsdalen
Lillehammer
Hamar
Elverum
Østerdalen
Mjøsa
Gjøvik
Valdres
Jotunheimen
2469 Galdhøpiggen
Sogndal
Sognefjorden
Voss
Odda
Hardangervidda
Hardangerfjorden
Folgefonni
Bergen
Haugesund
Stord
Bømlo
Stavanger
Sandnes
Bryne
Egersund
Flekkefjord
Kristiansand
Lista
Mandal
Farsund
Telemark
Gaustafjell 1883
Notodden
Kongsberg
Drammen
Oslo
Ski
Drøbak
Moss
Askim
Kongsvinger
Fredrikstad
Sarpsborg
Halden
Oslofjorden
Horten
Tønsberg
Sandefjord
Larvik
Skien
Porsgrunn
Arendal
Grimstad
Lillesand
Risør

DENMARK
København (Copenhagen)
Helsingør
Helsingborg
Roskilde
Køge
Næstved
Slagelse
Korsør
Kalundborg
Holbæk
Sjælland
Møn
Falster
Lolland
Langeland
Nykøbing
Gedser
Nakskov
Maribo
Svendborg
Odense
Nyborg
Store Bælt
Lille Bælt
Fyn
Kerteminde
Assens
Sønderborg
Aabenraa
Haderslev
Kolding
Vejle
Fredericia
Horsens
Silkeborg
Skanderborg
Århus
Randers
Hobro
Viborg
Aalborg
Hjørring
Frederikshavn
Skagen
Grenen
Thisted
Struer
Holstebro
Herning
Ringkøbing
Skjern
Esbjerg
Varde
Ribe
Tønder
Fanø
Rømø
Limfjorden
Læsø
Anholt
Samsø

GERMANY
Flensburg
Schleswig
Rendsburg
Kiel
Neumünster
Lübeck
Mecklenburger Bucht
Kieler Bucht
Fehmarn
Puttgarden
Rostock
Wismar
Rügen
Greifswald
Stralsund
Usedom
Sassnitz
Elbe
Cuxhaven
Itzehoe
Holstein
Helgoland
Ost-friesische Inseln
Nordfriesische Inseln
Sylt
Föhr
Deutsche Bucht

POLAND
Gdynia
Gdańsk
Sopot
Tczew
Starogard Gdański
Elbląg
Malbork
Wisła
Zalew Wiślany
Hel
Rumia
Wejherowo
Przylądek Rozewie
Łeba
Słupsk
Lębork
Bytów
Kościerzyna
Koszalin
Kołobrzeg
Darłowo
Białogard

East from Greenwich

Projection: Conical with two standard parallels

m 2000 1500 1000 500 200 0
ft 6000 4500 3000 1500 600 0
m 0 50-150 100-300 200-600 1000-3000 2000-6000
ft 0 150 300 600 1500 3000 6000

km scale: 10 0 10 20 30 40 50 60 70 80 90 km

miles scale: 10 0 10 20 30 40 50 60 miles

Gulf of Bothnia

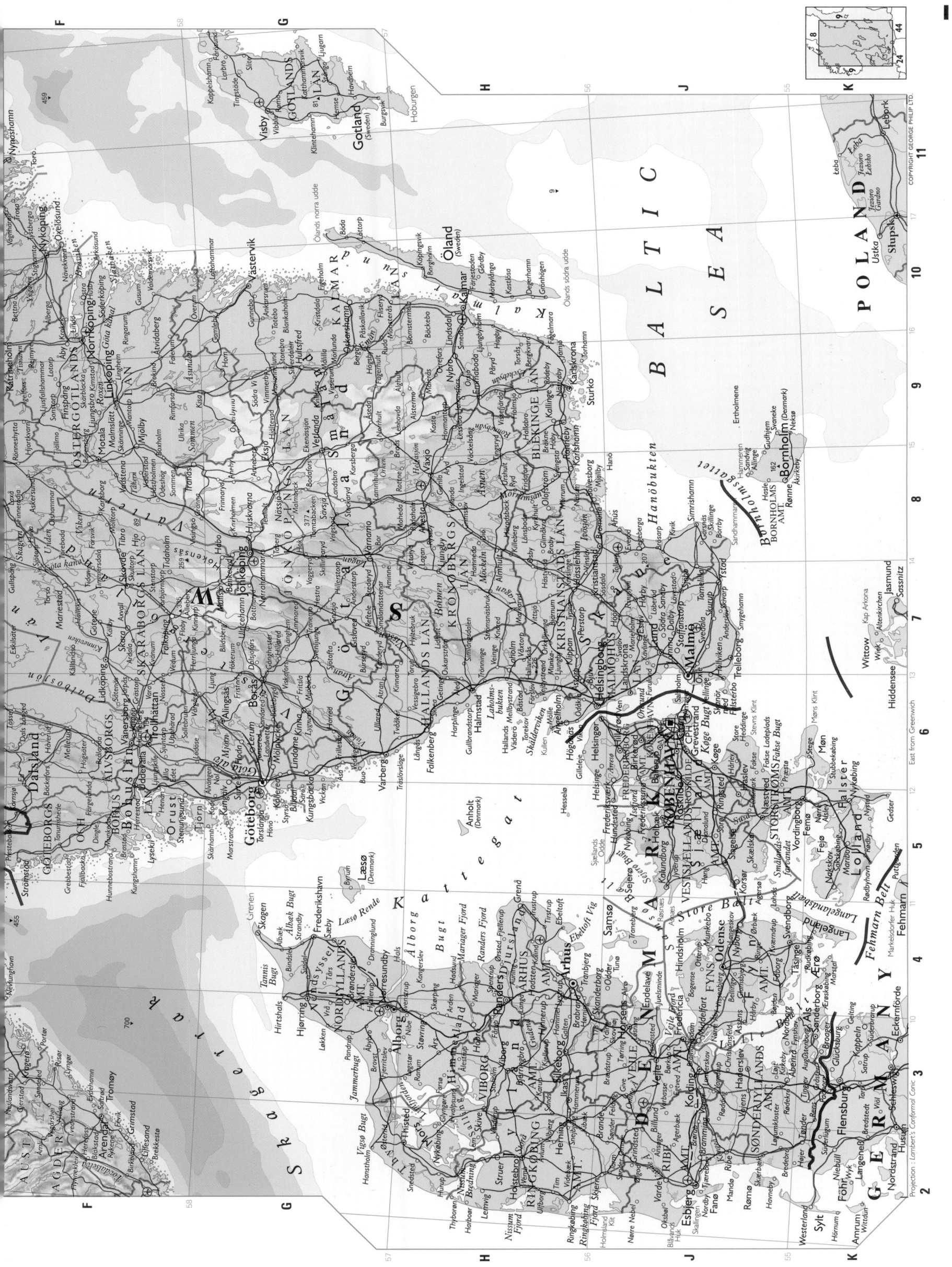

COPYRIGHT GEORGE PHILIP LTD.

Projection : Lambert's Conformal Conic
East from Greenwich

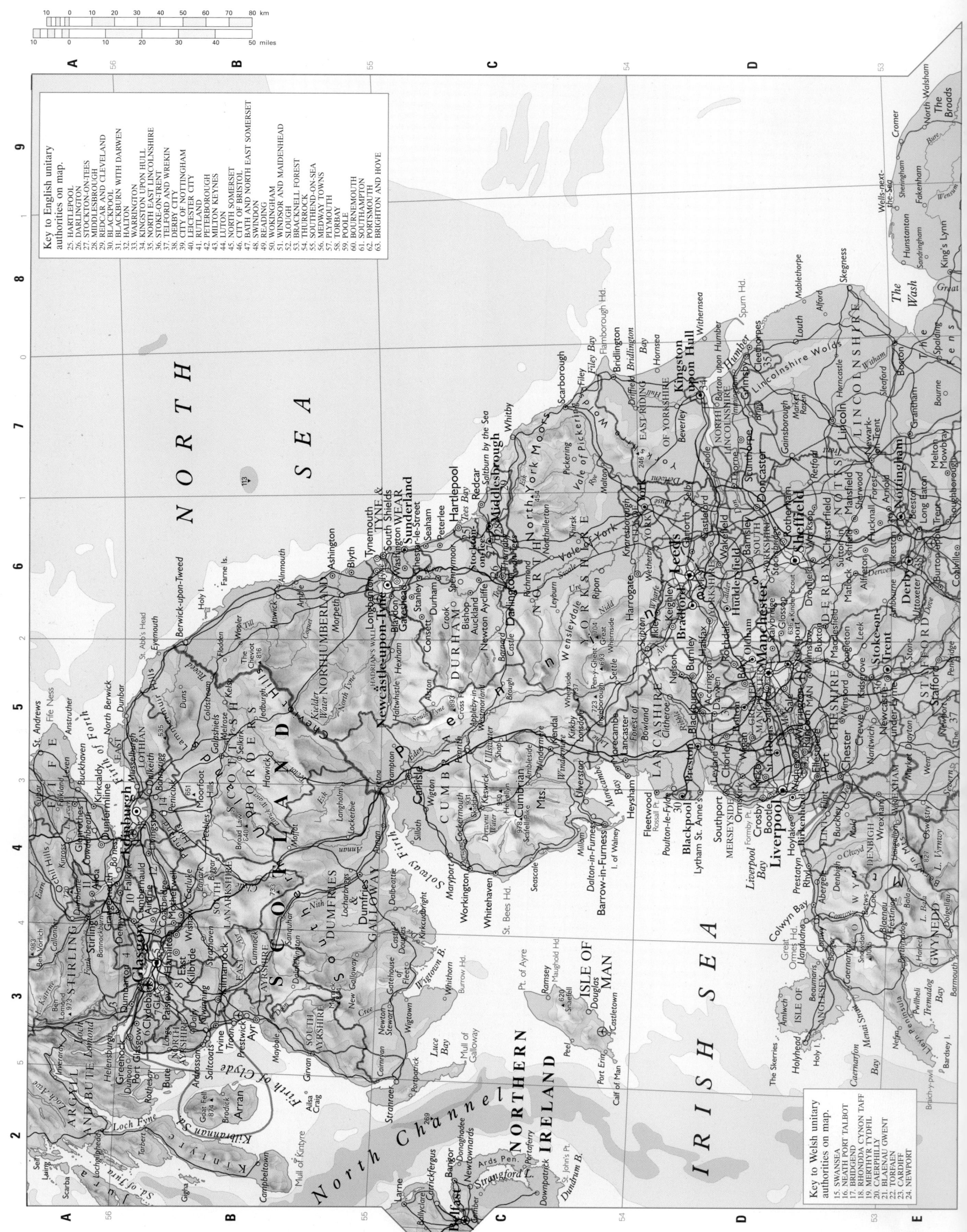

Key to English unitary authorities on map.

25. HARTLEPOOL
26. DARLINGTON
27. STOCKTON-ON-TEES
28. MIDDLESBROUGH
29. REDCAR AND CLEVELAND
30. BLACKPOOL
31. BLACKBURN WITH DARWEN
32. HALTON
33. WARRINGTON
34. KINGSTON UPON HULL
35. NORTH EAST LINCOLNSHIRE
36. NORTH LINCOLNSHIRE
37. TELFORD AND WREKIN
38. DERBY CITY
39. CITY OF NOTTINGHAM
40. LEICESTER CITY
41. RUTLAND
42. PETERBOROUGH
43. MILTON KEYNES
44. LUTON
45. NORTH SOMERSET
46. CITY OF BRISTOL
47. BATH AND NORTH EAST SOMERSET
48. SWINDON
49. READING
50. WOKINGHAM
51. WINDSOR AND MAIDENHEAD
52. SLOUGH
53. BRACKNELL FOREST
54. THURROCK
55. SOUTHEND-ON-SEA
56. MEDWAY TOWNS
57. PLYMOUTH
58. TORBAY
59. POOLE
60. BOURNEMOUTH
61. SOUTHAMPTON
62. PORTSMOUTH
63. BRIGHTON AND HOVE

Key to Welsh unitary authorities on map.

15. SWANSEA
16. NEATH PORT TALBOT
17. BRIDGEND
18. RHONDDA CYNON TAFF
19. MERTHYR TYDFIL
20. CAERPHILLY
21. BLAENAU GWENT
22. TORFAEN
23. CARDIFF
24. NEWPORT

NORTH SEA

IRISH SEA

North Channel

SCOTLAND

NORTHERN IRELAND

ISLE OF MAN

ENGLAND

WALES

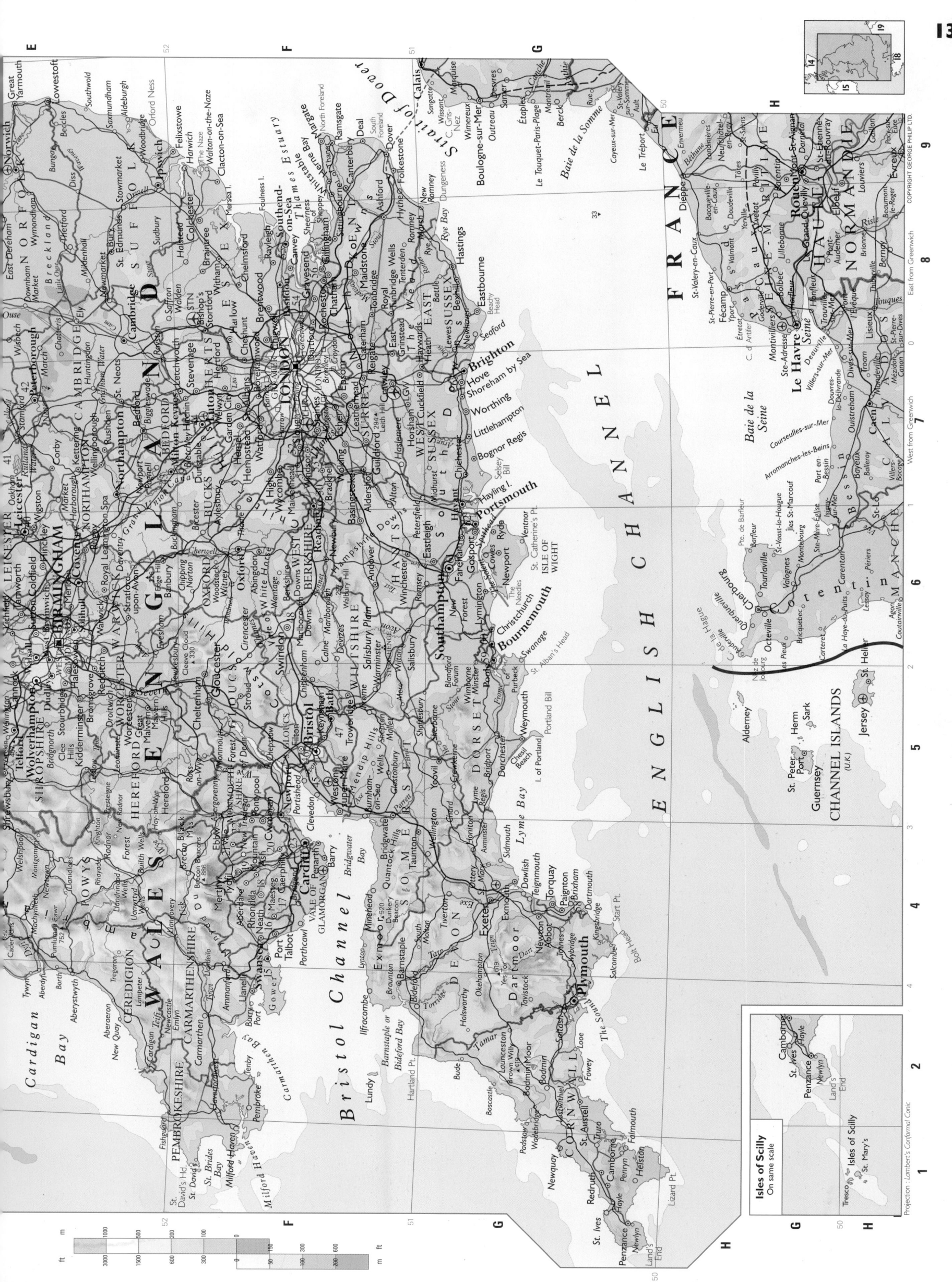

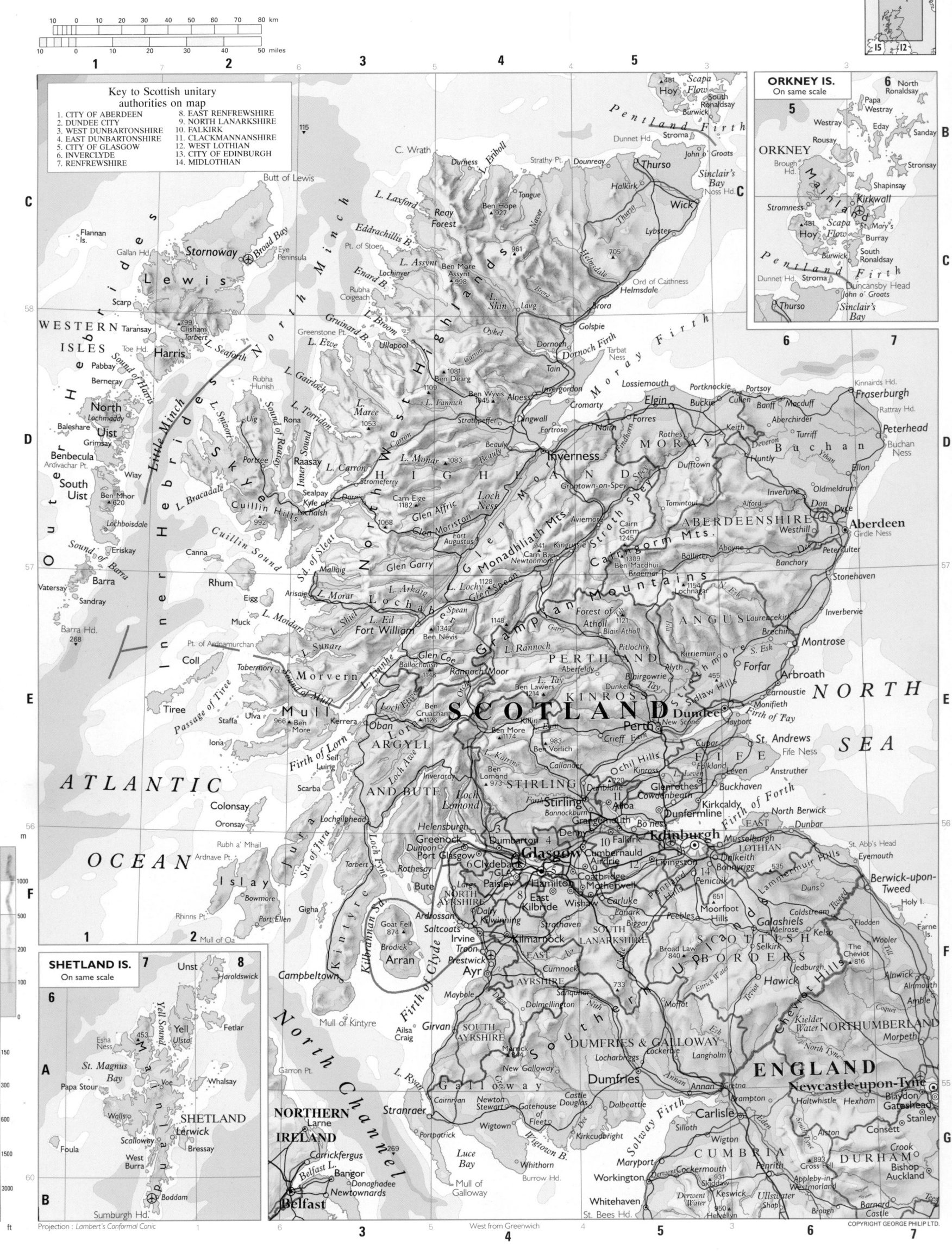

10 0 10 20 30 40 50 60 70 80 km
10 0 10 20 30 40 50 miles

Key to Scottish unitary authorities on map
1. CITY OF ABERDEEN 8. EAST RENFREWSHIRE
2. DUNDEE CITY 9. NORTH LANARKSHIRE
3. WEST DUNBARTONSHIRE 10. FALKIRK
4. EAST DUNBARTONSHIRE 11. CLACKMANNANSHIRE
5. CITY OF GLASGOW 12. WEST LOTHIAN
6. INVERCLYDE 13. CITY OF EDINBURGH
7. RENFREWSHIRE 14. MIDLOTHIAN

ORKNEY IS.
On same scale

ORKNEY

SHETLAND IS.
On same scale

SHETLAND

SCOTLAND

ATLANTIC OCEAN

NORTH SEA

ENGLAND

NORTHERN IRELAND

Projection : Lambert's Conformal Conic

West from Greenwich

COPYRIGHT GEORGE PHILIP LTD.

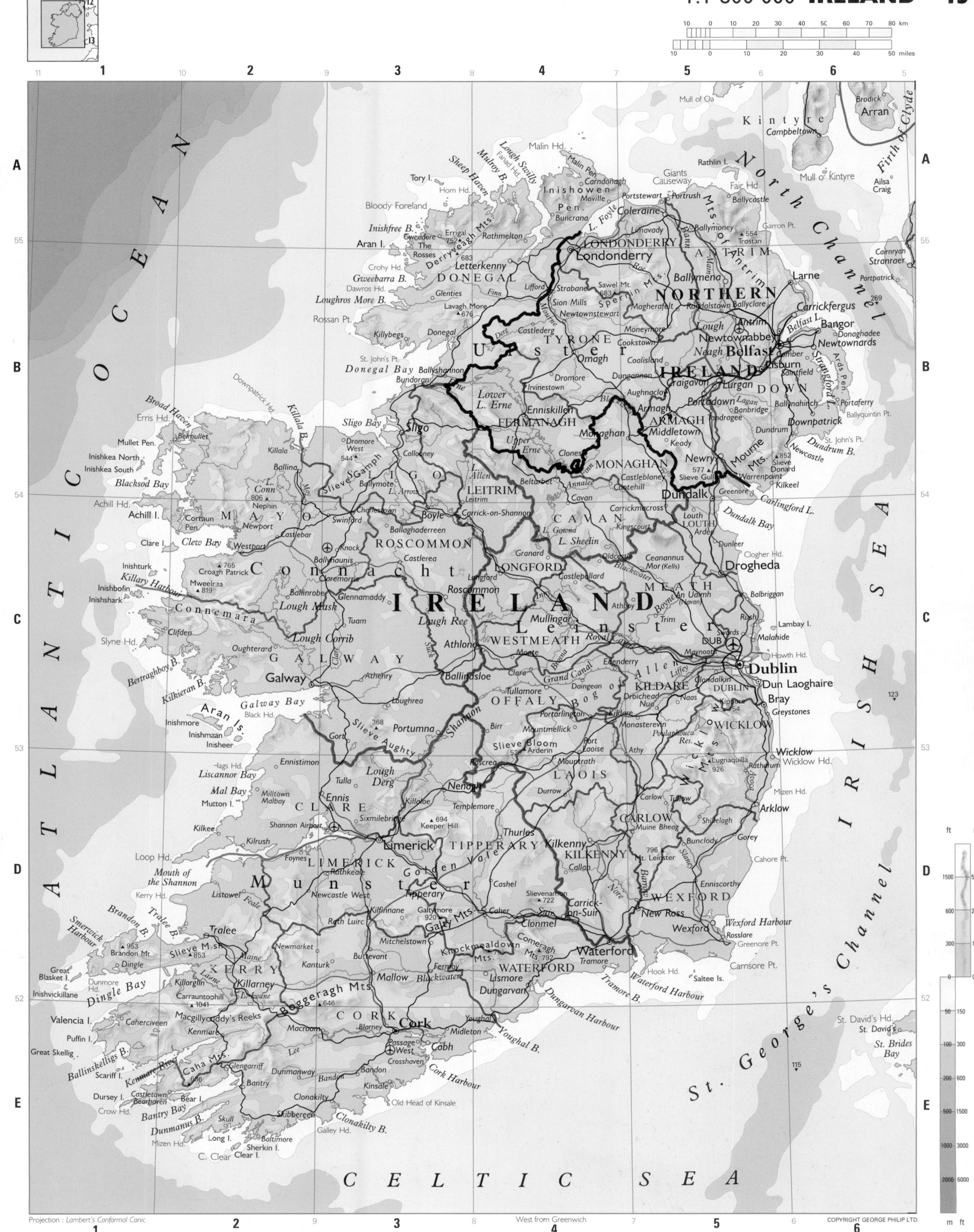

10 0 10 20 30 40 5C 60 70 80 km

10 0 10 20 30 40 50 miles

12
13

A

ATLANTIC OCEAN

Mull of Oa
Brodick
Arran
Kintyre
Campbeltown
Firth of Clyde

Malin Hd.
Fanad Hd.
Malin Pen.
Tory I.
Horn Hd.
Sheep Haven
Mutroy B.
Carndonagh
Moville
Giants Causeway
Rathlin I.
Ballycastle
Portstewart
Portrush
Mts. of Antrim
Fair Hd.
Mull o' Kintyre
Ailsa Craig

Bloody Foreland
Inishfree B.
Errigal
752
Gweedore
The Rosses
Rathmelton
683
Inishowen Pen.
Buncrana
L. Foyle
Limavady
Coleraine
Ballymoney
Garron Pt.
Cairnryan
Stranraer

55

Aran I.
Crohy Hd.
Derryveagh Mts.
Letterkenny
LONDONDERRY
Londonderry
Strabane
Sawel Mt.
683
ANTRIM
Ballymena
554
Trostan
269
55

Gweebarra B.
Dawros Hd.
DONEGAL
Glenties
Lifford
Sion Mills
Newtownstewart
Sperrin Mts.
Magherafelt
Moneymore
Randalstown Ballyclare
NORTHERN
Larne
Portpatrick

Loughros More B.
676
Lavagh More
Finn
Castlederg
TYRONE
Omagh
Coalisland
Dungannon
Antrim
L. Neagh
Newtownabbey
Belfast L.
Bangor
Donaghadee
Newtownards

B
Rossan Pt.
Killybegs
Donegal
Derg
Enniskillen
FERMANAGH
Irvinestown
Dromore
Aughnacloy
Monaghan
Craigavon
Lurgan
Portadown
Lagan
Banbridge
IRELAND
Belfast
Lisburn
DOWN
Ballynahinch
Portaferry
B

St. John's Pt.
Donegal Bay
Ballyshannon
Bundoran
Erne
Lower L. Erne
Upper L. Erne
Clones
MONAGHAN
Castleblaney
Keady
ARMAGH
Armagh
Middletown
Newry
577
Slieve Gullion
Downpatrick
Dundrum B.
St. John's Pt.

54
Downpatrick Hd.
Killala B.
Broad Haven
Erris Hd.
Sligo Bay
Sligo
SLIGO
Collooney
Ballymote
L. Arrow
L. Allen
Beltarbet
Annalee
Cootehill
Carrickmacross
Louth
Ardee
Dundalk
852
Slieve Donard
Newcastle
Kilkeel
Carlingford L.
Mourne Mts.
Warrenpoint
Greenore
54

Mullet Pen.
Inishkea North
Inishkea South
Blacksod Bay
Bellmullet
Killala
Ballina
Dromore West
544
Sligo
Slieve Gamph
Charlestown
Boyle
Carrick-on-Shannon
CAVAN
Cavan
L. Gowna
L. Sheelin
Kingscourt
Oldcastle
Ceanannus Mor (Kells)
Blackwater
Dunleer
Clogher Hd.
Dundalk Bay

C
Achill Hd.
Achill I.
Corraun Pen.
Clare I.
Newport
Castlebar
Knock
765
806
Nephin
L. Conn
MAYO
Swinford
Ballyhaunis
Ballaghaderreen
ROSCOMMON
Castlerea
LONGFORD
Granard
Longford
Castlepollard
MEATH
An Uaimh (Navan)
Boyne
Trim
Drogheda
Balbriggan
Lambay I.
C

Inishturk
Inishbofin
Inishshark
Croagh Patrick
819
Westport
Clew Bay
Claremorris
Castlebar
Knock
Ballinrobe
Lough Mask
Glennamaddy
Roscommon
Athboy
Royal Canal
Mullingar
WESTMEATH
Moate
Swords
DUB.
Malahide
Howth Hd.

GALWAY
Connacht
Tuam
Lough Corrib
Oughterard
Clifden
Slyne Hd.
Connemara
Lough Ree
Athlone
Moate
Brosna
IRELAND
Leinster
Enfield
Maynooth
DUBLIN
Dublin
Dun Laoghaire

Kilkieran B.
Bertraghboy B.
Aran Is.
Inishmore
Inishmaan
Inisheer
Galway Bay
Galway
Black Hd.
Slieve Aughty
368
Gort
Loughrea
Ballinasloe
Shannon
Clara
Grand Canal
Tullamore
Daingean
Allen Bog
KILDARE
Droichead Nua
Naas
Clondalkin
DUBLIN
Bray
Greystones
123

53
Inishmore
Liscannor Bay
Ennistimon
Tulla
Lough Derg
Portumna
Birr
OFFALY
Portarlington
Mountmellick
Slieve Bloom
529
Slieve Arderin
Port Laoise
Athy
Monasterevin
WICKLOW
Wicklow
Rathdrum
Wicklow Hd.
Mizen Hd.
53

Mal Bay
Mutton I.
CLARE
Ennis
Sixmilebridge
Killaloe
694
Keeper Hill
Templemore
Nenagh
Roscrea
Durrow
Mountrath
LAOIS
796
Mt. Leinster
Carlow
Tullow
Lugnaquilla
926
Rathvilly
Arklow

Loop Hd.
Kilrush
Kilkee
Shannon Airport
Foynes
Limerick
LIMERICK
Rathkeale
Golden Vale
TIPPERARY
Thurles
Kilkenny
KILKENNY
Callan
CARLOW
Muine Bheag
Bunclody
Gorey

D
Mouth of the Shannon
Kerry Hd.
Listowel
Feale
Munster
Tipperary
Cashel
Slievenamon
722
Carrick-on-Suir
Clonmel
Nore
Barrow
New Ross
WEXFORD
Enniscorthy
Cahore Pt.
D

Brandon B.
Tralee B.
Smerwick Harbour
Brandon Hd.
953
Brandon Mt.
Slieve Mish
853
Dingle
Dunmore Hd.
Maine
Newmarket
Kanturk
Mitchelstown
Fermoy
Galty Mts.
920
Galtymore
Kilfinnane
Newcastle West
Clonmel
Coleraine Mts.
Knockmealdown Mts.
792
WATERFORD
Waterford
Tramore
Wexford Harbour
Rosslare
Greenore Pt.
Carnsore Pt.

Great Blasket I.
Inishvickillane
Dingle Bay
KERRY
Killorglin
Killarney
Lough Leane
1041
Carrauntoohill
Macgillycuddy's Reeks
Kenmare
Mallow
Blackwater
Lismore
Dungarvan
Dungarvan Harbour
Tramore B.
Waterford Harbour
Hook Hd.
Saltee Is.
St. David's Hd.
St. David's

52
Valencia I.
Puffin I.
Great Skellig
Cahirciveen
Ballinskelligs B.
646
Caha Mts.
Glengarriff
Boggeragh Mts.
646
CORK
Macroom
Blarney
Cork
Lee
Midleton
Youghal
Youghal B.
St. Brides Bay
52

E
Scariff I.
Dursey I.
Crow Hd.
Castletown Bearhaven
Bear I.
Bantry Bay
Bantry
Dunmanway
Bandon
Bandon
Kinsale
Passage West
Crosshaven
Cork Harbour
Old Head of Kinsale
115
E

Mizen Hd.
Dunmanus B.
Skull
Long I.
Baltimore
Sherkin I.
Clear I.
C. Clear
Skibbereen
Clonakilty
Clonakilty B.
Galley Hd.

CELTIC SEA

NORTH CHANNEL

IRISH SEA

St. George's Channel

ft m
1500 500
600 200
300 100
0
150 300
600
260 1500
1000 3000
2000 6000
m ft

50   0 25 50 75 100 125 150 175 km
50   0   25   50   75   100 125 miles

ATLANTIC OCEAN

Shetland Is.
Yell Unst
Fetlar
Foula Mainland
Lerwick

Fair Isle

NORWAY
Bergen
Osøyra
Stord
Bømlo Leirvik
Haugesund
Kopervik
Åkrahamn
Sandnes Bryne
Stavanger
Nærbø
Boknafjorden

Orkney Is.
Westray Sanday
Stronsay
Mainland Kirkwall
Hoy South Ronaldsay

Pentland Firth
C. Wrath Thurso
Wick
Lewis Stornoway
Helmsdale

St. Kilda
North Harris
Uist Ullapool Lairg Golspie
Benbecula
South Uist
Outer Hebrides North West Highlands
Tain Moray Firth Buckie Banff Fraserburgh
Skye Portree Invergordon Dingwall Elgin Peterhead
L. Ness Inverness Spey Huntly Inverurie
Mallaig Rhum 1182 Aviemore Don Aberdeen
Eigg Fort William SCOTLAND Deen Ballater Stonehaven
Coll Ben Nevis 1342 Grampian Mts. 1311 Montrose
Tiree Mull Tobermory 1214 Forfar Arbroath
Oban Perth L. Lomond Dundee 238
Colonsay St. Andrews
L. Lomond 973 Glenrothes NORTH
Jura Stirling Kirkcaldy
Islay Greenock Dunfermline Dunbar SEA
Paisley Glasgow Edinburgh
East Kilbride Hamilton Berwick-upon-Tweed
Arran Kilmarnock Galashiels
Campbeltown Ayr Southern Uplands 840 Jedburgh 916 Alnwick
Malin Hd. Irvine Cheviot Hills
North Channel Girvan Dumfries Hawick
Aran I. Buncrana Coleraine Kirkcudbright Hexham 893 Newcastle-upon-Tyne
Letterkenny Ballymena Larne Annan Carlisle Gateshead South Shields Sunderland
Lifford NORTHERN IRELAND Antrim Bangor Workington Cumbrian Mts. Durham Hartlepool
Donegal Ulster Omagh Lough Belfast Whitehaven 978 Darlington Middlesbrough Redcar
Bundoran Lower L. Neagh Lisburn Lurgan Mull of Galloway Barrow- Stockton-on-Tees
Sligo Erne Enniskillen Portadown Armagh I. of Man in-Furness Scarborough
Ballina Clones Newry UNITED Douglas Lancaster Bridlington
Achill I. L. Conn Leitrim Cavan Castleblaney KINGDOM Pennines Harrogate
Castlebar Longford Ceanannus Mor Dundalk IRISH Blackpool Keighley York Beverley
Westport Roscommon Drogheda SEA Preston Leeds Kingston upon Hull
Connemara L. Mask Lough Ree Boyne Blackburn Burnley Bradford
Galway B. L. Corrib Athlone Mullingar Bolton Halifax Huddersfield Barnsley Grimsby
Galway Ballinasloe 636 Oldham Doncaster Rotherham Louth
Aran Is. Tullamore Lily Holyhead Liverpool Manchester Stockport Sheffield Lincoln
Ennis Birr Port Laoise Athy Anglesey Warrington Chesterfield Skegness
Nenagh Carlow Bangor Colwyn Bay Chester Crewe Mansfield The Wash Cromer
Kilrush IRELAND Thurles Kilkenny Wicklow Mts. 926 Snowdon Wrexham Nottingham Boston King's Lynn
Shannon Limerick Tipperary 1085 Pwllheli Stoke- Derby Grantham Norwich
953 Listowel Clonmel Carrick-on-Suir Cardigan Cambrian Mts. on-Trent Stafford Trent Great Yarmouth
1041 Tralee Wexford Bay Shrewsbury Telford ENGLAND Peterborough Lowestoft
Dingle Killarney Blackwater Rosslare Aberystwyth Welshpool Nuneaton Leicester Corby Thetford Bury St. Edmunds
Carrauntoohill Dungarvan Cambrian Mts. 886 Wolverhampton Coventry Rugby Northampton Ely Ipswich
Macgillycuddy's Reeks Waterford Fishguard BIRMINGHAM Redditch Royal Bedford Felixstowe Harwich
Valencia I. Cork Youghal Haverfordwest Carmarthen Brecon Worcester Leamington Spa Milton Keynes Cambridge Colchester
Bandon Cóbh Milford Haven Merthyr Tydfil Hereford Cotswold Hills Oxford Luton Harlow Chelmsford
Bantry Kinsale Pembroke Llanelli Neath WALES Cymbran Gloucester Cheltenham High Wycombe Hemel Hempstead Stevenage
C. Clear 99 Swansea Port Talbot Rhondda Newport Bristol Bath Swindon Newbury Reading LONDON Chatham Southend-on-Sea Margate
CELTIC Cardiff Barry Weston-super-Mare Salisbury Basingstoke Guildford Reigate Maidstone Dover Canterbury BELGIUM
SEA Bristol Channel Barnstaple Taunton Yeovil Southampton Fareham Crawley Ashford Folkestone Str. of Dover Dunkerque BRUSSEL
Exmoor Bude Exmouth 618 Bournemouth Winchester Havant Brighton Eastbourne Worthing Calais Boulogne-sur-Mer Gris-Nez (Bruxelles)
Newquay Dartmoor Weymouth Newport Portsmouth English Channel Le Touquet-Paris-Plage 33 St-Omer Béthune Lille Tournai
Truro Torbay Poole Isle of Wight Abbeville Bruay-la-Buissière Lens Valenciennes
Land's End Penzance St. Austell Plymouth Dieppe Le Tréport Amiens St-Quentin Cambrai
Falmouth Isles of Scilly FRANCE Picardie
C. de la Hague Pte. de Fécamp Pays de Rouen East from Greenwich
Alderney Barfleur Caux COPYRIGHT GEORGE PHILIP LTD.
Guernsey St. Peter Cherbourg Le Havre Bolbec Seine
Port Sark Valognes Trouville-sur-Mer Lisieux Elbeuf
Channel Is. St. Helier Jersey Cotentin Bayeux Caen
(U.K.) West from Greenwich

NETHERLANDS
's-Gravenhage
(Den Haag)
Hoek van Holland ROTTERDAM
Dordrecht
Texel
Den Helder
Alkmaar
Haarlem
Vlissingen
Zeebrugge Oostende
Antwerpen
Brugge Gent Mechelen

Projection: Conical with two standard parallels

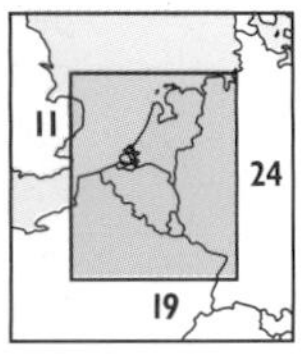

NORTH SEA

UNITED KINGDOM

NETHERLANDS

BELGIUM

GERMANY

FRANCE

LUXEMBOURG

Projection : Lambert's Conformal Conic

East from Greenwich

COPYRIGHT GEORGE PHILIP LTD.

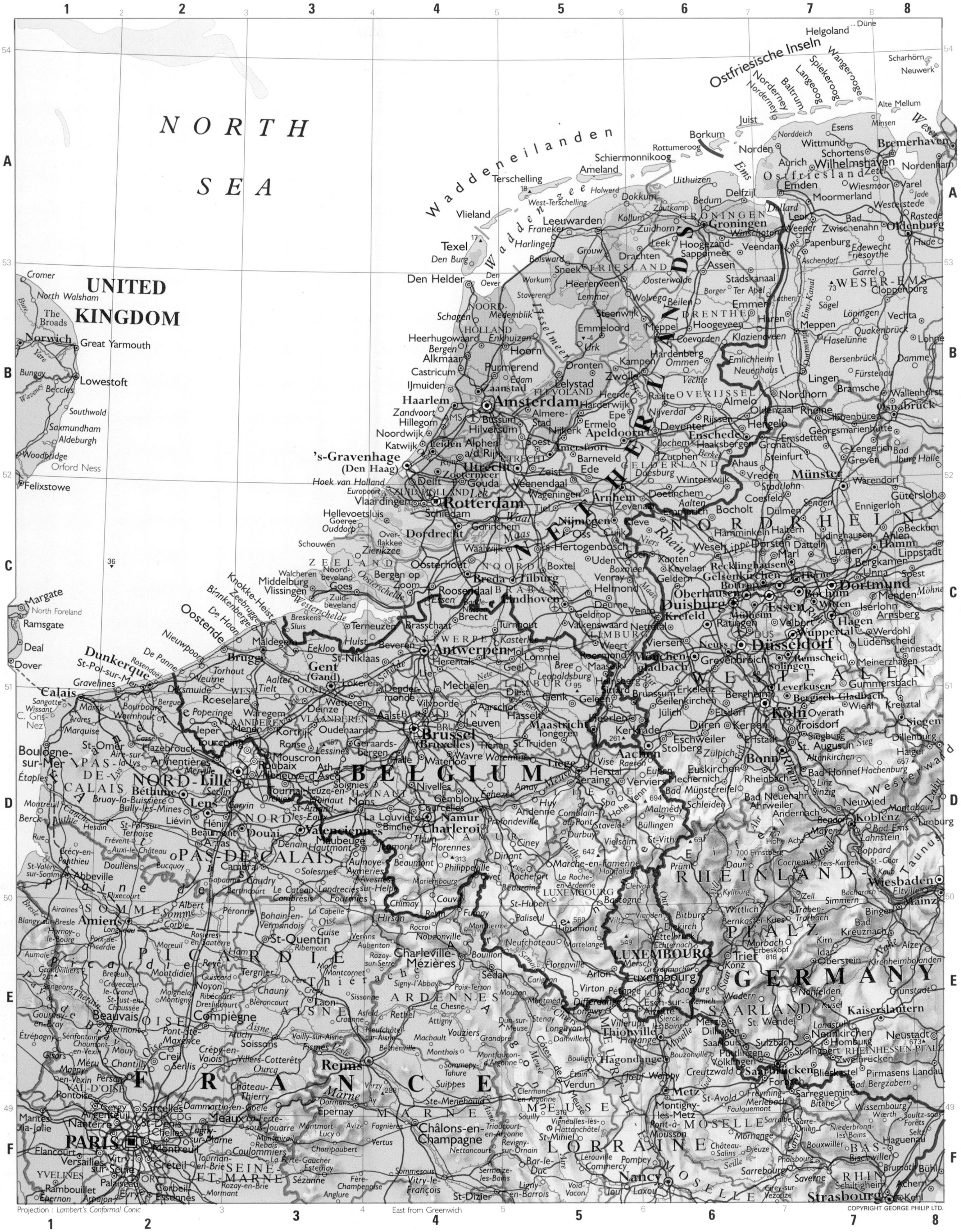

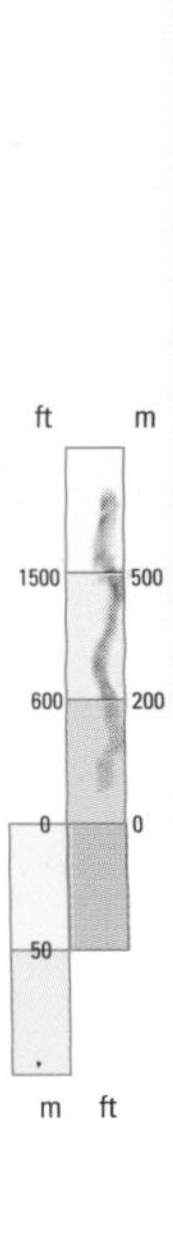

Underlined towns give their name to the
administrative area in which they stand.

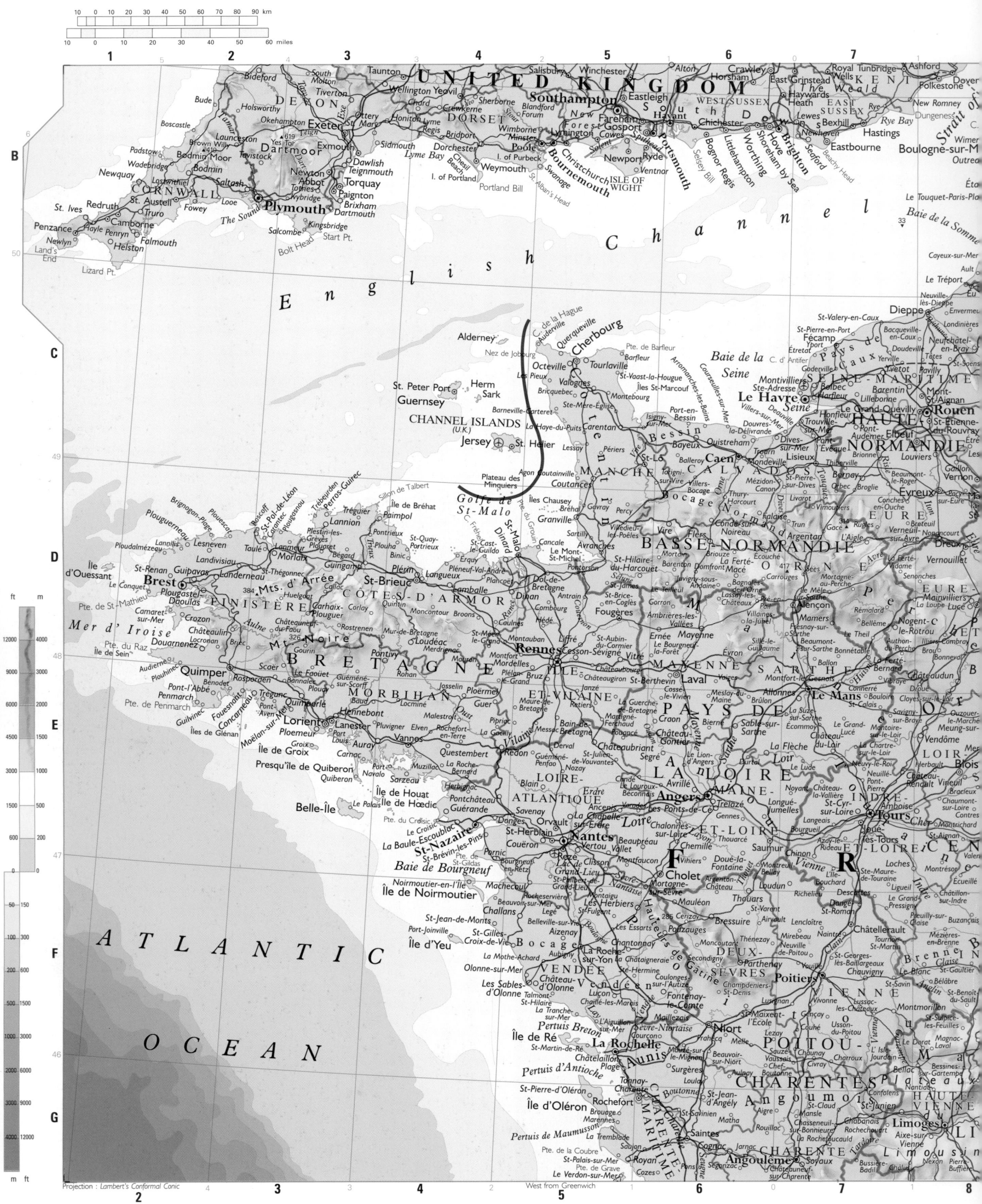

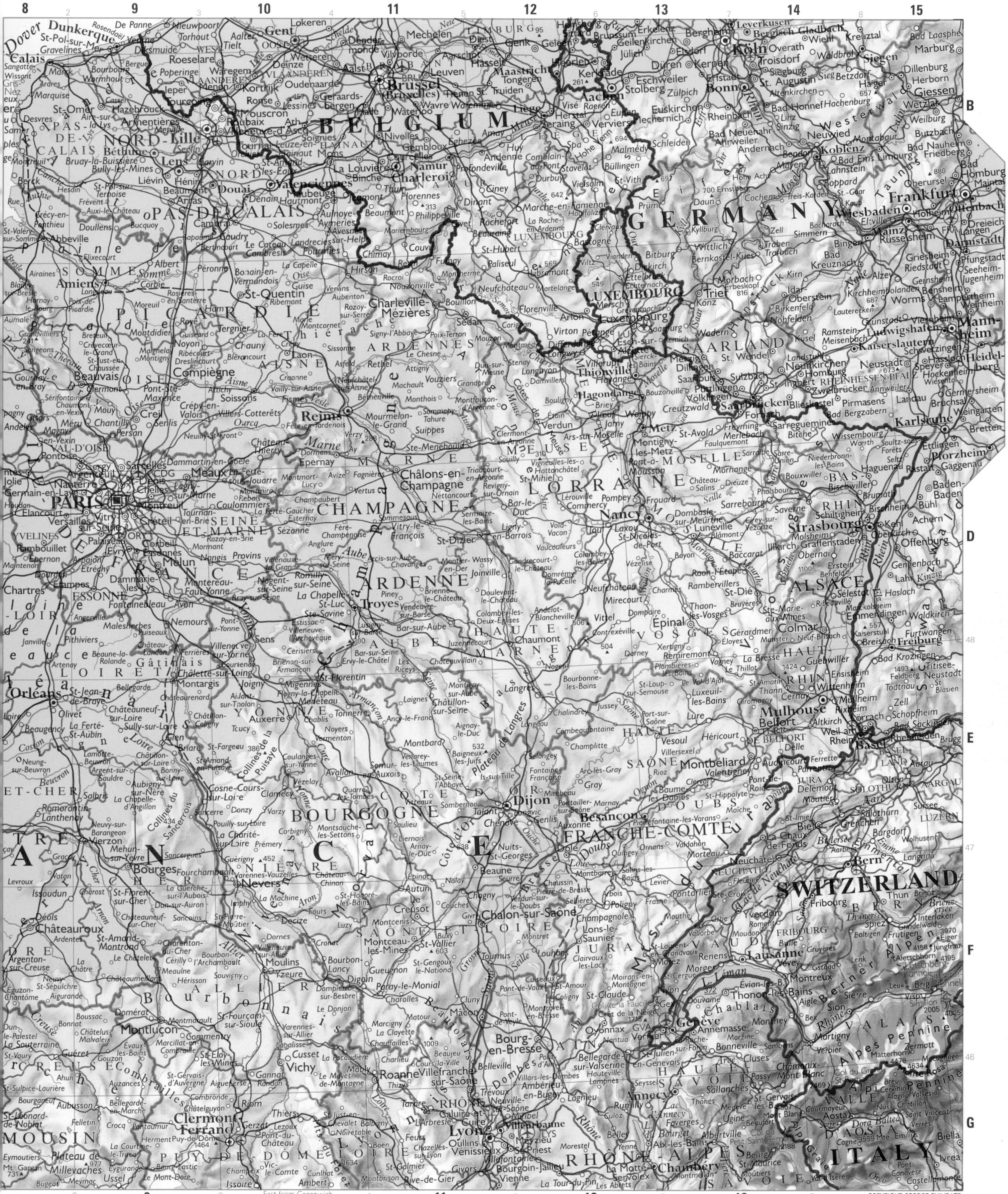

19

Underlined towns give their name to the
administrative area in which they stand.

COPYRIGHT GEORGE PHILIP LTD.

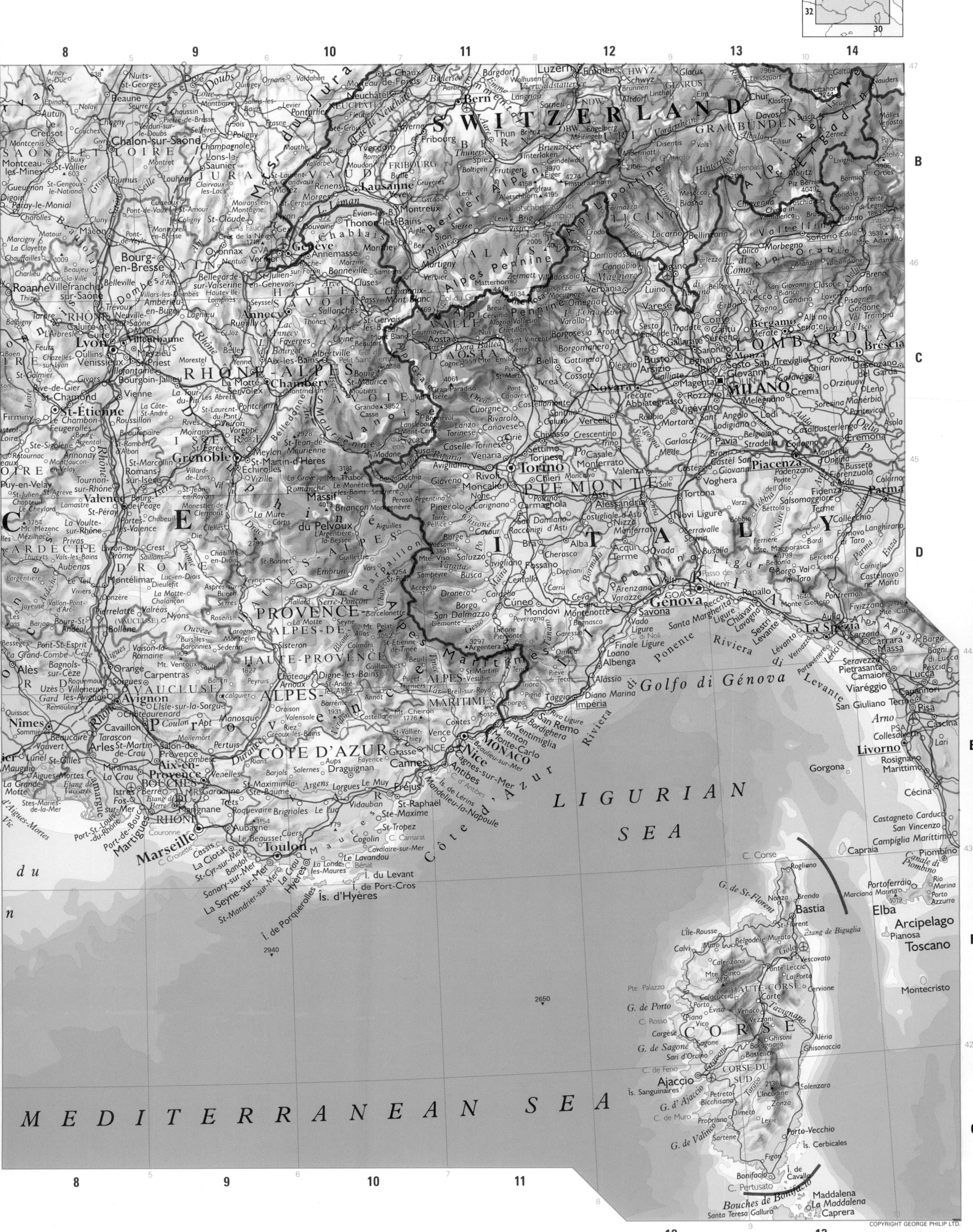

SWITZERLAND

SAÔNE-ET-LOIRE

JURA

VAUD

FRIBOURG

BERN

URI

GLARUS

SCHWYZ

GRAUBÜNDEN

TICINO

RHÔNE-ALPES

HAUTE-SAVOIE

SAVOIE

VALAIS

Alpes Pennine

LOMBARDIA

MILANO

ISÈRE

DRÔME

PROVENCE

ALPES-DE-HAUTE-PROVENCE

VAUCLUSE

ALPES-MARITIMES

PIEMONTE

ITALY

Lyon

St-Étienne

Grenoble

Valence

Avignon

Nîmes

Marseille

Toulon

Aix-en-Provence

CÔTE D'AZUR

Nice

MONACO

Cannes

Genève

Lausanne

Bern

Annecy

Chambéry

Torino

Génova

Savona

La Spezia

Livorno

Pisa

Lucca

Génova

GOLFO DI GÉNOVA

LIGURIAN
SEA

Riviera di Ponente

Riviera di Levante

Golfo di Génova

MEDITERRANEAN SEA

CORSE

HAUTE-CORSE

CORSE-DU-SUD

Bastia

Ajaccio

Calvi

Corte

Elba

Arcipelago Toscano

Pianosa

Montecristo

Bouches de Bonifacio

COPYRIGHT GEORGE PHILIP LTD.

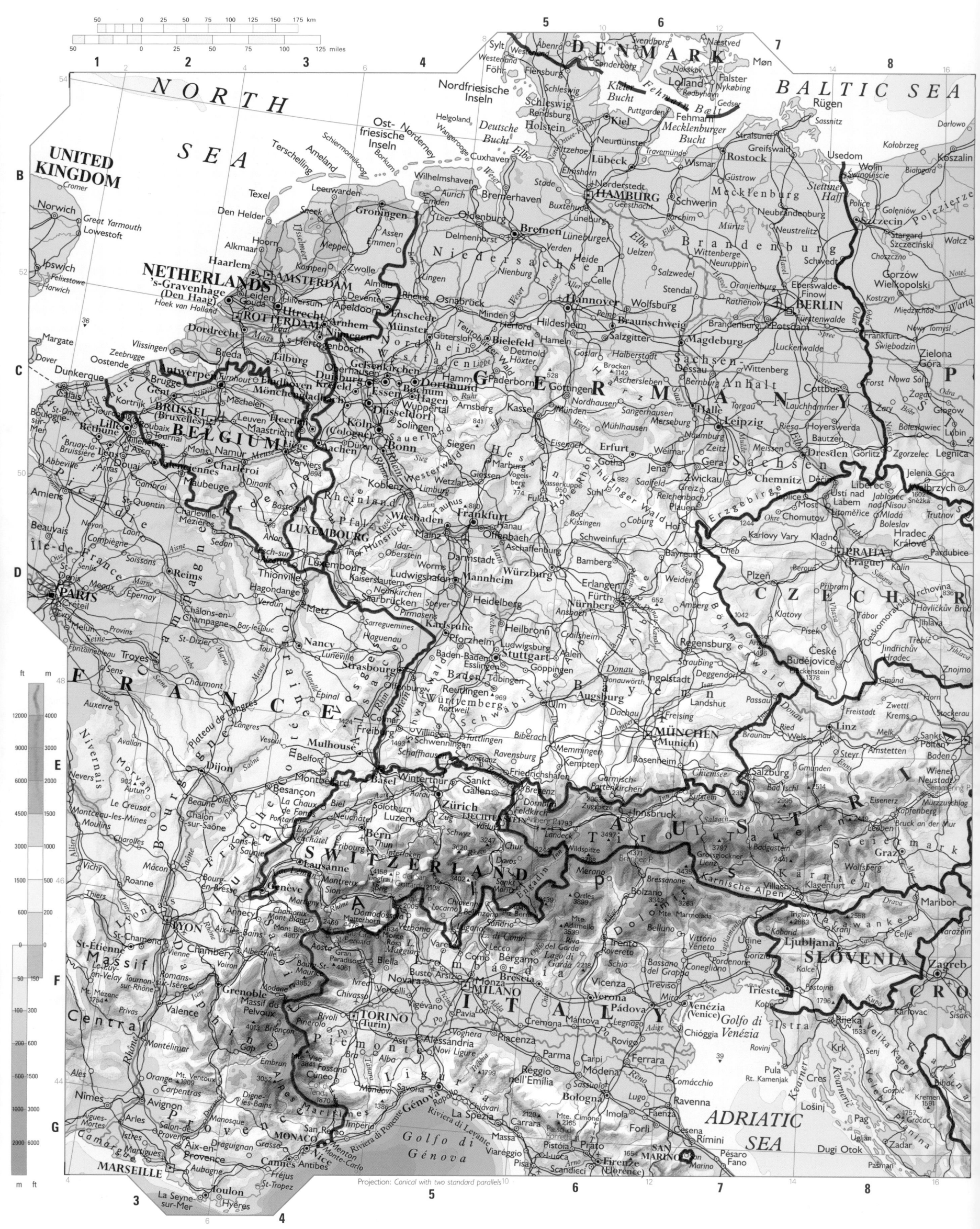

Projection: Conical with two standard parallels

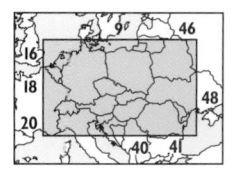

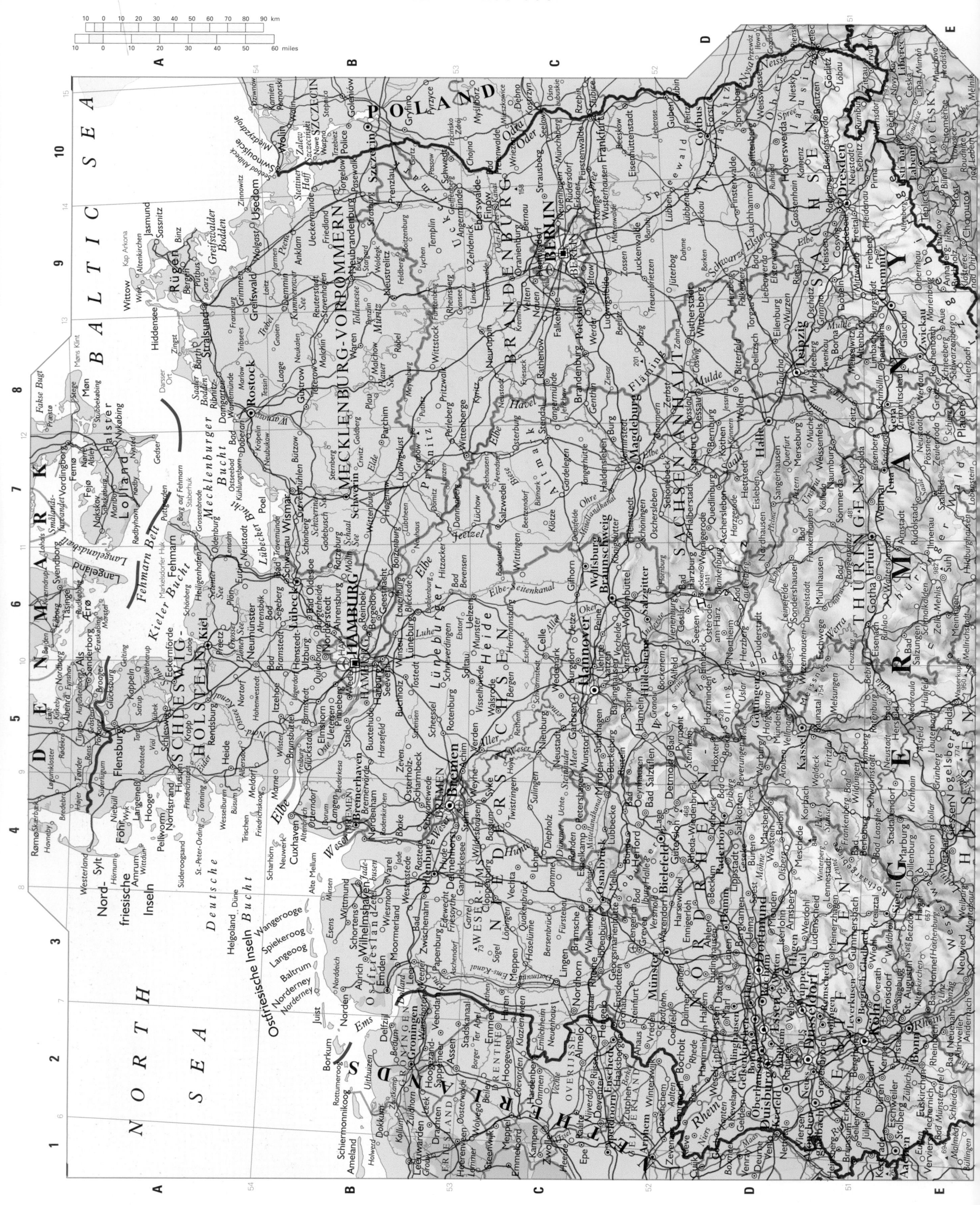

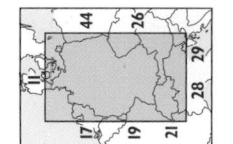

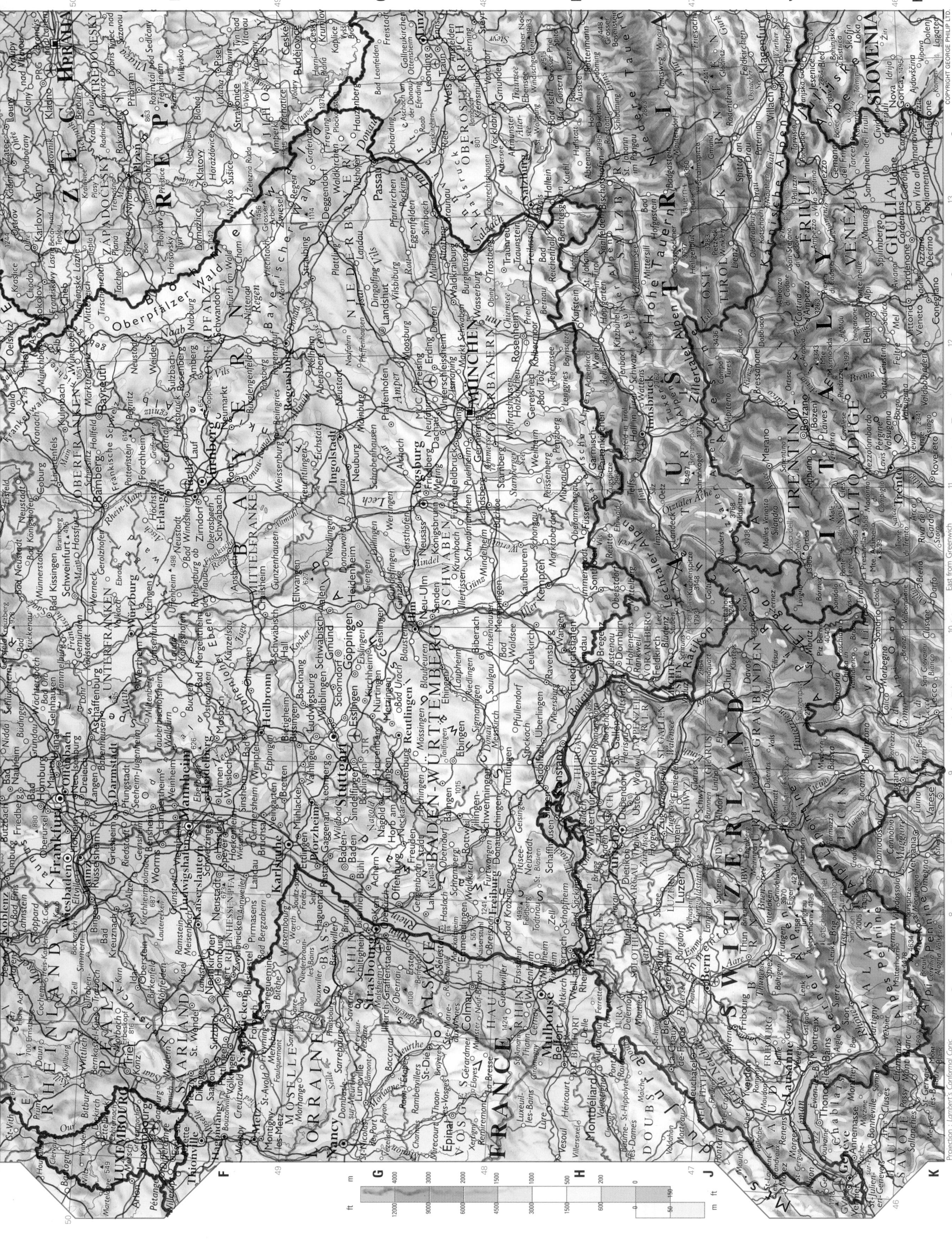

Underlined towns give their name to the administrative area in which they stand.

Projection : Lambert's Conformal Conic

East from Greenwich

COPYRIGHT GEORGE PHILIP LTD.

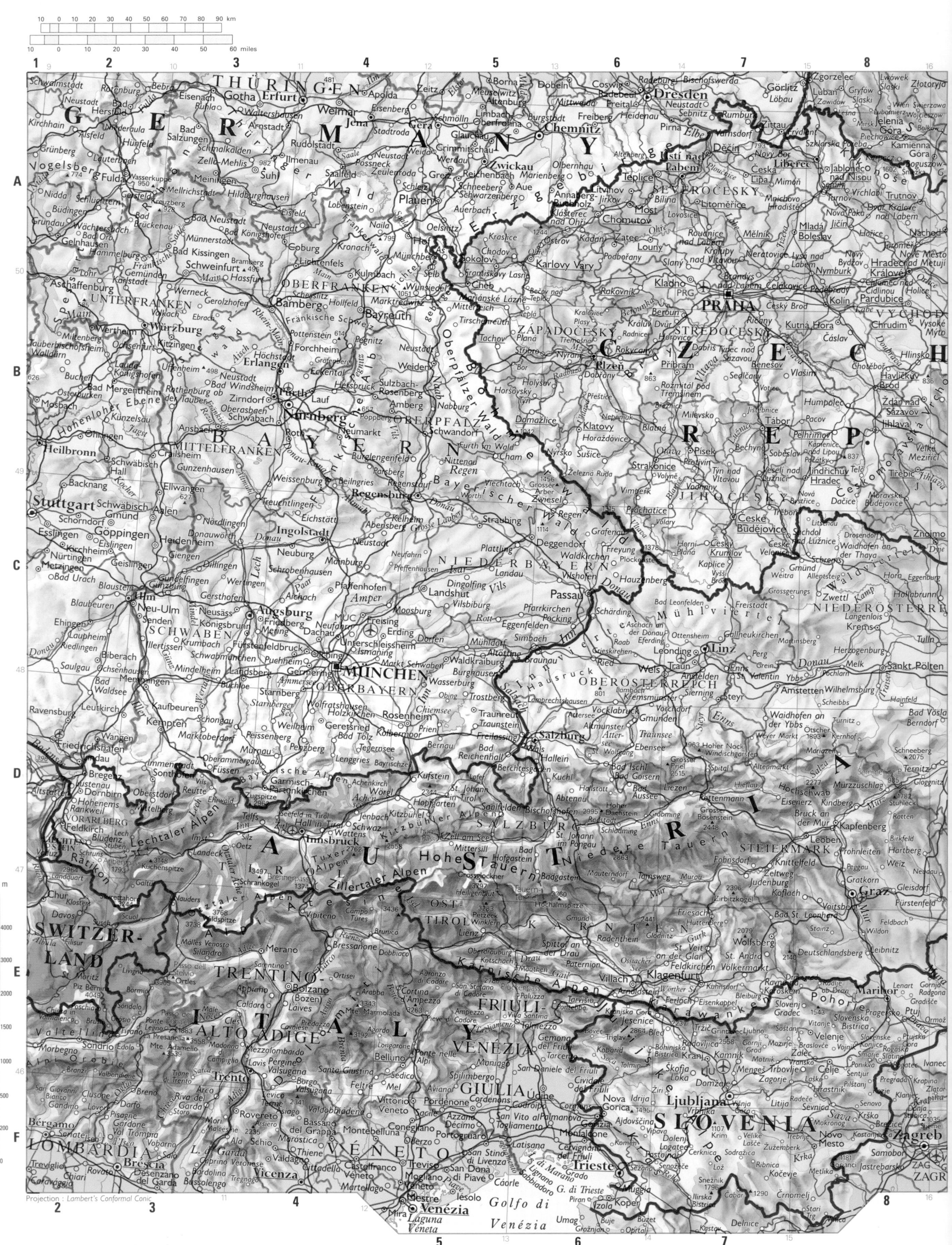

Underlined towns give their name to the
administrative area in which they stand.

Underlined towns give their name to the
administrative area in which they stand.

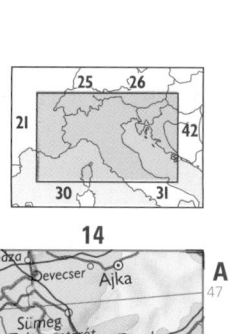

Administrative divisions in Croatia:

1. Brodsko-Posavska	4. Medimurska	8. Virovitičko-Podravska
2. Koprivničko-Križevačka	6. Požeško-Slavonska	10. Zagrebačka
3. Krapinsko-Zagorska	7. Varaždirska	

- - - - Inter-entity boundaries as agreed
at the 1995 Dayton Peace Agreement.

COPYRIGHT GEORGE PHILIP LTD.

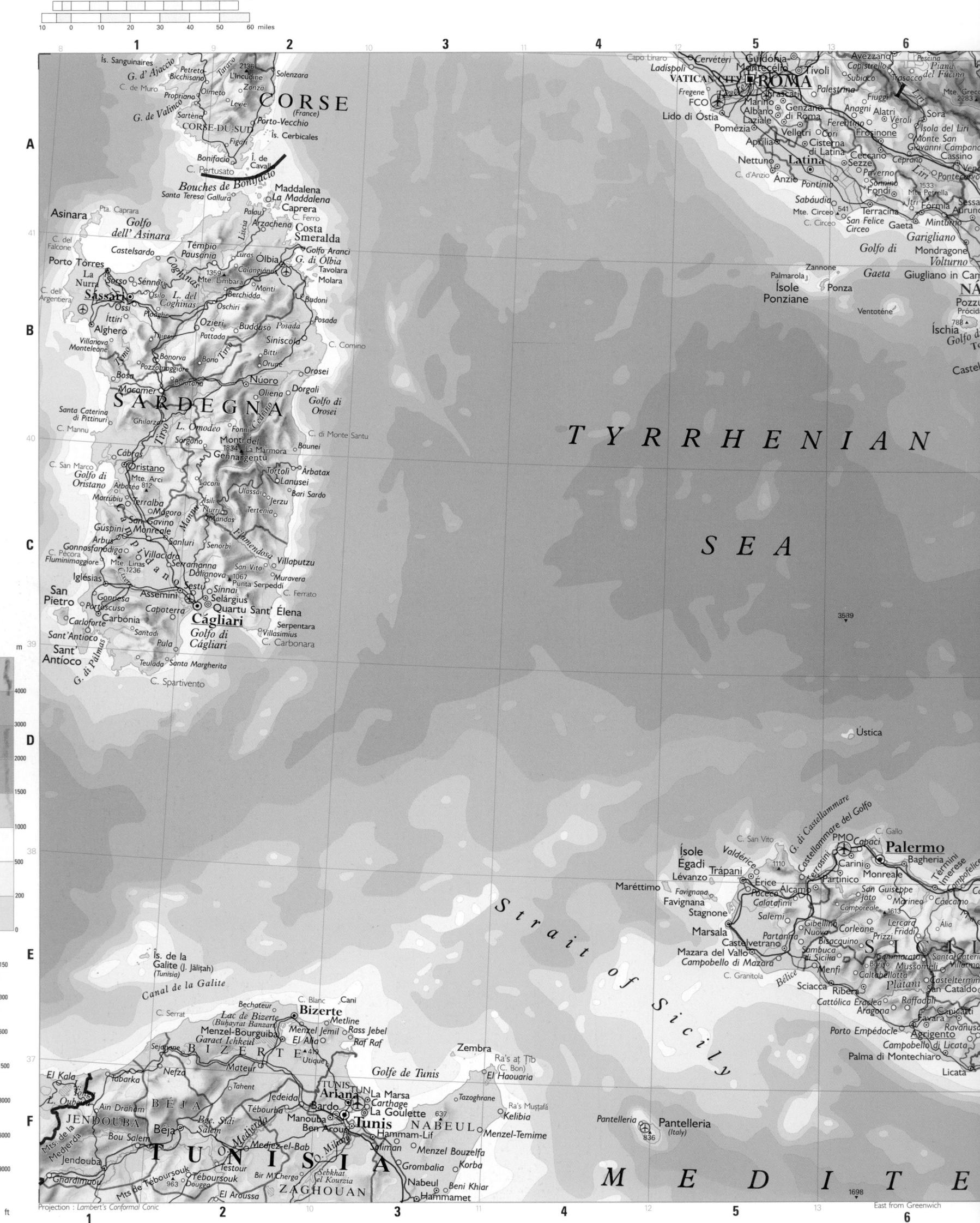

10 0 10 20 30 40 50 60 70 80 90 km
10 0 10 20 30 40 50 60 miles

CORSE
(France)

CORSE-DU-SUD

Ìs. Sanguinaires
G. d'Ajaccio
Petreto-Bicchisano
Propriano
Olmeto
G. de Valinco
Sartène
Levie
Zonza
Solenzara
Porto-Vecchio
Figari
Îs. Cerbicales
Bonifacio
Î. de Cavallo
C. Partusato
Bouches de Bonifacio

Maddalena
La Maddalena
Caprera
Santa Teresa Gallura
Palau
Arzachena
C. Ferro
Costa Smeralda

Asinara
Pta. Caprara
Golfo dell' Asinara
C. del Falcone
Castelsardo
Témpio Pausánia
Luras
Ólbia
Golfo Aranci
G. di Olbia
Tavolara
Molara

Porto Tórres
La Nurra
C. dell' Argentiera
Sorso
Sénnori
Sássari
Osilo
Osci
Coghinas
L. del Coghinas
Berchidda
Monti
Calangiánus
1359
Mte. Limbara

Ittiri
Alghero
Villanova Monteleone
Ploaghe
Ózieri
Buddusó
Pattada
Bitti
Orune
Posada
Siniscola

Bonorva
Bono
Núoro
Orosei
Bosa
Macomer
Pozzomaggiore
Orgosolo
Oliena
Dorgali
Golfo di Orosei

SARDEGNA

Santa Caterina di Pittinuri
C. Mannu
Ghilarza
L. Omodeo
Fonni
Sórgono
Monti del Gennargentu
1834 La Marmora
C. di Monte Santu
Baunei

Cábras
Oristano
Mte. Arci 812
Marrúbiu
Terralba
Mógoro
Làconi
Nurri
Tortolì
Árbatax
Lanusei
Jerzu
Bari Sardo
Tertenia
Ulassai

Güspini
San Gavino
Monreale
Sanluri
Senorbì
Mandas

Arbus
Gonnosfanádiga
Fluminimaggiore
Villacidro
Mte. Linas 1236
Dólianova
San Vito
1067
Muravera
Villaputzu
C. San Marco
Golfo di Oristano

C. Pécora
Iglésias
Serramanna
Sestu
Sínnai
Punta Serpeddi
C. Ferrato

San Pietro
Gonnesa
Assemini
Selárgius
Quartu Sant' Élena
Serpentara
Carloforte
Portoscuso
Capoterra
Cágliari
Villasimius

Sant'Antíoco
Santadi
Pula
Golfo di Cágliari
C. Carbonara

Sant' Antíoco
G. di Pálmas
Teulada
Santa Margherita
C. Spartivento

VATICAN CITY
FCO
ROMA
Capo Linaro
Ladíspoli
Cervéteri
Guidónia
Montecélio
Tivoli
Avezzano
Pescina
Piani del Fúcino
Mte. Greco 2283
Tarascio del Fúcino
Capistrello
Fregene
Frascati
Marino
Genzano di Roma
Subiaco
Palestrina
Sora
Albano
Lido di Óstia
Pomézia
Velletri
Laziale
Cisterna di Latina
Cori
Anagni Alatri
Ferentino
Véroli
Isola del Liri
Frosinone
Monte San Giovanni Campano
Nettuno
Ánzio
Aprília
Sezze
Ceccano
Ceprano
Cassino
C. d'Anzio
Pontínia
Sabáudia
541 Mte. Circeo
San Felice Circeo
Sónnino
Priverno
Terracina
1533 Mte. Petrella
Fondi
Itri
Pontecor
Gaeta
Fórmia
Minturno
Gariglíano
Golfo di Gaeta
Mondragone
Vólturno
Sessa Aurunca

Palmarola
Zannone
Ísole Ponziane
Ponza
Giugliano in Cam
NA
Ventoténe
Pózzu
788 Ìschia
Prócida
Golfo di
Castell

TYRRHENIAN
SEA

3539

Ústica

Íssole Égadi
Lévanzo
Maréttimo
Favignana
C. San Vito
Valdérice
Trápani
Érice
1110
Castellammare del Golfo
G. di Castellammare del Golfo
PMO
Cápaci
Carini
Monreale
Bagheria
Palermo
Términi Imerese
Cáccamo
Álcamo
Paceco
Partinico
San Giuseppe Jato
Marínea
Campofélice
Marsala
Calatafimi
Gibellina Nuova
Stagnone
Salemi
Partanna
Corleone
Prizzi
Lércara Friddi
1615
Ália
Castelvetrano
Bisacquino
Sámbuca di Sicília
S
Mazara del Vallo
Campobello di Mazara
Menfi
Caltabellotta
Mussomeli
Santa Caterir
Villalros
C. Granitola
Belice
Sciacca
Ribera
Plátani
Aragona
C. Blanc
Cani
Raffadali
San Cataldo

Strait of Sicily

Cattólica Erasclea
Porto Empédocle
Agrigento
Campobello di Licata
Palma di Montechiaro
Licata

MEDITE

Pantelleria
836 Pantelleria (Italy)
1698

Ís. de la Galite (J. Jālīṭah) (Tunisia)
Canal de la Galite

Bechateur
C. Blanc
Cani
C. Serrat
Lac de Bizerte (Buhayrat Banzart)
Garaet Ichkeul
Bizerte
Metline
Ras Jebel
Raf Raf
Menzel-Bourguiba
Menzel Jemil
El Alia
Mateur
412
Utique
Zembra
Ra's aṭ Ṭīb (C. Bon)
El Haouaria

Séjanane
Tahent
BIZERTE
Nefza
Tébourba
Jedeida
Golfe de Tunis
Tazoghrane
Ra's Muṣṭafá

El Kala
Tabarka
L. Oub
L. Oub
Ain Drâham
Mts. de la Medjerda
BÉJA
Béja
Bge. Sidi Salem
Testour
Manouba
Bardo
Ariana
TUNIS
Tunis
La Marsa
Carthage
La Goulette
UN
Kelibia
Menzel-Temime

JENDOUBA
Jendouba
Bou Salem
Medjez-el-Bab
Ben Arous
Hammam-Lif
NABEUL
Menzel Bouzelfa
Korba

Ghardimaou
Mts. de Téboursouk
963
Testour
Medjerda
Milian
Soliman
Grombalia
Beni Khiar
Nabeul

El Aroussa
Dougga
ZAGHOUAN
Bir M'Cherga
El Kourzia
Hammamet

TUNISIA

637

Projection : Lambert's Conformal Conic

East from Greenwich

ft m
12000 4000
9000 3000
6000 2000
4500 1500
3000 1000
1500 500
600 200
0 0

m ft
50 150
100 300
200 600
500 1500
1000 3000
2000 6000
3000 9000
m ft

28 29
40
78 38

7 8 9 10 11 12 20
15 16 17 18 19

A D R I A T I C

S E A

MOLISE
Términi
Campomarino
Montenero
di Bisaccia
Guglionesi
Trivento
Agnone
Castel
del Sangro
Castelmauro
Larino
Bojano
Riccia
Campobasso
Isernia
Piedimonte
Matese
Guardia
Sanframondi
Santa María
Marcianise
Caserta
Benevento
Montesárchio
Avellino
NAP
POLI
Aversa
Nola
Afragola
Pompei
Nocera Inferiore
Salerno
Cava de'
Tirreni
Sorrento
Battipáglia
Capri
Amalfi
Golfo di Salerno
Sele
Castellabate
Punta Licosa
Agrópoli
Póllica
Palinuro
C. Palinuro
Ascea
Camerota
Sapri
Maratea
Praia a Mare
Scalea
Diamante
Belvedere
Marittimo
San Marco Argentano
Cetraro
Fuscaldo
Páola
San Lúcido
Amantea

Campomarino
L. di Lésina
Lésina
Apricena
San Marco
in Lamis
San Severo
San Giovanni
Rotondo
Lucera
FÓGGIA
Orsara
di Puglia
Troia
Bovino
Ascoli
Satriano
Cerignola
Orta Nova
Candela
Lavello
Melfi
Rionero in Vulture
Venosa
Lioni
Calitri
Montella
Bella
Avigliano
POTENZA
Tito
Moliterno
Lagónegro
Mte. Sirino
Latrónico
Sinni
Lauria
Golfo di
Policastro
Mormanno
Morano
Cálabro
Castrovillari
Cassano allo Iónio
Trebisacce
Amendolara
Roggiano
Gravina
Spezzano
Albanese
Corigliano
Cálabro
Rossano
Bisignano
Acri
Luzzi
Montalto
Uffugo
Rende
Cosenza
Rogliano
Decollatura
BASILICATA
Matera
Grassano
Tricárico
Stigliano
Pisticci
Montalbano
Iónico
Nova Siri
Policoro
Senise
San Arcangelo
Agri
Tursi
Montescaglioso
Ferrandina
Pomarico
Bernalda
San Giórgio
Iónico
TÁRANTO

Vico del
Gargano
Vieste
Monte Sant' Ángelo
Manfredónia
Golfo di Manfredónia
Barletta
Biscéglie
Molfetta
Giovinazzo
Terlizzi
BARI
Mola di Bari
Polignano a Mare
Monópoli
Conversano
Putignano
Noci
Alberobello
Martina
Franca
Cisternino
Ostuni
Brindisi
San Vito dei Normanni
Mesagne
Francavilla
Grottaglie
Oria
Latiano
San Pietro
Vernótico
Squinzano
Trepuzzi
LECCE
Copertino
Leverano
Nardò
Galatina
Martano
Otranto
Gallípoli
Máglie
Poggiardo
Sant' Andrea
Casarano
Tricase
Taviano
Ugento
Presicce
Gagliano del Capo
C. Santa Maria di Léuca

S E A

Strait of Otranto

Shëngjin
Lezhë
MIRDITË
Rrëshen
Mat
Fushe-Krujë
Kruje
Durrës
TIRANË
Kavajë
Krrabë
Peqin
Elbasan
Cërrik
Lushnjë
Divjakë
Fier
Berat
Vlorë
Himarë
Girokastër
Sarandë
Finiq
GREECE

Golfo di
Táranto

KÉRKIRA
Kérkira
(Corfu)

I O N I A N

S E A

CALÁBRIA
Paola
Amantea
Nicastro
Golfo di
Sant' Eufémia
Pizzo
Vibo Valéntia
Tropea
Mileto
Rosarno
Gióia Tauro
Palmi
Scilla
Villa San Giovanni
Réggio di
Calábria
Mélito di
Porto Salvo
Bova
C. Spartivento
Crotone
Catanzaro
Golfo di Squillace
Soverato
Chiaravalle Centrale
Serra San Bruno
Guardavalle
Polístena
Cittanova
Caulónia
Roccella Iónica
Siderno
Locri
Bovalino Marina
Bianco

Ísole Eólie
Strómboli
Filicudi
Salina
Panarea
Lípari
Vulcano
Alicudi
Milazzo
Barcellona Pozzo di Gotto
Str. di Messina
Messina
Taormina
Giarre
Riposto
Acireale
Misterbianco
CATÁNIA
Golfo di
Catánia
Etna
Bronte
Randazzo
Adrano
Paternò
Biancavilla
Belpasso
Enna
Leonforte
Caltanissetta
Piazza
Armerina
Gela
Vittória
Cómiso
RAGUSA
Módica
Noto
Avola
Siracusa
Augusta
Melilli
C. Passero
C. Murro di Porco
Golfo di
Noto
Pachino

R R A N E A N   S E A

COPYRIGHT GEORGE PHILIP LTD.

7 8 9 10 11 12
15 16 17 18 19

Underlined towns give their name to the
administrative area in which they stand.

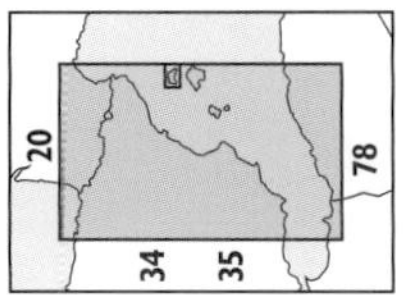

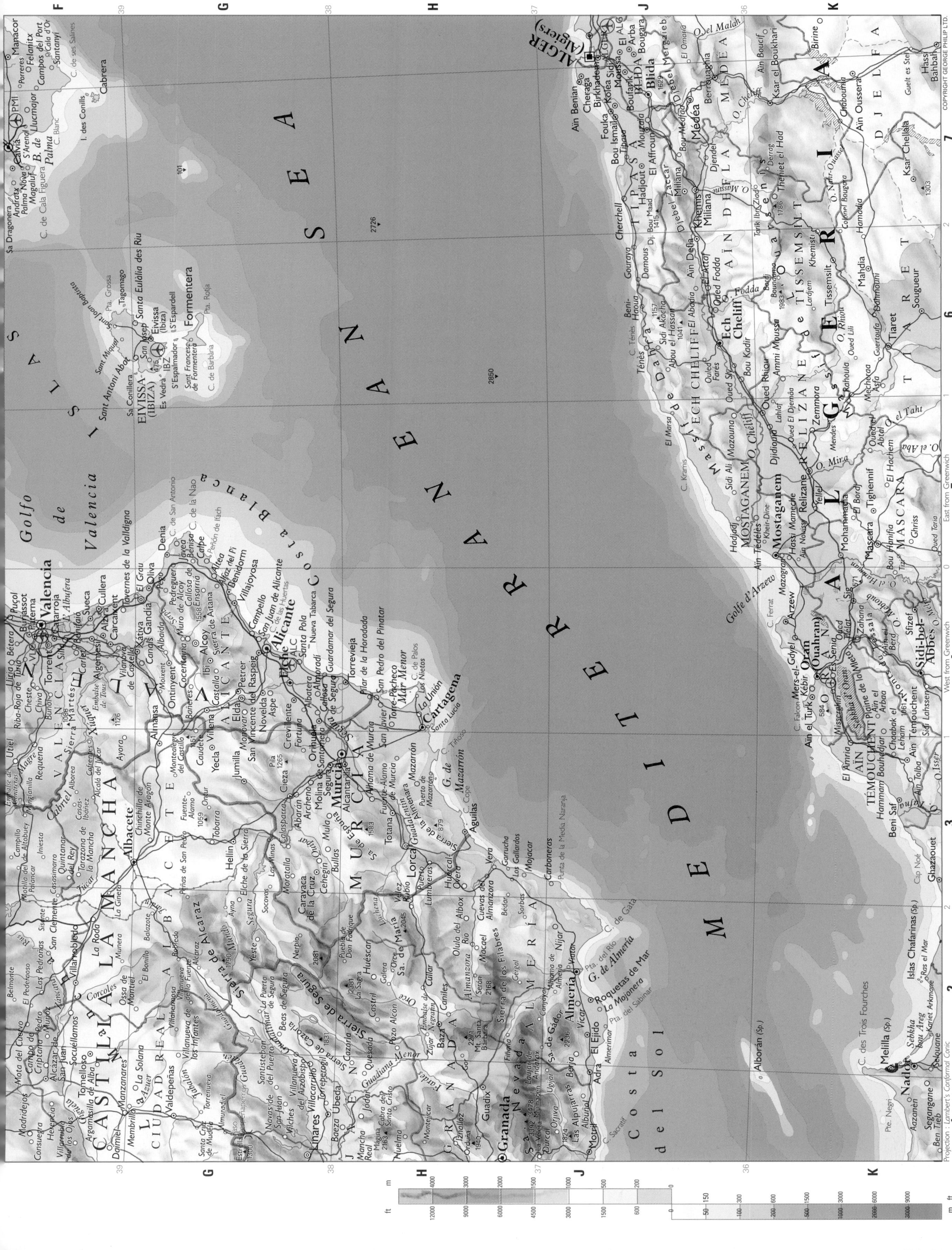

MEDITERRANEAN SEA

BALEARIC SEA

Islas Baleares

Golfo de Valencia

Costa Blanca

Costa del Sol

Spain

VALENCIA
Valencia
Alicante
Elche
Murcia
Cartagena
Lorca
Albacete
Granada
Almería
Melilla (Sp.)
Nador

CASTILLA-LA MANCHA
CIUDAD REAL
MURCIA
GRANADA
ALMERÍA
Sierra de Segura
Sierra Nevada

EIVISSA (IBIZA)
Formentera
Cabrera
Sa Dragonera

Algeria

ALGER (ALGIERS)
Blida
Médéa
Ech Cheliff
Mostaganem
Oran (Ouahran)
Mascara
Sidi-bel-Abbès
Tlemcen (TÉMOUCHENT)
Tiaret

MÉDÉA
ECH CHELIFF
RELIZANE
MOSTAGANEM
ORAN
MASCARA
GISELL (TISSEMSILT)
TIARET
DJELFA

Golfe d'Arzew

East from Greenwich

West from Greenwich

Projection: Lambert's Conformal Conic

COPYRIGHT GEORGE PHILIP LTD.

m / ft scale
4000 3000 2000 1500 1000 500 200 0 -50 -150 -300 -600 -1500 -3000 -6000
12000 9000 6000 4500 3000 1500 600 0

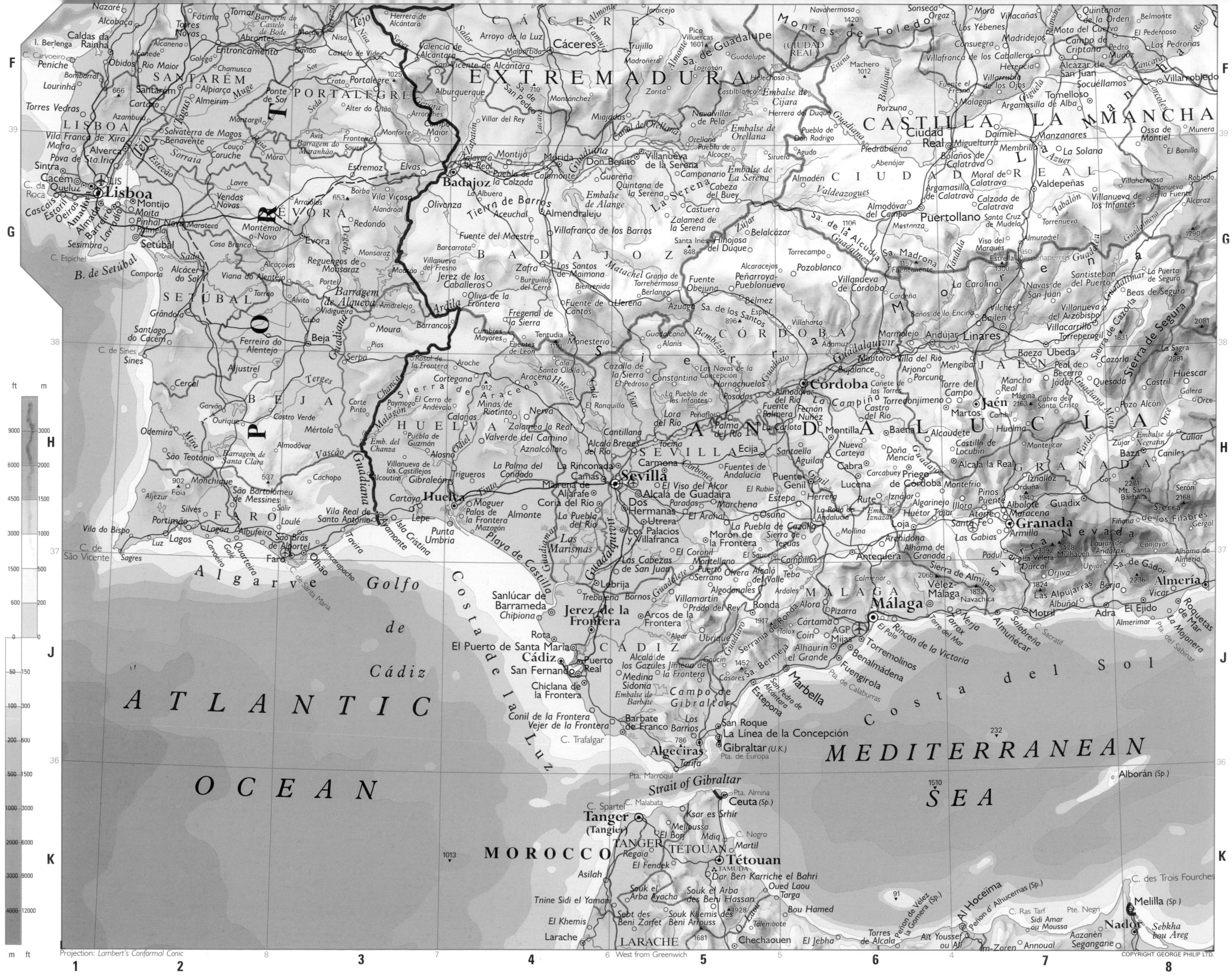

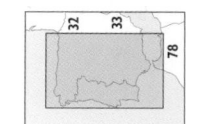

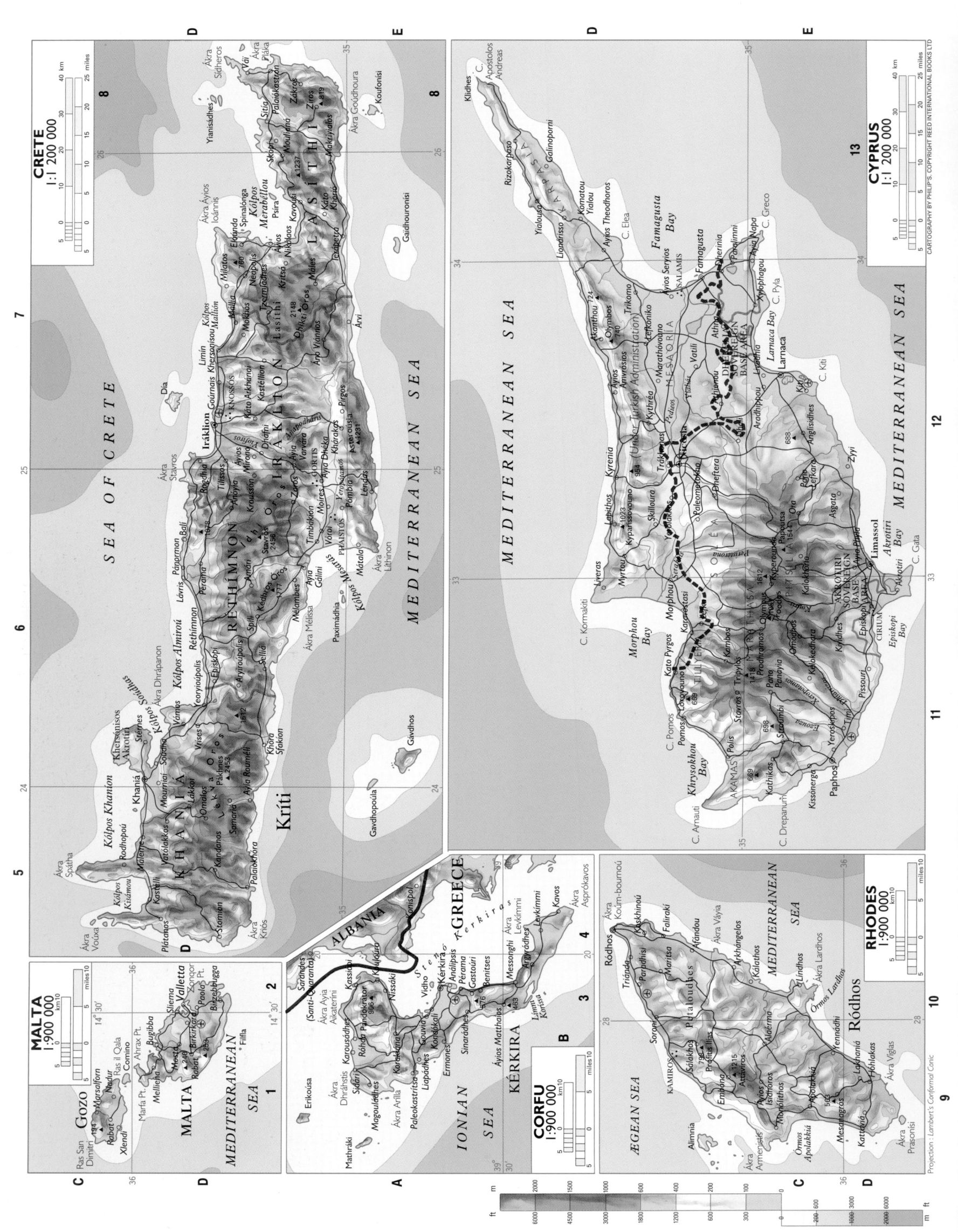

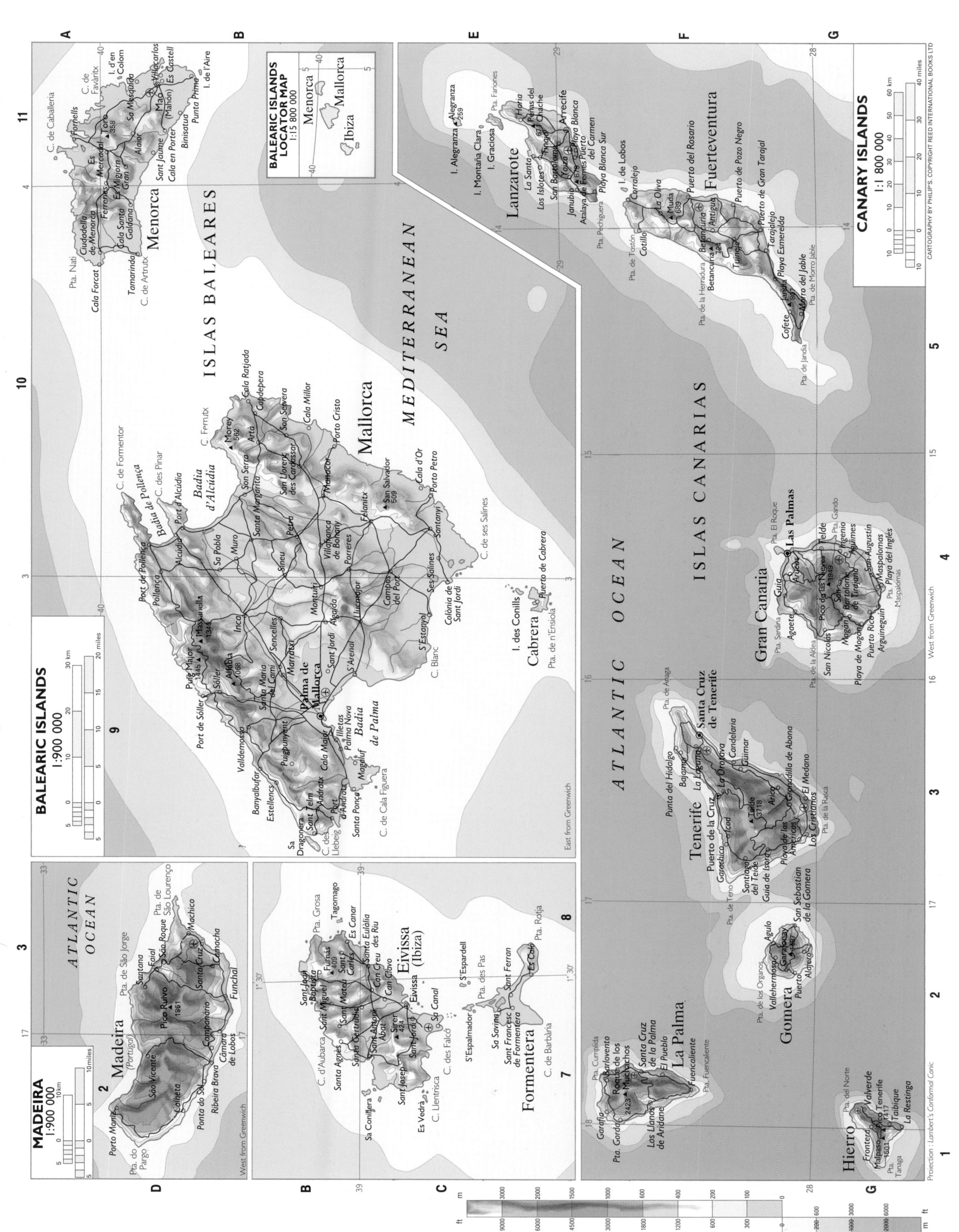

BALEARIC ISLANDS LOCATOR MAP
1:15 800 000

Menorca
Mallorca
Ibiza

BALEARIC ISLANDS
1:900 000

MADEIRA
1:900 000

CANARY ISLANDS
1:1 800 000

ISLAS BALEARES

MEDITERRANEAN SEA

Menorca

C. de Caballeria
Tornells
I. d'en Colom
C. de Favàritx
Es Mercadal
Fornells
Toro
358
Sa Mesquida
Maó (Mahón)
Villacarlos
Es Castell
Ferreries
Alaior
Ciudadella de Menorca
Sant Jaume
Cala en Porter
Binisatua
Punta Prima
I. de l'Aire
Cala Santa Galdana
Es Migjorn Gran
Pta. Nati
Cala Forcat
Tamarinda
C. de Artrutx

Mallorca

C. de Formentor
Port de Pollença
Pollença
Port de Sóller
Port de Sóller
Sóller
Badia de Pollença
Badia d'Alcúdia
Port d'Alcúdia
C. des Pinar
Alcúdia
Sa Pobla
Sa Dragonera
C. des Llebeig
Andratx
Port d'Andratx
Banyalbufar
Estellencs
Valldemossa
Puig Major
1445
Massanella
1348
Alfàbia
1068
Santa Maria del Camí
Inca
Muro
Santa Margarita
San Llorenç des Cardassar
Artà
Capdepera
Cala Ratjada
Morey
562
Son Servera
Cala Millor
Sant Telm
Santa Ponça
Magaluf
Palma Nova
Illetes
Cala Major
Sineu
Petra
Manacor
C. Ferrutx
Son Serra
Porto Cristo
Cala d'Or
Porto Petro
Cala Figuera
Badia de Palma
Palma de Mallorca
S'Arenal
S'Estanyol
Sant Jordi
Sa Cabaneta
Algaida
Montuïri
Llucmajor
Porreres
Felanitx
509
San Salvador
Campos del Port
Santanyí
Ses Salines
C. de ses Salines
C. Blanc
Colònia de Sant Jordi
I. des Conills
Puerto de Cabrera
Cabrera
I. de n'Ensiola
Pta. de n'Ensiola
Villafranca de Bonany
Sencelles
Marratxí
Vilademoscà
Puigpunyent

Madeira (Portugal)

ATLANTIC OCEAN
Porto Moniz
Pta. do Pargo
São Vicente
Seixal
Pta. de São Jorge
São Jorge
Santana
Faial
São Roque
Pta. de São Lourenço
Machico
Caniçal
Pico Ruivo
1861
Funchal
Santa Cruz
Câmara de Lobos
Ribeira Brava
Campanário
Ponta do Sol
Calheta
Canhas

Eivissa (Ibiza)

Pta. Grossa
Tagomago
Es Canar
Sant Joan Baptista
Sant Miguel
Santa Eulàlia del Riu
Santa Gertrudis
Fornàs
409
Sant Mateu
Sant Carles
Sant Antoni Abat
Sant Rafel
Can Clavo
Can Guasc
Eivissa
Sant Jordi
Sa Talaia
424
C. d'Aubarca
Santa Agnès
Sant Josep
Es Vedrà
C. Llentrisca
C. des Falcó
S'Espalmador
Sa Savina
Sant Francesc de Formentera
Sant Ferran
Es Caló
Pta. des Pas
S'Espardell
Pta. de Sa Creu des Riu

Formentera
Pta. Roija
C. de Barbària

Canary Islands
ISLAS CANARIAS

Lanzarote
I. Alegranza
Alegranza 259
I. Montaña Clara
I. Graciosa
Pta. Fanones
Haria
Palmas del Chache 671
Arrecife
La Santa
Los Islotes
Playa Blanca
San Bartolomé
Tinajo
Tiagua
Yaiza
Janubio
Atalaya de Femés 607
Pta. Pechiguera
Puerto del Carmen
I. de Lobos

Fuerteventura
Puerto del Rosario
Corralejo
La Oliva
Muda 689
Betancuria
Antigua
Tuineje
Tarajalejo
Puerto de Pozo Negro
Puerto de Gran Tarajal
Pta. de Tostón
Cotillo
Pta. de la Herradura
Betancuria
Pta. de Jandía
Morro del Jable
Pta. de Morro Jable
Playa del Jable
Cofete
Jandía
Playa Esmeralda

Gran Canaria
Las Palmas
Pta. El Roque
Guia
Pta. Sardina
Gáldar
Agaete
San Nicolás
Pta. de la Aldea
Mogán
Puerto de Mogán
Arguineguín
Puerto Rico
Playa de Mogán
Pico de las Nieves 1949
Teror
Telde
Ingenio
Agüimes
Santa Lucía
Arinaga
Bartolomé de Tirajana
San Agustín
Playa del Inglés
Maspalomas
Maspalomas

Tenerife
Santa Cruz de Tenerife
Puerto de la Cruz
La Orotava
La Laguna
Candelaria
Güímar
Teide 3718
Icod
Punta del Hidalgo
Pta. de Anaga
Bajamar
Pta. de Teno
Buenavista
Guía de Isora
Adeje
Granadilla de Abona
El Médano
Arico
Pta. de la Rasca
San Miguel
Los Cristianos
Playa de las Américas
Santiago del Teide
Pico de las Nieves

La Palma
Pta. Cumplida
Barlovento
Roque de los Muchachos 2423
Santa Cruz de la Palma
El Pueblo
Los Llanos de Aridane
Fuencaliente
Pta. Gorda
Garafía
Pta. de Fuencaliente
Sa Conillera

Gomera
San Sebastián de la Gomera
Agulo
Vallehermoso
Hermigua
Garajonay 1487
Chipude
Playa de Santiago
Pta. de los Órganos
Valle Gran Rey
Alajeró
Puerto

Hierro
Valverde
Pico de Tenerife 1417
Frontera
Taibique
La Restinga
Malpaso 1501
Pta. del Norte
Pta. de Orchilla
Pta. Tamaga

ATLANTIC OCEAN

East from Greenwich
West from Greenwich

CARTOGRAPHY BY PHILIP'S. COPYRIGHT REED INTERNATIONAL BOOKS LTD

Projection : Lambert's Conformal Conic

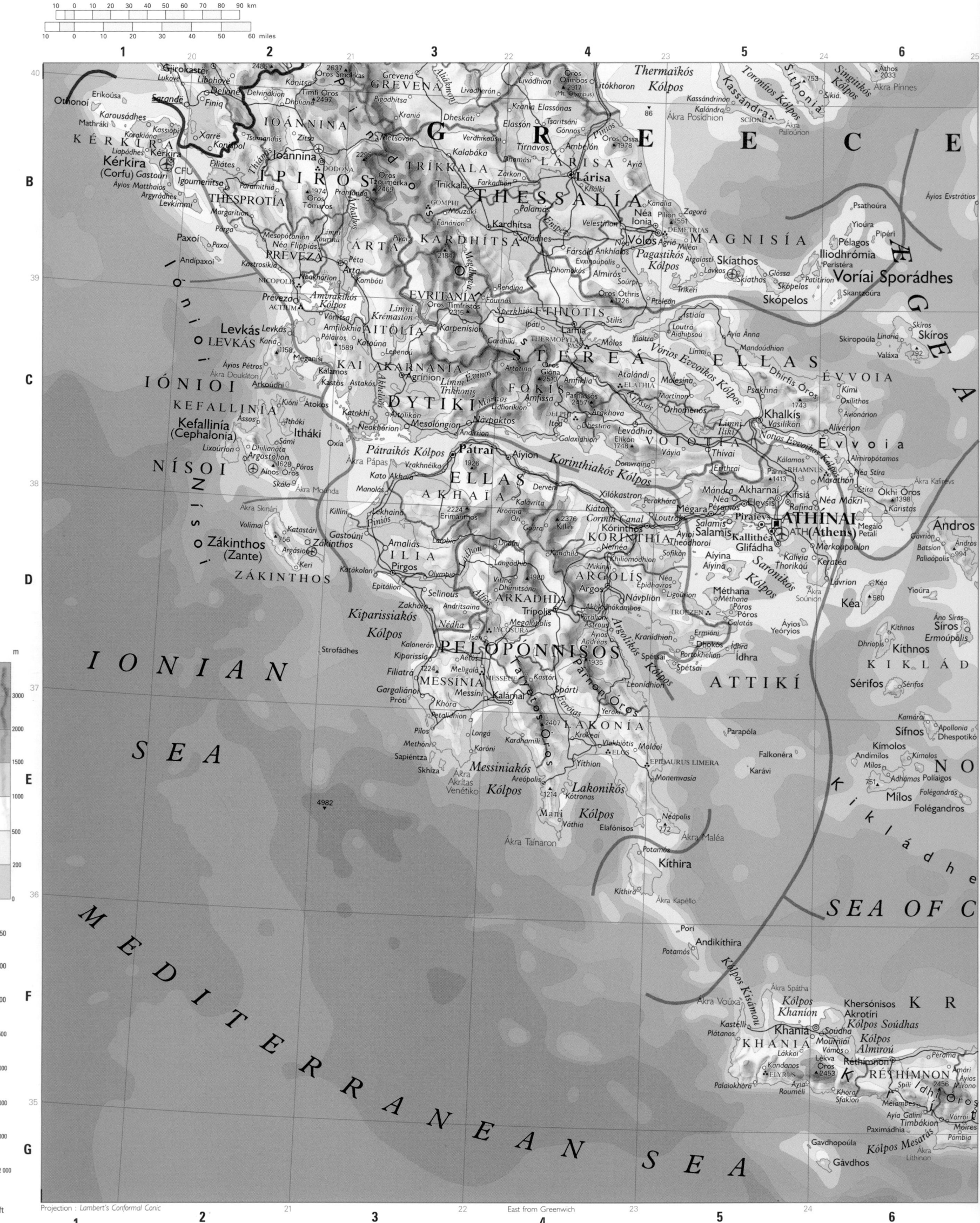

10 0 10 20 30 40 50 60 70 80 90 km
10 0 10 20 30 40 50 60 miles

IONIAN

SEA

MEDITERRANEAN SEA

GREECE

THESSALÍA

IPÍROS

IOÁNNINA

TRÍKKALA

LARISA

Lárisa

KARDHÍTSA

MAGNISÍA

Vólos

ÁRTA

PREVEZA

THESPROTÍA

Ioánnina

Kérkira
(Corfu)

KÉRKIRA

EVRITANÍA

FTHIÓTIS

STEREÁ

ELLAS

ÉVVOIA

FOKÍS

DYTIKÍ

AITOLÍA
KAI AKARNANÍA

VOIOTÍA

Khalkís

Évvoia

IÓNIOI

KEFALLINÍA

Kefallinía
(Cephalonia)

Ithháki

NÍSOI

Pátraikós Kólpos

Pátrai

Korinthiakós Kólpos

ELLAS

AKHAÍA

KORINTHÍA

ATHÍNAI
(Athens)

Piraiévs

Zákinthos
(Zante)

ZÁKINTHOS

ÍLIA

ARGOLÍS

ATTIKÍ

ARKADHÍA

PELOPÓNNISOS

KIKLÁD

MESSINÍA

LAKONÍA

Kalámai

Spárti

Messiniakós
Kólpos

Lakonikós
Kólpos

Máni

SEA OF C

Kíthira

KR

Kólpos
Khaníon

KHANÍA

Khaniá

Kólpos Soúdhas

RÉTHÍMNON

K

Kólpos Mesarás

Gávdhos

Projection : Lambert's Conformal Conic

East from Greenwich

ft m

9000 3000
6000 2000
4500 1500
3000 1000
1500 500
600 200
0 0

0 0
50 150
100 300
200 600
500 1500
1000 3000
2000 6000
3000 9000
4000 12 000
m ft

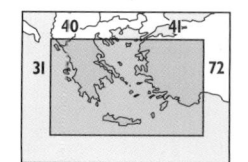

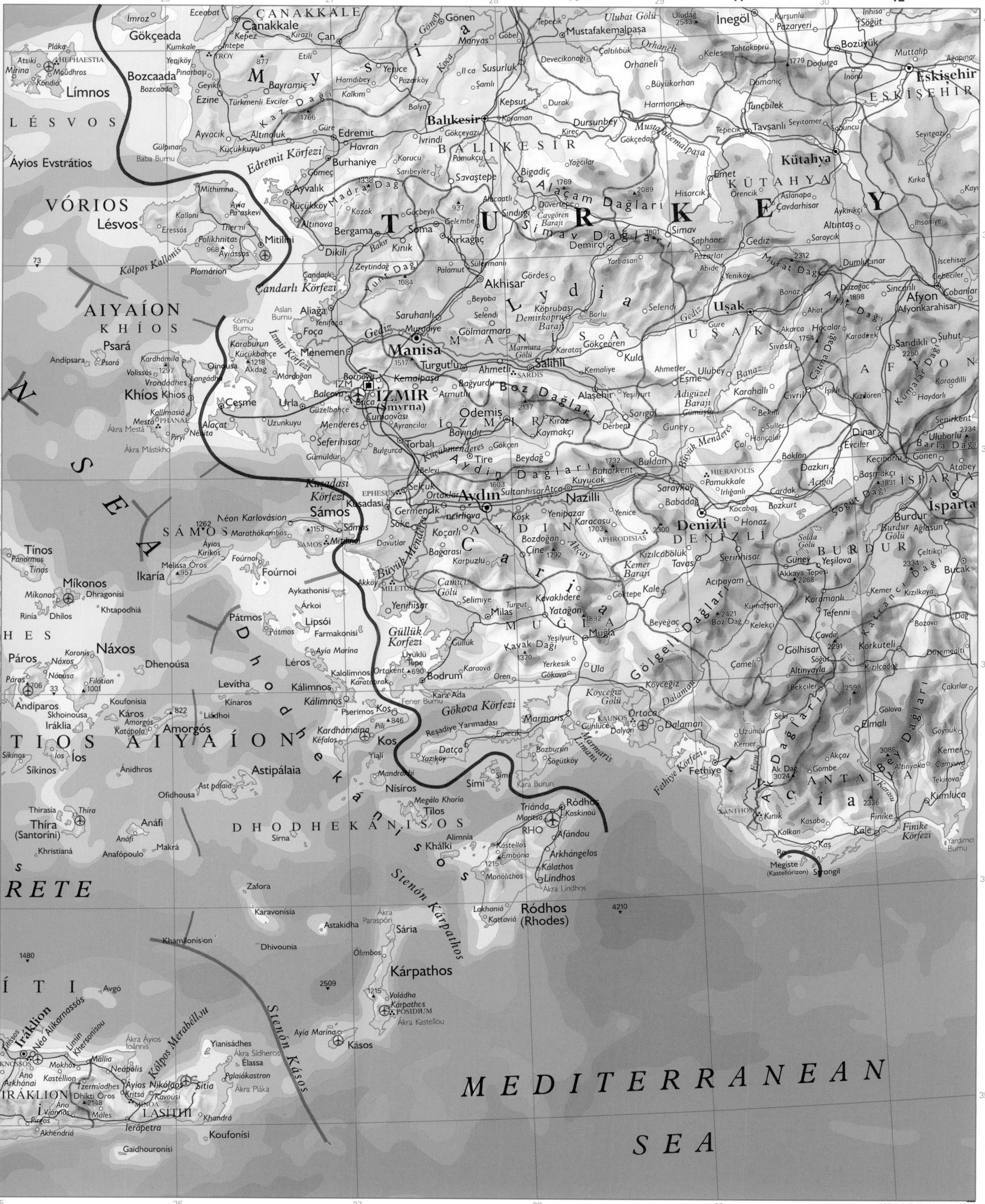

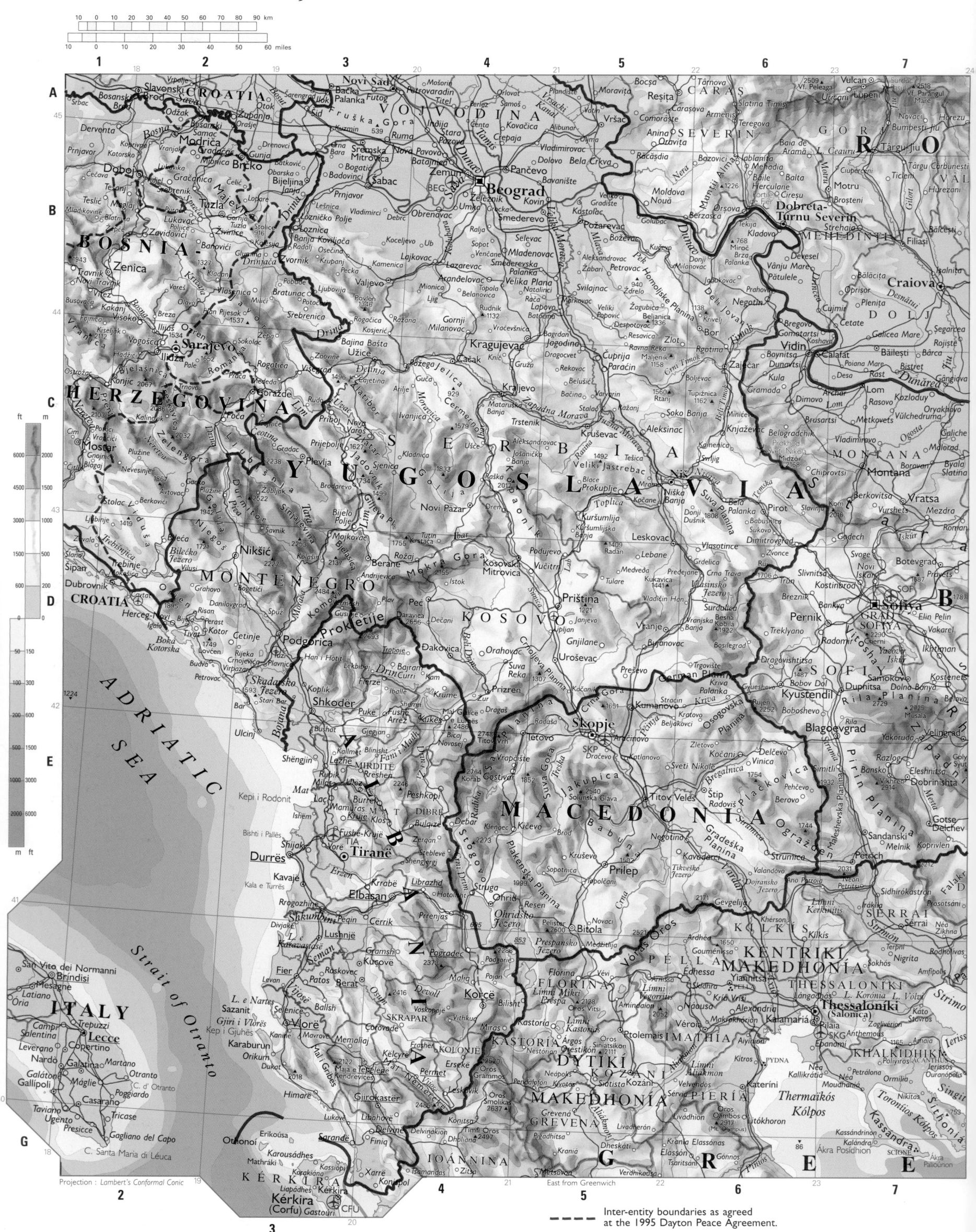

Projection : Lambert's Conformal Conic

East from Greenwich

Inter-entity boundaries as agreed
at the 1995 Dayton Peace Agreement.

Underlined towns give their name to the
administrative area in which they stand.

COPYRIGHT GEORGE PHILIP LTD.

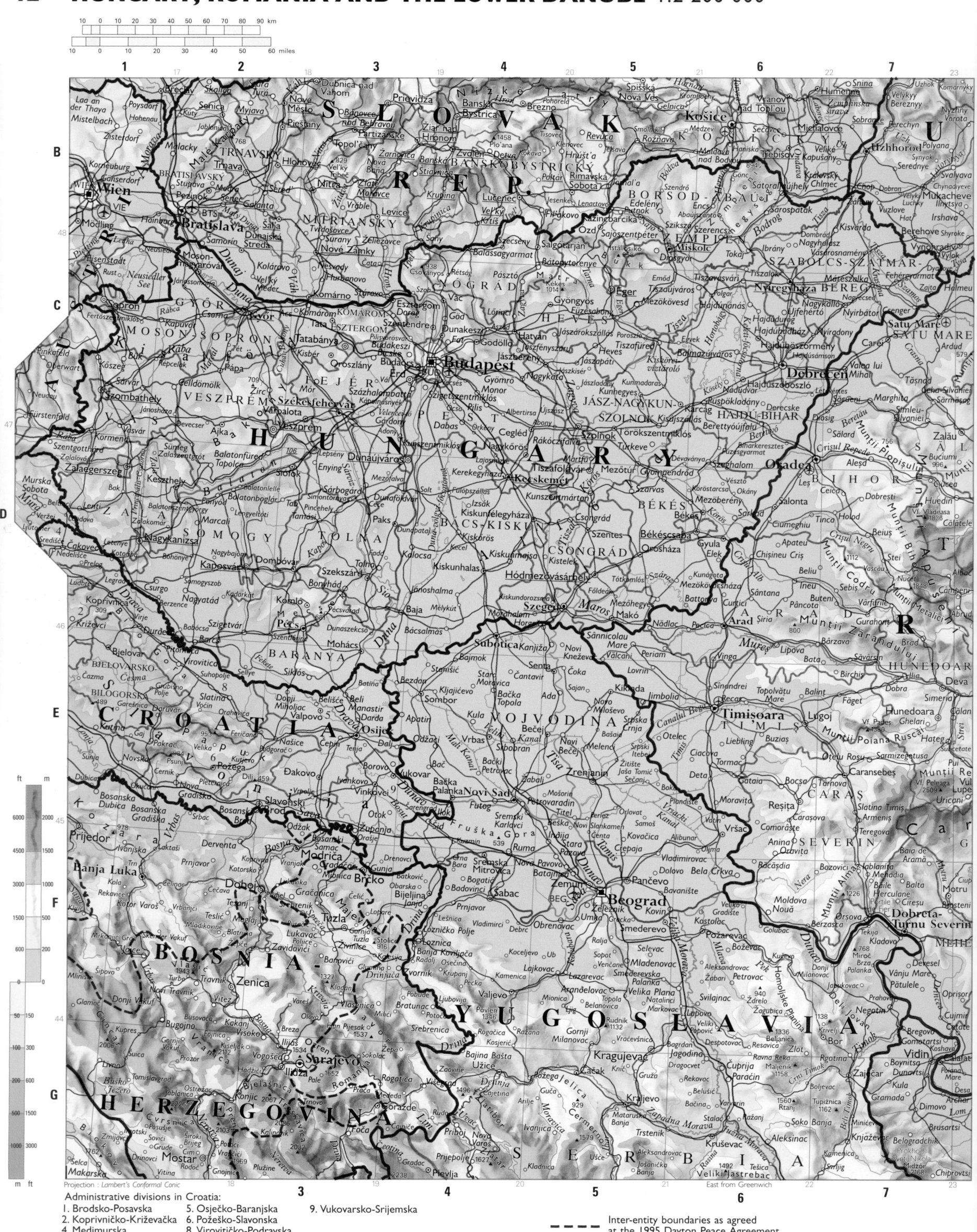

Administrative divisions in Croatia:
1. Brodsko-Posavska   5. Osječko-Baranjska   9. Vukovarsko-Srijemska
2. Koprivničko-Križevačka   6. Požeško-Slavonska
4. Medimurska   8. Virovitičko-Podravska

Projection : Lambert's Conformal Conic

Inter-entity boundaries as agreed
at the 1995 Dayton Peace Agreement.

East from Greenwich

Underlined towns give their name to the administrative area in which they stand.

COPYRIGHT GEORGE PHILIP LTD.

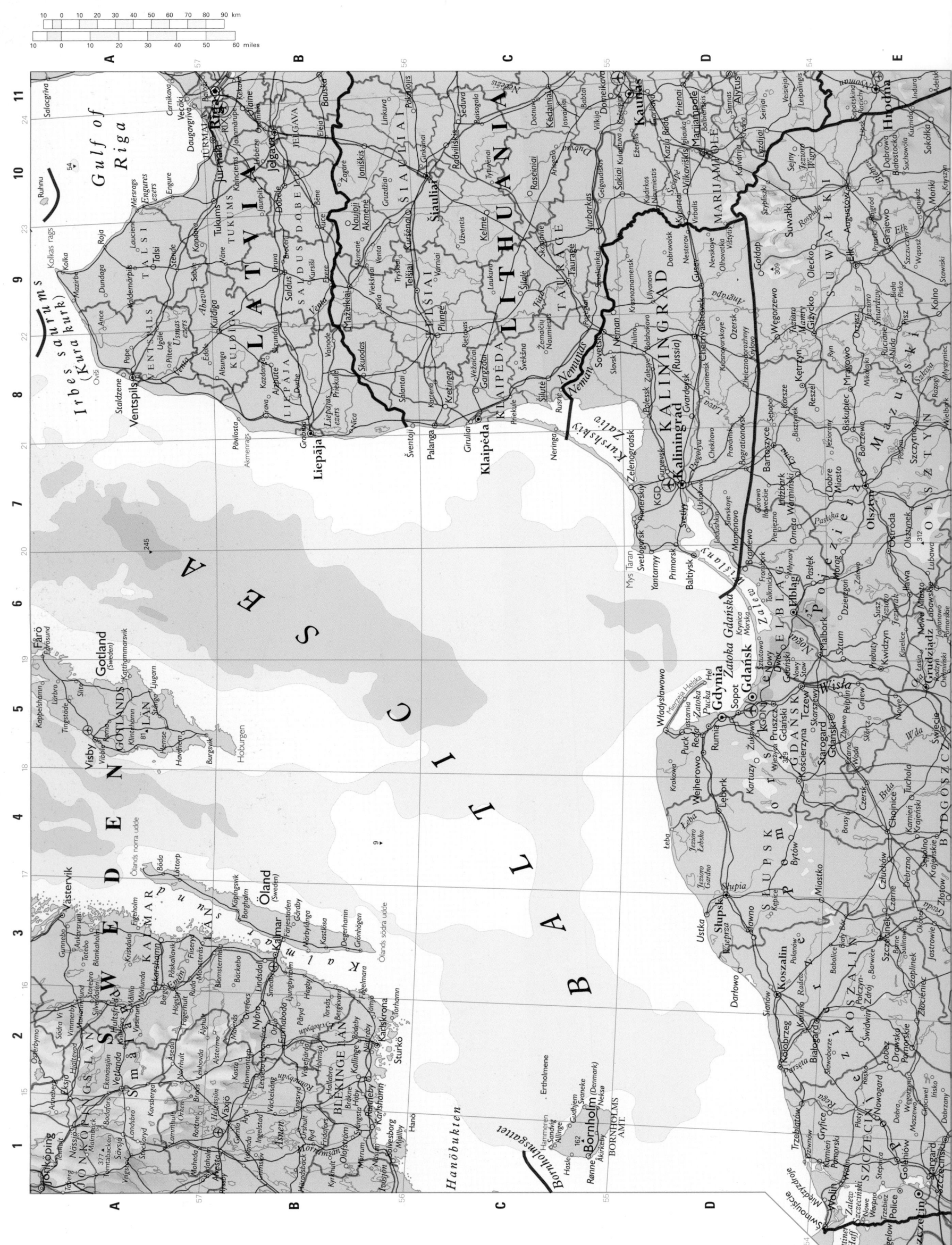

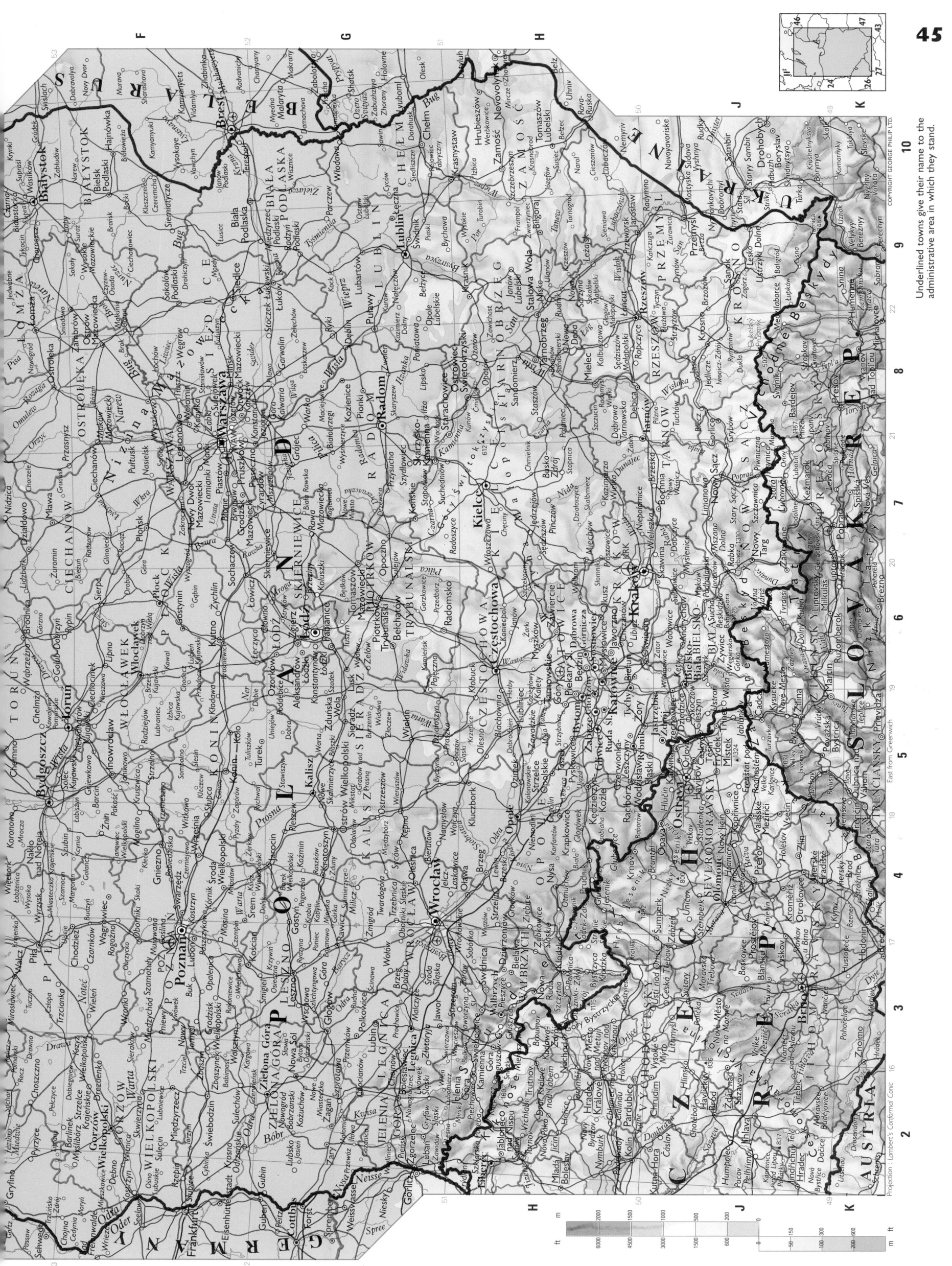

Underlined towns give their name to the
administrative area in which they stand.

COPYRIGHT GEORGE PHILIP LTD.

Projection: Lambert's Conformal Conic

East from Greenwich

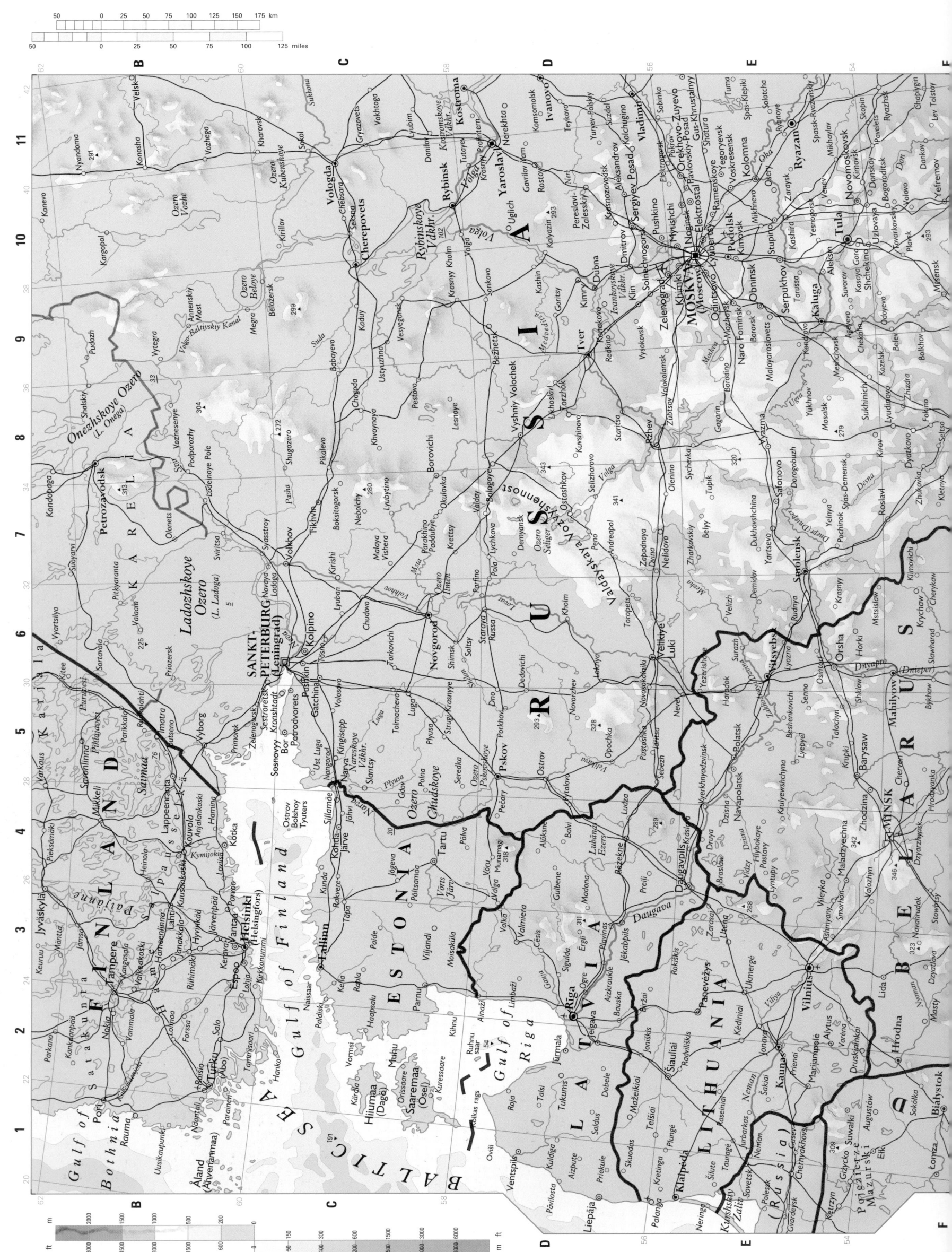

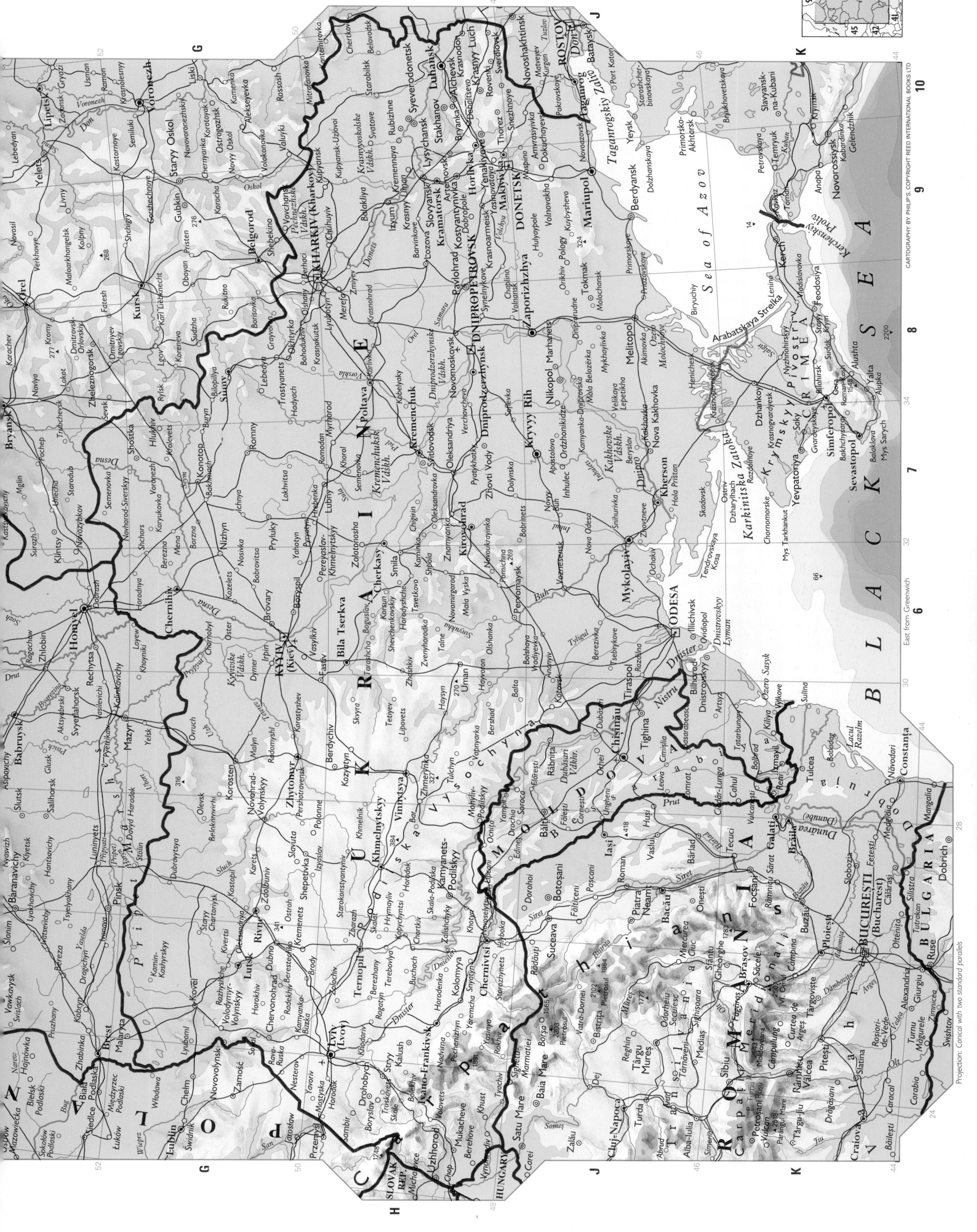

BLACK SEA

Sea of Azov

UKRAINE

ROMANIA

MOLDOVA

BULGARIA

SLOVAK REP.

HUNGARY

CRIMEA

KHARKIV (Kharkov)
KYYIV (Kiev)
ODESA
DNIPROPETROVSK
DONETSK
Luhansk
Mariupol
Zaporizhzhya
Kryvyy Rih
Mykolayiv
Kherson
Poltava
Sumy
Chernihiv
Lviv (Lvov)
Ternopil
Rivne
Lutsk
Zhytomyr
Vinnytsya
Khmelnytskyy
Kamyanets-Podilskyy
Chernivtsi
Ivano-Frankivsk
Uzhhorod
Kremenchuk
Kirovohrad
Cherkasy
Bila Tserkva
Simferopol
Sevastopol
Yalta
Kerch
Feodosiya
Yevpatoriya
Berdyansk
Melitopol
Nikopol

ROSTOV
Taganrog
Novoshakhtinsk
Novorossiysk
Anapa
Belgorod
Kursk
Orel
Bryansk
Homyel
Babruysk
Brest
Pinsk

CHIŞINĂU
Tiraspol
Tighina
BUCUREŞTI (Bucharest)
Constanţa
Galaţi
Brăila
Ploieşti
Bacău
Iaşi
Braşov
Sibiu
Cluj-Napoca
Craiova
Piteşti
Suceava

Danube (Dunărea)
Prut
Nistru
Dnister
Dnieper
Don
Desna
Pripet

Karkinitska Zatoka
Taganrogskiy Zaliv
Kerchenskiy Proliv
Arabatskaya Strelka

East from Greenwich

Projection: Conical with two standard parallels

CARTOGRAPHY BY PHILIP'S. COPYRIGHT REED INTERNATIONAL BOOKS LTD

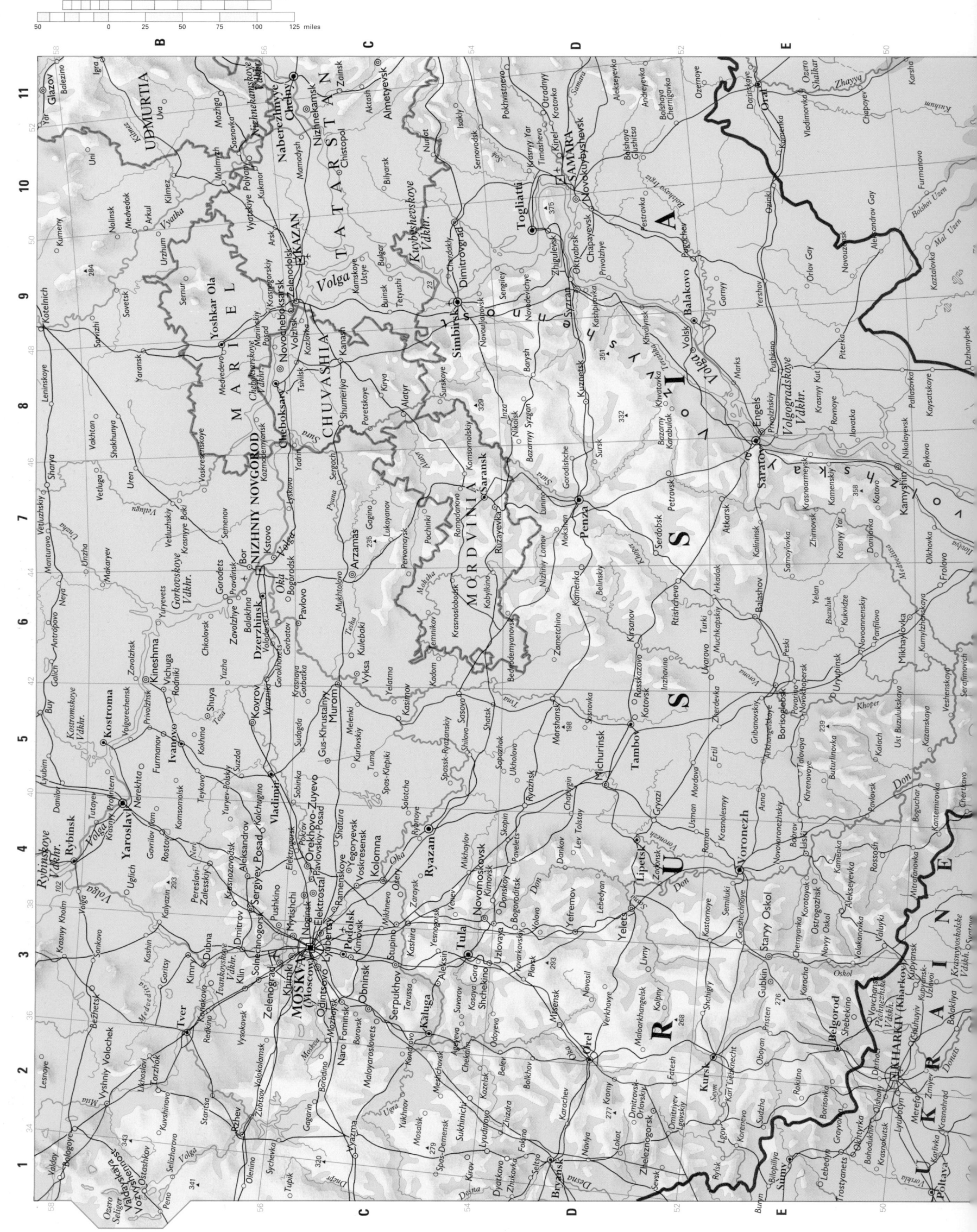

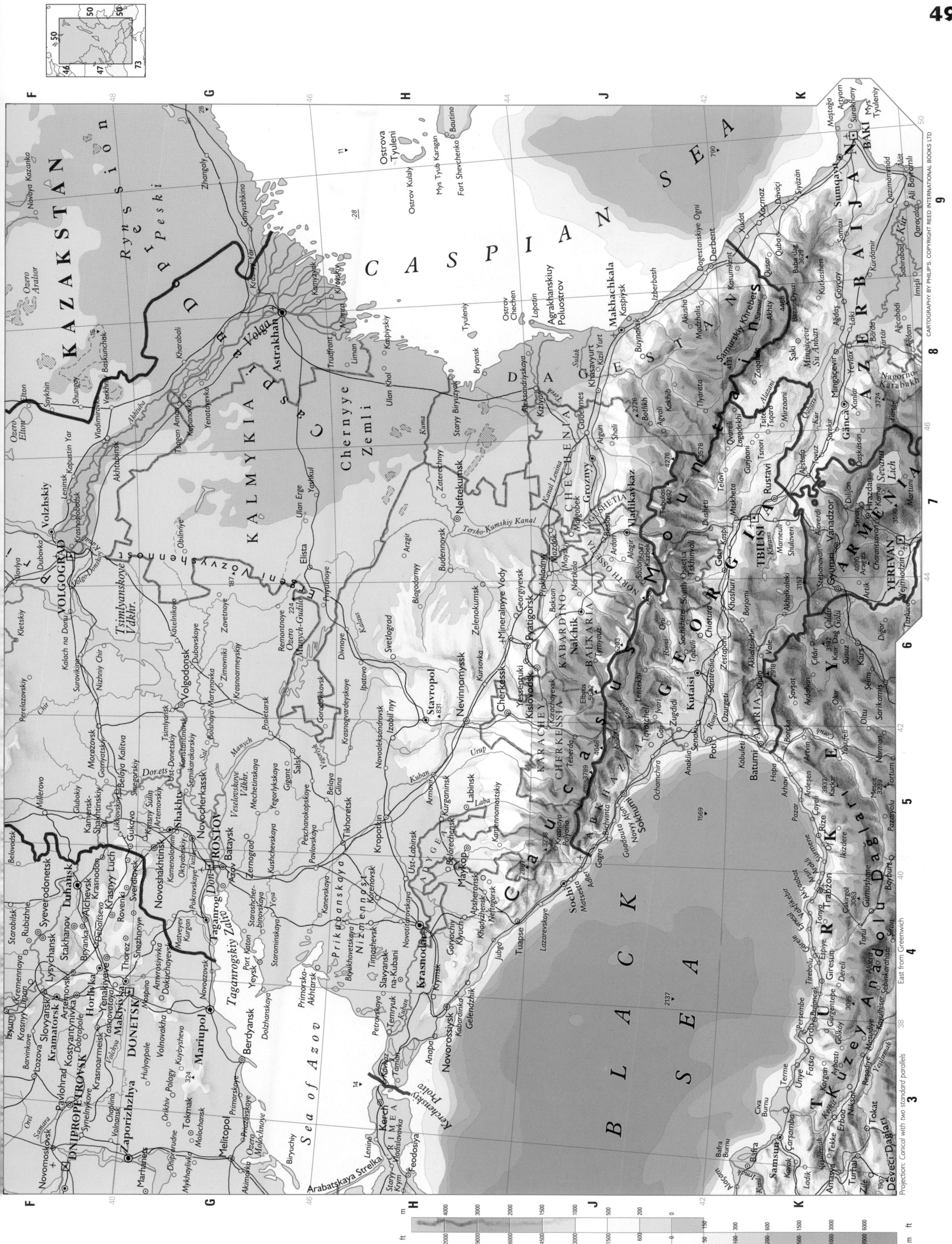

RUSSIA
1 Adygea
2 Karachey-Cherkessia
3 Kabardino-Balkaria
4 North Ossetia
5 Ingushetia
6 Chechenia
7 Dagestan
8 Mordvinia
9 Chuvashia
10 Mari El
11 Tatarstan
12 Udmurtia
13 Khakassia
AZERBAIJAN
14 Naxçıvan
GEORGIA   UKRAINE
15 Ajaria   17 Crimea
16 Abkhazia

East from Greenwich

CARTOGRAPHY BY PHILIP'S.
COPYRIGHT REED INTERNATIONAL BOOKS LTD.

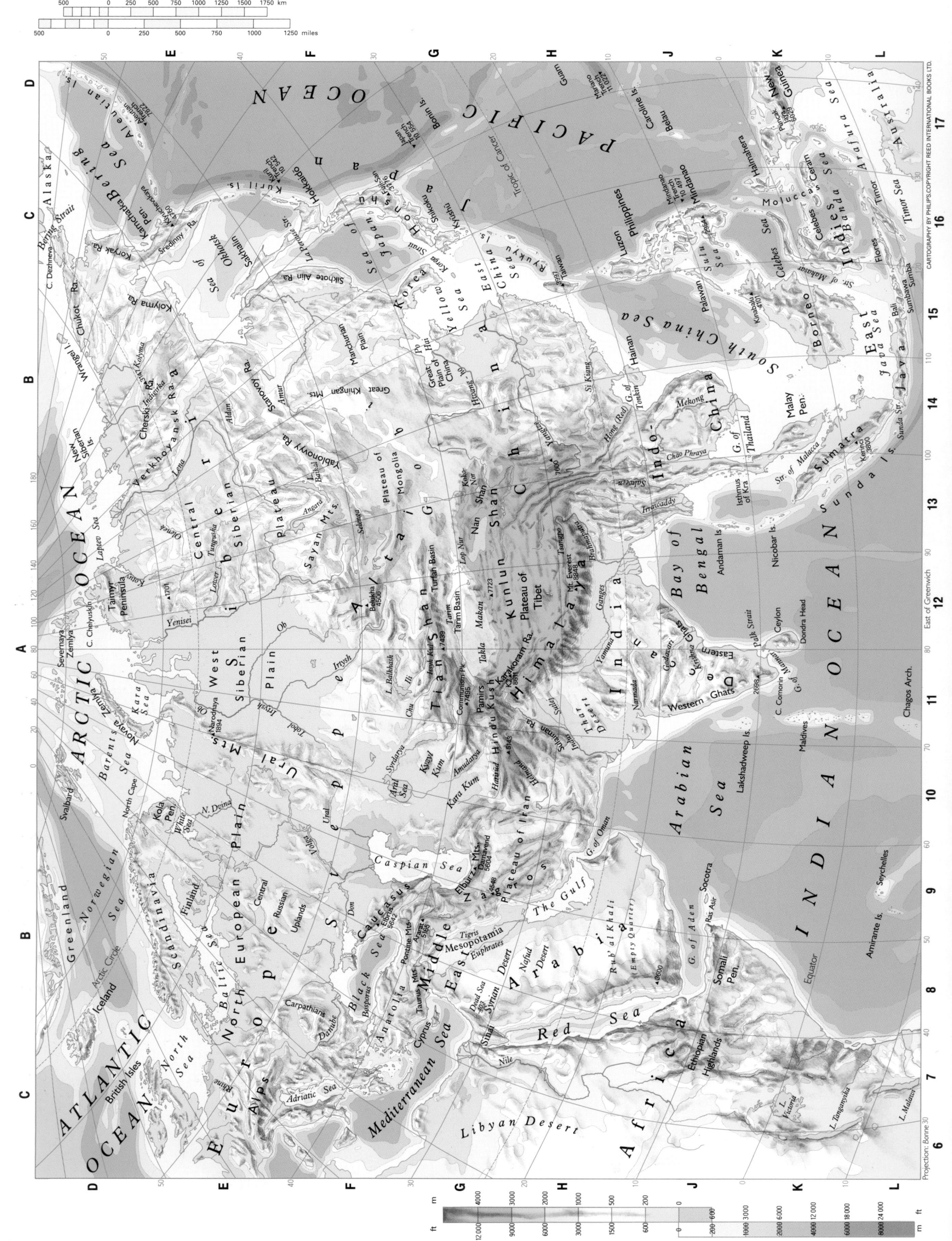

Projection: Bonne

CARTOGRAPHY BY PHILIP'S COPYRIGHT REED INTERNATIONAL BOOKS LTD.

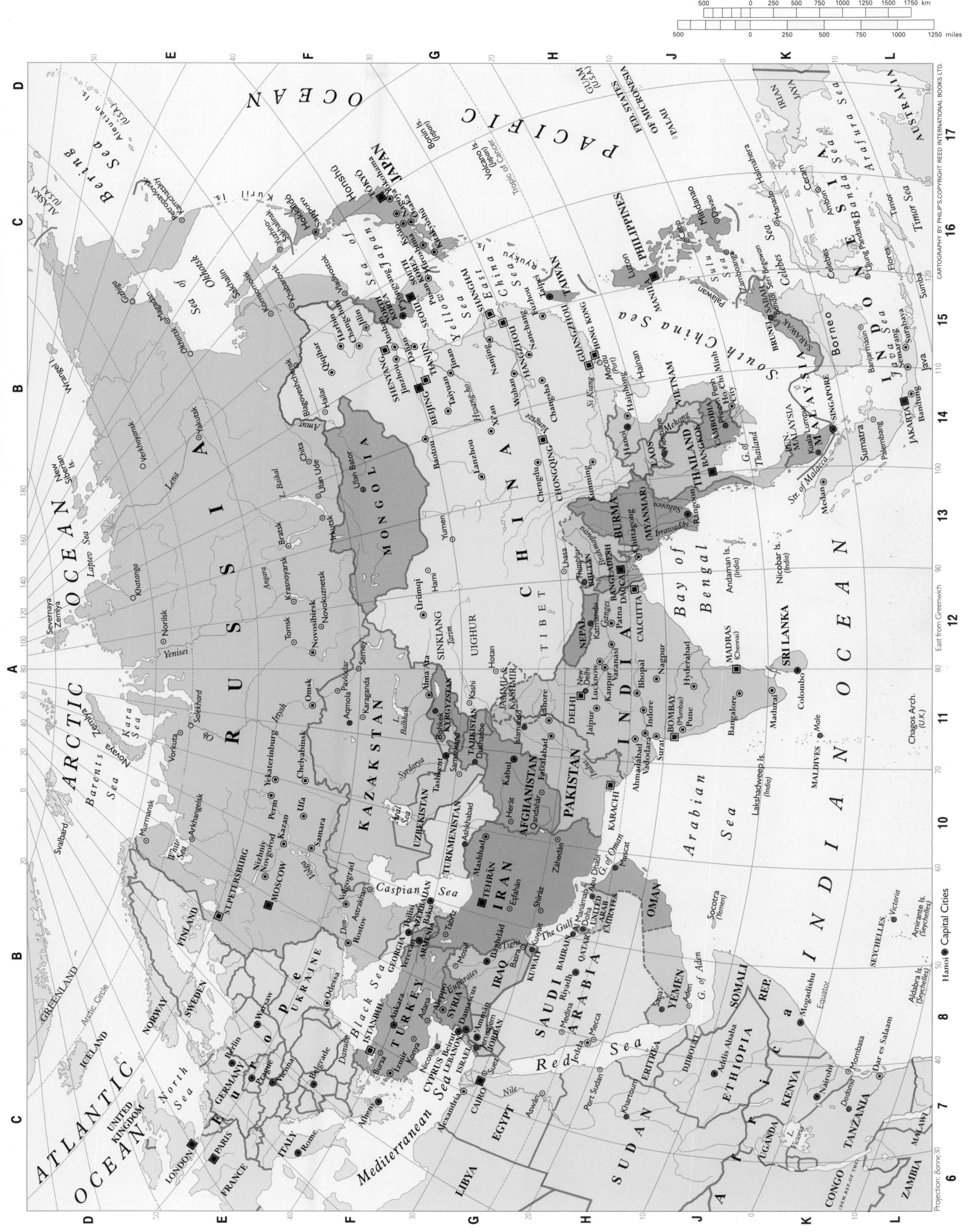

CARTOGRAPHY BY PHILIP'S COPYRIGHT REED INTERNATIONAL BOOKS LTD.

JAPAN 1:4 400 000

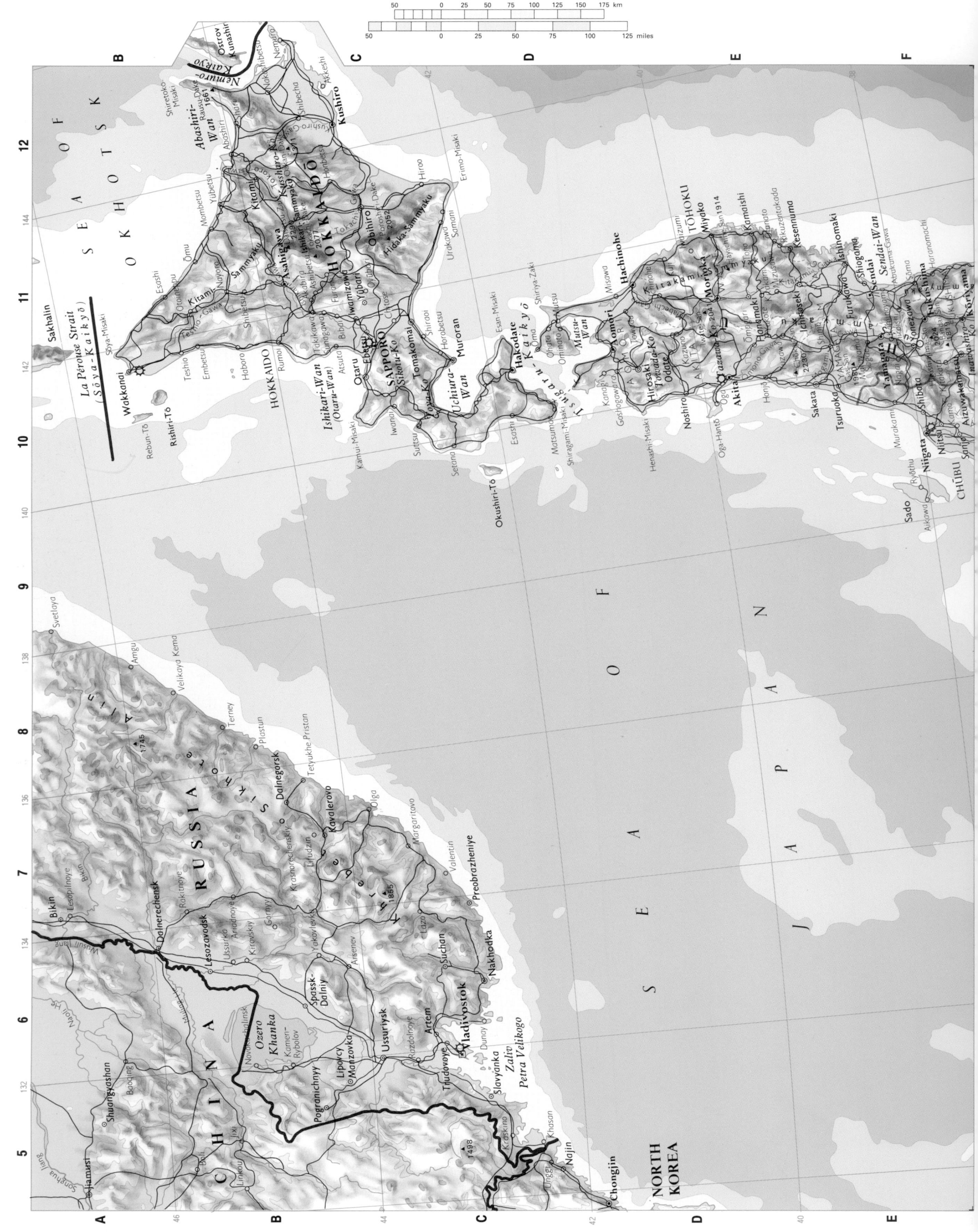

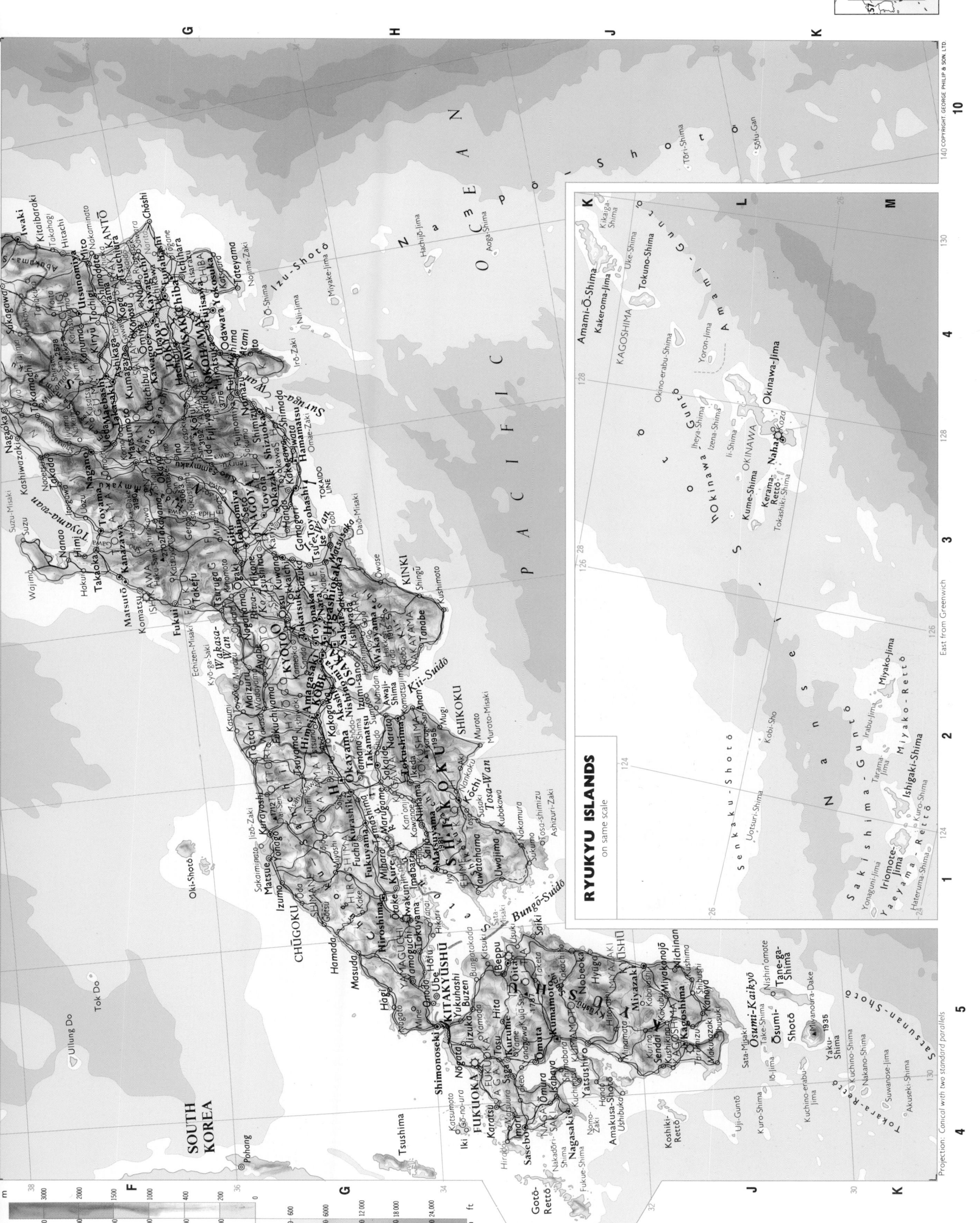

SOUTH
KOREA

PACIFIC OCEAN

CHŪGOKU

SHIKOKU

KINKI

KYOTO

KITAKYŪSHŪ

FUKUOKA

KAGOSHIMA

Tsushima

RYUKYU ISLANDS
on same scale

Amami-Ō-Shima

Kakeroma-Jima

KAGOSHIMA

Okino-erabu-Shima

Tokuno-Shima

Uke-Shima

Yoron-Jima

OKINAWA

Kume-Shima

Okinawa-Jima

Naha

Koza

Kerama-Retto

Tokashiki-Shima

YOKINAWA

Iheya-Shima

Izena-Shima

Ii-Shima

Iriomote-Jima

Ishigaki-Shima

Miyako-Jima

Miyako-Rettō

Sakishima-Guntō

Yaeyama-Rettō

Senkaku-Shotō

Nansei-Shotō

Tokara-Rettō

Satsunan-Shotō

Ōsumi-Kaikyō

Ōsumi-Shotō

Tane-ga-Shima

Yaku-Shima

Koshiki-Rettō

Gotō-Rettō

Nagasaki

Sasebo

Kumamoto

Sendai

Miyazaki

East from Greenwich

Projection: Conical with two standard parallels

COPYRIGHT GEORGE PHILIP & SON, LTD.

m ft
38 3000
     2000
     1500
     1000
     600
     400
     200
     0

ft m
9000 3000
6000 2000
4500 1500
3000 1000
1200 400
600   200
0   0
      −200 −600
      2000 6000
      4000 12000
      6000 18000
      8000 24000

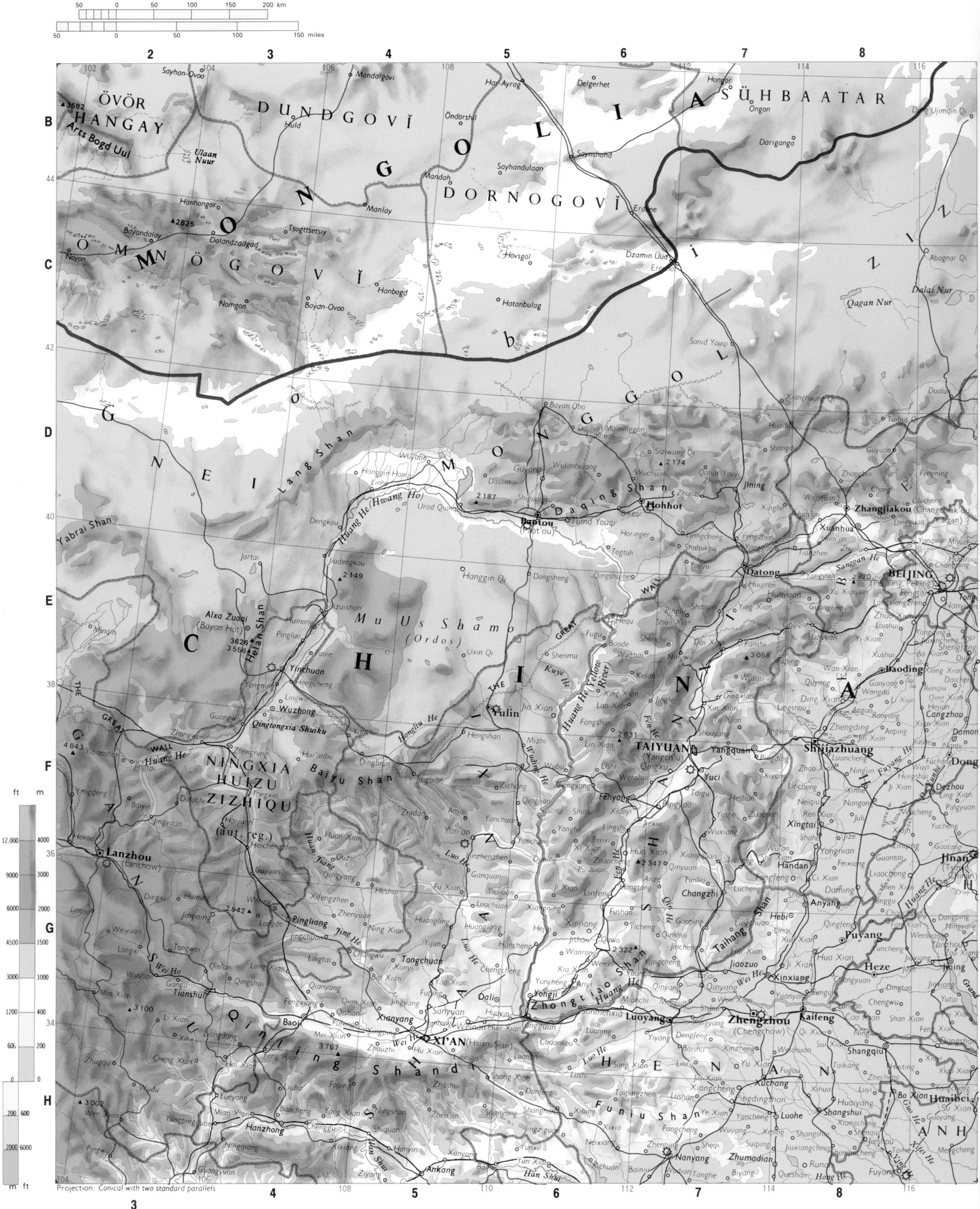

50 0 50 100 150 200 km
50 0 50 100 150 miles

ft m
12 000 4000
9000 3000
6000 2000
4500 1500
3000 1000
1200 400
600 200
0 0
200 600
2000 6000
m ft

ÖVÖR HANGAY
▲3582
Arts Bogd Uul

DUNDGOVI
Sayhan-Ovoo
Mandalgovi
Huld
Ulaan Nuur
Hanhongor
▲2825
Bayandalay
Dalandzadgad
Noyon
Nomgon
Hanbogd
Bayan-Ovoo
Tsogttsetsiy

Ö M Ö G O V I

M O N G O L I A
Har-Ayrag
Delgerhet
Hongor
Ongon
Onodrshil
Ondorshil
Sayhandulaan
Mandah
Manlay
Hövsgöl
Hatanbulag

DORNOGOVI
Erdene
Sainshand
Dzamin Üüd
Ereenhot

SÜHBAATAR
Dariganga
Dalai Nur
Qagan Nur
Abagnar Qi

Z I Z
Dong Ujimqin Qi
Xanghad
Duolun

N E I M O N G G O L
Bayan Obo
Darhan-Muminggan Lianheqi
▲2174
Siziwang Qi
Qahar Youyi Zhongqi
Jining
Zhangjiakou (Changchiak'ou Or Kalgan)
Xuanhua
Datong
Huairen
Yu Xian
Hunyuan
Yingxian
Ying Xian
▲2820

BEIJING
(Peiping)
Fengtai

Lang Shan
Wuyuan
Hanggin Houqi
Linhe
Dengkou
Urad Qianqi
Daqing Shan
Baotou (Pao t'ou)
Tumd Youqi
Hohhot
Horinger
Togtoh
Qingshuihe
Shahukou
Yanggao
Tianzhen
Zuoyun

Huang He Hwang Ho
2187
Shiguaikou
Dashetai
Güyang
Wulanbulang
Wuchuan

Mu Us Shamo (Ordos)
2149
Jiudengkou
Jizuishan
Hanggin Qi
Dongsheng
Uxin Qi
Yulin
Shenmu
Hengshan
Wuzhai
Kelan

C H I N A
Hanggin Qi
Hequ
Baode
Wuzhai
Kelan
Lan Xian

THE
Huang He Yellow River
Kuye He
Jia Xian
Mizhi
Suide
2831
Lin Xian

GREAT
Fugu
Shenmu
Jingle
Dingxiang

WALL

TAIYUAN (Yangch'ü)
Qingxu
Yuci
Yangquan
Pingyao
Fenyang
Jiexiu
Lingshi

S H A N X I
Xiaoyi
Taigu
Yushe
Heshun
Wuxiang

Alxa Zuoqi (Bayan Hot)
Huinong
3626
3556
Pingluo
Yinchuan
Hengcheng
Wuzhong
Lingwu
Yanchi
Dingbian

Helan Shan
Pingluo

NINGXIA HUIZU ZIZHIQU (aut. reg.)
Qingtongxia Shuiku
Zhongning
Zhongwei
Hur'anbu
Haiyuan
Xiji
Guyuan
Pingchuan

Baiyu Shan

Jing He
Tongxin

THE
GREAT
4 843
WALL
Huang He
Jingtai
Yingdeng
Baiyin
Jingyuan
Hekou
Dingxi

Lanzhou (Lanchow)
Huining
Dingxi
Weiyuan
Longxi
Jingning
Pingliang
2 942
Longde
Lintao
Weiyuan

N
Wushan
3 100
Min Xian
Li Xian
Lixian

Tianshui
Qin'an
Qingshui
Zhangjiachuan
Longxian
Long Xian
Qianyang
Qian'an
Fengxiang
Qishan

Qinling Shan
Baoji
Meixian
Feng Xian
3 767
Liuba
Huixian
Lüeyang
Cheng Xian
Hui Xian

Baiyu Shan
Wuqi
Zhidan
Ansai
Yan'an
Ganquan
Fu Xian
Luochuan

S H A A N X I
Yanchang
Yanchuan
Qingjian
Zichang
Yanchi
Huangling
Heshui
Qingyang
Huan Xian
Huachi

Luo He
Hancheng
Heyang
Chengcheng
Pucheng
Dali
Dali
Heyang

Tongchuan
Chengcheng
Fuping
Sanyuan
Jingyang

XI'AN (Hsian, Sian)
Xianyang
Zhouzhi
Huxian
Weinan
Hua Xian
Lintong
Lantian

Wei He
Baoji
Meixian

Qinling Shandi
Foping
Yang Xian
Yangpingguan
Ningshan
Zhen'an

Hanzhong
Chenggu
Mian Xian
Lueyang
Xixiang
Shiquan

Han Shui
Ankang
Hanyin
Ziyang
Pingli
Zhenping

Huang He Yellow River
Hequ
Baode
Wuzhai

3058
Fushan
Wutai
Daixian
Dingxiang
Xinzhou

A
Wan Xian
Quyang
Gaoyang
Lishi
Xushui

Baoding
Mancheng
Wan Xian
Dingzhou
Anguo
Boye
Gaoyang
Renqiu

Shijiazhuang
Luancheng
Ningjin
Jinzhou
Zhao Xian
Ningjin
Julu

Huang He
Dezhou
Wucheng
Pingyuan

Jinan (Tsinan)
Qihe
Changqing

Handan
Daming
Feixiang
Guangping
Linxi
Wei He
Quzhou

Anyang
Neihuang
Tangyin
Hebi

Puyang
Changyuan
Nanle
Qingfeng

Xinxiang
Huojia
Yuanyang
Fengqiu

H E N A N
Jiaozuo
Xiuwu
Boai
Qinyang
Wuzhi

Zhengzhou (Chengchow)
Xingyang
Gongxian

Kaifeng
Lankao
Qi Xian
Weishi

Luoyang
Yanshi
Yiyang
Dengfeng
Yuzhou
Xinmi

Sanmenxia
Mianchi
Xin'an
Luoning
Lushi

Zhongtiao Shan
Yongji
Ruicheng
Pinglu

Huang He
Lingbao
Shan Xian
Mianchi

Funiu Shan
Song Xian
Luanchuan
Lushan
Xixia
Neixiang
Xichuan

Luohe
Ye Xian
Wuyang
Xiangcheng
Linying

Nanyang
Fangcheng
Sheqi
Tanghe
Biyang
Xinye
Zhenping
Dengxian

A N H
Bo Xian
Huaibei
Zhumadian
Runan
Queshan
Suiping

Han Shui
Guanghua
Xiangfan

Qinling Shandi
Ningshan
Foping

Projection: Conical with two standard parallels

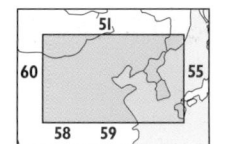

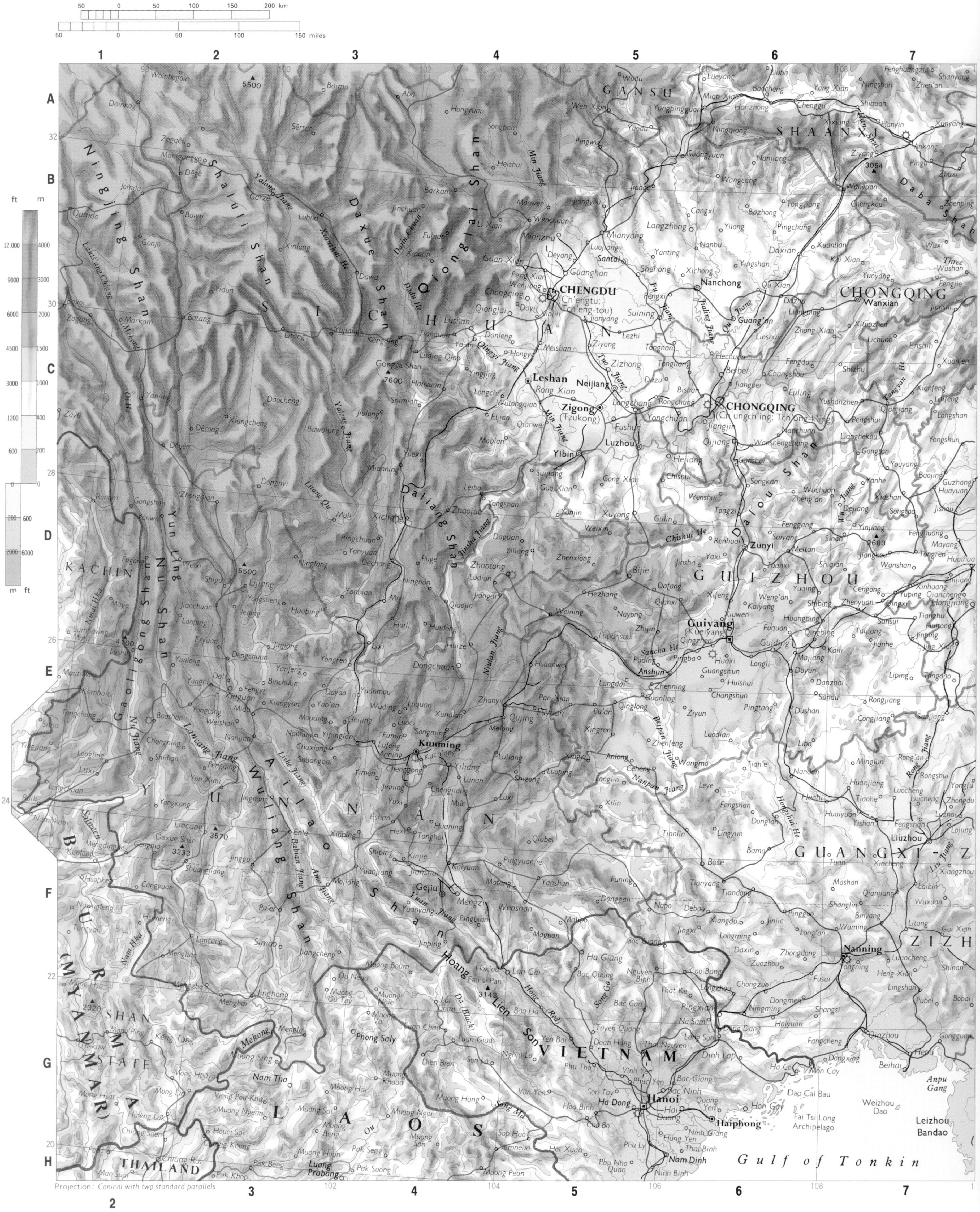

50 0 50 100 150 200 km
50 0 50 100 150 miles

ft m / ft m

12,000 4000
9000 3000
6000 2000
4500 1500
3000 1000
1200 400
600 200
m ft
200 600
2000 6000
m ft

SHAANXI
GANSU
SICHUAN
CHONGQING
GUIZHOU
YUNNAN
GUANGXI-ZIZH
KACHIN STATE
BURMA (MYANMAR)
THAILAND
LAOS
VIETNAM

Ningjing Shan
Shaluli Shan
Daxue Shan
Qionglai Shan
Daliang Shan
Nu Shan
Yun Ling
Gaoligong Shan
Wuliang Shan
Ailao Shan
Daba Shan
Dalou Shan
Hoang Lien Son

CHENGDU (Ch'engtu; Tch'eng-tou)
CHONGQING (Ch'ungch'ing; Tch'ong-k'ing)
Wanxian
Leshan
Zigong (Tzukong)
Neijiang
Yibin
Luzhou
Nanchong
Zunyi
Guiyang (Kueiyang)
Anshun
Kunming
Gejiu
Nanning
Liuzhou
Hanoi
Haiphong
Nam Dinh
Ha Dong
Luang Prabang

Yangtze / Jinsha Jiang
Yalong Jiang
Dadu He
Min Jiang
Tuo Jiang
Fujiang Jiang
Wu Jiang
Lancang Jiang (Mekong)
Nanpan Jiang
Beipan Jiang
Hongshui He
Yuan Jiang
Li Jiang
Nanxi Jiang
Hong (Red) / Hoang
Song Ma
Song Da (Black)

Gong'ga Shan 7600
5500
3054
2683
3149
3570
3233
2320

Gulf of Tonkin
Leizhou Bandao
Weizhou Dao
Anpu Gang
Fai Tsi Long Archipelago
Dap Cai Bau

Projection: Conical with two standard parallels

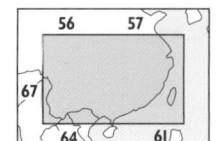

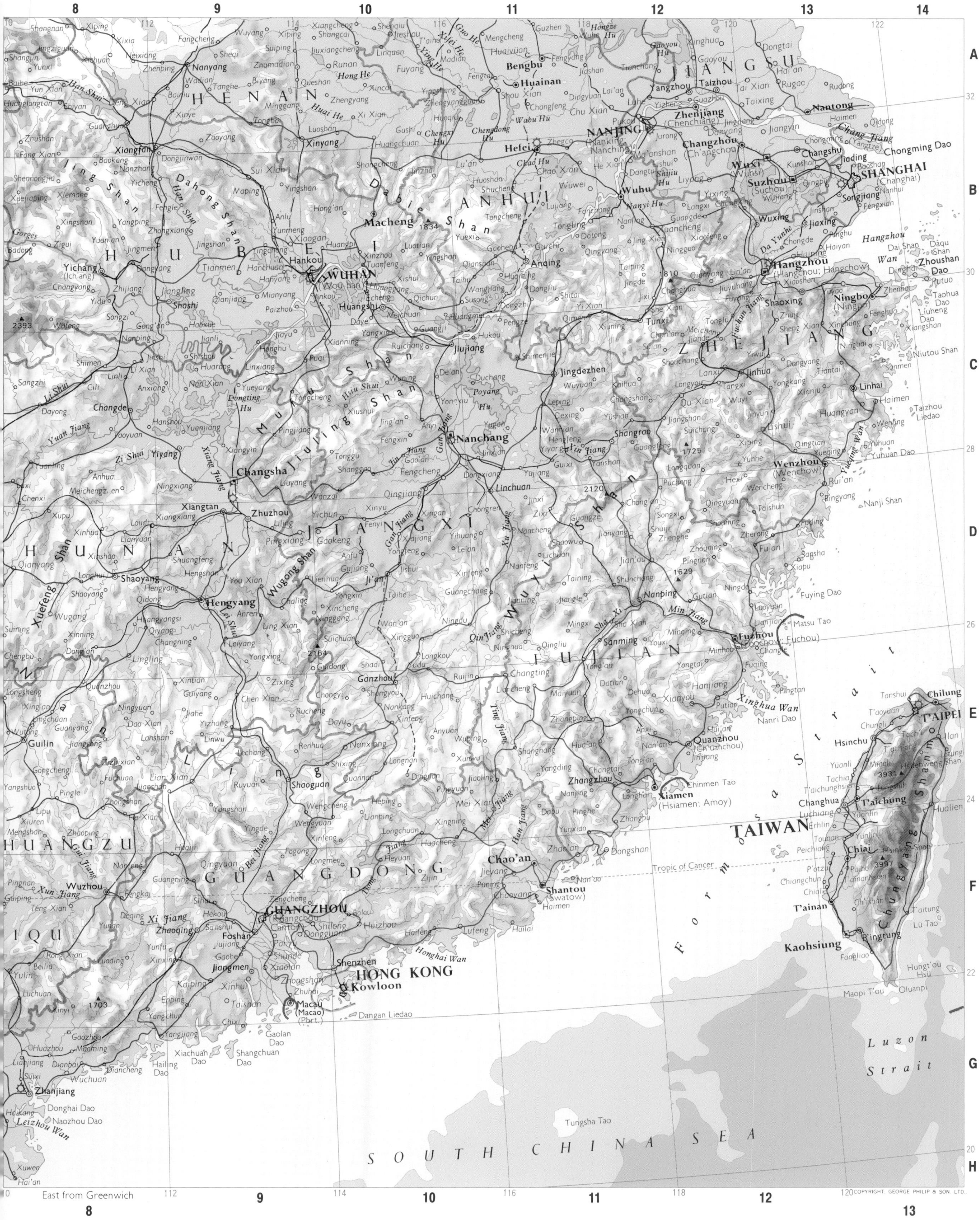

COPYRIGHT GEORGE PHILIP LTD.

50 0 100 150 200 250 300 km
50 0 50 100 150 200 miles

| | 1 | 2 | 3 | 4 | 5 | 6 | 7 | 8 |

116 118 120 122 124 126 128

A 20

Itbayat
Batanes Is.
Batan

Balintang Channel

B

Calayan
Babuyan

Dalupiri *Babuyan*
Babuyan Islands
Camiguin
Fuga
Mayraira Pt. *Babuyan Channel*
Bangui Claveria
Bacarra **Aparri** Port San Vicente
San Nicolas Ballesteros
Laoag Batuc Gonzaga
Butuc Kabugao Gattaran

C 18
Cabagao Banna 2360 Tuao Tuguegarao
Vigan Bangued Chico Naguil Cresta
Santa Maria Bontoc 1672
Candon Lubuagan *Sierra Madre*
Tagudin San Mateo Palanan Pt.
Luna Sabangan Santiago Palanan

P A C I F I C

San Fernando 2929 Solano
Lingayen **Baguio** Pulog Bayombong
Bolinao *Gulf* Anacuao 1860
Alaminos Lingayen **Dagupan** C. San Ildefonso
Rosario San Manuel

O C E A N

Santa Cruz San Carlos **Bayambang** **San Jose** Baler Bay
Camiling Moncada Cuyo Baler
Palawig 2038 Victoria **Cabanatuan** Bale
Tarlac Paz Dingalan
Iba Sapangbato Gapan
San Narciso **Angeles** **San Fernando** Polillo Is.
San Antonio Malaban Patnanongan
Olongapo Dinalongan Jomalig
Dani **Caloocan** Polillo Str.
Bataan *Manila* □ **Quezon City**
Cavite *Bay* ◉ **MANILA**

LUZON

D
Trece Martires Pasay *Lamon Bay* Paracale
Santa Cruz Labo
Tagaytay **Lucban** Alabat **Daet** San Miguel Bay
Nasugbu Balayan **San Pablo** Atimonan Pandan
Lipa **Lucena** Pagbilao
Batangas Lemery Lopez Catanauan
Lubang Tayabas Bay **Naga** Calabanga Callebo Catanduanes
Verde I. Pass. Lobo Boac **Iriga** **Nabua** Virac
C. Calavite Catalan Pola **Marinduque** *Lagonoy Gulf* Rapu Rapu
Mamburao Pinamalayan Ligao **Tabaco**
Bulan **Legazpi** Sorsogon
Baco Romblon Bugui Donsol Gubat

E 14
MINDORO 2488 *SIBUYAN* Sibuyan **Bulan** San Bernardino Str.
Sablayan Bongabong Tablas Irosin
Mindoro Strait Roxas *SEA* Ticao Looc
San Jose Odiongan Aroroy Mondragon Gamay
Tablas **Masbate** Catarman SAMAR
Busuanga Culion *Mandaon* **Masbate** Milagros Catbalogan
Calamian *Group* Placer Biliran Catbalogan Taft

F 12
Semirara Is. *Pandan* Kalibo Calbayog Borongan
Linapacan Str. **Roxas** *VISAYAN* Gutusan Sta. Rita
Libro Pt. Linapacan 2117 Sigma Estancia *SEA* Maydolong
Taytay Tibiao Ajuy Bantayan
Cuyo West Pass San Jose **PANAY** Cadiz Sagay Palompon General MacArthur
Pototan Sibuguan Bogo **Tacloban** Guiuan
Cuyo Is. de Buenavista **Iloilo** **Silay** **Victorias** *LEYTE* Hamohon
Cuyo East Pass Cuyo Jordan **Bacolod** San Carlos Dandoc Ormoc Dulag
Dumaran Guimaras 2465 Camotes Is. **Baybay** *Leyte Gulf*
Calling **Carlota** **Cebu** Camotes Abuyog
Cagayan Hinigaran Maasin Matalom Dinagat
PALAWAN Sipalay Binalbagan **Calamba** **Mandaue** Maasin Dinagat
Himamaylan Carcar *SEA* Surigao

G 10
1593 Kabankalan Argao **Bohol** Panaon Siargao
Baiso **Bohol** Malimono 10 497
Irahuan Honda B. Bayawan Baclayon Bucas Grande
Sibalay Oslob **Tagbilaran** Carrascal
Puerto Princesa **NEGROS** Tanjay **Dumaguete** *BOHOL* **Surigao**
Hinoba-an Siquijor Camiguin Cabadbaran Lanuza
Bayawan Zamboanguita Malaybalay 1857 **Mainit** Tandag
SULU Dapitan Cabadbaran Tago
Dipolog *SEA* Hinaghlong Butuan San Juan

G
Mantalingajan **Sandakan** Oroquieta Iligan Esperanza Lianga
2085 Manukan Bay Jasaan
C. Buliluyan Bugsuk *SEA* Sindangan **Ozamiz** **Cagayan de Oro** *Mindanao Trench*
Labason Maramag

H
Balabac
Balambangan Bangui Suba Tular. **Pagadian** *MINDANAO* Baganga
Langkon Kudat Turtle Is. 2896 L. Lanao Mangagoy
Rosok Siocon Malangas Cateel
Kota Belud Tenghilan Cagayan Sulu Malabang 2815 Midsayap Tagum Panabo
Tuaran 4101 Labuk Illana Parang Panabo
Kota Papar Bay Cotabato Bunawan Manay
Kinabalu Melalap Beluran Datu Piang Apo Matti
Kimanis Pangutaran Talayan Pikit 2954 **Davao**
Beaufort *Crocker Range* **SABAH** Group Basilan Str. Salaman Digos Davao

H
Melalap Langkupan **Zamboanga** Isabela Kabasalan Korondal *Davao Gulf*
Tenom Tampasak Tamor Basilan Kiamba C. San Agustin

J
Keningau Litang Jolo **Jolo** Samales Milbuk 2346 **General Santos**
Sapulut Lahad Datu Parang Group
Tambunan Laparan Siasi Tinaca Pt.
Kemabong Hog Pt. Tawitawi Tapul Group Sarangani Bay
Sook Lahag Datu Group Sarangani Is.
Darvel Bay **SULU ARCHIPELAGO** *CELEBES*
Tawitawi Group
Semporna Sibutu *SEA* Kawio Is. Talaud Is.

SOUTH CHINA SEA

SULU SEA

MORO GULF

CELEBES SEA

	ft	m
	9000	3000
	6000	2000
	4500	1500
	3000	1000
	1200	400
	600	200
	0	0
	600	200
	12 000	4000
	24 000	8000

m ft

100 0 100 200 300 400 500 km
100 0 50 100 150 200 250 300 350 miles

BURMA
(MYANMAR)
Letpadan
Tharrawaddy
Thoen
Insein
RANGOON
(YANGON)
Ma-ubin
Pyapon
G. of Martaban
Thaton
Moulmein
Kyaikkami
Kyaukse
Ye
Natkyizin
Tavoy
Maungmagan Islands
2075
Kadan Kyun
Mergui
Taninthari
Lenya
Myeik
Lambi Kyun
Kyungu Maliwun
Zadetkyi Kyun

THAILAND
Nong Khai
Uttaradit
Udon Thani
Nakhon Phanom
Sawankhalok
Loei
Muang Khammouan
Tak
Phitsanulok
Sakon Nakhon
Savannakhet
Phetchabun
Khon Kaen
Ubon Ratchathani
Nakhon Sawan
Chaiyaphum
Roi Et
Phra Nakhon Si Ayutthaya
Saraburi
Khu Khan
Sisaket
BANGKOK
Aranyaprathet
Kanchanaburi
Samut Songkhram
Nakhon Ratchasima
Somut Prakan
Chon Buri
Pattaya
Phet Buri
Hua Hin
Rayong
Chanthaburi
Ko Chang
Ko Kut
Prachuap Khiri Khan
Bang Saphan
Chumphon
Kho Khot Kra

VIETNAM
Nong Khai
Ba Don
Dong Hoi
Quang Tri
Hue
Hoi An
Da Nang
Quang Ngai
Kon Tum
Bong Son
2598
Binh Dinh
Qui Nhon
Song Cau
A Yun Pa
Pleiku
Nha Trang
Cam Ranh
2405
Buon Me Thuot
Da Lat
Phan Rang
Mui Dinh
Bien Hoa
Phan Thiet
PHANH BHO HO CHI MINH
Vung Tau

Paracel Is.

SOUTH CHINA SEA

Nanshan I.
4424
Loaita I.
Itu Aba I.
Sin Cowe I.
Spratly Is.
Amboyna Cay
Spratly I.

CAMBODIA
Cheom Ksan
Kulen
Siemreab
Tonle Sap
Batdambang
Pouthisat
1813
2190
Kampong Chhnang
Kampong Thom
Kracheh
Senmonorom
Phnom Penh (Phnum Penh)
Krong
Kaoh Kong
Sre Ambel
Kampong Cham
Prey Veng
Phumi Koh Kong
Takev
Svay Rieng
Kampot
Kampong Saom
Long Xuyen
My Tho
Hon Chong
Sa Dec
Can Tho
Rach Gia
Soc Trang
Bac Lieu
Ca Mau
Mui Ca Mau
Con Son

Gulf of Thailand
Ko Phangan
Ko Samui
Surat Thani
1835
Nakhon Si Thammarat
Pak Phanang
Thung Song
Phatthalung
Phangnga
Trang
Thale Luang
Phuket
Kantang

ANDAMAN SEA

Strait of Malacca
We
Sabang
Banda Aceh
Meureudu
Sigli
Bireuen
A C E H
Lhokseumawe
Langkawi
Alor Setar
Satun
Yala
Pattani
Narathiwat
Tumpat
Kota Baharu
Perhentian
Redang
Kuala Terengganu

MALAYSIA
Tarutao
George Town
Hat Yai
Songkhla
Idi
Peureulak
Takengon
G. Leuser
3381
Pangkalanbrandan
Belawan
MEDAN
Tebingtinggi
Kelang
KUALA LUMPUR
Tanjungbalai
PENINSULAR MALAYSIA
Taiping
Ipoh
Gunong Tahan
2190
Dungen
Kemaman
Teluk Intan
Kampar
Kuala Lipis
Temerloh
Kuantan
Tenggol
Port Dickson
Seremban
Segamat
Mersing
Pulau Tioman
Bagansiapiapi
Rantauprapat
Muar
Keluang
Kota Tinggi
SINGAPORE
Johor Baharu
Tanjungpinang
Bintan

SUMATRA
Lhokkruet
Calang
Meulaboh
Lhokseumawe
Sinabang
Simeulue
Pematangsiantar
Prapat
Danau Toba
Tarutung
Sibolga
Musala
Kepulauan Banyak
Lahewa
Gunungsitoli
Nias
Utara
Padangsidempuan
Telukdalam
Siaksriindrapura
Dumai
Bengkalis
Batu Pahat
Rupat
Pekanbaru
Bangkinang
Kuala
RIAU
Rengat
Lubuksikaping
Tanahmasa
Kepulauan Batu
Tanahbala
Bukittinggi
Payakumbuh
BARAT
Padangpanjang
Sawahlunto
3805
Solok
Kerinci
Pini
Pulau Pagai Utara
Siberut
Sipura
Sabulubbek
Pulau Pagai Selatan
Kepulauan Mentawai
Padang
Painan
Muarabungo
Sungaipenuh
Bangko
Solok
Sarolangun
Mukomuko
JAMBI
Jambi
Muaratembesi
Muaraenim
Lubuklinggau
Curup
SELATAN
Tebingtinggi
Bengkulu
Lahat
3159
Baturaja
Manna
Martapura
Menggala
PALEMBANG
Sekayu
Sungaigerong
Perabumulih
Muaraenim
Kotabumi
Tanjungkarang
Telukbetung
6073

LAMPUNG
Kotaagung
Kalianda
Kepulauan Seribu
JAKARTA
Serang
Bogor
Sukabumi
Panaitan
Pulau Rakata (Krakatau)
Teluk Pelabuhan Ratu
Merak
BANDUNG
Purwakarta
Cirebon
Tasikmalaya
Garut
Cilacap

INDIAN OCEAN

Java Trench
6650

MALAYSIA
Kepulauan Natuna Besar
Telukbutun
Natuna Besar
Binjai
Matak
Siantan
Subi
Kepulauan Natuna Selatan
Midai
Serasan
Kepulauan Anambas
Kepulauan Tambelan
Singkawang
Sambas
Kepulauan Riau
Kepulauan Lingga
Lingga
Pasirkuning
Singkep
Belinyu
Sungailiat
Pangkalpinang
Bangka
Muntok
Toboali
Manggar
Tanjungpandan
Dendang
Belitung
Tg. Lumut
Greater Sunda Islan

Selat Karimata
Kepulauan Karimata
Tanjung Sambar
Menjangan

Java Sea
Bawean
Kepulauan Karimunjawa
Sangkapura
Laut Kecil
Kepulauan Masalima

BRUNEI
Bandar Seri Begawan
Kuala Belait
Tutong
Miri
Seria
Niah
Bintulu
Mukah
Oya
SARAWAK
Sibu
Kanowit
Bintangor
Sarikei
Kapit
Gunung Hose
2988
Kuching
Bau
Lundu
Tanjung Datu
Sri Aman
Bandar Sri Aman
170
Tebedu
Ngabang
Serian
Betung
2240

KALIMANTAN
Putussibau
Semitau
Sintang
Sanggau
Nangapinoh
Sukadana
Ketapang
TENGAH
BARAT
Pontianak
Nangatayap
Nangapinoh
Sukaraja
Kualakurun
Kualakapuas
Palangkaraya
Sampit
Kumai
Pangkalanbuun
Kualapembuang
Semuda
Kuala
Pangkalanbuun
Mendawai
Tanjung Puting

SABAH
Kudat
Langkon
Kota Belud
Gunong Kinabalu
4101
Kota Kinabalu
Papar
Beaufort
Ranau
Pulau Labuan
Labuan
Keningau
Tenom
Melalap
Tawau
Balabac I.
Balabac Str.
Jemboringan
Beluran
Sandakan
Banjaran Brassey

TIMUR
Tanjungredeb
Tanjungselor
Tarakan
Tanjungbatu
Sangkulirang
Bontang
Muarakaman
Samarinda
Balikpapan
Tenggarong
Muaratewe
Longiram
Purukcahu
Barabai
Amuntai
Kandangan
1892
SELATAN
Banjarmasin
Martapura
Pelaihari
Rantau
Kotabaru
Satui
Pulau Laut
Pagatan
Sebuku
Karamba
Longnawan
Longpran
Muarajuloi
Tanjung
Kualakuayan
Tanahgrogot
Kepulauan Balabalangan
Selat

Greater Sunda Islan
Tanjung Selatan
Pulau Laut Kecil
Kepulauan Masalima

BALI
Negara
Singaraja
Denpasar
Agung
3142
Rinjani
3726
Lombok
Moyo
2851
Tambora
Sumbawa Besar
Ampenan
Mataram
Praya
Taliwang

JAVA
TIMUR
TENGAH
Pemalang
Tegal
Pekalongan
Kendal
SEMARANG
Bojonegoro
Gresik
Bangkalan
Sampang
Madura
Kepulauan Kangean
Tuban
Slamet
3428
Kudus
Magelang
Yogyakarta
Surakarta
Madiun
Kediri
3265
Tulungagung
Lawu
2563
Merbabu
Semeru
3670
Blitar
Malang
SURABAYA
Pasuruan
Probolinggo
Jember
Banyuwangi
Bondowoso

Lesser
Kepulauan Tengah
F L
NUSA TENGGARA BARAT

ft m
12 000 4000
9000 3000
6000 2000
4500 1500
3000 1000
1200 400
600 200
0 0
200 600
2000 6000
4000 12 000
6000 18 000
8000 24 000
m ft

105 110 115

1 2 3 4 5

Projection: Mercator
East from Greenwich

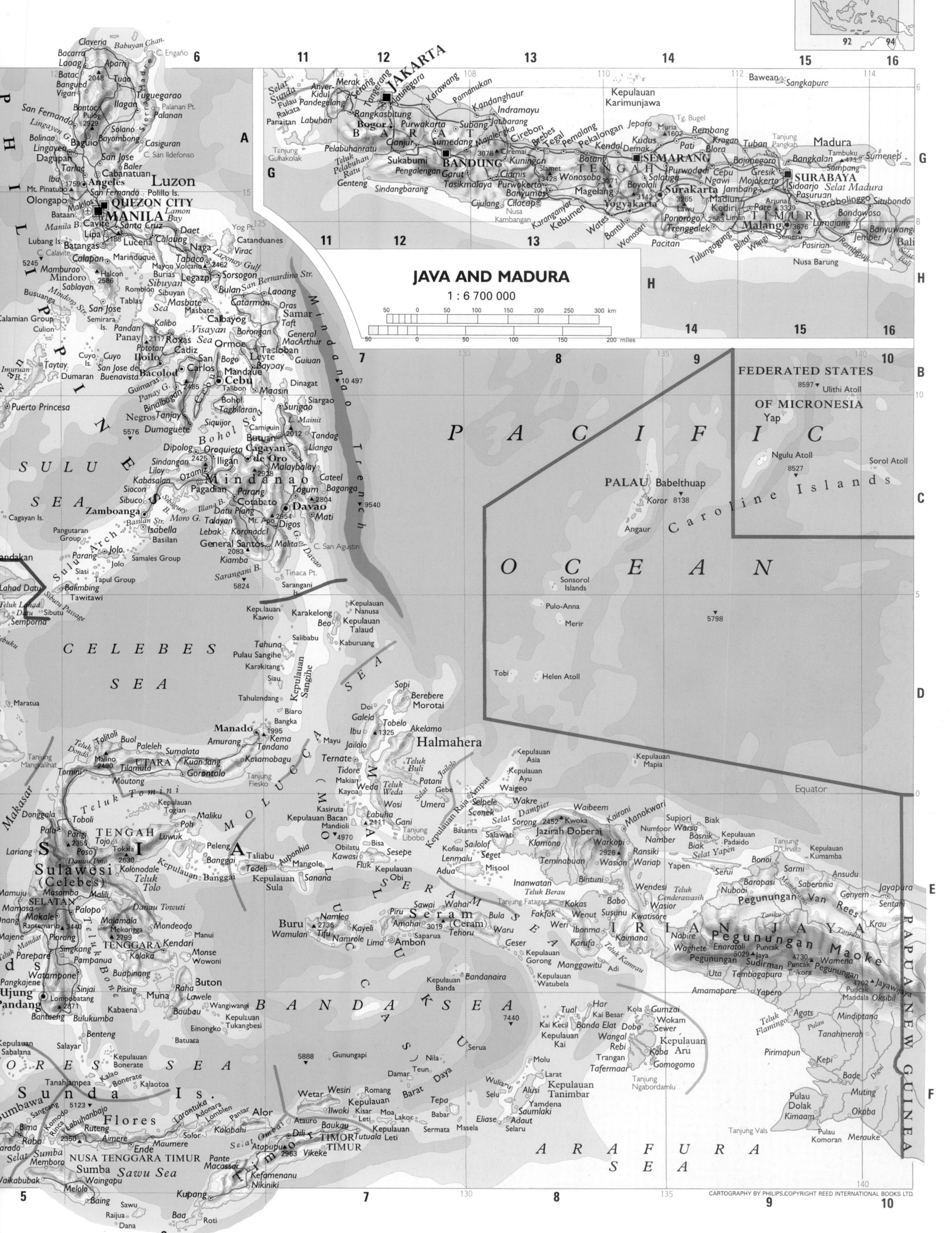

JAVA AND MADURA
1 : 6 700 000

CARTOGRAPHY BY PHILIP'S. COPYRIGHT REED INTERNATIONAL BOOKS LTD.

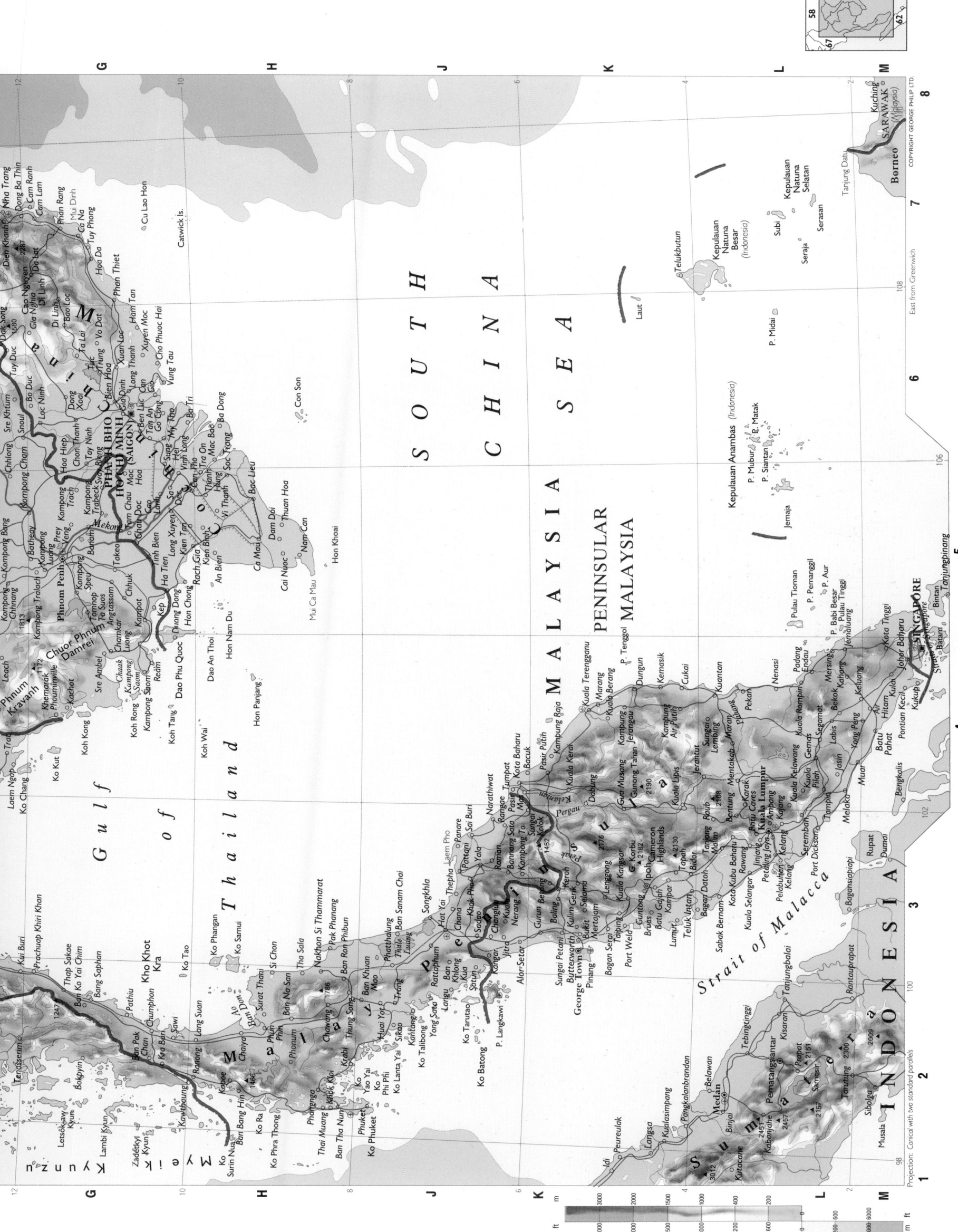

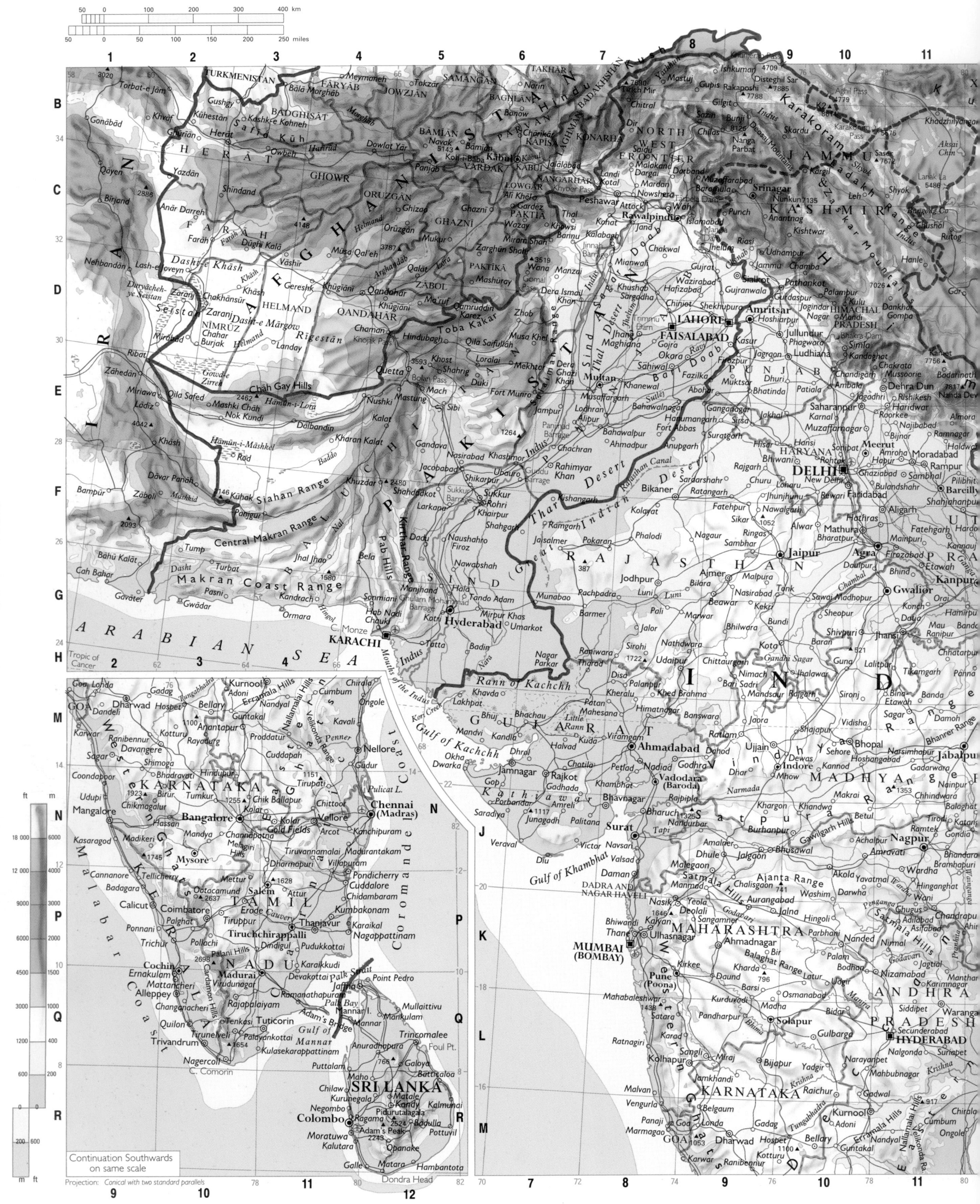

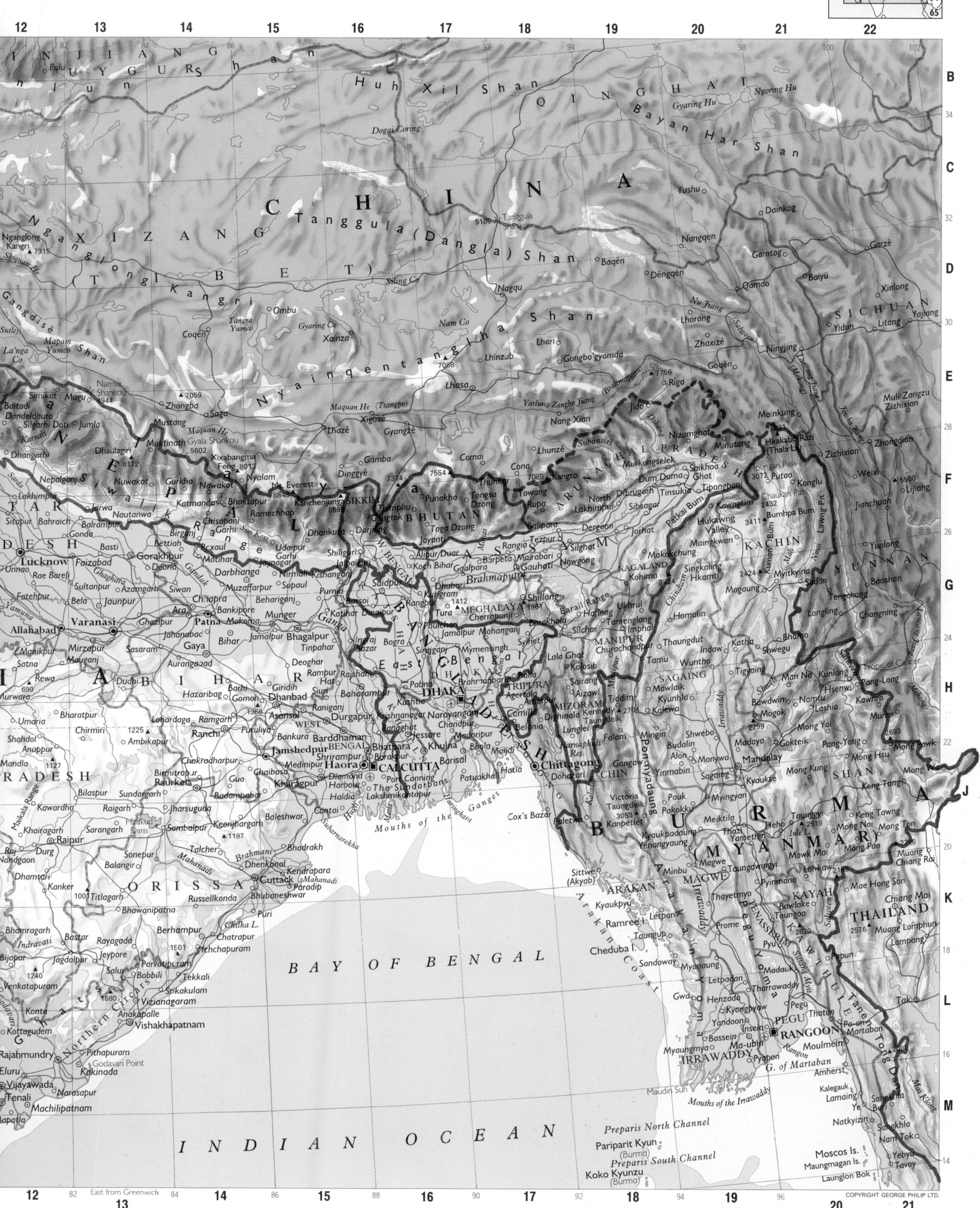

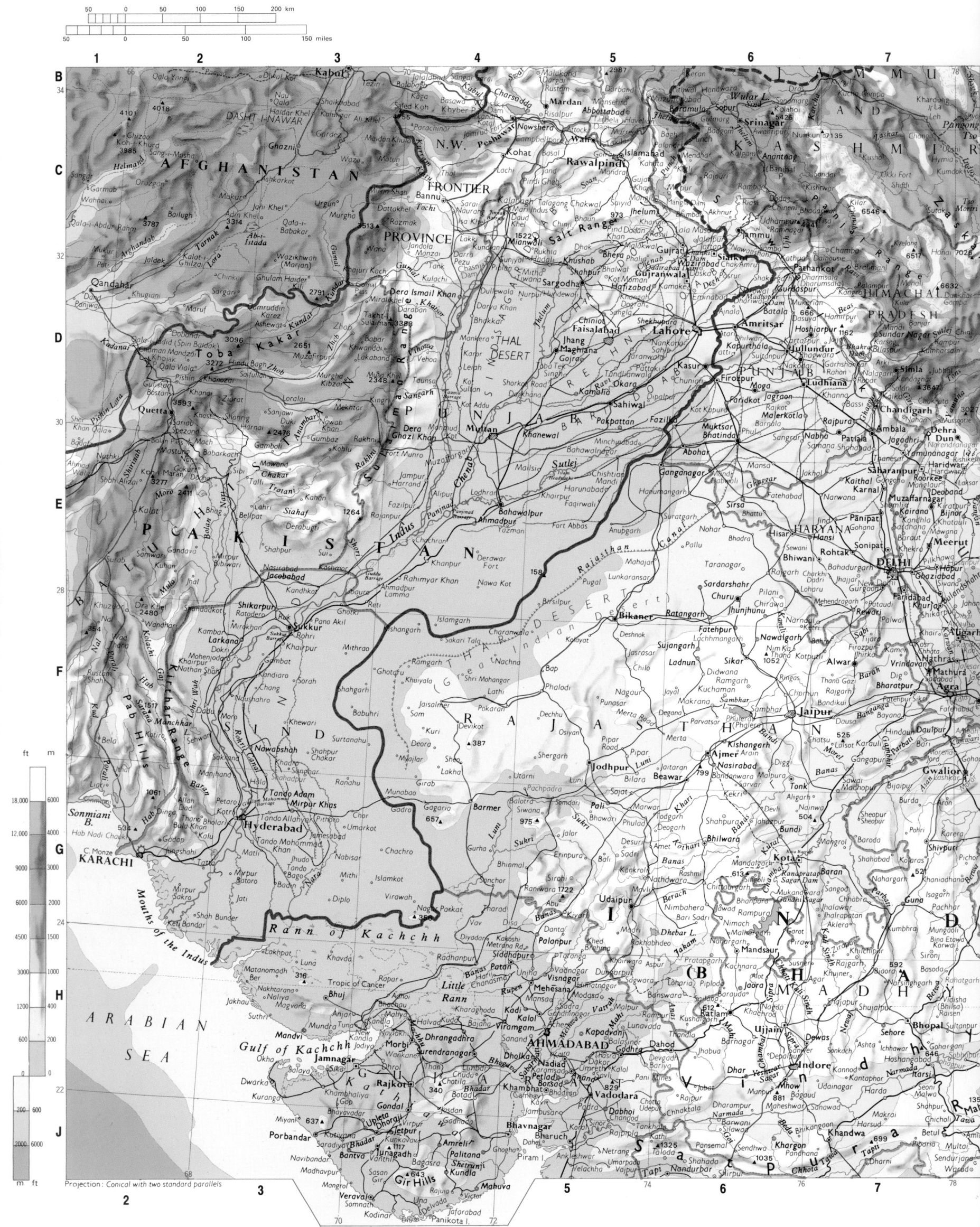

60
66
67
66

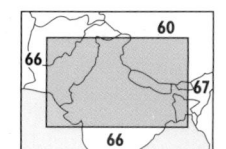

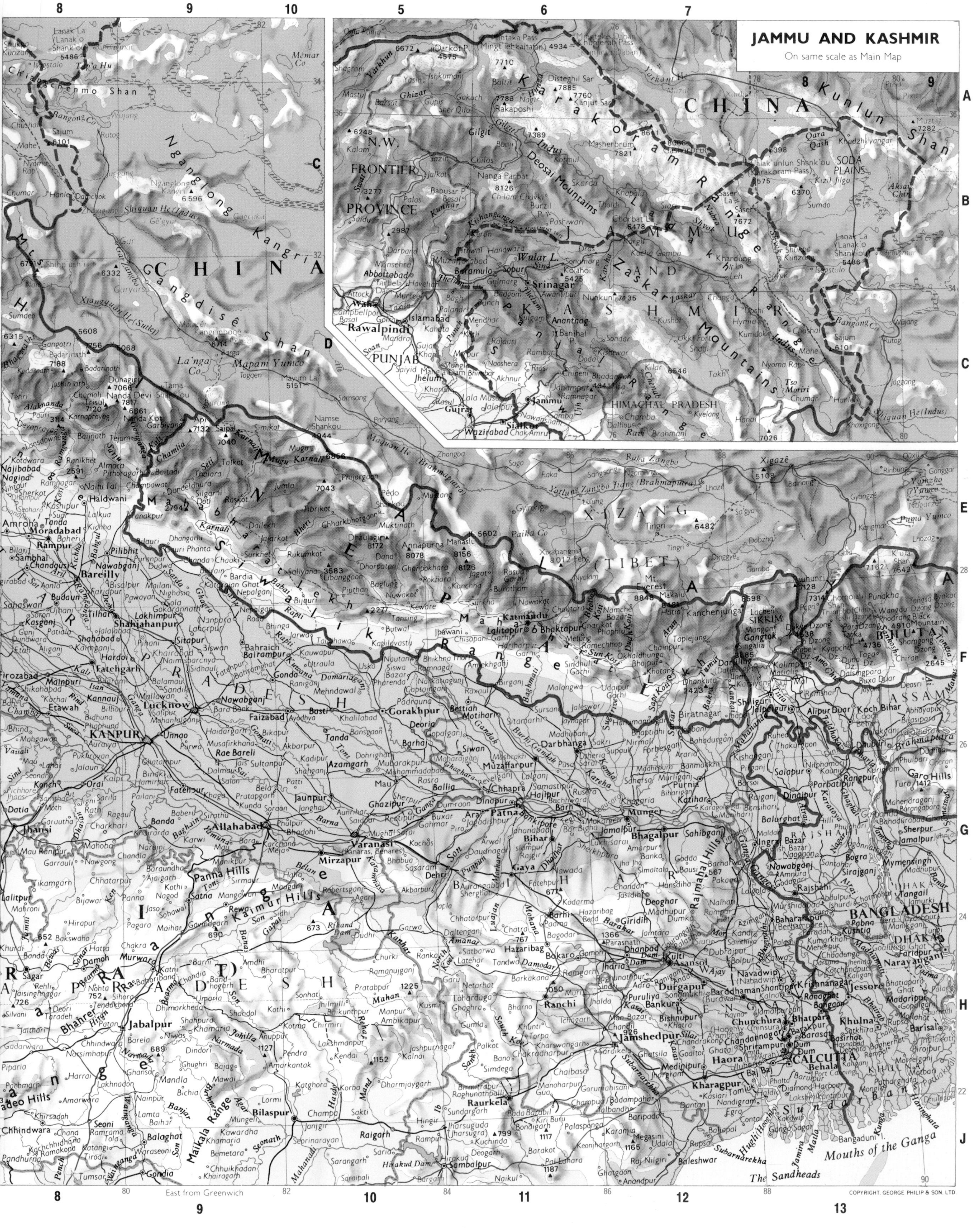

JAMMU AND KASHMIR
On same scale as Main Map
CHINA
Karakoram Range
Kunlun Shan
N.W. FRONTIER PROVINCE
PUNJAB
Rawalpindi
Islamabad
Abbottabad
Gilgit
Nanga Parbat 8126
Deosai Mountains
Srinagar
Wular L.
Jammu
Sialkot
Wazirabad
Jhelum
Gujrat
Ladakh Range
Zaskar Mountains
Leh
HIMACHAL PRADESH
Anantnag
Kishtwar
Karakoram Pass
Aksai Chin
SODA PLAINS
Nganglong Kangri
Gangdisê Shan
Mapam Yumco
La'nga Co
Xianggu'an He (Sutlej)
Nanda Devi 7817
NEPAL
Mahabharat Lekh
Dhaulagiri 8172
Annapurna 8078
Manaslu 8156
Katmandu
Bhaktapur
Lalitpur
Mt. Everest 8848
Makalu 8481
Kanchenjunga 8598
XIZANG (TIBET)
Yarlung Zangbo Jiang (Brahmaputra)
Xixabangma Feng 8012
Xigazê
SIKKIM
Gangtok
BHUTAN
Darjiling
ASSAM
Garo Hills
BANGLADESH
DHAKA
Narayanganj
Khulna
Jessore
Rajshahi
Barisal
Mymensingh
Tangail
UTTAR PRADESH
Lucknow
KANPUR
Allahabad
Varanasi
Mirzapur
Gorakhpur
Faizabad
Bareilly
Moradabad
Rampur
Shahjahanpur
Sitapur
Fatehgarh
Etawah
Jhansi
Orai
Banda
Jaunpur
Azamgarh
Ghazipur
Patna
Gaya
Bihar
Muzaffarpur
Darbhanga
Bhagalpur
Munger
Purnia
Katihar
Rajmahal Hills
Hazaribag
Ranchi
Dhanbad
Asansol
Durgapur
Bardhaman
Jamshedpur
Kharagpur
Medinipur
Haora
CALCUTTA
WEST BENGAL
Sundarbans
Mouths of the Ganga
The Sandheads
MADHYA PRADESH
Jabalpur
Satna
Rewa
Panna Hills
Kaimur Hills
Maikala Range
Bilaspur
Raigarh
Sambalpur
Raurkela
Seoni
Balaghat
Gondia
Chhindwara
Mandla
Damoh
Sagar
Mahadeo Hills
Hirakud Dam
East from Greenwich
COPYRIGHT. GEORGE PHILIP & SON, LTD.

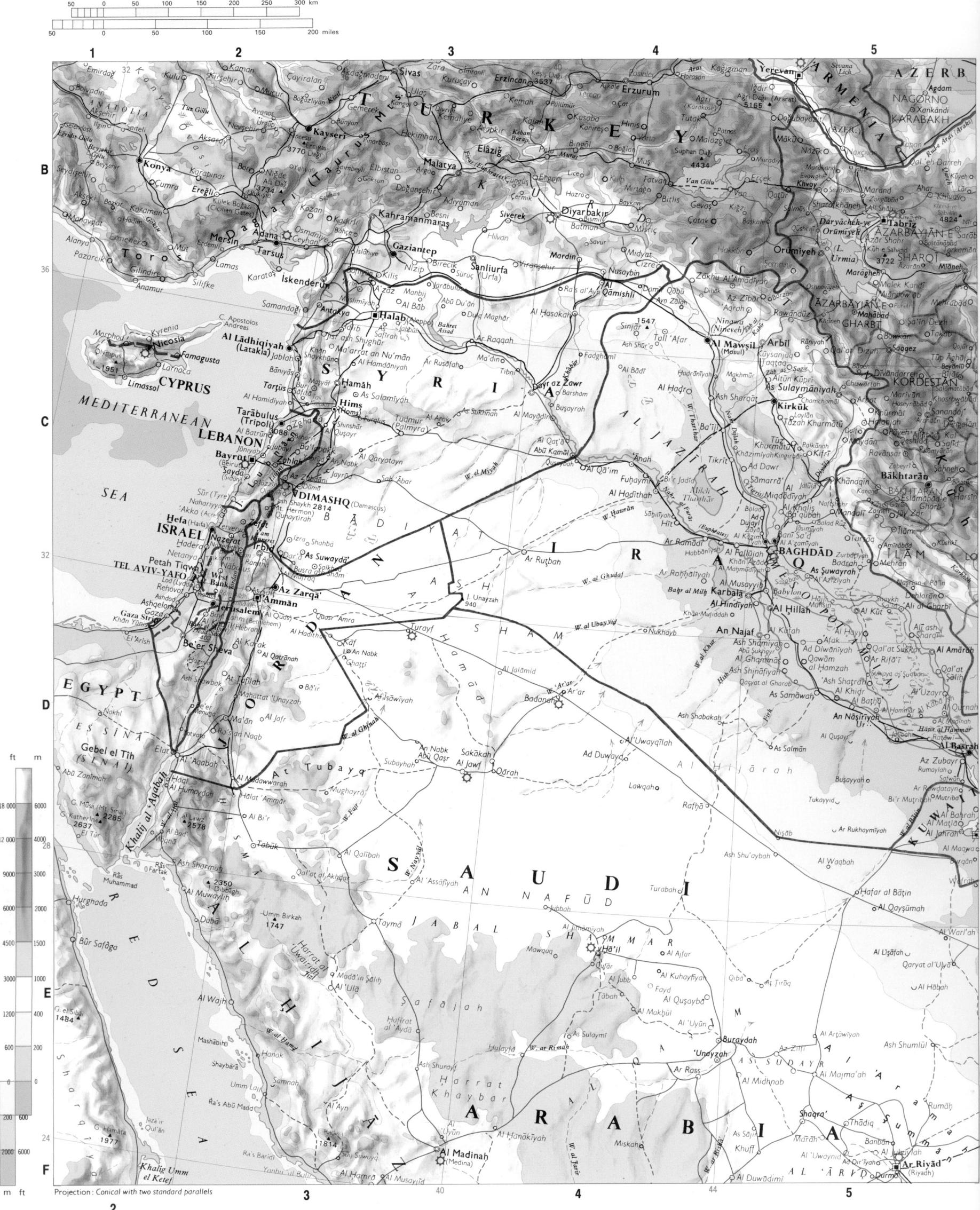

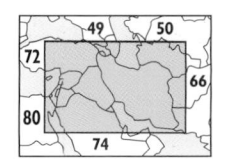

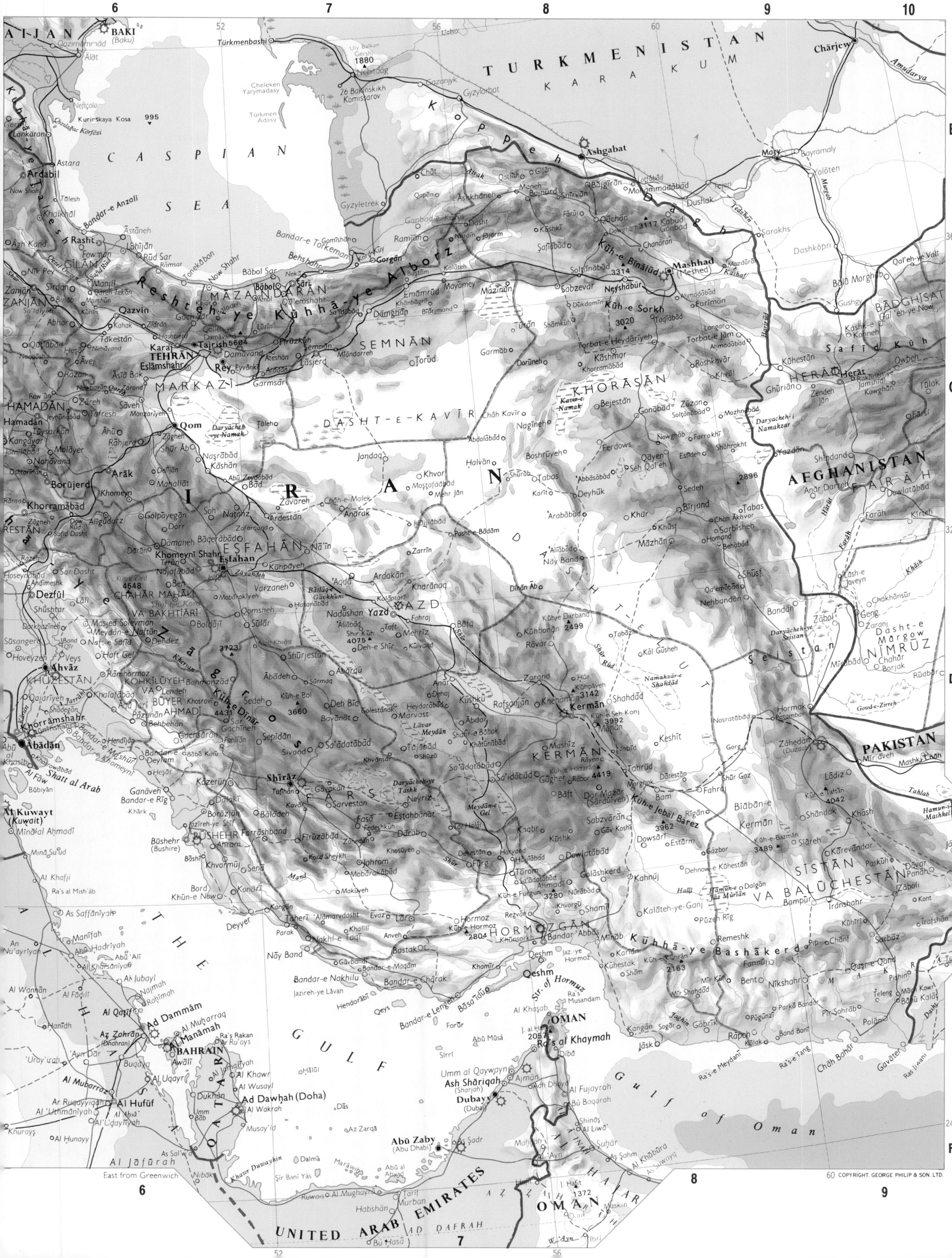

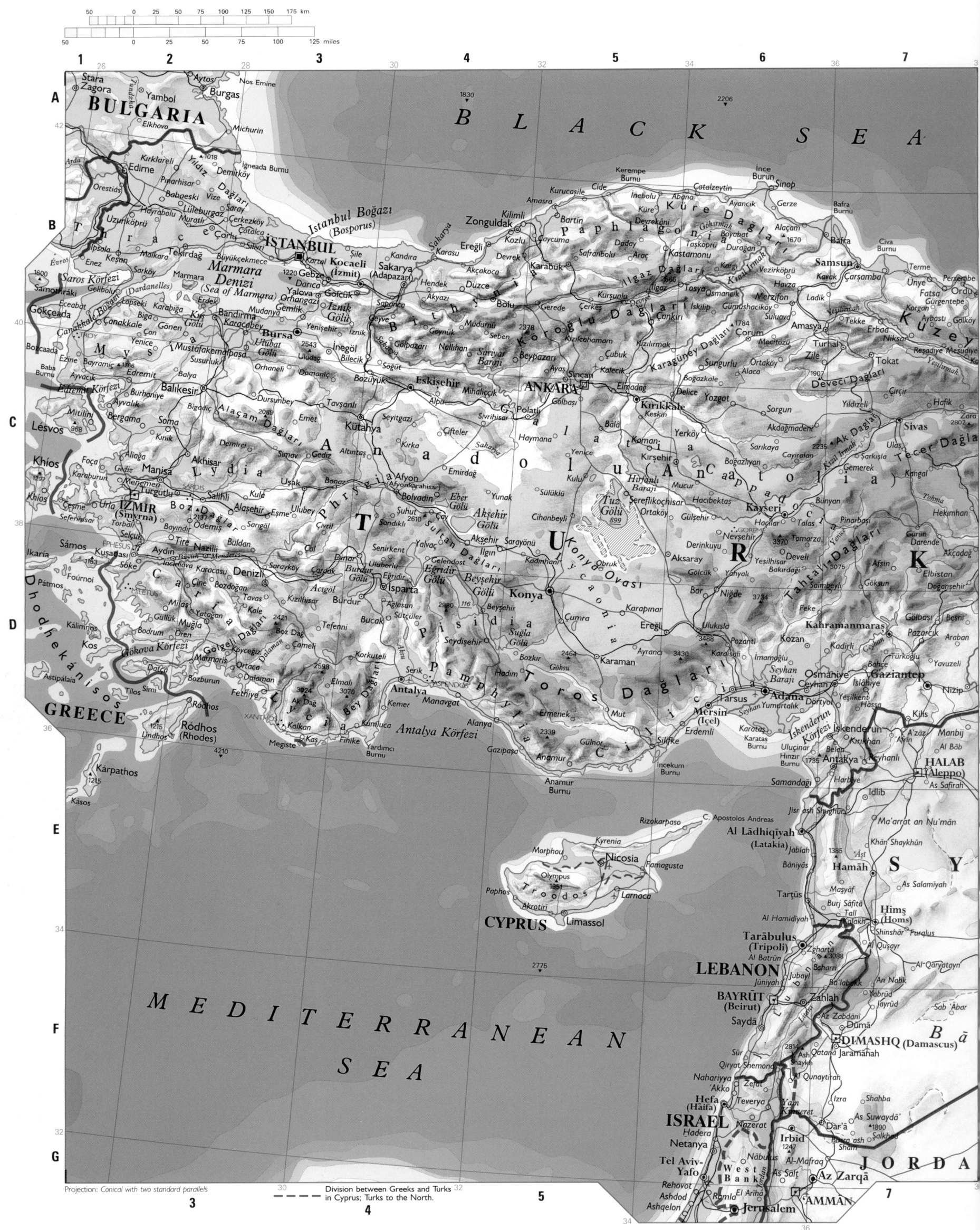

Projection: Conical with two standard parallels

Division between Greeks and Turks
in Cyprus; Turks to the North.

CASPIAN SEA

RUSSIA

GEORGIA

ARMENIA

AZERBAIJAN

IRAN

IRAQ

SYRIA

Caucasus Mountains

Anadolu Dağları

Güneydogu Toroslar

Hakkâri Dağları

Kurdistan

Al Jazirah (Mesopotamia)

Bingöl Dağları

NAXCIVAN (Azerbaijan)

KABARDINO-BALKARIA

NORTH OSSETIA

SOUTH OSSETIA

INGUSHETIA

CHECHENIA

DAGESTAN

ABKHAZIA

AJARIA

Cities and towns:

Sochi, Matsesta, Adler, Gagra, Bichvinta, Guadauta, Novyy Afon, Sokhumi, Ochamchira, Gali, Zugdidi, Anaklia, Senaki, Poti, Kobuleti, Batumi, Hopa, Arhavi, Pazar, Çayeli, Rize, Of, Trabzon, Tonya, Akçaabat, Arsin, Sürmene, İkizdere, Tirebolu, Espiye, Görele, Vakfıkebir, Giresun, Bulancak, Dereli, Alucra, Şebinkarahisar, Suşehri, Refahiye, İmranlı, Erzincan, Kelkit, Şiran, Bayburt, İspir, Torul, Gümüşhane, Kemah, İliç, Kemaliye, Divriği, Arapgir, Çemişgezek, Pertek, Tunceli, Pülümür, Karakoçan, Bingöl, Genç, Kulp, Muş, Varto, Hınıs, Karayazı, Tekman, Çat, Pasinler, Erzurum, Aşkale, Tercan, Narman, Oltu, Olur, Yusufeli, Ardanuç, Şavşat, Artvin, Ardahan, Çıldır, Susuz, Kars, Sarıkamış, Selim, Digor, Tuzluca, Iğdır, Doğubayazıt, Ağrı, Eleşkirt, Tutak, Patnos, Diyadin, Hamur, Malazgirt, Bulanık, Adilcevaz, Erciş, Muradiye, Ahlat, Tatvan, Bitlis, Kozluk, Siirt, Eruh, Şırnak, Silopi, Cizre, Zakhū, Beytüşşebap, Uludere, Şemdinli, Yüksekova, Hakkâri, Çatak, Başkale, Van, Özalp, Saray, Qotūr, Gevaş, Gürpınar

Elâzığ, Maden, Ergani, Çermik, Siverek, Diyarbakır, Batman, Bismil, Çınar, Mardin, Midyat, Nusaybin, Kızıltepe, Derik, Viranşehir, Şanlıurfa (Urfa), Siverek, Hilvan, Bozova, Suruç, Akçakale, Ceylânpınar, Birecik, Jarābulus, Abū Du'ān, Dulq Maghār

Al Qāmishlī, Ra's al 'Ayn, Al Ḥasakah, Dihōk, 'Aqrah, Al Amādīyah, Az Zibār, Aqrah, Tall 'Afar, Sinjār, Al Mawṣil (Mosul), Arbīl, Qal' at Dīzāh, Küysanjaq, Taqtaq, Altūn Küprī, Kirkūk, As Sulaymānīyah, Chamchamal, Ḥalabjah, Kifrī, Tūz Khurmātū, Ṭāzah Khurmātū, Makhmūr, Ash Sharqāṭ, Al Ḥaḍr, Fadghāmī, Al Mayādīn, Al Qā'im, Abū Kamāl, 'Ānah, Al Qaṭā, Buṣayrah, Khalāti, Tibnī, Barsham, Ma'dan, Ar Ruṣāfah, Dayr az Zawr, As Sukhnah, Al Arak, Tudmur (PALMYRA)

Ar Raqqah, Nahr al Furāt (Euphrates), Ar Ruṭbah, Nukhayb, 'Unāzah, W. Ḥawrān, W. al Ghudaf, W. al Ubayyiḍ, Ar Raḥḥālīyah, Ḥīt, Sāḥilīyah, Ḥabbānīyah, Ar Ramādī, Al Fallūjah, Al Ḥabbānīyah, Al Maḥmūdīyah, Karbalā', Al Ḥillah, BABYLON, Al Hindīyah, Al Kūfah, An Najaf, Al Qaṭā, Fuhaymī, Al Hadīthah

BAGHDAD, Ba'qūbah, Ad Dujayl, Balad, Sāmarrā, Ad Dawr, Tikrīt, Ba'ji, Al Miqdādīyah, Jalūlā, Khānaqīn, Mandalī, Balad Rūz, Jāsimīyah, Banī Sa'd, Al Khāliṣ, Al Kāẓimīyah, Al 'Azīzīyah, Al Kūt, Aş Şuwayrah, An Nu'mānīyah, Al Ḥayy, Qal' at Sukkar, Al 'Amārah, Badrah, Shaykh Sa'īd, 'Alī al Gharbī, Mehrān, Zurbāṭīyah, Tursāq

Kizil Yurt, Khasavyurt, Makhachkala, Kaspiysk, Izberbash, Derbent, Buynaksk, Botlikh, Agvali, Tlyarata, Akusha, Madzhalis, Dagestanskiye Ogni, Kakhib, Khunzakh, Khasmyurt

Groznyy, Argun, Shali, Achkhoy-Martan, Beslan, Vladikavkaz, Alagir, Ardon, Sadon, Kazbek, Tyrnyauz, Teberda, Elbrus

Kutaisi, Chiatura, Tqibuli, Sachkhere, Samtredia, Ozurgeti, Zestaponi, Khashuri, Gori, Kaspi, Mtskheta, TBILISI, Rustavi, Marneuli, Shulaveri, Gurjaani, Telavi, Logodekhi, Zaqatala, Qakh, Balakən, Tsnori, Tsiteli Tsqaro, Mirzaani, Akhaltsikhe, Borjomi, Akhalkalaki, Vale, Khulo, Stepanavan, Alaverdi, Vanadzor, Dilijan, Sevan, Hrazdan, Aparan, Gyumri, Artik, Aragats, Sevana Lich, Martuni, Vardenis, Chambarak, YEREVAN, Ejmiadzin, Kamo, Goris, Kapan, Kajaran, Meghri, Julfa, Ordubad, Naxçıvan, İlıchevsk, Kərkı, Makū, Qūshchī, Orūmiyeh (Urmia), Khvoy, Seydvān, Salmās, Marand, Tabrīz, Soufiān, Bostānābād, Āzar Shahr, Marāgheh, Mīāndowāb, Bonāb, Ajabshīr, Malek Kandī, Mehrābād, Naqādeh, Mahābād, Bowkān, Saqqez, Bāneh, Sa'in Dezh, Takāb, Shāhīn Dezh, Dīvāndarreh, Sanandaj, Marīvān, Qorveh, Dehgolān, Bījār, Hamadān, Asadābād, Tūysarkān, Malāyer, Nahāvand, Kangāvar, Sonqor, Bākhtarān, Harsin, Bīsotūn, Sahneh, Eslāmābād-e Gharb, Karand, Qaşr-e Shīrīn, Gīlān-e Gharb, Khorramābād, Borūjerd, Oshtorīnān, Jūy Zar, Dehlorān, Andīmeshk, Dezfūl, Shūsh, Sūsangerd

Ağstafa, Tovuz, Qazax, Şəmkir, Gəncə, Mingəçevir, Yevlax, Ağdaş, Göyçay, Zərdab, Sabirabad, İmişli, Ağcabədi, Bərdə, Tərtər, Xanlar, Daşkəsən, Xankəndi, Ağdam, Şuşa, Martuni, Fizuli, Cəbrayıl, Qaraçala, Salyan, Biləsuvar, Neftçala, Bilasuvar, Masallı, Cəlilabad, Lənkəran, Astara, Namīn, Ardabīl, Nīr, Sarāb, Khalkhāl, Āghkand, Hoseynābād, Bahār, Razan, Āsadābād, Khosrowābād, Qūtiābād, Tūp Āghāj, Abhar, Zanjān, Bināb, Takāb, Sirdān

Sumqayıt, Baki, Maştağa, Artyom, Suraxanı, Siyəzən, Dəvəçi, Quba, Xaçmaz, Xudat, Qusar, Qax, Şəki, Baş Qışlaq, Kutkashen, Şamaxı, Bazar Dyuzi, Baba dag, Mingəçevir Su Anbarı

Rasht, Bandar-e Anzalī, Fowman, Qezel Owzan, Manjīl, Tārom, Āstārā, Tālesh, Kūhhā-ye Sabalān, Kūhhā-ye Talesh, Kūh-e Sahand, Qızılağac Körfəzi, Kurinskaya Kosa, Port İlīç

Rivers, lakes & physical features:

Rūd-e Aras (Araks), Kür, Nahr al Furāt (Euphrates), Dicle Nehri, Dijlah (Tigris), Nahr Dijlah, Zāb al Kabīr, Zāb aş Şaghīr, W. ath Tharthar, Mileh Tharthār, Çıldır Gölü, Van Gölü 1720, Sevana Lich, Daryāchēh-ye Orūmīyeh (Lake Urmia), Keban Barajı, Atatürk Barajı, Bahret Assad, Bahr al Milh, Ḥawr al Ḥabbānīyah, Hawr as Sa'dīyah, Hawr ash Sharqī, Habbānīyah, Nahr al Furāt, Dicle Nehri (Euphrates), Suphan Dağı 4434, Ala Dağları, Ağrı Dağı 5165, Aragats 4090, Baba dag 3629, Bazar Dyuzi 4466, Kaçkar 3937, Mescit 3239, Kısır Dağ 3192, Cilo Dağı 4135, Kazbek, Elbrus 5633, Tebulos 4492, Uludoruk 4136, Cilo Dağı

Heights: 2137, 1569, 790, 2726, 4276, 3789, 4431, 3578, 3157, 3724, 3616, 3904, 3347, 4822, 2477, 1297, 3752, 3870, 3282, 3607, 3163, 3327, 3350, 3280, 2658, 1390, 940, 1460, 1957, 2545, 2967, 3660, 3537, 3095, 3063, 3239, 5203, 5047, 6047

East from Greenwich

CARTOGRAPHY BY PHILIP'S. COPYRIGHT REED INTERNATIONAL BOOKS LTD

ft   m
9000 3000
6000 2000
4500 1500
3000 1000
1500 500
600   200
0   0
150   50
300   100
600   200
1500 500
3000 1000
6000 2000
9000 3000
m   ft

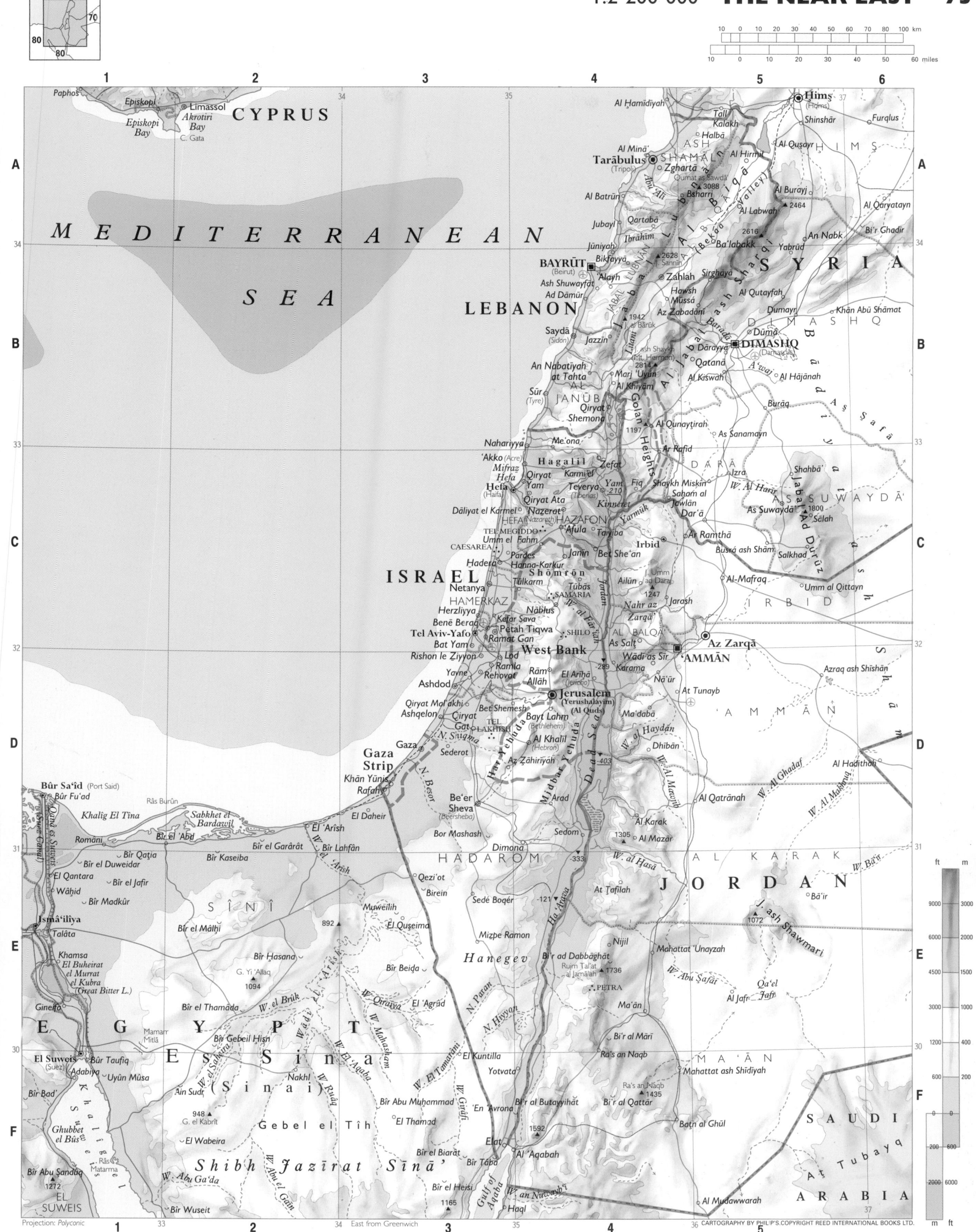

10 0 10 20 30 40 50 60 70 80 100 km

10 0 10 20 30 40 50 60 miles

CYPRUS

Paphos
Episkopi
Episkopi Bay
Akrotiri Bay
C. Gata
Limassol

M E D I T E R R A N E A N

S E A

Al Ḥamidiyah
Ṭall
Kalakh
Halba
Al Quṣayr
Shinshār
Furqlus

Ḥims (Homs)

ASH
SHAMAL
Al Minā'
Ṭarābulus (Tripoli)
Zgharta
Qumat as Sawdā'
3088
Bsharri
Al Buray
2464
Al Qaryatayn
Al Baṭrūn
Jubayl
Qartabā
2616
An Nabk
Bi'r Ghadir
Ibrāhīm
Jūniyah
2628
Sannin
Ba'labakk
Yabrūd

BAYRŪT (Beirut)
Bikfayyā
Zahlah
Sirghāyā
Al Qutayfah
Ash Shuwayfāt
Alayh
Ḥawsh Mūssá
Dumayr
Khān Abū Shāmat

LEBANON
Ad Dāmūr
Az Zabādānī
Baradá
A'waj
Al Ḥājānah

DIMASHQ
Saydā (Sidon)
Jazzin
1942
al Barūk
Darayyā
Qatanā
DIMASHQ (Damascus)
DŪMĀ

An Nabaṭīyah at Tahta
2814
(Jt. Hermon)
Marj 'Uyūn
Al Khiyām
Būrāq
Aṣ Ṣafā

Sūr (Tyre)
AL
JANŪB
Qiryat Shemona
Golan Heights
Al Qunayṭirah
As Sanamayn

Naharīyya
Me'ona
1197
Ar Rafid
DARA
Izra
Shahbā'

'Akko (Acre)
Ḥagalil
Zefat
Shaykh Miskin
As Suwaydā
1800
Sālah

Mifraz Ḥefa
Qiryat Yam
Karmi'el
Yam
-210
Fiq
Saḥam al Jawlān
Dar'ā
AS SUWAYDĀ

Ḥefa (Haifa)
Qiryat Ata
Teverya (Tiberias)
Kinneret
Jabal Ad Durūz

Dāliyat el Karmel
Nazerat
HEFA
(Nazareth)
HAZAFON
Yarmūk
Ramthā
Salkhad

TEL MEGIDDO
Afula
Tariyba
Irbid
Buṣrá ash Shām

CAESAREA
Umm el Faḥm
Janin
Bet She'an
Ailūn
J. Umm ad Dafar
Al-Mafraq
Umm al Qittayn

Hadera
Hanna-Karkur
Shōmrōn
Tūbās
1247
Jarash
IRBID

ISRAEL
Pardes
Ṭulkarm
SAMARIA
Nahr az Zarqā'

HAMERKAZ
Netanya
Nāblus
AL BALQĀ'
Jarash

Herzliyya
Kefar Sava
SHILO
As Salṭ
AMMĀN
Azraq ash Shishān

Benē Beraq
Petaḥ Tiqwa
WEST BANK
Wādī as Sir
AZ ZARQĀ'

Tel Aviv-Yafo
Ramat Gan
El 'Arīḥā (Jericho)
-289
Karāma
Nā'ūr
At Tunayb

Bat Yam
Rishon le Ziyyon
Rām Allāh
'AMMĀN

Yavne
Reḥovot
Lod
Ramla
Ma'dabā

Ashdod
Bet Shemesh
Jerusalem (Yerushalayim) (Al Quds)
W. al Ḥaydān

Qiryat Mal'akhi
Qiryat
Bayt Laḥm (Bethlehem)
Dhībān

Ashqelon
Gat
N. Shiqma
Al Khalil (Hebron)
403

Gaza
Gaza
Sederot
Az Ẓāhirīyah
Al Karak

Gaza Strip
Khān Yūnis
Rafaḥ
N. Besor
Be'er Sheva (Beersheba)
Arad
W. Al Mawjib

Bûr Sa'îd (Port Said)
Bûr Fu'ad
Rās Burūn
El Daheir
Bor Mashash
Sedom
Al Mazar
W. al Hasā

Khalîg El Tîna
Sabkhet el Bardawîl
El 'Arîsh
Dimona
-333
AL KARAK
Bā'ir

Romāni
Bîr el 'Abd
W. el 'Arîsh
Bîr Lahfân
Qezi'ot
Birein
Sedé Boqér
-121
A Ṭafīlah
1072

Bîr Qaṭia
Bîr el Garārât
W. al Hasā

El Qantara
Bîr el Duweidar
Bîr Kaseiba
Muweilih
El Quseima
Mizpe Ramon
Nijil
Mahaṭṭat 'Unayzah
W. ash Shawmari

Wâḥid
Bîr el Jafir
Bîr Madkûr
S Î N Î
892
Bi'r ad Dabbāghāt
W. Abū Ṣafāt
Qa'el Jafr

Ismâ'ilîya
Ṭalāta
Bîr el Malḥi
Bîr Ḥasana
Rujm Tal'at al Jamā'ah
1736

Khamsa
El Buheirat el Murrat el Kubra (Great Bitter L.)
G. Yi 'Allaq
1094
Bîr Beiḍa
H a n e g e v
PETRA
Ma'ān

Gineifa
Bîr el Thamâda
W. el Brûk
'Qraiya
El 'Agrád
N. Paran
Al Jafr

E G Y P T
Mamarr Mitlâ
G. el Kabrît
948
'Ain Sudr
W. Mahashem
Bi'r al Mārī
MA'ĀN

El Suweis (Suez)
Bûr Taufîq
Adabiya
Nakhl
El Thamad
El Kuntilla
Ra's an Naqb
Mahaṭṭat ash Shidiyah

Uyûn Mûsa
E s S i n a (Sinai)
W. El Aqaba
'En 'Avrona
Bi'r al Buṭayyiḥāt
Bi'r al Qaṭṭar
1435

Bîr Bad
Khalîg es Suweis
W. Ruaq
W. el Giráfi
Ra's an Naqb
1592
S A U D I

Ghubbet el Bûs
Râs Matarma
Gebel el Tîh
W. Abu el Gain
Bîr Abu Muhammad
Elat
Al 'Aqabah
Bi'r al Qaṭṭar
Boṭn el Ghûl

Bîr Abu Ṣandûq
1272
Shibh Jazîrat Sînā'
W. Abu Ga'da
Bîr el Biarât
Bîr Ṭāba
Al Mudawwarah
A R A B I A

EL SUWEIS
Bîr Wuseit
El Wabeira
Bîr el Heisi
1165
Ḥaql
W. an Nuwaybi
At Tubayq

J O R D A N

ISRAEL
HADAROM

Gulf of 'Aqaba

ft m
9000 3000
6000 2000
4500 1500
3000 1000
1200 400
600 200
0 0
200 600
2000 6000
m ft

═══ 1974 Cease Fire Lines

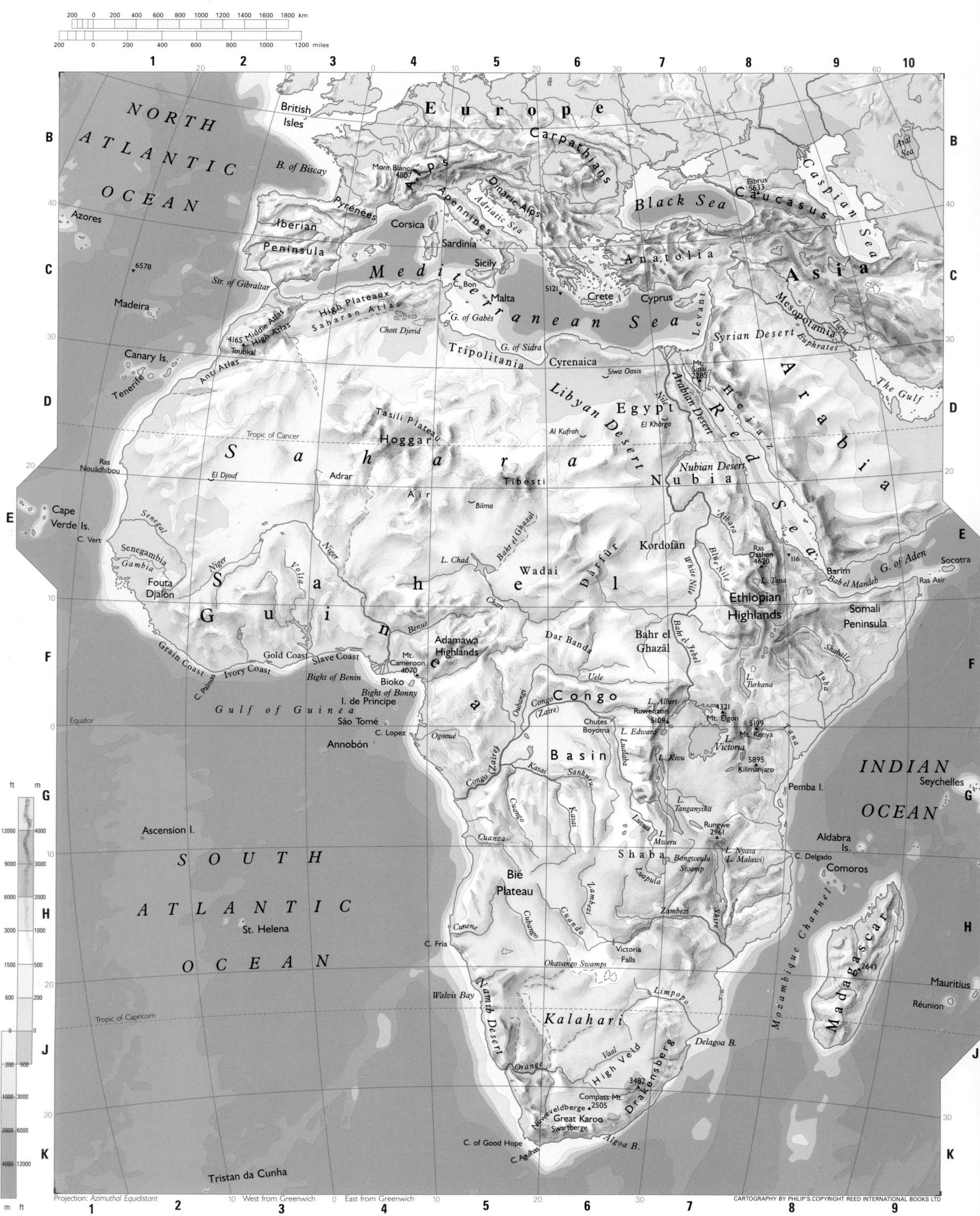

200 0 200 400 600 800 1000 1200 1400 1600 1800 km
200 0 200 400 600 800 1000 1200 miles

1   2   3   4   5   6   7   8   9   10

NORTH
ATLANTIC
OCEAN

Europe

British Isles

B. of Biscay

Alps
Mont Blanc
4807
Pyrénées
Apennines
Dinaric Alps
Adriatic Sea
Carpathians

Black Sea
Elbrus
5633
Caucasus
Aral Sea
Caspian Sea

Azores

Iberian
Peninsula
Corsica
Sardinia
Sicily

Anatolia

Asia

6578

Madeira
Str. of Gibraltar
C. Bon
Malta
5121
Crete
Cyprus

Mediterranean Sea

Levant

Mesopotamia
Tigris
Euphrates

The Gulf

Canary Is.
4165 Middle Atlas
High Atlas
Toubkal
High Plateaux
Saharan Atlas
G. of Gabès
Chott Djerid
Tripolitania
G. of Sidra
Cyrenaica
Siwa Oasis

Syrian Desert

Anti Atlas
Tenerife

Libyan Desert
Egypt
El Khârga

Mt.
Sinai
2285

Hejaz

Arabian Desert

Arabia

Ras
Nouâdhibou
Tropic of Cancer
Tasili Plateau
Hoggar
Adrar
Aïr
Tibesti

S a h a r a

El Djouf
Bilma
Nubian Desert
Nubia

Red Sea

Ras
Dashen
4620
116

Barim
Bab el Mandeb
G. of Aden
Socotra
Ras Asir

**Cape
Verde Is.**
C. Vert
Senegal
Senegambia
Gambia
Fouta
Djalon
Niger
Volta
Niger

S a h e l

L. Chad
Bahr el Ghazal
Wadai
Darfur
Kordofân
White Nile
Blue Nile
Atbara
L. Tana

**Ethiopian
Highlands**

**Somali
Peninsula**

G u i n e a

Grain Coast
Gold Coast
Ivory Coast
C. Palmas
Slave Coast
Bight of Benin
Benue
Mt.
Cameroon
4070
Bioko
Bight of Bonny
I. de Principe
São Tomé
Adamawa
Highlands
Chari
Dar Banda
Uele
Ubangi
Bahr el
Ghazâl
Bahr el Jebel

C a m e r o o n

Shaballe
L.
Turkana
Juba

Gulf of Guinea
Equator
C. Lopez
Annobón

Ogooué
Congo
(Zaïre)
Congo
Chutes
Boyoma
L. Albert
Ruwenzori
5094
L. Edward
Laudaba
L. Kivu
4321
Mt. Elgon
5199
Mt. Kenya
L.
Victoria
Tana

INDIAN

OCEAN

Seychelles

Ascension I.
Congo (Zaïre)
Kasai
Sankuru
Kasai
Basin
5895
Kilimanjaro

Pemba I.

SOUTH
Cuango
Cuanza
Shaba
L.
Tanganyika
L.
Mweru
Rungwe
2961
Bangweulu
Swamp
L. Nyasa
(L. Malawi)
Aldabra
Is.
C. Delgado
Comoros

ATLANTIC

St. Helena
Biè
Plateau
Cunene
Cubango
Luapula
Zambezi
Zambezi
Shire

Mozambique Channel

Madagascar
2643
Mauritius
Réunion

OCEAN

C. Fria
Cuando
Victoria
Falls
Okavango Swamps

Tropic of Capricorn
Namib Desert
Kalahari
Limpopo
Delagoa B.

Walvis Bay
Orange
Vaal
High Veld
Drakensberg
Algoa B.
3482
Compass Mt.
2505
Nuweveldberge
Great Karoo
Swartberge
C. of Good Hope
C. Agulhas

Tristan da Cunha

ft m
12000 4000
9000 3000
6000 2000
3000 1000
1500 500
600 200
0 0
200 500
1000 3000
2000 6000
4000 12000
m ft

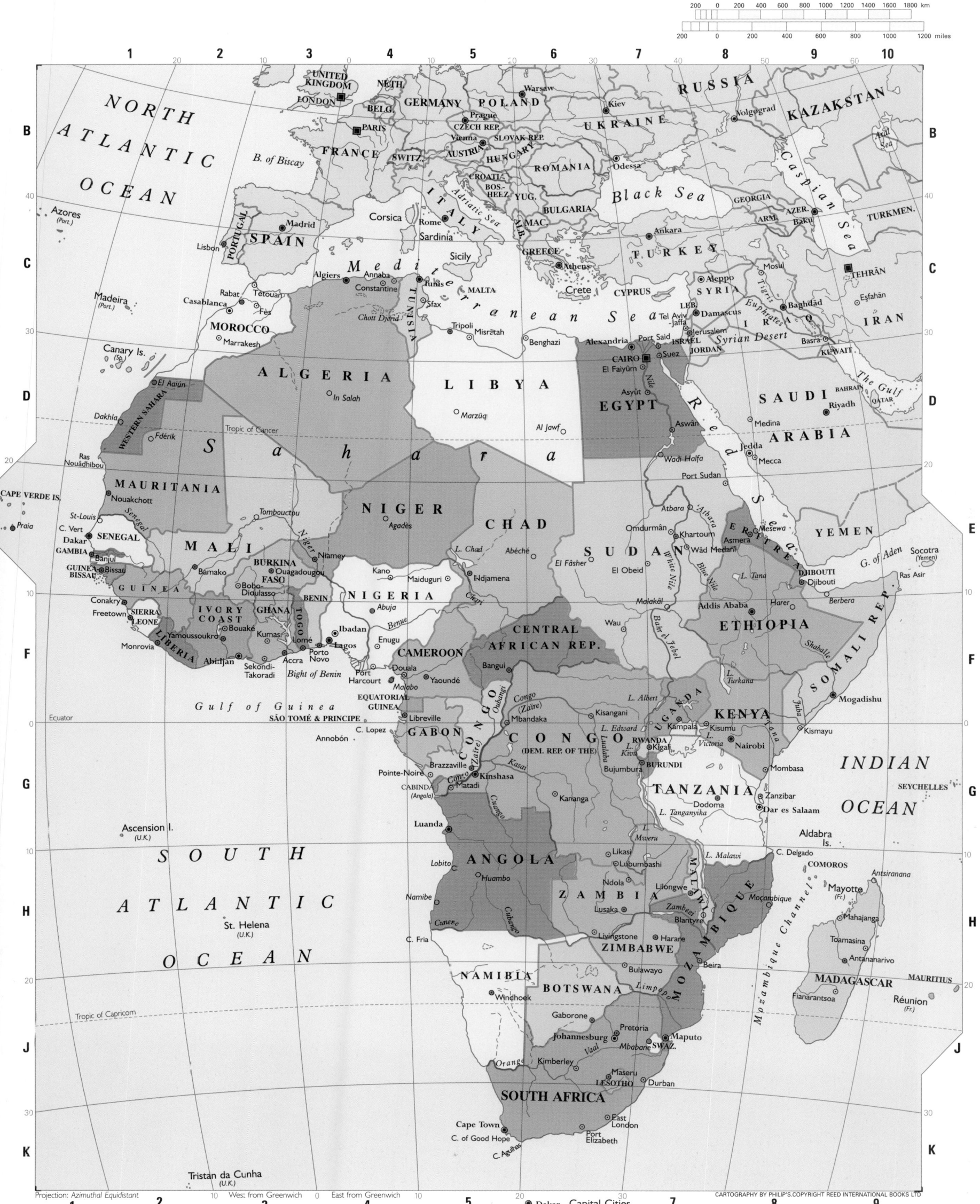

CARTOGRAPHY BY PHILIP'S.COPYRIGHT REED INTERNATIONAL BOOKS LTD

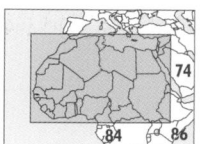

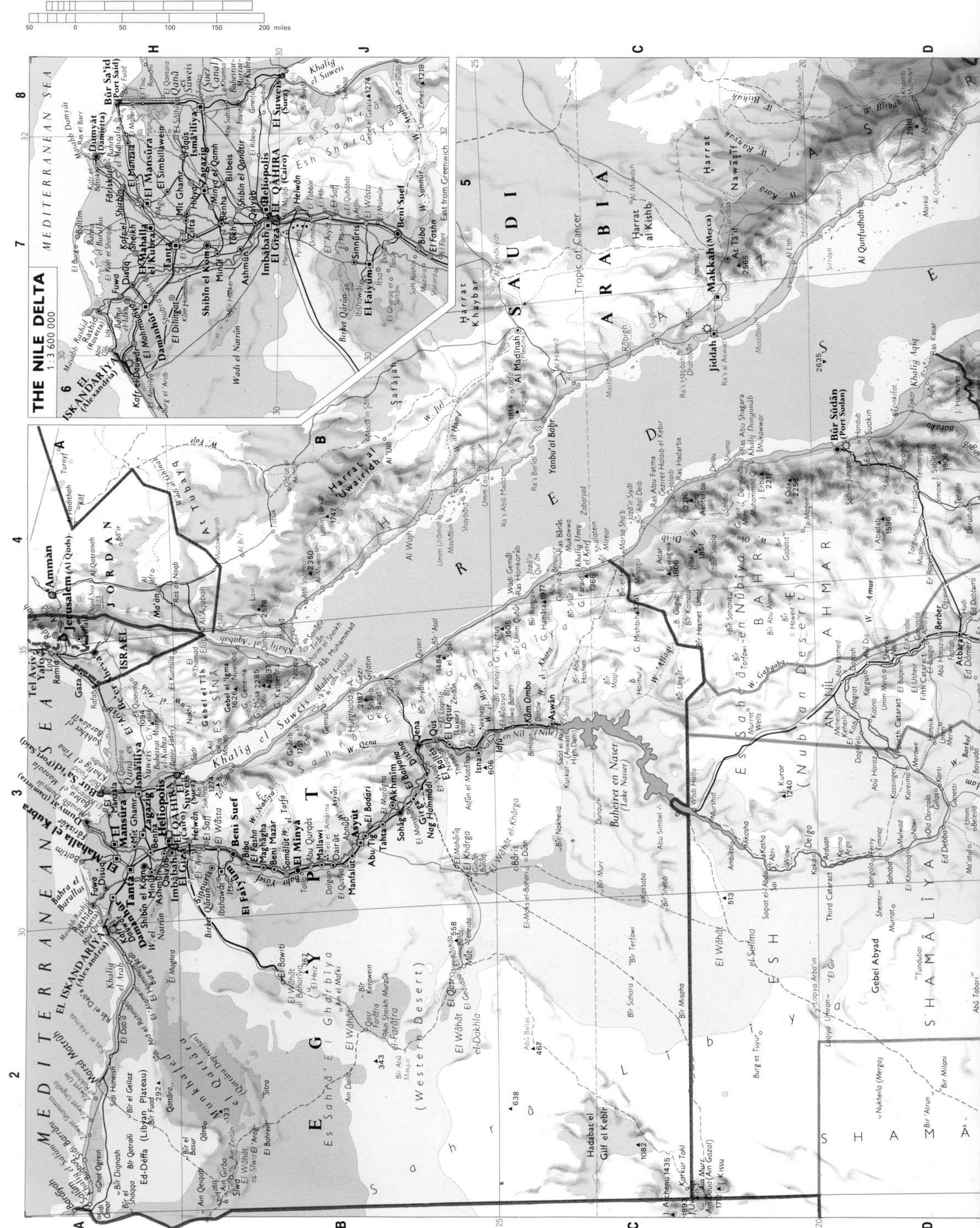

THE NILE DELTA
1:3 600 000

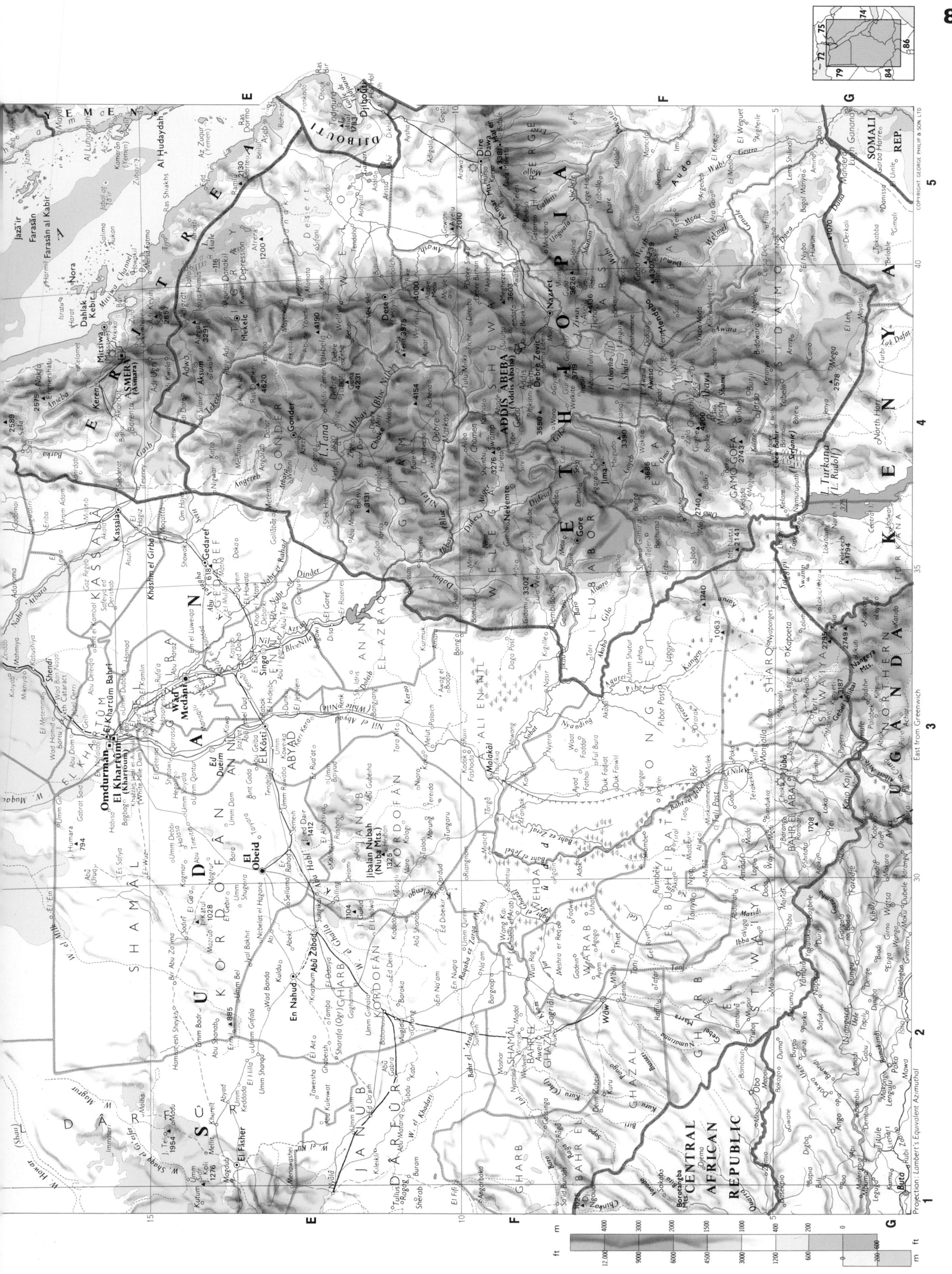

Projection: Lambert's Equivalent Azimuthal

West from Greenwich

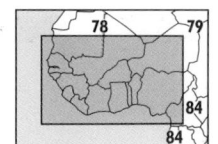

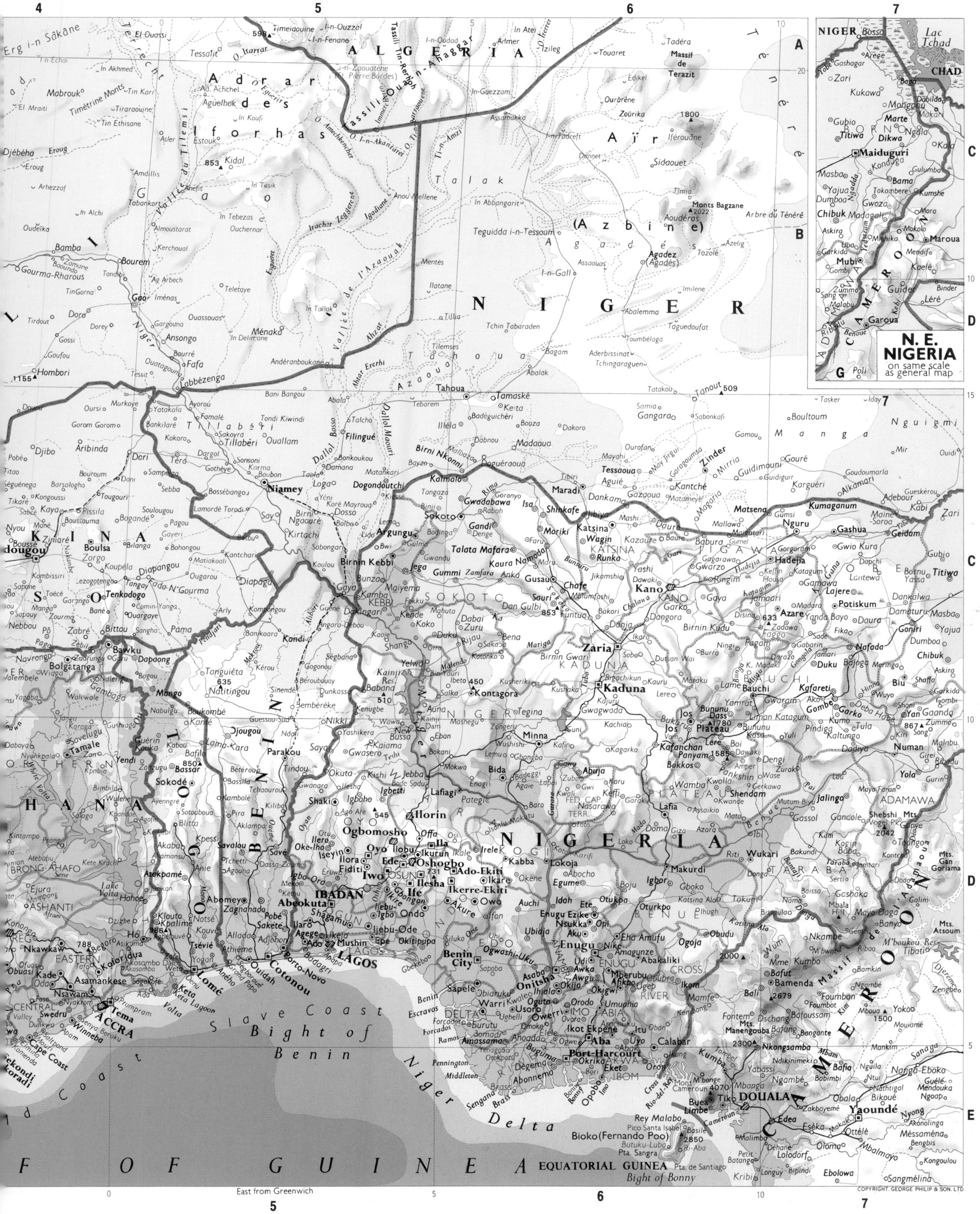

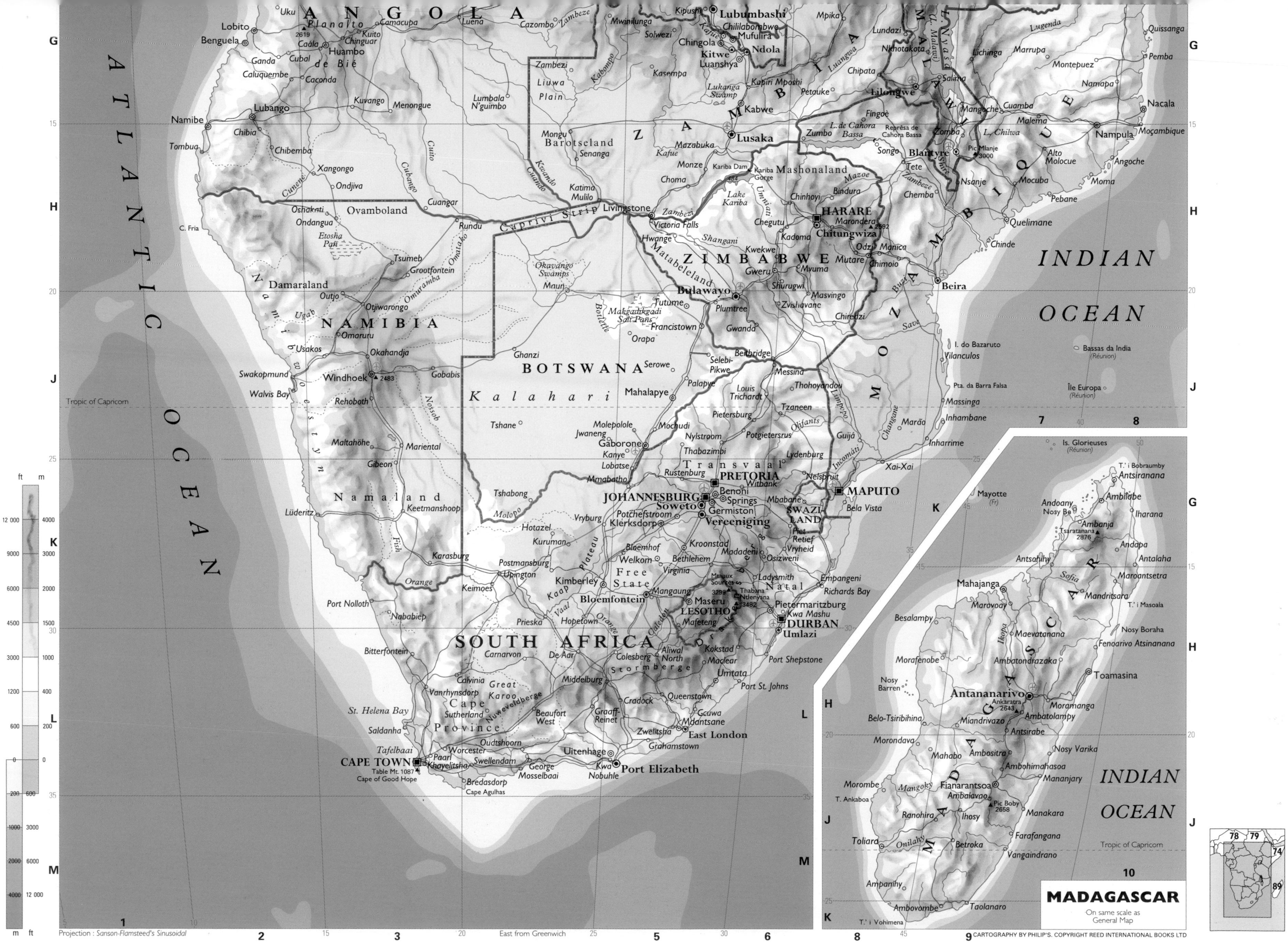

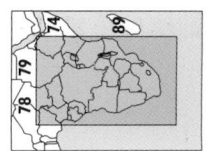

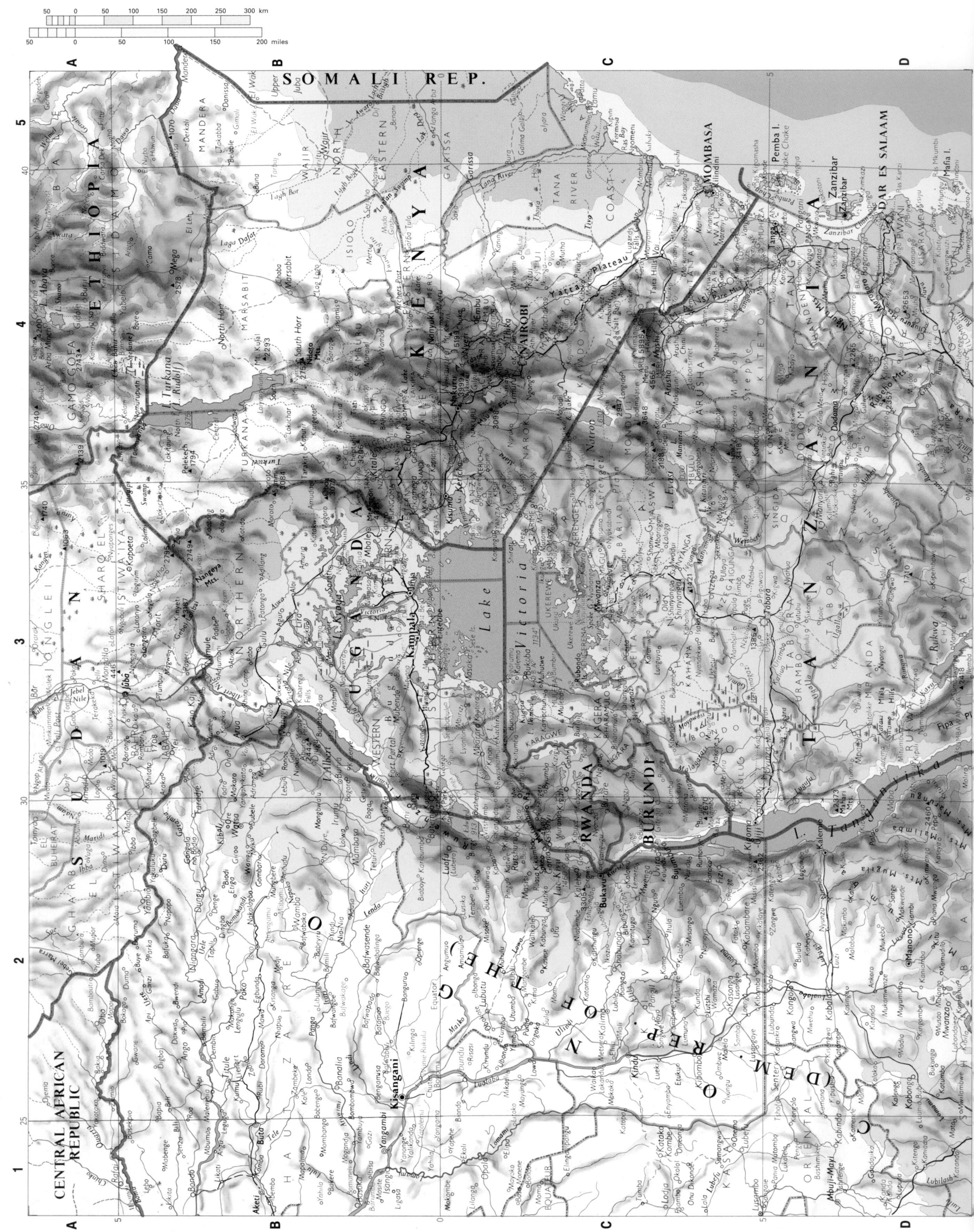

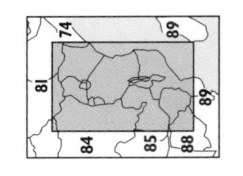

COPYRIGHT GEORGE PHILIP & SON LTD

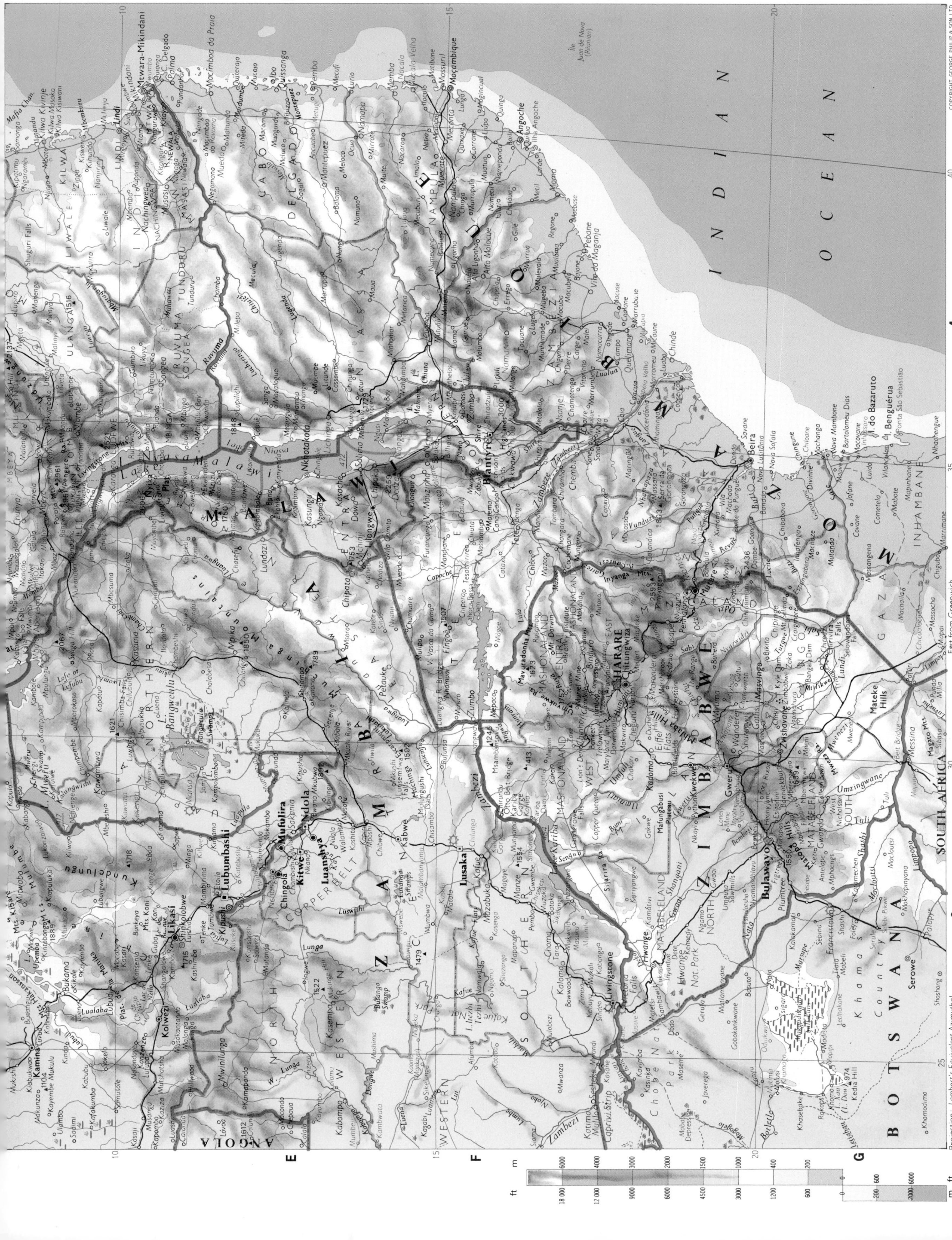

East from Greenwich

Projection: Lambert's Equivalent Azimuthal

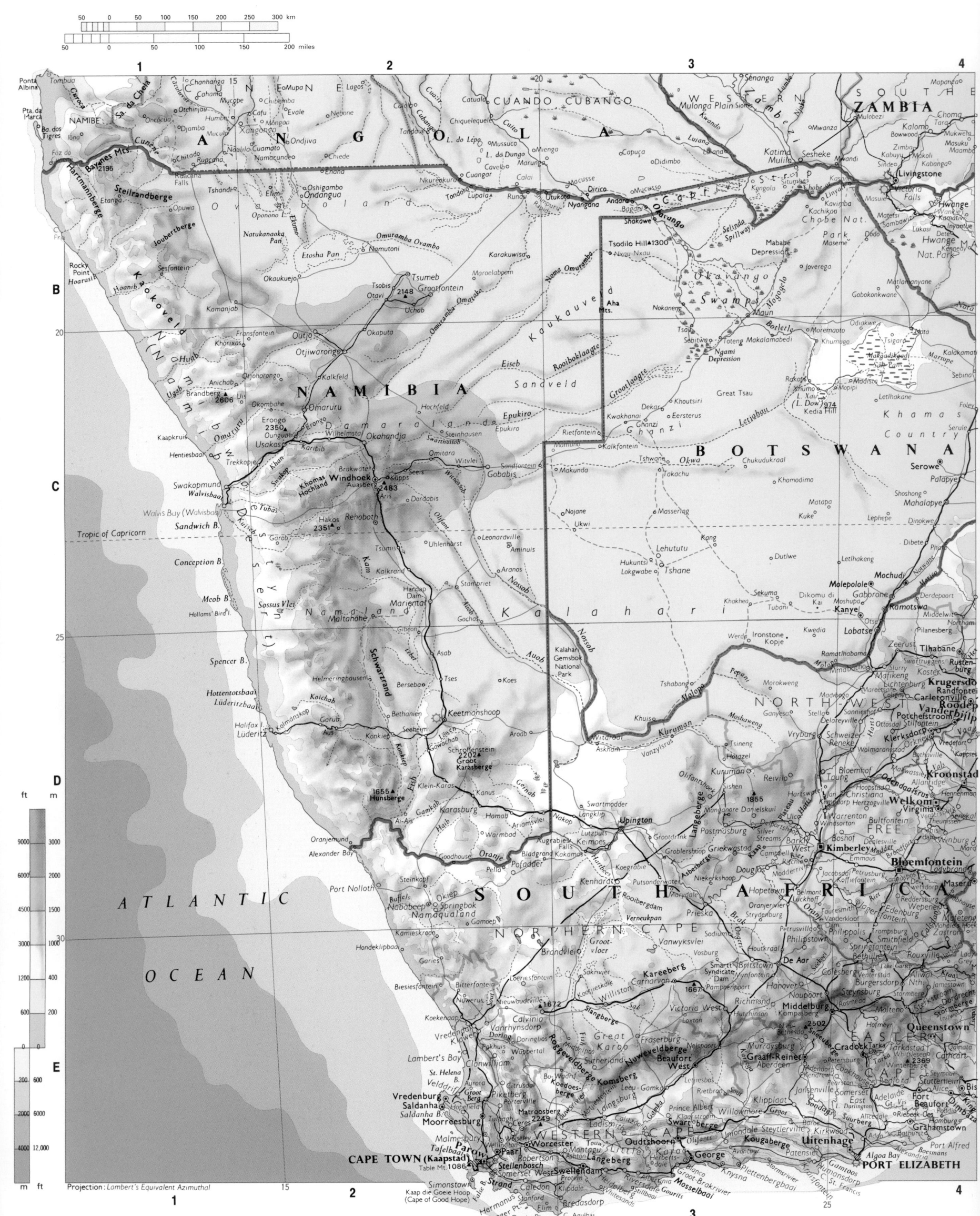

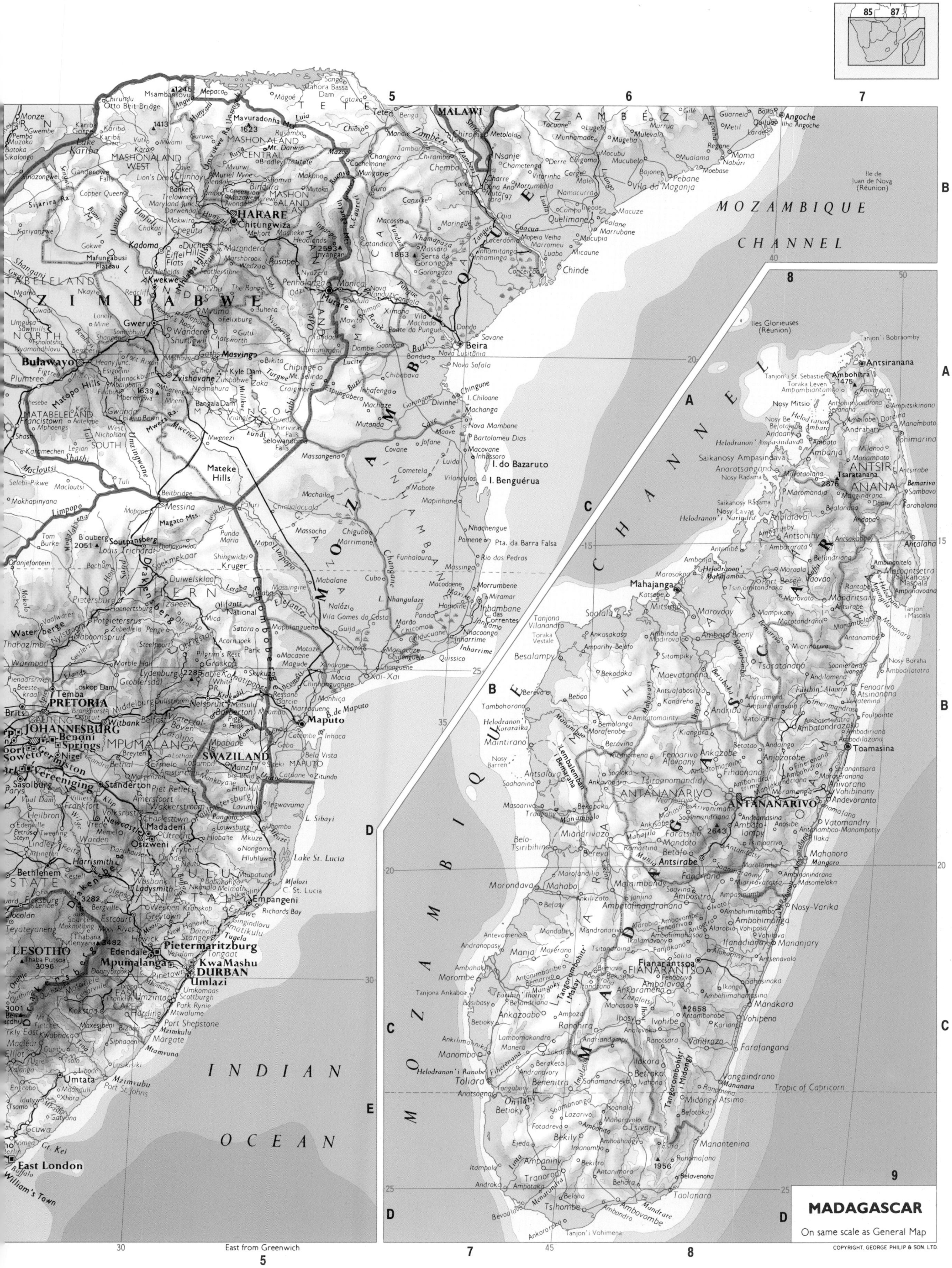

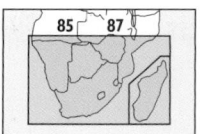
MADAGASCAR

On same scale as General Map

COPYRIGHT GEORGE PHILIP & SON LTD.

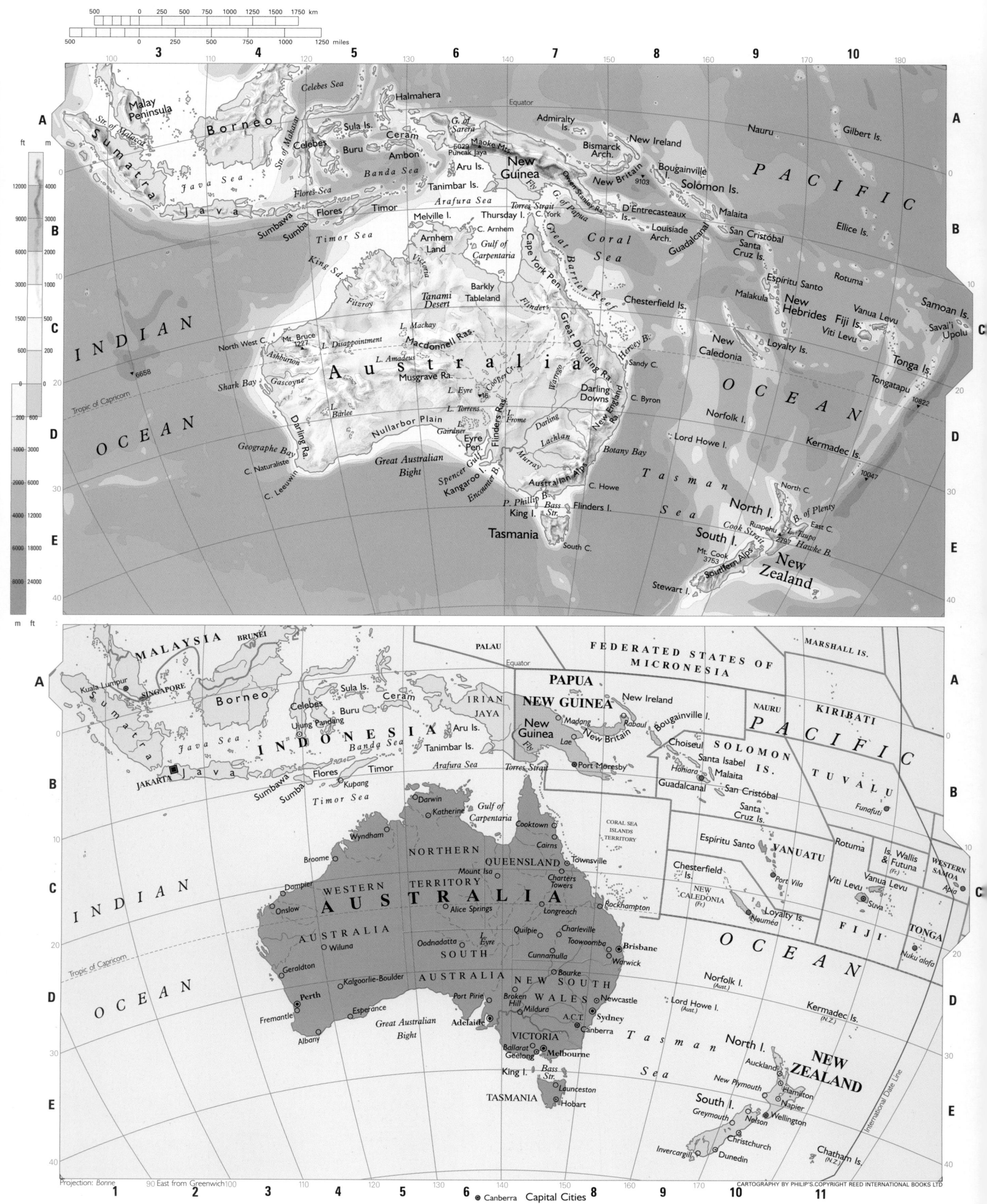

96
96 96
96

50   0   50   100   150   200 km
50   0   50   100   150 miles

1   2   3   4   5   6   7

PACIFIC

OCEAN

North C.
C. Reinga
C. Maria van Diemen
Houhora Heads
Rangaunu B.
Doubtless B.
Ahipara B.
Mongonui
Whangaroa Harb.
Kaitaia
Okahau
C. Brett
Tauroa Pt.
B. of Islands
Rawene
Kaikohe
Opua
Hokianga Harbour
Hikurangi
Whangarei
Whangarei Harb.
Donnelly's Crossing
Bream Hd.
Bream B.
Dargaville
Waipu
Little Barrier I.
Great Barrier I.
Warkworth
C. Rodney
Cuvier I.
Helensville
C. Colville
Kaipara Harbour
Hauraki Gulf
Coromandel
Devonport
Whitianga
Takapuna
AUCKLAND
Mayor I.
Manukau
Papakura
Thames
Whaihi
Waiuku
Pukekohe
Mercer
Tauranga Harb.
Waikato
Paeroa
Huntly
Te Aroha
White I.
C. Runaway
Morrinsville
Mount Maunganui

North Island

TASMAN

SEA

Raglan
Hamilton
Cambridge
Te Puke
Bay of Plenty
Te Awamutu
Tauranga
Whakatane
Opotiki
Mt. Hikurangi 1753
Kawhia Harbour
Putaruru
Rotorua
Waipiro
Otorohanga
Kinleith
Tikitere
Raukumara Ra.
Te Kuiti
Tokoroa
Kaingaroa
Murupara
Motu
Mokau
Mokau
Wairaker
Taupo
Forest
Ormond
Tolaga Bay
North Taranaki Bight
Ongarue
L. Taupo
Wairoa
Tarawera
Nuhaka
Poverty Bay
Waitara
Taumarunui
Turangi
Gisborne
New Plymouth
Whangamomona
Ruapehu 2797
Wairoa
Mahia Pen.
Inglewood
Mt. Egmont 2518
Stratford
Ohakune
Waiouru
Hawke Bay
C. Egmont
Opunake
Eltham
Raetihi
View
Kapuni
Hawera
Waverley
Taihape
Mangaweka
Napier
South Taranaki Bight
Patea
Wanganui
Marton
Hunterville
C. Kidnappers
Hastings
Halcombe
Danneverke
Waipawa
Bulls
Feilding
Waipukurau
Foxton
Palmerston North
Woodville
Shannon
Pahiatua
C. Turnagain
Levin
Eketahuna
Otaki
Paraparaumu
Kapiti I.
Masterton
Carterton
Upper Hutt
Greytown
C. Farewell
Featherston
Martinborough
Collingwood
Golden B.
D'Urville I.
Pelorus Sd.
L. Wairarapa
Takaka
Tasman B.
Petone
Tasman Mts.
Motueka
Lower Hutt
WELLINGTON
Karamea
Nelson
Havelock
Karamea Bight
Richmond
Picton
Seddonville
Wakefield
Blenheim
Cook Strait
Granity
Maitai Ra.
Westport
Lyell
Seddon
Murchison
Ward
Lewis
Tapuaenuku 2885 Mt.
Reefton
Rotoroa
Mt. Travers 2338
Spenser Mts.
Clarence

SAMOA ISLANDS
1:10 700 000

WESTERN SAMOA
AMERICAN SAMOA
Savai'i
Apia
Upolu
Pago Pago
Tutuila
12   13   14

Blackball
Runanga
Stillwater
Hanmer Springs
Greymouth
Kumara
Kaikoura
Hokitika
Jacksons
L. Brunner
Arnur
Waiau
Ross
Arthur's Pass
Waikari
Culverden
Waipara
Hurunui
Amberley
Oxford
Rangiora
Abut Hd.
Coleridge
Kaiapoi
Pegasus Bay
Springfield
New Brighton
Mt. Cook 3753
Whitecliffs
Christchurch
Methven
Riccarton
Lyttelton
Staveley
Lincoln
Banks Pen.
Mt. Aspiring 3027
Southbridge
Akaroa
Fairlie
Rakaia
Little River
Tekapo
Pukaki
Canterbury Plains
Ashburton Bight
Milford Sd.
Earnslaw 2818 Wanaka L.
Ohau
Temuka
Timaru
Bligh Sound
Wanaka
St. Andrews
George Sound
Arrowtown
Dunstan Mts.
Cromwell
Kurow
Waimate
Queenstown
Waitaki
Ngapara
South Island
Wakatipu L.
Naseby
Maheno
Clyde
Hampden
Secretary I.
Te Anau
Kingston
Alexandra
Oamaru
Doubtful Sd.
Roxburgh
Dunback
Palmerston
Manapouri
Lumsden
Mataura
Edievale
Kelso
Port Chalmers
Breaksea Sd.
Mossburn
Kaitangata
Otago Harbour
Resolution I.
Ohai
Waikouaiti
Saunders C.
Dusky Sd.
Nightcaps
Winton
Lawrence
Fairfield
Dunedin
Chalky Inlet
Tuatapere
Hedgehope
Clinton
Balclutha
Preservation Inlet
Orepuki
Gore
Mataura
Kaitangata
Te Waewae B.
Riverton
Wyndham
Nugget Pt.
Invercargill
Owaka
South Invercargill
Tokanui
Tahakopa
Bluff
Ruapuke I.
Halfmoon Bay
Foveaux Str.
Stewart I.
Southwest C.
Port Pegasus

FIJI AND TONGA ISLANDS
1:10 700 000
50   0   50   100   150   200 km
50   0   50   100   150 miles

Futuna
Wallis & Futuna (Fr.)
Niuafo'ou (Tonga)
Thikombia
Lambasa
Vanua Levu
FIJI
Vanua Mbalavu
Yasawa Group
Taveuni
Koro
Lautoka 1323
Levuka
Ovalau
TONGA (Friendly Is.)
Nandi
Viti Levu
Gau
Koro Sea
Lakemba
Lau Group
Vava'u
Suva
Moala
Kandavu
Vatoa
Tofua
Tongatapu
Nuku'alofa

ft   m
9000   3000
6000   2000
3000   1000
1200   400
600   200
0   0
200   600
2000   6000
4000   12 000
6000   18 000
m   ft

Projection : Conical with two standard parallels
CARTOGRAPHY BY PHILIP'S. COPYRIGHT REED INTERNATIONAL BOOKS LTD.

166   168   170   172   174   176   178

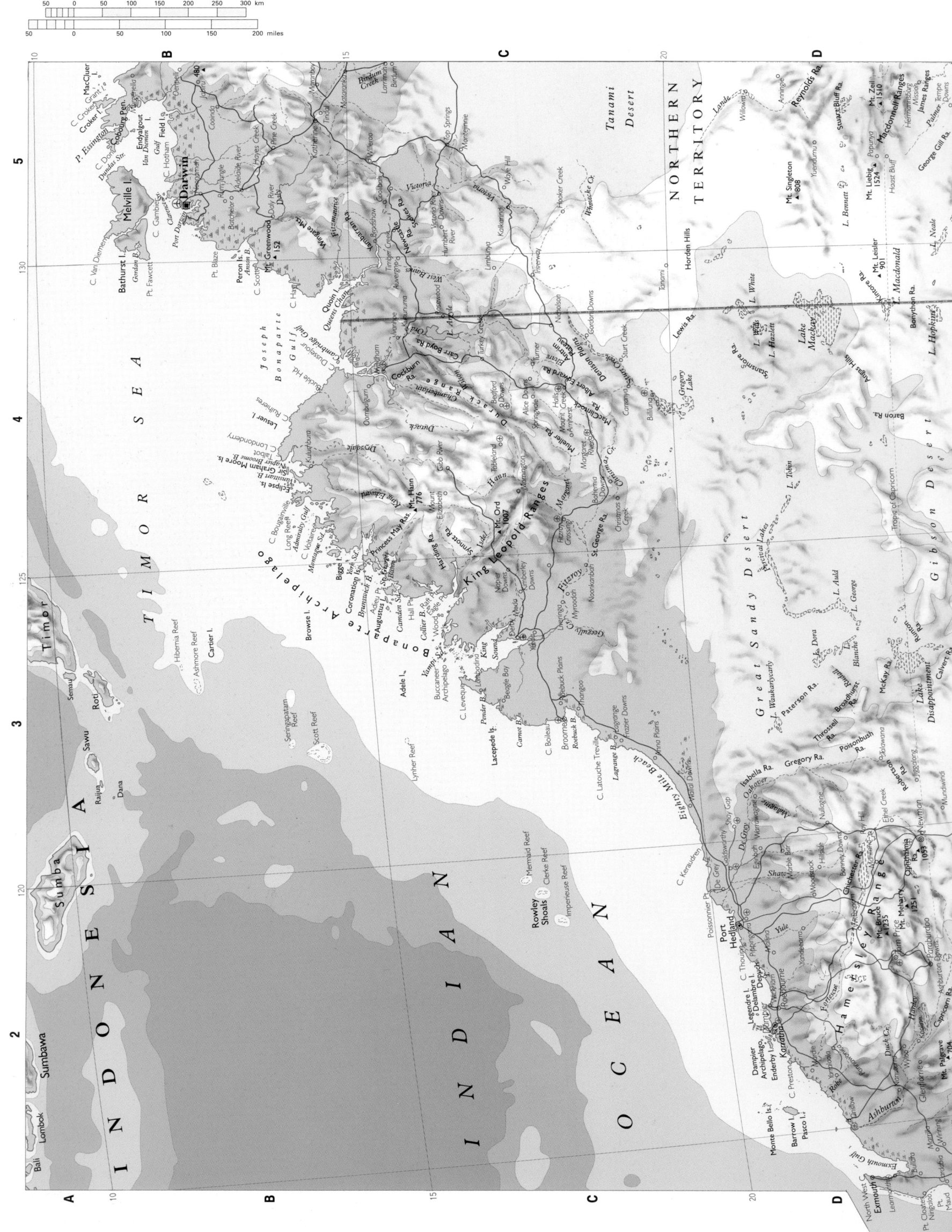

50 0 50 100 150 200 250 300 km
50 0 50 100 150 200 miles

NORTHERN TERRITORY

Reynolds Ra.
Mt. Zeil 1510
Macdonnell Ranges
Stuart Bluff Ra.
James Ranges
Hoast Bluff
George Gill Ra.
Mt. Liebig 1524
Mt. Leisler 901
L. Neale
L. Bennett
L. Macdonald
Boynthon Ra.
Angas Hills
L. Hopkins
Mt. Singleton 808

Tanami Desert

Darwin
Melville I.
Bathurst I.
C. Van Diemen
P. Essington
Coburg Pen.
Croker I.
C. Croker
C. Grant I.
MacCluer I.
Port Darwin
C. Hotham
Gulf
Endyalgout Ibn Diemen I.
Field Is.
Anson B.
Peron Is.
Pt. Blaze
C. Scott
C. Hay
Quoin
Queens Charlotte

TIMOR SEA

Joseph Bonaparte Gulf
Cambridge Gulf
Rulhieres
Lesueur I.
Eclipse Is.
Cape Bougainville
Long Reef
Admiralty Gulf
Montague Sd.
Bigge I.
York Sd.
Coronation Is.
Browse I.
Brunswick B.
Camden Sd.
Prince Regent R.
Augustus I.
Collier B.
Adele I.
C. Leveque
C. Borda
Pender B.
King Sd.
Yampi Sd.
Buccaneer Archipelago
Beagle Bay

TIMOR

Bali
Lombok
Sumbawa
Sumba
Sawu
Roti
Dana
Raijua
Semau

INDONESIA

Hibernia Reef
Cartier I.
Ashmore Reef
Scott Reef
Seringapatam Reef
Lynher Reef
Mermaid Reef
Clerke Reef
Imperieuse Reef
Rowley Shoals

Carr Boyd Ra.
Cockburn
Durack Range
Chamberlain
Bedford Downs
Bohemia
Mt. Hann 716
Mt. Ord 1007
King Leopold Ranges
Princess May Ras.
Harding R.
Fitzroy
Fitzroy Crossing
St. George Ra.
Derby
Meda
Liveringa
Myroodah
Noonkanbah
Lagrange B.
Frazier Downs
Anna Plains
Roebuck Plains
Broome
Roebuck B.
Lagrange
La Grange
Eighty Mile Beach
Wallal Downs

INDIAN OCEAN

Lewis Ra.
Gordon Downs
Sturt Creek
Denison Plains
Gregory Lake
Billiluna
Stansmore Ra.
L. White
L. Hazlett
Lake Mackay
Percival Lakes
L. Auld
L. George
L. Blanche
L. Dora
Dorra
Paterson Ra.
Throssell Ra.
Broadhurst Ra.
McKay Ra.
Poisonbush Ra.
Lake Disappointment
L. Waukarlycarly
Calvert Ra.

Great Sandy Desert

Gibson Desert

Tropic of Capricorn

Poissonnier Pt.
Port Hedland
De Grey
Goldsworthy
Shay Gap
Marble Bar
Nullagine
Bonney Downs
Roy Hill
Newman 1053
Mt. Bruce 1235
Mt. Meharry 1251
Hamersley Range
Ophthalmia Ra.
Chichester Ra.
Isabella Ra.
Gregory Ra.
Mt. Palgrave 704
Exmouth
North West C.
Exmouth Gulf
Monte Bello Is.
Barrow I.
Dampier Archipelago
Legendre I.
Delambre I.
Enderby I.
Karratha
Roebourne
C. Preston
Onslow
Ashburton

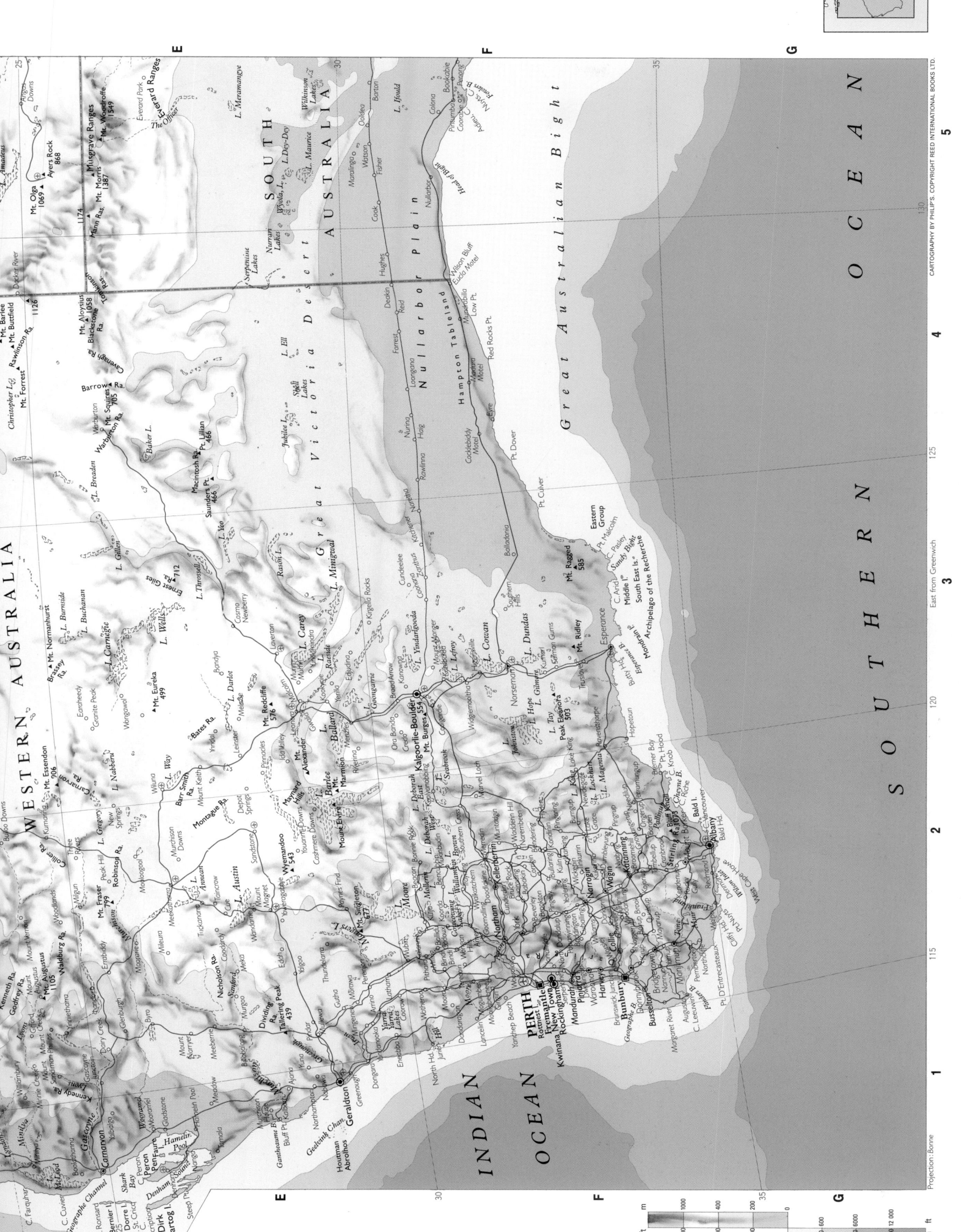

WESTERN AUSTRALIA

SOUTH AUSTRALIA

SOUTHERN OCEAN

INDIAN OCEAN

Great Australian Bight

Great Victoria Desert

Nullarbor Plain

Hampton Tableland

PERTH

Kalgoorlie-Boulder

Geraldton

Albany

Bunbury

Esperance

CARTOGRAPHY BY PHILIP'S. COPYRIGHT REED INTERNATIONAL BOOKS LTD.

Projection: Bonne

East from Greenwich

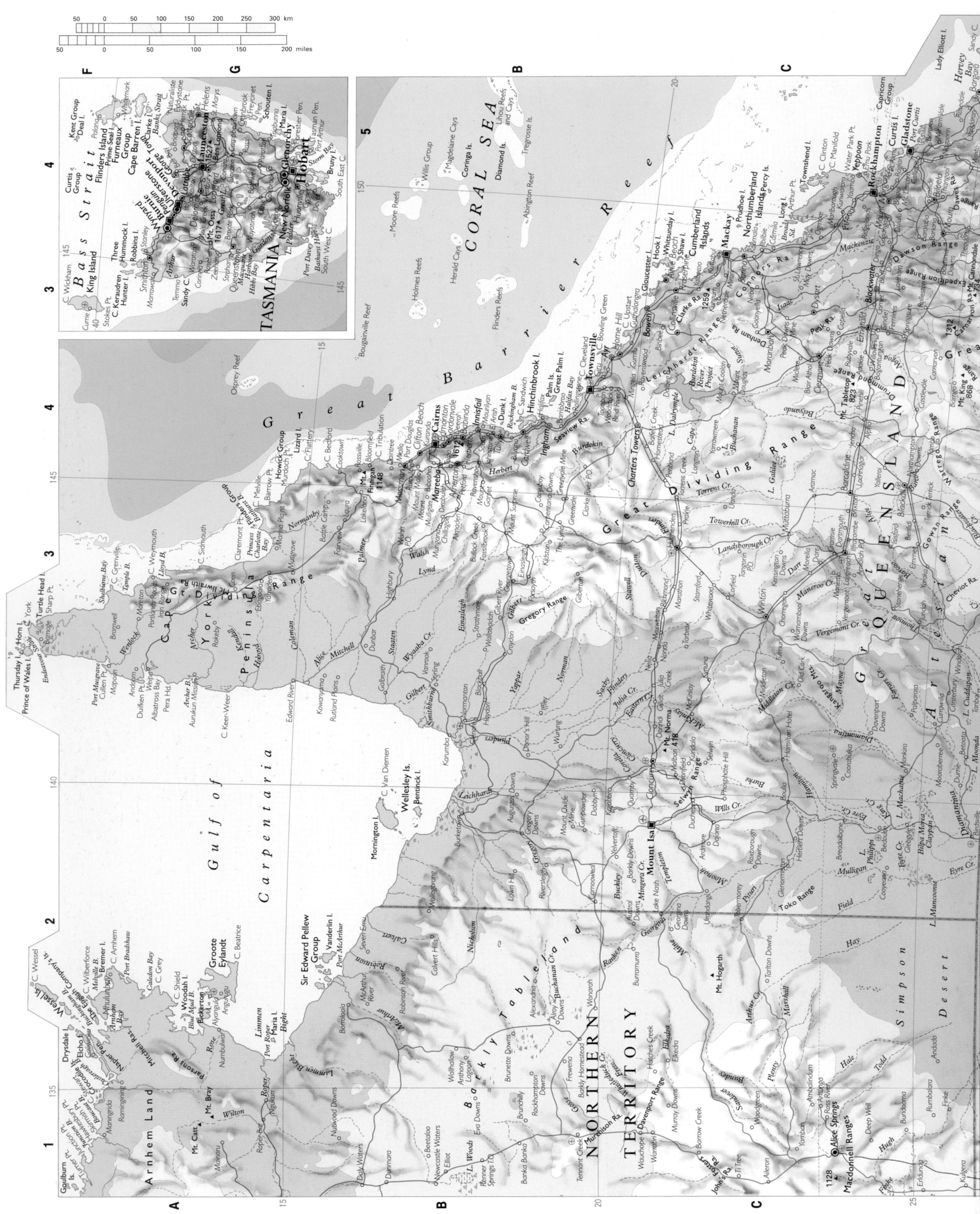

TASMANIA

CORAL SEA

Great Barrier Reef

Gulf of Carpentaria

QUEENSLAND

NORTHERN TERRITORY

Bass Strait

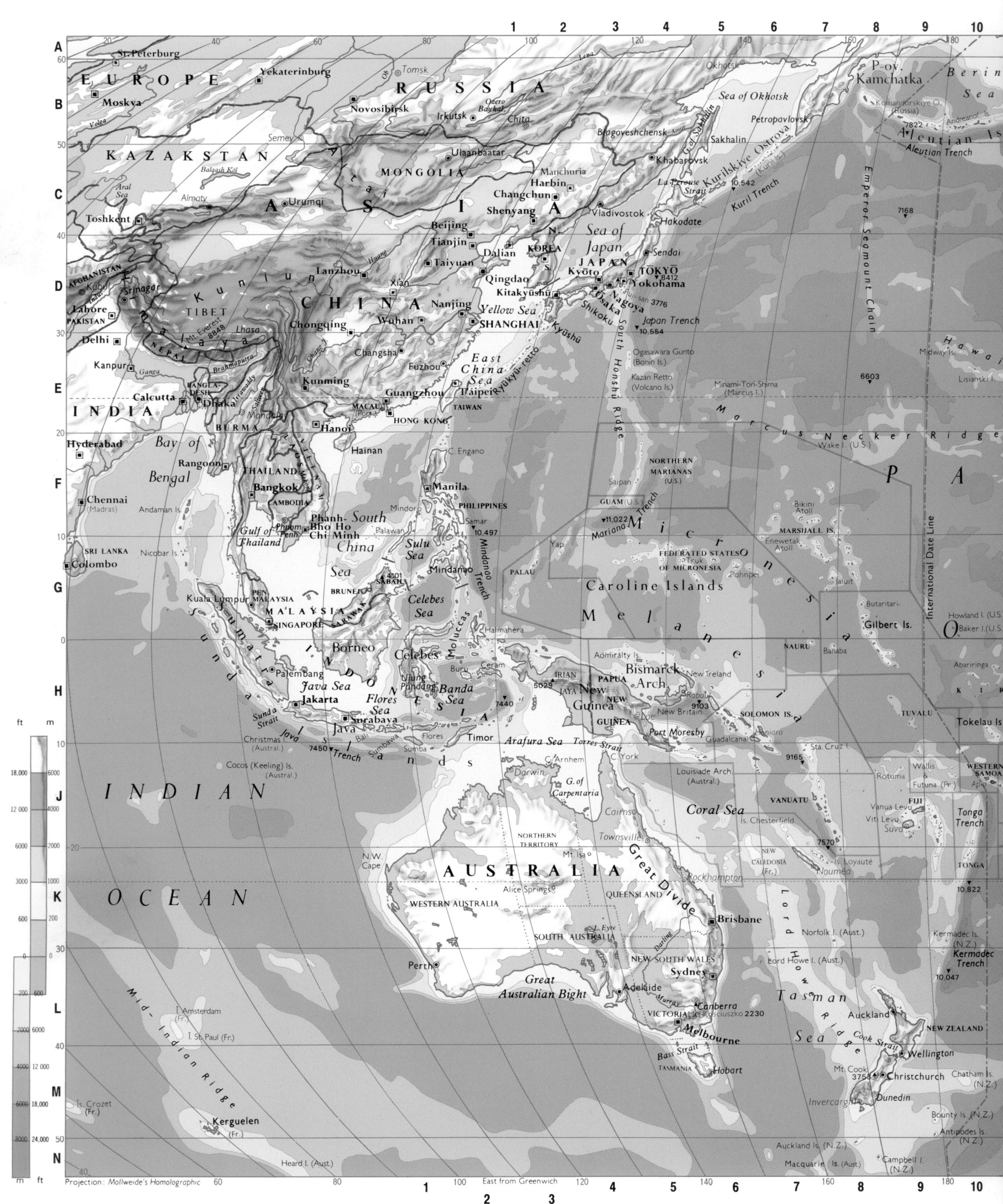

Projection: Mollweide's Homolographic

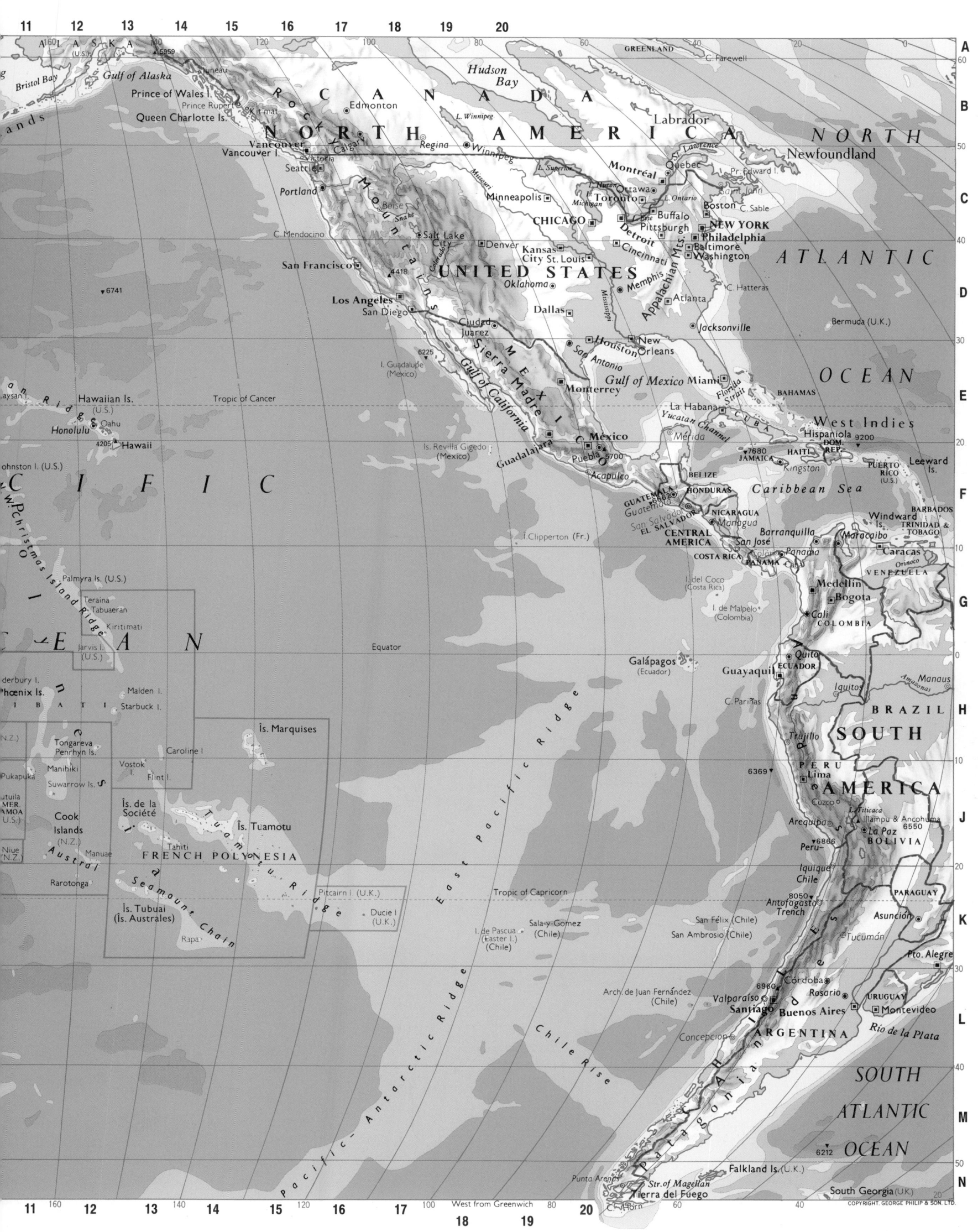

11 12 13 14 15 16 17 18 19 20

A L A S K A
(U.S.)
Bristol Bay
Gulf of Alaska
Prince of Wales I.
Queen Charlotte Is.
Vancouver
Vancouver I.
Seattle
Portland

▲5959
Juneau
Prince Rupert
Kitimat
R O C K Y
C A N A D A
Edmonton
NORTH AMERICA
Victoria
Calgary
Regina
Winnipeg
L. Winnipeg
Missouri
Minneapolis

Hudson Bay
GREENLAND
C. Farewell
NORTH
Labrador
Newfoundland
St. Lawrence
Montréal
Québec
Pr. Edward I.
Ottawa
Toronto
Saint John
Buffalo
Boston
C. Sable

C. Mendocino
Salt Lake City
Boise
Snake
Mountains
Colorado
Denver
Kansas City
St. Louis
CHICAGO
L. Superior
Huron
L. Michigan
L. Ontario
Detroit
Pittsburgh
Cincinnati
NEW YORK
Philadelphia
Baltimore
Washington
ATLANTIC

San Francisco
▲4418
UNITED STATES
Oklahoma
Memphis
Appalachian Mts.
Atlanta
C. Hatteras

Los Angeles
San Diego
Ciudad Juárez
Dallas
Houston
New Orleans
Jacksonville
Bermuda (U.K.)

6741
▼
Sierra Madre
I. Guadalupe
(Mexico)
6225
San Antonio
Monterrey
Gulf of Mexico
Miami
Florida Strait
OCEAN

Hawaiian Is.
(U.S.)
Honolulu
Oahu
Tropic of Cancer
Gulf of California
M E X I C O
BAHAMAS
CUBA
La Habana
Yucatan Channel
West Indies
Hispaniola
DOM. REP. 9200

4205
Hawaii
Is. Revilla Gigedo
(Mexico)
Guadalajara
México
Puebla 5700
Acapulco
Mérida
BELIZE
HAITI 7680
JAMAICA
Kingston
HONDURAS
PUERTO RICO
(U.S.)
Leeward Is.

C I F I C
I. Clipperton (Fr.)
GUATEMALA 4662
Guatemala
EL SALVADOR
San Salvador
NICARAGUA
Managua
CENTRAL AMERICA
Caribbean Sea
BARBADOS
Windward Is.
TRINIDAD & TOBAGO

Christmas Island Ridge
Palmyra Is. (U.S.)
Teraina
Tabuaeran
Kiritimati
Jarvis I.
(U.S.)
COSTA RICA
San José
Panama
Panama Canal
Maracaibo
Caracas
VENEZUELA
Orinoco

C E A N
Equator
I. del Coco
(Costa Rica)
I. de Malpelo
(Colombia)
Medellín
Bogotá
Cali
COLOMBIA

nderbury I.
Phoenix Is.
Malden I.
Starbuck I.
Galápagos
(Ecuador)
Quito
ECUADOR
Guayaquil
C. Pariñas
BRAZIL
SOUTH

Îs. Marquises
Tongareva
Penrhyn Is.
Manihiki
Pukapuka
Suwarrow Is.
Caroline I.
Vostok I.
Flint I.
Iquitos
Amazonas
Manaus

utuila
MER.
SAMOA
(U.S.)
Cook Islands
(N.Z.)
Îs. de la Société
Îs. Tuamotu
Trujillo
PERU
Lima
6369 ▼
AMERICA
Cuzco

Niue
(N.Z.)
Manuae
Tahiti
FRENCH POLYNESIA
Tuamotu
Arequipa
Illampu & Ancohuma 6550
Lago Titicaca
BOLIVIA
Peru- 6886
La Paz

Austral
Rarotonga
Îs. Tubuai
(Îs. Australes)
Rapa
Seamount Chain
Manuae
Pitcairn I. (U.K.)
Ducie I.
(U.K.)
Tropic of Capricorn
Iquique
Chile
PARAGUAY
Asunción

East Pacific Ridge
I. de Pascua
(Easter I.)
(Chile)
Sala-y-Gomez
(Chile)
San Félix (Chile)
San Ambrosio (Chile)
Antofagasta
8050 Trench
Tucumán
Pto. Alegre

Arch. de Juan Fernández
(Chile)
6960
Córdoba
Rosario
URUGUAY
Valparaíso
Santiago
Buenos Aires
Montevideo
Concepción
ANDES
ARGENTINA
Río de la Plata
SOUTH

Pacific - Antarctic Ridge
Chile Rise
Chonos
ATLANTIC
OCEAN
6212 ▼

Punta Arenas
Str. of Magellan
Tierra del Fuego
C. Horn
Falkland Is. (U.K.)
South Georgia (U.K.)
Patagonia

11 12 13 14 15 16 17 18 19 20
160 140 120 West from Greenwich 100 80 60 40

COPYRIGHT. GEORGE PHILIP & SON. LTD.

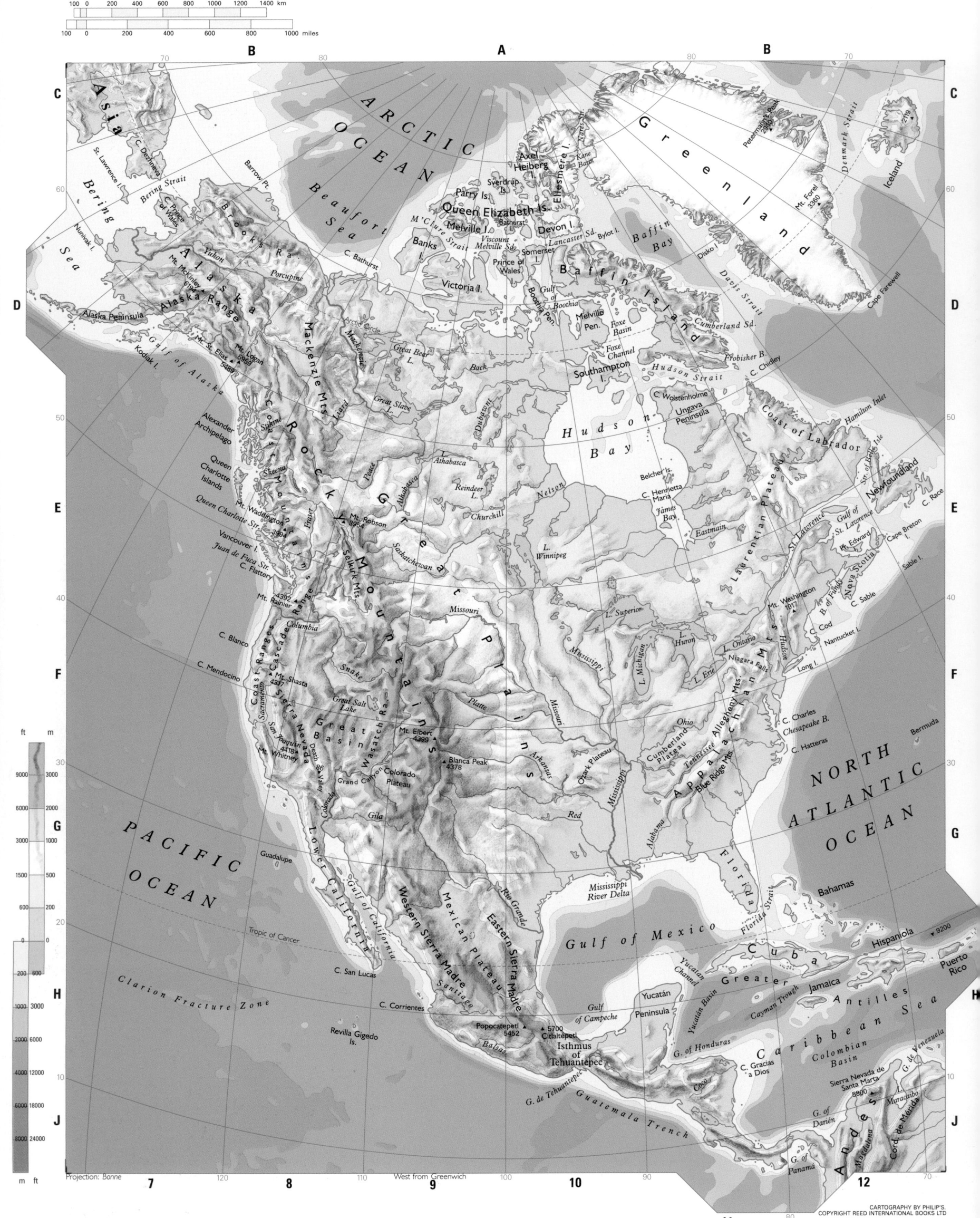

CARTOGRAPHY BY PHILIP'S
COPYRIGHT REED INTERNATIONAL BOOKS LTD

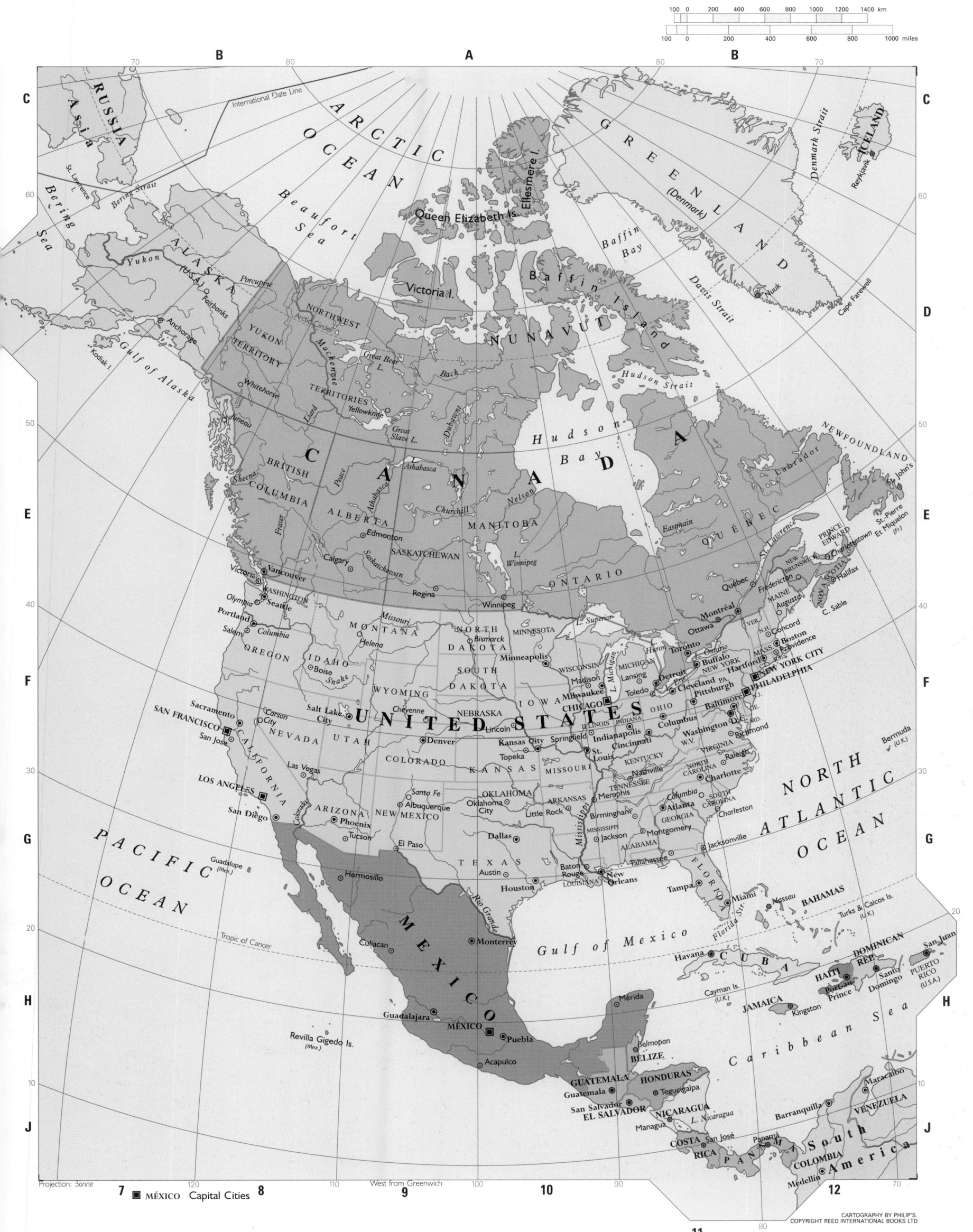

CARTOGRAPHY BY PHILIP'S.
COPYRIGHT REED INTERNATIONAL BOOKS LTD

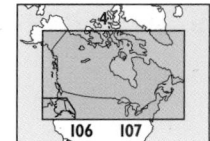

COPYRIGHT GEORGE PHILIP LTD.

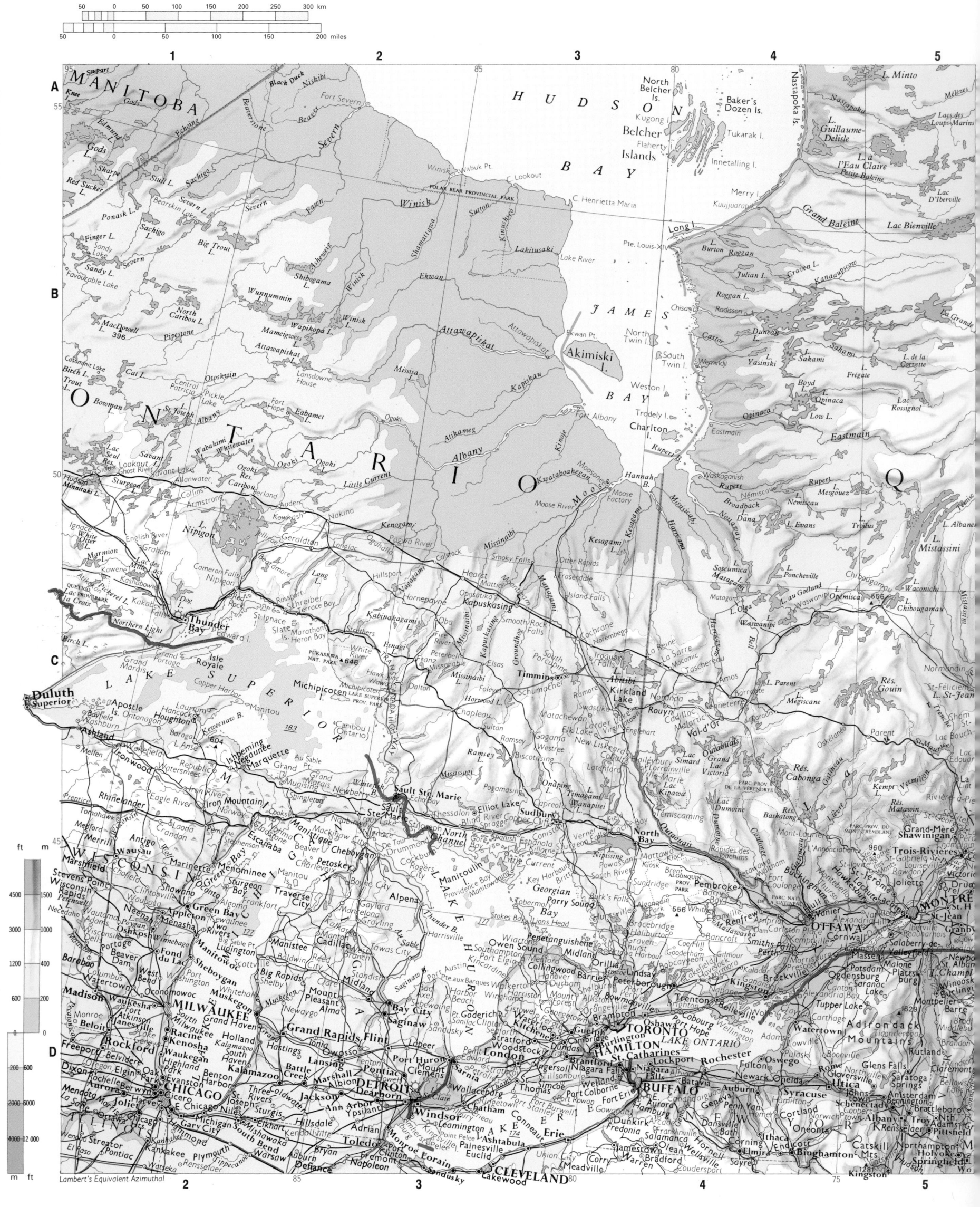

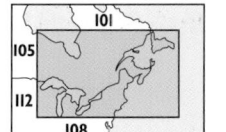

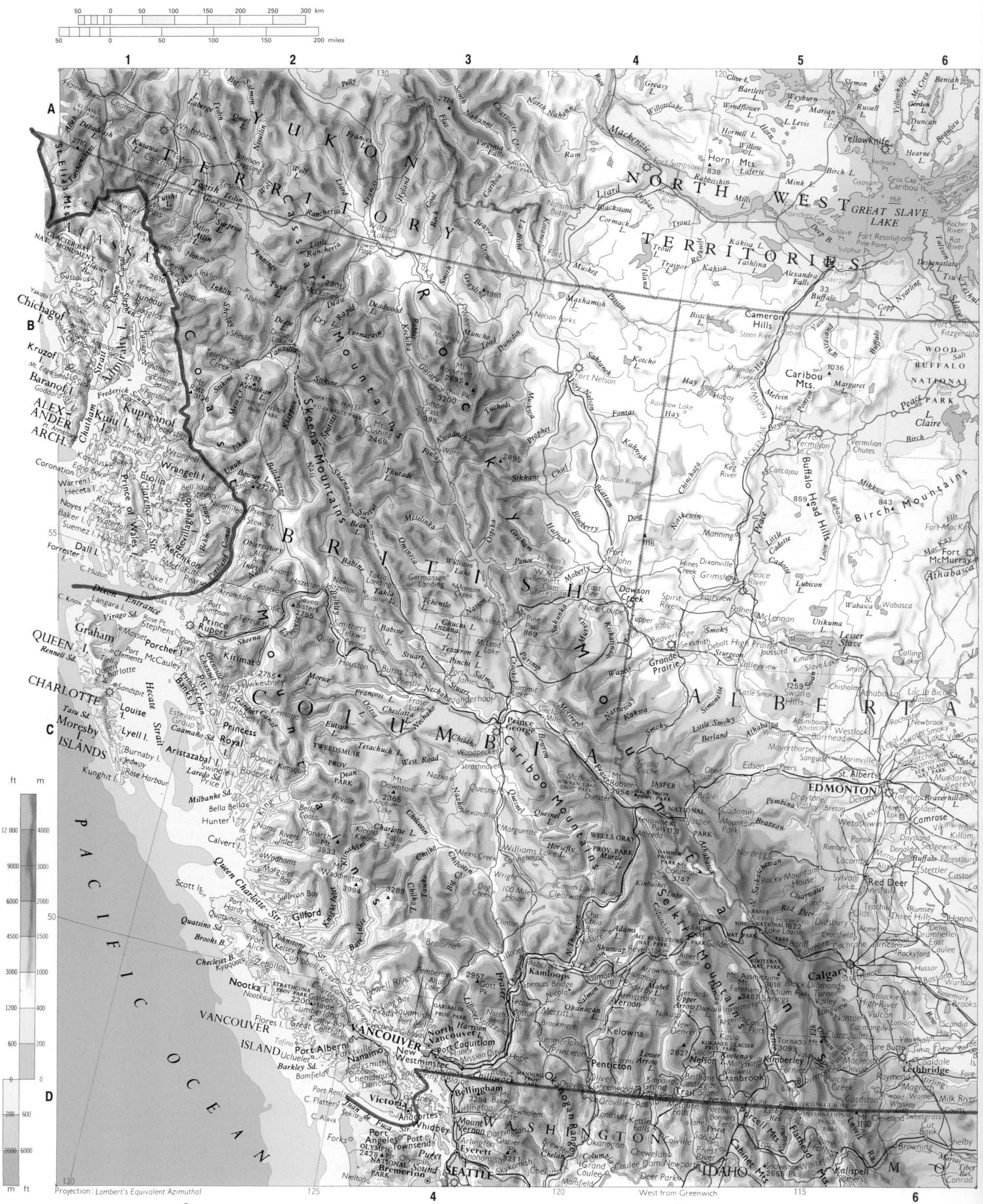

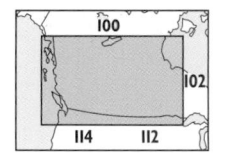

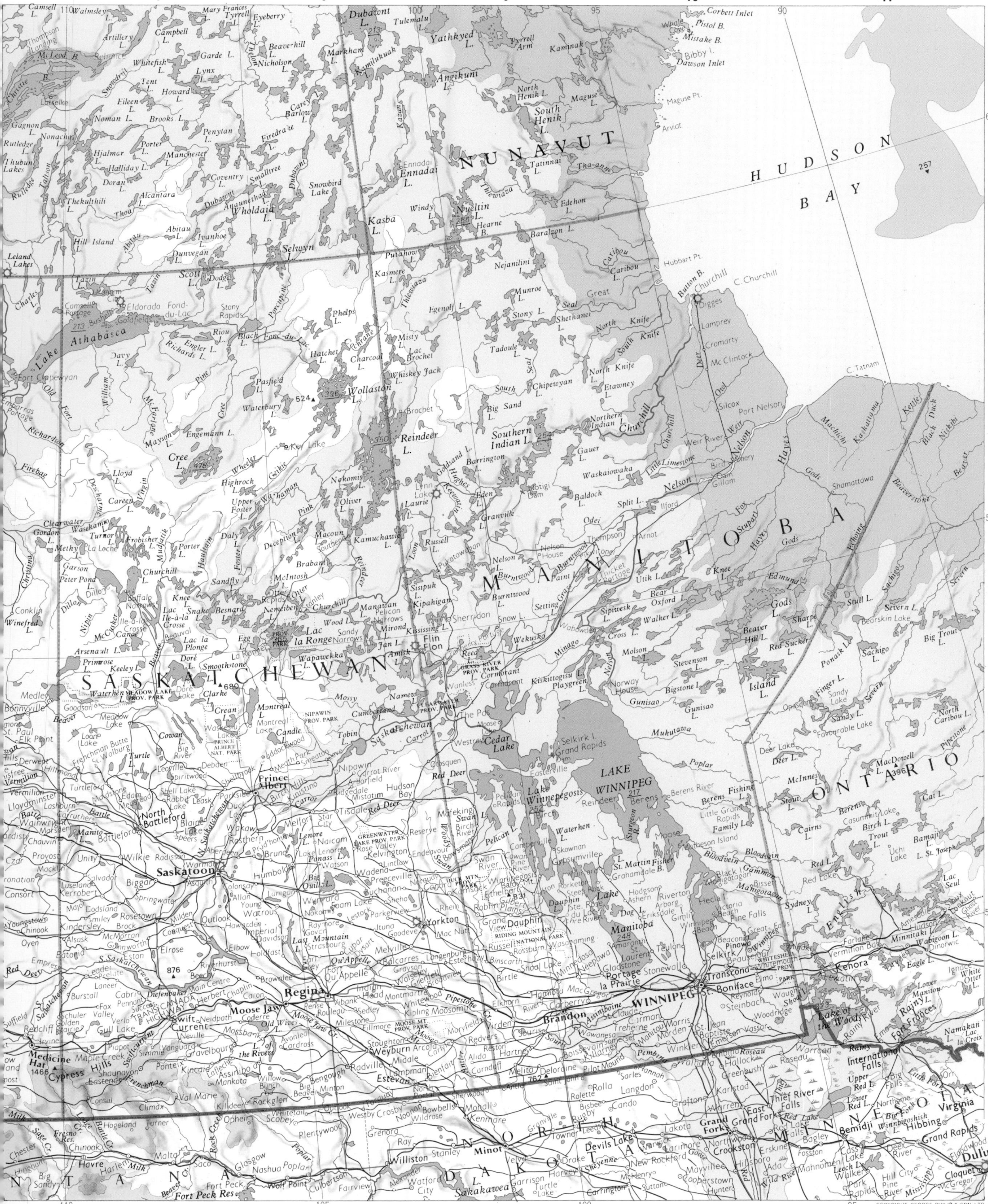

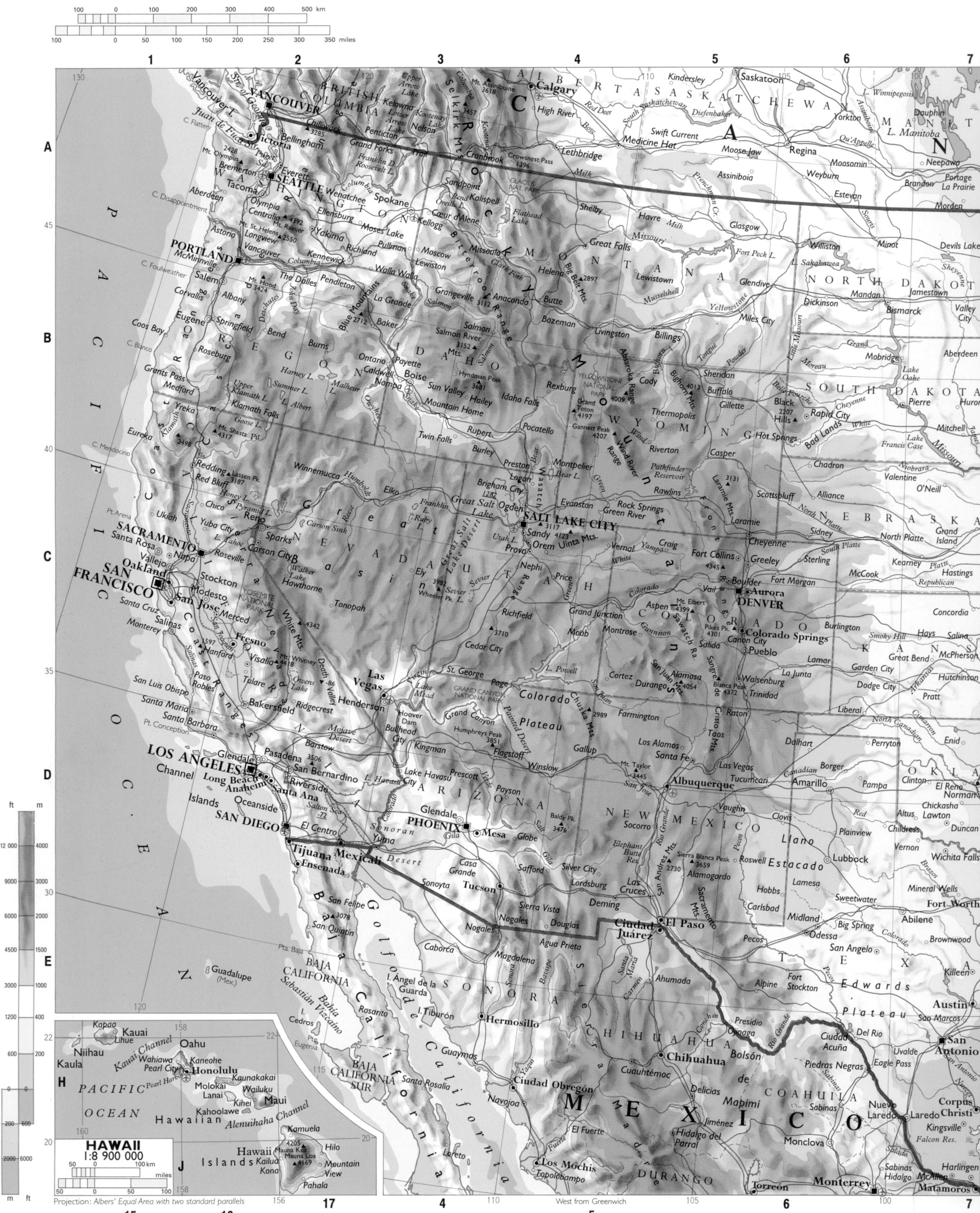

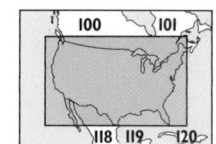

NORTH CAROLINA

SOUTH CAROLINA

GEORGIA

TENNESSEE

ALABAMA

MISSISSIPPI

FLORIDA

ATLANTIC OCEAN

GULF OF MEXICO

BAHAMAS

Great Abaco I.

Grand Bahama I.

Freeport

NEW HAMPSHIRE

MAINE

CANADA

Continuation Eastwards
On same scale.

Projection: Alber's Equal Area with two standard parallels

West from Greenwich

COPYRIGHT GEORGE PHILIP & SON LTD.

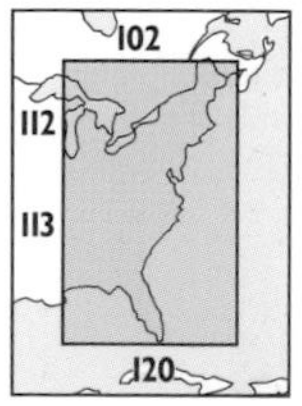

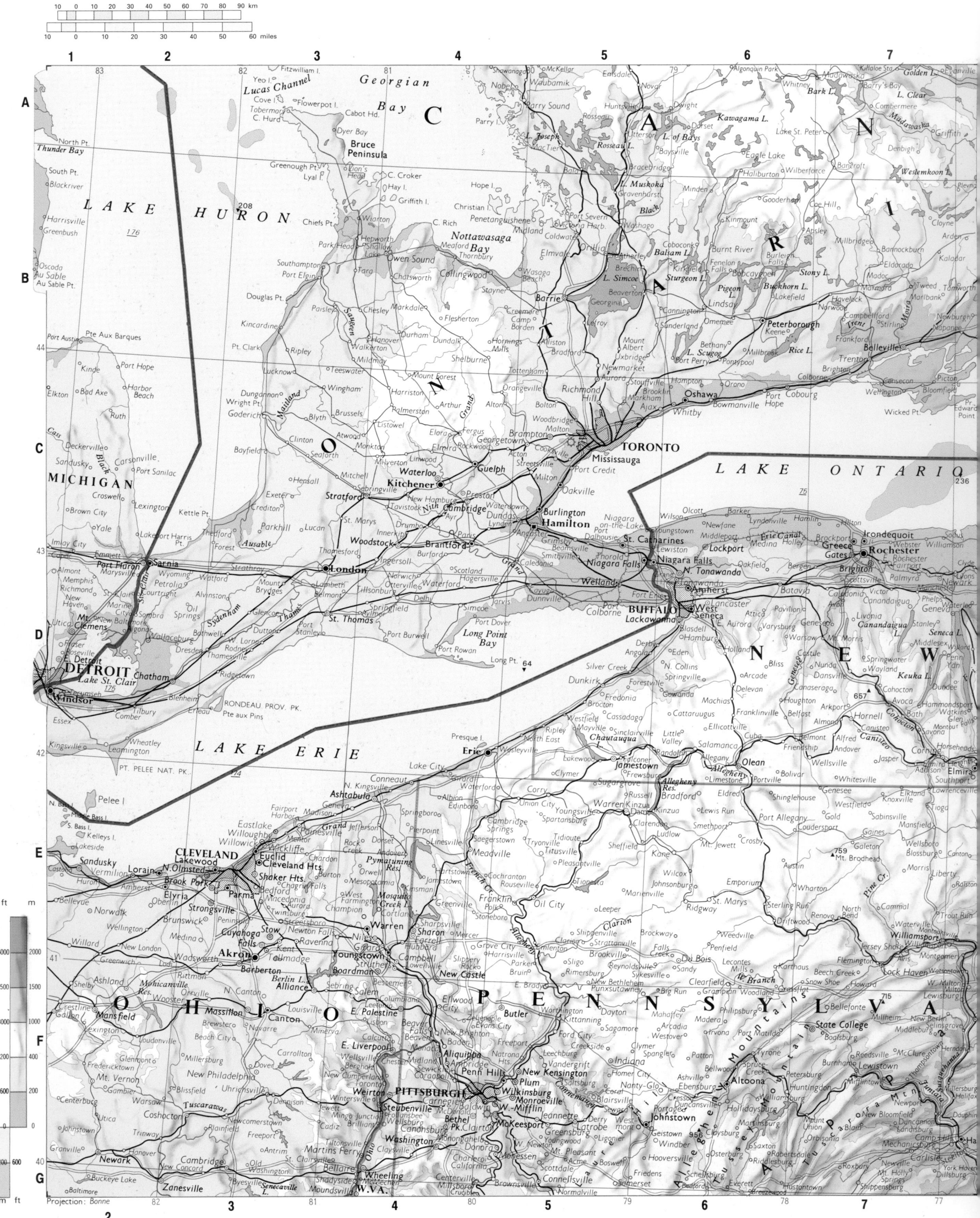

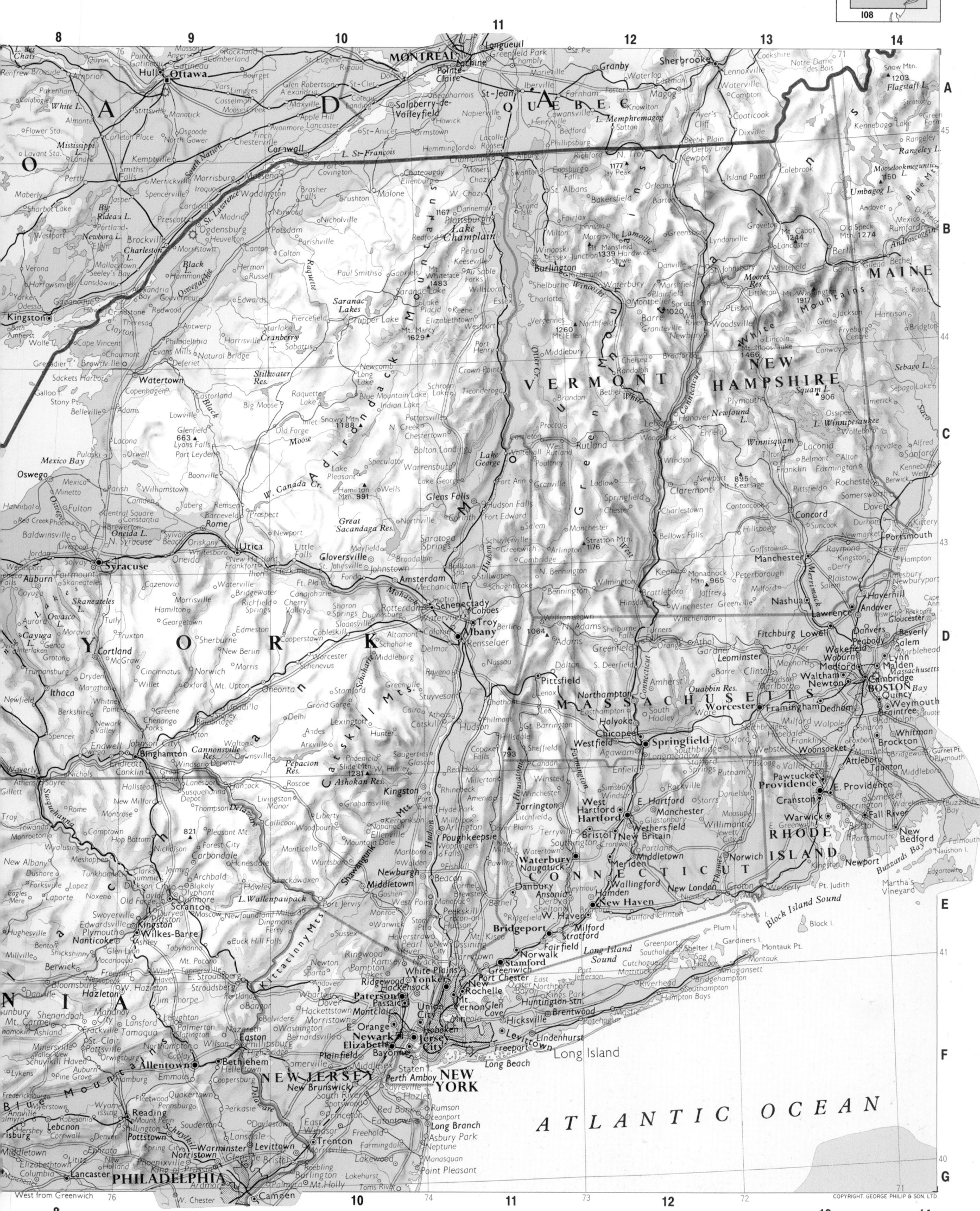

102
108
108

8 **9** **10** **11** **12** **13** **14**

MONTREAL

QUEBEC

MAINE

VERMONT

NEW HAMPSHIRE

NEW YORK

MASSACHUSETTS

CONNECTICUT

RHODE ISLAND

NEW JERSEY

NEW YORK

ATLANTIC OCEAN

Long Island

PHILADELPHIA

COPYRIGHT. GEORGE PHILIP & SON. LTD.

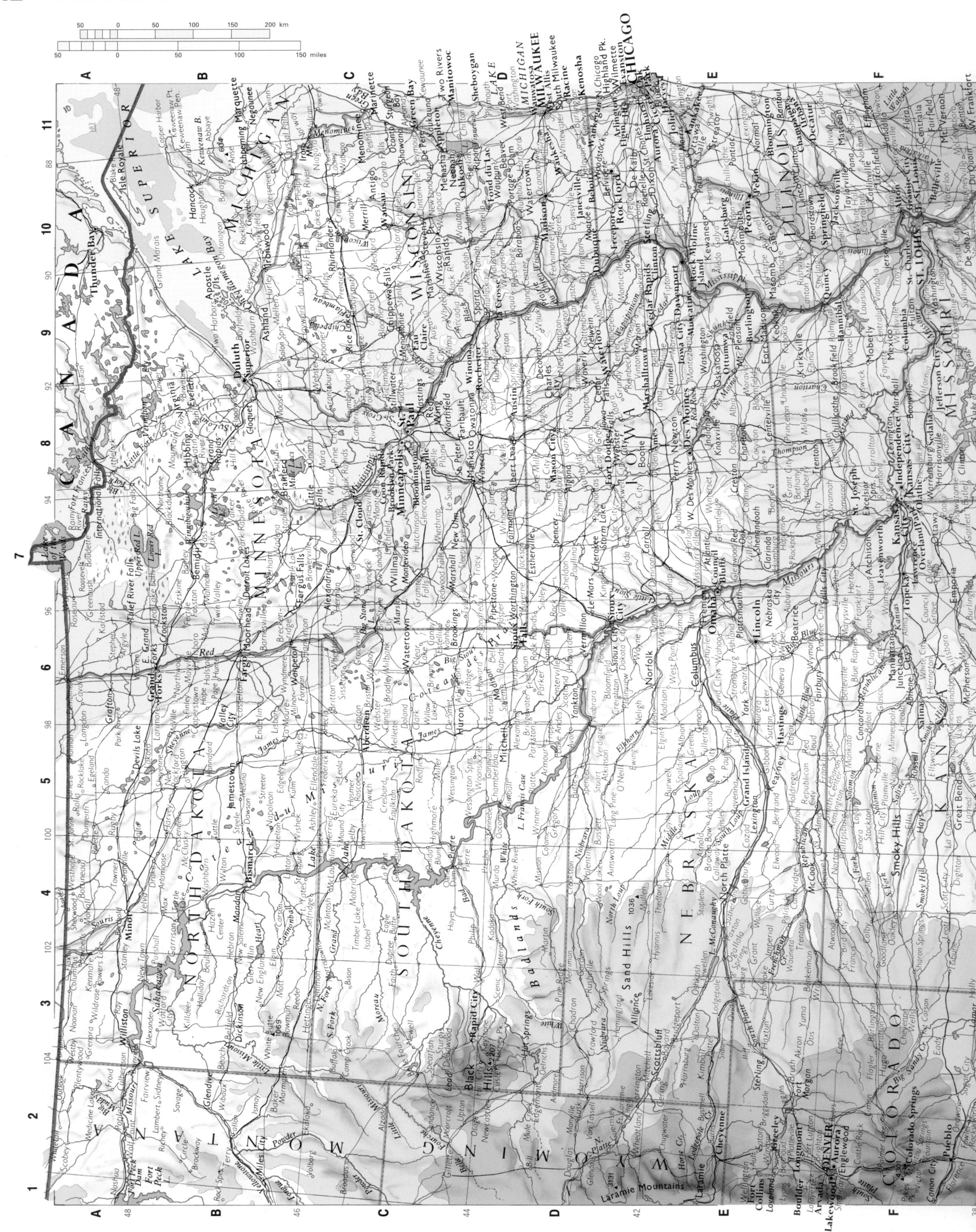

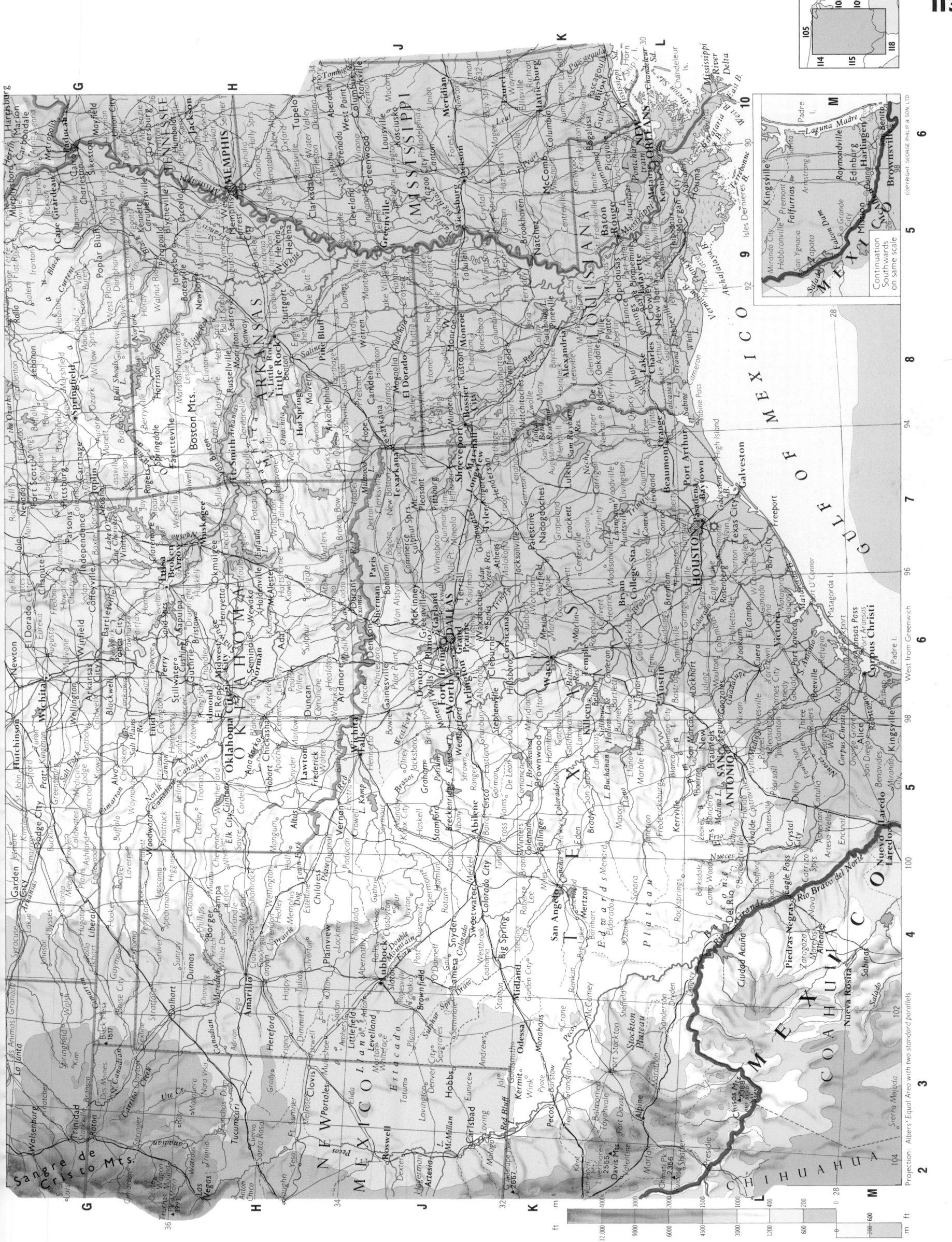

113

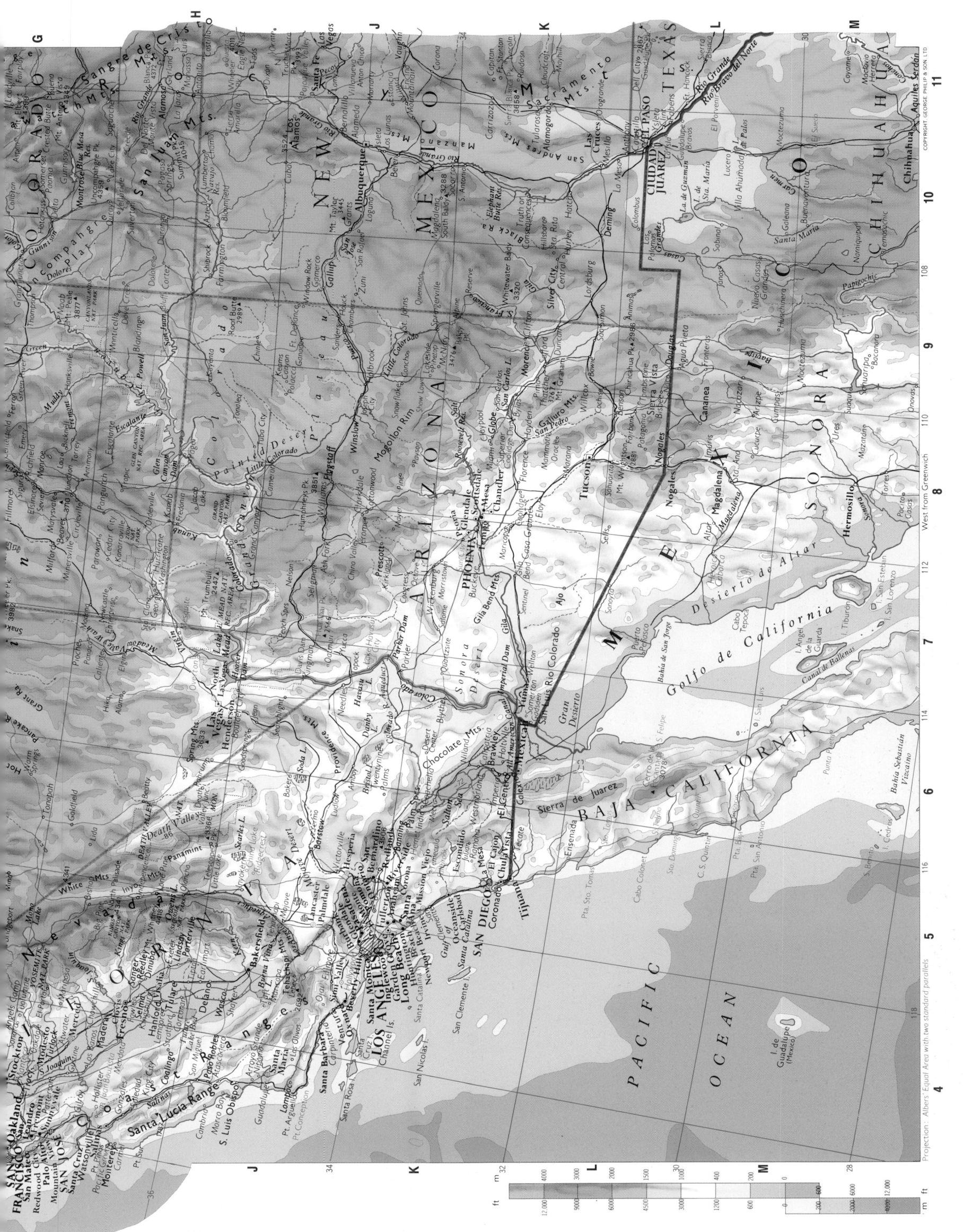

COPYRIGHT GEORGE PHILIP & SON, LTD

Projection: Albers' Equal Area with two standard parallels

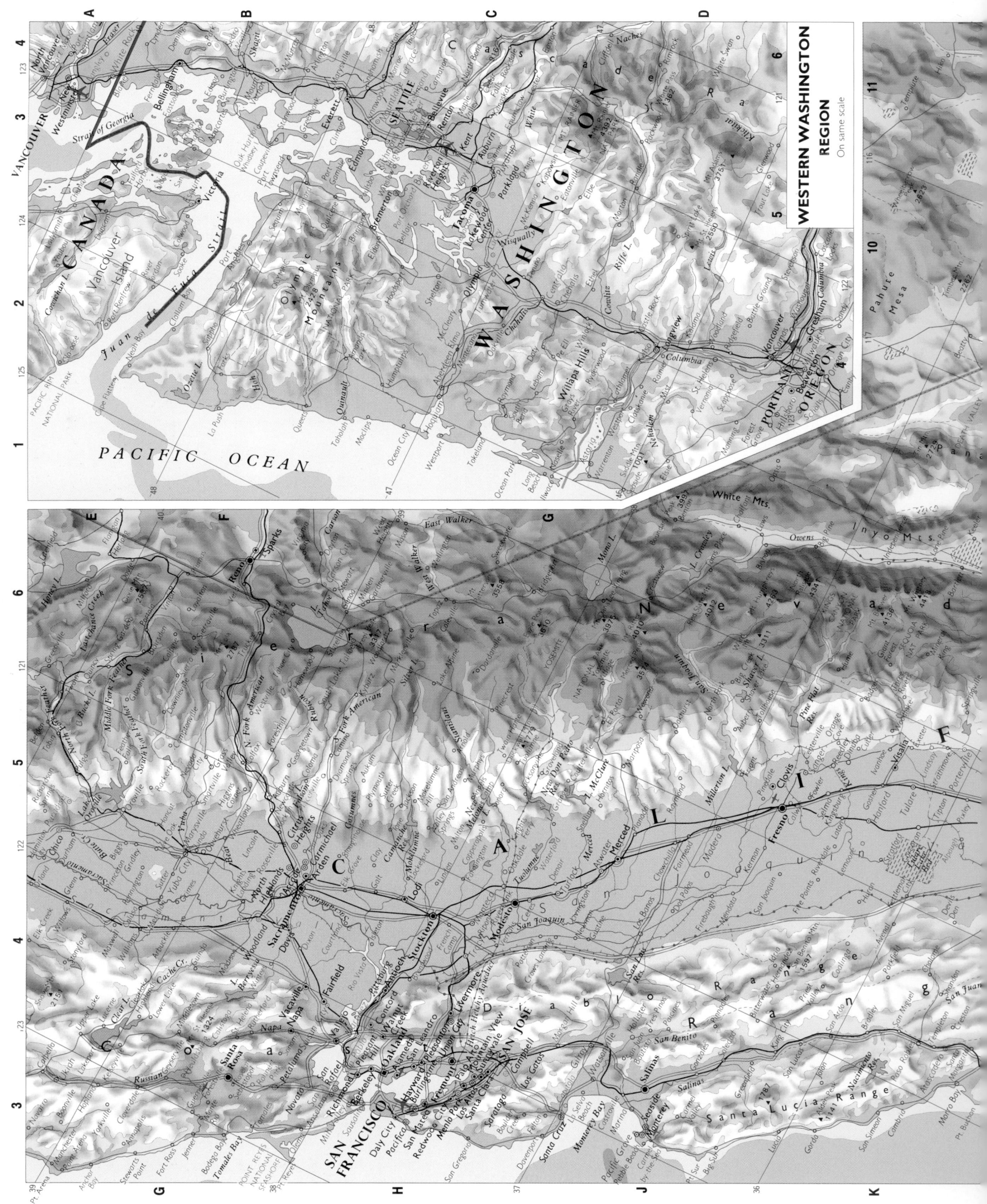

WESTERN WASHINGTON
REGION
On same scale

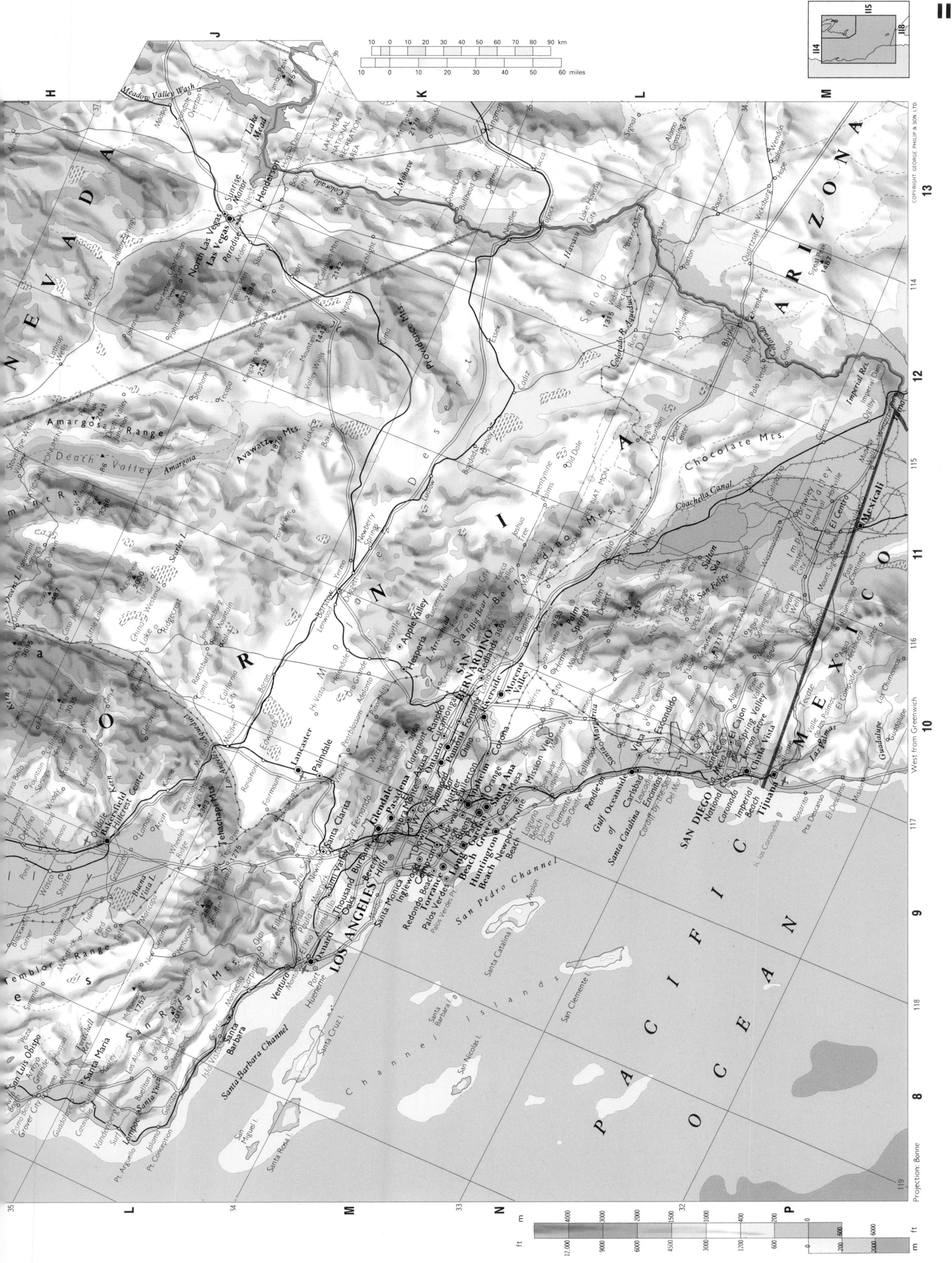

COPYRIGHT GEORGE PHILIP & SON LTD.

Projection: Bonne

50 0 50 100 150 200 250 300 km
50 0 50 100 150 200 miles

1   **2**   **3**   **4**

ft   m
12,000 4000
9000   3000
6000   2000
4500   1500
3000   1000
1200   400
600   200
0
200   600
2000   6000
4000   12,000
m ft

A B C D

Tijuana Mexicali Yuma San Luis Rio Colorado Globe Gila Gila Bend Elephant Butte Res. Roswell Lubbock

Ensenada I. Montague ARIZONA TUCSON San Pedro Lordsburg Deming Las Cruces Carlsbad Hobbs Big Spring Sweetwater

Santo Tomás Sierra de Juárez 3078 San Felipe B. de San Jorge Nogales Bisbee Douglas CIUDAD JUÁREZ EL PASO UNITE San Angelo

San Quintín BAJA El Desemboque Caborca Altar Cananea Agua Prieta La. de Guzmán Van Horn Alpine Pecos Sanderson

Pta. Baja Rosario Puerto Peñasco Concepción Imuris Santa Ana Magdalena Arizpe Nacozari Fronteras Ascensión Villa Ahumada Lucero El Porvenir Rio Bravo del Norte

CALIFORNIA El Dátil La Libertad Benjamin Hill Cumpas Moctezuma Janos Galeana Carmen El Sueco Presidio

I. Ángel de la Guarda I. San Luis SONORA Ures Mazatán Huachinera Nuevo Casas Grandes Moctezuma Ojinaga El Pueblito CHIHUAHUA

Santo Domingo C. Tepoca Canal de Ballenas HERMOSILLO Sonora Madera Buenaventura Conchos Aquiles Serdán CHIHUAHUA Acuña Del Río

Punta Prieta El Rosario I. Tiburón Kino Tecoripa Yécora Ciudad Guerrero Cusihuiriáchic Gen. Trías Julimes Meoqui Delicias San Carlos Eagle Pass

I. Cedros Bahía Sebastián Vizcaíno Desierto de Vizcaíno Pocito Casas Onavas Moris Creel Presa Fco. I. Madero Sateyó Saucillo COAHUILA Piedras Negras

Natividad Pta. Falsa San Ignacio Guaymas Empalme Yaqui Nuri Bocoyna Carichic San Pedro Nueva Rosita Zaragoza Nava Allende

Sierra Vizcaíno Laguna San Ignacio Santa Rosalía I. San Marcos Presa Álvaro Obregón Torín Alamos Urique Nonaava Boquilla Ciudad Camargo Sierra Mojada Melchor Múzquiz Progreso Villa Juárez

La Purísima Pta. Concepción Ciudad Obregón Presa Mocúzarí Chínipas Batopilas Valle de Zaragoza Jiménez San Buenaventura Villa Frontera Lampazos

I. Lobos Navojoa Huatabampo Yávaros Presa M. Hidalgo Choix Verde Oro Conejos Tlahualilo Escalón Cuatrociénegas Sabinas Hidalgo

BAJA CALIFORNIA SUR Santo Domingo Loreto I. Carmen Fuerte Topolobampo Ahome San Blas Agua Caliente Guanaceví El Palmito Villa Ocampo Bolsón de Mapimí Monclova

I. Santa Catalina Los Mochis Guasave El Fuerte Morelos El Palmito Mapimí Francisco I. Madero Saltillo MONTERREY

I. Santa Magdalena B. Magdalena I. San José B. de Santa María Guamúchil Sinaloa de Leyva DURANGO Symón San Pedro de las Colonias Sauceda Parras

I. Santa Margarita B. de la Paz I. Espíritu Santo Navolato Culiacán Altata Quilá Tepehuanes Gómez Palacio Matamoros Ramos Arizpe Saltillo

La Paz San Pedro I. Cerralvo Culiacán El Dorado Cosalá Presa Sanalona Santiago Papasquiaro Lerdo TORREÓN Nazas Laguna Santiaguillo

Tropic of Cancer San Lorenzo La Cruz Dimas El Salto Rio Grande Canatlán Francisco I. Madero Concepción del Oro

Todos Santos San Lucas Sa Concordia Villa Unión VICTORIA DE DURANGO Sombrerete San Juan del Río Camacho La Escondida

San Lucas San José del Cabo C. San Lucas Mazatlán Mezquital Valle de Guadiana Sombrerete Chalchihuites Matehuala

Rosario Escuinapa Valparaíso Jerez de García Charcas Charcas El Venado

PACIFIC Acaponeta Tecuala Jerez de García Salinas ZACATECAS Huizache

Santiago Ixcuintla Huejúcar Rincón de Romos San Luis Potosí Cerritos

I. Isabela San Pedro Ojocaliente Pinos 3352 SAN LUIS POTOSÍ

Santiago Tepic Huejúcar AGUASCALIENTES Asientos Cerritos

Islas Tres Marías Rio Grande de Santiago Ixtlán del Río Jalpa Encarnación de Díaz Lagos de Moreno S. Luis de la Paz Guanajuato

B. de Banderas Puerto Vallarta Compostela Etzatlán Mascota Ameca GUADALAJARA Irapuato LEÓN Los Lagos Celaya

C. Corrientes Talpa de Allende Orotlán Tlaquepaque Valle de Santiago Celaya Córdoba

Zacoalco La Barca La Piedad Zamora Morelón Acámbaro

Tomatlán Autlán L. de Chapala Sayula Jiquilpan Zacapu L. de Cuitzeo Morelia Pátzcuaro

Chamela Ciudad Guzmán Los Reyes Uruapan Paricutín Zitácuaro

Barra de Navidad Nevado de Colima Apatzingán Ario de Rosales Tacámbaro Huetamo

Manzanillo COLIMA Tecomán Coalcomán Tepalcatepec Cd. Altamirano Coyuca de Catalán

Is. de Revillagigedo (Mexico) San Benedicto Coahuayana Pomaro Arteaga Presa del Infiernillo

Roca Partida Socorro Las Truchas Balsas Zihuatanejo Petatlán

OCEAN

REFERENCE TO NUMBERS

1 Federal District   5 México
2 Aguascalientes   6 Morelos
3 Guanajuato   7 Querétaro
4 Hidalgo   8 Tlaxcala

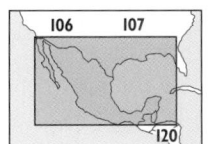

GULF OF MEXICO

U.S.A.

L. Okeechobee
West Palm Beach
Fort Myers
Boca Raton
Naples
Fort Lauderdale
C. Romano
Hialeah
MIAMI
Florida City
C. Sable
Florida Bay
Everglades
Dry Tortugas
Key West
Florida Keys

Little Abaco
Grand Bahama I.
Freeport
Hope Town
Great Abaco I.

BAH
Eleuthera
Nassau
New Providence
Governor's Harbour
Great Exuma I.
Exuma Sound
Jumentos Cays
Duncan Town

Bimini Is.
Berry Is.
Andros Town
Andros Island

Isla Desterrada
Isla Pérez

Canal de Yucatán

(Havana) LA HABANA
Guanabacoa
MARIANAO
San Antonio de los Baños
Guanajay
Matanzas
Bahía Honda
La Esperanza
Pinar del Río
Batabanó
Güines
Jagüey Grande
Colón
Cárdenas
Sagua la Grande
Santa Clara
Caibarién
CUBA
GREATER
Santa Cruz del Norte
Santa Cruz del Sur

Progreso
Dzilam de Bravo
Río Lagartos
C. Catoche
Pta. Yalkubul
Motul
Temax
Tizimín
Cancún
Pta. Juárez
El Díaz
MÉRIDA
Izamal
Espita
YUCATÁN
Ticul
Mayapán
Chichén Itzá
Valladolid
Peto
Puerto Morelos
Isla Cozumel

La Fé
San Luis
Isla de la Juventud
Nueva Gerona
Cienfuegos
Trinidad
Sancti-Spíritus
Júcaro
Ciego de Ávila
Morón
Cayo Romano
Nuevitas
Puerto Padre
Gibara
Holguín
Bayamo
Palma Soriano
SANTIAGO DE CUBA
Manzanillo
Victoria de las Tunas
Golfo de Guacanayabo
Sierra Maestra

Campeche
CAMPECHE
Champotón
Chenkán
Ciudad del Carmen
Laguna de Términos
Palizada

Hopelchén
Bolonchenticul
QUINTANA ROO
Felipe Carrillo Puerto
B. de la Ascensión
B. del Espíritu Santo
Vigía Chico
Banco Chinchorro

Chetumal
B. de Corozal
Ambergris Cay
Turneffe Is.

Uaxactún
Tikal
L. Petén Itzá
Flores
Orange Walk
Belmopan
BELIZE City
BELIZE
Dangriga
Middlesex
Benque Viejo
Maya Mts.
Monkey River
Punta Gorda

Cayman Islands (Br.)
Georgetown
Grand Cayman
Cayman Brac
Little Cayman

7680

Swan Islands (U.S.A. & Honduras)

Montego Bay
Lucea
Falmouth
St. Ann's Bay
Port Maria
Annotto Bay
Port Antonio
JAMAICA
South Negril Pt.
Savanna la Mar
Black River
Mandeville
May Pen
KINGSTON
Spanish Town
Morant Cays (Jamaica)
Pedro Cays (Jamaica)

GUATEMALA
Cobán
Huehuetenango
3993
Cuchumatanes
San Marcos
Totonicapán
Sololá
Antigua
GUATEMALA
Escuintla
Quezaltenango
Mazatenango
Retalhuleu
Coatepeque
Jalapa
Chiquimula
Sa. de las Minas
Zacapa
Santa Rosa de Copán
La Esperanza

L. de Izabal
Livingston
Puerto Barrios
Puerto Cortés
Tela
La Ceiba
Trujillo
Puerto Castilla
Balfate
Olanchito
Yoro
San Pedro Sula
El Progreso
Santa Bárbara
HONDURAS
Comayagua
Juticalpa
Catacamas
Tegucigalpa
Danlí
La Paz
Nacaome

Islas de la Bahía
Roatán
Golfo de Honduras

C. Camarón
Iriona
Pta. Patuca
Brus Laguna
Laguna Caratasca
Puerto Lempira
C. Falso
Mosquitia
Coco
Segovia
C. Gracias á Dios
Puerto Cabo Gracias á Dios
Kisalaya
Cayos Miskitos (Nicaragua)
Pta. Gorda
Puerto Cabezas

CARIB

Comitán
Comalapa
La Independencia
Usumacinta

Ahuachapán
Santa Ana
Suchitoto
Cojutepeque
SAN SALVADOR
Zacatecoluca
Usulután
SAN SALVADOR
San Miguel
EL SALVADOR
Golfo de Fonseca
Chinandega
León
Corinto
La Paz Centro
MANAGUA
Diriamba
Masaya
Granada
L. de Managua
Boaco
Juigalpa
Lago de Nicaragua
Isla de Ometepe
Rivas
San Juan del Sur
B. de Salinas

Esteli
Cord. Isabelia
Matagalpa
Jinotega
NICARAGUA
Bonanza
Siuna
Río Tuma
Tuma
Río Grande
Prinzapolca
Río Grande
Bluefields
El Bluff
Cord. de Yolaina
Bahía de San Juan del Norte
San Carlos
San Juan del Norte
San Juan

Pta. de Perlas
Islas del Maíz (Nicaragua, U.S.A.)

I. de Providencia (Colombia)
Cayos Roncador (U.S.A. & Colombia)
I. de San Andrés (Colombia)
Cayos de Albuquerque (Colombia)

COSTA RICA
Liberia
Cord. de Guanacaste
Santa Cruz
Nicoya
Pen. de Nicoya
C. Velas
Golfo de Papagayo
Puntarenas
C. Blanco
Alajuela
Cord. Central
SAN JOSÉ
Cartago
Guápiles
Siquirres
Limón
Pta. Mona

CARTAGE

Golfo de Nicoya
Pen. de Osa
Golfo Dulce
Bahía de Coronado
Quepos
Buenos Aires
Golfito
Puerto Armuelles
Pta. Burica
Golfo de Chiriqui
David
Boquete
Volcán Barú 3374
Remedios
Santiago
Chitré
Las Tablas
Pen. de Azuero
Pocrí
Pta. Mala

Cord. de Talamanca 3837
Bocas del Toro
Laguna de Chiriquí
Almirante
Serranía de Tabasará
Golfo de los Mosquitos
Nombre de Dios
Portobelo
Colón
Gatún L.
Balboa
PANAMÁ
La Chorrera
Penonomé
Aguadulce
Chimán
Golfo de Panamá
Arch. de las Perlas
San Miguel
I. del Rey

Archipiélago de San Blas
Sierranía del Darién
Golfo del Darién
G. de Morrosquillo
Lorica
Cereté
Monteria
Turbo
COR
Monte
La Palma
El Real
Garachiné
Jaque
Is. de San Bernardo

I. de Coiba
I. de Cebaco
I. Jicarón
Pta. Mariato

Projection: Bi-polar oblique Conical Orthomorphic

ATLANTIC

OCEAN

Tropic of Cancer

50 0 50 100 150 200 250 300 km
50 0 50 100 150 200 miles

5 6 7 8

AMAS

Arthur's Town

The Bight
Cat I.

Conception I.

San Salvador
(Watling I., Guanahani)

Rum Cay

Long I.

Sandy
Cay

Clarence
Town

Cay Verde

Richmond

Albert
Town

Snug
Corner

Crooked I.

Plana Cays

Acklins I.

Mira por vos Cay

Mayaguana I.

Caicos Passage

Cay Santa
Domingo

Hogsty Reefs

Little Inagua I.

Caicos
Islands
(Br.)

Turks Islands
(Br.)

Banes

Lake Rose

Matthew
Town

Great
Inagua I.

Antilla

Mayari

Moa

Baracoa

Pta. de
Maisi

I. de la
Tortue

Port-de-Paix

Cap-Haïtien

Jean-Rabel

Fort-Liberté

Monte Cristi

La Isabela

Puerto Plata

C. Frances Viejo

San Francisco de Macoris

Puerto Rico Trench

Milwaukee
Deep
9220

Guantánamo

Paso de
(Windward) les Vientos
Passage

Cap-à-Foux

Gonaïves

Hinche

Santiago de
los Caballeros

Vega

Nogua

Sánchez

Sabana de La Mar

San Juan

Virgin Gorda

Virgin Is.
(Br.)

Anegada

Sombrero (Anguilla)

Golfe de la
Gonâve

St.-Marc

San Juan

Central

317b

Aguadilla

Arecibo

Bayamón

SAN JUAN

Carolina

Virgin Is.

Road Town

Anegada Passage

Anguilla (Br.)

St.-Martin (Guad.)

Jérémie

Î. de la Gonâve

HAITI

DOMINICAN
REP.

San Pedro
de Macoris

Higüey

C. Engano

Mayagüez

Ponce

Fajardo

Caguas

St. Thomas

Charlotte Amalie

St. Croix

St.-Barthélemy (Fr.)

St. Maarten
(Neth.)

Saba (Neth.)

St. Eustatius
(Neth.)

Barbuda

Navassa I.
(U.S.A.)

Dame
Marie

PORT-
AU-PRINCE

San Juan

2280

Azua de
Compostela

Barahona

Bani

San Cristóbal

SANTO
DOMINGO

B. de
Yuma

La Romana

I. Saona

Canal de la
Mona

Isla
Mona
(U.S.A.)

PUERTO
RICO
(U.S.A.)

Guayama

Frederiksted

Christiansted

Anguilla

ST. KITTS
& NEVIS

Basseterre

Nevis

ANTIGUA
& BARBUDA

St. Johns

Antigua

Les Cayes

Massif de
la Hotte

Aquin

Jacmel

Pedernales

I. Beata

I. Beata

HISPANIOLA

ANTILLES

LEEWARD ISLANDS

Redonda

Montserrat

Pointe-à-Gravois

Î.-a-Vache

Guadeloupe Passage

Moule

Désirade

Ste-Rose

GUADELOUPE
(Fr.)

Basse-Terre

Pointe-à-Pitre

Marie-Galante (Fr.)

Grand-Bourg

BEAN SEA

I. de Aves (Bird I.)
(Venezuela)

Portsmouth

I. des Saintes
(Guad.)

Dominica Passage

DOMINICA

Roseau

Martinique Passage

Mt. Pelée
1397

Ste-Marie

François

Rivière-Pilote

LESSER ANTILLES

Fort-de-France

MARTINIQUE
(Fr.)

St. Lucia Channel

Castries

Soufrière

ST. LUCIA

St. Vincent Passage

Soufrière 1234

ST. VINCENT

Speightstown

WINDWARD ISLANDS

Kingstown

Bridgetown

THE BARBADOS

LESSER ANTILLES

Aruba
(Neth.)

Curaçao

Bonaire

NETH.
ANTILLES

Willemstad

I. Blanquilla (Ven.)

I. Los Hermanos
(Ven.)

The Grenadines

Hillsborough

GRENADINES

St. George's

GRENADA

Pta. Gallinas

C. San Román

Pen. de
Paraguana

Is. de Aves
(Ven.)

I. Orchila
(Ven.)

I. Los Testigos
(Ven.)

Tobago

Pta.
Espada

Pen. de la
Guajira

Punta
Cardón

Punto Fijo

Puerto
Cumarebo

Is. Los Roques
(Ven.)

I. Margarita

La Asunción

Pta. de Paria

Scarborough

Galera
Pt.

Ríohacha

Uribia

C. San Juan
de Guía

GUAJIRA

Coro

La Vela de Coro

NUEVA
ESPARTA

Porlamar

Carúpano

Río
Caribe

Port of
Spain

Arima

Trinidad

BARRAN-
QUILLA

Santa
Marta

Ciénaga

Golfo de
Venezuela

FALCON

Tucacas

Maiquetía

La Guaira

CARACAS

I. La Tortuga
(Ven.)

Güiria

TRINIDAD
& TOBAGO

Baranoa

Soledad

Sabanalarga

Sierra Nevada de
Santa Marta
5800

La
Concepción

Altagracia

Mene de Mauroa

Tocuyo

Puerto
Cabello

DISTRITO
FEDERAL

C. Codera

Higuerote

Río Chico

Cumaná

SUCRE

Caripito

San Fernando

Golfo de Paria

Río Claro

Serpent's Mouth

ATLANTICO

Fundación

Calamar

Valledupar

Villa del
Rosario

Santa Rita

Cabimas

San Felipe

YARACUY

Valencia

Los Teques

MIRANDA

San Juan de
los Morros

Altagracia

La Cruz

Barcelona

Anaco

MONAGAS

Maturín

DELTA

Carmen
de Bolívar

Plato

Agustín
Codazzi

Ciudad
Ojeda

Mene
Grande

Maracay

Tucupita

AMACUR

El Carmen
de Bolívar

MARACAIBO

Machiques

Lago de
Maracaibo

La Ceiba

Carora

LARA

BARQUISIMETO

Maritagua de
los Morros

Villa
de Cura

Aragua de
Barcelona

El Tigre

Sincé
lejo

Zambrano

TRUJILLO

Acarigua

El Tocuyo

San Carlos

Cantaura

Upata

Magangué

Mompos

CESAR

ZULIA

Betijoque

Trujillo

COJEDES

El Sombrero

Calabozo

GUARICO

Santa María
de Ipire

ANZOATEGUI

Soledad

Ciudad Guayana

Sincelejo

El Banco

San Carlos
del Zulia

Catatumbo

Encontrados

Valera

PORTUGUESA

El Baúl

Sierra Imataca

San
Marcos

Sahagún

Majagual

Ayapel

Ocaña

San
Rafael

MÉRIDA

Guanare

Portuguesa

Valle de la
Pascua

Uare

Pariaguan

El Pao

Planeta
Rica

NORTE

MÉRIDA

Barinas

Libertad

BARINAS

Mapire

Ciudad
Bolívar

Guasipati

El Callao

DOBA

BOLÍVAR

SANTANDER

TACHIRA

Cord.
de Mérida

Ciudad
Bolívar

Pto. de Nutrias

San Fernando
de Apure

Achaguas

Orinoco

Caicara

Emb. de Guri

Tumeremo

Cúcuta

Santa
Bárbara

VENEZUELA

Arauca

BARINAS

Apure

Bruzual

Caroní

75 70 6 65 7

West from Greenwich

5

COPYRIGHT. GEORGE PHILIP & SON. LTD.

ft m

12,000 4000

9000 3000

6000 2000

4500 1500

3000 1000

1200 400

600 200

0 0

200 600

2000 6000

4000 12,000

6000 18,000

8000 24,000

m ft

100 0 200 400 600 800 1000 1200 1400 km
100 0 200 400 600 800 1000 miles

1   90   2   80   3   4   70   5   60   6   50   7

Tropic of Cancer

A

Yucatán Channel
Cuba
Greater Antilles
Turks & Caicos Is.
Hispaniola
9200
Puerto Rico

NORTH

Gulf of Campeche
Yucatán Peninsula

Isthmus of Tehuantepec
G. de Honduras
Jamaica
Lesser Antilles
Guadeloupe
Dominica
Martinique
St. Lucia
Barbados
St. Vincent

ATLANTIC

B

Guatemala Trench
L. Nicaragua
Panama Canal
Coco
C. Gracias a Dios
Caribbean Sea
C. de la Aguja
5800
Sierra Nevada de Santa Marta
L. Maracaibo
I. Margarita
Grenada
Tobago
Trinidad

OCEAN

G. of Darién
Cord. de Merida
Orinoco
Llanos
Meta
Guiana Highlands
2810
Mt. Roraima
Sierra Pacaraima
Serra Tumucumaque
C. Orange

C

Cordillera Occidental
Cordillera Central
Cordillera Oriental
Guaviare
Caqueta
Branco
Negro
Equator

C. de San Francisco
Cotopaxi 5897
Chimborazo 6267
Napo
Putumayo
Japurá
Amazon
Amazon
Marajó I.

D

Galapagos Is.
G. of Guayaquil
Pta. Pariñas
Pta. Negra
Marañón
Ucayali
Huascarán 6768
S e l v a s
Juruá
Purus
Madeira
Madre de Dios
Tapajós
Xingu
Tocantins
Araguaia
São Francisco
Parnaíba
C. de São Roque
Plat. of Borborema

E

PACIFIC
Chincha Alta
Chile
L. Titicaca
Nevada Ancohuma 6580
Bolivian Plateau
L. de Poopó
Guaporé
Mamoré
Plateau of Mato Grosso
Brazilian Highlands

F

San Félix
San Ambrosio
Tropic of Capricorn
Peru
Atacama Desert
8050
Cerro Ojos del Salado 6863
Andes
Gran Chaco
Salinas Grandes
Paraguay
Pilcomayo
Paraná
Iguaçu Falls
Uruguay
Serra do Mar
2890
Serra da Mantiqueira
Pico da Bandeira
C. Frio
Abrolhos Bank

OCEAN
Trench

G

Arch. de Juan Fernández
Mt. Aconcagua 6960
Sierra de Córdoba
L. Mar Chiquita
Salado
Entre Ríos
Paraná
L. dos Patos
Rio de la Plata

SOUTH

Colorado
Bahía Blanca
Negro
G. San Matias
Valdés Peninsula

ATLANTIC

H

Chile Rise
Chiloé I.
Chonos Archipelago
Mre. San Valentin 4058
Taitao Peninsula
Gulf of Penas
Wellington I.
Madre de Dios I.
Magellan's Str.
Santa Inés I.
Gulf of San Jorge
Argentine Basin
6212

Patagonia

OCEAN

West Falkland
Falkland Is.
East Falkland
Tierra del Fuego
Staten I.
South Georgia
Canal Cockburn
Canal Beagle
C. Horn

ft m
12000 4000
9000 3000
6000 2000
3000 1000
1500 500
600 200
0
200 600
1000 3000
2000 6000
4000 12000
6000 18000
8000 24000
m ft

Projection: Lambert's Azimuthal Equal Area

1   90   2   80   3   4   70   5   60 West from Greenwich   50   6   40   7

30
20

CARTOGRAPHY BY PHILIP'S
COPYRIGHT REED INTERNATIONAL BOOKS LTD

■ LIMA Capital Cities

Projection: *Lambert's Azimuthal Equal Area*

CARTOGRAPHY BY PHILIP'S.
COPYRIGHT REED INTERNATIONAL BOOKS LTD

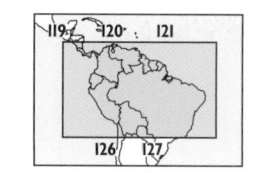

COPYRIGHT GEORGE PHILIP LTD.

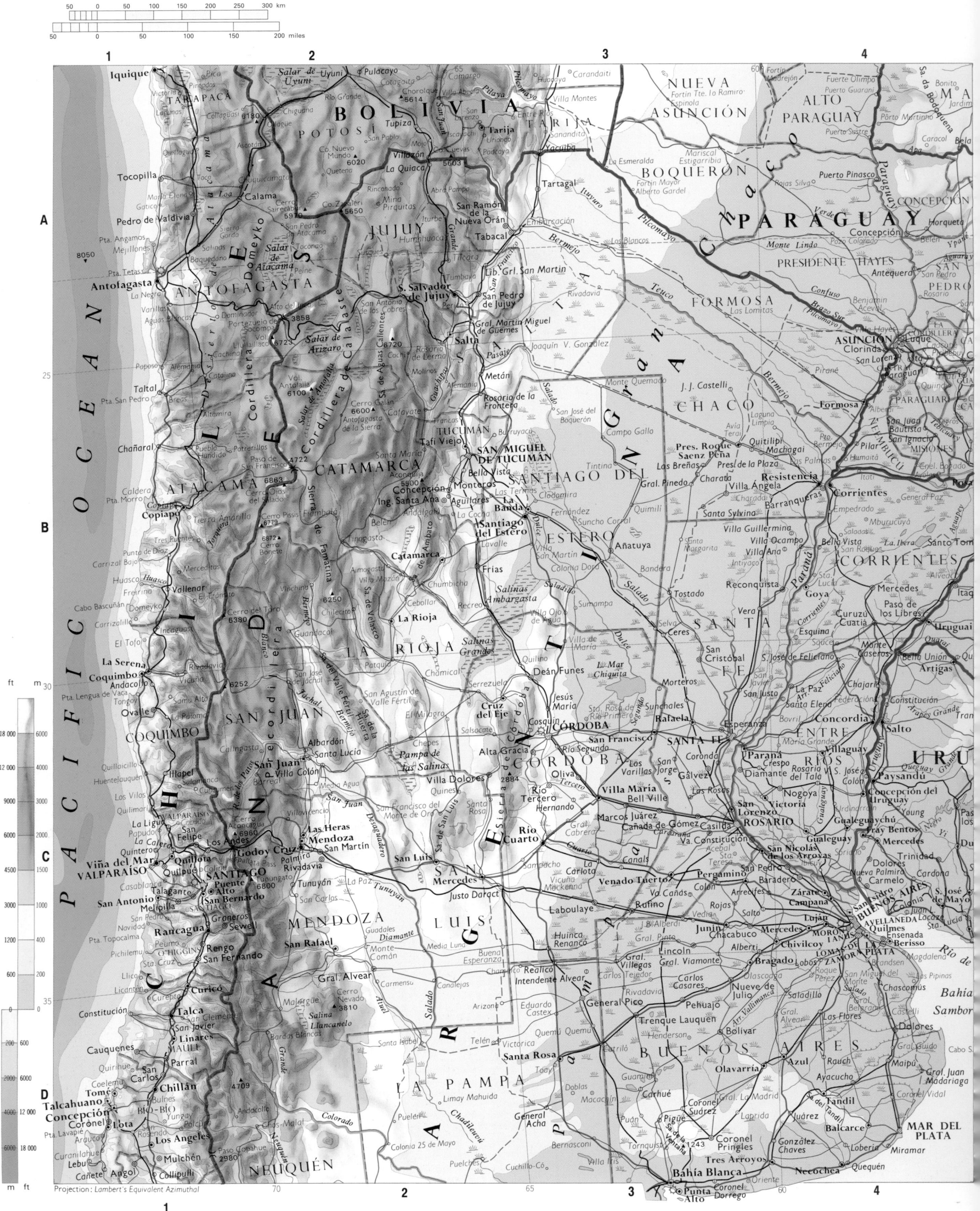

Projection: Lambert's Equivalent Azimuthal

BELO
HORIZONTE
Lima
Itabirito
Congonhas
Cons.
Lafaiete
Oliveira
Ouro
Prêto
Ponte Nova
VITÓRIA
Itaguaí
Vila
Velha
Guarapari

5 6 7

TO GROSSO
DO SUL
Nioaque
Guia Lopes
da Laguna
Maracaju
Ponta-Porá
Pedro Juan Caballero
Dourados
Amambai
Três Lagoas
Andradina
Mirandópolis
Xavantina
Panorama
Araçatuba
Birigui
Adamantina
Mirassol
Olímpia
S. José
do Rio Prêto
Catanduva
Batatais
Passos
Rebedouro
Ribeirão
Prêto
Jaboticabal
Mocóca
Casa
Branca
Guaxupé
São Seb
do Paraíso
Represa de
Furnas
Campo Belo
Três
Pontas
Lavras
Barbacena
Cataguases
Leopoldina
São João
del Rei
Ubá
Carangola
Muriaé
Alegre
Castelo
Cachoeiro
de Itapemirim
Tupã
Lins
Pirajuí
Casa
Branca
Poços de
Caldas
Alfenas
Varginha
Três
Corações
Santo
Dumont
Juiz de Fora
Além Paraiba
Campos
Cabo de
São Tomé

SÃO
PAULO
Presidente
Prudente
Adamantina
Martinópolis
Rancharia
Marília
Paraguaçu
Paulista
Garça
Bauru
Jaú
Araraquara
São
Carlos
da Boa Vista
Araras
Pinhal
Pouso
Alegre
Ouro Fino
Cruzeiro
Itajubá
Volta
Redonda
Barra do Pirai
Nova Friburgo
Macaé

Presidente
Epitácio
Pres.
Epitácio
Paranavaí
Centenário
do Oeste
Nova
Esperança
Sertanópolis
Assis
Cambará
Santa Cruz
do Rio Pardo
Piracicaba
CAMPINAS
Americana
Mogi-Mirim
Cruzeiro
2787
Guaratinguetá
Paraíba do Sul
RIO DE JANEIRO
Duque de Caxias
Nova Iguaçu
NITERÓI
São Gonçalo
Cabo Frio

Umuarama
Londrina
Maringá
Rolândia
Arapongas
Mandaguari
Apucarana
Jacarèzinho
Ourinhos
Avaré
Botucatu
Itu
Sorocaba
Jundiaí
Itapetininga
SÃO PAULO
São Bernardo
do Campo
SANTO ANDRÉ
Jacareí
S. J. dos Campos
Taubaté
Bragança
Paulista
Mansa
Angra dos Reis
La. de Araruama

PARANÁ
Cianorte
Cruzeiro
do Oeste
BRAZIL
Guaíra
Goio
Erê
Ivaí
Pto. Mendes
Pitanga
Castro
Sa da
Prudentópolis
Ponta Grossa
Palmeira
Irati
Lapa
CURITIBA
Antonina
Paranaguá
Guaratuba
Itararé
Itapeva
Apiaí
Paranapiacaba
São Vicente
SANTOS
Guarujá
Itanhaém
Registro
Iguape
Ilha Comprida
Ilha do Cardoso
Pta. do Boi
Ilha de São Sebastião
Tropic of Capricorn

ALTO
GUAZÚ
C. del Oviedo
Hernandarias
Foz do Iguaçu
Ciudad
del Este
PARANÁ
Represa de Itaipú
Cascavel
Guarapuava
Iguaçu
Laranjeiras
União da
Vitória
Pto. União
Mafra
Rio Negro
São Francisco do Sul
Joinville
1889

llarrica
ZAPÁ
ITAPÚA
an Pedro
el Paraná
Bernardo
de Irigoyen
Eldorado
San Pedro
Chopim
340
Palmas
Clevelândia
Caçador
Itajaí
Blumenau
Brusque
Rio do Sul

MISIONES
Corpus
al. Artíg
armen
Encarnación
Obera
San Javier
L. N. Alem
Santa Rosa
Montelucido
Chapecó
Joaçaba
Campos Novos
SANTA
CATARINA
Ilha de Santa Catarina
Florianópolis

Posadas
Candelaria
Santo Ângelo
São Luís
Gonzaga
Erechim
Lajes
1808

São Borja
San Javier
Santiago
Caràzinho
Passo Fundo
Vacaria
Tubarão
Laguna
Cabo Santa Marta Grande

RIO GRANDE
Santa
Maria
Santa Cruz
do Sul
Cruz Alta
Guaporé
Bento Gonçalves
Caxias do Sul
Criciúma
Araranguá

Alegrete
Rosário do Sul
Santana do
Livramento
São
Gabriel
Dom Pedrito
Bagé
Cachoeira do Sul
Montenegro
Taquara
Nôvo Hamburgo
São
Leopoldo
Canoas
Viamão
PORTO ALEGRE
Osorio
DO SUL

GUAY
Tacuarembó
Rivera
Melo
Jaguarão
Rio Branco
Santa Vitória do Palmar
Pelotas
Rio Grande
Lagoa dos Patos
Mostardes

ATLANTIC

MONTEVIDEO
San Gregorio
Treinta y Tres
José Batlle
y Ordóñez
Lascano
Aigua
Castillos
Lagoa Mangueira
Lagoa Mirim

OCEAN

5304

A

B

C

D

25

30

35

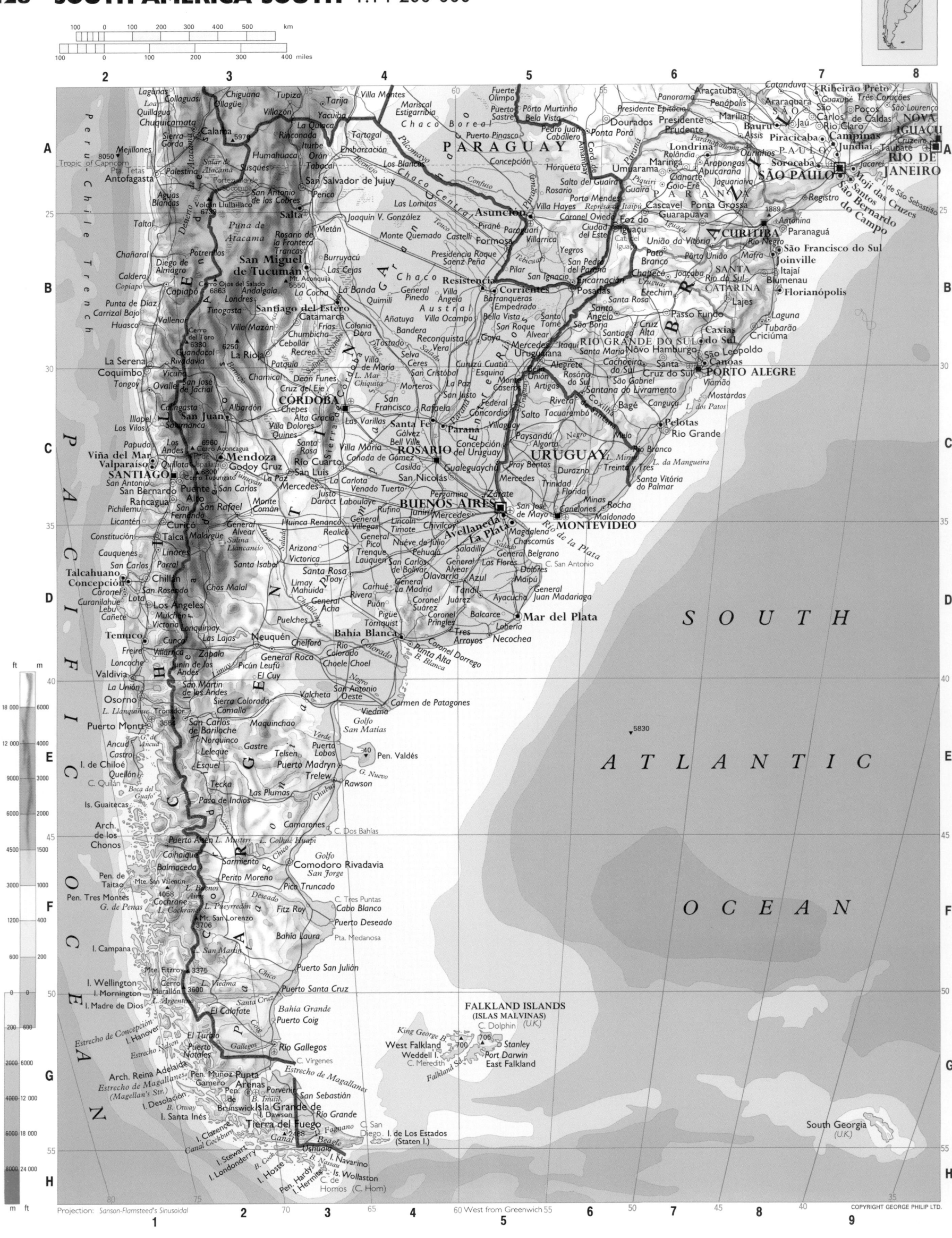

km
100 0 100 200 300 400 500
100 0 100 200 300 400 miles

126 127

ft m
18 000 6000
12 000 4000
9000 3000
6000 2000
4500 1500
3000 1000
1200 400
600 200
0 0
200 600
2000 6000
4000 12 000
6000 18 000
8000 24 000
m ft

Projection: Sanson-Flamsteed's Sinusoidal

COPYRIGHT GEORGE PHILIP LTD.

PARAGUAY
BRAZIL
ARGENTINA
URUGUAY
SÃO PAULO
RIO DE JANEIRO
CURITIBA
PORTO ALEGRE
ASUNCION
CORRIENTES
RESISTENCIA
CORDOBA
ROSARIO
Parana
SANTIAGO
Valparaiso
MENDOZA
BUENOS AIRES
La Plata
MONTEVIDEO
Mar del Plata
Bahía Blanca
Neuquén
Temuco
Valdivia
Puerto Montt
Talcahuano
Concepción

SOUTH
ATLANTIC
OCEAN

PACIFIC
OCEAN

FALKLAND ISLANDS
(ISLAS MALVINAS)
(U.K.)
West Falkland
East Falkland
Stanley
Port Darwin
King George B.
C. Dolphin
Weddell I.
C. Meredith
Falkland Sd.

South Georgia
(U.K.)

Tierra del Fuego
Ushuaia
C. Horn (C. de Hornos)
Estrecho de Magallanes
(Magellan's Str.)
Punta Arenas
Río Gallegos
Río Grande

Peru-Chile Trench

Tropic of Capricorn

60 West from Greenwich 55

INDEX

The index contains the names of all the principal places and features shown on the World Maps. Each name is followed by an additional entry in italics giving the country or region within which it is located. The alphabetical order of names composed of two or more words is governed primarily by the first word and then by the second. This is an example of the rule:

Mīr Kūh, *Iran*	**71**	**E8**
Mīr Shahdād, *Iran*	**71**	**E8**
Mira, *Italy*	**29**	**C9**
Mira por vos Cay, *Bahamas*	**121**	**B5**
Miraj, *India*	**66**	**L9**

Physical features composed of a proper name (Erie) and a description (Lake) are positioned alphabetically by the proper name. The description is positioned after the proper name and is usually abbreviated:

Erie, L., *N. Amer.*	**110**	**D4**

Where a description forms part of a settlement or administrative name however, it is always written in full and put in its true alphabetic position:

Mount Morris, *U.S.A.*	**110**	**D7**

Names beginning with M' and Mc are indexed as if they were spelled Mac. Names beginning St. are alphabetised under Saint, but Sankt, Sint, Sant', Santa and San are all spelt in full and are alphabetised accordingly. If the same place name occurs two or more times in the index and all are in the same country, each is followed by the name of the administrative subdivision in which it is located. The names are placed in the alphabetical order of the subdivisions. For example:

Jackson, *Ky., U.S.A.*	**108**	**G4**
Jackson, *Mich., U.S.A.*	**108**	**D3**
Jackson, *Minn., U.S.A.*	**112**	**D7**

The number in bold type which follows each name in the index refers to the number of the map page where that feature or place will be found. This is usually the largest scale at which the place or feature appears.

The letter and figure which are in bold type immediately after the page number give the grid square on the map page, within which the feature is situated. The letter represents the latitude and the figure the longitude.

In some cases the feature itself may fall within the specified square, while the name is outside. This is usually the case only with features which are larger than a grid square.

Rivers are indexed to their mouths or confluences, and carry the symbol → after their names. A solid square ■ follows the name of a country, while an open square □ refers to a first order administrative area.

ABBREVIATIONS USED IN THE INDEX

A.C.T. – Australian Capital Territory
Afghan. – Afghanistan
Ala. – Alabama
Alta. – Alberta
Amer. – America(n)
Arch. – Archipelago
Ariz. – Arizona
Ark. – Arkansas
Atl. Oc. – Atlantic Ocean
B. – Baie, Bahía, Bay, Bucht, Bugt
B.C. – British Columbia
Bangla. – Bangladesh
Barr. – Barrage
Bos.-H. – Bosnia-Herzegovina
C. – Cabo, Cap, Cape, Coast
C.A.R. – Central African Republic
C. Prov. – Cape Province
Calif. – California
Cent. – Central
Chan. – Channel
Colo. – Colorado
Conn. – Connecticut
Cord. – Cordillera
Cr. – Creek
Czech. – Czech Republic
D.C. – District of Columbia
Del. – Delaware
Dep. – Dependency
Des. – Desert
Dist. – District
Dj. – Djebel
Domin. – Dominica
Dom. Rep. – Dominican Republic
E. – East

E. Salv. – El Salvador
Eq. Guin. – Equatorial Guinea
Fla. – Florida
Falk. Is. – Falkland Is.
G. – Golfe, Golfo, Gulf, Guba, Gebel
Ga. – Georgia
Gt. – Great, Greater
Guinea-Biss. – Guinea-Bissau
H.K. – Hong Kong
H.P. – Himachal Pradesh
Hants. – Hampshire
Harb. – Harbor, Harbour
Hd. – Head
Hts. – Heights
I.(s). – Île, Ilha, Insel, Isla, Island, Isle
Ill. – Illinois
Ind. – Indiana
Ind. Oc. – Indian Ocean
Ivory C. – Ivory Coast
J. – Jabal, Jebel, Jazira
Junc. – Junction
K. – Kap, Kapp
Kans. – Kansas
Kep. – Kepulauan
Ky. – Kentucky
L. – Lac, Lacul, Lago, Lagoa, Lake, Limni, Loch, Lough
La. – Louisiana
Liech. – Liechtenstein
Lux. – Luxembourg
Mad. P. – Madhya Pradesh
Madag. – Madagascar
Man. – Manitoba
Mass. – Massachusetts

Md. – Maryland
Me. – Maine
Medit. S. – Mediterranean Sea
Mich. – Michigan
Minn. – Minnesota
Miss. – Mississippi
Mo. – Missouri
Mont. – Montana
Mozam. – Mozambique
Mt.(e) – Mont, Monte, Monti, Montaña, Mountain
N. – Nord, Norte, North, Northern, Nouveau
N.B. – New Brunswick
N.C. – North Carolina
N. Cal. – New Caledonia
N. Dak. – North Dakota
N.H. – New Hampshire
N.I. – North Island
N.J. – New Jersey
N. Mex. – New Mexico
N.S. – Nova Scotia
N.S.W. – New South Wales
N.W.T. – North West Territory
N.Y. – New York
N.Z. – New Zealand
Nebr. – Nebraska
Neths. – Netherlands
Nev. – Nevada
Nfld. – Newfoundland
Nic. – Nicaragua
O. – Oued, Ouadi
Occ. – Occidentale
Okla. – Oklahoma
Ont. – Ontario
Or. – Orientale

Oreg. – Oregon
Os. – Ostrov
Oz. – Ozero
P. – Pass, Passo, Pasul, Pulau
P.E.I. – Prince Edward Island
Pa. – Pennsylvania
Pac. Oc. – Pacific Ocean
Papua N.G. – Papua New Guinea
Pass. – Passage
Pen. – Peninsula, Péninsule
Phil. – Philippines
Pk. – Park, Peak
Plat. – Plateau
Prov. – Province, Provincial
Pt. – Point
Pta. – Ponta, Punta
Pte. – Pointe
Qué. – Québec
Queens. – Queensland
R. – Rio, River
R.I. – Rhode Island
Ra.(s). – Range(s)
Raj. – Rajasthan
Reg. – Region
Rep. – Republic
Res. – Reserve, Reservoir
S. – San, South, Sea
Si. Arabia – Saudi Arabia
S.C. – South Carolina
S. Dak. – South Dakota
S.I. – South Island
S. Leone – Sierra Leone
Sa. – Serra, Sierra
Sask. – Saskatchewan
Scot. – Scotland
Sd. – Sound

Sev. – Severnaya
Sib. – Siberia
Sprs. – Springs
St. – Saint
Sta. – Santa, Station
Ste. – Sainte
Sto. – Santo
Str. – Strait, Stretto
Switz. – Switzerland
Tas. – Tasmania
Tenn. – Tennessee
Tex. – Texas
Tg. – Tanjung
Trin. & Tob. – Trinidad & Tobago
U.A.E. – United Arab Emirates
U.K. – United Kingdom
U.S.A. – United States of America
Ut. P. – Uttar Pradesh
Va. – Virginia
Vdkhr. – Vodokhranilishche
Vf. – Vîrful
Vic. – Victoria
Vol. – Volcano
Vt. – Vermont
W. – Wadi, West
W. Va. – West Virginia
Wash. – Washington
Wis. – Wisconsin
Wlkp. – Wielkopolski
Wyo. – Wyoming
Yorks. – Yorkshire
Yug. – Yugoslavia

A

A Baña, Spain 34 C2
A Cañiza, Spain 34 C2
A Coruña, Spain 34 B2
A Estrada, Spain 34 C2
A Fonsagrada, Spain 34 B3
A Guarda, Spain 34 D2
A Gudiña, Spain 34 C3
A Rúa, Spain 34 C3
Aachen, Germany 24 E2
Aalborg = Ålborg, Denmark 11 G3
Aalen, Germany 25 G6
A'âli en Nîl □, Sudan ... 81 F3
Aalst, Belgium 17 D4
Aalten, Neths. 17 C6
Aalter, Belgium 17 C3
Äänekoski, Finland ... 9 E21
Aarau, Switz. 25 H4
Aarberg, Switz. 25 H3
Aare →, Switz. 25 H4
Aargau □, Switz. 25 H4
Aarhus = Århus, Denmark 11 H4
Aarschot, Belgium 17 D4
Aba, China 58 A3
Aba, Dem. Rep. of the Congo 86 B3
Aba, Nigeria 83 D6
Âbâ, Jazîrat, Sudan 81 E3
Ābādān, Iran 71 D6
Abade, Ethiopia 81 F4
Ābādeh, Iran 71 D7
Abadin, Spain 34 B3
Abadla, Algeria 78 B5
Abaetetuba, Brazil ... 125 D9
Abagnar Qi, China 56 C9
Abai, Paraguay 127 B4
Abak, Nigeria 83 E6
Abakaliki, Nigeria 83 D6
Abakan, Russia 51 D10
Abalemma, Niger 83 B6
Abana, Turkey 72 B6
Abancay, Peru 124 F4
Abano Terme, Italy 29 C8
Abarán, Spain 33 G3
Abariringa, Kiribati 96 H10
Abarqū, Iran 71 D7
Abashiri, Japan 54 C12
Abashiri-Wan, Japan 54 C12
Abaújszántó, Hungary ... 42 B6
Abava →, Latvia 44 A8
Abay, Kazakhstan 50 E8
Abaya, L., Ethiopia 81 F4
Abaza, Russia 50 D10
Abbadia San Salvatore, Italy 29 F8
'Abbāsābād, Iran 71 C8
Abbay = Nîl el Azraq →, Sudan 81 D3
Abbaye, Pt., U.S.A. 108 B1
Abbé, L., Ethiopia 81 E5
Abbeville, France 19 B8
Abbeville, La., U.S.A. ... 113 L8
Abbeville, S.C., U.S.A. .. 109 H4
Abbiategrasso, Italy 28 C5
Abbieglassie, Australia ... 95 D4
Abbot Ice Shelf, Antarctica . 5 D16
Abbotsford, Canada 104 D4
Abbotsford, U.S.A. 112 C9
Abbottabad, Pakistan 68 B5
Abd al Kūrī, Ind. Oc. 74 E5
Ābdār, Iran 71 D7
'Abdolābād, Iran 71 C8
Abéché, Chad 79 F10
Abejar, Spain 32 D2
Abekr, Sudan 81 E2
Abengourou, Ivory C. 82 D4
Abenójar, Spain 35 G6
Åbenrå, Denmark 11 J3
Abensberg, Germany 25 G7
Abeokuta, Nigeria 83 D5
Aber, Uganda 86 B3
Aberaeron, U.K. 13 E3
Aberayron = Aberaeron, U.K. 13 E3
Aberchirder, U.K. 14 D6
Abercorn = Mbala, Zambia 87 D3
Abercorn, Australia 95 D5
Aberdare, U.K. 13 F4
Aberdare Ra., Kenya 86 C4
Aberdeen, Australia 95 E5
Aberdeen, Canada 105 C7
Aberdeen, S. Africa 88 E3
Aberdeen, U.K. 14 D6
Aberdeen, Ala., U.S.A. ... 109 J1
Aberdeen, Idaho, U.S.A. ... 114 E7
Aberdeen, S. Dak., U.S.A. . 112 C5
Aberdeen, Wash., U.S.A. . 116 D3
Aberdeen, City of □, U.K. . 14 D6
Aberdeenshire □, U.K. ... 14 D6
Aberdovey = Aberdyfi, U.K. 13 E3
Aberdyfi, U.K. 13 E3
Aberfeldy, U.K. 14 E5
Abergavenny, U.K. 13 F4
Abergele, U.K. 12 D4
Abernathy, U.S.A. 113 J4
Abert, L., U.S.A. 114 E3
Aberystwyth, U.K. 13 E3
Abha, Si. Arabia 80 D5
Abhar, Iran 71 B6
Abhayapuri, India 69 F14
Abia □, Nigeria 83 D6
Abide, Turkey 39 C11

Abidiya, Sudan 80 D3
Abidjan, Ivory C. 82 D4
Abilene, Kans., U.S.A. 112 F6
Abilene, Tex., U.S.A. 113 J5
Abingdon, U.K. 13 F6
Abingdon, Ill., U.S.A. 112 E9
Abingdon, Va., U.S.A. 109 G5
Abington Reef, Australia . 94 B4
Abitau →, Canada 105 B7
Abitau L., Canada 105 A7
Abitibi L., Canada 102 C4
Abiy Adi, Ethiopia 81 E4
Abkhaz Republic □ = Abkhazia □, Georgia 49 J5
Abkhazia □, Georgia ... 49 J5
Abminga, Australia 95 D1
Abnûb, Egypt 80 B3
Åbo = Turku, Finland ... 9 F20
Abocho, Nigeria 83 D6
Abohar, India 68 D6
Aboisso, Ivory C. 82 D4
Abomey, Benin 83 D5
Abong-Mbang, Cameroon ... 84 D2
Abonnema, Nigeria 83 E6
Abony, Hungary 42 C5
Aboso, Ghana 82 D4
Abou-Deïa, Chad 79 F9
Aboyne, U.K. 14 D6
Abra Pampa, Argentina ... 126 A2
Abrantes, Portugal 35 F2
Abreojos, Pta., Mexico ... 118 B2
Abri, Esh Shamâliya, Sudan 80 C3
Abri, Janub Kordofân, Sudan 81 E3
Abrud, Romania 42 D8
Abruzzo □, Italy 29 F10
Absaroka Range, U.S.A. 114 D9
Abtenau, Austria 26 D6
Abū al Khaşīb, Iraq 71 D6
Abū 'Alī, Si. Arabia 71 E6
Abū 'Alī →, Lebanon ... 75 A4
Abū Ballas, Egypt 80 C2
Abu Deleiq, Sudan 81 D3
Abu Dhabi = Abū Ȥaby, U.A.E. 71 E7
Abū Dīs, Sudan 80 D3
Abū Dom, Sudan 81 D3
Abū Du'ān, Syria 70 B3
Abu el Gairi, W. →, Egypt 75 F2
Abū Gabra, Sudan 81 E2
Abu Ga'da, W. →, Egypt 75 F1
Abū Gubeiha, Sudan 81 E3
Abu Habl, Khawr →, Sudan 81 E3
Abū Ḥadrīyah, Si. Arabia 71 E6
Abu Hamed, Sudan 80 D3
Abu Haraz, An Nîl el Azraq, Sudan . 81 E3
Abū Haraz, Esh Shamâliya, Sudan 80 D3
Abū Higar, Sudan 81 E3
Abū Kamāl, Syria 70 C4
Abū Madd, Ra's, Si. Arabia 70 E3
Abu Matariq, Sudan 81 E2
Abu Qir, Egypt 80 H7
Abu Qireiya, Egypt 80 C4
Abu Qurqâs, Egypt 80 J7
Abū Şafāt, W. →, Jordan 75 E5
Abū Simbel, Egypt 80 C3
Abū Şukhayr, Iraq 70 D5
Abu Tig, Egypt 80 B3
Abu Tiga, Sudan 81 E3
Abū Zabad, Sudan 81 E2
Abū Ȥaby, U.A.E. 71 E7
Abū Zeydābād, Iran 71 C6
Abuja, Nigeria 83 D6
Abukuma-Gawa →, Japan 54 E10
Abukuma-Sammyaku, Japan 54 F10
Abunã, Brazil 124 E5
Abunã →, Brazil 124 E5
Aburo, Dem. Rep. of the Congo 86 B3
Abut Hd., N.Z. 91 K3
Abwong, Sudan 81 F3
Åby, Sweden 11 F10
Aby, Lagune, Ivory C. 82 D4
Åbybro, Denmark 11 G3
Açailândia, Brazil 125 D9
Acajutla, El Salv. 120 D2
Acámbaro, Mexico 118 D4
Acanthus, Greece 40 F7
Acaponeta, Mexico 118 C3
Acapulco, Mexico 119 D5
Acarai, Serra, Brazil 124 C7
Acarigua, Venezuela 124 B5
Acatlán, Mexico 119 D5
Acayucan, Mexico 119 D6
Accéglio, Italy 28 D4
Accomac, U.S.A. 108 G8
Accous, France 20 E3
Accra, Ghana 83 D4
Accrington, U.K. 12 D5
Acebal, Argentina 126 C3
Aceh □, Indonesia 62 D1
Acerra, Italy 31 B7
Aceuchal, Spain 35 G4
Achalpur, India 66 J10
Acheng, China 57 B14
Achenkirch, Austria 26 D4
Achensee, Austria 26 D4
Acher, India 68 H5
Achern, Germany 25 G4
Achill Hd., Ireland 15 C1

Achill I., Ireland 15 C1
Achim, Germany 24 B5
Achinsk, Russia 51 D10
Acıgöl, Turkey 39 D11
Acıpayam, Turkey 39 D11
Acireale, Italy 31 E8
Ackerman, U.S.A. 113 J10
Acklins I., Bahamas 121 B5
Acme, Canada 104 C6
Aconcagua, Cerro, Argentina 126 C2
Aconquija, Mt., Argentina 126 B2
Açores, Is. dos = Azores, Atl. Oc. 76 C1
Acquapendente, Italy 29 F8
Acquasanta Terme, Italy . 29 F10
Acquasparta, Italy 29 F9
Acquaviva delle Fonti, Italy 31 B9
Acqui Terme, Italy 28 D5
Acraman, L., Australia ... 95 E2
Acre = 'Akko, Israel 75 C4
Acre □, Brazil 124 E4
Acre →, Brazil 124 E5
Acri, Italy 31 C9
Acs, Hungary 42 C3
Actium, Greece 38 C2
Acton, Canada 110 C4
Ad Dammām, Si. Arabia ... 71 E6
Ad Dawḥah, Qatar 71 E6
Ad Dir'īyah, Si. Arabia ... 70 E5
Ad Dīwānīyah, Iraq 70 D5
Ad Dujayl, Iraq 70 C5
Ada, Ghana 83 D5
Ada, Serbia, Yug. 42 E5
Ada, Minn., U.S.A. 112 B6
Ada, Okla., U.S.A. 113 H6
Adaja →, Spain 34 D6
Adamawa, Massif de l', Cameroon 83 D7
Adamawa □, Nigeria = Adamaoua, Massif de l', Cameroon 83 D7
Adamawa Highlands = Adamaoua, Massif de l', Cameroon 83 D7
Adamello, Mte., Italy 28 B7
Adami Tulu, Ethiopia 81 F4
Adaminaby, Australia 95 F4
Adams, Mass., U.S.A. ... 111 D11
Adams, N.Y., U.S.A. ... 111 C8
Adams, Wis., U.S.A. ... 112 D10
Adam's Bridge, Sri Lanka 66 Q11
Adams L., Canada 104 C5
Adams Mt., U.S.A. 116 D5
Adam's Peak, Sri Lanka 66 R12
Adamuz, Spain 35 G6
Adana, Turkey 72 D6
Adanero, Spain 34 E6
Adapazarı, Turkey 72 B4
Adarama, Sudan 81 D3
Adare, C., Antarctica 5 D11
Adaut, Indonesia 63 F8
Adavale, Australia 95 D3
Adda →, Italy 28 C6
Addis Ababa = Addis Abeba, Ethiopia 81 F4
Addis Abeba, Ethiopia ... 81 F4
Addis Alem, Ethiopia 81 F4
Addison, U.S.A. 110 D7
Addo, S. Africa 88 E4
Adebour, Niger 83 C7
Ādeh, Iran 70 B5
Adel, U.S.A. 109 K4
Adelaide, Australia 95 E2
Adelaide, Bahamas 120 A4
Adelaide, S. Africa 88 E4
Adelaide I., Antarctica 5 C17
Adelaide Pen., Canada ... 100 B10
Adelaide River, Australia . 92 B5
Adelanto, U.S.A. 117 L9
Adele I., Australia 92 C3
Adélie, Terre, Antarctica 5 C10
Adélie Land = Adélie, Terre, Antarctica 5 C10
Ademuz, Spain 32 E3
Aden = Al 'Adan, Yemen 74 E4
Aden, G. of, Asia 74 E4
Adendorp, S. Africa 88 E3
Adh Dhayd, U.A.E. 71 E7
Adhoi, India 68 H4
Adi, Indonesia 63 E8
Adi Daro, Ethiopia 81 E4
Adi Keyih, Eritrea 81 E4
Adi Kwala, Eritrea 81 E4
Adi Ugri, Eritrea 81 E4
Adieu, C., Australia 93 F5
Adieu Pt., Australia 92 C3
Adigala, Ethiopia 81 E5
Adige →, Italy 29 C9
Adigrat, Ethiopia 81 E4
Adıgüzel Barajı, Turkey . 39 C11
Adilabad, India 66 K11
Adilcevaz, Turkey 73 C10
Adin, U.S.A. 114 F3
Adin Khel, Afghan. 66 C3
Adirondack Mts., U.S.A. . 111 C10
Adıyaman, Turkey 73 D8
Adjohon, Benin 83 D5
Adjud, Romania 43 D12
Adjumani, Uganda 86 B3
Adlavik Is., Canada 103 A8
Adler, Russia 49 J4
Admiralty G., Australia ... 92 B4
Admiralty I., U.S.A. 100 C6
Admiralty Inlet, U.S.A. ... 114 C2
Admiralty Is., Papua N. G. 96 H6
Ado, Nigeria 83 D5

Ado-Ekiti, Nigeria 83 D6
Adok, Sudan 81 F3
Adola, Ethiopia 81 E5
Adonara, Indonesia 63 F6
Adoni, India 66 M10
Adony, Hungary 42 C3
Adour →, France 20 E2
Adra, India 69 H12
Adra, Spain 35 J7
Adrano, Italy 31 E7
Adrar, Algeria 76 D4
Adrasan, Turkey 39 E12
Adria, Italy 29 C9
Adrian, Mich., U.S.A. 108 E3
Adrian, Tex., U.S.A. 113 H3
Adriatic Sea, Medit. S. 6 G9
Adua, Indonesia 63 E7
Adwa, Ethiopia 81 E4
Adygea □, Russia 49 H5
Adzhar Republic □ = Ajaria □, Georgia 49 K6
Adzopé, Ivory C. 82 D4
Ægean Sea, Medit. S. 39 C7
Aerhtai Shan, Mongolia ... 60 B4
Ærø, Denmark 11 K4
Ærøskøbing, Denmark 11 K4
Aëtós, Greece 38 D3
'Afak, Iraq 70 C5
Afandou, Greece 36 C10
Afghanistan ■, Asia 66 C4
Afikpo, Nigeria 83 D6
Aflou, Algeria 78 B6
Afogados da Ingàzeira, Brazil 125 E11
Afognak I., U.S.A. 100 C4
Afragóla, Italy 31 B7
Afrera, Ethiopia 81 E5
'Afrīn, Syria 70 B3
Afşin, Turkey 72 C7
Afton, U.S.A. 111 D9
Afuá, Brazil 125 D8
'Afula, Israel 75 C4
Afyon, Turkey 39 C12
Afyon □, Turkey 39 C12
Afyonkarahisar = Afyon, Turkey 39 C12
Aga, Egypt 80 H7
Agadès = Agadez, Niger . 83 B6
Agadez, Niger 83 B6
Agadir, Morocco 78 B4
Agaete, Canary Is. 37 F4
Ağapınar, Turkey 39 B12
Agar, India 68 H7
Agaro, Ethiopia 81 F4
Agartala, India 67 H17
Agăş, Romania 43 D11
Agassiz, Canada 104 D4
Agats, Indonesia 63 F9
Agbélouvé, Togo 83 D5
Agboville, Ivory C. 82 D4
Ağcabädi, Azerbaijan 49 K8
Ağdam, Azerbaijan 49 L8
Ağdaş, Azerbaijan 49 K8
Agde, France 20 E7
Agde, C. d', France 20 E7
Agdzhabedi = Ağcabädi, Azerbaijan 49 K8
Agen, France 20 D4
Agerbæk, Denmark 11 J2
Agersø, Denmark 11 J5
Ageyevo, Russia 46 E9
Āgh Kand, Iran 71 B6
Aghireşu, Romania 43 D8
Aginskoye, Russia 51 D12
Ağlasun, Turkey 39 D12
Agly →, France 20 F7
Agnibilékrou, Ivory C. 82 D4
Agnita, Romania 43 E9
Agnone, Italy 29 G11
Agofie, Ghana 83 D5
Agogna →, Italy 28 C5
Agogo, Sudan 81 F2
Agón, Sweden 10 C11
Agon Coutainville, France 18 C5
Agout →, France 20 E5
Agra, India 68 F7
Agrakhanskiy Poluostrov, Russia 49 J8
Agramunt, Spain 32 D6
Agreda, Spain 32 D3
Ağrı, Turkey 73 C10
Agri →, Italy 31 B9
Ağrı Dağı, Turkey 73 C11
Agriá, Greece 38 B5
Agrigento, Italy 30 E6
Agrínion, Greece 38 C3
Agrópoli, Italy 31 B7
Ağstafa, Azerbaijan 49 K7
Agua Caliente, Baja Calif., Mexico 117 N10
Agua Caliente, Sinaloa, Mexico 118 B3
Agua Caliente Springs, U.S.A. 117 N10
Água Clara, Brazil 125 H8
Agua Hechicero, Mexico . 117 N10
Agua Prieta, Mexico 118 A3
Aguadilla, Puerto Rico ... 121 C6
Aguadulce, Panama 120 E3
Aguanga, U.S.A. 117 M10
Aguanish, Canada 103 B7
Aguanus →, Canada 103 B7
Aguapey →, Argentina ... 126 B4
Aguaray Guazú →, Paraguay 126 A4
Aguarico →, Ecuador ... 124 D3
Aguas →, Spain 32 D4
Aguas Blancas, Chile 126 A2
Aguas Calientes, Sierra de, Argentina 126 B2
Aguascalientes, Mexico ... 118 C4

Aguascalientes □, Mexico 118 C4
Agudo, Spain 35 G6
Águeda, Portugal 34 E2
Águeda →, Spain 34 D4
Aguié, Niger 83 C6
Aguilafuente, Spain 34 D6
Aguilar, Spain 35 H6
Aguilar de Campóo, Spain 34 C6
Aguilares, Argentina 126 B2
Aguilas, Spain 33 H3
Agüímes, Canary Is. 37 G4
Aguja, C. de la, Colombia 122 A3
Agulaa, Ethiopia 81 E4
Agulhas, C., S. Africa 88 E3
Agulo, Canary Is. 37 F2
Agung, Indonesia 62 F5
Agur, Uganda 86 B3
Agusan →, Phil. 61 G6
Ağva, Turkey 41 E13
Agvali, Russia 49 J8
Aha Mts., Botswana 88 B3
Ahaggar, Algeria 78 D7
Ahamansu, Ghana 83 D5
Ahar, Iran 70 B5
Ahat, Turkey 39 C11
Ahaus, Germany 24 C2
Ahipara B., N.Z. 91 F4
Ahir Dağı, Turkey 39 C12
Ahiri, India 66 K12
Ahlat, Turkey 73 C10
Ahlen, Germany 24 D3
Ahmad Wal, Pakistan 68 E1
Ahmadabad, India 68 H5
Aḥmadābād, Khorāsān, Iran 71 C9
Aḥmadābād, Khorāsān, Iran 71 C8
Aḥmadī, Iran 71 E8
Ahmadnagar, India 66 K9
Ahmadpur, Pakistan 68 E4
Ahmar, Ethiopia 81 F5
Ahmedabad = Ahmadabad, India 68 H5
Ahmednagar = Ahmadnagar, India 66 K9
Ahmetbey, Turkey 41 E11
Ahmetler, Turkey 39 C11
Ahmetli, Turkey 39 C9
Ahoada, Nigeria 83 D6
Ahome, Mexico 118 B3
Ahr →, Germany 24 E3
Ahram, Iran 71 D6
Ahrax Pt., Malta 36 D1
Ahrensbök, Germany 24 A6
Ahrensburg, Germany 24 B6
Āhū, Iran 71 C6
Ahuachapán, El Salv. 120 D2
Ahun, France 19 F9
Åhus, Sweden 11 J8
Ahvāz, Iran 71 D6
Ahvenanmaa = Åland, Finland 9 F19
Aḥwar, Yemen 74 E4
Ahzar, Mali 83 B5
Aichach, Germany 25 G7
Aichi □, Japan 55 G8
Aigle, Switz. 25 J2
Aignay-le-Duc, France 19 E11
Aigoual, Mt., France 20 D7
Aigre, France 20 C4
Aigua, Uruguay 127 C5
Aigueperse, France 19 F10
Aigues →, France 21 D8
Aigues-Mortes, France ... 21 E8
Aigues-Mortes, G. d', France 21 E8
Aiguilles, France 21 D10
Aiguillon, France 20 D4
Aigurande, France 19 F8
Aihui, China 60 A7
Aija, Peru 124 E3
Aikawa, Japan 54 E9
Aiken, U.S.A. 109 J5
Ailao Shan, China 58 F3
Aillant-sur-Tholon, France 19 E10
Aillik, Canada 103 A8
Ailsa Craig, U.K. 14 F3
'Ailūn, Jordan 75 C4
Aim, Russia 51 D14
Aimere, Indonesia 63 F6
Aimogasta, Argentina 126 B2
Aimorés, Brazil 125 G10
Ain □, France 19 F12
Ain →, France 21 C9
Aïn Ben Tili, Mauritania . 78 C4
Aïn el Mafki, Egypt 80 B2
Ain Girba, Egypt 80 B2
Aïn Qeiqab, Egypt 80 B1
Aïn-Sefra, Algeria 78 B5
Aïn Sheikh Murzûk, Egypt 80 B2
'Ain Sudr, Egypt 75 F2
Ain Sukhna, Egypt 80 J8
Ain Zeitûn, Egypt 80 B2
Ainaži, Latvia 9 H21
Aínos Óros, Greece 38 C2
Ainsworth, U.S.A. 112 D5
Aiquile, Bolivia 124 G5
Air, Niger 83 B6
Air Hitam, Malaysia 65 M4
Airaines, France 19 C8
Airdrie, Canada 104 C6
Airdrie, U.K. 14 F5
Aire →, U.K. 12 D7
Aire, I. de l', Spain 37 B11
Aire-sur-la-Lys, France ... 19 B9
Aire-sur-l'Adour, France . 20 E3
Airlie Beach, Australia ... 94 C4

Airvault, *France* 18 F6
Aisch →, *Germany* 25 F6
Aisne ☐, *France* 19 C10
Aisne →, *France* 19 C9
Aitana, Sierra de, *Spain* .. 33 G4
Aitkin, *U.S.A.* 112 B8
Aitolía Kai Akarnanía ☐,
   Greece 38 C3
Aitolikón, *Greece* 38 C3
Aiud, *Romania* 43 D8
Aix-en-Provence, *France* .. 21 E9
Aix-la-Chapelle = Aachen,
   Germany 24 E2
Aix-les-Bains, *France* 21 C9
Aixe-sur-Vienne, *France* .. 20 C5
Aiyansh, *Canada* 104 B3
Aíyina, *Greece* 38 D5
Aiyínion, *Greece* 40 F6
Aíyion, *Greece* 38 C4
Aizawl, *India* 67 H18
Aizenay, *France* 18 F5
Aizkraukle, *Latvia* 9 H21
Aizpute, *Latvia* 9 H19
Aizuwakamatsu, *Japan* .. 54 F9
Ajaccio, *France* 21 G12
Ajaccio, G. d', *France* .. 21 G12
Ajalpan, *Mexico* 119 D5
Ajanta Ra., *India* 66 J9
Ajari Rep. = Ajaria ☐,
   Georgia 49 K6
Ajaria ☐, *Georgia* 49 K6
Ajax, *Canada* 110 C5
Ajdâbiyah, *Libya* 79 B10
Ajdovščina, *Slovenia* ... 29 C10
Ajibar, *Ethiopia* 81 E4
Ajka, *Hungary* 42 C2
'Ajman, *U.A.E.* 71 E7
Ajmer, *India* 68 F6
Ajo, *U.S.A.* 115 K7
Ajo, C. de, *Spain* 34 B7
Ajok, *Sudan* 81 F2
Ajuy, *Phil.* 61 F5
Ak Dağ, *Turkey* 39 E11
Ak Dağları, *Muğla, Turkey* 39 E11
Ak Dağları, *Sivas, Turkey* 72 C7
Akaba, *Togo* 83 D5
Akabira, *Japan* 54 C11
Akaki Beseka, *Ethiopia* .. 81 F4
Akala, *Sudan* 81 D4
Akamas ☐, *Cyprus* 36 D11
Akanthou, *Cyprus* 36 D12
Akarca, *Turkey* 39 C11
Akaroa, *N.Z.* 91 K4
Akasha, *Sudan* 80 C3
Akashi, *Japan* 55 G7
Akçaabat, *Turkey* 73 B8
Akçadağ, *Turkey* 72 C7
Akçakale, *Turkey* 73 D8
Akçakoca, *Turkey* 72 B4
Akçaova, *Turkey* 41 E13
Akçay, *Turkey* 39 E11
Akçay →, *Turkey* 39 D10
Akdağ, *Turkey* 39 C8
Akdağmadeni, *Turkey* ... 72 C6
Akelamo, *Indonesia* 63 D7
Åkers styckebruk, *Sweden* 10 E11
Åkersberga, *Sweden* 10 E12
Aketi,
   Dem. Rep. of the Congo 84 D4
Akhaïa ☐, *Greece* 38 C3
Akhalkalaki, *Georgia* 49 K6
Akhaltsikhe, *Georgia* 49 K6
Akharnaí, *Greece* 38 C5
Akhelóös →, *Greece* 38 C3
Akhendriá, *Greece* 39 G7
Akhisar, *Turkey* 39 C9
Akhladhókambos, *Greece* . 38 D4
Akhmîm, *Egypt* 80 B3
Akhnur, *India* 69 C6
Akhtopol, *Bulgaria* 41 D11
Akhtuba →, *Russia* 49 G8
Akhtubinsk, *Russia* 49 F8
Akhty, *Russia* 49 K8
Akhtyrka = Okhtyrka,
   Ukraine 47 G8
Aki, *Japan* 55 H6
Akimiski I., *Canada* 102 B3
Akimovka, *Ukraine* 47 J8
Åkirkeby, *Denmark* 11 J8
Akita, *Japan* 54 E10
Akita ☐, *Japan* 54 E10
Akjoujt, *Mauritania* 82 B2
Akkaya Tepesi, *Turkey* .. 39 D11
Akkeshi, *Japan* 54 C12
'Akko, *Israel* 75 C4
Akköy, *Turkey* 39 D9
Aklampa, *Benin* 83 D5
Aklavik, *Canada* 100 B6
Akmenė, *Lithuania* 44 B9
Akmenrags, *Latvia* 44 B8
Akmolinsk = Aqmola,
   Kazakhstan 50 D8
Akmonte = Almonte,
   Spain 35 H4
Akō, *Japan* 55 G7
Ako, *Nigeria* 83 C7
Akobo →, *Ethiopia* 81 F3
Akola, *India* 66 J10
Akonolinga, *Cameroon* .. 83 E7
Akordat, *Eritrea* 81 D4
Akosombo Dam, *Ghana* .. 83 D5
Akot, *Sudan* 81 F3
Akpatok I., *Canada* 101 B13
Åkrahamn, *Norway* 9 G11
Akranes, *Iceland* 8 D2
Akreïjit, *Mauritania* 82 B3

Akrítas Venétiko, Ákra,
   Greece 38 E3
Akron, *Colo., U.S.A.* 112 E3
Akron, *Ohio, U.S.A.* 110 E3
Akrotíri, *Cyprus* 36 E11
Akrotíri, Ákra, *Greece* ... 41 F9
Akrotiri Bay, *Cyprus* 36 E12
Aksai Chin, *India* 69 B8
Aksaray, *Turkey* 72 C6
Aksay, *Kazakstan* 50 D6
Akşehir, *Turkey* 72 C4
Akşehir Gölü, *Turkey* ... 72 C4
Akstafa = Ağstafa,
   Azerbaijan 49 K7
Aksu, *China* 60 B3
Aksu →, *Turkey* 72 D4
Aksum, *Ethiopia* 81 E4
Aktash, *Russia* 48 C11
Aktogay, *Kazakstan* 50 E8
Aktsyabrski, *Belarus* ... 47 F5
Aktyubinsk = Aqtöbe,
   Kazakstan 50 D6
Aku, *Nigeria* 83 D6
Akure, *Nigeria* 83 D6
Akureyri, *Iceland* 8 D4
Akuseki-Shima, *Japan* .. 55 K4
Akusha, *Russia* 49 J8
Akwa-Ibom ☐, *Nigeria* .. 83 E6
Akyab = Sittwe, *Burma* .. 67 J18
Akyazı, *Turkey* 72 B4
Al 'Adan, *Yemen* 74 E4
Al Aḥsā, *Si. Arabia* 71 E6
Al Ajfar, *Si. Arabia* 70 E4
Al Amādīyah, *Iraq* 70 B4
Al Amārah, *Iraq* 70 D5
Al 'Aqabah, *Jordan* 75 F4
Al Arak, *Syria* 70 C3
Al 'Aramah, *Si. Arabia* .. 70 E5
Al Arṭāwīyah, *Si. Arabia* . 70 E5
Al 'Āṣimah = 'Ammān ☐,
   Jordan 75 D5
Al 'Assāfiyah, *Si. Arabia* . 70 D3
Al 'Ayn, *Oman* 71 E7
Al 'Ayn, *Si. Arabia* 70 E3
Al A'zamīyah, *Iraq* 70 C5
Al 'Azīzīyah, *Iraq* 70 C5
Al Bāb, *Syria* 70 B3
Al Bad', *Si. Arabia* 70 D2
Al Bādī, *Iraq* 70 C4
Al Baḥrah, *Kuwait* 70 D5
Al Baḥral Mayyit = Dead
   Sea, *Asia* 75 D4
Al Balqā' ☐, *Jordan* 75 D4
Al Bārūk, J., *Lebanon* ... 75 B4
Al Baṣrah, *Iraq* 70 D5
Al Baṭḥā, *Iraq* 70 D5
Al Batrūn, *Lebanon* 75 A4
Al Baydā, *Libya* 79 B10
Al Biqā ☐, *Lebanon* 75 A5
Al Bi'r, *Si. Arabia* 70 D3
Al Burayj, *Syria* 75 A5
Al Fallūjah, *Iraq* 70 C4
Al Fāw, *Iraq* 71 D6
Al Fujayrah, *U.A.E.* 71 E8
Al Ghadaf, W. →, *Jordan* 75 D5
Al Ghammās, *Iraq* 70 D5
Al Hābah, *Si. Arabia* ... 70 E5
Al Ḥadīthah, *Iraq* 70 C4
Al Ḥadīthah, *Si. Arabia* . 70 D3
Al Ḥaḍr, *Iraq* 73 E10
Al Ḥājānah, *Syria* 75 B5
Al Ḥāmad, *Si. Arabia* ... 70 D3
Al Ḥamdāniyah, *Syria* .. 70 C3
Al Ḥamīdīyah, *Syria* ... 75 A4
Al Ḥammār, *Iraq* 70 D5
Al Ḥarīr, W. →, *Syria* ... 75 C4
Al Ḥasā, W. →, *Jordan* .. 75 D4
Al Ḥasakah, *Syria* 70 B4
Al Ḥaydān →, *Jordan* ... 75 D4
Al Ḥayy, *Iraq* 70 C5
Al Ḥillah, *Iraq* 70 C5
Al Hindīyah, *Iraq* 73 F11
Al Hirmil, *Lebanon* 75 A5
Al Hoceïma, *Morocco* .. 78 A5
Al Ḥudaydah, *Yemen* .. 74 E3
Al Ḥufūf, *Si. Arabia* 71 E6
Al Ḥumaydah, *Si. Arabia* . 70 D2
Al Ḥunayy, *Si Arabia* ... 71 E6
Al Īsāwīyah, *Si. Arabia* . 70 D3
Al Jafr, *Jordan* 75 E5
Al Jaghbūb, *Libya* 79 C10
Al Jahrah, *Kuwait* 70 D5
Al Jalāmīd, *Si. Arabia* .. 70 D3
Al Jamalīyah, *Qatar* 71 E6
Al Janūb ☐, *Lebanon* ... 75 B4
Al Jawf, *Libya* 79 D10
Al Jawf, *Si. Arabia* 70 D3
Al Jazirah, *Iraq* 70 C5
Al Jithāmīyah, *Si. Arabia* . 70 E4
Al Jubayl, *Si. Arabia* ... 71 E6
Al Jubaylah, *Si. Arabia* .. 70 E5
Al Jubb, *Si. Arabia* 70 E4
Al Junaynah, *Sudan* 79 F10
Al Kabā'ish, *Iraq* 70 D5
Al Karak, *Jordan* 75 D4
Al Karak ☐, *Jordan* 75 E5
Al Kāzim Tyab, *Iraq* 70 C5
Al Khalīl, *West Bank* ... 75 D4
Al Khāliṣ, *Iraq* 73 F11
Al Khawr, *Qatar* 71 E6
Al Khiḍr, *Iraq* 70 D5
Al Khiyām, *Lebanon* ... 75 B4
Al Kiswah, *Syria* 75 B5
Al Kūfah, *Iraq* 73 F11
Al Kufrah, *Libya* 79 D10
Al Kuhayfiyah, *Si. Arabia* 70 E4
Al Kūt, *Iraq* 70 C5

Al Kuwayt, *Kuwait* 70 D5
Al Labwah, *Lebanon* ... 75 A5
Al Lādhiqīyah, *Syria* 70 C2
Al Līth, *Si. Arabia* 80 C5
Al Liwā', *Oman* 71 E8
Al Luḥayyah, *Yemen* ... 74 D3
Al Madīnah, *Iraq* 70 D5
Al Madīnah, *Si. Arabia* .. 70 E3
Al Mafraq, *Jordan* 75 C5
Al Maḥmūdīyah, *Iraq* ... 70 C5
Al Majma'ah, *Si. Arabia* . 70 E5
Al Makhruq, W. →,
   Jordan 75 D6
Al Makḥūl, *Si. Arabia* ... 70 E4
Al Manāmah, *Bahrain* .. 71 E6
Al Maqwa', *Kuwait* 70 D5
Al Marj, *Libya* 79 B10
Al Maṭlā, *Kuwait* 70 D5
Al Mawjib, W. →, *Jordan* 75 D4
Al Mawṣil, *Iraq* 70 B4
Al Mayādin, *Syria* 70 C4
Al Mazār, *Jordan* 75 D4
Al Midhnab, *Si. Arabia* .. 70 E5
Al Minā', *Lebanon* 75 A4
Al Miqdādīyah, *Iraq* 70 C5
Al Mubarraz, *Si. Arabia* . 71 E6
Al Mughayrā', *U.A.E.* ... 71 E7
Al Muḥarraq, *Bahrain* .. 71 E6
Al Mukallā, *Yemen* 74 E4
Al Mukhā, *Yemen* 74 E3
Al Musayjīd, *Si. Arabia* .. 70 E3
Al Musayyib, *Iraq* 70 C5
Al Muwayliḥ, *Si. Arabia* . 70 E2
Al Owuho = Otukpa,
   Nigeria 83 D6
Al Qā'im, *Iraq* 70 C4
Al Qalībah, *Si. Arabia* ... 70 D3
Al Qāmishlī, *Syria* 73 D9
Al Qaryatayn, *Syria* 75 A6
Al Qaṭ'ā, *Syria* 70 C4
Al Qaṭīf, *Si. Arabia* 71 E6
Al Qaṭrānah, *Jordan* 75 D5
Al Qaṭrūn, *Libya* 79 D9
Al Qayṣūmah, *Si. Arabia* . 70 D5
Al Quds = Jerusalem,
   Israel 75 D4
Al Qunayṭirah, *Syria* ... 75 C4
Al Qunfudhah, *Si. Arabia* 80 D5
Al Qurnah, *Iraq* 70 D5
Al Quṣayr, *Iraq* 70 D5
Al Quṣayr, *Syria* 75 A5
Al Qutayfah, *Syria* 75 B5
Al 'Uḍaylīyah, *Si. Arabia* . 71 E6
Al 'Ulā, *Si. Arabia* 70 E3
Al Uqayr, *Si. Arabia* 71 E6
Al 'Uwaynid, *Si. Arabia* . 70 E5
Al 'Uwayqīlah, *Si. Arabia* 70 D4
Al 'Uyūn, *Ḥijāz, Si. Arabia* 70 E3
Al 'Uyūn, *Najd, Si. Arabia* 70 E4
Al 'Uzayr, *Iraq* 70 D5
Al Wajh, *Si. Arabia* 70 E3
Al Wakrah, *Qatar* 71 E6
Al Wannān, *Si. Arabia* .. 71 E6
Al Waqbah, *Si. Arabia* .. 70 D5
Al Wari'āh, *Si. Arabia* .. 70 E6
Al Wusayl, *Qatar* 71 E6
Ala, *Italy* 28 C8
Ala Dağ, *Turkey* 73 C10
Alabama ☐, *U.S.A.* 109 J2
Alabama →, *U.S.A.* 109 K2
Alaca, *Turkey* 72 B6
Alaçam, *Turkey* 72 B6
Alaçam Dağları, *Turkey* . 39 B10
Alaçatı, *Turkey* 39 C8
Alaejos, *Spain* 34 D5
Alaérma, *Greece* 36 C9
Alagir, *Russia* 49 J7
Alagna Valsésia, *Italy* .. 28 C4
Alagoa Grande, *Brazil* .. 125 E11
Alagoas ☐, *Brazil* 125 E11
Alagoinhas, *Brazil* 125 F11
Alagón, *Spain* 32 D3
Alagón →, *Spain* 34 F4
Alaior, *Spain* 37 B11
Alajero, *Canary Is.* 37 F2
Alajuela, *Costa Rica* ... 120 D3
Alakamisy, *Madag.* 89 C8
Alaminos, *Phil.* 61 C3
Alamo, *U.S.A.* 117 J11
Alamo Crossing, *U.S.A.* . 117 L13
Alamogordo, *U.S.A.* ... 115 K11
Alamos, *Mexico* 118 B3
Alamosa, *U.S.A.* 115 H11
Åland, *Finland* 9 F19
Alandroal, *Portugal* 35 G3
Ålands hav, *Sweden* ... 9 F18
Alandur, *India* 66 N12
Alange, Presa de, *Spain* . 35 G4
Alania = North Ossetia ☐,
   Russia 49 J7
Alanís, *Spain* 35 G5
Alanya, *Turkey* 72 D5
Alaotra, Farihin', *Madag.* . 89 B8
Alapayevsk, *Russia* 50 D7
Alar del Rey, *Spain* 34 C6
Alaraz, *Spain* 34 E5
Alaşehir, *Turkey* 39 C10
Alaska ☐, *U.S.A.* 100 B5
Alaska, G. of, *Pac. Oc.* .. 100 C5
Alaska Peninsula, *U.S.A.* 100 C4
Alaska Range, *U.S.A.* .. 100 B4
Alássio, *Italy* 28 D5
Älät, *Azerbaijan* 49 L9

Alataw Shankou, *China* .. 60 B3
Alatri, *Italy* 29 G10
Alatyr, *Russia* 48 C8
Alatyr →, *Russia* 48 C8
Alausi, *Ecuador* 124 D3
Álava ☐, *Spain* 32 C2
Alava, C., *U.S.A.* 114 B1
Alaverdi, *Armenia* 49 K7
Alavus, *Finland* 9 E20
Alawoona, *Australia* ... 95 E3
'Alayh, *Lebanon* 75 B4
Alba, *Italy* 28 D5
Alba ☐, *Romania* 43 D8
Alba Adriática, *Italy* ... 29 F10
Alba de Tormes, *Spain* .. 34 E5
Alba-Iulia, *Romania* ... 43 D8
Albac, *Romania* 42 D7
Albacete, *Spain* 33 F3
Albacete ☐, *Spain* 33 G3
Albacutya, L., *Australia* . 95 F3
Ålbæk, *Denmark* 11 G4
Ålbæk Bugt, *Denmark* .. 11 G4
Albalate de las Nogueras,
   Spain 32 E2
Albalate del Arzobispo,
   Spain 32 D4
Albania ■, *Europe* 40 E4
Albano Laziale, *Italy* ... 29 G9
Albany, *Australia* 93 G2
Albany, *Ga., U.S.A.* ... 109 K3
Albany, *N.Y., U.S.A.* .. 111 D11
Albany, *Oreg., U.S.A.* .. 114 D2
Albany, *Tex., U.S.A.* ... 113 J5
Albany →, *Canada* 102 B3
Albardón, *Argentina* ... 126 C2
Albarracín, *Spain* 32 E3
Albarracín, Sierra de, *Spain* 32 E3
Albatera, *Spain* 33 G4
Albatross B., *Australia* .. 94 A3
Albegna →, *Italy* 29 F8
Albemarle, *U.S.A.* 109 H5
Albemarle Sd., *U.S.A.* .. 109 H7
Albenga, *Italy* 28 D5
Alberche →, *Spain* 34 F6
Alberdi, *Paraguay* 126 B4
Alberes, Mts., *France* .. 20 F6
Ålberga, *Sweden* 11 F10
Albersdorf, *Germany* ... 24 A5
Albert, *France* 19 C9
Albert, L., *Australia* 95 F2
Albert Canyon, *Canada* . 104 C5
Albert Edward Ra.,
   Australia 92 C4
Albert L., *Africa* 86 B3
Albert Lea, *U.S.A.* 112 D8
Albert Nile →, *Uganda* . 86 B3
Albert Town, *Bahamas* . 121 B5
Alberta ☐, *Canada* 104 C6
Alberti, *Argentina* 126 D3
Albertinia, *S. Africa* 88 E3
Albertirsa, *Hungary* 42 C4
Alberton, *Canada* 103 C7
Albertville = Kalemie,
   Dem. Rep. of the Congo 86 D2
Albertville, *France* 21 C10
Albi, *France* 20 E6
Albia, *U.S.A.* 112 E8
Albina, *Surinam* 125 B8
Albina, Ponta, *Angola* .. 88 B1
Albino, *Italy* 28 C6
Albion, *Idaho, U.S.A.* .. 114 E7
Albion, *Mich., U.S.A.* .. 108 D3
Albion, *Nebr., U.S.A.* .. 112 E6
Albion, *Pa., U.S.A.* 110 E4
Alboán, Medit. *S.* 35 K7
Alborea, *Spain* 33 F3
Ålborg, *Denmark* 11 G3
Ålborg Bugt, *Denmark* .. 11 H4
Alborz, Reshteh-ye Kūhhā-
   ye, *Iran* 71 C7
Albox, *Spain* 33 H2
Albreda, *Canada* 104 C5
Albufeira, *Portugal* 35 H2
Albula →, *Switz.* 25 J5
Albuñol, *Spain* 35 J7
Albuquerque, *U.S.A.* ... 115 J10
Albuquerque, Cayos de,
   Caribbean 120 D3
Alburg, *U.S.A.* 111 B11
Alburno, Mte., *Italy* 31 B8
Alburquerque, *Spain* ... 35 F4
Albury, *Australia* 95 F4
Alcácer do Sal, *Portugal* . 35 G2
Alcáçovas, *Portugal* 35 G2
Alcalá de Chivert, *Spain* . 32 E5
Alcalá de Guadaira, *Spain* 35 H5
Alcalá de Henares, *Spain* . 34 E7
Alcalá de los Gazules,
   Spain 35 J5
Alcalá del Júcar, *Spain* .. 33 F3
Alcalá del Río, *Spain* ... 35 H5
Alcalá del Valle, *Spain* .. 35 J5
Alcalá la Real, *Spain* ... 35 H7
Álcamo, *Italy* 30 E6
Alcanadre, *Spain* 32 C2
Alcanar, *Spain* 32 E5
Alcanede, *Portugal* 35 F2
Alcanena, *Portugal* 35 F2
Alcanices, *Spain* 34 D4
Alcaniz, *Spain* 32 D4

Alcântara, *Brazil* 125 D10
Alcántara, *Spain* 34 F4
Alcántara, Embalse de,
   Spain 34 F4
Alcantara L., *Canada* ... 105 A7
Alcantarilla, *Spain* 33 H3
Alcaracejos, *Spain* 35 G6
Alcaraz, *Spain* 33 G2
Alcaraz, Sierra de, *Spain* . 33 G2
Alcaudete, *Spain* 35 H6
Alcázar de San Juan, *Spain* 35 F7
Alchevsk, *Ukraine* 47 H10
Alcira = Alzira, *Spain* .. 33 F4
Alcoa, *U.S.A.* 109 H4
Alcobaça, *Portugal* 35 F2
Alcobendas, *Spain* 34 E7
Alcolea del Pinar, *Spain* . 32 D2
Alcora, *Spain* 32 E4
Alcorcón, *Spain* 34 E7
Alcoutim, *Portugal* 35 H3
Alcova, *U.S.A.* 114 E10
Alcoy, *Spain* 33 G4
Alcubierre, Sierra de, *Spain* 32 D4
Alcublas, *Spain* 32 F4
Alcúdia, *Spain* 37 B10
Alcúdia, B. d', *Spain* ... 37 B10
Alcudia, Sierra de la, *Spain* 35 G6
Aldabra Is., *Seychelles* .. 77 G8
Aldama, *Mexico* 119 C5
Aldan, *Russia* 51 D13
Aldan →, *Russia* 51 C13
Aldea, Pta. de la,
   Canary Is. 37 G4
Aldeburgh, *U.K.* 13 E9
Alder, *U.S.A.* 114 D7
Alder Pk., *U.S.A.* 116 K5
Alderney, *U.K.* 13 H5
Aldershot, *U.K.* 13 F7
Åled, *Sweden* 11 H6
Aledo, *U.S.A.* 112 E9
Alefa, *Ethiopia* 81 E4
Aleg, *Mauritania* 82 B2
Alegranza, *Canary Is.* .. 37 E6
Alegranza, I., *Canary Is.* . 37 E6
Alegre, *Brazil* 127 A7
Alegrete, *Brazil* 127 B4
Aleisk, *Russia* 50 D9
Aleksandriya =
   Oleksandriya,
   Kirovohrad, Ukraine .. 47 H7
Aleksandriya =
   Oleksandriya, *Rivne,
   Ukraine* 47 G4
Aleksandriyskaya, *Russia* . 49 J8
Aleksandrov Gay, *Russia* . 48 E9
Aleksandrovac,
   Serbia, Yug. 40 C5
Aleksandrovac,
   Serbia, Yug. 40 B5
Aleksandrovka =
   Oleksandrivka, *Ukraine* 47 H7
Aleksandrovo, *Bulgaria* . 41 C8
Aleksandrovsk-
   Sakhalinskiy, *Russia* .. 51 D15
Aleksandrów Kujawski,
   Poland 45 F5
Aleksandrów Łódzki,
   Poland 45 G6
Alekseyevka, *Samara,
   Russia* 48 D10
Alekseyevka, *Voronezh,
   Russia* 47 G10
Aleksin, *Russia* 46 E9
Aleksinac, *Serbia, Yug.* . 40 C5
Além Paraíba, *Brazil* ... 127 A7
Alemania, *Argentina* ... 126 B2
Alemania, *Chile* 126 B2
Alençon, *France* 18 D7
Alenquer, *Brazil* 125 D8
Alenuihaha Channel,
   U.S.A. 106 H17
Aleppo = Ḥalab, *Syria* .. 70 B3
Aléria, *France* 21 F13
Alert Bay, *Canada* 104 C3
Alès, *France* 21 D8
Aleşd, *Romania* 42 C7
Alessándria, *Italy* 28 D5
Ålestrup, *Denmark* 11 H3
Ålesund, *Norway* 9 E12
Alet-les-Bains, *France* .. 20 F6
Aletschhorn, *Switz.* 25 J4
Aleutian Is., *Pac. Oc.* ... 100 C2
Aleutian Trench, *Pac. Oc.* 96 C10
Alexander, *U.S.A.* 112 B3
Alexander, Mt., *Australia* . 93 E3
Alexander Arch., *U.S.A.* 104 B2
Alexander B., *S. Africa* .. 88 D2
Alexander City, *U.S.A.* .. 109 J3
Alexander I., *Antarctica* . 5 C17
Alexandra, *Australia* ... 95 F4
Alexandra, *N.Z.* 91 L2
Alexandria = El
   Iskandarîya, *Egypt* ... 80 H7
Alexandria, *Australia* ... 94 B2
Alexandria, *B.C., Canada* 104 C4
Alexandria, *Ont., Canada* 111 A10
Alexandria, *Romania* ... 43 G10
Alexandria, *S. Africa* ... 88 E4
Alexandria, *U.K.* 14 F4
Alexandria, *Ind., U.S.A.* 108 E3
Alexandria, *La., U.S.A.* . 113 K8
Alexandria, *Minn., U.S.A.* 112 C7
Alexandria, *S. Dak.,
   U.S.A.* 112 D6
Alexandria, *Va., U.S.A.* . 108 F7

Alexandria Bay, *U.S.A.*	111	B9	
Alexandrina, L., *Australia*	95	F2	
Alexandroúpolis, *Greece*	41	F9	
Alexis →, *Canada*	103	B4	
Alexis Creek, *Canada*	104	C4	
Alfabia, *Spain*	37	B9	
Alfambra, *Spain*	32	E3	
Alfândega da Fé, *Portugal*	34	D4	
Alfaro, *Spain*	32	C3	
Alfatar, *Bulgaria*	41	C11	
Alfaz del Pi, *Spain*	33	G4	
Alfeld, *Germany*	24	D5	
Alfenas, *Brazil*	127	A6	
Alfiós →, *Greece*	38	D3	
Alföld, *Hungary*	42	D5	
Alfonsine, *Italy*	29	D9	
Alford, *Aberds., U.K.*	14	D6	
Alford, *Lincs., U.K.*	12	D8	
Alfred, *Maine, U.S.A.*	111	C14	
Alfred, *N.Y., U.S.A.*	110	D7	
Alfreton, *U.K.*	12	D6	
Alfta, *Sweden*	10	C10	
Alga, *Kazakstan*	50	E6	
Algaida, *Spain*	37	B9	
Algar, *Spain*	35	J5	
Ålgård, *Norway*	9	G11	
Algarinejo, *Spain*	35	H6	
Algarve, *Portugal*	35	J2	
Algeciras, *Spain*	35	J5	
Algemesí, *Spain*	33	F4	
Alger, *Algeria*	78	A6	
Algeria ■, *Africa*	78	C6	
Alghero, *Italy*	30	B1	
Älghult, *Sweden*	11	G9	
Algiers = Alger, *Algeria*	78	A6	
Algoa B., *S. Africa*	88	E4	
Algodonales, *Spain*	35	J5	
Algodor →, *Spain*	34	F7	
Algoma, *U.S.A.*	108	C2	
Algona, *U.S.A.*	112	D7	
Algonac, *U.S.A.*	110	D2	
Algorta, *Uruguay*	128	C5	
Alhama de Almería, *Spain*	35	J8	
Alhama de Aragón, *Spain*	32	D3	
Alhama de Granada, *Spain*	35	H7	
Alhama de Murcia, *Spain*	33	H3	
Alhambra, *U.S.A.*	117	L8	
Alhaurín el Grande, *Spain*	35	J6	
Alhucemas = Al Hoceïma, *Morocco*	78	A5	
'Alī al Gharbī, *Iraq*	70	C5	
'Alī ash Sharqī, *Iraq*	70	C5	
Äli Bayramlı, *Azerbaijan*	49	L9	
'Alī Khēl, *Afghan.*	68	C3	
Ali Sahîh, *Djibouti*	81	E5	
Alī Shāh, *Iran*	70	B5	
Ália, *Italy*	30	E6	
'Alīābād, *Khorāsān, Iran*	71	C8	
'Alīābād, *Kordestān, Iran*	70	C5	
'Alīābād, *Yazd, Iran*	71	D7	
Aliaga, *Spain*	32	E4	
Aliağa, *Turkey*	39	C8	
Aliákmon →, *Greece*	40	F6	
Alibo, *Ethiopia*	81	F4	
Alibunar, *Serbia, Yug.*	42	E5	
Alicante, *Spain*	33	G4	
Alicante □, *Spain*	33	G4	
Alice, *S. Africa*	88	E4	
Alice, *U.S.A.*	113	M5	
Alice →, *Queens., Australia*	94	C3	
Alice →, *Queens., Australia*	94	B3	
Alice, Punta, *Italy*	31	C10	
Alice Arm, *Canada*	104	B3	
Alice Downs, *Australia*	92	C4	
Alice Springs, *Australia*	94	C1	
Alicedale, *S. Africa*	88	E4	
Aliceville, *U.S.A.*	109	J1	
Alick Cr. →, *Australia*	94	C3	
Alicudi, *Italy*	31	D7	
Alida, *Canada*	105	D8	
Aligarh, *Raj., India*	68	G7	
Aligarh, *Ut. P., India*	68	F8	
Alīgūdarz, *Iran*	71	C6	
Alijó, *Portugal*	34	D3	
Alimnía, *Greece*	36	C9	
Alingsås, *Sweden*	11	G6	
Alipur, *Pakistan*	68	E4	
Alipur Duar, *India*	67	F16	
Aliquippa, *U.S.A.*	110	F4	
Aliste →, *Spain*	34	D5	
Alitus, *Lithuania*	9	J21	
Alivérion, *Greece*	38	C6	
Aliwal North, *S. Africa*	88	E4	
Alix, *Canada*	104	C6	
Aljezur, *Portugal*	35	H2	
Aljustrel, *Portugal*	35	H2	
Alkamari, *Niger*	83	C7	
Alkmaar, *Neths.*	17	B4	
All American Canal, *U.S.A.*	115	K6	
Allada, *Benin*	83	D5	
Allah Dad, *Pakistan*	68	G2	
Allahabad, *India*	69	G9	
Allan, *Canada*	105	C7	
Allanche, *France*	20	C6	
Allanmyo, *Burma*	67	K19	
Allanridge, *S. Africa*	88	D4	
Allanwater, *Canada*	102	B1	
Allaqi, Wadi →, *Egypt*	80	C3	
Allariz, *Spain*	34	C3	
Allassac, *France*	20	C5	
Ålleberg, *Sweden*	11	F7	
Allegan, *U.S.A.*	108	D3	
Allegany, *U.S.A.*	110	D6	
Allegheny →, *U.S.A.*	110	F5	

Allegheny Mts., *U.S.A.*	98	F11	
Allegheny Plateau, *U.S.A.*	108	G6	
Allegheny Reservoir, *U.S.A.*	110	E6	
Allègre, *France*	20	C7	
Allen, Bog of, *Ireland*	15	C5	
Allen, L., *Ireland*	15	B3	
Allende, *Mexico*	118	B4	
Allentown, *U.S.A.*	111	F9	
Allentsteig, *Austria*	26	C8	
Alleppey, *India*	66	Q10	
Allepuz, *Spain*	32	E4	
Aller →, *Germany*	24	C5	
Alliance, *Nebr., U.S.A.*	112	D3	
Alliance, *Ohio, U.S.A.*	110	F3	
Allier □, *France*	19	F9	
Allier →, *France*	19	F10	
Allinge, *Denmark*	11	J8	
Alliston, *Canada*	102	D4	
Alloa, *U.K.*	14	E5	
Allones, *France*	18	D8	
Allora, *Australia*	95	D5	
Allos, *France*	21	D10	
Alluitsup Paa = Sydprøven, *Greenland*	4	C5	
Alma, *Canada*	103	C5	
Alma, *Ga., U.S.A.*	109	K4	
Alma, *Kans., U.S.A.*	112	F6	
Alma, *Mich., U.S.A.*	108	D3	
Alma, *Nebr., U.S.A.*	112	E5	
Alma, *Wis., U.S.A.*	112	C9	
Alma Ata = Almaty, *Kazakstan*	50	E8	
Almacelles, *Spain*	32	D5	
Almada, *Portugal*	35	G1	
Almaden, *Australia*	94	B3	
Almadén, *Spain*	35	G6	
Almanor, L., *U.S.A.*	114	F3	
Almansa, *Spain*	33	G3	
Almanza, *Spain*	34	C5	
Almanzor, Pico, *Spain*	34	E5	
Almanzora →, *Spain*	33	H3	
Almaş, Munţii, *Romania*	42	F7	
Almassora, *Spain*	32	F4	
Almaty, *Kazakstan*	50	E8	
Almazán, *Spain*	32	D2	
Almeirim, *Brazil*	125	D8	
Almeirim, *Portugal*	35	F2	
Almelo, *Neths.*	17	B6	
Almenar de Soria, *Spain*	32	D2	
Almenara, *Spain*	32	F4	
Almenara, Sierra de la, *Spain*	33	H3	
Almendra, Embalse de, *Spain*	34	D4	
Almendralejo, *Spain*	35	G4	
Almere-Stad, *Neths.*	17	B5	
Almería, *Spain*	33	J8	
Almería □, *Spain*	33	H2	
Almería, G. de, *Spain*	33	J2	
Almetyevsk, *Russia*	48	C11	
Älmhult, *Sweden*	11	H8	
Almirante, *Panama*	120	E3	
Almiropótamos, *Greece*	38	C6	
Almirós, *Greece*	38	B4	
Almirou, Kólpos, *Greece*	36	D6	
Almodôvar, *Portugal*	35	H2	
Almodóvar del Campo, *Spain*	35	G6	
Almodóvar del Río, *Spain*	35	H5	
Almont, *U.S.A.*	110	D1	
Almonte, *Canada*	111	A8	
Almonte, *Spain*	35	H4	
Almora, *India*	69	E8	
Almoradí, *Spain*	33	G4	
Almorox, *Spain*	34	E6	
Almoustarat, *Mali*	83	B5	
Älmsta, *Sweden*	10	E12	
Almudévar, *Spain*	32	D4	
Almuñécar, *Spain*	35	J7	
Almunge, *Sweden*	10	E12	
Almuradiel, *Spain*	35	G7	
Alness, *U.K.*	14	D4	
Alnmouth, *U.K.*	12	B6	
Alnwick, *U.K.*	12	B6	
Aloi, *Uganda*	86	B3	
Alon, *Burma*	67	H19	
Alor, *Indonesia*	63	F6	
Alor Setar, *Malaysia*	65	J3	
Álora, *Spain*	35	J6	
Alosno, *Spain*	35	H3	
Aloysius, Mt., *Australia*	93	E4	
Alpaugh, *U.S.A.*	116	K7	
Alpedrinha, *Portugal*	34	E3	
Alpena, *U.S.A.*	108	C4	
Alpes-de-Haute-Provence □, *France*	21	D10	
Alpes-Maritimes □, *France*	21	E11	
Alpha, *Australia*	94	C4	
Alphen aan den Rijn, *Neths.*	17	B4	
Alpiarça, *Portugal*	35	F2	
Alpine, *Ariz., U.S.A.*	115	K9	
Alpine, *Calif., U.S.A.*	117	N10	
Alpine, *Tex., U.S.A.*	113	K3	
Alps, *Europe*	6	F7	
Alpu, *Turkey*	72	C4	
Alqueva, Barragem do, *Portugal*	35	G3	
Alrø, *Denmark*	11	J4	
Alroy Downs, *Australia*	94	B2	
Als, *Denmark*	11	K3	
Alsace, *France*	19	D14	
Alsask, *Canada*	105	C7	
Alsasua, *Spain*	32	C2	
Alsfeld, *Germany*	24	E5	
Alsten, *Norway*	8	D15	

Alstermo, *Sweden*	11	H9	
Alston, *U.K.*	12	C5	
Alta, *Norway*	8	B20	
Alta, Sierra, *Spain*	32	E3	
Alta Gracia, *Argentina*	126	C3	
Alta Lake, *Canada*	104	C4	
Alta Sierra, *U.S.A.*	117	K8	
Altaelva →, *Norway*	8	B20	
Altafjorden, *Norway*	8	A20	
Altai = Aerhtai Shan, *Mongolia*	60	B4	
Altamaha →, *U.S.A.*	109	K5	
Altamira, *Brazil*	125	D8	
Altamira, *Chile*	126	B2	
Altamira, *Mexico*	119	C5	
Altamira, Cuevas de, *Spain*	34	B6	
Altamont, *U.S.A.*	111	D10	
Altamura, *Italy*	31	B9	
Altanbulag, *Mongolia*	60	A5	
Altar, *Mexico*	118	A2	
Altata, *Mexico*	118	C3	
Altavista, *U.S.A.*	108	G6	
Altay, *China*	60	B3	
Altdorf, *Switz.*	25	J4	
Alte Mellum, *Germany*	24	B4	
Altea, *Spain*	33	G4	
Altenberg, *Germany*	24	E9	
Altenbruch, *Germany*	24	B4	
Altenburg, *Germany*	24	E8	
Altenkirchen, Mecklenburg-Vorpommern, *Germany*	24	A9	
Altenkirchen, Rhld.-Pfz., *Germany*	24	E3	
Altenmarkt, *Austria*	26	D7	
Alter do Chão, *Portugal*	35	F3	
Altinoluk, *Turkey*	39	B8	
Altinova, *Turkey*	39	B8	
Altıntaş, *Turkey*	39	B12	
Altınyaka, *Turkey*	39	E12	
Altınyayla, *Turkey*	39	D11	
Altkirch, *France*	19	E14	
Altmark, *Germany*	24	C7	
Altmühl →, *Germany*	25	G7	
Altmunster, *Austria*	26	D6	
Alto Adige = Trentino-Alto Adige □, *Italy*	29	B8	
Alto Araguaia, *Brazil*	125	G8	
Alto Cuchumatanes = Cuchumatanes, Sierra de los, *Guatemala*	120	C1	
Alto del Inca, *Chile*	126	A2	
Alto Ligonha, *Mozam.*	87	F4	
Alto Molocue, *Mozam.*	87	F4	
Alto Paraguai, *Brazil*	125	F7	
Alto Paraná □, *Paraguay*	127	B5	
Alton, *Canada*	110	C4	
Alton, *U.K.*	13	F7	
Alton, *U.S.A.*	112	F9	
Alton Downs, *Australia*	95	D2	
Altoona, *U.S.A.*	110	F6	
Altötting, *Germany*	25	G8	
Altstätten, *Switz.*	25	H5	
Altūn Kūprī, *Iraq*	70	C5	
Altun Shan, *China*	60	C3	
Alturas, *U.S.A.*	114	F3	
Altus, *U.S.A.*	113	H5	
Alubijid, *Phil.*	61	G6	
Alucra, *Turkey*	73	B8	
Alūksne, *Latvia*	9	H22	
Alunda, *Sweden*	10	D12	
Alunite, *U.S.A.*	117	K12	
Alupka, *Ukraine*	47	K8	
Alushta, *Ukraine*	47	K8	
Alusi, *Indonesia*	63	F8	
Alustante, *Spain*	32	E3	
Alva, *U.S.A.*	113	G5	
Alvaiázere, *Portugal*	34	F2	
Älvängen, *Sweden*	11	G6	
Alvarado, *Mexico*	119	D5	
Alvarado, *U.S.A.*	113	J6	
Alvaro Obregón, Presa, *Mexico*	118	B3	
Alvear, *Argentina*	126	B4	
Alverca, *Portugal*	35	G1	
Alvesta, *Sweden*	11	H8	
Alvie, *Australia*	95	F3	
Alvin, *U.S.A.*	113	L7	
Alvinston, *Canada*	110	D3	
Alvito, *Portugal*	35	G3	
Älvkarleby, *Sweden*	10	D11	
Älvros, *Sweden*	10	B8	
Älvsborgs län □, *Sweden*	11	F6	
Älvsbyn, *Sweden*	8	D19	
Alwar, *India*	68	F7	
Alxa Zuoqi, *China*	56	E3	
Alyata = Älät, *Azerbaijan*	49	L9	
Alyth, *U.K.*	14	E5	
Alytus, *Lithuania*	9	J21	
Alzada, *U.S.A.*	112	C2	
Alzey, *Germany*	25	F4	
Am-Timan, *Chad*	79	F10	
Amadeus, L., *Australia*	93	D5	
Amadi, Dem. Rep. of the Congo	86	B2	
Amâdi, *Sudan*	81	F3	
Amadjuak L., *Canada*	101	B12	
Amadora, *Portugal*	35	G1	
Amagasaki, *Japan*	55	G7	
Amagi, *Japan*	55	H5	
Amakusa-Shotō, *Japan*	55	H5	
Åmål, *Sweden*	10	E6	
Amalfi, *Italy*	31	B7	
Amaliás, *Greece*	38	D3	
Amalner, *India*	66	J9	

Amambaí, *Brazil*	127	A4	
Amambaí →, *Brazil*	127	A5	
Amambay □, *Paraguay*	127	A4	
Amambay, Cordillera de, *S. Amer.*	127	A4	
Amami-Guntō, *Japan*	55	L4	
Amami-Ō-Shima, *Japan*	55	L4	
Amaná, L., *Brazil*	124	D6	
Amanda Park, *U.S.A.*	116	C3	
Amangeldy, *Kazakstan*	50	D7	
Amantea, *Italy*	31	C9	
Amapá, *Brazil*	125	C8	
Amapá □, *Brazil*	125	C8	
Amara, *Sudan*	81	E3	
Amarante, *Brazil*	125	E10	
Amarante, *Portugal*	34	D2	
Amaranth, *Canada*	105	C9	
Amareleja, *Portugal*	35	G3	
Amargosa →, *U.S.A.*	117	J10	
Amargosa Range, *U.S.A.*	117	J10	
Amári, *Greece*	36	D6	
Amarillo, *U.S.A.*	113	H4	
Amaro, Mte., *Italy*	29	F11	
Amarpur, *India*	69	G12	
Amasra, *Turkey*	72	B5	
Amassama, *Nigeria*	83	D6	
Amasya, *Turkey*	72	B6	
Amatikulu, *S. Africa*	89	D5	
Amatitlán, *Guatemala*	120	D1	
Amatrice, *Italy*	29	F10	
Amay, *Belgium*	17	D5	
Amazon = Amazonas →, *S. Amer.*	122	D5	
Amazonas □, *Brazil*	124	E6	
Amazonas →, *S. Amer.*	122	D5	
Ambahakily, *Madag.*	89	C7	
Ambala, *India*	68	D7	
Ambalavao, *Madag.*	89	C8	
Ambalindum, *Australia*	94	C2	
Ambanja, *Madag.*	89	A8	
Ambarchik, *Russia*	51	C17	
Ambarijeby, *Madag.*	89	A8	
Ambaro, Helodranon', *Madag.*	89	A8	
Ambato, *Ecuador*	124	D3	
Ambato, Sierra de, *Argentina*	126	B2	
Ambato Boeny, *Madag.*	89	B8	
Ambatofinandrahana, *Madag.*	89	C8	
Ambatolampy, *Madag.*	89	B8	
Ambatondrazaka, *Madag.*	89	B8	
Ambatosoratra, *Madag.*	89	B8	
Ambelón, *Greece*	38	B4	
Ambenja, *Madag.*	89	B8	
Amberg, *Germany*	25	F7	
Ambergris Cay, *Belize*	119	D7	
Ambérieu-en-Bugey, *France*	21	C9	
Amberley, *N.Z.*	91	K4	
Ambert, *France*	20	C7	
Ambidédi, *Mali*	82	C2	
Ambikapur, *India*	69	H10	
Ambikol, *Sudan*	80	C3	
Ambilobé, *Madag.*	89	A8	
Ambinanindrano, *Madag.*	89	C8	
Amble, *U.K.*	12	B6	
Ambleside, *U.K.*	12	C5	
Ambo, *Ethiopia*	81	F4	
Ambo, *Peru*	124	F3	
Ambodifototra, *Madag.*	89	B8	
Ambodilazana, *Madag.*	89	B8	
Ambohimahasoa, *Madag.*	89	C8	
Ambohimanga, *Madag.*	89	C8	
Ambohitra, *Madag.*	89	A8	
Amboise, *France*	18	E8	
Amboseli, L., *Kenya*	86	C4	
Ambositra, *Madag.*	89	C8	
Ambovombé, *Madag.*	89	D8	
Amboy, *U.S.A.*	117	L11	
Amboyna Cay, S. China Sea	62	C4	
Ambridge, *U.S.A.*	110	F4	
Ambriz, *Angola*	84	F2	
Amby, *Australia*	95	D4	
Amchitka I., *U.S.A.*	100	C1	
Amderma, *Russia*	50	C7	
Ameca, *Mexico*	118	C4	
Ameca →, *Mexico*	118	C3	
Amecameca, *Mexico*	119	D5	
Ameland, *Neths.*	17	A5	
Amélia, *Italy*	29	F9	
Amendolara, *Italy*	31	C9	
American Falls, *U.S.A.*	114	E7	
American Falls Reservoir, *U.S.A.*	114	E7	
American Highland, *Antarctica*	5	D6	
American Samoa ■, Pac. Oc.	91	B13	
Americana, *Brazil*	127	A6	
Americus, *U.S.A.*	109	K3	
Amersfoort, *Neths.*	17	B5	
Amersfoort, *S. Africa*	89	D4	
Amery, *Australia*	93	F2	
Amery, *Canada*	105	B10	
Amery Ice Shelf, *Antarctica*	5	C6	
Ames, *Spain*	34	C2	
Ames, *U.S.A.*	112	E8	
Amesbury, *U.S.A.*	111	D14	
Amfíklia, *Greece*	38	C4	
Amfilokhía, *Greece*	38	C3	
Amfípolis, *Greece*	40	F7	
Amfissa, *Greece*	38	C4	
Amga, *Russia*	51	C14	
Amga →, *Russia*	51	C14	
Amgu, *Russia*	54	B8	

Amgun →, *Russia*	51	D14	
Amherst, *Burma*	67	L20	
Amherst, *Canada*	103	C7	
Amherst, *Mass., U.S.A.*	111	D12	
Amherst, *N.Y., U.S.A.*	110	D6	
Amherst, *Ohio, U.S.A.*	110	E2	
Amherst, *Tex., U.S.A.*	113	J3	
Amherst I., *Canada*	111	B8	
Amherstburg, *Canada*	102	D3	
Amiata, Mte., *Italy*	29	F8	
Amiens, *France*	19	C9	
Amindaion, *Greece*	40	F5	
Åminne, *Sweden*	11	G7	
Amīrābād, *Iran*	70	C5	
Amirante Is., *Seychelles*	52	K9	
Amisk L., *Canada*	105	C8	
Amistad, Presa de la, *Mexico*	118	B4	
Amite, *U.S.A.*	113	K9	
Amlwch, *U.K.*	12	D3	
Amm Adam, *Sudan*	81	D4	
'Ammān, *Jordan*	75	D4	
'Ammān □, *Jordan*	75	D5	
Ammanford, *U.K.*	13	F4	
Ammassalik = Angmagssalik, *Greenland*	4	C6	
Ammerån →, *Sweden*	10	A10	
Ammersee, *Germany*	25	G7	
Amnat Charoen, *Thailand*	64	E5	
Amo Jiang →, *China*	58	F3	
Åmol, *Iran*	71	B7	
Amorgós, *Greece*	39	E7	
Amory, *U.S.A.*	109	J1	
Amos, *Canada*	102	C4	
Åmot, *Norway*	9	G13	
Åmotfors, *Sweden*	10	E6	
Amoy = Xiamen, *China*	59	E12	
Ampang, *Malaysia*	65	L3	
Ampanihy, *Madag.*	89	C7	
Ampasinava, Helodranon', *Madag.*	89	A8	
Ampasindava, Saikanosy, *Madag.*	89	A8	
Ampenan, *Indonesia*	62	F5	
Amper, *Nigeria*	83	D6	
Amper →, *Germany*	25	G7	
Ampezzo, *Italy*	29	B9	
Amposta, *Spain*	32	E5	
Ampotaka, *Madag.*	89	D7	
Ampoza, *Madag.*	89	C7	
Amqui, *Canada*	103	C6	
Amravati, *India*	66	J10	
Amreli, *India*	68	J4	
Amritsar, *India*	68	D6	
Amroha, *India*	69	E8	
Amrum, *Germany*	24	A4	
Amsterdam, *Neths.*	17	B4	
Amsterdam, *U.S.A.*	111	D10	
Amsterdam, I., *Ind. Oc.*	3	F13	
Amstetten, *Austria*	26	C7	
Amudarya →, *Uzbekistan*	50	E6	
Amundsen Gulf, *Canada*	100	A7	
Amundsen Sea, *Antarctica*	5	D15	
Amungen, *Sweden*	10	C9	
Amuntai, *Indonesia*	62	E5	
Amur →, *Russia*	51	D15	
Amurang, *Indonesia*	63	D6	
Amuri Pass, *N.Z.*	91	K4	
Amurrio, *Spain*	32	B1	
Amursk, *Russia*	51	D14	
Amusco, *Spain*	34	C6	
Amvrakikós Kólpos, *Greece*	38	C2	
Amvrosiyivka, *Ukraine*	47	J10	
Amyderya = Amudarya →, *Uzbekistan*	50	E6	
An Bien, *Vietnam*	65	H5	
An Hoa, *Vietnam*	64	E7	
An Nabīyah at Tahta, *Lebanon*	75	B4	
An Nabk, *Si. Arabia*	70	D3	
An Nabk, *Syria*	75	A5	
An Nabk Abū Qaşr, *Si. Arabia*	70	D3	
An Nafūd, *Si. Arabia*	70	D4	
An Najaf, *Iraq*	70	C5	
An Nāşirīyah, *Iraq*	70	D5	
An Nhon, *Vietnam*	64	F7	
An Nîl □, *Sudan*	80	D3	
An Nîl el Abyad □, *Sudan*	81	E3	
An Nîl el Azraq □, *Sudan*	81	E3	
An Nu'ayrīyah, *Si. Arabia*	71	E6	
An Nuwayb'ī, W. →, *Si. Arabia*	75	B3	
An Thoi, Dao, *Vietnam*	65	H5	
An Uaimh, *Ireland*	15	C5	
Anabar →, *Russia*	51	B12	
'Anabtā, *West Bank*	75	C4	
Anaconda, *U.S.A.*	114	C7	
Anacortes, *U.S.A.*	116	B4	
Anacuao, Mt., *Phil.*	61	C4	
Anadarko, *U.S.A.*	113	H5	
Anadia, *Portugal*	34	E2	
Anadolu, *Turkey*	72	C5	
Anadyr, *Russia*	51	C18	
Anadyr →, *Russia*	51	C18	
Anadyrskiy Zaliv, *Russia*	51	C19	
Anáfi, *Greece*	39	E7	
Anafópolis, *Greece*	39	E7	
Anaga, Pta. de, *Canary Is.*	37	F3	
'Ānah, *Iraq*	70	C4	
Anaheim, *U.S.A.*	117	M9	
Anahim Lake, *Canada*	104	C3	
Anáhuac, *Mexico*	118	B4	
Anakapalle, *India*	67	L13	

Anakie, *Australia*	94	C4
Anaklia, *Georgia*	49	J5
Analalava, *Madag.*	89	A8
Análipsis, *Greece*	36	A3
Anambar →, *Pakistan*	68	D3
Anambas, Kepulauan, *Indonesia*	65	L6
Anambas Is. = Anambas, Kepulauan, *Indonesia*	65	L6
Anambra □, *Nigeria*	83	D6
Anamoose, *U.S.A.*	112	B4
Anamosa, *U.S.A.*	112	D9
Anamur, *Turkey*	72	D5
Anamur Burnu, *Turkey*	72	D5
Anan, *Japan*	55	H7
Anand, *India*	68	H5
Ánanes, *Greece*	38	E6
Anantnag, *India*	69	C6
Ananyiv, *Ukraine*	47	J5
Anapa, *Russia*	47	K9
Anapodháris →, *Greece*	36	E7
Anápolis, *Brazil*	125	G9
Anapu →, *Brazil*	125	D8
Anār, *Iran*	71	D7
Anārak, *Iran*	71	C7
Anarisfjällen, *Sweden*	10	A7
Anatolia = Anadolu, *Turkey*	72	C5
Anatone, *U.S.A.*	114	C5
Anatsogno, *Madag.*	89	C7
Añatuya, *Argentina*	126	B3
Anaunethad L., *Canada*	105	A8
Anbyŏn, *N. Korea*	57	E14
Ancares, Sierra de, *Spain*	34	C4
Ancenis, *France*	18	E5
Anchor Bay, *U.S.A.*	116	G3
Anchorage, *U.S.A.*	100	B5
Anci, *China*	56	E9
Ancohuma, Nevada, *Bolivia*	122	E4
Ancón, *Peru*	124	F3
Ancona, *Italy*	29	E10
Ancud, *Chile*	128	E2
Ancud, G. de, *Chile*	128	E2
Ancy-le-Franc, *France*	19	E11
Andacollo, *Argentina*	126	D1
Andacollo, *Chile*	126	C1
Andado, *Australia*	94	D2
Andalgalá, *Argentina*	126	B2
Åndalsnes, *Norway*	9	E12
Andalucía □, *Spain*	35	H6
Andalusia, *U.S.A.*	109	K2
Andalusia □ = Andalucía □, *Spain*	35	H6
Andaman Is., *Ind. Oc.*	52	H13
Andaman Sea, *Ind. Oc.*	62	B1
Andara, *Namibia*	88	B3
Andelot-Blancheville, *France*	19	D12
Andenes, *Norway*	8	B17
Andenne, *Belgium*	17	D5
Andéranboukane, *Mali*	83	B5
Andermatt, *Switz.*	25	J4
Andernos-les-Bains, *France*	20	D2
Andernach, *Germany*	24	E3
Anderslöv, *Sweden*	11	J7
Anderson, *Calif., U.S.A.*	114	F2
Anderson, *Ind., U.S.A.*	108	E3
Anderson, *Mo., U.S.A.*	113	G7
Anderson, *S.C., U.S.A.*	109	H4
Anderson →, *Canada*	100	B7
Anderstorp, *Sweden*	11	G7
Andes, Cord. de los, *S. Amer.*	122	F4
Andfjorden, *Norway*	8	B17
Andhra Pradesh □, *India*	66	L11
Andijon, *Uzbekistan*	50	E8
Andikíthira, *Greece*	38	F5
Andīmeshk, *Iran*	71	C6
Andímilos, *Greece*	38	E6
Andíparos, *Greece*	39	D7
Andípaxoi, *Greece*	38	B2
Andípsara, *Greece*	39	C7
Andírrion, *Greece*	38	C3
Andizhan = Andijon, *Uzbekistan*	50	E8
Andoain, *Spain*	32	B2
Andoany, *Madag.*	89	A8
Andong, *S. Korea*	57	F15
Andongwei, *China*	57	G10
Andorra, *Spain*	32	E4
Andorra ■, *Europe*	20	F5
Andorra La Vella, *Andorra*	20	F5
Andover, *U.K.*	13	F6
Andover, *Mass., U.S.A.*	111	D13
Andover, *N.Y., U.S.A.*	110	D7
Andover, *Ohio, U.S.A.*	110	E4
Andøya, *Norway*	8	B16
Andradina, *Brazil*	125	H8
Andraháry, Mt., *Madag.*	89	A8
Andramasina, *Madag.*	89	B8
Andranopasy, *Madag.*	89	C7
Andratx, *Spain*	37	B9
Andreanof Is., *U.S.A.*	100	C2
Andreapol, *Russia*	46	D7
Andrewilla, *Australia*	95	D2
Andrews, *S.C., U.S.A.*	109	J6
Andrews, *Tex., U.S.A.*	113	J3
Andreyevka, *Russia*	48	D10
Ándria, *Italy*	31	A9
Andriba, *Madag.*	89	B8
Andrijevica, *Montenegro, Yug.*	40	D3
Andrítsaina, *Greece*	38	D3
Androka, *Madag.*	89	C7
Andropov = Rybinsk, *Russia*	46	C10
Ándros, *Greece*	38	D6
Andros I., *Bahamas*	120	B4
Andros Town, *Bahamas*	120	B4
Andrychów, *Poland*	45	J6
Andselv, *Norway*	8	B18
Andújar, *Spain*	35	G6
Andulo, *Angola*	84	G3
Aneby, *Sweden*	11	G8
Anegada I., *Virgin Is.*	121	C7
Anegada Passage, *W. Indies*	121	C7
Aného, *Togo*	83	D5
Anenni-Noi, *Moldova*	43	D14
Aneto, Pico de, *Spain*	32	C5
Anfu, *China*	59	D10
Ang Thong, *Thailand*	64	E3
Angamos, Punta, *Chile*	126	A1
Ang'angxi, *China*	60	B7
Angara →, *Russia*	51	D10
Angarab, *Ethiopia*	81	E4
Angarsk, *Russia*	51	D11
Angas Downs, *Australia*	93	E5
Angas Hills, *Australia*	92	D4
Angaston, *Australia*	95	E2
Ånge, *Sweden*	10	B9
Ángel, Salto = Angel Falls, *Venezuela*	124	B6
Ángel de la Guarda, I., *Mexico*	118	B2
Angel Falls, *Venezuela*	124	B6
Angeles, *Phil.*	61	D4
Ängelholm, *Sweden*	11	H6
Angellala, *Australia*	95	D4
Angels Camp, *U.S.A.*	116	G6
Ängelsberg, *Sweden*	10	E10
Anger →, *Ethiopia*	81	F4
Angereb →, *Ethiopia*	81	E4
Ångermanälven →, *Sweden*	10	B11
Ångermanland, *Sweden*	8	E18
Angermünde, *Germany*	24	B9
Angers, *Canada*	111	A9
Angers, *France*	18	E6
Angerville, *France*	19	D9
Ängesån →, *Sweden*	8	C20
Angikuni L., *Canada*	105	A9
Angkor, *Cambodia*	64	F4
Anglès, *Spain*	32	D7
Anglesey, *U.K.*	12	D3
Anglesey, Isle of □, *U.K.*	12	D3
Anglet, *France*	20	E2
Angleton, *U.S.A.*	113	L7
Anglin →, *France*	20	B4
Anglisidhes, *Cyprus*	36	E12
Anglure, *France*	19	D10
Angmagssalik, *Greenland*	4	C6
Ango, *Dem. Rep. of the Congo*	86	B2
Angoche, *Mozam.*	87	F4
Angoche, I., *Mozam.*	87	F4
Angol, *Chile*	126	D1
Angola, *Ind., U.S.A.*	108	E3
Angola, *N.Y., U.S.A.*	110	D5
Angola ■, *Africa*	85	G3
Angoon, *U.S.A.*	104	B2
Angoulême, *France*	20	C4
Angoumois, *France*	20	C4
Angra dos Reis, *Brazil*	127	A7
Angren, *Uzbekistan*	50	E8
Anguang, *China*	57	B12
Anguilla ■, *W. Indies*	121	C7
Anguo, *China*	56	E8
Angurugu, *Australia*	94	A2
Angus, *U.K.*	14	E6
Anhanduí →, *Brazil*	127	A5
Anholt, *Denmark*	11	H5
Anhua, *China*	59	C8
Anhui □, *China*	59	B11
Anhwei □ = Anhui □, *China*	59	B11
Anichab, *Namibia*	88	C1
Ánidhros, *Greece*	39	E7
Anié, *Togo*	83	D5
Animas, *U.S.A.*	115	L9
Anina, *Romania*	42	E6
Aninoasa, *Romania*	43	F9
Anivorano, *Madag.*	89	B8
Anjalankoski, *Finland*	9	F22
Anjar, *India*	68	H4
Anjidiv I., *India*	66	M9
Anjou, *France*	18	E6
Anjozorobe, *Madag.*	89	B8
Anju, *N. Korea*	57	E13
Anka, *Nigeria*	83	C6
Ankaboa, Tanjona, *Madag.*	89	C7
Ankang, *China*	56	H5
Ankara, *Turkey*	72	C5
Ankaramena, *Madag.*	89	C8
Ankarsrum, *Sweden*	11	G10
Ankazoabo, *Madag.*	89	C7
Ankazobe, *Madag.*	89	B8
Ankisabe, *Madag.*	89	B8
Anklam, *Germany*	24	B9
Ankober, *Ethiopia*	81	F4
Ankoro, *Dem. Rep. of the Congo*	86	D2
Anlong, *China*	58	E5
Anlu, *China*	59	B9
Anmyŏn-do, *S. Korea*	57	F14
Ånn, *Sweden*	10	A6
Ann, C., *U.S.A.*	111	D14
Ann Arbor, *U.S.A.*	108	D4
Anna, *Russia*	48	E5
Anna, *U.S.A.*	113	G10
Anna Plains, *Australia*	92	C3
Annaba, *Algeria*	78	A7
Annaberg-Buchholz, *Germany*	24	E9
Annalee →, *Ireland*	15	B4
Annam, *Vietnam*	64	E7
Annamitique, Chaîne, *Asia*	64	D6
Annan, *U.K.*	14	G5
Annan →, *U.K.*	14	G5
Annapolis, *U.S.A.*	108	F7
Annapolis Royal, *Canada*	103	D6
Annapurna, *Nepal*	69	E10
Annean, L., *Australia*	93	E2
Anneberg, *Sweden*	11	G8
Annecy, *France*	21	C10
Annecy, L. d', *France*	21	C10
Annemasse, *France*	19	F13
Anning, *China*	58	E4
Anningie, *Australia*	92	D5
Anniston, *U.S.A.*	109	J3
Annobón, *Atl. Oc.*	77	G4
Annonay, *France*	21	C8
Annot, *France*	21	E10
Annotto Bay, *Jamaica*	120	C4
Ánnsjön, *Sweden*	10	A6
Annuello, *Australia*	95	E3
Annville, *U.S.A.*	111	F8
Annweiler, *Germany*	25	F3
Áno Arkhánai, *Greece*	39	F7
Áno Porróia, *Greece*	40	E7
Áno Síros, *Greece*	38	D6
Áno Viánnos, *Greece*	36	D7
Anorotsangana, *Madag.*	89	A8
Anóyia, *Greece*	36	D6
Anping, *Hebei, China*	56	E8
Anping, *Liaoning, China*	57	D12
Anpu Gang, *China*	58	G7
Anqing, *China*	59	B11
Anqiu, *China*	57	F10
Anren, *China*	59	D9
Ansager, *Denmark*	11	J2
Ansai, *China*	56	F5
Ansbach, *Germany*	25	F6
Anseba →, *Eritrea*	81	D4
Ansfelden, *Austria*	26	C7
Anshan, *China*	57	D12
Anshun, *China*	58	D5
Ansião, *Portugal*	34	F2
Ansley, *U.S.A.*	112	E5
Ansó, *Spain*	32	C4
Ansoain, *Spain*	32	C3
Anson, *U.S.A.*	113	J5
Anson B., *Australia*	92	B5
Ansongo, *Mali*	83	B5
Ansonia, *U.S.A.*	111	E11
Anstruther, *U.K.*	14	E6
Ansudu, *Indonesia*	63	E9
Antabamba, *Peru*	124	F4
Antakya, *Turkey*	72	D7
Antalaha, *Madag.*	89	A9
Antalya, *Turkey*	72	D4
Antalya □, *Turkey*	39	E12
Antalya Körfezi, *Turkey*	72	D4
Antananarivo, *Madag.*	89	B8
Antananarivo □, *Madag.*	89	B8
Antanimbaribe, *Madag.*	89	C7
Antarctic Pen., *Antarctica*	5	C18
Antarctica	5	E3
Antelope, *Zimbabwe*	87	G2
Antequera, *Paraguay*	126	A4
Antequera, *Spain*	35	H6
Antero, Mt., *U.S.A.*	115	G10
Anthemoús, *Greece*	40	F7
Anthony, *Kans., U.S.A.*	113	G5
Anthony, *N. Mex., U.S.A.*	115	K10
Anthony Lagoon, *Australia*	94	B2
Anti Atlas, *Morocco*	78	C4
Anti-Lebanon = Ash Sharqi, Al Jabal, *Lebanon*	75	B5
Antibes, *France*	21	E11
Antibes, C. d', *France*	21	E11
Anticosti, Î. d', *Canada*	103	C7
Antifer, C. d', *France*	18	C7
Antigo, *U.S.A.*	112	C10
Antigonish, *Canada*	103	C7
Antigua, *Canary Is.*	37	F5
Antigua, *Guatemala*	120	D1
Antigua ■, *W. Indies*	121	C7
Antigua & Barbuda ■, *W. Indies*	121	C7
Antigua Guatemala, *Guatemala*	120	D1
Antilla, *Cuba*	120	B4
Antimony, *U.S.A.*	115	G8
Antioch, *U.S.A.*	116	G5
Antioche, Pertuis d', *France*	20	B2
Antioquia, *Colombia*	124	B3
Antipodes Is., *Pac. Oc.*	96	M9
Antler, *U.S.A.*	112	A4
Antler →, *Canada*	105	D8
Antlers, *U.S.A.*	113	H7
Antofagasta, *Chile*	126	A1
Antofagasta □, *Chile*	126	A2
Antofagasta de la Sierra, *Argentina*	126	B2
Antofalla, *Argentina*	126	B2
Antofalla, Salar de, *Argentina*	126	B2
Anton, *U.S.A.*	113	J3
Anton Chico, *U.S.A.*	115	J11
Antongila, Helodrano, *Madag.*	89	B8
Antonibé, *Madag.*	89	B8
Antonibé, Presqu'île d', *Madag.*	89	A8
Antonina, *Brazil*	127	B6
Antonito, *U.S.A.*	115	H10
Antrain, *France*	18	D5
Antrim, *U.K.*	15	B5
Antrim □, *U.K.*	15	B5
Antrim, Mts. of, *U.K.*	15	A5
Antrim Plateau, *Australia*	92	C4
Antrodoco, *Italy*	29	F10
Antropovo, *Russia*	48	A6
Antsalova, *Madag.*	89	B7
Antsirabe, *Madag.*	89	B8
Antsiranana, *Madag.*	89	A8
Antsohihy, *Madag.*	89	A8
Antsohimbondrona Seranana, *Madag.*	89	A8
Antu, *China*	57	C15
Antwerp = Antwerpen, *Belgium*	17	C4
Antwerp, *U.S.A.*	111	B9
Antwerpen, *Belgium*	17	C4
Antwerpen □, *Belgium*	17	C4
Anupgarh, *India*	68	E5
Anuradhapura, *Sri Lanka*	66	Q12
Anveh, *Iran*	71	E7
Anvers = Antwerpen, *Belgium*	17	C4
Anvers I., *Antarctica*	5	C17
Anxi, *Fujian, China*	59	E12
Anxi, *Gansu, China*	60	B4
Anxiang, *China*	59	C9
Anxious B., *Australia*	95	E1
Anyama, *Ivory C.*	82	D4
Anyang, *China*	56	F8
Anyi, *Jiangxi, China*	59	C10
Anyi, *Shanxi, China*	56	G6
Anyuan, *China*	59	E10
Anza, *U.S.A.*	117	M10
Anze, *China*	56	F7
Anzhero-Sudzhensk, *Russia*	50	D9
Ánzio, *Italy*	30	A5
Aoga-Shima, *Japan*	55	H9
Aoiz, *Spain*	32	C3
Aomori, *Japan*	54	D10
Aomori □, *Japan*	54	D10
Aonla, *India*	69	E8
Aosta, *Italy*	28	C4
Aoudéras, *Niger*	83	B6
Aouker, *Mauritania*	82	B3
Apa →, *S. Amer.*	126	A4
Apache, *U.S.A.*	113	H5
Apalachee B., *U.S.A.*	109	L4
Apalachicola, *U.S.A.*	109	L3
Apalachicola →, *U.S.A.*	109	L3
Apapa, *Nigeria*	83	D5
Apaporis →, *Colombia*	124	D5
Aparri, *Phil.*	61	B4
Apateu, *Romania*	42	D6
Apatin, *Serbia, Yug.*	42	E4
Apatzingán, *Mexico*	118	D4
Apeldoorn, *Neths.*	17	B5
Apen, *Germany*	24	B3
Apennines = Appennini, *Italy*	28	E7
Aphrodisias, *Turkey*	39	D10
Apia, *W. Samoa*	91	A13
Apiacás, Serra dos, *Brazil*	124	E7
Apizaco, *Mexico*	119	D5
Aplao, *Peru*	124	G4
Apo, Mt., *Phil.*	63	C7
Apolakkiá, *Greece*	36	C9
Apolakkiá, Órmos, *Greece*	36	C9
Apolda, *Germany*	24	D7
Apollonia, *Greece*	38	E6
Apolo, *Bolivia*	124	F5
Aporé →, *Brazil*	125	G8
Apostle Is., *U.S.A.*	112	B9
Apóstoles, *Argentina*	127	B4
Apostolos Andreas, C., *Cyprus*	36	D13
Apostolovo, *Ukraine*	47	J7
Apoteri, *Guyana*	124	C7
Appalachian Mts., *U.S.A.*	108	G6
Äppelbo, *Sweden*	10	D8
Appennini, *Italy*	28	E7
Appennino Ligure, *Italy*	28	D6
Appenzell-Ausser Rhoden □, *Switz.*	25	H5
Appenzell-Inner Rhoden □, *Switz.*	25	H5
Appiano, *Italy*	29	B8
Apple Hill, *Canada*	111	A10
Apple Valley, *U.S.A.*	117	L9
Appleby-in-Westmorland, *U.K.*	12	C5
Appleton, *U.S.A.*	108	C1
Approuague →, *Fr. Guiana*	125	C8
Apricena, *Italy*	29	G12
Aprília, *Italy*	30	A5
Apsheronsk, *Russia*	49	H4
Apt, *France*	21	E9
Apuane, Alpi, *Italy*	28	D7
Apucarana, *Brazil*	127	A5
Apulia = Púglia □, *Italy*	31	A9
Apure →, *Venezuela*	124	B5
Apurímac →, *Peru*	124	F4
Apuseni, Munţii, *Romania*	42	D7
Aqaba = Al 'Aqabah, *Jordan*	75	F4
Aqaba, G. of, *Red Sea*	70	D2
'Aqabah, Khalīj al →, *Red Sea*	70	D2
Aqcheh, *Afghan.*	71	C7
Aqiq, *Sudan*	80	D4
Aqiq, Khalīg, *Sudan*	80	D4
Aqmola = Astana, *Kazakstan*	50	D8
Aqrah, *Iraq*	70	B4
Aqtöbe, *Kazakstan*	50	D6
Aquidauana, *Brazil*	125	H7
Aquiles Serdán, *Mexico*	118	B3
Aquin, *Haiti*	121	C5
Aquitaine □, *France*	20	D3
Ar Rachidiya, *Morocco*	78	B5
Ar Rafid, *Syria*	75	C4
Ar Raḥḥālīyah, *Iraq*	70	C4
Ar Ramādī, *Iraq*	70	C4
Ar Ramthā, *Jordan*	75	C5
Ar Raqqah, *Syria*	70	C3
Ar Rass, *Si. Arabia*	70	E4
Ar Rifā'ī, *Iraq*	70	D5
Ar Riyāḍ, *Si. Arabia*	70	E5
Ar Ru'ays, *Qatar*	71	E6
Ar Rukhaymīyah, *Iraq*	70	D5
Ar Ruqayyidah, *Si. Arabia*	71	E6
Ar Ruṣāfah, *Syria*	70	C3
Ar Ruṭbah, *Iraq*	70	C4
Ara, *India*	69	G11
'Arab, Bahr →, *Sudan*	81	F2
'Arabābād, *Iran*	71	C8
Araban, *Turkey*	72	D7
Arabatskaya Strelka, *Ukraine*	47	K8
Arabba, *Italy*	29	B8
Arabia, *Asia*	52	G8
Arabian Desert = Es Sahrâ' Esh Sharqîya, *Egypt*	80	B3
Arabian Gulf = Gulf, The, *Asia*	71	E6
Arabian Sea, *Ind. Oc.*	52	H10
Araç, *Turkey*	72	B5
Aracaju, *Brazil*	125	F11
Aracati, *Brazil*	125	D11
Araçatuba, *Brazil*	127	A5
Aracena, *Spain*	35	H4
Aracena, Sierra de, *Spain*	35	H4
Aračinovo, *Macedonia*	40	D5
Araçuaí, *Brazil*	125	G10
'Arad, *Israel*	75	D4
Arad, *Romania*	42	D6
Arad □, *Romania*	42	D6
Aradhippou, *Cyprus*	36	E12
Arafura Sea, *E. Indies*	63	F9
Aragats, *Armenia*	49	K7
Aragón □, *Spain*	32	C5
Aragona, *Italy*	30	E6
Araguacema, *Brazil*	125	E9
Araguaia →, *Brazil*	122	D6
Araguaína, *Brazil*	125	E9
Araguari, *Brazil*	125	G9
Araguari →, *Brazil*	125	C9
Arak, *Algeria*	78	C6
Arāk, *Iran*	71	C6
Arakan Coast, *Burma*	67	K19
Arakan Yoma, *Burma*	67	K19
Arákhova, *Greece*	38	C4
Arakli, *Turkey*	73	B8
Araks = Aras, Rūd-e →, *Azerbaijan*	70	B5
Aral, *Kazakstan*	50	E7
Aral Sea, *Asia*	50	E7
Aral Tengizi = Aral Sea, *Asia*	50	E7
Aralsk = Aral, *Kazakstan*	50	E7
Aralskoye More = Aral Sea, *Asia*	50	E7
Aralsor, Ozero, *Kazakstan*	49	F9
Aramac, *Australia*	94	C4
Arambag, *India*	69	H12
Aran I., *Ireland*	15	A3
Aran Is., *Ireland*	15	C2
Aranda de Duero, *Spain*	34	D7
Arandān, *Iran*	70	C5
Arandjelovac, *Serbia, Yug.*	40	B4
Aranjuez, *Spain*	34	E7
Aranos, *Namibia*	88	C2
Aransas Pass, *U.S.A.*	113	M6
Aranyaprathet, *Thailand*	64	F4
Araouane, *Mali*	82	B4
Arapahoe, *U.S.A.*	112	E5
Arapey Grande →, *Uruguay*	126	C4
Arapgir, *Turkey*	73	C8
Arapiraca, *Brazil*	125	E11
Arapongas, *Brazil*	127	A5
Ar'ar, *Si. Arabia*	70	D4
Araranguá, *Brazil*	127	B6
Araraquara, *Brazil*	125	H9
Ararás, Serra das, *Brazil*	127	B5
Ararat, *Armenia*	73	C11
Ararat, *Australia*	95	F3
Ararat, Mt. = Ağrı Dağı, *Turkey*	73	C11
Araria, *India*	69	F12
Araripe, Chapada do, *Brazil*	125	E11
Araruama, L. de, *Brazil*	127	A7
Aras, Rūd-e →, *Azerbaijan*	70	B5
Arauca, *Colombia*	124	B4
Arauca →, *Venezuela*	124	B5
Arauco, *Chile*	126	D1
Arauco □, *Chile*	126	D1
Arawa, *Ethiopia*	81	F5
Araxá, *Brazil*	125	G9
Araya, Pen. de, *Venezuela*	124	A6
Arba Minch, *Ethiopia*	81	F4
Arbaʼin, *Iraq*	70	C5
Árbatax, *Italy*	30	C2
Arbīl, *Iraq*	70	B5
Arboga, *Sweden*	10	E9
Arbois, *France*	19	F12

Arbore

Arbore, *Ethiopia* 81 F4
Arboréa, *Italy* 30 C1
Arborfield, *Canada* 105 C8
Arborg, *Canada* 105 C9
Arbroath, *U.K.* 14 E6
Arbuckle, *U.S.A.* 116 F4
Arbus, *Italy* 30 C1
Arc →, *France* 21 C10
Arc-lès-Gray, *France* 19 E12
Arcachon, *France* 20 D2
Arcachon, Bassin d', *France* 20 D2
Arcade, *U.S.A.* 110 D6
Arcadia, *Fla., U.S.A.* ... 109 M5
Arcadia, *La., U.S.A.* 113 J8
Arcadia, *Nebr., U.S.A.* ... 112 E5
Arcadia, *Pa., U.S.A.* 110 F6
Arcadia, *Wis., U.S.A.* ... 112 C9
Arcata, *U.S.A.* 114 F1
Arcévia, *Italy* 29 E9
Archangel = Arkhangelsk, *Russia* 50 C5
Archar, *Bulgaria* 40 C6
Archbald, *U.S.A.* 111 E9
Archena, *Spain* 33 G3
Archer →, *Australia* 94 A3
Archer B., *Australia* 94 A3
Archers Post, *Kenya* 86 B4
Archidona, *Spain* 35 H6
Arci, Mte., *Italy* 30 C1
Arcidosso, *Italy* 29 F8
Arcis-sur-Aube, *France* .. 19 D11
Arckaringa, *Australia* ... 95 D1
Arckaringa Cr. →, *Australia* 95 D2
Arco, *Italy* 28 C7
Arco, *U.S.A.* 114 E7
Arcola, *Canada* 105 D8
Arcos = Arcos de Jalón, *Spain* 32 D2
Arcos de Jalón, *Spain* ... 32 D2
Arcos de la Frontera, *Spain* 35 J5
Arcos de Valdevez, *Portugal* 34 D2
Arcot, *India* 66 N11
Arcozelo, *Portugal* 34 E3
Arctic Bay, *Canada* 101 A11
Arctic Ocean, *Arctic* 4 B18
Arda →, *Bulgaria* 41 E10
Arda →, *Italy* 28 C7
Ardabīl, *Iran* 71 B6
Ardakān = Sepīdān, *Iran* . 71 D7
Ardala, *Sweden* 11 F7
Ardales, *Spain* 35 J6
Ardèche □, *France* 21 D8
Ardèche →, *France* 21 D8
Ardee, *Ireland* 15 C5
Arden, *Canada* 110 B8
Arden, *Denmark* 11 H3
Arden, *Calif., U.S.A.* ... 116 G5
Arden, *Nev., U.S.A.* ... 117 J11
Ardenne, *Belgium* 6 F7
Ardennes = Ardenne, *Belgium* 6 F7
Ardennes □, *France* 19 C11
Ardentes, *France* 19 F8
Arderin, *Ireland* 15 C4
Ardeşen, *Turkey* 73 B9
Ardestān, *Iran* 71 C7
Árdhas →, *Greece* 41 E10
Ardhéa, *Greece* 40 F6
Ardila →, *Portugal* 35 G3
Ardino, *Bulgaria* 41 E9
Ardivachar Pt., *U.K.* 14 D1
Ardlethan, *Australia* 95 E4
Ardmore, *Australia* 94 C2
Ardmore, *Okla., U.S.A.* .. 113 H6
Ardmore, *Pa., U.S.A.* ... 111 G9
Ardmore, *S. Dak., U.S.A.* 112 D3
Ardnamurchan, Pt. of, *U.K.* 14 E2
Ardnave Pt., *U.K.* 14 F2
Ardon, *Russia* 49 J7
Ardore, *Italy* 31 D9
Ardres, *France* 19 B8
Ardrossan, *Australia* 95 E2
Ardrossan, *U.K.* 14 F4
Ards Pen., *U.K.* 15 B6
Ardud, *Romania* 42 C7
Åre, *Sweden* 10 A7
Arecibo, *Puerto Rico* 121 C6
Areia Branca, *Brazil* 125 E11
Arena, Pt., *U.S.A.* 116 G3
Arenas = Las Arenas, *Spain* 34 B6
Arenas de San Pedro, *Spain* 34 E5
Arendal, *Norway* 9 G13
Arendsee, *Germany* 24 C7
Arenys de Mar, *Spain* ... 32 D7
Arenzano, *Italy* 28 D5
Areópolis, *Greece* 38 E4
Arequipa, *Peru* 124 G4
Arero, *Ethiopia* 81 G4
Arès, *France* 20 D2
Arévalo, *Spain* 34 D6
Arezzo, *Italy* 29 E8
Arga →, *Spain* 32 C3
Argalastí, *Greece* 38 B5
Argamasilla de Alba, *Spain* 35 F7
Argamasilla de Calatrava, *Spain* 35 G6
Arganda, *Spain* 34 E7
Arganil, *Portugal* 34 E2
Argelès-Gazost, *France* .. 20 E3
Argelès-sur-Mer, *France* .. 20 F7

Argens →, *France* 21 E10
Argent-sur-Sauldre, *France* 19 E9
Argenta, *Italy* 29 D8
Argentan, *France* 18 D6
Argentário, Mte., *Italy* ... 29 F8
Argentat, *France* 20 C5
Argentera, *Italy* 28 D4
Argenteuil, *France* 19 D9
Argentia, *Canada* 103 C9
Argentina ■, *S. Amer.* ... 128 D3
Argentina Is., *Antarctica* . 5 C17
Argentino, L., *Argentina* . 128 G2
Argenton-Château, *France* 18 F6
Argenton-sur-Creuse, *France* 19 F8
Argeş □, *Romania* 43 F9
Argeş →, *Romania* 43 F11
Arghandab →, *Afghan.* .. 68 D1
Argo, *Sudan* 80 D3
Argolikós Kólpos, *Greece* . 38 D4
Argolís □, *Greece* 38 D4
Argonne, *France* 19 C12
Árgos, *Greece* 38 D4
Árgos Orestikón, *Greece* . 40 F5
Argostólion, *Greece* 38 C2
Arguedas, *Spain* 32 C3
Arguello, Pt., *U.S.A.* ... 117 L6
Arguineguín, *Canary Is.* . 37 G4
Argun →, *Russia* 49 J7
Argun →, *Russia* 51 D13
Argungu, *Nigeria* 83 C5
Argus Pk., *U.S.A.* 117 K9
Argyle, *U.S.A.* 112 A6
Argyle, L., *Australia* 92 C4
Argyll & Bute □, *U.K.* .. 14 E3
Arhavi, *Turkey* 73 B9
Århus, *Denmark* 11 H4
Århus Amtskommune □, *Denmark* 11 H4
Ariadnoye, *Russia* 54 B7
Ariamsvlei, *Namibia* 88 D2
Ariano Irpino, *Italy* 31 A8
Aribinda, *Burkina Faso* .. 83 C4
Arica, *Chile* 124 G4
Arica, *Colombia* 124 D4
Arico, *Canary Is.* 37 F3
Arid, C., *Australia* 93 F3
Arida, *Japan* 55 G7
Ariège □, *France* 20 F5
Ariège →, *France* 20 E5
Arieş →, *Romania* 43 D8
Arilje, *Serbia, Yug.* 40 C4
Arílla, Ákra, *Greece* 36 A3
Arima, *Trin. & Tob.* 121 D7
Arinos →, *Brazil* 122 F5
Ario de Rosales, *Mexico* . 118 D4
Aripuanã, *Brazil* 124 E6
Aripuanã →, *Brazil* 122 D4
Ariquemes, *Brazil* 124 E6
Arisaig, *U.K.* 14 E3
Arîsh, W. el →, *Egypt* .. 80 H8
Arissa, *Ethiopia* 81 E5
Aristazabal I., *Canada* ... 104 C3
Arivaca, *U.S.A.* 115 L8
Arivonimamo, *Madag.* .. 89 B8
Ariza, *Spain* 32 D2
Arizaro, Salar de, *Argentina* 126 A2
Arizona, *Argentina* 126 D2
Arizona □, *U.S.A.* 115 J8
Arizpe, *Mexico* 118 A2
Årjäng, *Sweden* 10 E6
Arjeplog, *Sweden* 8 D18
Arjona, *Colombia* 124 A3
Arjona, *Spain* 35 H6
Arjuna, *Indonesia* 63 G15
Arka, *Russia* 51 C15
Arkadak, *Russia* 48 E6
Arkadelphia, *U.S.A.* 113 H8
Arkadhía □, *Greece* 38 D4
Arkaig, L., *U.K.* 14 E3
Arkalyk = Arqalyk, *Kazakstan* 50 D7
Arkansas □, *U.S.A.* 113 H8
Arkansas →, *U.S.A.* ... 113 J9
Arkansas City, *U.S.A.* .. 113 G6
Árkathos →, *Greece* ... 38 B3
Arkhángelos, *Greece* ... 36 C10
Arkhangelsk, *Russia* 50 C5
Arkhangelskoye, *Russia* . 48 E5
Arkiko, *Eritrea* 81 D4
Arklow, *Ireland* 15 D5
Árkoi, *Greece* 39 D8
Arkona, Kap, *Germany* .. 24 A9
Arkösund, *Sweden* 11 F10
Arkoúdhi, *Greece* 38 C2
Arkticheskiy, Mys, *Russia* 51 A10
Arkul, *Russia* 48 B10
Árla, *Sweden* 10 E10
Arlanza →, *Spain* 34 C6
Arlanzón →, *Spain* 34 C6
Arlberggpass, *Austria* ... 26 D3
Arles, *France* 21 E8
Arlington, *S. Africa* 89 D4
Arlington, *Oreg., U.S.A.* . 114 D3
Arlington, *S. Dak., U.S.A.* 112 C6
Arlington, *Va., U.S.A.* .. 108 F7
Arlington, *Wash., U.S.A.* 116 B4
Arlington Heights, *U.S.A.* 108 D2
Arlon, *Belgium* 17 E5
Arly, *Burkina Faso* 83 C5
Armagh, *U.K.* 15 B5
Armagh □, *U.K.* 15 B5
Armagnac, *France* 20 E4

Armançon →, *France* ... 19 E10
Armavir, *Russia* 49 H5
Armenia, *Colombia* 124 C3
Armenia ■, *Asia* 49 K7
Armeniş, *Romania* 42 E7
Armenistís, Ákra, *Greece* . 36 C9
Armentières, *France* 19 B9
Armidale, *Australia* 95 E5
Armilla, *Spain* 35 H7
Armour, *U.S.A.* 112 D5
Armstrong, B.C., *Canada* 104 C5
Armstrong, Ont., *Canada* . 102 B2
Armstrong, *U.S.A.* 113 M6
Armutlu, *Bursa, Turkey* .. 41 F12
Armutlu, *İzmir, Turkey* .. 39 C9
Arnaía, *Greece* 40 F7
Arnarfjörður, *Iceland* ... 8 D2
Arnaud →, *Canada* 101 C13
Arnauti, C., *Cyprus* 36 D11
Arnay-le-Duc, *France* ... 19 E11
Arnedillo, *Spain* 32 C2
Arnedo, *Spain* 32 C2
Arnett, *U.S.A.* 113 G5
Arnhem, *Neths.* 17 C5
Arnhem, C., *Australia* ... 94 A2
Arnhem B., *Australia* ... 94 A2
Arnhem Land, *Australia* . 94 A1
Árnissa, *Greece* 40 F5
Arno →, *Italy* 28 E7
Arno Bay, *Australia* 95 E2
Arnold, *U.K.* 12 D6
Arnold, *Calif., U.S.A.* ... 116 G6
Arnold, *Nebr., U.S.A.* .. 112 E4
Arnoldstein, *Austria* 26 E6
Arnon →, *France* 19 E9
Arnot, *Canada* 105 B9
Arnøy, *Norway* 8 A19
Arnprior, *Canada* 102 C4
Arnsberg, *Germany* 24 D4
Arnstadt, *Germany* 24 E6
Aroab, *Namibia* 88 D2
Aroánia Óri, *Greece* 38 D4
Aroche, *Spain* 35 H4
Arolsen, *Germany* 24 D5
Aron →, *France* 19 F10
Arona, *Italy* 28 C5
Aroroy, *Phil.* 61 E5
Arosa, Ría de, *Spain* ... 34 C2
Arpajon, *France* 19 D9
Arpajon-sur-Cère, *France* . 20 D6
Arpaşu de Jos, *Romania* . 43 E9
Arqalyk, *Kazakstan* 50 D7
Arrabury, *Australia* 95 D3
Arrah = Ara, *India* 69 G11
Arraiolos, *Portugal* 35 G3
Arran, *U.K.* 14 F3
Arrandale, *Canada* 104 C3
Arras, *France* 19 B9
Arrasate, *Spain* 32 B2
Arrats →, *France* 20 D4
Arreau, *France* 20 F4
Arrecife, *Canary Is.* 37 F6
Arrecifes, *Argentina* 126 C3
Arrée, Mts. d', *France* ... 18 D3
Arresø, *Denmark* 11 J6
Arriaga, *Chiapas, Mexico* . 119 D6
Arriaga, *San Luis Potosí, Mexico* 118 C4
Arrilalah P.O., *Australia* . 94 C3
Arrino, *Australia* 93 E2
Arriondas, *Spain* 34 B5
Arromanches-les-Bains, *France* 18 C6
Arronches, *Portugal* 35 F3
Arros →, *France* 20 E3
Arrow, L., *Ireland* 15 B3
Arrow Rock Res., *U.S.A.* 114 E6
Arrowhead, *Canada* 104 C5
Arrowhead, L., *U.S.A.* .. 117 L9
Arrowtown, *N.Z.* 91 L2
Arroyo de la Luz, *Spain* . 35 F4
Arroyo Grande, *U.S.A.* . 117 K6
Ars, *Denmark* 11 H3
Ars, *Iran* 70 B5
Ars-sur-Moselle, *France* . 19 C13
Arsenault L., *Canada* ... 105 B7
Arsenev, *Russia* 54 B6
Arsi □, *Ethiopia* 81 F4
Arsiero, *Italy* 29 C8
Arsin, *Turkey* 73 B8
Arsk, *Russia* 48 B9
Årsunda, *Sweden* 10 D10
Árta, *Greece* 38 B3
Artà, *Spain* 37 B10
Árta □, *Greece* 38 B3
Arteaga, *Mexico* 118 D4
Arteche, *Phil.* 61 E6
Arteijo = Arteixo, *Spain* . 34 B2
Arteixo, *Spain* 34 B2
Artem = Artyom, *Azerbaijan* 49 K10
Artem, *Russia* 54 C6
Artemovsk, *Russia* 51 D10
Artemovsk, *Ukraine* 47 H9
Artemovskiy, *Russia* ... 49 G5
Artenay, *France* 19 D8
Artern, *Germany* 24 D7
Artesa de Segre, *Spain* .. 32 D6
Artesia = Mosomane, *Botswana* 88 C4
Artesia, *U.S.A.* 113 J2
Artesia Wells, *U.S.A.* .. 113 L5
Artesian, *U.S.A.* 112 C6
Arthington, *Liberia* 82 D2
Arthur →, *Australia* 94 G3
Arthur Cr. →, *Australia* . 94 C2

Arthur Pt., *Australia* 94 C5
Arthur's Pass, *N.Z.* 91 K3
Arthur's Town, *Bahamas* . 121 B4
Artigas, *Uruguay* 126 C4
Artik, *Armenia* 49 K6
Artillery L., *Canada* 105 A7
Artois, *France* 19 B9
Artotína, *Greece* 38 C4
Artrutx, C. de, *Spain* ... 37 B10
Artsyz, *Ukraine* 47 J5
Artvin, *Turkey* 73 B9
Artyom, *Azerbaijan* 49 K10
Aru, Kepulauan, *Indonesia* 63 F8
Aru Is. = Aru, Kepulauan, *Indonesia* 63 F8
Aru Meru □, *Tanzania* .. 86 C4
Arua, *Uganda* 86 B3
Aruanã, *Brazil* 125 F8
Aruba ■, *W. Indies* 121 D6
Arucas, *Canary Is.* 37 F4
Arudy, *France* 20 E3
Arumpo, *Australia* 95 E3
Arun →, *Nepal* 69 F12
Arun →, *U.K.* 13 G7
Arunachal Pradesh □, *India* 67 F19
Arusha, *Tanzania* 86 C4
Arusha □, *Tanzania* 86 C4
Arusha Chini, *Tanzania* . 86 C4
Aruwimi →, *Dem. Rep. of the Congo* 86 B1
Arvada, *U.S.A.* 114 D10
Arvayheer, *Mongolia* ... 60 B5
Arve →, *France* 19 F13
Árvi, *Greece* 36 E7
Arvida, *Canada* 103 C5
Arvidsjaur, *Sweden* 8 D18
Arvika, *Sweden* 10 E6
Arvin, *U.S.A.* 117 K8
Arxan, *China* 60 B6
Åryd, *Sweden* 11 H8
Arys, *Kazakstan* 50 E7
Arzachena, *Italy* 30 A2
Arzamas, *Russia* 48 C6
Arzgir, *Russia* 49 H7
Arzignano, *Italy* 29 C8
Arzúa, *Spain* 34 C2
Aş, *Czech Rep.* 26 A5
Ås, *Sweden* 10 A8
As Pontes de García Rodríguez, *Spain* 34 B3
Aş Şadr, *U.A.E.* 71 E7
Aş Şafā, *Syria* 75 B6
As Safirah, *Syria* 70 B3
Aş Şahm, *Oman* 71 E8
As Sājir, *Si. Arabia* 70 E5
As Salamīyah, *Syria* 70 C3
As Salţ, *Jordan* 75 C4
As Sal'w'a, *Qatar* 71 E6
As Samāwah, *Iraq* 70 D5
As Sanamayn, *Syria* 75 B5
As Sohar = Şuḥār, *Oman* 71 E8
As Sukhnah, *Syria* 70 C3
As Sulaymānīyah, *Iraq* .. 70 C5
As Sulaymī, *Si. Arabia* . 70 E4
As Summān, *Si. Arabia* . 70 E5
As Suwaydā, *Syria* 75 C5
As Suwaydā □, *Syria* ... 75 C5
As Suwayrah, *Iraq* 70 C5
Asab, *Namibia* 88 D2
Asaba, *Nigeria* 83 D6
Asadābād, *Iran* 73 E13
Asafo, *Ghana* 82 D4
Asahi-Gawa →, *Japan* .. 55 G6
Asahigawa, *Japan* 54 C11
Asale, L., *Ethiopia* 81 E5
Asamankese, *Ghana* 83 D4
Asansol, *India* 69 H12
Åsarna, *Sweden* 10 B8
Asbe Teferi, *Ethiopia* ... 81 F5
Asbesberg, *S. Africa* 88 D3
Asbestos, *Canada* 103 C5
Asbury Park, *U.S.A.* ... 111 F10
Ascensión, *Mexico* 118 A3
Ascensión, B. de la, *Mexico* 119 D7
Ascension I., *Atl. Oc.* 77 G2
Aschach an der Donau, *Austria* 26 C7
Aschaffenburg, *Germany* . 25 F5
Aschendorf, *Germany* ... 24 B3
Aschersleben, *Germany* . 24 D7
Asciano, *Italy* 29 E8
Asco, *France* 21 F13
Áscoli Piceno, *Italy* 29 F10
Áscoli Satriano, *Italy* ... 31 A8
Ascope, *Peru* 124 E3
Ascotán, *Chile* 126 A2
Aseb, *Eritrea* 81 E5
Aseda, *Sweden* 11 G9
Asela, *Ethiopia* 81 F4
Asen, *Sweden* 10 C7
Asenovgrad, *Bulgaria* ... 41 D8
Asfeld, *France* 19 C11
Asfûn el Matâ'na, *Egypt* . 80 B3
Asgata, *Cyprus* 36 E12
Ash Fork, *U.S.A.* 115 J7
Ash Grove, *U.S.A.* 113 G8
Ash Shām, Bādiyat, *Asia* . 52 F7
Ash Shamāl □, *Lebanon* . 75 A5
Ash Shāmīyah, *Iraq* 70 D5
Ash Shāriqah, *U.A.E.* .. 71 E7
Ash Sharmah, *Si. Arabia* . 70 D2

Ash Sharqāt, *Iraq* 70 C4
Ash Sharqi, Al Jabal, *Lebanon* 75 B5
Ash Shaṭrah, *Iraq* 70 D5
Ash Shawbak, *Jordan* ... 70 D2
Ash Shawmari, J., *Jordan* 75 E5
Ash Shaykh, J., *Lebanon* . 75 B4
Ash Shināfīyah, *Iraq* 70 D5
Ash Shu'aybah, *Si. Arabia* 70 E5
Ash Shumlūl, *Si. Arabia* . 70 E5
Ash Shūr'a, *Iraq* 70 C4
Ash Shurayf, *Si. Arabia* . 70 E3
Ash Shuwayfāt, *Lebanon* . 75 B4
Ashanti □, *Ghana* 83 D4
Ashau, *Vietnam* 64 D6
Ashbourne, *U.K.* 12 D6
Ashburn, *U.S.A.* 109 K4
Ashburton, *N.Z.* 91 K3
Ashburton →, *Australia* . 92 D1
Ashburton Downs, *Australia* 92 D2
Ashcroft, *Canada* 104 C4
Ashdod, *Israel* 75 D3
Asheboro, *U.S.A.* 109 H6
Asheville, *U.S.A.* 109 H4
Asheweig →, *Canada* ... 102 B2
Ashford, *Australia* 95 D5
Ashford, *U.K.* 13 F8
Ashford, *U.S.A.* 114 C2
Ashgabat, *Turkmenistan* . 50 F6
Ashibetsu, *Japan* 54 C11
Ashikaga, *Japan* 55 F9
Ashington, *U.K.* 12 B6
Ashizuri-Zaki, *Japan* 55 H6
Ashkarkot, *Afghan.* 68 C2
Ashkhabad = Ashgabat, *Turkmenistan* 50 F6
Ashland, *Kans., U.S.A.* .. 113 G5
Ashland, *Ky., U.S.A.* ... 108 F4
Ashland, *Maine, U.S.A.* . 103 C6
Ashland, *Mont., U.S.A.* . 114 D10
Ashland, *Nebr., U.S.A.* . 112 E6
Ashland, *Ohio, U.S.A.* .. 110 F2
Ashland, *Oreg., U.S.A.* . 114 E2
Ashland, *Pa., U.S.A.* ... 111 F8
Ashland, *Va., U.S.A.* ... 108 G7
Ashland, *Wis., U.S.A.* .. 112 B9
Ashley, *N. Dak., U.S.A.* . 112 B5
Ashley, *Pa., U.S.A.* 111 E9
Ashmont, *Canada* 104 C6
Ashmore Reef, *Australia* . 92 B3
Ashmûn, *Egypt* 80 H7
Ashmyany, *Belarus* 9 J21
Ashqelon, *Israel* 75 D3
Ashtabula, *U.S.A.* 110 E4
Ashton, *S. Africa* 88 E3
Ashton, *U.S.A.* 114 D8
Ashuanipi, L., *Canada* .. 103 B6
'Āşī →, *Asia* 72 D6
Asia, Kepulauan, *Indonesia* 63 D8
Āsīā Bak, *Iran* 71 C6
Asiago, *Italy* 29 C8
Asifabad, *India* 66 K11
Asinara, *Italy* 30 A1
Asinara, G. dell', *Italy* .. 30 A1
Asino, *Russia* 50 D9
Asipovichy, *Belarus* 46 F5
'Asīr □, *Si. Arabia* 74 D3
Asir, Ras, *Somali Rep.* .. 74 E5
Aşkale, *Turkey* 73 C9
Askersund, *Sweden* 11 F8
Askham, *S. Africa* 88 D3
Askim, *Norway* 9 G14
Askja, *Iceland* 8 D5
Askøy, *Norway* 9 F11
Asl, *Egypt* 80 J8
Aslan Burnu, *Turkey* ... 39 C8
Aslanapa, *Turkey* 39 B11
Asmara = Asmera, *Eritrea* 81 D4
Asmera, *Eritrea* 81 D4
Åsnæs, *Denmark* 11 J4
Åsnen, *Sweden* 11 H8
Ásola, *Italy* 28 C7
Asoteriba, Jebel, *Sudan* . 80 C4
Asotin, *U.S.A.* 114 C5
Aspe, *Spain* 33 G4
Aspen, *U.S.A.* 115 G10
Aspermont, *U.S.A.* 113 J4
Aspet, *France* 20 E4
Aspiring, Mt., *N.Z.* 91 L2
Aspres-sur-Buëch, *France* . 21 D9
Asprókavos, Ákra, *Greece* 36 B4
Aspromonte, *Italy* 31 D9
Aspur, *India* 68 H6
Asquith, *Canada* 105 C7
Assâba, *Mauritania* 82 B2
Assad, Bahret, *Syria* ... 70 C3
Assam □, *India* 67 G18
Assamakka, *Niger* 83 B6
Asse, *Belgium* 17 D4
Assémini, *Italy* 30 C1
Assen, *Neths.* 17 A6
Assens, *Denmark* 11 J3
Assini, *Ivory C.* 82 D4
Assiniboia, *Canada* 105 D7
Assiniboine →, *Canada* . 105 D9
Assis, *Brazil* 127 A5
Assisi, *Italy* 29 E9
Ássos, *Greece* 38 C2
Assynt, L., *U.K.* 14 C3
Astaffort, *France* 20 D4
Astakídha, *Greece* 39 F8
Astakós, *Greece* 38 C3
Astana = Aqmola, *Kazakstan* 50 D8

Bad Homburg

Astara, Azerbaijan 73 C13
Āstārā, Iran 73 C13
Asteroúsia, Greece 36 E7
Asti, Italy 28 D5
Astipálaia, Greece 39 E8
Astorga, Spain 34 C4
Astoria, U.S.A. 116 D3
Åstorp, Sweden 11 H6
Astrakhan, Russia 49 G9
Astudillo, Spain 34 C6
Asturias □, Spain 34 B5
Asunción, Paraguay 126 B4
Asunción Nochixtlán, Mexico 119 D5
Åsunden, Sweden 11 F9
Asutri, Sudan 81 D4
Aswa →, Uganda 86 B3
Aswad, Ras al, Si. Arabia 80 C4
Aswân, Egypt 80 C3
Aswân High Dam = Sadd el Aali, Egypt 80 C3
Asyût, Egypt 80 B3
Asyûti, Wadi →, Egypt 80 B3
Aszód, Hungary 42 C4
At Ţafīlah, Jordan 75 E4
Aţ Ţā'if, Si. Arabia 80 C5
Aţ Ţirāq, Si. Arabia 70 E5
Atabey, Turkey 39 D12
Atacama □, Chile 126 B2
Atacama, Desierto de, Chile 126 A2
Atacama, Salar de, Chile 126 A2
Atakpamé, Togo 83 D5
Atalándi, Greece 38 C4
Atalaya, Peru 124 F4
Atalaya de Femes, Canary Is. 37 F6
Atami, Japan 55 G9
Atapupu, Indonesia 63 F6
Atâr, Mauritania 78 D3
Atarfe, Spain 35 H7
Atascadero, U.S.A. 116 K6
Atasu, Kazakstan 50 E8
Atatürk Barajı, Turkey 73 D8
Atauro, Indonesia 63 F7
Atbara, Sudan 80 D3
'Atbara →, Sudan 80 D3
Atbasar, Kazakstan 50 D7
Atça, Turkey 39 D10
Atchafalaya B., U.S.A. 113 L9
Atchison, U.S.A. 112 F7
Atebubu, Ghana 83 D4
Ateca, Spain 32 D3
Aterno →, Italy 29 F10
Atesine, Alpi, Italy 29 B8
Atessa, Italy 29 F11
Ath, Belgium 17 D3
Athabasca, Canada 104 C6
Athabasca →, Canada 105 B6
Athabasca, L., Canada 105 B7
Athboy, Ireland 15 C5
Athenry, Ireland 15 C3
Athens = Athínai, Greece 38 D5
Athens, Ala., U.S.A. 109 H2
Athens, Ga., U.S.A. 109 J4
Athens, N.Y., U.S.A. 111 D11
Athens, Ohio, U.S.A. 108 F4
Athens, Pa., U.S.A. 111 E8
Athens, Tenn., U.S.A. 109 H3
Athens, Tex., U.S.A. 113 J7
Atherley, Canada 110 B5
Atherton, Australia 94 B4
Athiéme, Benin 83 D5
Athienou, Cyprus 36 D12
Athínai, Greece 38 D5
Athlone, Ireland 15 C4
Athna, Cyprus 36 D12
Atholl, Forest of, U.K. 14 E5
Atholville, Canada 103 C6
Áthos, Greece 41 F8
Athy, Ireland 15 C5
Ati, Chad 79 F9
Ati, Sudan 81 E2
Atiak, Uganda 86 B3
Atienza, Spain 32 D2
Atikokan, Canada 102 C1
Atikonak L., Canada 103 B7
Atimonan, Phil. 61 E4
Atka, Russia 51 C16
Atkarsk, Russia 48 E7
Atkinson, U.S.A. 112 D5
Atlanta, Ga., U.S.A. 109 J3
Atlanta, Tex., U.S.A. 113 J7
Atlantic, U.S.A. 112 E7
Atlantic City, U.S.A. 108 F8
Atlantic Ocean 2 E9
Atlas Mts. = Haut Atlas, Morocco 78 B4
Atlin, Canada 104 B2
Atlin, L., Canada 104 B2
Atmore, U.S.A. 109 K2
Atoka, U.S.A. 113 H6
Átokos, Greece 38 C2
Atolia, U.S.A. 117 K9
Atoyac →, Mexico 119 D5
Atrak → = Atrek →, Turkmenistan 71 B8
Ätran, Sweden 11 G6
Ätran →, Sweden 11 H6
Atrauli, India 68 E8
Atrek →, Turkmenistan 71 B8
Atri, Italy 29 F10
Atsbi, Ethiopia 81 E4
Atsikí, Greece 39 B7
Atsoum, Mts., Cameroon 83 D7
Atsuta, Japan 54 C10
Attalla, U.S.A. 109 H2
Attapu, Laos 64 E6
Attáviros, Greece 36 C9
Attawapiskat, Canada 102 B3
Attawapiskat →, Canada 102 B3
Attawapiskat, L., Canada 102 B2
Attersee, Austria 26 D6
Attica, U.S.A. 108 E2
Attichy, France 19 C10
Attigny, France 19 C11
Attikamagen L., Canada 103 B6
Attikí □, Greece 38 D5
Attleboro, U.S.A. 111 E13
Attock, Pakistan 68 C5
Attopeu = Attapu, Laos 64 E6
Attur, India 66 P11
Atuel →, Argentina 126 D2
Åtvidaberg, Sweden 11 F10
Atwater, U.S.A. 116 H6
Atwood, Canada 110 C3
Atwood, U.S.A. 112 F4
Atyraū, Kazakstan 50 E6
Au Sable →, U.S.A. 108 C4
Au Sable Pt., U.S.A. 102 C2
Aubagne, France 21 E9
Aubarca, C. d', Spain 37 B7
Aube □, France 19 D11
Aube →, France 19 D10
Aubenas, France 21 D8
Aubenton, France 19 C11
Auberry, U.S.A. 116 H7
Aubigny-sur-Nère, France 19 E9
Aubin, France 20 D6
Aubrac, Mts. d', France 20 D7
Auburn, Ala., U.S.A. 109 J3
Auburn, Calif., U.S.A. 116 G5
Auburn, Ind., U.S.A. 108 E3
Auburn, N.Y., U.S.A. 111 D8
Auburn, Nebr., U.S.A. 112 E7
Auburn, Wash., U.S.A. 116 C4
Auburn Ra., Australia 95 D5
Auburndale, U.S.A. 109 L5
Aubusson, France 20 C6
Auce, Latvia 44 B9
Auch, France 20 E4
Auchi, Nigeria 83 D6
Auckland, N.Z. 91 G5
Auckland Is., Pac. Oc. 96 N8
Aude □, France 20 E6
Aude →, France 20 E7
Auden, Canada 102 B2
Auderville, France 18 C5
Audierne, France 18 D2
Audincourt, France 19 E13
Audo, Ethiopia 81 F5
Audubon, U.S.A. 112 E7
Aue, Germany 24 E8
Auerbach, Germany 24 E8
Augathella, Australia 95 D4
Aughnacloy, U.K. 15 B5
Augrabies Falls, S. Africa 88 D3
Augsburg, Germany 25 G6
Augusta, Italy 31 E8
Augusta, Ark., U.S.A. 113 H9
Augusta, Ga., U.S.A. 109 J5
Augusta, Kans., U.S.A. 113 G6
Augusta, Maine, U.S.A. 103 D6
Augusta, Mont., U.S.A. 114 C7
Augusta, Wis., U.S.A. 112 C9
Augustenborg, Denmark 11 K3
Augustów, Poland 44 E9
Augustus, Mt., Australia 92 D2
Augustus Downs, Australia 94 B2
Augustus I., Australia 92 C3
Aukan, Eritrea 81 D5
Aukum, U.S.A. 116 G6
Auld, L., Australia 92 D3
Aulla, Italy 28 D6
Aulnay, France 20 B3
Aulne →, France 18 D2
Aulnoye-Aymeries, France 19 B10
Ault, France 18 B8
Ault, U.S.A. 112 E2
Aulus-les-Bains, France 20 F5
Aumale, France 19 C8
Aumont-Aubrac, France 20 D7
Auna, Nigeria 83 C5
Auning, Denmark 11 H4
Aunis, France 20 B3
Auponhia, Indonesia 63 E7
Aups, France 21 E10
Aur, Pulau, Malaysia 65 L5
Auraiya, India 69 F8
Aurangabad, Bihar, India 69 G11
Aurangabad, Maharashtra, India 66 K9
Auray, France 18 E4
Aurich, Germany 24 B3
Aurillac, France 20 D6
Auronzo di Cadore, Italy 29 B9
Aurora, Canada 110 C5
Aurora, S. Africa 88 E2
Aurora, Colo., U.S.A. 112 F2
Aurora, Ill., U.S.A. 108 E1
Aurora, Mo., U.S.A. 113 G8
Aurora, Nebr., U.S.A. 112 E6
Aurora, Ohio, U.S.A. 110 E3
Aurukun Mission, Australia 94 A3
Aus, Namibia 88 D2
Auschwitz = Oświęcim, Poland 45 H6
Austerlitz = Slavkov u Brna, Czech Rep. 27 B9
Austin, Minn., U.S.A. 112 D8
Austin, Nev., U.S.A. 114 G5
Austin, Pa., U.S.A. 110 E6
Austin, Tex., U.S.A. 113 K6
Austin, L., Australia 93 E2
Austra, Norway 8 D14
Austral Downs, Australia 94 C2
Austral Is. = Tubuai Is., Pac. Oc. 97 K13
Austral Seamount Chain, Pac. Oc. 97 K13
Australia ■, Oceania 96 K5
Australian Alps, Australia 95 F4
Australian Capital Territory □, Australia 95 F4
Austria ■, Europe 26 E7
Austvågøy, Norway 8 B16
Auterive, France 20 E5
Authie →, France 19 B8
Authon-du-Perche, France 18 D7
Autlán, Mexico 118 D4
Autun, France 19 F11
Auvergne, Australia 92 C5
Auvergne, France 20 C7
Auvergne, Mts. d', France 20 C6
Auvézère →, France 20 C4
Auxerre, France 19 E10
Auxi-le-Château, France 19 B9
Auxonne, France 19 E12
Auzances, France 19 F9
Avallon, France 19 E10
Avalon, U.S.A. 117 M8
Avalon Pen., Canada 103 C9
Avaré, Brazil 127 A6
Ávas, Greece 41 F9
Avawatz Mts., U.S.A. 117 K10
Avdan Dağı, Turkey 41 F13
Aveiro, Brazil 125 D7
Aveiro, Portugal 34 E2
Aveiro □, Portugal 34 E2
Āvej, Iran 71 C6
Avellaneda, Argentina 126 C4
Avellino, Italy 31 B7
Avenal, U.S.A. 116 K6
Aversa, Italy 31 B7
Avery, U.S.A. 114 C6
Aves, I. de, W. Indies 121 C7
Aves, Is. de, Venezuela 121 D6
Avesnes-sur-Helpe, France 19 B10
Avesta, Sweden 10 D10
Aveyron □, France 20 D6
Aveyron →, France 20 D5
Avezzano, Italy 29 F10
Avgó, Greece 39 F7
Aviá Terai, Argentina 126 B3
Aviano, Italy 29 B9
Aviemore, U.K. 14 D5
Avigliana, Italy 28 C4
Avigliano, Italy 31 B8
Avignon, France 21 E8
Ávila, Spain 34 E6
Ávila □, Spain 34 E6
Ávila, Sierra de, Spain 34 E5
Avila Beach, U.S.A. 117 K6
Avilés, Spain 34 B5
Avintes, Portugal 34 D2
Avionárion, Greece 38 C6
Avis, Portugal 35 F3
Avísio →, Italy 28 B8
Aviz = Avis, Portugal 35 F3
Avize, France 19 D11
Avlum, Denmark 11 H2
Avoca, U.S.A. 110 D7
Avoca →, Australia 95 F3
Avoca →, Ireland 15 D5
Avola, Canada 104 C5
Avola, Italy 31 F8
Avon, N.Y., U.S.A. 110 D7
Avon, S. Dak., U.S.A. 112 D5
Avon →, Australia 93 F2
Avon →, Bristol, U.K. 13 F5
Avon →, Dorset, U.K. 13 G6
Avon →, Warks., U.K. 13 E5
Avondale, Zimbabwe 87 F3
Avonlea, Canada 105 D8
Avonmore, Canada 111 A10
Avramov, Bulgaria 41 D10
Avranches, France 18 D5
Avre →, France 18 D8
Avrig, Romania 43 E9
Avrillé, France 18 E6
Avtovac, Bos.-H. 40 C2
Awag el Baqar, Sudan 81 E3
A'waj →, Syria 75 B5
Awaji-Shima, Japan 55 G7
'Awālī, Bahrain 71 E6
Awantipur, India 69 C6
Awasa, L., Ethiopia 81 F4
Awash, Ethiopia 81 F5
Awash →, Ethiopia 81 E5
Awaso, Ghana 82 D4
Awatere →, N.Z. 91 J5
Awbārī, Libya 79 C8
Awe, L., U.K. 14 E3
Aweil, Sudan 81 F2
Awgu, Nigeria 83 D6
Awjilah, Libya 79 C10
Ax-les-Thermes, France 20 F5
Axat, France 20 F6
Axe →, U.K. 13 F5
Axel Heiberg I., Canada 4 B3
Axim, Ghana 82 E4
Axintele, Romania 43 F11
Axiós →, Greece 40 F6
Axminster, U.K. 13 G4
Axvall, Sweden 11 F7
Ay, France 19 C11
Ayabaca, Peru 124 D3
Ayabe, Japan 55 G7
Ayacucho, Argentina 126 D4
Ayacucho, Peru 124 F4
Ayaguz, Kazakstan 50 E9
Ayamonte, Spain 35 H3
Ayan, Russia 51 D14
Ayancık, Turkey 72 B6
Ayas, Turkey 72 B5
Ayaviri, Peru 124 F4
Aybastı, Turkey 72 B7
Aydın, Turkey 72 D2
Aydin □, Turkey 39 D9
Aydin Dağları, Turkey 39 D10
Ayenngré, Togo 83 D5
Ayerbe, Spain 32 C4
Ayer's Cliff, Canada 111 A12
Ayers Rock, Australia 93 E5
Ayiá, Greece 38 B4
Ayia Aikateríni, Ákra, Greece 36 A3
Ayía Ánna, Greece 38 C5
Ayia Dhéka, Greece 36 D6
Ayia Gálini, Greece 36 D6
Ayía Marína, Kásos, Greece 39 F8
Ayía Marína, Léros, Greece 39 D8
Ayia Napa, Cyprus 36 E13
Ayía Paraskeví, Greece 39 B8
Ayia Phyla, Cyprus 36 E12
Ayía Rouméli, Greece 38 F5
Ayia Varvára, Greece 36 D7
Ayiássos, Greece 39 B8
Áyioi Theódhoroi, Greece 38 D5
Áyion Óros □, Greece 41 F8
Áyios Amvrósios, Cyprus 36 D12
Áyios Andréas, Greece 38 D4
Áyios Evstrátios, Greece 38 B6
Áyios Ioánnis, Ákra, Greece 36 D7
Áyios Isidhoros, Greece 36 C9
Áyios Kiríkos, Greece 39 D8
Áyios Matthaíos, Greece 36 B3
Áyios Mírono, Greece 39 F7
Áyios Nikólaos, Greece 36 D7
Áyios Pétros, Greece 38 C2
Áyios Seryios, Cyprus 36 D12
Ayios Theodhoros, Cyprus 36 D13
Áyios Yeóryios, Greece 38 D5
Aykathonisi, Greece 39 D8
Aykirikçi, Turkey 39 B12
Aylesbury, U.K. 13 F7
Aylmer, Canada 110 D4
Aylmer, L., Canada 100 B8
Ayn Zālah, Iraq 73 D10
Ayna, Spain 33 G2
Ayolas, Paraguay 126 B4
Ayom, Sudan 81 F2
Ayon, Ostrov, Russia 51 C17
Ayora, Spain 33 F3
Ayr, Australia 94 B4
Ayr, U.K. 14 F4
Ayr →, U.K. 14 F4
Ayrancı, Turkey 72 D5
Ayrancılar, Turkey 39 C9
Ayre, Pt. of, U.K. 12 C3
Aysha, Ethiopia 81 E5
Aytos, Bulgaria 41 D11
Aytoska Planina, Bulgaria 41 D11
Ayu, Kepulauan, Indonesia 63 D8
Ayutla, Guatemala 120 D1
Ayutla, Mexico 119 D5
Ayvacık, Turkey 72 C2
Ayvalık, Turkey 39 B8
Az Zabadānī, Syria 75 B5
Az̧ Z̧āhirīyah, West Bank 75 D3
Az̧ Z̧ahrān, Si. Arabia 71 E6
Az Zarqā, Jordan 75 C5
Az Zībār, Iraq 70 B5
Az-Zilfī, Si. Arabia 70 E5
Az Zubayr, Iraq 70 D5
Azambuja, Portugal 35 F2
Azamgarh, India 69 F10
Azangaro, Peru 124 F4
Azaouak, Vallée de l', Mali 83 B5
Āzār Shahr, Iran 70 B5
Azarān, Iran 73 D12
Azärbayjan = Azerbaijan ■, Asia 49 K9
Āzarbāyjān-e Gharbī □, Iran 70 B5
Āzarbāyjān-e Sharqī □, Iran 70 B5
Azare, Nigeria 83 C7
Azay-le-Rideau, France 18 E7
A'zāz, Syria 70 B3
Azbine = Aïr, Niger 83 B6
Azerbaijan ■, Asia 49 K9
Azerbaijchan = Azerbaijan ■, Asia 49 K9
Azezo, Ethiopia 81 E4
Azimganj, India 69 G13
Aznalcóllar, Spain 35 H4
Azogues, Ecuador 124 D3
Azores, Atl. Oc. 76 C1
Azov, Russia 47 J10
Azov, Sea of, Europe 47 J9
Azovskoye More = Azov, Sea of, Europe 47 J9
Azpeitia, Spain 32 B2
Aztec, U.S.A. 115 H10
Azúa, Dom. Rep. 121 C5
Azuaga, Spain 35 G5
Azuara, Spain 32 D4
Azuer →, Spain 35 F7
Azuero, Pen. de, Panama 120 E3
Azuga, Romania 43 E10
Azul, Argentina 126 D4
Azusa, U.S.A. 117 L9
Azzano Décimo, Italy 29 C9

B

Ba Don, Vietnam 64 D6
Ba Dong, Vietnam 65 H6
Ba Ngoi = Cam Lam, Vietnam 65 G7
Ba Tri, Vietnam 65 G6
Ba Xian, China 56 E9
Baa, Indonesia 63 F6
Baamonde, Spain 34 B3
Baarle-Nassau, Belgium 17 C4
Bab el Mandeb, Red Sea 74 E3
Baba, Bulgaria 40 D7
Baba Burnu, Turkey 39 B8
Baba dag, Azerbaijan 49 K9
Bābā Kalū, Iran 71 D6
Babadag, Romania 43 F13
Babadağ, Turkey 39 D10
Babadayhan, Turkmenistan 50 F7
Babaeski, Turkey 41 E11
Babahoyo, Ecuador 124 D3
Babakin, Australia 93 F2
Babana, Nigeria 83 C5
Babar, Indonesia 63 F7
Babar, Pakistan 68 D3
Babarkach, Pakistan 68 E3
Babayevo, Russia 46 C8
Babb, U.S.A. 114 B7
Babenhausen, Germany 25 F4
Băbeni, Romania 43 F9
Babi Besar, Pulau, Malaysia 65 L4
Babia Gora, Europe 45 J6
Babian Jiang →, China 58 F3
Babile, Ethiopia 81 F5
Babimost, Poland 45 F2
Babinda, Australia 94 B4
Babine, Canada 104 B3
Babine →, Canada 104 B3
Babine L., Canada 104 C3
Babo, Indonesia 63 E8
Babócsa, Hungary 42 D2
Bābol, Iran 71 B7
Bābol Sar, Iran 71 B7
Baborów, Poland 45 H5
Babruysk, Belarus 47 F5
Babuna, Macedonia 40 E5
Babura, Nigeria 83 C6
Babusar Pass, Pakistan 69 B5
Babušnica, Serbia, Yug. 40 C6
Babuyan Chan., Phil. 61 B4
Babuyan Is., Phil. 61 B4
Babylon, Iraq 70 C5
Bač, Serbia, Yug. 42 E4
Bâc →, Moldova 43 D14
Bac Can, Vietnam 64 A5
Bac Giang, Vietnam 64 B6
Bac Ninh, Vietnam 64 B6
Bac Phan, Vietnam 64 B5
Bac Quang, Vietnam 64 A5
Bacabal, Brazil 125 D10
Bacalar, Mexico 119 D7
Bacan, Kepulauan, Indonesia 63 E7
Bacarra, Phil. 61 B4
Bacău, Romania 43 D11
Bacău □, Romania 43 D11
Baccarat, France 19 D13
Bacerac, Mexico 118 A3
Băcești, Romania 43 D12
Bach Long Vi, Dao, Vietnam 64 B6
Bacharach, Germany 25 E3
Bachelina, Russia 50 D7
Bachuma, Ethiopia 81 F4
Bačina, Serbia, Yug. 40 C5
Back →, Canada 100 B9
Bačka Palanka, Serbia, Yug. 42 E4
Bačka Topola, Serbia, Yug. 42 E4
Bäckebo, Sweden 11 H10
Bäckefors, Sweden 11 F6
Bäckhammar, Sweden 10 E8
Bački Petrovac, Serbia, Yug. 42 E4
Backnang, Germany 25 G5
Backstairs Passage, Australia 95 F2
Baco, Mt., Phil. 61 E4
Bacolod, Phil. 61 F5
Bacqueville-en-Caux, France 18 C8
Bács-Kiskun □, Hungary 42 D4
Bácsalmás, Hungary 42 D4
Bacuag, Phil. 61 G6
Bacuk, Malaysia 65 J4
Bād, Iran 71 C7
Bad →, U.S.A. 112 C4
Bad Aussee, Austria 26 D6
Bad Axe, U.S.A. 110 C2
Bad Bergzabern, Germany 25 F3
Bad Berleburg, Germany 24 D4
Bad Bevensen, Germany 24 B6
Bad Bramstedt, Germany 24 B5
Bad Brückenau, Germany 25 E5
Bad Doberan, Germany 24 A7
Bad Driburg, Germany 24 D5
Bad Ems, Germany 25 E3
Bad Frankenhausen, Germany 24 D7
Bad Freienwalde, Germany 24 C10
Bad Goisern, Austria 26 D6
Bad Harzburg, Germany 24 D6
Bad Hersfeld, Germany 24 E5
Bad Hofgastein, Austria 26 D6
Bad Homburg, Germany 25 E4

Bad Honnef, *Germany* ... 24 E3
Bad Iburg, *Germany* 24 C4
Bad Ischl, *Austria* 26 D6
Bad Kissingen, *Germany* . 25 E6
Bad Königshofen, *Germany* 25 E6
Bad Kreuznach, *Germany* 25 F3
Bad Krozingen, *Germany* . 25 H3
Bad Laasphe, *Germany* .. 24 E4
Bad Lands, *U.S.A.* 112 D3
Bad Langensalza, *Germany* 24 D6
Bad Lauterberg, *Germany* 24 D6
Bad Leonfelden, *Austria* .. 26 C7
Bad Liebenwerda, *Germany* ... 24 D9
Bad Mergentheim, *Germany* ... 25 F5
Bad Münstereifel, *Germany* 24 E2
Bad Nauheim, *Germany* .. 25 E4
Bad Neuenahr-Ahrweiler, *Germany* ... 24 E3
Bad Neustadt, *Germany* .. 25 E6
Bad Oeynhausen, *Germany* 24 C4
Bad Oldesloe, *Germany* .. 24 B6
Bad Orb, *Germany* 25 E5
Bad Pyrmont, *Germany* .. 24 D5
Bad Reichenhall, *Germany* 25 H8
Bad Säckingen, *Germany* . 25 H3
Bad Salzuflen, *Germany* .. 24 C4
Bad Salzungen, *Germany* .. 24 E6
Bad Schwartau, *Germany* . 24 B6
Bad Segeberg, *Germany* .. 24 B6
Bad St. Leonhard, *Austria* 26 E7
Bad Tölz, *Germany* 25 H7
Bad Urach, *Germany* 25 G5
Bad Vöslau, *Austria* 27 D9
Bad Waldsee, *Germany* .. 25 H5
Bad Wildungen, *Germany* 24 D4
Bad Wimpfen, *Germany* . 25 F5
Bad Windsheim, *Germany* 25 F6
Bad Zwischenahn, *Germany* ... 24 B4
Badagara, *India* 66 P9
Badagri, *Nigeria* 83 D5
Badajós, L., *Brazil* 124 D6
Badajoz, *Spain* 35 G4
Badajoz □, *Spain* 35 G4
Badalona, *Spain* 32 D7
Badalzai, *Afghan.* 68 E1
Badampahar, *India* 67 H15
Badanah, *Si. Arabia* 70 D4
Badarinath, *India* 69 D8
Badas, Kepulauan, *Indonesia* ... 62 D3
Baddo →, *Pakistan* 66 F4
Bade, *Indonesia* 63 F9
Baden, *Austria* 27 C9
Baden, *Switz.* 25 H4
Baden-Baden, *Germany* . 25 G4
Baden-Württemberg □, *Germany* ... 25 G4
Badgastein, *Austria* 26 D6
Badger, *Canada* 103 C8
Badger, *U.S.A.* 116 J7
Bādghīsāt □, *Afghan.* .. 66 B3
Badgom, *India* 69 B6
Badia Polésine, *Italy* ... 29 C8
Badin, *Pakistan* 68 G3
Badogo, *Mali* 82 C3
Badong, *China* 59 B8
Badrah, *Iraq* 73 F11
Badulla, *Sri Lanka* 66 R12
Baena, *Spain* 35 H6
Baeza, *Spain* 35 H7
Bafang, *Cameroon* 83 D7
Bafatá, *Guinea-Biss.* ... 82 C2
Baffin B., *Canada* 4 B4
Baffin I., *Canada* 101 B12
Bafia, *Cameroon* 83 E7
Bafilo, *Togo* 83 D5
Bafing →, *Mali* 82 C2
Bafliyûn, *Syria* 70 B3
Bafoulabé, *Mali* 82 C2
Bafoussam, *Cameroon* .. 83 D7
Bāfq, *Iran* 71 D7
Bafra, *Turkey* 72 B6
Bafra Burnu, *Turkey* ... 72 B7
Bāft, *Iran* 71 D8
Bafut, *Cameroon* 83 D7
Bafwasende, *Dem. Rep. of the Congo* 86 B2
Bagamoyo, *Tanzania* ... 86 D4
Bagamoyo □, *Tanzania* .. 86 D4
Bagan Datoh, *Malaysia* . 65 L3
Bagan Serai, *Malaysia* .. 65 K3
Baganga, *Phil.* 61 H7
Bagani, *Namibia* 88 B3
Bagansiapiapi, *Indonesia* . 62 D2
Bagasra, *India* 68 J4
Bagawi, *Sudan* 81 E3
Bagdad, *U.S.A.* 117 L11
Bagdarin, *Russia* 51 D12
Bagé, *Brazil* 127 C5
Bagenalstown = Muine Bheag, *Ireland* ... 15 D5
Baggs, *U.S.A.* 114 F10
Bagh, *Pakistan* 69 C5
Baghdād, *Iraq* 70 C5
Bagheria, *Italy* 30 D6
Bagley, *U.S.A.* 112 B7
Bagnara Cálabra, *Italy* .. 31 D8
Bagnasco, *Italy* 28 D5
Bagnères-de-Bigorre, *France* ... 20 E4
Bagnères-de-Luchon, *France* ... 20 F4
Bagni di Lucca, *Italy* ... 28 D7

Bagno di Romagna, *Italy* . 29 E8
Bagnoles-de-l'Orne, *France* 18 D5
Bagnols-sur-Cèze, *France* . 21 D8
Bagnorégio, *Italy* 29 F9
Bagotville, *Canada* 103 C5
Bagrationovsk, *Russia* .. 9 J19
Bagrdan, *Serbia, Yug.* .. 40 B5
Baguio, *Phil.* 61 C4
Bahabón de Esgueva, *Spain* 34 D7
Bahadurgarh, *India* 68 E7
Bahama, Canal Viejo de, *W. Indies* ... 120 B4
Bahamas ■, *N. Amer.* .. 121 B5
Bahār, *Iran* 73 E13
Baharampur, *India* 69 G13
Baharîya, El Wâhât al, *Egypt* ... 80 J6
Bahawalnagar, *Pakistan* . 68 E5
Bahawalpur, *Pakistan* .. 68 E4
Bahçe, *Turkey* 72 D7
Bahçecik, *Turkey* 41 F13
Baheri, *India* 69 E8
Bahi, *Tanzania* 86 D4
Bahi Swamp, *Tanzania* . 86 D4
Bahía = Salvador, *Brazil* . 125 F11
Bahía □, *Brazil* 125 F10
Bahía, Is. de la, *Honduras* 120 C2
Bahía Blanca, *Argentina* . 126 D3
Bahía de Caráquez, *Ecuador* ... 124 D2
Bahía Honda, *Cuba* 120 B3
Bahía Laura, *Argentina* .. 128 F3
Bahía Negra, *Paraguay* .. 124 H7
Bahir Dar, *Ethiopia* 81 E4
Bahmanzād, *Iran* 71 D6
Bahr el Ahmar □, *Sudan* . 80 D4
Bahr el Ghazâl □, *Sudan* . 81 F2
Bahr Yûsef →, *Egypt* .. 80 J7
Bahra el Burullus, *Egypt* . 80 H7
Bahraich, *India* 69 F9
Bahrain ■, *Asia* 71 E6
Bahror, *India* 68 F7
Bāhū Kalāt, *Iran* 71 E9
Bai, *Mali* 82 C4
Bai Bung, Mui = Ca Mau, Mui, *Vietnam* ... 65 H5
Bai Duc, *Vietnam* 64 C5
Bai Thuong, *Vietnam* .. 64 C5
Baia de Aramă, *Romania* . 42 E7
Baia Mare, *Romania* ... 43 C8
Baia-Sprie, *Romania* ... 43 C8
Baião, *Brazil* 125 D9
Baïbokoum, *Chad* 79 G9
Baicheng, *China* 57 B12
Băicoi, *Romania* 43 E10
Baidoa, *Somali Rep.* ... 74 G3
Baie Comeau, *Canada* .. 103 C6
Baie-St-Paul, *Canada* ... 103 C5
Baie Trinité, *Canada* ... 103 C6
Baie Verte, *Canada* 103 C8
Baignes-Ste-Radegonde, *France* ... 20 C3
Baigneux-les-Juifs, *France* 19 E11
Baihe, *China* 56 H6
Ba'ījī, *Iraq* 70 C4
Baikal, L. = Baykal, Oz., *Russia* ... 51 D11
Baile Atha Cliath = Dublin, *Ireland* ... 15 C5
Băile Govora, *Romania* . 43 E9
Băile Herculane, *Romania* 42 F7
Băile Olănești, *Romania* . 43 E9
Băile Tuşnad, *Romania* . 43 D10
Bailei, *Ethiopia* 81 F5
Bailén, *Spain* 35 G7
Băilești, *Romania* 43 F8
Baima, *China* 58 A3
Bain-de-Bretagne, *France* 18 E5
Bainbridge, *Ga., U.S.A.* . 109 K3
Bainbridge, *N.Y., U.S.A.* 111 D9
Baing, *Indonesia* 63 F6
Bainiu, *China* 56 H7
Bainville, *U.S.A.* 112 A2
Baiona, *Spain* 34 C2
Bā'ir, *Jordan* 75 E5
Baird, *U.S.A.* 113 J5
Bairin Youqi, *China* ... 57 C10
Bairin Zuoqi, *China* ... 57 C10
Bairnsdale, *Australia* ... 95 F4
Bais, *Phil.* 61 G5
Baisha, *China* 56 G7
Baissa, *Nigeria* 83 D7
Baitadi, *Nepal* 69 E9
Baiyin, *China* 56 F3
Baiyü, *China* 58 B2
Baiyu Shan, *China* 56 F4
Baiyuda, *Sudan* 80 D3
Baj Baj, *India* 69 H13
Baja, *Hungary* 42 D3
Baja, Pta., *Mexico* 118 B1
Baja California, *Mexico* . 118 A1
Baja California □, *Mexico* 118 B2
Baja California Sur □, *Mexico* ... 118 B2
Bajamar, *Canary Is.* 37 F3
Bajana, *India* 68 H4
Bājgīrān, *Iran* 71 B8
Bajimba, Mt., *Australia* . 95 D5
Bajina Bašta, *Serbia, Yug.* 40 C3
Bajmok, *Serbia, Yug.* .. 42 E4
Bajo Nuevo, *Caribbean* . 120 C4
Bajoga, *Nigeria* 83 C7
Bajool, *Australia* 94 C5
Bak, *Hungary* 42 D1
Bakar, *Croatia* 29 C11
Bakel, *Senegal* 82 C2

Baker, *Calif., U.S.A.* ... 117 K10
Baker, *Mont., U.S.A.* .. 112 B2
Baker, *Oreg., U.S.A.* ... 114 D5
Baker, L., *Canada* 100 B10
Baker I., *Pac. Oc.* 96 G10
Baker I., *Australia* 93 E4
Baker Lake, *Canada* ... 100 B10
Baker Mt., *U.S.A.* 114 B3
Baker's Dozen Is., *Canada* 102 A4
Bakersfield, *Calif., U.S.A.* 117 K8
Bakersfield, *Vt., U.S.A.* . 111 B12
Bakhchysaray, *Ukraine* .. 47 K7
Bakhmach, *Ukraine* ... 47 G7
Bākhtarān, *Iran* 70 C5
Bākhtarān □, *Iran* 70 C5
Bakı, *Azerbaijan* 49 K9
Bakır →, *Turkey* 39 C9
Bakırdaği, *Turkey* 72 C6
Bakkafjörður, *Iceland* .. 8 C6
Baklan, *Turkey* 39 C11
Bakony, *Hungary* 42 C2
Bakony Forest = Bakony, *Hungary* ... 42 C2
Bakori, *Nigeria* 83 C6
Bakouma, *C.A.R.* 84 C4
Baksan, *Russia* 49 J6
Baku = Bakı, *Azerbaijan* 49 K9
Bakutis Coast, *Antarctica* 5 D15
Baky = Bakı, *Azerbaijan* . 49 K9
Bala, *Canada* 110 A5
Bâlâ, *Turkey* 72 C5
Bala, *U.K.* 12 E4
Bala, L., *U.K.* 12 E4
Balabac I., *Phil.* 61 H2
Balabac Str., *E. Indies* .. 62 C5
Balabagh, *Afghan.* 68 B4
Ba'labakk, *Lebanon* ... 75 B5
Balabalangan, Kepulauan, *Indonesia* ... 62 E5
Bălăciţa, *Romania* 43 F8
Balad, *Iraq* 70 C5
Balad Rūz, *Iraq* 70 C5
Bālādeh, *Fārs, Iran* 71 D6
Bālādeh, *Māzandaran, Iran* 71 B6
Balaghat, *India* 66 J12
Balaghat Ra., *India* 66 K10
Balaguer, *Spain* 32 D5
Balakhna, *Russia* 48 B6
Balaklava, *Australia* ... 95 E2
Balaklava, *Ukraine* 47 K7
Balakliya, *Ukraine* 47 H9
Balakovo, *Russia* 48 D8
Bālan, *Romania* 43 D10
Balancán, *Mexico* 119 D6
Balashov, *Russia* 48 E6
Balasinor, *India* 68 H5
Balasore = Baleshwar, *India* ... 67 J15
Balassagyarmat, *Hungary* . 42 B4
Balât, *Egypt* 80 B2
Balaton, *Hungary* 42 D2
Balatonboglár, *Hungary* . 42 D2
Balatonfüred, *Hungary* . 42 D2
Balatonszentgyörgy, *Hungary* ... 42 D2
Balayan, *Phil.* 61 E4
Balazote, *Spain* 33 G2
Balbieriškis, *Lithuania* .. 44 D10
Balbigny, *France* 21 C8
Balbina, Reprêsa de, *Brazil* 124 D7
Balboa, *Panama* 120 E4
Balbriggan, *Ireland* ... 15 C5
Balcarce, *Argentina* ... 126 D4
Balcarres, *Canada* 105 C8
Balchik, *Bulgaria* 41 C12
Balclutha, *N.Z.* 91 M2
Bald Hd., *Australia* 93 G2
Bald I., *Australia* 93 F2
Bald Knob, *U.S.A.* 113 H9
Baldock L., *Canada* ... 105 B9
Baldwin, *Fla., U.S.A.* .. 109 K4
Baldwin, *Mich., U.S.A.* . 108 D3
Baldwinsville, *U.S.A.* .. 111 C8
Baldy Peak, *U.S.A.* 115 K9
Bale, *Croatia* 29 C10
Bale □, *Ethiopia* 81 F5
Baleares, Is., *Spain* 37 B10
Balearic Is. = Baleares, Is., *Spain* ... 37 B10
Baleine = Whale →, *Canada* ... 103 A6
Băleni, *Romania* 43 E12
Baler, *Phil.* 61 D4
Baler Bay, *Phil.* 61 D4
Baleshare, *U.K.* 14 D1
Baleshwar, *India* 67 J15
Balezino, *Russia* 48 B11
Balfate, *Honduras* 120 C2
Balfe's Creek, *Australia* . 94 C4
Bali, *Cameroon* 83 D7
Balī, *Greece* 36 D6
Bali □, *Indonesia* 62 F5
Bali, Selat, *Indonesia* .. 63 H16
Baligród, *Poland* 45 J9
Balikeşir, *Turkey* 39 B9
Balıkesir □, *Turkey* 39 B9
Balıklıçeşme, *Turkey* ... 41 F11
Balikpapan, *Indonesia* . 62 E5
Balimbing, *Phil.* 63 C5
Baling, *Malaysia* 65 K3
Balingen, *Germany* 25 G4
Balinţ, *Romania* 42 E6
Balintang Channel, *Phil.* . 61 B4
Balipara, *India* 67 F18

Balkan Mts. = Stara Planina, *Bulgaria* ... 40 C7
Balkhash = Balqash, *Kazakstan* ... 50 E8
Balkhash, Ozero = Balqash Köl, *Kazakstan* ... 50 E8
Balla, *Bangla.* 67 G17
Ballachulish, *U.K.* 14 E3
Balladonia, *Australia* .. 93 F3
Ballaghaderreen, *Ireland* . 15 C3
Ballarat, *Australia* 95 F3
Ballard, L., *Australia* .. 93 E3
Ballater, *U.K.* 14 D5
Ballenas, Canal de, *Mexico* 118 B2
Balleny Is., *Antarctica* .. 5 C11
Balleroy, *France* 18 C6
Ballerup, *Denmark* 11 J6
Ballesteros, *Phil.* 61 B4
Ballı, *Turkey* 41 F11
Ballia, *India* 69 G11
Ballidu, *Australia* 93 F2
Ballina, *Australia* 95 D5
Ballina, *Ireland* 15 B2
Ballinasloe, *Ireland* ... 15 C3
Ballinger, *U.S.A.* 113 K5
Ballinrobe, *Ireland* ... 15 C2
Ballinskelligs B., *Ireland* . 15 E1
Ballon, *France* 18 D7
Ballsh, *Albania* 40 F3
Ballycastle, *U.K.* 15 A5
Ballyclare, *U.K.* 15 B5
Ballyhaunis, *Ireland* ... 15 C3
Ballymena, *U.K.* 15 B5
Ballymoney, *U.K.* 15 A5
Ballymote, *Ireland* 15 B3
Ballynahinch, *U.K.* 15 B6
Ballyquintin Pt., *U.K.* .. 15 B6
Ballyshannon, *Ireland* .. 15 B3
Balmaceda, *Chile* 128 F2
Balmazújváros, *Hungary* . 42 C6
Balmoral, *Australia* ... 95 F3
Balmorhea, *U.S.A.* 113 K3
Balonne →, *Australia* ... 95 D4
Balqash, *Kazakstan* ... 50 E8
Balqash Köl, *Kazakstan* . 50 E8
Balrampur, *India* 69 F10
Balranald, *Australia* ... 95 E3
Balş, *Romania* 43 F9
Balsas, *Mexico* 119 D5
Balsas →, *Brazil* 125 E9
Balsas →, *Mexico* 119 D5
Bålsta, *Sweden* 10 E11
Balston Spa, *U.S.A.* ... 111 D11
Balta, *Romania* 42 F7
Balta, *Ukraine* 47 H5
Balta, *U.S.A.* 112 A4
Baltanás, *Spain* 34 D6
Bălţi, *Moldova* 43 C12
Baltic Sea, *Europe* 9 H18
Baltîm, *Egypt* 80 H7
Baltimore, *Ireland* 15 E2
Baltimore, *U.S.A.* 108 F7
Baltit, *Pakistan* 69 A6
Baltiysk, *Russia* 9 J18
Baltrum, *Germany* 24 B3
Baluchistan □, *Pakistan* . 66 F4
Balurghat, *India* 69 G13
Balvi, *Latvia* 9 H22
Balya, *Turkey* 39 B9
Bam, *Iran* 71 D8
Bama, *China* 58 E6
Bama, *Nigeria* 83 C7
Bamako, *Mali* 82 C3
Bamba, *Mali* 83 B4
Bambari, *C.A.R.* 84 C4
Bambaroo, *Australia* .. 94 B4
Bamberg, *Germany* ... 25 F6
Bamberg, *U.S.A.* 109 J5
Bambesi, *Ethiopia* 81 F3
Bambey, *Senegal* 82 C1
Bambili, *Dem. Rep. of the Congo* 86 B2
Bamenda, *Cameroon* .. 83 D7
Bamfield, *Canada* 104 D3
Bamiancheng, *China* .. 57 C13
Bamkin, *Cameroon* ... 83 D7
Bāmīān □, *Afghan.* ... 66 B5
Bampūr, *Iran* 71 E9
Ban Ban, *Laos* 64 C4
Ban Bang Hin, *Thailand* . 65 H2
Ban Chiang Klang, *Thailand* ... 64 C3
Ban Chik, *Laos* 64 D4
Ban Choho, *Thailand* .. 64 E4
Ban Dan Lan Hoi, *Thailand* ... 64 D2
Ban Don = Surat Thani, *Thailand* ... 65 H2
Ban Don, *Vietnam* 64 F6
Ban Don, Ao →, *Thailand* 65 H2
Ban Dong, *Thailand* ... 64 C3
Ban Hong, *Thailand* .. 64 C2
Ban Kaeng, *Thailand* .. 64 D3
Ban Kantang, *Thailand* . 65 J2
Ban Keun, *Laos* 64 C4
Ban Khai, *Thailand* ... 64 F3
Ban Kheun, *Laos* 64 B3
Ban Khlong Kua, *Thailand* 65 J3
Ban Khuan Mao, *Thailand* 65 J2
Ban Ko Yai Chim, *Thailand* ... 65 G2
Ban Kok, *Thailand* ... 64 D4
Ban Laem, *Thailand* .. 64 F2
Ban Lao Ngam, *Laos* .. 64 E6
Ban Le Kathe, *Thailand* . 64 E2
Ban Mae Chedi, *Thailand* 64 C2

Ban Mae Laeng, *Thailand* 64 B2
Ban Mae Sariang, *Thailand* 64 C1
Ban Mê Thuot = Buon Ma Thuot, *Vietnam* 64 F7
Ban Mi, *Thailand* 64 E3
Ban Muong Mo, *Laos* .. 64 C4
Ban Na Mo, *Laos* 64 D5
Ban Na San, *Thailand* .. 65 H2
Ban Na Tong, *Laos* 64 B3
Ban Nam Ma, *Laos* ... 64 A3
Ban Ngang, *Laos* 64 E6
Ban Nong Bok, *Laos* .. 64 D5
Ban Nong Boua, *Laos* .. 64 E6
Ban Nong Pling, *Thailand* 64 E3
Ban Pak Chan, *Thailand* . 65 G2
Ban Phai, *Thailand* ... 64 D4
Ban Pong, *Thailand* ... 64 F2
Ban Ron Phibun, *Thailand* 65 H2
Ban Sanam Chai, *Thailand* 65 J3
Ban Sangkha, *Thailand* . 64 E4
Ban Tak, *Thailand* 64 D2
Ban Tako, *Thailand* ... 64 E4
Ban Tha Dua, *Thailand* . 64 D2
Ban Tha Li, *Thailand* .. 64 D3
Ban Tha Nun, *Thailand* . 65 H2
Ban Thahine, *Laos* 64 E5
Ban Xien Kok, *Laos* ... 64 B3
Ban Yen Nhan, *Vietnam* . 64 B6
Banaba, *Kiribati* 96 H8
Banalia, *Dem. Rep. of the Congo* 86 B2
Banam, *Cambodia* 65 G5
Banamba, *Mali* 82 C3
Banana, *Australia* 94 C5
Bananal, I. do, *Brazil* .. 125 F8
Banaras = Varanasi, *India* 69 G10
Banas →, *Gujarat, India* 68 H4
Banas →, *Mad. P., India* 69 G9
Bânâs, Ras, *Egypt* 80 C4
Banaz, *Turkey* 39 C11
Banaz →, *Turkey* 39 C11
Banbān, *Si. Arabia* 70 E5
Banbridge, *U.K.* 15 B5
Banbury, *U.K.* 13 E6
Banchory, *U.K.* 14 D6
Bancroft, *Canada* 102 C4
Band, *Romania* 43 D9
Band Boní, *Iran* 71 E8
Band Qīr, *Iran* 71 D6
Banda, *India* 69 G9
Banda, Kepulauan, *Indonesia* ... 63 E7
Banda Aceh, *Indonesia* . 62 C1
Banda Banda, Mt., *Australia* ... 95 E5
Banda Elat, *Indonesia* . 63 F8
Banda Is. = Banda, Kepulauan, *Indonesia* ... 63 E7
Banda Sea, *Indonesia* . 63 F8
Bandai-San, *Japan* 54 F10
Bandama →, *Ivory C.* .. 82 D3
Bandān, *Iran* 71 D9
Bandanaira, *Indonesia* . 63 E7
Bandanwara, *India* 68 F6
Bandar = Machilipatnam, *India* ... 67 L12
Bandār 'Abbās, *Iran* ... 71 E8
Bandar-e Anzalī, *Iran* .. 71 B6
Bandar-e Bushehr = Büshehr, *Iran* ... 71 D6
Bandar-e Chārak, *Iran* . 71 E7
Bandar-e Deylam, *Iran* . 71 D6
Bandar-e Khomeynī, *Iran* 71 D6
Bandar-e Lengeh, *Iran* . 71 E7
Bandar-e Ma'shur, *Iran* . 71 D6
Bandar-e Maqām, *Iran* . 71 E7
Bandar-e Nakhīlū, *Iran* . 71 E7
Bandar-e Rīg, *Iran* 71 D6
Bandar-e Torkeman, *Iran* . 71 B7
Bandar Maharani = Muar, *Malaysia* ... 65 L4
Bandar Penggaram = Batu Pahat, *Malaysia* ... 65 M4
Bandar Seri Begawan, *Brunei* ... 62 D5
Bandar Sri Aman, *Malaysia* 62 D4
Bandawe, *Malawi* 87 E3
Bande, *Spain* 34 C3
Bandeira, Pico da, *Brazil* 127 A7
Bandera, *Argentina* ... 126 B3
Bandera, *U.S.A.* 113 L5
Banderas, B. de, *Mexico* . 118 C3
Bandiagara, *Mali* 82 C4
Bandırma, *Turkey* 41 F11
Bandol, *France* 21 E9
Bandon, *Ireland* 15 E3
Bandon →, *Ireland* ... 15 E3
Bandula, *Mozam.* 87 F3
Bandundu, *Dem. Rep. of the Congo* 84 E3
Bandung, *Indonesia* ... 63 G12
Bandya, *Australia* 93 E3
Băneasa, *Romania* 43 E12
Bāneh, *Iran* 70 C5
Bañeres, *Spain* 33 G4
Banes, *Cuba* 121 B4
Banff, *Canada* 104 C5
Banff, *U.K.* 14 D6
Banff Nat. Park, *Canada* . 104 C5
Banfora, *Burkina Faso* .. 82 C4
Bang Fai →, *Laos* 64 D5
Bang Hieng →, *Laos* .. 64 D5
Bang Krathum, *Thailand* 64 D3
Bang Lamung, *Thailand* 64 F3
Bang Mun Nak, *Thailand* . 64 D3
Bang Pa In, *Thailand* ... 64 E3

Bayan Obo

Bang Rakam, *Thailand* ... 64 D3
Bang Saphan, *Thailand* ... 65 G2
Bangala Dam, *Zimbabwe* . 87 G3
Bangalore, *India* 66 N10
Bangangté, *Cameroon* 83 D7
Bangaon, *India* 69 H13
Bangassou, *C.A.R.* 84 D4
Banggai, Kepulauan, *Indonesia* 63 E6
Banggai Arch. = Banggai, Kepulauan, *Indonesia* .. 63 E6
Banggi, *Malaysia* 62 C5
Banghāzī, *Libya* 79 B10
Bangjang, *Sudan* 81 E3
Bangka, *Sulawesi, Indonesia* 63 D7
Bangka, *Sumatera, Indonesia* 62 E3
Bangka, Selat, *Indonesia* . 62 E3
Bangkalan, *Indonesia* 63 G15
Bangkinang, *Indonesia* ... 62 D2
Bangko, *Indonesia* 62 E2
Bangkok, *Thailand* 64 F3
Bangladesh ■, *Asia* 67 H17
Bangolo, *Ivory C.* 82 D3
Bangong Co, *India* 69 B8
Bangor, *Down, U.K.* 15 B6
Bangor, *Gwynedd, U.K.* .. 12 D3
Bangor, *Maine, U.S.A.* ... 103 D6
Bangor, *Pa., U.S.A.* 111 F9
Bangued, *Phil.* 61 C4
Bangui, *C.A.R.* 84 D3
Bangui, *Phil.* 61 B4
Banguru, *Dem. Rep. of the Congo* 86 B2
Bangweulu, L., *Zambia* .. 87 E3
Bangweulu Swamp, *Zambia* 87 E3
Bani, *Dom. Rep.* 121 C5
Bani →, *Mali* 82 C4
Bani Bangou, *Niger* 83 B5
Banī Sa'd, *Iraq* 70 C5
Bania, *Ivory C.* 82 D4
Banihal Pass, *India* 69 C6
Bāniyās, *Syria* 70 C3
Banja Luka, *Bos.-H.* 42 F2
Banjarmasin, *Indonesia* ... 62 E4
Banjul, *Gambia* 82 C1
Banka Banka, *Australia* .. 94 B1
Bankeryd, *Sweden* 11 G8
Banket, *Zimbabwe* 87 F3
Bankilaré, *Niger* 83 C5
Bankipore, *India* 69 G11
Banks I., *B.C., Canada* .. 104 C3
Banks I., *N.W.T., Canada* 4 B1
Banks Pen., *N.Z.* 91 K4
Banks Str., *Australia* 94 G4
Bankura, *India* 69 H12
Bankya, *Bulgaria* 40 D7
Bann →, *Arm., U.K.* 15 B5
Bann →, *L'derry., U.K.* . 15 A5
Banna, *Phil.* 61 C4
Bannalec, *France* 18 E3
Bannang Sata, *Thailand* .. 65 J3
Banning, *U.S.A.* 117 M10
Banningville = Bandundu, *Dem. Rep. of the Congo* 84 E3
Bannockburn, *Canada* 110 B7
Bannockburn, *U.K.* 14 E5
Bannockburn, *Zimbabwe* . 87 G2
Bannu, *Pakistan* 66 C7
Bañolas = Banyoles, *Spain* 32 C7
Banon, *France* 21 D9
Baños de la Encina, *Spain* 35 G7
Baños de Molgas, *Spain* .. 34 C3
Bánovce nad Bebravou, *Slovak Rep.* 27 C11
Banovići, *Bos.-H.* 42 F3
Banská Bystrica, *Slovak Rep.* 27 C12
Banská Štiavnica, *Slovak Rep.* 27 C11
Bansko, *Bulgaria* 40 E7
Banskobystrický □, *Slovak Rep.* 27 C12
Banswara, *India* 68 H6
Bantayan, *Phil.* 61 F5
Bantry, *Ireland* 15 E2
Bantry B., *Ireland* 15 E2
Bantul, *Indonesia* 63 G14
Bantva, *India* 68 J4
Banu, *Afghan.* 66 B6
Banya, *Bulgaria* 41 D8
Banyak, Kepulauan, *Indonesia* 62 D1
Banyalbufar, *Spain* 37 B9
Banyo, *Cameroon* 83 D7
Banyoles, *Spain* 32 C7
Banyuls-sur-Mer, *France* .. 20 F7
Banyumas, *Indonesia* 63 G13
Banyuwangi, *Indonesia* ... 63 H16
Banzare Coast, *Antarctica* 5 C9
Banzyville = Mobayi, *Dem. Rep. of the Congo* 84 D4
Bao Ha, *Vietnam* 64 A5
Bao Lac, *Vietnam* 64 A5
Bao Loc, *Vietnam* 65 G6
Bao'an = Shenzhen, *China* 59 F10
Baocheng, *China* 56 H4
Baode, *China* 56 E6
Baodi, *China* 57 E9
Baoding, *China* 56 E8
Baoji, *China* 56 G4
Baojing, *China* 58 C7
Baokang, *China* 59 B8
Baoshan, *Shanghai, China* 59 B13
Baoshan, *Yunnan, China* . 58 E2
Baotou, *China* 56 D6
Baoying, *China* 57 H10
Bap, *India* 68 F5
Bapatla, *India* 67 M12
Bapaume, *France* 19 B9
Bāqerābād, *Iran* 71 C6
Ba'qūbah, *Iraq* 70 C5
Baquedano, *Chile* 126 A2
Bar, *Montenegro, Yug.* ... 40 D3
Bar, *Ukraine* 47 H4
Bar Bigha, *India* 69 G11
Bar Harbor, *U.S.A.* 103 D6
Bar-le-Duc, *France* 19 D12
Bar-sur-Aube, *France* 19 D11
Bar-sur-Seine, *France* 19 D11
Bâra, *Romania* 43 C12
Barabai, *Indonesia* 62 E5
Baraboo, *U.S.A.* 112 D10
Baracoa, *Cuba* 121 B5
Baradā →, *Syria* 75 B5
Baradero, *Argentina* 126 C4
Baraga, *U.S.A.* 112 B10
Bărăganul, *Romania* 43 F12
Barahona, *Dom. Rep.* 121 C5
Barahona, *Spain* 32 D2
Barail Range, *India* 67 G18
Baraka →, *Sudan* 80 D4
Barakaldo, *Spain* 32 B2
Barakhola, *India* 67 G18
Barakot, *India* 69 J11
Barakpur, *India* 69 H13
Barakula, *Australia* 95 D5
Baralaba, *Australia* 94 C4
Baralla, *Spain* 34 C3
Baralzon L., *Canada* 105 B9
Barameiya, *Sudan* 80 D4
Baramula, *India* 69 B6
Baran, *India* 68 G7
Barañain, *Spain* 32 C3
Baranavichy, *Belarus* 47 F4
Baranof I., *U.S.A.* 104 B1
Baranów Sandomierski, *Poland* 45 H8
Baranya □, *Hungary* 42 E3
Baraolt, *Romania* 43 D10
Barapasi, *Indonesia* 63 E9
Barasat, *India* 69 H13
Barat Daya, Kepulauan, *Indonesia* 63 F7
Barataria B., *U.S.A.* 113 L10
Baraut, *India* 68 E7
Barbacena, *Brazil* 127 A7
Barbados ■, *W. Indies* ... 121 D8
Barban, *Croatia* 29 C11
Barbària, C. de, *Spain* ... 37 C7
Barbaros, *Turkey* 41 F11
Barbastro, *Spain* 32 C5
Barbate = Barbate de Franco, *Spain* 35 J5
Barbate de Franco, *Spain* . 35 J5
Barberino di Mugello, *Italy* 29 E8
Barberton, *S. Africa* 89 D5
Barberton, *U.S.A.* 110 E3
Barbezieux-St-Hilaire, *France* 20 C3
Barbosa, *Colombia* 124 B4
Barbourville, *U.S.A.* 109 G4
Barbuda, *W. Indies* 121 C7
Bârca, *Romania* 43 G8
Barcaldine, *Australia* 94 C4
Barcarrota, *Spain* 35 G4
Barcellona Pozzo di Gotto, *Italy* 31 D8
Barcelona, *Spain* 32 D7
Barcelona, *Venezuela* 124 A6
Barcelona □, *Spain* 32 D7
Barcelonette, *France* 21 D10
Barcelos, *Brazil* 124 D6
Barcin, *Poland* 45 F4
Barcoo →, *Australia* 94 D3
Barcs, *Hungary* 42 E2
Barczewo, *Poland* 44 E7
Bärdä, *Azerbaijan* 49 K8
Bardaï, *Chad* 79 D9
Bardas Blancas, *Argentina* 126 D2
Barddhaman, *India* 69 H12
Bardejov, *Slovak Rep.* 27 B14
Bardera, *Somali Rep.* 74 G3
Bardi, *Italy* 28 D6
Bardīyah, *Libya* 79 B10
Bardolino, *Italy* 28 C7
Bardonécchia, *Italy* 28 C3
Bardsey I., *U.K.* 12 E3
Bardstown, *U.S.A.* 108 G3
Bareilly, *India* 69 E8
Barentin, *France* 18 C7
Barenton, *France* 18 D6
Barents Sea, *Arctic* 4 B9
Barentu, *Eritrea* 81 D4
Barfleur, *France* 18 C5
Barfleur, Pte. de, *France* . 18 C5
Barga, *China* 60 C3
Barga, *Italy* 28 D7
Bargara, *Australia* 94 C5
Bargas, *Spain* 34 F6
Bârgăului Bistriţa, *Romania* 43 C9
Barge, *Italy* 28 D4
Bargnop, *Sudan* 81 F2
Bargteheide, *Germany* ... 24 B6
Barguzin, *Russia* 51 D11
Barh, *India* 69 G11
Barhaj, *India* 69 F10
Barhi, *India* 69 G11
Bari, *India* 68 F7
Bari, *Italy* 31 A9
Bari Doab, *Pakistan* 68 D5
Bari Sardo, *Italy* 30 C2
Bariadi □, *Tanzania* 86 C3
Barīm, *Yemen* 76 E8
Barinas, *Venezuela* 124 B4
Baring, C., *Canada* 100 B8
Baringo, *Kenya* 86 B4
Baringo □, *Kenya* 86 B4
Baringo, L., *Kenya* 86 B4
Bârîs, *Egypt* 80 C3
Barisal, *Bangla.* 67 H17
Barisan, Bukit, *Indonesia* . 62 E2
Barito →, *Indonesia* 62 E4
Barjac, *France* 21 D8
Barjols, *France* 21 E10
Bark L., *Canada* 110 A7
Barka = Baraka →, *Sudan* 80 D4
Barkam, *China* 58 B4
Barker, *U.S.A.* 110 C6
Barkley Sound, *Canada* .. 104 D3
Barkly Downs, *Australia* .. 94 C2
Barkly East, *S. Africa* 88 E4
Barkly Tableland, *Australia* 94 B2
Barkly West, *S. Africa* ... 88 D3
Barkol, Wadi →, *Sudan* . 80 D3
Barksdale, *U.S.A.* 113 L4
Barla Dağı, *Turkey* 39 C12
Bârlad, *Romania* 43 D12
Bârlad →, *Romania* 43 E12
Barlee, L., *Australia* 93 E2
Barlee, Mt., *Australia* 93 D4
Barletta, *Italy* 31 A9
Barlinek, *Poland* 45 F2
Barlovento, *Canary Is.* ... 37 F2
Barlow L., *Canada* 105 A8
Barmedman, *Australia* 95 E4
Barmer, *India* 68 G4
Barmera, *Australia* 95 E3
Barmouth, *U.K.* 12 E3
Barmstedt, *Germany* 24 B5
Barnagar, *India* 68 H6
Barnard Castle, *U.K.* 12 C6
Barnato, *Australia* 95 E4
Barnaul, *Russia* 50 D9
Barnesville, *U.S.A.* 109 J3
Barnet, *U.K.* 13 F7
Barneveld, *Neths.* 17 B5
Barneveld, *U.S.A.* 111 C9
Barneville-Cartevert, *France* 18 C5
Barngo, *Australia* 94 D4
Barnhart, *U.S.A.* 113 K4
Barnsley, *U.K.* 12 D6
Barnstaple, *U.K.* 13 F3
Barnstaple Bay = Bideford Bay, *U.K.* 13 F3
Barnsville, *U.S.A.* 112 B6
Baro, *Nigeria* 83 D6
Baro →, *Ethiopia* 81 F3
Baroda = Vadodara, *India* 68 H5
Baroda, *India* 68 G7
Baroe, *S. Africa* 88 E3
Baron Ra., *Australia* 92 D4
Barpeta, *India* 67 F17
Barques, Pt. Aux, *U.S.A.* 108 C4
Barquísimeto, *Venezuela* .. 124 A5
Barra, *Brazil* 125 F10
Barra, *U.K.* 14 E1
Barra, Sd. of, *U.K.* 14 D1
Barra de Navidad, *Mexico* 118 D4
Barra do Corda, *Brazil* ... 125 E9
Barra do Piraí, *Brazil* 127 A7
Barra Falsa, Pta. da, *Mozam.* 89 C6
Barra Hd., *U.K.* 14 E1
Barra Mansa, *Brazil* 127 A7
Barraba, *Australia* 95 E5
Barrackpur = Barakpur, *India* 69 H13
Barrafranca, *Italy* 31 E7
Barraigh = Barra, *U.K.* .. 14 E1
Barranca, *Lima, Peru* 124 F3
Barranca, *Loreto, Peru* ... 124 D3
Barrancabermeja, *Colombia* 124 B4
Barrancas, *Venezuela* 124 B6
Barrancos, *Portugal* 35 G4
Barranqueras, *Argentina* .. 126 B4
Barranquilla, *Colombia* ... 124 A4
Barraute, *Canada* 102 C4
Barre, *Mass., U.S.A.* 111 D12
Barre, *Vt., U.S.A.* 111 B12
Barreal, *Argentina* 126 C2
Barreiras, *Brazil* 125 F10
Barreirinhas, *Brazil* 125 D10
Barreiro, *Portugal* 35 G1
Barrême, *France* 21 E10
Barren, Nosy, *Madag.* 89 B7
Barretos, *Brazil* 125 H9
Barrhead, *Canada* 104 C6
Barrie, *Canada* 102 D4
Barrier Ra., *Australia* 95 E3
Barrière, *Canada* 104 C4
Barrington, *U.S.A.* 111 E13
Barrington L., *Canada* ... 105 B8
Barrington Tops, *Australia* 95 E5
Barringun, *Australia* 95 D4
Barro do Garças, *Brazil* .. 125 G8
Barrow, *U.S.A.* 100 A4
Barrow →, *Ireland* 15 D5
Barrow Creek, *Australia* .. 94 C1
Barrow I., *Australia* 92 D2
Barrow-in-Furness, *U.K.* . 12 C4
Barrow Pt., *Australia* 94 A3
Barrow Pt., *U.S.A.* 98 B4
Barrow Ra., *Australia* 93 E4
Barrow Str., *Canada* 4 B3
Barruecopardo, *Spain* 34 D4
Barruelo de Santullán, *Spain* 34 C6
Barry, *U.K.* 13 F4
Barry's Bay, *Canada* 102 C4
Barsalogho, *Burkina Faso* 83 C4
Barsat, *Pakistan* 69 A5
Barsham, *Syria* 70 C4
Barsi, *India* 66 K9
Barsinghausen, *Germany* . 24 C5
Barsoi, *India* 67 G15
Barstow, *Calif., U.S.A.* ... 117 L9
Barstow, *Tex., U.S.A.* 113 K3
Barth, *Germany* 24 A8
Barthélemy, Col, *Vietnam* 64 C5
Bartica, *Guyana* 124 B7
Bartin, *Turkey* 72 B5
Bartlesville, *U.S.A.* 113 G7
Bartlett, *Calif., U.S.A.* ... 116 J8
Bartlett, *Tex., U.S.A.* 113 K6
Bartlett, L., *Canada* 104 A5
Bartolomeu Dias, *Mozam.* 87 G4
Barton, *Australia* 93 F5
Barton upon Humber, *U.K.* 12 D7
Bartoszyce, *Poland* 44 D7
Bartow, *U.S.A.* 109 M5
Barú, Volcan, *Panama* ... 120 E3
Barumba, *Dem. Rep. of the Congo* 86 B1
Baruth, *Germany* 24 C9
Barvinkove, *Ukraine* 47 H9
Barwani, *India* 68 H6
Barwice, *Poland* 44 E3
Barycz →, *Poland* 45 G3
Barysaw, *Belarus* 46 E5
Barysh, *Russia* 48 D8
Barzān, *Iraq* 70 B5
Bârzava, *Romania* 42 D6
Bas-Rhin □, *France* 19 D14
Bašaid, *Serbia, Yug.* 42 E5
Bāsa'idū, *Iran* 71 E7
Basal, *Pakistan* 68 C5
Basankusa, *Dem. Rep. of the Congo* 84 D3
Basarabeasca, *Moldova* ... 43 D13
Basarabi, *Romania* 43 F13
Basauri, *Spain* 32 B2
Basawa, *Afghan.* 68 B4
Bascuñán, C., *Chile* 126 B1
Basel, *Switz.* 25 H3
Baselland □, *Switz.* 25 H3
Basento →, *Italy* 31 B9
Bāshī, *Iran* 71 D6
Bashi Channel, *Phil.* 60 D7
Bashkir Republic = Bashkortostan □, *Russia* 50 D6
Bashkortostan □, *Russia* .. 50 D6
Basilan, *Phil.* 61 H5
Basilan Str., *Phil.* 61 H5
Basildon, *U.K.* 13 F8
Basilicata □, *Italy* 31 B9
Basim = Washim, *India* .. 66 J10
Basin, *U.S.A.* 114 D9
Basingstoke, *U.K.* 13 F6
Baška, *Croatia* 29 D11
Başkale, *Turkey* 73 C10
Baskatong, Rés., *Canada* . 102 C4
Basle = Basel, *Switz.* 25 H3
Başmakçı, *Turkey* 39 D12
Basoda, *India* 68 H7
Basoka, *Dem. Rep. of the Congo* 86 B1
Basque, Pays, *France* 20 E2
Basque Provinces = País Vasco □, *Spain* 32 C2
Basra = Al Başrah, *Iraq* .. 70 D5
Bass Str., *Australia* 94 F4
Bassano, *Canada* 104 C6
Bassano del Grappa, *Italy* 29 C8
Bassar, *Togo* 83 D5
Bassas da India, *Ind. Oc.* . 85 J7
Basse-Normandie □, *France* 18 D6
Basse Santa-Su, *Gambia* .. 82 C2
Basse-Terre, *Guadeloupe* . 121 C7
Bassein, *Burma* 67 L19
Basseterre, *St. Kitts & Nevis* 121 C7
Bassett, *Nebr., U.S.A.* ... 112 D5
Bassett, *Va., U.S.A.* 109 G6
Bassi, *India* 68 D7
Bassigny, *France* 19 E12
Bassikounou, *Mauritania* . 82 B3
Bassum, *Germany* 24 C4
Båstad, *Sweden* 11 H6
Bastak, *Iran* 71 E7
Baştām, *Iran* 71 B7
Bastar, *India* 67 K12
Bastelica, *France* 21 F13
Basti, *India* 69 F10
Bastia, *France* 21 F13
Bastogne, *Belgium* 17 D5
Bastrop, *U.S.A.* 113 K6
Bat Yam, *Israel* 75 C3
Bata, *Eq. Guin.* 84 D1
Bata, *Romania* 42 D7
Bataan, *Phil.* 61 D4
Batabanó, *Cuba* 120 B3
Batabanó, G. de, *Cuba* ... 120 B3
Batac, *Phil.* 61 B4
Batagai, *Russia* 51 C14
Batajnica, *Serbia, Yug.* ... 40 B4
Batak, *Bulgaria* 41 E8
Batalha, *Portugal* 34 F2
Batama, *Dem. Rep. of the Congo* 86 B2
Batamay, *Russia* 51 C13
Batan I., *Phil.* 61 A4
Batanes Is., *Phil.* 61 A4
Batang, *China* 58 B2
Batang, *Indonesia* 63 G13
Batangas, *Phil.* 61 E4
Batanta, *Indonesia* 63 E8
Batatais, *Brazil* 127 A6
Batavia, *U.S.A.* 110 D6
Bataysk, *Russia* 47 J10
Batchelor, *Australia* 92 B5
Batdambang, *Cambodia* .. 64 F4
Bateman's B., *Australia* .. 95 F5
Batemans Bay, *Australia* .. 95 F5
Bates Ra., *Australia* 93 E3
Batesburg, *U.S.A.* 109 J5
Batesville, *Ark., U.S.A.* .. 113 H9
Batesville, *Miss., U.S.A.* . 113 H10
Batesville, *Tex., U.S.A.* .. 113 L5
Bath, *U.K.* 13 F5
Bath, *Maine, U.S.A.* 103 D6
Bath, *N.Y., U.S.A.* 110 D7
Bath & North East Somerset □, *U.K.* 13 F5
Batheay, *Cambodia* 65 G5
Bathurst = Banjul, *Gambia* 82 C1
Bathurst, *Australia* 95 E4
Bathurst, *Canada* 103 C6
Bathurst, *S. Africa* 88 E4
Bathurst, C., *Canada* 4 B1
Bathurst B., *Australia* ... 94 A3
Bathurst Harb., *Australia* . 94 G4
Bathurst I., *Australia* 92 B5
Bathurst I., *Canada* 4 B2
Bathurst Inlet, *Canada* ... 100 B9
Batie, *Burkina Faso* 82 D4
Batlow, *Australia* 95 F4
Batman, *Turkey* 73 D9
Batna, *Algeria* 78 A7
Batobato, *Phil.* 61 H7
Batočina, *Serbia, Yug.* ... 40 B5
Batoka, *Zambia* 87 F2
Baton Rouge, *U.S.A.* 113 K9
Batong, Ko, *Thailand* 65 J2
Bátonyterenye, *Hungary* .. 42 C4
Batopilas, *Mexico* 118 B3
Batouri, *Cameroon* 84 D2
Båtsfjord, *Norway* 8 A23
Battambang = Batdambang, *Cambodia* 64 F4
Batticaloa, *Sri Lanka* 66 R12
Battipáglia, *Italy* 31 B7
Battle, *U.K.* 13 G8
Battle →, *Canada* 105 C7
Battle Camp, *Australia* ... 94 B3
Battle Creek, *U.S.A.* 108 D3
Battle Ground, *U.S.A.* ... 116 E4
Battle Harbour, *Canada* .. 103 B8
Battle Lake, *U.S.A.* 112 B7
Battle Mountain, *U.S.A.* . 114 F5
Battlefields, *Zimbabwe* ... 87 F2
Battleford, *Canada* 105 C7
Battonya, *Hungary* 42 D6
Batu, Kepulauan, *Indonesia* 62 E1
Batu, Mt., *Ethiopia* 81 F4
Batu Caves, *Malaysia* 65 L3
Batu Gajah, *Malaysia* 65 K3
Batu Is. = Batu, Kepulauan, *Indonesia* .. 62 E1
Batu Pahat, *Malaysia* 65 M4
Batuata, *Indonesia* 63 F6
Batumi, *Georgia* 49 K5
Baturaja, *Indonesia* 62 E2
Baturité, *Brazil* 125 D11
Bau, *Malaysia* 62 D4
Baubau, *Indonesia* 63 F6
Bauchi, *Nigeria* 83 C6
Bauchi □, *Nigeria* 83 C7
Baud, *France* 18 E3
Baudette, *U.S.A.* 112 A7
Bauer, C., *Australia* 95 E1
Bauhinia Downs, *Australia* 94 C4
Baukau, *Indonesia* 63 F7
Baume-les-Dames, *France* 19 E13
Baunatal, *Germany* 24 D5
Baunei, *Italy* 30 B2
Bauru, *Brazil* 127 A6
Bauska, *Latvia* 9 H21
Bautino, *Kazakstan* 49 H10
Bautzen, *Germany* 24 D10
Bavānāt, *Iran* 71 D7
Bavanište, *Serbia, Yug.* ... 42 F5
Bavaria = Bayern □, *Germany* 25 G7
Båven, *Sweden* 10 E10
Bavi Sadri, *India* 68 G6
Bavispe →, *Mexico* 118 B3
Bawdwin, *Burma* 67 H20
Bawean, *Indonesia* 62 F4
Bawku, *Ghana* 83 C4
Bawlake, *Burma* 67 K20
Bawolung, *China* 58 C3
Baxley, *U.S.A.* 109 K4
Baxoi, *China* 58 B1
Baxter Springs, *U.S.A.* ... 113 G7
Bay Bulls, *Canada* 103 C9
Bay City, *Mich., U.S.A.* .. 108 D4
Bay City, *Oreg., U.S.A.* .. 114 D2
Bay City, *Tex., U.S.A.* ... 113 L7
Bay de Verde, *Canada* 103 C9
Bay Minette, *U.S.A.* 109 K2
Bay St. Louis, *U.S.A.* 113 K10
Bay Springs, *U.S.A.* 113 K10
Bay View, *N.Z.* 91 H6
Baya, *Dem. Rep. of the Congo* 87 E2
Bayamo, *Cuba* 120 B4
Bayamón, *Puerto Rico* ... 121 C6
Bayan Har Shan, *China* .. 60 C4
Bayan Hot = Alxa Zuoqi, *China* 56 E3
Bayan Obo, *China* 56 D5

Bayan-Ovoo, *Mongolia* ... 56 C4
Bayana, *India* 68 F7
Bayanaūyl, *Kazakstan* .. 50 D8
Bayandalay, *Mongolia* 56 C2
Bayanhongor, *Mongolia* .. 60 B5
Bayard, *U.S.A.* 112 E3
Bayawan, *Phil.* 61 G5
Baybay, *Phil.* 61 F6
Bayburt, *Turkey* 73 B9
Bayerische Alpen,
  Germany 25 H7
Bayerischer Wald,
  Germany 25 G8
Bayern □, *Germany* 25 G7
Bayeux, *France* 18 C6
Bayfield, *Canada* 110 C3
Bayfield, *U.S.A.* 112 B9
Bayındır, *Turkey* 39 C9
Baykal, Oz., *Russia* 51 D11
Baykonur = Bayqongyr,
  Kazakstan 50 E7
Baynes Mts., *Namibia* .. 88 B1
Bayombong, *Phil.* 61 C4
Bayon, *France* 19 D13
Bayona = Baiona, *Spain* . 34 C2
Bayonne, *France* 20 E2
Bayonne, *U.S.A.* 111 F10
Bayovar, *Peru* 124 E2
Bayqongyr, *Kazakstan* .. 50 E7
Bayram-Ali = Bayramaly,
  Turkmenistan 50 F7
Bayramaly, *Turkmenistan* 50 F7
Bayramiç, *Turkey* 39 B8
Bayreuth, *Germany* 25 F7
Bayrischzell, *Germany* .. 25 H8
Bayrūt, *Lebanon* 75 B4
Bayt Lahm, *West Bank* ... 75 D4
Baytown, *U.S.A.* 113 L7
Bayzo, *Niger* 83 C5
Baza, *Spain* 35 H8
Bazar Dyuzi, *Russia* 49 K8
Bazardüzü = Bazar Dyuzi,
  Russia 49 K8
Bazarny Karabulak, *Russia* 48 D8
Bazarny Syzgan, *Russia* .. 48 D8
Bazaruto, I. do, *Mozam.* . 89 C6
Bazas, *France* 20 D3
Bazhong, *China* 58 B6
Bazmān, Kūh-e, *Iran* 71 D9
Beach, *U.S.A.* 112 B3
Beach City, *U.S.A.* 110 F3
Beachport, *Australia* 95 F3
Beachy Hd., *U.K.* 13 G8
Beacon, *Australia* 93 F2
Beacon, *U.S.A.* 111 E11
Beaconia, *Canada* 105 C9
Beagle, Canal, *S. Amer.* .. 122 J4
Beagle Bay, *Australia* ... 92 C3
Bealanana, *Madag.* 89 A8
Beamsville, *Canada* 110 C5
Bear →, *U.S.A.* 116 G5
Béar, C., *France* 20 F7
Bear I., *Ireland* 15 E2
Bear L., *B.C., Canada* .. 104 B3
Bear L., *Man., Canada* .. 105 B9
Bear L., *U.S.A.* 114 F8
Bearcreek, *U.S.A.* 114 D9
Beardmore, *Canada* 102 C2
Beardmore Glacier,
  Antarctica 5 E11
Beardstown, *U.S.A.* ... 112 F9
Béarn, *France* 20 E3
Bearpaw Mts., *U.S.A.* .. 114 B9
Bearskin Lake, *Canada* .. 102 B1
Beas de Segura, *Spain* 35 G8
Beasain, *Spain* 32 B2
Beata, C., *Dom. Rep.* ... 121 C5
Beata, I., *Dom. Rep.* ... 121 C5
Beatrice, *U.S.A.* 112 E6
Beatrice, *Zimbabwe* 87 F3
Beatrice, C., *Australia* .. 94 A2
Beatton →, *Canada* 104 B4
Beatton River, *Canada* .. 104 B4
Beatty, *U.S.A.* 116 J10
Beaucaire, *France* 21 E8
Beauce, Plaine de la,
  France 19 D8
Beauceville, *Canada* 103 C5
Beaudesert, *Australia* ... 95 D5
Beaufort, *France* 21 C10
Beaufort, *Malaysia* 62 C5
Beaufort, *N.C., U.S.A.* ... 109 H7
Beaufort, *S.C., U.S.A.* ... 109 J5
Beaufort Sea, *Arctic* 4 B1
Beaufort West, *S. Africa* . 88 E3
Beaugency, *France* 19 E8
Beauharnois, *Canada* ... 102 C5
Beaujeu, *France* 19 F11
Beaujolais, *France* 19 F11
Beaulieu →, *Canada* 104 A6
Beaulieu-sur-Dordogne,
  France 20 D5
Beaulieu-sur-Mer, *France* . 21 E11
Beauly, *U.K.* 14 D4
Beauly →, *U.K.* 14 D4
Beaumaris, *U.K.* 12 D3
Beaumont, *Belgium* 17 D4
Beaumont, *France* 20 D4
Beaumont, *U.S.A.* 113 K7
Beaumont-de-Lomagne,
  France 20 E5
Beaumont-le-Roger, *France* 18 C7
Beaumont-sur-Sarthe,
  France 18 D7
Beaune, *France* 19 E11
Beaune-la-Rolande, *France* 19 D9
Beaupréau, *France* 18 E6

Beauraing, *Belgium* 17 D4
Beaurepaire, *France* 21 C9
Beauséjour, *Canada* 105 C9
Beauvais, *France* 19 C9
Beauval, *Canada* 105 B7
Beauvoir-sur-Mer, *France* . 18 F4
Beauvoir-sur-Niort, *France* 20 B3
Beaver, *Okla., U.S.A.* ... 113 G4
Beaver, *Pa., U.S.A.* 110 F4
Beaver, *Utah, U.S.A.* ... 115 G7
Beaver →, *B.C., Canada* 104 B4
Beaver →, *Ont., Canada* 102 A2
Beaver →, *Sask., Canada* 105 B7
Beaver City, *U.S.A.* 112 E5
Beaver Dam, *U.S.A.* ... 112 D10
Beaver Falls, *U.S.A.* ... 110 F4
Beaver Hill L., *Canada* .. 105 C10
Beaver I., *U.S.A.* 108 C3
Beaverhill L., *Alta.,
  Canada* 104 C6
Beaverhill L., *N.W.T.,
  Canada* 105 A8
Beaverlodge, *Canada* ... 104 B5
Beavermouth, *Canada* .. 104 C5
Beaverstone →, *Canada* . 102 B2
Beaverton, *Canada* 110 B5
Beaverton, *U.S.A.* 116 E4
Beawar, *India* 68 F6
Bebedouro, *Brazil* 127 A6
Beboa, *Madag.* 89 B7
Bebra, *Germany* 24 E5
Beccles, *U.K.* 13 E9
Bečej, *Serbia, Yug.* 42 E5
Beceni, *Romania* 43 E11
Becerreá, *Spain* 34 C3
Béchar, *Algeria* 78 B5
Bechyně, *Czech Rep.* 26 B7
Beckley, *U.S.A.* 108 G5
Beckum, *Germany* 24 D4
Beclean, *Romania* 43 C9
Bečov nad Teplou,
  Czech Rep. 26 A5
Bečva →, *Czech Rep.* ... 27 B10
Bédar, *Spain* 33 H3
Bédarieux, *France* 20 E7
Bedele, *Ethiopia* 81 F4
Bederkesa, *Germany* ... 24 B4
Bedeso, *Ethiopia* 81 F5
Bedford, *Canada* 102 C5
Bedford, *S. Africa* 88 E4
Bedford, *U.K.* 13 E7
Bedford, *Ind., U.S.A.* ... 108 F2
Bedford, *Iowa, U.S.A.* .. 112 E7
Bedford, *Ohio, U.S.A.* .. 110 E3
Bedford, *Pa., U.S.A.* ... 110 F6
Bedford, *Va., U.S.A.* ... 108 G6
Bedford, C., *Australia* ... 94 B4
Bedford Downs, *Australia* 92 C4
Bedfordshire □, *U.K.* ... 13 E7
Będków, *Poland* 45 G6
Bednja →, *Croatia* 29 B13
Bednodemyanovsk, *Russia* 48 D6
Bedónia, *Italy* 28 D6
Bedourie, *Australia* 94 C2
Bedum, *Neths.* 17 A6
Będzin, *Poland* 45 H6
Beech Grove, *U.S.A.* ... 108 F2
Beechy, *Canada* 105 C7
Beelitz, *Germany* 24 C8
Beenleigh, *Australia* 95 D5
Be'er Menuha, *Israel* ... 70 D2
Be'er Sheva, *Israel* 75 D3
Beersheba = Be'er Sheva,
  Israel 75 D3
Beeskow, *Germany* 24 C10
Beeston, *U.K.* 12 E6
Beetaloo, *Australia* 94 B1
Beetzendorf, *Germany* .. 24 C7
Beeville, *U.S.A.* 113 L6
Befale,
  Dem. Rep. of the Congo 84 D4
Befandriana, *Madag.* ... 89 C7
Befotaka, *Madag.* 89 C8
Bega, *Australia* 95 F4
Bega, Canalul, *Romania* . 42 E5
Bégard, *France* 18 D3
Beğendik, *Turkey* 41 F10
Begusarai, *India* 69 G12
Behābād, *Iran* 71 C8
Behara, *Madag.* 89 C8
Behbehān, *Iran* 71 D6
Behshahr, *Iran* 71 B7
Bei Jiang →, *China* 59 F9
Bei'an, *China* 60 B7
Beibei, *China* 60 D5
Beihai, *China* 58 G7
Beijing, *China* 56 E9
Beijing □, *China* 56 E9
Beilen, *Neths.* 17 B6
Beiliu, *China* 59 F8
Beilngries, *Germany* 25 G7
Beilpajah, *Australia* 95 E3
Beilul, *Eritrea* 81 E5
Beinn na Faoghla =
  Benbecula, *U.K.* 14 D1
Beipiao, *China* 57 D11
Beira, *Mozam.* 87 F3
Beirut = Bayrūt, *Lebanon* 75 B4
Beitaolaizhao, *China* 57 B13
Beitbridge, *Zimbabwe* ... 87 G3
Beiuş, *Romania* 42 D7
Beizhen, *Liaoning, China* 57 D11
Beizhen, *Shandong, China* 57 F10
Beizhengzhen, *China* 57 B12
Beja, *Portugal* 35 G3
Béja, *Tunisia* 79 A7
Beja □, *Portugal* 35 H3

Bejaia, *Algeria* 78 A7
Béjar, *Spain* 34 E5
Bejestān, *Iran* 71 C8
Bekçiler, *Turkey* 39 E11
Békés, *Hungary* 42 D6
Békés □, *Hungary* 42 D6
Békéscsaba, *Hungary* ... 42 D6
Bekilli, *Turkey* 39 C11
Bekily, *Madag.* 89 C8
Bekoji, *Ethiopia* 81 F4
Bekok, *Malaysia* 65 L4
Bekwai, *Ghana* 83 D4
Bela, *India* 69 G10
Bela, *Pakistan* 68 F2
Bela Crkva, *Serbia, Yug.* 42 F6
Bela Palanka, *Serbia, Yug.* 40 C6
Bela Vista, *Brazil* 126 A4
Bela Vista, *Mozam.* 89 D5
Bélâbre, *France* 20 B5
Belalcázar, *Spain* 35 G5
Belanovica, *Serbia, Yug.* .. 40 B4
Belau = Palau ■, *Pac. Oc.* 96 G5
Belavenona, *Madag.* 89 C8
Belawan, *Indonesia* 62 D1
Belaya, *Ethiopia* 81 E4
Belaya Glina, *Russia* 49 G5
Belaya Kalitva, *Russia* .. 49 F5
Belaya Tserkov = Bila
  Tserkva, *Ukraine* ... 47 H6
Belcești, *Romania* 43 C12
Belchatów, *Poland* 45 G6
Belcher Is., *Canada* 101 C12
Belchite, *Spain* 32 D4
Belden, *U.S.A.* 116 E5
Belém, *Brazil* 125 D9
Belén, *Argentina* 126 B2
Belén, *Paraguay* 126 A4
Belen, *U.S.A.* 115 J10
Belene, *Bulgaria* 41 C9
Beleni, *Turkey* 72 D7
Belet Uen, *Somali Rep.* . 74 G4
Belev, *Russia* 46 F9
Belevi, *Turkey* 39 C9
Belfair, *U.S.A.* 116 C4
Belfast, *S. Africa* 89 D5
Belfast, *U.K.* 15 B6
Belfast, *Maine, U.S.A.* .. 103 D6
Belfast, *N.Y., U.S.A.* ... 110 D6
Belfast L., *U.K.* 15 B6
Belfield, *U.S.A.* 112 B3
Belfort, *France* 19 E13
Belfort, Territoire de □,
  France 19 E13
Belfry, *U.S.A.* 114 D9
Belgaum, *India* 66 M9
Belgioioso, *Italy* 28 C6
Belgium ■, *Europe* 17 D4
Belgodère, *France* 21 F13
Belgorod, *Russia* 47 G7
Belgorod-Dnestrovskiy =
  Bilhorod-Dnistrovskyy,
  Ukraine 47 J6
Belgrade = Beograd,
  Serbia, Yug. 40 B4
Belgrade, *U.S.A.* 114 D8
Belhaven, *U.S.A.* 109 H7
Beli Drim →, *Europe* ... 40 D4
Beli Manastir, *Croatia* ... 42 E3
Beli Timok →,
  Serbia, Yug. 40 C6
Bélice →, *Italy* 30 E5
Belinskiy, *Russia* 48 D5
Belinyu, *Indonesia* 62 E3
Beliton Is. = Belitung,
  Indonesia 62 E3
Belitung, *Indonesia* 62 E3
Beliu, *Romania* 42 D6
Belize ■, *Cent. Amer.* .. 119 D7
Belize City, *Belize* 119 D7
Beljakovci, *Macedonia* .. 40 D5
Beljanica, *Serbia, Yug.* .. 40 B5
Belkovskiy, Ostrov, *Russia* 51 B14
Bell →, *Canada* 102 C4
Bell Bay, *Australia* 94 G4
Bell I., *Canada* 103 B8
Bell-Irving →, *Canada* .. 104 B3
Bell Peninsula, *Canada* .. 101 B11
Bell Ville, *Argentina* 126 C3
Bella, *Italy* 31 B8
Bella Bella, *Canada* 104 C3
Bella Coola, *Canada* 104 C3
Bella Unión, *Uruguay* ... 126 C4
Bella Vista, Corrientes,
  Argentina 126 B4
Bella Vista, Tucuman,
  Argentina 126 B2
Bellac, *France* 20 B5
Bellágio, *Italy* 28 C6
Bellaire, *U.S.A.* 110 F4
Bellária, *Italy* 29 D9
Bellary, *India* 66 M10
Bellata, *Australia* 95 D4
Belle Fourche, *U.S.A.* .. 112 C3
Belle Fourche →, *U.S.A.* 112 C3
Belle Glade, *U.S.A.* 109 M5
Belle-Île, *France* 18 E3
Belle Isle, *Canada* 103 B8
Belle Isle, Str. of, *Canada* 103 B8
Belle Plaine, *Iowa, U.S.A.* 112 E8
Belle Plaine, *Minn., U.S.A.* 112 C8
Belle Yella, *Liberia* 82 D3
Belledonne, *France* 21 C10
Belledune, *Canada* 103 C6
Bellefontaine, *U.S.A.* ... 108 E4
Bellefonte, *U.S.A.* 110 F7

Bellegarde, *France* 19 E9
Bellegarde-en-Marche,
  France 20 C6
Bellegarde-sur-Valserine,
  France 19 F12
Bellême, *France* 18 D7
Belleoram, *Canada* 103 C8
Belleville, *Canada* 102 D4
Belleville, *France* 19 F11
Belleville, *Ill., U.S.A.* .. 112 F10
Belleville, *Kans., U.S.A.* . 112 F6
Belleville, *N.Y., U.S.A.* .. 111 C8
Belleville-sur-Vie, *France* . 18 F5
Bellevue, *Canada* 104 D6
Bellevue, *Idaho, U.S.A.* . 114 E6
Bellevue, *Ohio, U.S.A.* .. 110 E2
Bellevue, *Wash., U.S.A.* . 116 C4
Belley, *France* 21 C9
Bellin = Kangirsuk,
  Canada 101 C13
Bellinge, *Denmark* 11 J4
Bellingen, *Australia* 95 E5
Bellingham, *U.S.A.* 116 B4
Bellingshausen Sea,
  Antarctica 5 C17
Bellinzona, *Switz.* 25 J5
Bello, *Colombia* 124 B3
Bellows Falls, *U.S.A.* ... 111 C12
Bellpat, *Pakistan* 68 E3
Bellpuig d'Urgell, *Spain* . 32 D6
Belluno, *Italy* 29 B9
Bellville, *U.S.A.* 113 L6
Bellwood, *U.S.A.* 110 F6
Bélmez, *Spain* 35 G5
Belmont, *Australia* 95 E5
Belmont, *Canada* 110 D3
Belmont, *S. Africa* 88 D3
Belmont, *U.S.A.* 110 D6
Belmonte, *Brazil* 125 G11
Belmonte, *Portugal* 34 E3
Belmonte, *Spain* 33 F2
Belmopan, *Belize* 119 D7
Belmullet, *Ireland* 15 B2
Belo Horizonte, *Brazil* .. 125 G10
Belo-sur-Mer, *Madag.* .. 89 C7
Belo-Tsiribihina, *Madag.* 89 B7
Belogorsk = Bilohirsk,
  Ukraine 47 K8
Belogorsk, *Russia* 51 D13
Belogradchik, *Bulgaria* .. 40 C6
Beloha, *Madag.* 89 D8
Beloit, *Kans., U.S.A.* ... 112 F5
Beloit, *Wis., U.S.A.* 112 D10
Belokorovichi, *Ukraine* .. 47 G5
Belomorsk, *Russia* 50 C4
Belonia, *India* 67 H17
Belopolye = Bilopillya,
  Ukraine 47 G8
Belorechensk, *Russia* ... 49 H4
Belorussia = Belarus ■,
  Europe 46 F4
Beloslav, *Bulgaria* 41 C11
Belovo, *Bulgaria* 41 D8
Belovo, *Russia* 50 D9
Belovodsk, *Ukraine* 47 H10
Beloye, Ozero, *Russia* .. 46 B9
Beloye More, *Russia* ... 50 C4
Belozem, *Bulgaria* 41 D9
Belozersk, *Russia* 46 B9
Belpasso, *Italy* 31 E7
Beltana, *Australia* 95 E2
Belterra, *Brazil* 125 D8
Beltinci, *Slovenia* 29 B13
Belton, *S.C., U.S.A.* 109 H4
Belton, *Tex., U.S.A.* 113 K6
Belton Res., *U.S.A.* 113 K6
Beltsy = Bălți, *Moldova* . 43 C12
Belturbet, *Ireland* 15 B4
Belukha, *Russia* 50 E9
Beluran, *Malaysia* 62 C5
Beluša, *Slovak Rep.* 27 B11
Belušić, *Serbia, Yug.* 40 C5
Belvedere Maríttimo, *Italy* 31 C8
Belvès, *France* 20 D5
Belvidere, *Ill., U.S.A.* .. 112 D10
Belvidere, *N.J., U.S.A.* .. 111 F9
Belvis de la Jara, *Spain* .. 34 F6
Belyando →, *Australia* .. 94 C4
Belyy, *Russia* 46 E7
Belyy, Ostrov, *Russia* ... 50 B8
Belyy Yar, *Russia* 50 D9
Belzec, *Poland* 45 H10
Belzig, *Germany* 24 C8
Belzoni, *U.S.A.* 113 J9
Bełżyce, *Poland* 45 G9
Bemaraha, Lembalemban'
  i, *Madag.* 89 B7
Bemarivo, *Madag.* 89 B8
Bemarivo →, *Madag.* ... 89 C8
Bemavo, *Madag.* 89 C8
Bembéréke, *Benin* 83 C5
Bembesi, *Zimbabwe* 87 G2
Bembesi →, *Zimbabwe* .. 87 F2
Bembibre, *Spain* 34 C4
Bemidji, *U.S.A.* 112 B7
Ben, *Iran* 71 C6
Ben Cruachan, *U.K.* 14 E3
Ben Dearg, *U.K.* 14 D4
Ben Hope, *U.K.* 14 C4
Ben Lawers, *U.K.* 14 E4
Ben Lomond, *N.S.W.,
  Australia* 95 E5
Ben Lomond, *Tas.,
  Australia* 94 G4
Ben Lomond, *U.K.* 14 E4

Ben Luc, *Vietnam* 65 G6
Ben Macdhui, *U.K.* 14 D5
Ben Mhor, *U.K.* 14 D1
Ben More, *Arg. & Bute,
  U.K.* 14 E2
Ben More, *Stirl., U.K.* .. 14 E4
Ben More Assynt, *U.K.* . 14 C4
Ben Nevis, *U.K.* 14 E3
Ben Quang, *Vietnam* ... 64 D6
Ben Vorlich, *U.K.* 14 E4
Ben Wyvis, *U.K.* 14 D4
Bena, *Nigeria* 83 C6
Benāb, *Iran* 73 D12
Benagerie, *Australia* 95 E3
Benalla, *Australia* 95 F4
Benalmádena, *Spain* 35 J6
Benambra, Mt., *Australia* . 95 F4
Benares = Varanasi, *India* 69 G10
Bénat, C., *France* 21 E10
Benavente, *Portugal* 35 G2
Benavente, *Spain* 34 C5
Benavides, *U.S.A.* 113 M5
Benavides de Órbigo, *Spain* 34 C5
Benbecula, *U.K.* 14 D1
Benbonyathe, *Australia* .. 95 E2
Bencubbin, *Australia* ... 93 F2
Bend, *U.S.A.* 114 D3
Bender Beila, *Somali Rep.* 74 F5
Bendering, *Australia* 93 F2
Bendery = Tighina,
  Moldova 43 D14
Bendigo, *Australia* 95 F3
Bendorf, *Germany* 24 E3
Benē Beraq, *Israel* 75 C3
Bénéna, *Mali* 82 C4
Benenitra, *Madag.* 89 C8
Benešov, *Czech Rep.* ... 26 B7
Benevento, *Italy* 31 A7
Benfeld, *France* 19 D14
Benga, *Mozam.* 87 F3
Bengal, Bay of, *Ind. Oc.* . 67 M17
Bengbu, *China* 57 H9
Benghazi = Banghāzī,
  Libya 79 B10
Bengkalis, *Indonesia* 62 D2
Bengkulu, *Indonesia* 62 E2
Bengkulu □, *Indonesia* .. 62 E2
Bengough, *Canada* 105 D7
Bengtsfors, *Sweden* 10 E6
Benguela, *Angola* 85 G2
Benguérua, I., *Mozam.* .. 89 C6
Benha, *Egypt* 80 H7
Beni,
  Dem. Rep. of the Congo 86 B2
Beni →, *Bolivia* 124 F5
Beni Mazâr, *Egypt* 80 J7
Beni Mellal, *Morocco* ... 78 B4
Beni Suef, *Egypt* 80 J7
Beniah L., *Canada* 104 A6
Benicarló, *Spain* 32 E5
Benicàssim, *Spain* 32 E5
Benicia, *U.S.A.* 116 G4
Benidorm, *Spain* 33 G4
Benin ■, *Africa* 83 D5
Benin, Bight of, *W. Afr.* . 83 E5
Benin City, *Nigeria* 83 D6
Benisa, *Spain* 33 G5
Benitses, *Greece* 36 A3
Benjamin Aceval, *Paraguay* 126 A4
Benjamin Constant, *Brazil* 124 D4
Benjamin Hill, *Mexico* .. 118 A2
Benkelman, *U.S.A.* 112 E4
Benkovac, *Croatia* 29 D12
Benlidi, *Australia* 94 C3
Bennett, *Canada* 104 B2
Bennett, L., *Australia* ... 92 D5
Bennetta, Ostrov, *Russia* . 51 B15
Bennettsville, *U.S.A.* ... 109 H6
Bennington, *U.S.A.* 111 D11
Bénodet, *France* 18 E2
Benoni, *S. Africa* 89 D4
Benque Viejo, *Belize* 119 D7
Bensheim, *Germany* 25 F4
Benson, *U.S.A.* 115 L8
Bent, *Iran* 71 E8
Benteng, *Indonesia* 63 F6
Bentinck I., *Australia* ... 94 B2
Bentiu, *Sudan* 81 F2
Bento Gonçalves, *Brazil* . 127 B5
Benton, *Calif., U.S.A.* ... 116 H8
Benton, *Ill., U.S.A.* 112 G10
Benton Harbor, *U.S.A.* . 108 D2
Benton Liben, *Ethiopia* . 81 F4
Bentung, *Malaysia* 65 L3
Benue □, *Nigeria* 83 D6
Benue →, *Nigeria* 83 D6
Benxi, *China* 57 D12
Beo, *Indonesia* 63 D7
Beograd, *Serbia, Yug.* .. 40 B4
Beowawe, *U.S.A.* 114 F5
Bepan Jiang →, *China* .. 58 E6
Beppu, *Japan* 55 H5
Beqaa Valley = Al Biqā □,
  Lebanon 75 A5
Berane, *Montenegro, Yug.* 40 D3
Berati, *Albania* 40 F4
Berau, Teluk, *Indonesia* . 63 E8
Berber, *Sudan* 80 D3
Berbera, *Somali Rep.* ... 74 E4
Berbérati, *C.A.R.* 84 D3
Berbice →, *Guyana* 124 B7
Berchida, *Italy* 28 D6
Berchtesgaden, *Germany* . 25 H8
Berck, *France* 19 B8

Biratnagar

Berdichev = Berdychiv, *Ukraine* 47 H5
Berdsk, *Russia* 50 D9
Berdyansk, *Ukraine* 47 J9
Berdychiv, *Ukraine* 47 H5
Berea, *U.S.A.* 108 G3
Berebere, *Indonesia* 63 D7
Bereda, *Somali Rep.* 74 E5
Berehove, *Ukraine* 47 H2
Berekum, *Ghana* 82 D4
Berenice, *Egypt* 80 C4
Berens →, *Canada* 105 C9
Berens I., *Canada* 105 C9
Berens River, *Canada* 105 C9
Berestechko, *Ukraine* 47 G3
Bereşti, *Romania* 43 D12
Beretău →, *Romania* 42 C6
Berettyó →, *Hungary* 42 D6
Berettyóújfalu, *Hungary* 42 C6
Berevo, *Mahajanga, Madag.* 89 B7
Berevo, *Toliara, Madag.* 89 B7
Bereza, *Belarus* 47 F3
Berezhany, *Ukraine* 47 H3
Berezina = Byarezina →, *Belarus* 47 F6
Berezivka, *Ukraine* 47 J6
Berezna, *Ukraine* 47 G6
Berezniki, *Russia* 50 D6
Berezovo, *Russia* 50 C7
Berga, *Spain* 32 C6
Berga, *Sweden* 11 G10
Bergama, *Turkey* 39 B9
Bérgamo, *Italy* 28 C6
Bergara, *Spain* 32 B2
Bergby, *Sweden* 10 D11
Bergedorf, *Germany* 24 B6
Bergeforsen, *Sweden* 10 B11
Bergen, *Mecklenburg-Vorpommern, Germany* 24 A9
Bergen, *Niedersachsen, Germany* 24 C5
Bergen, *Neths.* 17 B4
Bergen, *Norway* 9 F11
Bergen, *U.S.A.* 110 C7
Bergen op Zoom, *Neths.* 17 C4
Bergerac, *France* 20 D4
Bergheim, *Germany* 24 E2
Bergisch Gladbach, *Germany* 24 E3
Bergkamen, *Germany* 24 D3
Bergkvara, *Sweden* 11 H10
Bergshamra, *Sweden* 10 E12
Bergsjö, *Sweden* 10 C11
Bergues, *France* 19 B9
Bergviken, *Sweden* 10 C10
Bergville, *S. Africa* 89 D4
Berhala, Selat, *Indonesia* 62 E2
Berhampore = Baharampur, *India* 69 G13
Berhampur = Brahmapur, *India* 67 K14
Berheci →, *Romania* 43 E12
Bering Sea, *Pac. Oc.* 100 C1
Bering Strait, *Pac. Oc.* 4 C17
Beringovskiy, *Russia* 51 C18
Berisso, *Argentina* 126 C4
Berja, *Spain* 35 J8
Berkeley, *U.S.A.* 116 H4
Berkeley Springs, *U.S.A.* 108 F6
Berkner I., *Antarctica* 5 D18
Berkovitsa, *Bulgaria* 40 C7
Berkshire Downs, *U.K.* 13 F6
Berland →, *Canada* 104 C5
Berlanga, *Spain* 35 G5
Berlenga, I., *Portugal* 35 F1
Berlin, *Germany* 24 C9
Berlin, *Md., U.S.A.* 108 F8
Berlin, *N.H., U.S.A.* 111 B13
Berlin, *Wis., U.S.A.* 108 D1
Berlin □, *Germany* 24 C9
Bermeja, Sierra, *Spain* 35 J5
Bermejo →, *Formosa, Argentina* 126 B4
Bermejo →, *San Juan, Argentina* 126 C2
Bermeo, *Spain* 32 B2
Bermillo de Sayago, *Spain* 34 D4
Bermuda ■, *Atl. Oc.* 98 F13
Bern, *Switz.* 25 J3
Bern □, *Switz.* 25 J3
Bernado, *U.S.A.* 115 J10
Bernalda, *Italy* 31 B9
Bernalillo, *U.S.A.* 115 J10
Bernardo de Irigoyen, *Argentina* 127 B5
Bernardo O'Higgins □, *Chile* 126 C1
Bernasconi, *Argentina* 126 D3
Bernau, *Bayern, Germany* 25 H8
Bernau, *Brandenburg, Germany* 24 C9
Bernay, *France* 18 C7
Bernburg, *Germany* 24 D7
Berndorf, *Austria* 26 D9
Berne = Bern, *Switz.* 25 J3
Berne = Bern □, *Switz.* 25 J3
Berner Alpen, *Switz.* 25 J3
Berneray, *U.K.* 14 D1
Bernier I., *Australia* 93 D1
Bernina, Piz, *Switz.* 25 J5
Bernkastel-Kues, *Germany* 25 F3
Beroroha, *Madag.* 89 C8
Béroubouay, *Benin* 83 C5
Beroun, *Czech Rep.* 26 B7
Berounka →, *Czech Rep.* 26 B7
Berovo, *Macedonia* 40 E6
Berre, Étang de, *France* 21 E9
Berre-l'Étang, *France* 21 E9
Berri, *Australia* 95 E3
Berry, *Australia* 95 E5
Berry, *France* 19 F8
Berry Is., *Bahamas* 120 A4
Berryessa L., *U.S.A.* 116 G4
Berryville, *U.S.A.* 113 G8
Bersenbrück, *Germany* 24 C3
Bershad, *Ukraine* 47 H5
Berthold, *U.S.A.* 112 A4
Berthoud, *U.S.A.* 112 E2
Bertincourt, *France* 19 B9
Bertoua, *Cameroon* 84 D2
Bertraghboy B., *Ireland* 15 C2
Bertrand, *U.S.A.* 112 E5
Berwick, *U.S.A.* 111 E8
Berwick-upon-Tweed, *U.K.* 12 B6
Berwyn Mts., *U.K.* 12 E4
Beryslav, *Ukraine* 47 J7
Berzasca, *Romania* 42 F6
Berzence, *Hungary* 42 D2
Besal, *Pakistan* 69 B5
Besalampy, *Madag.* 89 B7
Besançon, *France* 19 E13
Besar, *Indonesia* 62 E5
Beshenkovichi, *Belarus* 46 E5
Beška, *Serbia, Yug.* 42 E5
Beslan, *Russia* 49 J7
Besna Kobila, *Serbia, Yug.* 40 D6
Besnard L., *Canada* 105 B7
Besni, *Turkey* 72 D7
Besor, N. →, *Egypt* 75 D3
Bessarabiya, *Moldova* 47 J5
Bessarabka = Basarabeasca, *Moldova* 43 D13
Bessèges, *France* 21 D8
Bessemer, *Ala., U.S.A.* 109 J2
Bessemer, *Mich., U.S.A.* 112 B9
Bessin, *France* 18 C6
Bessines-sur-Gartempe, *France* 20 B5
Bet She'an, *Israel* 75 C4
Bet Shemesh, *Israel* 75 D4
Betafo, *Madag.* 89 B8
Betancuria, *Canary Is.* 37 F5
Betanzos, *Spain* 34 B2
Bétaré Oya, *Cameroon* 84 C2
Bétera, *Spain* 33 F4
Bethal, *S. Africa* 89 D4
Bethanien, *Namibia* 88 D2
Bethany, *U.S.A.* 112 E7
Bethel, *Alaska, U.S.A.* 100 B3
Bethel, *Vt., U.S.A.* 111 C12
Bethel Park, *U.S.A.* 110 F4
Béthenville, *France* 19 C11
Bethlehem = Bayt Lahm, *West Bank* 75 D4
Bethlehem, *S. Africa* 89 D4
Bethlehem, *U.S.A.* 111 F9
Bethulie, *S. Africa* 88 E4
Béthune, *France* 19 B9
Béthune →, *France* 18 C8
Bethungra, *Australia* 95 E4
Betioky, *Madag.* 89 C7
Betong, *Thailand* 65 K3
Betoota, *Australia* 94 D3
Betroka, *Madag.* 89 C8
Betsiamites, *Canada* 103 C6
Betsiamites →, *Canada* 103 C6
Betsiboka →, *Madag.* 89 B8
Bettiah, *India* 69 F11
Bettna, *Sweden* 11 F10
Béttola, *Italy* 28 D6
Betul, *India* 66 J10
Betung, *Malaysia* 62 D4
Betws-y-Coed, *U.K.* 12 D4
Betxi, *Spain* 32 F4
Betzdorf, *Germany* 24 E3
Beuil, *France* 21 D10
Beulah, *U.S.A.* 112 B4
Beuvron →, *France* 18 E8
Beveren, *Belgium* 17 C4
Beverley, *Australia* 93 F2
Beverley, *U.K.* 12 D7
Beverly, *Mass., U.S.A.* 111 D14
Beverly, *Wash., U.S.A.* 114 C4
Beverly Hills, *U.S.A.* 117 L8
Beverungen, *Germany* 24 D5
Bex, *Switz.* 25 J3
Bexhill, *U.K.* 13 G8
Bey Dağları, *Turkey* 39 E12
Beyānlū, *Iran* 70 C5
Beyazköy, *Turkey* 41 E11
Beyçayırı, *Turkey* 41 F10
Beydağ, *Turkey* 39 C10
Beyeğaç, *Turkey* 39 D10
Beyin, *Ghana* 82 D4
Beykoz, *Turkey* 41 E13
Beyla, *Guinea* 82 D3
Beynat, *France* 20 C5
Beyneu, *Kazakstan* 50 E6
Beyoba, *Turkey* 39 C9
Beyoğlu, *Turkey* 41 E12
Beypazarı, *Turkey* 72 B4
Beyşehir, *Turkey* 72 D4
Beyşehir Gölü, *Turkey* 72 D4
Beytüşşebap, *Turkey* 73 D10
Bezdan, *Serbia, Yug.* 42 E3
Bezhetsk, *Russia* 46 D9
Béziers, *France* 20 E7
Bezwada = Vijayawada, *India* 67 L12
Bhachau, *India* 66 H7
Bhadarwah, *India* 69 C6
Bhadrakh, *India* 67 J15
Bhadravati, *India* 66 N9
Bhagalpur, *India* 69 G12
Bhakkar, *Pakistan* 68 D4
Bhakra Dam, *India* 68 D7
Bhamo, *Burma* 67 G20
Bhandara, *India* 66 J11
Bhanrer Ra., *India* 68 H8
Bharat = India ■, *Asia* 66 K11
Bharatpur, *India* 68 F7
Bhatinda, *India* 68 D6
Bhatpara, *India* 69 H13
Bhaun, *Pakistan* 68 C5
Bhaunagar = Bhavnagar, *India* 68 J5
Bhavnagar, *India* 68 J5
Bhawanipatna, *India* 67 K12
Bhera, *Pakistan* 68 C5
Bhilsa = Vidisha, *India* 68 H7
Bhilwara, *India* 68 G6
Bhima →, *India* 66 L10
Bhimavaram, *India* 67 L12
Bhimbar, *Pakistan* 69 C6
Bhind, *India* 69 F8
Bhiwandi, *India* 66 K8
Bhiwani, *India* 68 E7
Bhola, *Bangla.* 67 H17
Bhopal, *India* 68 H7
Bhubaneshwar, *India* 67 J14
Bhuj, *India* 68 H3
Bhusaval, *India* 66 J9
Bhutan ■, *Asia* 67 F17
Biafra, B. of = Bonny, Bight of, *Africa* 83 E6
Biak, *Indonesia* 63 E9
Biała, *Poland* 45 H4
Biała →, *Poland* 45 H7
Biała Piska, *Poland* 44 E9
Biała Podlaska, *Poland* 45 F10
Biała Podlaska □, *Poland* 45 G10
Biała Rawska, *Poland* 45 G7
Białobrzegi, *Poland* 45 G7
Białogard, *Poland* 44 D2
Białowieża, *Poland* 45 F10
Biały Bór, *Poland* 44 E3
Białystok, *Poland* 45 E10
Białystok □, *Poland* 45 E10
Biancavilla, *Italy* 31 E7
Bianco, *Italy* 31 D9
Bīārjmand, *Iran* 71 B7
Biaro, *Indonesia* 63 D7
Biarritz, *France* 20 E2
Biasca, *Switz.* 25 J4
Biba, *Egypt* 80 J7
Bibai, *Japan* 54 C10
Bibbiena, *Italy* 29 E8
Bibby I., *Canada* 105 A10
Bibel →, *Spain* 34 C3
Biberach, *Germany* 25 G5
Bibiani, *Ghana* 82 D4
Biboohra, *Australia* 94 B4
Bibungwa, *Dem. Rep. of the Congo* 86 C2
Bic, *Canada* 103 C6
Bicaj, *Albania* 40 E4
Bicaz, *Romania* 43 D11
Bicazu Ardelean, *Romania* 43 D10
Bíccari, *Italy* 31 A8
Bicester, *U.K.* 13 F6
Bichena, *Ethiopia* 81 E4
Bichvinta, *Georgia* 49 J5
Bickerton I., *Australia* 94 A2
Bicknell, *Ind., U.S.A.* 108 F2
Bicknell, *Utah, U.S.A.* 115 G8
Bicske, *Hungary* 42 C3
Bida, *Nigeria* 83 D6
Bidar, *India* 66 L10
Biddeford, *U.S.A.* 103 D5
Biddwara, *Ethiopia* 81 F4
Bideford, *U.K.* 13 F3
Bideford Bay, *U.K.* 13 F3
Bidor, *Malaysia* 65 K3
Bie, *Sweden* 10 E10
Bié, Planalto de, *Angola* 85 G3
Bieber, *U.S.A.* 114 F3
Biebrza →, *Poland* 45 E9
Biecz, *Poland* 45 J8
Biel, *Switz.* 25 H3
Bielawa, *Poland* 45 H3
Bielefeld, *Germany* 24 C4
Bielersee, *Switz.* 25 H3
Biella, *Italy* 28 C5
Bielsk Podlaski, *Poland* 45 F10
Bielsko-Biała, *Poland* 45 J6
Bielsko-Biała □, *Poland* 45 J6
Bien Hoa, *Vietnam* 65 G6
Bienfait, *Canada* 105 D8
Bienne = Biel, *Switz.* 25 H3
Bienvenida, *Spain* 35 G4
Bienville, L., *Canada* 102 A5
Bierné, *France* 18 E6
Bierun, *Poland* 45 H6
Bierutów, *Poland* 45 G4
Biescas, *Spain* 32 C4
Biese →, *Germany* 24 C7
Biesiesfontein, *S. Africa* 88 E2
Bietigheim-Bissingen, *Germany* 25 G5
Bieżuń, *Poland* 45 F6
Biferno →, *Italy* 29 G12
Big →, *Canada* 103 B8
Big B., *Canada* 103 A7
Big Bear City, *U.S.A.* 117 L10
Big Bear Lake, *U.S.A.* 117 L10
Big Beaver, *Canada* 105 D7
Big Belt Mts., *U.S.A.* 114 C8
Big Bend, *Swaziland* 89 D5
Big Bend National Park, *U.S.A.* 113 L3
Big Black →, *U.S.A.* 113 K9
Big Blue →, *U.S.A.* 112 F6
Big Cr. →, *Canada* 104 C4
Big Creek, *U.S.A.* 116 H7
Big Cypress Swamp, *U.S.A.* 109 M5
Big Falls, *U.S.A.* 112 A8
Big Fork →, *U.S.A.* 112 A8
Big Horn Mts. = Bighorn Mts., *U.S.A.* 114 D10
Big Lake, *U.S.A.* 113 K4
Big Moose, *U.S.A.* 111 C10
Big Muddy Cr. →, *U.S.A.* 112 A2
Big Pine, *U.S.A.* 116 H8
Big Piney, *U.S.A.* 114 E8
Big Quill L., *Canada* 105 C8
Big Rapids, *U.S.A.* 108 D3
Big River, *Canada* 105 C7
Big Run, *U.S.A.* 110 F6
Big Sable Pt., *U.S.A.* 108 C2
Big Sand L., *Canada* 105 B9
Big Sandy, *U.S.A.* 114 B8
Big Sandy Cr. →, *U.S.A.* 112 F3
Big Sioux →, *U.S.A.* 112 D6
Big Spring, *U.S.A.* 113 J4
Big Springs, *U.S.A.* 112 E3
Big Stone City, *U.S.A.* 112 C6
Big Stone Gap, *U.S.A.* 109 G4
Big Stone L., *U.S.A.* 112 C6
Big Sur, *U.S.A.* 116 J5
Big Timber, *U.S.A.* 114 D9
Big Trout L., *Canada* 102 B2
Biğa, *Turkey* 41 F11
Biga →, *Turkey* 41 F11
Bigadiç, *Turkey* 39 B10
Biganos, *France* 20 D3
Bigfork, *U.S.A.* 114 B6
Biggar, *Canada* 105 C7
Biggar, *U.K.* 14 F5
Bigge I., *Australia* 92 B4
Biggenden, *Australia* 95 D5
Biggleswade, *U.K.* 13 E7
Biggs, *U.S.A.* 116 F5
Bighorn, *U.S.A.* 114 C10
Bighorn →, *U.S.A.* 114 C10
Bighorn Mts., *U.S.A.* 114 D10
Bignona, *Senegal* 82 C1
Bigorre, *France* 20 E4
Bigstone L., *Canada* 105 C9
Biguglia, Étang de, *France* 21 F13
Bigwa, *Tanzania* 86 D4
Bihać, *Bos.-H.* 29 D12
Bihar, *India* 69 G11
Bihar □, *India* 69 G12
Biharamulo, *Tanzania* 86 C3
Biharamulo □, *Tanzania* 86 C3
Biharkeresztes, *Hungary* 42 C6
Bihor □, *Romania* 42 D7
Bihor, Munţii, *Romania* 42 D7
Bijagós, Arquipélago dos, *Guinea-Biss.* 82 C1
Bijaipur, *India* 68 F7
Bijapur, *Karnataka, India* 66 L9
Bijapur, *Mad. P., India* 67 K12
Bījār, *Iran* 70 C5
Bijeljina, *Bos.-H.* 42 F4
Bijelo Polje, *Montenegro, Yug.* 40 C3
Bijie, *China* 58 D5
Bijnor, *India* 68 E8
Bikaner, *India* 68 E5
Bikapur, *India* 69 F10
Bikeqi, *China* 56 D6
Bikfayyā, *Lebanon* 75 B4
Bikin, *Russia* 51 E14
Bikin →, *Russia* 54 A7
Bikini Atoll, *Pac. Oc.* 96 F8
Bikoué, *Cameroon* 83 E7
Bila Tserkva, *Ukraine* 47 H6
Bilara, *India* 68 F5
Bilaspur, *Mad. P., India* 69 H10
Bilaspur, *Punjab, India* 68 D7
Biläsuvar, *Azerbaijan* 73 C13
Bilauk Taungdan, *Thailand* 64 F2
Bilbao, *Spain* 32 B2
Bilbeis, *Egypt* 80 H7
Bilbo = Bilbao, *Spain* 32 B2
Bilbor, *Romania* 43 C10
Bilciureşti, *Romania* 43 F10
Bíldudalur, *Iceland* 8 D2
Bílé Karpaty, *Europe* 27 B11
Bileća, *Bos.-H.* 40 D2
Bilecik, *Turkey* 72 B4
Biłgoraj, *Poland* 45 H9
Bilhorod-Dnistrovskyy, *Ukraine* 47 J6
Bilibino, *Russia* 51 C17
Bilibiza, *Mozam.* 87 E5
Biliran I., *Phil.* 61 F6
Bilishti, *Albania* 40 F5
Bill, *U.S.A.* 112 D2
Billabalong, *Australia* 93 E2
Billdal, *Sweden* 11 G5
Billiluna, *Australia* 92 C4
Billings, *U.S.A.* 114 D9
Billiton Is. = Belitung, *Indonesia* 62 E3
Billsta, *Sweden* 10 A12
Billund, *Denmark* 11 J3
Bilma, *Niger* 79 E8
Bilo Gora, *Croatia* 42 E2
Biloela, *Australia* 94 C5
Bilohirsk, *Ukraine* 47 K8
Bilopillya, *Ukraine* 47 G8
Biloxi, *U.S.A.* 113 K10
Bilpa Morea Claypan, *Australia* 94 D3
Biltine, *Chad* 79 F10
Bilyana, *Australia* 94 B4
Bilyarsk, *Russia* 48 C10
Bima, *Indonesia* 63 F5
Bimban, *Egypt* 80 C3
Bimbila, *Ghana* 83 D5
Bimini Is., *Bahamas* 120 A4
Bin Xian, *Heilongjiang, China* 57 B14
Bin Xian, *Shaanxi, China* 56 G5
Bina-Etawah, *India* 68 G8
Bināb, *Iran* 71 B6
Binalbagan, *Phil.* 61 F5
Binalong, *Australia* 95 E4
Bīnālūd, Kūh-e, *Iran* 71 B8
Binatang = Bintangor, *Malaysia* 62 D4
Binbee, *Australia* 94 C4
Binche, *Belgium* 17 D4
Binchuan, *China* 58 E3
Binda, *Australia* 95 D4
Bindle, *Australia* 95 D4
Bindslev, *Denmark* 11 G4
Bindura, *Zimbabwe* 87 F3
Binefar, *Spain* 32 D5
Bingara, *N.S.W., Australia* 95 D5
Bingara, *Queens., Australia* 95 D3
Bingen, *Germany* 25 F3
Bingerville, *Ivory C.* 82 D4
Bingham, *U.S.A.* 103 C6
Bingham Canyon, *U.S.A.* 114 F7
Binghamton, *U.S.A.* 111 D9
Bingöl, *Turkey* 73 C9
Bingöl Dağları, *Turkey* 73 C9
Bingsjö, *Sweden* 10 C9
Binh Dinh = An Nhon, *Vietnam* 64 F7
Binh Khe, *Vietnam* 64 F7
Binh Son, *Vietnam* 64 E7
Binhai, *China* 57 G10
Binic, *France* 18 D4
Binisatua, *Spain* 37 B11
Binjai, *Indonesia* 62 D1
Binnaway, *Australia* 95 E4
Binongko, *Indonesia* 63 F6
Binscarth, *Canada* 105 C8
Bintan, *Indonesia* 62 D2
Bintangor, *Malaysia* 62 D4
Bintulu, *Malaysia* 62 D4
Bintuni, *Indonesia* 63 E8
Binyang, *China* 58 F7
Binz, *Germany* 24 A9
Binzert = Bizerte, *Tunisia* 79 A7
Bío Bío □, *Chile* 126 D1
Biograd na Moru, *Croatia* 29 E12
Bioko, *Eq. Guin.* 83 E6
Biokovo, *Croatia* 29 E14
Bir, *India* 66 K9
Bir, Ras, *Djibouti* 81 E5
Bîr Abu Hashim, *Egypt* 80 C3
Bîr Abu M'nqar, *Egypt* 80 B2
Bîr Abu Muḩammad, *Egypt* 75 F3
Bi'r ad Dabbāghāt, *Jordan* 75 E4
Bîr Adal Deib, *Sudan* 80 C4
Bi'r al Butayyihāt, *Jordan* 75 F4
Bi'r al Mārī, *Jordan* 75 E4
Bi'r al Qattār, *Jordan* 75 F4
Bîr 'Asal, *Egypt* 80 B3
Bîr Autrun, *Sudan* 80 D2
Bîr Beiḑa, *Egypt* 75 E3
Bîr Diqnash, *Egypt* 80 A2
Bîr el 'Abd, *Egypt* 75 D2
Bîr el Basur, *Egypt* 80 B2
Bîr el Biarât, *Egypt* 75 F3
Bîr el Duweidar, *Egypt* 75 E1
Bîr el Garârât, *Egypt* 75 D2
Bîr el Gellaz, *Egypt* 80 A2
Bîr el Heisi, *Egypt* 75 F3
Bîr el Jafir, *Egypt* 75 E1
Bîr el Mâlḩi, *Egypt* 75 E2
Bîr el Shaqqa, *Egypt* 80 A2
Bîr el Thamâda, *Egypt* 75 E2
Bîr Fuad, *Egypt* 80 A2
Bîr Gebeil Ḩişn, *Egypt* 75 E2
Bi'r Ghadīr, *Syria* 75 A6
Bîr Haimur, *Egypt* 80 C3
Bîr Ḩasana, *Egypt* 75 E2
Bi'r Jadīd, *Iraq* 70 C4
Bîr Kanayis, *Egypt* 80 C3
Bîr Kaseiba, *Egypt* 75 E2
Bîr Kerawein, *Egypt* 80 B2
Bîr Lahfân, *Egypt* 75 E2
Bîr Madkûr, *Egypt* 75 E1
Bîr Maql, *Egypt* 80 C3
Bîr Misaha, *Egypt* 80 C2
Bîr Mogreïn, *Mauritania* 78 C3
Bîr Murr, *Egypt* 80 C3
Bi'r Muţribah, *Kuwait* 70 D5
Bîr Nakheila, *Egypt* 80 C3
Bîr Qaţia, *Egypt* 75 E1
Bîr Qatrani, *Egypt* 80 A2
Bîr Ranga, *Egypt* 80 C4
Bîr Sahara, *Egypt* 80 C2
Bîr Seiyâla, *Egypt* 80 B3
Bîr Shalatein, *Egypt* 80 C4
Bîr Shebb, *Egypt* 80 C2
Bîr Shût, *Egypt* 80 C4
Bîr Terfawi, *Egypt* 80 C2
Bîr Umm Qubûr, *Egypt* 80 C3
Bîr Ungât, *Egypt* 80 C3
Bîr Za'farâna, *Egypt* 80 J8
Bîr Zeidûn, *Egypt* 80 B3
Biramféro, *Guinea* 82 C3
Biratnagar, *Nepal* 69 F12

Birawa,
  Dem. Rep. of the Congo 86 C2
Birch Hills, Canada ... 105 C7
Birch I., Canada ... 105 C9
Birch L., N.W.T., Canada 104 A5
Birch L., Ont., Canada .. 102 B1
Birch L., U.S.A. ... 102 C1
Birch Mts., Canada ... 104 B6
Birch River, Canada ... 105 C8
Birchip, Australia ... 95 F3
Birchiş, Romania ... 42 E7
Bird, Canada ... 105 B10
Bird City, U.S.A. ... 112 F4
Bird I. = Aves, I. de,
  W. Indies ... 121 C7
Birdsville, Australia ... 94 D2
Birdum, Australia ... 92 C5
Birecik, Turkey ... 73 D8
Birein, Israel ... 75 E3
Bireuen, Indonesia ... 62 C1
Birifo, Gambia ... 82 C2
Birigui, Brazil ... 127 A5
Birkenfeld, Germany ... 25 F3
Birkenhead, U.K. ... 12 D4
Birkerød, Denmark ... 11 J6
Birket Qârûn, Egypt ... 80 J7
Birkfeld, Austria ... 26 D8
Bîrlad = Bârlad, Romania 43 D12
Birmingham, U.K. ... 13 E6
Birmingham, U.S.A. ... 109 J2
Birmitrapur, India ... 67 H14
Birni Ngaouré, Niger ... 83 C5
Birni Nkonni, Niger ... 83 C6
Birnin Gwari, Nigeria ... 83 C6
Birnin Kebbi, Nigeria ... 83 C5
Birnin Kudu, Nigeria ... 83 C6
Birobidzhan, Russia ... 51 E14
Birr, Ireland ... 15 C4
Birrie →, Australia ... 95 D4
Birsilpur, India ... 68 E5
Birsk, Russia ... 50 D6
Birštonas, Lithuania ... 44 D11
Birtle, Canada ... 105 C8
Birur, India ... 66 N9
Biryuchiy, Ukraine ... 47 J8
Biržai, Lithuania ... 9 H21
Birzebbuġa, Malta ... 36 D2
Bisa, Indonesia ... 63 E7
Bisáccia, Italy ... 31 A8
Bisacquino, Italy ... 30 E6
Bisalpur, India ... 69 E8
Bisbee, U.S.A. ... 115 L9
Biscarrosse, France ... 20 D2
Biscarrosse et de Parentis,
  Étang de, France ... 20 D2
Biscay, B. of, Atl. Oc. ... 6 F5
Biscayne, B., U.S.A. ... 109 N5
Biscéglie, Italy ... 31 A9
Bischheim, France ... 19 D14
Bischofshofen, Austria ... 26 D6
Bischofswerda, Germany . 24 D10
Bischwiller, France ... 19 D14
Biscoe Bay, Antarctica ... 5 D13
Biscoe Is., Antarctica ... 5 C17
Biscostasing, Canada ... 102 C3
Biševo, Croatia ... 29 F13
Bisha, Eritrea ... 81 D4
Bishah, W. →, Si. Arabia 80 C5
Bishan, China ... 58 C6
Bishkek, Kyrgyzstan ... 50 E8
Bishnupur, India ... 69 H12
Bisho, S. Africa ... 89 E4
Bishop, Calif., U.S.A. ... 116 H8
Bishop, Tex., U.S.A. ... 113 M6
Bishop Auckland, U.K. ... 12 C6
Bishop's Falls, Canada ... 103 C8
Bishop's Stortford, U.K. . 13 F8
Bisignano, Italy ... 31 C9
Bisina, L., Uganda ... 86 B3
Biskra, Algeria ... 78 B7
Biskupiec, Poland ... 44 E7
Bismarck, U.S.A. ... 112 B4
Bismarck Arch.,
  Papua N. G. ... 96 H7
Bismark, Germany ... 24 C7
Bismil, Turkey ... 73 D9
Biso, Uganda ... 86 B3
Bison, U.S.A. ... 112 C3
Bīsotūn, Iran ... 70 C5
Bispgården, Sweden ... 10 A10
Bissagos = Bijagós,
  Arquipélago dos,
  Guinea-Biss. ... 82 C1
Bissau, Guinea-Biss. ... 82 C1
Bissett, Canada ... 105 C9
Bissikrima, Guinea ... 82 C2
Bistcho L., Canada ... 104 B5
Bistreţ, Romania ... 43 G8
Bistrica = Ilirska-Bistrica,
  Slovenia ... 29 C11
Bistrița, Romania ... 43 C9
Bistrița →, Romania ... 43 D11
Bistrița Năsăud □,
  Romania ... 43 C9
Bistriţei, Munţii, Romania 43 C10
Biswan, India ... 69 F9
Bisztynek, Poland ... 44 D7
Bitburg, Germany ... 25 F2
Bitche, France ... 19 C14
Bithynia, Turkey ... 72 B4
Bitlis, Turkey ... 73 C10
Bitola, Macedonia ... 40 E5
Bitolj = Bitola, Macedonia 40 E5
Bitonto, Italy ... 31 A9
Bitter Creek, U.S.A. ... 114 F9
Bitter L. = Buheirat-
  Murrat-el-Kubra, Egypt 80 H8

Bitterfeld, Germany ... 24 D8
Bitterfontein, S. Africa ... 88 E2
Bitterroot →, U.S.A. ... 114 C6
Bitterroot Range, U.S.A. . 114 D6
Bitterwater, U.S.A. ... 116 J6
Bitti, Italy ... 30 B2
Bittou, Burkina Faso ... 83 C4
Biu, Nigeria ... 83 C7
Bivolari, Romania ... 43 C12
Bivolu, Vf., Romania ... 43 C10
Biwa-Ko, Japan ... 55 G8
Biwabik, U.S.A. ... 112 B8
Bixad, Romania ... 43 C8
Biyang, China ... 56 H7
Bizana, S. Africa ... 89 E4
Bizen, Japan ... 55 G7
Bizerte, Tunisia ... 79 A7
Bjargtangar, Iceland ... 8 D1
Bjärnum, Sweden ... 11 H7
Bjästa, Sweden ... 10 A12
Bjelasica,
  Montenegro, Yug. ... 40 D3
Bjelašnica, Bos.-H. ... 42 G3
Bjelovar, Croatia ... 29 C13
Bjerringbro, Denmark ... 11 H3
Björbo, Sweden ... 10 D8
Björklinge, Sweden ... 10 D11
Björneborg, Sweden ... 10 E8
Bjørnevatn, Norway ... 8 B23
Bjørnøya, Arctic ... 4 B8
Bjursås, Sweden ... 10 D9
Bjuv, Sweden ... 11 H6
Blace, Serbia, Yug. ... 40 C5
Black = Da →, Vietnam . 64 B5
Black →, Canada ... 110 B5
Black →, Ark., U.S.A. ... 113 H9
Black →, N.Y., U.S.A. . 111 C8
Black →, Wis., U.S.A. . 112 D9
Black Diamond, Canada . 104 C6
Black Forest =
  Schwarzwald, Germany . 25 G4
Black Hd., Ireland ... 15 C2
Black Hills, U.S.A. ... 112 D3
Black I., Canada ... 105 C9
Black L., Canada ... 105 B7
Black L., U.S.A. ... 108 C3
Black Mesa, U.S.A. ... 113 G3
Black Mt. = Mynydd Du,
  U.K. ... 13 F4
Black Mts., U.K. ... 13 F4
Black Range, U.S.A. ... 115 K10
Black River, Jamaica ... 120 C4
Black River Falls, U.S.A. . 112 C9
Black Sea, Eurasia ... 6 G12
Black Volta →, Africa ... 82 D4
Black Warrior →, U.S.A. . 109 J2
Blackall, Australia ... 94 C4
Blackball, N.Z. ... 91 K3
Blackbull, Australia ... 94 B3
Blackburn, U.K. ... 12 D5
Blackburn with Darwen □,
  U.K. ... 12 D5
Blackduck, U.S.A. ... 112 B7
Blackfoot, U.S.A. ... 114 E7
Blackfoot →, U.S.A. ... 114 C7
Blackfoot River Reservoir,
  U.S.A. ... 114 E8
Blackie, Canada ... 104 C6
Blackpool, U.K. ... 12 D4
Blackpool □, U.K. ... 12 D4
Blackriver, U.S.A. ... 110 B1
Blacks Harbour, Canada . 103 C6
Blacksburg, U.S.A. ... 108 G5
Blacksod B., Ireland ... 15 B1
Blackstone, U.S.A. ... 108 G7
Blackstone →, Canada . 104 A4
Blackstone Ra., Australia 93 E4
Blackville, Canada ... 103 C6
Blackwater, Australia ... 94 C4
Blackwater →, Meath,
  Ireland ... 15 C4
Blackwater →, Waterford,
  Ireland ... 15 D4
Blackwater →, U.K. ... 15 B5
Blackwater Cr. →,
  Australia ... 95 D3
Blackwell, U.S.A. ... 113 G6
Blackwells Corner, U.S.A. 117 K7
Blaenau Ffestiniog, U.K. . 12 E4
Blaenau Gwent □, U.K. . 13 F4
Blagaj, Bos.-H. ... 40 C1
Blagnac, France ... 20 E5
Blagodarnyy, Russia ... 49 H6
Blagoevgrad, Bulgaria ... 40 D7
Blagoveshchensk, Russia . 51 D13
Blain, France ... 18 E5
Blaine, U.S.A. ... 116 B4
Blaine Lake, Canada ... 105 C7
Blair, U.S.A. ... 112 E6
Blair Athol, Australia ... 94 C4
Blair Atholl, U.K. ... 14 E5
Blairgowrie, U.K. ... 14 E5
Blairmore, Canada ... 104 D6
Blairsden, U.S.A. ... 116 F6
Blairsville, U.S.A. ... 110 F5
Blaj, Romania ... 43 D8
Blake Pt., U.S.A. ... 112 A10
Blâmont, France ... 19 D13
Blanc, C., Tunisia ... 37 B9
Blanc, Mont, Alps ... 21 C10
Blanca, B., Argentina ... 122 H4
Blanca Peak, U.S.A. ... 115 H11
Blanchard, U.S.A. ... 113 H6
Blanche, C., Australia ... 95 E1

Blanche, L., S. Austral.,
  Australia ... 95 D2
Blanche, L., W. Austral.,
  Australia ... 92 D3
Blanco, S. Africa ... 88 E3
Blanco, U.S.A. ... 113 K5
Blanco →, Argentina ... 126 C2
Blanco, C., Costa Rica ... 120 E2
Blanco, C., U.S.A. ... 114 E1
Blanda →, Iceland ... 8 D3
Blandford Forum, U.K. ... 13 G5
Blanding, U.S.A. ... 115 H9
Blanes, Spain ... 32 D7
Blangy-sur-Bresle, France . 19 C8
Blanice →, Czech Rep. . 26 B7
Blankaholm, Sweden ... 11 G10
Blankenberge, Belgium ... 17 C3
Blankenburg, Germany ... 24 D6
Blanquefort, France ... 20 D3
Blanquillo, Uruguay ... 127 C4
Blansko, Czech Rep. ... 27 B9
Blantyre, Malawi ... 87 F4
Blarney, Ireland ... 15 E3
Błaszki, Poland ... 45 G5
Blatná, Czech Rep. ... 26 B6
Blato, Croatia ... 29 F13
Blaubeuren, Germany ... 25 G5
Blaustein, Germany ... 25 G5
Blåvands Huk, Denmark . 11 J2
Blaydon, U.K. ... 12 C6
Blaye, France ... 20 C3
Blaye-les-Mines, France . 20 D6
Blayney, Australia ... 95 E4
Blaze, Pt., Australia ... 92 B5
Bleckede, Germany ... 24 B6
Bled, Slovenia ... 29 B11
Bleiburg, Austria ... 26 E7
Blejeşti, Romania ... 43 F10
Blekinge, Sweden ... 9 H16
Blekinge län □, Sweden . 11 H9
Blenheim, Canada ... 110 D3
Blenheim, N.Z. ... 91 J4
Bléone →, France ... 21 D10
Blérancourt, France ... 19 C10
Bletchley, U.K. ... 13 F7
Blida, Algeria ... 78 A6
Blidö, Sweden ... 10 E12
Blidsberg, Sweden ... 11 G7
Blieskastel, Germany ... 25 F3
Bligh Sound, N.Z. ... 91 L1
Blind River, Canada ... 102 C3
Blinishti, Albania ... 40 E3
Blitar, Indonesia ... 63 H15
Blitta, Togo ... 83 D5
Block I., U.S.A. ... 111 E13
Block Island Sd., U.S.A. . 111 E13
Blodgett Iceberg Tongue,
  Antarctica ... 5 C9
Bloemfontein, S. Africa ... 88 D4
Bloemhof, S. Africa ... 88 D4
Blois, France ... 18 E8
Blomskog, Sweden ... 10 E6
Blomstermåla, Sweden ... 11 H10
Blönduós, Iceland ... 8 D3
Błonie, Poland ... 45 F7
Bloodvein →, Canada . 105 C9
Bloody Foreland, Ireland . 15 A3
Bloomer, U.S.A. ... 112 C9
Bloomfield, Australia ... 94 B4
Bloomfield, Canada ... 110 C7
Bloomfield, Iowa, U.S.A. . 112 E8
Bloomfield, N. Mex.,
  U.S.A. ... 115 H10
Bloomfield, Nebr., U.S.A. 112 D6
Bloomington, Ill., U.S.A. . 112 E10
Bloomington, Ind., U.S.A. 108 F2
Bloomington, Minn.,
  U.S.A. ... 112 C8
Bloomsburg, U.S.A. ... 111 F8
Blora, Indonesia ... 63 G14
Blossburg, U.S.A. ... 110 E7
Blouberg, S. Africa ... 89 C4
Blountstown, U.S.A. ... 109 K3
Bludenz, Austria ... 26 D2
Blue Island, U.S.A. ... 108 E2
Blue Lake, U.S.A. ... 114 F2
Blue Mesa Reservoir,
  U.S.A. ... 115 G10
Blue Mts., Oreg., U.S.A. . 114 D4
Blue Mts., Pa., U.S.A. ... 111 F8
Blue Mud B., Australia ... 94 A2
Blue Nile = Nîl el
  Azraq →, Sudan ... 81 D3
Blue Rapids, U.S.A. ... 112 F6
Blue Ridge Mts., U.S.A. . 109 G5
Blueberry →, Canada . 104 B4
Bluefield, U.S.A. ... 108 G5
Bluefields, Nic. ... 120 D3
Bluff, Australia ... 94 C4
Bluff, N.Z. ... 91 M2
Bluff, U.S.A. ... 115 H9
Bluff Knoll, Australia ... 93 F2
Bluff Pt., Australia ... 93 E1
Bluffton, U.S.A. ... 108 E3
Blumenau, Brazil ... 127 B6
Blunt, U.S.A. ... 112 C4
Bly, U.S.A. ... 114 E3
Blyth, Canada ... 110 C3
Blyth, U.K. ... 12 B6
Blythe, U.S.A. ... 117 M12
Blytheville, U.S.A. ... 113 H10
Bo, S. Leone ... 82 D2
Bo Duc, Vietnam ... 65 G6
Bo Hai, China ... 57 E10
Bo Xian, China ... 56 H9
Boa Vista, Brazil ... 124 C6
Boac, Phil. ... 61 E4

Boaco, Nic. ... 120 D2
Bo'ai, China ... 56 G7
Boal, Spain ... 34 B4
Boardman, U.S.A. ... 110 E4
Boatman, Australia ... 95 D4
Bobadah, Australia ... 95 E4
Bobai, China ... 58 F7
Bobbili, India ... 67 K13
Bóbbio, Italy ... 28 D6
Bobcaygeon, Canada ... 102 D4
Bobo-Dioulasso,
  Burkina Faso ... 82 C4
Bobolice, Poland ... 44 E3
Boboshevo, Bulgaria ... 40 D7
Bobov Dol, Bulgaria ... 40 D6
Bóbr →, Poland ... 45 F2
Bobraomby, Tanjon' i,
  Madag. ... 89 A8
Bobrinets, Ukraine ... 47 H7
Bobrov, Russia ... 48 E5
Bobrovitsa, Ukraine ... 47 G6
Bobruysk = Babruysk,
  Belarus ... 47 F5
Bôca do Acre, Brazil ... 124 E5
Boca Raton, U.S.A. ... 109 M5
Bocanda, Ivory C. ... 82 D4
Bocas del Toro, Panama . 120 E3
Boceguillas, Spain ... 34 D7
Bochnia, Poland ... 45 J7
Bocholt, Germany ... 24 D2
Bochum, Germany ... 24 D3
Bockenem, Germany ... 24 C5
Boćki, Poland ... 45 F10
Bocognano, France ... 21 F13
Bocoyna, Mexico ... 118 B3
Bocşa, Romania ... 42 E6
Böda, Sweden ... 11 G11
Boda, Kopparberg, Sweden 10 C9
Boda, Västernorrland,
  Sweden ... 10 B10
Bodafors, Sweden ... 11 G8
Bodaybo, Russia ... 51 D12
Boddam, U.K. ... 14 B7
Boddington, Australia ... 93 F2
Bodega Bay, U.S.A. ... 116 G3
Boden, Sweden ... 8 D19
Bodensee, Europe ... 25 H5
Bodenteich, Germany ... 24 C6
Bodhan, India ... 66 K10
Bodinga, Nigeria ... 83 C6
Bodmin, U.K. ... 13 G3
Bodmin Moor, U.K. ... 13 G3
Bodø, Norway ... 8 C16
Bodrog →, Hungary ... 42 B6
Bodrum, Turkey ... 39 D9
Bódva →, Hungary ... 42 B5
Boën, France ... 21 C8
Boende,
  Dem. Rep. of the Congo 84 E4
Boerne, U.S.A. ... 113 L5
Boffa, Guinea ... 82 C2
Bogalusa, U.S.A. ... 113 K10
Bogan Gate, Australia ... 95 E4
Bogantungan, Australia . 94 C4
Bogata, U.S.A. ... 113 J7
Bogatić, Serbia, Yug. ... 40 B3
Boğazkale, Turkey ... 72 B6
Boğazlıyan, Turkey ... 72 C6
Bogen, Sweden ... 10 D6
Bogense, Denmark ... 11 J4
Bogetići, Montenegro, Yug. 40 D2
Boggabilla, Australia ... 95 D5
Boggabri, Australia ... 95 E5
Boggeragh Mts., Ireland . 15 D3
Bognor Regis, U.K. ... 13 G7
Bogo, Phil. ... 61 F6
Bogodukhov, Ukraine ... 47 G8
Bogong, Mt., Australia ... 95 F4
Bogor, Indonesia ... 63 G12
Bogoroditsk, Russia ... 46 F10
Bogorodsk, Russia ... 48 B6
Bogoso, Ghana ... 82 D4
Bogotá, Colombia ... 124 C4
Bogotol, Russia ... 50 D9
Bogra, Bangla. ... 67 G16
Boguchany, Russia ... 51 D10
Boguchar, Russia ... 48 F5
Bogué, Mauritania ... 82 B2
Boguslav, Ukraine ... 47 H6
Boguszów-Gorce, Poland . 45 H3
Bohain-en-Vermandois,
  France ... 19 C10
Bohemia Downs, Australia 92 C4
Bohemian Forest =
  Böhmerwald, Germany . 25 F9
Bohena Cr. →, Australia 95 E4
Bohinjska Bistrica, Slovenia 29 B11
Böhmerwald, Germany ... 25 F9
Bohmte, Germany ... 24 C4
Bohodukhiv, Ukraine ... 47 G8
Bohol, Phil. ... 61 G6
Bohol Sea, Phil. ... 63 C6
Böhönye, Hungary ... 42 D2
Bohuslän, Sweden ... 11 F5
Boi, Nigeria ... 83 D6
Boi, Pta. de, Brazil ... 127 A6
Boiaçu, Brazil ... 124 D6
Boileau, C., Australia ... 92 C3
Boiro, Spain ... 34 C2
Boise, U.S.A. ... 114 E5
Boise City, U.S.A. ... 113 G3
Boissevain, Canada ... 105 D8
Bóite →, Italy ... 29 B9

Bojador C., W. Sahara ... 78 C3
Bojana →, Albania ... 40 E3
Bojano, Italy ... 31 A7
Bojanowo, Poland ... 45 G3
Bøjden, Denmark ... 11 J4
Bojnūrd, Iran ... 71 B8
Bojonegoro, Indonesia . 63 G14
Boju, Nigeria ... 83 D6
Boka, Serbia, Yug. ... 42 E5
Boka Kotorska,
  Montenegro, Yug. ... 40 D2
Bokala, Ivory C. ... 82 D4
Boké, Guinea ... 82 C2
Bokhara →, Australia ... 95 D4
Bokkos, Nigeria ... 83 D6
Boknafjorden, Norway ... 9 G11
Bokoro, Chad ... 79 F9
Bokpyin, Burma ... 65 G2
Boksitogorsk, Russia ... 46 C7
Bol, Croatia ... 29 E13
Bolama, Guinea-Biss. ... 82 C1
Bolan Pass, Pakistan ... 66 E5
Bolaños →, Mexico ... 118 C4
Bolaños de Calatrava,
  Spain ... 35 G7
Bolayır, Turkey ... 41 F10
Bolbec, France ... 18 C7
Boldājī, Iran ... 71 D6
Boldeşti-Scăeni, Romania . 43 E11
Bole, China ... 60 B3
Bole, Ethiopia ... 81 F4
Bolekhiv, Ukraine ... 47 H2
Bolesławiec, Poland ... 45 G2
Bolgatanga, Ghana ... 83 C4
Bolgrad = Bolhrad,
  Ukraine ... 47 K5
Bolhrad, Ukraine ... 47 K5
Boli, Sudan ... 81 F2
Bolinao, Phil. ... 61 C3
Bolintin-Vale, Romania . 43 F10
Bolívar, Argentina ... 126 D3
Bolivar, Mo., U.S.A. ... 113 G8
Bolivar, Tenn., U.S.A. ... 113 H10
Bolivia ■, S. Amer. ... 124 G6
Bolivian Plateau, S. Amer. 122 E4
Boljevac, Serbia, Yug. ... 40 C5
Bolkhov, Russia ... 46 F9
Bolków, Poland ... 45 H3
Bollebygd, Sweden ... 11 G6
Bollène, France ... 21 D8
Bollnäs, Sweden ... 10 C10
Bollon, Australia ... 95 D4
Bollstabruk, Sweden ... 10 B11
Bolmen, Sweden ... 11 H7
Bolobo,
  Dem. Rep. of the Congo 84 E3
Bologna, Italy ... 29 D8
Bologoye, Russia ... 46 D8
Bolonchenticul, Mexico . 119 D7
Bolótana, Italy ... 30 B1
Boloven, Cao Nguyen,
  Laos ... 64 E6
Bolpur, India ... 69 H12
Bolsena, Italy ... 29 F8
Bolsena, L. di, Italy ... 29 F8
Bolshaya Chernigovka,
  Russia ... 48 D10
Bolshaya Glushitsa, Russia 48 D10
Bolshaya Martynovka,
  Russia ... 49 G5
Bolshaya Vradiyevka,
  Ukraine ... 47 J6
Bolshevik, Ostrov, Russia . 51 B11
Bolshoi Kavkas = Caucasus
  Mountains, Eurasia ... 49 J7
Bolshoy Anyuy →, Russia 51 C17
Bolshoy Begichev, Ostrov,
  Russia ... 51 B12
Bolshoy Lyakhovskiy,
  Ostrov, Russia ... 51 B15
Bolshoy Tokmak =
  Tokmak, Ukraine ... 47 J8
Bolshoy Tyuters, Ostrov,
  Russia ... 9 G22
Bolsward, Neths. ... 17 A5
Bolt Head, U.K. ... 13 G4
Boltaña, Spain ... 32 C5
Boltigen, Switz. ... 25 J3
Bolton, Canada ... 110 C5
Bolton, U.K. ... 12 D5
Bolu, Turkey ... 72 B4
Bolungavík, Iceland ... 8 C2
Boluo, China ... 59 F10
Bolvadin, Turkey ... 72 C4
Bolzano, Italy ... 29 B8
Bom Jesus da Lapa, Brazil 125 F10
Boma,
  Dem. Rep. of the Congo 84 F2
Bomaderry, Australia ... 95 E5
Bombala, Australia ... 95 F4
Bombarral, Portugal ... 35 F1
Bombay = Mumbai, India 66 K8
Bomboma,
  Dem. Rep. of the Congo 84 D3
Bombowa,
  Dem. Rep. of the Congo 86 B2
Bomi Hills, Liberia ... 82 D2
Bomili,
  Dem. Rep. of the Congo 86 B2
Bømlo, Norway ... 9 G11
Bomokandi →,
  Dem. Rep. of the Congo 86 B2
Bomu →, C.A.R. ... 84 D4
Bon, C., Tunisia ... 76 C5
Bon Sar Pa, Vietnam ... 64 F6
Bonaire, Neth. Ant. ... 121 D6
Bonang, Australia ... 95 F4

Bonanza, Nic. ... 120 D3
Bonaparte Arch., Australia 92 B3
Boñar, Spain ... 34 C5
Bonaventure, Canada ... 103 C6
Bonavista, Canada ... 103 C9
Bonavista, C., Canada ... 103 C9
Bonawan, Phil. ... 61 G5
Bondeno, Italy ... 29 D8
Bondo,
  Dem. Rep. of the Congo 86 B1
Bondoukou, Ivory C. ... 82 D4
Bondowoso, Indonesia ... 63 G15
Bone, Teluk, Indonesia ... 63 E6
Bonerate, Indonesia ... 63 F6
Bonerate, Kepulauan,
  Indonesia ... 63 F6
Bo'ness, U.K. ... 14 E5
Bonete, Cerro, Argentina . 126 B2
Bong Son = Hoai Nhon,
  Vietnam ... 64 E7
Bongabong, Phil. ... 61 E4
Bongor, Chad ... 79 F9
Bongouanou, Ivory C. ... 82 D4
Bonham, U.S.A. ... 113 J6
Bonifacio, France ... 21 G13
Bonifacio, Bouches de,
  Medit. S. ... 30 A2
Bonin Is. = Ogasawara
  Gunto, Pac. Oc. ... 96 E6
Bonke, Ethiopia ... 81 F4
Bonn, Germany ... 24 E3
Bonnat, France ... 19 F8
Bonne Terre, U.S.A. ... 113 G9
Bonners Ferry, U.S.A. ... 114 B5
Bonnétable, France ... 18 D7
Bonneval, Eure-et-Loir,
  France ... 18 D8
Bonneval, Savoie, France . 21 C11
Bonneville, France ... 19 F13
Bonney, L., Australia ... 95 F3
Bonnie Downs, Australia . 94 C3
Bonnie Rock, Australia ... 93 F2
Bonny, Nigeria ... 83 E6
Bonny →, Nigeria ... 83 E6
Bonny, Bight of, Africa ... 83 E6
Bonny-sur-Loire, France . 19 E9
Bonnyrigg, U.K. ... 14 F5
Bonnyville, Canada ... 105 C6
Bono, Italy ... 30 B2
Bonoi, Indonesia ... 63 E9
Bonorva, Italy ... 30 B1
Bonsall, U.S.A. ... 117 M9
Bontang, Indonesia ... 62 D5
Bonthe, S. Leone ... 82 D2
Bontoc, Phil. ... 61 C4
Bonyeri, Ghana ... 82 D4
Bonyhád, Hungary ... 42 D3
Bonython Ra., Australia .. 92 D4
Bookabie, Australia ... 93 F5
Booker, U.S.A. ... 113 G4
Boolaboolka L., Australia 95 E3
Booligal, Australia ... 95 E3
Boonah, Australia ... 95 D5
Boone, Iowa, U.S.A. ... 112 D8
Boone, N.C., U.S.A. ... 109 G5
Booneville, Ark., U.S.A. . 113 H8
Booneville, Miss., U.S.A. 109 H1
Boonville, Calif., U.S.A. . 116 F3
Boonville, Ind., U.S.A. ... 108 F2
Boonville, Mo., U.S.A. ... 112 F8
Boonville, N.Y., U.S.A. .. 111 C9
Boorindal, Australia ... 95 E4
Boorowa, Australia ... 95 E4
Boothia, Gulf of, Canada . 4 B3
Boothia Pen., Canada ... 100 A10
Bootle, U.K. ... 12 D4
Booué, Gabon ... 84 E2
Boppard, Germany ... 25 E3
Boquete, Panama ... 120 E3
Boquilla, Presa de la,
  Mexico ... 118 B3
Boquillas del Carmen,
  Mexico ... 118 B4
Bor, Czech Rep. ... 26 B5
Bor, Russia ... 48 B7
Bor, Serbia, Yug. ... 40 B6
Bôr, Sudan ... 81 F3
Bor, Sweden ... 11 G8
Bor, Turkey ... 72 D6
Bor Mashash, Israel ... 75 D3
Borah Peak, U.S.A. ... 114 D7
Borang, Sudan ... 81 G3
Borås, Sweden ... 11 G6
Borāzjān, Iran ... 71 D6
Borba, Brazil ... 124 D7
Borba, Portugal ... 35 G3
Borborema, Planalto da,
  Brazil ... 122 D7
Borcea, Romania ... 43 F12
Borça, Turkey ... 73 B9
Bord Khūn-e Now, Iran .. 71 D6
Borda, C., Australia ... 95 F2
Bordeaux, France ... 20 D3
Borden, Australia ... 93 F2
Borden, Canada ... 103 C7
Borden I., Canada ... 4 B2
Bordertown, Australia ... 95 F3
Bordeyri, Iceland ... 8 D3
Bordighera, Italy ... 28 E4
Bordj Fly Ste. Marie,
  Algeria ... 78 C5
Bordj-in-Eker, Algeria ... 78 D7
Bordj Omar Driss, Algeria 78 C7
Borehamwood, U.K. ... 13 F7
Borek Wielkopolski,
  Poland ... 45 G4
Borensberg, Sweden ... 11 F9

Borgå = Porvoo, Finland . 9 F21
Borgarfjörður, Iceland ... 8 D7
Borgarnes, Iceland ... 8 D3
Børgefjellet, Norway ... 8 D15
Borger, Neths. ... 17 B6
Borger, U.S.A. ... 113 H4
Borgholm, Sweden ... 11 H10
Bórgia, Italy ... 31 D9
Borgo San Dalmazzo, Italy 28 D4
Borgo San Lorenzo, Italy . 29 E8
Borgo Val di Taro, Italy .. 28 D6
Borgo Valsugana, Italy ... 29 B8
Borgomanero, Italy ... 28 C5
Borgorose, Italy ... 29 F10
Borgosésia, Italy ... 28 C5
Borikhane, Laos ... 64 C4
Borisoglebsk, Russia ... 48 E6
Borisov = Barysaw,
  Belarus ... 46 E5
Borisovka, Russia ... 47 G9
Borja, Peru ... 124 D3
Borja, Spain ... 32 D3
Borjas Blancas = Les
  Borges Blanques, Spain 32 D5
Borjomi, Georgia ... 49 K6
Borken, Germany ... 24 D9
Børkop, Denmark ... 11 J3
Borkou, Chad ... 79 E9
Borkum, Germany ... 24 B2
Borlänge, Sweden ... 10 D9
Borley, C., Antarctica ... 5 C5
Borlu, Turkey ... 39 C10
Bormida →, Italy ... 28 D5
Bórmio, Italy ... 28 B7
Borna, Germany ... 24 D8
Borne Sulinowo, Poland .. 44 E3
Bornholm, Denmark ... 11 J8
Bornholms
  Amtskommune □,
  Denmark ... 11 J8
Bornholmsgattet, Europe . 11 J8
Borno □, Nigeria ... 83 C7
Bornos, Spain ... 35 J5
Bornova, Turkey ... 39 C9
Bornu Yassa, Nigeria ... 83 C7
Borodino, Russia ... 46 E8
Borogontsy, Russia ... 51 C14
Boromo, Burkina Faso ... 82 C4
Boron, U.S.A. ... 117 L9
Borongan, Phil. ... 61 F6
Bororen, Australia ... 94 C5
Borotangba Mts., C.A.R. . 81 F2
Borovan, Bulgaria ... 40 C7
Borovichi, Russia ... 46 C7
Borovsk, Russia ... 46 E9
Borrby, Sweden ... 11 J8
Borrego Springs, U.S.A. .. 117 M10
Borriol, Spain ... 32 E4
Borroloola, Australia ... 94 B2
Borşa, Cluj, Romania ... 43 D8
Borşa, Maramureş,
  Romania ... 43 C9
Borsec, Romania ... 43 D10
Borsod-Abaúj-Zemplén □,
  Hungary ... 42 B6
Bort-les-Orgues, France ... 20 C6
Borth, U.K. ... 13 E3
Börtnan, Sweden ... 10 B7
Borūjerd, Iran ... 71 C6
Boryslav, Ukraine ... 47 H2
Boryspil, Ukraine ... 47 G6
Borzhomi = Borjomi,
  Georgia ... 49 K6
Borzna, Ukraine ... 47 G7
Borzya, Russia ... 51 D12
Bosa, Italy ... 30 B1
Bosanska Dubica, Bos.-H. 29 C13
Bosanska Gradiška,
  Bos.-H. ... 42 E2
Bosanska Kostajnica,
  Bos.-H. ... 29 C13
Bosanska Krupa, Bos.-H. . 29 D13
Bosanski Brod, Bos.-H. ... 42 E2
Bosanski Novi, Bos.-H. ... 29 C13
Bosanski Petrovac, Bos.-H. 29 D13
Bosanski Šamac, Bos.-H. . 42 E3
Bosansko Grahovo,
  Bos.-H. ... 29 D13
Bosaso, Somali Rep. ... 74 E4
Boscastle, U.K. ... 13 G3
Bose, China ... 58 F6
Boshan, China ... 57 F9
Boshof, S. Africa ... 88 D4
Boshrūyeh, Iran ... 71 C8
Bosilegrad, Serbia, Yug. .. 40 D6
Bosna →, Bos.-H. ... 42 E3
Bosna i Hercegovina =
  Bosnia-Herzegovina ■,
  Europe ... 42 G2
Bosnia-Herzegovina ■,
  Europe ... 42 G2
Bosnik, Indonesia ... 63 E9
Bosobolo,
  Dem. Rep. of the Congo 84 D3
Bosporus = İstanbul
  Boğazı, Turkey ... 41 E13
Bossangoa, C.A.R. ... 84 C3
Bossier City, U.S.A. ... 113 J8
Bosso, Niger ... 83 C7
Bostānābād, Iran ... 70 B5
Bosten Hu, China ... 60 B3
Boston, U.K. ... 12 E7
Boston, U.S.A. ... 111 D13
Boston Bar, Canada ... 104 D4
Bosut →, Croatia ... 42 E3

Boswell, Canada ... 104 D5
Boswell, Okla., U.S.A. ... 113 H7
Boswell, Pa., U.S.A. ... 110 F5
Botad, India ... 68 H4
Botan →, Turkey ... 73 D10
Botany B., Australia ... 95 E5
Botene, Laos ... 64 D3
Botev, Bulgaria ... 41 D8
Botevgrad, Bulgaria ... 40 D7
Bothaville, S. Africa ... 88 D4
Bothnia, G. of, Europe ... 8 E19
Bothwell, Australia ... 94 G4
Bothwell, Canada ... 110 D3
Boticas, Portugal ... 34 D3
Botletle →, Botswana ... 88 C3
Botlikh, Russia ... 49 J8
Botna →, Moldova ... 43 D14
Botoroaga, Romania ... 43 F10
Botoşani, Romania ... 43 C11
Botoşani □, Romania ... 43 C11
Botricello, Italy ... 31 D9
Botro, Ivory C. ... 82 D3
Botswana ■, Africa ... 88 C3
Bottineau, U.S.A. ... 112 A4
Bottnaryd, Sweden ... 11 G7
Bottrop, Germany ... 24 D2
Botucatu, Brazil ... 127 A6
Botwood, Canada ... 103 C8
Bou Djébéha, Mali ... 82 B4
Bouaflé, Ivory C. ... 82 D3
Bouaké, Ivory C. ... 82 D3
Bouar, C.A.R. ... 84 C3
Bouârfa, Morocco ... 78 B5
Boucaut B., Australia ... 94 A1
Bouches-du-Rhône □,
  France ... 21 E9
Bougainville, C., Australia 92 B4
Bougainville Reef,
  Australia ... 94 B4
Bougie = Bejaia, Algeria . 78 A7
Bougouni, Mali ... 82 C3
Bouillon, Belgium ... 17 E5
Boulazac, France ... 20 C4
Boulder, Colo., U.S.A. ... 112 E2
Boulder, Mont., U.S.A. ... 114 C7
Boulder City, U.S.A. ... 117 K12
Boulder Creek, U.S.A. ... 116 H4
Boulder Dam = Hoover
  Dam, U.S.A. ... 117 K12
Bouli, Mauritania ... 82 B2
Boulia, Australia ... 94 C2
Bouligny, France ... 19 C12
Boulogne →, France ... 18 E5
Boulogne-sur-Gesse, France 20 E4
Boulogne-sur-Mer, France 19 B8
Bouloire, France ... 18 E7
Boulsa, Burkina Faso ... 83 C4
Boultoum, Niger ... 83 C7
Boun Neua, Laos ... 64 B3
Boun Tai, Laos ... 64 B3
Bouna, Ivory C. ... 82 D4
Boundary Peak, U.S.A. ... 116 H8
Boundiali, Ivory C. ... 82 D3
Bountiful, U.S.A. ... 114 F8
Bounty Is., Pac. Oc. ... 96 M9
Bourbon-Lancy, France ... 19 F10
Bourbon-l'Archambault,
  France ... 19 F10
Bourbonnais, France ... 19 F10
Bourbonne-les-Bains,
  France ... 19 E12
Bourbourg, France ... 19 B9
Bourem, Mali ... 83 B4
Bourg, France ... 20 C3
Bourg-Argental, France .. 21 C8
Bourg-de-Péage, France .. 21 C9
Bourg-en-Bresse, France .. 19 F12
Bourg-Lastic, France ... 20 C6
Bourg-Madame, France ... 20 F5
Bourg-St-Andéol, France . 21 D8
Bourg-St-Maurice, France . 21 C10
Bourganeuf, France ... 20 C5
Bourges, France ... 19 E9
Bourget, Canada ... 111 A9
Bourget, L. du, France ... 21 C9
Bourgneuf, B. de, France . 18 E4
Bourgneuf-en-Retz, France 18 E5
Bourgogne, France ... 19 F11
Bourgoin-Jallieu, France .. 21 C9
Bourgueil, France ... 18 E7
Bourke, Australia ... 95 E4
Bourne, U.K. ... 12 E7
Bournemouth, U.K. ... 13 G6
Bournemouth □, U.K. ... 13 G6
Bouse, U.S.A. ... 117 M13
Boussac, France ... 19 F9
Boutilimit, Mauritania ... 82 B2
Boutonne →, France ... 20 C3
Bouvet I. = Bouvetøya,
  Antarctica ... 3 G10
Bouvetøya, Antarctica ... 3 G10
Bouxwiller, France ... 19 D14
Bouznika, Morocco ... 19 C13
Bova Marina, Italy ... 31 E8
Bovalino Marina, Italy ... 31 D9
Bovec, Slovenia ... 29 B10
Bovill, U.S.A. ... 114 C5
Bovino, Italy ... 31 A8
Bow Island, Canada ... 104 D6
Bowbells, U.S.A. ... 112 A3
Bowdle, U.S.A. ... 112 C5
Bowelling, Australia ... 93 F2
Bowen, Australia ... 94 C4
Bowen Mts., Australia ... 95 F4
Bowie, Ariz., U.S.A. ... 115 K9
Bowie, Tex., U.S.A. ... 113 J6
Bowkān, Iran ... 70 B5

Bowland, Forest of, U.K. . 12 D5
Bowling Green, Ky.,
  U.S.A. ... 108 G2
Bowling Green, Ohio,
  U.S.A. ... 108 E4
Bowling Green, C.,
  Australia ... 94 B4
Bowman, U.S.A. ... 112 B3
Bowman I., Antarctica ... 5 C8
Bowmans, Australia ... 95 E2
Bowmanville, Canada ... 102 D4
Bowmore, U.K. ... 14 F2
Bowral, Australia ... 95 E5
Bowraville, Australia ... 95 E5
Bowron →, Canada ... 104 C4
Bowser L., Canada ... 104 B3
Bowsman, Canada ... 105 C8
Bowwood, Zambia ... 87 F2
Boxholm, Sweden ... 11 F9
Boxmeer, Neths. ... 17 C5
Boxtel, Neths. ... 17 C5
Boyabat, Turkey ... 72 B6
Boyalıca, Turkey ... 41 F13
Boyce, U.S.A. ... 113 K8
Boyer →, Canada ... 104 B5
Boyne →, Ireland ... 15 C5
Boyne City, U.S.A. ... 108 C3
Boynitsa, Bulgaria ... 40 C6
Boynton Beach, U.S.A. .. 109 M5
Boyoma, Chutes,
  Dem. Rep. of the Congo 86 B2
Boyuibe, Bolivia ... 124 G6
Boyup Brook, Australia .. 93 F2
Boz Dağ, Turkey ... 39 D11
Boz Dağları, Turkey ... 39 C10
Bozburun, Turkey ... 39 E10
Bozcaada, Turkey ... 39 B8
Bozdoğan, Turkey ... 39 D10
Bozeman, U.S.A. ... 114 D8
Bozen = Bolzano, Italy ... 29 B8
Boževac, Serbia, Yug. ... 40 B5
Bozkır, Turkey ... 72 D5
Bozkurt, Turkey ... 39 D11
Bozouls, France ... 20 D6
Bozoum, C.A.R. ... 84 C3
Bozova, Antalya, Turkey . 39 D12
Bozova, Sanlıurfa, Turkey 73 D8
Bozovici, Romania ... 42 F7
Bozüyük, Turkey ... 39 B12
Bra, Italy ... 28 D4
Braås, Sweden ... 11 G9
Brabant □, Belgium ... 17 D4
Brabant L., Canada ... 105 B8
Brabrand, Denmark ... 11 H4
Brač, Croatia ... 29 E13
Bracadale, L., U.K. ... 14 D2
Bracciano, Italy ... 29 F9
Bracciano, L. di, Italy ... 29 F9
Bracebridge, Canada ... 102 C4
Brach, Libya ... 79 C8
Bracieux, France ... 18 E8
Bräcke, Sweden ... 10 B9
Brackettville, U.S.A. ... 113 L4
Bracknell, U.K. ... 13 F7
Bracknell Forest □, U.K. . 13 F7
Brad, Romania ... 42 D7
Brádano →, Italy ... 31 B9
Bradenton, U.S.A. ... 109 M4
Bradford, Canada ... 110 B5
Bradford, U.K. ... 12 D6
Bradford, Pa., U.S.A. ... 110 E6
Bradford, Vt., U.S.A. ... 111 C12
Bradley, Ark., U.S.A. ... 113 J8
Bradley, Calif., U.S.A. ... 116 K6
Bradley, S. Dak., U.S.A. . 112 C6
Bradley Institute,
  Zimbabwe ... 87 F3
Bradore Bay, Canada ... 103 B8
Bradshaw, Australia ... 92 C5
Brady, U.S.A. ... 113 K5
Braemar, Australia ... 95 E2
Braemar, U.K. ... 14 D5
Braeside, Canada ... 111 A8
Braga, Portugal ... 34 D2
Braga □, Portugal ... 34 D2
Bragadiru, Romania ... 43 G10
Bragado, Argentina ... 126 D3
Bragança, Brazil ... 125 D9
Bragança, Portugal ... 34 D4
Bragança □, Portugal ... 34 D4
Bragança Paulista, Brazil . 127 A6
Brahmanbaria, Bangla. ... 67 H17
Brahmani →, India ... 67 J15
Brahmapur, India ... 67 K14
Brahmaputra →, India ... 69 H13
Braich-y-pwll, U.K. ... 12 E3
Braidwood, Australia ... 95 F4
Brăila, Romania ... 43 E12
Brăila □, Romania ... 43 E12
Brainerd, U.S.A. ... 112 B7
Braintree, U.K. ... 13 F8
Braintree, U.S.A. ... 111 D14
Brak →, S. Africa ... 88 D3
Brake, Germany ... 24 B4
Brakel, Germany ... 24 D5
Bräkne-Hoby, Sweden ... 11 H9
Brakwater, Namibia ... 88 C2
Brålanda, Sweden ... 11 F6
Bralorne, Canada ... 104 C4
Bramberg, Germany ... 25 E6
Bramdrupdam, Denmark . 11 J3
Bramming, Denmark ... 11 J2
Brämön, Sweden ... 10 B11

Brampton, Canada ... 102 D4
Brampton, U.K. ... 12 C5
Bramsche, Germany ... 24 C3
Bramwell, Australia ... 94 A3
Branco →, Brazil ... 122 D4
Brande, Denmark ... 11 J3
Brandenburg =
  Neubrandenburg,
  Germany ... 24 B9
Brandenburg, Germany ... 24 C8
Brandenburg □, Germany 24 C9
Brandfort, S. Africa ... 88 D4
Brandon, France ... 21 F13
Brandon, Canada ... 105 D9
Brandon, U.S.A. ... 111 C11
Brandon B., Ireland ... 15 D1
Brandon Mt., Ireland ... 15 D1
Brandsen, Argentina ... 126 D4
Brandvlei, S. Africa ... 88 E3
Brandýs nad Labem,
  Czech Rep. ... 26 A7
Brăneşti, Romania ... 43 F11
Branford, U.S.A. ... 111 E12
Braniewo, Poland ... 44 D6
Bransfield Str., Antarctica 5 C18
Brańsk, Poland ... 45 F9
Branson, Colo., U.S.A. ... 113 G3
Branson, Mo., U.S.A. ... 113 G8
Brantford, Canada ... 102 D3
Brantôme, France ... 20 C4
Branxholme, Australia ... 95 F3
Branzi, Italy ... 28 B6
Bras d'Or, L., Canada ... 103 C7
Brasil, Planalto, Brazil ... 122 E6
Brasiléia, Brazil ... 124 F5
Brasília, Brazil ... 125 G9
Brasília Legal, Brazil ... 125 D7
Braslaw, Belarus ... 9 J22
Braslovče, Slovenia ... 29 B12
Braşov, Romania ... 43 E10
Braşov □, Romania ... 43 E10
Brass, Nigeria ... 83 E6
Brass →, Nigeria ... 83 E6
Brassac-les-Mines, France . 20 C7
Brasschaat, Belgium ... 17 C4
Brassey, Banjaran,
  Malaysia ... 62 D5
Brassey Ra., Australia ... 93 E3
Brasstown Bald, U.S.A. .. 109 H4
Brastad, Sweden ... 11 F5
Brastavăţu, Romania ... 43 G9
Bratan = Morozov,
  Bulgaria ... 41 D9
Brateş, Romania ... 43 E11
Bratislava, Slovak Rep. ... 27 C10
Bratislavský □, Slovak Rep. 27 C10
Bratsigovo, Bulgaria ... 41 D8
Bratsk, Russia ... 51 D11
Brattleboro, U.S.A. ... 111 D12
Bratunac, Bos.-H. ... 42 F4
Braunau, Austria ... 26 C6
Braunschweig, Germany .. 24 C6
Braunton, U.K. ... 13 F3
Bravicea, Moldova ... 43 C13
Bråviken, Sweden ... 11 F10
Bravo del Norte →,
  Mexico ... 118 B5
Bravo del Norte, Rio → =
  Grande, Rio →, U.S.A. 113 N6
Brawley, U.S.A. ... 117 N11
Bray, Ireland ... 15 C5
Bray, Mt., Australia ... 94 A1
Bray-sur-Seine, France ... 19 D10
Brazeau →, Canada ... 104 C5
Brazil, U.S.A. ... 108 F2
Brazil ■, S. Amer. ... 125 F9
Brazilian Highlands =
  Brasil, Planalto, Brazil . 122 E6
Brazo Sur →, S. Amer. .. 126 B4
Brazos →, U.S.A. ... 113 L7
Brazzaville, Congo ... 84 E3
Brčko, Bos.-H. ... 42 F3
Brda →, Poland ... 44 E5
Brdy, Czech Rep. ... 26 B6
Breadalbane, Australia ... 94 C2
Breaden, L., Australia ... 93 E4
Breaksea Sd., N.Z. ... 91 L1
Bream B., N.Z. ... 91 F5
Bream Hd., N.Z. ... 91 F5
Breas, Chile ... 126 B1
Breaza, Romania ... 43 E10
Brebes, Indonesia ... 63 G13
Brechin, Canada ... 110 B5
Brechin, U.K. ... 14 E6
Brecht, Belgium ... 17 C4
Breckenridge, Colo.,
  U.S.A. ... 114 G10
Breckenridge, Minn.,
  U.S.A. ... 112 B6
Breckenridge, Tex., U.S.A. 113 J5
Breckland, U.K. ... 13 E8
Břeclav, Czech Rep. ... 27 C9
Brecon, U.K. ... 13 F4
Brecon Beacons, U.K. ... 13 F4
Breda, Neths. ... 17 C4
Bredaryd, Sweden ... 11 G7
Bredasdorp, S. Africa ... 88 E3
Bredbo, Australia ... 95 F4
Bredebro, Denmark ... 11 J2
Bredstedt, Germany ... 11 J2
Bree, Belgium ... 17 C5
Breganica →, Macedonia 40 E8
Bregenz, Austria ... 26 D2
Bregovo, Bulgaria ... 40 B6
Bréhal, France ... 18 D5
Bréhat, Î. de, France ... 18 D4
Breiðafjörður, Iceland ... 8 D2

Breil-sur-Roya, France ... 21 E11
Breisach, Germany 25 G3
Brejo, Brazil 125 D10
Bremen, Germany 24 B4
Bremen □, Germany 24 B4
Bremerhaven, Germany ... 24 B4
Bremer I., Australia 94 A2
Bremervörde, Germany ... 24 B5
Brenes, Spain 35 H5
Brenham, U.S.A. 113 K6
Brenne, France 20 B5
Brennerpass, Austria 26 D4
Breno, Italy 28 C7
Brent, Canada 102 C4
Brenta →, Italy 29 C9
Brentwood, U.K. 13 F8
Brentwood, U.S.A. 111 F11
Bréscia, Italy 28 C7
Breskens, Neths. 17 C3
Breslau = Wrocław, Poland 45 G4
Bresle →, France 18 B8
Bressanone, Italy 29 B8
Bressay, U.K. 14 A7
Bresse, France 19 F12
Bressuire, France 18 F6
Brest, Belarus 47 F2
Brest, France 18 D2
Brest-Litovsk = Brest,
  Belarus 47 F2
Bretagne, France 18 D3
Bretçu, Romania 43 D11
Bretenoux, France 20 D5
Breteuil, Eure, France ... 18 D7
Breteuil, Oise, France ... 19 C9
Breton, Canada 104 C6
Breton, Pertuis, France .. 20 B2
Breton Sd., U.S.A. 113 L10
Brett, C., N.Z. 91 F5
Bretten, Germany 25 F4
Breuil-Cervínia, Italy ... 28 C4
Brevard, U.S.A. 109 H4
Breves, Brazil 125 D8
Brewarrina, Australia ... 95 E4
Brewer, U.S.A. 103 D6
Brewer, Mt., U.S.A. ... 116 J8
Brewster, N.Y., U.S.A. . 111 E11
Brewster, Wash., U.S.A. . 114 B4
Brewster, Kap, Greenland 4 B6
Brewton, U.S.A. 109 K2
Breyten, S. Africa 89 D5
Breza, Bos.-H. 42 F3
Brezhnev = Naberezhnyye
  Chelny, Russia 48 C11
Brežice, Slovenia 29 C12
Březnice, Czech Rep. 26 B6
Breznik, Bulgaria 40 D6
Brezno, Slovak Rep. 27 C12
Brezoi, Romania 43 E9
Brezovo, Bulgaria 41 D9
Briançon, France 21 D10
Briare, France 19 E9
Briático, Italy 31 D9
Bribie I., Australia 95 D5
Briceni, Moldova 43 B12
Bricquebec, France 18 C5
Bridgehampton, U.S.A. . 111 F12
Bridgend, U.K. 13 F4
Bridgend □, U.K. 13 F4
Bridgeport, Calif., U.S.A. 116 G7
Bridgeport, Conn., U.S.A. 111 E11
Bridgeport, Nebr., U.S.A. 112 E3
Bridgeport, Tex., U.S.A. 113 J6
Bridger, U.S.A. 114 D9
Bridgeton, U.S.A. 108 F8
Bridgetown, Australia ... 93 F2
Bridgetown, Barbados ... 121 D8
Bridgetown, Canada 103 D6
Bridgewater, Canada 103 D7
Bridgewater, Mass., U.S.A. 111 E14
Bridgewater, S. Dak.,
  U.S.A. 112 D6
Bridgewater, C., Australia 95 F3
Bridgnorth, U.K. 13 E5
Bridgton, U.S.A. 111 B14
Bridgwater, U.K. 13 F5
Bridgwater B., U.K. 13 F4
Bridlington, U.K. 12 C7
Bridlington B., U.K. 12 C7
Bridport, Australia 94 G4
Bridport, U.K. 13 G5
Briec, France 18 D2
Brienne-le-Château, France 19 D11
Brienon-sur-Armançon,
  France 19 E10
Brienz, Switz. 25 J4
Brienzersee, Switz. 25 J3
Brig, Switz. 25 J3
Brigg, U.K. 12 D7
Briggsdale, U.S.A. 112 E2
Brigham City, U.S.A. ... 114 F7
Bright, Australia 95 F4
Brighton, Australia 95 F2
Brighton, Canada 102 D4
Brighton, U.K. 13 G7
Brighton, U.S.A. 112 F2
Brignogan-Plage, France . 18 D2
Brignoles, France 21 E10
Brihuega, Spain 32 E2
Brikama, Gambia 82 C1
Brilliant, Canada 104 D5
Brilliant, U.S.A. 110 F4
Brilon, Germany 24 D4
Bríndisi, Italy 31 B10
Brinje, Croatia 29 D12
Brinkley, U.S.A. 113 H9
Brinkworth, Australia ... 95 E2

Brinnon, U.S.A. 116 C4
Brion, I., Canada 103 C7
Brionne, France 18 C7
Brionski, Croatia 29 D10
Brioude, France 20 C7
Briouze, France 18 D6
Brisbane, Australia 95 D5
Brisbane →, Australia ... 95 D5
Brisighella, Italy 29 D8
Bristol, U.K. 13 F5
Bristol, Conn., U.S.A. .. 111 E12
Bristol, Pa., U.S.A. 111 F10
Bristol, R.I., U.S.A. 111 E13
Bristol, S. Dak., U.S.A. . 112 C6
Bristol, Tenn., U.S.A. .. 109 G4
Bristol, City of □, U.K. . 13 F5
Bristol B., U.S.A. 100 C4
Bristol Channel, U.K. ... 13 F3
Bristol I., Antarctica 5 B1
Bristol L., U.S.A. 115 J5
Bristow, U.S.A. 113 H6
British Columbia □,
  Canada 104 C3
British Isles, Europe 6 E5
Brits, S. Africa 89 D4
Britstown, S. Africa 88 E3
Britt, Canada 102 C3
Brittany = Bretagne,
  France 18 D3
Britton, U.S.A. 112 C6
Brive-la-Gaillarde, France 20 C5
Briviesca, Spain 34 C7
Brixen = Bressanone, Italy 29 B8
Brixham, U.K. 13 G4
Brixton, Australia 94 C3
Brnaze, Croatia 29 E13
Brno, Czech Rep. 27 B9
Broad →, U.S.A. 109 J5
Broad Arrow, Australia . 93 F3
Broad B., U.K. 14 C2
Broad Haven, Ireland ... 15 B2
Broad Law, U.K. 14 F5
Broad Sd., Australia 94 C4
Broadhurst Ra., Australia . 92 D3
Broads, The, U.K. 12 E9
Broadus, U.S.A. 112 C2
Broadview, Canada 105 C8
Broager, Denmark 11 K3
Brocēni, Latvia 44 B9
Brochet, Canada 105 B8
Brochet, L., Canada 105 B8
Brock, Canada 105 C7
Brocken, Germany 24 D6
Brockport, U.S.A. 110 C7
Brockton, U.S.A. 111 D13
Brockville, Canada 102 D4
Brockway, Mont., U.S.A. 112 B2
Brockway, Pa., U.S.A. .. 110 E6
Brocton, U.S.A. 110 D5
Brod, Macedonia 40 E5
Brodarevo, Serbia, Yug. . 40 C3
Brodeur Pen., Canada .. 101 A11
Brodick, U.K. 14 F3
Brodnica, Poland 45 E6
Brody, Ukraine 47 G3
Brogan, U.S.A. 114 D5
Broglie, France 18 C7
Brok, Poland 45 F8
Broken Arrow, U.S.A. .. 113 G7
Broken Bow, Nebr.,
  U.S.A. 112 E5
Broken Bow, Okla.,
  U.S.A. 113 H7
Broken Hill = Kabwe,
  Zambia 87 E2
Broken Hill, Australia ... 95 E3
Brokind, Sweden 11 F9
Bromley, U.K. 13 F8
Bromölla, Sweden 11 H8
Bromsgrove, U.K. 13 E5
Brønderslev, Denmark .. 11 G3
Brong-Ahafo □, Ghana . 82 D4
Broni, Italy 28 C6
Bronkhorstspruit, S. Africa 89 D4
Brønnøysund, Norway .. 8 D15
Bronte, Italy 31 E7
Bronte, U.S.A. 113 K4
Bronte Park, Australia .. 94 G4
Brook Park, U.S.A. 110 E4
Brookfield, U.S.A. 112 F8
Brookhaven, U.S.A. 113 K9
Brookings, Oreg., U.S.A. 114 E1
Brookings, S. Dak., U.S.A. 112 C6
Brooklin, Canada 110 C6
Brooklyn Park, U.S.A. .. 112 C8
Brookmere, Canada 104 D4
Brooks, Canada 104 C6
Brooks B., Canada 104 C3
Brooks L., Canada 105 B8
Brooks Range, U.S.A. .. 100 B5
Brooksville, U.S.A. 109 L4
Brookville, U.S.A. 108 F3
Brooloo, Australia 95 D5
Broom, L., U.K. 14 D3
Broome, Australia 92 C3
Broomehill, Australia ... 93 F2
Broons, France 18 D4
Brora, U.K. 14 C5
Brora →, U.K. 14 C5
Brørup, Denmark 11 J2
Brösarp, Sweden 11 J8
Brosna →, Ireland 15 C4
Broșteni, Mehedinți,
  Romania 42 F7
Broșteni, Suceava, Romania 43 C10
Brothers, U.S.A. 114 E3

Brou, France 18 D8
Brouage, France 20 C2
Brough, U.K. 12 C5
Brough Hd., U.K. 14 B5
Broughton Island, Canada 101 B13
Broumov, Czech Rep. ... 27 A9
Brovary, Ukraine 47 G6
Brovst, Denmark 11 G3
Browerville, U.S.A. 112 B7
Brown, Pt., Australia ... 95 E1
Brown Willy, U.K. 13 G3
Brownfield, U.S.A. 113 J3
Browning, U.S.A. 114 B7
Brownlee, Canada 105 C7
Brownsville, Oreg., U.S.A. 114 D2
Brownsville, Tenn., U.S.A. 113 H10
Brownsville, Tex., U.S.A. 113 N6
Brownwood, U.S.A. 113 K5
Brownwood, L., U.S.A. . 113 K5
Browse I., Australia 92 B3
Bruas, Malaysia 65 K3
Bruay-la-Buissière, France 19 B9
Bruce, Mt., Australia ... 92 D2
Bruce Pen., Canada 110 B3
Bruce Rock, Australia ... 93 F2
Bruche →, France 19 D14
Bruchsal, Germany 25 F4
Bruck an der Leitha,
  Austria 27 C9
Bruck an der Mur, Austria 26 D8
Brue →, U.K. 13 F5
Bruges = Brugge, Belgium 17 C3
Brugg, Switz. 25 H4
Brugge, Belgium 17 C3
Brûlé, Canada 104 C5
Brûlon, France 18 E6
Brumado, Brazil 125 F10
Brumath, France 19 D14
Brumunddal, Norway .. 9 F14
Brunchilly, Australia ... 94 B1
Brundidge, U.S.A. 109 K3
Bruneau, U.S.A. 114 E6
Bruneau →, U.S.A. 114 E6
Bruneck = Brunico, Italy . 29 B8
Brunei = Bandar Seri
  Begawan, Brunei 62 D5
Brunei ■, Asia 62 D5
Brunette Downs, Australia 94 B2
Brunflo, Sweden 10 A8
Brunico, Italy 29 B8
Brunna, Sweden 10 E11
Brunnen, Switz. 25 J4
Brunner, L., N.Z. 91 K3
Bruno, Canada 105 C7
Brunsbüttel, Germany .. 24 B5
Brunssum, Neths. 17 D5
Brunswick =
  Braunschweig, Germany 24 C6
Brunswick, Ga., U.S.A. . 109 K5
Brunswick, Maine, U.S.A. 103 D6
Brunswick, Md., U.S.A. . 108 F7
Brunswick, Mo., U.S.A. . 112 F8
Brunswick, Ohio, U.S.A. . 110 E3
Brunswick, Pen. de, Chile 128 G2
Brunswick B., Australia . 92 C3
Brunswick Junction,
  Australia 93 F2
Bruntál, Czech Rep. 27 B10
Bruny I., Australia 94 G4
Brus Laguna, Honduras . 120 C3
Brusartsi, Bulgaria 40 C7
Brush, U.S.A. 112 E3
Brushton, U.S.A. 111 B10
Brusio, Switz. 25 J6
Brusque, Brazil 127 B6
Brussel, Belgium 17 D4
Brussels = Brussel,
  Belgium 17 D4
Brussels, Canada 110 C3
Brusy, Poland 44 E4
Bruthen, Australia 95 F4
Bruxelles = Brussel,
  Belgium 17 D4
Bruyères, France 19 D13
Bruz, France 18 D5
Brwinów, Poland 45 F7
Bryagovo, Bulgaria 41 E9
Bryan, Ohio, U.S.A. ... 108 E3
Bryan, Tex., U.S.A. 113 K6
Bryan, Mt., Australia ... 95 E2
Bryanka, Ukraine 47 H10
Bryansk, Bryansk, Russia . 47 F8
Bryansk, Dagestan, Russia 49 H8
Bryanskoye = Bryansk,
  Russia 49 H8
Bryant, U.S.A. 112 C6
Bryne, Norway 9 G11
Bryson City, U.S.A. 109 H4
Bryukhovetskaya, Russia . 47 K10
Brza Palanka, Serbia, Yug. 40 B6
Brzeg, Poland 45 H4
Brzeg Dolny, Poland ... 45 G3
Brześć Kujawski, Poland . 45 F5
Brzesko, Poland 45 J7
Brzeziny, Poland 45 G6
Brzozów, Poland 45 J9
Bsharri, Lebanon 75 A5
Bū Baqarah, U.A.E. 71 E8
Bu Craa, W. Sahara 78 C3
Bū Ḩasā, U.A.E. 71 F7
Bua, Sweden 11 G6
Bua Yai, Thailand 64 E4
Buapinang, Indonesia ... 63 E6
Buba, Guinea-Biss. 82 C2
Bubanza, Burundi 86 C2
Būbiyān, Kuwait 71 D6
Buca, Turkey 39 C9

Bucak, Turkey 39 D12
Bucaramanga, Colombia . 124 B4
Bucas Grande I., Phil. ... 61 G6
Buccaneer Arch., Australia 92 C3
Buccino, Italy 31 B8
Bucecea, Romania 43 C11
Buchach, Ukraine 47 H3
Buchan, U.K. 14 D6
Buchan Ness, U.K. 14 D7
Buchanan, Canada 105 C8
Buchanan, Liberia 82 D2
Buchanan, L., Queens.,
  Australia 94 C4
Buchanan, L., W. Austral.,
  Australia 93 E3
Buchanan, L., U.S.A. ... 113 K5
Buchanan Cr. →, Australia 94 B2
Buchans, Canada 103 C8
Bucharest = București,
  Romania 43 F11
Buchen, Germany 25 F5
Buchholz, Germany 24 B5
Buchloe, Germany 25 G6
Buchon, Pt., U.S.A. 116 K6
Buciumi, Romania 42 C8
Buck, L., U.S.A. 111 C11
Buckeye, U.S.A. 115 K7
Buckhannon, U.S.A. ... 108 F5
Buckhaven, U.K. 14 E5
Buckie, U.K. 14 D6
Buckingham, Canada ... 102 C4
Buckingham, U.K. 13 F7
Buckingham B., Australia 94 A2
Buckinghamshire □, U.K. 13 F7
Buckle Hd., Australia ... 92 B4
Buckleboo, Australia ... 95 E2
Buckley, U.K. 12 D4
Buckley →, Australia ... 94 C2
Buckley, U.S.A. 114 C2
Bucks L., U.S.A. 116 F5
Bucquoy, France 19 B9
Buctouche, Canada 103 C7
București, Romania 43 F11
Bucyrus, U.S.A. 108 E4
Budacu, Vf., Romania .. 43 C10
Budalin, Burma 67 H19
Budaörs, Hungary 42 C3
Budapest, Hungary 42 C4
Budapest □, Hungary .. 42 C4
Budaun, India 69 E8
Budd Coast, Antarctica . 5 C8
Buddusò, Italy 30 B2
Bude, U.K. 13 G3
Budennovsk, Russia 49 H7
Budești, Romania 43 F11
Budge Budge = Baj Baj,
  India 69 H13
Budgewoi, Australia ... 95 E5
Budia, Spain 32 E2
Budingen, Germany ... 25 E5
Budjala,
  Dem. Rep. of the Congo 84 D3
Budoni, Italy 30 B2
Búdrio, Italy 29 D8
Budva, Montenegro, Yug. 40 D2
Budzyń, Poland 45 F3
Buea, Cameroon 83 E6
Buellton, U.S.A. 117 L6
Buena Park, U.S.A. 117 M9
Buena Vista, Colo., U.S.A. 115 G10
Buena Vista, Va., U.S.A. . 108 G6
Buena Vista L., U.S.A. .. 117 K7
Buenaventura, Colombia . 124 C3
Buenaventura, Mexico ... 118 B3
Buendía, Embalse de,
  Spain 32 E2
Buenos Aires, Argentina . 126 C4
Buenos Aires, Costa Rica 120 E3
Buenos Aires □, Argentina 126 D4
Buenos Aires, L., Chile .. 128 F2
Buffalo, Mo., U.S.A. ... 113 G8
Buffalo, N.Y., U.S.A. ... 110 D6
Buffalo, Okla., U.S.A. .. 113 G5
Buffalo, S. Dak., U.S.A. . 112 C3
Buffalo, Wyo., U.S.A. .. 114 D10
Buffalo →, Canada 104 A5
Buffalo Head Hills, Canada 104 B5
Buffalo L., Canada 104 C6
Buffalo Narrows, Canada . 105 B7
Buffels →, S. Africa 88 D2
Buford, U.S.A. 109 H4
Bug →, Buh →,
  Ukraine 47 J6
Bug →, Poland 45 F8
Buga, Colombia 124 C3
Buganda, Uganda 86 C3
Buganga, Uganda 86 C3
Bugasong, Phil. 61 F5
Bugeat, France 20 C5
Bugel, Tanjung, Indonesia 63 G14
Bugibba, Malta 36 D1
Bugojno, Bos.-H. 42 F2
Bugsuk, Phil. 61 G2
Buguma, Nigeria 83 E6
Bugun Shara, Mongolia . 60 B5
Buguruslan, Russia 50 D6
Buh →, Ukraine 47 J6
Buharkent, Turkey 39 D10
Buheirat-Murrat-el-Kubra,
  Egypt 80 H8
Bühl, Germany 25 G4
Buhl, Idaho, U.S.A. 114 E6
Buhl, Minn., U.S.A. 112 B8
Buhuşi, Romania 43 D11
Buick, U.S.A. 113 G9
Builth Wells, U.K. 13 E4

Buinsk, Russia 48 C9
Buir Nur, Mongolia 60 B6
Buis-les-Baronnies, France 21 D9
Buitrago = Buitrago del
  Lozoya, Spain 34 E7
Buitrago del Lozoya, Spain 34 E7
Bujalance, Spain 35 H6
Bujaraloz, Spain 32 D4
Buje, Croatia 29 C10
Bujumbura, Burundi ... 86 C2
Bük, Hungary 42 C1
Buk, Poland 45 F3
Bukachacha, Russia 51 D12
Bukama,
  Dem. Rep. of the Congo 87 D2
Bukavu,
  Dem. Rep. of the Congo 86 C2
Bukene, Tanzania 86 C3
Bukhara = Bukhoro,
  Uzbekistan 50 F7
Bukhoro, Uzbekistan ... 50 F7
Bukima, Tanzania 86 C3
Bukit Mertajam, Malaysia 65 K3
Bukittinggi, Indonesia .. 62 E2
Bükk, Hungary 42 B5
Bukoba, Tanzania 86 C3
Bukoba □, Tanzania 86 C3
Bukuru, Nigeria 83 D6
Bukuya, Uganda 86 B3
Bula, Guinea-Biss. 82 C1
Bula, Indonesia 63 E8
Bülach, Switz. 25 H4
Bulahdelah, Australia ... 95 E5
Bulan, Phil. 61 E5
Bulancak, Turkey 73 B8
Bulandshahr, India 68 E7
Bulanık, Turkey 73 C10
Bûlâq, Egypt 80 B3
Bulawayo, Zimbabwe .. 87 G2
Buldan, Turkey 39 C10
Bulgan, Mongolia 60 B5
Bulgar, Russia 48 C9
Bulgaria ■, Europe 41 D9
Bulgheria, Monte, Italy . 31 B8
Bulgroo, Australia 95 D3
Bulgunnia, Australia ... 95 E1
Bulgurca, Turkey 39 C9
Buli, Teluk, Indonesia .. 63 D7
Buliluyan, C., Phil. 61 G2
Bulki, Ethiopia 81 F4
Bulkley →, Canada 104 B3
Bull Shoals L., U.S.A. .. 113 G8
Bullaque →, Spain 35 G6
Bullara, Australia 92 D1
Bullaring, Australia 93 F2
Bullas, Spain 33 G3
Bulle, Switz. 25 J3
Bulli, Australia 95 E5
Büllingen, Belgium 17 D6
Bullock Creek, Australia . 94 B3
Bulloo →, Australia 95 D3
Bulloo Downs, Queens.,
  Australia 95 D3
Bulloo Downs, W. Austral.,
  Australia 92 D2
Bulloo L., Australia 95 D3
Bulls, N.Z. 91 J5
Bully-les-Mines, France . 19 B9
Bulnes, Chile 126 D1
Bulqiza, Albania 40 E4
Bulsar = Valsad, India .. 66 J8
Bultfontein, S. Africa ... 88 D4
Bulukumba, Indonesia .. 63 F6
Bulun, Russia 51 B13
Bumba,
  Dem. Rep. of the Congo 84 D4
Bumbești-Jiu, Romania . 43 E8
Bumbiri I., Tanzania ... 86 C3
Bumhpa Bum, Burma .. 67 F20
Bumi →, Zimbabwe ... 87 F2
Buna, Kenya 86 B4
Bunawan, Agusan del S.,
  Phil. 61 G6
Bunawan, Davao del S.,
  Phil. 61 H6
Bunazi, Tanzania 86 C3
Bunbury, Australia 93 F2
Bunclody, Ireland 15 D5
Buncrana, Ireland 15 A4
Bundaberg, Australia ... 95 C5
Bünde, Germany 24 C4
Bundey →, Australia ... 94 C2
Bundi, India 68 G6
Bundooma, Australia ... 94 C1
Bundoran, Ireland 15 B3
Bundukia, Sudan 81 F3
Bung Kan, Thailand ... 64 C4
Bungay, U.K. 13 E9
Bungil Cr. →, Australia . 94 D4
Bungo-Suidō, Japan ... 55 H6
Bungoma, Kenya 86 B3
Bungu, Tanzania 86 D4
Bunia,
  Dem. Rep. of the Congo 86 B3
Bunji, Pakistan 69 B6
Bunkie, U.S.A. 113 K8
Bunnell, U.S.A. 109 L5
Buñol, Spain 33 F4
Buntok, Indonesia 62 E4
Bununu, Nigeria 83 D6
Bununu Dass, Nigeria .. 83 C6
Bünyan, Turkey 72 C6
Bunyu, Indonesia 62 D5
Bunza, Nigeria 83 C5
Buol, Indonesia 63 D6

Buon Brieng, *Vietnam* 64 F7
Buon Ma Thuot, *Vietnam* . 64 F7
Buong Long, *Cambodia* .. 64 F6
Buorkhaya, Mys, *Russia* . 51 B14
Buqayq, *Si. Arabia* 71 E6
Buqbuq, *Egypt* 80 A2
Bur Acaba, *Somali Rep.* .. 74 G3
Bûr Fuad, *Egypt* 80 H8
Bûr Safâga, *Egypt* 80 B3
Bûr Sa'îd, *Egypt* 80 H8
Bûr Sûdân, *Sudan* 80 D4
Bûr Taufiq, *Egypt* 80 J8
Bura, *Kenya* 86 C4
Burao, *Somali Rep.* 74 F4
Burāq, *Syria* 75 B5
Buras, *U.S.A.* 113 L10
Buraydah, *Si. Arabia* 70 E5
Burbank, *U.S.A.* 117 L8
Burcher, *Australia* 95 E4
Burdekin →, *Australia* .. 94 B4
Burdett, *Canada* 104 D6
Burdur, *Turkey* 39 D12
Burdur □, *Turkey* 39 D12
Burdur Gölü, *Turkey* 39 D12
Burdwan = Barddhaman,
  India 69 H12
Bure, *Ethiopia* 81 E4
Bure →, *U.K.* 12 E9
Büren, *Germany* 24 D4
Bureya →, *Russia* 51 E13
Burford, *Canada* 110 C4
Burg, *Germany* 24 C7
Burg auf Fehmarn,
  Germany 24 A7
Burg el Arab, *Egypt* 80 H6
Burg et Tuyur, *Sudan* ... 80 C2
Burg Stargard, *Germany* . 24 B9
Burgas, *Bulgaria* 41 D11
Burgas □, *Bulgaria* 41 D10
Burgaski Zaliv, *Bulgaria* . 41 D11
Burgdorf, *Germany* 24 C6
Burgdorf, *Switz.* 25 H3
Burgenland □, *Austria* .. 27 D9
Burgeo, *Canada* 103 C8
Burgersdorp, *S. Africa* .. 88 E4
Burges, Mt., *Australia* ... 93 F3
Burghausen, *Germany* ... 25 G8
Búrgio, *Italy* 30 E6
Burglengenfeld, *Germany* . 25 F8
Burgohondo, *Spain* 34 E6
Burgos, *Spain* 34 C7
Burgos □, *Spain* 34 C7
Burgstädt, *Germany* 24 E8
Burgsvik, *Sweden* 11 G12
Burguillos del Cerro, *Spain* 35 G4
Burgundy = Bourgogne,
  France 19 F11
Burhaniye, *Turkey* 39 B8
Burhanpur, *India* 66 J10
Buri Pen., *Eritrea* 81 D4
Burias, *Phil.* 61 E5
Burica, Pta., *Costa Rica* . 120 E3
Burigi, L., *Tanzania* 86 C3
Burin, *Canada* 103 C8
Buriram, *Thailand* 64 E4
Burj Sāfitā, *Syria* 70 C3
Burji, *Ethiopia* 81 F4
Burkburnett, *U.S.A.* 113 H5
Burke, *U.S.A.* 114 C6
Burke →, *Australia* 94 C2
Burketown, *Australia* 94 B2
Burkina Faso ■, *Africa* .. 82 C4
Burk's Falls, *Canada* 102 C4
Burlada, *Spain* 32 C3
Burley, *U.S.A.* 114 E7
Burlingame, *U.S.A.* 116 H4
Burlington, *Canada* 110 C5
Burlington, Colo., *U.S.A.* . 112 F3
Burlington, Iowa, *U.S.A.* . 112 E9
Burlington, Kans., *U.S.A.* . 112 F7
Burlington, N.C., *U.S.A.* . 109 G6
Burlington, N.J., *U.S.A.* . 111 F10
Burlington, Vt., *U.S.A.* ... 111 B11
Burlington, Wash., *U.S.A.* . 116 B4
Burlington, Wis., *U.S.A.* . 108 D1
Burlyu-Tyube, *Kazakstan* . 50 E8
Burma ■, *Asia* 67 J20
Burnaby I., *Canada* 104 C2
Burnet, *U.S.A.* 113 K5
Burney, *U.S.A.* 114 F3
Burngup, *Australia* 93 F2
Burnham, *U.S.A.* 110 F7
Burnham-on-Sea, *U.K.* .. 13 F5
Burnie, *Australia* 94 G4
Burnley, *U.K.* 12 D5
Burns, Oreg., *U.S.A.* 114 E4
Burns, Wyo., *U.S.A.* 112 E2
Burns Lake, *Canada* 104 C3
Burnside →, *Canada* 100 B9
Burnside, L., *Australia* ... 93 E3
Burnsville, *U.S.A.* 112 C8
Burnt River, *Canada* 110 B6
Burntwood →, *Canada* .. 105 B9
Burntwood L., *Canada* ... 105 B8
Burqān, *Kuwait* 70 D5
Burqin, *China* 60 B3
Burra, *Australia* 95 E2
Burramurra, *Australia* ... 94 C2
Burray, *U.K.* 14 C6
Burreli, *Albania* 40 E4
Burren Junction, *Australia* 95 E4
Burrendong Dam, *Australia* 95 E4
Burro, Serranías del,
  Mexico 118 B4
Burrow Hd., *U.K.* 14 G4

Burruyacú, *Argentina* ... 126 B3
Burry Port, *U.K.* 13 F3
Bursa, *Turkey* 41 F13
Burseryd, *Sweden* 11 G7
Burstall, *Canada* 105 C7
Burton L., *Canada* 102 B4
Burton upon Trent, *U.K.* . 12 E6
Burtundy, *Australia* 95 E3
Buru, *Indonesia* 63 E7
Burullus, Bahra el, *Egypt* . 80 H7
Burûn, Râs, *Egypt* 75 D2
Burundi ■, *Africa* 86 C3
Bururi, *Burundi* 86 C2
Burutu, *Nigeria* 83 D6
Burwell, *U.S.A.* 112 E5
Burwick, *U.K.* 14 C5
Bury, *U.K.* 12 D5
Bury St. Edmunds, *U.K.* . 13 E8
Buryatia □, *Russia* 51 D12
Buryn, *Ukraine* 47 G7
Burzenin, *Poland* 45 G5
Busalla, *Italy* 28 D5
Busango Swamp, *Zambia* . 87 E2
Buşayrah, *Syria* 70 C4
Buşayyah, *Iraq* 70 D5
Busca, *Italy* 28 D4
Bushati, *Albania* 40 E3
Büshehr, *Iran* 71 D6
Büshehr □, *Iran* 71 D6
Bushell, *Canada* 105 B7
Bushenyi, *Uganda* 86 C3
Bushire = Büshehr, *Iran* . 71 D6
Bushnell, Ill., *U.S.A.* 112 E9
Bushnell, Nebr., *U.S.A.* .. 112 E3
Busia □, *Kenya* 86 B3
Busie, *Ghana* 82 C4
Businga,
  Dem. Rep. of the Congo 84 D4
Busko-Zdrój, *Poland* 45 H7
Busovača, *Bos.-H.* 42 F2
Buşra ash Shām, *Syria* ... 75 C5
Busselton, *Australia* 93 F2
Busseto, *Italy* 28 D7
Bussière-Badil, *France* ... 20 C4
Bussolengo, *Italy* 28 C7
Bussum, *Neths.* 17 B5
Buşteni, *Romania* 43 E10
Busto, C., *Spain* 34 B4
Busto Arsízio, *Italy* 28 C5
Busu-Djanoa,
  Dem. Rep. of the Congo 84 D4
Büsum, *Germany* 24 A4
Buta,
  Dem. Rep. of the Congo 86 B1
Butare, *Rwanda* 86 C2
Butaritari, *Kiribati* 96 G9
Bute, *U.K.* 14 F3
Bute Inlet, *Canada* 104 C4
Butemba, *Uganda* 86 B3
Butembo,
  Dem. Rep. of the Congo 86 B2
Buteni, *Romania* 42 D7
Butera, *Italy* 31 E7
Butha Qi, *China* 60 B7
Butiaba, *Uganda* 86 B3
Butler, Mo., *U.S.A.* 112 F7
Butler, Pa., *U.S.A.* 110 F5
Buton, *Indonesia* 63 F6
Butte, Mont., *U.S.A.* 114 C7
Butte, Nebr., *U.S.A.* 112 D5
Butte Creek →, *U.S.A.* .. 116 F5
Butterworth,
  S. Africa 89 E4
Butterworth, *Malaysia* ... 65 K3
Buttevant, *Ireland* 15 D3
Buttfield, Mt., *Australia* .. 93 D4
Button B., *Canada* 105 B10
Buttonwillow, *U.S.A.* 117 K7
Butty Hd., *Australia* 93 F3
Butuan, *Phil.* 61 G6
Butuku-Luba, *Eq. Guin.* . 83 E6
Butung = Buton, *Indonesia* 63 F6
Buturlinovka, *Russia* 48 E5
Butzbach, *Germany* 25 E4
Bützow, *Germany* 24 B7
Buxar, *India* 69 G10
Buxtehude, *Germany* 24 B5
Buxton, *U.K.* 12 D6
Buxy, *France* 19 F11
Buy, *Russia* 48 A5
Buynaksk, *Russia* 49 J8
Büyük Menderes →,
  Turkey 39 D9
Büyükçekmece, *Turkey* .. 41 E12
Büyükkarıştıran, *Turkey* . 41 E11
Büyükkemikli Burnu,
  Turkey 41 F10
Büyükorhan, *Turkey* 39 B10
Büyükyoncalı, *Turkey* ... 41 E11
Buzançais, *France* 18 F8
Buzău, *Romania* 43 E11
Buzău □, *Romania* 43 E11
Buzău →, *Romania* 43 E11
Buzău, Pasul, *Romania* .. 43 E11
Buzen, *Japan* 55 H5
Buzet, *Croatia* 29 C10
Buzi →, *Mozam.* 87 F3
Buziaş, *Romania* 42 E6
Buzuluk, *Russia* 50 D6
Buzuluk →, *Russia* 48 E6
Buzzards Bay, *U.S.A.* ... 111 E14
Bwana Mkubwe,
  Dem. Rep. of the Congo 87 E2
Byala, Ruse, *Bulgaria* 41 C9
Byala, Varna, *Bulgaria* ... 41 D11
Byala Slatina, *Bulgaria* .. 40 C7
Byarezina →, *Belarus* ... 47 F6

Bychawa, *Poland* 45 G9
Byczyna, *Poland* 45 G5
Bydgoszcz, *Poland* 45 E5
Bydgoszcz □, *Poland* 45 E4
Byelarus = Belarus ■,
  Europe 46 F4
Byelorussia = Belarus ■,
  Europe 46 F4
Byers, *U.S.A.* 112 F2
Byesville, *U.S.A.* 110 G3
Byhalia, *U.S.A.* 113 H10
Byhaw, *Belarus* 46 F6
Bykhov = Byhaw, *Belarus* 46 F6
Bykovo, *Russia* 48 E7
Bylas, *U.S.A.* 115 K8
Bylot I., *Canada* 101 A12
Byrd, C., *Antarctica* 5 C17
Byro, *Australia* 93 E2
Byrock, *Australia* 95 E4
Byron Bay, *Australia* 95 D5
Byrranga, Gory, *Russia* .. 51 B11
Byrranga Mts. = Byrranga,
  Gory, *Russia* 51 B11
Byrum, *Denmark* 11 G5
Byske, *Sweden* 8 D19
Byske älv →, *Sweden* ... 8 D19
Bystrzyca →, Lublin,
  Poland 45 G9
Bystrzyca →, Wrocław,
  Poland 45 G3
Bystrzyca Kłodzka, *Poland* 45 H3
Bytča, *Slovak Rep.* 27 B11
Bytom, *Poland* 45 H5
Bytom Odrzański, *Poland* . 45 G2
Bytów, *Poland* 44 D4
Byumba, *Rwanda* 86 C3
Bzenec, *Czech Rep.* 27 C10
Bzura →, *Poland* 45 F7

C

Ca →, *Vietnam* 64 C5
Ca Mau, *Vietnam* 65 H5
Ca Mau, Mui, *Vietnam* .. 65 H5
Ca Na, *Vietnam* 65 G7
Caacupé, *Paraguay* 126 B4
Caála, *Angola* 85 G3
Caamano Sd., *Canada* ... 104 C3
Caazapá, *Paraguay* 126 B4
Caazapá □, *Paraguay* 127 B4
Cabadbaran, *Phil.* 61 G6
Cabalian, *Phil.* 61 F6
Cabana, *Spain* 34 B2
Cabañaquinta, *Spain* 34 B5
Cabanatuan, *Phil.* 61 D4
Cabanes, *Spain* 32 E5
Cabano, *Canada* 103 C6
Čabar, *Croatia* 29 C11
Cabazon, *U.S.A.* 117 M10
Cabedelo, *Brazil* 125 E12
Cabeza del Buey, *Spain* .. 35 G5
Cabezón de la Sal, *Spain* . 34 B6
Cabildo, *Chile* 126 C1
Cabimas, *Venezuela* 124 A4
Cabinda, *Angola* 84 F2
Cabinda □, *Angola* 84 F2
Cabinet Mts., *U.S.A.* 114 C6
Cabo Blanco, *Argentina* . 128 F3
Cabo Frio, *Brazil* 127 A7
Cabo Pantoja, *Peru* 124 D3
Cabonga, Réservoir,
  Canada 102 C4
Cabool, *U.S.A.* 113 G8
Caboolture, *Australia* 95 D5
Cabora Bassa Dam =
  Cahora Bassa, Reprêsa
  de, *Mozam.* 87 F3
Caborca, *Mexico* 118 A2
Cabot, Mt., *U.S.A.* 111 B13
Cabot Str., *Canada* 103 C8
Cabra, *Spain* 35 H6
Cabra del Santo Cristo,
  Spain 35 H7
Cábras, *Italy* 30 C1
Cabrera, *Spain* 37 B9
Cabrera, Sierra, *Spain* ... 34 C4
Cabri, *Canada* 105 C7
Cabriel →, *Spain* 33 F3
Cabugao, *Phil.* 61 C4
Cacabelos, *Spain* 34 C4
Čačak, *Serbia, Yug.* 40 C4
Cáccamo, *Italy* 30 E6
Cacém, *Portugal* 35 G1
Cáceres, *Brazil* 124 G7
Cáceres, *Spain* 35 F4
Cáceres □, *Spain* 34 F5
Cache Bay, *Canada* 102 C4
Cache Cr. →, *U.S.A.* 116 G5
Cacheu, *Guinea-Biss.* 82 C1
Cachi, *Argentina* 126 B2
Cachimbo, Serra do, *Brazil* 125 E7
Cachoeira, *Brazil* 125 F11
Cachoeira de Itapemirim,
  Brazil 127 A7
Cachoeira do Sul, *Brazil* . 127 C5
Cachopo, *Portugal* 35 H3
Cacoal, *Brazil* 124 F6
Cacólo, *Angola* 84 G3
Caconda, *Angola* 85 G3
Čadan, *Romania* 42 E7
Cádis, *Slovak Rep.* 27 B11
Caddo, *U.S.A.* 113 H6
Cadell Cr. →, *Australia* .. 94 C3
Cader Idris, *U.K.* 13 E4
Cadí, Sierra del, *Spain* ... 32 C6

Cadibarrawirracanna, L.,
  Australia 95 D2
Cadillac, *Canada* 102 C4
Cadillac, *France* 20 D3
Cadillac, *U.S.A.* 108 C3
Cadiz, *Phil.* 61 F5
Cádiz, *Spain* 35 J4
Cadiz, *U.S.A.* 110 F4
Cádiz □, *Spain* 35 J5
Cádiz, G. de, *Spain* 35 J3
Cadney Park, *Australia* .. 95 D1
Cadomin, *Canada* 104 C5
Cadotte →, *Canada* 104 B5
Cadours, *France* 20 E5
Cadoux, *Australia* 93 F2
Caen, *France* 18 C6
Caernarfon, *U.K.* 12 D3
Caernarfon B., *U.K.* 12 D3
Caernarvon = Caernarfon,
  U.K. 12 D3
Caerphilly, *U.K.* 13 F4
Caerphilly □, *U.K.* 13 F4
Caesarea, *Israel* 75 C3
Caetité, *Brazil* 125 F10
Cafayate, *Argentina* 126 B2
Cafu, *Angola* 88 B2
Cagayan →, *Phil.* 61 B4
Cagayan de Oro, *Phil.* ... 61 G6
Cagayan Is., *Phil.* 61 G4
Cagayan Sulu I., *Phil.* ... 61 H3
Cagli, *Italy* 29 E9
Cágliari, *Italy* 30 C2
Cágliari, G. di, *Italy* 30 C2
Cagnano Varano, *Italy* ... 29 G12
Cagnes-sur-Mer, *France* . 21 E11
Caguán →, *Colombia* 124 D4
Caguas, *Puerto Rico* 121 C6
Caha Mts., *Ireland* 15 E2
Caher, *Ireland* 15 D4
Caherciveen, *Ireland* 15 E1
Cahora Bassa, Reprêsa de,
  Mozam. 87 F3
Cahore Pt., *Ireland* 15 D5
Cahors, *France* 20 D5
Cahul, *Moldova* 43 E13
Cai Bau, Dao, *Vietnam* .. 64 B6
Cai Nuoc, *Vietnam* 65 H5
Caia, *Mozam.* 87 F4
Caianda, *Angola* 87 E1
Caibarién, *Cuba* 120 B4
Caibiran, *Phil.* 61 F6
Caicara, *Venezuela* 124 B5
Caicó, *Brazil* 125 E11
Caicos Is., *W. Indies* 121 B5
Caicos Passage, *W. Indies* 121 B5
Cǎinari, *Moldova* 43 D14
Caird Coast, *Antarctica* .. 5 D1
Cairn Gorm, *U.K.* 14 D5
Cairngorm Mts., *U.K.* ... 14 D5
Cairnryan, *U.K.* 14 G3
Cairns, *Australia* 94 B4
Cairo = El Qâhira, *Egypt* . 80 H7
Cairo, Ga., *U.S.A.* 109 K3
Cairo, Ill., *U.S.A.* 113 G10
Cairo Montenotte, *Italy* .. 28 D5
Caithness, Ord of, *U.K.* .. 14 C5
Cajamarca, *Peru* 124 E3
Cajarc, *France* 20 D5
Cajàzeiras, *Brazil* 125 E11
Čajetina, *Serbia, Yug.* ... 40 C3
Çakirgöl, *Turkey* 73 B8
Çakırlar, *Turkey* 39 E12
Čakovec, *Croatia* 29 B13
Çal, *Turkey* 39 C11
Cala, *Spain* 35 H4
Cala →, *Spain* 35 H4
Cala Cadolar, Punta de =
  Rotja, Pta., *Spain* 33 G6
Cala d'Or, *Spain* 37 B10
Cala en Porter, *Spain* 37 B11
Cala Figuera, C. de, *Spain* 37 B9
Cala Forcat, *Spain* 37 B10
Cala Major, *Spain* 37 B9
Cala Mezquida = Sa
  Mesquida, *Spain* 37 B11
Cala Millor, *Spain* 37 B10
Cala Ratjada, *Spain* 37 B10
Cala Santa Galdana, *Spain* 37 B10
Calabanga, *Phil.* 61 E5
Calabar, *Nigeria* 83 E6
Calabozo, *Venezuela* 124 B5
Calábria □, *Italy* 31 C9
Calaburras, Pta. de, *Spain* 35 J6
Calacuccia, *France* 21 F13
Calafat, *Romania* 42 G7
Calafate, *Argentina* 128 G2
Calafell, *Spain* 32 D6
Calahorra, *Spain* 32 C3
Calais, *France* 19 B8
Calais, *U.S.A.* 103 C6
Calalaste, Cord. de,
  Argentina 126 B2
Calama, *Brazil* 124 E6
Calama, *Chile* 126 A2
Calamar, *Colombia* 124 A4
Calamba, *Phil.* 61 F5
Calamian Group, *Phil.* ... 61 F3
Calamocha, *Spain* 32 E3
Calamonte, *Spain* 35 G4
Calañas, *Spain* 35 H4
Calanda, *Spain* 32 E4
Calang, *Indonesia* 62 D1
Calangiánus, *Italy* 30 B2
Calapan, *Phil.* 61 E4

Cǎlǎrasi, *Moldova* 43 C13
Cǎlǎraşi, *Romania* 43 F12
Cǎlǎraşi □, *Romania* 43 F12
Calasparra, *Spain* 33 G3
Calatafimi, *Italy* 30 E5
Calatayud, *Spain* 32 D3
Cǎlǎţele, *Romania* 42 D8
Calato = Kálathos, *Greece* 39 E10
Calauag, *Phil.* 61 E5
Calavà, C., *Italy* 31 D7
Calavite, C., *Phil.* 61 E4
Calayan, *Phil.* 61 B4
Calbayog, *Phil.* 61 E6
Calca, *Peru* 124 F4
Calcasieu L., *U.S.A.* 113 L8
Calcutta, *India* 69 H13
Caldaro, *Italy* 29 B8
Caldas da Rainha, *Portugal* 35 F1
Caldas de Reis, *Spain* 34 C2
Calder →, *U.K.* 12 D6
Caldera, *Chile* 126 B1
Caldwell, Idaho, *U.S.A.* .. 114 E5
Caldwell, Kans., *U.S.A.* .. 113 G6
Caldwell, Tex., *U.S.A.* ... 113 K6
Caledon, *S. Africa* 88 E2
Caledon →, *S. Africa* 88 E4
Caledon B., *Australia* 94 A2
Caledonia, *Canada* 110 C5
Caledonia, *U.S.A.* 110 D7
Calella, *Spain* 32 D7
Calemba, *Angola* 88 B2
Calenzana, *France* 21 F12
Calexico, *U.S.A.* 117 N11
Calf of Man, *U.K.* 12 C3
Calgary, *Canada* 104 C6
Calheta, *Madeira* 37 D2
Calhoun, *U.S.A.* 109 H3
Cali, *Colombia* 124 C3
Calicut, *India* 66 P9
California, Mo., *U.S.A.* .. 112 F8
California, Pa., *U.S.A.* ... 110 F5
California □, *U.S.A.* 115 H4
California, Baja, *Mexico* .. 118 A1
California, Baja, T.N. □ =
  Baja California □,
  Mexico 118 B2
California, Baja, T.S. □ =
  Baja California Sur □,
  Mexico 118 B2
California, G. de, *Mexico* . 118 B2
California City, *U.S.A.* ... 117 K9
California Hot Springs,
  U.S.A. 117 K8
Cǎlimǎneşti, *Romania* ... 43 E9
Cǎlimani, Munţii, *Romania* 43 C10
Calingasta, *Argentina* ... 126 C2
Calipatria, *U.S.A.* 117 M11
Calistoga, *U.S.A.* 116 G4
Calitri, *Italy* 31 B8
Calitzdorp, *S. Africa* 88 E3
Callabonna, L., *Australia* . 95 D3
Callac, *France* 18 D3
Callan, *Ireland* 15 D4
Callander, *U.K.* 14 E4
Callao, *Peru* 124 F3
Callaway, *U.S.A.* 112 E5
Calles, *Mexico* 119 C5
Callide, *Australia* 94 C5
Calling Lake, *Canada* 104 B6
Calliope, *Australia* 94 C5
Callosa de Ensarriá, *Spain* 33 G4
Callosa de Segura, *Spain* . 33 G4
Calne, *U.K.* 13 F6
Calola, *Angola* 88 B2
Calolbon, *Phil.* 61 E6
Calonge, *Spain* 32 D8
Caloocan, *Phil.* 61 D4
Calore →, *Italy* 31 A7
Caloundra, *Australia* 95 D5
Calpe, *Spain* 33 G5
Calpella, *U.S.A.* 116 F3
Calpine, *U.S.A.* 116 F6
Calstock, *Canada* 102 C3
Caltabellotta, *Italy* 30 E6
Caltagirone, *Italy* 31 E7
Caltanissetta, *Italy* 31 E7
Çaltılıbük, *Turkey* 41 G12
Caluire-et-Cuire, *France* . 19 G11
Calulo, *Angola* 84 G2
Calumet, *U.S.A.* 108 B1
Caluso, *Italy* 28 C4
Calvados □, *France* 18 C6
Calvert, *U.S.A.* 113 K6
Calvert →, *Australia* 94 B2
Calvert Hills, *Australia* ... 94 B2
Calvert I., *Canada* 104 C3
Calvert Ra., *Australia* 92 D3
Calvi, *France* 21 F12
Calviá, *Spain* 37 B9
Calvillo, *Mexico* 118 C4
Calvinia, *S. Africa* 88 E2
Calvo = Calvo, Mte., *Italy* 29 G12
Calvo, Mte., *Italy* 29 G12
Calwa, *U.S.A.* 116 J7
Calzada Almuradiel =
  Almuradiel, *Spain* 35 G7
Calzada de Calatrava,
  Spain 35 G7
Cam →, *U.K.* 13 E8
Cam Lam, *Vietnam* 65 G7
Cam Pha, *Vietnam* 64 B6
Cam Ranh, *Vietnam* 65 G7
Cam Xuyen, *Vietnam* 64 C6
Camabatela, *Angola* 84 F3
Camacha, *Madeira* 37 D3
Camacho, *Mexico* 118 C4

143

Camacupa, *Angola* 85 G3
Camagüey, *Cuba* 120 B4
Camaiore, *Italy* 28 E7
Camaná, *Peru* 124 G4
Camanche Reservoir,
  U.S.A. 116 G6
Camaquã ➔, *Brazil* 127 C5
Câmara de Lobos, *Madeira* 37 D3
Camarat, C., *France* 21 E10
Camarès, *France* 20 E6
Camaret-sur-Mer, *France* . 18 D2
Camargue, *France* 21 E8
Camarillo, *U.S.A.* 117 L7
Camariñas, *Spain* 34 B1
Camarón, C., *Honduras* .. 120 C2
Camarones, *Argentina* .. 128 E3
Camas, *Spain* 35 H4
Camas, *U.S.A.* 116 E4
Camas Valley, *U.S.A.* 114 E2
Cambará, *Brazil* 127 A5
Cambay = Khambhat,
  India 68 H5
Cambay, G. of =
  Khambhat, G. of, *India* 68 J5
Cambil, *Spain* 35 H7
Cambo-les-Bains, *France* . 20 E2
Cambodia ■, *Asia* 64 F5
Camborne, *U.K.* 13 G2
Cambrai, *France* 19 B10
Cambre, *Spain* 34 B2
Cambria, *U.S.A.* 116 K5
Cambrian Mts., *U.K.* 13 E4
Cambridge, *Canada* 102 D3
Cambridge, *Jamaica* 120 C4
Cambridge, *N.Z.* 91 G5
Cambridge, *U.K.* 13 E8
Cambridge, *Idaho, U.S.A.* 114 D5
Cambridge, *Mass., U.S.A.* 111 D13
Cambridge, *Md., U.S.A.* . 108 F7
Cambridge, *Minn., U.S.A.* 112 C8
Cambridge, *Nebr., U.S.A.* 112 E4
Cambridge, *N.Y., U.S.A.* . 111 C11
Cambridge, *Ohio, U.S.A.* . 110 F3
Cambridge G., *Australia* . 92 B4
Cambridge Springs, *U.S.A.* 110 E4
Cambrils, *Spain* 32 D6
Cambridgeshire □, *U.K.* . 13 E7
Cambuci, *Brazil* 127 A7
Cambundi-Catembo,
  Angola 84 G3
Camden, *Ala., U.S.A.* 109 K2
Camden, *Ark., U.S.A.* ... 113 J8
Camden, *Maine, U.S.A.* .. 103 D6
Camden, *N.J., U.S.A.* 111 G9
Camden, *S.C., U.S.A.* ... 109 H5
Camden Sd., *Australia* .. 92 C3
Camdenton, *U.S.A.* 113 F8
Çameli, *Turkey* 39 D11
Camenca, *Moldova* 43 B13
Camerino, *Italy* 29 E10
Cameron, *Ariz., U.S.A.* .. 115 J8
Cameron, *La., U.S.A.* 113 L8
Cameron, *Mo., U.S.A.* ... 112 F7
Cameron, *Tex., U.S.A.* ... 113 K6
Cameron Falls, *Canada* .. 102 C2
Cameron Highlands,
  Malaysia 65 K3
Cameron Hills, *Canada* .. 104 B5
Cameroon ■, *Africa* 84 C2
Camerota, *Italy* 31 B8
Cameroun = *Cameroon* . 83 E6
Cameroun, Mt., *Cameroon* 83 E6
Cametá, *Brazil* 125 D9
Çamiçi Gölü, *Turkey* 39 D9
Camiguin □, *Phil.* 61 G6
Camiguin I., *Phil.* 61 B4
Camiling, *Phil.* 61 D4
Caminha, *Portugal* 34 D2
Camino, *U.S.A.* 116 G6
Camira Creek, *Australia* . 95 D5
Cammal, *U.S.A.* 110 E7
Camocim, *Brazil* 125 D10
Camooweal, *Australia* ... 94 B2
Camopi, *Fr. Guiana* 125 C8
Camotes Is., *Phil.* 61 F6
Camotes Sea, *Phil.* 61 F6
Camp Crook, *U.S.A.* 112 C3
Camp Nelson, *U.S.A.* ... 117 J8
Camp Wood, *U.S.A.* 113 L5
Campagna, *Italy* 31 B8
Campana, *Argentina* 126 C4
Campana, I., *Chile* 128 F1
Campanário, *Madeira* ... 37 D2
Campanario, *Spain* 35 G5
Campánia □, *Italy* 31 B7
Campbell, *S. Africa* 88 D3
Campbell, *Calif., U.S.A.* . 116 H5
Campbell, *Ohio, U.S.A.* . 110 E4
Campbell I., *Pac. Oc.* 96 N8
Campbell L., *Canada* 105 A7
Campbell River, *Canada* . 104 C3
Campbell Town, *Australia* 94 G4
Campbellford, *Canada* ... 110 B7
Campbellpur, *Pakistan* .. 68 C5
Campbellsville, *U.S.A.* ... 108 G3
Campbellton, *Canada* ... 103 C6
Campbelltown, *Australia* . 95 E5
Campbeltown, *U.K.* 14 F3
Campeche, *Mexico* 119 D6
Campeche □, *Mexico* 119 D6
Campeche, B. de, *Mexico* 119 D6
Campello, *Spain* 33 G4
Câmpeni, *Romania* 42 D8
Camperdown, *Australia* . 95 F3
Camperville, *Canada* 105 C8
Campi Salentina, *Italy* ... 31 B11

Câmpia Turzii, *Romania* .. 43 D8
Campidano, *Italy* 30 C1
Campíglia Maríttima, *Italy* 28 E7
Campillo de Altobuey,
  Spain 33 F3
Campillos, *Spain* 35 H6
Câmpina, *Romania* 43 E10
Campina Grande, *Brazil* . 125 E11
Campinas, *Brazil* 127 A6
Campli, *Italy* 29 F10
Campo, *Spain* 32 C5
Campo de Criptana, *Spain* 35 F7
Campo de Gibraltar, *Spain* 35 J5
Campo Grande, *Brazil* ... 125 H8
Campo Maíor, *Brazil* 125 D10
Campo Maior, *Portugal* .. 35 F3
Campo Mourão, *Brazil* .. 127 A5
Campo Túres, *Italy* 29 B8
Campobasso, *Italy* 31 A7
Campobello di Licata, *Italy* 30 E6
Campobello di Mazara,
  Italy 30 E5
Campofelice di Roccella,
  Italy 30 E6
Campomarino, *Italy* 29 G12
Camporeale, *Italy* 30 E6
Camporrobles, *Spain* 32 F3
Campos, *Brazil* 127 A7
Campos Belos, *Brazil* 125 F9
Campos del Puerto, *Spain* 37 B10
Campos Novos, *Brazil* ... 127 B5
Camprodón, *Spain* 32 C7
Camptonville, *U.S.A.* 116 F5
Câmpulung, *Argeş,
  Romania* 43 E10
Câmpulung, *Suceava,
  Romania* 43 C10
Câmpuri, *Romania* 43 D11
Camrose, *Canada* 104 C6
Camsell Portage, *Canada* . 105 B7
Çamyuva, *Turkey* 39 E12
Çan, *Turkey* 41 F11
Can Clavo, *Spain* 37 C7
Can Creu, *Spain* 37 C7
Can Gio, *Vietnam* 65 G6
Can Tho, *Vietnam* 65 G5
Canaan, *U.S.A.* 111 D11
Canada ■, *N. Amer.* 100 C10
Cañada de Gómez,
  Argentina 126 C3
Canadian, *U.S.A.* 113 H4
Canadian ➔, *U.S.A.* 113 H7
Çanakkale, *Turkey* 41 F10
Çanakkale □, *Turkey* 41 F10
Çanakkale Boğazı, *Turkey* 41 F10
Canal Flats, *Canada* 104 C5
Canalejas, *Argentina* 126 D2
Canals, *Argentina* 126 C3
Canals, *Spain* 33 G4
Canandaigua, *U.S.A.* 110 D7
Cananea, *Mexico* 118 A2
Canarias, Is., *Atl. Oc.* 37 F4
Canarreos, Arch. de los,
  Cuba 120 B3
Canary Is. = Canarias, Is.,
  Atl. Oc. 37 F4
Canatlán, *Mexico* 118 C4
Canaveral, C., *U.S.A.* 109 L5
Cañaveruelas, *Spain* 32 E2
Canavieiras, *Brazil* 125 G11
Canbelego, *Australia* 95 E4
Canberra, *Australia* 95 F4
Canby, *Calif., U.S.A.* 114 F3
Canby, *Minn., U.S.A.* 112 C6
Canby, *Oreg., U.S.A.* 116 E4
Cancale, *France* 18 D5
Canche ➔, *France* 19 B8
Cancún, *Mexico* 119 C7
Candanchu, *Spain* 32 C4
Çandarlı, *Turkey* 39 C8
Çandarlı Körfezi, *Turkey* . 39 C8
Candas, *Spain* 34 B5
Candé, *France* 18 E5
Candela, *Italy* 31 A8
Candelaria, *Argentina* ... 127 B4
Candelaria, *Canary Is.* ... 37 F3
Candeleda, *Spain* 34 E5
Candelo, *Australia* 95 F4
Candia = Iráklion, *Greece* 36 D7
Candia, Sea of = Crete,
  Sea of, *Greece* 39 E7
Candle L., *Canada* 105 C7
Candlemas I., *Antarctica* . 5 B1
Cando, *U.S.A.* 112 A5
Candon, *Phil.* 61 C4
Canea = Khaniá, *Greece* . 36 D6
Canelli, *Italy* 28 D5
Canelones, *Uruguay* 127 C4
Canet-Plage, *France* 20 F7
Cañete, *Chile* 126 D1
Cañete, *Peru* 124 F3
Cañete, *Spain* 32 E3
Cañete de las Torres, *Spain* 35 H6
Cangas, *Spain* 34 C2
Cangas de Narcea, *Spain* . 34 B4
Cangas de Onís, *Spain* ... 34 B5
Canguaretama, *Brazil* ... 125 E11
Canguçu, *Brazil* 127 C5
Cangxi, *China* 58 B5
Cangyuan, *China* 58 F2
Cangzhou, *China* 56 E9
Caniapiscau =
  Kaniapiskau ➔, *Canada* 103 A6
Caniapiscau, L. =
  Kaniapiskau L., *Canada* 103 B6
Canicattì, *Italy* 30 E6
Canicattini Bagni, *Italy* ... 31 E8

Caniles, *Spain* 35 H8
Canim Lake, *Canada* 104 C4
Canindeyu □, *Paraguay* .. 127 A5
Canino, *Italy* 29 F8
Canisteo, *U.S.A.* 110 D7
Canisteo ➔, *U.S.A.* 110 D7
Cañitas, *Mexico* 118 C4
Cañizal, *Spain* 34 D5
Canjáyar, *Spain* 35 H8
Çankırı, *Turkey* 72 B5
Cankuzo, *Burundi* 86 C3
Canmore, *Canada* 104 C5
Cann River, *Australia* 95 F4
Canna, *U.K.* 14 D2
Cannanore, *India* 66 P9
Cannes, *France* 21 E11
Canning Town = Port
  Canning, *India* 69 H13
Cannington, *Canada* 110 B5
Cannóbio, *Italy* 28 B5
Cannock, *U.K.* 13 E5
Cannon Ball ➔, *U.S.A.* ... 112 B4
Cannondale Mt., *Australia* 94 D4
Canoas, *Brazil* 127 B5
Canoe L., *Canada* 105 B7
Canon City, *U.S.A.* 112 F2
Canora, *Canada* 105 C8
Canosa di Púglia, *Italy* ... 31 A9
Canowindra, *Australia* ... 95 E4
Canso, *Canada* 103 C7
Cantabria □, *Spain* 34 B7
Cantabria, Sierra de, *Spain* 32 C2
Cantabrian Mts. =
  Cantábrica, Cordillera,
  Spain 34 C5
Cantábrica, Cordillera,
  Spain 34 C5
Cantal □, *France* 20 C6
Cantal, Plomb du, *France* . 20 C6
Cantanhede, *Portugal* ... 34 E2
Cantavieja, *Spain* 32 E4
Čantavir, *Serbia, Yug.* ... 42 E4
Cantemir, *Moldova* 43 D13
Canterbury, *Australia* 94 D3
Canterbury, *U.K.* 13 F9
Canterbury □, *N.Z.* 91 K3
Canterbury Bight, *N.Z.* ... 91 L3
Canterbury Plains, *N.Z.* .. 91 K3
Cantil, *U.S.A.* 117 K9
Cantillana, *Spain* 35 H5
Canton = Guangzhou,
  China 59 F9
Canton, *Ga., U.S.A.* 109 H3
Canton, *Ill., U.S.A.* 112 E9
Canton, *Miss., U.S.A.* ... 113 J9
Canton, *Mo., U.S.A.* 112 E9
Canton, *N.Y., U.S.A.* 111 B9
Canton, *Ohio, U.S.A.* 110 F3
Canton, *Okla., U.S.A.* ... 113 G5
Canton, *S. Dak., U.S.A.* .. 112 D6
Canton L., *U.S.A.* 113 G5
Cantù, *Italy* 28 C6
Canudos, *Brazil* 124 E7
Canumã ➔, *Brazil* 124 D7
Canutama, *Brazil* 124 E6
Canutillo, *U.S.A.* 115 L10
Canvey, *U.K.* 13 F8
Canyon, *Tex., U.S.A.* 113 H4
Canyon, *Wyo., U.S.A.* ... 114 D8
Canyonlands National Park,
  U.S.A. 115 G9
Canyonville, *U.S.A.* 114 E2
Cao Bang, *Vietnam* 64 A6
Cao He ➔, *China* 57 D13
Cao Lanh, *Vietnam* 65 G5
Cao Xian, *China* 56 G8
Cáorle, *Italy* 29 C9
Cap-aux-Meules, *Canada* . 103 C7
Cap-Chat, *Canada* 103 C6
Cap-de-la-Madeleine,
  Canada 102 C5
Cap-Haïtien, *Haiti* 121 C5
Capácio, *Italy* 31 B8
Capaci, *Italy* 30 D6
Capanaparo ➔, *Venezuela* 124 B5
Capánnori, *Italy* 28 E7
Capbreton, *France* 20 E2
Capdenac, *France* 20 D6
Capdepera, *Spain* 32 F8
Cape ➔, *Australia* 94 C4
Cape Barren I., *Australia* . 94 G4
Cape Breton Highlands
  Nat. Park, *Canada* 103 C7
Cape Breton I., *Canada* .. 103 C7
Cape Charles, *U.S.A.* 108 G8
Cape Coast, *Ghana* 83 D4
Cape Coral, *U.S.A.* 109 M5
Cape Dorset, *Canada* 101 B12
Cape Fear ➔, *U.S.A.* 109 H6
Cape Girardeau, *U.S.A.* .. 113 G10
Cape Jervis, *Australia* 95 F2
Cape May, *U.S.A.* 108 F8
Cape May Point, *U.S.A.* .. 107 C12
Cape Palmas, *Liberia* 82 E3
Cape Town, *S. Africa* 88 E2
Cape Verde Is. ■, *Atl. Oc.* 77 E1
Cape Vincent, *U.S.A.* 111 B8
Cape York Peninsula,
  Australia 94 A3
Capela, *Brazil* 125 F11
Capella, *Australia* 94 C4
Capendu, *France* 20 E6
Capestang, *France* 20 E7
Capim ➔, *Brazil* 125 D9
Capistrello, *Italy* 29 G10
Capitan, *U.S.A.* 115 K11

Capitola, *U.S.A.* 116 J5
Capizzi, *Italy* 31 E7
Capoche ➔, *Mozam.* 87 F3
Cappadocia, *Turkey* 72 C6
Capraia, *Italy* 28 E6
Caprara, Pta., *Italy* 30 A1
Caprarola, *Italy* 29 F9
Capreol, *Canada* 102 C3
Caprera, *Italy* 30 A2
Capri, *Italy* 31 B7
Capricorn Group, *Australia* 94 C5
Capricorn Ra., *Australia* .. 92 D2
Caprino Veronese, *Italy* .. 28 C7
Caprivi Strip, *Namibia* ... 88 B3
Captainganj, *India* 69 F10
Captain's Flat, *Australia* .. 95 F4
Captieux, *France* 20 D3
Caquetá ➔, *Colombia* 122 D4
Caracal, *Romania* 43 F9
Caracas, *Venezuela* 124 A5
Caracol, *Brazil* 125 E10
Caradoc, *Australia* 95 E3
Caráglio, *Italy* 28 D4
Carajas, *Brazil* 125 E8
Carajás, Serra dos, *Brazil* . 125 E8
Carangola, *Brazil* 127 A7
Carani, *Australia* 93 F2
Caransebeş, *Romania* 42 E7
Carantec, *France* 18 D3
Caras, *Peru* 124 E3
Caraş Severin □, *Romania* 42 E7
Caraşova, *Romania* 42 E6
Caratasca, L., *Honduras* .. 120 C3
Caratinga, *Brazil* 125 G10
Caraúbas, *Brazil* 125 E11
Caravaca = Caravaca de la
  Cruz, *Spain* 33 G3
Caravaca de la Cruz, *Spain* 33 G3
Caravággio, *Italy* 28 C6
Caravelas, *Brazil* 125 G11
Caraveli, *Peru* 124 G4
Caràzinho, *Brazil* 127 B5
Carballino = O Carballiño,
  Spain 34 C2
Carballo, *Spain* 34 B2
Carberry, *Canada* 105 D9
Carbó, *Mexico* 118 B2
Carbon, *Canada* 104 C6
Carbonara, C., *Italy* 30 C2
Carbondale, *Colo., U.S.A.* 114 G10
Carbondale, *Ill., U.S.A.* .. 113 G10
Carbondale, *Pa., U.S.A.* .. 111 E9
Carbonear, *Canada* 103 C9
Carboneras, *Spain* 33 J3
Carboneras de Guadazón,
  Spain 32 F3
Carbónia, *Italy* 30 C1
Carcabuey, *Spain* 35 H6
Carcagente = Carcaixent,
  Spain 33 F4
Carcaixent, *Spain* 33 F4
Carcajou, *Canada* 104 B5
Carcar, *Phil.* 61 F5
Carcasse, C., *Haiti* 121 C5
Carcassonne, *France* 20 E6
Carcross, *Canada* 100 B6
Cardabia, *Australia* 92 D1
Çardak, *Çanakkale, Turkey* 41 F10
Çardak, *Denizli, Turkey* .. 39 D11
Cardamon Hills, *India* ... 66 Q10
Cardeña, *Spain* 35 G6
Cárdenas, *Cuba* 120 B3
Cárdenas, *San Luis Potosí,
  Mexico* 119 C5
Cárdenas, *Tabasco, Mexico* 119 D6
Cardenete, *Spain* 32 F3
Cardiff, *U.K.* 13 F4
Cardiff □, *U.K.* 13 F4
Cardiff-by-the-Sea, *U.S.A.* 117 M9
Cardigan, *U.K.* 13 E3
Cardigan B., *U.K.* 13 E3
Cardinal, *Canada* 111 B9
Cardona, *Spain* 32 D6
Cardona, *Uruguay* 126 C4
Cardoner ➔, *Spain* 32 D6
Cardross, *Canada* 105 D7
Cardston, *Canada* 104 D6
Cardwell, *Australia* 94 B4
Careen L., *Canada* 105 B7
Carei, *Romania* 42 C7
Careme = Ciremai,
  Indonesia 63 G13
Carentan, *France* 18 C5
Carey, *Idaho, U.S.A.* 114 E7
Carey, *Ohio, U.S.A.* 108 E4
Carey, L., *Australia* 93 E3
Carey L., *Canada* 105 A8
Careysburg, *Liberia* 82 D2
Cargèse, *France* 21 F12
Carhaix-Plouguer, *France* . 18 D3
Carhué, *Argentina* 126 D3
Caria, *Turkey* 39 D10
Cariacica, *Brazil* 125 H10
Cariati, *Italy* 31 C9
Caribbean Sea, *W. Indies* . 121 D5
Cariboo Mts., *Canada* ... 104 C4
Caribou, *U.S.A.* 103 C6
Caribou ➔, *Man., Canada* 105 B10
Caribou ➔, *N.W.T.,
  Canada* 104 A3
Caribou I., *Canada* 102 C2
Caribou Is., *Canada* 104 A6
Caribou L., *Man., Canada* 105 B9
Caribou L., *Ont., Canada* . 102 B2
Caribou Mts., *Canada* ... 104 B5

Carigara, *Phil.* 61 F6
Carignan, *France* 19 C12
Carignano, *Italy* 28 D4
Carinda, *Australia* 95 E4
Cariñena, *Spain* 32 D3
Carinhanha, *Brazil* 125 F10
Carinhanha ➔, *Brazil* 125 F10
Carini, *Italy* 30 D6
Cariño, *Spain* 34 B3
Carínola, *Italy* 30 A6
Carinthia □ = Kärnten □,
  Austria 26 E6
Caripito, *Venezuela* 124 A6
Carlbrod = Dimitrovgrad,
  Serbia, Yug. 40 C6
Carlet, *Spain* 33 F4
Carleton Place, *Canada* .. 102 C4
Carletonville, *S. Africa* ... 88 D4
Cârlibaba, *Romania* 43 C10
Carlin, *U.S.A.* 114 F5
Carlingford L., *U.K.* 15 B5
Carlinville, *U.S.A.* 112 F10
Carlisle, *U.K.* 12 C5
Carlisle, *U.S.A.* 110 F7
Carlit, Pic, *France* 20 F5
Carloforte, *Italy* 30 C1
Carlos Casares, *Argentina* . 126 D3
Carlos Tejedor, *Argentina* . 126 D3
Carlow, *Ireland* 15 D5
Carlow □, *Ireland* 15 D5
Carlsbad, *Calif., U.S.A.* .. 117 M9
Carlsbad, *N. Mex., U.S.A.* 113 J2
Carluke, *U.K.* 14 F5
Carlyle, *Canada* 105 D8
Carlyle, *U.S.A.* 112 F10
Carmacks, *Canada* 100 B4
Carmagnola, *Italy* 28 D4
Carman, *Canada* 105 D9
Carmangay, *Canada* 104 C6
Carmanville, *Canada* 103 C9
Carmarthen, *U.K.* 13 F3
Carmarthen B., *U.K.* 13 F3
Carmarthenshire □, *U.K.* . 13 F3
Carmaux, *France* 20 D6
Carmel, *U.S.A.* 111 E11
Carmel-by-the-Sea, *U.S.A.* 116 J5
Carmel Valley, *U.S.A.* ... 116 J5
Carmelo, *Uruguay* 126 C4
Carmen, *Colombia* 124 B3
Carmen, *Paraguay* 127 B4
Carmen ➔, *Mexico* 118 A3
Carmen, I., *Mexico* 118 B2
Carmen de Patagones,
  Argentina 128 E4
Cármenes, *Spain* 34 C5
Carmensa, *Argentina* 126 D2
Carmi, *U.S.A.* 108 F1
Carmichael, *U.S.A.* 116 G5
Carmila, *Australia* 94 C4
Carmona, *Spain* 35 H5
Carn Ban, *U.K.* 14 D4
Carn Eige, *U.K.* 14 D3
Carnarvon, *Queens.,
  Australia* 94 C4
Carnarvon, *W. Austral.,
  Australia* 93 D1
Carnarvon, *S. Africa* 88 E3
Carnarvon Ra., *Queens.,
  Australia* 94 D4
Carnarvon Ra.,
  W. Austral., Australia .. 93 E3
Carnation, *U.S.A.* 116 C5
Carndonagh, *Ireland* 15 A4
Carnduff, *Canada* 105 D8
Carnegie, *U.S.A.* 110 F4
Carnegie, L., *Australia* ... 93 E3
Carnic Alps = Karnische
  Alpen, *Europe* 26 E6
Carniche Alpi = Karnische
  Alpen, *Europe* 26 E6
Carnot, C.A.R. 84 D3
Carnot, C., *Australia* 95 E2
Carnot B., *Australia* 92 C3
Carnoustie, *U.K.* 14 E6
Carnsore Pt., *Ireland* 15 D5
Caro, *U.S.A.* 108 D4
Carol City, *U.S.A.* 109 N5
Carolina, *Brazil* 125 E9
Carolina, *Puerto Rico* ... 121 C6
Carolina, *S. Africa* 89 D5
Caroline I., *Kiribati* 97 H12
Caroline Is., *Pac. Oc.* 96 G7
Caron, *Canada* 105 C7
Caroní ➔, *Venezuela* 124 B6
Caronie = Nébrodi, Monti,
  Italy 31 E7
Caroona, *Australia* 95 E5
Carpathians, *Europe* 6 F10
Carpaţi Meridionali,
  Romania 43 E9
Carpentaria, G. of,
  Australia 94 A2
Carpentaria Downs,
  Australia 94 B3
Carpentras, *France* 21 D9
Cârpineni, *Moldova* 43 D13
Carpinteria, *U.S.A.* 117 L7
Carpio, *Spain* 34 D5
Carpolac = Morea,
  Australia 95 F3
Carr Boyd Ra., *Australia* . 92 C4
Carrabelle, *U.S.A.* 109 L3
Carral, *Spain* 34 B2
Carranya, *Australia* 92 C4
Carrara, *Italy* 28 D7

Carrascal, *Phil.* 61 G6
Carrascosa del Campo,
  Spain 32 E2
Carrauntoohill, *Ireland* ... 15 D2
Carrick-on-Shannon,
  Ireland 15 C3
Carrick-on-Suir, *Ireland* .. 15 D4
Carrickfergus, *U.K.* 15 B6
Carrickmacross, *Ireland* .. 15 C5
Carrieton, *Australia* 95 E2
Carrington, *U.S.A.* 112 B5
Carrión →, *Spain* 34 D6
Carrión de los Condes,
  Spain 34 C6
Carrizal Bajo, *Chile* 126 B1
Carrizalillo, *Chile* 126 B1
Carrizo Cr. →, *U.S.A.* 113 G3
Carrizo Springs, *U.S.A.* .. 113 L5
Carrizozo, *U.S.A.* 115 K11
Carroll, *U.S.A.* 112 D7
Carrollton, *Ga., U.S.A.* ... 109 J3
Carrollton, *Ill., U.S.A.* ... 112 F9
Carrollton, *Ky., U.S.A.* ... 108 F3
Carrollton, *Mo., U.S.A.* .. 112 F8
Carrollton, *Ohio, U.S.A.* .. 110 F3
Carron →, *U.K.* 14 D4
Carron, L., *U.K.* 14 D3
Carrot →, *Canada* 105 C8
Carrot River, *Canada* 105 C8
Carrouges, *France* 18 D6
Carrù, *Italy* 28 D4
Carruthers, *Canada* 105 C7
Çarşamba, *Turkey* 72 B7
Carsóli, *Italy* 29 F10
Carson, *Calif., U.S.A.* 117 M8
Carson, *N. Dak., U.S.A.* .. 112 B4
Carson →, *U.S.A.* 116 F8
Carson City, *U.S.A.* 116 F7
Carson Sink, *U.S.A.* 114 G4
Cartagena, *Colombia* 124 A3
Cartagena, *Spain* 33 H4
Cartago, *Colombia* 124 C3
Cartago, *Costa Rica* 120 E3
Cártama, *Spain* 35 J6
Cartaxo, *Portugal* 35 F2
Cartaya, *Spain* 35 H3
Cartersville, *U.S.A.* 109 H3
Carterton, *N.Z.* 91 J5
Carthage, *Ark., U.S.A.* ... 113 H8
Carthage, *Ill., U.S.A.* 112 E9
Carthage, *Mo., U.S.A.* ... 113 G7
Carthage, *S. Dak., U.S.A.* 112 C6
Carthage, *Tex., U.S.A.* ... 113 J7
Cartier I., *Australia* 92 B3
Cartwright, *Canada* 103 B8
Caruaru, *Brazil* 125 E11
Carúpano, *Venezuela* 124 A6
Caruthersville, *U.S.A.* 113 G10
Carvin, *France* 19 B9
Carvoeiro, *Brazil* 124 D6
Carvoeiro, C., *Portugal* .. 35 F1
Cary, *U.S.A.* 109 H6
Casa Branca, *Portugal* ... 35 G2
Casa Grande, *U.S.A.* 115 K8
Casablanca, *Chile* 126 C1
Casablanca, *Morocco* 78 B4
Casacalenda, *Italy* 29 G11
Casalbordino, *Italy* 29 F11
Casale Monferrato, *Italy* .. 28 C5
Casalmaggiore, *Italy* 28 D7
Casalpusterlengo, *Italy* ... 28 C6
Casamance →, *Senegal* ... 82 C1
Casarano, *Italy* 31 B11
Casares, *Spain* 35 J5
Casas Grandes, *Mexico* ... 118 A3
Casas Ibáñez, *Spain* 33 F3
Casasimarro, *Spain* 33 F2
Casatejada, *Spain* 34 F5
Casavieja, *Spain* 34 E6
Cascade, *Idaho, U.S.A.* ... 114 D5
Cascade, *Mont., U.S.A.* .. 114 C8
Cascade Locks, *U.S.A.* ... 116 E5
Cascade Ra., *U.S.A.* 116 D5
Cascais, *Portugal* 35 G1
Cascavel, *Brazil* 127 A5
Cáscina, *Italy* 28 E7
Caselle Torinese, *Italy* ... 28 C4
Caserta, *Italy* 31 A7
Cashel, *Ireland* 15 D4
Cashmere, *U.S.A.* 114 C3
Cashmere Downs, *Australia* 93 E2
Casiguran, *Phil.* 61 C5
Casilda, *Argentina* 126 C3
Casimcea, *Romania* 43 F13
Casino, *Australia* 95 D5
Casiquiare →, *Venezuela* .. 124 C5
Caslan, *Canada* 104 C6
Čáslav, *Czech Rep.* 26 B8
Casma, *Peru* 124 E3
Casmalia, *U.S.A.* 117 L6
Cásola Valsénio, *Italy* 29 D8
Cásoli, *Italy* 29 F11
Caspe, *Spain* 32 D4
Casper, *U.S.A.* 114 E10
Caspian Depression,
  Eurasia 49 G9
Caspian Sea, *Eurasia* 50 E6
Cass City, *U.S.A.* 108 D4
Cass Lake, *U.S.A.* 112 B7
Cassà de la Selva, *Spain* .. 32 D7
Cassano allo Iónio, *Italy* .. 31 C9
Casse, Grande, *France* ... 21 C10
Cassel, *France* 19 B9
Casselman, *Canada* 111 A9
Casselton, *U.S.A.* 112 B6
Cassiar, *Canada* 104 B3
Cassiar Mts., *Canada* 104 B2

Cassino, *Italy* 30 A6
Cassis, *France* 21 E9
Cassville, *U.S.A.* 113 G8
Castagneto Carducci, *Italy* 28 E7
Castaic, *U.S.A.* 117 L8
Castanhal, *Brazil* 125 D9
Castéggio, *Italy* 28 C6
Castejón de Monegros,
  Spain 32 D4
Castèl di Sangro, *Italy* 29 G11
Castèl San Giovanni, *Italy* 28 C6
Castèl San Pietro Terme,
  Italy 29 D8
Castelbuono, *Italy* 31 E7
Castelfidardo, *Italy* 29 E10
Castelfiorentino, *Italy* 28 E7
Castelfranco Emília, *Italy* . 28 D8
Castelfranco Véneto, *Italy* 29 C8
Casteljaloux, *France* 20 D4
Castellabate, *Italy* 31 B7
Castellammare, *Italy* 30 D5
Castellammare del Golfo,
  Italy 30 D5
Castellammare di Stábia,
  Italy 31 B7
Castellamonte, *Italy* 28 C4
Castellane, *France* 21 E10
Castellaneta, *Italy* 31 B9
Castelli, *Argentina* 126 D4
Castelló de la Plana, *Spain* 32 F4
Castellón de la Plana □,
  Spain 32 E4
Castellote, *Spain* 32 E4
Castelmáuro, *Italy* 29 G11
Castelnau-de-Médoc,
  France 20 C3
Castelnau-Magnoac, *France* 20 E4
Castelnaudary, *France* 20 E5
Castelnovo ne' Monti, *Italy* 28 D7
Castelnuovo di Val di
  Cécina, *Italy* 28 E7
Castelo, *Brazil* 127 A7
Castelo Branco, *Portugal* . 34 F3
Castelo Branco □, *Portugal* 34 F3
Castelo de Paiva, *Portugal* 34 D2
Castelo de Vide, *Portugal* . 35 F3
Castelsardo, *Italy* 30 B1
Castelsarrasin, *France* 20 D5
Casteltérmini, *Italy* 30 E6
Castelvetrano, *Italy* 30 E5
Casterton, *Australia* 95 F3
Castets, *France* 20 E2
Castiglion Fiorentino, *Italy* 29 E8
Castiglione del Lago, *Italy* 29 E9
Castiglione della Pescáia,
  Italy 28 F7
Castiglione delle Stiviere,
  Italy 28 C7
Castilblanco, *Spain* 35 F5
Castilla, Playa de, *Spain* . 35 J4
Castilla-La Mancha □,
  Spain 6 H5
Castilla y Leon □, *Spain* .. 34 D6
Castillo de Locubín, *Spain* 35 H7
Castillon-en-Couserans,
  France 20 F5
Castillonès, *France* 20 D4
Castillos, *Uruguay* 127 C5
Castle Dale, *U.S.A.* 114 G8
Castle Douglas, *U.K.* 14 G5
Castle Rock, *Colo., U.S.A.* 112 F2
Castle Rock, *Wash.,
  U.S.A.* 116 D4
Castlebar, *Ireland* 15 C2
Castleblaney, *Ireland* 15 B5
Castlederg, *U.K.* 15 B4
Castleford, *U.K.* 12 D6
Castlegar, *Canada* 104 D5
Castlemaine, *Australia* 95 F3
Castlepollard, *Ireland* 15 C4
Castlerea, *Ireland* 15 C3
Castlereagh →, *Australia* .. 95 E4
Castlereagh B., *Australia* . 94 A2
Castletown, *I. of Man* 12 C3
Castletown Bearhaven,
  Ireland 15 E2
Castlevale, *Australia* 94 C4
Castor, *Canada* 104 C6
Castres, *France* 20 E6
Castricum, *Neths.* 17 B4
Castries, *St. Lucia* 121 D7
Castril, *Spain* 35 H8
Castro, *Brazil* 127 A6
Castro, *Chile* 128 E2
Castro Alves, *Brazil* 125 F11
Castro del Río, *Spain* 35 H6
Castro-Urdiales, *Spain* ... 34 B7
Castro Verde, *Portugal* ... 35 H2
Castrojeriz, *Spain* 34 C6
Castropol, *Spain* 34 B4
Castroreale, *Italy* 31 D8
Castrovíllari, *Italy* 31 C9
Castroville, *Calif., U.S.A.* 116 J5
Castroville, *Tex., U.S.A.* .. 113 L5
Castuera, *Spain* 35 G5
Casummit Lake, *Canada* .. 102 B1
Çat, *Turkey* 73 C9
Cat Ba, Dao, *Vietnam* 64 B6
Cat I., *Bahamas* 121 B4
Cat I., *U.S.A.* 113 K10
Cat L., *Canada* 102 B1
Cata, *Slovak Rep.* 27 D11
Catacamas, *Honduras* 120 D2
Cataguases, *Brazil* 127 A7
Catahoula L., *U.S.A.* 113 K8
Catalão, *Brazil* 125 G9

Çatalca, *Turkey* 41 E12
Catalina, *Canada* 103 C9
Catalonia = Cataluña □,
  Spain 32 D6
Cataluña □, *Spain* 32 D6
Çatalzeytin, *Turkey* 72 B6
Catamarca, *Argentina* ... 126 B2
Catamarca □, *Argentina* .. 126 B2
Catanauan, *Phil.* 61 E5
Catanduanes, *Phil.* 61 E6
Catanduva, *Brazil* 127 A6
Catánia, *Italy* 31 E8
Catánia, G. di, *Italy* 31 E8
Catanzaro, *Italy* 31 D9
Catarman, *Phil.* 61 E6
Catbalogan, *Phil.* 61 F6
Cateel, *Phil.* 61 H7
Caterham, *U.K.* 13 F7
Cathcart, *S. Africa* 88 E4
Cathlamet, *U.S.A.* 116 D3
Catio, *Guinea-Biss.* 82 C1
Catlettsburg, *U.S.A.* 108 F4
Çatma Dağı, *Turkey* 39 C11
Catoche, C., *Mexico* 119 C7
Cátria, Mte., *Italy* 29 E9
Catrimani, *Brazil* 124 C6
Catrimani →, *Brazil* 124 C6
Catskill, *U.S.A.* 111 D11
Catskill Mts., *U.S.A.* 111 D10
Catt, Mt., *Australia* 94 A1
Cattaraugus, *U.S.A.* 110 D6
Cáttólica, *Italy* 29 E9
Cáttólica Eraclea, *Italy* .. 30 E6
Catuala, *Angola* 88 B2
Catur, *Mozam.* 87 E4
Catwick Is., *Vietnam* 65 H7
Cauca →, *Colombia* 124 B4
Caucaia, *Brazil* 125 D11
Caucasus Mountains,
  Eurasia 49 J7
Caudete, *Spain* 33 G3
Caudry, *France* 19 B10
Caulnes, *France* 18 D4
Caulónia, *Italy* 31 D9
Caungula, *Angola* 84 F3
Cauquenes, *Chile* 126 D1
Caura →, *Venezuela* 124 B6
Cauresi →, *Mozam.* 87 F3
Căuşani, *Moldova* 43 D14
Causapscal, *Canada* 103 C6
Caussade, *France* 20 D5
Causse-Méjean, *France* ... 20 D7
Cauterets, *France* 20 F3
Cauvery →, *India* 66 P11
Caux, Pays de, *France* ... 18 C7
Cava de' Tirreni, *Italy* ... 31 B7
Cávado →, *Portugal* 34 D2
Cavaillon, *France* 21 E9
Cavalaire-sur-Mer, *France* 21 E10
Cavalese, *Italy* 29 B8
Cavalier, *U.S.A.* 112 A6
Cavalla = Cavally →,
  Africa 82 E3
Cavalleria, C. de, *Spain* .. 37 A11
Cavallo, I. de, *France* 21 G13
Cavally →, *Africa* 82 E3
Cavan, *Ireland* 15 B4
Cavan □, *Ireland* 15 C4
Cavárzere, *Italy* 29 C9
Çavdarhisar, *Turkey* 39 B11
Çavdır, *Turkey* 39 D11
Cave City, *U.S.A.* 108 G3
Cavenagh Ra., *Australia* .. 93 E4
Cavendish, *Australia* 95 F3
Caviana, I., *Brazil* 125 C8
Cavite, *Phil.* 61 D4
Cavnic, *Romania* 43 C8
Cavour, *Italy* 28 D4
Cavtat, *Croatia* 40 D2
Cawndilla L., *Australia* ... 95 E3
Cawnpore = Kanpur, *India* 69 F9
Caxias, *Brazil* 125 D10
Caxias do Sul, *Brazil* 127 B5
Çay, *Turkey* 72 C4
Cay Sal Bank, *Bahamas* .. 120 B4
Cayambe, *Ecuador* 124 C3
Çaycuma, *Turkey* 72 B5
Çayeli, *Turkey* 73 B9
Cayenne, *Fr. Guiana* 125 B8
Caygören Barajı, *Turkey* .. 39 B10
Çayıralan, *Turkey* 72 C6
Çaylus, *France* 20 D5
Cayman Brac, *Cayman Is.* 120 C4
Cayman Is. ■, *W. Indies* . 120 C3
Cayo Romano, *Cuba* 121 B4
Cayres, *France* 20 D7
Cayuga, *Canada* 110 D5
Cayuga, *U.S.A.* 111 D8
Cayuga L., *U.S.A.* 111 D8
Cazalla de la Sierra, *Spain* 35 H5
Căzăneşti, *Romania* 43 F12
Cazaubon, *France* 20 E3
Cazaux et de Sanguinet,
  Étang de, *France* 20 D2
Cazères, *France* 20 E5
Cazin, *Bos.-H.* 29 D12
Čazma, *Croatia* 29 C13
Cazombo, *Angola* 85 G4
Cazorla, *Spain* 35 H7
Cazorla, Sierra de, *Spain* . 35 G8
Cea →, *Spain* 34 C5
Ceamurlia de Jos, *Romania* 43 F13
Ceanannus Mor, *Ireland* .. 15 C5
Ceará = Fortaleza, *Brazil* 125 D11
Ceará □, *Brazil* 125 E11
Ceará Mirim, *Brazil* 125 E11
Cearu, L., *Romania* 43 F8

Cebaco, I. de, *Panama* ... 120 E3
Cebollar, *Argentina* 126 B2
Cebollera, Sierra de, *Spain* 32 D2
Cebreros, *Spain* 34 E6
Cebu, *Phil.* 61 F5
Čečava, *Bos.-H.* 42 F2
Ceccano, *Italy* 30 A6
Cece, *Hungary* 42 D3
Cechi, *Ivory C.* 82 D4
Cecil Plains, *Australia* 95 D5
Cécina, *Italy* 28 E7
Cécina →, *Italy* 28 E7
Ceclavín, *Spain* 34 F4
Cedar →, *U.S.A.* 112 E9
Cedar City, *U.S.A.* 115 H7
Cedar Creek Reservoir,
  U.S.A. 113 J6
Cedar Falls, *Iowa, U.S.A.* 112 D8
Cedar Falls, *Wash., U.S.A.* 116 C5
Cedar Key, *U.S.A.* 109 L4
Cedar L., *Canada* 105 C9
Cedar Rapids, *U.S.A.* 112 E9
Cedartown, *U.S.A.* 109 H3
Cedarvale, *Canada* 104 B3
Cedarville, *S. Africa* 89 E4
Cedarville, *U.S.A.* 114 F3
Cedeira, *Spain* 34 B2
Cedral, *Mexico* 118 C4
Cedrino →, *Italy* 30 B2
Cedro, *Brazil* 125 E11
Cedros, I. de, *Mexico* 118 B1
Ceduna, *Australia* 95 E1
Cée, *Spain* 34 C1
Cefalù, *Italy* 31 D7
Cega →, *Spain* 34 D6
Cegléd, *Hungary* 42 C4
Céglie Messápico, *Italy* ... 31 B10
Cehegín, *Spain* 33 G3
Ceheng, *China* 58 E5
Cehu-Silvaniei, *Romania* .. 43 C8
Ceica, *Romania* 42 D7
Ceira →, *Portugal* 34 E2
Čelákovice, *Czech Rep.* .. 26 A7
Celano, *Italy* 29 F10
Celanova, *Spain* 34 C3
Celaya, *Mexico* 118 C4
Celebes = Sulawesi □,
  Indonesia 63 E6
Celebes Sea, *Indonesia* ... 63 D6
Čelić, *Bos.-H.* 42 F3
Celina, *U.S.A.* 108 E3
Celinac, *Bos.-H.* 42 F2
Celje, *Slovenia* 29 B12
Celldömölk, *Hungary* 42 C2
Celle, *Germany* 24 C6
Celorico da Beira, *Portugal* 34 E3
Çeltikçi, *Turkey* 39 D12
Cement, *U.S.A.* 113 H5
Çemişgezek, *Turkey* 73 C8
Cengong, *China* 58 D7
Ceno →, *Italy* 28 D7
Centallo, *Italy* 28 D4
Centelles, *Spain* 32 D7
Center, *N. Dak., U.S.A.* .. 112 B4
Center, *Tex., U.S.A.* 113 K7
Centerfield, *U.S.A.* 115 G8
Centerville, *Calif., U.S.A.* 116 J7
Centerville, *Iowa, U.S.A.* . 112 E8
Centerville, *Pa., U.S.A.* ... 110 F5
Centerville, *S. Dak.,
  U.S.A.* 112 D6
Centerville, *Tenn., U.S.A.* 109 H2
Centerville, *Tex., U.S.A.* . 113 K7
Cento, *Italy* 29 D8
Central, *U.S.A.* 115 K9
Central □, *Kenya* 86 C4
Central □, *Malawi* 87 E3
Central □, *Zambia* 87 E2
Central, Cordillera,
  Colombia 122 C3
Central, Cordillera,
  Costa Rica 120 D3
Central, Cordillera,
  Dom. Rep. 121 C5
Central, Cordillera, *Phil.* . 61 C4
Central African Rep. ■,
  Africa 84 C4
Central City, *Ky., U.S.A.* . 108 G2
Central City, *Nebr., U.S.A.* 112 E6
Central I., *Kenya* 86 B4
Central Makran Range,
  Pakistan 66 F4
Central Patricia, *Canada* .. 102 B1
Central Russian Uplands,
  Europe 6 E13
Central Siberian Plateau,
  Russia 52 C14
Centralia, *Ill., U.S.A.* 112 F10
Centralia, *Mo., U.S.A.* ... 112 F8
Centralia, *Wash., U.S.A.* .. 116 D4
Centreville, *Ala., U.S.A.* .. 109 J2
Centreville, *Miss., U.S.A.* 113 K9
Ceotina →, *Bos.-H.* 40 C2
Cephalonia = Kefallinía,
  Greece 38 C2
Čepin, *Croatia* 42 E3
Ceprano, *Italy* 30 A6
Ceptura, *Romania* 43 E11
Cepu, *Indonesia* 63 G14
Ceram = Seram, *Indonesia* 63 E7
Ceram Sea = Seram Sea,
  Indonesia 63 E7

Cère →, *France* 20 D5
Cerea, *Italy* 29 C8
Ceredigion □, *U.K.* 13 E3
Ceres, *Argentina* 126 B3
Ceres, *S. Africa* 88 E2
Ceres, *U.S.A.* 116 H6
Céret, *France* 20 F6
Cergy, *France* 19 C9
Cerignola, *Italy* 31 A8
Cerigo = Kíthira, *Greece* . 38 E5
Cérilly, *France* 19 F9
Cerisiers, *France* 19 D10
Cerizay, *France* 18 F6
Çerkeş, *Turkey* 72 B5
Çerkezköy, *Turkey* 41 E12
Čerknica, *Slovenia* 29 C11
Cerkovica, *Bulgaria* 41 C8
Cermerno, *Serbia, Yug.* ... 40 C4
Çermik, *Turkey* 73 C8
Cerna, *Romania* 43 E13
Cerna →, *Romania* 43 F8
Cernavodă, *Romania* 43 F13
Cernay, *France* 19 E14
Černik, *Croatia* 42 E2
Cerralvo, I., *Mexico* 118 C3
Čërrik, *Albania* 40 E3
Cerritos, *Mexico* 118 C4
Certaldo, *Italy* 28 E8
Cervaro →, *Italy* 31 A8
Cervera, *Spain* 32 D6
Cervera de Pisuerga, *Spain* 34 C6
Cervera del Río Alhama,
  Spain 32 C3
Cervéteri, *Italy* 29 F9
Cérvia, *Italy* 29 D9
Cervignano del Friuli, *Italy* 29 C10
Cervinara, *Italy* 31 A7
Cervione, *France* 21 F13
Cervo, *Spain* 34 B3
Cesarò, *Italy* 31 E7
Cesena, *Italy* 29 D9
Cesenático, *Italy* 29 D9
Cēsis, *Latvia* 9 H21
Česká Lípa, *Czech Rep.* .. 26 A7
Česká Třebová, *Czech Rep.* 27 B9
České Budějovice,
  Czech Rep. 26 C7
České Velenice,
  Czech Rep. 26 C7
Českomoravská Vrchovina,
  Czech Rep. 26 B8
Český Brod, *Czech Rep.* .. 26 A7
Český Krumlov,
  Czech Rep. 26 C7
Český Těšín, *Czech Rep.* .. 27 B11
Česma →, *Croatia* 29 C13
Çeşme, *Turkey* 39 C8
Cessnock, *Australia* 95 E5
Cesson-Sévigné, *France* .. 18 D5
Cestas, *France* 20 D3
Cestos →, *Liberia* 82 D3
Cetate, *Romania* 42 F8
Cetin Grad, *Croatia* 29 C12
Cetina →, *Croatia* 29 E13
Cetinje, *Montenegro, Yug.* 40 D2
Cetraro, *Italy* 31 C8
Ceuta, *N. Afr.* 78 A4
Ceva, *Italy* 28 D5
Cévennes, *France* 20 D7
Ceyhan, *Turkey* 72 D6
Ceyhan →, *Turkey* 72 D6
Ceylânpınar, *Turkey* 73 D9
Ceylon = Sri Lanka ■,
  Asia 66 R12
Cèze →, *France* 21 D8
Cha-am, *Thailand* 64 F2
Cha Pa, *Vietnam* 64 A4
Chabanais, *France* 20 C4
Chabeuil, *France* 21 D9
Chablais, *France* 19 F13
Chablis, *France* 19 E10
Chacabuco, *Argentina* 126 C3
Chachapoyas, *Peru* 124 E3
Chachoengsao, *Thailand* .. 64 F3
Chachran, *Pakistan* 66 E7
Chachro, *Pakistan* 68 G4
Chaco □, *Argentina* 126 B3
Chaco □, *Paraguay* 126 B4
Chaco Austral, *S. Amer.* .. 128 B4
Chaco Boreal, *S. Amer.* .. 128 A4
Chaco Central, *S. Amer.* .. 128 A4
Chad ■, *Africa* 79 F8
Chad, L. = Tchad, L.,
  Chad 79 F8
Chadan, *Russia* 51 D10
Chadileuvú →, *Argentina* . 126 D2
Chadiza, *Zambia* 87 E3
Chadron, *U.S.A.* 112 D3
Chadyr-Lunga = Ciadâr-
  Lunga, *Moldova* 43 D13
Chae Hom, *Thailand* 64 C2
Chaem →, *Thailand* 64 C2
Chaeryŏng, *N. Korea* 57 E13
Chagai Hills, *Afghan.* 66 E3
Chagda, *Russia* 53 D14
Chagny, *France* 19 F11
Chagoda, *Russia* 46 C8
Chagos Arch., *Ind. Oc.* ... 52 K11
Chāh Ākhvor, *Iran* 71 C8
Chāh Bahār, *Iran* 71 E9
Chāh-e-Malek, *Iran* 71 D8
Chāh Kavīr, *Iran* 71 D7
Chahar Burjak, *Afghan.* .. 66 D3
Chaibasa, *India* 67 H14
Chaillé-les-Marais, *France* 20 B2
Chainat, *Thailand* 64 E3

Chaiya, *Thailand* 65 H2
Chaj Doab, *Pakistan* 68 C5
Chajari, *Argentina* 126 C4
Chake Chake, *Tanzania* .. 86 D4
Chakhānsūr, *Afghan.* 66 D3
Chakonipau, L., *Canada* .. 103 A6
Chakradharpur, *India* 69 H11
Chakwal, *Pakistan* 68 C5
Chala, *Peru* 124 G4
Chalais, *France* 20 C4
Chalchihuites, *Mexico* .. 118 C4
Chalcis = Khalkís, *Greece* . 38 C5
Châlette-sur-Loing, *France* 19 D9
Chaleur B., *Canada* 103 C6
Chalfant, *U.S.A.* 116 H4
Chalhuanca, *Peru* 124 F4
Chalindrey, *France* 19 E12
Chaling, *China* 59 D9
Chalisgaon, *India* 66 J9
Chalky Inlet, *N.Z.* 91 M1
Challans, *France* 18 F5
Challapata, *Bolivia* 124 G5
Challis, *U.S.A.* 114 D6
Chalna, *India* 69 H13
Chalon-sur-Saône, *France* . 19 F11
Chalonnes-sur-Loire, *France* 18 E6
Châlons-en-Champagne, *France* 19 D11
Châlus, *France* 20 C4
Chalyaphum, *Thailand* 64 E4
Cham, *Germany* 25 F8
Cham, Cu Lao, *Vietnam* .. 64 E7
Chama, *U.S.A.* 115 H10
Chaman, *Pakistan* 66 D5
Chamba, *India* 68 C7
Chamba, *Tanzania* 87 E4
Chambal →, *India* 69 F8
Chamberlain, *U.S.A.* 112 D5
Chamberlain →, *Australia* 92 C4
Chambers, *U.S.A.* 115 J9
Chambersburg, *U.S.A.* .. 108 F7
Chambéry, *France* 21 C9
Chambly, *Canada* 111 A11
Chambord, *Canada* 103 C5
Chamboulive, *France* 20 C5
Chamchamal, *Iraq* 70 C5
Chamela, *Mexico* 118 D3
Chamical, *Argentina* 126 C2
Chamkar Luong, *Cambodia* 65 G4
Chamonix-Mont Blanc, *France* 21 C10
Champa, *India* 69 H10
Champagne, *Canada* 104 A1
Champagne, *France* 19 D11
Champagnole, *France* 19 F12
Champaign, *U.S.A.* 108 E1
Champassak, *Laos* 64 E5
Champaubert, *France* 19 D10
Champdeniers-St-Denis, *France* 20 B3
Champeix, *France* 20 C7
Champlain, *Canada* 108 B9
Champlain, *U.S.A.* 111 B11
Champlain, L., *U.S.A.* .. 111 B11
Champlitte, *France* 19 E12
Champotón, *Mexico* 119 D6
Chamusca, *Portugal* 35 F2
Chana, *Thailand* 65 J3
Chañaral, *Chile* 126 B1
Chanārān, *Iran* 71 B8
Chanasma, *India* 68 H5
Chandannagar, *India* 69 H13
Chandausi, *India* 69 E8
Chandeleur Is., *U.S.A.* .. 113 L10
Chandeleur Sd., *U.S.A.* . 113 L10
Chandigarh, *India* 68 D7
Chandler, *Australia* 95 D1
Chandler, *Canada* 103 C7
Chandler, *Ariz., U.S.A.* .. 115 K8
Chandler, *Okla., U.S.A.* .. 113 H6
Chandmani, *Mongolia* .. 60 B4
Chandpur, *Bangla.* 67 H17
Chandpur, *India* 68 E8
Chandrapur, *India* 66 K11
Chānf, *Iran* 71 E9
Chang, *Pakistan* 68 F3
Chang, Ko, *Thailand* 65 G4
Ch'ang Chiang = Chang Jiang →, *China* 59 B13
Chang Jiang →, *China* .. 59 B13
Changa, *India* 69 C7
Changanacheri, *India* .. 66 Q10
Changane →, *Mozam.* .. 89 C5
Changbai, *China* 57 D15
Changbai Shan, *China* .. 57 C15
Changchiak'ou = Zhangjiakou, *China* 56 D8
Changchun, *China* 57 C13
Changchunling, *China* .. 57 B13
Changde, *China* 59 C8
Changdo-ri, *N. Korea* .. 57 E14
Changfeng, *China* 59 A11
Changhai = Shanghai, *China* 59 B13
Changhua, *China* 59 B12
Changhua, *Taiwan* 59 F13
Changhǔng, *S. Korea* .. 57 G14
Changhǔngni, *N. Korea* . 57 D15
Changjiang, *China* 60 E5
Changjin, *N. Korea* 57 D14
Changjin-chǒsuji, *N. Korea* 57 D14
Changle, *China* 59 E12
Changli, *China* 57 E10
Changling, *China* 57 B12

Changlun, *Malaysia* 65 J3
Changning, *Hunan, China* 59 D9
Changning, *Yunnan, China* 58 E2
Changping, *China* 56 D9
Changsha, *China* 59 C9
Changshan, *China* 59 C12
Changshou, *China* 58 C6
Changshu, *China* 59 B13
Changshun, *China* 58 D6
Changtai, *China* 59 E11
Changting, *China* 59 E11
Changwu, *China* 56 G4
Changxing, *China* 59 B12
Changyang, *China* 59 B8
Changyi, *China* 57 F10
Changyǒn, *N. Korea* 57 E13
Changyuan, *China* 56 G8
Changzhi, *China* 56 F7
Changzhou, *China* 59 B12
Chanhanga, *Angola* 88 B1
Chanlar = Xanlar, *Azerbaijan* 49 K8
Channapatna, *India* 66 N10
Channel Is., *U.K.* 13 H5
Channel Is., *U.S.A.* 117 M7
Channel-Port aux Basques, *Canada* 103 C8
Channing, *Mich., U.S.A.* . 108 B1
Channing, *Tex., U.S.A.* .. 113 H3
Chantada, *Spain* 34 C3
Chanthaburi, *Thailand* .. 64 F4
Chantilly, *France* 19 C9
Chantonnay, *France* 18 F5
Chantrey Inlet, *Canada* .. 100 B10
Chanute, *U.S.A.* 113 G7
Chanza →, *Spain* 35 H3
Chao Hu, *China* 59 B11
Chao Phraya →, *Thailand* 64 F3
Chao Phraya Lowlands, *Thailand* 64 E3
Chao Xian, *China* 59 B11
Chao'an, *China* 59 F11
Chaocheng, *China* 56 F8
Chaoyang, *Guangdong, China* 59 F11
Chaoyang, *Liaoning, China* 57 D11
Chapala, *Mozam.* 87 F4
Chapala, L. de, *Mexico* .. 118 C4
Chapayev, *Kazakstan* 48 E10
Chapayevsk, *Russia* 48 D9
Chapecó, *Brazil* 127 B5
Chapel Hill, *U.S.A.* 109 H6
Chapleau, *Canada* 102 C3
Chaplin, *Canada* 105 C7
Chaplino, *Ukraine* 47 H9
Chaplygin, *Russia* 46 F11
Chapra = Chhapra, *India* . 69 G11
Chara, *Russia* 51 D12
Charadai, *Argentina* 126 B4
Charagua, *Bolivia* 124 G6
Charambirá, Punta, *Colombia* 124 C3
Charaña, *Bolivia* 124 G5
Charantsavan, *Armenia* .. 49 K7
Charata, *Argentina* 126 B3
Charcas, *Mexico* 118 C4
Charcoal L., *Canada* 105 B8
Chard, *U.K.* 13 G5
Chardon, *U.S.A.* 110 E3
Chardzhou = Chärjew, *Turkmenistan* 50 F7
Charente □, *France* 20 C4
Charente →, *France* 20 C2
Charente-Maritime □, *France* 20 C3
Charenton-du-Cher, *France* 19 F9
Chari →, *Chad* 79 F8
Chārīkār, *Afghan.* 66 B6
Chariton →, *U.S.A.* 112 F8
Chärjew, *Turkmenistan* .. 50 F7
Charkhari, *India* 69 G8
Charkhi Dadri, *India* 68 E7
Charleroi, *Belgium* 17 D4
Charleroi, *U.S.A.* 110 F5
Charles, C., *U.S.A.* 108 G8
Charles City, *U.S.A.* 112 D8
Charles L., *Canada* 105 B6
Charles Town, *U.S.A.* .. 108 F7
Charleston, *Ill., U.S.A.* .. 108 F1
Charleston, *Miss., U.S.A.* 113 H9
Charleston, *Mo., U.S.A.* . 113 G10
Charleston, *S.C., U.S.A.* . 109 J6
Charleston, *W. Va., U.S.A.* 108 F5
Charleston Peak, *U.S.A.* . 117 J11
Charlestown, *Ireland* 15 C3
Charlestown, *S. Africa* .. 89 D4
Charlestown, *U.S.A.* 108 F3
Charleville = Rath Luirc, *Ireland* 15 D3
Charleville, *Australia* 95 D4
Charleville-Mézières, *France* 19 C11
Charlevoix, *U.S.A.* 108 C3
Charlieu, *France* 19 F11
Charlotte, *Mich., U.S.A.* . 108 D3
Charlotte, *N.C., U.S.A.* .. 109 H5
Charlotte Amalie, *Virgin Is.* 121 C7
Charlotte Harbor, *U.S.A.* 109 M4
Charlottenberg, *Sweden* .. 10 E6
Charlottesville, *U.S.A.* .. 108 F6
Charlottetown, *Canada* .. 103 C7
Charlton, *Australia* 95 F3
Charlton, *U.S.A.* 112 E8
Charlton I., *Canada* 102 B4
Charmes, *France* 19 D13
Charny, *Canada* 103 C5

Charolles, *France* 19 F11
Chârost, *France* 19 F9
Charre, *Mozam.* 87 F4
Charroux, *France* 20 B4
Charsadda, *Pakistan* 68 B4
Charters Towers, *Australia* 94 C4
Chartres, *France* 18 D8
Chascomús, *Argentina* .. 126 D4
Chasefu, *Zambia* 87 E3
Chasseneuil-sur-Bonnieure, *France* 20 C4
Chāt, *Iran* 71 B7
Chatal Balkan = Udvoy Balkan, *Bulgaria* 41 D10
Château-Arnoux, *France* . 21 D10
Château-Chinon, *France* . 19 E10
Château-d'Olonne, *France* 20 B2
Château-du-Loir, *France* . 18 E7
Château-Gontier, *France* . 18 E6
Château-la-Vallière, *France* 18 E7
Château-Renault, *France* . 18 E7
Château-Salins, *France* .. 19 D13
Château-Thierry, *France* . 19 C10
Châteaubourg, *France* .. 18 D5
Châteaubriant, *France* .. 18 E5
Châteaudun, *France* 18 D8
Châteaugiron, *France* .. 18 D5
Châteaulin, *France* 18 D2
Châteaumeillant, *France* . 19 F9
Châteauneuf-du-Faou, *France* 18 D3
Châteauneuf-sur-Charente, *France* 20 C3
Châteauneuf-sur-Cher, *France* 19 F9
Châteauneuf-sur-Loire, *France* 19 E9
Châteaurenard, *Bouches-du-Rhône, France* 21 E8
Châteaurenard, *Loiret, France* 19 E9
Châteauroux, *France* 19 F8
Châteauvillain, *France* .. 19 D11
Châtelaillon-Plage, *France* 20 B2
Châtelguyon, *France* 20 C7
Châtellerault, *France* 18 F7
Châtelus-Malvaleix, *France* 19 F9
Chatfield, *U.S.A.* 112 D9
Chatham, *N.B., Canada* . 103 C6
Chatham, *Ont., Canada* . 102 D3
Chatham, *U.K.* 13 F8
Chatham, *La., U.S.A.* 113 J8
Chatham, *N.Y., U.S.A.* .. 111 D11
Chatham Is., *Pac. Oc.* .. 96 M10
Chatham Str., *U.S.A.* 104 B2
Châtillon, *Italy* 28 C4
Châtillon-Coligny, *France* . 19 E9
Châtillon-en-Bazois, *France* 19 E10
Châtillon-sur-Indre, *France* 18 F8
Châtillon-sur-Seine, *France* 19 E11
Chatmohar, *Bangla.* 69 G13
Chatra, *India* 69 G11
Chatrapur, *India* 67 K14
Chats, L. des, *Canada* .. 111 A8
Chatsworth, *Canada* 110 B4
Chatsworth, *Zimbabwe* . 87 F3
Chattahoochee →, *U.S.A.* 109 K3
Chattanooga, *U.S.A.* 109 H3
Chatteris, *U.K.* 13 E8
Chaturat, *Thailand* 64 E3
Chau Doc, *Vietnam* 65 G5
Chaudes-Aigues, *France* . 20 D7
Chauffailles, *France* 19 F11
Chauk, *Burma* 67 J19
Chaukan La, *Burma* 67 F20
Chaumont, *France* 19 D12
Chaumont, *U.S.A.* 111 B8
Chaumont-en-Vexin, *France* 19 C8
Chaumont-sur-Loire, *France* 18 E8
Chaunay, *France* 20 B4
Chauny, *France* 19 C10
Chausey, Îs., *France* 18 D5
Chaussin, *France* 19 F12
Chautauqua L., *U.S.A.* .. 110 D5
Chauvigny, *France* 18 F7
Chauvin, *Canada* 105 C6
Chavanges, *France* 19 D11
Chaves, *Brazil* 125 D9
Chaves, *Portugal* 34 D3
Chawang, *Thailand* 65 H2
Chazelles-sur-Lyon, *France* 21 C8
Chazy, *U.S.A.* 111 B11
Cheb, *Czech Rep.* 26 A5
Cheboksarskoye Vdkhr., *Russia* 48 B8
Cheboksary, *Russia* 48 B8
Cheboygan, *U.S.A.* 108 C3
Chebsara, *Russia* 46 C10
Chech, Erg, *Africa* 78 D5
Chechen, Ostrov, *Russia* . 49 H8
Chechenia □, *Russia* 49 J7
Checheno-Ingush Republic = Chechenia □, *Russia* 49 J7
Chechnya = Chechenia □, *Russia* 49 J7
Chechon, *S. Korea* 57 F15
Chęciny, *Poland* 45 H7
Checleset B., *Canada* 104 C3
Checotah, *U.S.A.* 113 H7
Cheduba I., *Burma* 67 K18

Cheepie, *Australia* 95 D4
Chef-Boutonne, *France* .. 20 B3
Chegdomyn, *Russia* 51 D14
Chegga, *Mauritania* 78 C4
Chegutu, *Zimbabwe* 87 F3
Chehalis, *U.S.A.* 116 D4
Cheiron, Mt., *France* 21 E10
Cheju Do, *S. Korea* 57 H14
Chekalin, *Russia* 46 E9
Chekiang = Zhejiang □, *China* 59 C13
Chel = Kuru, Bahr el →, *Sudan* 81 F2
Chela, Sa. da, *Angola* .. 88 B1
Chelan, *U.S.A.* 114 C4
Chelan, L., *U.S.A.* 114 B3
Cheleken, *Turkmenistan* . 50 F6
Chelforó, *Argentina* 128 D3
Chelkar = Shalqar, *Kazakstan* 50 E6
Chelkar Tengiz, Solonchak, *Kazakstan* 50 E7
Chelles, *France* 19 D9
Chełm, *Poland* 45 G10
Chełm □, *Poland* 45 G10
Chełmno, *Poland* 45 E5
Chelmsford, *U.K.* 13 F8
Chełmża, *Poland* 45 E5
Chelsea, *Okla., U.S.A.* .. 113 G7
Chelsea, *Vt., U.S.A.* 111 C12
Cheltenham, *U.K.* 13 F5
Chelva, *Spain* 32 F4
Chelyabinsk, *Russia* 50 D7
Chelyuskin, C., *Russia* .. 52 B14
Chembar = Belinskiy, *Russia* 48 D6
Chemillé, *France* 18 E6
Chemnitz, *Germany* 24 E8
Chemult, *U.S.A.* 114 E3
Chen, Gora, *Russia* 51 C15
Chen Xian, *China* 59 E9
Chenab →, *Pakistan* 68 D4
Chenango Forks, *U.S.A.* 111 D9
Chencha, *Ethiopia* 81 F4
Chenchiang = Zhenjiang, *China* 59 A12
Cheney, *U.S.A.* 114 C5
Cheng Xian, *China* 56 H3
Chengbu, *China* 59 D8
Chengcheng, *China* 56 G5
Chengchou = Zhengzhou, *China* 56 G7
Chengde, *China* 57 D9
Chengdong Hu, *China* .. 59 A11
Chengdu, *China* 58 B5
Chenggong, *China* 58 E4
Chengjiang, *China* 58 E4
Chengjiang, *China* 58 E4
Chengkou, *China* 58 B7
Ch'engtu = Chengdu, *China* 58 B5
Chengwu, *China* 56 G8
Chengxi Hu, *China* 59 A11
Chengyang, *China* 57 F11
Chenjiagang, *China* 57 G10
Chenkán, *Mexico* 119 D6
Chennai, *India* 66 N12
Chenôve, *France* 19 E12
Chenxi, *China* 59 C8
Cheom Ksan, *Cambodia* . 64 E5
Chepelare, *Bulgaria* 41 E8
Chepén, *Peru* 124 E3
Chepes, *Argentina* 126 C2
Chepo, *Panama* 120 E4
Chepstow, *U.K.* 13 F5
Chequamegon B., *U.S.A.* 112 B9
Cher □, *France* 19 E9
Cher →, *France* 18 E7
Chéradi, *Italy* 31 B10
Cherasco, *Italy* 28 D4
Cheraw, *U.S.A.* 109 H6
Cherbourg, *France* 18 C5
Cherdakly, *Russia* 48 C9
Cherdyn, *Russia* 50 C6
Cheremkhovo, *Russia* .. 51 D11
Cherepanovo, *Russia* .. 50 D9
Cherepovets, *Russia* 46 C10
Chergui, Chott ech, *Algeria* 78 B6
Cherikov = Cherykaw, *Belarus* 46 F6
Cherkasy, *Ukraine* 47 H7
Cherkessk, *Russia* 49 H6
Cherlak, *Russia* 50 D8
Chernaya, *Russia* 51 B9
Cherni, *Bulgaria* 40 D7
Chernigov = Chernihiv, *Ukraine* 47 G6
Chernihiv, *Ukraine* 47 G6
Chernivtsi, *Ukraine* 47 H3
Chernobyl = Chornobyl, *Ukraine* 47 G6
Chernogorsk, *Russia* 51 D10
Chernomorskoye = Chornomorske, *Ukraine* 47 K7
Chernovtsy = Chernivtsi, *Ukraine* 47 H3
Chernyakhovsk, *Russia* . 9 J19
Chernyanka, *Russia* 47 G9
Chernysheyskiy, *Russia* . 51 C12
Chernyye Zemli, *Russia* . 49 H8
Cherokee, *Iowa, U.S.A.* . 112 D7
Cherokee, *Okla., U.S.A.* . 113 G5
Cherokees, Lake O' The, *U.S.A.* 113 G7
Cherrapunji, *India* 67 G17

Cherry Creek, *U.S.A.* 114 G6
Cherry Valley, *U.S.A.* .. 117 M10
Cherryvale, *U.S.A.* 113 G7
Cherskiy, *Russia* 51 C17
Cherskogo Khrebet, *Russia* 51 C15
Chertkovo, *Russia* 47 H11
Cherven, *Belarus* 46 F5
Cherven-Bryag, *Bulgaria* . 41 C8
Chervonohrad, *Ukraine* .. 47 G3
Cherwell →, *U.K.* 13 F6
Cherykaw, *Belarus* 46 F6
Chesapeake, *U.S.A.* 108 G7
Chesapeake B., *U.S.A.* .. 108 G7
Cheshire □, *U.K.* 12 D5
Cheshskaya Guba, *Russia* . 50 C5
Cheshunt, *U.K.* 13 F7
Chesil Beach, *U.K.* 13 G5
Cheslatta L., *Canada* 104 C3
Chesley, *Canada* 110 B3
Cheste, *Spain* 33 F4
Chester, *U.K.* 12 D5
Chester, *Calif., U.S.A.* .. 114 F3
Chester, *Ill., U.S.A.* 113 G10
Chester, *Mont., U.S.A.* .. 114 B8
Chester, *Pa., U.S.A.* 108 F8
Chester, *S.C., U.S.A.* 109 H5
Chester-le-Street, *U.K.* .. 12 C6
Chesterfield, *U.K.* 12 D6
Chesterfield, Is., *N. Cal.* . 96 J7
Chesterton Ra., *Australia* . 95 D4
Chesterville, *Canada* 111 A9
Chesuncook L., *U.S.A.* .. 103 C6
Chéticamp, *Canada* 103 C7
Chetrosu, *Moldova* 43 B12
Chetumal, B. de, *Mexico* . 119 D7
Chetwynd, *Canada* 104 B4
Chevanceaux, *France* .. 20 C3
Cheviot, The, *U.K.* 12 B5
Cheviot Hills, *U.K.* 12 B5
Cheviot Ra., *Australia* .. 94 D3
Chew Bahir, *Ethiopia* .. 81 G4
Chewelah, *U.S.A.* 114 B5
Cheyenne, *Okla., U.S.A.* . 113 H5
Cheyenne, *Wyo., U.S.A.* . 112 E2
Cheyenne →, *U.S.A.* 112 C4
Cheyenne Wells, *U.S.A.* . 112 F3
Cheyne B., *Australia* 93 F2
Chhabra, *India* 68 G7
Chhapra, *India* 69 G11
Chhata, *India* 68 F7
Chhatarpur, *India* 69 G8
Chhep, *Cambodia* 64 F5
Chhindwara, *India* 69 H8
Chhlong, *Cambodia* 65 F5
Chhuk, *Cambodia* 65 G5
Chi →, *Thailand* 64 E5
Chiai, *Taiwan* 59 F13
Chiali, *Taiwan* 59 F13
Chiamussu = Jiamusi, *China* 60 B8
Chianciano Terme, *Italy* . 29 E8
Chiang Dao, *Thailand* .. 64 C2
Chiang Kham, *Thailand* . 64 C3
Chiang Khan, *Thailand* .. 64 D3
Chiang Khong, *Thailand* . 64 B3
Chiang Mai, *Thailand* .. 64 C2
Chiang Saen, *Thailand* .. 64 B3
Chiapa →, *Mexico* 119 D6
Chiapa de Corzo, *Mexico* . 119 D6
Chiapas □, *Mexico* 119 D6
Chiaramonte Gulfi, *Italy* . 31 E7
Chiaravalle, *Italy* 29 E10
Chiaravalle Centrale, *Italy* 31 D9
Chiari, *Italy* 28 C6
Chiatura, *Georgia* 49 J6
Chiautla, *Mexico* 119 D5
Chiávari, *Italy* 28 D6
Chiavenna, *Italy* 28 B6
Chiba, *Japan* 55 G10
Chibabava, *Mozam.* 89 C5
Chibemba, *Cunene, Angola* 85 H2
Chibemba, *Huíla, Angola* . 88 B2
Chibia, *Angola* 85 H2
Chibougamau, *Canada* .. 102 C5
Chibougamau L., *Canada* . 102 C5
Chibuk, *Nigeria* 83 C7
Chic-Chocs, Mts., *Canada* 103 C6
Chicacole = Srikakulam, *India* 67 K13
Chicago, *U.S.A.* 108 E2
Chicago Heights, *U.S.A.* . 108 E2
Chichagof I., *U.S.A.* 104 B1
Chicheng, *China* 56 D8
Chichester, *U.K.* 13 G7
Chichibu, *Japan* 55 F9
Ch'ich'ihaerh = Qiqihar, *China* 60 B7
Chickasha, *U.S.A.* 113 H6
Chiclana de la Frontera, *Spain* 35 J4
Chiclayo, *Peru* 124 E3
Chico, *U.S.A.* 116 F5
Chico →, *Chubut, Argentina* 128 E3
Chico →, *Santa Cruz, Argentina* 128 G3
Chicomo, *Mozam.* 89 C5
Chicontepec, *Mexico* .. 119 C5
Chicopee, *U.S.A.* 111 D12
Chicoutimi, *Canada* 103 C5
Chicualacuala, *Mozam.* . 89 C5
Chidambaram, *India* 66 P11
Chidenguele, *Mozam.* .. 89 C5
Chidley, C., *Canada* 4 C5
Chiede, *Angola* 88 B2
Chiefs Pt., *Canada* 110 B3

Chiem Hoa, Vietnam 64 A5
Chiemsee, Germany 25 H8
Chiengi, Zambia 87 D2
Chiengmai = Chiang Mai,
  Thailand 64 C2
Chienti →, Italy 29 E10
Chieri, Italy 28 C4
Chiers →, France 19 C11
Chiesa in Valmalenco, Italy 28 B6
Chiese →, Italy 28 C7
Chieti, Italy 29 F11
Chifeng, China 57 C10
Chigirin, Ukraine 47 H7
Chignecto B., Canada ... 103 C7
Chiguana, Bolivia 126 A2
Chigwell, U.K. 13 F8
Chiha-ri, N. Korea 57 E14
Chihli, G. of = Bo Hai,
  China 57 E10
Chihuahua, Mexico 118 B3
Chihuahua □, Mexico ... 118 B3
Chiili, Kazakstan 50 E7
Chik Bollapur, India 66 N10
Chikmagalur, India 66 N9
Chikwawa, Malawi 87 F3
Chilac, Mexico 119 D5
Chilako →, Canada 104 C4
Chilam Chavki, Pakistan . 69 B6
Chilanga, Zambia 87 F2
Chilapa, Mexico 119 D5
Chilas, Pakistan 69 B6
Chilaw, Sri Lanka 66 R11
Chilcotin →, Canada 104 C4
Childers, Australia 95 D5
Childress, U.S.A. 113 H4
Chile ■, S. Amer. 128 D2
Chile Rise, Pac. Oc. 97 L18
Chilecito, Argentina 126 B2
Chilete, Peru 124 E3
Chilia, Brațul →, Romania 43 E14
Chililabombwe, Zambia . 87 E2
Chilin = Jilin, China 57 C14
Chilka L., India 67 K14
Chilko →, Canada 104 C4
Chilko L., Canada 104 C4
Chillagoe, Australia 94 B3
Chillán, Chile 126 D1
Chillicothe, Ill., U.S.A. .. 112 E10
Chillicothe, Mo., U.S.A. . 112 F8
Chillicothe, Ohio, U.S.A. 108 F4
Chilliwack, Canada 104 D4
Chilo, India 68 F5
Chiloane, I., Mozam. 89 C5
Chiloé, I. de, Chile 122 H3
Chilpancingo, Mexico ... 119 D5
Chiltern Hills, U.K. 13 F7
Chilton, U.S.A. 108 C1
Chilubi, Zambia 87 E2
Chilubula, Zambia 87 E3
Chilumba, Malawi 87 E3
Chilung, Taiwan 59 E13
Chilwa, L., Malawi 87 F4
Chimaltitán, Mexico 118 C4
Chimán, Panama 120 E4
Chimay, Belgium 17 D4
Chimbay, Uzbekistan 50 E6
Chimborazo, Ecuador ... 122 D3
Chimbote, Peru 124 E3
Chimkent = Shymkent,
  Kazakstan 50 E7
Chimoio, Mozam. 87 F3
Chimpembe, Zambia 87 D2
Chin □, Burma 67 J18
Chin Ling Shan = Qinling
  Shandi, China 56 H5
China, Mexico 119 B5
China ■, Asia 56 E3
China Lake, U.S.A. 117 K9
Chinan = Jinan, China .. 56 F9
Chinandega, Nic. 120 D2
Chinati Peak, U.S.A. 113 L2
Chincha Alta, Peru 122 E3
Chinchilla, Australia 95 D5
Chinchilla de Monte
  Aragón, Spain 33 G3
Chinchorro, Banco, Mexico 119 D7
Chinchou = Jinzhou, China 57 D11
Chincoteague, U.S.A. ... 108 G8
Chinde, Mozam. 87 F4
Chindo, S. Korea 57 G14
Chindwin →, Burma 67 J19
Chineni, India 69 C6
Chinga, Mozam. 87 F4
Chingola, Zambia 87 E2
Chingole, Malawi 87 E3
Ch'ingtao = Qingdao,
  China 57 F11
Chinguetti, Mauritania .. 78 D3
Chingune, Mozam. 89 C5
Chinhae, S. Korea 57 G15
Chinhanguanine, Mozam. 89 D5
Chinhoyi, Zimbabwe 87 F3
Chiniot, Pakistan 68 D5
Chínipas, Mexico 118 B3
Chinju, S. Korea 57 G15
Chinle, U.S.A. 115 H9
Chinmen, Taiwan 59 E13
Chinmen Tao, Taiwan ... 59 E13
Chinnampo = Nampo,
  N. Korea 57 E13
Chino, Japan 55 G9
Chino, U.S.A. 117 L9
Chino Valley, U.S.A. 115 J7
Chinon, France 18 E7
Chinook, Canada 105 C6
Chinook, U.S.A. 114 B9
Chinsali, Zambia 87 E3

Chióggia, Italy 29 C9
Chipata, Zambia 87 E3
Chiperceni, Moldova 43 C13
Chipewyan L., Canada .. 105 B9
Chipinge, Zimbabwe 87 G3
Chipiona, Spain 35 J4
Chipley, U.S.A. 109 K3
Chipman, Canada 103 C6
Chipoka, Malawi 87 E3
Chippenham, U.K. 13 F5
Chippewa →, U.S.A. ... 112 C8
Chippewa Falls, U.S.A. . 112 C9
Chipping Norton, U.K. .. 13 F6
Chiprovtsi, Bulgaria 40 C6
Chiquián, Peru 124 F3
Chiquimula, Guatemala . 120 D2
Chiquinquira, Colombia . 124 B4
Chir →, Russia 49 F6
Chirala, India 66 M12
Chiramba, Mozam. 87 F3
Chirawa, India 68 E6
Chirchiq, Uzbekistan ... 50 E7
Chiredzi, Zimbabwe 89 C5
Chiricahua Peak, U.S.A. 115 L9
Chiriquí, G. de, Panama . 120 E3
Chiriquí, L. de, Panama . 120 E3
Chirivira Falls, Zimbabwe 87 G3
Chirmiri, India 67 H13
Chirnogi, Romania 43 F11
Chirpan, Bulgaria 41 D9
Chirripó Grande, Cerro,
  Costa Rica 120 E3
Chisamba, Zambia 87 E2
Chisapani Garhi, Nepal . 67 F14
Chisasibi, Canada 102 B4
Chisholm, Canada 104 C6
Ch'ishan, Taiwan 59 F13
Chishtian Mandi, Pakistan 68 E5
Chishui, China 58 C5
Chishui He →, China ... 58 C5
Chisimaio, Somali Rep. . 77 G8
Chisimba Falls, Zambia . 87 E3
Chișinău, Moldova 43 C13
Chișineu Criș, Romania . 42 D6
Chisone →, Italy 28 D4
Chisos Mts., U.S.A. 113 L3
Chistopol, Russia 48 C10
Chita, Russia 51 D12
Chitipa, Malawi 87 D3
Chitose, Japan 54 C10
Chitral, Pakistan 66 B7
Chitré, Panama 120 E3
Chittagong, Bangla. 67 H17
Chittagong □, Bangla. .. 67 G17
Chittaurgarh, India 68 G6
Chittoor, India 66 N11
Chitungwiza, Zimbabwe . 87 F3
Chiusi, Italy 29 E8
Chiva, Spain 33 F4
Chivasso, Italy 28 C4
Chivhu, Zimbabwe 87 F3
Chivilcoy, Argentina 126 C4
Chiwanda, Tanzania 87 E3
Chixi, China 59 G9
Chizera, Zambia 87 E2
Chkalov = Orenburg,
  Russia 50 D6
Chkolovsk, Russia 48 B6
Chloride, U.S.A. 117 K12
Chlumec nad Cidlinou,
  Czech Rep. 26 A8
Chmielnik, Poland 45 H7
Cho Bo, Vietnam 64 B5
Cho-do, N. Korea 57 E13
Cho Phuoc Hai, Vietnam 65 G6
Choba, Kenya 86 B4
Chobe National Park,
  Botswana 88 B4
Chochiwŏn, S. Korea ... 57 F14
Chocianów, Poland 45 G2
Chociwel, Poland 44 E2
Choctawhatchee B., U.S.A. 107 D9
Chodecz, Poland 45 F6
Chodov, Czech Rep. 26 A5
Chodziez, Poland 45 F3
Choele Choel, Argentina 128 D3
Choix, Mexico 118 B3
Chojna, Poland 45 F1
Chojnice, Poland 44 E4
Chojnów, Poland 45 G2
Chōkai-San, Japan 54 E10
Choke, Ethiopia 81 E4
Chokurdakh, Russia 51 B15
Cholame, U.S.A. 116 K6
Cholet, France 18 E6
Choluteca, Honduras ... 120 D2
Choluteca →, Honduras 120 D2
Chom Bung, Thailand .. 64 F2
Chom Thong, Thailand . 64 C2
Choma, Zambia 87 F2
Chomen Swamp, Ethiopia 81 F4
Chomun, India 68 F6
Chomutov, Czech Rep. .. 26 A6
Chon Buri, Thailand ... 64 F3
Chon Thanh, Vietnam .. 65 G6
Chonan, S. Korea 57 F14
Chone, Ecuador 124 D3
Chong Kai, Cambodia .. 64 F4
Chong Mek, Thailand .. 64 E5
Chong'an, China 59 D12
Chongde, China 59 B13
Chongdo, S. Korea 57 G15
Chŏngha, S. Korea 57 F15
Chŏngjin, N. Korea 57 D15
Chŏngju, N. Korea 57 E13
Chŏngju, S. Korea 57 F14
Chongli, China 56 D8

Chongming, China 59 B13
Chongming Dao, China . 59 B13
Chongqing, Chongqing,
  China 58 C6
Chongqing, Sichuan, China 58 B4
Chongqing □, China 58 B7
Chongren, China 59 D11
Chongzuo, China 58 F6
Chŏnju, S. Korea 57 G14
Chonos, Arch. de los, Chile 122 H3
Chop, Ukraine 47 H2
Chopim →, Brazil 127 B5
Chorbat La, India 69 B7
Chorley, U.K. 12 D5
Chornobyl, Ukraine 47 G6
Chornomorske, Ukraine . 47 K7
Chorolque, Cerro, Bolivia 126 A2
Choroszcz, Poland 45 E9
Chorregon, Australia ... 94 C3
Chortkiv, Ukraine 47 H3
Chŏrwŏn, S. Korea 57 E14
Chorzele, Poland 45 E7
Chorzów, Poland 45 H5
Chos-Malal, Argentina .. 126 D1
Chosan, N. Korea 57 D13
Choszczno, Poland 45 E2
Choteau, U.S.A. 114 C7
Chotěboř, Czech Rep. .. 26 B8
Chotila, India 68 H4
Chowchilla, U.S.A. 116 H6
Choybalsan, Mongolia .. 60 B6
Christchurch, N.Z. 91 K4
Christchurch, U.K. 13 G6
Christian I., Canada 110 B4
Christiana, S. Africa 88 D4
Christiansfeld, Denmark . 11 J3
Christiansted, Virgin Is. . 121 C7
Christie B., Canada 105 A6
Christina →, Canada ... 105 B6
Christmas Cr. →, Australia 92 C4
Christmas Creek, Australia 92 C4
Christmas I. = Kiritimati,
  Kiribati 97 G12
Christmas I., Ind. Oc. .. 96 J2
Christopher L., Australia 93 D4
Chrudim, Czech Rep. ... 26 B8
Chrzanów, Poland 45 H6
Chtimba, Malawi 87 E3
Chu →, Kazakstan 50 E8
Chu = Shu, Kazakstan .. 50 E8
Chu →= Shu →,
  Kazakstan 52 E10
Chu →, Vietnam 64 C5
Chu Chua, Canada 104 C4
Chu Lai, Vietnam 64 E7
Chu Xian, China 59 A12
Ch'uanchou = Quanzhou,
  China 59 E12
Chuankou, China 56 G6
Chūbu □, Japan 55 F8
Chubut →, Argentina .. 122 H4
Chuchi L., Canada 104 B4
Chudovo, Russia 46 C6
Chudskoye, Oz., Russia . 9 G22
Chūgoku □, Japan 55 G6
Chūgoku-Sanchi, Japan . 55 G6
Chuguyev = Chuhuyiv,
  Ukraine 47 H9
Chugwater, U.S.A. 112 E2
Chuhuyiv, Ukraine 47 H9
Chukchi Sea, Russia ... 51 C19
Chukotskoye Nagorye,
  Russia 51 C18
Chula Vista, U.S.A. 117 N9
Chulman, Russia 51 D13
Chulucanas, Peru 124 E2
Chulym →, Russia 50 D9
Chum Phae, Thailand .. 64 D4
Chum Saeng, Thailand . 64 E3
Chumar, India 69 C8
Chumbicha, Argentina .. 126 B2
Chumerna, Bulgaria 41 D9
Chumikan, Russia 51 D14
Chumphon, Thailand ... 65 G2
Chumuare, Mozam. 87 E3
Chumunjin, S. Korea ... 57 F15
Chuna →, Russia 51 D10
Chun'an, China 59 C12
Chunchŏn, S. Korea ... 57 F14
Chunchura, India 69 H13
Chunga, Zambia 87 F2
Chunggang-ŭp, N. Korea 57 D14
Chunghwa, N. Korea ... 57 E13
Chungju, S. Korea 57 F14
Chungking = Chongqing,
  China 58 C6
Chungli, Taiwan 59 E13
Chungmu, S. Korea 57 G15
Chungt'iaoshan =
  Zhongtiao Shan, China 56 G6
Chungyang Shanmo,
  Taiwan 59 F13
Chunian, Pakistan 68 D6
Chunya, Tanzania 87 D3
Chunya □, Tanzania 86 D3
Chunyang, China 57 C15
Chuquibamba, Peru 124 G4
Chuquicamata, Chile ... 126 A2
Chur, Switz. 25 J5
Churachandpur, India .. 67 G18
Churchill →, Man.,
  Canada 105 B10
Churchill →, Nfld.,
  Canada 103 B7
Churchill, C., Canada .. 105 B10
Churchill Falls, Canada . 103 B7
Churchill L., Canada ... 105 B7

Churchill Pk., Canada .. 104 B3
Churu, India 68 E6
Churún Merú = Angel
  Falls, Venezuela 124 B6
Chushal, India 69 C8
Chusovoy, Russia 50 D6
Chuuronjang, N. Korea . 57 D15
Chuvash Republic □ =
  Chuvashia □, Russia . 48 C8
Chuvashia □, Russia ... 48 C8
Chuwārtah, Iraq 70 C5
Chuxiong, China 58 E3
Ci Xian, China 56 F8
Ciacova, Romania 42 E6
Ciadâr-Lunga, Moldova . 43 D13
Ciamis, Indonesia 63 G13
Cianjur, Indonesia 63 G12
Cianorte, Brazil 128 B6
Cibola, U.S.A. 117 M12
Cicero, U.S.A. 108 E2
Cidacos →, Spain 32 C3
Cide, Turkey 72 B5
Ciechanów, Poland 45 F7
Ciechanów □, Poland .. 45 E7
Ciechanowiec, Poland .. 45 F9
Ciechocinek, Poland ... 45 F5
Ciego de Avila, Cuba ... 120 B4
Ciénaga, Colombia 124 A4
Cienfuegos, Cuba 120 B3
Cierp, France 20 F4
Cíes, Is →, Spain 34 C2
Cieszanów, Poland 45 H10
Cieszyn, Poland 45 J5
Cieza, Spain 33 G3
Cihanbeyli, Turkey 72 C5
Cihuatlán, Mexico 118 D4
Cijara, Embalse de, Spain 35 F6
Cijulang, Indonesia 63 G13
Cilacap, Indonesia 63 G13
Çıldır, Turkey 73 B10
Çıldır Gölü, Turkey 73 B10
Cíli, China 59 C8
Cilibia, Romania 43 E12
Cilicia, Turkey 72 D5
Cill Chainnigh = Kilkenny,
  Ireland 15 D4
Cilo Dağı, Turkey 73 D10
Cima, U.S.A. 117 K11
Cimarron, Kans., U.S.A. 113 G4
Cimarron, N. Mex., U.S.A. 113 G2
Cimarron →, U.S.A. ... 113 G6
Cimișlia, Moldova 43 D13
Cimone, Mte., Italy 28 D7
Çınar, Turkey 73 D9
Çınarcık, Turkey 41 F13
Cinca →, Spain 32 D5
Cincar, Bos.-H. 42 G2
Cincinnati, U.S.A. 108 F3
Çine, Turkey 39 D10
Ciney, Belgium 17 D5
Cíngoli, Italy 29 E10
Cinigiano, Italy 29 F8
Cinto, Mte., France 21 F12
Cintruénigo, Spain 32 C3
Ciolănești din Deal,
  Romania 43 F10
Ciorani, Romania 43 F11
Ciovo, Croatia 29 E13
Circeo, Mte., Italy 30 A6
Çірçir, Turkey 72 C7
Circle, Alaska, U.S.A. .. 100 B5
Circle, Mont., U.S.A. ... 112 B2
Circleville, Ohio, U.S.A. . 108 F4
Circleville, Utah, U.S.A. 115 G7
Cirebon, Indonesia 63 G13
Ciremai, Indonesia 63 G13
Cirencester, U.K. 13 F6
Cireșu, Romania 42 F7
Cirey-sur-Vezouze, France 19 D13
Ciriè, Italy 28 C4
Cirium, Cyprus 36 E11
Ciró, Italy 31 C10
Ciró Marina, Italy 31 C10
Ciron →, France 20 D3
Cisco, U.S.A. 113 J5
Cislău, Romania 43 E11
Cisnădie, Romania 43 E9
Cisna, Poland 45 J9
Cisterna di Latina, Italy . 30 A5
Cisternino, Italy 31 B10
Cistierna, Spain 34 C5
Citeli-Ckaro = Tsiteli-
  Tsqaro, Georgia 49 K8
Citlaltépetl, Mexico 119 D5
Citrus Heights, U.S.A. .. 116 G5
Citrusdal, S. Africa 88 E2
Città della Pieve, Italy .. 29 F9
Città di Castello, Italy .. 29 E9
Città Sant' Angelo, Italy 29 F11
Cittadella, Italy 29 C8
Cittaducale, Italy 29 F9
Cittanova, Italy 31 D9
City of Edinburgh □, U.K. 14 F5
City of Glasgow □, U.K. 14 F4
Ciuc, Munții, Romania .. 43 D11
Ciucaş, Vf., Romania ... 43 E10
Ciuciuleni, Moldova 43 C13
Ciudad Altamirano, Mexico 118 D4
Ciudad Bolívar, Venezuela 124 B6
Ciudad Camargo, Mexico 118 B3
Ciudad Chetumal, Mexico 119 D7
Ciudad de Valles, Mexico 119 C5

Ciudad del Carmen, Mexico 119 D6
Ciudad del Este, Paraguay 127 B5
Ciudad Delicias = Delicias,
  Mexico 118 B3
Ciudad Guayana,
  Venezuela 124 B6
Ciudad Guerrero, Mexico 118 B3
Ciudad Guzmán, Mexico 118 D4
Ciudad Juárez, Mexico .. 118 A3
Ciudad Madero, Mexico 119 C5
Ciudad Mante, Mexico . 119 C5
Ciudad Obregón, Mexico 118 B3
Ciudad Real, Spain 35 G7
Ciudad Real □, Spain .. 35 G7
Ciudad Rodrigo, Spain . 34 E4
Ciudad Trujillo = Santo
  Domingo, Dom. Rep. . 121 C6
Ciudad Victoria, Mexico . 119 C5
Ciudadela, Spain 37 B10
Ciulnița, Romania 43 F12
Ciumeghiu, Romania ... 42 D6
Ciuperceni, Romania ... 42 F8
Civa Burnu, Turkey 72 B7
Cividale del Friuli, Italy . 29 B10
Cívita Castellana, Italy . 29 F9
Civitanova Marche, Italy 29 E10
Civitavécchia, Italy 29 F8
Civray, France 20 B4
Çivril, Turkey 39 C11
Cixerri →, Italy 30 C1
Cizre, Turkey 73 D10
Cizur Mayor, Spain 32 C3
Clackmannanshire □, U.K. 14 E5
Clacton-on-Sea, U.K. ... 13 F9
Clain →, France 18 F7
Claire, L., Canada 104 B6
Clairemont, U.S.A. 113 J4
Clairton, U.S.A. 110 F5
Clairvaux-les-Lacs, France 19 F12
Claise →, France 20 B5
Clallam Bay, U.S.A. 116 B2
Clamecy, France 19 E10
Clanton, U.S.A. 109 J2
Clanwilliam, S. Africa .. 88 E2
Clara, Ireland 15 C4
Clara →, Australia 94 B3
Claraville, U.S.A. 117 K8
Clare, Australia 95 E2
Clare, U.S.A. 108 D3
Clare □, Ireland 15 D3
Clare →, Ireland 15 C2
Clare I., Ireland 15 C1
Claremont, Calif., U.S.A. 117 L9
Claremont, N.H., U.S.A. 111 C12
Claremont Pt., Australia 94 A3
Claremore, U.S.A. 113 G7
Claremorris, Ireland ... 15 C3
Clarence →, Australia . 95 D5
Clarence →, N.Z. 91 K4
Clarence, I., Chile 128 G2
Clarence I., Antarctica .. 5 C18
Clarence Str., Australia . 92 B5
Clarence Str., U.S.A. ... 104 B2
Clarence Town, Bahamas 121 B5
Clarendon, Ark., U.S.A. 113 H9
Clarendon, Tex., U.S.A. 113 H4
Clarenville, Canada 103 C9
Claresholm, Canada 104 D6
Clarie Coast, Antarctica . 5 C9
Clarinda, U.S.A. 112 E7
Clarion, Iowa, U.S.A. .. 112 D8
Clarion, Pa., U.S.A. 110 E5
Clarion →, U.S.A. 110 E5
Clark, U.S.A. 112 C6
Clark, Pt., Canada 110 B3
Clark Fork, U.S.A. 114 B5
Clark Fork →, U.S.A. .. 114 B5
Clark Hill L., U.S.A. 109 J4
Clarkdale, U.S.A. 115 J7
Clarke City, Canada 103 B6
Clarke I., Australia 94 G4
Clarke Ra., Australia ... 94 C4
Clark's Fork →, U.S.A. 114 D9
Clark's Harbour, Canada 103 D6
Clarks Summit, U.S.A. . 111 E9
Clarksburg, U.S.A. 108 F5
Clarksdale, U.S.A. 113 H9
Clarkston, U.S.A. 114 C5
Clarksville, Ark., U.S.A. 113 H8
Clarksville, Tenn., U.S.A. 109 G2
Clarksville, Tex., U.S.A. 113 J7
Clatskanie, U.S.A. 116 D3
Claude, U.S.A. 113 H4
Claveria, Phil. 61 B4
Clay, U.S.A. 116 G5
Clay Center, U.S.A. 112 F6
Claypool, U.S.A. 115 K8
Claysville, U.S.A. 110 F4
Clayton, Idaho, U.S.A. . 114 D6
Clayton, N. Mex., U.S.A. 113 G3
Cle Elum, U.S.A. 114 C3
Clear, C., Ireland 15 E2
Clear, L., Canada 110 A7
Clear I., Ireland 15 E2
Clear L., U.S.A. 116 F2
Clear Lake, S. Dak.,
  U.S.A. 112 C6
Clear Lake, Wash., U.S.A. 114 B2
Clear Lake Reservoir,
  U.S.A. 114 F3
Clearfield, Pa., U.S.A. . 108 E6
Clearfield, Utah, U.S.A. 114 F8
Clearlake Highlands,
  U.S.A. 116 G4
Clearmont, U.S.A. 114 D10
Clearwater, Canada 104 C4
Clearwater, U.S.A. 109 M4

Clearwater →, *Alta., Canada*	104	C6
Clearwater →, *Alta., Canada*	105	B6
Clearwater Cr. →, *Canada*	104	A3
Clearwater Mts., *U.S.A.*	114	C6
Clearwater Prov. Park, *Canada*	105	C8
Cleburne, *U.S.A.*	113	J6
Clee Hills, *U.K.*	13	E5
Cleethorpes, *U.K.*	12	D7
Cleeve Cloud, *U.K.*	13	F6
Clelles, *France*	21	D9
Clerke Reef, *Australia*	92	C2
Clermont, *Australia*	94	C4
Clermont, *France*	19	C9
Clermont-en-Argonne, *France*	19	C12
Clermont-Ferrand, *France*	20	C7
Clermont-l'Hérault, *France*	20	E7
Clerval, *France*	19	E13
Clervaux, *Lux.*	17	D6
Cles, *Italy*	28	B8
Clevedon, *U.K.*	13	F5
Cleveland, *Australia*	95	D5
Cleveland, *Miss., U.S.A.*	113	J9
Cleveland, *Ohio, U.S.A.*	110	E3
Cleveland, *Okla., U.S.A.*	113	G6
Cleveland, *Tenn., U.S.A.*	109	H3
Cleveland, *Tex., U.S.A.*	113	K7
Cleveland, *C., Australia*	94	B4
Cleveland Heights, *U.S.A.*	110	E3
Cleveländia, *Brazil*	127	B5
Clew B., *Ireland*	15	C2
Clewiston, *U.S.A.*	109	M5
Clifden, *Ireland*	15	C1
Clifden, *N.Z.*	91	M1
Cliffdell, *U.S.A.*	116	D5
Clifton, *Australia*	95	D5
Clifton, *Ariz., U.S.A.*	115	K9
Clifton, *Tex., U.S.A.*	113	K6
Clifton Beach, *Australia*	94	B4
Clifton Forge, *U.S.A.*	108	G6
Clifton Hills, *Australia*	95	D2
Climax, *Canada*	105	D7
Clinch →, *U.S.A.*	109	H3
Clingmans Dome, *U.S.A.*	109	H4
Clint, *U.S.A.*	115	L10
Clinton, *B.C., Canada*	104	C4
Clinton, *Ont., Canada*	102	D3
Clinton, *N.Z.*	91	M2
Clinton, *Ark., U.S.A.*	113	H8
Clinton, *Ill., U.S.A.*	112	E10
Clinton, *Ind., U.S.A.*	108	F2
Clinton, *Iowa, U.S.A.*	112	E9
Clinton, *Mass., U.S.A.*	111	D13
Clinton, *Mo., U.S.A.*	112	F8
Clinton, *N.C., U.S.A.*	109	H6
Clinton, *Okla., U.S.A.*	113	H5
Clinton, *S.C., U.S.A.*	109	H5
Clinton, *Tenn., U.S.A.*	109	G3
Clinton, *Wash., U.S.A.*	116	C4
Clinton C., *Australia*	94	C5
Clinton Colden L., *Canada*	100	B9
Clintonville, *U.S.A.*	112	C10
Clipperton, I., *Pac. Oc.*	97	F17
Clisham, *U.K.*	14	D2
Clisson, *France*	18	E5
Clitheroe, *U.K.*	12	D5
Clive L., *Canada*	104	A5
Cloates, Pt., *Australia*	92	D1
Clocolan, *S. Africa*	89	D4
Clodomira, *Argentina*	126	B3
Clogher Hd., *Ireland*	15	C5
Clonakilty, *Ireland*	15	E3
Clonakilty B., *Ireland*	15	E3
Cloncurry, *Australia*	94	C3
Cloncurry →, *Australia*	94	B3
Clondalkin, *Ireland*	15	C5
Clones, *Ireland*	15	B4
Clonmel, *Ireland*	15	D4
Cloppenburg, *Germany*	24	C4
Cloquet, *U.S.A.*	112	B8
Clorinda, *Argentina*	126	B4
Cloud Peak, *U.S.A.*	114	D10
Cloudcroft, *U.S.A.*	115	K11
Cloverdale, *U.S.A.*	116	G4
Clovis, *Calif., U.S.A.*	116	J7
Clovis, *N. Mex., U.S.A.*	113	H3
Cloyes-sur-le-Loir, *France*	18	E8
Cluj □, *Romania*	43	D8
Cluj-Napoca, *Romania*	43	D8
Clunes, *Australia*	95	F3
Cluny, *France*	19	F11
Cluses, *France*	19	F13
Clusone, *Italy*	28	C6
Clutha →, *N.Z.*	91	M2
Clwyd □, *U.K.*	12	D4
Clyde, *N.Z.*	91	L2
Clyde, *U.S.A.*	110	C8
Clyde →, *U.K.*	14	F4
Clyde, Firth of, *U.K.*	14	F3
Clyde River, *Canada*	101	A13
Clydebank, *U.K.*	14	F4
Clymer, *U.S.A.*	110	D5
Ćmielów, *Poland*	45	H8
Côa →, *Portugal*	34	D3
Coachella, *U.S.A.*	117	M10
Coachella Canal, *U.S.A.*	117	N12
Coahoma, *U.S.A.*	113	J4
Coahuayana →, *Mexico*	118	D4
Coahuayutla, *Mexico*	118	D4
Coahuila □, *Mexico*	118	B4
Coal →, *Canada*	104	B3
Coalane, *Mozam.*	87	F4
Coalcomán, *Mexico*	118	D4
Coaldale, *Canada*	104	D6
Coalgate, *U.S.A.*	113	H6
Coalinga, *U.S.A.*	116	J6
Coalisland, *U.K.*	15	B5
Coalville, *U.K.*	12	E6
Coalville, *U.S.A.*	114	F8
Coari, *Brazil*	124	D6
Coast □, *Kenya*	86	C4
Coast Mts., *Canada*	104	C3
Coast Ranges, *U.S.A.*	116	G4
Coatbridge, *U.K.*	14	F4
Coatepec, *Mexico*	119	D5
Coatepeque, *Guatemala*	120	D1
Coatesville, *U.S.A.*	108	F8
Coaticook, *Canada*	103	C5
Coats I., *Canada*	101	B11
Coats Land, *Antarctica*	5	D1
Coatzacoalcos, *Mexico*	119	D6
Cobadin, *Romania*	43	F13
Cobalt, *Canada*	102	C4
Cobán, *Guatemala*	120	C1
Çobanlar, *Turkey*	39	C12
Cobar, *Australia*	95	E4
Cóbh, *Ireland*	15	E3
Cobham, *Australia*	95	E3
Cobija, *Bolivia*	124	F5
Cobleskill, *U.S.A.*	111	D10
Coboconk, *Canada*	110	B6
Cobourg, *Canada*	102	D4
Cobourg Pen., *Australia*	92	B5
Cobram, *Australia*	95	F4
Cobre, *U.S.A.*	114	F6
Cóbué, *Mozam.*	87	E3
Coburg, *Germany*	25	E6
Coca, *Spain*	34	D6
Cocanada = Kakinada, *India*	67	L13
Cocentaina, *Spain*	33	G4
Cochabamba, *Bolivia*	124	G5
Cochem, *Germany*	25	E3
Cochemane, *Mozam.*	87	F3
Cochin, *India*	66	Q10
Cochin China, *Vietnam*	65	G6
Cochise, *U.S.A.*	115	K9
Cochran, *U.S.A.*	109	J4
Cochrane, *Alta., Canada*	104	C6
Cochrane, *Ont., Canada*	102	C3
Cochrane, *Chile*	128	F2
Cochrane →, *Canada*	105	B8
Cochrane, L., *Chile*	128	F2
Cockburn, *Australia*	95	E3
Cockburn, Canal, *Chile*	122	J3
Cockburn I., *Canada*	102	C3
Cockburn Ra., *Australia*	92	C4
Cockermouth, *U.K.*	12	C4
Cocklebiddy Motel, *Australia*	93	F4
Coco →, *Cent. Amer.*	120	D3
Cocoa, *U.S.A.*	109	L5
Cocobeach, *Gabon*	84	D1
Cocora, *Romania*	43	F12
Cocos, I. del, *Pac. Oc.*	97	G19
Cocos Is., *Ind. Oc.*	96	J1
Cod, C., *U.S.A.*	107	B12
Codajás, *Brazil*	124	D6
Coderre, *Canada*	105	C7
Codigoro, *Italy*	29	D9
Codlea, *Romania*	43	E10
Codó, *Brazil*	125	D10
Codogno, *Italy*	28	C6
Codróipo, *Italy*	29	C10
Codru, Munţii, *Romania*	42	D7
Cody, *U.S.A.*	114	D9
Coe Hill, *Canada*	102	D4
Coelemu, *Chile*	126	D1
Coen, *Australia*	94	A3
Coesfeld, *Germany*	24	D3
Cœur d'Alene, *U.S.A.*	114	C5
Cœur d'Alene L., *U.S.A.*	114	C5
Coevorden, *Neths.*	17	B6
Cofete, *Canary Is.*	37	F5
Coffeyville, *U.S.A.*	113	G7
Coffin B., *Australia*	95	E2
Coffin Bay Peninsula, *Australia*	95	E2
Coffs Harbour, *Australia*	95	E5
Cofrentes, *Spain*	33	F3
Cogalnic →, *Moldova*	43	E14
Cogealac, *Romania*	43	F13
Coghinas →, *Italy*	30	B1
Coghinas, L. del, *Italy*	30	B2
Cognac, *France*	20	C3
Cogne, *Italy*	28	C4
Cogolin, *France*	21	E10
Cogolludo, *Spain*	32	E1
Cohagen, *U.S.A.*	114	C10
Cohoes, *U.S.A.*	111	D11
Cohuna, *Australia*	95	F3
Coiba, I., *Panama*	120	E3
Coig →, *Argentina*	128	G3
Coigeach, Rubha, *U.K.*	14	C3
Coihaique, *Chile*	128	F2
Coimbatore, *India*	66	P10
Coimbra, *Brazil*	124	G7
Coimbra, *Portugal*	34	E2
Coimbra □, *Portugal*	34	E2
Coín, *Spain*	35	J6
Coipasa, Salar de, *Bolivia*	124	G5
Cojimies, *Ecuador*	124	C3
Cojocna, *Romania*	43	D8
Cojutepequé, *El Salv.*	120	D2
Čoka, *Serbia, Yug.*	42	E5
Cokeville, *U.S.A.*	114	E8
Colac, *Australia*	95	F3
Colatina, *Brazil*	125	G10
Colbeck, C., *Antarctica*	5	D13
Colbinabbin, *Australia*	95	F3
Colborne, *Canada*	110	C7
Colby, *U.S.A.*	112	F4
Colchagua □, *Chile*	126	C1
Colchester, *U.K.*	13	F8
Coldstream, *Canada*	104	C5
Coldwater, *Canada*	110	B5
Coldwater, *U.S.A.*	113	G5
Colebrook, *Australia*	94	G4
Colebrook, *U.S.A.*	111	B13
Coleman, *Canada*	104	D6
Coleman, *U.S.A.*	113	K5
Coleman →, *Australia*	94	B3
Colenso, *S. Africa*	89	D4
Coleraine, *Australia*	95	F3
Coleraine, *U.K.*	15	A5
Coleridge, L., *N.Z.*	91	K3
Colesberg, *S. Africa*	88	E4
Coleville, *U.S.A.*	116	G7
Colfax, *Calif., U.S.A.*	116	F6
Colfax, *La., U.S.A.*	113	K8
Colfax, *Wash., U.S.A.*	114	C5
Colhué Huapi, L., *Argentina*	128	F3
Colibaşi, *Moldova*	43	E13
Colibaşi, *Romania*	43	F9
Cólico, *Italy*	28	B6
Coligny, *France*	19	F12
Coligny, *S. Africa*	89	D4
Colima, *Mexico*	118	D4
Colima □, *Mexico*	118	D4
Colima, Nevado de, *Mexico*	118	D4
Colina, *Chile*	126	C1
Colina do Norte, *Guinea-Biss.*	82	C2
Colinas, *Brazil*	125	E10
Colindres, *Spain*	34	B7
Coll, *U.K.*	14	E2
Collaguasi, *Chile*	126	A2
Collarada, Peña, *Spain*	32	C4
Collarenebri, *Australia*	95	D4
Collbran, *U.S.A.*	115	G10
Colle di Val d'Elsa, *Italy*	28	E8
Collécchio, *Italy*	28	D7
Colleen Bawn, *Zimbabwe*	87	G2
College Park, *U.S.A.*	109	J3
College Station, *U.S.A.*	113	K6
Collesalvetti, *Italy*	28	E7
Collette, *Canada*	103	C6
Collie, *Australia*	93	F2
Collier B., *Australia*	92	C3
Collier Ra., *Australia*	92	D2
Collina, Passo di, *Italy*	28	D7
Collingwood, *Canada*	102	B2
Collingwood, *N.Z.*	91	J4
Collins, *Canada*	102	B2
Collinsville, *Australia*	94	C4
Collipulli, *Chile*	126	D1
Collooney, *Ireland*	15	B3
Colmar, *France*	19	D14
Colmars, *France*	21	D10
Colmenar, *Spain*	35	J6
Colmenar de Oreja, *Spain*	34	E7
Colmenar Viejo, *Spain*	34	E7
Colo →, *Australia*	95	E5
Cologne = Köln, *Germany*	24	E2
Colom, I. d'en, *Spain*	37	B11
Coloma, *U.S.A.*	116	G6
Colomb-Béchar = Béchar, *Algeria*	78	B5
Colombey-les-Belles, *France*	19	D12
Colombey-les-Deux-Églises, *France*	19	D11
Colombia ■, *S. Amer.*	124	C4
Colombian Basin, *S. Amer.*	98	H12
Colombo, *Sri Lanka*	66	R11
Colome, *U.S.A.*	112	D5
Colomiers, *France*	20	E5
Colón, *Argentina*	126	C4
Colón, *Cuba*	120	B3
Colón, *Panama*	120	E4
Colona, *Australia*	93	F5
Colonia de Sant Jordi, *Spain*	37	B9
Colonia del Sacramento, *Uruguay*	126	C4
Colonia Dora, *Argentina*	126	B3
Colonial Heights, *U.S.A.*	108	G7
Colonna, C., *Italy*	31	C10
Colonsay, *Canada*	105	C7
Colonsay, *U.K.*	14	E2
Colorado □, *U.S.A.*	115	G10
Colorado →, *Argentina*	128	D4
Colorado →, *N. Amer.*	115	L6
Colorado →, *U.S.A.*	113	L7
Colorado City, *U.S.A.*	113	J4
Colorado Desert, *U.S.A.*	106	D3
Colorado Plateau, *U.S.A.*	115	H8
Colorado River Aqueduct, *U.S.A.*	117	L12
Colorado Springs, *U.S.A.*	112	F2
Colorno, *Italy*	28	D7
Colotlán, *Mexico*	118	C4
Colton, *N.Y., U.S.A.*	111	B10
Colton, *Wash., U.S.A.*	114	C5
Columbia, *La., U.S.A.*	113	J8
Columbia, *Miss., U.S.A.*	113	K10
Columbia, *Mo., U.S.A.*	112	F8
Columbia, *Pa., U.S.A.*	111	F8
Columbia, *S.C., U.S.A.*	109	J5
Columbia, *Tenn., U.S.A.*	109	H2
Columbia →, *U.S.A.*	114	C1
Columbia, C., *Canada*	4	A4
Columbia, District of □, *U.S.A.*	108	F7
Columbia, Mt., *Canada*	104	C5
Columbia Basin, *U.S.A.*	114	C4
Columbia Falls, *U.S.A.*	114	B6
Columbia Heights, *U.S.A.*	112	C8
Columbiana, *U.S.A.*	110	F4
Columbretes, Is., *Spain*	32	F5
Columbus, *Ga., U.S.A.*	109	J3
Columbus, *Ind., U.S.A.*	108	F3
Columbus, *Kans., U.S.A.*	113	G7
Columbus, *Miss., U.S.A.*	109	J1
Columbus, *Mont., U.S.A.*	114	D9
Columbus, *N. Dak., U.S.A.*	112	A3
Columbus, *N. Mex., U.S.A.*	115	L10
Columbus, *Nebr., U.S.A.*	112	E6
Columbus, *Ohio, U.S.A.*	108	F4
Columbus, *Tex., U.S.A.*	113	L6
Columbus, *Wis., U.S.A.*	112	D10
Colunga, *Spain*	34	B5
Colusa, *U.S.A.*	116	F4
Colville, *U.S.A.*	114	B5
Colville →, *U.S.A.*	100	A4
Colville, C., *N.Z.*	91	G5
Colwyn Bay, *U.K.*	12	D4
Coma, *Ethiopia*	81	F4
Comácchio, *Italy*	29	D9
Comalcalco, *Mexico*	119	D6
Comallo, *Argentina*	128	E2
Comana, *Romania*	43	F11
Comanche, *Okla., U.S.A.*	113	H6
Comanche, *Tex., U.S.A.*	113	K5
Comăneşti, *Romania*	43	D11
Comarnic, *Romania*	43	E10
Comayagua, *Honduras*	120	D2
Combahee →, *U.S.A.*	109	J5
Combeaufontaine, *France*	19	E12
Comber, *Canada*	110	D2
Comber, *U.K.*	15	B6
Comblain-au-Pont, *Belgium*	17	D5
Combourg, *France*	18	D5
Combrailles, *France*	19	F9
Combronde, *France*	20	C7
Comeragh Mts., *Ireland*	15	D4
Comet, *Australia*	94	C4
Comilla, *Bangla.*	67	H17
Comino, *Malta*	36	C1
Comino, C., *Italy*	30	B2
Cómiso, *Italy*	31	F7
Comitán, *Mexico*	119	D6
Commentry, *France*	19	F9
Commerce, *Ga., U.S.A.*	109	H4
Commerce, *Tex., U.S.A.*	113	J7
Commercy, *France*	19	D12
Committee B., *Canada*	101	B11
Commonwealth B., *Antarctica*	5	C10
Commoron Cr. →, *Australia*	95	D5
Communism Pk. = Kommunizma, Pik, *Tajikistan*	50	F8
Como, *Italy*	28	C6
Como, L. di, *Italy*	28	B6
Comodoro Rivadavia, *Argentina*	128	F3
Comorâşte, *Romania*	42	E6
Comorin, C., *India*	66	Q10
Comoro Is. = Comoros ■, *Ind. Oc.*	77	H8
Comoros ■, *Ind. Oc.*	77	H8
Comox, *Canada*	104	D4
Compiègne, *France*	19	C9
Comporta, *Portugal*	35	G2
Compostela, *Mexico*	118	C4
Comprida, I., *Brazil*	127	A6
Compton, *U.S.A.*	117	M8
Compton Downs, *Australia*	95	E4
Comrat, *Moldova*	43	E13
Con Cuong, *Vietnam*	64	C5
Con Son, *Vietnam*	65	H6
Conakry, *Guinea*	82	D2
Conara Junction, *Australia*	94	G4
Concarneau, *France*	18	E3
Conceição, *Mozam.*	87	F4
Conceição da Barra, *Brazil*	125	G11
Conceição do Araguaia, *Brazil*	125	E9
Concepción, *Argentina*	126	B2
Concepción, *Bolivia*	124	G6
Concepción, *Chile*	126	D1
Concepción, *Mexico*	119	D6
Concepción, *Paraguay*	126	A4
Concepción □, *Chile*	126	D1
Concepción →, *Mexico*	118	A2
Concepción, Est. de, *Chile*	128	G2
Concepción, L., *Bolivia*	124	G6
Concepción, Punta, *Mexico*	118	B2
Concepción del Oro, *Mexico*	118	C4
Concepción del Uruguay, *Argentina*	126	C4
Conception, Pt., *U.S.A.*	117	L6
Conception B., *Namibia*	88	C1
Conception I., *Bahamas*	121	B4
Concession, *Zimbabwe*	87	F3
Conchas Dam, *U.S.A.*	113	H2
Conche, *Canada*	103	B8
Concho, *U.S.A.*	115	J9
Concho →, *U.S.A.*	113	K5
Conchos →, *Chihuahua, Mexico*	118	B4
Conchos →, *Tamaulipas, Mexico*	119	B5
Concord, *Calif., U.S.A.*	116	H4
Concord, *N.C., U.S.A.*	109	H5
Concord, *N.H., U.S.A.*	111	C13
Concordia, *Argentina*	126	C4
Concórdia, *Brazil*	124	D5
Concordia, *Mexico*	118	C3
Concordia, *U.S.A.*	112	F6
Concrete, *U.S.A.*	114	B3
Condamine, *Australia*	95	D5
Condat, *France*	20	C6
Conde, *U.S.A.*	112	C5
Condé-sur-Noireau, *France*	18	D6
Condeúba, *Brazil*	125	F10
Condobolin, *Australia*	95	E4
Condom, *France*	20	E4
Condon, *U.S.A.*	114	D3
Conegliano, *Italy*	29	C9
Conejera, I. = Conills, I. des, *Spain*	37	B9
Conejos, *Mexico*	118	B4
Confolens, *France*	20	B4
Confuso →, *Paraguay*	126	B4
Congaz, *Moldova*	43	D13
Congjiang, *China*	58	E7
Congleton, *U.K.*	12	D5
Congo (Kinshasa) = Congo, Dem. Rep. of the ■, *Africa*	84	E4
Congo ■, *Africa*	84	E3
Congo →, *Africa*	84	F2
Congo, Dem. Rep. of the ■, *Africa*	84	E4
Congo Basin, *Africa*	76	G6
Congonhas, *Brazil*	127	A7
Congress, *U.S.A.*	115	J7
Conil = Conil de la Frontera, *Spain*	35	J4
Conil de la Frontera, *Spain*	35	J4
Conills, I. des, *Spain*	37	B9
Coniston, *Canada*	102	C3
Conjeeveram = Kanchipuram, *India*	66	N11
Conjuboy, *Australia*	94	B3
Conklin, *Canada*	105	B6
Conlea, *Australia*	95	E3
Conn, L., *Ireland*	15	B2
Connacht □, *Ireland*	15	C2
Conneaut, *U.S.A.*	110	E4
Connecticut □, *U.S.A.*	111	E12
Connecticut →, *U.S.A.*	111	E12
Connell, *U.S.A.*	114	C4
Connellsville, *U.S.A.*	110	F5
Connemara, *Ireland*	15	C2
Connemaugh →, *U.S.A.*	110	F5
Connerré, *France*	18	D7
Connersville, *U.S.A.*	108	F3
Connors Ra., *Australia*	94	C4
Conoble, *Australia*	95	E3
Conques, *France*	20	D6
Conquest, *Canada*	105	C7
Conrad, *U.S.A.*	114	B8
Conran, C., *Australia*	95	F4
Conroe, *U.S.A.*	113	K7
Conselheiro Lafaiete, *Brazil*	127	A7
Conselve, *Italy*	29	C8
Consett, *U.K.*	12	C6
Consort, *Canada*	105	C6
Constance = Konstanz, *Germany*	25	H5
Constance, L. = Bodensee, *Europe*	25	H5
Constanţa, *Romania*	43	F13
Constanţa □, *Romania*	43	F13
Constantina, *Spain*	35	H5
Constantine, *Algeria*	78	A7
Constitución, *Chile*	126	D1
Constitución, *Uruguay*	126	C4
Consuegra, *Spain*	35	F7
Consul, *Canada*	105	D7
Contact, *U.S.A.*	114	F6
Contai, *India*	69	J12
Contamana, *Peru*	124	E4
Contarina, *Italy*	29	C9
Contas →, *Brazil*	125	F11
Contes, *France*	21	E11
Contoocook, *U.S.A.*	111	C13
Contra Costa, *Mozam.*	89	D5
Contres, *France*	18	E8
Contrexéville, *France*	19	D12
Conversano, *Italy*	31	B10
Conway = Conwy, *U.K.*	12	D4
Conway = Conwy →, *U.K.*	12	D4
Conway, *Ark., U.S.A.*	113	H8
Conway, *N.H., U.S.A.*	111	C13
Conway, *S.C., U.S.A.*	109	J6
Conway, L., *Australia*	95	D2
Conwy, *U.K.*	12	D4
Conwy →, *U.K.*	12	D4
Conwy □, *U.K.*	12	D4
Coober Pedy, *Australia*	95	D1
Cooch Behar = Koch Bihar, *India*	67	F16
Coodardy, *Australia*	93	E2
Cook, *Australia*	93	F5
Cook, *U.S.A.*	112	B8
Cook, B., *Chile*	128	H3
Cook, Mt., *N.Z.*	91	K3
Cook Inlet, *U.S.A.*	100	C4
Cook Is., *Pac. Oc.*	97	J12
Cook Strait, *N.Z.*	91	J5
Cookeville, *U.S.A.*	109	G3
Cookhouse, *S. Africa*	88	E4
Cookshire, *Canada*	111	A13
Cookstown, *U.K.*	15	B5
Cooksville, *Canada*	110	C5
Cooktown, *Australia*	94	B4
Coolabah, *Australia*	95	E4
Cooladdi, *Australia*	95	D4
Coolah, *Australia*	95	E4
Coolamon, *Australia*	95	E4

Coolangatta, *Australia* 95 D5
Coolgardie, *Australia* 93 F3
Coolibah, *Australia* 92 C5
Coolidge, *U.S.A.* 115 K8
Coolidge Dam, *U.S.A.* ... 115 K8
Cooma, *Australia* 95 F4
Coon Rapids, *U.S.A.* 112 C8
Coonabarabran, *Australia* . 95 E4
Coonamble, *Australia* 95 E4
Coonana, *Australia* 93 F3
Coondapoor, *India* 66 N9
Coongie, *Australia* 95 D3
Coongoola, *Australia* 95 D4
Cooninie, L., *Australia* ... 95 D2
Cooper, *U.S.A.* 113 J7
Cooper →, *U.S.A.* 109 J4
Cooper Cr. →, *Australia* . 95 D2
Cooperstown, *N. Dak.,*
  U.S.A. 112 B5
Cooperstown, *N.Y., U.S.A.* 111 D10
Coorabie, *Australia* 93 F5
Coorabulka, *Australia* 94 C3
Coorow, *Australia* 93 E2
Cooroy, *Australia* 95 D5
Coos Bay, *U.S.A.* 114 E1
Cootamundra, *Australia* .. 95 E4
Cootehill, *Ireland* 15 B4
Cooyar, *Australia* 95 D5
Cooyeana, *Australia* 94 C2
Copahue Paso, *Argentina* . 126 D1
Copainalá, *Mexico* 119 D6
Copalnic Mănăştur,
  Romania 43 C8
Copán, *Honduras* 120 D2
Cope, *U.S.A.* 112 F3
Cope, C., *Spain* 33 H3
Copenhagen = København,
  Denmark 11 J6
Copertino, *Italy* 31 B11
Copiapó, *Chile* 126 B1
Copiapó →, *Chile* 126 B1
Copley, *Australia* 95 E2
Copp L., *Canada* 104 A6
Copparo, *Italy* 29 D8
Coppename →, *Surinam* . 125 B7
Copper Cliff, *Canada* 102 C3
Copper Harbor, *U.S.A.* .. 108 B2
Copper Queen, *Zimbabwe* 87 F2
Copperbelt □, *Zambia* ... 87 E2
Coppermine = Kugluktuk,
  Canada 100 B8
Coppermine →, *Canada* .. 100 B8
Copperopolis, *U.S.A.* 116 H6
Copşa Mică, *Romania* 43 D9
Coquet →, *U.K.* 12 B6
Coquilhatville =
  Mbandaka,
  Dem. Rep. of the Congo 84 D3
Coquille, *U.S.A.* 114 E1
Coquimbo, *Chile* 126 C1
Coquimbo □, *Chile* 126 C1
Corabia, *Romania* 43 G9
Coracora, *Peru* 124 G4
Coral Gables, *U.S.A.* 109 N5
Coral Sea, *Pac. Oc.* 96 J7
Coral Springs, *U.S.A.* ... 109 M5
Coraopolis, *U.S.A.* 110 F4
Corato, *Italy* 31 A9
Corbeil-Essonnes, *France* . 19 D9
Corbie, *France* 19 C9
Corbières, *France* 20 F6
Corbigny, *France* 19 E10
Corbin, *U.S.A.* 108 G3
Corbones →, *Spain* 35 H5
Corby, *U.K.* 13 E7
Corcaigh = Cork, *Ireland* . 15 E3
Corcoran, *U.S.A.* 116 J7
Cordele, *U.S.A.* 109 K4
Cordell, *U.S.A.* 113 H5
Cordenòns, *Italy* 29 C9
Cordes, *France* 20 D5
Córdoba, *Argentina* 126 C3
Córdoba, *Mexico* 119 D5
Córdoba, *Spain* 35 H6
Córdoba □, *Argentina* ... 126 C3
Córdoba □, *Spain* 35 G6
Córdoba, Sierra de,
  Argentina 126 C3
Cordon, *Phil.* 61 C4
Cordova, *Ala., U.S.A.* ... 109 J2
Cordova, *Alaska, U.S.A.* . 100 B5
Corella, *Spain* 32 C3
Corella →, *Australia* 94 B3
Corfield, *Australia* 94 C3
Corfu, Str. of, *Greece* ... 36 A4
Corgo = O Corgo, *Spain* . 34 C3
Cori, *Italy* 30 A5
Coria, *Spain* 34 F4
Coria del Río, *Spain* 35 H4
Coriglíano Cálabro, *Italy* . 31 C9
Coringa Is., *Australia* 94 B4
Corinna, *Australia* 94 G4
Corinth = Kórinthos,
  Greece 38 D4
Corinth, *Miss., U.S.A.* ... 109 H1
Corinth, *N.Y., U.S.A.* ... 111 C11
Corinth, G. of =
  Korinthiakós Kólpos,
  Greece 38 C4
Corinth Canal, *Greece* ... 38 D4
Corinto, *Brazil* 125 G10
Corinto, *Nic.* 120 D2
Cork, *Ireland* 15 E3
Cork □, *Ireland* 15 E3
Cork Harbour, *Ireland* ... 15 E3
Corlay, *France* 18 D3

Corleone, *Italy* 30 E6
Corleto Perticara, *Italy* ... 31 B9
Çorlu, *Turkey* 41 E11
Cormack L., *Canada* 104 A4
Cormòns, *Italy* 29 C10
Cormorant, *Canada* 105 C8
Cormorant L., *Canada* ... 105 C8
Corn Is. = Maíz, Is. del,
  Nic. 120 D3
Cornélio Procópio, *Brazil* . 127 A5
Cornell, *U.S.A.* 112 C9
Corner Brook, *Canada* ... 103 C8
Corneşti, *Moldova* 43 C13
Corníglio, *Italy* 28 D7
Corning, *Ark., U.S.A.* ... 113 G9
Corning, *Calif., U.S.A.* .. 114 G2
Corning, *Iowa, U.S.A.* .. 112 E7
Corning, *N.Y., U.S.A.* ... 110 D7
Corno Grande, *Italy* 29 F10
Cornwall, *Canada* 102 C5
Cornwall □, *U.K.* 13 G3
Corny Pt., *Australia* 95 E2
Coro, *Venezuela* 124 A5
Coroatá, *Brazil* 125 D10
Corocoro, *Bolivia* 124 G5
Coroico, *Bolivia* 124 G5
Coromandel, *N.Z.* 91 G5
Coromandel Coast, *India* . 66 N12
Corona, *Australia* 95 E3
Corona, *Calif., U.S.A.* ... 117 M9
Corona, *N. Mex., U.S.A.* 117 J11
Coronado, *U.S.A.* 117 N9
Coronado, B. de
  Costa Rica 120 E3
Coronados, Is. los, *U.S.A.* 117 N9
Coronation, *Canada* 104 C6
Coronation Gulf, *Canada* . 100 B9
Coronation I., *Antarctica* . 5 C18
Coronation I., *U.S.A.* 104 B2
Coronation Is., *Australia* . 92 B3
Coronda, *Argentina* 126 C3
Coronel, *Chile* 126 D1
Coronel Bogado, *Paraguay* 126 B4
Coronel Dorrego,
  Argentina 126 D3
Coronel Oviedo, *Paraguay* 126 B4
Coronel Pringles, *Argentina* 126 D3
Coronel Suárez, *Argentina* 126 D3
Coronel Vidal, *Argentina* . 126 D4
Coropuna, Nevado, *Peru* . 124 G4
Çorovoda, *Albania* 40 F4
Corowa, *Australia* 95 F4
Corozal, *Belize* 119 D7
Corps, *France* 21 D9
Corpus, *Argentina* 127 B4
Corpus Christi, *U.S.A.* ... 113 M6
Corpus Christi, L., *U.S.A.* 113 L6
Corral de Almaguer, *Spain* 34 F7
Corralejo, *Canary Is.* 37 F6
Corraun Pen., *Ireland* 15 C2
Corréggio, *Italy* 28 D7
Correntes →, *France* 20 C5
Corrèze □, *France* 20 C5
Corrèze →, *France* 20 C5
Corrib, L., *Ireland* 15 C2
Corridónia, *Italy* 29 E10
Corrientes, *Argentina* 126 B4
Corrientes □, *Argentina* .. 126 B4
Corrientes →, *Argentina* .. 126 C4
Corrientes →, *Peru* 124 D4
Corrientes, C., *Colombia* . 124 B3
Corrientes, C., *Cuba* 120 B3
Corrientes, C., *Mexico* ... 118 C3
Corrigan, *U.S.A.* 113 K7
Corrigin, *Australia* 93 F2
Corry, *U.S.A.* 110 E5
Corse, *France* 21 G13
Corse, C., *France* 21 E13
Corse-du-Sud □, *France* . 21 G13
Corsica = Corse, *France* . 21 G13
Corsicana, *U.S.A.* 113 J6
Corte, *France* 21 F13
Corte Pinto, *Portugal* 35 H3
Cortegana, *Spain* 35 H4
Cortez, *U.S.A.* 115 H9
Cortina d'Ampezzo, *Italy* . 29 B9
Cortland, *U.S.A.* 111 D8
Cortona, *Italy* 29 E8
Coruche, *Portugal* 35 G2
Çoruh →, *Turkey* 49 K5
Çorum, *Turkey* 72 B6
Corumbá, *Brazil* 124 G7
Corund, *Romania* 43 D10
Corunna = A Coruña,
  Spain 34 B2
Corvallis, *U.S.A.* 114 D2
Corvette, L. de la, *Canada* 102 B5
Corydon, *U.S.A.* 112 E8
Cosalá, *Mexico* 118 C3
Cosamaloapan, *Mexico* ... 119 D5
Cosenza, *Italy* 31 C9
Coşereni, *Romania* 43 F11
Coshocton, *U.S.A.* 110 F3
Cosmo Newberry, *Australia* 93 E3
Cosne-Cours-sur-Loire,
  France 19 E9
Coso Junction, *U.S.A.* ... 117 J9
Coso Pk., *U.S.A.* 117 J9
Cospeito, *Spain* 34 B3
Cosquín, *Argentina* 126 C3
Cossato, *Italy* 28 C5
Cossé-le-Vivien, *France* ... 18 E6
Cosson →, *France* 18 E8
Costa Blanca, *Spain* 33 G4
Costa Brava, *Spain* 32 D8
Costa del Sol, *Spain* 35 J6
Costa Dorada, *Spain* 32 D6

Costa Mesa, *U.S.A.* 117 M9
Costa Rica ■, *Cent. Amer.* 120 E3
Costa Smeralda, *Italy* 30 A2
Costeşti, *Romania* 43 F9
Costigliole d'Asti, *Italy* ... 28 D5
Costilla, *U.S.A.* 115 H11
Cosumnes →, *U.S.A.* ... 116 G5
Coswig, *Sachsen, Germany* 24 D9
Coswig, *Sachsen-Anhalt,*
  Germany 24 D8
Cotabato, *Phil.* 61 H6
Cotagaita, *Bolivia* 126 A2
Côte d'Azur, *France* 21 E11
Côte-d'Ivoire = Ivory
  Coast ■, *Africa* 82 D4
Côte-d'Or □, *France* 19 E11
Côte-d'Or □, *France* 19 E11
Coteau des Prairies, *U.S.A.* 112 C6
Coteau du Missouri, *U.S.A.* 112 B4
Coteau Landing, *Canada* . 111 A10
Cotentin, *France* 18 C5
Côtes-d'Armor □, *France* . 18 D4
Côtes de Meuse, *France* .. 19 C12
Côtes-du-Nord = Côtes-
  d'Armor □, *France* 18 D4
Cotiella, *Spain* 32 C5
Cotillo, *Canary Is.* 37 F5
Cotiujeni, *Moldova* 43 C13
Cotonou, *Benin* 83 D5
Cotopaxi, *Ecuador* 122 D3
Cotronei, *Italy* 31 C9
Cotswold Hills, *U.K.* 13 F5
Cottage Grove, *U.S.A.* ... 114 E2
Cottbus, *Germany* 24 D10
Cottonwood, *U.S.A.* 115 J7
Cotulla, *U.S.A.* 113 L5
Coubre, Pte. de la, *France* 20 C2
Couches, *France* 19 F11
Couço, *Portugal* 35 G2
Coudersport, *U.S.A.* 110 E6
Couedic, C. du, *Australia* . 95 F2
Couëron, *France* 18 E5
Couesnon →, *France* 18 D5
Couhé, *France* 20 B4
Coulanges-sur-Yonne,
  France 19 E10
Coulee City, *U.S.A.* 114 C4
Coulman I., *Antarctica* ... 5 D11
Coulommiers, *France* 19 D10
Coulon →, *France* 21 E9
Coulonge →, *Canada* 102 C4
Coulonges-sur-l'Autize,
  France 20 B3
Coulounieix-Chamiers,
  France 20 C4
Coulterville, *U.S.A.* 116 H6
Council, *U.S.A.* 114 D5
Council Bluffs, *U.S.A.* ... 112 E7
Council Grove, *U.S.A.* ... 112 F6
Coupeville, *U.S.A.* 116 B4
Courantyne →, *S. Amer.* . 122 C5
Courcelles, *Belgium* 17 D4
Courcon, *France* 20 B3
Courmayeur, *Italy* 28 C3
Couronne, C., *France* 21 E9
Cours-la-Ville, *France* 19 F11
Coursan, *France* 20 E7
Courseulles-sur-Mer,
  France 18 C6
Courtenay, *Canada* 104 D4
Courtenay, *France* 19 D10
Courtland, *U.S.A.* 116 G5
Courtrai = Kortrijk,
  Belgium 17 D3
Courtright, *Canada* 110 D2
Coushatta, *U.S.A.* 113 J8
Coutances, *France* 18 C5
Coutras, *France* 20 C3
Coutts, *Canada* 104 D6
Couvin, *Belgium* 17 D4
Covarrubias, *Spain* 34 C1
Covasna, *Romania* 43 E11
Covasna □, *Romania* 43 E10
Coventry, *U.K.* 13 E6
Coventry L., *Canada* 105 A7
Covilhã, *Portugal* 34 E3
Covington, *Ga., U.S.A.* .. 109 J4
Covington, *Ky., U.S.A.* .. 108 F3
Covington, *Okla., U.S.A.* . 113 G6
Covington, *Tenn., U.S.A.* . 113 H10
Cowal, L., *Australia* 95 E4
Cowan, *Canada* 105 C8
Cowan, L., *Australia* 93 F3
Cowan L., *Canada* 105 C7
Cowangie, *Australia* 95 F3
Cowansville, *Canada* 111 A12
Cowarie, *Australia* 95 D2
Cowcowing Lakes,
  Australia 93 F2
Cowdenbeath, *U.K.* 14 E5
Cowell, *Australia* 95 E2
Cowes, *U.K.* 13 G6
Cowlitz →, *U.S.A.* 116 D4
Cowra, *Australia* 95 E4
Cox →, *Australia* 95 G4
Coxilha Grande, *Brazil* .. 127 B5
Coxim, *Brazil* 125 G8
Cox's Bazar, *Bangla.* 67 J17
Cox's Cove, *Canada* 103 C8
Coyame, *Mexico* 118 B3
Coyote Wells, *U.S.A.* 117 N11
Coyuca de Benítez, *Mexico* 119 D4
Coyuca de Catalan, *Mexico* 119 D4
Cozad, *U.S.A.* 112 E5
Cozes, *France* 20 C3
Cozumel, *Mexico* 119 C7
Cozumel, I. de, *Mexico* ... 119 C7

Craboon, *Australia* 95 E4
Cracow = Kraków, *Poland* 45 H6
Cracow, *Australia* 95 D5
Cradock, *S. Africa* 88 E4
Craig, *Alaska, U.S.A.* 104 B2
Craig, *Colo., U.S.A.* 114 F10
Craigavon, *U.K.* 15 B5
Craigmore, *Zimbabwe* ... 87 G3
Craik, *Canada* 105 C7
Crailsheim, *Germany* 25 F6
Craiova, *Romania* 43 F8
Cramsie, *Australia* 94 C3
Cranberry Portage, *Canada* 105 C8
Cranbrook, *Tas., Australia* 94 G4
Cranbrook, *W. Austral.,*
  Australia 93 F2
Cranbrook, *Canada* 104 D5
Crandon, *U.S.A.* 112 C10
Crane, *Oreg., U.S.A.* 114 E4
Crane, *Tex., U.S.A.* 113 K3
Cranston, *U.S.A.* 111 E13
Craon, *France* 18 E6
Craonne, *France* 19 C10
Craponne-sur-Arzon,
  France 20 C7
Crasna, *Romania* 43 D12
Crasna →, *Romania* 42 C7
Crasnei, Munţii, *Romania* 43 C8
Crater L., *U.S.A.* 114 E2
Crateús, *Brazil* 125 E10
Crati →, *Italy* 31 C9
Crato, *Brazil* 125 E11
Crato, *Portugal* 35 F3
Crawford, *U.S.A.* 112 D3
Crawfordsville, *U.S.A.* ... 108 E2
Crawley, *U.K.* 13 F7
Crean L., *Canada* 105 C7
Crécy-la-Ponthieu, *France* 19 B8
Crediton, *Canada* 110 C3
Credo, *Australia* 93 F3
Cree →, *Canada* 105 B7
Cree →, *U.K.* 14 G4
Cree L., *Canada* 105 B7
Creede, *U.S.A.* 115 H10
Creel, *Mexico* 118 B3
Creighton, *U.S.A.* 112 D6
Creil, *France* 19 C9
Crema, *Italy* 28 C6
Cremona, *Italy* 28 C7
Crepaja, *Serbia, Yug.* 42 E5
Crépy, *France* 19 C10
Crépy-en-Valois, *France* .. 19 C9
Cres, *Croatia* 29 D11
Cresbard, *U.S.A.* 112 C5
Crescent, *Okla., U.S.A.* .. 113 H6
Crescent, *Oreg., U.S.A.* .. 114 E3
Crescent City, *U.S.A.* 114 F1
Crescentino, *Italy* 28 C5
Crespino, *Italy* 28 C5
Crespo, *Argentina* 126 C3
Cressy, *Australia* 95 F3
Crest, *France* 21 D9
Crested Butte, *U.S.A.* 115 G10
Crestline, *Calif., U.S.A.* .. 117 L9
Crestline, *Ohio, U.S.A.* .. 110 F2
Creston, *Canada* 104 D5
Creston, *Calif., U.S.A.* ... 116 K6
Creston, *Iowa, U.S.A.* ... 112 E7
Creston, *Wash., U.S.A.* .. 114 C4
Crestview, *Calif., U.S.A.* . 116 H8
Crestview, *Fla., U.S.A.* ... 109 K2
Crêt de la Neige, *France* .. 19 F12
Crete = Kríti, *Greece* 36 D7
Crete, *U.S.A.* 112 E6
Crete, Sea of, *Greece* 39 E7
Créteil, *France* 19 D9
Creus, C. de, *Spain* 32 C8
Creuse □, *France* 19 F9
Creuse →, *France* 20 B4
Creutzwald, *France* 19 C13
Creuzburg, *Germany* 24 D6
Crèvecœur-le-Grand,
  France 19 C9
Crevillente, *Spain* 33 G4
Crewe, *U.K.* 12 D5
Crewkerne, *U.K.* 13 G5
Criciúma, *Brazil* 127 B6
Cricova, *Moldova* 43 C13
Crieff, *U.K.* 14 E5
Crikvenica, *Croatia* 29 C11
Crimea □, *Ukraine* 47 K8
Crimean Pen. = Krymskyy
  Pivostriv, *Ukraine* 47 K8
Crimmitschau, *Germany* . 24 E8
Cristuru Secuiesc, *Romania* 43 D10
Crişul Alb →, *Romania* .. 42 D6
Crişul Negru →, *Romania* 42 D6
Crişul Repede →,
  Romania 42 D5
Criuleni, *Moldova* 43 C14
Crivitz, *Germany* 24 B7
Crna →, *Macedonia* 40 E5
Crna Gora =
  Montenegro □,
  Yugoslavia 40 D3
Crna Gora, *Macedonia* .. 40 D5
Crna Reka = Crna →,
  Macedonia 40 E5
Crna Trava, *Serbia, Yug.* . 40 D6
Crni Drim →, *Macedonia* 40 E4
Crni Timok →,
  Serbia, Yug. 40 C6
Crnoljeva Planina,
  Serbia, Yug. 40 D5
Črnomelj, *Slovenia* 29 C12
Croagh Patrick, *Ireland* .. 15 C2
Croatia ■, *Europe* 29 C13

Crocker, Banjaran,
  Malaysia 62 C5
Crockett, *U.S.A.* 113 K7
Crocodile = Krokodil →,
  Mozam. 89 D5
Crocodile Is., *Australia* ... 94 A1
Crocq, *France* 20 C6
Crodo, *Italy* 28 B5
Crohy Hd., *Ireland* 15 B3
Croisette, C., *France* 21 E9
Croisic, Pte. du, *France* .. 18 E4
Croix, L. La, *Canada* 102 C1
Croker, C., *Australia* 92 B5
Croker I., *Australia* 92 B5
Cromarty, *Canada* 105 B10
Cromarty, *U.K.* 14 D4
Cromer, *U.K.* 12 E9
Cromwell, *N.Z.* 91 L2
Cronat, *France* 19 F10
Cronulla, *Australia* 95 E5
Crook, *U.K.* 12 C6
Crooked →, *Canada* 104 C4
Crooked →, *U.S.A.* 114 D3
Crooked I., *Bahamas* 121 B5
Crooked Island Passage,
  Bahamas 121 B5
Crookston, *Minn., U.S.A.* 112 B6
Crookston, *Nebr., U.S.A.* 112 D4
Crooksville, *U.S.A.* 108 F4
Crosby, *U.K.* 12 D4
Crosby, *Minn., U.S.A.* ... 112 B8
Crosby, *N. Dak., U.S.A.* . 105 D8
Crosby, *Pa., U.S.A.* 110 E6
Crosbyton, *U.S.A.* 113 J4
Crosía, *Italy* 31 C9
Cross →, *Nigeria* 83 E6
Cross City, *U.S.A.* 109 L4
Cross Fell, *U.K.* 12 C5
Cross L., *Canada* 105 C9
Cross Plains, *U.S.A.* 113 J5
Cross River □, *Nigeria* ... 83 D6
Cross Sound, *U.S.A.* 100 C6
Crossett, *U.S.A.* 113 J9
Crossfield, *Canada* 104 C6
Crosshaven, *Ireland* 15 E3
Croton-on-Hudson, *U.S.A.* 111 E11
Crotone, *Italy* 31 C10
Crow →, *Canada* 104 B4
Crow Agency, *U.S.A.* ... 114 D10
Crow Hd., *Ireland* 15 E1
Crowell, *U.S.A.* 113 J5
Crowley, *U.S.A.* 113 K8
Crowley, L., *U.S.A.* 116 H8
Crown Point, *U.S.A.* 108 E2
Crows Landing, *U.S.A.* .. 116 H5
Crows Nest, *Australia* ... 95 D5
Crowsnest Pass, *Canada* . 104 D6
Croydon, *Australia* 94 B3
Croydon, *U.K.* 13 F7
Crozet Is., *Ind. Oc.* 3 G12
Crozon, *France* 18 D2
Cruz, C., *Cuba* 120 C4
Cruz Alta, *Brazil* 127 B5
Cruz de Incio, *Spain* 34 C3
Cruz del Eje, *Argentina* .. 126 C3
Cruzeiro, *Brazil* 127 A7
Cruzeiro do Oeste, *Brazil* . 127 A5
Cruzeiro do Sul, *Brazil* .. 124 E4
Cry L., *Canada* 104 B3
Crystal Bay, *U.S.A.* 116 F7
Crystal Brook, *Australia* .. 95 E2
Crystal City, *Mo., U.S.A.* 112 F9
Crystal City, *Tex., U.S.A.* 113 L5
Crystal Falls, *U.S.A.* 108 B1
Crystal River, *U.S.A.* 109 L4
Crystal Springs, *U.S.A.* .. 113 K9
Csenger, *Hungary* 42 C7
Csongrád, *Hungary* 42 D5
Csongrád □, *Hungary* ... 42 D5
Csorna, *Hungary* 42 C2
Csurgo, *Hungary* 42 D2
Cu Lao Hon, *Vietnam* ... 65 G7
Cua Rao, *Vietnam* 64 C5
Cuácua →, *Mozam.* 87 F4
Cuamato, *Angola* 88 B2
Cuamba, *Mozam.* 87 E4
Cuando →, *Angola* 85 H4
Cuando Cubango □,
  Angola 88 B3
Cuangar, *Angola* 88 B2
Cuanza →, *Angola* 76 G5
Cuarto →, *Argentina* ... 126 C3
Cuatrociénegas, *Mexico* .. 118 B4
Cuauhtémoc, *Mexico* 118 B3
Cuba, *Portugal* 35 G3
Cuba, *N. Mex., U.S.A.* .. 115 J10
Cuba, *N.Y., U.S.A.* 110 D6
Cuba ■, *W. Indies* 120 B4
Cuballing, *Australia* 93 F2
Cubango →, *Africa* 88 B3
Çubuk, *Turkey* 72 B5
Cuchumatanes, Sierra de
  los, *Guatemala* 120 C1
Cuckfield, *U.K.* 13 F7
Cucuí, *Brazil* 124 C5
Cucurpe, *Mexico* 118 A2
Cúcuta, *Colombia* 124 B4
Cudalbi, *Romania* 43 E12
Cuddalore, *India* 66 P11
Cuddapah, *India* 66 M11
Cuddapan, L., *Australia* .. 94 D3
Cudgewa, *Australia* 95 F4
Cudillero, *Spain* 34 B4
Cue, *Australia* 93 E2
Cuéllar, *Spain* 34 D6
Cuenca, *Ecuador* 124 D3

Cuenca, *Spain* 32 E2
Cuenca □, *Spain* 32 F3
Cuenca, Serranía de, *Spain* 32 F3
Cuerdo del Pozo, Embalse
de la, *Spain* 32 D2
Cuernavaca, *Mexico* 119 D5
Cuero, *U.S.A.* 113 L6
Cuervo, *U.S.A.* 113 H2
Cuevas del Almanzora,
Spain 33 H3
Cuevo, *Bolivia* 124 H6
Cugir, *Romania* 43 E8
Cugnaux, *France* 20 E5
Cuhai-Bakony →, *Hungary* 42 C2
Cuiabá, *Brazil* 125 G7
Cuiabá →, *Brazil* 125 G7
Cuijk, *Neths.* 17 C5
Cuilco, *Guatemala* 120 C1
Cuillin Hills, *U.K.* 14 D2
Cuillin Sd., *U.K.* 14 D2
Cuiseaux, *France* 19 F12
Cuito →, *Angola* 88 B3
Cuitzeo, L. de, *Mexico* .. 118 D4
Cujmir, *Romania* 42 F7
Cukai, *Malaysia* 65 K4
Culbertson, *U.S.A.* 112 A2
Culcairn, *Australia* 95 F4
Culebra, Sierra de la, *Spain* 34 D4
Culfa, *Azerbaijan* 73 C11
Culgoa →, *Australia* 95 D4
Culiacán, *Mexico* 118 C3
Culiacán →, *Mexico* 118 C3
Culion, *Phil.* 61 F4
Cúllar, *Spain* 35 H8
Cullarin Ra., *Australia* ... 95 E4
Cullen, *U.K.* 14 D6
Cullen Pt., *Australia* 94 A3
Cullera, *Spain* 33 F4
Cullman, *U.S.A.* 109 H2
Culoz, *France* 21 C9
Culpeper, *U.S.A.* 108 F7
Culuene →, *Brazil* 125 F8
Culver, Pt., *Australia* 93 F3
Culverden, *N.Z.* 91 K4
Cumaná, *Venezuela* 124 A6
Cumaovası, *Turkey* 39 C9
Cumberland, *Canada* 104 D4
Cumberland, *Md.*, *U.S.A.* 108 F6
Cumberland, *Wis.*, *U.S.A.* 112 C8
Cumberland →, *U.S.A.* ... 109 G2
Cumberland I., *U.S.A.* 109 K5
Cumberland Is., *Australia* . 94 C4
Cumberland L., *Canada* .. 105 C8
Cumberland Pen., *Canada* 101 B13
Cumberland Plateau,
U.S.A. 109 H3
Cumberland Sd., *Canada* . 101 B13
Cumbernauld, *U.K.* 14 F5
Cumborah, *Australia* 95 D4
Cumbres Mayores, *Spain* . 35 G4
Cumbria □, *U.K.* 12 C5
Cumbrian Mts., *U.K.* 12 C5
Cumbum, *India* 66 M11
Cuminá →, *Brazil* 125 D7
Cummings Mt., *U.S.A.* ... 117 K8
Cummins, *Australia* 95 E2
Cumnock, *Australia* 95 E4
Cumnock, *U.K.* 14 F4
Cumpas, *Mexico* 118 B3
Cumplida, Pta., *Canary Is.* 37 F2
Çumra, *Turkey* 72 D5
Cunco, *Chile* 128 D2
Cuncumén, *Chile* 126 C1
Cundeelee, *Australia* 93 F3
Cunderdin, *Australia* 93 F2
Cunene →, *Angola* 88 B1
Cúneo, *Italy* 28 D4
Cunillera, I. = Sa
Conillera, *Spain* 37 C7
Cunlhat, *France* 20 C7
Cunnamulla, *Australia* 95 D4
Cuorgnè, *Italy* 28 C4
Cupar, *Canada* 105 C8
Cupar, *U.K.* 14 E5
Cupcini, *Moldova* 43 B12
Cupica, G. de, *Colombia* . 124 B3
Ćuprija, *Serbia, Yug.* 40 C5
Curaçao, *Neth. Ant.* 121 D6
Curanilahue, *Chile* 126 D1
Curaray →, *Peru* 124 D4
Cure →, *France* 19 E10
Curepto, *Chile* 126 D1
Curiapo, *Venezuela* 124 B6
Curicó, *Chile* 126 C1
Curicó □, *Chile* 126 C1
Curinga, *Italy* 31 D9
Curitiba, *Brazil* 127 B6
Currabubula, *Australia* ... 95 E5
Currais Novos, *Brazil* ... 125 E11
Curralinho, *Brazil* 125 D9
Currant, *U.S.A.* 114 G6
Curraweena, *Australia* ... 95 E4
Currawilla, *Australia* 94 D3
Current →, *U.S.A.* 113 G9
Currie, *Australia* 94 F3
Currie, *U.S.A.* 114 F6
Currituck Sd., *U.S.A.* 109 G8
Curtea de Argeş, *Romania* 43 E9
Curtici, *Romania* 42 D6
Curtis, *U.S.A.* 112 E4
Curtis Group, *Australia* .. 94 F4
Curtis I., *Australia* 94 C5
Curuápanema →, *Brazil* . 125 D7
Curuçá, *Brazil* 125 D9
Curuguaty, *Paraguay* 127 A4
Curup, *Indonesia* 62 E2

Cururupu, *Brazil* 125 D10
Curuzú Cuatiá, *Argentina* . 126 B4
Curvelo, *Brazil* 125 G10
Cushing, *U.S.A.* 113 H6
Cushing, Mt., *Canada* ... 104 B3
Cusihuiriáchic, *Mexico* .. 118 B3
Cusna, Mte., *Italy* 28 D7
Cusset, *France* 19 F10
Custer, *U.S.A.* 112 D3
Cut Bank, *U.S.A.* 114 B7
Cuthbert, *U.S.A.* 109 K3
Cutler, *U.S.A.* 116 J7
Cutro, *Italy* 31 C9
Cuttaburra →, *Australia* . 95 D3
Cuttack, *India* 67 J14
Cuvier, C., *Australia* 93 D1
Cuvier I., *N.Z.* 91 G5
Cuxhaven, *Germany* 24 B4
Cuyahoga Falls, *U.S.A.* .. 110 E3
Cuyapo, *Phil.* 61 D4
Cuyo, *Phil.* 61 F4
Cuyo East Pass, *Phil.* 61 F4
Cuyo West Pass, *Phil.* ... 61 F4
Cuyuni →, *Guyana* 124 B7
Cuzco, *Bolivia* 124 H5
Cuzco, *Peru* 124 F4
Čvrsnica, *Bos.-H.* 42 G2
Cwmbran, *U.K.* 13 F4
Cyangugu, *Rwanda* 86 C2
Cybinka, *Poland* 45 F1
Cyclades = Kikládhes,
Greece 38 E6
Cygnet, *Australia* 94 G4
Cynthiana, *U.S.A.* 108 F3
Cypress Hills, *Canada* ... 105 D7
Cyprus ■, *Asia* 36 E12
Cyrenaica, *Libya* 79 C10
Czaplinek, *Poland* 44 E3
Czar, *Canada* 105 C6
Czarna →,
Piotrkow Trybunalski,
Poland 45 G6
Czarna →, *Tarnobrzeg,*
Poland 45 H8
Czarna Białostocka, *Poland* 45 E10
Czarna Woda, *Poland* ... 44 E5
Czarne, *Poland* 44 E3
Czarnków, *Poland* 45 F3
Czech Rep. ■, *Europe* ... 26 B8
Czechowice-Dziedzice,
Poland 45 J5
Czempiń, *Poland* 45 F3
Czeremcha, *Poland* 45 F10
Czerniejewo, *Poland* 45 F4
Czersk, *Poland* 44 E4
Czerwieńsk, *Poland* 45 F2
Czerwionka-Leszczyny,
Poland 45 H5
Częstochowa, *Poland* ... 45 H6
Częstochowa □, *Poland* . 45 H6
Człopa, *Poland* 45 E3
Człuchów, *Poland* 44 E4
Czyżew-Osada, *Poland* .. 45 F9

D

Da →, *Vietnam* 64 B5
Da Hinggan Ling, *China* .. 60 B7
Da Lat, *Vietnam* 65 G7
Da Nang, *Vietnam* 64 D7
Da Qaidam, *China* 60 C4
Da Yunhe →, *China* 57 G11
Da'an, *China* 57 B13
Dab'a, Râs el, *Egypt* 80 H6
Daba Shan, *China* 58 B7
Dabai, *Nigeria* 83 C6
Dabakala, *Ivory C.* 82 D4
Dabas, *Hungary* 42 C4
Dabhoi, *India* 68 H5
Dąbie, *Poland* 45 F5
Dabie Shan, *China* 59 B10
Dabo = Pasirkuning,
Indonesia 62 E2
Dabola, *Guinea* 82 C2
Dabou, *Ivory C.* 82 D4
Daboya, *Ghana* 83 D4
Dąbrowa Białostocka,
Poland 44 E10
Dąbrowa Górnicza, *Poland* 45 H6
Dąbrowa Tarnowska,
Poland 45 H7
Dabu, *China* 59 E11
Dabung, *Malaysia* 65 K4
Dabus →, *Ethiopia* 81 E4
Dacato →, *Ethiopia* 81 F5
Dacca = Dhaka, *Bangla.* . 69 H14
Dacca = Dhaka □, *Bangla.* 69 G14
Dachau, *Germany* 25 G7
Dachstein, Hoher, *Austria* 26 D6
Dačice, *Czech Rep.* 26 B8
Dadanawa, *Guyana* 124 C7
Daday, *Turkey* 72 B5
Dade City, *U.S.A.* 109 L4
Dadiya, *Nigeria* 83 D7
Dadra & Nagar Haveli □,
India 66 J8
Dadri = Charkhi Dadri,
India 68 E7
Dadu, *Pakistan* 68 F2
Dadu He →, *China* 58 C4
Daet, *Phil.* 61 D5
Dafang, *China* 58 D5
Dağ, *Turkey* 39 D12
Dagana, *Senegal* 82 B1

Dagash, *Sudan* 80 D3
Dagestan □, *Russia* 49 J8
Dagestanskiye Ogni, *Russia* 49 J9
Daggett, *U.S.A.* 117 L10
Daghestan Republic =
Dagestan □, *Russia* ... 49 J8
Daghfeli, *Sudan* 80 D3
Dağlıq Qarabağ =
Nagorno-Karabakh,
Azerbaijan 73 C12
Dagö = Hiiumaa, *Estonia* 9 G20
Dagu, *China* 57 E9
Daguan, *China* 58 D4
Dagupan, *Phil.* 61 C4
Dahab, *Egypt* 80 B3
Dahlak Kebir, *Eritrea* 81 D5
Dahlenburg, *Germany* ... 24 B6
Dahlonega, *U.S.A.* 109 H4
Dahme, *Germany* 24 D9
Dahod, *India* 68 H6
Dahomey = Benin ■,
Africa 83 D5
Dahong Shan, *China* 59 B9
Dahra, *Senegal* 82 B1
Dai Hao, *Vietnam* 64 C6
Dai-Sen, *Japan* 55 G6
Dai Shan, *China* 59 B14
Dai Xian, *China* 56 E7
Daicheng, *China* 56 E9
Daimiel, *Spain* 35 F7
Daingean, *Ireland* 15 C4
Dainkog, *China* 58 A1
Daintree, *Australia* 94 B4
Daiō-Misaki, *Japan* 55 G8
Dairût, *Egypt* 80 B3
Daisetsu-Zan, *Japan* 54 C11
Dajarra, *Australia* 94 C2
Dajin Chuan →, *China* .. 58 B3
Dak Dam, *Cambodia* 64 F6
Dak Nhe, *Vietnam* 64 E6
Dak Pek, *Vietnam* 64 E6
Dak Song, *Vietnam* 65 F6
Dak Sui, *Vietnam* 64 E6
Dakar, *Senegal* 82 C1
Dakhla, *W. Sahara* 78 D2
Dakhla, El Wâhât el-,
Egypt 80 B2
Dakingari, *Nigeria* 83 C5
Dakor, *India* 68 H5
Dakoro, *Niger* 83 C6
Dakota City, *U.S.A.* 112 D6
Đakovica, *Serbia, Yug.* .. 40 D4
Đakovo, *Croatia* 42 E3
Dalaba, *Guinea* 82 C2
Dalachi, *China* 56 F3
Dalai Nur, *China* 56 C9
Dālakī, *Iran* 71 D6
Dalälven, *Sweden* 10 D10
Dalaman, *Turkey* 39 E10
Dalaman →, *Turkey* 39 E10
Dalandzadgad, *Mongolia* . 56 C3
Dalarna, *Sweden* 10 D8
Dālbandīn, *Pakistan* 66 E4
Dalbeattie, *U.K.* 14 G5
Dalbosjön, *Sweden* 11 F6
Dalby, *Australia* 95 D5
Dalby, *Sweden* 11 J7
Dalga, *Egypt* 80 B3
Dalgān, *Iran* 71 E8
Dalhart, *U.S.A.* 113 G3
Dalhousie, *Canada* 103 C6
Dalhousie, *India* 68 C6
Dali, *Shaanxi, China* 56 G5
Dali, *Yunnan, China* 58 E3
Dalian, *China* 57 E11
Daliang Shan, *China* 58 D4
Daling He →, *China* 57 D11
Dāliyat el Karmel, *Israel* . 75 C4
Dalj, *Croatia* 42 E3
Dalkeith, *U.K.* 14 F5
Dall I., *U.S.A.* 104 C2
Dallarnil, *Australia* 95 D5
Dallas, *Oreg., U.S.A.* 114 D2
Dallas, *Tex., U.S.A.* 113 J6
Dalmacija, *Croatia* 29 E13
Dalmatia = Dalmacija,
Croatia 29 E13
Dalmellington, *U.K.* 14 F4
Dalnegorsk, *Russia* 54 B7
Dalnerechensk, *Russia* .. 54 B6
Daloa, *Ivory C.* 82 D3
Dalou Shan, *China* 58 D6
Dalry, *U.K.* 14 F4
Dals Långed, *Sweden* ... 11 F6
Dalsjöfors, *Sweden* 11 G7
Dalsland, *Sweden* 11 F6
Daltenganj, *India* 69 H11
Dalton, *Canada* 102 C3
Dalton, *Ga., U.S.A.* 109 H3
Dalton, *Mass., U.S.A.* ... 111 D11
Dalton, *Nebr., U.S.A.* ... 112 E3
Dalton Iceberg Tongue,
Antarctica 5 C9
Dalton-in-Furness, *U.K.* .. 12 C4
Dalupiri I., *Phil.* 61 B4
Daly →, *Australia* 92 B5
Daly City, *U.S.A.* 116 H4
Daly L., *Canada* 105 B7
Daly Waters, *Australia* ... 94 B1
Dalyan, *Turkey* 39 E10
Dam Doi, *Vietnam* 65 H5
Dam Ha, *Vietnam* 64 B6
Daman, *India* 66 J8
Dāmaneh, *Iran* 71 C6
Damanhûr, *Egypt* 80 H7

Damanzhuang, *China* ... 56 E9
Damar, *Indonesia* 63 F7
Damaraland, *Namibia* ... 88 C2
Damascus = Dimashq,
Syria 75 B5
Damaturu, *Nigeria* 83 C7
Damāvand, *Iran* 71 C7
Damāvand, Qolleh-ye, *Iran* 71 C7
Damba, *Angola* 84 F3
Dame Marie, *Haiti* 121 C5
Dāmghān, *Iran* 71 B7
Damiel → = Dumyât, *Egypt* 80 H7
Daming, *China* 56 F8
Damīr Qābū, *Syria* 70 B4
Dammam = Ad Dammām,
Si. Arabia 71 E6
Dammartin-les-Lys, *France* 19 D9
Dammartin-en-Goële,
France 19 C9
Damme, *Germany* 24 C4
Damodar →, *India* 69 H12
Damoh, *India* 69 H8
Dampier, *Australia* 92 D2
Dampier, Selat, *Indonesia* 63 E8
Dampier Arch., *Australia* . 92 D2
Damrei, Chuor Phnum,
Cambodia 65 G4
Damvillers, *France* 19 C12
Dan-Gulbi, *Nigeria* 83 C6
Dan Xian, *China* 64 C7
Dana, *Indonesia* 63 F6
Dana, L., *Canada* 102 B4
Dana, Mt., *U.S.A.* 116 H7
Danakil Depression,
Ethiopia 81 E5
Danao, *Phil.* 61 F6
Danbury, *U.S.A.* 111 E11
Danby L., *U.S.A.* 115 J6
Dand, *Afghan.* 68 D1
Dandaragan, *Australia* ... 93 F2
Dandeldhura, *Nepal* 69 E9
Dandeli, *India* 66 M9
Dandenong, *Australia* ... 95 F4
Dandong, *China* 57 D13
Danfeng, *China* 56 H6
Danforth, *U.S.A.* 103 C6
Dangan Liedao, *China* ... 59 F10
Dangé-St-Roman, *France* . 20 B4
Dângení, *Romania* 43 C11
Danger Is. = Pukapuka,
Cook Is. 97 J11
Danger Pt., *S. Africa* 88 E2
Dangla, *Ethiopia* 81 E4
Dangla Shan = Tanggula
Shan, *China* 60 C4
Dangora, *Nigeria* 83 C6
Dangrek, Phnom, *Thailand* 64 E5
Dangriga, *Belize* 119 D7
Dangshan, *China* 56 G9
Dangtu, *China* 59 B12
Dangyang, *China* 59 B8
Daniel, *U.S.A.* 114 E8
Daniel's Harbour, *Canada* 103 B8
Danielskuil, *S. Africa* 88 D3
Danielson, *U.S.A.* 111 E13
Danilov, *Russia* 46 C11
Danilovgrad,
Montenegro, Yug. ... 40 D3
Danilovka, *Russia* 48 E7
Daning, *China* 56 F6
Danissa, *Kenya* 86 B5
Danja, *Nigeria* 83 C6
Dankalwa, *Nigeria* 83 C7
Dankama, *Nigeria* 83 C6
Dankhar Gompa, *India* .. 66 C11
Dankov, *Russia* 46 F10
Danleng, *China* 58 B4
Danlí, *Honduras* 120 D2
Dannemora, *U.S.A.* 111 B11
Dannenberg, *Germany* .. 24 B7
Dannevirke, *N.Z.* 91 J6
Dannhauser, *S. Africa* ... 89 D5
Dansville, *U.S.A.* 110 D7
Dantan, *India* 69 J12
Dante, *Somali Rep.* 74 E5
Danube = Dunărea →,
Europe 43 E14
Danville, *Ill., U.S.A.* 108 E2
Danville, *Ky., U.S.A.* 108 G3
Danville, *Va., U.S.A.* 109 G6
Danyang, *China* 59 B12
Danzhai, *China* 58 D6
Danzig = Gdańsk, *Poland* 44 D5
Dão →, *Portugal* 34 E2
Dao Xian, *China* 59 E8
Daocheng, *China* 58 C3
Daosa = Dausa, *India* ... 68 F7
Daoud = Aïn Beïda,
Algeria 78 A7
Dapaong, *Togo* 83 C5
Dapitan, *Phil.* 61 G5
Daqing Shan, *China* 56 D6
Daqu Shan, *China* 59 B14
Dar Banda, *Africa* 76 F6
Dar el Beida = Casablanca,
Morocco 78 B4
Dar es Salaam, *Tanzania* . 86 D4
Dar Mazār, *Iran* 71 D8
Dar'ā, *Syria* 75 C5
Dar'ā □, *Syria* 75 C5
Dārāb, *Iran* 71 D7
Darabani, *Romania* 43 B11
Daraj, *Libya* 79 B8
Dāmaneh, *Iran* 71 C6
Daravica, *Serbia, Yug.* ... 40 D4

Draw, *Egypt* 80 C3
Dārayyā, *Syria* 75 B5
Darazo, *Nigeria* 83 C7
Darband, *Pakistan* 68 B5
Darband, Kūh-e, *Iran* 71 D8
Darbhanga, *India* 69 F11
Darby, *U.S.A.* 114 C6
Darda, *Croatia* 42 E3
Dardanelle, *Ark., U.S.A.* . 113 H8
Dardanelle, *Calif., U.S.A.* 116 G7
Dardanelles = Çanakkale
Boğazı, *Turkey* 41 F10
Darende, *Turkey* 72 C7
Dārestān, *Iran* 71 D8
Darfo, *Italy* 28 C7
Dârfûr, *Sudan* 79 F10
Dargai, *Pakistan* 68 B4
Dargan Ata, *Uzbekistan* . 50 E7
Dargaville, *N.Z.* 91 F4
Darhan Muminggan
Lianheqi, *China* 56 D6
Dari, *Sudan* 81 F3
Darıca, *Turkey* 72 B3
Darién, G. del, *Colombia* . 122 C3
Dariganga, *Mongolia* 56 B7
Darinskoye, *Kazakstan* .. 48 E10
Darjeeling = Darjiling,
India 69 F13
Darjiling, *India* 69 F13
Dark Cove, *Canada* 103 C9
Darkan, *Australia* 93 F2
Darkhazīneh, *Iran* 71 D6
Darkot Pass, *Pakistan* ... 69 A5
Darling →, *Australia* 95 E3
Darling Downs, *Australia* . 95 D5
Darling Ra., *Australia* 93 F2
Darlington, *U.K.* 12 C6
Darlington, *S.C., U.S.A.* . 109 H6
Darlington, *Wis., U.S.A.* . 112 D9
Darlington □, *U.K.* 12 C6
Darlington, L., *S. Africa* .. 88 E4
Darlot, L., *Australia* 93 E3
Darłowo, *Poland* 44 D3
Dărmăneşti, *Bacău,*
Romania 43 D11
Dărmăneşti, *Suceava,*
Romania 43 C11
Darmstadt, *Germany* 25 F4
Darnah, *Libya* 79 B10
Darnall, *S. Africa* 89 D5
Darney, *France* 19 D13
Darnley, C., *Antarctica* .. 5 C6
Darnley B., *Canada* 100 B7
Daroca, *Spain* 32 D3
Darr, *Australia* 94 C3
Darr →, *Australia* 94 C3
Darrington, *U.S.A.* 114 B3
Darsser Ort, *Germany* ... 24 A8
Dart →, *U.K.* 13 G4
Dart, C., *Antarctica* 5 D14
Dartford, *U.K.* 13 F8
Dartmoor, *U.K.* 13 G4
Dartmouth, *Australia* 94 C3
Dartmouth, *Canada* 103 D7
Dartmouth, *U.K.* 13 G4
Dartmouth, L., *Australia* . 95 D4
Dartuch, C. = Artrutx, C.
de, *Spain* 37 B10
Daruvar, *Croatia* 42 E2
Darvaza, *Turkmenistan* .. 50 E6
Darvel, Teluk = Lahad
Datu, Teluk, *Malaysia* . 63 D5
Darwen, *U.K.* 12 D5
Darwha, *India* 66 J10
Darwin, *Australia* 92 B5
Darwin, *U.S.A.* 117 J9
Darwin River, *Australia* .. 92 B5
Daryoi Amu =
Amudarya →,
Uzbekistan 50 E6
Dās, *U.A.E.* 71 E7
Dashetai, *China* 56 D5
Dashhowuz, *Turkmenistan* 50 E6
Dashkesan = Daşkäsän,
Azerbaijan 49 K7
Dasht, *Iran* 71 B8
Dasht →, *Pakistan* 66 G2
Dasht-e Mārgow, *Afghan.* 66 D3
Dasht-i-Nawar, *Afghan.* . 68 C3
Daska, *Pakistan* 68 C6
Daşkäsän, *Azerbaijan* ... 49 K7
Dassa, *Benin* 83 D5
Datça, *Turkey* 39 E9
Datia, *India* 69 G8
Datian, *China* 59 E11
Datong, *Anhui, China* ... 59 B11
Datong, *Shanxi, China* .. 56 D7
Datteln, *Germany* 24 D3
Datu, Tanjung, *Indonesia* . 62 D3
Datu Piang, *Phil.* 61 H6
Daugava →, *Latvia* 9 H21
Daugavpils, *Latvia* 9 J22
Daulpur, *India* 68 F7
Daun, *Germany* 25 E2
Dauphin, *Canada* 105 C8
Dauphin I., *U.S.A.* 109 K1
Dauphin L., *Canada* 105 C9
Dauphiné, *France* 21 C9
Daura, *Borno, Nigeria* ... 83 C7
Daura, *Kaduna, Nigeria* . 83 C6
Dausa, *India* 68 F7
Davangere, *India* 66 M9
Davao, *Phil.* 61 H6
Davao, G. of, *Phil.* 61 H6
Dāvar Panāh, *Iran* 71 E9
Davenport, *Calif., U.S.A.* 116 H4

Davenport, *Iowa, U.S.A.* . 112 E9
Davenport, *Wash., U.S.A.* 114 C4
Davenport Downs,
  Australia 94 C3
Davenport Ra., *Australia* . 94 C1
Daventry, *U.K.* 13 E6
David, *Panama* 120 E3
David City, *U.S.A.* 112 E6
David Gorodok = Davyd
  Haradok, *Belarus* 47 F4
Davidson, *Canada* 105 C7
Davis, *U.S.A.* 116 G5
Davis Dam, *U.S.A.* 117 K12
Davis Inlet, *Canada* 103 A7
Davis Mts., *U.S.A.* 113 K2
Davis Sea, *Antarctica* 5 C7
Davis Str., *N. Amer.* ... 101 B14
Davos, *Switz.* 25 J5
Davutlar, *Turkey* 39 D9
Davy L., *Canada* 105 B7
Davyd Haradok, *Belarus* . 47 F4
Dawa →, *Ethiopia* 81 G5
Dawaki, *Bauchi, Nigeria* .. 83 D6
Dawaki, *Kano, Nigeria* .. 83 C6
Dawei, *Burma* 64 E2
Dawes Ra., *Australia* 94 C5
Dawlish, *U.K.* 13 G4
Dawros Hd., *Ireland* 15 B3
Dawson, *Canada* 100 B6
Dawson, *Ga., U.S.A.* 109 K3
Dawson, *N. Dak., U.S.A.* 112 B5
Dawson, I., *Chile* 128 G2
Dawson Creek, *Canada* .. 104 B4
Dawson Inlet, *Canada* ... 105 A10
Dawson Ra., *Australia* ... 94 C4
Dawu, *China* 58 B3
Dax, *France* 20 E2
Daxian, *China* 58 B6
Daxin, *China* 58 F6
Daxindian, *China* 57 F11
Daxinggou, *China* 57 C15
Daxue Shan, *Sichuan,*
  China 58 B3
Daxue Shan, *Yunnan,*
  China 58 F2
Dayao, *China* 58 E3
Daye, *China* 59 B10
Dayi, *China* 58 B4
Daylesford, *Australia* 95 F3
Dayong, *China* 59 C8
Dayr az Zawr, *Syria* 70 C4
Daysland, *Canada* 104 C6
Dayton, *Nev., U.S.A.* 116 F7
Dayton, *Ohio, U.S.A.* ... 108 F3
Dayton, *Pa., U.S.A.* 110 F5
Dayton, *Tenn., U.S.A.* ... 109 H3
Dayton, *Wash., U.S.A.* .. 114 C4
Daytona Beach, *U.S.A.* .. 109 L5
Dayu, *China* 59 E10
Dayville, *U.S.A.* 114 D4
Dazhu, *China* 58 B6
Dazkırı, *Turkey* 39 D11
Dazu, *China* 58 C5
De Aar, *S. Africa* 88 E3
De Funiak Springs, *U.S.A.* 109 K2
De Grey, *Australia* 92 D2
De Grey →, *Australia* ... 92 D2
De Haan, *Belgium* 17 C3
De Kalb, *U.S.A.* 112 E10
De Land, *U.S.A.* 109 L5
De Leon, *U.S.A.* 113 J5
De Panne, *Belgium* 17 C2
De Pere, *U.S.A.* 108 C1
De Queen, *U.S.A.* 113 H7
De Quincy, *U.S.A.* 113 K8
De Ridder, *U.S.A.* 113 K8
De Smet, *U.S.A.* 112 C6
De Soto, *U.S.A.* 112 F9
De Tour Village, *U.S.A.* .. 108 C4
De Witt, *U.S.A.* 113 H9
Dead Sea, *Asia* 75 D4
Deadwood, *U.S.A.* 112 C3
Deadwood L., *Canada* ... 104 B3
Deakin, *Australia* 93 F4
Deal, *U.K.* 13 F9
Deal I., *Australia* 94 F4
Dealesville, *S. Africa* 88 D4
De'an, *China* 59 C10
Dean, Forest of, *U.K.* ... 13 F5
Dearborn, *U.S.A.* 102 D3
Dease →, *Canada* 104 B3
Dease L., *Canada* 104 B2
Dease Lake, *Canada* 104 B2
Death Valley, *U.S.A.* 117 J10
Death Valley Junction,
  U.S.A. 117 J10
Death Valley National
  Monument, *U.S.A.* ... 117 J10
Deauville, *France* 18 C7
Deba, *Spain* 32 B2
Deba Habe, *Nigeria* 83 C7
Debalt'sevo, *Ukraine* 47 H10
Debao, *China* 58 F6
Debar, *Macedonia* 40 E4
Debden, *Canada* 105 C7
Dębica, *Poland* 45 H8
Dęblin, *Poland* 45 G8
Dębno, *Poland* 45 F1
Débo, L., *Mali* 82 C4
Debolt, *Canada* 104 B5
Deborah East, L., *Australia* 93 F2
Deborah West, L.,
  Australia 93 F2
Debrc, *Serbia, Yug.* 40 B3
Debre Birhan, *Ethiopia* .. 81 F4
Debre Markos, *Ethiopia* .. 81 E4

Debre May, *Ethiopia* 81 E4
Debre Sina, *Ethiopia* 81 F4
Debre Tabor, *Ethiopia* ... 81 E4
Debre Zebit, *Ethiopia* 81 E4
Debrecen, *Hungary* 42 C6
Debrzno, *Poland* 44 E4
Dečani, *Serbia, Yug.* 40 D4
Decatur, *Ala., U.S.A.* 109 H2
Decatur, *Ga., U.S.A.* 109 H3
Decatur, *Ill., U.S.A.* 112 F10
Decatur, *Ind., U.S.A.* 108 E3
Decatur, *Tex., U.S.A.* 113 J6
Decazeville, *France* 20 D6
Deccan, *India* 66 L11
Deception L., *Canada* ... 105 B8
Dechang, *China* 58 D4
Děčín, *Czech Rep.* 26 A7
Decize, *France* 19 F10
Deckerville, *U.S.A.* 110 C2
Decollatura, *Italy* 31 C9
Decorah, *U.S.A.* 112 D9
Deda, *Romania* 43 D9
Dedéagach =
  Alexandroúpolis, *Greece* 41 F9
Dedham, *U.S.A.* 111 D13
Dédougou, *Burkina Faso* . 82 C4
Dedovichi, *Russia* 46 D5
Dedza, *Malawi* 87 E3
Dee →, *Aberds., U.K.* ... 14 D6
Dee →, *Dumf. & Gall.,*
  U.K. 14 G4
Dee →, *Wales, U.K.* 12 D4
Deep B., *Canada* 104 A5
Deep Well, *Australia* 94 C1
Deepwater, *Australia* 95 D5
Deer →, *Canada* 105 B10
Deer Lake, *Nfld., Canada* . 103 C8
Deer Lake, *Ont., Canada* . 105 C10
Deer Lodge, *U.S.A.* 114 C7
Deer Park, *U.S.A.* 114 C5
Deer River, *U.S.A.* 112 B8
Deeral, *Australia* 94 B4
Deerdepoort, *S. Africa* ... 88 C4
Deferiet, *U.S.A.* 111 B9
Defiance, *U.S.A.* 108 E3
Dêgê, *China* 58 B2
Degebe →, *Portugal* 35 G3
Degeberga, *Sweden* 11 J8
Degema, *Nigeria* 83 E6
Degerfors, *Sweden* 10 E8
Degerhamn, *Sweden* 11 H10
Deggendorf, *Germany* ... 25 G8
Değirmendere, *Turkey* ... 41 F13
Deh Bīd, *Iran* 71 D7
Deh-e Shīr, *Iran* 71 D7
Dehaj, *Iran* 71 D7
Dehdez, *Iran* 71 D6
Dehestān, *Iran* 71 D7
Dehgolān, *Iran* 70 C5
Dehi Titan, *Afghan.* 66 C3
Dehibat, *Tunisia* 79 B8
Dehlorān, *Iran* 70 C5
Dehnow-e Kühestān, *Iran* 71 E8
Dehra Dun, *India* 68 D8
Dehri, *India* 69 G11
Dehua, *China* 59 E12
Dehui, *China* 57 B13
Deinze, *Belgium* 17 D3
Dej, *Romania* 43 C8
Deje, *Sweden* 10 E7
Dejiang, *China* 58 C7
Dekemhare, *Eritrea* 81 E4
Dekese,
  Dem. Rep. of the Congo 84 E4
Del Mar, *U.S.A.* 117 N9
Del Norte, *U.S.A.* 115 H10
Del Rio, *U.S.A.* 113 L4
Delai, *Sudan* 80 D4
Delano, *U.S.A.* 117 K7
Delareyville, *S. Africa* 88 D4
Delavan, *U.S.A.* 112 D10
Delaware, *U.S.A.* 108 E4
Delaware □, *U.S.A.* 108 F8
Delaware →, *U.S.A.* 108 F8
Delaware B., *U.S.A.* 107 C12
Delbrück, *Germany* 24 D4
Delčevo, *Macedonia* 40 E6
Delegate, *Australia* 95 F4
Delémont, *Switz.* 25 H3
Delft, *Neths.* 17 B4
Delfzijl, *Neths.* 17 A6
Delgado, C., *Mozam.* 87 E5
Delgerhet, *Mongolia* 56 B6
Delgo, *Sudan* 80 C3
Delhi, *Canada* 110 D4
Delhi, *India* 68 E7
Delhi, *U.S.A.* 111 D10
Deli Jovan, *Serbia, Yug.* .. 40 B6
Delia, *Canada* 104 C6
Delice, *Turkey* 72 C6
Delicias, *Mexico* 118 B3
Delījān, *Iran* 71 C6
Déline, *Canada* 100 B7
Dell City, *U.S.A.* 115 L11
Dell Rapids, *U.S.A.* 112 D6
Delmar, *U.S.A.* 111 D11
Delmenhorst, *Germany* .. 24 B4
Delnice, *Croatia* 29 C11
Delong, Ostrova, *Russia* .. 51 B15
Deloraine, *Australia* 94 G4
Deloraine, *Canada* 105 D8
Delphi, *Greece* 38 C4
Delphi, *U.S.A.* 108 E2
Delphos, *U.S.A.* 108 E3
Delportshoop, *S. Africa* .. 88 D3

Delray Beach, *U.S.A.* 109 M5
Delsbo, *Sweden* 10 C10
Delta, *Colo., U.S.A.* 115 G9
Delta, *Utah, U.S.A.* 114 G7
Delta □, *Nigeria* 83 D6
Delungra, *Australia* 95 D5
Delvinákion, *Greece* 38 B2
Delvinë, *Albania* 40 G4
Demanda, Sierra de la,
  Spain 32 C2
Demavand = Damāvand,
  Iran 71 C7
Dembecha, *Ethiopia* 81 E4
Dembi, *Ethiopia* 81 F4
Dembia,
  Dem. Rep. of the Congo 86 B2
Dembidolo, *Ethiopia* 81 F3
Demer →, *Belgium* 17 D4
Demetrias, *Greece* 38 B5
Deming, *N. Mex., U.S.A.* 115 K10
Deming, *Wash., U.S.A.* .. 116 B4
Demini →, *Brazil* 124 D6
Demirci, *Turkey* 39 B10
Demirköprü Barajı, *Turkey* 39 C10
Demirköy, *Turkey* 41 E11
Demmin, *Germany* 24 B9
Demonte, *Italy* 28 D4
Demopolis, *U.S.A.* 109 J2
Demyansk, *Russia* 46 D7
Den Burg, *Neths.* 17 A4
Den Chai, *Thailand* 64 D3
Den Haag = 's-
  Gravenhage, *Neths.* 17 B4
Den Helder, *Neths.* 17 B4
Den Oever, *Neths.* 17 B5
Denain, *France* 19 B10
Denair, *U.S.A.* 116 H6
Denau, *Uzbekistan* 50 F7
Denbigh, *U.K.* 12 D4
Denbighshire □, *U.K.* 12 D4
Dendang, *Indonesia* 62 E3
Dendermonde, *Belgium* .. 17 C4
Deneba, *Ethiopia* 81 F4
Deng Xian, *China* 59 A9
Dengchuan, *China* 58 E3
Denge, *Nigeria* 83 C6
Dengfeng, *China* 56 G7
Dengi, *Nigeria* 83 D6
Dengkou, *China* 56 D4
Denham, *Australia* 93 E1
Denham Ra., *Australia* ... 94 C4
Denham Sd., *Australia* ... 93 E1
Denia, *Spain* 33 G5
Denial B., *Australia* 95 E1
Deniliquin, *Australia* 95 F3
Denison, *Iowa, U.S.A.* ... 112 E7
Denison, *Tex., U.S.A.* ... 113 J6
Denison Plains, *Australia* . 92 C4
Denizli, *Turkey* 39 D11
Denizli □, *Turkey* 39 D11
Denman Glacier, *Antarctica* 5 C7
Denmark, *Australia* 93 F2
Denmark ■, *Europe* 11 J3
Denmark Str., *Atl. Oc.* ... 4 C6
Dennison, *U.S.A.* 110 F3
Denny, *U.K.* 14 E5
Denpasar, *Indonesia* 62 F5
Denton, *Mont., U.S.A.* ... 114 C9
Denton, *Tex., U.S.A.* 113 J6
D'Entrecasteaux, Pt.,
  Australia 93 F2
Denu, *Ghana* 83 D5
Denver, *U.S.A.* 112 F2
Denver City, *U.S.A.* 113 J3
Deoband, *India* 68 E7
Deogarh, *India* 69 G12
Deoghar, *India* 69 G12
Deolali, *India* 66 K8
Deoli = Devli, *India* 68 G6
Deoria, *India* 69 F10
Deosai Mts., *Pakistan* 69 B6
Deping, *China* 57 F9
Deposit, *U.S.A.* 111 D9
Depot Springs, *Australia* . 93 E3
Deputatskiy, *Russia* 51 C14
Dêqên, *China* 58 C2
Deqing, *China* 59 F8
Dera Ghazi Khan, *Pakistan* 68 D4
Dera Ismail Khan, *Pakistan* 68 D4
Derbent, *Russia* 49 J9
Derbent, *Turkey* 39 C10
Derby, *Australia* 92 C3
Derby, *U.K.* 12 E6
Derby, *Conn., U.S.A.* 111 E11
Derby, *N.Y., U.S.A.* 110 D6
Derby City □, *U.K.* 12 E6
Derbyshire □, *U.K.* 12 E6
Derecske, *Hungary* 42 C6
Dereköy, *Turkey* 41 E11
Dereli, *Turkey* 73 B8
Derg →, *U.K.* 15 B4
Derg, L., *Ireland* 15 D3
Dergachi = Derhaci,
  Ukraine 47 G9
Dergaon, *India* 67 F19
Derhaci, *Ukraine* 47 G9
Derik, *Turkey* 73 D9
Dermantsi, *Bulgaria* 41 C8
Dernieres, Isles, *U.S.A.* .. 113 L9
Dêrong, *China* 58 C2
Derry = Londonderry,
  U.K. 15 B4
Derry = Londonderry □,
  U.K. 15 B4
Derryveagh Mts., *Ireland* . 15 B3

Derudub, *Sudan* 80 D4
Derval, *France* 18 E5
Dervéni, *Greece* 38 C4
Derventa, *Bos.-H.* 42 F2
Derwent, *Canada* 105 C6
Derwent →, *Cumb., U.K.* 12 C4
Derwent →, *Derby, U.K.* . 12 E6
Derwent →, *N. Yorks.,*
  U.K. 12 D7
Derwent Water, *U.K.* 12 C4
Des Moines, *Iowa, U.S.A.* 112 E8
Des Moines, *N. Mex.,*
  U.S.A. 113 G3
Des Moines →, *U.S.A.* .. 112 E9
Desa, *Romania* 42 G8
Desaguadero →, *Argentina* 126 C2
Desaguadero →, *Bolivia* . 124 G5
Descanso, Pta., *Mexico* ... 117 N9
Descartes, *France* 20 B4
Deschaillons, *Canada* ... 103 C5
Descharme →, *Canada* .. 105 B7
Deschutes →, *U.S.A.* 114 D3
Dese, *Ethiopia* 81 E4
Deseado →, *Argentina* .. 128 F3
Desenzano del Garda, *Italy* 28 C7
Desert Center, *U.S.A.* ... 117 M11
Desert Hot Springs, *U.S.A.* 117 M10
Désirade, I., *Guadeloupe* . 121 C7
Deskenatlata L., *Canada* . 104 A6
Desna →, *Ukraine* 47 G6
Desnăţui →, *Romania* ... 43 G8
Desolación, I., *Chile* 128 G2
Despeñaperros, Paso, *Spain* 35 G7
Despotovac, *Serbia, Yug.* . 40 B5
Dessau, *Germany* 24 D8
Dessye = Dese, *Ethiopia* . 81 E4
D'Estrees B., *Australia* ... 95 F2
Desuri, *India* 68 G5
Desvres, *France* 19 B8
Det Udom, *Thailand* 64 E5
Deta, *Romania* 42 E6
Dete, *Zimbabwe* 87 F2
Đetinja →, *Serbia, Yug.* .. 40 C4
Detmold, *Germany* 24 D4
Detour, Pt., *U.S.A.* 108 C2
Detroit, *Mich., U.S.A.* ... 102 D3
Detroit, *Tex., U.S.A.* 113 J7
Detroit Lakes, *U.S.A.* 112 B7
Detva, *Slovak Rep.* 27 C12
Deurne, *Neths.* 17 C5
Deutsche Bucht, *Germany* 24 A4
Deutschlandsberg, *Austria* 26 E8
Deux-Sèvres □, *France* .. 18 F6
Deva, *Romania* 42 E7
Devakottai, *India* 66 Q11
Devaprayag, *India* 69 D8
Dévaványa, *Hungary* 42 C5
Deveci Dağları, *Turkey* ... 72 B7
Devecser, *Hungary* 42 C2
Develi, *Turkey* 72 C6
Deventer, *Neths.* 17 B6
Deveron →, *U.K.* 14 D6
Devesel, *Romania* 42 F7
Devgadh Bariya, *India* ... 68 H5
Devils Den, *U.S.A.* 116 K7
Devils Lake, *U.S.A.* 112 A5
Devils Paw, *Canada* 104 B2
Devin, *Bulgaria* 41 E8
Devizes, *U.K.* 13 F6
Devli, *India* 68 G6
Devnya, *Bulgaria* 41 C11
Devolii →, *Albania* 40 F4
Devon, *Canada* 104 C6
Devon □, *U.K.* 13 G4
Devon I., *Canada* 4 B3
Devonport, *Australia* 94 G4
Devonport, *N.Z.* 91 G5
Devrek, *Turkey* 72 B4
Devrekâni, *Turkey* 72 B5
Devrez →, *Turkey* 72 B6
Dewas, *India* 68 H7
Dewetsdorp, *S. Africa* ... 88 D4
Dexing, *China* 59 C11
Dexter, *Mo., U.S.A.* 113 G10
Dexter, *N. Mex., U.S.A.* .. 113 J2
Dey-Dey, L., *Australia* ... 93 E5
Deyang, *China* 58 B5
Deyhūk, *Iran* 71 C8
Deyyer, *Iran* 71 E6
Dezadeash L., *Canada* ... 104 A1
Dezfūl, *Iran* 71 C6
Dezhneva, Mys, *Russia* .. 51 C19
Dezhou, *China* 56 F9
Dháfni, *Kríti, Greece* 36 D7
Dháfni,
  Pelopónnisos,
  Greece 38 D4
Dhahaban, *Si. Arabia* 80 C4
Dhahiriya = Aẕ Ẕāhirīyah,
  West Bank 75 D3
Dhahran = Aẕ Ẕahrān,
  Si. Arabia 71 E6
Dhaka, *Bangla.* 69 H14
Dhaka □, *Bangla.* 69 G14
Dhali, *Cyprus* 36 D12
Dhamási, *Greece* 38 B4
Dhampur, *India* 69 E8
Dhamtari, *India* 67 J12
Dhanbad, *India* 69 H12
Dhangarhi, *Nepal* 67 E12
Dhankuta, *Nepal* 69 F12
Dhar, *India* 68 H6
Dharampur, *India* 68 H6
Dharamsala = Dharmsala,
  India 68 C7
Dharmapuri, *India* 66 N11
Dharmsala, *India* 68 C7

Dharwad, *India* 66 M9
Dhaulagiri, *Nepal* 69 E10
Dhebar, L., *India* 68 G6
Dheftera, *Cyprus* 36 D12
Dhenkanal, *India* 67 J14
Dhenoúsa, *Greece* 39 D7
Dherinia, *Cyprus* 36 D12
Dheskáti, *Greece* 40 G5
Dhespotikó, *Greece* 38 E6
Dhestina, *Greece* 38 C4
Dhiarrizos →, *Cyprus* ... 36 E11
Dhībān, *Jordan* 75 D4
Dhidhimótikhon, *Greece* . 41 E10
Dhíkti Óros, *Greece* 36 D7
Dhilianáta, *Greece* 38 C2
Dhílos, *Greece* 39 D7
Dhimitsána, *Greece* 38 D4
Dhírfis = Dhírfis Óros,
  Greece 38 C5
Dhírfis Óros, *Greece* 38 C5
Dhodhekánisos, *Greece* .. 39 E8
Dhodhekánisos □, *Greece* 39 E8
Dhokós, *Greece* 38 D5
Dholiana, *Greece* 38 B2
Dholka, *India* 68 H5
Dhomokós, *Greece* 38 B4
Dhoraji, *India* 68 J4
Dhoxáton, *Greece* 41 E8
Dragonísi, *Greece* 39 D7
Dráhstis, Ákra, *Greece* ... 36 A3
Dhrangadhra, *India* 68 H4
Dhrápanon, Ákra, *Greece* 36 D6
Dhriopís, *Greece* 38 D6
Dhrol, *India* 68 H4
Dhuburi, *India* 67 F16
Dhule, *India* 66 J9
Di Linh, *Vietnam* 65 G7
Di Linh, Cao Nguyen,
  Vietnam 65 G7
Día, *Greece* 36 D7
Diablo, Mt., *U.S.A.* 116 H5
Diablo Range, *U.S.A.* 116 J5
Diafarabé, *Mali* 82 C4
Diala, *Mali* 82 C3
Dialakoro, *Mali* 82 C3
Diallassagou, *Mali* 82 C4
Diamante, *Argentina* 126 C3
Diamante, *Italy* 31 C8
Diamante →, *Argentina* .. 126 C2
Diamantina, *Brazil* 125 G10
Diamantina →, *Australia* . 95 D2
Diamantino, *Brazil* 125 F7
Diamond Bar, *U.S.A.* 117 L9
Diamond Harbour, *India* . 69 H13
Diamond Is., *Australia* ... 94 B5
Diamond Mts., *U.S.A.* ... 114 G6
Diamond Springs, *U.S.A.* . 116 G6
Diamondville, *U.S.A.* 114 F8
Dianalund, *Denmark* 11 J5
Dianbai, *China* 59 G8
Diancheng, *China* 59 G8
Diano Marina, *Italy* 28 E5
Dianra, *Ivory C.* 82 D3
Diapaga, *Burkina Faso* ... 83 C5
Diapangou, *Burkina Faso* . 83 C5
Diariguila, *Guinea* 82 C2
Dībā, *Oman* 71 E8
Dibaya-Lubue,
  Dem. Rep. of the Congo 84 E3
Dibbi, *Ethiopia* 81 G5
Dibete, *Botswana* 88 C4
Dibrugarh, *India* 67 F19
Dickinson, *U.S.A.* 112 B3
Dickson = Dikson, *Russia* 50 B9
Dickson, *U.S.A.* 109 G2
Dickson City, *U.S.A.* 111 E9
Dicle Nehri →, *Turkey* ... 73 D9
Dicomano, *Italy* 29 E8
Didesa →, *Ethiopia* 81 E4
Didiéni, *Mali* 82 C3
Didsbury, *Canada* 104 C6
Didwana, *India* 68 F6
Die, *France* 21 D9
Diébougou, *Burkina Faso* . 82 C4
Diefenbaker L., *Canada* .. 105 C7
Diego de Almagro, *Chile* . 128 B2
Diego Garcia, *Ind. Oc.* ... 3 E13
Diekirch, *Lux.* 17 E6
Diéma, *Mali* 82 C3
Diembéring, *Senegal* 82 C1
Dien Ban, *Vietnam* 64 E7
Dien Bien, *Vietnam* 64 B4
Dien Khanh, *Vietnam* 65 F7
Diepholz, *Germany* 24 C4
Dieppe, *France* 18 C8
Dierks, *U.S.A.* 113 H8
Diest, *Belgium* 17 D5
Dietikon, *Switz.* 25 H4
Dieulefit, *France* 21 D9
Dieuze, *France* 19 D13
Differdange, *Lux.* 17 E5
Dig, *India* 68 F7
Digba,
  Dem. Rep. of the Congo 86 B2
Digby, *Canada* 103 D6
Digges, *Canada* 105 B10
Dighinala, *Bangla.* 67 H18
Dighton, *U.S.A.* 112 F4
Digne-les-Bains, *France* .. 21 D10
Digoin, *France* 19 F11
Digor, *Turkey* 73 B10
Digos, *Phil.* 61 H6
Digranes, *Iceland* 8 C6
Digul →, *Indonesia* 63 F9
Dihang →, *India* 67 F19
Dīhōk, *Iraq* 70 B3
Dijlah, Nahr →, *Asia* 70 D5

Dijon, *France* 19 E12
Dikala, *Sudan* 81 G3
Dikili, *Turkey* 39 B8
Dikkil, *Djibouti* 81 E5
Dikomu di Kai, *Botswana* 88 C3
Diksmuide, *Belgium* 17 C2
Dikson, *Russia* 50 B9
Dikwa, *Nigeria* 83 C7
Dila, *Ethiopia* 81 F4
Dili, *Indonesia* 63 F7
Dilijan, *Armenia* 49 K7
Dilizhan = Dilijan,
  Armenia 49 K7
Dilj, *Croatia* 42 E3
Dillenburg, *Germany* 24 E4
Dilley, *U.S.A.* 113 L5
Dilling, *Sudan* 81 E2
Dillingen, *Bayern,*
  Germany 25 G6
Dillingen, *Saarland,*
  Germany 25 F2
Dillingham, *U.S.A.* 100 C4
Dillon, *Canada* 105 B7
Dillon, *Mont., U.S.A.* 114 D7
Dillon, *S.C., U.S.A.* 109 H6
Dillon →, *Canada* 105 B7
Dilolo,
  Dem. Rep. of the Congo 84 G4
Dilston, *Australia* 94 G4
Dimas, *Mexico* 118 C3
Dimashq, *Syria* 75 B5
Dimashq □, *Syria* 75 B5
Dimbaza, *S. Africa* 89 E4
Dimbokro, *Ivory C.* 82 D4
Dimboola, *Australia* 95 F3
Dîmboviţa =
  Dâmboviţa →, *Romania* 43 F11
Dimbulah, *Australia* 94 B4
Dimitrovgrad, *Bulgaria* . . . 41 D9
Dimitrovgrad, *Russia* 48 C9
Dimitrovgrad, *Serbia, Yug.* 40 C6
Dimitrovo = Pernik,
  Bulgaria 40 D7
Dimmitt, *U.S.A.* 113 H3
Dimo, *Sudan* 81 F2
Dimona, *Israel* 75 D4
Dimovo, *Bulgaria* 40 C6
Dinagat, *Phil.* 61 F6
Dinajpur, *Bangla.* 67 G16
Dinan, *France* 18 D4
Dīnān Āb, *Iran* 71 C8
Dinant, *Belgium* 17 D4
Dinapur, *India* 69 G11
Dinar, *Turkey* 39 C12
Dīnār, Kūh-e, *Iran* 71 D6
Dinara Planina, *Croatia* . . 29 D13
Dinard, *France* 18 D4
Dinaric Alps = Dinara
  Planina, *Croatia* 29 D13
Dinder, Nahr ed →, *Sudan* 81 E3
Dindigul, *India* 66 P11
Ding Xian, *China* 56 E8
Dingalan, *Phil.* 61 D4
Dingbian, *China* 56 F4
Dingelstädt, *Germany* 24 D6
Dinghai, *China* 59 B14
Dingle, *Ireland* 15 D1
Dingle, *Sweden* 11 F5
Dingle B., *Ireland* 15 D1
Dingmans Ferry, *U.S.A.* . . 111 E10
Dingnan, *China* 59 E10
Dingo, *Australia* 94 C4
Dingolfing, *Germany* 25 G8
Dingtao, *China* 56 G8
Dinguiraye, *Guinea* 82 C2
Dingwall, *U.K.* 14 D4
Dingxi, *China* 56 G3
Dingxiang, *China* 56 E7
Dingyuan, *China* 59 A11
Dinh, Mui, *Vietnam* 65 G7
Dinh Lap, *Vietnam* 64 B6
Dinokwe, *Botswana* 88 C4
Dinosaur National
  Monument, *U.S.A.* 114 F9
Dinuba, *U.S.A.* 116 J7
Diö, *Sweden* 11 H8
Diósgyör, *Hungary* 42 B5
Diosig, *Romania* 42 C7
Diourbel, *Senegal* 82 C1
Diplo, *Pakistan* 68 G3
Dipolog, *Phil.* 61 G5
Dir, *Pakistan* 66 B7
Diré, *Mali* 82 B4
Dire Dawa, *Ethiopia* 81 F5
Diriamba, *Nic.* 120 D2
Dirk Hartog I., *Australia* . . 93 E1
Dirranbandi, *Australia* . . . 95 D4
Disa, *India* 68 G5
Disa, *Sudan* 81 E3
Disappointment, C.,
  U.S.A. 114 C2
Disappointment, L.,
  Australia 92 D3
Disaster B., *Australia* 95 F4
Discovery B., *Australia* . . . 95 F3
Disentis, *Switz.* 25 J4
Dishna, *Egypt* 80 B3
Disina, *Nigeria* 83 C6
Disko, *Greenland* 4 C5
Disko Bugt, *Greenland* . . . 4 C5
Disna = Dzisna →,
  Belarus 46 E5
Diss, *U.K.* 13 E9
Disteghil Sar, *Pakistan* . . . 69 A6
Distrito Federal □, *Brazil* 125 G9
Disûq, *Egypt* 80 H7
Diu, *India* 68 J4

Dīvāndarreh, *Iran* 70 C5
Dives →, *France* 18 C6
Dives-sur-Mer, *France* . . . 18 C6
Divichi = Däväçi,
  Azerbaijan 49 K9
Divide, *U.S.A.* 114 D7
Dividing Ra., *Australia* . . . 93 E2
Divinópolis, *Brazil* 125 H10
Divjake, *Albania* 40 F3
Divnoye, *Russia* 49 H6
Divo, *Ivory C.* 82 D3
Divriği, *Turkey* 73 C8
Dīwāl Kol, *Afghan.* 68 B2
Dixie Mt., *U.S.A.* 116 F6
Dixon, *Calif., U.S.A.* 116 G5
Dixon, *Ill., U.S.A.* 112 E10
Dixon, *Mont., U.S.A.* 114 C6
Dixon, *N. Mex., U.S.A.* . . 115 H11
Dixon Entrance, *U.S.A.* . . 104 C2
Dixonville, *Canada* 104 B5
Diyadin, *Turkey* 73 C10
Diyālā →, *Iraq* 73 F11
Diyarbakır, *Turkey* 73 D9
Djakarta = Jakarta,
  Indonesia 63 G12
Djamba, *Angola* 88 B1
Djambala, *Congo* 84 E2
Djanet, *Algeria* 78 D7
Djawa = Jawa, *Indonesia* 63 G14
Djelfa, *Algeria* 78 B6
Djema, *C.A.R.* 86 A2
Djenné, *Mali* 82 C4
Djerba, I. de, *Tunisia* 79 B8
Djerid, Chott, *Tunisia* 78 B7
Djibo, *Burkina Faso* 83 C4
Djibouti, *Djibouti* 81 E5
Djibouti ■, *Africa* 81 E5
Djolu,
  Dem. Rep. of the Congo 84 D4
Djougou, *Benin* 83 D5
Djoum, *Cameroon* 84 D2
Djourab, Erg du, *Chad* . . . 79 E9
Djugu,
  Dem. Rep. of the Congo 86 B3
Djúpivogur, *Iceland* 8 D6
Djurås, *Sweden* 10 D9
Djursland, *Denmark* 11 H4
Dmitriya Lapteva, Proliv,
  Russia 51 B15
Dmitriyev Lgovskiy, *Russia* 47 F8
Dmitrov, *Russia* 46 D9
Dmitrovsk-Orlovskiy,
  Russia 47 F8
Dnepr → = Dnipro →,
  Ukraine 47 J7
Dneprodzerzhinsk =
  Dniprodzerzhynsk,
  Ukraine 47 H8
Dneprodzerzhinskoye
  Vdkhr. =
  Dniprodzerzhynske
  Vdskh., *Ukraine* 47 H8
Dnepropetrovsk =
  Dnipropetrovsk, *Ukraine* 47 H8
Dneprorudnoye =
  Dniprorudne, *Ukraine* . . 47 J8
Dnestr → = Dnister →,
  Europe 47 J6
Dnestrovski = Belgorod,
  Russia 47 G9
Dnieper = Dnipro →,
  Ukraine 47 J7
Dniester = Dnister →,
  Europe 47 J6
Dnipro →, *Ukraine* 47 J7
Dniprodzerzhynsk, *Ukraine* 47 H8
Dniprodzerzhynske Vdskh.,
  Ukraine 47 H8
Dnipropetrovsk, *Ukraine* . 47 H8
Dniprorudne, *Ukraine* . . . 47 J8
Dnister →, *Europe* 47 J6
Dnistrovskyy Lyman,
  Ukraine 47 J6
Dno, *Russia* 46 D5
Dnyapro = Dnipro →,
  Ukraine 47 J7
Doan Hung, *Vietnam* 64 B5
Doba, *Chad* 79 G9
Dobbiaco, *Italy* 29 B9
Dobbyn, *Australia* 94 B3
Dobczyce, *Poland* 45 J7
Dobele, *Latvia* 9 H20
Dobele □, *Latvia* 44 B10
Döbeln, *Germany* 24 D9
Doberai, Jazirah, *Indonesia* 63 E8
Dobiegniew, *Poland* 45 F2
Doblas, *Argentina* 126 D3
Dobo, *Indonesia* 63 F8
Doboj, *Bos.-H.* 42 F3
Dobra, Konin, *Poland* 45 G5
Dobra, Szczecin, *Poland* . . 44 E2
Dobra, Dîmbovita,
  Romania 43 F10
Dobra, Hunedoara,
  Romania 42 E7
Dobre Miasto, *Poland* 44 E7
Dobreşti, *Romania* 42 D7
Dobreta-Turnu Severin,
  Romania 42 F7
Dobrich, *Bulgaria* 41 C11
Dobrinishta, *Bulgaria* 40 E7
Dobříš, *Czech Rep.* 26 B7
Dobrodzień, *Poland* 45 H5
Dobropole, *Ukraine* 47 H9
Dobruja, *Europe* 43 F13
Dobrush, *Belarus* 47 F6
Dobrzany, *Poland* 44 E2

Dobrzyń nad Wisłą, *Poland* 45 F6
Dobtong, *Sudan* 81 F3
Doc, Mui, *Vietnam* 64 D6
Docksta, *Sweden* 10 A12
Doda, *India* 69 C6
Dodecanese =
  Dhodhekánisos, *Greece* . 39 E8
Dodge Center, *U.S.A.* . . . 112 C8
Dodge City, *U.S.A.* 113 G5
Dodge L., *Canada* 105 B7
Dodgeville, *U.S.A.* 112 D9
Dodo, *Sudan* 81 F2
Dodola, *Ethiopia* 81 F4
Dodoma, *Tanzania* 86 D4
Dodoma □, *Tanzania* 86 D4
Dodona, *Greece* 38 B2
Dodsland, *Canada* 105 C7
Dodson, *U.S.A.* 114 B9
Dodurga, *Turkey* 39 B11
Doesburg, *Neths.* 17 B6
Doetinchem, *Neths.* 17 C6
Dog Creek, *Canada* 104 C4
Dog L., *Man., Canada* . . . 105 C9
Dog L., *Ont., Canada* . . . 102 C2
Dogansehir, *Turkey* 72 C7
Dogi, *Afghan.* 66 C3
Dogliani, *Italy* 28 D4
Dogondoutchi, *Niger* 83 C5
Dogran, *Pakistan* 68 D5
Doğubayazıt, *Turkey* 73 C11
Dogué raoua, *Niger* 83 C6
Doha = Ad Dawhah, *Qatar* 71 E6
Dohazari, *Bangla.* 67 H18
Doi, *Indonesia* 63 D7
Doi Luang, *Thailand* 64 C3
Doi Saket, *Thailand* 64 C2
Doig →, *Canada* 104 B4
Dois Irmãos, Sa., *Brazil* . 125 E10
Dojransko Jezero,
  Macedonia 40 E6
Dokkum, *Neths.* 17 A5
Dokri, *Pakistan* 68 F3
Dokuchayevsk, *Ukraine* . . 47 J9
Dol-de-Bretagne, *France* . . 18 D5
Dolak, Pulau, *Indonesia* . . 63 F9
Doland, *U.S.A.* 112 C5
Dolbeau, *Canada* 103 C5
Dole, *France* 19 E12
Doleib, Wadi →, *Sudan* . 81 E3
Dolenji Logatec, *Slovenia* . 29 C11
Dolgellau, *U.K.* 12 E4
Dolgelley = Dolgellau,
  U.K. 12 E4
Dolhasca, *Romania* 43 C11
Dolianova, *Italy* 30 C2
Dolj □, *Romania* 43 F8
Dollard, *Neths.* 17 A7
Dolna Banya, *Bulgaria* . . . 40 D7
Dolni Chiflik, *Bulgaria* . . . 41 D11
Dolni Dŭbnik, *Bulgaria* . . 41 C8
Dolný Kubín, *Slovak Rep.* . 27 B12
Dolo, *Ethiopia* 81 G5
Dolo, *Italy* 29 C9
Dolomites = Dolomiti,
  Italy 29 B8
Dolomiti, *Italy* 29 B8
Dolores, *Argentina* 126 D4
Dolores, *Uruguay* 126 C4
Dolores, *U.S.A.* 115 H9
Dolores →, *U.S.A.* 115 G9
Dolovo, *Serbia, Yug.* 42 F5
Dolphin, C., *Falk. Is.* 128 G5
Dolphin and Union Str.,
  Canada 100 B8
Dolsk, *Poland* 45 G4
Dolynska, *Ukraine* 47 H7
Dolzhanskaya, *Russia* . . . 47 J9
Dom Pedrito, *Brazil* 127 C5
Doma, *Nigeria* 83 D6
Domaniç, *Turkey* 39 B11
Domasi, *Malawi* 87 F4
Domažlice, *Czech Rep.* . . . 26 B5
Dombarovskiy, *Russia* . . . 50 D6
Dombås, *Norway* 9 E13
Dombasle-sur-Meurthe,
  France 19 D13
Dombes, *France* 21 C9
Dombóvár, *Hungary* 42 D3
Dombrád, *Hungary* 42 B6
Domel I. = Letsôk-aw
  Kyun, *Burma* 65 G2
Domérat, *France* 19 F9
Domeyko, *Chile* 126 B1
Domeyko, Cordillera, *Chile* 126 A2
Domfront, *France* 18 D6
Dominador, *Chile* 126 A2
Dominica ■, *W. Indies* . . . 121 C7
Dominica Passage,
  W. Indies 121 C7
Dominican Rep. ■,
  W. Indies 121 C5
Dömitz, *Germany* 24 B7
Domme, *France* 20 D5
Domnești, *Romania* 43 E9
Domodóssola, *Italy* 28 B4
Dompaire, *France* 19 D13
Dompierre-sur-Besbre,
  France 19 F10
Dompim, *Ghana* 82 D4
Domrémy-la-Pucelle,
  France 19 D12
Domville, Mt., *Australia* . . 95 D5
Domvraína, *Greece* 38 C4
Domžale, *Slovenia* 29 B11
Don →, *Russia* 47 J10

Don →, *Aberds., U.K.* . . 14 D6
Don →, *S. Yorks., U.K.* . . 12 D7
Don, C., *Australia* 92 B5
Don Benito, *Spain* 35 G5
Don Martín, Presa de,
  Mexico 118 B4
Dona Ana = Nhamaabué,
  Mozam. 87 F4
Doña Mencía, *Spain* 35 H6
Donaghadee, *U.K.* 15 B6
Donald, *Australia* 95 F3
Donalda, *Canada* 104 C6
Donaldsonville, *U.S.A.* . . . 113 K9
Donalsonville, *U.S.A.* 109 K3
Donau = Dunărea →,
  Europe 43 E14
Donau →, *Austria* 27 C10
Donaueschingen, *Germany* 25 H4
Donauwörth, *Germany* . . . 25 G6
Doncaster, *U.K.* 12 D6
Dondo, *Mozam.* 87 F3
Dondo, Teluk, *Indonesia* . 63 D6
Dondra Head, *Sri Lanka* . 66 S12
Donduşeni, *Moldova* 43 B12
Donegal, *Ireland* 15 B3
Donegal □, *Ireland* 15 B4
Donegal B., *Ireland* 15 B3
Donets →, *Russia* 49 G5
Donetsk, *Ukraine* 47 J9
Dong Ba Thin, *Vietnam* . . 65 F7
Dong Dang, *Vietnam* 64 B6
Dong Giam, *Vietnam* 64 C5
Dong Ha, *Vietnam* 64 D6
Dong Hene, *Laos* 64 D5
Dong Hoi, *Vietnam* 64 D6
Dong Jiang →, *China* 59 F10
Dong Khe, *Vietnam* 64 A6
Dong Ujimqin Qi, *China* . . 56 B9
Dong Van, *Vietnam* 64 A5
Dong Xoai, *Vietnam* 65 G6
Donga, *Nigeria* 83 D7
Dong'an, *China* 59 D8
Dongara, *Australia* 93 E1
Dongbei, *China* 57 D13
Dongchuan, *China* 58 D4
Dongfang, *China* 64 C7
Dongfeng, *China* 57 C13
Donggala, *Indonesia* 63 E5
Donggan, *China* 58 F5
Donggou, *China* 57 E13
Dongguan, *China* 59 F9
Dongguang, *China* 56 F9
Donghai Dao, *China* 59 G8
Dongjingcheng, *China* . . . 57 B15
Donglan, *China* 58 E6
Dongliu, *China* 59 B11
Dongmen, *China* 58 F6
Dongning, *China* 57 B16
Dongnyi, *China* 58 C3
Dongping, *China* 56 G9
Dongshan, *China* 59 F11
Dongsheng, *China* 56 E6
Dongtai, *China* 57 H11
Dongting Hu, *China* 59 C9
Dongxiang, *China* 59 C11
Dongxing, *China* 58 G7
Dongyang, *China* 59 C13
Dongzhi, *China* 59 B11
Donington, C., *Australia* . . 95 E2
Doniphan, *U.S.A.* 113 G9
Donja Stubica, *Croatia* . . . 29 C12
Donji Dušnik, *Serbia, Yug.* 40 C6
Donji Miholjac, *Croatia* . . 42 E3
Donji Milanovac,
  Serbia, Yug. 40 B6
Donji Vakuf, *Bos.-H.* 42 F2
Dønna, *Norway* 8 C15
Donna, *U.S.A.* 113 M5
Donnaconna, *Canada* 103 C5
Donnelly's Crossing, *N.Z.* . 91 F4
Donnybrook, *Australia* . . . 93 F2
Donnybrook, *S. Africa* . . . 89 D4
Donora, *U.S.A.* 110 F5
Donor's Hill, *Australia* . . . 94 B3
Donostia = Donostia-San
  Sebastián, *Spain* 32 B3
Donostia-San Sebastián,
  Spain 32 B3
Donskoy, *Russia* 46 F10
Donsol, *Phil.* 61 E5
Donzère, *France* 21 D8
Donzy, *France* 19 E10
Doon →, *U.K.* 14 F4
Dora, L., *Australia* 92 D3
Dora Báltea →, *Italy* 28 C5
Dora Ripária →, *Italy* 28 C4
Doran L., *Canada* 105 A7
Dorchester, *U.K.* 13 G5
Dorchester, C., *Canada* . . 101 B12
Dordogne □, *France* 20 C4
Dordogne →, *France* 20 C3
Dordrecht, *Neths.* 17 C4
Dordrecht, *S. Africa* 88 E4
Dore →, *France* 20 C7
Doré, Mts., *France* 20 C7
Doré L., *Canada* 105 C7
Doré Lake, *Canada* 105 C7
Dorfen, *Germany* 25 G8
Dorgali, *Italy* 30 B2
Dori, *Burkina Faso* 83 C4
Doring →, *S. Africa* 88 E2
Doringbos, *S. Africa* 88 E2
Dorion, *Canada* 102 C5
Dormaa-Ahenkro, *Ghana* . 82 D4

Dormo, Ras, *Eritrea* 81 E5
Dornbirn, *Austria* 26 D2
Dornes, *France* 19 F10
Dorneşti, *Romania* 43 C11
Dornie, *U.K.* 14 D3
Dornoch, *U.K.* 14 D4
Dornoch Firth, *U.K.* 14 D4
Dornogovĭ □, *Mongolia* . . 56 C6
Doro, *Mali* 83 B4
Dorog, *Hungary* 42 C3
Dorogobuzh, *Russia* 46 E7
Dorohoi, *Romania* 43 C11
Döröö Nuur, *Mongolia* . . . 60 B4
Dorr, *Iran* 71 C6
Dorre I., *Australia* 93 E1
Dorrigo, *Australia* 95 E5
Dorris, *U.S.A.* 114 F3
Dorset, *Canada* 110 A6
Dorset, *U.S.A.* 110 E4
Dorset □, *U.K.* 13 G5
Dorsten, *Germany* 24 D2
Dortmund, *Germany* 24 D3
Dortmund-Ems-Kanal →,
  Germany 24 D3
Dörtyol, *Turkey* 72 D7
Dorum, *Germany* 24 B4
Doruma,
  Dem. Rep. of the Congo 86 B2
Dorūneh, *Iran* 71 C8
Dos Bahías, C., *Argentina* 128 E3
Dos Hermanas, *Spain* 35 H5
Dos Palos, *U.S.A.* 116 J6
Döşemealtı, *Turkey* 39 D12
Dosso, *Niger* 83 C5
Dothan, *U.S.A.* 109 K3
Doty, *U.S.A.* 116 D3
Douai, *France* 19 B10
Douala, *Cameroon* 83 E6
Douarnenez, *France* 18 D2
Double Island Pt., *Australia* 95 D5
Doubrava →, *Czech Rep.* . 26 A8
Doubs □, *France* 19 E13
Doubs →, *France* 19 F12
Doubtful Sd., *N.Z.* 91 L1
Doubtless B., *N.Z.* 91 F4
Doudeville, *France* 18 C7
Doué-la-Fontaine, *France* . 18 E6
Douentza, *Mali* 82 C4
Douglas, *S. Africa* 88 D3
Douglas, *U.K.* 12 C3
Douglas, *Alaska, U.S.A.* . 104 B2
Douglas, *Ariz., U.S.A.* . . . 115 L9
Douglas, *Ga., U.S.A.* 109 K4
Douglas, *Wyo., U.S.A.* . . . 112 D2
Douglastown, *Canada* . . . 103 C7
Douglasville, *U.S.A.* 109 J3
Doukáton, Ákra, *Greece* . 38 C2
Doulevant-le-Château,
  France 19 D11
Doullens, *France* 19 B9
Douna, *Mali* 82 C3
Dounreay, *U.K.* 14 C5
Dourada, Serra, *Brazil* . . . 125 F9
Dourados, *Brazil* 127 A5
Dourados →, *Brazil* 127 A5
Dourdan, *France* 19 D9
Douro →, *Europe* 34 D2
Douvaine, *France* 19 F13
Douvres-la-Délivrande,
  France 18 C6
Douze →, *France* 20 E3
Dove →, *U.K.* 12 E6
Dove Creek, *U.S.A.* 115 H9
Dover, *Australia* 94 G4
Dover, *U.K.* 13 F9
Dover, *Del., U.S.A.* 108 F8
Dover, *N.H., U.S.A.* 111 C14
Dover, *N.J., U.S.A.* 111 F10
Dover, *Ohio, U.S.A.* 110 F3
Dover, Pt., *Australia* 93 F4
Dover, Str. of, *Europe* . . . 13 G9
Dover-Foxcroft, *U.S.A.* . . . 103 C6
Dover Plains, *U.S.A.* 111 E11
Dovey = Dyfi →, *U.K.* . . . 13 E3
Dovrefjell, *Norway* 9 E13
Dow Rūd, *Iran* 71 C6
Dowa, *Malawi* 87 E3
Dowagiac, *U.S.A.* 108 E2
Dowgha'i, *Iran* 71 B8
Dowlatābād, *Iran* 71 D8
Down □, *U.K.* 15 B5
Downey, *Calif., U.S.A.* . . . 117 M8
Downey, *Idaho, U.S.A.* . . . 114 E7
Downham Market, *U.K.* . . 13 E8
Downieville, *U.S.A.* 116 F6
Downpatrick, *U.K.* 15 B6
Downpatrick Hd., *Ireland* . 15 B2
Dowsārī, *Iran* 71 D8
Doyle, *U.S.A.* 116 E6
Doylestown, *U.S.A.* 111 F9
Drac →, *France* 21 C9
Dračevo, *Macedonia* 40 E5
Drachten, *Neths.* 17 A6
Drăgănești, *Moldova* 43 C13
Drăgănești-Olt, *Romania* . 43 F9
Drăgănești-Vlașca,
  Romania 43 F10
Dragaš, *Serbia, Yug.* 40 D4
Drăgășani, *Romania* 43 F9
Dragichyn, *Belarus* 47 F3
Dragocvet, *Serbia, Yug.* . . 40 C5
Dragovishtitsa, *Bulgaria* . . 40 D6
Draguignan, *France* 21 E10
Drain, *U.S.A.* 114 E2
Drake, *Australia* 95 D5
Drake, *U.S.A.* 112 B4
Drake Passage, *S. Ocean* . 5 B17

Drakensberg, S. Africa ... 89 E4
Dráma, Greece 41 E8
Dráma □, Greece 41 E8
Drammen, Norway 9 G14
Drangajökull, Iceland 8 C2
Dranov, Ostrov, Romania 43 F14
Dras, India 69 B6
Drau = Drava →, Croatia 42 E3
Drava →, Croatia 42 E3
Dravograd, Slovenia 29 B12
Drawa →, Poland 45 E2
Drawno, Poland 45 E2
Drawsko Pomorskie,
  Poland 44 E2
Drayton Valley, Canada .. 104 C6
Dreieich, Germany 25 E4
Dren, Serbia, Yug. 40 C4
Drenthe □, Neths. 17 B6
Drepanum, C., Cyprus ... 36 E11
Dresden, Canada 110 D2
Dresden, Germany 24 D9
Dreux, France 18 D8
Drezdenko, Poland 45 F2
Driffield, U.K. 12 C7
Driftwood, U.S.A. 110 E6
Driggs, U.S.A. 114 E8
Drin i Zi →, Albania 40 E4
Drina →, Bos.-H. 40 B3
Drincea →, Romania 42 F7
Drini →, Albania 40 D3
Drinjača →, Bos.-H. ... 42 F4
Drissa =
  Vyerkhnyadzvinsk,
  Belarus 46 E4
Drniš, Croatia 29 E13
Drøbak, Norway 9 G14
Drobin, Poland 45 F6
Drochia, Moldova 43 B12
Drogheda, Ireland 15 C5
Drogichin = Dragichyn,
  Belarus 47 F3
Drogobych = Drohobych,
  Ukraine 47 H2
Drohiczyn, Poland 45 F9
Drohobych, Ukraine 47 H2
Droichead Atha =
  Drogheda, Ireland 15 C5
Droichead Nua, Ireland .. 15 C5
Droitwich, U.K. 13 E5
Drôme □, France 21 D9
Drôme →, France 21 D8
Dromedary, C., Australia . 95 F5
Dromore, U.K. 15 B4
Dromore West, Ireland ... 15 B3
Dronero, Italy 28 D4
Dronfield, Australia 94 C3
Dronfield, U.K. 12 D6
Dronne →, France 20 C3
Dronning Ingrid, Denmark 11 G4
Dronten, Neths. 17 B5
Dropt →, France 20 D3
Drosendorf, Austria 26 C8
Droué, France 18 D8
Drumbo, Canada 110 C4
Drumheller, Canada 104 C6
Drummond, U.S.A. 114 C7
Drummond I., U.S.A. ... 102 C3
Drummond Pt., Australia . 95 E2
Drummond Ra., Australia 94 C4
Drummondville, Canada .. 102 C5
Drumright, U.S.A. 113 H6
Druskininkai, Lithuania .. 9 J20
Drut →, Belarus 47 F6
Druya, Belarus 46 E4
Druzhba, Bulgaria 41 C12
Druzhina, Russia 51 C15
Drvar, Bos.-H. 29 D13
Drvenik, Croatia 29 E13
Drwęca →, Poland 45 E6
Dry Tortugas, U.S.A. ... 120 B3
Dryanovo, Bulgaria 41 D9
Dryden, Canada 105 D10
Dryden, U.S.A. 113 K3
Drygalski I., Antarctica .. 5 C7
Drysdale →, Australia .. 92 B4
Drysdale I., Australia ... 94 A2
Drzewica, Poland 45 G7
Drzewiczka →, Poland . 45 G7
Dschang, Cameroon 83 D7
Du Bois, U.S.A. 110 E6
Du Quoin, U.S.A. 112 G10
Duanesburg, U.S.A. 111 D10
Duaringa, Australia 94 C4
Dubā, Si. Arabia 70 E2
Dubai = Dubayy, U.A.E. . 71 E7
Dubăsari, Moldova 43 C14
Dubăsari Vdkhr., Moldova 43 C13
Dubawnt →, Canada ... 105 A8
Dubawnt, L., Canada ... 105 A8
Dubayy, U.A.E. 71 E7
Dubbo, Australia 95 E4
Dubele,
  Dem. Rep. of the Congo 86 B2
Dübendorf, Switz. 25 H4
Dubica, Croatia 29 C13
Dublin, Ireland 15 C5
Dublin, Ga., U.S.A. 109 J4
Dublin, Tex., U.S.A. 113 J5
Dublin □, Ireland 15 C5
Dubna, Russia 46 D9
Dubnica nad Váhom,
  Slovak Rep. 27 C11
Dubno, Ukraine 47 G3
Dubois, U.S.A. 114 D7
Dubossary = Dubăsari,
  Moldova 43 C14

Dubossary Vdkhr. =
  Dubăsari Vdkhr.,
  Moldova 43 C13
Dubovka, Russia 49 F7
Dubovskoye, Russia 49 G6
Dubrajpur, India 69 H12
Dubréka, Guinea 82 D2
Dubrovitsa = Dubrovytsa,
  Ukraine 47 G4
Dubrovnik, Croatia 40 D2
Dubrovytsa, Ukraine 47 G4
Dubuque, U.S.A. 112 D9
Dubysa →, Lithuania .. 44 C10
Duchang, China 59 C11
Duchesne, U.S.A. 114 F8
Duchess, Australia 94 C2
Ducie I., Pac. Oc. 97 K15
Duck Cr. →, Australia .. 92 D2
Duck Lake, Canada 105 C7
Duck Mountain Prov. Park,
  Canada 105 C8
Duckwall, Mt., U.S.A. .. 116 H6
Duderstadt, Germany ... 24 D6
Dudhi, India 67 G13
Dudinka, Russia 51 C9
Dudley, U.K. 13 E5
Dueñas, Spain 34 D6
Duero = Douro →,
  Europe 34 D2
Dufftown, U.K. 14 D5
Dufourspitz, Switz. 25 K3
Dugi Otok, Croatia 29 D11
Dugo Selo, Croatia 29 C13
Duifken Pt., Australia ... 94 A3
Duisburg, Germany 24 D2
Duiwelskloof, S. Africa .. 89 C5
Dukati, Albania 40 F3
Dükdamïn, Iran 71 C8
Duke I., U.S.A. 104 C2
Dukelský Průsm˅k,
  Slovak Rep. 27 B14
Dukhān, Qatar 71 E6
Dukhovshchina, Russia .. 46 E7
Duki, Pakistan 66 D6
Dukla, Poland 45 J8
Dulag, Phil. 61 F6
Dulce, →, Argentina ... 126 C3
Dulce, G., Costa Rica ... 120 E3
Dulf, Iraq 70 C5
Dŭlgopol, Bulgaria 41 C11
Dulit, Banjaran, Malaysia . 62 D4
Duliu, China 56 E9
Dullewala, Pakistan 68 D4
Dülmen, Germany 24 D3
Dulovo, Bulgaria 41 C11
Dulq Maghār, Syria 70 B3
Dululu, Australia 94 C5
Duluth, U.S.A. 112 B8
Dum Dum, India 69 H13
Dum Duma, India 67 F19
Dūmā, Syria 75 B5
Dumaguete, Phil. 61 G5
Dumai, Indonesia 62 D2
Dumaran, Phil. 61 F3
Dumas, Ark., U.S.A. ... 113 J9
Dumas, Tex., U.S.A. ... 113 H4
Dumbarton, U.K. 14 F4
Dumbier, Slovak Rep. ... 27 C12
Dumbleyung, Australia .. 93 F2
Dumbrăveni, Romania .. 43 D9
Dumfries, U.K. 14 F5
Dumfries & Gallcway □,
  U.K. 14 F5
Dumitreşti, Romania 43 E11
Dumka, India 69 G12
Dumlupınar, Turkey 39 C12
Dümmer, German, ... 24 C4
Dumoine →, Canada ... 102 C4
Dumoine, L., Canada ... 102 C4
Dumraon, India 69 G11
Dumyât, Egypt 80 H7
Dumyât, Masabb, Egypt . 80 H7
Dún Dealgan = Dundalk,
  Ireland 15 B5
Dun Laoghaire, Ireland .. 15 C5
Dun-le-Palestel, France .. 19 F8
Dun-sur-Auron, France .. 19 F9
Dun-sur-Meuse, France . 19 C12
Duna = Dunărea →,
  Europe 43 E14
Duna →, Hungary 42 E3
Duna-völgyi-főcsatorna,
  Hungary 42 D4
Dunaföldvár, Hungary .. 42 D3
Dunaj = Dunărea →,
  Europe 43 E14
Dunaj →, Slovak Rep. .. 27 D11
Dunajec →, Poland 45 H7
Dunajská Streda,
  Slovak Rep. 27 C10
Dunakeszi, Hungary 42 C4
Dunapataj, Hungary 42 D4
Dunărea →, Europe 43 E14
Dunaszekcső, Hungary .. 42 E3
Dunaújváros, Hungary .. 42 D3
Dunav = Dunărea →,
  Europe 43 E14
Dunavătu de Jos, Romania 43 F14
Dunavtsi, Bulgaria 40 C6
Dunay, Russia 54 C6
Dunback, N.Z. 91 L3
Dunbar, Australia 94 B3
Dunbar, U.K. 14 E6
Dunblane, U.K. 14 E5
Duncan, Canada 104 D4

Duncan, Ariz., U.S.A. ... 115 K9
Duncan, Okla., U.S.A. ... 113 H6
Duncan, L., Canada 102 B4
Duncan L., Canada 104 A6
Duncan Town, Bahamas .. 120 B4
Duncannon, U.S.A. 110 F7
Duncansby Head, U.K. .. 14 C5
Dundaga, Latvia 44 A9
Dundalk, Canada 110 B4
Dundalk, Ireland 15 B5
Dundalk Bay, Ireland ... 15 C5
Dundas, Canada 102 D4
Dundas, L., Australia ... 93 F3
Dundas I., Canada 104 C2
Dundas Str., Australia .. 92 B5
Dundee, S. Africa 89 D5
Dundee, U.K. 14 E6
Dundee City □, U.K. ... 14 E6
Dundgovı □, Mongolia .. 56 B4
Dundoo, Australia 95 D3
Dundrum, U.K. 15 B6
Dundrum B., U.K. 15 B6
Dundwara, India 69 F8
Dunedin, N.Z. 91 L3
Dunedin, U.S.A. 109 L4
Dunedin →, Canada ... 104 B4
Dunfermline, U.K. 14 E5
Dungannon, Canada 110 C3
Dungannon, U.K. 15 B5
Dungarpur, India 68 H5
Dungarvan, Ireland 15 D4
Dungarvan Harbour,
  Ireland 15 D4
Dungeness, U.K. 13 G8
Dungo, L. do, Angola ... 88 B2
Dungog, Australia 95 E5
Dungu,
  Dem. Rep. of the Congo 86 B2
Dungun, Malaysia 65 K4
Dungunâb, Sudan 80 C4
Dungunâb, Khalij, Sudan . 80 C4
Dunhua, China 57 C15
Dunhuang, China 60 B4
Dunk I., Australia 94 B4
Dunkeld, U.K. 14 E5
Dunkerque, France 19 A9
Dunkery Beacon, U.K. .. 13 F4
Dunkirk = Dunkerque,
  France 19 A9
Dunkirk, U.S.A. 110 D5
Dunkuj, Sudan 81 E3
Dunkwa, Central, Ghana . 82 D4
Dunkwa, Central, Ghana . 83 D4
Dunlap, U.S.A. 112 E7
Dúnleary = Dun
  Laoghaire, Ireland 15 C5
Dunleer, Ireland 15 C5
Dunmanus B., Ireland ... 15 E2
Dunmanway, Ireland ... 15 E2
Dunmara, Australia 94 B1
Dunmore, U.S.A. 111 E9
Dunmore Hd., Ireland ... 15 D1
Dunmore Town, Bahamas 120 A4
Dunn, U.S.A. 109 H6
Dunnellon, U.S.A. 109 L4
Dunnet Hd., U.K. 14 C5
Dunning, U.S.A. 112 E4
Dunnville, Canada 110 D5
Dunolly, Australia 95 F3
Dunoon, U.K. 14 F4
Dunqul, Egypt 80 C3
Duns, U.K. 14 F6
Dunseith, U.S.A. 112 A4
Dunsmuir, U.S.A. 114 F2
Dunstable, U.K. 13 F7
Dunstan Mts., N.Z. 91 L2
Dunster, Canada 104 C5
Dunvegan L., Canada ... 105 A7
Duolun, China 56 C9
Duong Dong, Vietnam .. 65 G4
Dupree, U.S.A. 112 C4
Dupuyer, U.S.A. 114 B7
Duque de Caxias, Brazil . 127 A7
Durack →, Australia ... 92 C4
Durack Ra., Australia ... 92 C4
Durağan, Turkey 72 B6
Durak, Turkey 39 B10
Durance →, France ... 21 E8
Durand, U.S.A. 108 D4
Durango, Mexico 118 C4
Durango, U.S.A. 115 H10
Durango □, Mexico 118 C4
Duranillin, Australia ... 93 F2
Durant, U.S.A. 113 J6
Duratón →, Spain 34 D6
Durazno, Uruguay 126 C4
Durazzo = Durrësi,
  Albania 40 E3
Durban, France 20 F6
Durban, S. Africa 89 D5
Durbuy, Belgium 17 D5
Dúrcal, Spain 35 J7
Đurđevac, Croatia 29 C13
Düren, Germany 24 E2
Durg, India 67 J12
Durgapur, India 69 H12
Durham, Canada 102 D3
Durham, U.K. 12 C6
Durham, Calif., U.S.A. .. 116 F5
Durham, N.C., U.S.A. .. 109 H6
Durham □, U.K. 12 C6
Durham Downs, Australia 95 D4
Durleşti, Moldova 43 C13
Durmitor,
  Montenegro, Yug. 40 C2
Durness, U.K. 14 C4

Durrësi, Albania 40 E3
Durrie, Australia 94 D3
Durrow, Ireland 15 D4
Dursey I., Ireland 15 E1
Dursunbey, Turkey 39 B10
Durtal, France 18 E6
Duru,
  Dem. Rep. of the Congo 86 B2
Duru Gölü, Turkey 41 E12
Durusu, Turkey 41 E12
Durūz, Jabal ad, Jordan .. 75 C5
D'Urville, Tanjung,
  Indonesia 63 E9
D'Urville I., N.Z. 91 J4
Duryea, U.S.A. 111 E9
Dûsh, Egypt 80 C3
Dushak, Turkmenistan .. 50 F7
Dushan, China 58 E6
Dushanbe, Tajikistan ... 50 F7
Dusheti, Georgia 49 J7
Dusky Sd., N.Z. 91 L1
Dussejour, C., Australia .. 92 B4
Düsseldorf, Germany ... 24 D2
Duszniki-Zdrój, Poland . 45 H3
Dutch Harbor, U.S.A. .. 100 C3
Dutlwe, Botswana 88 C3
Dutton, Canada 110 D3
Dutton →, Australia ... 94 C3
Duved, Sweden 10 A6
Düvertepe, Turkey 39 B10
Duyun, China 58 D6
Düzağaç, Turkey 39 C12
Düzce, Turkey 72 B4
Dve Mogili, Bulgaria ... 41 C9
Dvina, Severnaya →,
  Russia 50 C5
Dvinsk = Daugavpils,
  Latvia 9 J22
Dvor, Croatia 29 C13
Dvůr Králové nad Labem,
  Czech Rep. 26 A8
Dwarka, India 68 H3
Dwellingup, Australia .. 93 F2
Dwight, Canada 110 A5
Dwight, U.S.A. 108 E1
Dyatkovo, Russia 46 F8
Dyatlovo = Dzyatlava,
  Belarus 46 F3
Dyce, U.K. 14 D6
Dyer, C., Canada 101 B13
Dyer Plateau, Antarctica . 5 D17
Dyersburg, U.S.A. 113 G10
Dyfi →, U.K. 13 E3
Dyje →, Czech Rep. ... 27 C9
Dymer, Ukraine 47 G6
Dynevor Downs, Australia 95 D3
Dynów, Poland 45 J9
Dysart, Canada 105 C8
Dzamin Üüd, Mongolia .. 56 C6
Dzerzhinsk, Russia 48 B6
Dzhalinda, Russia 51 D13
Dzhambul = Zhambyl,
  Kazakstan 50 E8
Dzhankoy, Ukraine 47 K8
Dzhanybek, Kazakstan .. 49 F8
Dzharylhach, Ostriv,
  Ukraine 47 J7
Dzhezkazgan =
  Zhezqazghan, Kazakstan 50 E7
Dzhizak = Jizzakh,
  Uzbekistan 50 E7
Dzhugdzur, Khrebet,
  Russia 51 D14
Dzhvari = Jvari, Georgia . 49 J6
Działdowo, Poland 45 E7
Działoszyce, Poland 45 H7
Działoszyn, Poland 45 G5
Dzierzgoń, Poland 44 E6
Dzierżoniów, Poland ... 45 H3
Dzilam de Bravo, Mexico . 119 C7
Dzisna, Belarus 46 E5
Dzisna →, Belarus 46 E5
Dziwnów, Poland 44 D1
Dzungaria = Junggar
  Pendi, China 60 B3
Dzungarian Gate = Alataw
  Shankou, China 60 B3
Dzuumod, Mongolia ... 60 B5
Dzyarzhynsk, Belarus .. 46 F4
Dzyatlava, Belarus 46 F3

Earlimart, U.S.A. 117 K7
Earn →, U.K. 14 E5
Earn, L., U.K. 14 E4
Earnslaw, Mt., N.Z. 91 L2
Earth, U.S.A. 113 H3
Easley, U.S.A. 109 H4
East Angus, Canada 103 C5
East Aurora, U.S.A. 110 D6
East Ayrshire □, U.K. .. 14 F4
East B., U.S.A. 113 L10
East Bengal, Bangla. 67 H17
East Beskids = Vychodné
  Beskydy, Europe 27 B15
East Brady, U.S.A. 110 F5
East C., N.Z. 91 G7
East Chicago, U.S.A. ... 108 E2
East China Sea, Asia 60 C7
East Coulee, Canada 104 C6
East Dereham, U.K. 13 E8
East Dunbartonshire □,
  U.K. 14 F4
East Falkland, Falk. Is. .. 122 J5
East Grand Forks, U.S.A. 112 B6
East Greenwich, U.S.A. . 111 E13
East Grinstead, U.K. 13 F8
East Hartford, U.S.A. ... 111 E12
East Helena, U.S.A. 114 C8
East Indies, Asia 52 K15
East Jordan, U.S.A. 108 C3
East Kilbride, U.K. 14 F4
East Lansing, U.S.A. 108 D3
East Liverpool, U.S.A. .. 110 F4
East London, S. Africa .. 89 E4
East Lothian □, U.K. ... 14 F6
East Main = Eastmain,
  Canada 102 B4
East Orange, U.S.A. 111 F10
East Pacific Ridge,
  Pac. Oc. 97 J17
East Palestine, U.S.A. ... 110 F4
East Pine, Canada 104 B4
East Point, U.S.A. 109 J3
East Providence, U.S.A. . 111 E13
East Pt., Canada 103 C7
East Renfrewshire □, U.K. 14 F4
East Retford = Retford,
  U.K. 12 D7
East Riding of
  Yorkshire □, U.K. 12 D7
East St. Louis, U.S.A. ... 112 F9
East Schelde =
  Oosterschelde, Neths. .. 17 C4
East Siberian Sea, Russia . 51 B17
East Stroudsburg, U.S.A. . 111 E9
East Sussex □, U.K. 13 G8
East Tawas, U.S.A. 108 C4
East Toorale, Australia .. 95 E4
East Walker →, U.S.A. .. 116 G7
Eastbourne, N.Z. 91 J5
Eastbourne, U.K. 13 G8
Eastend, Canada 105 D7
Easter Islands = Pascua, I.
  de, Pac. Oc. 97 K17
Eastern □, Kenya 86 C4
Eastern □, Uganda 86 B3
Eastern Cape □, S. Africa 88 E4
Eastern Cr. →, Australia 94 C3
Eastern Ghats, India 66 N11
Eastern Group = Lau
  Group, Fiji 91 C9
Eastern Group, Australia . 93 F3
Eastern Province □,
  S. Leone 82 D2
Eastern Transvaal =
  Mpumalanga □, S. Africa 89 B5
Easterville, Canada 105 C9
Easthampton, U.S.A. ... 111 D12
Eastland, U.S.A. 113 J5
Eastleigh, U.K. 13 G6
Eastmain, Canada 102 B4
Eastmain →, Canada .. 102 B4
Eastman, Canada 111 A12
Eastman, U.S.A. 109 J4
Easton, Md., U.S.A. 108 F7
Easton, Pa., U.S.A. 111 F9
Easton, Wash., U.S.A. .. 116 C5
Eastport, U.S.A. 103 D6
Eastsound, U.S.A. 116 B4
Eaton, U.S.A. 112 E2
Eatonia, Canada 105 C7
Eatonton, U.S.A. 109 J4
Eatontown, U.S.A. 111 F10
Eatonville, U.S.A. 116 D4
Eau Claire, U.S.A. 112 C9
Eauze, France 20 E4
Ebagoola, Australia 94 A3
Eban, Nigeria 83 D5
Ebbw Vale, U.K. 13 F4
Ebeltoft, Denmark 11 H4
Ebeltoft Vig, Denmark .. 11 H4
Ebensburg, U.S.A. 110 F6
Ebensee, Austria 26 D6
Eber Gölü, Turkey 72 C4
Eberbach, Germany 25 F4
Eberswalde-Finow,
  Germany 24 C9
Ebetsu, Japan 54 C10
Ebian, China 58 C4
Ebingen, Germany 25 G5
Éboli, Italy 31 B8
Ebolowa, Cameroon 83 E7
Ebrach, Germany 25 F6
Ébrié, Lagune, Ivory C. .. 82 D4
Ebro →, Spain 32 E5
Ebro, Embalse del, Spain . 34 C7
Ebstorf, Germany 24 B6
Eceabat, Turkey 41 F10

Ech Cheliff, *Algeria* 78 A6
Echeng, *China* 59 B10
Echigo-Sammyaku, *Japan* . 55 F9
Échirolles, *France* 21 C9
Echizen-Misaki, *Japan* 55 G7
Echmiadzin = Yejmiadzin, *Armenia* 49 K7
Echo Bay, *N.W.T., Canada* 100 B8
Echo Bay, *Ont., Canada* . 102 C3
Echoing →, *Canada* 105 B10
Echternach, *Lux.* 17 E6
Echuca, *Australia* 95 F3
Ecija, *Spain* 35 H5
Eckental, *Germany* 25 F7
Eckernförde, *Germany* ... 24 A5
Eclipse Is., *Australia* 92 B4
Écommoy, *France* 18 E7
Écouché, *France* 18 D6
Ecuador ■, *S. Amer.* ... 124 D3
Écueillé, *France* 18 E8
Ed, *Sweden* 11 F5
Ed Dabbura, *Sudan* 80 D3
Ed Dâmer, *Sudan* 80 D3
Ed Debba, *Sudan* 80 D3
Ed-Déffa, *Egypt* 80 A2
Ed Deim, *Sudan* 81 E2
Ed Dueim, *Sudan* 81 E3
Edah, *Australia* 93 E2
Edam, *Canada* 105 C7
Edam, *Neths.* 17 B5
Edane, *Sweden* 10 E6
Eday, *U.K.* 14 B6
Edd, *Eritrea* 81 E5
Eddrachillis B., *U.K.* 14 C3
Eddystone Pt., *Australia* . . 94 G4
Ede, *Neths.* 17 B5
Ede, *Nigeria* 83 D5
Édéa, *Cameroon* 83 E7
Edebäck, *Sweden* 10 D7
Edehon L., *Canada* 105 A9
Edelény, *Hungary* 42 B5
Eden, *Australia* 95 F4
Eden, *N.C., U.S.A.* 109 G6
Eden, *N.Y., U.S.A.* 110 D6
Eden, *Tex., U.S.A.* 113 K5
Eden, *Wyo., U.S.A.* 114 E9
Eden →, *U.K.* 12 C4
Eden L., *Canada* 105 B8
Edenburg, *S. Africa* 88 D4
Edendale, *S. Africa* 89 D5
Edenderry, *Ireland* 15 C4
Edenton, *U.S.A.* 109 G7
Edenville, *S. Africa* 89 D4
Eder →, *Germany* 24 D5
Eder-Stausee, *Germany* . 24 D4
Edewecht, *Germany* 24 B3
Edgar, *U.S.A.* 112 E6
Edgartown, *U.S.A.* 111 E14
Edge Hill, *U.K.* 13 E6
Edgefield, *U.S.A.* 109 J5
Edgeley, *U.S.A.* 112 B5
Edgemont, *U.S.A.* 112 D3
Edgeøya, *Svalbard* 4 B9
Édhessa, *Greece* 40 F6
Edievale, *N.Z.* 91 L2
Edina, *Liberia* 82 D2
Edina, *U.S.A.* 112 E8
Edinburg, *U.S.A.* 113 M5
Edinburgh, *U.K.* 14 F5
Edineţ, *Moldova* 43 B12
Edirne, *Turkey* 41 E10
Edirne □, *Turkey* 41 E10
Edison, *U.S.A.* 116 B4
Edithburgh, *Australia* .. 95 F2
Edjudina, *Australia* ... 93 E3
Edmeston, *U.S.A.* 111 D9
Edmond, *U.S.A.* 113 H6
Edmonds, *U.S.A.* 116 C4
Edmonton, *Australia* .. 94 B4
Edmonton, *Canada* ... 104 C6
Edmund L., *Canada* ... 105 C10
Edmundston, *Canada* .. 103 C6
Edna, *U.S.A.* 113 L6
Edna Bay, *U.S.A.* 104 B2
Edo □, *Nigeria* 83 D6
Edolo, *Italy* 28 B7
Edremit, *Turkey* 39 B9
Edremit Körfezi, *Turkey* 39 B8
Edsbro, *Sweden* 10 E12
Edsbyn, *Sweden* 10 C9
Edson, *Canada* 104 C5
Eduardo Castex, *Argentina* 126 D3
Edward →, *Australia* .. 95 F3
Edward →, *Africa* 86 C2
Edward I., *Canada* ... 102 C2
Edward River, *Australia* . . 94 A3
Edward VII Land, *Antarctica* 5 E13
Edwards, *U.S.A.* 117 L9
Edwards Plateau, *U.S.A.* 113 K4
Edwardsville, *U.S.A.* .. 111 E9
Edzo, *Canada* 104 A5
Eeklo, *Belgium* 17 C3
Eferding, *Austria* 26 C7
Effingham, *U.S.A.* ... 108 F1
Eforie, *Romania* 43 F13
Ega →, *Spain* 32 C3
Égadi, Ísole, *Italy* ... 30 E5
Egeland, *U.S.A.* 112 A5
Egenolf L., *Canada* ... 105 B9
Eger = Cheb, *Czech Rep.* 26 A5
Eger, *Hungary* 42 C5
Eger →, *Hungary* 42 C5
Egersund, *Norway* ... 9 G12
Egg L., *Canada* 105 B7
Eggenburg, *Austria* ... 26 C8

Eggenfelden, *Germany* .. 25 G8
Éghezée, *Belgium* 17 D4
Eginbah, *Australia* 92 D2
Égletons, *France* 20 C6
Egmont, C., *N.Z.* 91 H4
Egmont, Mt., *N.Z.* 91 H5
Eğridir, *Turkey* 72 D4
Eğridir Gölü, *Turkey* ... 72 D4
Egtved, *Denmark* 11 J3
Egume, *Nigeria* 83 D6
Éguzon-Chantôme, *France* 19 F8
Egvekinot, *Russia* 51 C19
Egyek, *Hungary* 42 C5
Egypt ■, *Africa* 80 J7
Eha Amufu, *Nigeria* ... 83 D6
Ehime □, *Japan* 55 H6
Ehingen, *Germany* 25 G5
Ehrenberg, *U.S.A.* ... 117 M12
Ehrwald, *Austria* 26 D3
Eibar, *Spain* 32 B2
Eichstätt, *Germany* ... 25 G7
Eider →, *Germany* ... 24 A4
Eidsvold, *Australia* ... 95 D5
Eidsvoll, *Norway* 9 F14
Eifel, *Germany* 25 E2
Eiffel Flats, *Zimbabwe* . 87 F3
Eiger, *Switz.* 25 B5
Eigg, *U.K.* 14 E2
Eighty Mile Beach, *Australia* 92 C3
Eil, *Somali Rep.* 74 F4
Eil, L., *U.K.* 14 E3
Eildon, *Australia* 95 F4
Eildon, L., *Australia* .. 95 F4
Eileen L., *Canada* ... 105 A7
Eilenburg, *Germany* .. 24 D8
Ein el Luweiqa, *Sudan* . 81 E3
Einasleigh, *Australia* .. 94 B3
Einasleigh →, *Australia* . 94 B3
Einbeck, *Germany* ... 24 D5
Eindhoven, *Neths.* ... 17 C5
Einsiedeln, *Switz.* ... 25 H4
Eire = Ireland ■, *Europe* 15 C4
Eiríksjökull, *Iceland* .. 8 D3
Eirunepé, *Brazil* 124 E5
Eisenach, *Germany* ... 24 E6
Eisenberg, *Germany* .. 24 E7
Eisenerz, *Austria* ... 26 D7
Eisenhüttenstadt, *Germany* 24 C10
Eisenkappel, *Austria* .. 26 E7
Eisenstadt, *Austria* ... 27 D9
Eisfeld, *Germany* ... 25 E6
Eisleben, *Germany* ... 24 D7
Eislingen, *Germany* .. 25 G5
Eivissa, *Spain* 37 C7
Eixe, Serra do, *Spain* . 34 C4
Ejea de los Caballeros, *Spain* 32 C3
Ejutla, *Mexico* 119 D5
Ekalaka, *U.S.A.* 112 C2
Ekenässjön, *Sweden* .. 11 G9
Ekerö, *Sweden* 10 E11
Eket, *Nigeria* 83 E6
Eketahuna, *N.Z.* 91 J5
Ekhínos, *Greece* 41 E9
Ekibastuz, *Kazakhstan* . 50 D8
Ekoli, *Dem. Rep. of the Congo* 86 C1
Ekoln, *Sweden* 10 E11
Ekshärad, *Sweden* ... 10 D7
Eksjö, *Sweden* 11 G8
Ekwan →, *Canada* ... 102 B3
Ekwan Pt., *Canada* ... 102 B3
El Aaiún, *W. Sahara* . 78 C3
El 'Agrûd, *Egypt* ... 75 E3
El 'Aiyat, *Egypt* 80 J7
El Alamein, *Egypt* ... 80 H6
El 'Aqaba, W. →, *Egypt* 75 E2
El 'Arag, *Egypt* 80 B2
El Arahal, *Spain* ... 35 H5
El Arīḥā, *West Bank* . 75 D4
El Arish, *Australia* ... 94 B4
El 'Arîsh, *Egypt* 75 D2
El 'Arîsh, W. →, *Egypt* 75 D2
El Asnam = Ech Cheliff, *Algeria* 78 A6
El Astillero, *Spain* ... 34 B7
El Badâri, *Egypt* ... 80 B3
El Bahrein, *Egypt* ... 80 B2
El Ballâs, *Egypt* 80 B3
El Balyana, *Egypt* ... 80 B3
El Baqeir, *Sudan* ... 80 D3
El Barco de Ávila, *Spain* 34 E5
El Barco de Valdeorras = O Barco, *Spain* ... 34 C4
El Bauga, *Sudan* ... 80 D3
El Bawiti, *Egypt* 80 J6
El Bayadh, *Algeria* .. 78 B6
El Bierzo, *Spain* 34 C4
El Bluff, *Nic.* 120 D3
El Bonillo, *Spain* ... 33 G2
El Brûk, W. →, *Egypt* 75 E2
El Buheirat □, *Sudan* . 81 F3
El Burgo de Osma, *Spain* 32 D1
El Cajon, *U.S.A.* ... 117 N10
El Campo, *U.S.A.* ... 113 L6
El Centro, *U.S.A.* ... 117 N11
El Cerro, *Bolivia* ... 124 G6
El Cerro de Andévalo, *Spain* 35 H4
El Compadre, *Mexico* . 117 N10
El Coronil, *Spain* ... 35 H5
El Cuy, *Argentina* ... 128 D3
El Cuyo, *Mexico* ... 119 C7
El Dab'a, *Egypt* 80 H6
El Daheir, *Egypt* 75 D3
El Deir, *Egypt* 80 B3
El Dere, *Somali Rep.* .. 74 G4

El Descanso, *Mexico* 117 N10
El Desemboque, *Mexico* .. 118 A2
El Dilingat, *Egypt* 80 H7
El Diviso, *Colombia* ... 124 C3
El Djouf, *Mauritania* ... 76 D3
El Dorado, *Ark., U.S.A.* . 113 J8
El Dorado, *Kans., U.S.A.* 113 G6
El Dorado, *Venezuela* ... 124 B6
El Ejido, *Spain* 35 J8
El Escorial, *Spain* 34 E6
El Espinar, *Spain* 34 D6
El Faiyûm, *Egypt* 80 J7
El Fâsher, *Sudan* 81 E2
El Fashn, *Egypt* 80 J7
El Ferrol = Ferrol, *Spain* . 34 B2
El Fifi, *Sudan* 81 E2
El Fuerte, *Mexico* 118 B3
El Gal, *Somali Rep.* ... 74 E5
El Gebir, *Sudan* 81 E2
El Gedida, *Egypt* 80 B2
El Geneina = Al Junaynah, *Sudan* 79 F10
El Geteina, *Sudan* 81 E3
El Gezira □, *Sudan* ... 81 E3
El Gîza, *Egypt* 80 J7
El Grau, *Spain* 33 G4
El Hagiz, *Sudan* 81 D4
El Hammam, *Egypt* ... 80 H6
El Hawata, *Sudan* ... 81 E3
El Heiz, *Egypt* 80 B2
El 'Idisât, *Egypt* 80 B3
El Iskandarîya, *Egypt* .. 80 H7
El Jadida, *Morocco* ... 78 B4
El Jebelein, *Sudan* ... 81 E3
El Kab, *Sudan* 80 D3
El Kabrît, G., *Egypt* .. 75 F2
El Kamlin, *Sudan* 81 D3
El Karaba, *Sudan* 80 D3
El Khandaq, *Sudan* ... 80 D3
El Khârga, *Egypt* 80 B3
El Khartûm, *Sudan* ... 81 D3
El Khartûm □, *Sudan* .. 81 D3
El Khartûm Bahrî, *Sudan* 81 D3
El Kuntilla, *Egypt* ... 75 E3
El Laqâwa, *Sudan* ... 81 E2
El Laqeita, *Egypt* 80 B3
El Leiya, *Sudan* 81 D4
El Maestrazgo, *Spain* .. 32 E4
El Mafâza, *Sudan* ... 81 E3
El Mahalla el Kubra, *Egypt* 80 H7
El Mahârîq, *Egypt* ... 80 B3
El Mahmûdîya, *Egypt* .. 80 H7
El Maks el-Bahari, *Egypt* . 80 C3
El Manshah, *Egypt* ... 80 B3
El Mansûra, *Egypt* ... 80 H7
El Manzala, *Egypt* ... 80 H7
El Marâgha, *Egypt* ... 80 B3
El Masid, *Sudan* 81 D3
El Masnou, *Spain* ... 32 D7
El Matariya, *Egypt* ... 80 H8
El Medano, *Canary Is.* . 37 F3
El Metemma, *Sudan* .. 81 D3
El Milagro, *Argentina* . 126 C2
El Minyâ, *Egypt* 80 J7
El Monte, *U.S.A.* ... 117 L8
El Montseny, *Spain* .. 32 D7
El Mreyye, *Mauritania* . 82 B3
El Obeid, *Sudan* 81 E3
El Odaiya, *Sudan* ... 81 E2
El Oro, *Mexico* 119 D4
El Oued, *Algeria* 78 B7
El Palmito, Presa, *Mexico* 118 B3
El Paso, *U.S.A.* 115 L10
El Paso Robles, *U.S.A.* . 116 K6
El Pedernoso, *Spain* .. 33 F2
El Pedroso, *Spain* ... 35 H5
El Pobo de Dueñas, *Spain* 32 E3
El Portal, *U.S.A.* ... 116 H7
El Porvenir, *Mexico* ... 118 A3
El Prat de Llobregat, *Spain* 32 D7
El Progreso, *Honduras* . 120 C2
El Pueblito, *Mexico* .. 118 B3
El Pueblo, *Canary Is.* . 37 F2
El Puente del Arzobispo, *Spain* 34 F5
El Puerto de Santa María, *Spain* 35 J4
El Qâhira, *Egypt* ... 80 H7
El Qantara, *Egypt* ... 75 E1
El Qasr, *Egypt* 80 B2
El Quseima, *Egypt* ... 75 E3
El Quşîya, *Egypt* 80 B3
El Râshda, *Egypt* ... 80 B2
El Real, *Panama* 124 B3
El Reno, *U.S.A.* 113 H6
El Rîdisiya, *Egypt* ... 80 C3
El Rio, *U.S.A.* 117 L7
El Ronquillo, *Spain* .. 35 H4
El Roque, Pta., *Canary Is.* 37 F4
El Rosarito, *Mexico* .. 118 B2
El Rubio, *Spain* 35 H5
El Saff, *Egypt* 80 J7
El Saheira, W. →, *Egypt* . 75 E2
El Salto, *Mexico* 118 C3
El Salvador ■, *Cent. Amer.* 120 D2
El Sauce, *Nic.* 120 D2
El Saucejo, *Spain* ... 35 H5
El Shallal, *Egypt* 80 C3
El Simbillawein, *Egypt* . 80 H7
El Suweis, *Egypt* ... 80 J8
El Thamad, *Egypt* ... 75 F3
El Tigre, *Venezuela* .. 124 B6
El Tîh, *Egypt* 75 F2
El Tîna, Khalîg, *Egypt* . 75 D1
El Tofo, *Chile* 126 B1
El Tránsito, *Chile* ... 126 B1

El Tûr, *Egypt* 80 J8
El Turbio, *Argentina* 128 G2
El Uqsur, *Egypt* 80 B3
El Venado, *Mexico* 118 C4
El Vendrell, *Spain* 32 D6
El Vigía, *Venezuela* 124 B4
El Viso del Alcor, *Spain* . 35 H5
El Wabeira, *Egypt* 75 F2
El Wak, *Kenya* 86 B5
El Waqf, *Egypt* 80 B3
El Weguet, *Ethiopia* ... 81 F5
El Wuz, *Sudan* 81 D3
Elafónisos, *Greece* 38 E4
Élancourt, *France* 19 D8
Élassa, *Greece* 39 F8
Elassón, *Greece* 38 B4
Elat, *Israel* 75 F3
Eláthia, *Greece* 38 C4
Elâzığ, *Turkey* 73 C8
Elba, *Italy* 28 F7
Elba, *U.S.A.* 109 K2
Elbasani, *Albania* 40 E4
Elbe, *U.S.A.* 116 D4
Elbe →, *Europe* 24 B4
Elbe-Seitenkanal, *Germany* 24 C6
Elbert, Mt., *U.S.A.* ... 115 G10
Elberta, *U.S.A.* 108 C2
Elberton, *U.S.A.* 109 H4
Elbeuf, *France* 18 C8
Elbing = Elbląg, *Poland* . 44 D6
Elbistan, *Turkey* 72 C7
Elbląg, *Poland* 44 D6
Elbląg □, *Poland* 44 D6
Elbow, *Canada* 105 C7
Elbrus, *Asia* 49 J6
Elburz Mts. = Alborz, Reshteh-ye Kūhhā-ye, *Iran* 71 C7
Elche, *Spain* 33 G4
Elche de la Sierra, *Spain* . 33 G2
Elcho I., *Australia* 94 A2
Elda, *Spain* 33 G4
Elde →, *Germany* 24 B7
Eldon, *Mo., U.S.A.* ... 112 F8
Eldon, *Wash., U.S.A.* .. 116 C3
Eldora, *U.S.A.* 112 D8
Eldorado, *Argentina* .. 127 B5
Eldorado, *Canada* ... 105 B7
Eldorado, *Mexico* ... 118 C3
Eldorado, *Ill., U.S.A.* . 108 G1
Eldorado, *Tex., U.S.A.* . 113 K4
Eldorado Springs, *U.S.A.* 113 G8
Eldoret, *Kenya* 86 B4
Eldred, *U.S.A.* 110 E6
Elea, C., *Cyprus* 36 D13
Electra, *U.S.A.* 113 H5
Elefantes →, *Mozam.* . 89 C5
Elefsís, *Greece* 38 C5
Elektrogorsk, *Russia* .. 46 E10
Elektrostal, *Russia* ... 46 E10
Elele, *Nigeria* 83 D6
Elena, *Bulgaria* 41 D9
Elephant Butte Reservoir, *U.S.A.* 115 K10
Elephant I., *Antarctica* . 5 C18
Eleshnitsa, *Bulgaria* .. 40 E7
Eleuthera, *Bahamas* .. 120 B4
Elevsís, *Greece* 38 C5
Elevtheroúpolis, *Greece* . 41 F8
Elgeyo-Marakwet □, *Kenya* 86 B4
Elgin, *N.B., Canada* .. 103 C6
Elgin, *Ont., Canada* .. 111 B8
Elgin, *U.K.* 14 D5
Elgin, *Ill., U.S.A.* ... 108 D1
Elgin, *N. Dak., U.S.A.* . 112 B4
Elgin, *Nebr., U.S.A.* .. 112 E5
Elgin, *Nev., U.S.A.* .. 115 H6
Elgin, *Oreg., U.S.A.* .. 114 D5
Elgin, *Tex., U.S.A.* .. 113 K6
Elgoibar, *Spain* 32 B2
Elgon, Mt., *Africa* ... 86 B3
Eliase, *Indonesia* 63 F8
Elida, *U.S.A.* 113 J3
Elikón, *Greece* 38 C4
Elim, *S. Africa* 88 E2
Elin Pelin, *Bulgaria* .. 40 D7
Elisabethville = Lubumbashi, *Dem. Rep. of the Congo* 87 E2
Elista, *Russia* 49 G7
Elizabeth, *Australia* .. 95 E2
Elizabeth, *U.S.A.* ... 111 F10
Elizabeth City, *U.S.A.* . 109 G7
Elizabethton, *U.S.A.* .. 109 G4
Elizabethtown, *Ky., U.S.A.* 108 G3
Elizabethtown, *N.Y., U.S.A.* 111 B11
Elizabethtown, *Pa., U.S.A.* 111 F8
Elizondo, *Spain* 32 B3
Elk, *Poland* 44 E9
Elk →, *Poland* 44 E9
Elk City, *U.S.A.* 113 H5
Elk Creek, *U.S.A.* ... 116 F4
Elk Grove, *U.S.A.* ... 116 G5
Elk Island Nat. Park, *Canada* 104 C6
Elk Lake, *Canada* ... 102 C3
Elk Point, *Canada* ... 105 C6
Elk River, *Idaho, U.S.A.* 114 C5
Elk River, *Minn., U.S.A.* 112 C8
Elkedra, *Australia* ... 94 C2
Elkedra →, *Australia* . 94 C2
Elkhart, *Ind., U.S.A.* . 108 E3
Elkhart, *Kans., U.S.A.* . 113 G4
Elkhorn, *Canada* 105 D8
Elkhorn →, *U.S.A.* .. 112 E6

Elkhovo, *Bulgaria* 41 D10
Elkin, *U.S.A.* 109 G5
Elkins, *U.S.A.* 108 F7
Elko, *Canada* 104 D5
Elko, *U.S.A.* 114 F6
Ell, L., *Australia* 93 E4
Ellef Ringnes I., *Canada* . 4 B2
Ellendale, *Australia* ... 92 C3
Ellendale, *U.S.A.* 112 B5
Ellensburg, *U.S.A.* ... 114 C3
Ellenville, *U.S.A.* 111 E10
Ellery, Mt., *Australia* .. 95 F4
Ellesmere, L., *N.Z.* 91 M4
Ellesmere I., *Canada* ... 4 B4
Ellesmere Port, *U.K.* ... 12 D5
Ellice Is. = Tuvalu ■, *Pac. Oc.* 96 H9
Ellinwood, *U.S.A.* 112 F5
Elliot, *Australia* 94 B1
Elliot, *S. Africa* 89 E4
Elliot Lake, *Canada* ... 102 C3
Elliotdale = Xhora, *S. Africa* 89 E4
Ellis, *U.S.A.* 112 F5
Elliston, *Australia* 95 E1
Ellisville, *U.S.A.* 113 K10
Ellon, *U.K.* 14 D6
Ellore = Eluru, *India* .. 67 L12
Ells →, *Canada* 104 B6
Ellsworth, *U.S.A.* 112 F5
Ellsworth Land, *Antarctica* 5 D16
Ellsworth Mts., *Antarctica* 5 D16
Ellwangen, *Germany* .. 25 G6
Ellwood City, *U.S.A.* .. 110 F4
Elm, *Switz.* 25 J5
Elma, *Canada* 105 D9
Elma, *U.S.A.* 116 D3
Elmadağ, *Turkey* 72 C5
Elmalı, *Turkey* 39 E11
Elmhurst, *U.S.A.* 108 E2
Elmina, *Ghana* 83 D4
Elmira, *Canada* 110 C4
Elmira, *U.S.A.* 110 D8
Elmore, *Australia* 95 F3
Elmore, *U.S.A.* 117 M11
Elmshorn, *Germany* .. 24 B5
Elmvale, *Canada* 110 B5
Elne, *France* 20 F6
Elora, *Canada* 110 C4
Elos, *Greece* 38 E4
Eloúnda, *Greece* 36 D7
Eloy, *U.S.A.* 115 K8
Éloyes, *France* 19 D13
Elrose, *Canada* 105 C7
Elsas, *Canada* 102 C3
Elsdorf, *Germany* ... 24 E2
Elsie, *U.S.A.* 116 E3
Elsinore = Helsingør, *Denmark* 11 H6
Elsinore, *U.S.A.* 115 G7
Elster →, *Germany* .. 24 D7
Elsterwerda, *Germany* . 24 D9
Eltham, *N.Z.* 91 H5
Elton, *Russia* 49 F8
Elton, Ozero, *Russia* .. 49 F8
Eltville, *Germany* ... 25 E4
Eluru, *India* 67 L12
Elvas, *Portugal* 35 G3
Elven, *France* 18 E4
Elverum, *Norway* ... 9 F14
Elvire →, *Australia* .. 92 C4
Elvo →, *Italy* 28 C5
Elwood, *Ind., U.S.A.* .. 108 E3
Elwood, *Nebr., U.S.A.* . 112 E5
Elx = Elche, *Spain* ... 33 G4
Ely, *U.K.* 13 E8
Ely, *Minn., U.S.A.* ... 112 B9
Ely, *Nev., U.S.A.* ... 114 G6
Elyria, *U.S.A.* 110 E2
Elyrus, *Greece* 38 F5
Elz →, *Germany* ... 25 G3
Emådalen, *Sweden* .. 10 C8
Emāmrūd, *Iran* 71 B7
Emån →, *Sweden* ... 11 G10
Emba, *Kazakhstan* ... 50 E6
Embarcación, *Argentina* 126 A3
Embarras Portage, *Canada* 105 B6
Embetsu, *Japan* 54 B10
Embi = Emba, *Kazakhstan* 50 E6
Embi = Emba →, *Kazakhstan* 50 E6
Embóna, *Greece* 36 C9
Embrun, *France* 21 D10
Embu, *Kenya* 86 C4
Embu □, *Kenya* 86 C4
Emden, *Germany* ... 24 B3
Emecik, *Turkey* 39 E9
Emerald, *Australia* .. 94 C4
Emerald, *U.S.A.* 117 M11
Emerson, *Canada* ... 105 D9
Emery, *U.S.A.* 115 G8
Emet, *Turkey* 39 B11
Emi Koussi, *Chad* ... 79 E9
Emília-Romagna □, *Italy* . 28 D8
Emilius, Mte., *Italy* .. 28 C4
Eminabad, *Pakistan* .. 68 C6
Emine, Nos, *Bulgaria* . 41 D11
Emirdağ, *Turkey* ... 72 C4
Emlenton, *U.S.A.* ... 110 E5
Emlichheim, *Germany* . 24 C2
Emmaboda, *Sweden* . 11 H9
Emme →, *Switz.* ... 25 H3
Emmeloord, *Neths.* .. 17 B5
Emmen, *Neths.* 17 B6
Emmen, *Switz.* 25 H4
Emmendingen, *Germany* 25 G3
Emmental, *Switz.* ... 25 J3

Emmerich, *Germany* 24 D2
Emmet, *Australia* 94 C3
Emmetsburg, *U.S.A.* 112 D7
Emmett, *U.S.A.* 114 E5
Emőd, *Hungary* 42 C5
Emona, *Bulgaria* 41 D11
Empalme, *Mexico* 118 B2
Empangeni, *S. Africa* 89 D5
Empedrado, *Argentina* .. 126 B4
Emperor Seamount Chain,
  Pac. Oc. 96 D9
Empoli, *Italy* 28 E7
Emporia, *Kans., U.S.A.* .. 112 F6
Emporia, *Va., U.S.A* ... 109 G7
Emporium, *U.S.A.* 110 E6
Empress, *Canada* 105 C7
Empty Quarter = Rub' al
  Khālī, *Si. Arabia* 74 D4
Ems →, *Germany* 24 B3
Emsdale, *Canada* 110 A5
Emsdetten, *Germany* 24 C3
Emu, *China* 57 C15
Emu Park, *Australia* 94 C5
'En 'Avrona, *Israel* 75 F4
En Nahud, *Sudan* 81 E2
Ena, *Japan* 55 G8
Enana, *Namibia* 88 B2
Enånger, *Sweden* 10 C11
Enaratoli, *Indonesia* 63 E9
Enard B., *U.K.* 14 C3
Enare = Inarijärvi, *Finland* 8 B22
Encantadas, Serra, *Brazil* 127 C5
Encarnación, *Paraguay* .. 127 B4
Encarnación de Diaz,
  Mexico 118 C4
Enchi, *Ghana* 82 D4
Encinal, *U.S.A.* 113 L5
Encinitas, *U.S.A.* 117 M9
Encino, *U.S.A.* 115 J11
Encounter B., *Australia* . 95 F2
Encs, *Hungary* 42 B6
Ende, *Indonesia* 63 F6
Endeavour, *Canada* 105 C8
Endeavour Str., *Australia* 94 A3
Endelave, *Denmark* 11 J4
Enderbury I., *Kiribati* ... 96 H10
Enderby, *Canada* 104 C5
Enderby I., *Australia* ... 92 D2
Enderby Land, *Antarctica* 5 C5
Enderlin, *U.S.A.* 112 B6
Endicott, *N.Y., U.S.A.* .. 111 D8
Endicott, *Wash., U.S.A.* . 114 C5
Endyalgout I., *Australia* . 92 B5
Enewetak Atoll, *Pac. Oc.* 96 F8
Enez, *Turkey* 41 F10
Engadin, *Switz.* 25 J6
Engaño, C., *Dom. Rep.* . 121 C6
Engaño, C., *Phil.* 63 A6
Engcobo, *S. Africa* 89 E4
Engelberg, *Switz.* 25 J4
Engels, *Russia* 48 E8
Engemann L., *Canada* .. 105 B7
Enggano, *Indonesia* 62 F2
England, *U.S.A.* 113 H9
England □, *U.K.* 12 D7
Englee, *Canada* 103 B8
Englehart, *Canada* 102 C4
Engler L., *Canada* 105 B7
Englewood, *Colo., U.S.A.* 112 F2
Englewood, *Kans., U.S.A.* 113 G5
English →, *Canada* 105 C10
English Bazar = Ingraj
  Bazar, *India* 69 G13
English Channel, *Europe* . 13 G6
English River, *Canada* .. 102 C1
Engures ezers, *Latvia* ... 44 A10
Enguri →, *Georgia* 49 J5
Enid, *U.S.A.* 113 G6
Enipévs →, *Greece* 38 B4
Enkhuizen, *Neths.* 17 B5
Enköping, *Sweden* 10 E11
Enle, *China* 58 F3
Enna, *Italy* 31 E7
Ennadai, *Canada* 105 A8
Ennadai L., *Canada* 105 A8
Ennedi, *Chad* 79 E10
Enngonia, *Australia* 95 D4
Ennigerloh, *Germany* ... 24 D4
Ennis, *Ireland* 15 D3
Ennis, *Mont., U.S.A.* ... 114 D8
Ennis, *Tex., U.S.A.* 113 J6
Enniscorthy, *Ireland* ... 15 D5
Enniskillen, *U.K.* 15 B4
Ennistimon, *Ireland* ... 15 D2
Enns, *Austria* 26 C7
Enns →, *Austria* 26 C7
Enontekiö, *Finland* 8 B20
Enping, *China* 59 F9
Enriquillo, L., *Dom. Rep.* 121 C5
Enschede, *Neths.* 17 B6
Ensenada, *Argentina* ... 126 C4
Ensenada, *Mexico* 118 A1
Enshi, *China* 58 B7
Ensiola, Pta. de n', *Spain* 37 B9
Ensisheim, *France* 19 E14
Entebbe, *Uganda* 86 B3
Enterprise, *Canada* 104 A5
Enterprise, *Oreg., U.S.A.* 114 D5
Enterprise, *Utah, U.S.A.* 115 H7
Entraygues-sur-Truyère,
  France 20 D6
Entre Ríos, *Bolivia* 126 A3
Entre Ríos □, *Argentina* . 126 C4
Entrepeñas, Embalse de,
  Spain 32 E2
Entroncamento, *Portugal* 35 F2
Enugu, *Nigeria* 83 D6

Enugu □, *Nigeria* 83 D6
Enugu Ezike, *Nigeria* ... 83 D6
Enumclaw, *U.S.A.* 116 C5
Envermeu, *France* 18 C8
Enviken, *Sweden* 10 D9
Enying, *Hungary* 42 D3
Enza →, *Italy* 28 D7
Eólie, Ís., *Italy* 31 D7
Epanomí, *Greece* 40 F6
Epe, *Neths.* 17 B5
Epe, *Nigeria* 83 D5
Épernay, *France* 19 C10
Épernon, *France* 19 D8
Ephesus, *Turkey* 39 D9
Ephraim, *U.S.A.* 114 G8
Ephrata, *U.S.A.* 114 C4
Epidaurus Limera, *Greece* 38 E5
Épila, *Spain* 32 D3
Épinac, *France* 19 F11
Épinal, *France* 19 D13
Episkopi, *Cyprus* 36 E11
Episkopí, *Greece* 36 D6
Episkopi Bay, *Cyprus* ... 36 E11
Epitálion, *Greece* 38 D3
Eppan = Appiano, *Italy* . 29 B8
Eppingen, *Germany* 25 F4
Epsom, *U.K.* 13 F7
Epukiro, *Namibia* 88 C2
Equatorial Guinea ■,
  Africa 84 D1
Er Rahad, *Sudan* 81 E3
Er Rif, *Morocco* 78 A5
Er Roseires, *Sudan* 81 E3
Eraclea, *Italy* 29 C9
Erāwadī Myit =
  Irrawaddy →, *Burma* . 67 M19
Erba, *Italy* 28 C6
Erba, *Sudan* 80 D4
Erbaa, *Turkey* 72 B7
Erbeskopf, *Germany* ... 25 F3
Erbil = Arbīl, *Iraq* 70 B5
Erçiş, *Turkey* 73 C10
Érd, *Hungary* 42 C3
Erdao Jiang →, *China* .. 57 C14
Erdek, *Turkey* 41 F11
Erdemli, *Turkey* 72 D6
Erdene, *Mongolia* 56 B6
Erding, *Germany* 25 G7
Erdre →, *France* 18 E5
Erebus, Mt., *Antarctica* . 5 D11
Erechim, *Brazil* 127 B5
Ereğli, *Konya, Turkey* ... 72 D6
Ereğli, *Zonguldak, Turkey* 72 B4
Erei, Monti, *Italy* 31 E7
Erenhot, *China* 56 C7
Eresma →, *Spain* 34 D6
Eressós, *Greece* 39 B7
Erewadi Myitwanya, *Burma* 67 M19
Erfenisdam, *S. Africa* ... 88 D4
Erfstadt, *Germany* 24 E2
Erft →, *Germany* 24 D2
Erfurt, *Germany* 24 E6
Ergani, *Turkey* 73 C8
Ergene →, *Turkey* 41 E10
Ergeni Vozvyshennost,
  Russia 49 G7
Érgli, *Latvia* 9 H21
Erhlin, *Taiwan* 59 F13
Eria →, *Spain* 34 C5
Eriba, *Sudan* 81 D4
Eriboll, L., *U.K.* 14 C4
Érice, *Italy* 30 D5
Erie, *U.S.A.* 110 D4
Erie, L., *N. Amer.* 110 D4
Erie Canal, *U.S.A.* 110 C7
Erieau, *Canada* 110 D3
Erigavo, *Somali Rep.* ... 74 E4
Erikoúsa, *Greece* 36 A3
Eriksdale, *Canada* 105 C9
Erímanthos, *Greece* 38 D3
Erimo-misaki, *Japan* ... 54 D11
Eriskay, *U.K.* 14 D1
Erithraí, *Greece* 38 C5
Eritrea ■, *Africa* 81 E4
Erjas →, *Portugal* 34 F3
Erkelenz, *Germany* 24 D2
Erkner, *Germany* 24 C9
Erlangen, *Germany* 25 F6
Erldunda, *Australia* 94 D1
Ermelo, *Neths.* 17 B5
Ermelo, *S. Africa* 89 D4
Ermenek, *Turkey* 72 D5
Ermióni, *Greece* 38 D5
Ermones, *Greece* 36 A3
Ernakulam = Cochin, *India* 66 Q10
Erne →, *Ireland* 15 B3
Erne, Lower L., *U.K.* ... 15 B4
Erne, Upper L., *U.K.* ... 15 B4
Ernée, *France* 18 D6
Ernest Giles Ra., *Australia* 93 E3
Ernstberg, *Germany* ... 25 E2
Erode, *India* 66 P10
Eromanga, *Australia* ... 95 D3
Erongo, *Namibia* 88 C2
Erquy, *France* 18 D4
Errabiddy, *Australia* ... 93 E2
Erramala Hills, *India* ... 66 M11
Errer →, *Ethiopia* 81 F5
Errigal, *Ireland* 15 A3
Erris Hd., *Ireland* 15 B1
Erseka, *Albania* 40 F4
Erskine, *U.S.A.* 112 B7
Ertholmene, *Denmark* .. 11 J9
Ertil, *Russia* 48 E5
Ertis = Irtysh →,
  Russia 50 C7

Eruh, *Turkey* 73 D10
Eruwa, *Nigeria* 83 D5
Ervy-le-Châtel, *France* ... 19 D10
Erwin, *U.S.A.* 109 G4
Eryuan, *China* 58 D2
Erzgebirge, *Germany* ... 24 E8
Erzin, *Russia* 51 D10
Erzincan, *Turkey* 73 C8
Erzurum, *Turkey* 73 C9
Es Caló, *Spain* 37 C8
Es Canar, *Spain* 37 B8
Es Mercadal, *Spain* 37 B11
Es Migjorn Gran, *Spain* . 37 B11
Es Sahrâ' Esh Sharqîya,
  Egypt 80 B3
Es Sînâ', *Egypt* 80 J8
Es Sûkî, *Sudan* 81 E3
Es Vedrà, *Spain* 37 C7
Esambo,
  Dem. Rep. of the Congo 86 C1
Esan-Misaki, *Japan* 54 D10
Esashi, *Hokkaidō, Japan* 54 B11
Esashi, *Hokkaidō, Japan* 54 D10
Esbjerg, *Denmark* 11 J2
Escalante, *U.S.A.* 115 H8
Escalante →, *U.S.A.* ... 115 H8
Escalón, *Mexico* 118 B4
Escambia →, *U.S.A.* .. 109 K2
Escanaba, *U.S.A.* 108 C2
Esch-sur-Alzette, *Lux.* .. 17 E6
Eschede, *Germany* 24 C6
Eschwege, *Germany* ... 24 D6
Eschweiler, *Germany* .. 24 E2
Escondido, *U.S.A.* 117 M9
Escuinapa, *Mexico* 118 C3
Escuintla, *Guatemala* ... 120 D1
Eséka, *Cameroon* 83 E7
Eşen →, *Turkey* 39 E11
Esens, *Germany* 24 B3
Esenyurt, *Turkey* 41 E12
Esera →, *Spain* 32 C5
Eşfahān, *Iran* 71 C6
Esfīdeh, *Iran* 71 C8
Esgueva →, *Spain* 34 D6
Esh Sham = Dimashq,
  Syria 75 B5
Esh Shamâlîya □, *Sudan* . 80 D2
Esha Ness, *U.K.* 14 A7
Eshan, *China* 58 E4
Esher, *U.K.* 13 F7
Eshowe, *S. Africa* 89 D5
Esiama, *Ghana* 82 E4
Esil →= Ishim →, *Russia* 50 D8
Esino →, *Italy* 29 E10
Esk →, *Cumb., U.K.* ... 14 G5
Esk →, *N. Yorks., U.K.* . 12 C7
Esla →, *Spain* 34 D4
Eslāmābād-e Gharb, *Iran* 70 C5
Eslöv, *Sweden* 11 J7
Eşme, *Turkey* 39 C10
Esmeraldas, *Ecuador* ... 124 C3
Espalion, *France* 20 D6
Espanola, *Canada* 102 C3
Esparreguera, *Spain* ... 32 D6
Esparta, *Costa Rica* 120 E3
Espelkamp, *Germany* .. 24 C4
Esperance, *Australia* ... 93 F3
Esperance B., *Australia* . 93 F3
Esperanza, *Argentina* ... 126 C3
Esperanza, *Phil.* 61 G6
Espéraza, *France* 20 F6
Espichel, C., *Portugal* .. 35 G1
Espiel, *Spain* 35 G5
Espigão, Serra do, *Brazil* 127 B5
Espinazo, Sierra del =
  Espinhaço, Serra do,
  Brazil 125 G10
Espinhaço, Serra do, *Brazil* 125 G10
Espinho, *Portugal* 34 D2
Espinilho, Serra do, *Brazil* 127 B5
Espinosa de los Monteros,
  Spain 34 B7
Espírito Santo □, *Brazil* . 125 H10
Espíritu Santo, B. del,
  Mexico 119 D7
Espíritu Santo, I., *Mexico* 118 C2
Espita, *Mexico* 119 C7
Espiye, *Turkey* 73 B8
Espluga de Francolí, *Spain* 32 D6
Espoo, *Finland* 9 F21
Espuña, Sierra de, *Spain* 33 H3
Espungabera, *Mozam.* .. 89 C5
Esquel, *Argentina* 128 E2
Esquina, *Argentina* 126 C4
Essaouira, *Morocco* 78 B4
Essebie,
  Dem. Rep. of the Congo 86 B3
Essen, *Belgium* 17 C4
Essen, *Germany* 24 D3
Essendon, Mt., *Australia* 93 E3
Essequibo →, *Guyana* .. 122 C5
Essex, *Canada* 110 D2
Essex, *Calif., U.S.A.* ... 117 L11
Essex, *N.Y., U.S.A.* 111 B11
Essex □, *U.K.* 13 F8
Esslingen, *Germany* ... 25 G5
Essonne □, *France* 19 D9
Estaca de Bares, C. de,
  Spain 34 B3

Estadilla, *Spain* 32 C5
Estados, I. de Los,
  Argentina 122 J4
Estagel, *France* 20 F6
Eşţahbānāt, *Iran* 71 D7
Estância, *Brazil* 125 F11
Estancia, *U.S.A.* 115 J10
Estārm, *Iran* 71 D8
Estarreja, *Portugal* 34 E2
Estats, Pic d', *Spain* ... 32 C6
Estcourt, *S. Africa* 89 D4
Este, *Italy* 29 C8
Estelí, *Nic.* 120 D2
Estella, *Spain* 32 C2
Estellencs, *Spain* 37 B9
Estelline, *S. Dak., U.S.A.* 112 C6
Estelline, *Tex., U.S.A.* .. 113 H4
Estena →, *Spain* 35 F6
Estepa, *Spain* 35 H6
Estepona, *Spain* 35 J5
Esterhazy, *Canada* 105 C8
Esternay, *France* 19 D10
Esterri d'Aneu, *Spain* .. 32 C6
Estevan, *Canada* 105 D8
Estevan Group, *Canada* . 104 C3
Estherville, *U.S.A.* 112 D7
Estissac, *France* 19 D10
Eston, *Canada* 105 C7
Estonia ■, *Europe* 9 G21
Estoril, *Portugal* 35 G1
Estrela, Serra da, *Portugal* 34 E3
Estrella, *Spain* 35 G7
Estremoz, *Portugal* 35 G3
Estrondo, Serra do, *Brazil* 125 E9
Esztergom, *Hungary* ... 42 C3
Et Tîdra, *Mauritania* ... 82 B1
Etadunna, *Australia* ... 95 D2
Etah, *India* 69 F8
Étain, *France* 19 C12
Étampes, *France* 19 D9
Etanga, *Namibia* 88 B1
Étaples, *France* 19 B8
Etawah, *India* 69 F8
Etawah →, *U.S.A.* 109 H3
Etawney L., *Canada* ... 105 B9
Ete, *Nigeria* 83 D6
Ethel, *U.S.A.* 116 D4
Ethel Creek, *Australia* . 92 D3
Ethelbert, *Canada* 105 C8
Ethiopia ■, *Africa* 74 F3
Ethiopian Highlands,
  Ethiopia 52 J7
Etili, *Turkey* 41 G10
Etive, L., *U.K.* 14 E3
Etna, *Italy* 31 E7
Etoile,
  Dem. Rep. of the Congo 87 E2
Etolin I., *U.S.A.* 104 B2
Etosha Pan, *Namibia* .. 88 B2
Etowah, *U.S.A.* 109 H3
Étréchy, *France* 19 D9
Étrépagny, *France* 19 C8
Étretat, *France* 18 C7
Etropole, *Bulgaria* 41 D8
Ettelbruck, *Lux.* 17 E6
Ettlingen, *Germany* ... 25 G4
Ettrick Water →, *U.K.* . 14 F6
Etuku,
  Dem. Rep. of the Congo 86 C2
Etulia, *Moldova* 43 E13
Etzatlán, *Mexico* 118 C4
Eu, *France* 18 B8
Euboea = Évvoia, *Greece* 38 C6
Eucla Motel, *Australia* . 93 F4
Euclid, *U.S.A.* 110 E3
Eucumbene, L., *Australia* 95 F4
Eudora, *U.S.A.* 113 J9
Eudunda, *Australia* 95 E2
Eufaula, *Ala., U.S.A.* ... 109 K3
Eufaula, *Okla., U.S.A.* .. 113 H7
Eufaula L., *U.S.A.* 113 H7
Eugene, *U.S.A.* 114 E2
Eugowra, *Australia* 95 E4
Eulo, *Australia* 95 D4
Eunice, *La., U.S.A.* 113 K8
Eunice, *N. Mex., U.S.A.* . 113 J3
Eupen, *Belgium* 17 D6
Euphrates = Furāt, Nahr
  al →, *Asia* 70 D5
Eure □, *France* 18 C8
Eure →, *France* 18 C8
Eure-et-Loir □, *France* . 18 D8
Eureka, *Canada* 4 B3
Eureka, *Calif., U.S.A.* .. 114 F1
Eureka, *Kans., U.S.A.* .. 113 G6
Eureka, *Mont., U.S.A.* .. 114 B6
Eureka, *Nev., U.S.A.* ... 114 G5
Eureka, *S. Dak., U.S.A.* . 112 C4
Eureka, *Utah, U.S.A.* ... 114 G7
Eureka, Mt., *Australia* . 93 E3
Euroa, *Australia* 95 F4
Europa, Île, *Ind. Oc.* .. 85 J8
Europa, Picos de, *Spain* . 34 B6
Europa, Pta. de, *Gib.* .. 35 J5
Europoort, *Neths.* 17 C4
Euskirchen, *Germany* .. 24 E2
Eustis, *U.S.A.* 109 L5
Eutin, *Germany* 24 A6
Eutsuk L., *Canada* 104 C3
Eva Downs, *Australia* .. 94 B1
Evale, *Angola* 88 B2
Evans, *U.S.A.* 112 E2
Evans Head, *Australia* . 95 D5
Evans L., *Canada* 102 B4
Evans Mills, *U.S.A.* 111 B9

Evanston, *Ill., U.S.A.* .. 108 E2
Evanston, *Wyo., U.S.A.* . 114 F8
Evansville, *Ind., U.S.A.* . 108 G2
Evansville, *Wis., U.S.A.* . 112 D10
Évaux-les-Bains, *France* . 19 F9
Eveleth, *U.S.A.* 112 B8
Evensk, *Russia* 51 C16
Everard, L., *Australia* .. 95 E2
Everard Park, *Australia* . 93 E5
Everard Ranges, *Australia* 93 E5
Everest, Mt., *Nepal* 69 F12
Everett, *Pa., U.S.A.* 110 F6
Everett, *Wash., U.S.A.* . 116 C4
Everglades, The, *U.S.A.* . 109 N5
Everglades City, *U.S.A.* . 109 N5
Everglades National Park,
  U.S.A. 109 N5
Evergreen, *U.S.A.* 109 K2
Everöd, *Sweden* 11 J8
Everson, *U.S.A.* 114 B2
Evertsberg, *Sweden* ... 10 C7
Evesham, *U.K.* 13 E6
Évian-les-Bains, *France* . 19 F13
Évinos →, *Greece* 38 C3
Évisa, *France* 21 F12
Evje, *Norway* 9 G12
Évora, *Portugal* 35 G3
Évora □, *Portugal* 35 G3
Évreux, *France* 18 C8
Evritanía □, *Greece* ... 38 C3
Évron, *France* 18 D6
Évros □, *Greece* 41 E10
Évros □, *Bulgaria* 72 B2
Evrótas →, *Greece* 38 E4
Évry, *France* 19 D9
Évvoia, *Greece* 38 C6
Évvoia □, *Greece* 38 C5
Evxinoúpolis, *Greece* .. 38 B4
Ewe, L., *U.K.* 14 D3
Ewing, *U.S.A.* 112 D5
Ewo, *Congo* 84 E2
Exaltación, *Bolivia* 124 F5
Excelsior Springs, *U.S.A.* 112 F7
Excideuil, *France* 20 C5
Exe →, *U.K.* 13 G4
Exeter, *Canada* 110 C3
Exeter, *U.K.* 13 G4
Exeter, *Calif., U.S.A.* ... 116 J7
Exeter, *N.H., U.S.A.* ... 111 D14
Exeter, *Nebr., U.S.A.* .. 112 E6
Exmoor, *U.K.* 13 F4
Exmouth, *Australia* ... 92 D1
Exmouth, *U.K.* 13 G4
Exmouth G., *Australia* . 92 D1
Expedition Ra., *Australia* 94 C4
Extremadura □, *Spain* . 35 F4
Exuma Sound, *Bahamas* 120 B4
Eyasi, L., *Tanzania* 86 C4
Eye, Pen., *U.K.* 14 C2
Eyeberry L., *Canada* ... 105 A8
Eyemouth, *U.K.* 14 F6
Eygurande, *France* 19 G9
Eyjafjörður, *Iceland* 8 D4
Eymet, *France* 20 D4
Eymoutiers, *France* ... 20 C5
Eynesil, *Turkey* 73 B8
Eyre, *Australia* 93 F4
Eyre (North), L., *Australia* 95 D2
Eyre (South), L., *Australia* 95 D2
Eyre Cr. →, *Australia* . 95 D2
Eyre Mts., *N.Z.* 91 L2
Eyre Pen., *Australia* ... 95 E2
Eysturoy, *Færoe Is.* 8 E9
Eyvānkī, *Iran* 71 C6
Ez Zeidab, *Sudan* 80 D3
Ezcaray, *Spain* 32 C1
Eẑerelis, *Lithuania* 44 D10
Ezine, *Turkey* 39 B8
Ezouza →, *Cyprus* 36 E11

F

F.Y.R.O.M. =
  Macedonia ■, *Europe* . 40 E5
Fabens, *U.S.A.* 115 L10
Fabero, *Spain* 34 C4
Fåborg, *Denmark* 11 J4
Fabriano, *Italy* 29 E9
Făcăeni, *Romania* 43 F12
Fachi, *Niger* 79 E8
Fada, *Chad* 79 E10
Fada-n-Gourma,
  Burkina Faso 83 C5
Fadd, *Hungary* 42 D3
Faddeyevskiy, Ostrov,
  Russia 51 B15
Fadghāmī, *Syria* 70 C4
Fadlab, *Sudan* 80 D3
Faenza, *Italy* 29 D8
Færoe Is. = Føroyar,
  Atl. Oc. 8 F9
Fafa, *Mali* 83 B5
Fafe, *Portugal* 34 D2
Fagam, *Nigeria* 83 C7
Făgăras, *Romania* 43 E9
Făgăras, Munţii, *Romania* 43 E9
Fågelmara, *Sweden* ... 11 H9
Fagerhult, *Sweden* 11 H8
Fagersta, *Sweden* 10 D9
Făget, *Romania* 42 E7

Făget, Munţii, *Romania* .. 43 C8
Fagnano, L., *Argentina* ... 128 G3
Fagnières, *France* 19 D11
Fahlīān, *Iran* 71 D6
Fahraj, *Kermān, Iran* 71 D8
Fahraj, *Yazd, Iran* 71 D7
Faial, *Madeira* 37 D3
Fair Hd., *U.K.* 15 A5
Fair Oaks, *U.S.A.* 116 G5
Fairbank, *U.S.A.* 115 L8
Fairbanks, *U.S.A.* 100 B5
Fairbury, *U.S.A.* 112 E6
Fairfax, *U.S.A.* 113 G6
Fairfield, *Ala., U.S.A.* ... 109 J2
Fairfield, *Calif., U.S.A.* . 116 G4
Fairfield, *Conn., U.S.A.* .. 111 E11
Fairfield, *Idaho, U.S.A.* .. 114 E6
Fairfield, *Ill., U.S.A.* 108 F1
Fairfield, *Iowa, U.S.A.* ... 112 E9
Fairfield, *Mont., U.S.A.* .. 114 C8
Fairfield, *Tex., U.S.A.* ... 113 K7
Fairford, *Canada* 105 C9
Fairhope, *U.S.A.* 109 K2
Fairlie, *N.Z.* 91 L3
Fairmead, *U.S.A.* 116 H6
Fairmont, *Minn., U.S.A.* .. 112 D7
Fairmont, *W. Va., U.S.A.* . 108 F5
Fairmount, *U.S.A.* 117 L8
Fairplay, *U.S.A.* 115 G11
Fairport, *U.S.A.* 110 C7
Fairport Harbor, *U.S.A.* .. 110 E3
Fairview, *Australia* 94 B3
Fairview, *Canada* 104 B5
Fairview, *Mont., U.S.A.* .. 112 B2
Fairview, *Okla., U.S.A.* .. 113 G5
Fairview, *Utah, U.S.A.* ... 114 G8
Fairweather, Mt., *U.S.A.* . 100 C6
Faisalabad, *Pakistan* 68 D5
Faith, *U.S.A.* 112 C3
Faizabad, *India* 69 F10
Fajardo, *Puerto Rico* 121 C6
Fakenham, *U.K.* 12 E8
Fåker, *Sweden* 10 A8
Fakfak, *Indonesia* 63 E8
Fakiya, *Bulgaria* 41 D11
Fakobli, *Ivory C.* 82 D3
Fakse, *Denmark* 11 J6
Fakse Bugt, *Denmark* 11 J6
Fakse Ladeplads, *Denmark* . 11 J6
Faku, *China* 57 C12
Falaise, *France* 18 D6
Falaise, Mui, *Vietnam* 64 C5
Falakrón Óros, *Greece* 40 E7
Falam, *Burma* 67 H18
Falces, *Spain* 32 C3
Fălciu, *Romania* 43 D13
Falcó, C. des, *Spain* 37 C7
Falcon Dam, *U.S.A.* 113 M5
Falconara Maríttima, *Italy* . 29 E10
Falcone, C. del, *Italy* 30 B1
Falconer, *U.S.A.* 110 D5
Faléa, *Mali* 82 C2
Falerum, *Sweden* 11 F10
Faleshty = Fălești,
  Moldova 43 C12
Fălești, *Moldova* 43 C12
Falfurrias, *U.S.A.* 113 M5
Falher, *Canada* 104 B5
Falirakí, *Greece* 36 C10
Falkenberg, *Germany* 24 D9
Falkenberg, *Sweden* 11 H6
Falkensee, *Germany* 24 C9
Falkirk, *U.K.* 14 F5
Falkirk □, *U.K.* 14 F5
Falkland, *U.K.* 14 E5
Falkland Is. □, *Atl. Oc.* .. 128 G5
Falkland Sd., *Falk. Is.* ... 128 G5
Falkonéra, *Greece* 38 E5
Falköping, *Sweden* 11 F7
Fall River, *U.S.A.* 111 E13
Fall River Mills, *U.S.A.* .. 114 F3
Fallbrook, *U.S.A.* 115 K5
Fallbrook, *Calif., U.S.A.* . 117 M9
Fallon, *Mont., U.S.A.* 112 B2
Fallon, *Nev., U.S.A.* 114 G4
Falls City, *Nebr., U.S.A.* . 112 E7
Falls City, *Oreg., U.S.A.* . 114 D2
Falls Creek, *U.S.A.* 110 E6
Falmouth, *Jamaica* 120 C4
Falmouth, *U.K.* 13 G2
Falmouth, *U.S.A.* 108 F3
False B., *S. Africa* 88 E2
Falso, C., *Honduras* 120 C3
Falster, *Denmark* 11 K5
Falsterbo, *Sweden* 9 J15
Fălticeni, *Romania* 43 C11
Falun, *Sweden* 10 D9
Famagusta, *Cyprus* 36 D12
Famagusta Bay, *Cyprus* ... 36 D13
Famatina, Sierra de,
  Argentina 126 B2
Family L., *Canada* 105 C9
Famoso, *U.S.A.* 117 K7
Fan Xian, *China* 56 G8
Fana, *Mali* 82 C3
Fanad Hd., *Ireland* 15 A4
Fanárion, *Greece* 38 B3
Fandriana, *Madag.* 89 C8
Fang, *Thailand* 64 C2
Fang Xian, *China* 59 A8
Fangchang, *China* 59 B12
Fangcheng,
  *Guangxi Zhuangzu,
  China* 58 G7
Fangcheng, *Henan, China* . 56 H7
Fangliao, *Taiwan* 59 F13
Fangshan, *China* 56 E6

Fangzi, *China* 57 F10
Fani i Madh →, *Albania* . 40 E4
Fanjiatun, *China* 57 C13
Fannich, L., *U.K.* 14 D4
Fannūj, *Iran* 71 E8
Fanny Bay, *Canada* 104 D4
Fanø, *Denmark* 11 J2
Fano, *Italy* 29 E10
Fanshaw, *U.S.A.* 104 B2
Fanshi, *China* 56 E7
Fao = Al Fāw, *Iraq* 71 D6
Faqirwali, *Pakistan* 68 E5
Fara in Sabina, *Italy* 29 F9
Faradje,
  Dem. Rep. of the Congo 86 B2
Farafangana, *Madag.* 89 C8
Farâfra, El Wâhât el-,
  Egypt 80 B2
Farāh, *Afghan.* 66 C3
Farāh □, *Afghan.* 66 C3
Farahalana, *Madag.* 89 A9
Faraid, Gebel, *Egypt* 80 C4
Faramana, *Burkina Faso* .. 82 C4
Faranah, *Guinea* 82 C2
Farasān, Jazā'ir, *Si. Arabia* 74 D3
Farasan Is. = Farasān,
  Jazā'ir, *Si. Arabia* 74 D3
Faratsiho, *Madag.* 89 B8
Fardes →, *Spain* 35 H7
Fareham, *U.K.* 13 G6
Farewell, *U.S.A.* 91 J4
Farewell C. = Farvel, Kap,
  Greenland 4 D5
Färgelanda, *Sweden* 11 F5
Farghona, *Uzbekistan* 50 E8
Fargo, *U.S.A.* 112 B6
Fār'iah, W. al →,
  West Bank 75 C4
Faribault, *U.S.A.* 112 C8
Faridkot, *India* 68 D6
Faridpur, *Bangla.* 69 H13
Färila, *Sweden* 10 C9
Farim, *Guinea-Biss.* 82 C1
Farīmān, *Iran* 71 C8
Farina, *Australia* 95 E2
Fariones, Pta., *Canary Is.* . 37 E6
Fâriskûr, *Egypt* 80 H7
Färjestaden, *Sweden* 11 H10
Farkadhón, *Greece* 38 B4
Farmakonisi, *Greece* 39 D9
Farmerville, *U.S.A.* 113 J8
Farmington, *Calif., U.S.A.* 116 H6
Farmington, *N.H., U.S.A.* 111 C13
Farmington, *N. Mex.,
  U.S.A.* 115 H9
Farmington, *Utah, U.S.A.* 114 F8
Farmington →, *U.S.A.* .. 111 E12
Farmville, *U.S.A.* 108 G6
Färnäs, *Sweden* 10 D8
Farne Is., *U.K.* 12 B6
Farnham, *Canada* 111 A12
Farnville, *U.S.A.* 108 G6
Faro, *Brazil* 125 D7
Fårö, *Sweden* 9 H18
Faro, *Portugal* 35 H3
Faro □, *Portugal* 35 H2
Fårösund, *Sweden* 11 G13
Farquhar, C., *Australia* ... 93 D1
Farrars Cr. →, *Australia* . 94 D3
Farrāshband, *Iran* 71 D7
Farrell, *U.S.A.* 110 E4
Farrell Flat, *Australia* 95 E2
Farrokhī, *Iran* 71 C8
Farruch, C. = Ferrutx, C.,
  Spain 37 B10
Farrukhabad-cum-
  Fatehgarh, *India* 69 F8
Fārs □, *Iran* 71 D7
Fársala, *Greece* 38 B4
Farsø, *Denmark* 11 H3
Farsund, *Norway* 9 G12
Fartak, Râs, *Si. Arabia* ... 70 D2
Fârţăneşti, *Romania* 43 E12
Fartura, Serra da, *Brazil* .. 127 B5
Faru, *Nigeria* 83 C6
Fārūj, *Iran* 71 B8
Fårup, *Denmark* 11 H3
Farvel, Kap, *Greenland* ... 4 D5
Farwell, *U.S.A.* 113 H3
Fasā, *Iran* 71 D7
Fasano, *Italy* 31 B10
Fashoda, *Sudan* 81 F3
Fastiv, *Ukraine* 47 G5
Fastov = Fastiv, *Ukraine* . 47 G5
Fatagar, Tanjung, *Indonesia* 63 E8
Fatehgarh, *India* 69 F8
Fatehpur, *Raj., India* 68 F6
Fatehpur, *Ut. P., India* ... 69 G9
Fatesh, *Russia* 47 F8
Fatick, *Senegal* 82 C1
Fatima, *Canada* 103 C7
Fátima, *Portugal* 35 F2
Fatoya, *Guinea* 82 C3
Fatsa, *Turkey* 72 B7
Faucille, Col de la, *France* 19 F13
Faulkton, *U.S.A.* 112 C5
Faulquemont, *France* 19 C13
Fauresmith, *S. Africa* 88 D4
Fauske, *Norway* 8 C16
Favara, *Italy* 30 E6
Faváritx, C. de, *Spain* 37 B11
Faverges, *France* 21 C10
Favignana, *Italy* 30 E5
Favignana, I., *Italy* 30 E5
Favourable Lake, *Canada* . 102 B1
Fawn →, *Canada* 102 A2

Fawnskin, *U.S.A.* 117 L10
Faxaflói, *Iceland* 8 D2
Faxälven →, *Sweden* 10 A10
Faya-Largeau, *Chad* 79 E9
Fayd, *Si. Arabia* 70 E4
Fayence, *France* 21 E10
Fayette, *Ala., U.S.A.* 109 J2
Fayette, *Mo., U.S.A.* 112 F8
Fayetteville, *Ark., U.S.A.* . 113 G7
Fayetteville, *N.C., U.S.A.* . 109 H6
Fayetteville, *Tenn., U.S.A.* 109 H2
Fayón, *Spain* 32 D5
Fazilka, *India* 68 D6
Fazilpur, *Pakistan* 68 E4
Fdérik, *Mauritania* 78 D3
Feale →, *Ireland* 15 D2
Fear, C., *U.S.A.* 109 J7
Feather →, *U.S.A.* 114 G3
Feather Falls, *U.S.A.* 116 F5
Featherston, *N.Z.* 91 J5
Featherstone, *Zimbabwe* .. 87 F3
Fécamp, *France* 18 C7
Federación, *Argentina* 126 C4
Féderal, *Argentina* 128 C5
Fedeshkūh, *Iran* 71 D7
Fehérgyarmat, *Hungary* ... 42 C7
Fehmarn, *Germany* 24 A7
Fehmarn Bælt, *Europe* ... 11 K5
Fehmarn Belt = Fehmarn
  Bælt, *Europe* 11 K5
Fei Xian, *China* 57 G9
Feijó, *Brazil* 124 E4
Feilding, *N.Z.* 91 J5
Feira de Santana, *Brazil* .. 125 F11
Feixiang, *China* 56 F8
Fejér □, *Hungary* 42 C3
Fejø, *Denmark* 11 K5
Feke, *Turkey* 72 D6
Fekete →, *Hungary* 42 E3
Felanitx, *Spain* 37 B10
Feldbach, *Austria* 26 E8
Feldberg, *Baden-W.,
  Germany* 25 H3
Feldberg,
  *Mecklenburg-Vorpommern,
  Germany* 24 B9
Feldkirch, *Austria* 26 D2
Feldkirchen, *Austria* 26 E7
Felipe Carrillo Puerto,
  Mexico 119 D7
Felixstowe, *U.K.* 13 F9
Felletin, *France* 20 C6
Fellingsbro, *Sweden* 10 E9
Felton, *U.S.A.* 116 H4
Feltre, *Italy* 29 B8
Femer Bælt = Fehmarn
  Bælt, *Europe* 11 K5
Femø, *Denmark* 11 K5
Femunden, *Norway* 9 E14
Fen He →, *China* 56 G6
Fene, *Spain* 34 B2
Fenelon Falls, *Canada* 110 B6
Fener Burnu, *Turkey* 39 E9
Feneroa, *Ethiopia* 81 E4
Feng Xian, *Jiangsu, China* 56 G9
Feng Xian, *Shaanxi, China* 56 H4
Fengári, *Greece* 41 F8
Fengcheng, *Jiangxi, China* 59 C10
Fengcheng, *Liaoning,
  China* 57 D13
Fengdu, *China* 58 C6
Fengfeng, *China* 56 F8
Fenggang, *China* 58 D6
Fenghua, *China* 59 C13
Fenghuang, *China* 58 D7
Fenghuangzui, *China* 58 A7
Fengjie, *China* 58 B7
Fengkai, *China* 59 F8
Fengle, *China* 59 B9
Fengning, *China* 56 D9
Fengqing, *China* 58 E2
Fengqiu, *China* 56 G8
Fengrun, *China* 57 E10
Fengshan,
  *Guangxi Zhuangzu,
  China* 58 E7
Fengshan,
  *Guangxi Zhuangzu,
  China* 58 E6
Fengtai, *Anhui, China* 59 A11
Fengtai, *Beijing, China* ... 56 E9
Fengxian, *China* 59 B13
Fengxiang, *China* 56 G4
Fengxin, *China* 59 C10
Fengyang, *China* 57 H9
Fengyi, *China* 58 E3
Fengzhen, *China* 56 D7
Fennimore, *U.S.A.* 112 D9
Feno, C. de, *France* 21 G12
Fenoarivo Afovoany,
  Madag. 89 B8
Fenoarivo Atsinanana,
  Madag. 89 B8
Fens, The, *U.K.* 12 E7
Fensmark, *Denmark* 11 J5
Fenton, *U.S.A.* 108 D4
Fenxi, *China* 56 F6
Fenyang, *China* 56 F6
Fenyi, *China* 59 D10
Feodosiya, *Ukraine* 47 K8
Ferdows, *Iran* 71 C8
Fère-Champenoise, *France* 19 D10
Fère-en-Tardenois, *France* 19 C10
Ferentino, *Italy* 29 G10
Ferfer, *Somali Rep.* 74 F4
Fergana = Farghona,
  Uzbekistan 50 E8

Fergus, *Canada* 102 D3
Fergus Falls, *U.S.A.* 112 B6
Feričanci, *Croatia* 42 E2
Ferkéssédougou, *Ivory C.* . 82 D3
Ferlach, *Austria* 26 E7
Ferland, *Canada* 102 B2
Ferlo, Vallée du, *Senegal* . 82 B2
Fermanagh □, *U.K.* 15 B4
Fermo, *Italy* 29 E10
Fermoselle, *Spain* 34 D4
Fermoy, *Ireland* 15 D3
Fernán Nuñéz, *Spain* 35 H6
Fernández, *Argentina* 126 B3
Fernandina Beach, *U.S.A.* 109 K5
Fernando de Noronha,
  Brazil 125 D12
Fernando Póo = Bioko,
  Eq. Guin. 83 E6
Ferndale, *Calif., U.S.A.* .. 114 F1
Ferndale, *Wash., U.S.A.* .. 116 B4
Fernie, *Canada* 104 D5
Fernlees, *Australia* 94 C4
Fernley, *U.S.A.* 114 G4
Ferozepore = Firozpur,
  India 68 D6
Férrai, *Greece* 41 F10
Ferrandina, *Italy* 31 B9
Ferrara, *Italy* 29 D8
Ferrato, C., *Italy* 30 C2
Ferreira do Alentejo,
  Portugal 35 G2
Ferreñafe, *Peru* 124 E3
Ferrerías, *Spain* 37 B11
Ferret, C., *France* 20 D2
Ferrette, *France* 19 E14
Ferriday, *U.S.A.* 113 K9
Ferrière, *Italy* 28 D6
Ferrières, *France* 19 D9
Ferro, Capo, *Italy* 30 A2
Ferrol, *Spain* 34 B2
Ferron, *U.S.A.* 115 G8
Ferrutx, C., *Spain* 37 B10
Ferryland, *Canada* 103 C9
Fertile, *U.S.A.* 112 B6
Fertőszentmiklós, *Hungary* 42 C1
Fès, *Morocco* 78 B5
Fessenden, *U.S.A.* 112 B5
Feteşti, *Romania* 43 F12
Fethiye, *Turkey* 39 E11
Fethiye Körfezi, *Turkey* .. 39 E10
Fetlar, *U.K.* 14 A8
Feuilles →, *Canada* 101 C12
Feurs, *France* 21 C8
Fezzan, *Libya* 79 C8
Fiambalá, *Argentina* 126 B2
Fianarantsoa, *Madag.* 89 C8
Fianarantsoa □, *Madag.* ... 89 B8
Fichtelgebirge, *Germany* .. 25 E7
Ficksburg, *S. Africa* 89 D4
Fidenza, *Italy* 28 D7
Fiditi, *Nigeria* 83 D5
Field, *Canada* 102 C3
Field →, *Australia* 94 C2
Field I., *Australia* 92 B5
Fieni, *Romania* 43 E10
Fier, *Albania* 40 F3
Fierzë, *Albania* 40 D4
Fife □, *U.K.* 14 E5
Fife Ness, *U.K.* 14 E6
Fifth Cataract, *Sudan* 80 D3
Figari, *France* 21 G13
Figeac, *France* 20 D6
Figeholm, *Sweden* 11 H10
Figline Valdarno, *Italy* 29 E8
Figtree, *Zimbabwe* 87 G2
Figueira Castelo Rodrigo,
  Portugal 34 E4
Figueira da Foz, *Portugal* . 34 E2
Figueiró dos Vinhos,
  Portugal 34 F2
Figueres, *Spain* 32 C7
Figuig, *Morocco* 78 B5
Fihaonana, *Madag.* 89 B8
Fiherenana, *Madag.* 89 C7
Fiherenana →, *Madag.* ... 89 C7
Fiji ■, *Pac. Oc.* 91 C8
Fika, *Nigeria* 83 C7
Filabres, Sierra de los,
  Spain 35 H8
Filadélfia, *Italy* 31 D9
Fil'akovo, *Slovak Rep.* ... 27 C12
Filer, *U.S.A.* 114 E6
Filey, *U.K.* 12 C7
Filey B., *U.K.* 12 C7
Filfla, *Malta* 36 D1
Filiaşi, *Romania* 43 F8
Filiátes, *Greece* 38 B2
Filiatrá, *Greece* 38 D3
Filicudi, *Italy* 31 D7
Filingué, *Niger* 83 C5
Filiourí →, *Greece* 41 E9
Filipstad, *Sweden* 10 E8
Filisur, *Switz.* 25 J5
Fillmore, *Calif., U.S.A.* ... 117 L8
Fillmore, *Utah, U.S.A.* ... 115 G7
Filótion, *Greece* 39 D7
Filottrano, *Italy* 29 E10
Finale Emília, *Italy* 29 D8
Finale Lígure, *Italy* 28 D5
Fiñana, *Spain* 35 H8
Findhorn →, *U.K.* 14 D5
Findlay, *U.S.A.* 108 E4
Finger L., *Canada* 105 C10
Fíngoè, *Mozam.* 87 E3
Finike, *Turkey* 39 E12

Finike Körfezi, *Turkey* ... 39 E12
Finiq, *Albania* 40 G4
Finistère □, *France* 18 D3
Finisterre = Fisterra, *Spain* 34 C1
Finisterre, C. = Fisterra,
  C., *Spain* 34 C1
Finke, *Australia* 94 D1
Finke →, *Australia* 95 D2
Finland ■, *Europe* 8 E22
Finland, G. of, *Europe* ... 9 G21
Finlay →, *Canada* 104 B3
Finley, *Australia* 95 F4
Finley, *U.S.A.* 112 B6
Finn →, *Ireland* 15 B4
Finnerödja, *Sweden* 11 F8
Finnigan, Mt., *Australia* .. 94 B4
Finniss, C., *Australia* 95 E1
Finnmark, *Norway* 8 B20
Finnsnes, *Norway* 8 B18
Finspång, *Sweden* 11 F9
Finsteraarhorn, *Switz.* 25 J4
Finsterwalde, *Germany* ... 24 D9
Fiora →, *Italy* 29 F8
Fiordland △, *N.Z.* 91 L1
Fiorenzuola d'Arda, *Italy* . 28 D6
Fīq, *Syria* 75 C4
Firat = Furāt, Nahr al →,
  Asia 70 D5
Fire River, *Canada* 102 C3
Firebag →, *Canada* 105 B6
Firebaugh, *U.S.A.* 116 J6
Firedrake L., *Canada* 105 A8
Firenze, *Italy* 29 E8
Firenzuola, *Italy* 29 D8
Firk →, *Iraq* 70 D5
Firmi, *France* 20 D6
Firminy, *France* 21 C8
Firozabad, *India* 69 F8
Firozpur, *India* 68 D6
Firozabad, *Iran* 71 D7
Fīrūzābād, *Iran* 71 C7
Fīrūzkūh, *Iran* 71 C7
Firvale, *Canada* 104 C3
Fish →, *Namibia* 88 D2
Fish →, *S. Africa* 88 E3
Fisher, *Australia* 93 F5
Fisher B., *Canada* 105 C9
Fishguard, *U.K.* 13 E3
Fishing L., *Canada* 105 C9
Fismes, *France* 19 C10
Fisterra, *Spain* 34 C1
Fisterra, C., *Spain* 34 C1
Fitchburg, *U.S.A.* 111 D13
Fitz Roy, *Argentina* 128 F3
Fitzgerald, *Canada* 104 B6
Fitzgerald, *U.S.A.* 109 K4
Fitzmaurice →, *Australia* . 92 B5
Fitzroy →, *Queens.,
  Australia* 94 C5
Fitzroy →, *W. Austral.,
  Australia* 92 C3
Fitzroy, Mte., *Argentina* .. 128 F2
Fitzroy Crossing, *Australia* 92 C4
Fitzwilliam I., *Canada* 110 A3
Fiuggi, *Italy* 29 G10
Fiume = Rijeka, *Croatia* .. 29 C11
Five Points, *U.S.A.* 116 J6
Fivizzano, *Italy* 28 D7
Fizi,
  Dem. Rep. of the Congo 86 C2
Fjällbacka, *Sweden* 11 F5
Fjärdhundra, *Sweden* 10 E10
Fjellerup, *Denmark* 11 H4
Fjerritslev, *Denmark* 11 G3
Fjugesta, *Sweden* 10 E8
Flagler, *U.S.A.* 112 F3
Flagstaff, *U.S.A.* 115 J8
Flaherty I., *Canada* 102 A4
Flåm, *Norway* 9 F12
Flambeau →, *U.S.A.* 112 C9
Flamborough Hd., *U.K.* .. 12 C7
Fläming, *Germany* 24 C8
Flaming Gorge Dam,
  U.S.A. 114 F9
Flaming Gorge Reservoir,
  U.S.A. 114 F9
Flamingo, Teluk, *Indonesia* 63 F9
Flanders = Flandre,
  Europe 19 B9
Flandre, *Europe* 19 B9
Flandre Occidentale =
  West-Vlaanderen □,
  Belgium 17 D2
Flandre Orientale = Oost-
  Vlaanderen □, *Belgium* 17 C3
Flandreau, *U.S.A.* 112 C6
Flanigan, *U.S.A.* 116 E7
Flannan Is., *U.K.* 14 C1
Flåsjön, *Sweden* 8 D16
Flat →, *Canada* 104 A3
Flat River, *U.S.A.* 113 G9
Flathead L., *U.S.A.* 114 C7
Flattery, C., *Australia* 94 A4
Flattery, C., *U.S.A.* 116 B2
Flaxton, *U.S.A.* 112 A3
Fleetwood, *U.K.* 12 D4
Flekkefjord, *Norway* 9 G12
Flemington, *U.S.A.* 110 E7
Flen, *Sweden* 10 E10
Flensburg, *Germany* 24 A5
Flers, *France* 18 D6
Flesherton, *Canada* 110 B4
Flesko, Tanjung, *Indonesia* 63 D6
Fleurance, *France* 20 E4
Fleurier, *Switz.* 25 J2
Flevoland □, *Neths.* 17 B5
Flin Flon, *Canada* 105 C8
Flinders →, *Australia* 94 B3
Flinders B., *Australia* 93 F2

Flinders Group, *Australia*	94	A3
Flinders I., *Australia*	94	G4
Flinders Ranges, *Australia*	95	E2
Flinders Reefs, *Australia*	94	B4
Flint, *U.K.*	12	D4
Flint, *U.S.A.*	108	D4
Flint ➤, *U.S.A.*	109	K3
Flint I., *Kiribati*	97	J12
Flinton, *Australia*	95	D4
Flintshire □, *U.K.*	12	D4
Fliseryd, *Sweden*	11	G10
Flix, *Spain*	32	D5
Flixecourt, *France*	19	B9
Floby, *Sweden*	11	F7
Floda, *Sweden*	11	G6
Flodden, *U.K.*	12	B5
Flogny-la-Chapelle, *France*	19	E10
Floodwood, *U.S.A.*	112	B8
Flora, *U.S.A.*	108	F1
Florac, *France*	20	D7
Florala, *U.S.A.*	109	K2
Florence = Firenze, *Italy*	29	E8
Florence, *Ala., U.S.A.*	109	H2
Florence, *Ariz., U.S.A.*	115	K8
Florence, *Colo., U.S.A.*	112	F2
Florence, *Oreg., U.S.A.*	114	E1
Florence, *S.C., U.S.A.*	109	H6
Florence, L., *Australia*	95	D2
Florencia, *Colombia*	124	
Florennes, *Belgium*	17	D4
Florensac, *France*	20	E7
Florenville, *Belgium*	17	E5
Flores, *Guatemala*	120	C2
Flores, *Indonesia*	63	F6
Flores I., *Canada*	104	D3
Flores Sea, *Indonesia*	63	F6
Florești, *Moldova*	43	C13
Floresville, *U.S.A.*	113	L5
Floriano, *Brazil*	125	E10
Florianópolis, *Brazil*	127	B6
Florida, *Cuba*	120	B4
Florida, *Uruguay*	127	C4
Florida □, *U.S.A.*	109	L5
Florida, Straits of, *U.S.A.*	120	B3
Florida B., *U.S.A.*	120	B3
Florida Keys, *U.S.A.*	107	F10
Florídia, *Italy*	31	E8
Flórina, *Greece*	40	F5
Flórina □, *Greece*	40	F5
Florø, *Norway*	9	F11
Flower Station, *Canada*	111	A8
Flower's Cove, *Canada*	103	B8
Floydada, *U.S.A.*	113	J4
Fluk, *Indonesia*	63	E7
Flúmen ➤, *Spain*	32	D4
Flumendosa ➤, *Italy*	30	C2
Fluminimaggiore, *Italy*	30	C1
Flushing = Vlissingen, *Neths.*	17	C3
Fluviá ➤, *Spain*	32	C8
Flying Fish, C., *Antarctica*	5	D15
Foam Lake, *Canada*	105	C8
Foča, *Bos.-H.*	40	C2
Foça, *Turkey*	39	C8
Focșani, *Romania*	43	E12
Fogang, *China*	59	F9
Fóggia, *Italy*	31	A8
Foggo, *Nigeria*	83	C6
Foglia ➤, *Italy*	29	E9
Fogo, *Canada*	103	C9
Fogo I., *Canada*	103	C9
Fohnsdorf, *Austria*	26	D7
Föhr, *Germany*	24	A4
Foia, *Portugal*	35	H2
Foix, *France*	20	E5
Fojnica, *Bos.-H.*	42	G2
Fokino, *Russia*	46	F8
Fokís □, *Greece*	38	C4
Folda, *Nord-Trøndelag, Norway*	8	D14
Folda, *Nordland, Norway*	8	C16
Földeák, *Hungary*	42	D5
Folégandros, *Greece*	38	E6
Foleyet, *Canada*	102	C3
Folgefonni, *Norway*	9	F12
Foligno, *Italy*	29	F9
Folkestone, *U.K.*	13	F9
Folkston, *U.S.A.*	109	K5
Follett, *U.S.A.*	113	G4
Follónica, *Italy*	28	F7
Follónica, G. di, *Italy*	28	F7
Folsom Res., *U.S.A.*	116	G5
Foltești, *Romania*	43	E13
Fond-du-Lac, *Canada*	105	B7
Fond du Lac, *U.S.A.*	112	D10
Fond-du-Lac ➤, *Canada*	105	B7
Fonda, *U.S.A.*	111	D10
Fondi, *Italy*	30	A6
Fonfría, *Spain*	34	D4
Fonni, *Italy*	30	B2
Fonsagrada = A Fonsagrada, *Spain*	34	B3
Fonseca, G. de, *Cent. Amer.*	120	D2
Font-Romeu, *France*	20	F5
Fontaine-Française, *France*	19	E12
Fontainebleau, *France*	19	D9
Fontana, *U.S.A.*	117	L9
Fontas ➤, *Canada*	104	B4
Fonte Boa, *Brazil*	124	D5
Fontem, *Cameroon*	83	D6
Fontenay-le-Comte, *France*	20	B3
Fontur, *Iceland*	8	C6
Fonyód, *Hungary*	42	D2
Foochow = Fuzhou, *China*	59	D12
Foping, *China*	56	H5
Forbach, *France*	19	C13

Forbes, *Australia*	95	E4
Forbesganj, *India*	69	F12
Forcados, *Nigeria*	83	D6
Forcados ➤, *Nigeria*	83	D6
Forcalquier, *France*	21	E9
Forchheim, *Germany*	25	F7
Ford City, *Calif., U.S.A.*	117	K7
Ford City, *Pa., U.S.A.*	110	F5
Førde, *Norway*	9	F11
Ford's Bridge, *Australia*	95	D4
Fordyce, *U.S.A.*	113	J8
Forécariah, *Guinea*	82	D2
Forel, Mt., *Greenland*	4	C6
Foremost, *Canada*	104	D6
Forest, *Canada*	110	C3
Forest, *U.S.A.*	113	J10
Forest City, *Iowa, U.S.A.*	112	D8
Forest City, *N.C., U.S.A.*	109	H5
Forest City, *Pa., U.S.A.*	111	E9
Forest Grove, *U.S.A.*	116	E3
Forestburg, *Canada*	104	C6
Foresthill, *U.S.A.*	116	F6
Forestier Pen., *Australia*	94	G4
Forestville, *Canada*	103	C6
Forestville, *Calif., U.S.A.*	116	G4
Forestville, *Wis., U.S.A.*	108	C2
Forez, Mts. du, *France*	20	C7
Forfar, *U.K.*	14	E6
Forks, *U.S.A.*	116	C2
Forlì, *Italy*	29	D9
Forman, *U.S.A.*	112	B6
Formby Pt., *U.K.*	12	D4
Formazza, *Italy*	28	B5
Formentera, *Spain*	37	C7
Formentor, C. de, *Spain*	37	B10
Former Yugoslav Republic of Macedonia = Macedonia ■, *Europe*	40	E5
Fórmia, *Italy*	30	A6
Formígine, *Italy*	28	D7
Formosa = Taiwan ■, *Asia*	59	F13
Formosa, *Argentina*	126	B4
Formosa, *Brazil*	125	G9
Formosa □, *Argentina*	126	B4
Formosa, Serra, *Brazil*	125	F8
Formosa Bay, *Kenya*	86	C5
Formosa Strait, *Asia*	59	E12
Fornells, *Spain*	37	A11
Fornos de Algodres, *Portugal*	34	E3
Fornovo di Taro, *Italy*	28	D7
Føroyar, *Atl. Oc.*	8	F9
Forres, *U.K.*	14	D5
Forrest, *Vic., Australia*	95	F3
Forrest, *W. Austral., Australia*	93	F4
Forrest, Mt., *Australia*	93	D4
Forrest City, *U.S.A.*	113	H9
Fors, *Sweden*	10	D10
Forsayth, *Australia*	94	B3
Forshaga, *Sweden*	10	E7
Förslöv, *Sweden*	11	H6
Forsmo, *Sweden*	10	A11
Forssa, *Finland*	9	F20
Forst, *Germany*	24	D10
Forster, *Australia*	95	E5
Forsvik, *Sweden*	11	F8
Forsyth, *Ga., U.S.A.*	109	J4
Forsyth, *Mont., U.S.A.*	114	C10
Fort Albany, *Canada*	102	B3
Fort Apache, *U.S.A.*	115	K9
Fort Assiniboine, *Canada*	104	C6
Fort Augustus, *U.K.*	14	D4
Fort Beaufort, *S. Africa*	88	E4
Fort Benton, *U.S.A.*	114	C8
Fort Bragg, *U.S.A.*	114	G2
Fort Bridger, *U.S.A.*	114	F8
Fort Chipewyan, *Canada*	105	B6
Fort Collins, *U.S.A.*	112	E2
Fort-Coulonge, *Canada*	102	C4
Fort Davis, *U.S.A.*	113	K3
Fort-de-France, *Martinique*	121	D7
Fort Defiance, *U.S.A.*	115	J9
Fort Dodge, *U.S.A.*	112	D7
Fort Edward, *U.S.A.*	111	C11
Fort Frances, *Canada*	105	D10
Fort Garland, *U.S.A.*	115	H11
Fort George = Chisasibi, *Canada*	102	B4
Fort Good-Hope, *Canada*	100	B7
Fort Hancock, *U.S.A.*	115	L11
Fort Hertz = Putao, *Burma*	67	F20
Fort Hope, *Canada*	102	B2
Fort Irwin, *U.S.A.*	117	K10
Fort Jameson = Chipata, *Zambia*	87	E3
Fort Kent, *U.S.A.*	103	C6
Fort Klamath, *U.S.A.*	114	E3
Fort-Lamy = Ndjamena, *Chad*	79	F8
Fort Laramie, *U.S.A.*	112	D2
Fort Lauderdale, *U.S.A.*	109	M5
Fort Liard, *Canada*	104	A4
Fort Liberté, *Haiti*	121	C5
Fort Lupton, *U.S.A.*	112	E2
Fort Mackay, *Canada*	104	B6
Fort McKenzie, *Canada*	103	A6
Fort Macleod, *Canada*	104	D6
Fort McMurray, *Canada*	104	B6
Fort McPherson, *Canada*	100	B6
Fort Madison, *U.S.A.*	112	E9
Fort Meade, *U.S.A.*	109	M5
Fort Morgan, *U.S.A.*	112	E3
Fort Myers, *U.S.A.*	109	M5
Fort Nelson, *Canada*	104	B4
Fort Nelson ➤, *Canada*	104	B4

Fort Norman = Tulita, *Canada*	100	B7
Fort Payne, *U.S.A.*	109	H3
Fort Peck, *U.S.A.*	114	B10
Fort Peck Dam, *U.S.A.*	114	C10
Fort Peck L., *U.S.A.*	114	C10
Fort Pierce, *U.S.A.*	109	M5
Fort Pierre, *U.S.A.*	112	C4
Fort Plain, *U.S.A.*	111	D10
Fort Portal, *Uganda*	86	B3
Fort Providence, *Canada*	104	A5
Fort Qu'Appelle, *Canada*	105	C8
Fort Resolution, *Canada*	104	A6
Fort Rixon, *Zimbabwe*	87	G2
Fort Roseberry = Mansa, *Zambia*	87	E2
Fort Ross, *U.S.A.*	116	G3
Fort Rupert = Waskaganish, *Canada*	102	B4
Fort St. James, *Canada*	104	C4
Fort St. John, *Canada*	104	B4
Fort Sandeman = Zhob, *Pakistan*	68	D3
Fort Saskatchewan, *Canada*	104	C6
Fort Scott, *U.S.A.*	113	G7
Fort Severn, *Canada*	102	A2
Fort Shevchenko, *Kazakstan*	49	H10
Fort Simpson, *Canada*	104	A4
Fort Smith, *Canada*	104	B6
Fort Smith, *U.S.A.*	113	H7
Fort Stanton, *U.S.A.*	115	K11
Fort Stockton, *U.S.A.*	113	K3
Fort Sumner, *U.S.A.*	113	H2
Fort Trinquet = Bir Mogreïn, *Mauritania*	78	C3
Fort Valley, *U.S.A.*	109	J4
Fort Vermilion, *Canada*	104	B5
Fort Walton Beach, *U.S.A.*	109	K2
Fort Wayne, *U.S.A.*	108	E3
Fort William, *U.K.*	14	E3
Fort Worth, *U.S.A.*	113	J6
Fort Yates, *U.S.A.*	112	B4
Fort Yukon, *U.S.A.*	100	B5
Fortaleza, *Brazil*	125	D11
Forteau, *Canada*	103	B8
Forth ➤, *U.K.*	14	E5
Forth, Firth of, *U.K.*	14	E6
Fortore ➤, *Italy*	29	G12
Fortrose, *U.K.*	14	D4
Fortuna, *Spain*	33	G3
Fortuna, *Calif., U.S.A.*	114	F1
Fortuna, *N. Dak., U.S.A.*	112	A3
Fortune B., *Canada*	103	C8
Fosnavåg, *Norway*	9	E12
Fos-sur-Mer, *France*	21	E8
Foshan, *China*	59	F9
Fosna, *Norway*	8	E14
Fosnavåg, *Norway*	9	E11
Fossano, *Italy*	28	D4
Fossil, *U.S.A.*	114	D3
Fossilbrook, *Australia*	94	B3
Fossombrone, *Italy*	29	E9
Fosston, *U.S.A.*	112	B7
Foster, *Canada*	111	A12
Foster ➤, *Canada*	105	B7
Fosters Ra., *Australia*	94	C1
Fostoria, *U.S.A.*	108	E4
Fouesnant, *France*	18	E2
Fougères, *France*	18	D5
Foul Pt., *Sri Lanka*	66	Q12
Foula, *U.K.*	14	A6
Foulness I., *U.K.*	13	F8
Foulpointe, *Madag.*	89	B8
Fouman, *Cameroon*	83	D7
Foundiougne, *Senegal*	82	C1
Fountain, *Colo., U.S.A.*	112	F2
Fountain, *Utah, U.S.A.*	114	G8
Fountain Springs, *U.S.A.*	117	K8
Fourchambault, *France*	19	E10
Fourchu, *Canada*	103	C7
Fouriesburg, *S. Africa*	88	D4
Fourmies, *France*	19	B11
Fournás, *Greece*	38	B3
Foúrnoi, *Greece*	39	D8
Fours, *France*	19	F10
Fouta Djalon, *Guinea*	82	C2
Foux, Cap-à-, *Haiti*	121	C5
Foveaux Str., *N.Z.*	91	M2
Fowey, *U.K.*	13	G3
Fowler, *Calif., U.S.A.*	116	J7
Fowler, *Colo., U.S.A.*	112	F3
Fowler, *Kans., U.S.A.*	113	G4
Fowlers B., *Australia*	93	F5
Fowlerton, *U.S.A.*	113	L5
Fowman, *Iran*	73	D13
Fox ➤, *Canada*	105	B10
Fox Valley, *Canada*	105	C7
Foxe Basin, *Canada*	4	C4
Foxe Chan., *Canada*	101	B12
Foxe Pen., *Canada*	101	B12
Foxen, *Sweden*	10	E5
Foxton, *N.Z.*	91	J5
Foyle, Lough, *U.K.*	15	A4
Foynes, *Ireland*	15	D2
Foz, *Spain*	34	B3
Fóz do Cúnene, *Angola*	88	B1
Foz do Iguaçu, *Brazil*	127	B5
Fraga, *Spain*	32	D5
Framingham, *U.S.A.*	111	D13
Frampol, *Poland*	45	H9
Franca, *Brazil*	125	H9
Francavilla al Mare, *Italy*	29	F11
Francavilla Fontana, *Italy*	31	B10
France ■, *Europe*	7	F6
Frances, *Australia*	95	F3

Frances ➤, *Canada*	104	A3
Frances L., *Canada*	104	A3
Franceville, *Gabon*	84	E2
Franche-Comté, *France*	19	F12
Francisco I. Madero, *Coahuila, Mexico*	118	B4
Francisco I. Madero, *Durango, Mexico*	118	C4
Francistown, *Botswana*	89	C4
Francofonte, *Italy*	31	E7
François, *Canada*	103	C8
François L., *Canada*	104	C3
Franeker, *Neths.*	17	A5
Frankado, *Djibouti*	81	E5
Frankenberg, *Germany*	24	D4
Frankenwald, *Germany*	25	E7
Frankfort, *S. Africa*	89	D4
Frankfort, *Ind., U.S.A.*	108	E2
Frankfort, *Kans., U.S.A.*	112	F6
Frankfort, *Ky., U.S.A.*	108	F3
Frankfort, *Mich., U.S.A.*	108	C2
Frankfurt, *Brandenburg, Germany*	24	C10
Frankfurt, *Hessen, Germany*	25	E4
Fränkische Alb, *Germany*	25	F7
Fränkische Rezat ➤, *Germany*	25	F7
Fränkische Saale ➤, *Germany*	25	E5
Fränkische Schweiz, *Germany*	25	F7
Frankland ➤, *Australia*	93	G2
Franklin, *Ky., U.S.A.*	109	G2
Franklin, *La., U.S.A.*	113	L9
Franklin, *Mass., U.S.A.*	111	D13
Franklin, *N.H., U.S.A.*	111	C13
Franklin, *Nebr., U.S.A.*	112	E5
Franklin, *Pa., U.S.A.*	110	E5
Franklin, *Tenn., U.S.A.*	109	H2
Franklin, *Va., U.S.A.*	109	G7
Franklin B., *Canada*	100	B7
Franklin, *W. Va., U.S.A.*	108	F6
Franklin I., *Antarctica*	5	D11
Franklin L., *U.S.A.*	114	F6
Franklin Mts., *Canada*	100	B7
Franklin Str., *Canada*	100	A10
Franklinton, *U.S.A.*	113	K9
Franklinville, *U.S.A.*	110	D6
Franks Pk., *U.S.A.*	114	E9
Frankston, *Australia*	95	F4
Frånö, *Sweden*	10	B11
Fränsta, *Sweden*	10	B10
Frantsa Iosifa, Zemlya, *Russia*	4	A10
Franz, *Canada*	102	C3
Franz Josef Land = Frantsa Iosifa, Zemlya, *Russia*	4	A10
Franzburg, *Germany*	24	A8
Frascati, *Italy*	29	G9
Fraser ➤, *B.C., Canada*	104	D4
Fraser ➤, *Nfld., Canada*	103	A7
Fraser, Mt., *Australia*	93	E2
Fraser I., *Australia*	95	D5
Fraser Lake, *Canada*	104	C4
Fraserburg, *S. Africa*	88	E3
Fraserburgh, *U.K.*	14	D6
Fraserdale, *Canada*	102	C3
Frashëri, *Albania*	40	F4
Frasne, *France*	19	F13
Frătești, *Romania*	43	G10
Frauenfeld, *Switz.*	25	H4
Fray Bentos, *Uruguay*	126	C4
Frazier Downs, *Australia*	92	C3
Frechilla, *Spain*	34	C6
Fredericia, *Denmark*	11	J3
Frederick, *Md., U.S.A.*	108	F7
Frederick, *Okla., U.S.A.*	113	H5
Frederick, *S. Dak., U.S.A.*	112	C5
Frederick Sd., *U.S.A.*	104	B2
Fredericksburg, *Tex., U.S.A.*	113	K5
Fredericksburg, *Va., U.S.A.*	108	F7
Fredericktown, *U.S.A.*	113	G9
Frederico I. Madero, Presa, *Mexico*	118	B3
Fredericton, *Canada*	103	C6
Fredericton Junc., *Canada*	103	C6
Frederiksborg Amtskommune □, *Denmark*	11	J6
Frederikshåb, *Greenland*	4	C5
Frederikshavn, *Denmark*	11	H4
Frederikssund, *Denmark*	11	J6
Frederiksted, *Virgin Is.*	121	C7
Frederiksværk, *Denmark*	11	J6
Fredonia, *Ariz., U.S.A.*	115	H7
Fredonia, *Kans., U.S.A.*	113	G7
Fredonia, *N.Y., U.S.A.*	110	D5
Fredriksberg, *Sweden*	10	D8
Fredrikstad, *Norway*	9	G14
Free State □, *S. Africa*	88	D4
Freehold, *U.S.A.*	111	F10
Freel Peak, *U.S.A.*	116	G7
Freeland, *U.S.A.*	111	E9
Freels, C., *Canada*	103	C9
Freeman, *Calif., U.S.A.*	117	K9
Freeman, *S. Dak., U.S.A.*	112	D6
Freeport, *Bahamas*	120	A4
Freeport, *Canada*	103	D6
Freeport, *Ill., U.S.A.*	112	D10
Freeport, *N.Y., U.S.A.*	111	F11

Freeport, *Tex., U.S.A.*	113	L7
Freetown, *S. Leone*	82	D2
Frégate, L., *Canada*	102	B5
Fregenal de la Sierra, *Spain*	35	G4
Fregene, *Italy*	29	G9
Fréhel, C., *France*	18	D4
Freiberg, *Germany*	24	E9
Freibourg = Fribourg, *Switz.*	25	J3
Freiburg, *Baden-W., Germany*	25	H3
Freiburg, *Niedersachsen, Germany*	24	B5
Freilassing, *Germany*	25	H8
Freire, *Chile*	128	D2
Freirina, *Chile*	126	B1
Freising, *Germany*	25	G7
Freistadt, *Austria*	26	C7
Freital, *Germany*	24	D9
Fréjus, *France*	21	E10
Fremantle, *Australia*	93	F2
Fremont, *Calif., U.S.A.*	116	H4
Fremont, *Mich., U.S.A.*	108	D3
Fremont, *Nebr., U.S.A.*	112	E6
Fremont, *Ohio, U.S.A.*	108	E4
Fremont ➤, *U.S.A.*	115	G8
Fremont L., *U.S.A.*	114	E9
French Camp, *U.S.A.*	116	H5
French Creek ➤, *U.S.A.*	110	E5
French Guiana ■, *S. Amer.*	125	C8
French Pass, *N.Z.*	91	J4
French Polynesia ■, *Pac. Oc.*	97	K13
Frenchglen, *U.S.A.*	114	E4
Frenchman Butte, *Canada*	105	C7
Frenchman Cr. ➤, *Mont., U.S.A.*	114	B10
Frenchman Cr. ➤, *Nebr., U.S.A.*	112	E4
Frenštát pod Radhoštěm, *Czech Rep.*	27	B11
Fresco ➤, *Brazil*	125	E8
Freshfield, C., *Antarctica*	5	C10
Fresnay-sur-Sarthe, *France*	18	D7
Fresnillo, *Mexico*	118	C4
Fresno, *U.S.A.*	116	J7
Fresno Alhandiga, *Spain*	34	E5
Fresno Reservoir, *U.S.A.*	114	B9
Freudenstadt, *Germany*	25	G4
Frévent, *France*	19	B9
Frew ➤, *Australia*	94	C2
Frewena, *Australia*	94	B2
Freycinet Pen., *Australia*	94	G4
Freyming-Merlebach, *France*	19	C13
Freyung, *Germany*	25	G9
Fria, *Guinea*	82	C2
Fria, C., *Namibia*	88	B1
Friant, *U.S.A.*	116	J7
Frías, *Argentina*	126	B2
Fribourg, *Switz.*	25	J3
Fribourg □, *Switz.*	25	J3
Fridafors, *Sweden*	11	H8
Friday Harbor, *U.S.A.*	116	B3
Friedberg, *Bayern, Germany*	25	G6
Friedberg, *Hessen, Germany*	25	E4
Friedland, *Germany*	24	B9
Friedrichshafen, *Germany*	25	H5
Friedrichskoog, *Germany*	24	A5
Friedrichstadt, *Germany*	24	A5
Friendly Is. = Tonga ■, *Pac. Oc.*	91	D11
Friesach, *Austria*	26	E7
Friesack, *Germany*	24	C8
Friesoythe, *Germany*	24	B3
Friggesund, *Sweden*	10	C10
Frillesås, *Sweden*	11	G6
Frinnaryd, *Sweden*	11	G8
Frio ➤, *U.S.A.*	113	L5
Frio, C., *Brazil*	122	F6
Friol, *Spain*	34	B3
Friona, *U.S.A.*	113	H3
Fristad, *Sweden*	11	G6
Fritch, *U.S.A.*	113	H4
Fritsla, *Sweden*	11	G6
Fritzlar, *Germany*	24	D5
Friuli-Venézia Giulia □, *Italy*	29	B9
Frobisher B., *Canada*	101	B13
Frobisher Bay = Iqaluit, *Canada*	101	B13
Frobisher L., *Canada*	105	B7
Frohavet, *Norway*	8	E13
Frohnleiten, *Austria*	26	D8
Froid, *U.S.A.*	112	A2
Frolovo, *Russia*	48	F6
Fromberg, *U.S.A.*	114	D9
Frombork, *Poland*	44	D6
Frome, *U.K.*	13	F5
Frome ➤, *U.K.*	13	G5
Frome, L., *Australia*	95	E2
Frome Downs, *Australia*	95	E2
Frómista, *Spain*	34	C6
Front Range, *U.S.A.*	114	G11
Front Royal, *U.S.A.*	108	F6
Frontera, *Canary Is.*	37	G2
Frontera, *Mexico*	119	D6
Frontignan, *France*	20	E7
Frosinone, *Italy*	30	A6
Frostburg, *U.S.A.*	108	F6
Frostisen, *Norway*	8	B17
Frouard, *France*	19	D13
Frövi, *Sweden*	10	E9

Frøya, *Norway* 8 E13
Frumoasa, *Romania* 43 D10
Frunze = Bishkek,
  Kyrgyzstan 50 E8
Fruška Gora, *Serbia, Yug.* 42 E4
Frutal, *Brazil* 125 H9
Frutigen, *Switz.* 25 J3
Frýdek-Místek, *Czech Rep.* 27 B11
Frýdlant, *Czech Rep.* ... 26 A8
Fryvaldov = Jeseník,
  Czech Rep. 27 A10
Fthiótis □, *Greece* 38 C4
Fu Jiang →, *China* 58 C6
Fu Xian, *Liaoning, China* 57 E11
Fu Xian, *Shaanxi, China* . 56 G5
Fu'an, *China* 59 D12
Fubian, *China* 58 B4
Fucécchio, *Italy* 28 E7
Fucheng, *China* 56 F9
Fuchou = Fuzhou, *China* 59 D12
Fuchū, *Japan* 55 G6
Fuchuan, *China* 59 E8
Fuchun Jiang →, *China* . 59 B13
Fúcino, Piana del, *Italy* . 29 F10
Fuding, *China* 59 D13
Fuencaliente, *Canary Is.* 37 F2
Fuencaliente, *Spain* 35 G6
Fuencaliente, Pta.,
  Canary Is. 37 F2
Fuengirola, *Spain* 35 J6
Fuenlabrada, *Spain* 34 E7
Fuensalida, *Spain* 34 E6
Fuente-Alamo, *Spain* ... 33 G3
Fuente-Álamo de Murcia,
  Spain 33 H3
Fuente de Cantos, *Spain* . 35 G4
Fuente del Maestre, *Spain* 35 G4
Fuente el Fresno, *Spain* . 35 F7
Fuente Obejuna, *Spain* ... 35 G5
Fuente Palmera, *Spain* . 35 H5
Fuentes de Andalucía,
  Spain 35 H5
Fuentes de Ebro, *Spain* . 32 D4
Fuentes de León, *Spain* . 35 G4
Fuentes de Oñoro, *Spain* . 34 E4
Fuentesaúco, *Spain* 34 D5
Fuerte →, *Mexico* 118 B3
Fuerte Olimpo, *Paraguay* . 126 A4
Fuerteventura, *Canary Is.* . 37 F6
Fufeng, *China* 56 G5
Fuga I., *Phil.* 61 B4
Fugong, *China* 58 D2
Fugou, *China* 56 G8
Fugu, *China* 56 E6
Fuhai, *China* 60 B3
Fuḥaymī, *Iraq* 70 C4
Fuji, *Japan* 55 G9
Fuji-San, *Japan* 55 G9
Fuji-yoshida, *Japan* 55 G9
Fujian □, *China* 59 E12
Fujinomiya, *Japan* 55 G9
Fujisawa, *Japan* 55 G9
Fukien = Fujian □, *China* 59 E12
Fukuchiyama, *Japan* 55 G7
Fukue-Shima, *Japan* 55 H4
Fukui, *Japan* 55 F8
Fukui □, *Japan* 55 G8
Fukuoka, *Japan* 55 H5
Fukuoka □, *Japan* 55 H5
Fukushima, *Japan* 54 F10
Fukushima □, *Japan* 54 F10
Fukuyama, *Japan* 55 G6
Fulda, *Germany* 24 E5
Fulda →, *Germany* 24 D5
Fuling, *China* 58 C6
Fullerton, *Calif., U.S.A.* . 117 M9
Fullerton, *Nebr., U.S.A.* . 112 E6
Fulongquan, *China* 57 B13
Fülöpszállás, *Hungary* .. 42 D4
Fulton, *Mo., U.S.A.* 112 F9
Fulton, *N.Y., U.S.A.* 111 C8
Fulton, *Tenn., U.S.A.* ... 109 G1
Fuluälven →, *Sweden* .. 10 C7
Fulufjället, *Sweden* 10 C6
Fumay, *France* 19 C11
Fumel, *France* 20 D4
Fumin, *China* 58 E4
Funabashi, *Japan* 55 G10
Funchal, *Madeira* 37 D3
Fundación, *Colombia* ... 124 A4
Fundão, *Portugal* 34 E3
Fundu Moldovei, *Romania* 43 C10
Fundulea, *Romania* 43 F11
Fundy, B. of, *Canada* ... 103 D6
Funing, *Hebei, China* 57 E10
Funing, *Jiangsu, China* .. 57 H10
Funing, *Yunnan, China* . 58 F5
Funiu Shan, *China* 56 H7
Funsi, *Ghana* 82 C4
Funtua, *Nigeria* 83 C6
Fuping, *Hebei, China* 56 E8
Fuping, *Shaanxi, China* . 56 G5
Fuqing, *China* 59 E12
Fuquan, *China* 58 D6
Furano, *Japan* 54 C11
Furāt, Nahr al →, *Asia* . 70 D5
Fürg, *Iran* 71 D7
Furmanov, *Russia* 48 B5
Furmanovo, *Kazakstan* .. 48 F9
Furnás, *Spain* 37 B8
Furnas, Reprêsa de, *Brazil* 127 A6
Furneaux Group, *Australia* 94 G4
Furqlus, *Syria* 75 A6
Fürstenau, *Germany* 24 C3
Fürstenberg, *Germany* ... 24 B9
Fürstenfeld, *Austria* 26 D9
Fürstenfeldbruck, *Germany* 25 G7
Fürstenwalde, *Germany* .. 24 C10
Fürth, *Germany* 25 F6
Furth im Wald, *Germany* . 25 F8
Furtwangen, *Germany* ... 25 G4
Furudal, *Sweden* 10 C9
Furukawa, *Japan* 54 E10
Furulund, *Sweden* 11 J7
Fury and Hecla Str.,
  Canada 101 B11
Fusagasuga, *Colombia* .. 124 C4
Fuscaldo, *Italy* 31 C9
Fushan, *Shandong, China* 57 F11
Fushan, *Shanxi, China* .. 56 G6
Fushë Arrëzi, *Albania* ... 40 D4
Fushë-Krujë, *Albania* 40 E3
Fushun, *Liaoning, China* . 57 D12
Fushun, *Sichuan, China* . 58 C5
Fusong, *China* 57 C14
Füssen, *Germany* 25 H6
Fusui, *China* 58 F6
Futog, *Yugoslavia* 42 E4
Futuna, *Wall. & F. Is.* .. 91 B8
Fuwa, *Egypt* 80 H7
Fuxin, *China* 57 C11
Fuyang, *Anhui, China* ... 56 H8
Fuyang, *Zhejiang, China* . 59 B12
Fuyang He →, *China* 56 E9
Fuying Dao, *China* 59 D13
Fuyu, *China* 57 B13
Fuyuan, *Heilongjiang,*
  China 60 B8
Fuyuan, *Yunnan, China* . 58 E5
Füzesgyarmat, *Hungary* . 42 C6
Fuzhou, *China* 59 D12
Fylde, *U.K.* 12 D5
Fyn, *Denmark* 11 J4
Fyne, L., *U.K.* 14 F3
Fyns Amtskommune □,
  Denmark 11 J4
Fynshav, *Denmark* 11 K3

G

Gaanda, *Nigeria* 83 C7
Gabarin, *Nigeria* 83 C7
Gabas →, *France* 20 E3
Gabela, *Angola* 84 G2
Gabès, *Tunisia* 79 B8
Gabès, G. de, *Tunisia* ... 79 B8
Gabgaba, W. →, *Egypt* .. 80 C3
Gabin, *Poland* 45 F6
Gabon ■, *Africa* 84 E2
Gaborone, *Botswana* 88 C4
Gabriels, *U.S.A.* 111 B10
Gābrīk, *Iran* 71 E8
Gabrovo, *Bulgaria* 41 D9
Gacé, *France* 18 D7
Gāch Sār, *Iran* 71 B6
Gachsārān, *Iran* 71 D6
Gacko, *Bos.-H.* 40 C2
Gadag, *India* 66 M9
Gadamai, *Sudan* 81 D4
Gadap, *Pakistan* 68 G2
Gadarwara, *India* 69 H8
Gadebusch, *Germany* 24 B7
Gadein, *Sudan* 81 F2
Gadhada, *India* 68 J4
Gádor, Sierra de, *Spain* . 35 J8
Gadsden, *Ala., U.S.A.* ... 109 H3
Gadsden, *Ariz., U.S.A.* .. 115 K6
Gadwal, *India* 66 L10
Gadyach = Hadyach,
  Ukraine 47 G8
Găeşti, *Romania* 43 F10
Gaeta, *Italy* 30 A6
Gaeta, G. di, *Italy* 30 A6
Gaffney, *U.S.A.* 109 H5
Gafsa, *Tunisia* 78 B7
Gagarin, *Russia* 46 E8
Gagetown, *Canada* 103 C6
Gaggenau, *Germany* 25 G4
Gagino, *Russia* 48 C7
Gagliano del Capo, *Italy* . 31 C11
Gagnef, *Sweden* 10 D9
Gagnoa, *Ivory C.* 82 D3
Gagnon, *Canada* 103 B6
Gagnon, L., *Canada* 105 A6
Gagra, *Georgia* 49 J5
Gahini, *Rwanda* 86 C3
Gahmar, *India* 69 G10
Gai Xian, *China* 57 D12
Gaïdhouronísi, *Greece* ... 36 E7
Gail, *U.S.A.* 113 J4
Gail →, *Austria* 26 E6
Gaillac, *France* 20 E5
Gaillimh = Galway, *Ireland* 15 C2
Gaillon, *France* 18 C8
Gaines, *U.S.A.* 110 E7
Gainesville, *Fla., U.S.A.* . 109 L4
Gainesville, *Ga., U.S.A.* . 109 H4
Gainesville, *Mo., U.S.A.* . 113 G8
Gainesville, *Tex., U.S.A.* . 113 J6
Gainsborough, *U.K.* 12 D7
Gairdner, L., *Australia* ... 95 E2
Gairloch, *U.K.* 14 D3
Gaj, *Croatia* 42 E2
Gakuch, *Pakistan* 69 A5
Galán, Cerro, *Argentina* . 126 B2
Galana →, *Kenya* 86 C5
Galanta, *Slovak Rep.* 27 C10
Galapagar, *Spain* 34 E7
Galápagos, *Pac. Oc.* ... 122 D1
Galashiels, *U.K.* 14 F6

Galatás, *Greece* 38 D5
Galaţi, *Romania* 43 E13
Galaţi □, *Romania* 43 E12
Galatia, *Turkey* 72 C5
Galátone, *Italy* 31 B11
Galax, *U.S.A.* 109 G5
Galaxídhion, *Greece* 38 C4
Galbraith, *Australia* 94 B3
Galcaio, *Somali Rep.* 74 F4
Galdhøpiggen, *Norway* .. 9 F12
Galeana, *Mexico* 118 C4
Galela, *Indonesia* 63 D7
Galera, *Spain* 33 H2
Galera Point, *Trin. & Tob.* 121 D7
Galesburg, *U.S.A.* 112 E9
Galeton, *U.S.A.* 110 E7
Gali, *Georgia* 49 J5
Galicea Mare, *Romania* . 43 F8
Galich, *Russia* 48 A6
Galiche, *Bulgaria* 40 C7
Galicia □, *Spain* 34 C3
Galilee = Hagalil, *Israel* . 75 C4
Galilee, L., *Australia* 94 C4
Galilee, Sea of = Yam
  Kinneret, *Israel* 75 C4
Galinoporni, *Cyprus* 36 D13
Galion, *U.S.A.* 110 F2
Galiuro Mts., *U.S.A.* 115 K8
Gallabat, *Sudan* 81 E4
Gallan Hd., *U.K.* 14 C1
Gallarate, *Italy* 28 C5
Galle, *Sri Lanka* 66 R12
Gállego →, *Spain* 32 D4
Gallegos →, *Argentina* .. 128 G3
Galley Hd., *Ireland* 15 E3
Galliate, *Italy* 28 C5
Gallinas, Pta., *Colombia* . 124 A4
Gallipoli = Gelibolu,
  Turkey 41 F10
Gallípoli, *Italy* 31 B10
Gallipolis, *U.S.A.* 108 F4
Gällivare, *Sweden* 8 C19
Gallneukirchen, *Austria* . 26 C7
Gällö, *Sweden* 10 B9
Gallo →, *Italy* 30 D6
Gallocanta, L. de, *Spain* . 32 E3
Galloway, *U.K.* 14 F4
Galloway, Mull of, *U.K.* . 14 G4
Gallup, *U.S.A.* 115 J9
Gallur, *Spain* 32 D3
Galong, *Australia* 95 E4
Galoya, *Sri Lanka* 66 Q12
Galt, *U.S.A.* 116 G5
Galten, *Denmark* 11 H3
Galtür, *Austria* 26 E3
Galty Mts., *Ireland* 15 D3
Galtymore, *Ireland* 15 D3
Galva, *U.S.A.* 112 E9
Galve de Sorbe, *Spain* .. 32 D1
Galveston, *U.S.A.* 113 L7
Galveston B., *U.S.A.* 113 L7
Gálvez, *Argentina* 126 C3
Galway, *Ireland* 15 C2
Galway □, *Ireland* 15 C2
Galway B., *Ireland* 15 C2
Gam →, *Vietnam* 64 B5
Gamagori, *Japan* 55 G8
Gamari, L., *Ethiopia* 81 E5
Gamawa, *Nigeria* 83 C7
Gamay, *Phil.* 61 E6
Gambaga, *Ghana* 83 C4
Gambat, *Pakistan* 68 F3
Gambela, *Ethiopia* 81 F3
Gambia ■, *W. Afr.* 82 C1
Gambia →, *W. Afr.* 82 C1
Gambier, C., *Australia* .. 92 B5
Gambier Is., *Australia* ... 95 F2
Gamboli, *Pakistan* 68 E3
Gamboma, *Congo* 84 E3
Gamerco, *U.S.A.* 115 J9
Gamla Uppsala, *Sweden* . 10 E11
Gamlakarleby = Kokkola,
  Finland 8 E20
Gamleby, *Sweden* 11 G10
Gammon →, *Canada* 105 C9
Gamu-Gofa □, *Ethiopia* . 81 F4
Gan, *France* 20 E3
Gan Jiang →, *China* 59 C11
Ganado, *Ariz., U.S.A.* ... 115 J9
Ganado, *Tex., U.S.A.* 113 L6
Gananoque, *Canada* 102 D4
Ganāveh, *Iran* 71 D6
Gäncä, *Azerbaijan* 49 K8
Gancheng, *China* 64 C7
Gand = Gent, *Belgium* .. 17 C3
Ganda, *Angola* 85 G2
Gandak →, *India* 69 G11
Gandava, *Pakistan* 68 E2
Gander, *Canada* 103 C9
Gander L., *Canada* 103 C9
Ganderkesee, *Germany* . 24 B4
Ganderowe Falls,
  Zimbabwe 87 F2
Gandesa, *Spain* 32 D5
Gandhi Sagar, *India* 68 G6
Gandi, *Nigeria* 83 C6
Gandía, *Spain* 33 G4
Gandino, *Italy* 28 C6
Gando, Pta., *Canary Is.* . 37 G4
Gandole, *Nigeria* 83 D7

Ganga →, *India* 69 H14
Ganganagar, *India* 68 E5
Gangapur, *India* 68 F7
Gangara, *Niger* 83 C6
Gangaw, *Burma* 67 H19
Gangdisê Shan, *China* .. 67 D12
Ganges = Ganga →, *India* 69 H14
Ganges, *France* 20 E7
Ganges, Mouths of the,
  India 69 J14
Gånghester, *Sweden* 11 G7
Gangi, *Italy* 31 E7
Gângiova, *Romania* 43 G8
Gangoh, *India* 68 E7
Gangtok, *India* 67 F16
Gangu, *China* 56 G3
Gangyao, *China* 57 B14
Gani, *Indonesia* 63 E7
Ganj, *India* 69 F8
Gannat, *France* 19 F10
Gannett Peak, *U.S.A.* ... 114 E9
Gannvalley, *U.S.A.* 112 C5
Ganquan, *China* 56 F5
Gänserdorf, *Austria* 27 C9
Ganshui, *China* 58 C6
Gansu □, *China* 56 G3
Ganta, *Liberia* 82 D3
Gantheaume, C., *Australia* 95 F2
Gantheaume B., *Australia* 93 E1
Gantsevichi = Hantsavichy,
  Belarus 47 F4
Ganyem = Genyem,
  Indonesia 63 E10
Ganyu, *China* 57 G10
Ganyushkino, *Kazakstan* . 49 G9
Ganzhou, *China* 59 E10
Gao, *Mali* 83 B5
Gao Xian, *China* 58 C5
Gao'an, *China* 59 C10
Gaohe, *China* 59 F9
Gaohebu, *China* 59 B11
Gaokeng, *China* 59 D9
Gaolan Dao, *China* 59 G9
Gaoligong Shan, *China* . 58 E2
Gaomi, *China* 57 F10
Gaoping, *China* 56 G7
Gaotang, *China* 56 F9
Gaoua, *Burkina Faso* ... 82 C4
Gaoual, *Guinea* 82 C2
Gaoxiong = Kaohsiung,
  Taiwan 59 F13
Gaoyang, *China* 56 E9
Gaoyou, *China* 59 A12
Gaoyou Hu, *China* 57 H10
Gaoyuan, *China* 57 F9
Gaozhou, *China* 59 G8
Gap, *France* 21 D10
Gapan, *Phil.* 61 D4
Gar, *China* 60 C2
Garabogazköl Aylagy,
  Turkmenistan 50 E6
Garachico, *Canary Is.* ... 37 F3
Garachiné, *Panama* 120 E4
Garafia, *Canary Is.* 37 F2
Garajonay, *Canary Is.* ... 37 F2
Garanhuns, *Brazil* 125 E11
Garawe, *Liberia* 82 E3
Garba Tula, *Kenya* 86 B4
Garber, *U.S.A.* 113 G6
Garberville, *U.S.A.* 114 F2
Garbsen, *Germany* 24 C4
Gard □, *France* 21 D8
Gard →, *France* 21 E8
Garda, L. di, *Italy* 28 C7
Gardanne, *France* 21 E9
Garde L., *Canada* 105 A7
Gardelegen, *Germany* ... 24 C7
Garden City, *Kans., U.S.A.* 113 G4
Garden City, *Tex., U.S.A.* 113 K4
Garden Grove, *U.S.A.* ... 117 M9
Gardēz, *Afghan.* 68 C3
Gardiner, *U.S.A.* 114 D8
Gardiners I., *U.S.A.* 111 E12
Gardner, *U.S.A.* 111 D13
Gardner Canal, *Canada* . 104 C3
Gardnerville, *U.S.A.* 116 G7
Gardno, Jezioro, *Poland* . 44 D4
Gardo, *Somali Rep.* 74 F4
Gardone Val Trómpia, *Italy* 28 C7
Gárdony, *Hungary* 42 C3
Garey, *U.S.A.* 117 L6
Garfield, *U.S.A.* 114 C5
Garforth, *U.K.* 12 D6
Gargaliánoi, *Greece* 38 D3
Gargan, Mt., *France* 20 C5
Gargano, *Italy* 30 A6
Gargždai, *Lithuania* 44 C8
Garhshankar, *India* 68 D7
Garibaldi Prov. Park,
  Canada 104 D4
Garies, *S. Africa* 88 E2
Garigliano →, *Italy* 30 A6
Garissa, *Kenya* 86 C4
Garissa □, *Kenya* 86 C5
Garkida, *Nigeria* 83 C7
Garko, *Nigeria* 83 C6
Garland, *Tex., U.S.A.* ... 113 J6
Garland, *Utah, U.S.A.* .. 114 F7
Garlasco, *Italy* 28 C5
Garlin, *France* 20 E3
Garliava, *Lithuania* 44 D10
Garm, *Tajikistan* 50 F8
Garmāb, *Iran* 71 C8

Garmisch-Partenkirchen,
  Germany 25 H7
Garmsār, *Iran* 71 C7
Garner, *U.S.A.* 112 D8
Garnett, *U.S.A.* 112 F7
Garo Hills, *India* 69 G14
Garoe, *Somali Rep.* 74 F4
Garonne →, *France* 20 C3
Garonne, Canal Latéral à
  la, *France* 20 D4
Garoua, *Cameroon* 83 D7
Garpenberg, *Sweden* 10 D10
Garphyttan, *Sweden* 10 E8
Garrel, *Germany* 24 C4
Garrigue = Garrigues,
  France 20 E7
Garrigues, *France* 20 E7
Garrison, *Mont., U.S.A.* . 114 C7
Garrison, *N. Dak., U.S.A.* 112 B4
Garrison, *Tex., U.S.A.* ... 113 K7
Garrison Res. =
  Sakakawea, L., *U.S.A.* 112 B4
Garron Pt., *U.K.* 15 A6
Garrovillas, *Spain* 35 F4
Garrucha, *Spain* 33 H3
Garry →, *U.K.* 14 E5
Garry, L., *Canada* 100 B9
Garsen, *Kenya* 86 C5
Gärsnäs, *Sweden* 11 J8
Garson L., *Canada* 105 B6
Gartempe →, *France* 20 B4
Gartz, *Germany* 24 B10
Garu, *Ghana* 83 C4
Garub, *Namibia* 88 D2
Garut, *Indonesia* 63 G12
Garvão, *Portugal* 35 H2
Garvie Mts., *N.Z.* 91 L2
Garwa = Garoua,
  Cameroon 83 D7
Garwa, *India* 69 G10
Garwolin, *Poland* 45 G8
Gary, *U.S.A.* 108 E2
Garz, *Germany* 24 A9
Garzê, *China* 58 B3
Garzón, *Colombia* 124 C3
Gas-San, *Japan* 54 E10
Gasan Kuli = Esenguly,
  Turkmenistan 50 F6
Gascogne, *France* 20 E4
Gascogne, G. de, *Europe* . 20 E2
Gascony = Gascogne,
  France 20 E4
Gascoyne →, *Australia* .. 93 D1
Gascoyne Junc. T.O.,
  Australia 93 E2
Gascueña, *Spain* 32 E2
Gash, Wadi →, *Ethiopia* . 81 E4
Gashaka, *Nigeria* 83 D7
Gasherbrum, *Pakistan* .. 69 B7
Gashua, *Nigeria* 83 C7
Gaspé, *Canada* 103 C7
Gaspé, C. de, *Canada* ... 103 C7
Gaspé, Pén. de, *Canada* . 103 C6
Gaspésie, Parc Prov. de la,
  Canada 103 C6
Gassaway, *U.S.A.* 108 F5
Gassol, *Nigeria* 83 D7
Gasteiz = Vitoria-Gasteiz,
  Spain 32 C2
Gastonia, *U.S.A.* 109 H5
Gastoúni, *Greece* 38 D3
Gastoúri, *Greece* 38 B1
Gastre, *Argentina* 128 E3
Gästrikland, *Sweden* 10 D10
Gata, *Cyprus* 36 E12
Gata, C. de, *Spain* 33 J2
Gata, Sierra de, *Spain* .. 34 E4
Gataga →, *Canada* 104 B3
Gătaia, *Romania* 42 E6
Gatchina, *Russia* 46 C6
Gatehouse of Fleet, *U.K.* 14 G4
Gates, *U.S.A.* 110 C7
Gateshead, *U.K.* 12 C6
Gatesville, *U.S.A.* 113 K6
Gaths, *Zimbabwe* 87 G3
Gatico, *Chile* 126 A1
Gâtinais, *France* 19 D9
Gâtine, Hauteurs de,
  France 20 B3
Gatineau, *Canada* 102 C4
Gatineau, Parc de la,
  Canada 102 C4
Gattaran, *Phil.* 61 B4
Gattinara, *Italy* 28 C5
Gatun, L., *Panama* 120 E4
Gatyana, *S. Africa* 89 E4
Gau, *Fiji* 91 D8
Gaucín, *Spain* 35 J5
Gauer L., *Canada* 105 B9
Gauhati, *India* 69 F14
Gauja →, *Latvia* 9 H21
Gaula →, *Norway* 8 E14
Gausta, *Norway* 9 G13
Gauteng □, *S. Africa* 89 D4
Gāv Koshī, *Iran* 71 D8
Gāvakān, *Iran* 71 D7
Gavarnie, *France* 20 F3
Gāvāter, *Iran* 71 E9
Gāvbandī, *Iran* 71 E7
Gavdhopoúla, *Greece* ... 36 E6
Gávdhos, *Greece* 36 E6
Gavi, *Italy* 28 D5
Gavião, *Portugal* 35 F3
Gaviota, *U.S.A.* 117 L6
Gävle, *Sweden* 10 D11
Gävleborgs län □, *Sweden* 10 C10
Gävlebukten, *Sweden* ... 10 D11

Gavorrano, *Italy* 28 F7
Gavray, *France* 18 D5
Gavrilov Yam, *Russia* 46 D10
Gávrion, *Greece* 38 D6
Gawachab, *Namibia* 88 D2
Gawilgarh Hills, *India* ... 66 J10
Gawler, *Australia* 95 E2
Gaxun Nur, *China* 60 B5
Gaya, *India* 69 G11
Gaya, *Niger* 83 C5
Gaya, *Nigeria* 83 C6
Gaylord, *U.S.A.* 108 C3
Gayndah, *Australia* 95 D5
Gaysin = Haysyn, *Ukraine* 47 H5
Gayvoron = Hayvoron,
    Ukraine 47 H5
Gaza, *Gaza Strip* 75 D3
Gaza □, *Mozam.* 89 C5
Gaza Strip □, *Asia* 75 D3
Gazaoua, *Niger* 83 C6
Gāzbor, *Iran* 71 D8
Gazi,
    Dem. Rep. of the Congo 86 B1
Gaziantep, *Turkey* 72 D7
Gazipaşa, *Turkey* 72 D5
Gbarnga, *Liberia* 82 D3
Gbekebo, *Nigeria* 83 D5
Gboko, *Nigeria* 83 D6
Gbongan, *Nigeria* 83 D5
Gcuwa, *S. Africa* 89 E4
Gdańsk, *Poland* 44 D5
Gdańsk □, *Poland* 44 D5
Gdańska, Zatoka, *Poland* . 44 D6
Gdov, *Russia* 9 G22
Gdynia, *Poland* 44 D5
Gebe, *Indonesia* 63 D7
Gebeciler, *Turkey* 39 C12
Gebeit Mine, *Sudan* 80 C4
Gebze, *Turkey* 41 F13
Gecha, *Ethiopia* 81 F4
Gedaref, *Sudan* 81 E4
Gediz, *Turkey* 39 B11
Gediz →, *Turkey* 39 C8
Gedo, *Ethiopia* 81 F4
Gèdre, *France* 20 F4
Gedser, *Denmark* 11 K5
Geegully Cr. →, *Australia* 92 C3
Geel, *Belgium* 17 C4
Geelong, *Australia* 95 F3
Geelvink Chan., *Australia* 93 E1
Geesthacht, *Germany* 24 B6
Geidam, *Nigeria* 83 C7
Geikie →, *Canada* 105 B8
Geilenkirchen, *Germany* .. 24 E2
Geili, *Sudan* 81 D3
Geisingen, *Germany* 25 H4
Geislingen, *Germany* 25 G5
Geita, *Tanzania* 86 C3
Geita □, *Tanzania* 86 C3
Gejiu, *China* 58 F4
Gel →, *Sudan* 81 F2
Gel River, *Sudan* 81 F2
Gela, *Italy* 31 E7
Gela, G. di, *Italy* 31 F7
Gelderland □, *Neths.* ... 17 B6
Geldern, *Germany* 24 D2
Geldrop, *Neths.* 17 C5
Geleen, *Neths.* 17 D5
Gelehun, *S. Leone* 82 D2
Gelembe, *Turkey* 39 B9
Gelendost, *Turkey* 72 C4
Gelendzhik, *Russia* 47 K10
Gelibolu, *Turkey* 41 F10
Gelibolu Yarımadası,
    Turkey 41 F10
Gelidonya Burnu, *Turkey* . 72 D4
Gelnhausen, *Germany* ... 25 E5
Gelnica, *Slovak Rep.* 27 C13
Gelsenkirchen, *Germany* .. 24 D3
Gelting, *Germany* 24 A5
Gemas, *Malaysia* 65 L4
Gembloux, *Belgium* 17 D4
Gemena,
    Dem. Rep. of the Congo 84 D3
Gemerek, *Turkey* 72 C7
Gemla, *Sweden* 11 H8
Gemlik, *Turkey* 41 F13
Gemlik Körfezi, *Turkey* .. 41 F12
Gemona del Friuli, *Italy* .. 29 B10
Gemsa, *Egypt* 80 B3
Gemünden, *Germany* ... 25 E5
Genale, *Ethiopia* 81 F4
Genç, *Turkey* 73 C9
Gençay, *France* 20 B4
Geneina, Gebel, *Egypt* .. 80 J8
General Acha, *Argentina* . 126 D3
General Alvear,
    Buenos Aires, Argentina 126 D4
General Alvear, *Mendoza,
    Argentina* 126 D2
General Artigas, *Paraguay* . 126 B4
General Belgrano,
    Argentina 126 D4
General Cabrera, *Argentina* 126 C3
General Cepeda, *Mexico* . 118 B4
General Guido, *Argentina* 126 D4
General Juan Madariaga,
    Argentina 126 D4
General La Madrid,
    Argentina 126 D3
General MacArthur, *Phil.* . 61 F6
General Martin Miguel de
    Güemes, *Argentina* ... 126 A3
General Paz, *Argentina* .. 126 B4
General Pico, *Argentina* .. 126 D3
General Pinedo, *Argentina* 126 B3

General Pinto, *Argentina* . 126 C3
General Roca, *Argentina* . 128 D3
General Santos, *Phil.* 61 H6
General Toshevo, *Bulgaria* 41 C12
General Trevino, *Mexico* . 119 B5
General Trías, *Mexico* 118 B3
General Viamonte,
    Argentina · 126 D3
General Villegas, *Argentina* 126 D3
Genesee, *Idaho, U.S.A.* .. 114 C5
Genesee, *Pa., U.S.A.* ... 110 E7
Genesee →, *U.S.A.* 110 C7
Geneseo, *Ill., U.S.A.* ... 112 E9
Geneseo, *Kans., U.S.A.* .. 112 F5
Geneseo, *N.Y., U.S.A.* .. 110 D7
Geneva = Genève, *Switz.* 25 J2
Geneva, *Ala., U.S.A.* ... 109 K3
Geneva, *N.Y., U.S.A.* ... 110 D8
Geneva, *Nebr., U.S.A.* .. 112 E6
Geneva, *Ohio, U.S.A.* ... 110 E4
Geneva, L. = Léman, L.,
    Europe 19 F13
Geneva, L., *U.S.A.* 108 D1
Genève, *Switz.* 25 J2
Gengenbach, *Germany* .. 25 G4
Gengma, *China* 58 F2
Genichesk = Henichesk,
    Ukraine 47 J8
Genil →, *Spain* 35 H5
Genk, *Belgium* 17 D5
Genlis, *France* 19 E12
Gennargentu, Mti. del,
    Italy 30 B2
Gennes, *France* 18 E6
Genoa = Génova, *Italy* ... 28 D5
Genoa, *Australia* 95 F4
Genoa, *N.Y., U.S.A.* ... 111 D8
Genoa, *Nebr., U.S.A.* .. 112 E6
Genoa, *Nev., U.S.A.* ... 116 F7
Génova, *Italy* 28 D5
Génova, G. di, *Italy* 28 D6
Genriyetty, Ostrov, *Russia* 51 B16
Gent, *Belgium* 17 C3
Genthin, *Germany* 24 C8
Genyem, *Indonesia* 63 E10
Genzano di Lucánia, *Italy* 31 B9
Genzano di Roma, *Italy* . 29 G9
Geoagiu, *Romania* 43 E8
Geographe B., *Australia* . 93 F2
Geographe Chan., *Australia* 93 D1
Geokchay = Göyçay,
    Azerbaijan 49 K8
Georga, Zemlya, *Russia* .. 50 A5
George, *S. Africa* 88 E3
George →, *Canada* 103 A6
George, L., *N.S.W.,
    Australia* 95 F4
George, L., *S. Austral.,
    Australia* 95 F3
George, L., *W. Austral.,
    Australia* 92 D3
George, L., *Uganda* 86 B3
George, L., *Fla., U.S.A.* . 109 L5
George, L., *N.Y., U.S.A.* 111 C11
George Gill Ra., *Australia* 92 D5
George River =
    Kangiqsualujjuaq,
    Canada 101 C13
George Sound, *N.Z.* 91 L1
George Town, *Bahamas* . 120 B4
George Town, *Malaysia* .. 65 K3
George V Land, *Antarctica* 5 C10
George VI Sound,
    Antarctica 5 D17
George West, *U.S.A.* ... 113 L5
Georgetown, *Australia* .. 94 B3
Georgetown, *Ont., Canada* 102 D4
Georgetown, *P.E.I.,
    Canada* 103 C7
Georgetown, *Cayman Is.* . 120 C3
Georgetown, *Gambia* ... 82 C2
Georgetown, *Guyana* ... 124 B7
Georgetown, *Calif., U.S.A.* 116 G6
Georgetown, *Colo., U.S.A.* 114 G11
Georgetown, *Ky., U.S.A.* 108 F3
Georgetown, *S.C., U.S.A.* 109 J6
Georgetown, *Tex., U.S.A.* 113 K6
Georgia □, *U.S.A.* 109 K5
Georgia ■, *Asia* 49 J6
Georgia, Str. of, *Canada* . 104 D4
Georgian B., *Canada* ... 102 C3
Georgina →, *Australia* .. 94 C2
Georgina Downs, *Australia* 94 C2
Georgiu-Dezh = Liski,
    Russia 47 G10
Georgiyevsk, *Russia* 49 H6
Georgsmarienhütte,
    Germany 24 C4
Gera, *Germany* 24 E8
Geraardsbergen, *Belgium* . 17 D3
Geral, Serra, *Brazil* 127 B6
Geral de Goiás, Serra,
    Brazil 125 F9
Geraldine, *U.S.A.* 114 C8
Geraldton, *Australia* 93 E1
Geraldton, *Canada* 102 C2
Gérardmer, *France* 19 D13
Gercüş, *Turkey* 73 D9
Gerede, *Turkey* 72 B5
Gerês, Sierra do, *Portugal* 34 D3
Gereshk, *Afghan.* 66 D4
Geretsried, *Germany* 25 H7
Gérgal, *Spain* 33 H2
Gerik, *Malaysia* 65 K3
Gering, *U.S.A.* 112 E3
Gerlach, *U.S.A.* 114 F4

Gerlachovský štit,
    Slovak Rep. 27 B13
German Planina,
    Macedonia 40 D6
Germansen Landing,
    Canada 104 B4
Germany ■, *Europe* 24 E6
Germencik, *Turkey* 39 D9
Germering, *Germany* 25 G7
Germersheim, *Germany* .. 25 F4
Germi, *Iran* 73 C13
Germiston, *S. Africa* 89 D4
Gernika-Lumo, *Spain* ... 32 B2
Gernsheim, *Germany* 25 F4
Gero, *Japan* 55 G8
Gerolzhofen, *Germany* ... 25 F6
Gerona = Girona, *Spain* . 32 D7
Gerrard, *Canada* 104 C5
Gers □, *France* 20 E4
Gers →, *France* 20 D4
Gersfeld, *Germany* 24 E5
Gersthofen, *Germany* ... 25 G6
Gerzat, *France* 20 C7
Gerze, *Turkey* 72 B6
Geseke, *Germany* 24 D4
Geser, *Indonesia* 63 E8
Gesso →, *Italy* 28 D4
Gestro, Wabi →, *Ethiopia* 81 G5
Getafe, *Spain* 34 E7
Gethsémani, *Canada* ... 103 B7
Getinge, *Sweden* 11 H6
Gettysburg, *Pa., U.S.A.* . 108 F7
Gettysburg, *S. Dak.,
    U.S.A.* 112 C5
Getxo, *Spain* 32 B2
Getz Ice Shelf, *Antarctica* . 5 D14
Gevaş, *Turkey* 73 C10
Gévaudan, *France* 20 D7
Gevgelija, *Macedonia* ... 40 E6
Gévora →, *Spain* 35 G4
Gex, *France* 19 F13
Geyikli, *Turkey* 39 B8
Geyser, *U.S.A.* 114 C8
Geyserville, *U.S.A.* 116 G4
Geyve, *Turkey* 72 B4
Ghâbat el Arab = Wang
    Kai, *Sudan* 81 F2
Ghaghara →, *India* 69 G11
Ghalla, Wadi el →, *Sudan* 81 E2
Ghana ■, *W. Afr.* 83 D4
Ghansor, *India* 69 H9
Ghanzi, *Botswana* 88 C3
Ghanzi □, *Botswana* ... 88 C3
Gharb el Istiwa'iya □,
    Sudan 81 G3
Gharb Bahr el →, *Chad* 79 F9
Gharbîya, Es Sahrâ el,
    Egypt 80 B2
Ghard Abû Muharik, *Egypt* 80 B3
Ghardaïa, *Algeria* 78 B6
Ghârib, G., *Egypt* 80 J8
Gharyān, *Libya* 79 B8
Ghatal, *India* 69 H12
Ghatampur, *India* 69 F9
Ghaṭṭī, *Si. Arabia* 70 D3
Ghawdex = Gozo, *Malta* 36 C1
Ghazal, Bahr el →, *Chad* 79 F9
Ghazâl, Bahr el →, *Sudan* 81 F3
Ghaziabad, *India* 68 E7
Ghazipur, *India* 69 G10
Ghaznī, *Afghan.* 68 C3
Ghaznī □, *Afghan.* 66 C6
Ghedi, *Italy* 28 C7
Ghelari, *Romania* 42 E7
Ghent = Gent, *Belgium* . 17 C3
Gheorghe Gheorghiu-
    Dej = Oneşti, *Romania* 43 D11
Gheorgheni, *Romania* ... 43 D10
Gherla, *Romania* 43 C8
Ghidigeni, *Romania* 43 D12
Ghilarza, *Italy* 30 B1
Ghimeş-Făget, *Romania* . 43 D11
Ghisonaccia, *France* 21 F13
Ghisoni, *France* 21 F13
Ghizao, *Afghan.* 68 C1
Ghizar →, *Pakistan* 69 A5
Ghogha, *India* 68 J5
Ghot Ogrein, *Egypt* 80 A2
Ghotaru, *India* 68 F4
Ghotki, *Pakistan* 68 E3
Ghowr □, *Afghan.* 66 C4
Ghudāf, W. al →, *Iraq* . 70 C4
Ghudāmis, *Libya* 77 C4
Ghughri, *India* 69 H9
Ghugus, *India* 66 K11
Ghulam Mohammad
    Barrage, *Pakistan* ... 68 G3
Ghūrīān, *Afghan.* 66 B2
Gia Dinh, *Vietnam* 65 G6
Gia Lai = Plei Ku, *Vietnam* 64 F7
Gia Nghia, *Vietnam* 65 G6
Gia Ngoc, *Vietnam* 64 E7
Gia Vuc, *Vietnam* 64 E7
Giannutri, *Italy* 28 F4
Giant Forest, *U.S.A.* ... 116 J8
Giant Mts. = Krkonoše,
    Czech Rep. 26 A8
Giants Causeway, *U.K.* .. 15 A5
Giarabub = Al Jaghbūb,
    Libya 79 C10
Giarre, *Italy* 31 E8
Giaveno, *Italy* 28 C4
Gibara, *Cuba* 120 B4
Gibb River, *Australia* ... 92 C4
Gibbon, *U.S.A.* 112 E5
Gibe →, *Ethiopia* 81 F4

Gibellina Nuova, *Italy* ... 30 E5
Gibraléon, *Spain* 35 H4
Gibraltar ■, *Europe* 35 J5
Gibraltar, Str. of, *Medit. S.* 35 K5
Gibson Desert, *Australia* . 92 D4
Gibsons, *Canada* 104 D4
Gibsonville, *U.S.A.* 116 F6
Giddings, *U.S.A.* 113 K6
Gidole, *Ethiopia* 81 F4
Gien, *France* 19 E9
Giengen, *Germany* 25 G6
Giessen, *Germany* 24 E4
Gifan, *Iran* 71 B8
Gifatin, Geziret, *Egypt* .. 80 B3
Gifford Creek, *Australia* . 92 D2
Gifhorn, *Germany* 24 C6
Gifu, *Japan* 55 G8
Gifu □, *Japan* 55 G8
Gigant, *Russia* 49 G5
Giganta, Sa. de la, *Mexico* 118 B2
Gigen, *Bulgaria* 41 C8
Gigha, *U.K.* 14 F3
Gíglio, *Italy* 28 F4
Gignac, *France* 20 E7
Gigüela →, *Spain* 35 F7
Gijón, *Spain* 34 B5
Gil I., *Canada* 104 C3
Gila →, *U.S.A.* 115 K6
Gila Bend, *U.S.A.* 115 K7
Gila Bend Mts., *U.S.A.* . 115 K7
Gīlān □, *Iran* 71 B6
Gilău, *Romania* 43 D8
Gilbert →, *Australia* ... 94 B3
Gilbert Is., *Kiribati* 96 G9
Gilbert Plains, *Canada* .. 105 C8
Gilbert River, *Australia* .. 94 B3
Gilberton, *Australia* 94 B3
Gilf el Kebîr, Hadabat el,
    Egypt 80 C2
Gilford I., *Canada* 104 C3
Gilgandra, *Australia* 95 E4
Gilgil, *Kenya* 86 C4
Gilgit, *India* 69 B6
Gilgit →, *Pakistan* 69 B6
Giljeva Planina,
    Serbia, Yug. 40 C3
Gillam, *Canada* 105 B10
Gilleleje, *Denmark* 11 H6
Gillen, L., *Australia* 93 E3
Gilles, L., *Australia* 95 E2
Gillette, *U.S.A.* 112 C2
Gilliat, *Australia* 94 C3
Gillingham, *U.K.* 13 F8
Gilmer, *U.S.A.* 113 J7
Gilmore, *Australia* 95 F4
Gilmore, L., *Australia* ... 93 F3
Gilmour, *Canada* 102 D4
Gilo →, *Ethiopia* 81 F3
Gilort →, *Romania* 43 F8
Gilroy, *U.S.A.* 116 H5
Gimbi, *Ethiopia* 81 F4
Gimli, *Canada* 105 C9
Gimo, *Sweden* 10 D12
Gimone →, *France* 20 E5
Gimont, *France* 20 E4
Gin Gin, *Australia* 95 D5
Ginâh, *Egypt* 80 B3
Gindie, *Australia* 94 C4
Gingin, *Australia* 93 F2
Ginir, *Ethiopia* 81 F5
Ginosa, *Italy* 31 B9
Ginzo de Limia = Xinzo de
    Limia, *Spain* 34 C3
Gióia, G. di, *Italy* 31 D8
Gióia del Colle, *Italy* ... 31 B9
Gióia Táuro, *Italy* 31 D8
Gioiosa Iónica, *Italy* 31 D9
Gioiosa Marea, *Italy* 31 D7
Gióna, Óros, *Greece* ... 38 C4
Giovi, Passo dei, *Italy* .. 28 D5
Giovinazzo, *Italy* 31 A9
Gir Hills, *India* 68 J4
Girab, *India* 68 F4
Girâfi, W. →, *Egypt* ... 75 F3
Giraltovce, *Slovak Rep.* .. 27 B14
Girard, *Kans., U.S.A.* ... 113 G7
Girard, *Ohio, U.S.A.* ... 110 E4
Girard, *Pa., U.S.A.* 110 D4
Girdle Ness, *U.K.* 14 D6
Giresun, *Turkey* 73 B8
Girga, *Egypt* 80 B3
Giridih, *India* 69 G12
Girifalco, *Italy* 31 D9
Girilambone, *Australia* .. 95 E4
Girne = Kyrenia, *Cyprus* 36 D12
Giro, *Nigeria* 83 C5
Giromagny, *France* 19 E13
Girona, *Spain* 32 D7
Girona □, *Spain* 32 C7
Gironde □, *France* 20 D3
Gironde →, *France* 20 C2
Gironella, *Spain* 32 C6
Giru, *Australia* 94 B4
Girvan, *U.K.* 14 F4
Gisborne, *N.Z.* 91 H7
Gisenyi, *Rwanda* 86 C2
Gislaved, *Sweden* 11 H7
Gisors, *France* 19 C8
Gitega, *Burundi* 86 C2
Giuba →, *Somali Rep.* .. 74 G3
Giugliano in Campania,
    Italy 31 B7
Giulianova, *Italy* 29 F10
Giurgeni, *Romania* 43 F12
Giurgiu, *Romania* 43 G10
Giurgiu □, *Romania* ... 43 F10

Giurgiuleşti, *Moldova* 43 E13
Give, *Denmark* 11 J3
Givet, *France* 19 B11
Givors, *France* 21 C8
Givry, *France* 19 F11
Giyon, *Ethiopia* 81 F4
Giza = El Gîza, *Egypt* .. 80 J7
Gizhiga, *Russia* 51 C17
Gizhiginskaya Guba, *Russia* 51 C16
Giżycko, *Poland* 44 D8
Gizzeria, *Italy* 31 D9
Gjalicës e Lumës, Mal,
    Albania 40 D4
Gjegjani, *Albania* 40 E4
Gjirokastra, *Albania* 40 F4
Gjoa Haven, *Canada* ... 100 B10
Gjøvik, *Norway* 9 F14
Gjuhës, Kep i, *Albania* .. 40 F3
Glace Bay, *Canada* 103 C8
Glacier Bay, *U.S.A.* 104 B1
Glacier Nat. Park, *Canada* 104 C5
Glacier Park, *U.S.A.* ... 114 B7
Glacier Peak, *U.S.A.* ... 114 B3
Gladewater, *U.S.A.* 113 J7
Gladstone, *Queens.,
    Australia* 94 C5
Gladstone, *S. Austral.,
    Australia* 95 E2
Gladstone, *W. Austral.,
    Australia* 93 E1
Gladstone, *Canada* 105 C9
Gladstone, *U.S.A.* 108 C2
Gladwin, *U.S.A.* 108 D3
Gladys L., *Canada* 104 B2
Glafsfjorden, *Sweden* ... 10 E6
Głogów Małopolski, *Poland* 45 H8
Głâma = Glomma →,
    Norway 9 G14
Gláma, *Iceland* 8 D2
Glamis, *U.S.A.* 117 N11
Glamoč, *Bos.-H.* 29 D13
Glamsbjerg, *Denmark* ... 11 J4
Glarus, *Switz.* 25 H5
Glarus □, *Switz.* 25 J5
Glasco, *Kans., U.S.A.* .. 112 F6
Glasco, *N.Y., U.S.A.* ... 111 D11
Glasgow, *U.K.* 14 F4
Glasgow, *Ky., U.S.A.* .. 108 G3
Glasgow, *Mont., U.S.A.* . 114 B10
Glastonbury, *U.K.* 13 F5
Glastonbury, *U.S.A.* ... 111 E12
Glauchau, *Germany* 24 E8
Glava, *Sweden* 10 E6
Glavice, *Croatia* 29 E13
Glazov, *Russia* 48 A11
Gleisdorf, *Austria* 26 D8
Gleiwitz = Gliwice, *Poland* 45 H5
Glen, *U.S.A.* 111 B13
Glen Affric, *U.K.* 14 D3
Glen Canyon Dam, *U.S.A.* 115 H8
Glen Canyon National
    Recreation Area, *U.S.A.* 115 H8
Glen Coe, *U.K.* 14 E3
Glen Cove, *U.S.A.* 111 F11
Glen Garry, *U.K.* 14 D3
Glen Innes, *Australia* ... 95 D5
Glen Lyon, *U.S.A.* 111 E8
Glen Mor, *U.K.* 14 D4
Glen Moriston, *U.K.* ... 14 D4
Glen Spean, *U.K.* 14 E4
Glen Ullin, *U.S.A.* 112 B4
Glénan, Îs. de, *France* .. 18 E3
Glenburgh, *Australia* ... 93 E2
Glencoe, *Canada* 110 D3
Glencoe, *S. Africa* 89 D5
Glencoe, *U.S.A.* 112 C7
Glendale, *Ariz., U.S.A.* . 115 K7
Glendale, *Calif., U.S.A.* . 117 L8
Glendale, *Oreg., U.S.A.* . 114 E2
Glendale, *Zimbabwe* ... 87 F3
Glendive, *U.S.A.* 112 B2
Glendo, *U.S.A.* 112 D2
Glenelg, *Australia* 95 E2
Glenelg →, *Australia* ... 95 F3
Glenflorrie, *Australia* ... 92 D2
Glengarriff, *Ireland* 15 E2
Glengyle, *Australia* 94 C2
Glenmora, *U.S.A.* 113 K8
Glenmorgan, *Australia* .. 95 D4
Glenn, *U.S.A.* 116 F4
Glennamaddy, *Ireland* .. 15 C3
Glenns Ferry, *U.S.A.* ... 114 E6
Glenorchy, *Australia* ... 94 G4
Glenore, *Australia* 94 B3
Glenormiston, *Australia* . 94 C2
Glenreagh, *Australia* ... 95 E5
Glenrock, *U.S.A.* 114 E11
Glenrothes, *U.K.* 14 E5
Glens Falls, *U.S.A.* 111 C11
Glenties, *Ireland* 15 B3
Glenville, *U.S.A.* 108 F5
Glenwood, *Nfld., Canada* . 103 C9
Glenwood, *Ark., U.S.A.* . 113 H8
Glenwood, *Hawaii, U.S.A.* 106 J17
Glenwood, *Iowa, U.S.A.* . 112 E7
Glenwood, *Minn., U.S.A.* 112 C7
Glenwood, *Wash., U.S.A.* 116 D5
Glenwood Springs, *U.S.A.* 114 G10
Glettinganes, *Iceland* ... 8 D7
Glifádha, *Greece* 38 D5
Glímakra, *Sweden* 11 H8
Glina, *Croatia* 29 C13
Glinojeck, *Poland* 45 F7
Gliwice, *Poland* 45 H5
Globe, *U.S.A.* 115 K8

Glodeanu Siliştea, *Romania* 43 F11
Glodeni, *Moldova* 43 C12
Glödnitz, *Austria* 26 E7
Gloggnitz, *Austria* 26 D8
Głogów, *Poland* 45 G3
Głogówek, *Poland* 45 H4
Glomma →, *Norway* 9 G14
Glóssa, *Greece* 38 B5
Glossop, *U.K.* 12 D6
Gloucester, *Australia* 95 E5
Gloucester, *U.K.* 13 F5
Gloucester, *U.S.A.* 111 D14
Gloucester I., *Australia* .. 94 C4
Gloucestershire □, *U.K.* .. 13 F5
Gloversville, *U.S.A.* 111 C10
Glovertown, *Canada* 103 C9
Głowno, *Poland* 45 G6
Głubczyce, *Poland* 45 H4
Glubokiy, *Russia* 49 F5
Glubokoye = Hlybokaye,
  Belarus 46 E4
Głuchołazy, *Poland* 45 H4
Glücksburg, *Germany* ... 24 A5
Glückstadt, *Germany* 24 B5
Glukhov = Hlukhiv,
  Ukraine 47 G7
Glusk, *Belarus* 47 F5
Głuszyca, *Poland* 45 H3
Glyngøre, *Denmark* 11 H2
Gmünd, *Kärnten, Austria* . 26 E6
Gmünd, *Niederösterreich,*
  Austria 26 C8
Gmunden, *Austria* 26 D6
Gnarp, *Sweden* 10 B11
Gnesta, *Sweden* 10 E11
Gniew, *Poland* 44 E5
Gniewkowo, *Poland* 45 F5
Gniezno, *Poland* 45 F4
Gnjilane, *Serbia, Yug.* ... 40 D5
Gnoien, *Germany* 24 B8
Gnosjö, *Sweden* 11 G7
Gnowangerup, *Australia* . 93 F2
Go Cong, *Vietnam* 65 G6
Gō-no-ura, *Japan* 55 H4
Goa, *India* 66 M8
Goa □, *India* 66 M8
Goalen Hd., *Australia* ... 95 F5
Goalpara, *India* 67 F17
Goalundo Ghat, *Bangla.* . 69 H13
Goaso, *Ghana* 82 D4
Goat Fell, *U.K.* 14 F3
Goba, *Ethiopia* 81 F4
Goba, *Mozam.* 89 D5
Gobabis, *Namibia* 88 C2
Göbel, *Turkey* 41 F12
Gobi, *Asia* 56 C6
Gobō, *Japan* 55 H7
Gobo, *Sudan* 81 F3
Göçbeyli, *Turkey* 39 B9
Goch, *Germany* 24 D2
Gochas, *Namibia* 88 C2
Godavari →, *India* 67 L13
Godavari Point, *India* ... 67 L13
Godbout, *Canada* 103 C6
Godda, *India* 69 G12
Godech, *Bulgaria* 40 C7
Goderich, *Canada* 102 D3
Goderville, *France* 18 C7
Godhavn, *Greenland* 4 C5
Godhra, *India* 68 H5
Gödöllő, *Hungary* 42 C4
Godoy Cruz, *Argentina* .. 126 C2
Gods →, *Canada* 105 B10
Gods L., *Canada* 105 C10
Godthåb = Nuuk,
  Greenland 4 C5
Godwin Austen = K2,
  Pakistan 69 B7
Goeie Hoop, Kaap die =
  Good Hope, C. of,
  S. Africa 88 E2
Goéland, L. au, *Canada* . 102 C4
Goeree, *Neths.* 17 C3
Goes, *Neths.* 17 C3
Gogama, *Canada* 102 C3
Gogango, *Australia* 94 C5
Gogebic, L., *U.S.A.* 112 B10
Gogolin, *Poland* 45 H5
Gogra = Ghaghara →,
  India 69 G11
Gogriâl, *Sudan* 81 F2
Goiânia, *Brazil* 125 G9
Goiás, *Brazil* 125 G8
Goiás □, *Brazil* 125 F9
Goio-Ere, *Brazil* 127 A5
Góis, *Portugal* 34 E2
Gojam □, *Ethiopia* 81 E4
Gojeb, Wabi →, *Ethiopia* 81 F4
Gojō, *Japan* 55 G7
Gojra, *Pakistan* 68 D5
Gokarannath, *India* 69 F9
Gökçeada, *Turkey* 41 F9
Gökçedağ, *Turkey* 39 B10
Gökçen, *Turkey* 39 C9
Gökçeören, *Turkey* 39 C10
Gökçeyazı, *Turkey* 39 B9
Gökırmak →, *Turkey* 72 B6
Gökova, *Turkey* 39 D10
Gökova Körfezi, *Turkey* . 39 E9
Göksu →, *Turkey* 72 D5
Göksun, *Turkey* 72 C7
Gokteik, *Burma* 67 H20
Göktepe, *Turkey* 39 D10
Gokurt, *Pakistan* 68 E2
Gola, *India* 69 E9

Golakganj, *India* 69 F13
Golan Heights = Hagolan,
  Syria 75 C4
Gołańcz, *Poland* 45 F4
Golāshkerd, *Iran* 71 E8
Golaya Pristen = Hola
  Pristan, *Ukraine* 47 J7
Gölbaşı, *Adiyaman, Turkey* 72 D7
Gölbaşı, *Ankara, Turkey* . 72 C5
Golchikha, *Russia* 4 B12
Golconda, *U.S.A.* 114 F5
Gölcük, *Kocaeli, Turkey* . 41 F13
Gölcük, *Niğde, Turkey* .. 72 C6
Gold Beach, *U.S.A.* 114 E1
Gold Coast, *Australia* ... 95 D5
Gold Coast, *W. Afr.* 83 E4
Gold Hill, *U.S.A.* 114 E2
Gołdap, *Poland* 44 D9
Goldberg, *Germany* 24 B8
Golden, *Canada* 104 C5
Golden, *U.S.A.* 112 F2
Golden B., *N.Z.* 91 J4
Golden Gate, *U.S.A.* 114 H4
Golden Hinde, *Canada* .. 104 D3
Golden Lake, *Canada* ... 110 A7
Golden Prairie, *Canada* . 105 C7
Golden Vale, *Ireland* 15 D3
Goldendale, *U.S.A.* 114 D3
Goldfield, *U.S.A.* 115 H5
Goldfields, *Canada* 105 B7
Goldsand L., *Canada* 105 B8
Goldsboro, *U.S.A.* 109 H7
Goldsmith, *U.S.A.* 113 K3
Goldsworthy, *Australia* . 92 D2
Goldthwaite, *U.S.A.* 113 K5
Golegã, *Portugal* 35 F2
Goleniów, *Poland* 44 E1
Golestānak, *Iran* 71 D7
Goleta, *U.S.A.* 117 L7
Golfito, *Costa Rica* 120 E3
Golfo Aranci, *Italy* 30 B2
Gölgeli Dağları, *Turkey* . 39 D10
Gölhisar, *Turkey* 39 D11
Goliad, *U.S.A.* 113 L6
Golija, *Montenegro, Yug.* 40 C2
Golija, *Serbia, Yug.* 40 C4
Golina, *Poland* 45 F5
Gölköy, *Turkey* 72 B7
Göllersdorf, *Austria* 26 C9
Gölmarmara, *Turkey* 39 C9
Golo →, *France* 21 F13
Gölova, *Turkey* 39 E12
Golpāyegān, *Iran* 71 C6
Gölpazarı, *Turkey* 72 B4
Golra, *Pakistan* 68 C5
Golspie, *U.K.* 14 D5
Golub-Dobrzyń, *Poland* . 45 E6
Golubac, *Serbia, Yug.* ... 40 B5
Golyam Perelik, *Bulgaria* 41 E8
Golyama Kamchiya →,
  Bulgaria 41 C11
Goma,
  Dem. Rep. of the Congo 86 C2
Gomati →, *India* 69 G10
Gombari,
  Dem. Rep. of the Congo 86 B2
Gombe, *Nigeria* 83 C7
Gömbe, *Turkey* 39 E11
Gombe →, *Tanzania* 86 C3
Gombi, *Nigeria* 83 C7
Gomel = Homyel, *Belarus* 47 F6
Gomera, *Canary Is.* 37 F2
Gómez Palacio, *Mexico* . 118 B4
Gomīshān, *Iran* 71 B7
Gommern, *Germany* 24 C7
Gomogomo, *Indonesia* .. 63 F8
Gomoh, *India* 67 H15
Gomotartsi, *Bulgaria* ... 40 B6
Gompa = Ganta, *Liberia* 82 D3
Gomphi, *Greece* 38 B3
Gonābād, *Iran* 71 C8
Gonaïves, *Haiti* 121 C5
Gonâve, G. de la, *Haiti* . 121 C5
Gonâve, I. de la, *Haiti* .. 121 C5
Gonbad-e Kāvūs, *Iran* .. 71 B7
Gönc, *Hungary* 42 B6
Gonda, *India* 69 F9
Gondal, *India* 68 J4
Gonder, *Ethiopia* 81 E4
Gonder □, *Ethiopia* 81 E4
Gondia, *India* 66 J12
Gondola, *Mozam.* 87 F3
Gondomar, *Portugal* 34 D2
Gondrecourt-le-Château,
  France 19 D12
Gönen, *Balıkesir, Turkey* 41 F11
Gönen, *Isparta, Turkey* . 39 D12
Gönen →, *Turkey* 41 F11
Gong Xian, *China* 58 C5
Gong'an, *China* 59 B9
Gongcheng, *China* 59 E8
Gongguan, *China* 58 G7
Gonghe, *China* 60 C5
Gongola →, *Nigeria* 83 D7
Gongolgon, *Australia* ... 95 E4
Gongshan, *China* 58 D2
Goniadz, *Poland* 44 E9
Goniri, *Nigeria* 83 C7
Gonjo, *China* 58 B2
Gonnesa, *Italy* 30 C1
Gónnos, *Greece* 38 B4
Gonnosfanádiga, *Italy* .. 30 C1
Gonzaga, *Phil.* 61 B5
Gonzales, *Calif., U.S.A.* . 116 J5

Gonzales, *Tex., U.S.A.* .. 113 L6
González Chaves,
  Argentina 126 D3
Good Hope, C. of,
  S. Africa 88 E2
Gooderham, *Canada* 102 D4
Goodeve, *Canada* 105 C8
Gooding, *U.S.A.* 114 E6
Goodland, *U.S.A.* 112 F4
Goodnight, *U.S.A.* 113 H4
Goodooga, *Australia* 95 D4
Goodsoil, *Canada* 105 C7
Goodsprings, *U.S.A.* 115 J6
Goole, *U.K.* 12 D7
Goolgowi, *Australia* 95 E4
Goomalling, *Australia* ... 93 F2
Goombalie, *Australia* ... 95 D4
Goonda, *Mozam.* 87 F3
Goondiwindi, *Australia* .. 95 D5
Goongarrie, L., *Australia* . 93 F3
Goonyella, *Australia* 94 C4
Gooray, *Australia* 95 D5
Goose →, *Canada* 103 B7
Goose L., *U.S.A.* 114 F3
Gop, *India* 66 H6
Gopalganj, *India* 69 F11
Göppingen, *Germany* ... 25 G5
Gor, *Spain* 35 H8
Góra, *Leszno, Poland* ... 45 G3
Góra, *Płock, Poland* 45 F7
Góra Kalwaria, *Poland* .. 45 G8
Gorakhpur, *India* 69 F10
Goražde, *Bos.-H.* 42 G3
Gorbatov, *Russia* 48 B6
Gorbea, Peña, *Spain* 32 B2
Gorda, *U.S.A.* 116 K5
Gorda, Pta., *Canary Is.* . 37 F2
Gorda, Pta., *Nic.* 120 D3
Gordan B., *Australia* 92 B5
Gördes, *Turkey* 39 C10
Gordon, *U.S.A.* 112 D3
Gordon →, *Australia* 94 G4
Gordon Downs, *Australia* 92 C4
Gordon L., *Alta., Canada* 105 B6
Gordon L., *N.W.T.,*
  Canada 104 A6
Gordonvale, *Australia* ... 94 B4
Gore, *Australia* 95 D5
Gore, *Ethiopia* 81 F4
Gore, *N.Z.* 91 M2
Gore Bay, *Canada* 102 C3
Görele, *Turkey* 73 B8
Goreme, *Turkey* 72 C6
Gorey, *Ireland* 15 D5
Gorg, *Iran* 71 D8
Gorgān, *Iran* 71 B7
Gorgona, *Italy* 28 E6
Gorgona, I., *Colombia* .. 124 C3
Gorgora, *Ethiopia* 81 E4
Gorham, *U.S.A.* 111 B13
Gori, *Georgia* 49 J7
Gorinchem, *Neths.* 17 C4
Goris, *Armenia* 73 C12
Goritsy, *Russia* 46 D9
Gorízia, *Italy* 29 C10
Gorj □, *Romania* 43 E8
Gorki = Horki, *Belarus* .. 46 E6
Gorkiy = Nizhniy
  Novgorod, *Russia* 48 B7
Gorkovskoye Vdkhr.,
  Russia 48 B6
Gorlice, *Poland* 45 J8
Görlitz, *Germany* 24 D10
Gorlovka = Horlivka,
  Ukraine 47 H10
Gorman, *Calif., U.S.A.* . 117 L8
Gorman, *Tex., U.S.A.* ... 113 J5
Gorna Dzhumayo =
  Blagoevgrad, *Bulgaria* 40 D7
Gorna Oryakhovitsa,
  Bulgaria 41 C9
Gornja Radgona, *Slovenia* 29 B13
Gornja Tuzla, *Bos.-H.* ... 42 F3
Gornji Grad, *Slovenia* ... 29 B11
Gornji Milanovac,
  Serbia, Yug. 40 B4
Gornji Vakuf, *Bos.-H.* ... 42 G2
Gorno Ablanovo, *Bulgaria* 41 C9
Gorno-Altay □, *Russia* .. 50 D9
Gorno-Altaysk, *Russia* .. 50 D9
Gornyatskiy, *Russia* 49 F5
Gornyi, *Russia* 54 B6
Gornyy, *Russia* 48 E9
Gorodenka = Horodenka,
  Ukraine 47 H3
Gorodets, *Russia* 48 B6
Gorodishche =
  Horodyshche, *Ukraine* . 47 H6
Gorodishche, *Russia* 48 D7
Gorodnya = Horodnya,
  Ukraine 47 G6
Gorodok = Haradok,
  Belarus 46 E6
Gorodok = Horodok,
  Ukraine 47 H2
Gorodovikovsk, *Russia* . 49 G5
Gorokhov = Horokhiv,
  Ukraine 47 G3
Gorokhovets, *Russia* 48 B6
Gorom Gorom,
  Burkina Faso 83 C4
Goromonzi, *Zimbabwe* . 87 F3
Gorongose →, *Mozam.* . 89 C5
Gorongoza, *Mozam.* 87 F3

Gorongoza, Sa. da,
  Mozam. 87 F3
Gorontalo, *Indonesia* ... 63 D6
Goronyo, *Nigeria* 83 C6
Górowo Iławeckie, *Poland* 44 D7
Gorron, *France* 18 D6
Gorshechnoye, *Russia* .. 47 G10
Gort, *Ireland* 15 C3
Gortis, *Greece* 36 D6
Góry Bystrzyckie, *Poland* . 45 H3
Goryachiy Klyuch, *Russia* 49 H4
Gorzkowice, *Poland* 45 G6
Górzno, *Poland* 45 E6
Gorzów Śląski, *Poland* .. 45 G5
Gorzów Wielkopolski,
  Poland 45 F2
Gorzów Wielkopolski □,
  Poland 45 F2
Gosford, *Australia* 95 E5
Goshen, *Calif., U.S.A.* .. 116 J7
Goshen, *Ind., U.S.A.* ... 108 E3
Goshen, *N.Y., U.S.A.* ... 111 E10
Goshogawara, *Japan* ... 54 D10
Goslar, *Germany* 24 D6
Gospič, *Croatia* 29 D12
Gosport, *U.K.* 13 G6
Gosse →, *Australia* 94 B1
Gostivar, *Macedonia* 40 E4
Gostyń, *Poland* 45 G4
Gostynin, *Poland* 45 F6
Göta älv →, *Sweden* 11 G5
Göta kanal, *Sweden* 11 F9
Götaland, *Sweden* 11 G8
Göteborg, *Sweden* 11 G5
Göteborgs och Bohus
  län □, *Sweden* 11 F5
Götene, *Sweden* 11 F7
Goteşti, *Moldova* 43 D13
Gotha, *Germany* 24 E6
Gothenburg = Göteborg,
  Sweden 11 G5
Gothenburg, *U.S.A.* 112 E4
Gotland, *Sweden* 11 G12
Gotlands län □, *Sweden* . 11 G12
Gotse Delchev, *Bulgaria* 40 E7
Gotska Sandön, *Sweden* 9 G18
Götsu, *Japan* 55 G6
Göttero, Monte, *Italy* ... 28 D6
Göttingen, *Germany* 24 D5
Gottwaldov = Zmiyev,
  Ukraine 47 H9
Gottwaldov = Zlín,
  Czech Rep. 27 B10
Goubangzi, *China* 57 D11
Gouda, *Neths.* 17 B4
Goúdhoura, Ákra, *Greece* 36 E8
Goudiry, *Senegal* 82 C2
Gough I., *Atl. Oc.* 2 G9
Gouin, Rés., *Canada* 102 C5
Goulburn, *Australia* 95 E4
Goulburn Is., *Australia* .. 94 A1
Goulia, *Ivory C.* 82 C3
Gouménissa, *Greece* 40 F6
Gourdon, *France* 20 D5
Gouré, *Niger* 83 C7
Gouri, *France* 18 D3
Gourits →, *S. Africa* 88 E3
Gourma Rharous, *Mali* . 83 B4
Goúrnais, *Greece* 36 D7
Gournay-en-Bray, *France* 19 C8
Gourock Ra., *Australia* .. 95 F4
Goursi, *Burkina Faso* ... 82 C4
Gouverneur, *U.S.A.* 111 B9
Gouviá, *Greece* 36 A3
Gouzon, *France* 19 F9
Govan, *Canada* 105 C8
Governador Valadares,
  Brazil 125 G10
Governor's Harbour,
  Bahamas 120 A4
Gowan Ra., *Australia* ... 94 D4
Gowanda, *U.S.A.* 110 D6
Gowd-e Zirreh, *Afghan.* . 66 E3
Gower, *U.K.* 13 F3
Gowna, L., *Ireland* 15 C4
Goya, *Argentina* 126 B4
Göyçay, *Azerbaijan* 49 K8
Goyder Lagoon, *Australia* 95 D2
Goyllarisquisga, *Peru* ... 124 F3
Göynük, *Antalya, Turkey* 39 E12
Göynük, *Bolu, Turkey* ... 72 B4
Goz Beïda, *Chad* 79 F10
Goz Regeb, *Sudan* 81 D4
Gozdnica, *Poland* 45 G2
Gozo, *Malta* 36 C1
Graaff-Reinet, *S. Africa* . 88 E3
Grabow, *Germany* 24 B7
Grabów nad Prosną,
  Poland 45 G5
Gračac, *Croatia* 29 D12
Gračanica, *Bos.-H.* 42 F3
Graçay, *France* 19 E8
Grace, *U.S.A.* 114 E8
Graceville, *U.S.A.* 112 C6
Gracias a Dios, C.,
  Honduras 120 D3
Graciosa, I., *Canary Is.* . 37 E6
Grad Sofiya □, *Bulgaria* . 40 D7
Gradac, *Montenegro, Yug.* 40 C3
Gradačac, *Bos.-H.* 42 F3
Gradeška Planina,
  Macedonia 40 E5
Gradets, *Bulgaria* 41 D10
Gradišče, *Slovenia* 29 B12

Grădiştea de Munte,
  Romania 43 E8
Grado, *Italy* 29 C10
Grado, *Spain* 34 B4
Gradule, *Australia* 95 D4
Grady, *U.S.A.* 113 H3
Graeca, Lacul, *Romania* . 43 F11
Grafenau, *Germany* 25 G9
Gräfenberg, *Germany* ... 25 F7
Grafham Water, *U.K.* 13 E7
Grafton, *Australia* 95 D5
Grafton, *U.S.A.* 112 A6
Graham, *Canada* 102 C1
Graham, *N.C., U.S.A.* ... 109 H6
Graham, *Tex., U.S.A.* ... 113 J5
Graham →, *Canada* 104 B4
Graham, Mt., *U.S.A.* 115 K9
Graham Bell, Ostrov =
  Greem-Bell, Ostrov,
  Russia 50 A7
Graham I., *Canada* 104 C2
Graham Land, *Antarctica* 5 C17
Grahamdale, *Canada* ... 105 C9
Grahamstown, *S. Africa* . 88 E4
Grahovo,
  Montenegro, Yug. 40 D2
Graie, Alpi, *Europe* 21 C11
Grain Coast, *W. Afr.* 82 E3
Grajaú, *Brazil* 125 E9
Grajaú →, *Brazil* 125 D10
Grajewo, *Poland* 44 E9
Gramada, *Bulgaria* 40 C6
Gramat, *France* 20 D5
Grammichele, *Italy* 31 E7
Grámmos, Óros, *Greece* . 40 F4
Grampian Highlands =
  Grampian Mts., *U.K.* .. 14 E5
Grampian Mts., *U.K.* 14 E5
Gramsh, *Albania* 40 F4
Gran Chaco, *S. Amer.* .. 126 B3
Gran Paradiso, *Italy* 28 C4
Gran Sasso d'Itália, *Italy* 29 F10
Granada, *Nic.* 120 D2
Granada, *Spain* 35 H7
Granada, *U.S.A.* 113 F3
Granada □, *Spain* 35 H7
Granadilla de Abona,
  Canary Is. 37 F3
Granard, *Ireland* 15 C4
Granbury, *U.S.A.* 113 J6
Granby, *Canada* 102 C5
Grand →, *Mo., U.S.A.* .. 112 F8
Grand →, *S. Dak., U.S.A.* 112 C4
Grand Bahama, *Bahamas* 120 A4
Grand Bank, *Canada* 103 C8
Grand Bassam, *Ivory C.* . 82 D4
Grand Béréby, *Ivory C.* .. 82 E3
Grand-Bourg, *Guadeloupe* 121 C7
Grand Canal = Yun
  Ho →, *China* 57 E9
Grand Canyon, *U.S.A.* .. 115 H7
Grand Canyon National
  Park, *U.S.A.* 115 H7
Grand Cayman, *Cayman Is.* 120 C3
Grand Cess, *Liberia* 82 E3
Grand Coulee, *U.S.A.* ... 114 C4
Grand Coulee Dam,
  U.S.A. 114 C4
Grand Falls, *Canada* 103 C8
Grand Forks, *Canada* ... 104 D5
Grand Forks, *U.S.A.* 112 B6
Grand Haven, *U.S.A.* ... 108 D2
Grand I., *U.S.A.* 108 B2
Grand Island, *U.S.A.* ... 112 E5
Grand Isle, *U.S.A.* 113 L10
Grand Junction, *U.S.A.* . 115 G9
Grand L., *N.B., Canada* . 103 C6
Grand L., *Nfld., Canada* . 103 C8
Grand L., *Nfld., Canada* . 103 B7
Grand L., *U.S.A.* 113 L8
Grand Lac Victoria,
  Canada 102 C4
Grand Lahou, *Ivory C.* .. 82 D3
Grand Lake, *U.S.A.* 114 F11
Grand-Lieu, L. de, *France* 18 E5
Grand Manan I., *Canada* 103 D6
Grand Marais, *Canada* .. 112 B9
Grand Marais, *U.S.A.* ... 108 B3
Grand-Mère, *Canada* ... 102 C5
Grand Popo, *Benin* 83 D5
Grand Portage, *U.S.A.* .. 102 C2
Grand Prairie, *U.S.A.* ... 113 J6
Grand Rapids, *Canada* .. 105 C9
Grand Rapids, *Mich.,*
  U.S.A. 108 D2
Grand Rapids, *Minn.,*
  U.S.A. 112 B8
Grand St-Bernard, Col du,
  Europe 25 K3
Grand Teton, *U.S.A.* 114 E8
Grand Union Canal, *U.K.* 13 E7
Grand View, *Canada* ... 105 C8
Grandas de Salime, *Spain* 34 B4
Grande →, *Jujuy,*
  Argentina 126 A2
Grande →, *Mendoza,*
  Argentina 126 D2
Grande →, *Bolivia* 124 G6
Grande →, *Bahia, Brazil* 125 F10
Grande →, *Minas Gerais,*
  Brazil 125 H8
Grande, B., *Argentina* .. 128 G3
Grande, Rio →, *U.S.A.* . 113 N6
Grande Baie, *Canada* ... 103 C5

Guernsey

Grande Baleine, R. de la →, *Canada* 102 A4
Grande Cache, *Canada* 104 C5
Grande de Santiago →, *Mexico* 118 C3
Grande-Entrée, *Canada* 103 C7
Grande Prairie, *Canada* 104 B5
Grande-Rivière, *Canada* 103 C7
Grande-Vallée, *Canada* 103 C6
Grandes-Bergeronnes, *Canada* 103 C6
Grandfalls, *U.S.A.* 113 K3
Grandoe Mines, *Canada* 104 B3
Grândola, *Portugal* 35 G2
Grandpré, *France* 19 C11
Grandview, *U.S.A.* 114 C4
Grandvilliers, *France* 19 C8
Graneros, *Chile* 126 C1
Grangemouth, *U.K.* 14 E5
Granger, *Wash., U.S.A.* 114 C3
Granger, *Wyo., U.S.A.* 114 F9
Grängesberg, *Sweden* 10 D9
Grangeville, *U.S.A.* 114 D5
Granite City, *U.S.A.* 112 F9
Granite Falls, *U.S.A.* 112 C7
Granite Mt., *U.S.A.* 117 M10
Granite Peak, *Australia* 93 E3
Granite Peak, *U.S.A.* 114 D9
Granitola, C., *Italy* 30 E5
Granity, *N.Z.* 91 J3
Granja, *Brazil* 125 D10
Granja de Moreruela, *Spain* 34 D5
Granja de Torrehermosa, *Spain* 35 G5
Gränna, *Sweden* 11 F8
Granollers, *Spain* 32 D7
Gransee, *Germany* 24 B9
Grant, *U.S.A.* 112 E4
Grant, Mt., *U.S.A.* 114 G4
Grant City, *U.S.A.* 112 E7
Grant I., *Australia* 92 B5
Grant Range, *U.S.A.* 115 G6
Grantham, *U.K.* 12 E7
Grantown-on-Spey, *U.K.* 14 D5
Grants, *U.S.A.* 115 J10
Grants Pass, *U.S.A.* 114 E2
Grantsburg, *U.S.A.* 112 C8
Grantsville, *U.S.A.* 114 F7
Granville, *France* 18 D5
Granville, *N. Dak., U.S.A.* 112 A4
Granville, *N.Y., U.S.A.* 108 D9
Granville L., *Canada* 105 B8
Grapeland, *U.S.A.* 113 K7
Graskop, *S. Africa* 89 C5
Gräsö, *Sweden* 10 D12
Grass →, *Canada* 105 B9
Grass Range, *U.S.A.* 114 C9
Grass River Prov. Park, *Canada* 105 C8
Grass Valley, *Calif., U.S.A.* 116 F6
Grass Valley, *Oreg., U.S.A.* 114 D3
Grassano, *Italy* 31 B9
Grasse, *France* 21 E10
Grassmere, *Australia* 95 E3
Gråsten, *Denmark* 11 K3
Grästorp, *Sweden* 11 F6
Gratkorn, *Austria* 26 D8
Graubünden □, *Switz.* 25 J5
Graulhet, *France* 20 E5
Graus, *Spain* 32 C5
Grave, Pte. de, *France* 20 C2
Gravelbourg, *Canada* 105 D7
Gravelines, *France* 19 A9
's-Gravenhage, *Neths.* 17 B4
Gravenhurst, *Canada* 110 B5
Gravesend, *Australia* 95 D5
Gravesend, *U.K.* 13 F8
Gravina in Púglia, *Italy* 31 B9
Gravois, Pointe-à-, *Haiti* 121 C5
Gravone →, *France* 21 G12
Gray, *France* 19 E12
Grayling, *U.S.A.* 108 C3
Grayling →, *Canada* 104 B4
Grays Harbor, *U.S.A.* 114 C1
Grays L., *U.S.A.* 114 E8
Grays River, *U.S.A.* 116 D3
Grayson, *Canada* 105 C8
Grayvoron, *Russia* 47 G8
Graz, *Austria* 26 D8
Grdelica, *Serbia, Yug.* 40 D6
Greasy L., *Canada* 104 A4
Great Abaco I., *Bahamas* 120 A4
Great Artesian Basin, *Australia* 94 C3
Great Australian Bight, *Australia* 93 F5
Great Bahama Bank, *Bahamas* 120 B4
Great Barrier I., *N.Z.* 91 G5
Great Barrier Reef, *Australia* 94 B4
Great Barrington, *U.S.A.* 111 D11
Great Basin, *U.S.A.* 114 G5
Great Bear →, *Canada* 100 B7
Great Bear L., *Canada* 100 B8
Great Belt = Store Bælt, *Denmark* 11 J4
Great Bend, *Kans., U.S.A.* 112 F5
Great Bend, *Pa., U.S.A.* 111 E9
Great Blasket I., *Ireland* 15 D1
Great Britain, *Europe* 6 E5
Great Central, *Canada* 104 D3
Great Dividing Ra., *Australia* 94 C4
Great Driffield = Driffield, *U.K.* 12 C7
Great Exuma I., *Bahamas* 120 B4
Great Falls, *Canada* 105 C9
Great Falls, *U.S.A.* 114 C8
Great Fish = Groot Vis →, *S. Africa* 88 E4
Great Guana Cay, *Bahamas* 120 B4
Great Harbour Deep, *Canada* 103 B8
Great I., *Canada* 105 B9
Great Inagua I., *Bahamas* 121 B5
Great Indian Desert = Thar Desert, *India* 68 F5
Great Karoo, *S. Africa* 88 E3
Great Lake, *Australia* 94 G4
Great Malvern, *U.K.* 13 E5
Great Ormes Head, *U.K.* 12 D4
Great Ouse →, *U.K.* 12 E8
Great Palm I., *Australia* 94 B4
Great Plains, *N. Amer.* 106 A6
Great Ruaha →, *Tanzania* 86 D4
Great Saint Bernard Pass = Grand St-Bernard, Col du, *Europe* 25 K3
Great Salt L., *U.S.A.* 114 F7
Great Salt Lake Desert, *U.S.A.* 114 F7
Great Salt Plains L., *U.S.A.* 113 G5
Great Sandy Desert, *Australia* 92 D3
Great Sangi = Sangihe, Pulau, *Indonesia* 63 D7
Great Scarcies →, *S. Leone* 82 D2
Great Skellig, *Ireland* 15 E1
Great Slave L., *Canada* 104 A5
Great Smoky Mts. Nat. Park, *U.S.A.* 109 H4
Great Stour = Stour →, *U.K.* 13 F9
Great Victoria Desert, *Australia* 93 E4
Great Wall, *China* 56 E5
Great Whernside, *U.K.* 12 C6
Great Yarmouth, *U.K.* 13 E9
Greater Antilles, *W. Indies* 121 C5
Greater London □, *U.K.* 13 F7
Greater Manchester □, *U.K.* 12 D5
Greater Sunda Is., *Indonesia* 62 F4
Grebbestad, *Sweden* 11 F5
Grebenka = Hrebenka, *Ukraine* 47 G7
Greco, C., *Cyprus* 36 E13
Greco, Mte., *Italy* 29 G10
Gredos, Sierra de, *Spain* 34 E6
Greece, *U.S.A.* 110 C7
Greece ■, *Europe* 38 B3
Greeley, *Colo., U.S.A.* 112 E2
Greeley, *Nebr., U.S.A.* 112 E5
Greem-Bell, Ostrov, *Russia* 50 A7
Green →, *Ky., U.S.A.* 108 G2
Green →, *Utah, U.S.A.* 115 G9
Green B., *U.S.A.* 108 C2
Green Bay, *U.S.A.* 108 C2
Green C., *Australia* 95 F5
Green Cove Springs, *U.S.A.* 109 L5
Green River, *U.S.A.* 115 G8
Greenbank, *U.S.A.* 116 B4
Greenbush, *Mich., U.S.A.* 110 B1
Greenbush, *Minn., U.S.A.* 112 A6
Greencastle, *U.S.A.* 108 F2
Greene, *U.S.A.* 111 D9
Greenfield, *Calif., U.S.A.* 116 J5
Greenfield, *Calif., U.S.A.* 117 K8
Greenfield, *Ind., U.S.A.* 108 F3
Greenfield, *Iowa, U.S.A.* 112 E7
Greenfield, *Mass., U.S.A.* 111 D12
Greenfield, *Mo., U.S.A.* 113 G8
Greenfield Park, *Canada* 111 A11
Greenland ■, *N. Amer.* 4 C5
Greenland Sea, *Arctic* 4 B7
Greenock, *U.K.* 14 F4
Greenore, *Ireland* 15 B5
Greenore Pt., *Ireland* 15 D5
Greenough →, *Australia* 93 E1
Greenport, *U.S.A.* 111 E12
Greensboro, *Ga., U.S.A.* 109 J4
Greensboro, *N.C., U.S.A.* 109 G6
Greensburg, *Ind., U.S.A.* 108 F3
Greensburg, *Kans., U.S.A.* 113 G5
Greensburg, *Pa., U.S.A.* 110 F5
Greenstone Pt., *U.K.* 14 D3
Greenville, *Liberia* 82 D3
Greenville, *Ala., U.S.A.* 109 K2
Greenville, *Calif., U.S.A.* 116 E6
Greenville, *Ill., U.S.A.* 112 F10
Greenville, *Maine, U.S.A.* 103 C6
Greenville, *Mich., U.S.A.* 108 D3
Greenville, *Miss., U.S.A.* 113 J9
Greenville, *N.C., U.S.A.* 109 H7
Greenville, *Ohio, U.S.A.* 108 E3
Greenville, *Pa., U.S.A.* 110 E4
Greenville, *S.C., U.S.A.* 109 H4
Greenville, *Tenn., U.S.A.* 109 G4
Greenville, *Tex., U.S.A.* 113 J6
Greenwater Lake Prov. Park, *Canada* 105 C8
Greenwich, *U.K.* 13 F8
Greenwich, *Conn., U.S.A.* 111 E11
Greenwich, *N.Y., U.S.A.* 111 C11
Greenwich, *Ohio, U.S.A.* 110 E2
Greenwood, *Canada* 104 D5
Greenwood, *Miss., U.S.A.* 113 J9
Greenwood, *S.C., U.S.A.* 109 H4
Greenwood, Mt., *Australia* 92 B5
Gregory, *U.S.A.* 112 D5
Gregory →, *Australia* 94 B2
Gregory, L., *S. Austral., Australia* 95 D2
Gregory, L., *W. Austral., Australia* 93 E2
Gregory Downs, *Australia* 94 B2
Gregory L., *Australia* 92 D4
Gregory Ra., *Queens., Australia* 94 B3
Gregory Ra., *W. Austral., Australia* 92 D3
Greiffenberg, *Germany* 24 B9
Greifswald, *Germany* 24 A9
Greifswalder Bodden, *Germany* 24 A9
Grein, *Austria* 26 C7
Greiz, *Germany* 24 E8
Gremikha, *Russia* 50 C4
Grenå, *Denmark* 11 H4
Grenada, *U.S.A.* 113 J10
Grenada ■, *W. Indies* 121 D7
Grenade, *France* 20 E5
Grenadines, *W. Indies* 121 D7
Grenchen, *Switz.* 25 H3
Grenen, *Denmark* 11 G4
Grenfell, *Australia* 95 E4
Grenfell, *Canada* 105 C8
Grenoble, *France* 21 C9
Grenora, *U.S.A.* 112 A3
Grenville, C., *Australia* 94 A3
Grenville Chan., *Canada* 104 C3
Gréoux-les-Bains, *France* 21 E9
Gresham, *U.S.A.* 116 E4
Gresik, *Indonesia* 63 G15
Gretna, *U.K.* 14 F5
Greven, *Germany* 24 C3
Grevená, *Greece* 40 F5
Grevená □, *Greece* 40 F5
Grevenbroich, *Germany* 24 D2
Grevenmacher, *Lux.* 17 E6
Grevesmühlen, *Germany* 24 B7
Grevestrand, *Denmark* 11 J6
Grey →, *N.Z.* 91 K3
Grey, C., *Australia* 94 A2
Grey Ra., *Australia* 95 D3
Grey Res., *Canada* 103 C8
Greybull, *U.S.A.* 114 D9
Greymouth, *N.Z.* 91 K3
Greystones, *Ireland* 15 C5
Greytown, *N.Z.* 91 J5
Greytown, *S. Africa* 89 D5
Gribanovskiy, *Russia* 48 E5
Gribbell I., *Canada* 104 C3
Gribës, Mal i, *Albania* 40 F3
Gridley, *U.S.A.* 116 F5
Griekwastad, *S. Africa* 88 D3
Griesheim, *Germany* 25 F4
Grieskirchen, *Austria* 26 C6
Griffin, *U.S.A.* 109 J3
Griffith, *Australia* 95 E4
Grignols, *France* 20 D3
Grigoriopol, *Moldova* 43 C14
Grimaylov = Hrymayliv, *Ukraine* 47 H4
Grimes, *U.S.A.* 116 F5
Grimma, *Germany* 24 D8
Grimmen, *Germany* 24 A9
Grimsay, *U.K.* 14 D1
Grimsby, *Canada* 110 C5
Grimsby, *U.K.* 12 D7
Grímsey, *Iceland* 8 C5
Grimshaw, *Canada* 104 B5
Grimslöv, *Sweden* 11 H8
Grimstad, *Norway* 9 G13
Grindelwald, *Switz.* 25 J4
Grindsted, *Denmark* 11 J2
Grindu, *Romania* 43 F11
Grinnell, *U.S.A.* 112 E8
Grintavec, *Slovenia* 29 B11
Gris-Nez, C., *France* 19 B8
Grisolles, *France* 20 E5
Grisons = Graubünden □, *Switz.* 25 J5
Grisslehamn, *Sweden* 10 D12
Grmeč Planina, *Bos.-H.* 29 D13
Groais I., *Canada* 103 B8
Grobiņa, *Latvia* 44 B8
Groblersdal, *S. Africa* 89 D4
Grobming, *Austria* 26 D6
Grocka, *Serbia, Yug.* 40 B4
Gródek, *Poland* 45 E10
Grodków, *Poland* 45 H4
Grodno = Hrodna, *Belarus* 46 F2
Grodzisk Mazowiecki, *Poland* 45 F7
Grodzisk Wielkopolski, *Poland* 45 F3
Grodzyanka = Hrodzyanka, *Belarus* 46 F5
Groesbeck, *U.S.A.* 113 K6
Groix, *France* 18 E3
Groix, Î. de, *France* 18 E3
Grójec, *Poland* 45 G7
Gronau, *Niedersachsen, Germany* 24 C5
Gronau, *Nordrhein-Westfalen, Germany* 24 C3
Grong, *Norway* 8 D15
Grönhögen, *Sweden* 11 H10
Groningen, *Neths.* 17 A6
Groningen □, *Neths.* 17 A6
Groom, *U.S.A.* 113 H4
Groot →, *S. Africa* 88 E3
Groot Berg →, *S. Africa* 88 E2
Groot-Brakrivier, *S. Africa* 88 E3
Groot-Kei →, *S. Africa* 89 E4
Groot Vis →, *S. Africa* 88 E4
Groote Eylandt, *Australia* 94 A2
Grootfontein, *Namibia* 88 B2
Grootlaagte →, *Africa* 88 C3
Grootvloer, *S. Africa* 88 E3
Gros C., *Canada* 104 A6
Grósio, *Italy* 28 B7
Grosne →, *France* 19 F11
Grossa, Pta., *Spain* 37 B8
Grossenbrode, *Germany* 24 A7
Grossenhain, *Germany* 24 D9
Grosser Arber, *Germany* 25 F9
Grosser Plöner See, *Germany* 24 A6
Grosseto, *Italy* 29 F8
Grossgerungs, *Austria* 26 C7
Grossglockner, *Austria* 26 D5
Groswater B., *Canada* 103 B8
Groton, *Conn., U.S.A.* 111 E12
Groton, *S. Dak., U.S.A.* 112 C5
Grottáglie, *Italy* 31 B10
Grottaminarda, *Italy* 31 A8
Grottammare, *Italy* 29 F10
Grouard Mission, *Canada* 104 B5
Grouin, Pte. du, *France* 18 D5
Groundhog →, *Canada* 102 C3
Grouse Creek, *U.S.A.* 114 F7
Grouw, *Neths.* 17 A5
Grove City, *U.S.A.* 110 E4
Groveland, *U.S.A.* 116 H6
Grover City, *U.S.A.* 117 K6
Groveton, *N.H., U.S.A.* 111 B13
Groveton, *Tex., U.S.A.* 113 K7
Grožnjan, *Croatia* 29 C10
Groznyy, *Russia* 49 J7
Grubišno Polje, *Croatia* 42 E2
Grudovo, *Bulgaria* 41 D11
Grudusk, *Poland* 45 E7
Grudziądz, *Poland* 44 E5
Gruinard B., *U.K.* 14 D3
Gruissan, *France* 20 E7
Grumo Áppula, *Italy* 31 A9
Grums, *Sweden* 10 E7
Grünberg, *Germany* 24 E4
Gründau, *Germany* 25 E5
Grundy Center, *U.S.A.* 112 D8
Grünstadt, *Germany* 25 F4
Gruvberget, *Sweden* 10 C10
Gruver, *U.S.A.* 113 G4
Gruyères, *Switz.* 25 J3
Gruža, *Serbia, Yug.* 40 C4
Gryazi, *Russia* 47 F10
Gryazovets, *Russia* 46 C11
Grybów, *Poland* 45 J7
Grycksbo, *Sweden* 10 D9
Gryfice, *Poland* 44 E2
Gryfino, *Poland* 45 E1
Gryfów Śląski, *Poland* 45 G2
Grythyttan, *Sweden* 10 E8
Gstaad, *Switz.* 25 J3
Gua, *India* 67 H14
Gua Musang, *Malaysia* 65 K3
Guacanayabo, G. de, *Cuba* 120 B4
Guachípas →, *Argentina* 126 B2
Guadajoz →, *Spain* 35 H6
Guadalajara, *Mexico* 118 C4
Guadalajara, *Spain* 32 E1
Guadalajara □, *Spain* 32 E2
Guadalcanal, *Solomon Is.* 96 H8
Guadalcanal, *Spain* 35 G5
Guadalén →, *Spain* 35 G7
Guadales, *Argentina* 126 C2
Guadalete →, *Spain* 35 J4
Guadalimar →, *Spain* 35 G7
Guadalmena →, *Spain* 35 G8
Guadalmez →, *Spain* 35 G5
Guadalope →, *Spain* 32 D4
Guadalquivir →, *Spain* 35 J4
Guadalupe = Guadeloupe ■, *W. Indies* 121 C7
Guadalupe, *Mexico* 117 N10
Guadalupe, *Spain* 35 F5
Guadalupe, *U.S.A.* 117 L6
Guadalupe →, *Mexico* 117 N10
Guadalupe →, *U.S.A.* 113 L6
Guadalupe, Sierra de, *Spain* 35 F5
Guadalupe Bravos, *Mexico* 118 A3
Guadalupe I., *Pac. Oc.* 98 G8
Guadalupe Peak, *U.S.A.* 115 L11
Guadalupe y Calvo, *Mexico* 118 B3
Guadarrama, Sierra de, *Spain* 34 E7
Guadauta, *Georgia* 49 J5
Guadeloupe ■, *W. Indies* 121 C7
Guadeloupe Passage, *W. Indies* 121 C7
Guadiamar →, *Spain* 35 J4
Guadiana →, *Portugal* 35 H3
Guadiana Menor →, *Spain* 35 H7
Guadiaro →, *Spain* 35 J5
Guadiato →, *Spain* 35 H5
Guadiela →, *Spain* 32 E2
Guadix, *Spain* 35 H7
Guafo, Boca del, *Chile* 128 E2
Guainía →, *Colombia* 124 C5
Guaíra, *Brazil* 127 A5
Guaitecas, Is., *Chile* 128 E2
Guajará-Mirim, *Brazil* 124 F5
Guajira, Pen. de la, *Colombia* 124 A4
Gualán, *Guatemala* 120 C2
Gualdo Tadino, *Italy* 29 E9
Gualeguay, *Argentina* 126 C4
Gualeguaychú, *Argentina* 126 C4
Guam ■, *Pac. Oc.* 96 F6
Guaminí, *Argentina* 126 D3
Guamúchil, *Mexico* 118 B3
Guan Xian, *China* 58 B4
Guanabacoa, *Cuba* 120 B3
Guanacaste, Cordillera del, *Costa Rica* 120 D2
Guanaceví, *Mexico* 118 B3
Guanahani = San Salvador, *Bahamas* 121 B5
Guanajay, *Cuba* 120 B3
Guanajuato, *Mexico* 118 C4
Guanajuato □, *Mexico* 118 C4
Guandacol, *Argentina* 126 B2
Guane, *Cuba* 120 B3
Guang'an, *China* 58 B6
Guangchang, *China* 59 D11
Guangde, *China* 59 B12
Guangdong □, *China* 59 F9
Guangfeng, *China* 59 C12
Guanghan, *China* 58 B5
Guanghua, *China* 59 A8
Guangji, *China* 59 C10
Guangling, *China* 56 E8
Guangning, *China* 59 F9
Guangrao, *China* 57 F10
Guangshun, *China* 58 D6
Guangwu, *China* 56 F3
Guangxi Zhuangzu Zizhiqu □, *China* 58 F7
Guangyuan, *China* 58 A5
Guangze, *China* 59 D11
Guangzhou, *China* 59 F9
Guanipa →, *Venezuela* 124 B6
Guanling, *China* 58 E5
Guannan, *China* 57 G10
Guantánamo, *Cuba* 121 B4
Guantao, *China* 56 F8
Guanyang, *China* 59 E8
Guanyun, *China* 57 G10
Guápiles, *Costa Rica* 120 D3
Guaporé →, *Brazil* 122 E4
Guaqui, *Bolivia* 124 G5
Guara, Sierra de, *Spain* 32 C4
Guarapari, *Brazil* 127 A7
Guarapuava, *Brazil* 127 B5
Guaratinguetá, *Brazil* 127 A6
Guaratuba, *Brazil* 127 B6
Guarda, *Portugal* 34 E3
Guarda □, *Portugal* 34 E3
Guardafui, C. = Asir, Ras, *Somali Rep.* 74 E5
Guardamar del Segura, *Spain* 33 G4
Guardavalle, *Italy* 31 D9
Guárdia Sanframondi, *Italy* 31 A7
Guardiagrele, *Italy* 29 F11
Guardo, *Spain* 34 C6
Guareña, *Spain* 35 G4
Guareña →, *Spain* 34 D5
Guaria □, *Paraguay* 126 B4
Guárico □, *Venezuela* 124 B5
Guarujá, *Brazil* 127 A6
Guarus, *Brazil* 127 A7
Guasave, *Mexico* 118 B3
Guasdualito, *Venezuela* 124 B4
Guastalla, *Italy* 28 D7
Guatemala, *Guatemala* 120 D1
Guatemala ■, *Cent. Amer.* 120 C1
Guaviare →, *Colombia* 122 C4
Guaxupé, *Brazil* 127 A6
Guayama, *Puerto Rico* 121 C6
Guayaquil, *Ecuador* 124 D3
Guayaquil, G. de, *Ecuador* 122 D2
Guaymas, *Mexico* 118 B2
Guazhou, *China* 59 A12
Guba, *Dem. Rep. of the Congo* 87 E2
Gûbâl, Madîq, *Egypt* 80 B3
Gubat, *Phil.* 61 E6
Gúbbio, *Italy* 29 E9
Guben, *Germany* 24 D10
Gubin, *Poland* 45 G1
Gubio, *Nigeria* 83 C7
Gubkin, *Russia* 47 G9
Guča, *Serbia, Yug.* 40 C4
Gudata = Guadauta, *Georgia* 49 J5
Gudbrandsdalen, *Norway* 9 F14
Guddu Barrage, *Pakistan* 66 E6
Gudenå →, *Denmark* 11 H4
Gudermes, *Russia* 49 J8
Gudhjem, *Denmark* 11 J8
Gudivada, *India* 67 L12
Gudur, *India* 66 M11
Guebwiller, *France* 19 E14
Guecho = Getxo, *Spain* 32 B2
Guékédou, *Guinea* 82 D2
Guelph, *Canada* 102 D3
Guéméné-Penfao, *France* 18 E5
Guéméné-sur-Scorff, *France* 18 D3
Guéné, *Benin* 83 C5
Guer, *France* 18 E4
Guérande, *France* 18 E4
Guéret, *France* 19 F8
Guérigny, *France* 19 E10
Guerneville, *U.S.A.* 116 G4
Guernica = Gernika-Lumo, *Spain* 32 B2
Guernsey, *U.K.* 13 H5

Guernsey

Guernsey, *U.S.A.* 112 D2
Guerrero □, *Mexico* 119 D5
Gueugnon, *France* 19 F11
Gueydan, *U.S.A.* 113 K8
Gūgher, *Iran* 71 D8
Guglionesi, *Italy* 29 G11
Gui Jiang →, *China* 59 F8
Gui Xian, *China* 58 F7
Guia, *Canary Is.* 37 F4
Guia de Isora, *Canary Is.* 37 F3
Guia Lopes da Laguna, *Brazil* 127 A4
Guiana, *S. Amer.* 122 C4
Guichi, *China* 59 B11
Guider, *Cameroon* 83 D7
Guidimouni, *Niger* 83 C6
Guiding, *China* 58 D6
Guidong, *China* 59 D9
Guidónia-Montecélio, *Italy* 29 F9
Guiglo, *Ivory C.* 82 D3
Guijá, *Mozam.* 89 C5
Guijuelo, *Spain* 34 E5
Guildford, *U.K.* 13 F7
Guilford, *U.S.A.* 103 C6
Guilin, *China* 59 E8
Guillaumes, *France* 21 D10
Guillestre, *France* 21 D10
Guilvinec, *France* 18 E2
Güimar, *Canary Is.* 37 F3
Guimarães, *Portugal* 34 D2
Guimaras, *Phil.* 61 F5
Guinda, *U.S.A.* 116 G4
Guinea, *Africa* 76 F4
Guinea ■, *W. Afr.* 82 C2
Guinea, Gulf of, *Atl. Oc.* 83 E5
Guinea-Bissau ■, *Africa* 82 C2
Güines, *Cuba* 120 B3
Guingamp, *France* 18 D3
Guipavas, *France* 18 D2
Guiping, *China* 59 F8
Guipúzcoa □, *Spain* 32 B2
Güiria, *Venezuela* 124 A6
Guiscard, *France* 19 C10
Guise, *France* 19 C10
Guitiriz, *Spain* 34 B3
Guiuan, *Phil.* 61 F6
Guixi, *China* 59 C11
Guiyang, *Guizhou, China* 58 D6
Guiyang, *Hunan, China* 59 E9
Guizhou □, *China* 58 D6
Gujan-Mestras, *France* 20 D2
Gujarat □, *India* 68 H4
Gujiang, *China* 59 D10
Gujranwala, *Pakistan* 68 C6
Gujrat, *Pakistan* 68 C6
Gukovo, *Russia* 49 F5
Gulbarga, *India* 66 L10
Gulbene, *Latvia* 9 H22
Gulf, The, *Asia* 71 E6
Gulfport, *U.S.A.* 113 K10
Gulgong, *Australia* 95 E4
Gulin, *China* 58 C5
Gulistan, *Pakistan* 68 D2
Gull Lake, *Canada* 105 C7
Gullbrandstorp, *Sweden* 11 H6
Gullspång, *Sweden* 11 F8
Güllük, *Turkey* 39 D9
Güllük Korfezi, *Turkey* 39 D9
Gulma, *Nigeria* 83 C5
Gulmarg, *India* 69 B6
Gülnar, *Turkey* 72 D5
Gülpınar, *Turkey* 39 B8
Gülşehir, *Turkey* 72 C6
Gulshad, *Kazakstan* 50 E8
Gulu, *Uganda* 86 B3
Gŭlŭbovo, *Bulgaria* 41 D9
Gulwe, *Tanzania* 86 D4
Gulyaypole = Hulyaypole, *Ukraine* 47 J9
Gum Lake, *Australia* 95 E3
Gumal →, *Pakistan* 68 D4
Gumbaz, *Pakistan* 68 D3
Gumel, *Nigeria* 83 C6
Gumiel de Hizán, *Spain* 34 D7
Gumlu, *Australia* 94 B4
Gumma □, *Japan* 55 F9
Gummersbach, *Germany* 24 D3
Gummi, *Nigeria* 83 C6
Gümüldür, *Turkey* 39 C9
Gümüşçay, *Turkey* 41 F11
Gümüşhaciköy, *Turkey* 72 B6
Gümüşhane, *Turkey* 73 B8
Gümüşsu, *Turkey* 39 C11
Gumzai, *Indonesia* 63 F8
Guna, *Ethiopia* 81 E4
Guna, *India* 68 G7
Gundagai, *Australia* 95 F4
Gundelfingen, *Germany* 25 G6
Güney, *Burdur, Turkey* 39 D11
Güney, *Denizli, Turkey* 39 C11
Güneydoğu Toroslar, *Turkey* 73 C9
Gunisao →, *Canada* 105 C9
Gunisao L., *Canada* 105 C9
Günlüce, *Turkey* 39 E10
Gunnarskog, *Sweden* 10 E6
Gunnbjørn Fjeld, *Greenland* 4 C6
Gunnebo, *Sweden* 11 G10
Gunnedah, *Australia* 95 E5
Gunningbar Cr. →, *Australia* 95 E4
Gunnison, *Colo., U.S.A.* 115 G10
Gunnison, *Utah, U.S.A.* 114 G8
Gunnison →, *U.S.A.* 115 G9
Gunpowder, *Australia* 94 B2
Guntakal, *India* 66 M10
Guntersville, *U.S.A.* 109 H2
Guntong, *Malaysia* 65 K3
Guntur, *India* 67 L12
Gunungapi, *Indonesia* 63 F7
Gunungsitoli, *Indonesia* 62 D1
Günz →, *Germany* 25 G6
Gunza, *Angola* 84 G2
Günzburg, *Germany* 25 G6
Gunzenhausen, *Germany* 25 F6
Guo He →, *China* 57 H9
Guoyang, *China* 56 H9
Gupis, *Pakistan* 69 A5
Gura Humorului, *Romania* 43 C10
Gura-Teghii, *Romania* 43 E11
Gurag, *Ethiopia* 81 F4
Gurahonţ, *Romania* 42 D7
Gurdaspur, *India* 68 C6
Gurdon, *U.S.A.* 113 J8
Güre, *Balıkesir, Turkey* 39 B8
Güre, *Uşak, Turkey* 39 C11
Gurgaon, *India* 68 E7
Gürgentepe, *Turkey* 72 B7
Gurghiu, Munţii, *Romania* 43 D10
Gurgueia →, *Brazil* 125 E10
Gurha, *India* 68 G4
Guri, Embalse de, *Venezuela* 124 B6
Gurjaani, *Georgia* 49 K7
Gurk →, *Austria* 26 E7
Gurkha, *Nepal* 69 E11
Gurley, *Australia* 95 D4
Gürpınar, *İst., Turkey* 41 F12
Gürpınar, *Van, Turkey* 73 C10
Gürsu, *Turkey* 41 F13
Gurué, *Mozam.* 87 F4
Gurun, *Malaysia* 65 K3
Gürün, *Turkey* 72 C7
Gurupá, *Brazil* 125 D8
Gurupá, I. Grande de, *Brazil* 125 D8
Gurupi, *Brazil* 125 F9
Gurupi →, *Brazil* 125 D9
Guryev = Atyraū, *Kazakstan* 50 E6
Gus-Khrustalnyy, *Russia* 48 C5
Gusau, *Nigeria* 83 C6
Gusev, *Russia* 9 J20
Gushan, *China* 57 E12
Gushgy, *Turkmenistan* 50 F7
Gushi, *China* 59 A10
Gushiago, *Ghana* 83 D4
Gusinje, *Montenegro, Yug.* 40 D3
Gusinoozersk, *Russia* 51 D11
Gúspini, *Italy* 30 C1
Güssing, *Austria* 27 D9
Gustavsberg, *Sweden* 10 E12
Gustine, *U.S.A.* 116 H6
Güstrow, *Germany* 24 B8
Gusum, *Sweden* 11 F10
Guta = Kolárovo, *Slovak Rep.* 27 D10
Gütersloh, *Germany* 24 D4
Gutha, *Australia* 93 E2
Guthalongra, *Australia* 94 B4
Guthrie, *U.S.A.* 113 H6
Gutian, *China* 59 D12
Guttenberg, *U.S.A.* 112 D9
Guyana ■, *S. Amer.* 124 C7
Guyane française = French Guiana ■, *S. Amer.* 125 C8
Guyang, *China* 56 D6
Guyenne, *France* 20 D4
Guymon, *U.S.A.* 113 G4
Guyra, *Australia* 95 E5
Guyuan, *Hebei, China* 56 D8
Guyuan, *Ningxia Huizu, China* 56 G4
Güzelbahçe, *Turkey* 39 C8
Guzhang, *China* 58 C7
Guzhen, *China* 57 H9
Guzmán, L. de, *Mexico* 118 A3
Gvardeysk, *Russia* 9 J19
Gvardeyskoye, *Ukraine* 47 K8
Gwa, *Burma* 67 L19
Gwaai, *Zimbabwe* 87 F2
Gwabegar, *Australia* 95 E4
Gwadabawa, *Nigeria* 83 C6
Gwādar, *Pakistan* 66 G3
Gwagwada, *Nigeria* 83 C6
Gwalia, *Australia* 93 E3
Gwalior, *India* 68 F8
Gwanda, *Zimbabwe* 87 G2
Gwandu, *Nigeria* 83 C5
Gwane, *Dem. Rep. of the Congo* 86 B2
Gwaram, *Nigeria* 83 C7
Gwarzo, *Nigeria* 83 C6
Gwda →, *Poland* 45 E3
Gweebarra B., *Ireland* 15 B3
Gweedore, *Ireland* 15 A3
Gweru, *Zimbabwe* 87 F2
Gwi, *Nigeria* 83 D6
Gwinn, *U.S.A.* 108 B2
Gwio Kura, *Nigeria* 83 C7
Gwol, *Ghana* 82 C4
Gwoza, *Nigeria* 83 C7
Gwydir →, *Australia* 95 D4
Gwynedd □, *U.K.* 12 E3
Gyandzha = Gäncä, *Azerbaijan* 49 K8
Gyaring Hu, *China* 60 C4
Gydanskiy Poluostrov, *Russia* 50 C8
Gympie, *Australia* 95 D5
Gyomaendrőd, *Hungary* 42 D5
Gyöngyös, *Hungary* 42 C4
Győr, *Hungary* 42 C2
Győr-Moson-Sopron □, *Hungary* 42 C2
Gypsum Pt., *Canada* 104 A6
Gypsumville, *Canada* 105 C9
Gyueshevo, *Bulgaria* 40 D6
Gyula, *Hungary* 42 D6
Gyumri, *Armenia* 49 K6
Gyzylarbat, *Turkmenistan* 50 F6
Gzhatsk = Gagarin, *Russia* 46 E8

H

Ha 'Arava →, *Israel* 75 E4
Ha Coi, *Vietnam* 64 B6
Ha Dong, *Vietnam* 64 B5
Ha Giang, *Vietnam* 64 A5
Ha Tien, *Vietnam* 65 G5
Ha Tinh, *Vietnam* 64 C5
Ha Trung, *Vietnam* 64 C5
Haaksbergen, *Neths.* 17 B6
Haapsalu, *Estonia* 9 G20
Haarlem, *Neths.* 17 B4
Haast →, *N.Z.* 91 K2
Haast Bluff, *Australia* 92 D5
Hab Nadi Chauki, *Pakistan* 68 G2
Habaswein, *Kenya* 86 B4
Habay, *Canada* 104 B5
Ḩabbānīyah, *Iraq* 70 C4
Ḩabbānīyah, Hawr al, *Iraq* 73 F10
Habo, *Sweden* 11 G8
Haboro, *Japan* 54 B10
Hachenburg, *Germany* 24 E3
Hachijō-Jima, *Japan* 55 H9
Hachinohe, *Japan* 54 D10
Hachiōji, *Japan* 55 G9
Hachŏn, *N. Korea* 57 D15
Hacıbektaş, *Turkey* 72 C6
Hacılar, *Turkey* 72 C6
Hackås, *Sweden* 10 B8
Hackensack, *U.S.A.* 111 F10
Hadali, *Pakistan* 68 C5
Hadarba, Ras, *Sudan* 80 C4
Hadarom □, *Israel* 75 E4
Hadejia, *Nigeria* 83 C7
Hadejia →, *Nigeria* 83 C7
Haden, *Australia* 95 D5
Hadera, *Israel* 75 C3
Hadera, N. →, *Israel* 75 C3
Haderslev, *Denmark* 11 J3
Hadhramaut = Ḩaḑramawt, *Yemen* 74 D4
Hadım, *Turkey* 72 D5
Hadong, *S. Korea* 57 G14
Ḩaḑramawt, *Yemen* 74 D4
Ḩadrānīyah, *Iraq* 70 C4
Hadrian's Wall, *U.K.* 12 B5
Hadsten, *Denmark* 11 H4
Hadsund, *Denmark* 11 H4
Hadyach, *Ukraine* 47 G8
Haeju, *N. Korea* 57 E13
Haenam, *S. Korea* 57 G14
Haerhpin = Harbin, *China* 57 B14
Hafar al Bāţin, *Si. Arabia* 70 D5
Hafik, *Turkey* 72 C7
Ḩafīrat al 'Aydā, *Si. Arabia* 70 E3
Hafizabad, *Pakistan* 68 C5
Haflong, *India* 67 G18
Hafnarfjörður, *Iceland* 8 D3
Hafun, Ras, *Somali Rep.* 74 E5
Hagalil, *Israel* 75 C4
Hagby, *Sweden* 11 H10
Hagen, *Germany* 24 D3
Hagenow, *Germany* 24 B7
Hagerman, *U.S.A.* 113 J2
Hagerstown, *U.S.A.* 108 F7
Hagetmau, *France* 20 E3
Hagfors, *Sweden* 10 D7
Hagi, *Japan* 55 G5
Hagolan, *Syria* 75 C4
Hagondange, *France* 19 C13
Hags Hd., *Ireland* 15 D2
Hague, C. de la, *France* 18 C5
Hague, The = 's-Gravenhage, *Neths.* 17 B4
Haguenau, *France* 19 D14
Hai □, *Tanzania* 86 C4
Hai Duong, *Vietnam* 64 B6
Hai'an, *Guangdong, China* 59 G8
Hai'an, *Jiangsu, China* 59 A13
Haicheng, *Fujian, China* 59 E11
Haicheng, *Liaoning, China* 57 D12
Haidar Khel, *Afghan.* 68 C3
Haifa = Ḩefa, *Israel* 75 C4
Haifeng, *China* 59 F10
Haig, *Australia* 93 F4
Haiger, *Germany* 24 E4
Haikang, *China* 59 G8
Haikou, *China* 60 D6
Ḩā'il, *Si. Arabia* 70 E4
Hailar, *China* 60 B6
Hailey, *U.S.A.* 114 E6
Haileybury, *Canada* 102 C4
Hailin, *China* 57 B15
Hailing Dao, *China* 59 G8
Hailong, *China* 57 C13
Hailun, *China* 60 B7
Hailuoto, *Finland* 8 D21
Haimen, *Guangdong, China* 59 F11
Haimen, *Jiangsu, China* 59 B13
Haimen, *Zhejiang, China* 59 C13
Hainan □, *China* 60 E5
Hainaut □, *Belgium* 17 D4
Hainburg, *Austria* 27 C9
Haines, *U.S.A.* 114 D5
Haines City, *U.S.A.* 109 L5
Haines Junction, *Canada* 104 A1
Hainfeld, *Austria* 26 C8
Haining, *China* 59 B13
Haiphong, *Vietnam* 60 D5
Haiti ■, *W. Indies* 121 C5
Haiya, *Sudan* 80 D4
Haiyan, *China* 59 B13
Haiyang, *China* 57 F11
Haiyuan, *Guangxi Zhuangzu, China* 58 F6
Haiyuan, *Ningxia Huizu, China* 56 F3
Haizhou, *China* 57 G10
Haizhou Wan, *China* 57 G10
Hajdú-Bihar □, *Hungary* 42 C6
Hajdúböszörmény, *Hungary* 42 C6
Hajdúdurog, *Hungary* 42 C6
Hajdúhadház, *Hungary* 42 C6
Hajdúnánás, *Hungary* 42 C6
Hajdúsámson, *Hungary* 42 C6
Hajdúszoboszló, *Hungary* 42 C6
Hajipur, *India* 69 G11
Ḩājjī Muḩsin, *Iraq* 70 C5
Ḩājjīābād, *Eşfahan, Iran* 71 C7
Ḩājjīābād, *Hormozgān, Iran* 71 D7
Hajnówka, *Poland* 45 F10
Hakansson, Mts., *Dem. Rep. of the Congo* 87 D2
Hakkâri, *Turkey* 73 D10
Hakkâri Dağları, *Turkey* 73 C10
Hakken-Zan, *Japan* 55 G7
Hakodate, *Japan* 54 D10
Håksberg, *Sweden* 10 D9
Haku-San, *Japan* 55 F8
Hakui, *Japan* 55 F8
Hala, *Pakistan* 66 G6
Ḩalab, *Syria* 70 B3
Ḩalabjah, *Iraq* 70 C5
Halaib, *Sudan* 80 C4
Hālat 'Ammār, *Si. Arabia* 70 D3
Halbā, *Lebanon* 75 A5
Halberstadt, *Germany* 24 D7
Halcombe, *N.Z.* 91 J5
Halcon, *Phil.* 63 B6
Halden, *Norway* 9 G14
Haldensleben, *Germany* 24 C7
Haldia, *India* 67 H16
Haldwani, *India* 69 E8
Hale →, *Australia* 94 C2
Haleakala Crater, *U.S.A.* 106 H16
Halesowen, *U.K.* 13 E5
Haleyville, *U.S.A.* 109 H2
Half Assini, *Ghana* 82 D4
Halfway →, *Canada* 104 B4
Haliburton, *Canada* 102 C4
Halifax, *Australia* 94 B4
Halifax, *Canada* 103 D7
Halifax, *U.K.* 12 D6
Halifax B., *Australia* 94 B4
Halifax I., *Namibia* 88 D2
Halīl →, *Iran* 71 E8
Halkirk, *U.K.* 14 C5
Hall in Tirol, *Austria* 26 D4
Hall Pt., *Australia* 92 C3
Hallabro, *Sweden* 11 H9
Halland, *Sweden* 9 H15
Hallands län □, *Sweden* 11 H6
Hallands Väderö, *Sweden* 11 H6
Hallandsås, *Sweden* 11 H7
Hällbybrunn, *Sweden* 10 E10
Halle, *Belgium* 17 D4
Halle, *Nordrhein-Westfalen, Germany* 24 C4
Halle, *Sachsen-Anhalt, Germany* 24 D7
Hällefors, *Sweden* 10 E8
Hälleforsnäs, *Sweden* 10 E10
Hallein, *Austria* 26 D6
Hällekis, *Sweden* 11 F7
Hallen, *Sweden* 10 A8
Hallett, *Australia* 95 E2
Hallettsville, *U.S.A.* 113 L6
Halliday, *U.S.A.* 112 B3
Halliday L., *Canada* 105 A7
Hallim, *S. Korea* 57 H14
Hallingdalselvi →, *Norway* 9 F13
Hallock, *U.S.A.* 105 D9
Halls Creek, *Australia* 92 C4
Hallsberg, *Sweden* 10 E9
Hallstahammar, *Sweden* 10 E10
Hallstatt, *Austria* 26 D6
Hallstavik, *Sweden* 10 D12
Hallstead, *U.S.A.* 111 E9
Halmahera, *Indonesia* 63 D7
Halmeu, *Romania* 42 C8
Halmstad, *Sweden* 11 H6
Hals, *Denmark* 11 H4
Hälsingborg = Helsingborg, *Sweden* 11 H6
Hälsingland, *Sweden* 10 C10
Halstad, *U.S.A.* 112 B6
Halstead, *U.K.* 13 F8
Haltern, *Germany* 24 D3
Halti, *Finland* 8 B19
Halton □, *U.K.* 12 D5
Haltwhistle, *U.K.* 12 C5
Halul, *Qatar* 71 E7
Ḩalvān, *Iran* 71 C8
Ham, *France* 19 C10
Ham Tan, *Vietnam* 65 G6
Ham Yen, *Vietnam* 64 A5
Hamab, *Namibia* 88 D2
Hamad, *Sudan* 81 D3
Hamada, *Japan* 55 G6
Hamadān, *Iran* 71 C6
Hamadān □, *Iran* 71 C6
Ḩamāh, *Syria* 70 C3
Hamamatsu, *Japan* 55 G8
Hamar, *Norway* 9 F14
Hamâta, Gebel, *Egypt* 80 C4
Hambantota, *Sri Lanka* 66 R12
Hamber Prov. Park, *Canada* 104 C5
Hamburg, *Germany* 24 B5
Hamburg, *Ark., U.S.A.* 113 J9
Hamburg, *Iowa, U.S.A.* 112 E7
Hamburg, *N.Y., U.S.A.* 110 D6
Hamburg, *Pa., U.S.A.* 111 F9
Hamburg □, *Germany* 24 B5
Ḩamḑ, W. al →, *Si. Arabia* 70 E3
Hamden, *U.S.A.* 111 E12
Hamdibey, *Turkey* 39 B9
Häme, *Finland* 9 F20
Hämeenlinna, *Finland* 9 F21
Hamélé, *Ghana* 82 C4
Hamelin Pool, *Australia* 93 E1
Hameln, *Germany* 24 C5
Hamer Koke, *Ethiopia* 81 F4
Hamerkaz □, *Israel* 75 C3
Hamersley Ra., *Australia* 92 D2
Hamhung, *N. Korea* 57 E14
Hami, *China* 60 B4
Hamilton, *Australia* 95 F3
Hamilton, *Canada* 102 D4
Hamilton, *N.Z.* 91 G5
Hamilton, *U.K.* 14 F4
Hamilton, *Mo., U.S.A.* 112 F8
Hamilton, *Mont., U.S.A.* 114 C6
Hamilton, *N.Y., U.S.A.* 111 D9
Hamilton, *Ohio, U.S.A.* 108 F3
Hamilton, *Tex., U.S.A.* 113 K5
Hamilton →, *Australia* 94 C2
Hamilton City, *U.S.A.* 116 F4
Hamilton Hotel, *Australia* 94 C3
Hamilton Inlet, *Canada* 103 B8
Hamina, *Finland* 9 F22
Hamiota, *Canada* 105 C8
Hamitabat, *Turkey* 41 E11
Hamlet, *U.S.A.* 109 H6
Hamley Bridge, *Australia* 95 E2
Hamlin = Hameln, *Germany* 24 C5
Hamlin, *N.Y., U.S.A.* 110 C7
Hamlin, *Tex., U.S.A.* 113 J4
Hamm, *Germany* 24 D3
Hammarstrand, *Sweden* 10 A10
Hammelburg, *Germany* 25 E5
Hammeren, *Denmark* 11 J8
Hammerfest, *Norway* 8 A20
Hammerum, *Denmark* 11 H3
Hamminkeln, *Germany* 24 D2
Hammond, *Ind., U.S.A.* 108 E2
Hammond, *La., U.S.A.* 113 K9
Hammonton, *U.S.A.* 108 F8
Hamneda, *Sweden* 11 H7
Hamoyet, Jebel, *Sudan* 80 D4
Hampden, *N.Z.* 91 L3
Hampshire □, *U.K.* 13 F6
Hampshire Downs, *U.K.* 13 F6
Hampton, *Ark., U.S.A.* 113 J8
Hampton, *Iowa, U.S.A.* 112 D8
Hampton, *N.H., U.S.A.* 111 D14
Hampton, *S.C., U.S.A.* 109 J5
Hampton, *Va., U.S.A.* 108 G7
Hampton Tableland, *Australia* 93 F4
Hamra, *Sweden* 10 C8
Hamrat esh Sheykh, *Sudan* 81 E2
Hamur, *Turkey* 73 C10
Hamyang, *S. Korea* 57 G14
Han Jiang →, *China* 59 F11
Han Shui →, *China* 59 B10
Hana, *U.S.A.* 106 H17
Hanak, *Si. Arabia* 70 E3
Hanamaki, *Japan* 54 E10
Hanang, *Tanzania* 86 C4
Hanau, *Germany* 25 E4
Hanbogd, *Mongolia* 56 C4
Hançalar, *Turkey* 39 C11
Hâncești, *Moldova* 43 D13
Hancheng, *China* 56 G6
Hanchuan, *China* 59 B9
Hancock, *Mich., U.S.A.* 112 B10
Hancock, *Minn., U.S.A.* 112 C7
Hancock, *N.Y., U.S.A.* 111 E9
Handa, *Japan* 55 G8
Handan, *China* 56 F8
Handeni, *Tanzania* 86 D4
Handeni □, *Tanzania* 86 D4
Handlová, *Slovak Rep.* 27 C11
Handub, *Sudan* 80 D4
Handwara, *India* 69 B6
Hanegev, *Israel* 75 E4
Haney, *Canada* 104 D4
Hanford, *U.S.A.* 116 J7
Hang Chat, *Thailand* 64 C2
Hang Dong, *Thailand* 64 C2
Hangang →, *S. Korea* 57 F14
Hangayn Nuruu, *Mongolia* 60 B4
Hangchou = Hangzhou, *China* 59 B13
Hanggin Houqi, *China* 56 D4
Hanggin Qi, *China* 56 E5
Hangu, *China* 57 E9

Hermannsburg

Hangzhou, *China* 59 B13
Hangzhou Wan, *China* 59 B13
Hanhongor, *Mongolia* 56 C3
Ḥanīdh, *Si. Arabia* 71 E6
Ḥanīsh, *Yemen* 74 E3
Haniska, *Slovak Rep.* 27 C14
Hanjiang, *China* 59 E12
Hankinson, *U.S.A.* 112 B6
Hanko, *Finland* 9 G20
Hankou, *China* 59 B10
Hanksville, *U.S.A.* 115 G8
Hanle, *India* 69 C8
Hanmer Springs, *N.Z.* 91 K4
Hann →, *Australia* 92 C4
Hann, Mt., *Australia* 92 C4
Hanna, *Canada* 104 C6
Hannaford, *U.S.A.* 112 B5
Hannah, *U.S.A.* 112 A5
Hannah B., *Canada* 102 B4
Hannibal, *U.S.A.* 112 F9
Hannik, *Sudan* 80 D3
Hannover, *Germany* 24 C5
Hanö, *Sweden* 11 H8
Hanöbukten, *Sweden* 11 J8
Hanoi, *Vietnam* 60 D5
Hanover = Hannover, *Germany* 24 C5
Hanover, *Canada* 110 B3
Hanover, *S. Africa* 88 E3
Hanover, *N.H., U.S.A.* 111 C12
Hanover, *Ohio, U.S.A.* 110 F2
Hanover, *Pa., U.S.A.* 108 F7
Hanover, I., *Chile* 128 G2
Hanshou, *China* 59 C8
Hansi, *India* 68 E6
Hanson, L., *Australia* 95 E2
Hanstholm, *Denmark* 11 G2
Hantsavichy, *Belarus* 47 F4
Hanyang, *China* 59 B10
Hanyin, *China* 58 A7
Hanyuan, *China* 58 C4
Hanzhong, *China* 56 H4
Hanzhuang, *China* 57 G9
Haora, *India* 69 H13
Haoxue, *China* 59 B9
Haparanda, *Sweden* 8 D21
Happy, *U.S.A.* 113 H4
Happy Camp, *U.S.A.* 114 F2
Happy Valley-Goose Bay, *Canada* 103 B7
Hapsu, *N. Korea* 57 D15
Hapur, *India* 68 E7
Ḥaql, *Si. Arabia* 75 F3
Har, *Indonesia* 63 F8
Har-Ayrag, *Mongolia* 56 B5
Har Hu, *China* 60 C4
Har Us Nuur, *Mongolia* 60 B4
Har Yehuda, *Israel* 75 D3
Ḥaraḍ, *Si. Arabia* 74 C4
Haradok, *Belarus* 46 E6
Häradsbäck, *Sweden* 11 H8
Haranomachi, *Japan* 54 F10
Harare, *Zimbabwe* 87 F3
Harat, *Eritrea* 81 D4
Harbin, *China* 57 B14
Harbiye, *Turkey* 72 D7
Harbo, *Sweden* 10 D11
Harboør, *Denmark* 11 H2
Harbor Beach, *U.S.A.* 108 D4
Harbor Springs, *U.S.A.* 108 C3
Harbour Breton, *Canada* 103 C8
Harbour Grace, *Canada* 103 C9
Harburg, *Germany* 24 B5
Hårby, *Denmark* 11 J4
Harda, *India* 68 H7
Hardangerfjorden, *Norway* 9 F12
Hardangervidda, *Norway* 9 F12
Hardap Dam, *Namibia* 88 C2
Hardenberg, *Neths.* 17 B6
Harderwijk, *Neths.* 17 B5
Hardey →, *Australia* 92 D2
Hardin, *U.S.A.* 114 D10
Harding, *S. Africa* 89 E4
Harding Ra., *Australia* 92 C3
Hardisty, *Canada* 104 C6
Hardman, *U.S.A.* 114 D4
Hardoi, *India* 69 F9
Hardwar = Haridwar, *India* 68 E8
Hardwick, *U.S.A.* 111 B12
Hardy, *U.S.A.* 113 G9
Hardy, Pen., *Chile* 128 H3
Hare B., *Canada* 103 B8
Hareid, *Norway* 9 E12
Haren, *Germany* 24 C3
Harer, *Ethiopia* 81 F5
Harerge □, *Ethiopia* 81 F5
Hareto, *Ethiopia* 81 F4
Harfleur, *France* 18 C7
Hargeisa, *Somali Rep.* 74 F3
Harghita □, *Romania* 43 D10
Harghita, Munţii, *Romania* 43 D10
Hargshamn, *Sweden* 10 D12
Hari →, *Indonesia* 62 E2
Haria, *Canary Is.* 37 E6
Haridwar, *India* 68 E8
Haringhata →, *Bangla.* 67 J16
Harīrūd →, *Asia* 66 A2
Härjedalen, *Sweden* 10 B7
Harlan, *Iowa, U.S.A.* 112 E7
Harlan, *Ky., U.S.A.* 109 G4
Hârlău, *Romania* 43 C11
Harlech, *U.K.* 12 E3
Harlem, *U.S.A.* 114 B9
Hårlev, *Denmark* 11 J6
Harlingen, *Neths.* 17 A5
Harlingen, *U.S.A.* 113 M6
Harlow, *U.K.* 13 F8
Harlowton, *U.S.A.* 114 C9
Harmancık, *Turkey* 39 B11
Harmånger, *Sweden* 10 C11
Harmil, *Eritrea* 81 D5
Harney Basin, *U.S.A.* 114 E4
Harney L., *U.S.A.* 114 E4
Harney Peak, *U.S.A.* 112 D3
Härnön, *Sweden* 10 B12
Härnösand, *Sweden* 10 B11
Haro, *Spain* 32 C2
Haroldswick, *U.K.* 14 A8
Harp L., *Canada* 103 A7
Harper, *Liberia* 82 E3
Harplinge, *Sweden* 11 H6
Harrand, *Pakistan* 68 E4
Harriman, *U.S.A.* 109 H3
Harrington Harbour, *Canada* 103 B8
Harris, *U.K.* 14 D2
Harris, Sd. of, *U.K.* 14 D1
Harris L., *Australia* 95 E2
Harrisburg, *Ill., U.S.A.* 113 G10
Harrisburg, *Nebr., U.S.A.* 112 E3
Harrisburg, *Oreg., U.S.A.* 114 D2
Harrisburg, *Pa., U.S.A.* 110 F8
Harrismith, *S. Africa* 89 D4
Harrison, *Ark., U.S.A.* 113 G8
Harrison, *Idaho, U.S.A.* 114 C5
Harrison, *Nebr., U.S.A.* 112 D3
Harrison, C., *Canada* 103 B8
Harrison L., *Canada* 104 D4
Harrisonburg, *U.S.A.* 108 F6
Harrisonville, *U.S.A.* 112 F7
Harriston, *Canada* 102 D3
Harrisville, *U.S.A.* 110 B1
Harrogate, *U.K.* 12 C6
Harrow, *U.K.* 13 F7
Harsefeld, *Germany* 24 B5
Harsewinkel, *Germany* 24 D4
Harsīn, *Iran* 70 C5
Hârşova, *Romania* 43 F12
Harstad, *Norway* 8 B17
Hart, *U.S.A.* 108 D2
Hart, L., *Australia* 95 E2
Hartbees →, *S. Africa* 88 D3
Hartberg, *Austria* 26 D8
Hartford, *Conn., U.S.A.* 111 E12
Hartford, *Ky., U.S.A.* 108 G2
Hartford, *S. Dak., U.S.A.* 112 D6
Hartford, *Wis., U.S.A.* 112 D10
Hartford City, *U.S.A.* 108 E3
Hartland, *Canada* 103 C6
Hartland Pt., *U.K.* 13 F3
Hartlepool, *U.K.* 12 C6
Hartlepool □, *U.K.* 12 C6
Hartley Bay, *Canada* 104 C3
Hartmannberge, *Namibia* 88 B1
Hartney, *Canada* 105 D8
Hârtop, *Moldova* 43 D13
Harts →, *S. Africa* 88 D3
Hartselle, *U.S.A.* 109 H2
Hartshorne, *U.S.A.* 113 H7
Hartsville, *U.S.A.* 109 H5
Hartwell, *U.S.A.* 109 H4
Harunabad, *Pakistan* 68 E5
Harvand, *Iran* 71 D7
Harvey, *Australia* 93 F2
Harvey, *Ill., U.S.A.* 108 E2
Harvey, *N. Dak., U.S.A.* 112 B5
Harwich, *U.K.* 13 F9
Haryana □, *India* 68 E7
Haryn →, *Belarus* 47 F4
Harz, *Germany* 24 D6
Harzgerode, *Germany* 24 D7
Hasaheisa, *Sudan* 81 E3
Hasan Kīādeh, *Iran* 71 B6
Ḥasanābād, *Iran* 71 C7
Hasanpur, *India* 68 E8
Haselünne, *Germany* 24 C3
Hashimoto, *Japan* 55 G7
Hashtjerd, *Iran* 71 C6
Haskell, *Okla., U.S.A.* 113 H7
Haskell, *Tex., U.S.A.* 113 J5
Hasköy, *Turkey* 41 E10
Haslach, *Germany* 25 G4
Hasle, *Denmark* 11 J8
Haslemere, *U.K.* 13 F7
Haslev, *Denmark* 11 J5
Hasparren, *France* 20 E2
Hassa, *Turkey* 72 D7
Hassela, *Sweden* 10 B10
Hasselt, *Belgium* 17 D5
Hassfurt, *Germany* 25 E6
Hassi Messaoud, *Algeria* 78 B7
Hässleholm, *Sweden* 11 H7
Hassloch, *Germany* 25 F4
Hästholmen, *Sweden* 11 F8
Hastings, *N.Z.* 91 H6
Hastings, *U.K.* 13 G8
Hastings, *Mich., U.S.A.* 108 D3
Hastings, *Minn., U.S.A.* 112 C8
Hastings, *Nebr., U.S.A.* 112 E5
Hastings Ra., *Australia* 95 E5
Hästveda, *Sweden* 11 H7
Hat Yai, *Thailand* 65 J3
Hatanbulag, *Mongolia* 56 C5
Hatay = Antalya, *Turkey* 72 D4
Hatch, *U.S.A.* 115 K10
Hatches Creek, *Australia* 94 C2
Hatchet L., *Canada* 105 B8
Haţeg, *Romania* 42 E7
Hateruma-Shima, *Japan* 55 M1
Hatfield P.O., *Australia* 95 E3
Hatgal, *Mongolia* 60 A5
Hathras, *India* 68 F8
Hatia, *Bangla.* 67 H17
Hato Mayor, *Dom. Rep.* 121 C6
Hattah, *Australia* 95 E3
Hatteras, C., *U.S.A.* 109 H8
Hattiesburg, *U.S.A.* 113 K10
Hatvan, *Hungary* 42 C4
Hau Duc, *Vietnam* 64 E7
Haugesund, *Norway* 9 G11
Haukipudas, *Finland* 8 D21
Haultain →, *Canada* 105 B7
Hauraki G., *N.Z.* 91 G5
Hausruck, *Austria* 26 C6
Haut Atlas, *Morocco* 78 B4
Haut-Rhin □, *France* 19 E14
Haut-Zaïre □, *Dem. Rep. of the Congo* 86 B2
Haute-Corse □, *France* 21 F13
Haute-Garonne □, *France* 20 E5
Haute-Loire □, *France* 20 C7
Haute-Marne □, *France* 19 D12
Haute-Normandie □, *France* 18 C7
Haute-Saône □, *France* 19 E13
Haute-Savoie □, *France* 21 C10
Haute-Vienne □, *France* 20 C5
Hauterive, *Canada* 103 C6
Hautes-Alpes □, *France* 21 D10
Hautes Fagnes = Hohe Venn, *Belgium* 17 D6
Hautes-Pyrénées □, *France* 20 F4
Hauteville-Lompnès, *France* 21 C9
Hautmont, *France* 19 B10
Hauts-de-Seine □, *France* 19 D9
Hauts Plateaux, *Algeria* 76 C4
Hauzenberg, *Germany* 25 G9
Havana = La Habana, *Cuba* 120 B3
Havana, *U.S.A.* 112 E9
Havant, *U.K.* 13 G7
Havârna, *Romania* 43 B11
Havasu, L., *U.S.A.* 117 L12
Havdhem, *Sweden* 11 G12
Havel →, *Germany* 24 C8
Havelian, *Pakistan* 68 B5
Havelock, *N.B., Canada* 103 C6
Havelock, *Ont., Canada* 102 D4
Havelock, *N.Z.* 91 J4
Haverfordwest, *U.K.* 13 F3
Haverhill, *U.S.A.* 111 D13
Haverstraw, *U.S.A.* 111 E11
Håverud, *Sweden* 11 F6
Havířov, *Czech.* 27 B11
Havlíčkův Brod, *Czech Rep.* 26 B8
Havneby, *Denmark* 11 J2
Havran, *Turkey* 39 B9
Havre, *U.S.A.* 114 B9
Havre-Aubert, *Canada* 103 C7
Havre-St.-Pierre, *Canada* 103 B7
Havsa, *Turkey* 41 E10
Havza, *Turkey* 72 B6
Haw →, *U.S.A.* 109 H6
Hawaii □, *U.S.A.* 106 H16
Hawaii I., *Pac. Oc.* 106 J17
Hawaiian Is., *Pac. Oc.* 106 H17
Hawaiian Ridge, *Pac. Oc.* 97 E11
Hawarden, *Canada* 105 C7
Hawarden, *U.S.A.* 112 D6
Hawea, L., *N.Z.* 91 L2
Hawera, *N.Z.* 91 H5
Hawick, *U.K.* 14 F6
Hawk Junction, *Canada* 102 C3
Hawke B., *N.Z.* 91 H6
Hawker, *Australia* 95 E2
Hawkesbury, *Canada* 102 C5
Hawkesbury I., *Canada* 104 C3
Hawkesbury Pt., *Australia* 94 A1
Hawkinsville, *U.S.A.* 109 J4
Hawkwood, *Australia* 95 D5
Hawley, *U.S.A.* 112 B6
Hawrān, *Syria* 70 C3
Ḥawrān, W. →, *Iraq* 73 F10
Hawsh Mūssá, *Lebanon* 75 B4
Hawthorne, *U.S.A.* 114 G4
Hawzen, *Ethiopia* 81 E4
Haxtun, *U.S.A.* 112 E3
Hay, *Australia* 95 E3
Hay →, *Australia* 94 C2
Hay →, *Canada* 104 A5
Hay, C., *Australia* 92 B4
Hay L., *Canada* 104 B5
Hay Lakes, *Canada* 104 C6
Hay-on-Wye, *U.K.* 13 E4
Hay River, *Canada* 104 A5
Hay Springs, *U.S.A.* 112 D3
Haya = Tehoru, *Indonesia* 63 E7
Hayachine-San, *Japan* 54 E10
Hayange, *France* 19 C13
Haydarlı, *Turkey* 39 C12
Hayden, *Ariz., U.S.A.* 115 K8
Hayden, *Colo., U.S.A.* 114 F10
Haydon, *Australia* 94 B3
Hayes, *U.S.A.* 112 C4
Hayes →, *Canada* 105 B10
Hayle, *U.K.* 13 G2
Hayling I., *U.K.* 13 G7
Haymana, *Turkey* 72 C5
Haynesville, *U.S.A.* 113 J8
Hayrabolu, *Turkey* 41 E11
Hays, *Canada* 104 C6
Hays, *U.S.A.* 112 F5
Haysyn, *Ukraine* 47 H5
Hayvoron, *Ukraine* 47 H5
Hayward, *Calif., U.S.A.* 116 H4
Hayward, *Wis., U.S.A.* 112 B9
Haywards Heath, *U.K.* 13 G7
Hazafon □, *Israel* 75 C4
Hazarām, Kūh-e, *Iran* 71 D8
Hazard, *U.S.A.* 108 G4
Hazaribag, *India* 69 H11
Hazaribag Road, *India* 69 G11
Hazebrouck, *France* 19 B9
Hazelton, *Canada* 104 B3
Hazelton, *U.S.A.* 112 B4
Hazen, *N. Dak., U.S.A.* 112 B4
Hazen, *Nev., U.S.A.* 114 G4
Hazlehurst, *Ga., U.S.A.* 109 K4
Hazlehurst, *Miss., U.S.A.* 113 K9
Hazleton, *U.S.A.* 111 F9
Hazlett, L., *Australia* 92 D4
He Xian, *Anhui, China* 59 B12
He Xian, *Guangxi Zhuangzu, China* 59 E8
Head of Bight, *Australia* 93 F5
Headlands, *Zimbabwe* 87 F3
Healdsburg, *U.S.A.* 116 G4
Healdton, *U.S.A.* 113 H6
Healesville, *Australia* 95 F4
Heard I., *Ind. Oc.* 3 G13
Hearne, *U.S.A.* 113 K6
Hearne B., *Canada* 105 A9
Hearne L., *Canada* 104 A6
Hearst, *Canada* 102 C3
Heart →, *U.S.A.* 112 B4
Heart's Content, *Canada* 103 C9
Heath Pt., *Canada* 103 C7
Heath Steele, *Canada* 103 C6
Heavener, *U.S.A.* 113 H7
Hebbronville, *U.S.A.* 113 M5
Hebei □, *China* 56 E9
Hebel, *Australia* 95 D4
Heber, *U.S.A.* 117 N11
Heber Springs, *U.S.A.* 113 H9
Hebert, *Canada* 105 C7
Hebgen L., *U.S.A.* 114 D8
Hebi, *China* 56 G8
Hebrides, *U.K.* 6 D4
Hebron = Al Khalīl, *West Bank* 75 D4
Hebron, *Canada* 101 C13
Hebron, *N. Dak., U.S.A.* 112 B3
Hebron, *Nebr., U.S.A.* 112 E6
Heby, *Sweden* 10 E10
Hecate Str., *Canada* 104 C2
Hechi, *China* 58 E7
Hechingen, *Germany* 25 G4
Hechuan, *China* 58 B6
Hecla, *U.S.A.* 112 C5
Hecla I., *Canada* 105 C9
Hédé, *France* 18 D5
Hede, *Sweden* 10 B7
Hedemora, *Sweden* 10 D9
Hedensted, *Denmark* 11 J3
Hedesunda, *Sweden* 10 D10
Hedley, *U.S.A.* 113 H4
Heerde, *Neths.* 17 B6
Heerenveen, *Neths.* 17 B5
Heerhugowaard, *Neths.* 17 B4
Heerlen, *Neths.* 17 D5
Ḥefa, *Israel* 75 C4
Ḥefa □, *Israel* 75 C4
Hefei, *China* 59 B11
Hegang, *China* 60 B8
Heichengzhen, *China* 56 F4
Heide, *Germany* 24 A5
Heidelberg, *Germany* 25 F4
Heidelberg, *S. Africa* 88 E3
Heidenau, *Germany* 24 E9
Heidenheim, *Germany* 25 G6
Heijing, *China* 58 E3
Heilbad Heiligenstadt, *Germany* 24 D6
Heilbron, *S. Africa* 89 D4
Heilbronn, *Germany* 25 F5
Heiligenblut, *Austria* 26 D5
Heiligenhafen, *Germany* 24 A6
Heilongjiang □, *China* 57 A14
Heilunkiang = Heilongjiang □, *China* 57 A14
Heimaey, *Iceland* 8 E3
Heinola, *Finland* 9 F22
Heinsberg, *Germany* 24 D2
Heinze Is., *Burma* 67 M20
Heishan, *China* 57 D12
Heishui, *Liaoning, China* 57 C10
Heishui, *Sichuan, China* 58 A4
Hejaz = Ḥijāz □, *Si. Arabia* 80 C5
Hejian, *China* 56 E9
Hejiang, *China* 58 C5
Hejin, *China* 56 G6
Hekımhan, *Turkey* 72 C7
Hekla, *Iceland* 8 E4
Hekou, *Gansu, China* 56 F2
Hekou, *Guangdong, China* 59 F9
Hekou, *Yunnan, China* 60 D5
Hel, *Poland* 44 D5
Helagsfjället, *Sweden* 10 B6
Helan Shan, *China* 56 E3
Helechosa, *Spain* 35 F6
Helena, *Ark., U.S.A.* 113 H9
Helena, *Mont., U.S.A.* 114 C7
Helendale, *U.S.A.* 117 L9
Helensburgh, *U.K.* 14 E4
Helensville, *N.Z.* 91 G5
Helgasjön, *Sweden* 11 H8
Helgeland, *Norway* 8 C15
Helgoland, *Germany* 24 A3
Heligoland = Helgoland, *Germany* 24 A3
Heligoland B. = Deutsche Bucht, *Germany* 24 A4
Heliopolis, *Egypt* 80 H7
Hella, *Iceland* 8 E3
Hellevoetsluis, *Neths.* 17 C4
Hellín, *Spain* 33 G3
Helmand □, *Afghan.* 66 D4
Helmand →, *Afghan.* 66 D2
Helme →, *Germany* 24 D7
Helmond, *Neths.* 17 C5
Helmsdale, *U.K.* 14 C5
Helmsdale →, *U.K.* 14 C5
Helmstedt, *Germany* 24 C7
Helong, *China* 57 C15
Helper, *U.S.A.* 114 G8
Helsingborg, *Sweden* 11 H6
Helsinge, *Denmark* 11 H6
Helsingfors = Helsinki, *Finland* 9 F21
Helsingør, *Denmark* 11 H6
Helsinki, *Finland* 9 F21
Helska, Mierzeja, *Poland* 44 D5
Helston, *U.K.* 13 G2
Helvellyn, *U.K.* 12 C4
Helwân, *Egypt* 80 J7
Hemel Hempstead, *U.K.* 13 F7
Hemet, *U.S.A.* 117 M10
Hemingford, *U.S.A.* 112 D3
Hemphill, *U.S.A.* 113 K8
Hempstead, *U.S.A.* 113 K6
Hemse, *Sweden* 11 G12
Hemsön, *Sweden* 10 B12
Henån, *Sweden* 11 F5
Henan □, *China* 56 H8
Henares →, *Spain* 34 E7
Henashi-Misaki, *Japan* 54 D9
Hendaye, *France* 20 E2
Hendek, *Turkey* 72 B4
Henderson, *Argentina* 126 D3
Henderson, *Ky., U.S.A.* 108 G2
Henderson, *N.C., U.S.A.* 109 G6
Henderson, *Nev., U.S.A.* 117 J12
Henderson, *Tenn., U.S.A.* 109 H1
Henderson, *Tex., U.S.A.* 113 J7
Hendersonville, *U.S.A.* 109 H4
Hendījān, *Iran* 71 D6
Hendon, *Australia* 95 D5
Heng Xian, *China* 58 F7
Hengcheng, *China* 56 E4
Hengdaohezi, *China* 57 B15
Hengelo, *Neths.* 17 B6
Hengfeng, *China* 59 C10
Hengshan, *Hunan, China* 59 D9
Hengshan, *Shaanxi, China* 56 F5
Hengshui, *China* 56 F8
Hengyang, *Hunan, China* 59 D9
Hengyang, *Hunan, China* 59 D9
Henichesk, *Ukraine* 47 J8
Hénin-Beaumont, *France* 19 B9
Henlopen, C., *U.S.A.* 108 F8
Hennan, *Sweden* 10 B9
Hennebont, *France* 18 E3
Hennenman, *S. Africa* 88 D4
Hennessey, *U.S.A.* 113 G6
Hennigsdorf, *Germany* 24 C9
Henrietta, *U.S.A.* 113 J5
Henrietta, Ostrov = Genriyetty, Ostrov, *Russia* 51 B16
Henrietta Maria, C., *Canada* 102 A3
Henry, *U.S.A.* 112 E10
Henryetta, *U.S.A.* 113 H7
Hensall, *Canada* 110 C3
Henstedt-Ulzburg, *Germany* 24 B6
Hentiyn Nuruu, *Mongolia* 60 B5
Henty, *Australia* 95 F4
Henzada, *Burma* 67 L19
Hephaestia, *Greece* 39 B7
Heping, *China* 59 E10
Heppner, *U.S.A.* 114 D4
Hepu, *China* 58 G7
Hepworth, *Canada* 110 B3
Heqing, *China* 58 D3
Hequ, *China* 56 E6
Héraðsflói, *Iceland* 8 D6
Héraðsvötn →, *Iceland* 8 D4
Herald Cays, *Australia* 94 B4
Herāt, *Afghan.* 66 B3
Herāt □, *Afghan.* 66 B3
Hérault □, *France* 20 E7
Hérault →, *France* 20 E7
Herbault, *France* 18 E8
Herbert →, *Australia* 94 B4
Herbert Downs, *Australia* 94 C2
Herberton, *Australia* 94 B4
Herbignac, *France* 18 E4
Herborn, *Germany* 24 E4
Herby, *Poland* 45 H5
Herceg-Novi, *Montenegro, Yug.* 40 D2
Herðubreið, *Iceland* 8 D5
Hereford, *U.K.* 13 E5
Hereford, *U.S.A.* 113 H3
Herefordshire □, *U.K.* 13 E5
Hereke, *Turkey* 41 F13
Herencia, *Spain* 35 F7
Herentals, *Belgium* 17 C4
Herford, *Germany* 24 C4
Héricourt, *France* 19 E13
Herington, *U.S.A.* 112 F6
Herisau, *Switz.* 25 H5
Hérisson, *France* 19 F9
Herkimer, *U.S.A.* 111 D10
Herlong, *U.S.A.* 116 E6
Herm, *U.K.* 13 H5
Herman, *U.S.A.* 112 C6
Hermann, *U.S.A.* 112 F9
Hermannsburg, *Germany* 24 C6

Hermannsburg Mission, *Australia* 92 D5
Hermanus, *S. Africa* 88 E2
Herment, *France* 20 C6
Hermidale, *Australia* 95 E4
Hermiston, *U.S.A.* 114 D4
Hermitage, *N.Z.* 91 K3
Hermite, I., *Chile* 128 H3
Hermon, Mt. = Ash Shaykh, J., *Lebanon* 75 B4
Hermosillo, *Mexico* 118 B2
Hernád →, *Hungary* 42 C6
Hernandarias, *Paraguay* 127 B5
Hernandez, *U.S.A.* 116 J6
Hernando, *Argentina* 126 C3
Hernando, *U.S.A.* 113 H10
Hernani, *Spain* 32 B3
Herne, *Germany* 24 D3
Herne Bay, *U.K.* 13 F9
Herning, *Denmark* 11 H2
Heroica = Caborca, *Mexico* 118 A2
Heroica Nogales = Nogales, *Mexico* 118 A2
Heron Bay, *Canada* 102 C2
Herradura, Pta. de la, *Canary Is.* 37 F5
Herreid, *U.S.A.* 112 C4
Herrenberg, *Germany* ... 25 G4
Herrera, *Spain* 35 H6
Herrera de Alcántara, *Spain* 35 F3
Herrera de Pisuerga, *Spain* 34 C6
Herrera del Duque, *Spain* 35 F5
Herrestad, *Sweden* 11 F5
Herrick, *Australia* 94 G4
Herrin, *U.S.A.* 113 G10
Herrljunga, *Sweden* 11 F7
Hersbruck, *Germany* 25 F7
Hersonissos, *Greece* 36 D7
Herstal, *Belgium* 17 D5
Hertford, *U.K.* 13 F7
Hertfordshire □, *U.K.* ... 13 F7
's-Hertogenbosch, *Neths.* .. 17 C5
Hertzogville, *S. Africa* ... 88 D4
Hervás, *Spain* 34 E5
Herzberg, *Brandenburg, Germany* 24 D9
Herzberg, *Niedersachsen, Germany* 24 D6
Herzliyya, *Israel* 75 C3
Herzogenburg, *Austria* .. 26 C8
Ḥeşar, *Fārs, Iran* 71 D6
Ḥeşar, *Markazī, Iran* ... 71 C6
Hesdin, *France* 19 B9
Heshui, *China* 56 G5
Heshun, *China* 56 F7
Hesperia, *U.S.A.* 117 L9
Hesse = Hessen □, *Germany* 24 E4
Hessen □, *Germany* 24 E4
Hestra, *Sweden* 11 G7
Hetch Hetchy Aqueduct, *U.S.A.* 116 H5
Hettinger, *U.S.A.* 112 C3
Hettstedt, *Germany* 24 D7
Heves, *Hungary* 42 C5
Heves □, *Hungary* 42 C5
Hexham, *U.K.* 12 C5
Hexi, *Yunnan, China* ... 58 E4
Hexi, *Zhejiang, China* ... 59 D12
Hexigten Qi, *China* 57 C9
Ḥeydarābād, *Iran* 71 D7
Heyfield, *Australia* 95 F4
Heysham, *U.K.* 12 C5
Heyuan, *China* 59 F10
Heywood, *Australia* 95 F3
Heze, *China* 56 G8
Hezhang, *China* 58 D5
Hi Vista, *U.S.A.* 117 L9
Hialeah, *U.S.A.* 109 N5
Hiawatha, *Kans., U.S.A.* 112 F7
Hiawatha, *Utah, U.S.A.* 114 G8
Hibbing, *U.S.A.* 112 B8
Hibbs B., *Australia* 94 G4
Hibernia Reef, *Australia* .. 92 B3
Hickory, *U.S.A.* 109 H5
Hicks, Pt., *Australia* 95 F4
Hicksville, *U.S.A.* 111 F11
Hida, *Romania* 43 C8
Hida-Gawa →, *Japan* ... 55 G8
Hida-Sammyaku, *Japan* .. 55 F8
Hidaka-Sammyaku, *Japan* 54 C11
Hidalgo, *Mexico* 119 C5
Hidalgo □, *Mexico* 119 C5
Hidalgo, Presa M., *Mexico* 118 B3
Hidalgo, Pta. del, *Canary Is.* 37 F3
Hidalgo del Parral, *Mexico* 118 B3
Hiddensee, *Germany* ... 24 A9
Hieflau, *Austria* 26 D7
Hiendelaencina, *Spain* ... 32 D2
Hierro, *Canary Is.* 37 G1
Higashiajima-San, *Japan* .. 54 F10
Higashiōsaka, *Japan* 55 G7
Higgins, *U.S.A.* 113 G4
Higgins Corner, *U.S.A.* .. 116 F5
Higginsville, *Australia* 93 F3
High Atlas = Haut Atlas, *Morocco* 78 B4
High I., *Canada* 103 A7
High Island, *U.S.A.* 113 L7
High Level, *Canada* 104 B5
High Point, *U.S.A.* 109 H6
High Prairie, *Canada* 104 B5
High River, *Canada* 104 C6
High Springs, *U.S.A.* 109 L4

High Tatra = Tatry, *Slovak Rep.* 27 B13
High Veld, *Africa* 76 J6
High Wycombe, *U.K.* 13 F7
Highbury, *Australia* 94 B3
Highland □, *U.K.* 14 D4
Highland Park, *U.S.A.* ... 108 D2
Highmore, *U.S.A.* 112 C5
Highrock L., *Canada* 105 B7
Higüey, *Dom. Rep.* 121 C6
Hihya, *Egypt* 80 H7
Hiiumaa, *Estonia* 9 G20
Híjar, *Spain* 32 D4
Ḥijāz □, *Si. Arabia* 80 C5
Hijo = Tagum, *Phil.* 61 H6
Hikari, *Japan* 55 H5
Hikone, *Japan* 55 G8
Hiko, *U.S.A.* 116 H11
Hikurangi, *N.Z.* 91 F5
Hikurangi, Mt., *N.Z.* ... 91 H6
Hildburghausen, *Germany* 24 E6
Hildesheim, *Germany* ... 24 C5
Hill →, *Australia* 93 F2
Hill City, *Idaho, U.S.A.* .. 114 E6
Hill City, *Kans., U.S.A.* .. 112 F5
Hill City, *Minn., U.S.A.* .. 112 B8
Hill City, *S. Dak., U.S.A.* 112 D3
Hill Island L., *Canada* ... 105 A7
Hillared, *Sweden* 11 G7
Hillcrest Center, *U.S.A.* .. 117 K8
Hillegom, *Neths.* 17 B4
Hillerød, *Denmark* 11 J6
Hillerstorp, *Sweden* 11 G7
Hillman, *U.S.A.* 108 C4
Hillmond, *Canada* 105 C7
Hillsboro, *Kans., U.S.A.* . 112 F6
Hillsboro, *N. Dak., U.S.A.* 112 B6
Hillsboro, *N.H., U.S.A.* .. 111 C13
Hillsboro, *N. Mex., U.S.A.* 115 K10
Hillsboro, *Oreg., U.S.A.* .. 116 E4
Hillsboro, *Tex., U.S.A.* .. 113 J6
Hillsborough, *Grenada* .. 121 D7
Hillsdale, *Mich., U.S.A.* .. 108 E3
Hillsdale, *N.Y., U.S.A.* .. 111 D11
Hillside, *Australia* 92 D2
Hillsport, *Canada* 102 C2
Hillston, *Australia* 95 E4
Hilo, *U.S.A.* 106 J17
Hilton, *U.S.A.* 110 C7
Hilvan, *Turkey* 73 D8
Hilversum, *Neths.* 17 B5
Himachal Pradesh □, *India* 68 D7
Himalaya, *Asia* 69 E11
Himamaylan, *Phil.* 61 F5
Himara, *Albania* 40 F3
Himatnagar, *India* 66 H8
Himeji, *Japan* 55 G7
Himi, *Japan* 55 F8
Himmerland, *Denmark* .. 11 H3
Ḥimṣ, *Syria* 75 A5
Ḥimṣ □, *Syria* 75 A6
Hinche, *Haiti* 121 C5
Hinchinbrook I., *Australia* 94 B4
Hinckley, *U.K.* 13 E6
Hinckley, *U.S.A.* 114 G7
Hindaun, *India* 68 F7
Hindmarsh, L., *Australia* . 95 F3
Hindsholm, *Denmark* ... 11 J4
Hindu Bagh, *Pakistan* ... 68 D2
Hindu Kush, *Asia* 66 B7
Hindubagh, *Pakistan* ... 66 D5
Hindupur, *India* 66 N10
Hines Creek, *Canada* ... 104 B5
Hinganghat, *India* 66 J11
Hingham, *U.S.A.* 114 B8
Hingoli, *India* 66 K10
Hinigaran, *Phil.* 61 F5
Hinis, *Turkey* 73 C9
Hinna = Imi, *Ethiopia* ... 81 F5
Hinna, *Nigeria* 83 C7
Hinnerup, *Denmark* 11 H4
Hinnøya, *Norway* 8 B16
Hinojosa del Duque, *Spain* 35 G5
Hinsdale, *U.S.A.* 114 B10
Hinterrhein →, *Switz.* ... 25 J5
Hinton, *Canada* 104 C5
Hinton, *U.S.A.* 108 G5
Hınzır Burnu, *Turkey* ... 72 D6
Hirado, *Japan* 55 H4
Hirakud Dam, *India* 67 J13
Hiratsuka, *Japan* 55 G9
Hirfanlı Barajı, *Turkey* .. 72 C5
Hiroo, *Japan* 54 C11
Hirosaki, *Japan* 54 D10
Hiroshima, *Japan* 55 G6
Hiroshima □, *Japan* 55 G6
Hirson, *France* 19 C11
Hirtshals, *Denmark* 11 G3
Hisar, *India* 68 E6
Hisarcık, *Turkey* 39 B11
Hisaria, *Bulgaria* 41 D8
Hisb →, *Iraq* 70 D5
Ḥismā, *Si. Arabia* 70 D3
Hispaniola, *W. Indies* ... 121 C5
Hīt, *Iraq* 70 C4
Hita, *Japan* 55 H5
Hitachi, *Japan* 55 F10
Hitchin, *U.K.* 13 F7
Hitoyoshi, *Japan* 55 H5
Hitra, *Norway* 8 E13
Hitzacker, *Germany* 24 B7
Hiyyon, N. →, *Israel* ... 75 E4
Hjalmar L., *Canada* 105 A7
Hjälmaren, *Sweden* 10 E9
Hjältevad, *Sweden* 11 G9
Hjo, *Sweden* 11 F8
Hjørring, *Denmark* 11 G3

Hjortkvarn, *Sweden* 11 F9
Hlinsko, *Czech Rep.* 26 B8
Hlohovec, *Slovak Rep.* .. 27 C10
Hlučín, *Czech Rep.* 27 B11
Hluhluwe, *S. Africa* 89 D5
Hlukhiv, *Ukraine* 47 G7
Hlyboka, *Ukraine* 47 H3
Hlybokaye, *Belarus* 46 E4
Hnúšťa, *Slovak Rep.* 27 C12
Ho, *Ghana* 83 D5
Ho Chi Minh City = Phanh Bho Ho Chi Minh, *Vietnam* 65 G6
Ho Thuong, *Vietnam* ... 64 C5
Hoa Binh, *Vietnam* 64 B5
Hoa Da, *Vietnam* 65 G7
Hoa Hiep, *Vietnam* 65 G5
Hoai Nhon, *Vietnam* ... 64 E7
Hoang Lien Son, *Vietnam* 64 A4
Hobart, *Australia* 94 G4
Hobart, *U.S.A.* 113 H5
Hobbs, *U.S.A.* 113 J3
Hobbs Coast, *Antarctica* 5 D14
Hoboken, *U.S.A.* 111 F10
Hobro, *Denmark* 11 H3
Hoburgen, *Sweden* 11 H12
Hocalar, *Turkey* 39 C11
Hochschwab, *Austria* ... 26 D8
Höchstadt, *Germany* 25 F6
Hockenheim, *Germany* .. 25 F4
Hodaka-Dake, *Japan* ... 55 F8
Hodgson, *Canada* 105 C9
Hódmezővásárhely, *Hungary* 42 D5
Hodna, Chott el, *Algeria* . 78 A6
Hodonín, *Czech Rep.* ... 27 C10
Hoeamdong, *N. Korea* .. 57 C16
Hoek van Holland, *Neths.* 17 C4
Hoengsŏng, *S. Korea* ... 57 F14
Hoeryong, *N. Korea* 57 C15
Hoeyang, *N. Korea* 57 E14
Hof, *Germany* 25 E7
Hofgeismar, *Germany* ... 24 D5
Hofheim, *Germany* 25 E4
Hofmeyr, *S. Africa* 88 E4
Höfn, *Iceland* 8 D6
Hofors, *Sweden* 10 D10
Hofsjökull, *Iceland* 8 D4
Hōfu, *Japan* 55 G5
Hogan Group, *Australia* .. 94 F4
Höganäs, *Sweden* 11 H6
Hogansville, *U.S.A.* 109 J3
Hogeland, *U.S.A.* 114 B9
Hoggar = Ahaggar, *Algeria* 78 D7
Högsäter, *Sweden* 11 F6
Högsby, *Sweden* 11 G10
Högsjö, *Sweden* 10 E9
Hogsty Reef, *Bahamas* .. 121 B5
Hoh →, *U.S.A.* 116 C2
Hoh Xil Shan, *China* 60 C3
Hohe Acht, *Germany* ... 25 E3
Hohe Tauern, *Austria* ... 26 D5
Hohe Venn, *Belgium* 17 D6
Hohenau, *Austria* 27 C9
Hohenems, *Austria* 26 D2
Hohenloher Ebene, *Germany* 25 F5
Hohenwald, *U.S.A.* 109 H2
Hohenwestedt, *Germany* . 24 A5
Hohhot, *China* 56 D6
Hóhlakas, *Greece* 36 D9
Hohoe, *Ghana* 83 D5
Hoi An, *Vietnam* 64 E7
Hoi Xuan, *Vietnam* 64 B5
Hoisington, *U.S.A.* 112 F5
Højer, *Denmark* 11 K2
Hōjō, *Japan* 55 H6
Hok, *Sweden* 11 G8
Hökensås, *Sweden* 11 F8
Hökerum, *Sweden* 11 G7
Hokianga Harbour, *N.Z.* 91 F4
Hokitika, *N.Z.* 91 K3
Hokkaidō □, *Japan* 54 C11
Hol-Hol, *Djibouti* 81 E5
Hola Pristan, *Ukraine* ... 47 J7
Holbæk, *Denmark* 11 J5
Holbrook, *Australia* 95 F4
Holbrook, *U.S.A.* 115 J8
Holden, *Canada* 104 C6
Holden, *U.S.A.* 114 G7
Holdenville, *U.S.A.* 113 H6
Holdfast, *Canada* 105 C7
Holdrege, *U.S.A.* 112 E5
Holešov, *Czech Rep.* 27 B10
Holguín, *Cuba* 120 B4
Holíč, *Slovak Rep.* 27 C10
Holice, *Czech Rep.* 26 A8
Höljes, *Sweden* 10 D6
Hollabrunn, *Austria* 26 C9
Hollams Bird I., *Namibia* 88 C1
Holland, *U.S.A.* 108 D2
Hollandia = Jayapura, *Indonesia* 63 E10
Hollfeld, *Germany* 25 F7
Hollidaysburg, *U.S.A.* .. 110 F6
Hollis, *U.S.A.* 113 H5
Hollister, *Calif., U.S.A.* .. 116 J5
Hollister, *Idaho, U.S.A.* .. 114 E6
Höllviken, *Sweden* 11 J6
Holly, *U.S.A.* 112 F3
Holly Hill, *U.S.A.* 109 L5
Holly Springs, *U.S.A.* ... 113 H10
Hollywood, *Calif., U.S.A.* 106 K8
Hollywood, *Fla., U.S.A.* . 109 N5
Holman, *Canada* 100 A8
Hólmavík, *Iceland* 8 D3

Holmes Reefs, *Australia* .. 94 B4
Holmsjö, *Sweden* 11 H9
Holmsjön, *Västernorrland, Sweden* 10 B10
Holmsjön, *Västernorrland, Sweden* 10 B9
Holmsland Klit, *Denmark* 11 J2
Holmsund, *Sweden* 8 E19
Holod, *Romania* 42 D7
Holroyd →, *Australia* ... 94 A3
Holstebro, *Denmark* 11 H2
Holsworthy, *U.K.* 13 G3
Holton, *Canada* 103 B8
Holton, *U.S.A.* 112 F7
Holtville, *U.S.A.* 117 N11
Holwerd, *Neths.* 17 A5
Holy I., *Angl., U.K.* 12 D3
Holy I., *Northumb., U.K.* 12 B6
Holyhead, *U.K.* 12 D3
Holyoke, *Colo., U.S.A.* .. 112 E3
Holyoke, *Mass., U.S.A.* . 111 D12
Holyrood, *Canada* 103 C9
Holzkirchen, *Germany* .. 25 H7
Holzminden, *Germany* .. 24 D5
Homa Bay, *Kenya* 86 C3
Homa Bay □, *Kenya* ... 86 C3
Homalin, *Burma* 67 G19
Homand, *Iran* 71 C8
Homberg, *Germany* 24 D5
Hombori, *Mali* 83 B4
Homburg, *Germany* 25 F3
Home B., *Canada* 101 B13
Home Hill, *Australia* 94 B4
Homedale, *U.S.A.* 114 E5
Homer, *Alaska, U.S.A.* .. 100 C4
Homer, *La., U.S.A.* 113 J8
Homestead, *Australia* ... 94 C4
Homestead, *Fla., U.S.A.* 109 N5
Homestead, *Oreg., U.S.A.* 114 D5
Homewood, *U.S.A.* 116 F6
Hominy, *U.S.A.* 113 G6
Homoine, *Mozam.* 89 C6
Homoljske Planina, *Serbia, Yug.* 40 B5
Homorod, *Romania* 43 D10
Homs = Ḥimṣ, *Syria* ... 75 A5
Homyel, *Belarus* 47 F6
Hon Chong, *Vietnam* ... 65 G5
Hon Me, *Vietnam* 64 C5
Honan = Henan □, *China* 56 H8
Honaz, *Turkey* 39 D11
Honbetsu, *Japan* 54 C11
Honcut, *U.S.A.* 116 F5
Honda Bay, *Phil.* 61 G3
Hondarribia, *Spain* 32 B3
Hondeklipbaai, *S. Africa* . 88 E2
Hondo, *Japan* 55 H5
Hondo, *U.S.A.* 113 L5
Hondo →, *Belize* 119 D7
Hondo, *Belize* 119 D7
Honduras ■, *Cent. Amer.* 120 D2
Honduras, G. de, *Caribbean* 120 C2
Hønefoss, *Norway* 9 F14
Honesdale, *U.S.A.* 111 E9
Honey L., *U.S.A.* 116 E6
Honfleur, *France* 18 C7
Høng, *Denmark* 11 J5
Hong Gai, *Vietnam* 64 B6
Hong He →, *China* 56 H8
Hong Kong □, *China* ... 59 F10
Hong'an, *China* 59 B10
Hongch'ŏn, *S. Korea* ... 57 F14
Honghai Wan, *China* ... 59 F10
Honghu, *China* 59 C9
Hongjiang, *China* 58 D7
Hongliu He →, *China* ... 56 F5
Hongor, *Mongolia* 56 B7
Hongsa, *Laos* 64 C3
Hongshui He →, *China* .. 58 F7
Hongsŏng, *S. Korea* 57 F14
Hongtong, *China* 56 F6
Honguedo, Détroit d', *Canada* 103 C7
Hongwon, *N. Korea* 57 E14
Hongya, *China* 58 C4
Hongyuan, *China* 58 A4
Hongze Hu, *China* 57 H10
Honiara, *Solomon Is.* ... 96 H7
Honiton, *U.K.* 13 G4
Honjō, *Japan* 54 E10
Honkorâb, Ras, *Egypt* .. 80 C4
Honningsvåg, *Norway* .. 8 A21
Hönö, *Sweden* 11 G5
Honolulu, *U.S.A.* 106 H16
Honshū, *Japan* 55 G9
Hontoria del Pinar, *Spain* 32 D1
Hood, Mt., *U.S.A.* 114 D3
Hood, Pt., *Australia* 93 F2
Hood River, *U.S.A.* 114 D3
Hoodsport, *U.S.A.* 116 C3
Hooge, *Germany* 24 A4
Hoogeveen, *Neths.* 17 B6
Hoogezand-Sappemeer, *Neths.* 17 A6
Hooghly → = Hugli →, *India* 69 J13
Hooghly-Chinsura = Chunchura, *India* ... 69 H13
Hook Hd., *Ireland* 15 D5
Hook I., *Australia* 94 C4
Hook of Holland = Hoek van Holland, *Neths.* .. 17 C4
Hooker, *U.S.A.* 113 G4
Hooker Creek, *Australia* 92 C5
Hoopeston, *U.S.A.* 108 E2
Hoopstad, *S. Africa* 88 D4

Hoorn, *Neths.* 17 B5
Hoover Dam, *U.S.A.* ... 117 K12
Hooversville, *U.S.A.* 110 F6
Hop Bottom, *U.S.A.* ... 111 E9
Hopa, *Turkey* 73 B9
Hope, *Canada* 104 D4
Hope, *Ariz., U.S.A.* 117 M13
Hope, *Ark., U.S.A.* 113 J8
Hope, *N. Dak., U.S.A.* . 112 B6
Hope, L., *Australia* 95 D2
Hope Town, *Bahamas* .. 120 A4
Hopedale, *Canada* 103 A7
Hopefield, *S. Africa* 88 E2
Hopei = Hebei □, *China* 56 E9
Hopelchén, *Mexico* 119 D7
Hopetoun, *Vic., Australia* 95 F3
Hopetoun, *W. Austral., Australia* 93 F3
Hopetown, *S. Africa* ... 88 D3
Hopfgarten, *Austria* 26 D5
Hopkins, *U.S.A.* 112 E7
Hopkins, L., *Australia* ... 92 D4
Hopkinsville, *U.S.A.* 109 G2
Hopland, *U.S.A.* 116 G3
Hoquiam, *U.S.A.* 116 D3
Horasan, *Turkey* 73 B10
Horažďovice, *Czech Rep.* . 26 B6
Horb, *Germany* 25 G4
Hörby, *Sweden* 11 J7
Horcajo de Santiago, *Spain* 32 F1
Horden Hills, *Australia* .. 92 D5
Horezu, *Romania* 43 E8
Horgen, *Switz.* 25 H4
Horgoš, *Serbia, Yug.* ... 42 D4
Hořice, *Czech Rep.* 26 A8
Horinger, *China* 56 D6
Horki, *Belarus* 46 E6
Horlick Mts., *Antarctica* . 5 E15
Horlivka, *Ukraine* 47 H10
Hormoz, *Iran* 71 E7
Hormoz, Jaz. ye, *Iran* .. 71 E8
Hormuz, Str. of, *The Gulf* 71 E8
Horn, *Austria* 26 C8
Horn, *Iceland* 8 C2
Horn, *Sweden* 11 G9
Horn →, *Canada* 104 A5
Horn, Cape = Hornos, C. de, *Chile* 122 J4
Horn Head, *Ireland* 15 A3
Horn I., *Australia* 94 A3
Horn I., *U.S.A.* 109 K1
Horn Mts., *Canada* 104 A5
Hornachuelos, *Spain* ... 35 H5
Hornavan, *Sweden* 8 C17
Hornbeck, *U.S.A.* 113 K8
Hornbrook, *U.S.A.* 114 F2
Hornburg, *Germany* ... 24 C6
Horncastle, *U.K.* 12 D7
Horndal, *Sweden* 10 D10
Hornell, *U.S.A.* 110 D7
Hornell L., *Canada* 104 A5
Hornepayne, *Canada* ... 102 C3
Horní Planá, *Czech Rep.* . 26 C7
Hornitos, *U.S.A.* 116 H6
Hornos, C. de, *Chile* ... 122 J4
Hornoy-le-Bourg, *France* 19 C8
Hornsby, *Australia* 95 E5
Hornsea, *U.K.* 12 D7
Hornslandet, *Sweden* ... 10 C11
Hörnum, *Germany* 24 A4
Horobetsu, *Japan* 54 C10
Horodenka, *Ukraine* ... 47 H3
Horodnya, *Ukraine* 47 G6
Horodok, *Khmelnytskyy, Ukraine* 47 H4
Horodok, *Lviv, Ukraine* . 47 H2
Horodyshche, *Ukraine* .. 47 H6
Horokhiv, *Ukraine* 47 G3
Horovice, *Czech Rep.* ... 26 B6
Horqin Youyi Qianqi, *China* 57 A12
Horqueta, *Paraguay* 126 A4
Horred, *Sweden* 11 G6
Horse Creek, *U.S.A.* ... 112 E3
Horse Is., *Canada* 103 B8
Horsefly L., *Canada* 104 C4
Horsens, *Denmark* 11 J3
Horsham, *Australia* 95 F3
Horsham, *U.K.* 13 F7
Horšovský Týn, *Czech Rep.* 26 B5
Horten, *Norway* 9 G14
Hortobágy →, *Hungary* . 42 C6
Horton, *U.S.A.* 112 F7
Horton →, *Canada* 100 B7
Horwood, L., *Canada* ... 102 C3
Hosaina, *Ethiopia* 81 F4
Hose, Gunung-Gunung, *Malaysia* 62 D4
Ḥoseynābād, *Khuzestān, Iran* 71 C6
Ḥoseynābād, *Kordestān, Iran* 70 C5
Hoshangabad, *India* 68 H7
Hoshiarpur, *India* 68 D6
Hosmer, *U.S.A.* 112 C5
Hospet, *India* 66 M10
Hospitalet, I., *Chile* 128 C2
Hostens, *France* 20 D3
Hot, *Thailand* 64 C2
Hot Creek Range, *U.S.A.* 114 G6
Hot Springs, *Ark., U.S.A.* 113 H8
Hot Springs, *S. Dak., U.S.A.* 112 D3
Hotagen, *Sweden* 8 E16
Hotan, *China* 60 C2
Hotazel, *S. Africa* 88 D3
Hotchkiss, *U.S.A.* 115 G10

Hotham, C., Australia 92 B5
Hoting, Sweden 8 D17
Hotolishti, Albania 40 E4
Hotte, Massif de la, Haiti . 121 C5
Hottentotsbaai, Namibia .. 88 D1
Houat, Î. de, France 18 E4
Houck, U.S.A. 115 J9
Houdan, France 19 D8
Houei Sai, Laos 64 B3
Houeillès, France 20 D4
Houffalize, Belgium 17 D5
Houghton, U.S.A. 112 B10
Houghton L., U.S.A. 108 C3
Houhora Heads, N.Z. 91 F4
Houlton, U.S.A. 103 C6
Houma, U.S.A. 113 L9
Houndé, Burkina Faso ... 82 C4
Hourtin, France 20 C2
Hourtin-Carcans, Étang d', France ... 20 C2
Houston, Canada 104 C3
Houston, Mo., U.S.A. ... 113 G9
Houston, Tex., U.S.A. ... 113 L7
Houtman Abrolhos, Australia ... 93 E1
Hovd, Mongolia 60 B4
Hove, U.K. 13 G7
Hoveyzeh, Iran 71 D6
Hovmantorp, Sweden 11 H9
Hövsgöl, Mongolia 56 C5
Hövsgöl Nuur, Mongolia . 60 A5
Hovsta, Sweden 10 E9
Howakil, Eritrea 81 D5
Howar, Wadi →, Sudan . 81 D2
Howard, Australia 95 D5
Howard, Kans., U.S.A. .. 113 G6
Howard, Pa., U.S.A. 110 F7
Howard, S. Dak., U.S.A. . 112 C6
Howard I., Australia 94 A2
Howard L., Canada 105 A7
Howe, U.S.A. 114 E7
Howe, C., Australia 95 F5
Howell, U.S.A. 108 D4
Howick, Canada 111 A11
Howick, S. Africa 89 D5
Howick Group, Australia . 94 A4
Howitt, L., Australia 95 D2
Howland I., Pac. Oc. 96 G10
Howley, Canada 103 C8
Howrah = Haora, India .. 69 H13
Howth Hd., Ireland 15 C5
Höxter, Germany 24 D5
Hoy, U.K. 14 C5
Hoya, Germany 24 C5
Høyanger, Norway 9 F12
Hoyerswerda, Germany .. 24 D10
Hoylake, U.K. 12 D4
Hoyos, Spain 34 E4
Hpungan Pass, Burma 67 F20
Hradec Králové, Czech Rep. ... 26 A8
Hrádek, Czech Rep. 27 C9
Hranice, Czech Rep. 27 B10
Hrazdan, Armenia 49 K7
Hrebenka, Ukraine 47 G7
Hrodna, Belarus 46 F2
Hrodzyanka, Belarus 46 F5
Hron →, Slovak Rep. 27 D11
Hrubieszów, Poland 45 H10
Hrubý Jeseník, Czech Rep. 27 A10
Hrvatska = Croatia ■, Europe ... 29 C13
Hrymayliv, Ukraine 47 H4
Hsenwi, Burma 67 H20
Hsiamen = Xiamen, China 59 E12
Hsian = Xi'an, China 56 G5
Hsinchu, Taiwan 59 E13
Hsinhailien = Lianyungang, China ... 57 G10
Hsüchou = Xuzhou, China 57 G9
Hu Xian, China 56 G5
Hua Hin, Thailand 64 F2
Hua Xian, Henan, China . 56 G8
Hua Xian, Shaanxi, China 56 G5
Hua'an, China 59 E11
Huacheng, China 59 E10
Huachinera, Mexico 118 A3
Huacho, Peru 124 F3
Huade, China 56 D7
Huadian, China 57 C14
Huai He →, China 59 A12
Huai Yot, Thailand 65 J2
Huai'an, Hebei, China ... 56 D8
Huai'an, Jiangsu, China .. 57 H10
Huaibei, China 56 G9
Huaide, China 57 C13
Huaidezhen, China 57 C13
Huaihua, China 58 D7
Huaiji, China 59 F9
Huainan, China 59 A11
Huaining, China 59 B11
Huairen, China 56 E7
Huairou, China 56 D9
Huaiyang, China 56 H8
Huaiyuan, Anhui, China . 57 H9
Huaiyuan, Guangxi Zhuangzu, China ... 58 E7
Huajianzi, China 57 D13
Huajuapan de Leon, Mexico ... 119 D5
Hualapai Peak, U.S.A. .. 115 J7
Hualien, Taiwan 59 E13
Huallaga →, Peru 124 E3
Huambo, Angola 85 G3
Huan Jiang →, China ... 56 G5
Huan Xian, China 56 F4

Huancabamba, Peru 124 E3
Huancane, Peru 124 G5
Huancavelica, Peru 124 F3
Huancayo, Peru 124 F3
Huanchaca, Bolivia 124 H5
Huang Hai = Yellow Sea, China ... 57 G12
Huang He →, China 57 F10
Huang Xian, China 57 F11
Huangchuan, China 59 A10
Huanggang, China 59 B10
Huangling, China 56 G5
Huangliu, China 60 E5
Huanglong, China 56 G5
Huanglongtan, China 59 A8
Huangmei, China 59 B10
Huangpi, China 59 B10
Huangshi, China 59 B10
Huangsongdian, China ... 57 C14
Huangyan, China 59 C13
Huangyangsi, China 59 D8
Huaning, China 58 E4
Huanjiang, China 58 E7
Huantai, China 57 F9
Huánuco, Peru 124 E3
Huaping, China 58 D3
Huaraz, Peru 124 E3
Huarmey, Peru 124 F3
Huarong, China 59 C9
Huascarán, Peru 122 D3
Huasco, Chile 126 B1
Huasco →, Chile 126 B1
Huasna, U.S.A. 117 K6
Huatabampo, Mexico ... 118 B3
Huauchinango, Mexico .. 119 C5
Huautla de Jiménez, Mexico ... 119 D5
Huaxi, China 58 D6
Huay Namota, Mexico .. 118 C4
Huayin, China 56 G6
Huayuan, China 58 C7
Huazhou, China 59 G8
Hubbard, U.S.A. 113 K6
Hubbart Pt., Canada 105 B10
Hubei □, China 59 B9
Hubli-Dharwad = Dharwad, India ... 66 M9
Hucknall, U.K. 12 D6
Huddersfield, U.K. 12 D6
Hude, Germany 24 B4
Hudi, Sudan 80 D3
Hudiksvall, Sweden 10 C11
Hudson, Canada 105 C10
Hudson, Mass., U.S.A. .. 111 D13
Hudson, Mich., U.S.A. .. 108 E3
Hudson, N.Y., U.S.A. ... 111 D11
Hudson, Wis., U.S.A. ... 112 C8
Hudson, Wyo., U.S.A. .. 114 E9
Hudson →, U.S.A. 111 F10
Hudson Bay, N.W.T., Canada ... 101 C11
Hudson Bay, Sask., Canada 105 C8
Hudson Falls, U.S.A. ... 111 C11
Hudson Mts., Antarctica . 5 D16
Hudson Str., Canada 101 B13
Hudson's Hope, Canada . 104 B4
Hue, Vietnam 64 D6
Huebra →, Spain 34 D4
Huedin, Romania 42 D8
Huehuetenango, Guatemala 120 C1
Huejúcar, Mexico 118 C4
Huélamo, Spain 32 E3
Huelgoat, France 18 D3
Huelma, Spain 35 H7
Huelva, Spain 35 H4
Huelva □, Spain 35 H4
Huelva →, Spain 35 H5
Huentelauquén, Chile ... 126 C1
Huércal-Overa, Spain ... 33 H3
Huerta, Sa. de la, Argentina ... 126 C2
Huertas, C. de las, Spain . 33 G4
Huerva →, Spain 32 D4
Huesca, Spain 32 C4
Huesca □, Spain 32 C5
Huéscar, Spain 33 H2
Huetamo, Mexico 118 D4
Huete, Spain 32 E2
Hugh →, Australia 94 D1
Hughenden, Australia .. 94 C3
Hughes, Australia 93 F4
Hugli →, India 69 J13
Hugo, U.S.A. 112 F3
Hugoton, U.S.A. 113 G4
Hui Xian, Gansu, China . 56 H4
Hui Xian, Henan, China . 56 G7
Hui'an, China 59 E12
Hui'anbu, China 56 F4
Huichang, China 59 E10
Huichapán, Mexico 119 C5
Huidong, China 58 D4
Huifa He →, China 57 C14
Huila, Nevado del, Colombia ... 124 C3
Huilai, China 59 F11
Huili, China 58 D4
Huimin, China 57 F9
Huinan, China 57 C14
Huinca Renancó, Argentina 126 C3
Huining, China 56 G3
Huinong, China 56 E4
Huisne →, France 18 E7
Huiting, China 56 G9
Huitong, China 58 D7

Huixtla, Mexico 119 D6
Huize, China 58 D4
Huizhou, China 59 F10
Hukawng Valley, Burma . 67 F20
Hukou, China 59 C11
Hukuntsi, Botswana 88 C3
Hula, Ethiopia 81 F4
Hulan, China 60 B7
Hulayfā', Si. Arabia 70 E4
Huld, Mongolia 56 B3
Hulin He →, China 57 B12
Hull = Kingston upon Hull, U.K. ... 12 D7
Hull, Canada 102 C4
Hull →, U.K. 12 D7
Hulst, Neths. 17 C4
Hultsfred, Sweden 11 G9
Hulun Nur, China 60 B6
Hulyaypole, Ukraine ... 47 J9
Humahuaca, Argentina .. 126 A2
Humaitá, Brazil 124 E6
Humaitá, Paraguay 126 B4
Humansdorp, S. Africa .. 88 E3
Humbe, Angola 88 B1
Humber →, U.K. 12 D7
Humbert River, Australia . 92 C5
Humble, U.S.A. 113 L8
Humboldt, Canada 105 C7
Humboldt, Iowa, U.S.A. . 112 D7
Humboldt, Tenn., U.S.A. . 113 H10
Humboldt →, U.S.A. .. 114 F4
Humboldt Gletscher, Greenland ... 4 B4
Hume, U.S.A. 116 J8
Hume, L., Australia 95 F4
Humenné, Slovak Rep. .. 27 C14
Hummelsta, Sweden 10 E10
Humphreys, Mt., U.S.A. . 116 J8
Humphreys Peak, U.S.A. . 115 J8
Humpolec, Czech Rep. .. 26 B8
Humptulips, U.S.A. 116 C3
Hūn, Libya 79 C9
Hun Jiang →, China ... 57 D13
Húnaflói, Iceland 8 D3
Hunan □, China 59 D9
Hunchun, China 57 C16
Hundested, Denmark ... 11 J5
Hundred Mile House, Canada ... 104 C4
Hunedoara, Romania ... 42 E7
Hunedoara □, Romania . 42 E7
Hünfeld, Germany 24 E5
Hung Yen, Vietnam 64 B6
Hungary ■, Europe 27 D12
Hungary, Plain of, Europe 6 F10
Hungerford, Australia .. 95 D3
Hüngnam, N. Korea 57 E14
Huni Valley, Ghana 82 D4
Hunneberg, Sweden 11 F6
Hunnebostrand, Sweden . 11 F5
Hunsberge, Namibia ... 88 D2
Hunsrück, Germany 25 F3
Hunstanton, U.K. 12 E8
Hunte →, Germany 24 B4
Hunter, N. Dak., U.S.A. . 112 B6
Hunter, N.Y., U.S.A. ... 111 D10
Hunter I., Australia 94 G3
Hunter I., Canada 104 C3
Hunter Ra., Australia ... 95 E5
Hunters Road, Zimbabwe 87 F2
Hunterville, N.Z. 91 H5
Huntingburg, U.S.A. ... 108 F2
Huntingdon, Canada ... 102 C5
Huntingdon, U.K. 13 E7
Huntington, U.S.A. 110 F6
Huntington, Ind., U.S.A. . 108 E3
Huntington, N.Y., U.S.A. 111 F11
Huntington, Oreg., U.S.A. 114 D5
Huntington, Utah, U.S.A. 114 G8
Huntington, W. Va., U.S.A. ... 108 F4
Huntington Beach, U.S.A. 117 M9
Huntington Park, U.S.A. . 115 K4
Huntly, N.Z. 91 G5
Huntly, U.K. 14 D6
Huntsville, Canada 102 C4
Huntsville, Ala., U.S.A. . 109 H2
Huntsville, Tex., U.S.A. . 113 K7
Hunyani →, Zimbabwe . 87 F3
Hunyuan, China 56 E7
Huo Xian, China 56 F6
Huong Hoa, Vietnam ... 64 D6
Huong Khe, Vietnam ... 64 C5
Huonville, Australia 94 G4
Huoqiu, China 59 A11
Huoshan, Anhui, China . 59 A12
Huoshan, Anhui, China . 59 B11
Hupeh = Hubei □, China 59 B9
Hūr, Iran 71 D8
Hurbanovo, Slovak Rep. . 27 D11
Hure Qi, China 57 C11
Hurezani, Romania 43 F8
Hurghada, Egypt 80 B3
Hurley, N. Mex., U.S.A. . 115 K9
Hurley, Wis., U.S.A. ... 112 B9
Huron, Calif., U.S.A. ... 116 J6
Huron, Ohio, U.S.A. ... 110 E2
Huron, S. Dak., U.S.A. . 112 C5
Huron, L., U.S.A. 110 B2
Hurricane, U.S.A. 115 H7
Hurso, Ethiopia 81 F5
Hurunui →, N.Z. 91 K4
Hurup, Denmark 11 H2
Húsavík, Iceland 8 C5
Huşi, Romania 43 D13
Huskvarna, Sweden 11 G8

Hussar, Canada 104 C6
Hustadvika, Norway 8 E12
Hustopeče, Czech Rep. .. 27 C9
Husum, Germany 24 A5
Husum, Sweden 10 A13
Hutchinson, Kans., U.S.A. 113 F6
Hutchinson, Minn., U.S.A. 112 C7
Hüttenberg, Austria 26 E7
Huttig, U.S.A. 113 J8
Hutton, Mt., Australia .. 95 D4
Huwun, Ethiopia 81 G5
Huy, Belgium 17 D5
Hvalpsund, Denmark ... 11 H3
Hvammstangi, Iceland .. 8 D3
Hvar, Croatia 29 E13
Hvarski Kanal, Croatia .. 29 E13
Hvítá →, Iceland 8 D3
Hwachon-chosuji, S. Korea 57 E14
Hwang Ho = Huang He →, China ... 57 F10
Hwange, Zimbabwe 87 F2
Hwange Nat. Park, Zimbabwe ... 88 B4
Hyannis, U.S.A. 112 E4
Hyargas Nuur, Mongolia 60 B4
Hybo, Sweden 10 C10
Hyden, Australia 93 F2
Hyderabad, India 66 L11
Hyderabad, Pakistan ... 68 G3
Hyères, France 21 E10
Hyères, Îs. d', France .. 21 F10
Hyesan, N. Korea 57 D15
Hyland →, Canada 104 B3
Hyltebruk, Sweden 11 H7
Hymia, India 69 C8
Hyndman Peak, U.S.A. . 114 E6
Hyōgo □, Japan 55 G7
Hyrum, U.S.A. 114 F8
Hysham, U.S.A. 114 C10
Hythe, U.K. 13 F9
Hyūga, Japan 55 H5
Hyvinge = Hyvinkää, Finland ... 9 F21
Hyvinkää, Finland 9 F21

I

I-n-Gall, Niger 83 B6
Iablaniţa, Romania 42 F7
Iaco →, Brazil 124 E5
Iacobeni, Romania 43 C10
Iakora, Madag. 89 C8
Ialomiţa □, Romania ... 43 F12
Ialomiţa →, Romania .. 43 F12
Ialoveni, Moldova 43 D13
Ialpug →, Moldova ... 43 F13
Ianca, Romania 43 E12
Iara, Romania 43 D8
Iargara, Moldova 43 D13
Iaşi, Romania 43 C12
Iaşi □, Romania 43 C12
Íasmos, Greece 41 E9
Iba, Phil. 61 D4
Ibadan, Nigeria 83 D5
Ibagué, Colombia 124 C3
Iballja, Albania 40 D4
Ibăneşti, Botoşani, Romania ... 43 B11
Ibăneşti, Mureş, Romania . 43 D9
Ibar →, Serbia, Yug. .. 40 C4
Ibaraki □, Japan 55 F10
Ibarra, Ecuador 124 C3
Ibba, Sudan 81 G2
Ibba, Bahr el →, Sudan . 81 F2
Ibbenbüren, Germany .. 24 C3
Ibembo, Dem. Rep. of the Congo 86 B1
Ibera, L., Argentina ... 126 B4
Iberian Peninsula, Europe 6 H5
Iberville, Canada 102 C5
Iberville, Lac d', Canada . 102 A5
Ibi, Nigeria 83 D6
Ibi, Spain 33 G4
Ibiá, Brazil 125 G9
Ibicuy, Argentina 126 C4
Ibioapaba, Sa. da, Brazil . 125 D10
Ibiza = Eivissa, Spain .. 37 C7
Íblei, Monti, Italy 31 E7
Ibo, Mozam. 87 E5
Ibonma, Indonesia 63 E8
Ibotirama, Brazil 125 F10
Ibrāhīm →, Lebanon .. 75 A4
İbriktepe, Turkey 41 E10
Ibshawâi, Egypt 80 J7
Ibu, Indonesia 63 D7
Ibusuki, Japan 55 J5
Ica, Peru 124 F3
Içana, Brazil 124 C5
Içana →, Brazil 124 C5
İçel = Mersin, Turkey ... 72 D6
Iceland ■, Europe 8 D4
Ich'ang = Yichang, China 59 B8
Ichchapuram, India ... 67 K14
Ichihara, Japan 55 G10
Ichikawa, Japan 55 G9
Ichilo →, Bolivia 124 G6
Ichinohe, Japan 54 D10
Ichinomiya, Japan 55 G8
Ichinoseki, Japan 54 E10
Ichnya, Ukraine 47 G7
Ichŏn, S. Korea 57 F14
Icod, Canary Is. 37 F3
Icy Str., U.S.A. 104 B1

Ida Grove, U.S.A. 112 D7
Ida Valley, Australia ... 93 E3
Idabel, U.S.A. 113 J7
Idaga Hamus, Ethiopia . 81 E4
Idah, Nigeria 83 D6
Idaho □, U.S.A. 114 D7
Idaho City, U.S.A. 114 E6
Idaho Falls, U.S.A. 114 E7
Idaho Springs, U.S.A. . 114 G11
Idanha-a-Nova, Portugal . 34 F3
Idar-Oberstein, Germany . 25 F3
Idfû, Egypt 80 C3
Ídhi Óros, Greece 36 D6
Ídhra, Greece 38 D5
Idi, Indonesia 62 C1
Idiofa, Dem. Rep. of the Congo 84 E3
Idkerberget, Sweden ... 10 D9
Idku, Bahra el, Egypt .. 80 H7
Idlib, Syria 70 C3
Idre, Sweden 10 C6
Idria, U.S.A. 116 J6
Idrija, Slovenia 29 C11
Idritsa, Russia 46 D5
Idutywa, S. Africa 89 E4
Ieper, Belgium 17 D2
Ierápetra, Greece 36 E7
Ierissós, Greece 40 F7
Ierissoú Kólpos, Greece . 40 F7
Iernut, Romania 43 D9
Iesi, Italy 29 E10
Íesolo, Italy 29 C9
Ifach, Peñón de, Spain . 33 G5
'Ifāl, W. al →, Si. Arabia 70 D2
Ifanadiana, Madag. 89 C8
Ife, Nigeria 83 D5
Iférouâne, Niger 83 B6
Iffley, Australia 94 B3
Ifni, Morocco 78 C3
Ifon, Nigeria 83 D6
Iforas, Adrar des, Mali . 83 B5
Ifould, L., Australia ... 93 F5
Iganga, Uganda 86 B3
Igarapava, Brazil 125 H9
Igarka, Russia 50 C9
Igatimi, Paraguay 127 A4
Igbetti, Nigeria 83 D5
Igbo-Ora, Nigeria 83 D5
Igboho, Nigeria 83 D5
Iğdır, Turkey 73 C11
Igelfors, Sweden 11 F9
Iggesund, Sweden 10 C11
Iglésias, Italy 30 C1
Igloolik, Canada 101 B11
Igma, Gebel el, Egypt .. 80 J8
Ignace, Canada 102 C1
Iğneada, Turkey 41 E11
Iğneada Burnu, Turkey . 41 E12
Igoumenítsa, Greece ... 38 B2
Igra, Russia 48 B11
Iguaçu →, Brazil 127 B5
Iguaçu, Cat. del, Brazil . 127 B5
Iguaçu Falls = Iguaçu, Cat. del, Brazil ... 127 B5
Iguala, Mexico 119 D5
Igualada, Spain 32 D6
Iguassu = Iguaçu →, Brazil ... 127 B5
Iguatu, Brazil 125 E11
Igunga □, Tanzania 86 C3
Iharana, Madag. 89 A9
Iheya-Shima, Japan ... 55 L3
Ihiala, Nigeria 83 D6
Ihosy, Madag. 89 C8
Ihotry, L., Madag. 89 C7
Ii, Finland 8 D21
Ii-Shima, Japan 55 L3
Iida, Japan 55 G8
Iijoki →, Finland 8 D21
Iisalmi, Finland 8 E22
Iiyama, Japan 55 F9
Iizuka, Japan 55 H5
Ijebu-Igbo, Nigeria ... 83 D5
Ijebu-Ode, Nigeria ... 83 D5
IJmuiden, Neths. 17 B4
IJssel →, Neths. 17 B5
IJsselmeer, Neths. 17 B5
Ijuí →, Brazil 127 B4
Ikale, Nigeria 83 D6
Ikare, Nigeria 83 D6
Ikaría, Greece 39 D8
Ikast, Denmark 11 H3
Ikeda, Japan 55 G6
Ikeja, Nigeria 83 D5
Ikela, Dem. Rep. of the Congo 84 E4
Ikerre-Ekiti, Nigeria .. 83 D6
Ikhtiman, Bulgaria ... 40 D7
Iki, Japan 55 H4
Ikimba L., Tanzania ... 86 C3
Ikire, Nigeria 83 D5
Ikizdere, Turkey 73 B9
Ikom, Nigeria 83 D6
Ikopa →, Madag. 89 B8
Ikot Ekpene, Nigeria .. 83 D6
Ikungu, Tanzania 86 C3
Ikurun, Nigeria 83 D5
Ila, Nigeria 83 D5
Ilagan, Phil. 61 C4
Ïlâm, Iran 70 C5
Ilam, Nepal 69 F12
Ilanskiy, Russia 51 D10
Ilaro, Nigeria 83 D5
Ilbilbie, Australia 94 C4
Ile-à-la-Crosse, Canada ... 105 B7

Ile-à-la-Crosse, Lac,
  Canada 105 B7
Île-de-France □, France . 19 D9
Ileanda, Romania 43 C8
Ilebo,
  Dem. Rep. of the Congo 84 E4
Ileje □, Tanzania 87 D3
Ilek, Russia 50 D6
Ilero, Nigeria 83 D5
Ilesha, Kwara, Nigeria ... 83 D5
Ilesha, Oyo, Nigeria 83 D5
Ilford, Canada 105 B9
Ilfracombe, Australia ... 94 C3
Ilfracombe, U.K. 13 F3
Ilgaz, Turkey 72 B5
Ilgaz Dağları, Turkey ... 72 B5
Ilgın, Turkey 72 C4
Ílhavo, Portugal 34 E2
Ilhéus, Brazil 125 F11
Ili →, Kazakstan 50 E8
Ilia, Romania 42 E7
Ilia □, Greece 38 D3
Iliç, Turkey 73 C8
Ilıca, Turkey 39 B9
Ilichevsk, Azerbaijan ... 73 C11
Iliff, U.S.A. 112 E3
Iligan, Phil. 61 G6
Iligan Bay, Phil. 61 G6
Ilíkí, L., Greece 38 C5
Ilin I., Phil. 61 E4
Iliodhrómia, Greece 38 B5
Ilion, U.S.A. 111 D9
Ilirska-Bistrica, Slovenia 29 C11
Ilkeston, U.K. 12 E6
Ilkley, U.K. 12 D6
Illampu = Ancohuma,
  Nevada, Bolivia 122 E4
Illana B., Phil. 61 H5
Illapel, Chile 126 C1
Ille-et-Vilaine □, France . 18 D5
Ille-sur-Têt, France ... 20 F6
Iller →, Germany 25 G5
Illertissen, Germany ... 25 G6
Illescas, Spain 34 E7
Illetas, Spain 37 B9
Illichivsk, Ukraine 47 J6
Illiers-Combray, France ... 18 D8
Illimani, Bolivia 124 G5
Illinois □, U.S.A. 107 B9
Illinois →, U.S.A. 107 C8
Illium = Troy, Turkey 39 B8
Illkirch-Graffenstaden,
  France 19 D14
Íllora, Spain 35 H7
Ilm →, Germany 24 D7
Ilmajoki, Finland 9 E20
Ilmen, Ozero, Russia ... 46 C6
Ilmenau, Germany 24 E6
Ilo, Peru 124 G4
Ilobu, Nigeria 83 D5
Iloilo, Phil. 61 F5
Ilora, Nigeria 83 D5
Ilorin, Nigeria 83 D5
Ilovatka, Russia 48 E7
Ilovlya, Russia 49 F7
Ilovlya →, Russia 49 F7
Iłowa, Poland 45 G2
Ilubabor □, Ethiopia ... 81 F4
Ilva Mică, Romania 43 C9
Ilwaco, U.S.A. 116 D2
Ilwaki, Indonesia 63 F7
Ilyichevsk = Illichivsk,
  Ukraine 47 J6
Iłża, Poland 45 G8
Iłżanka →, Poland 45 G8
Imabari, Japan 55 G6
Imaloto →, Madag. 89 C8
İmamoğlu, Turkey 72 D6
Imandra, Ozero, Russia . 50 C4
Imari, Japan 55 H4
Imasa, Sudan 80 D4
Imathía □, Greece 40 F6
Imatra, Finland 46 B5
Imbâbah, Egypt 80 H7
Imbler, U.S.A. 114 D5
imeni 26 Bakinskikh
  Komissarov = Neftçala,
  Azerbaijan 73 C13
Imeri, Serra, Brazil ... 124 C5
Imerimandroso, Madag. .. 89 B8
Imi, Ethiopia 81 F5
Imishly = Imişli,
  Azerbaijan 49 L9
Imişli, Azerbaijan 49 L9
Imlay, U.S.A. 114 F4
Imlay City, U.S.A. 110 D1
Immenstadt, Germany 25 H6
Immingham, U.K. 12 D7
Immokalee, U.S.A. 109 M5
Imo □, Nigeria 83 D6
Ímola, Italy 29 D8
Imotski, Croatia 29 E14
Imperatriz, Brazil 125 E9
Impéria, Italy 28 E5
Imperial, Canada 105 C7
Imperial, Calif., U.S.A. . 117 N11
Imperial, Nebr., U.S.A. . 112 E4
Imperial Beach, U.S.A. . 117 N9
Imperial Dam, U.S.A. ... 117 N12
Imperial Reservoir, U.S.A. 117 N12
Imperial Valley, U.S.A. . 117 N11
Imperieuse Reef, Australia 92 C2
Impfondo, Congo 84 D3
Imphal, India 67 G18
Imphy, France 19 F10
İmranlı, Turkey 73 C8
Imroz = Gökçeada, Turkey 41 F9

İmroz, Turkey 41 F9
Imst, Austria 26 D3
Imuruan B., Phil. 63 B5
In Delimane, Mali 83 B5
In Salah, Algeria 78 C6
In Tallak, Mali 83 B5
Ina, Japan 55 G8
Inangahua Junction, N.Z. . 91 J3
Inanwatan, Indonesia ... 63 E8
Iñapari, Peru 124 F5
Inari, Finland 8 B22
Inarijärvi, Finland 8 B22
Inawashiro-Ko, Japan ... 54 F10
Inca, Spain 37 B9
Incaguasi, Chile 126 B1
İnce Burun, Turkey 72 A6
Incekum Burnu, Turkey .. 72 D5
Inch'ŏn, S. Korea 57 F14
Incio = Cruz de Incio,
  Spain 34 C3
İncirliova, Turkey 39 D9
Incomáti →, Mozam. ... 89 D5
Inda Silase, Ethiopia .. 81 E4
Indal, Sweden 10 B11
Indalsälven →, Sweden . 10 B11
Indaw, Burma 67 G20
Indbir, Ethiopia 81 F4
Independence, Calif.,
  U.S.A. 116 J8
Independence, Iowa,
  U.S.A. 112 D9
Independence, Kans.,
  U.S.A. 113 G7
Independence, Mo., U.S.A. 112 F7
Independence, Oreg.,
  U.S.A. 114 D2
Independence Fjord,
  Greenland 4 A6
Independence Mts., U.S.A. 114 F5
Independenţa, Romania .. 43 E12
Index, U.S.A. 116 C5
India ■, Asia 66 K11
Indian →, U.S.A. 109 M5
Indian Cabins, Canada .. 104 B5
Indian Harbour, Canada . 103 B8
Indian Head, Canada ... 105 C8
Indian Ocean 52 K11
Indian Springs, U.S.A. . 117 J11
Indiana, U.S.A. 110 F5
Indiana □, U.S.A. 108 F3
Indianapolis, U.S.A. ... 108 F2
Indianola, Iowa, U.S.A. . 112 E8
Indianola, Miss., U.S.A. 113 J9
Indigirka →, Russia ... 51 B15
Indija, Serbia, Yug. ... 42 E5
Indio, U.S.A. 117 M10
Indonesia ■, Asia 62 F5
Indore, India 68 H6
Indramayu, Indonesia ... 63 G13
Indravati →, India 67 K12
Indre □, France 19 F8
Indre →, France 18 E7
Indre-et-Loire □, France . 18 E7
Indus →, Pakistan 68 G2
Indus, Mouth of the,
  Pakistan 68 H3
İnebolu, Turkey 72 B5
İnecik, Turkey 41 F11
İnegöl, Turkey 41 F13
Ineu, Romania 42 D6
Infantes = Villanueva de
  los Infantes, Spain .. 35 G7
Infiernillo, Presa del,
  Mexico 118 D4
Infiesto, Spain 34 B5
Ingelstad, Sweden 11 H8
Ingenio, Canary Is. ... 37 G4
Ingenio Santa Ana,
  Argentina 126 B2
Ingersoll, Canada 110 C4
Ingham, Australia 94 B4
Ingleborough, U.K. 12 C5
Inglewood, Queens.,
  Australia 95 D5
Inglewood, Vic., Australia 95 F3
Inglewood, N.Z. 91 H5
Inglewood, U.S.A. 117 M8
Ingólfshöfði, Iceland .. 8 E5
Ingomar, U.S.A. 114 C10
Ingonish, Canada 103 C7
Ingore, Guinea-Biss. ... 82 C1
Ingraj Bazar, India ... 69 G13
Ingrid Christensen Coast,
  Antarctica 5 C6
Ingul → = Inhul →,
  Ukraine 47 J7
Ingulec = Inhulec, Ukraine 47 J7
Ingulets → = Inhulets →,
  Ukraine 47 J7
Inguri → = Enguri →,
  Georgia 49 J5
Ingushetia □, Russia ... 49 J7
Ingwavuma, S. Africa ... 89 D5
Inhaca, I., Mozam. 89 D5
Inhafenga, Mozam. 89 C5
Inhambane, Mozam. 89 C6
Inhambane □, Mozam. ... 89 C5
Inhaminga, Mozam. 87 F4
Inharrime, Mozam. 89 C6
Inharrime →, Mozam. .. 89 C6
Inhisar, Turkey 39 A12
Inhul →, Ukraine 47 J7
Inhulec, Ukraine 47 J7
Inhulets →, Ukraine ... 47 J7
Iniesta, Spain 33 F3
Ining = Yining, China .. 60 B3

Inírida →, Colombia ... 124 C5
Inishbofin, Ireland 15 C1
Inisheer, Ireland 15 C2
Inishfree B., Ireland .. 15 A3
Inishkea North, Ireland . 15 B1
Inishkea South, Ireland . 15 B1
Inishmaan, Ireland 15 C2
Inishmore, Ireland 15 C2
Inishowen Pen., Ireland . 15 A4
Inishshark, Ireland 15 C1
Inishturk, Ireland 15 C1
Inishvickillane, Ireland 15 D1
Injune, Australia 95 D4
Inklin, Canada 104 B2
Inklin →, Canada 104 B2
Inkom, U.S.A. 114 E7
Inle L., Burma 67 J20
Inn →, Austria 26 C6
Innamincka, Australia .. 95 D3
Inner Hebrides, U.K. ... 14 E2
Inner Mongolia = Nei
  Monggol Zizhiqu □,
  China 56 D7
Inner Sound, U.K. 14 D3
Innerkip, Canada 110 C4
Innetalling I., Canada . 102 A4
Innisfail, Australia ... 94 B4
Innisfail, Canada 104 C6
In'no-shima, Japan 55 G6
Innsbruck, Austria 26 D4
Innviertel, Austria ... 26 C6
Inny →, Ireland 15 C4
Inongo,
  Dem. Rep. of the Congo 84 E3
İnönü, Turkey 39 B12
Inoucdjouac = Inukjuak,
  Canada 101 C12
Inowrocław, Poland 45 F5
Inpundong, N. Korea ... 57 D14
Inscription, C., Australia 93 E1
Insein, Burma 67 L20
Insjön, Sweden 10 D9
Ínsko, Poland 44 E2
Însurăţei, Romania 43 F12
Intendente Alvear,
  Argentina 126 D3
İntepe, Turkey 39 A8
Interior, U.S.A. 112 D4
Interlaken, Switz. 25 J3
International Falls, U.S.A. 112 A8
Intiyaco, Argentina ... 126 B3
Întorsura Buzăului,
  Romania 43 E11
Inukjuak, Canada 101 C12
Inútil, B., Chile 128 G2
Inuvik, Canada 100 B6
Inveraray, U.K. 14 E3
Inverbervie, U.K. 14 E6
Invercargill, N.Z. 91 M2
Inverclyde □, U.K. 14 F4
Inverell, Australia ... 95 D5
Invergordon, U.K. 14 D4
Invermere, Canada 104 C5
Inverness, Canada 103 C7
Inverness, U.K. 14 D4
Inverness, U.S.A. 109 L4
Inverurie, U.K. 14 D6
Inverway, Australia ... 92 C4
Investigator Group,
  Australia 95 E1
Investigator Str., Australia 95 F2
Inya, Russia 50 D9
Inyanga, Zimbabwe 87 F3
Inyangani, Zimbabwe ... 87 F3
Inyantue, Zimbabwe 87 F2
Inyo Mts., U.S.A. 115 H5
Inyokern, U.S.A. 117 K9
Inza, Russia 48 D8
Inzhavino, Russia 48 D6
Iō-Jima, Japan 55 J5
Ioánnina, Greece 38 B2
Ioánnina □, Greece 38 B2
Iola, U.S.A. 113 G7
Ion Corvin, Romania ... 43 F12
Iona, U.K. 14 E2
Ione, Calif., U.S.A. .. 116 G6
Ione, Wash., U.S.A. ... 114 B5
Ionia, U.S.A. 108 D3
Ionian Sea, Medit. S. . 6 H9
Iónioi Nísoi □, Greece . 38 C2
Íos, Greece 39 E7
Iowa □, U.S.A. 112 D8
Iowa City, U.S.A. 112 E9
Iowa Falls, U.S.A. 112 D8
Ipala, Tanzania 86 C3
Ipameri, Brazil 125 G9
Ípáti, Greece 38 C4
Ipatinga, Brazil 125 G10
Ipatovo, Russia 49 H6
Ipel' →, Europe 27 D11
Ipiales, Colombia 124 C3
Ipin = Yibin, China ... 58 C5
Ipíros □, Greece 38 B2
Ipixuna, Brazil 124 E4
Ipoh, Malaysia 65 K3
Ippy, C.A.R. 84 C4
Ipsala, Turkey 41 F10
Ipsárion, Óros, Greece . 41 F8
Ipswich, Australia 95 D5
Ipswich, U.K. 13 E9
Ipswich, Mass., U.S.A. . 111 D14
Ipswich, S. Dak., U.S.A. 112 C5
Ipu, Brazil 125 D10
Iqaluit, Canada 101 B13
Iquique, Chile 124 H4
Iquitos, Peru 124 D4
Irabu-Jima, Japan 55 M2

Iracoubo, Fr. Guiana ... 125 B8
Īrafshān, Iran 71 E9
Irahuan, Phil. 61 G3
Iráklia, Kikládhes, Greece 39 E7
Iráklia, Sérrai, Greece . 40 E7
Iráklion, Greece 36 D7
Iráklion □, Greece 36 D7
Irala, Paraguay 127 B5
Iramba □, Tanzania 86 C3
Iran ■, Asia 71 C7
Iran, Gunung-Gunung,
  Malaysia 62 D4
Iran, Plateau of, Asia . 52 F9
Iran Ra. = Iran, Gunung-
  Gunung, Malaysia 62 D4
Īrānshahr, Iran 71 E9
Irapuato, Mexico 118 C4
Iraq ■, Asia 70 C5
Irati, Brazil 127 B5
Irbes saurums, Latvia . 44 A9
Irbid, Jordan 75 C4
Irbid □, Jordan 75 C4
Iregua →, Spain 32 C7
Ireland ■, Europe 15 C4
Irele, Nigeria 83 D6
Irgiz, Bolshaya →, Russia 48 D9
Irhyangdong, N. Korea . 57 D15
Iri, S. Korea 57 G14
Irian Jaya □, Indonesia 63 E9
Irié, Guinea 82 D3
Iriga, Phil. 61 E5
Iringa, Tanzania 86 D4
Iringa □, Tanzania 86 D4
Iriomote-Jima, Japan .. 55 M1
Iriona, Honduras 120 C2
Iriri →, Brazil 125 D8
Irish Republic ■, Europe 15 C3
Irish Sea, U.K. 12 D3
Irkutsk, Russia 51 D11
Irlığanlı, Turkey 39 D11
Irma, Canada 105 C6
Irō-Zaki, Japan 55 G9
Iroise, Mer d', France . 18 D2
Iron Baron, Australia . 95 E2
Iron Gate = Portile de
  Fier, Europe 42 F7
Iron Knob, Australia .. 95 E2
Iron Mountain, U.S.A. . 108 C1
Iron Ra., Australia ... 94 A3
Iron River, U.S.A. 112 B10
Irondequoit, U.S.A. ... 110 C7
Ironstone Kopje, Botswana 88 D3
Ironton, Mo., U.S.A. .. 113 G9
Ironton, Ohio, U.S.A. . 108 F4
Ironwood, U.S.A. 112 B9
Iroquois Falls, Canada . 102 C3
Irosin, Phil. 61 E6
Irpin, Ukraine 47 G6
Irrara Cr. →, Australia 95 D4
Irrawaddy □, Burma 67 L19
Irrawaddy →, Burma ... 67 M19
Irsina, Italy 31 B9
Irtysh →, Russia 50 C7
Irumu,
  Dem. Rep. of the Congo 86 B2
Irún, Spain 32 B3
Irunea = Pamplona, Spain 32 C3
Irurzun, Spain 32 C3
Irvine, Canada 105 D6
Irvine, U.K. 14 F4
Irvine, Calif., U.S.A. . 117 M9
Irvine, Ky., U.S.A. ... 108 G4
Irvinestown, U.K. 15 B4
Irving, U.S.A. 113 J6
Irvona, U.S.A. 110 F6
Irwin →, Australia ... 93 E1
Irymple, Australia 95 E3
Is-sur-Tille, France .. 19 E12
Isa, Nigeria 83 C6
Isaac →, Australia ... 94 C4
Isabel, U.S.A. 112 C4
Isabela, I., Mexico ... 118 C3
Isabela, Phil. 61 H5
Isabela, Cord., Nic. .. 120 D2
Isabella Ra., Australia 92 D3
Isaccea, Romania 43 E13
Isafjarðardjúp, Iceland 8 C2
Ísafjörður, Iceland ... 8 C2
Isagarh, India 68 G7
Isahaya, Japan 55 H5
Isaka, Tanzania 86 C3
Isakly, Russia 48 C10
Isaltis, Romania 43 F8
Isana = Içana →, Brazil 124 C5
Isar →, Germany 25 G8
Isarco →, Italy 29 B8
Ísari, Greece 38 D3
Íscar, Spain 34 D6
İscehisar, Turkey 39 C12
Íschia, Italy 30 B6
Isdell →, Australia ... 92 C3
Ise, Japan 55 G8
Ise-Wan, Japan 55 G8
Isefjord, Denmark 11 J5
Isel →, Austria 26 E5
Iseo, Italy 28 C7
Iseo, L. d', Italy 28 C7
Iseramagazi, Tanzania . 86 C3
Isère □, France 21 C9
Isère →, France 21 D8
Iserlohn, Germany 24 D3
Isérnia, Italy 31 A7
Iseyin, Nigeria 83 D5
Ishigaki-Shima, Japan . 55 M2
Ishikari-Gawa →, Japan 54 C10
Ishikari-Sammyaku, Japan 54 C11
Ishikari-Wan, Japan ... 54 C10

Ishikawa □, Japan 55 F8
Ishim, Russia 50 D7
Ishim →, Russia 50 D8
Ishinomaki, Japan 54 E10
Ishioka, Japan 55 F10
Ishkuman, Pakistan 69 A5
Ishmi, Albania 40 E3
Ishpeming, U.S.A. 108 B2
Isigny-sur-Mer, France . 18 C5
Isıklar Dağı, Turkey .. 41 F11
Işıklı, Turkey 39 C11
Isil Kul, Russia 50 D8
Ísili, Italy 30 C2
Isiolo, Kenya 86 B4
Isiolo □, Kenya 86 B4
Isiro,
  Dem. Rep. of the Congo 86 B2
Isisford, Australia ... 94 C3
İskenderun, Turkey 72 D7
İskenderun Körfezi, Turkey 72 D6
İskilip, Turkey 72 B6
Iskůr →, Bulgaria 41 C8
Iskůr, Yazovir, Bulgaria 40 D7
Iskut →, Canada 104 B2
Isla →, U.K. 14 E5
Isla Cristina, Spain .. 35 H3
Isla Vista, U.S.A. 117 L7
Islâhiye, Turkey 72 D7
Islamabad, Pakistan ... 68 C5
Islamkot, Pakistan 68 G4
Island →, Canada 104 A4
Island Falls, Canada .. 102 C3
Island Falls, U.S.A. .. 103 C6
Island L., Canada 105 C10
Island Lagoon, Australia 95 E2
Island Pond, U.S.A. ... 111 B13
Islands, B. of, Canada . 103 C8
Islay, U.K. 14 F2
Isle →, France 20 D3
Isle aux Morts, Canada . 103 C8
Isle of Wight □, U.K. . 13 G6
Isle Royale, U.S.A. ... 112 B10
Isleta, U.S.A. 115 J10
Isleton, U.S.A. 116 G5
Ismail = Izmayil, Ukraine 47 K5
Ismâ'ilîya, Egypt 80 H8
Ismaning, Germany 25 G7
Isna, Egypt 80 B3
Isogstalo, India 69 B8
Ísola del Liri, Italy . 29 G10
Ísola della Scala, Italy 28 C7
Ísola di Capo Rizzuto, Italy 31 D10
Isparta, Turkey 39 D12
Isperikh, Bulgaria 41 C10
Íspica, Italy 31 F7
Israel ■, Asia 75 D3
Issia, Ivory C. 82 D3
Issoire, France 20 C7
Issoudun, France 19 F8
Issyk-Kul = Ysyk-Köl,
  Kyrgyzstan 52 E11
Issyk-Kul, Ozero = Ysyk-
  Köl, Ozero, Kyrgyzstan 52 E11
Ist, Croatia 29 D11
Istaihah, U.A.E. 71 F7
Istállós-kő, Hungary .. 42 D6
İstanbul, Turkey 41 E12
İstanbul □, Turkey 41 E12
İstanbul Boğazı, Turkey 41 E13
Istiaía, Greece 38 C5
Istok, Serbia, Yug. ... 40 D4
Istokpoga, L., U.S.A. . 109 M5
Istra, Croatia 29 C10
Istres, France 21 E8
Istria = Istra, Croatia 29 C10
Itá, Paraguay 126 B4
Itaberaba, Brazil 125 F10
Itabira, Brazil 125 G10
Itabirito, Brazil 127 A7
Itabuna, Brazil 125 F11
Itacaunas →, Brazil .. 125 E9
Itacoatiara, Brazil ... 124 D7
Itaipú, Reprêsa de, Brazil 127 B5
Itaituba, Brazil 125 D7
Itajaí, Brazil 127 B6
Itajubá, Brazil 127 A6
Itaka, Tanzania 87 D3
Italy ■, Europe 7 G8
Itamaraju, Brazil 125 G11
Itampolo, Madag. 89 C7
Itapecuru-Mirim, Brazil 125 D10
Itaperuna, Brazil 127 A7
Itapetininga, Brazil .. 127 A6
Itapeva, Brazil 127 A6
Itapicuru →, Bahia, Brazil 125 F11
Itapicuru →, Maranhão,
  Brazil 125 D10
Itapipoca, Brazil 125 D11
Itaquari □, Paraguay .. 127 B4
Itaquari, Brazil 127 A7
Itaqui, Brazil 126 B4
Itararé, Brazil 127 A6
Itchen →, U.K. 13 G6
Itéa, Greece 38 C4
Itezhi Tezhi, L., Zambia 87 F2
Ithaca = Itháki, Greece 38 C2
Ithaca, U.S.A. 111 D8
Itháki, Greece 38 C2
Ito, Japan 55 G9
Itoigawa, Japan 55 F8
Iton →, France 18 C8
Itonamas →, Bolivia .. 124 F6

Itri, Italy 30 A6
Itsa, Egypt 80 J7
Íttiri, Italy 30 B1
Ittoqqortoormiit =
  Scoresbysund, Greenland 4 B6
Itu, Brazil 127 A6
Itu, Nigeria 83 D6
Ituiutaba, Brazil 125 G9
Itumbiara, Brazil 125 G9
Ituna, Canada 105 C8
Itunge Port, Tanzania 87 D3
Iturbe, Argentina 126 A2
Ituri →,
  Dem. Rep. of the Congo 86 B2
Iturup, Ostrov, Russia ... 51 E15
Ituxi →, Brazil 124 E6
Ituyuro →, Argentina 126 A3
Itzehoe, Germany 24 B5
Ivaí →, Brazil 127 A5
Ivalo, Finland 8 B22
Ivalojoki →, Finland 8 B22
Ivanava, Belarus 47 F3
Ivančice, Czech Rep. 27 B9
Ivăneşti, Romania 43 D12
Ivangorod, Russia 46 C5
Ivanhoe, N.S.W., Australia 95 E3
Ivanhoe, W. Austral.,
  Australia 92 C4
Ivanhoe, U.S.A. 116 J7
Ivanhoe L., Canada 105 A7
Ivanić Grad, Croatia 29 C13
Ivanjica, Serbia, Yug. ... 40 C4
Ivanjska, Bos.-H. 42 F2
Ivankoyskoye Vdkhr.,
  Russia 46 D9
Ivano-Frankivsk, Ukraine . 47 H3
Ivano-Frankovsk = Ivano-
  Frankivsk, Ukraine 47 H3
Ivanovo = Ivanava, Belarus 47 F3
Ivanovo, Russia 46 D11
Ivanščica, Croatia 29 B13
Ivato, Madag. 89 C8
Ivatsevichy, Belarus 47 F3
Ivaylovgrad, Bulgaria 41 E10
Ivinheima →, Brazil 127 A5
Ivohibe, Madag. 89 C8
Ivory Coast ■, Africa ... 82 D4
Ivösjön, Sweden 11 H8
Ivrea, Italy 28 C4
Ivrindi, Turkey 39 B9
Ivujivik, Canada 101 B12
Ivybridge, U.K. 13 G4
Iwaizumi, Japan 54 E10
Iwaki, Japan 55 F10
Iwakuni, Japan 55 G6
Iwamizawa, Japan 54 C10
Iwanai, Japan 54 C10
Iwata, Japan 55 G8
Iwate □, Japan 54 E10
Iwate-San, Japan 54 E10
Iwo, Nigeria 83 D5
Iwonicz-Zdrój, Poland ... 45 J8
Ixiamas, Bolivia 124 F5
Ixopo, S. Africa 89 E5
Ixtepec, Mexico 119 D5
Ixtlán del Río, Mexico ... 118 C4
Iyo, Japan 55 H6
Izabal, L. de, Guatemala . 120 C2
Izamal, Mexico 119 C7
Izberbash, Russia 49 J8
Izbica, Poland 45 H10
Izbica Kujawska, Poland . 45 F5
Izbiceni, Romania 43 G9
Izena-Shima, Japan 55 L3
Izgrev, Bulgaria 41 C10
Izhevsk, Russia 50 D6
Izmayil, Ukraine 47 K5
Izmir, Turkey 39 C9
Izmir □, Turkey 39 C9
İzmir Körfezi, Turkey ... 39 C9
Izmit = Kocaeli, Turkey . 41 F13
Iznájar, Spain 35 H6
Iznalloz, Spain 35 H7
Iznik, Turkey 72 B3
Iznik Gölü, Turkey 41 F13
Izobil'nyy, Russia 49 H5
Izola, Slovenia 29 C10
Izra, Syria 75 C5
Iztochni Rodopi, Bulgaria 41 E9
Izu-Shotō, Japan 55 G10
Izumi-sano, Japan 55 G7
Izumo, Japan 55 G6
Izyaslav, Ukraine 47 G4
Izyum, Ukraine 47 H9

J

Jaba, Ethiopia 81 F4
Jabal el Awlīya, Sudan .. 81 D3
Jabalón →, Spain 35 G6
Jabalpur, India 69 H8
Jabbūl, Syria 70 B3
Jablah, Syria 70 C3
Jablanac, Croatia 29 D11
Jablanica, Bos.-H. 42 G2
Jablonec nad Nisou,
  Czech Rep. 26 A8
Jablonica, Slovak Rep. .. 27 C10
Jabłonowo Pomorskie,
  Poland 44 E6
Jablunkov, Czech Rep. ... 27 B11
Jaboatão, Brazil 125 E11
Jaboticabal, Brazil 127 A6
Jabukovac, Serbia, Yug. .. 40 B6

Jaca, Spain 32 C4
Jacareí, Brazil 127 A6
Jacarèzinho, Brazil 127 A6
Jackman, U.S.A. 103 C5
Jacksboro, U.S.A. 113 J5
Jackson, Australia 95 D4
Jackson, Ala., U.S.A. ... 109 K2
Jackson, Calif., U.S.A. .. 116 G6
Jackson, Ky., U.S.A. 108 G4
Jackson, Mich., U.S.A. .. 108 D3
Jackson, Minn. U.S.A. .. 112 D7
Jackson, Miss., U.S.A. .. 113 J9
Jackson, Mo., U.S.A. ... 113 G10
Jackson, Ohio, U.S.A. ... 108 F4
Jackson, Tenn., U.S.A. .. 109 H1
Jackson, Wyo., U.S.A. .. 114 E8
Jackson B., N.Z. 91 K2
Jackson L., U.S.A. 114 E8
Jacksons, N.Z. 91 K3
Jacksonville, Ala., U.S.A. 109 J3
Jacksonville, Calif., U.S.A. 116 H6
Jacksonville, Fla., U.S.A. 109 K5
Jacksonville, Ill., U.S.A. 112 F9
Jacksonville, N.C., U.S.A. 109 H7
Jacksonville, Oreg., U.S.A. 114 E2
Jacksonville, Tex., U.S.A. 113 K7
Jacksonville Beach, U.S.A. 109 K5
Jacmel, Haiti 121 C5
Jacob Lake, U.S.A. 115 H7
Jacobabad, Pakistan 68 E3
Jacobina, Brazil 125 F10
Jacques-Cartier, Mt.,
  Canada 103 C6
Jacqueville, Ivory C. 82 D4
Jacuí →, Brazil 127 C5
Jacumba, U.S.A. 117 N10
Jacundá →, Brazil 125 D8
Jade, Germany 24 B4
Jadebusen, Germany 24 B4
Jadotville = Likasi,
  Dem. Rep. of the Congo 87 E2
Jadovnik, Serbia, Yug. ... 40 C3
Jadraque, Spain 32 E2
Jaén, Peru 124 E3
Jaén, Spain 35 H7
Jaén □, Spain 35 H7
Jaffa = Tel Aviv-Yafo,
  Israel 75 C3
Jaffa, C., Australia 95 F2
Jaffna, Sri Lanka 66 Q12
Jagadhri, India 68 D7
Jagadishpur, India 69 G11
Jagdalpur, India 67 K13
Jagersfontein, S. Africa . 88 D4
Jagodina, Serbia, Yug. ... 40 B5
Jagraon, India 66 D9
Jagst →, Germany 25 F5
Jagtial, India 66 K11
Jaguariaíva, Brazil 127 A6
Jaguaribe →, Brazil 125 D11
Jagüey Grande, Cuba 120 B3
Jahangirabad, India 68 E8
Jahrom, Iran 71 D7
Jailolo, Indonesia 63 D7
Jailolo, Selat, Indonesia . 63 D7
Jaipur, India 68 F6
Jajarm, Iran 71 B8
Jajce, Bos.-H. 42 F2
Jakarta, Indonesia 63 G12
Jakobstad = Pietarsaari,
  Finland 8 E20
Jakupica, Macedonia 40 E5
Jal, U.S.A. 113 J3
Jalalabad, Afghan. 68 B4
Jalalabad, India 69 F8
Jalalpur Jattan, Pakistan . 68 C6
Jalama, U.S.A. 117 L6
Jalapa, Guatemala 120 D2
Jalapa Enríquez, Mexico . 119 D5
Jalasjärvi, Finland 9 E20
Jalaun, India 69 F8
Jaleswar, Nepal 69 F11
Jalgaon, Maharashtra, India 66 J10
Jalgaon, Maharashtra, India 66 J9
Jalībah, Iraq 70 D5
Jalingo, Nigeria 83 D7
Jalisco □, Mexico 118 D4
Jalkot, Pakistan 69 B5
Jallas →, Spain 34 C1
Jalna, India 66 K9
Jalón →, Spain 32 D3
Jalpa, Mexico 118 C4
Jalpaiguri, India 67 F16
Jaluit I., Pac. Oc. 96 G8
Jalūlā, Iraq 70 C5
Jamaari, Nigeria 83 C6
Jamaica ■, W. Indies ... 120 C4
Jamalpur, Bangla. 67 G16
Jamalpur, India 69 G12
Jamalpurganj, India 69 H13
Jamanxim →, Brazil 125 D7
Jambi, Indonesia 62 E2
Jambi □, Indonesia 62 E2
Jambusar, India 68 H5
James →, U.S.A. 112 D6
James B., Canada 101 C12
James Ranges, Australia . 92 D5
James Ross I., Antarctica . 5 C18
Jamestown, Australia 95 E2
Jamestown, S. Africa 88 E4
Jamestown, Ky., U.S.A. . 108 G3
Jamestown, N. Dak.,
  U.S.A. 112 B5
Jamestown, N.Y., U.S.A. . 110 D5
Jamestown, Pa., U.S.A. .. 110 E4
Jamestown, Tenn., U.S.A. 109 G3
Jamīlābād, Iran 71 C6

Jamiltepec, Mexico 119 D5
Jämjö, Sweden 11 H9
Jamkhandi, India 66 L9
Jammerbugt, Denmark ... 11 G3
Jammu, India 68 C6
Jammu & Kashmir □, India 69 B7
Jamnagar, India 68 H4
Jampur, Pakistan 68 E4
Jamrud, Pakistan 68 C4
Jämsä, Finland 9 F21
Jamshedpur, India 69 H12
Jamtara, India 69 H12
Jämtland, Sweden 8 E15
Jämtlands län □, Sweden . 10 B7
Jan L., Canada 105 C8
Jan Mayen, Arctic 4 B7
Janakkala, Finland 9 F21
Janaúba, Brazil 125 G10
Jand, Pakistan 68 C5
Jandaq, Iran 71 C7
Jandia, Canary Is. 37 F5
Jandia, Pta. de, Canary Is. 37 F5
Jandola, Pakistan 68 C4
Jandowae, Australia 95 D5
Jándula →, Spain 35 G6
Janesville, U.S.A. 112 D10
Janga, Ghana 83 C4
Janikowo, Poland 45 F5
Janin, West Bank 75 C4
Janinà = Ioánnina □,
  Greece 38 B2
Janja, Bos.-H. 42 F4
Janjevo, Serbia, Yug. 40 D5
Janjina, Croatia 29 F14
Janos, Mexico 118 A3
Jánoshalma, Hungary ... 42 D4
Jánosháza, Hungary 42 C2
Jánossomorja, Hungary .. 42 C1
Janów, Poland 45 H6
Janów Lubelski, Poland .. 45 H9
Janów Podlaski, Poland .. 45 F10
Janowiec Wielkopolski,
  Poland 45 F4
Januária, Brazil 125 G10
Janub Dârfûr □, Sudan .. 81 E2
Janub Kordofân □, Sudan 81 E3
Janubio, Canary Is. 37 F6
Janville, France 19 D8
Janzé, France 18 E5
Jaora, India 66 H6
Japan ■, Asia 55 G8
Japan, Sea of, Asia 54 E7
Japan Trench, Pac. Oc. .. 96 D6
Japen = Yapen, Indonesia 63 E9
Japurá →, Brazil 122 D4
Jaqué, Panama 124 B3
Jarābulus, Syria 70 B3
Jaraicejo, Spain 35 F5
Jaraíz de la Vera, Spain . 34 E5
Jarama →, Spain 34 E7
Jaramānah, Syria 72 F7
Jarandilla, Spain 34 E5
Jaranwala, Pakistan 68 D5
Jarash, Jordan 75 C4
Järbo, Sweden 10 D10
Jardim, Brazil 126 A4
Jardín □, Mexico 33 G2
Jardines de la Reina, Is.,
  Cuba 120 B4
Jargalang, China 57 C12
Jargalant = Hovd,
  Mongolia 60 B4
Jari →, Brazil 125 D8
Jarīr, W. al →, Si. Arabia 70 E4
Järlåsa, Sweden 10 E11
Jarmen, Germany 24 B9
Järna, Kopparberg, Sweden 10 D8
Järna, Stockholm, Sweden 10 E11
Jarnac, France 20 C3
Jarny, France 19 C12
Jarocin, Poland 45 G4
Jaroměř, Czech Rep. 26 A8
Jarosław, Poland 45 H9
Järpås, Sweden 11 F6
Järpen, Sweden 10 A7
Jarrahdale, Australia 93 F2
Jarres, Plaine des, Laos . 64 C4
Jarso, Ethiopia 81 F4
Jartai, China 56 E3
Jarud Qi, China 57 B11
Järvenpää, Finland 9 F21
Jarvis, Canada 110 D4
Jarvis I., Pac. Oc. 97 H12
Jarvornník, Czech Rep. .. 27 A10
Järvsö, Sweden 10 C10
Jarwa, India 69 F10
Jaša Tomić, Serbia, Yug. . 42 E5
Jasień, Poland 45 G2
Jāsimīyah, Iraq 70 C5
Jasin, Malaysia 65 L4
Jāsk, Iran 71 E8
Jasło, Poland 45 J8
Jasmund, Germany 24 A9
Jasper, Alta., Canada ... 104 C5
Jasper, Ont., Canada 111 B9
Jasper, Ala., U.S.A. 109 J2
Jasper, Fla., U.S.A. 109 K4
Jasper, Tex., U.S.A. 113 K8
Jasper Nat. Park, Canada 104 C5
Jastarnia, Poland 44 D5
Jastrebarsko, Croatia ... 29 C12
Jastrowie, Poland 44 E3
Jastrzębie Zdrój, Poland . 45 J5
Jász-Nagykun-Szolnok □,
  Hungary 42 C5
Jászapáti, Hungary 42 C5

Jászárokszállás, Hungary . 42 C4
Jászberény, Hungary 42 C4
Jászkisér, Hungary 42 C5
Jászladány, Hungary 42 C5
Jatai, Brazil 125 G8
Jati, Pakistan 68 G3
Jatibarang, Indonesia ... 63 G13
Jatinegara, Indonesia ... 63 G12
Játiva = Xàtiva, Spain .. 33 G4
Jättendal, Sweden 10 C11
Jaú, Brazil 127 A6
Jaunpur, India 69 G10
Java = Jawa, Indonesia .. 63 G14
Java Sea, Indonesia 62 E3
Java Trench, Ind. Oc. ... 96 H2
Javalambre, Sa. de, Spain 32 E4
Jávea, Spain 33 G5
Javhlant = Ulyasutay,
  Mongolia 60 B4
Jawa, Indonesia 63 G14
Jawor, Poland 45 G3
Jaworzno, Poland 45 H6
Jaworzyna Śląska, Poland . 45 H3
Jay, U.S.A. 113 G7
Jaya, Puncak, Indonesia . 63 E9
Jayanti, India 67 F16
Jayapura, Indonesia 63 E10
Jayawijaya, Pegunungan,
  Indonesia 63 F9
Jaynagar, India 67 F15
Jayrūd, Syria 70 C3
Jayton, U.S.A. 113 J4
Jāzgīn-ye Shīf, Iran 71 D6
Jazminal, Mexico 118 C4
Jazzīn, Lebanon 75 B4
Jean, U.S.A. 117 K11
Jean Marie River, Canada 104 A4
Jean Rabel, Haiti 121 C5
Jeanerette, U.S.A. 113 L9
Jeanette, Ostrov =
  Zhannetty, Ostrov,
  Russia 51 B16
Jeannette, U.S.A. 110 F5
Jebba, Nigeria 83 D5
Jebel, Bahr el →, Sudan . 81 F3
Jebel Qerri, Sudan 81 D3
Jedburgh, U.K. 14 F6
Jedda = Jiddah, Si. Arabia 74 C2
Jedlicze, Poland 45 J8
Jędrzejów, Poland 45 H7
Jedwabne, Poland 45 E9
Jedway, Canada 104 C2
Jeetzel →, Germany 24 B7
Jefferson, Iowa, U.S.A. .. 112 D7
Jefferson, Ohio, U.S.A. .. 110 E4
Jefferson, Tex., U.S.A. .. 113 J7
Jefferson, Wis., U.S.A. .. 112 D10
Jefferson, Mt., Nev.,
  U.S.A. 114 G5
Jefferson, Mt., Oreg.,
  U.S.A. 114 D3
Jefferson City, Mo., U.S.A. 112 F8
Jefferson City, Tenn.,
  U.S.A. 109 G4
Jeffersonville, U.S.A. 108 F3
Jega, Nigeria 83 C5
Jēkabpils, Latvia 9 H21
Jelcz-Laskowice, Poland . 45 G4
Jelenia Góra, Poland 45 H2
Jelenia Góra □, Poland .. 45 G2
Jelgava, Latvia 9 H20
Jelgava □, Latvia 44 B10
Jelica, Serbia, Yug. 40 C4
Jelli, Sudan 81 F3
Jellicoe, Canada 102 C2
Jemaja, Indonesia 65 L5
Jelšava, Slovak Rep. 27 C13
Jemaluang, Malaysia 65 L4
Jember, Indonesia 63 H15
Jembongan, Malaysia ... 62 C5
Jena, Germany 24 E7
Jena, U.S.A. 113 K8
Jenbach, Austria 26 D4
Jenkins, U.S.A. 108 G4
Jenner, U.S.A. 116 G3
Jennings, U.S.A. 113 K8
Jennings →, Canada 104 B2
Jeparit, Australia 95 F3
Jequié, Brazil 125 F10
Jequitinhonha, Brazil ... 125 G10
Jequitinhonha →, Brazil . 125 G11
Jerantut, Malaysia 65 L4
Jérémie, Haiti 121 C5
Jerez, Punta, Mexico ... 119 C5
Jerez de García Salinas,
  Mexico 118 C4
Jerez de la Frontera, Spain 35 J4
Jerez de los Caballeros,
  Spain 35 G4
Jericho = El Arīḥā,
  West Bank 75 D4
Jericho, Australia 94 C4
Jerichow, Germany 24 C8
Jerilderie, Australia 95 F4
Jermyn, U.S.A. 111 E9
Jerome, U.S.A. 115 J8
Jersey, U.K. 13 H5
Jersey City, U.S.A. 111 F10
Jersey Shore, U.S.A. 110 E7
Jerseyville, U.S.A. 112 F9
Jerusalem, Israel 75 D4
Jervis B., Australia 95 F5
Jerzu, Italy 30 C2
Jesenice, Slovenia 29 B11
Jeseník, Czech Rep. 27 A10
Jesenké, Slovak Rep. 27 C13

Jesselton = Kota Kinabalu,
  Malaysia 62 C5
Jessnitz, Germany 24 D8
Jessore, Bangla. 67 H16
Jesup, U.S.A. 109 K5
Jesús Carranza, Mexico . 119 D5
Jesús María, Argentina . 126 C3
Jetmore, U.S.A. 113 F5
Jetpur, India 68 J4
Jeumont, France 19 B11
Jevnaker, Norway 9 F14
Jewett, Ohio, U.S.A. 110 F3
Jewett, Tex., U.S.A. 113 K6
Jewett City, U.S.A. 111 E13
Jeyḥūnābād, Iran 71 C6
Jeypore, India 67 K13
Jeziorak, Jezioro, Poland . 44 E6
Jeziorany, Poland 44 E7
Jeziorka →, Poland 45 F8
Jhajjar, India 68 E7
Jhal Jhao, Pakistan 66 F4
Jhalawar, India 68 G7
Jhang Maghiana, Pakistan 68 D5
Jhansi, India 69 G8
Jharia, India 69 H12
Jharsuguda, India 67 J14
Jhelum, Pakistan 68 C5
Jhelum →, Pakistan 68 D5
Jhunjhunu, India 68 E6
Ji-Paraná, Brazil 124 F6
Ji Xian, Hebei, China ... 56 F8
Ji Xian, Henan, China .. 56 G8
Ji Xian, Shanxi, China .. 56 F6
Jia Xian, Henan, China . 56 H7
Jia Xian, Shaanxi, China . 56 E6
Jiading, China 59 B13
Jiahe, China 59 E9
Jialing Jiang →, China .. 58 C6
Jiamusi, China 60 B8
Ji'an, Jiangxi, China 59 D10
Ji'an, Jilin, China 57 D14
Jianchang, China 57 D11
Jianchangying, China ... 57 D10
Jianchuan, China 58 D2
Jiangbei, China 58 C6
Jiangcheng, China 58 F3
Jiangdi, China 58 D4
Jiange, China 58 A5
Jiangjin, China 58 C6
Jiangkou, China 58 D7
Jiangle, China 59 D11
Jiangling, China 59 B9
Jiangmen, China 59 F9
Jiangshan, China 59 C12
Jiangsu □, China 57 H11
Jiangxi □, China 59 D11
Jiangyin, China 59 B13
Jiangyong, China 59 E8
Jiangyou, China 58 B5
Jianhe, China 58 D7
Jianli, China 59 C9
Jianning, China 59 D11
Jian'ou, China 59 D12
Jianshi, China 58 B7
Jianshui, China 58 F4
Jianyang, Fujian, China . 59 D12
Jianyang, Sichuan, China . 58 B5
Jiao Xian, China 57 F11
Jiaohe, Hebei, China 56 E9
Jiaohe, Jilin, China 57 C14
Jiaoling, China 59 E11
Jiaozhou Wan, China ... 57 F11
Jiaozuo, China 56 G7
Jiashan, China 59 A11
Jiawang, China 57 G9
Jiaxiang, China 56 G9
Jiaxing, China 59 B13
Jiayi = Chiai, Taiwan ... 59 F13
Jiayu, China 59 C9
Jibiya, Nigeria 83 C6
Jibou, Romania 43 C8
Jibuti = Djibouti ■, Africa 81 E5
Jicarón, I., Panama 120 E3
Jičín, Czech Rep. 26 A8
Jiddah, Si. Arabia 74 C2
Jido, India 67 E19
Jieshou, China 56 H8
Jiexiu, China 56 F6
Jieyang, China 59 F11
Jigawa □, Nigeria 83 C6
Jiggalong, Australia 92 D3
Jihlava, Czech Rep. 26 B8
Jihlava →, Czech Rep. .. 27 C9
Jihočeský □, Czech Rep. . 26 B7
Jihomoravský □,
  Czech Rep. 27 B9
Jijiga, Ethiopia 74 F3
Jikamshi, Nigeria 83 C6
Jilin, China 57 C14
Jilin □, China 57 C14
Jiloca →, Spain 32 D3
Jilong = Chilung, Taiwan . 59 E13
Jima, Ethiopia 81 F4
Jimbolia, Romania 42 E5
Jimena de la Frontera,
  Spain 35 J5
Jiménez, Mexico 118 B4
Jimo, China 57 F11
Jin Jiang →, China 59 C10
Jin Xian, Hebei, China .. 56 E8
Jin Xian, Liaoning, China 57 E11
Jinan, China 56 F9
Jincheng, China 56 G7
Jinchuan, China 58 B4
Jind, India 68 E7
Jindabyne, Australia 95 F4

Jindřichův Hradec, Czech Rep. 26 B8
Jing He →, China 56 G5
Jing Shan, China 59 B8
Jing Xian, Anhui, China 59 B12
Jing Xian, Hunan, China 58 D7
Jing'an, China 59 C10
Jingbian, China 56 F5
Jingchuan, China 56 G4
Jingde, China 59 B12
Jingdezhen, China 59 C11
Jingdong, China 58 E3
Jinggu, China 58 F3
Jinghai, China 56 E9
Jinghong, China 58 G3
Jingjiang, China 59 A13
Jingle, China 56 E6
Jingmen, China 59 B9
Jingning, China 56 G3
Jingpo Hu, China 57 C15
Jingshan, China 56 B9
Jingtai, China 56 F3
Jingxi, China 58 F6
Jingxing, China 56 E8
Jingyang, China 56 G5
Jingyu, China 57 C14
Jingyuan, China 56 F3
Jingziguan, China 56 H6
Jinhua, China 59 C12
Jining, Nei Mongol Zizhiqu, China 56 D7
Jining, Shandong, China 56 G9
Jinja, Uganda 86 B3
Jinjang, Malaysia 65 L3
Jinji, China 56 F4
Jinjiang, Fujian, China 59 E12
Jinjiang, Yunnan, China 58 D3
Jinjie, China 58 F6
Jinjini, Ghana 82 D4
Jinkou, China 59 B10
Jinmen Dao, China 59 E12
Jinnah Barrage, Pakistan 66 C7
Jinning, China 58 E4
Jinotega, Nic. 120 D2
Jinotepe, Nic. 120 D2
Jinping, Guizhou, China 58 D7
Jinping, Yunnan, China 58 F4
Jinsha, China 58 D6
Jinsha Jiang →, China 58 C5
Jinshan, China 59 B13
Jinshi, China 59 C8
Jintan, China 59 B12
Jinxi, Jiangxi, China 59 D11
Jinxi, Liaoning, China 57 D11
Jinxian, China 59 C11
Jinxiang, China 56 G9
Jinyun, China 59 C13
Jinzhai, China 59 B10
Jinzhou, China 57 D11
Jiparaná →, Brazil 124 E6
Jipijapa, Ecuador 124 D2
Jiquilpan, Mexico 118 D4
Jishan, China 56 G6
Jishou, China 58 C7
Jishui, China 59 D10
Jisr ash Shughūr, Syria 70 C3
Jitarning, Australia 93 F2
Jitra, Malaysia 65 J3
Jiu →, Romania 43 G8
Jiudengkou, China 56 E4
Jiujiang, Guangdong, China 59 F9
Jiujiang, Jiangxi, China 59 C10
Jiuling Shan, China 59 C10
Jiulong, China 58 C3
Jiuquan, China 60 C4
Jiutai, China 57 B13
Jiuxiangcheng, China 56 H8
Jiuxincheng, China 56 E8
Jiuyuhang, China 59 B12
Jixi, Anhui, China 59 B12
Jixi, Heilongjiang, China 57 B16
Jiyang, China 57 F9
Jīzān, Si. Arabia 74 D3
Jize, China 56 F8
Jizera →, Czech Rep. 26 A7
Jizō-Zaki, Japan 55 G6
Jizzakh, Uzbekistan 50 E7
Joaçaba, Brazil 127 B5
João Pessoa, Brazil 125 E12
Joaquín V. González, Argentina 126 B3
Jobourg, Nez de, France 18 C5
Jódar, Spain 35 H7
Jodhpur, India 68 F5
Jœuf, France 19 C12
Jofane, Mozam. 89 C5
Jõgeva, Estonia 9 G22
Joggins, Canada 103 C7
Jogjakarta = Yogyakarta, Indonesia 63 G14
Johannesburg, S. Africa 89 D4
Johannesburg, U.S.A. 117 K9
Johansfors, Sweden 11 H9
John Day, U.S.A. 114 D4
John Day →, U.S.A. 114 D3
John H. Kerr Reservoir, U.S.A. 109 G6
John o' Groats, U.K. 14 C5
John's Ra., Australia 94 C1
Johnson, U.S.A. 113 G4
Johnson City, N.Y., U.S.A. 111 D9
Johnson City, Tenn., U.S.A. 109 G4
Johnson City, Tex., U.S.A. 113 K5
Johnsonburg, U.S.A. 110 E6

Johnsondale, U.S.A. 117 K8
Johnson's Crossing, Canada 104 A2
Johnston, L., Australia 93 F3
Johnston Falls = Mambilima Falls, Zambia 87 E2
Johnston I., Pac. Oc. 97 F11
Johnstone Str., Canada 104 C3
Johnstown, N.Y., U.S.A. 111 C10
Johnstown, Pa., U.S.A. 110 F6
Johor Baharu, Malaysia 65 M4
Jõhvi, Estonia 9 G22
Joigny, France 19 E10
Joinville, Brazil 127 B6
Joinville, France 19 D12
Joinville I., Antarctica 5 C18
Jojutla, Mexico 119 D5
Jokkmokk, Sweden 8 C18
Jökulsá á Bru →, Iceland 8 D6
Jökulsá á Fjöllum →, Iceland 8 C5
Jolfā, Āzarbājān-e Sharqī, Iran 70 B5
Jolfā, Esfahan, Iran 71 C6
Joliet, U.S.A. 108 E1
Joliette, Canada 102 C5
Jolo, Phil. 61 J4
Jolon, U.S.A. 116 K5
Jomalig, Phil. 61 D5
Jombang, Indonesia 63 G15
Jomda, China 58 B2
Jonava, Lithuania 9 J21
Jones Sound, Canada 4 B3
Jonesboro, Ark., U.S.A. 113 H9
Jonesboro, Ill., U.S.A. 113 G10
Jonesboro, La., U.S.A. 113 J8
Jonesport, U.S.A. 103 D6
Jonglei, Sudan 81 F3
Jonglei □, Sudan 81 F3
Joniškis, Lithuania 9 H20
Jönköping, Sweden 11 G8
Jönköpings län □, Sweden 11 G8
Jonquière, Canada 103 C5
Jonsered, Sweden 11 G6
Jonzac, France 20 C3
Joplin, U.S.A. 113 G7
Jordan, U.S.A. 114 C10
Jordan ■, Asia 75 E5
Jordan →, Asia 75 D4
Jordan Valley, U.S.A. 114 E5
Jordanów, Poland 45 J6
Jorhat, India 67 F19
Jörn, Sweden 8 D19
Jorong, Indonesia 62 E4
Jørpeland, Norway 9 G11
Jorquera →, Chile 126 B2
Jos, Nigeria 83 D6
Jošanička Banja, Serbia, Yug. 40 C4
José Batlle y Ordóñez, Uruguay 127 C4
Joseni, Romania 43 D10
Joseph, U.S.A. 114 D5
Joseph, L., Nfld., Canada 103 B6
Joseph, L., Ont., Canada 110 A5
Joseph Bonaparte G., Australia 92 B4
Joseph City, U.S.A. 115 J8
Joshua Tree, U.S.A. 117 L10
Joshua Tree National Monument, U.S.A. 117 M10
Josselin, France 18 E4
Jostedalsbreen, Norway 9 F12
Jotunheimen, Norway 9 F13
Joué-lès-Tours, France 18 E7
Jourdanton, U.S.A. 113 L5
Joussard, Canada 104 B5
Joutseno, Finland 46 B5
Jovellanos, Cuba 120 B3
Joyeuse, France 21 D8
Józefów, Warszawa, Poland 45 F8
Józefów, Zamość, Poland 45 H10
Ju Xian, China 57 F10
Juan Aldama, Mexico 118 C4
Juan Bautista Alberdi, Argentina 126 C3
Juan de Fuca Str., Canada 116 B3
Juan de Nova, Ind. Oc. 89 B7
Juan Fernández, Arch. de, Pac. Oc. 122 G2
Juan José Castelli, Argentina 126 B3
Juan L. Lacaze, Uruguay 126 C4
Juankoski, Finland 8 E23
Juárez, Argentina 126 D4
Juárez, Mexico 117 N11
Juárez, Sierra de, Mexico 118 A1
Juàzeiro, Brazil 125 E10
Juàzeiro do Norte, Brazil 125 E11
Jûbâ, Sudan 81 G3
Jubayl, Lebanon 75 A4
Jubbah, Si. Arabia 70 D4
Jubbulpore = Jabalpur, India 69 H8
Jübek, Germany 24 A5
Jubga, Russia 49 H4
Jubilee L., Australia 93 E4
Juby, C., Morocco 78 C3
Júcar = Xúquer →, Spain 33 F4
Júcaro, Cuba 120 B4
Juchitán, Mexico 119 D5
Judaea = Har Yehuda, Israel 75 D3
Judenburg, Austria 26 D7
Judith →, U.S.A. 114 C9
Judith, Pt., U.S.A. 111 E13
Judith Gap, U.S.A. 114 C9
Juelsminde, Denmark 11 J4

Jugoslavia = Yugoslavia ■, Europe 40 C4
Juigalpa, Nic. 120 D2
Juillac, France 20 C5
Juist, Germany 24 B2
Juiz de Fora, Brazil 127 A7
Jujuy □, Argentina 126 A2
Juli, Peru 124 G5
Julia Cr. →, Australia 94 C3
Julia Creek, Australia 94 C3
Juliaca, Peru 124 G4
Julian, U.S.A. 117 M10
Julian Alps = Julijske Alpe, Slovenia 29 B11
Julianatop, Surinam 125 C7
Julianehåb, Greenland 4 C5
Jülich, Germany 24 E2
Julijske Alpe, Slovenia 29 B11
Julimes, Mexico 118 B3
Jullundur, India 68 D6
Julu, China 56 F8
Jumbo, Zimbabwe 87 F3
Jumbo Pk., U.S.A. 117 J12
Jumentos Cays, Bahamas 121 B4
Jumilla, Spain 33 G3
Jumla, Nepal 69 E10
Jumna = Yamuna →, India 69 G9
Junagadh, India 68 J4
Junction, Tex., U.S.A. 113 K5
Junction, Utah, U.S.A. 115 G7
Junction B., Australia 94 A1
Junction City, Kans., U.S.A. 112 F6
Junction City, Oreg., U.S.A. 114 D2
Junction Pt., Australia 94 A1
Jundah, Australia 94 C3
Jundiaí, Brazil 127 A6
Juneau, U.S.A. 100 C6
Junee, Australia 95 E4
Jungfrau, Switz. 25 J3
Junggar Pendi, China 60 B3
Jungshahi, Pakistan 68 G2
Juniata →, U.S.A. 110 F7
Junín, Argentina 126 C3
Junín de los Andes, Argentina 128 D2
Jūniyah, Lebanon 75 B4
Juntura, U.S.A. 114 E4
Jupiter →, Canada 103 C7
Jur, Nahr el →, Sudan 81 F2
Jura = Jura, Mts. du, Europe 19 F13
Jura = Schwäbische Alb, Germany 25 G5
Jura, U.K. 14 F3
Jura □, France 19 F12
Jura □, Switz. 25 H3
Jūra →, Lithuania 44 C9
Jura, Mts. du, Europe 19 F13
Jura, Sd. of, U.K. 14 F3
Jurbarkas, Lithuania 44 C9
Jurilovca, Romania 43 F13
Jūrmala, Latvia 9 H20
Jurong, China 59 B12
Juruá →, Brazil 122 D4
Juruena, Brazil 124 F7
Juruena →, Brazil 124 E7
Juruti, Brazil 125 D7
Jussey, France 19 E12
Justo Daract, Argentina 126 C2
Jutaí →, Brazil 124 D5
Jüterbog, Germany 24 D9
Juticalpa, Honduras 120 D2
Jutland = Jylland, Denmark 11 H3
Juventud, I. de la, Cuba 120 B3
Juvigny-sous-Andaine, France 18 D6
Juwain, Afghan. 66 D2
Jūy Zar, Iran 70 C5
Juye, China 56 G9
Juzennecourt, France 19 D11
Jvari, Georgia 49 J6
Jyderup, Denmark 11 J5
Jylland, Denmark 11 H3
Jyväskylä, Finland 9 E21

K

K2, Pakistan 69 B7
Kaap Plateau, S. Africa 88 D3
Kaapkruis, Namibia 88 C1
Kaapstad = Cape Town, S. Africa 88 E2
Kabaena, Indonesia 63 F6
Kabala, S. Leone 82 D2
Kabale, Uganda 86 C3
Kabalo, Dem. Rep. of the Congo 86 D2
Kabambare, Dem. Rep. of the Congo 86 C2
Kabango, Dem. Rep. of the Congo 87 D2
Kabanjahe, Indonesia 62 D1
Kabankalan, Phil. 61 G5
Kabara, Mali 82 B4
Kabardinka, Russia 47 K10
Kabardino-Balkar Republic = Kabardino-Balkaria □, Russia 49 J6

Kabardino-Balkaria □, Russia 49 J6
Kabarega Falls = Murchison Falls, Uganda 86 B3
Kabasalan, Phil. 61 H5
Kabba, Nigeria 83 D6
Kabinakagami L., Canada 102 C3
Kabna, Sudan 80 D3
Kabompo, Zambia 87 E1
Kabompo →, Zambia 85 G4
Kabondo, Dem. Rep. of the Congo 87 D2
Kabongo, Dem. Rep. of the Congo 86 D2
Kabou, Togo 83 D5
Kabra, Australia 94 C5
Kabūd Gonbad, Iran 71 B8
Kabugao, Phil. 61 B4
Kābul, Afghan. 68 B3
Kābul □, Afghan. 66 B6
Kabul →, Pakistan 68 C5
Kabunga, Dem. Rep. of the Congo 86 C2
Kaburuang, Indonesia 63 D7
Kabushiya, Sudan 81 D3
Kabwe, Zambia 87 E2
Kačanik, Serbia, Yug. 40 D5
Kačerginė, Lithuania 44 D10
Kachchh, Gulf of, India 68 H3
Kachchh, Rann of, India 68 H4
Kachebera, Zambia 87 E3
Kachin □, Burma 67 G20
Kachira, L., Uganda 86 C3
Kachiry, Kazakstan 50 D8
Kachisi, Ethiopia 81 F4
Kachot, Cambodia 65 G4
Kaçkar, Turkey 73 B9
Kadan, Czech Rep. 26 A6
Kadan Kyun, Burma 64 F2
Kadanai →, Afghan. 68 D1
Kadarkút, Hungary 42 D2
Kade, Ghana 83 D4
Kadi, India 68 H5
Kadina, Australia 95 E2
Kadınhanı, Turkey 72 C5
Kadirli, Turkey 72 D7
Kadiyevka = Stakhanov, Ukraine 47 H10
Kadoka, U.S.A. 112 D4
Kadom, Russia 48 C6
Kadoma, Zimbabwe 87 F2
Kâdugli, Sudan 81 E2
Kaduna, Nigeria 83 C6
Kaduna □, Nigeria 83 C6
Kaduy, Russia 46 C9
Kaédi, Mauritania 82 B2
Kaélé, Cameroon 83 C7
Kaeng Khoï, Thailand 64 E3
Kaesŏng, N. Korea 57 F14
Kāf, Si. Arabia 70 D3
Kafan = Kapan, Armenia 73 C12
Kafanchan, Nigeria 83 D6
Kafareti, Nigeria 83 C7
Kaffrine, Senegal 82 C1
Kafinda, Zambia 87 E3
Kafirévs, Ákra, Greece 38 C6
Kafr el Dauwâr, Egypt 80 H7
Kafr el Sheikh, Egypt 80 H7
Kafue, Zambia 87 F2
Kafue →, Zambia 85 H5
Kafue Flats, Zambia 87 F2
Kafue Nat. Park, Zambia 87 F2
Kafulwe, Zambia 87 D2
Kaga, Afghan. 68 B4
Kaga Bandoro, C.A.R. 84 C3
Kagan, Uzbekistan 50 F7
Kagawa □, Japan 55 G7
Kagera □, Tanzania 86 C3
Kagera →, Uganda 86 C3
Kağızman, Turkey 73 B10
Kagoshima, Japan 55 J5
Kagoshima □, Japan 55 J5
Kagul = Cahul, Moldova 43 E13
Kahak, Iran 71 B6
Kahama, Tanzania 86 C3
Kahama □, Tanzania 86 C3
Kahang, Malaysia 65 L4
Kahayan →, Indonesia 62 E4
Kahe, Tanzania 86 C4
Kahniah →, Canada 104 B4
Kahnūj, Iran 71 E8
Kahoka, U.S.A. 112 E9
Kahoolawe, U.S.A. 106 H16
Kahramanmaraş, Turkey 72 D7
Kâhta, Turkey 73 D8
Kahuta, Pakistan 68 C5
Kai, Kepulauan, Indonesia 63 F8
Kai Besar, Indonesia 63 F8
Kai Is. = Kai, Kepulauan, Indonesia 63 F8
Kai Kecil, Indonesia 63 F8
Kai Xian, China 58 B7
Kaiama, Nigeria 83 D5
Kaiapoi, N.Z. 91 K4
Kaieteur Falls, Guyana 124 B7
Kaifeng, China 56 G8
Kaihua, China 59 C12
Kaikohe, N.Z. 91 F4
Kaikoura, N.Z. 91 K4
Kaikoura Ra., N.Z. 91 J4
Kaili, China 58 D6
Kailu, China 57 C11
Kailua Kona, U.S.A. 106 J17
Kaimana, Indonesia 63 E8
Kaimanawa Mts., N.Z. 91 H5

Kaimganj, India 69 F8
Kaimur Hills, India 69 G10
Kaingaroa Forest, N.Z. 91 H6
Kainji Res., Nigeria 83 C5
Kainuu, Finland 8 D23
Kaipara Harbour, N.Z. 91 G5
Kaiping, China 59 F9
Kaipokok B., Canada 103 B8
Kaironi, Indonesia 63 E8
Kairouan, Tunisia 79 A8
Kaiserslautern, Germany 25 F3
Kaiserstuhl, Germany 25 G3
Kaitaia, N.Z. 91 F4
Kaitangata, N.Z. 91 M2
Kaithal, India 68 E7
Kaitu →, Pakistan 68 C4
Kaiwi Channel, U.S.A. 106 H16
Kaiyang, China 58 D6
Kaiyuan, Liaoning, China 57 C13
Kaiyuan, Yunnan, China 58 F4
Kajaani, Finland 8 D22
Kajabbi, Australia 94 C3
Kajana = Kajaani, Finland 8 D22
Kajang, Malaysia 65 L3
Kajaran, Armenia 73 C12
Kajiado, Kenya 86 C4
Kajiado □, Kenya 86 C4
Kajo Kaji, Sudan 81 G3
Kaka, Sudan 81 E3
Kakabeka Falls, Canada 102 C2
Kakamas, S. Africa 88 D3
Kakamega, Kenya 86 B3
Kakamega □, Kenya 86 B3
Kakanj, Bos.-H. 42 F3
Kakanui Mts., N.Z. 91 L3
Kake, Japan 55 G6
Kakegawa, Japan 55 G9
Kakeroma-Jima, Japan 55 K4
Kakhib, Russia 49 J8
Kakhovka, Ukraine 47 J7
Kakhovske Vdskh., Ukraine 47 J7
Kakinada, India 67 L13
Kakisa →, Canada 104 A5
Kakisa L., Canada 104 A5
Kakogawa, Japan 55 G7
Kakwa →, Canada 104 C5
Kāl Gūsheh, Iran 71 D8
Kal Safid, Iran 70 C5
Kala, Nigeria 83 C7
Kalabagh, Pakistan 68 C4
Kalabahi, Indonesia 63 F6
Kalábáka, Greece 38 B3
Kalach, Russia 48 E5
Kalach na Donu, Russia 49 F6
Kaladan →, Burma 67 J18
Kaladar, Canada 110 B7
Kalahari, Africa 88 C3
Kalahari Gemsbok Nat. Park, S. Africa 88 D3
Kalajoki, Finland 8 D20
Kālak, Iran 71 E8
Kalakamati, Botswana 89 C4
Kalakan, Russia 51 D12
Kalakh, Syria 70 C3
K'alak'unlun Shank'ou, Pakistan 69 B7
Kalam, Pakistan 69 B5
Kalama, Dem. Rep. of the Congo 86 C2
Kalama, U.S.A. 116 E4
Kalámai, Greece 38 D4
Kalamariá, Greece 40 F6
Kalamata = Kalámai, Greece 38 D4
Kalamazoo, U.S.A. 108 D3
Kalamazoo →, U.S.A. 108 D2
Kalambo Falls, Tanzania 87 D3
Kálamos, Attikí, Greece 38 C5
Kálamos, Iónioi Nísoi, Greece 38 C2
Kalannie, Australia 93 F2
Kalāntarī, Iran 71 C7
Kalao, Indonesia 63 F6
Kalaotoa, Indonesia 63 F6
Kälarne, Sweden 10 B10
Kalasin, Thailand 64 D4
Kalat, Pakistan 66 E5
Kalāteh, Iran 71 B7
Kalāteh-ye-Ganj, Iran 71 E8
Kálathos, Greece 39 E10
Kalaus →, Russia 49 H7
Kalávrita, Greece 38 C4
Kalbarri, Australia 93 E1
Kale, Antalya, Turkey 39 E12
Kale, Denizli, Turkey 39 D10
Kalecik, Turkey 72 B5
Kalegauk Kyun, Burma 67 M20
Kalehe, Dem. Rep. of the Congo 86 C2
Kalema, Tanzania 86 C3
Kalemie, Dem. Rep. of the Congo 86 D2
Kalety, Poland 45 H6
Kalewa, Burma 67 H19
Kalgan = Zhangjiakou, China 56 D8
Kalgoorlie-Boulder, Australia 93 F3
Kaliakra, Nos, Bulgaria 41 C12
Kalianda, Indonesia 62 F3
Kalibo, Phil. 61 F5
Kaliganj, Bangla. 69 H13
Kalima, Dem. Rep. of the Congo 86 C2
Kalimantan □, Indonesia 62 E4

Kalimantan Barat □, Indonesia ... 62 E4
Kalimantan Selatan □, Indonesia ... 62 E5
Kalimantan Tengah □, Indonesia ... 62 E4
Kalimantan Timur □, Indonesia ... 62 D5
Kálimnos, Greece ... 39 E8
Kalimpong, India ... 69 F13
Kalinin = Tver, Russia ... 46 D8
Kaliningrad, Russia ... 9 J19
Kalininsk, Russia ... 48 E7
Kalinkavichy, Belarus ... 47 F5
Kalinkovichi = Kalinkavichy, Belarus ... 47 F5
Kalinovik, Bos.-H. ... 40 C2
Kalipetrovo, Bulgaria ... 41 B11
Kaliro, Uganda ... 86 B3
Kalirrákhi, Greece ... 41 F8
Kalispell, U.S.A. ... 114 A6
Kalisz, Poland ... 45 G5
Kalisz □, Poland ... 45 G4
Kalisz Pomorski, Poland ... 45 E2
Kaliua, Tanzania ... 86 D3
Kalívia Thorikoú, Greece ... 38 D5
Kalix, Sweden ... 8 D20
Kalix →, Sweden ... 8 D20
Kalka, India ... 68 D7
Kalkan, Turkey ... 39 E11
Kalkaska, U.S.A. ... 108 C3
Kalkfeld, Namibia ... 88 C2
Kalkfontein, Botswana ... 88 C3
Kalkım, Turkey ... 39 B9
Kalkrand, Namibia ... 88 C2
Kållandsö, Sweden ... 11 F7
Kallavesi, Finland ... 8 E22
Källby, Sweden ... 11 F7
Kållered, Sweden ... 11 G6
Kallimasiá, Greece ... 39 C8
Kallinge, Sweden ... 11 H9
Kallithéa, Greece ... 38 D5
Kallmeti, Albania ... 40 E3
Kalloní, Greece ... 39 B8
Kallonís, Kólpos, Greece ... 39 B8
Kallsjön, Sweden ... 8 E15
Kalmalo, Nigeria ... 83 C6
Kalmar, Sweden ... 11 H10
Kalmar län □, Sweden ... 11 G10
Kalmar sund, Sweden ... 11 H10
Kalmyk Republic = Kalmykia □, Russia ... 49 G8
Kalmykia □, Russia ... 49 G8
Kalmykovo, Kazakstan ... 50 E6
Kalna, Russia ... 69 H13
Kalocsa, Hungary ... 42 D4
Kalofer, Bulgaria ... 41 D8
Kalokhorio, Cyprus ... 36 E12
Kaloko, Dem. Rep. of the Congo ... 86 D2
Kalol, Gujarat, India ... 68 H5
Kalol, Gujarat, India ... 68 H5
Kalolímnos, Greece ... 39 D9
Kalomo, Zambia ... 87 F2
Kalonerón, Greece ... 38 D3
Kalpi, India ... 69 F8
Kaltern = Caldaro, Italy ... 29 B8
Kaltungo, Nigeria ... 83 D7
Kalu, Pakistan ... 68 G2
Kaluga, Russia ... 46 E9
Kalulushi, Zambia ... 87 E2
Kalundborg, Denmark ... 11 J5
Kalush, Ukraine ... 47 H3
Kałuszyn, Poland ... 45 F8
Kalutara, Sri Lanka ... 66 R12
Kalvarija, Lithuania ... 44 D10
Kalyazin, Russia ... 46 D9
Kama, Dem. Rep. of the Congo ... 86 C2
Kama →, Russia ... 6 D16
Kamachumu, Tanzania ... 86 C3
Kamaishi, Japan ... 54 E10
Kamalia, Pakistan ... 68 D5
Kaman, Turkey ... 72 C5
Kamapanda, Zambia ... 87 E1
Kamaran, Yemen ... 74 D3
Kamativi, Zimbabwe ... 87 F2
Kamba, Nigeria ... 83 C5
Kambalda, Australia ... 93 F3
Kambar, Pakistan ... 68 F3
Kambia, S. Leone ... 82 D2
Kambolé, Zambia ... 87 D3
Kambos, Cyprus ... 36 D11
Kambove, Dem. Rep. of the Congo ... 87 E2
Kamchatka, Poluostrov, Russia ... 51 D17
Kamchatka Pen. = Kamchatka, Poluostrov, Russia ... 51 D17
Kamchiya →, Bulgaria ... 41 C11
Kamen, Russia ... 50 D9
Kamen-Rybolov, Russia ... 54 B6
Kamenica, Serbia, Yug. ... 40 C4
Kamenica, Serbia, Yug. ... 40 B3
Kamenice nad Lipou, Czech Rep. ... 26 B8
Kamenjak, Rt., Croatia ... 29 D10
Kamenka = Kaminka, Ukraine ... 47 H7
Kamenka, Kazakstan ... 48 E10
Kamenka, Penza, Russia ... 48 D6
Kamenka, Voronezh, Russia ... 47 G10
Kamenka Bugskaya = Kamyanka-Buzka, Ukraine ... 47 G3

Kamenka Dneprovskaya = Kamyanka-Dniprovska, Ukraine ... 47 J8
Kamennomostskiy, Russia ... 49 H5
Kameno, Bulgaria ... 41 D11
Kamenolomini, Russia ... 49 G5
Kamensk-Shakhtinskiy, Russia ... 49 F5
Kamensk Uralskiy, Russia ... 50 D7
Kamenskiy, Russia ... 48 E7
Kamenskoye, Russia ... 51 C17
Kamenyak, Bulgaria ... 41 C10
Kamenz, Germany ... 24 D10
Kameoka, Japan ... 55 G7
Kami, Albania ... 40 D4
Kamiah, U.S.A. ... 114 C5
Kamień Krajeński, Poland ... 44 E4
Kamień Pomorski, Poland ... 44 E1
Kamienna →, Poland ... 45 G8
Kamienna Góra, Poland ... 45 H3
Kamieńsk, Poland ... 45 G6
Kamieskroon, S. Africa ... 88 E2
Kamilukuak, L., Canada ... 105 A8
Kamin-Kashyrskyy, Ukraine ... 47 G3
Kamina, Dem. Rep. of the Congo ... 87 D2
Kaminak L., Canada ... 105 A10
Kaminka, Ukraine ... 47 H7
Kaminoyama, Japan ... 54 E10
Kamiros, Greece ... 36 C9
Kamituga, Dem. Rep. of the Congo ... 86 C2
Kamloops, Canada ... 104 C4
Kamnik, Slovenia ... 29 B11
Kamo, Armenia ... 49 K7
Kamo, Japan ... 54 F9
Kamoke, Pakistan ... 68 C6
Kamp →, Austria ... 26 C8
Kampala, Uganda ... 86 B3
Kampang Chhnang, Cambodia ... 65 F5
Kampar, Malaysia ... 65 K3
Kampar →, Indonesia ... 62 D2
Kampen, Neths. ... 17 B5
Kamphaeng Phet, Thailand ... 64 D2
Kampolombo, L., Zambia ... 87 E2
Kampong Saom, Cambodia ... 65 G4
Kampong Saom, Chaak, Cambodia ... 65 G4
Kampong To, Thailand ... 65 J3
Kampot, Cambodia ... 65 G5
Kampti, Burkina Faso ... 82 C4
Kampuchea = Cambodia ■, Asia ... 64 F5
Kampung Air Putih, Malaysia ... 65 K4
Kampung Jerangau, Malaysia ... 65 K4
Kampung Raja, Malaysia ... 65 K4
Kampungbaru = Tolitoli, Indonesia ... 63 D6
Kamrau, Teluk, Indonesia ... 63 E8
Kamsack, Canada ... 105 C8
Kamskoye Ustye, Russia ... 48 C9
Kamuchawie L., Canada ... 105 B8
Kamui-Misaki, Japan ... 54 C10
Kamyanets-Podilskyy, Ukraine ... 47 H4
Kamyanka-Buzka, Ukraine ... 47 G3
Kamyanka-Dniprovska, Ukraine ... 47 J8
Kāmyārān, Iran ... 70 C5
Kamyshin, Russia ... 48 E7
Kamyzyak, Russia ... 49 G9
Kanaaupscow, Canada ... 102 B4
Kanaaupscow →, Canada ... 101 C12
Kanab, U.S.A. ... 115 H7
Kanab →, U.S.A. ... 115 H7
Kanagi, Japan ... 54 D10
Kanairiktok →, Canada ... 103 A7
Kanália, Greece ... 38 B4
Kananga, Dem. Rep. of the Congo ... 84 F4
Kanarraville, U.S.A. ... 115 H7
Kanash, Russia ... 48 C8
Kanaskat, U.S.A. ... 116 C5
Kanastraíon, Ákra = Palioúrion, Ákra, Greece ... 40 G7
Kanawha →, U.S.A. ... 108 F4
Kanazawa, Japan ... 55 F8
Kanchanaburi, Thailand ... 64 E2
Kanchenjunga, Nepal ... 69 F13
Kanchipuram, India ... 66 N11
Kańczuga, Poland ... 45 J9
Kandahar = Qandahār, Afghan. ... 66 D4
Kandalaksha, Russia ... 50 C4
Kandalu, Afghan. ... 66 E3
Kandangan, Indonesia ... 62 E5
Kandanos, Greece ... 36 D5
Kandava, Latvia ... 44 A9
Kandhíla, Greece ... 38 D4
Kandhkot, Pakistan ... 68 E3
Kandhla, India ... 68 E7
Kandi, Benin ... 83 C5
Kandi, India ... 69 H13
Kandra, Turkey ... 72 B4
Kandla, India ... 68 H4
Kandos, Australia ... 95 E4
Kandy, Sri Lanka ... 66 R12
Kane, U.S.A. ... 110 E6
Kane Basin, Greenland ... 4 B4
Kanevskaya, Russia ... 49 G4
Kanfanar, Croatia ... 29 C10
Kangaba, Mali ... 82 C3
Kangal, Turkey ... 72 C7
Kangān, Fārs, Iran ... 71 E7

Kangān, Hormozgān, Iran ... 71 E8
Kangar, Malaysia ... 65 J3
Kangaroo I., Australia ... 95 F2
Kangasala, Finland ... 9 F21
Kangāvar, Iran ... 71 C6
Kangding, China ... 58 B3
Kangdong, N. Korea ... 57 E14
Kangean, Kepulauan, Indonesia ... 62 F5
Kangean Is. = Kangean, Kepulauan ... 62 F5
Kanggye, N. Korea ... 57 D14
Kanggyŏng, S. Korea ... 57 F14
Kanghwa, S. Korea ... 57 F14
Kangiqsualujjuaq, Canada ... 101 C13
Kangiqsujuaq, Canada ... 101 B12
Kangirsuk, Canada ... 101 C13
Kangnŭng, S. Korea ... 57 F15
Kangping, China ... 57 C12
Kangto, India ... 67 F18
Kani, Ivory C. ... 82 D3
Kaniama, Dem. Rep. of the Congo ... 86 D1
Kaniapiskau →, Canada ... 103 A6
Kaniapiskau L., Canada ... 103 B6
Kanin, Poluostrov, Russia ... 50 C5
Kanin Nos, Mys, Russia ... 50 C5
Kanin Pen. = Kanin, Poluostrov, Russia ... 50 C5
Kanina, Albania ... 40 F3
Kaniva, Australia ... 95 F3
Kanjiža, Serbia, Yug. ... 42 D5
Kanjut Sar, Pakistan ... 69 A6
Kankaanpää, Finland ... 9 F20
Kankakee, U.S.A. ... 108 E2
Kankakee →, U.S.A. ... 108 E1
Kankan, Guinea ... 82 C3
Kankendy = Xankändi, Azerbaijan ... 73 C12
Kanker, India ... 67 J12
Kannapolis, U.S.A. ... 109 H5
Kannauj, India ... 69 F8
Kannod, India ... 66 H10
Kano, Nigeria ... 83 C6
Kano □, Nigeria ... 83 C6
Kan'onji, Japan ... 55 G6
Kanoroba, Ivory C. ... 82 D3
Kanowit, Malaysia ... 62 D4
Kanowna, Australia ... 93 F3
Kanoya, Japan ... 55 J5
Kanpetlet, Burma ... 67 J18
Kanpur, India ... 69 F9
Kansas □, U.S.A. ... 112 F6
Kansas →, U.S.A. ... 112 F7
Kansas City, Kans., U.S.A. ... 112 F7
Kansas City, Mo., U.S.A. ... 112 F7
Kansenia, Dem. Rep. of the Congo ... 87 E2
Kansk, Russia ... 51 D10
Kansŏng, S. Korea ... 57 E15
Kansu = Gansu □, China ... 56 G3
Kantché, Niger ... 83 C6
Kanté, Togo ... 83 D5
Kantemirovka, Russia ... 47 H10
Kantharalak, Thailand ... 64 E5
Kantō □, Japan ... 55 F9
Kantō-Sanchi, Japan ... 55 G9
Kanturk, Ireland ... 15 D3
Kanuma, Japan ... 55 F9
Kanus, Namibia ... 88 D2
Kanye, Botswana ... 88 C4
Kanzenze, Dem. Rep. of the Congo ... 87 E2
Kanzi, Ras, Tanzania ... 86 D4
Kaohsiung, Taiwan ... 59 F13
Kaokoveld, Namibia ... 88 B1
Kaolack, Senegal ... 82 C1
Kaoshan, China ... 57 B13
Kapadvanj, India ... 68 H5
Kapaklı, Turkey ... 41 E11
Kapan, Armenia ... 73 C12
Kapanga, Dem. Rep. of the Congo ... 84 F4
Kapchagai = Qapshaghay, Kazakstan ... 50 E8
Kapela = Velika Kapela, Croatia ... 29 C12
Kapéllo, Ákra, Greece ... 38 E5
Kapema, Dem. Rep. of the Congo ... 87 E2
Kapfenberg, Austria ... 26 D8
Kapı Dağı, Turkey ... 41 F11
Kapiri Mposhi, Zambia ... 87 E2
Kapiskau →, Canada ... 102 B3
Kapit, Malaysia ... 62 D4
Kapiti I., N.Z. ... 91 J5
Kaplice, Czech Rep. ... 26 C7
Kapoe, Thailand ... 65 H2
Kapoeta, Sudan ... 81 G3
Kapos →, Hungary ... 42 D3
Kaposvár, Hungary ... 42 D2
Kapowsin, U.S.A. ... 116 D4
Kappeln, Germany ... 24 A5
Kappelshamn, Sweden ... 11 G12
Kapsan, N. Korea ... 57 D15
Kapsukas = Marijampolė, Lithuania ... 9 J20
Kapuas →, Indonesia ... 62 E3
Kapuas Hulu, Pegunungan, Malaysia ... 62 D4
Kapuas Hulu Ra. = Kapuas Hulu, Pegunungan, Malaysia ... 62 D4

Kapulo, Dem. Rep. of the Congo ... 87 D2
Kapunda, Australia ... 95 E2
Kapuni, N.Z. ... 91 H5
Kapurthala, India ... 68 D6
Kapuskasing, Canada ... 102 C3
Kapuskasing →, Canada ... 102 C3
Kaputar, Australia ... 95 E5
Kaputir, Kenya ... 86 B4
Kapuvár, Hungary ... 42 C2
Kara, Russia ... 50 C7
Kara Bogaz Gol, Zaliv = Garabogazköl Aylagy, Turkmenistan ... 50 E6
Kara Burun, Turkey ... 39 E9
Kara Kalpak Republic = Karakalpakstan □, Uzbekistan ... 50 E6
Kara Kum, Turkmenistan ... 50 F7
Kara Sea, Russia ... 50 B8
Karaadilli, Turkey ... 39 C12
Karabiğa, Turkey ... 41 F11
Karabük, Turkey ... 72 B5
Karaburun, Turkey ... 39 C8
Karaburuni, Albania ... 40 F3
Karabutak = Qarabutaq, Kazakstan ... 50 E7
Karacabey, Turkey ... 41 F12
Karacakılavuz, Turkey ... 41 E11
Karacaköy, Turkey ... 41 E12
Karacasu, Turkey ... 39 D10
Karachala = Qaraçala, Azerbaijan ... 49 L9
Karachayevsk, Russia ... 49 J5
Karachev, Russia ... 47 F8
Karachi, Pakistan ... 68 G2
Karad, India ... 66 L9
Karadirek, Turkey ... 39 C12
Karaga, Ghana ... 83 D4
Karaganda = Qaraghandy, Kazakstan ... 50 E8
Karagayly, Kazakstan ... 50 E8
Karaginskiy, Ostrov, Russia ... 51 D17
Karagüney Dağları, Turkey ... 72 B6
Karagwe □, Tanzania ... 86 C3
Karahallı, Turkey ... 39 C11
Karaikal, India ... 66 P11
Karaikkudi, India ... 66 P11
Karaisalı, Turkey ... 72 D6
Karaj, Iran ... 71 C6
Karak, Malaysia ... 65 L4
Karakalpakstan □, Uzbekistan ... 50 E6
Karakelong, Indonesia ... 63 D7
Karakitang, Indonesia ... 63 D7
Karaklis = Vanadzor, Armenia ... 49 K7
Karakoçan, Turkey ... 73 C9
Karakoram Pass, Pakistan ... 69 B7
Karakoram Ra., Pakistan ... 69 B7
Karakurt, Turkey ... 73 B10
Karalon, Russia ... 51 D12
Karaman, Balıkesir, Turkey ... 39 B9
Karaman, Konya, Turkey ... 72 D5
Karamanlı, Turkey ... 39 D11
Karamay, China ... 60 B3
Karambu, Indonesia ... 62 E5
Karamea Bight, N.Z. ... 91 J3
Karamsad, India ... 68 H5
Karamürsel, Turkey ... 41 F13
Karand, Iran ... 70 C5
Karanganyar, Indonesia ... 63 G13
Karaova, Turkey ... 39 D9
Karapınar, Turkey ... 72 D5
Karasburg, Namibia ... 88 D2
Karasino, Russia ... 50 C9
Karasjok, Norway ... 8 B21
Karasu, Turkey ... 72 B4
Karasu →, Turkey ... 39 E12
Karasuk, Russia ... 50 D8
Karasuyama, Japan ... 55 F10
Karataş, Adana, Turkey ... 72 D6
Karataş, Manisa, Turkey ... 39 C10
Karataş Burnu, Turkey ... 72 D6
Karatau = Qarataū, Kazakstan ... 50 E8
Karatau, Khrebet, Kazakstan ... 50 E7
Karatoprak, Turkey ... 39 D9
Karauli, India ... 68 F7
Karavastasë, L. e, Albania ... 40 F3
Karávi, Greece ... 38 E5
Karawang, Indonesia ... 63 G12
Karawanken, Europe ... 26 E7
Karayazı, Turkey ... 73 C10
Karazhal, Kazakstan ... 50 E8
Karbalā, Iraq ... 70 C5
Kårböle, Sweden ... 10 C9
Karcag, Hungary ... 42 C5
Karcha →, Pakistan ... 69 B7
Karczew, Poland ... 45 F8
Kardam, Bulgaria ... 41 C12
Kardeljevo = Ploče, Croatia ... 29 E14
Kardhámdli, Greece ... 38 E4
Kardhítsa, Greece ... 38 B3
Kardhítsa □, Greece ... 38 B3
Kärdla, Estonia ... 9 G20
Kareeberge, S. Africa ... 88 E3
Kareima, Sudan ... 80 D3
Karelia □, Russia ... 50 C4

Karelian Republic □ = Karelia □, Russia ... 50 C4
Kārevāndar, Iran ... 71 E9
Kargasok, Russia ... 50 D9
Kargat, Russia ... 50 D9
Kargı, Turkey ... 72 B6
Kargil, India ... 69 B7
Kargopol, Russia ... 46 B10
Kargowa, Poland ... 45 F2
Karguéri, Niger ... 83 C7
Kariá, Greece ... 38 C2
Kariaí, Greece ... 41 F8
Kariān, Iran ... 71 E8
Kariba, Zimbabwe ... 87 F2
Kariba, L., Zimbabwe ... 87 F2
Kariba Dam, Zimbabwe ... 87 F2
Kariba Gorge, Zambia ... 87 F2
Karibib, Namibia ... 88 C2
Karimata, Kepulauan, Indonesia ... 62 E3
Karimata, Selat, Indonesia ... 62 E3
Karimata Is. = Karimata, Kepulauan, Indonesia ... 62 E3
Karimnagar, India ... 66 K11
Karimunjawa, Kepulauan, Indonesia ... 62 F4
Karin, Somali Rep. ... 74 E4
Káristos, Greece ... 38 C6
Karīt, Iran ... 71 C8
Kariya, Japan ... 55 G8
Karjala, Finland ... 46 A5
Karkaralinsk = Qarqaraly, Kazakstan ... 50 E8
Karkinitska Zatoka, Ukraine ... 47 K7
Karkinitskiy Zaliv = Karkinitska Zatoka, Ukraine ... 47 K7
Karkur Tohl, Egypt ... 80 C2
Karl Liebknecht, Russia ... 47 G8
Karl-Marx-Stadt = Chemnitz, Germany ... 24 E8
Karlholmsbruk, Sweden ... 10 D11
Karlino, Poland ... 44 D2
Karlivka, Ukraine ... 47 H8
Karlobag, Croatia ... 29 D12
Karlovac, Croatia ... 29 C12
Karlovka = Karlivka, Ukraine ... 47 H8
Karlovo, Bulgaria ... 41 D8
Karlovy Vary, Czech Rep. ... 26 A5
Karlsbad = Karlovy Vary, Czech Rep. ... 26 A5
Karlsborg, Sweden ... 11 F8
Karlshamn, Sweden ... 11 H8
Karlskoga, Sweden ... 10 E8
Karlskrona, Sweden ... 11 H9
Karlsruhe, Germany ... 25 F4
Karlstad, Sweden ... 10 E7
Karlstad, U.S.A. ... 112 A6
Karlstadt, Germany ... 25 F5
Karmélava, Lithuania ... 44 D11
Karnal, India ... 68 E7
Karnali →, Nepal ... 69 E9
Karnaphuli Res., Bangla. ... 67 H18
Karnataka □, India ... 66 N10
Karnes City, U.S.A. ... 113 L6
Karnische Alpen, Europe ... 26 E6
Karnobat, Bulgaria ... 41 D10
Kärnten □, Austria ... 26 E6
Karo, Mali ... 82 C4
Karoi, Zimbabwe ... 87 F2
Karonga, Malawi ... 87 D3
Karoonda, Australia ... 95 F2
Karora, Sudan ... 80 D4
Káros, Greece ... 39 E7
Karousádhes, Greece ... 38 B1
Karpacz, Poland ... 45 H2
Karpasia □, Cyprus ... 36 D13
Kárpathos, Greece ... 39 F8
Kárpathos, Stenón, Greece ... 39 F8
Karpenísion, Greece ... 38 C3
Karpuz Burnu = Apostolos Andreas, C., Cyprus ... 36 D13
Karpuzlu, Turkey ... 39 D9
Kars, Turkey ... 73 B10
Karsakpay, Kazakstan ... 50 E7
Karsha, Kazakstan ... 48 F10
Karshi = Qarshi, Uzbekistan ... 50 F7
Karsiyang, India ... 69 F13
Karst = Kras, Croatia ... 29 C10
Kartal, Turkey ... 41 F13
Kartál Óros, Greece ... 41 E9
Kartaly, Russia ... 50 D7
Kartapur, India ... 68 D6
Karthaus, U.S.A. ... 110 E6
Kartuzy, Poland ... 44 D5
Karufa, Indonesia ... 63 E8
Karumba, Australia ... 94 B3
Karumo, Tanzania ... 86 C3
Karumwa, Tanzania ... 86 C3
Karungu, Kenya ... 86 C3
Karup, Denmark ... 11 H3
Karviná, Czech Rep. ... 27 B11
Karwar, India ... 66 M9
Karwi, India ... 69 G9
Kaş, Turkey ... 39 E11
Kasaba, Turkey ... 39 E11
Kasama, Malawi ... 87 E3
Kasai →, Dem. Rep. of the Congo ... 84 E3
Kasai Oriental □, Dem. Rep. of the Congo ... 86 D1
Kasaji, Dem. Rep. of the Congo ... 87 E1
Kasama, Zambia ... 87 E3

Kasan-dong

Kasan-dong, N. Korea 57 D14
Kasane, Namibia 88 B3
Kasanga, Tanzania 87 D3
Kasaragod, India 66 N9
Kasba L., Canada 105 A8
Kāseh Garān, Iran 70 C5
Kasempa, Zambia 87 E2
Kasenga,
  Dem. Rep. of the Congo 87 E2
Kasese, Uganda 86 B3
Kasewa, Zambia 87 E2
Kasganj, India 69 F8
Kashabowie, Canada 102 C1
Kāshān, Iran 71 C6
Kashi, China 60 C2
Kashimbo,
  Dem. Rep. of the Congo 87 E2
Kashin, Russia 46 D9
Kashipur, India 69 E8
Kashira, Russia 46 E10
Kashiwazaki, Japan 55 F9
Kashk-e Kohneh, Afghan. 66 B3
Kāshmar, Iran 71 C8
Kashmir, Asia 69 C7
Kashmor, Pakistan 68 E3
Kashpirovka, Russia 48 D9
Kashun Noerh = Gaxun
  Nur, China 60 B5
Kasimov, Russia 48 C5
Kasinge,
  Dem. Rep. of the Congo 86 D2
Kasiruta, Indonesia 63 E7
Kaskaskia →, U.S.A. 112 G10
Kaskattama →, Canada .. 105 B10
Kaskinen, Finland 9 E19
Kaslo, Canada 104 D5
Kasmere L., Canada 105 B8
Kasongo,
  Dem. Rep. of the Congo 86 C2
Kasongo Lunda,
  Dem. Rep. of the Congo 84 F3
Kásos, Greece 39 F8
Kásos, Stenón, Greece ... 39 F8
Kaspi, Georgia 49 K7
Kaspichan, Bulgaria 41 C11
Kaspiysk, Russia 49 J8
Kaspiyskiy, Russia 49 H8
Kassab ed Doleib, Sudan . 81 E3
Kassaba, Egypt 80 C2
Kassalâ, Sudan 81 D4
Kassalâ □, Sudan 81 D4
Kassándra, Greece 40 F7
Kassándrinon, Greece ... 40 F7
Kassel, Germany 24 D5
Kassinger, Sudan 80 D3
Kassiópi, Greece 36 A3
Kastamonu, Turkey 72 B5
Kastav, Croatia 29 C11
Kastéli, Greece 36 D5
Kastéllion, Greece 36 D7
Kastellórizon = Megiste,
  Greece 39 E11
Kástellos, Greece 39 E9
Kastéllou, Ákra, Greece .. 39 F9
Kasterlee, Belgium 17 C4
Kastlösa, Sweden 11 H10
Kastóri, Greece 38 D4
Kastoría, Greece 40 F5
Kastoría □, Greece 40 F5
Kastoría, Límni, Greece . 40 F5
Kastornoye, Russia 47 G10
Kastós, Greece 38 C2
Kastrosikiá, Greece 38 B2
Kastsyukovichy, Belarus . 46 F7
Kasulu, Tanzania 86 C3
Kasulu □, Tanzania 86 C3
Kasumi, Japan 55 G7
Kasumkent, Russia 49 K9
Kasungu, Malawi 87 E3
Kasur, Pakistan 68 D6
Kataba, Zambia 87 F2
Katako Kombe,
  Dem. Rep. of the Congo 86 C1
Katákolon, Greece 38 D3
Katale, Tanzania 86 C3
Katamatite, Australia 95 F4
Katanda, Kivu,
  Dem. Rep. of the Congo 86 C2
Katanda, Shaba,
  Dem. Rep. of the Congo 86 D1
Katanga = Shaba □,
  Dem. Rep. of the Congo 86 D2
Katangi, India 66 J11
Katastári, Greece 38 D2
Katavi Swamp, Tanzania . 86 D3
Katerini, Greece 40 F6
Katha, Burma 67 G20
Katherîna, Gebel, Egypt . 80 J8
Katherine, Australia 92 B5
Kathiawar, India 68 H4
Kathikas, Cyprus 36 E11
Kati, Mali 82 C3
Katihar, India 69 G12
Katima Mulilo, Zambia .. 88 B3
Katimbira, Malawi 87 E3
Katingan = Mendawai →,
  Indonesia 62 E4
Katiola, Ivory C. 82 D3
Katlanovo, Macedonia ... 40 E5
Katmandu, Nepal 69 F11
Kato Akhaïa, Greece 38 C3
Káto Arkhánai, Greece .. 36 D7
Káto Khorió, Greece 36 D7
Kato Pyrgos, Cyprus 36 D11
Káto Stavros, Greece 40 F7
Katokhí, Greece 38 C3

Katompe,
  Dem. Rep. of the Congo 86 D2
Katonga →, Uganda 86 B3
Katoomba, Australia 95 E5
Katoúna, Greece 38 C3
Katowice, Poland 45 H6
Katowice □, Poland 45 H6
Katrancı Dağı, Turkey .. 39 D12
Katrine, L., U.K. 14 E4
Katrineholm, Sweden ... 11 E10
Katsepe, Madag. 89 B8
Katsina, Nigeria 83 C6
Katsina □, Nigeria 83 C6
Katsina Ala →, Nigeria . 83 D6
Katsumoto, Japan 55 H4
Katsuura, Japan 55 G10
Katsuyama, Japan 55 F8
Kattaviá, Greece 36 D9
Kattegat, Denmark 11 H5
Katthammarsvik, Sweden . 11 G12
Katumba,
  Dem. Rep. of the Congo 86 D2
Katungu, Kenya 86 C5
Katwa, India 69 H13
Katwijk, Neths. 17 B4
Kąty Wrocławskie, Poland 45 G3
Kauai, U.S.A. 106 H15
Kauai Channel, U.S.A. .. 106 H16
Kaub, Germany 25 E3
Kaufbeuren, Germany ... 25 H6
Kaufman, U.S.A. 113 J6
Kauhajoki, Finland 9 E20
Kaukauna, U.S.A. 108 C1
Kaukauveld, Namibia .. 88 C3
Kaunas, Lithuania 9 J20
Kaunos, Turkey 39 E10
Kaura Namoda, Nigeria . 83 C6
Kautokeino, Norway ... 8 B20
Kavacha, Russia 51 C17
Kavadarci, Macedonia .. 40 E6
Kavaja, Albania 40 E3
Kavak, Turkey 72 B7
Kavak Dağı, Turkey ... 39 D10
Kavaklı, Turkey 41 E11
Kavaklıdere, Turkey ... 39 D10
Kavali, India 66 M12
Kaválla, Greece 41 E8
Kaválla □, Greece 41 E8
Kaválla Kólpos, Greece . 41 F8
Kavār, Iran 71 D7
Kavarna, Bulgaria 41 C12
Kavkaz, Russia 47 K9
Kavos, Greece 36 B4
Kavoúsi, Greece 39 F7
Kaw, Fr. Guiana 125 C8
Kawa, Sudan 81 E3
Kawagama L., Canada .. 110 A6
Kawagoe, Japan 55 G9
Kawaguchi, Japan 55 G9
Kawaihae, U.S.A. 106 H17
Kawambwa, Zambia ... 87 D2
Kawanoe, Japan 55 G6
Kawardha, India 69 J9
Kawasaki, Japan 55 G9
Kawasi, Indonesia 63 E7
Kawene, Canada 102 C1
Kawerau, N.Z. 91 H6
Kawhia Harbour, N.Z. .. 91 H5
Kawio, Kepulauan,
  Indonesia 63 D7
Kawnro, Burma 67 H21
Kawthaung, Burma 65 H2
Kawthoolei = Kawthule □,
  Burma 67 L20
Kawthule □, Burma ... 67 L20
Kaxholmen, Sweden ... 11 G8
Kaya, Burkina Faso ... 83 C4
Kayah □, Burma 67 K20
Kayalıköy Barajı, Turkey . 41 E11
Kayan →, Indonesia .. 62 D5
Kaycee, U.S.A. 114 E10
Kayeli, Indonesia 63 E7
Kayenta, U.S.A. 115 H8
Kayes, Mali 82 C2
Kayı, Turkey 39 B12
Kayima, S. Leone 82 D2
Kaymakçı, Turkey 39 C10
Kayoa, Indonesia 63 D7
Kayomba, Zambia 87 E1
Kayoro, Ghana 83 C4
Kayrunnera, Australia .. 95 E3
Kaysatskoye, Russia ... 48 F8
Kayseri, Turkey 72 C6
Kaysville, U.S.A. 114 F8
Kaz Dağı, Turkey 39 B8
Kazachye, Russia 51 B14
Kazakstan ■, Asia 50 E8
Kazan, Russia 48 C9
Kazan-Rettō, Pac. Oc. .. 96 E6
Kazanluk, Bulgaria ... 41 D9
Kazanskaya, Russia ... 48 F5
Kazatin = Kozyatyn,
  Ukraine 47 H5
Kazbek, Russia 49 J7
Kazerūn, Iran 71 D6
Kazi Magomed =
  Qazimämmäd,
  Azerbaijan 49 K9
Kazimierz Dolny, Poland . 45 G8
Kazimierza Wielka, Poland 45 H7
Kazincbarcika, Hungary .. 42 B5
Kazlų Rūda, Lithuania .. 44 D10
Kaztalovka, Kazakstan .. 48 F9
Kazuno, Japan 54 D10
Kazym →, Russia 50 C7

Kcynia, Poland 45 F4
Ké-Macina, Mali 82 C3
Kéa, Greece 38 D6
Keady, U.K. 15 B5
Keams Canyon, U.S.A. . 115 J8
Kearney, U.S.A. 112 E5
Keban, Turkey 73 C8
Keban Baraji, Turkey .. 73 C8
Kebbi □, Nigeria 83 C6
Kebnekaise, Sweden ... 8 C18
Kebri Dehar, Ethiopia .. 74 F3
Kebumen, Indonesia ... 63 G13
Kecel, Hungary 42 D4
Kechika →, Canada ... 104 B3
Keçiborlu, Turkey 39 D12
Kecskemét, Hungary .. 42 D4
Kedada, Ethiopia 81 F4
Kėdainiai, Lithuania .. 9 J21
Kedgwick, Canada 103 C6
Kédhros Óros, Greece .. 36 D6
Kedia Hill, Botswana .. 88 C3
Kediri, Indonesia 63 G15
Kédougou, Senegal ... 82 C2
Katwa, India 69 H13
Keeley L., Canada 105 C7
Keeling Is. = Cocos Is.,
  Ind. Oc. 96 J1
Keene, Calif., U.S.A. .. 117 K8
Keene, N.H., U.S.A. ... 111 D12
Keeper Hill, Ireland ... 15 D3
Keer-Weer, C., Australia 94 A3
Keeseville, U.S.A. 111 B11
Keetmanshoop, Namibia 88 D2
Keewatin, U.S.A. 112 B8
Keewatin □, Canada .. 105 A10
Keewatin →, Canada .. 105 B8
Kefa □, Ethiopia 81 F4
Kefallinía, Greece 38 C2
Kefallinía □, Greece .. 38 C2
Kéfalos, Greece 39 E8
Kefamenanu, Indonesia . 63 F6
Keffi, Nigeria 83 D6
Keflavík, Iceland 8 D2
Keg River, Canada ... 104 B5
Kegaska, Canada 103 B7
Kehl, Germany 25 G3
Keighley, U.K. 12 D6
Keila, Estonia 9 G21
Keimoes, S. Africa 88 D3
Keita, Niger 83 C6
Keitele, Finland 8 E22
Keith, Australia 95 F3
Keith, U.K. 14 D6
Kejser Franz Joseph
  Fjord = Kong Franz
  Joseph Fd., Greenland . 4 B6
Kekri, India 68 G6
Kelamet, Eritrea 81 D4
Kelan, China 56 E6
Kelang, Malaysia 65 L3
Kelantan □, Malaysia .. 65 J4
Kelantan →, Malaysia . 65 J4
Kělcyra, Albania 40 F4
Kelekçi, Turkey 39 D11
Keles, Turkey 41 G13
Keleti-főcsatorna, Hungary 42 C6
Kelheim, Germany 25 G7
Kelkit, Turkey 73 B8
Kelkit →, Turkey 72 B7
Kellerberrin, Australia .. 93 F2
Kellett, C., Canada ... 4 B1
Kelleys I., U.S.A. 110 E2
Kellogg, U.S.A. 114 C5
Kells = Ceanannus Mor,
  Ireland 15 C5
Kelmė, Lithuania 44 C9
Kelokedhara, Cyprus .. 36 E11
Kelowna, Canada 104 D5
Kelsey Bay, Canada ... 104 C3
Kelseyville, U.S.A. ... 116 G4
Kelso, N.Z. 91 L2
Kelso, U.K. 14 F6
Kelso, U.S.A. 116 D4
Keluang, Malaysia ... 65 L4
Kelvington, Canada ... 105 C8
Kem, Russia 50 C4
Kema, Indonesia 63 D7
Kemah, Turkey 73 C8
Kemaliye, Erzincan,
  Turkey 73 C8
Kemaliye, Manisa, Turkey 39 C10
Kemalpaşa, Turkey ... 39 C9
Kemano, Canada 104 C3
Kemasik, Malaysia ... 65 K4
Kembolcha, Ethiopia .. 81 E4
Kemer, Antalya, Turkey . 39 E12
Kemer, Burdur, Turkey . 39 D12
Kemer, Muğla, Turkey . 39 E11
Kemer Barajı, Turkey .. 39 D10
Kemerovo, Russia 50 D9
Kemi, Finland 8 D21
Kemi älv = Kemijoki →,
  Finland 8 D21
Kemijärvi, Finland ... 8 C22
Kemijoki →, Finland . 8 D21
Kemmerer, U.S.A. ... 114 F8
Kemmuna = Comino,
  Malta 36 C1
Kemp, L., U.S.A. 113 J5
Kemp Land, Antarctica . 5 C5
Kempsey, Australia ... 95 E5
Kempt, L., Canada ... 102 C5
Kempten, Germany ... 25 H6
Kemptville, Canada ... 102 D4
Kendal, Indonesia 63 G14

Kendal, U.K. 12 C5
Kendall, Australia 95 E5
Kendall →, Australia .. 94 A3
Kendallville, U.S.A. .. 108 E3
Kendari, Indonesia ... 63 E6
Kendawangan, Indonesia . 62 E4
Kende, Nigeria 83 C5
Kendenup, Australia .. 93 F2
Kendrapara, India 67 J15
Kendrew, S. Africa ... 88 E3
Kendrick, U.S.A. 114 C5
Kene Thao, Laos 64 D3
Kenedy, U.S.A. 113 L6
Kenema, S. Leone 82 D2
Keng Kok, Laos 64 D5
Keng Tawng, Burma .. 67 J21
Keng Tung, Burma ... 67 J21
Kengeja, Tanzania 86 D4
Kenhardt, S. Africa ... 88 D3
Kenitra, Morocco 78 B4
Kenli, China 57 F10
Kenmare, Ireland 15 E2
Kenmare, U.S.A. 112 A3
Kenmare River, Ireland . 15 E2
Kennebec, U.S.A. 112 D5
Kennebec →, U.S.A. .. 111 D11
Kennedy, Zimbabwe .. 87 F2
Kennedy Ra., Australia . 93 D2
Kennedy Taungdeik,
  Burma 67 H18
Kenner, U.S.A. 113 L9
Kennet →, U.K. 13 F7
Kenneth Ra., Australia . 92 D2
Kennett, U.S.A. 113 G9
Kennewick, U.S.A. ... 114 C4
Kénogami, Canada ... 103 C5
Kenogami →, Canada . 102 B3
Kenora, Canada 105 D10
Kenosha, U.S.A. 108 D2
Kensington, Canada .. 103 C7
Kensington, U.S.A. ... 112 F5
Kensington Downs,
  Australia 94 C3
Kent, Ohio, U.S.A. ... 110 E3
Kent, Oreg., U.S.A. .. 114 D3
Kent, Tex., U.S.A. ... 113 K2
Kent, Wash., U.S.A. .. 116 C4
Kent □, U.K. 13 F8
Kent Group, Australia . 94 F4
Kent Pen., Canada ... 100 B9
Kentau, Kazakstan ... 50 E7
Kentland, U.S.A. 108 E2
Kenton, U.S.A. 108 E4
Kentucky □, U.S.A. .. 108 G3
Kentucky →, U.S.A. .. 108 F3
Kentucky L., U.S.A. .. 109 G2
Kentville, Canada 103 C7
Kentwood, U.S.A. 113 K9
Kenya ■, Africa 86 B4
Kenya, Mt., Kenya ... 86 C4
Keo Neua, Deo, Vietnam 64 C5
Keokuk, U.S.A. 112 E9
Kep, Cambodia 65 G5
Kep, Vietnam 58 B6
Kepez, Turkey 41 F10
Kepi, Indonesia 63 F9
Kepice, Poland 44 D3
Kępno, Poland 45 G4
Kepsut, Turkey 39 B10
Kerala □, India 66 P10
Kerama-Rettō, Japan .. 55 L3
Keran, Pakistan 69 B5
Kerang, Australia 95 F3
Keratéa, Greece 38 D5
Keraudren, C., Australia 92 C2
Kerava, Finland 9 F21
Kerch, Ukraine 47 K9
Kerchenskiy Proliv,
  Black Sea 47 K9
Kerchoual, Mali 83 B5
Kerempe Burnu, Turkey . 72 A5
Keren, Eritrea 81 D4
Kerewan, Gambia 82 C1
Kerguelen, Ind. Oc. .. 3 G13
Keri, Greece 38 D2
Keri Kera, Sudan 81 E3
Kericho, Kenya 86 C4
Kericho □, Kenya 86 C4
Kerinci, Indonesia ... 62 E2
Kerki, Turkmenistan .. 50 F7
Kerkinítis, Límni, Greece . 40 E7
Kérkira, Greece 38 B1
Kérkira □, Greece 38 B1
Kerkrade, Neths. 17 D6
Kerma, Sudan 80 D3
Kermadec Is., Pac. Oc. . 96 L10
Kermadec Trench, Pac. Oc. 96 L10
Kermān, Iran 71 D8
Kerman, U.S.A. 116 J6
Kermān □, Iran 71 D8
Kermānshāh = Bākhtarān,
  Iran 70 C5
Kermen, Bulgaria 41 D10
Kermit, U.S.A. 113 K3
Kern →, U.S.A. 117 K7
Kernhof, Austria 26 D8
Kernville, U.S.A. 117 K8
Keroh, Malaysia 65 K3
Kerpen, Germany 24 E2
Kerrera, U.K. 14 E3
Kerrobert, Canada ... 105 C7
Kerrville, U.S.A. 113 K5
Kerry □, Ireland 15 D2
Kerry Hd., Ireland ... 15 D2
Kersa, Ethiopia 81 F5
Kerulen →, Asia 60 B6

Kerzaz, Algeria 78 C5
Kesagami →, Canada .. 102 B4
Kesagami L., Canada .. 102 B3
Keşan, Turkey 41 F10
Kesennuma, Japan 54 E10
Keshit, Iran 71 D8
Keşiş Dağ, Turkey ... 73 C8
Keskin, Turkey 72 C5
Kestell, S. Africa 89 D4
Kestenga, Russia 50 C4
Keswick, U.K. 12 C4
Keszthely, Hungary .. 42 D2
Ket →, Russia 50 D9
Keta, Ghana 83 D5
Ketapang, Indonesia .. 62 E4
Ketchikan, U.S.A. 100 C6
Ketchum, U.S.A. 114 E6
Kete Krachi, Ghana ... 83 D4
Ketef, Khalîg Umm el,
  Egypt 80 C4
Keti Bandar, Pakistan . 68 G2
Ketri, India 68 E6
Kętrzyn, Poland 44 D8
Kettering, U.K. 13 E7
Kettering, U.S.A. 108 F3
Kettle →, Canada 105 B11
Kettle Falls, U.S.A. .. 114 B4
Kettleman City, U.S.A. . 116 J7
Kęty, Poland 45 J6
Keuruu, Finland 9 E21
Kevelaer, Germany ... 24 D2
Kevin, U.S.A. 114 B8
Kewanee, U.S.A. 112 E10
Kewaunee, U.S.A. 108 C2
Keweenaw B., U.S.A. . 108 B1
Keweenaw Pen., U.S.A. . 108 B2
Keweenaw Pt., U.S.A. . 108 B2
Key Harbour, Canada . 102 C3
Key West, U.S.A. 107 F10
Keynsham, U.K. 13 F5
Keyser, U.S.A. 108 F6
Keystone, U.S.A. 112 D3
Kezhma, Russia 51 D11
Kežmarok, Slovak Rep. . 27 B13
Khabarovsk, Russia .. 51 E14
Khabr, Iran 71 D8
Khābūr →, Syria 70 C4
Khachmas = Xaçmaz,
  Azerbaijan 49 K9
Khachrod, India 68 H6
Khadari, W. el →, Sudan . 81 E2
Khadro, Pakistan 68 F3
Khadyzhensk, Russia . 49 H4
Khadzhilyangar, India . 69 B8
Khagaria, India 69 G12
Khaipur, Bahawalpur,
  Pakistan 68 E5
Khaipur, Hyderabad,
  Pakistan 68 F3
Khair, India 68 F7
Khairabad, India 69 F9
Khairagarh, India 69 J9
Khairpur, Pakistan ... 68 F3
Khakassia □, Russia .. 50 D9
Khakhea, Botswana .. 88 C3
Khalafābād, Iran 71 D6
Khalilabad, India 69 F10
Khalīlī, Iran 71 E7
Khalkhāl, Iran 71 B6
Khálki, Dhodhekánisos,
  Greece 39 E9
Khálki, Thessalía, Greece . 38 B4
Khalkidhikí □, Greece . 40 F7
Khalkís, Greece 38 C5
Khalmer-Sede = Tazovskiy,
  Russia 50 C8
Khalmer Yu, Russia .. 50 C7
Khalūf, Oman 74 C6
Kham Keut, Laos 64 C5
Khamas Country, Botswana 88 C4
Khambhaliya, India .. 68 H3
Khambhat, India 68 H5
Khambhat, G. of, India . 68 J5
Khamilonísion, Greece . 39 F8
Khamir, Iran 71 E7
Khamir, Yemen 74 D3
Khamsa, Egypt 75 E1
Khān Abū Shāmat, Syria . 75 B5
Khān Āzād, Iraq 70 C5
Khān Mujiddah, Iraq .. 70 C4
Khān Shaykhūn, Syria . 70 C3
Khān Yūnis, Gaza Strip . 75 D3
Khānaqīn, Iraq 70 C5
Khānbāghī, Iran 71 B7
Khandrá, Greece 39 F8
Khandwa, India 66 J10
Khandyga, Russia 51 C14
Khāneh, Iran 70 B5
Khanewal, Pakistan .. 68 D4
Khanh Duong, Vietnam . 64 F7
Khaniá, Greece 36 D6
Khaniá □, Greece 36 D6
Khaníon, Kólpos, Greece . 36 D5
Khanka, L., Asia 54 B6
Khankendy = Xankändi,
  Azerbaijan 73 C12
Khanna, India 68 D7
Khanpur, Pakistan ... 68 E4
Khanty-Mansiysk, Russia . 50 C7
Khapalu, Pakistan ... 69 B7
Khapcheranga, Russia . 51 E12
Kharabali, Russia 49 G8
Kharagpur, India 69 H12
Khárakas, Greece 36 D7
Kharan Kalat, Pakistan . 66 F4
Kharānaq, Iran 71 C7
Kharda, India 66 K9

Khardung La, India 69 B7
Khârga, El Wâhât el, Egypt 80 B3
Khargon, India 66 J9
Kharit, Wadi el →, Egypt 80 C3
Khärk, Jazireh, Iran 71 D6
Kharkiv, Ukraine 47 H9
Kharkov = Kharkiv,
  Ukraine 47 H9
Kharmanli, Bulgaria 41 E9
Kharovsk, Russia 46 C11
Kharta, Turkey 72 B3
Khartoum = El Khartûm,
  Sudan 81 D3
Khasan, Russia 54 C5
Khasavyurt, Russia 49 J8
Khāsh, Iran 66 E2
Khashm el Girba, Sudan .. 81 E4
Khashuri, Georgia 49 J6
Khaskovo, Bulgaria 41 E9
Khaskovo □, Bulgaria ... 41 E9
Khatanga, Russia 51 B11
Khatanga →, Russia 51 B11
Khatauli, India 68 E7
Khātūnābād, Iran 71 C6
Khatyrka, Russia 51 C18
Khaybar, Harrat,
  Si. Arabia 70 E4
Khāzimiyah, Iraq 70 C4
Khazzan Jabal el Awliyâ,
  Sudan 81 D3
Khe Bo, Vietnam 64 C5
Khe Long, Vietnam 64 B5
Khed Brahma, India 66 G8
Khekra, India 68 E7
Khemarak Phouminville,
  Cambodia 65 G4
Khemmarat, Thailand 64 D5
Khenāmān, Iran 71 D8
Khenchela, Algeria 78 A7
Khérson, Greece 40 E6
Kherson, Ukraine 47 J7
Khersónisos Akrotíri,
  Greece 36 D6
Kheta →, Russia 51 B11
Khiliomódhion, Greece .. 38 D4
Khilok, Russia 51 D12
Khimki, Russia 46 E9
Khíos, Greece 39 C8
Khíos □, Greece 39 C8
Khiuma = Hiiumaa,
  Estonia 9 G20
Khiva, Uzbekistan 50 E7
Khīyāv, Iran 70 B5
Khlebarovo, Bulgaria ... 41 C10
Khlong Khlung, Thailand 64 D2
Khmelnik, Ukraine 47 H4
Khmelnitskiy =
  Khmelnytskyy, Ukraine . 47 H4
Khmelnytskyy, Ukraine ... 47 H4
Khmer Rep. =
  Cambodia ■, Asia 64 F5
Khoai, Hon, Vietnam 65 H5
Khodorivv, Ukraine 47 H3
Khodzent = Khudzhand,
  Tajikistan 50 E7
Khojak Pass, Afghan. ... 66 D5
Khok Kloi, Thailand 65 H2
Khok Pho, Thailand 65 J3
Kholm, Russia 46 D6
Kholmsk, Russia 51 E15
Khomas Hochland,
  Namibia 88 C2
Khomeyn, Iran 71 C6
Khon Kaen, Thailand 64 D4
Khong →, Cambodia 64 F5
Khong Sedone, Laos 64 E5
Khonuu, Russia 51 C15
Khoper →, Russia 48 F6
Khor 'Atash, Sudan 81 E3
Khóra, Greece 38 D3
Khóra Sfakíon, Greece .. 36 D6
Khorāsān □, Iran 71 C8
Khorat = Nakhon
  Ratchasima, Thailand . 64 E4
Khorat, Cao Nguyen,
  Thailand 64 E4
Khorixas, Namibia 88 C1
Khorol, Ukraine 47 H7
Khorramābād, Khorāsān,
  Iran 71 C8
Khorramābād, Lorestān,
  Iran 71 C6
Khorrāmshahr, Iran 71 D6
Khorugh, Tajikistan 50 F8
Khosravī, Iran 71 D6
Khosrowābād, Khuzestān,
  Iran 71 D6
Khosrowābād, Kordestān,
  Iran 70 C5
Khosūyeh, Iran 71 D7
Khotyn, Ukraine 47 H4
Khouribga, Morocco 78 B4
Khowai, Bangla. 67 G17
Khoyniki, Belarus 47 G5
Khrami →, Georgia 49 K7
Khrenovoye, Russia 48 E5
Khrisoúpolis, Greece ... 41 F8
Khristianá, Greece 39 E7
Khrysokhou B., Cyprus .. 36 D11
Khtapodhiá, Greece 39 D7
Khu Khan, Thailand 64 E5
Khudzhand, Tajikistan .. 50 E7
Khuff, Si. Arabia 70 E5
Khūgīānī, Afghan. 68 D1
Khulna, Bangla. 67 H16
Khulna □, Bangla. 67 H16
Khulo, Georgia 49 K6

Khumago, Botswana 88 C3
Khūnsorkh, Iran 71 E8
Khūr, Iran 71 C8
Khurai, India 68 G8
Khurayş, Si. Arabia 71 E6
Khurīyā Murīyā, Jazā 'ir,
  Oman 74 D6
Khurja, India 68 E7
Khūsf, Iran 71 C8
Khush, Afghan. 66 C3
Khust, Ukraine 47 H2
Khuzdar, Pakistan 68 F2
Khūzestān □, Iran 71 D6
Khvājeh, Iran 70 B5
Khvalynsk, Russia 48 D9
Khvānsār, Iran 71 D7
Khvatovka, Russia 48 D8
Khvor, Iran 71 C7
Khvorgū, Iran 71 E8
Khvormūj, Iran 71 D6
Khvoy, Iran 70 B5
Khvoynaya, Russia 46 C8
Khyber Pass, Afghan. ... 68 B4
Kiabukwa,
  Dem. Rep. of the Congo 87 D1
Kiama, Australia 95 E5
Kiamba, Phil. 61 H6
Kiambi,
  Dem. Rep. of the Congo 86 D2
Kiambu, Kenya 86 C4
Kiangsi = Jiangxi □, China 59 D11
Kiangsu = Jiangsu □,
  China 57 H11
Kiáton, Greece 38 C4
Kibæk, Denmark 11 H2
Kibanga Port, Uganda ... 86 B3
Kibara, Tanzania 86 C3
Kibare, Mts.,
  Dem. Rep. of the Congo 86 D2
Kibombo,
  Dem. Rep. of the Congo 86 C2
Kibondo, Tanzania 86 C3
Kibondo □, Tanzania 86 C3
Kibumbu, Burundi 86 C2
Kibungo, Rwanda 86 C3
Kibuye, Burundi 86 C2
Kibuye, Rwanda 86 C2
Kibwesa, Tanzania 86 D2
Kibwezi, Kenya 86 C4
Kicasalih, Turkey 41 E10
Kičevo, Macedonia 40 E4
Kicking Horse Pass,
  Canada 104 C5
Kidal, Mali 83 B5
Kidderminster, U.K. 13 E5
Kidete, Tanzania 86 D4
Kidira, Senegal 82 C2
Kidnappers, C., N.Z. ... 91 H6
Kidsgrove, U.K. 12 D5
Kidston, Australia 94 B3
Kidugallo, Tanzania 86 D4
Kiel, Germany 24 A6
Kiel Canal = Nord-Ostsee-
  Kanal, Germany 24 A5
Kielce, Poland 45 H7
Kielce □, Poland 45 H7
Kielder Water, U.K. 12 B5
Kieler Bucht, Germany .. 24 A6
Kien Binh, Vietnam 65 H5
Kien Tan, Vietnam 65 G5
Kienge,
  Dem. Rep. of the Congo 87 E2
Kiessé, Niger 83 C5
Kiev = Kyyiv, Ukraine .. 47 G6
Kiffa, Mauritania 82 B2
Kifisiá, Greece 38 C5
Kifissós →, Greece 38 C5
Kifrī, Iraq 70 C5
Kigali, Rwanda 86 C3
Kigarama, Tanzania 86 C3
Kigoma □, Tanzania 86 D3
Kigoma-Ujiji, Tanzania . 86 C2
Kigomasha, Ras, Tanzania 86 C4
Kihee, Australia 95 D3
Kihnu, Estonia 9 G21
Kii-Sanchi, Japan 55 G8
Kii-Suidō, Japan 55 H7
Kikaiga-Shima, Japan ... 55 K4
Kikinda, Serbia, Yug. .. 42 E5
Kikládhes, Greece 38 E6
Kikládhes □, Greece 38 D6
Kikwit,
  Dem. Rep. of the Congo 84 F3
Kil, Sweden 10 E7
Kilafors, Sweden 10 C10
Kilauea Crater, U.S.A. . 106 J17
Kilbrannan Sd., U.K. ... 14 F3
Kilchu, N. Korea 57 D15
Kilcoy, Australia 95 D5
Kildare, Ireland 15 C5
Kildare □, Ireland 15 C5
Kilfinnane, Ireland 15 D3
Kilgore, U.S.A. 113 J7
Kilifi, Kenya 86 C4
Kilimanjaro, Tanzania .. 86 C4
Kilimanjaro □, Tanzania 86 C4
Kilimli, Turkey 72 B4
Kilindini, Kenya 86 C4
Kiliya, Ukraine 47 K5
Kilkee, Ireland 15 D2
Kilkeel, U.K. 15 B5
Kilkenny, Ireland 15 D4
Kilkenny □, Ireland 15 D4
Kilkieran B., Ireland .. 15 C2

Kilkís, Greece 40 F6
Kilkís □, Greece 40 E6
Killala, Ireland 15 B2
Killala B., Ireland 15 B2
Killaloe, Ireland 15 D3
Killaloe Sta., Canada .. 110 A7
Killam, Canada 104 C6
Killarney, Australia ... 95 D5
Killarney, Canada 102 C3
Killarney, Ireland 15 D2
Killary Harbour, Ireland 15 C2
Killdeer, Canada 105 D7
Killdeer, U.S.A. 112 B3
Killeberg, Sweden 11 H8
Killeen, U.S.A. 113 K6
Killin, U.K. 14 E4
Killíni, Ilía, Greece .. 38 D3
Killíni, Korinthía, Greece 38 D4
Killorglin, Ireland 15 D2
Killybegs, Ireland 15 B3
Kilmarnock, U.K. 14 F4
Kilmez, Russia 48 B10
Kilmez →, Russia 48 B10
Kilmore, Australia 95 F3
Kilondo, Tanzania 87 D3
Kilosa, Tanzania 86 D4
Kilosa □, Tanzania 86 D4
Kilrush, Ireland 15 D2
Kilwa □, Tanzania 87 D4
Kilwa Kisiwani, Tanzania 87 D4
Kilwa Kivinje, Tanzania 87 D4
Kilwa Masoko, Tanzania . 87 D4
Kilwinning, U.K. 14 F4
Kim, U.S.A. 113 G3
Kimaam, Indonesia 63 F9
Kimamba, Tanzania 86 D4
Kimba, Australia 95 E2
Kimball, Nebr., U.S.A. . 112 E3
Kimball, S. Dak., U.S.A. 112 D5
Kimberley, Canada 104 D5
Kimberley, S. Africa ... 88 D3
Kimberley Downs,
  Australia 92 C3
Kimberly, U.S.A. 114 E6
Kimchaek, N. Korea 57 D15
Kimchŏn, S. Korea 57 F15
Kími, Greece 38 C6
Kimje, S. Korea 57 G14
Kimmirut, Canada 101 B13
Kímolos, Greece 38 E6
Kimovsk, Moskva, Russia 46 E9
Kimovsk, Tula, Russia .. 46 E10
Kimparana, Mali 82 C4
Kimry, Russia 46 D9
Kimsquit, Canada 104 C3
Kimstad, Sweden 11 F9
Kinabalu, Gunong,
  Malaysia 62 C5
Kínaros, Greece 39 E8
Kinaskan L., Canada 104 B2
Kinbasket L., Canada ... 104 C5
Kincaid, Canada 105 D7
Kincardine, Canada 102 D3
Kinda,
  Dem. Rep. of the Congo 87 D2
Kindberg, Austria 26 D8
Kinder Scout, U.K. 12 D6
Kindersley, Canada 105 C7
Kindia, Guinea 82 D2
Kindu,
  Dem. Rep. of the Congo 86 C2
Kinel, Russia 48 D10
Kineshma, Russia 48 B6
Kinesi, Tanzania 86 C3
King, L., Australia 93 F2
King, Mt., Australia ... 94 D4
King City, U.S.A. 116 J5
King Cr. →, Australia .. 94 C2
King Edward →, Australia 92 B4
King Frederick VI Land =
  Kong Frederik VI.s Kyst,
  Greenland 4 C5
King George B., Falk. Is. 128 G4
King George I., Antarctica 5 C18
King George Is., Canada 101 C11
King I. = Kadan Kyun,
  Burma 64 F2
King I., Australia 94 F3
King I., Canada 104 C3
King Leopold Ranges,
  Australia 92 C4
King Sd., Australia 92 C3
King William I., Canada 100 B10
King William's Town,
  S. Africa 88 E4
Kingaroy, Australia 95 D5
Kingfisher, U.S.A. 113 H6
Kingirbān, Iraq 70 C5
Kingisepp = Kuressaare,
  Estonia 9 G20
Kingisepp, Russia 46 C4
Kingman, Ariz., U.S.A. . 117 K12
Kingman, Kans., U.S.A. . 113 G5
Kingoonya, Australia ... 95 E2
Kings →, U.S.A. 116 J7
Kings Canyon National
  Park, U.S.A. 116 J8
King's Lynn, U.K. 12 E8
Kings Mountain, U.S.A. . 109 H5
King's Peak, U.S.A. 114 F8
Kingsbridge, U.K. 13 G4
Kingsburg, U.S.A. 116 J7
Kingscote, Australia ... 95 F2
Kingscourt, Ireland 15 C5
Kingsley, U.S.A. 112 D7
Kingsport, U.S.A. 109 G4
Kingston, Canada 102 D4

Kingston, Jamaica 120 C4
Kingston, N.Z. 91 L2
Kingston, N.Y., U.S.A. . 111 E11
Kingston, Pa., U.S.A. .. 111 E9
Kingston, R.I., U.S.A. . 111 E13
Kingston Pk., U.S.A. ... 117 K11
Kingston South East,
  Australia 95 F2
Kingston upon Hull, U.K. 12 D7
Kingston upon Hull □,
  U.K. 12 D7
Kingston-upon-Thames,
  U.K. 13 F7
Kingstown, St. Vincent . 121 D7
Kingstree, U.S.A. 109 J6
Kingsville, Canada 102 D3
Kingsville, U.S.A. 113 M6
Kingussie, U.K. 14 D4
Kiník, Antalya, Turkey . 39 E11
Kiník, Izmir, Turkey ... 39 B9
Kinistino, Canada 105 C7
Kinkala, Congo 84 E2
Kinki □, Japan 55 H8
Kinleith, N.Z. 91 H5
Kinmount, Canada 110 B6
Kinna, Sweden 11 G6
Kinnaird, Canada 104 D5
Kinnairds Hd., U.K. 14 D6
Kinnared, Sweden 11 G7
Kinnarodden, Norway 6 A11
Kinnarp, Sweden 11 F7
Kinneviken, Sweden 11 F7
Kino, Mexico 118 B2
Kinoje →, Canada 102 B3
Kinomoto, Japan 55 G8
Kinoni, Uganda 86 C3
Kinross, U.K. 14 E5
Kinsale, Ireland 15 E3
Kinsale, Old Hd. of,
  Ireland 15 E3
Kinsha = Chang Jiang →,
  China 59 B13
Kinshasa,
  Dem. Rep. of the Congo 84 E3
Kinsley, U.S.A. 113 G5
Kinston, U.S.A. 109 H7
Kintampo, Ghana 83 D4
Kintore Ra., Australia . 92 D4
Kintyre, U.K. 14 F3
Kintyre, Mull of, U.K. . 14 F3
Kinushseo →, Canada 102 A3
Kinuso, Canada 104 B5
Kinyangiri, Tanzania ... 86 C3
Kinzia →, Germany 25 G3
Kinzua, U.S.A. 110 E6
Kinzua Dam, U.S.A. 110 E6
Kióni, Greece 38 C2
Kiosk, Canada 102 C4
Kiowa, Kans., U.S.A. ... 113 G5
Kiowa, Okla., U.S.A. ... 113 H7
Kipahigan L., Canada ... 105 B8
Kipanga, Tanzania 86 D4
Kiparissía, Greece 38 D3
Kiparissiakós Kólpos,
  Greece 38 D3
Kipembawe, Tanzania 86 D3
Kipengere Ra., Tanzania 87 D3
Kipili, Tanzania 86 D3
Kipini, Kenya 86 C5
Kipling, Canada 105 C8
Kippure, Ireland 15 C5
Kipushi,
  Dem. Rep. of the Congo 87 E2
Kiratpur, India 68 E8
Kiraz, Turkey 39 C10
Kirazlı, Turkey 41 F10
Kirchhain, Germany 24 E4
Kirchheim, Germany 25 G5
Kirchheimbolanden,
  Germany 25 F3
Kirchschlag, Austria ... 27 D9
Kireç, Turkey 39 B10
Kirensk, Russia 51 D11
Kirgella Rocks, Australia 93 F3
Kirghizia = Kyrgyzstan ■,
  Asia 50 E8
Kirghizstan =
  Kyrgyzstan ■, Asia ... 50 E8
Kiribati ■, Pac. Oc. ... 96 H10
Kırıkhan, Turkey 72 D7
Kırıkkale, Turkey 72 C5
Kirillov, Russia 46 C10
Kirin = Jilin, China ... 57 C14
Kirishi, Russia 46 C6
Kiritimati, Kiribati ... 97 G12
Kırka, Turkey 39 B12
Kırkağaç, Turkey 39 B9
Kirkby, U.K. 12 D5
Kirkby Lonsdale, U.K. .. 12 C5
Kirkcaldy, U.K. 14 E5
Kirkcudbright, U.K. 14 G4
Kirkee, India 66 K8
Kirkenes, Norway 8 B23
Kirkjubæjarklaustur,
  Iceland 8 E4
Kirkkonummi, Finland ... 9 F21
Kirkland, U.S.A. 115 J7
Kirkland Lake, Canada .. 102 C3
Kirklareli, Turkey 41 E11
Kirklareli □, Turkey ... 41 E11
Kirksville, U.S.A. 112 E8
Kirkūk, Iraq 70 C5
Kirkwall, U.K. 14 C6
Kirkwood, S. Africa 88 E4
Kirov, Kaluga, Russia .. 46 E8
Kirov, Kirov, Russia ... 50 D5

Kirovabad = Gäncä,
  Azerbaijan 49 K8
Kirovakan = Vanadzor,
  Armenia 49 K7
Kirovograd = Kirovohrad,
  Ukraine 47 H7
Kirovohrad, Ukraine 47 H7
Kirovsk = Babadayhan,
  Turkmenistan 50 F7
Kirovskiy, Astrakhan,
  Russia 49 H9
Kirovskiy, Kamchatka,
  Russia 51 D16
Kirovskiy, Primorsk, Russia 54 B6
Kirriemuir, U.K. 14 E5
Kirsanov, Russia 48 D6
Kırşehir, Turkey 72 C6
Kirtachi, Niger 83 C5
Kirthar Range, Pakistan 68 F2
Kiruna, Sweden 8 C19
Kirundu,
  Dem. Rep. of the Congo 86 C2
Kirup, Australia 93 F2
Kirya, Russia 48 C8
Kiryū, Japan 55 F9
Kisa, Sweden 11 G9
Kisaga, Tanzania 86 C3
Kisalaya, Nic. 120 D3
Kisanga,
  Dem. Rep. of the Congo 86 B2
Kisangani,
  Dem. Rep. of the Congo 86 B2
Kisar, Indonesia 63 F7
Kisarawe, Tanzania 86 D4
Kisarawe □, Tanzania ... 86 D4
Kisarazu, Japan 55 G9
Kisbér, Hungary 42 C3
Kishanganga →, Pakistan 69 B5
Kishanganj, India 69 F13
Kishangarh, India 68 F4
Kishi, Nigeria 83 D5
Kishinev = Chişinău,
  Moldova 43 C13
Kishiwada, Japan 55 G7
Kishtwar, India 69 C6
Kisielice, Poland 44 E6
Kisii, Kenya 86 C3
Kisii □, Kenya 86 C3
Kisiju, Tanzania 86 D4
Kisir, Turkey 73 B10
Kisizi, Uganda 86 C2
Kiskatinaw →, Canada ... 104 B4
Kiskittogisu L., Canada 105 C9
Kiskomárom = Zalakomár,
  Hungary 42 D2
Kiskörei-Víztároló, Hungary 42 C5
Kiskőrös, Hungary 42 D4
Kiskundorozsma, Hungary 42 D5
Kiskunfélegyháza, Hungary 42 D4
Kiskunhalas, Hungary ... 42 D4
Kiskunmajsa, Hungary ... 42 D4
Kislovodsk, Russia 49 J6
Kismayu = Chisimaio,
  Somali Rep. 77 G8
Kiso-Gawa →, Japan 55 G8
Kiso-Sammyaku, Japan ... 55 G8
Kisofukushima, Japan ... 55 G8
Kisoro, Uganda 86 C2
Kissidougou, Guinea 82 D2
Kissimmee, U.S.A. 109 L5
Kissimmee →, U.S.A. 109 M5
Kississing L., Canada .. 105 B8
Kissónerga, Cyprus 36 E11
Kistanje, Croatia 29 E12
Kisújszállás, Hungary .. 42 C5
Kisumu, Kenya 86 C3
Kisvárda, Hungary 42 B7
Kiswani, Tanzania 86 C4
Kiswere, Tanzania 87 D4
Kit Carson, U.S.A. 112 F3
Kita, Mali 82 C3
Kitaibaraki, Japan 55 F10
Kitakami, Japan 54 E10
Kitakami-Gawa →, Japan . 54 E10
Kitakami-Sammyaku, Japan 54 E10
Kitakata, Japan 54 F9
Kitakyūshū, Japan 55 H5
Kitale, Kenya 86 B4
Kitami, Japan 54 C11
Kitami-Sammyaku, Japan . 54 B11
Kitangiri, L., Tanzania 86 C3
Kitaya, Tanzania 87 E5
Kitchener, Australia ... 93 F3
Kitchener, Canada 102 D3
Kitee, Finland 46 A6
Kitega = Gitega, Burundi 86 C2
Kitengo,
  Dem. Rep. of the Congo 86 D1
Kiteto □, Tanzania 86 D4
Kitgum, Uganda 86 B3
Kíthira, Greece 38 E5
Kíthnos, Greece 38 D6
Kiti, Cyprus 36 E12
Kiti, C., Cyprus 36 E12
Kitimat, Canada 104 C3
Kitinen →, Finland 8 C22
Kitiyab, Sudan 81 D3
Kítros, Greece 40 F6
Kitsuki, Japan 55 H5
Kittakittaooloo, L.,
  Australia 95 D2
Kittanning, U.S.A. 110 F5
Kittatinny Mts., U.S.A. 111 F10
Kittery, U.S.A. 109 D10
Kittilä, Finland 8 C21

Kitui, *Kenya* 86 C4
Kitui □, *Kenya* 86 C4
Kitwe, *Zambia* 87 E2
Kitzbühel, *Austria* 26 D5
Kitzbühler Alpen, *Austria* 26 D5
Kitzingen, *Germany* 25 F6
Kivarli, *India* 68 G5
Kivertsi, *Ukraine* 47 G3
Kivides, *Cyprus* 36 E11
Kivik, *Sweden* 11 J8
Kivotós, *Greece* 40 F5
Kivu, L.,
  Dem. Rep. of the Congo 86 C2
Kivu □,
  Dem. Rep. of the Congo 86 C2
Kiyev = Kyyiv, *Ukraine* .. 47 G6
Kiyevskoye Vdkhr. =
  Kyyivske Vdskh.,
  Ukraine 47 G6
Kıyıköy, *Turkey* 41 E12
Kiziguru, *Rwanda* 86 C3
Kızıl Adalar, *Turkey* 41 F13
Kızıl Irmak →, *Turkey* ... 72 B6
Kizil Jilga, *India* 69 B8
Kizil Yurt, *Russia* 49 J8
Kızılcabölük, *Turkey* 39 D11
Kızılcadağ, *Turkey* 39 D11
Kızılcahamam, *Turkey* ... 72 B5
Kızılhisar, *Turkey* 72 D3
Kızılırmak, *Turkey* 72 B5
Kızılkaya, *Turkey* 39 D12
Kızılören, *Turkey* 39 C12
Kızıltepe, *Turkey* 73 D9
Kizimkazi, *Tanzania* 86 D4
Kizlyar, *Russia* 49 J8
Kizyl-Arvat = Gyzylarbat,
  Turkmenistan 50 F6
Kjellerup, *Denmark* 11 H3
Kjölur, *Iceland* 8 D4
Kladanj, *Bos.-H.* 42 F3
Kladnica, *Serbia, Yug.* .. 40 C4
Kladno, *Czech Rep.* 26 A7
Kladovo, *Serbia, Yug.* ... 40 B6
Klaeng, *Thailand* 64 F3
Klagenfurt, *Austria* 26 E7
Klaipėda, *Lithuania* 9 J19
Klaipėda □, *Lithuania* ... 44 C8
Klaksvík, *Færoe Is.* 8 E9
Klamath →, *U.S.A.* 114 F1
Klamath Falls, *U.S.A.* ... 114 E3
Klamath Mts., *U.S.A.* ... 114 F2
Klanjec, *Croatia* 29 B12
Klappan →, *Canada* 104 B3
Klarälven →, *Sweden* ... 10 E7
Klässbol, *Sweden* 10 E6
Klatovy, *Czech Rep.* 26 B6
Klawer, *S. Africa* 88 E2
Klawock, *U.S.A.* 104 B2
Klazienaveen, *Neths.* ... 17 B6
Klecko, *Poland* 45 F4
Kleczew, *Poland* 45 F5
Kleena Kleene, *Canada* .. 104 C4
Klein, *U.S.A.* 114 C9
Klein-Karas, *Namibia* ... 88 D2
Klekovača, *Bos.-H.* 29 D13
Klenoec, *Macedonia* 40 E4
Klenovec, *Slovak Rep.* .. 27 C12
Klerksdorp, *S. Africa* ... 88 D4
Kleszczele, *Poland* 45 F10
Kletnya, *Russia* 46 F7
Kletsk = Klyetsk, *Belarus* 47 F4
Kletskiy, *Russia* 49 F6
Kleve, *Germany* 24 D2
Klickitat, *U.S.A.* 114 D3
Klickitat →, *U.S.A.* 116 E5
Klidhes, *Cyprus* 36 D13
Klimovichi, *Belarus* 46 F6
Klin, *Russia* 46 D9
Klinaklini →, *Canada* ... 104 C3
Klintehamn, *Sweden* 11 G12
Klintsy, *Russia* 47 F7
Klipdale, *S. Africa* 88 E2
Klippan, *Sweden* 11 H7
Klipplaat, *S. Africa* 88 E3
Klisura, *Bulgaria* 41 D8
Kljajićevo, *Serbia, Yug.* . 42 E4
Ključ, *Bos.-H.* 29 D13
Kłobuck, *Poland* 45 H5
Klockestrand, *Sweden* .. 10 B11
Kłodawa, *Poland* 45 F5
Kłodzko, *Poland* 45 H3
Klosi, *Albania* 40 E4
Klosterneuburg, *Austria* . 27 C9
Klosters, *Switz.* 25 J5
Klötze, *Germany* 24 C7
Klouto, *Togo* 83 D5
Kluane L., *Canada* 100 B6
Kluczbork, *Poland* 45 H5
Klyetsk, *Belarus* 47 F4
Klyuchevskaya, Gora,
  Russia 51 D17
Knäred, *Sweden* 11 H7
Knaresborough, *U.K.* ... 12 C6
Knee L., *Man., Canada* . 105 B10
Knee L., *Sask., Canada* . 105 B7
Knezha, *Bulgaria* 41 C8
Knić, *Serbia, Yug.* 40 C4
Knight Inlet, *Canada* 104 C3
Knighton, *U.K.* 13 E4
Knights Ferry, *U.S.A.* ... 116 H6
Knights Landing, *U.S.A.* . 116 G5
Knin, *Croatia* 29 D13
Knislinge, *Sweden* 11 H8
Knittelfeld, *Austria* 26 D7
Knivsta, *Sweden* 10 E11
Knob, C., *Australia* 93 F2

Knock, *Ireland* 15 C3
Knockmealdown Mts.,
  Ireland 15 D4
Knokke-Heist, *Belgium* .. 17 C3
Knossós, *Greece* 36 D7
Knox, *U.S.A.* 108 E2
Knox, C., *Canada* 104 C2
Knox City, *U.S.A.* 113 J5
Knox Coast, *Antarctica* .. 5 C8
Knoxville, *Iowa, U.S.A.* . 112 E8
Knoxville, *Tenn., U.S.A.* . 109 H4
Knysna, *S. Africa* 88 E3
Knyszyn, *Poland* 44 E9
Ko Kha, *Thailand* 64 C2
Koartac = Quaqtaq,
  Canada 101 B13
Koba, *Indonesia* 63 F8
Kobarid, *Slovenia* 29 B10
Kobayashi, *Japan* 55 J5
Kobdo = Hovd, *Mongolia* 60 B4
Kōbe, *Japan* 55 G7
Kobelyaky, *Ukraine* 47 H8
København, *Denmark* ... 11 J6
Københavns
  Amtskommune □,
  Denmark 11 J6
Kōbi-Sho, *Japan* 55 M1
Koblenz, *Germany* 25 E3
Kobo, *Ethiopia* 81 E4
Kobryn, *Belarus* 47 F3
Kobuleti, *Georgia* 49 K5
Kobylin, *Poland* 45 G4
Kobyłka, *Poland* 45 F8
Kobylkino, *Russia* 48 C6
Koca →, *Turkey* 41 F11
Kocabaş, *Turkey* 39 D11
Kocaeli, *Turkey* 41 F13
Kocaeli □, *Turkey* 41 F13
Kočane, *Serbia, Yug.* ... 40 C5
Kočani, *Macedonia* 40 E6
Koçarlı, *Turkey* 39 D9
Koceljevo, *Serbia, Yug.* . 40 B3
Kočevje, *Slovenia* 29 C11
Koch Bihar, *India* 67 F16
Kochang, *S. Korea* 57 G14
Kochas, *India* 69 G10
Kocher →, *Germany* 25 F5
Kōchi, *Japan* 55 H6
Kōchi □, *Japan* 55 H6
Kochiu = Gejiu, *China* .. 58 F4
Kock, *Poland* 45 G9
Kode, *Sweden* 11 G5
Kodiak, *U.S.A.* 100 C4
Kodiak I., *U.S.A.* 100 C4
Kodinar, *India* 68 J4
Kodori →, *Georgia* 49 J5
Koes, *Namibia* 88 D2
Kofçaz, *Turkey* 41 E11
Koffiefontein, *S. Africa* .. 88 D4
Kofiau, *Indonesia* 63 E7
Köflach, *Austria* 26 D8
Koforidua, *Ghana* 83 D4
Kōfu, *Japan* 55 G9
Koga, *Japan* 55 F9
Kogaluk →, *Canada* 103 A7
Kogan, *Australia* 95 D5
Køge, *Denmark* 11 J6
Køge Bugt, *Denmark* ... 11 J6
Kogi □, *Nigeria* 83 D6
Kogin Baba, *Nigeria* 83 D7
Koh-i-Bābā, *Afghan.* ... 66 B5
Koh-i-Khurd, *Afghan.* .. 68 C1
Kohat, *Pakistan* 68 C4
Kohima, *India* 67 G19
Kohkīlūyeh va Būyer
  Aḥmadi □, *Iran* 71 D6
Kohler Ra., *Antarctica* .. 5 D15
Kohtla-Järve, *Estonia* ... 9 G22
Koillismaa, *Finland* 8 D23
Koin-dong, *N. Korea* 57 D14
Koinare, *Bulgaria* 41 C8
Kojetín, *Czech Rep.* 27 B10
Kojŏ, *N. Korea* 57 E14
Kojonup, *Australia* 93 F2
Kojūr, *Iran* 71 B6
Koka, *Sudan* 80 C3
Kokand = Qŭqon,
  Uzbekistan 50 E8
Kokanee Glacier Prov.
  Park, *Canada* 104 D5
Kokas, *Indonesia* 63 E8
Kokava, *Slovak Rep.* 27 C12
Kokchetav = Kökshetaū,
  Kazakstan 50 D7
Kokemäenjoki →, *Finland* 9 F19
Kokhma, *Russia* 48 B5
Kokkola, *Finland* 8 E20
Koko, *Nigeria* 83 C5
Koko Kyunzu, *Burma* ... 67 M18
Kokolopozo, *Ivory C.* ... 82 D3
Kokomo, *U.S.A.* 108 E2
Kokoro, *Niger* 83 C5
Koksan, *N. Korea* 57 E14
Kökshetaū, *Kazakstan* ... 50 D7
Koksoak →, *Canada* 101 C13
Kokstad, *S. Africa* 89 E4
Kokubu, *Japan* 55 J5
Kola, *Indonesia* 63 F8
Kola Pen. = Kolskiy
  Poluostrov, *Russia* 50 C4
Kolahoi, *India* 69 B6
Kolahun, *Liberia* 82 D2
Kolaka, *Indonesia* 63 E6
Kolar, *India* 66 N11
Kolar Gold Fields, *India* . 66 N11
Kolari, *Finland* 8 C20
Kolárovo, *Slovak Rep.* ... 27 D10

Kolašin, *Montenegro, Yug.* 40 D3
Kolayat, *India* 66 F8
Kolbäck, *Sweden* 10 E10
Kolbäcksån →, *Sweden* . 10 E10
Kolbermoor, *Germany* .. 25 H8
Kolbuszowa, *Poland* 45 H8
Kolchugino = Leninsk-
  Kuznetskiy, *Russia* 50 D9
Kolchugino, *Russia* 46 D10
Kolda, *Senegal* 82 C2
Kolding, *Denmark* 11 J3
Kolepom = Dolak, Pulau,
  Indonesia 63 F9
Kolguyev, Ostrov, *Russia* 50 C5
Kolhapur, *India* 66 L9
Kolia, *Ivory C.* 82 D3
Kolín, *Czech Rep.* 26 A8
Kolind, *Denmark* 11 H4
Kolkas rags, *Latvia* 9 H20
Kölleda, *Germany* 24 D7
Kollum, *Neths.* 17 A6
Kolmanskop, *Namibia* .. 88 D2
Köln, *Germany* 24 E2
Kolno, *Poland* 44 E8
Koło, *Poland* 45 F5
Kołobrzeg, *Poland* 44 D2
Kolokani, *Mali* 82 C3
Kolomna, *Russia* 46 E10
Kolomyya, *Ukraine* 47 H3
Kolondiéba, *Mali* 82 C3
Kolonodale, *Indonesia* .. 63 E6
Kolonowskie, *Poland* ... 45 H5
Kolosib, *India* 67 G18
Kolpashevo, *Russia* 50 D9
Kolpino, *Russia* 46 C6
Kolpny, *Russia* 47 F9
Kolskiy Poluostrov, *Russia* 50 C4
Kolsva, *Sweden* 10 E9
Kolubara →, *Serbia, Yug.* 40 B4
Koluszki, *Poland* 45 G6
Kolwezi,
  Dem. Rep. of the Congo 87 E2
Kolyma →, *Russia* 51 C17
Kolymskoye Nagorye,
  Russia 51 C16
Kôm Ombo, *Egypt* 80 C3
Komandorskiye Is. =
  Komandorskiye Ostrova,
  Russia 51 D17
Komandorskiye Ostrova,
  Russia 51 D17
Komárno, *Slovak Rep.* .. 27 D11
Komárom, *Hungary* 42 C3
Komárom-Esztergom □,
  Hungary 42 C3
Komatipoort, *S. Africa* .. 89 D5
Komatou Yialou, *Cyprus* 36 D13
Komatsu, *Japan* 55 F8
Komatsujima, *Japan* 55 H7
Kombissiri, *Burkina Faso* 83 C4
Kombori, *Burkina Faso* . 82 C4
Kombóti, *Greece* 38 B3
Komen, *Slovenia* 29 C10
Komenda, *Ghana* 83 D4
Komi □, *Russia* 50 C6
Komiža, *Croatia* 29 E13
Komló, *Hungary* 42 D3
Kommunarsk = Alchevsk,
  Ukraine 47 H10
Kommunizma, Pik,
  Tajikistan 50 F8
Komodo, *Indonesia* 63 F5
Komoé →, *Ivory C.* 82 D4
Komoran, Pulau, *Indonesia* 63 F9
Komoro, *Japan* 55 F9
Komotini, *Greece* 41 E9
Komovi, *Montenegro, Yug.* 40 D3
Kompasberg, *S. Africa* .. 88 E3
Kompong Bang, *Cambodia* 65 F5
Kompong Cham, *Cambodia* 65 G5
Kompong Chhnang =
  Kampang Chhnang,
  Cambodia 65 F5
Kompong Chikreng,
  Cambodia 64 F5
Kompong Kleang,
  Cambodia 64 F5
Kompong Luong,
  Cambodia 65 G5
Kompong Pranak,
  Cambodia 64 F5
Kompong Som = Kampong
  Saom, *Cambodia* 65 G4
Kompong Som, Chhung =
  Kampong Saom, Chaak,
  Cambodia 65 G4
Kompong Speu, *Cambodia* 65 G5
Kompong Sralao,
  Cambodia 64 E5
Kompong Thom, *Cambodia* 64 F5
Kompong Trabeck,
  Cambodia 64 F5
Kompong Trabeck,
  Cambodia 65 G5
Kompong Trach, *Cambodia* 65 G5
Kompong Tralach,
  Cambodia 65 G5
Komrat = Comrat,
  Moldova 43 D13
Komsberg, *S. Africa* 88 E3
Komsomolets, Ostrov,
  Russia 51 A10
Komsomolsk, *Amur, Russia* 51 D14
Komsomolsk, *Ivanovo,
  Russia* 46 D11
Komsomolskiy, *Russia* .. 48 C7
Kömür Burnu, *Turkey* ... 39 C8

Kon Tum, *Vietnam* 64 E7
Kon Tum, Plateau du,
  Vietnam 64 E7
Konakovo, *Russia* 46 D9
Konarhá □, *Afghan.* 66 B7
Konārī, *Iran* 71 D6
Konawa, *U.S.A.* 113 H6
Konch, *India* 69 G8
Kondinin, *Australia* 93 F2
Kondoa, *Tanzania* 86 C4
Kondoa □, *Tanzania* 86 D4
Kondókali, *Greece* 36 A3
Kondopaga, *Russia* 46 A8
Kondratyevo, *Russia* 51 D10
Kondrovo, *Russia* 46 E8
Konduga, *Nigeria* 83 C7
Köneürgench,
  Turkmenistan 50 E6
Konevo, *Russia* 46 A10
Kong, *Ivory C.* 82 D4
Kong = Khong →,
  Cambodia 64 F5
Kong, Koh, *Cambodia* ... 65 G4
Kong Christian IX.s Land,
  Greenland 4 C6
Kong Christian X.s Land,
  Greenland 4 B6
Kong Franz Joseph Fd.,
  Greenland 4 B6
Kong Frederik IX.s Land,
  Greenland 4 C5
Kong Frederik VI.s Kyst,
  Greenland 4 C5
Kong Frederik VIII.s Land,
  Greenland 4 B6
Kong Oscar Fjord,
  Greenland 4 B6
Kongeå →, *Denmark* 11 J2
Kongerslev, *Denmark* ... 11 H4
Kongju, *S. Korea* 57 F14
Konglu, *Burma* 67 F20
Kongolo, *Kasai Or.,
  Dem. Rep. of the Congo* 86 D1
Kongolo, *Shaba,
  Dem. Rep. of the Congo* 86 D2
Kongor, *Sudan* 81 F3
Kongoussi, *Burkina Faso* 83 C4
Kongsberg, *Norway* 9 G13
Kongsvinger, *Norway* ... 9 F15
Kongwa, *Tanzania* 86 D4
Koni,
  Dem. Rep. of the Congo 87 E2
Koni, Mts.,
  Dem. Rep. of the Congo 87 E2
Koniecpol, *Poland* 45 H6
Königs Wusterhausen,
  Germany 24 C9
Königsberg = Kaliningrad,
  Russia 9 J19
Königsbrunn, *Germany* . 25 G6
Königslutter, *Germany* .. 24 C6
Konin, *Poland* 45 F5
Konin □, *Poland* 45 F5
Konispoli, *Albania* 40 G4
Kónitsa, *Greece* 38 A2
Konjic, *Bos.-H.* 42 G2
Konkiep, *Namibia* 88 D2
Konkouré →, *Guinea* ... 82 D2
Könnern, *Germany* 24 D7
Kono, *S. Leone* 82 D2
Konongo, *Ghana* 83 D4
Konosha, *Russia* 48 B11
Kōnosu, *Japan* 55 F9
Konotop, *Ukraine* 47 G7
Konqi He →, *China* 60 B4
Końskie, *Poland* 45 G7
Konstancin-Jeziorna,
  Poland 45 F8
Konstantinovka =
  Kostyantynivka, *Ukraine* 47 H9
Konstantinovsk, *Russia* . 49 G5
Konstantynów Łódźki,
  Poland 45 G6
Konstanz, *Germany* 25 H5
Kont, *Iran* 71 E9
Kontagora, *Nigeria* 83 C6
Kontum, *Vietnam* 64 E7
Konya, *Turkey* 72 D5
Konya Ovası, *Turkey* ... 72 C5
Konz, *Germany* 25 F2
Konza, *Kenya* 86 C4
Kookynie, *Australia* 93 E3
Kooline, *Australia* 92 D2
Kooloonong, *Australia* .. 95 E3
Koolyanobbing, *Australia* 93 F2
Koondrook, *Australia* ... 95 F3
Koonibba, *Australia* 95 E1
Koorawatha, *Australia* .. 95 E4
Koorda, *Australia* 93 F2
Kooskia, *U.S.A.* 114 C6
Kootenai →, *U.S.A.* 114 B5
Kootenay L., *Canada* 104 D5
Kootenay Nat. Park,
  Canada 104 C5
Kootjieskolk, *S. Africa* .. 88 E3
Kopanovka, *Russia* 49 G8
Kopaonik, *Serbia, Yug.* . 40 C4
Kópavogur, *Iceland* 8 D3
Koper, *Slovenia* 29 C10
Kopervik, *Norway* 9 G11
Kopi, *Australia* 95 E2
Köping, *Sweden* 10 E10
Köpingsvik, *Sweden* 11 H10
Kopište, *Croatia* 29 F13
Koplik, *Albania* 40 D3
Köpmanholmen, *Sweden* 10 A12

Kopparberg, *Sweden* 10 E9
Kopparbergs län □, *Sweden* 10 C8
Koppeh Dāgh, *Asia* 71 B8
Koppies, *S. Africa* 89 D4
Koppom, *Sweden* 10 E6
Koprivlen, *Bulgaria* 40 E7
Koprivnica, *Croatia* 29 B13
Kopřivnice, *Czech Rep.* . 27 B11
Koprivshtitsa, *Bulgaria* .. 41 D8
Köprübaşı, *Turkey* 39 C10
Kopychyntsi, *Ukraine* ... 47 H3
Korab, *Macedonia* 40 E4
Korakiána, *Greece* 36 A3
Korba, *India* 69 H10
Korbach, *Germany* 24 D4
Korbu, G., *Malaysia* 65 K3
Korça, *Albania* 40 F4
Korce = Korça, *Albania* .. 40 F4
Korčula, *Croatia* 29 F13
Korčulanski Kanal, *Croatia* 29 E13
Kord Kūy, *Iran* 71 B7
Kord Sheykh, *Iran* 71 D7
Kordestān □, *Iran* 70 C5
Kordofān, *Sudan* 79 F11
Korea, North ■, *Asia* ... 57 E14
Korea, South ■, *Asia* ... 57 G15
Korea Bay, *Korea* 57 E13
Korea Strait, *Asia* 57 H15
Korenevo, *Russia* 47 G8
Korenovsk, *Russia* 49 H4
Korets, *Ukraine* 47 G4
Korfantów, *Poland* 45 H4
Korgan, *Turkey* 72 B7
Korgus, *Sudan* 80 D3
Korhogo, *Ivory C.* 82 D3
Koribundu, *S. Leone* 82 D2
Korinthía □, *Greece* 38 D4
Korinthiakós Kólpos,
  Greece 38 C4
Kórinthos, *Greece* 38 D4
Korioumé, *Mali* 82 B4
Koríssa, Límni, *Greece* .. 36 B3
Kōriyama, *Japan* 54 F10
Korkuteli, *Turkey* 39 D12
Kormakiti, C., *Cyprus* ... 36 D11
Körmend, *Hungary* 42 C1
Kornat, *Croatia* 29 E12
Korneshty = Corneşti,
  Moldova 43 C13
Korneuburg, *Austria* 27 C9
Kórnik, *Poland* 45 F4
Koro, *Fiji* 91 C8
Koro, *Ivory C.* 82 D3
Koro, *Mali* 82 C4
Koro Sea, *Fiji* 91 C9
Korocha, *Russia* 47 G9
Köroğlu Dağları, *Turkey* . 72 B5
Korogwe, *Tanzania* 86 D4
Korogwe □, *Tanzania* ... 86 D4
Koroit, *Australia* 95 F3
Koronadal, *Phil.* 61 H6
Koróni, *Greece* 38 E3
Korónia, Limni, *Greece* .. 40 F7
Koronís, *Greece* 39 D7
Koronowo, *Poland* 45 E4
Koror, *Pac. Oc.* 63 C8
Körös →, *Hungary* 42 D5
Köröstarcsa, *Hungary* ... 42 D6
Korosten, *Ukraine* 47 G5
Korostyshev, *Ukraine* ... 47 G5
Korotoyak, *Russia* 47 G10
Korraraika, Helodranon' i,
  Madag. 89 B7
Korsakov, *Russia* 51 E15
Korsberga, *Sweden* 11 G9
Korshunovo, *Russia* 51 D12
Korsør, *Denmark* 11 J5
Korsun Shevchenkovskiy,
  Ukraine 47 H6
Korsze, *Poland* 44 D8
Korti, *Sudan* 80 D3
Kortrijk, *Belgium* 17 D3
Korucu, *Turkey* 39 B9
Korwai, *India* 68 G8
Koryakskoye Nagorye,
  Russia 51 C18
Koryŏng, *S. Korea* 57 G15
Koryukovka, *Ukraine* ... 47 G7
Kos, *Greece* 39 E9
Kosa, *Ethiopia* 81 F4
Kosaya Gora, *Russia* 46 E9
Kościan, *Poland* 45 F3
Kościerzyna, *Poland* 44 D5
Kosciusko, *U.S.A.* 113 J10
Kosciusko I., *U.S.A.* 104 B2
Kosciuszko, Mt., *Australia* 95 F4
Kösély →, *Hungary* 42 C6
Kosha, *Sudan* 80 C3
Koshava, *Bulgaria* 40 B7
K'oshih = Kashi, *China* .. 60 C2
Koshiki-Rettō, *Japan* 55 J4
Kosi, *India* 68 F7
Košice, *Slovak Rep.* 27 C14
Košický □, *Slovak Rep.* . 27 C14
Kosjerić, *Serbia, Yug.* ... 40 B3
Köşk, *Turkey* 39 D10
Koskhinoú, *Greece* 36 C10
Kosŏng, *N. Korea* 57 E15
Kosovo □, *Serbia, Yug.* . 40 D4
Kosovska Mitrovica,
  Serbia, Yug. 40 D4
Kossou, L. de, *Ivory C.* .. 82 D3
Kosta, *Sweden* 11 H9
Kostajnica, *Croatia* 29 C13
Kostanjevica, *Slovenia* .. 29 C12
Kostenets, *Bulgaria* 40 D7
Koster, *S. Africa* 88 D4

Kôstî, Sudan 81 E3
Kostinbrod, Bulgaria 40 D7
Kostolac, Serbia, Yug. 40 B5
Kostopil, Ukraine 47 G4
Kostroma, Russia 46 D11
Kostromskoye Vdkhr.,
 Russia 46 D11
Kostrzyn, Gorzow Wlkp.,
 Poland 45 F1
Kostrzyn, Poznań, Poland 45 F4
Kostyantynivka, Ukraine .. 47 H9
Kostyukovichi =
 Kastsyukovichy, Belarus 46 F7
Koszalin, Poland 44 D3
Koszalin □, Poland 44 E3
Kőszeg, Hungary 42 C1
Kot Addu, Pakistan 68 D4
Kot Moman, Pakistan 68 C5
Kota, India 68 G6
Kota Baharu, Malaysia ... 65 J4
Kota Belud, Malaysia 62 C5
Kota Kinabalu, Malaysia .. 62 C5
Kota Kubu Baharu,
 Malaysia 65 L3
Kota Tinggi, Malaysia ... 65 M4
Kotaagung, Indonesia 62 F2
Kotabaru, Indonesia 62 E5
Kotabumi, Indonesia 62 E2
Kotamobagu, Indonesia ... 63 D6
Kotaneelee →, Canada .. 104 A4
Kotcho L., Canada 104 B4
Kotel, Bulgaria 41 D10
Kotelnich, Russia 48 A9
Kotelnikovo, Russia 49 G6
Kotelnyy, Ostrov, Russia . 51 B14
Köthen, Germany 24 D7
Kothi, India 69 G9
Kotiro, Pakistan 68 F2
Kotka, Finland 9 F22
Kotlas, Russia 50 C5
Kotlenska Planina, Bulgaria 41 D10
Kotli, Pakistan 68 C5
Kotmul, Pakistan 69 B6
Kotonkoro, Nigeria 83 C6
Kotor, Montenegro, Yug. . 40 D2
Kotor Varoš, Bos.-H. 42 F2
Kotoriba, Croatia 29 B13
Kotovo, Russia 48 E7
Kotovsk, Russia 48 D5
Kotovsk, Ukraine 47 J5
Kotputli, India 68 F7
Kotri, Pakistan 68 G3
Kótronas, Greece 38 E4
Kötschach-Mauthen,
 Austria 26 E6
Kottayam, India 66 Q10
Kotturu, India 66 M10
Kotuy →, Russia 51 B11
Kotzebue, U.S.A. 100 B3
Koudougou, Burkina Faso 82 C4
Koufonísi, Greece 36 E8
Koufonísia, Greece 39 E7
Kougaberge, S. Africa ... 88 E3
Kouibli, Ivory C. 82 D3
Kouilou →, Congo 84 E2
Koula Moutou, Gabon ... 84 E2
Koulen = Kulen,
 Cambodia 64 F5
Koulikoro, Mali 82 C3
Kouloúra, Greece 36 A3
Koúm-bournoú, Ákra,
 Greece 36 C10
Koumala, Australia 94 C4
Koumankou, Mali 82 C3
Koumbia, Burkina Faso . 82 C4
Koumbia, Guinea 82 C2
Koumboum, Guinea 82 C2
Koumpenntoum, Senegal . 82 C2
Koumra, Chad 79 G9
Koundara, Guinea 82 C2
Kounradskiy, Kazakstan . 50 E8
Kountze, U.S.A. 113 K7
Koupéla, Burkina Faso .. 83 C4
Kouris →, Cyprus 36 E11
Kourou, Fr. Guiana 125 B8
Kouroussa, Guinea 82 C3
Koussané, Mali 82 C2
Kousséri, Cameroon ... 79 F8
Koutiala, Mali 82 C3
Kouto, Ivory C. 82 D3
Kouvé, Togo 83 D5
Kovačica, Serbia, Yug. .. 42 E5
Kovel, Ukraine 47 G3
Kovin, Serbia, Yug. 42 F5
Kovrov, Russia 48 B5
Kowal, Poland 45 F6
Kowalewo Pomorskie,
 Poland 45 E5
Kowanyama, Australia .. 94 B3
Kowkash, Canada 102 B2
Kowloon, H.K. 59 F10
Kowŏn, N. Korea 57 E14
Köyceğiz, Turkey 39 E10
Köyceğiz Gölü, Turkey .. 39 E10
Koyulhisar, Turkey 72 B7
Koyunyeri, Turkey 41 F10
Koza, Japan 55 L3
Kozak, Turkey 39 B9
Kozan, Turkey 72 D6
Kozáni, Greece 40 F5
Kozáni □, Greece 40 F5
Kozara, Bos.-H. 29 D14
Kozarac, Bos.-H. 29 D13
Kozelets, Ukraine 47 G6
Kozelsk, Russia 46 E8
Kozhikode = Calicut, India 66 P9

Koziegłowy, Poland 45 H6
Kozienice, Poland 45 G8
Kozje, Slovenia 29 B12
Kozloduy, Bulgaria 40 C7
Kozlovets, Bulgaria 41 C9
Kozlovka, Russia 48 C9
Kozlu, Turkey 72 B4
Kozluk, Turkey 73 C9
Koźmin, Poland 45 G4
Kozmodemyansk, Russia . 48 B8
Kożuchów, Poland 45 G2
Kozyatyn, Ukraine 47 H5
Kpabia, Ghana 83 D4
Kpalimé, Togo 83 D5
Kpandae, Ghana 83 D4
Kpessi, Togo 83 D5
Kra, Isthmus of = Kra,
 Kho Khot, Thailand ... 65 G2
Kra, Kho Khot, Thailand . 65 G2
Kra Buri, Thailand 65 G2
Krabi, Thailand 65 H2
Kracheh, Cambodia 64 F6
Kragan, Indonesia 63 G14
Kragerø, Norway 9 G13
Kragujevac, Serbia, Yug. . 40 B4
Krajenka, Poland 45 E3
Krajina, Bos.-H. 29 D13
Krakatau = Rakata, Pulau,
 Indonesia 62 F3
Krakor, Cambodia 64 F5
Kraków, Poland 45 H6
Kraków □, Poland 45 H6
Kralanh, Cambodia 64 F4
Králíky, Czech Rep. 27 A9
Kraljevo, Serbia, Yug. ... 40 C4
Královský Chlmec,
 Slovak Rep. 27 C14
Kralupy nad Vltavou,
 Czech Rep. 26 A7
Kramatorsk, Ukraine 47 H9
Kramfors, Sweden 10 B11
Kraniá, Greece 40 G5
Kranía Elassóna, Greece . 38 B4
Kranídhion, Greece 38 D5
Kranj, Slovenia 29 B11
Kranjska Gora, Slovenia . 29 B10
Krankskop, S. Africa 89 D5
Krapina, Croatia 29 B12
Krapina →, Croatia 29 C12
Krapkowice, Poland 45 H4
Kras, Croatia 29 C10
Kraskino, Russia 54 C5
Kráslava, Latvia 46 E4
Kraslice, Czech Rep. 26 A5
Krasnaya Gorbatka, Russia 48 C5
Krasnaya Polyana, Russia . 49 J5
Kraśnik, Poland 45 H9
Krasnoarmeisk, Ukraine . 47 H9
Krasnoarmeysk, Russia .. 48 E7
Krasnoarmeyskiy, Russia . 49 G6
Krasnobrod, Poland 45 H10
Krasnodar, Russia 49 H4
Krasnodon, Ukraine 47 H10
Krasnogorskiy, Russia ... 48 B9
Krasnograd = Krasnohrad,
 Ukraine 47 H8
Krasnogvardeyskoye,
 Russia 49 H5
Krasnogvardyeysk, Ukraine 47 K8
Krasnohrad, Ukraine 47 H8
Krasnokutsk, Ukraine ... 47 G8
Krasnolesnyy, Russia 47 G10
Krasnoperekopsk, Ukraine 47 J7
Krasnorechenskiy, Russia . 54 B7
Krasnoselkup, Russia 50 C9
Krasnoslobodsk,
 Mordvinia, Russia 48 C6
Krasnoslobodsk,
 Volgograd, Russia 49 F7
Krasnoturinsk, Russia ... 50 D7
Krasnovodsk =
 Türkmenbashi,
 Turkmenistan 50 F6
Krasnoyarsk, Russia 51 D10
Krasnoye = Krasnyy,
 Russia 46 E6
Krasnozavodsk, Russia .. 46 D10
Krasny Sulin, Russia 47 J11
Krasnystaw, Poland 45 H10
Krasnyy, Russia 46 E6
Krasnyy Kholm, Russia .. 46 C9
Krasnyy Kut, Russia 48 E8
Krasnyy Liman, Ukraine . 47 H9
Krasnyy Luch, Ukraine .. 47 H10
Krasnyy Profintern, Russia 46 D11
Krasnyy Yar, Astrakhan,
 Russia 49 G9
Krasnyy Yar, Samara,
 Russia 48 D10
Krasnyy Yar, Volgograd,
 Russia 48 E7
Krasnyye Baki, Russia ... 48 B7
Krasnyyoskolske Vdskh.,
 Ukraine 47 H9
Kraszna →, Hungary ... 42 B7
Kratie = Kracheh,
 Cambodia 64 F6
Kratovo, Macedonia 40 D6
Krau, Indonesia 63 E10
Kravanh, Chuor Phnum,
 Cambodia 65 G4
Krawang, Indonesia 63 G13
Krefeld, Germany 24 D2
Krémaston, Límni, Greece 38 C3
Kremen, Croatia 29 D12
Kremenchug =
 Kremenchuk, Ukraine . 47 H7
Kremenchuk, Ukraine 47 H7

Kremenchuksk Vdskh.,
 Ukraine 47 H7
Kremenets, Ukraine 47 G3
Kremennaya, Ukraine ... 47 H10
Kremges = Svitlovodsk,
 Ukraine 47 H7
Kremmen, Germany 24 C9
Kremmling, U.S.A. 114 F10
Kremnica, Slovak Rep. ... 27 C11
Krems, Austria 26 C8
Kremsmünster, Austria ... 26 C7
Kretinga, Lithuania 9 J19
Krettsy, Russia 46 C7
Kreuzberg, Germany 25 E5
Kreuztal, Germany 24 E4
Kría Vrísi, Greece 40 F6
Kribi, Cameroon 83 E6
Krichem, Bulgaria 41 D8
Krichev = Krychaw,
 Belarus 46 F6
Krim, Slovenia 29 C11
Kriós, Ákra, Greece 36 D5
Krishna →, India 67 M12
Krishnanagar, India 69 H13
Kristdala, Sweden 11 G10
Kristiansand, Norway ... 9 G13
Kristianstad, Sweden 11 H8
Kristianstads län □, Sweden 11 H7
Kristiansund, Norway ... 8 E12
Kristiinankaupunki, Finland 9 E19
Kristinehamn, Sweden ... 10 E8
Kristinestad =
 Kristiinankaupunki,
 Finland 9 E19
Kríti, Greece 36 D7
Kritsá, Greece 36 D7
Kriva →, Macedonia ... 40 D5
Kriva Palanka, Macedonia 40 D6
Krivaja →, Bos.-H. 42 F3
Krivelj, Serbia, Yug. 40 B6
Krivoy Rog = Kryvyy Rih,
 Ukraine 47 J7
Križevci, Croatia 29 B13
Krk, Croatia 29 C11
Krka →, Slovenia 29 C12
Krkonoše, Czech Rep. ... 26 A8
Krnov, Czech Rep. 27 A10
Krobia, Poland 45 G3
Krokeaí, Greece 38 E4
Krokek, Sweden 11 F10
Krokodil →, Mozam. ... 89 D5
Krokom, Sweden 10 A8
Krokowa, Poland 44 D5
Krolevets, Ukraine 47 G7
Kroměříž, Czech Rep. ... 27 B10
Krompachy, Slovak Rep. . 27 C13
Kromy, Russia 47 F8
Kronach, Germany 25 E7
Kronobergs län □, Sweden 11 H8
Kronprins Olav Kyst,
 Antarctica 5 C5
Kronshtadt, Russia 46 C5
Kroonstad, S. Africa 88 D4
Krôpelin, Germany 24 A7
Kropotkin, Russia 49 H5
Kropp, Germany 24 A5
Krosna, Lithuania 44 D10
Krośniewice, Poland 45 F6
Krosno, Poland 45 J8
Krosno □, Poland 45 J9
Krosno Odrzańskie, Poland 45 F2
Krotoszyn, Poland 45 G4
Krotovka, Russia 48 D10
Kroussón, Greece 36 D6
Krrabë, Albania 40 E3
Krško, Slovenia 29 C12
Krstača, Serbia, Yug. 40 D4
Kruger Nat. Park, S. Africa 89 C5
Krugersdorp, S. Africa .. 89 D4
Kruisfontein, S. Africa .. 88 E3
Kruja, Albania 40 E3
Krulevshchina =
 Krulyewshchyna, Belarus 46 E4
Krulyewshchyna, Belarus . 46 E4
Kruma, Albania 40 D4
Krumbach, Germany 25 G6
Krumovgrad, Bulgaria ... 41 E9
Krung Thep = Bangkok,
 Thailand 64 F3
Krupanj, Serbia, Yug. ... 40 B3
Krupina, Slovak Rep. 27 C12
Krupinica →, Slovak Rep. 27 C11
Krupki, Belarus 46 E5
Kruševac, Serbia, Yug. ... 40 C5
Kruševo, Macedonia 40 E5
Kruszwica, Poland 45 F5
Kruzof I., U.S.A. 104 B1
Krychaw, Belarus 46 F6
Krymsk, Russia 47 K10
Krymskiy Poluostrov =
 Krymskyy Pivostriv,
 Ukraine 47 K8
Krymskyy Pivostriv,
 Ukraine 47 K8
Krynica, Poland 45 J7
Krynica Morska, Poland . 44 D6
Krynki, Poland 45 E10
Kryvyy Rih, Ukraine 47 J7
Krzepice, Poland 45 H5
Krzeszyn, Poland 45 H9
Krzna →, Poland 45 F10
Krzywiń, Poland 45 G3
Krzyż Wielkopolski, Poland 45 F2

Kstovo, Russia 48 B7
Kuala Berang, Malaysia .. 65 K4
Kuala Dungun = Dungun,
 Malaysia 65 K4
Kuala Kangsar, Malaysia . 65 K3
Kuala Kelawang, Malaysia 65 L4
Kuala Kerai, Malaysia ... 65 K4
Kuala Lipis, Malaysia 65 K4
Kuala Lumpur, Malaysia . 65 L3
Kuala Nerang, Malaysia . 65 J3
Kuala Pilah, Malaysia 65 L4
Kuala Rompin, Malaysia . 65 L4
Kuala Selangor, Malaysia . 65 L3
Kuala Sepetang, Malaysia . 65 K3
Kuala Terengganu,
 Malaysia 65 K4
Kualajelai, Indonesia 62 E4
Kualakapuas, Indonesia .. 62 E4
Kualakurun, Indonesia ... 62 E4
Kualapembuang, Indonesia 62 E4
Kualasimpang, Indonesia . 62 D1
Kuancheng, China 57 D10
Kuandang, Indonesia 63 D6
Kuandian, China 57 D13
Kuangchou = Guangzhou,
 China 59 F9
Kuantan, Malaysia 65 L4
Kuba = Quba, Azerbaijan 49 K9
Kuban →, Russia 47 K9
Kubenskoye, Ozero, Russia 46 C10
Kubokawa, Japan 55 H6
Kubrat, Bulgaria 41 C10
Kučevo, Serbia, Yug. 40 B5
Kucha Gompa, India 69 B7
Kuchaman, India 68 F6
Kuchenspitze, Austria ... 26 D3
Kuching, Malaysia 62 D4
Kuchino-eruba-Jima, Japan 55 J5
Kuchino-Shima, Japan ... 55 K4
Kuchinotsu, Japan 55 H5
Kuchl, Austria 26 D6
Kucing = Kuching,
 Malaysia 62 D4
Kuçovë, Albania 40 F3
Küçükbahçe, Turkey 39 C8
Küçükköy, Turkey 39 B8
Küçükkuyu, Turkey 39 B8
Küçükmenderes →,
 Turkey 39 D9
Kud →, Pakistan 68 F2
Kuda, India 66 H7
Kudat, Malaysia 62 C5
Kudirkos Naumiestis,
 Lithuania 44 D9
Kudowa-Zdrój, Poland .. 45 H3
Kudus, Indonesia 63 G14
Kudymkar, Russia 50 D6
Kueiyang = Guiyang,
 China 58 D6
Kufra Oasis = Al Kufrah,
 Libya 79 D10
Kufstein, Austria 26 D5
Kugluktuk, Canada 100 B8
Kugong 1., Canada 102 A4
Küh-e-Hazārān, Iran 71 D8
Kühak, Iran 66 F3
Kühbonān, Iran 71 D8
Kūhestak, Iran 71 E8
Kühīn, Iran 71 C6
Kühīrī, Iran 71 E9
Kuhnsdorf, Austria 26 E7
Kühpāyeh, Esfahan, Iran . 71 C7
Kühpāyeh, Kermān, Iran . 71 D8
Kui Buri, Thailand 65 F2
Kuito, Angola 85 G3
Kujang, N. Korea 57 E14
Kuji, Japan 54 D10
Kujū-San, Japan 55 H5
Kukavica, Serbia, Yug. .. 40 D5
Kukawa, Nigeria 83 C7
Kukerin, Australia 93 F2
Kukësi, Albania 40 D4
Kukmor, Russia 48 B10
Kukup, Malaysia 65 M4
Kukvidze, Russia 48 E6
Kula, Bulgaria 40 C6
Kula, Serbia, Yug. 42 E4
Kula, Turkey 39 C10
Kulai, Malaysia 65 M4
Kulal, Mt., Kenya 86 B4
Kulaly, Ostrov, Kazakstan 49 H10
Kulasekarappattinam, India 66 Q11
Kulautuva, Lithuania 44 D10
Kuldīga, Latvia 9 H19
Kuldīga □, Latvia 44 B8
Kuldja = Yining, China .. 60 B3
Kuldu, Sudan 81 E2
Kulebaki, Russia 48 C6
Kulen, Cambodia 64 F5
Kulen Vakuf, Bos.-H. ... 29 D13
Kulgam, India 69 C6
Kulim, Malaysia 65 K3
Kulin, Australia 93 F2
Kulja, Australia 93 F2
Kulm, U.S.A. 112 B5
Kulmbach, Germany 25 E7
Kulp, Turkey 73 C9
Kulsary, Kazakstan 50 E6
Kulti, India 69 H12
Kulu, Turkey 72 C5
Kulumbura, Australia ... 92 B4
Kulunda, Russia 50 D8
Kulungar, Afghan. 68 C3
Kulvand, Iran 71 D7
Kulwin, Australia 95 F3

Kulyab = Külob, Tajikistan 50 F7
Kuma →, Russia 49 H8
Kumafşarı, Turkey 39 D11
Kumaganum, Nigeria ... 83 C7
Kumagaya, Japan 55 F9
Kumai, Indonesia 62 E4
Kumamba, Kepulauan,
 Indonesia 63 E9
Kumamoto, Japan 55 H5
Kumamoto □, Japan ... 55 H5
Kumanovo, Macedonia .. 40 D5
Kumara, N.Z. 91 K3
Kumarl, Australia 93 F3
Kumasi, Ghana 82 D4
Kumayri = Gyumri,
 Armenia 49 K6
Kumba, Cameroon 83 E6
Kumbağ, Turkey 41 F11
Kumbakonam, India 66 P11
Kumbarilla, Australia ... 95 D5
Kumbo, Cameroon 83 D7
Kŭmchŏn, N. Korea 57 E14
Kumdok, India 69 C8
Kume-Shima, Japan 55 L3
Kumeny, Russia 48 A9
Kumertau, Russia 50 D6
Kumguri, Australia 94 C4
Kumhar →, Pakistan ... 69 B5
Kumheyges, Hungary ... 42 C5
Kuningan, Indonesia 63 G13
Kunlong, Burma 67 H21
Kunlun Shan, Asia 60 C3
Kunmadaras, Hungary .. 42 C5
Kunming, China 58 E4
Kunów, Poland 45 H8
Kunsan, S. Korea 57 G14
Kunshan, China 59 B13
Kunszentmárton, Hungary 42 D5
Kunszentmiklós, Hungary . 42 C4
Kununurra, Australia ... 92 C4
Kunwarara, Australia ... 94 C5
Kunya-Urgench =
 Köneürgench,
 Turkmenistan 50 E6
Künzelsau, Germany ... 25 F5
Kuopio, Finland 8 E22
Kupa →, Croatia 29 C13
Kupang, Indonesia 63 F6
Kupres, Bos.-H. 42 G2
Kupyansk, Ukraine 47 H9
Kupyansk-Uzlovoi, Ukraine 47 H9
Kuqa, China 60 B3
Kür = Kür →,
 Azerbaijan 73 C13
Kura = Kür →,
 Azerbaijan 73 C13
Kuranda, Australia 94 B4
Kurashiki, Japan 55 G6
Kurayoshi, Japan 55 G6
Kürdämir, Azerbaijan ... 49 K9
Kurdistan, Asia 73 D10
Kure, Japan 55 G6
Küre, Turkey 72 B5
Küre Dağları, Turkey ... 72 B5
Kuressaare, Estonia 9 G20
Kurgaldzhino = Kurganaya,
 Russia 49 H5
Kurgan, Russia 50 D7
Kurgannaya = Kurganinsk,
 Russia 49 H5
Kuria Maria Is. = Khurīyā
 Mūrīyā, Jazā 'ir, Oman . 74 D6
Kuridala, Australia 94 C3
Kurigram, Bangla. 67 G16
Kurikka, Finland 9 E20
Kuril Is. = Kurilskiye
 Ostrova, Russia 51 E16
Kuril Trench, Pac. Oc. .. 96 C7
Kurilsk, Russia 51 E15
Kurilskiye Ostrova, Russia 51 E16
Kurino, Japan 55 J5
Kurinskaya Kosa,
 Azerbaijan 73 C13
Kurkur, Egypt 80 C3
Kurlovskiy, Russia 48 C5
Kurmuk, Sudan 81 E3
Kurnool, India 66 M11
Kuro-Shima, Kagoshima,
 Japan 55 J4
Kuro-Shima, Okinawa,
 Japan 55 M2
Kurow, N.Z. 91 L3

Kurów, *Poland* 45 G9
Kurrajong, *Australia* 95 E5
Kurram →, *Pakistan* 68 C4
Kurri Kurri, *Australia* ... 95 E5
Kursavka, *Russia* 49 H6
Kuršėnai, *Lithuania* 44 B9
Kurshskiy Zaliv, *Russia* .. 9 J19
Kursk, *Russia* 47 G9
Kuršumlija, *Serbia, Yug.* .. 40 C5
Kuršumlijska Banja,
   Serbia, Yug. 40 C5
Kurşunlu, *Bursa, Turkey* . 41 F13
Kurşunlu, *Çankırı, Turkey* 72 B5
Kurtalan, *Turkey* 73 D9
Kurtbey, *Turkey* 41 E10
Kuru Bahr →, *Sudan* 81 F2
Kurucaşile, *Turkey* 72 B5
Kuruktag, *China* 60 B3
Kuruman, *S. Africa* 88 D3
Kuruman →, *S. Africa* ... 88 D3
Kurume, *Japan* 55 H5
Kurunegala, *Sri Lanka* ... 66 R12
Kus Gölü, *Turkey* 41 F11
Kuşadası, *Turkey* 72 D2
Kuşadası Körfezi, *Turkey* . 39 D8
Kusatsu, *Japan* 55 F9
Kusawa L., *Canada* 104 A1
Kusel, *Germany* 25 F3
Kushchevskaya, *Russia* ... 49 G4
Kushikino, *Japan* 55 J5
Kushima, *Japan* 55 J5
Kushimoto, *Japan* 55 H7
Kushiro, *Japan* 54 C12
Kushiro →, *Japan* 54 C12
Kūshk, *Iran* 71 D8
Kushka = Gushgy,
   Turkmenistan 50 F7
Kūshkī, *Īlām, Iran* 70 C5
Kūshkī, *Khorāsān, Iran* .. 71 B8
Kūshkū, *Iran* 71 E7
Kushol, *India* 69 C7
Kushtia, *Bangla.* 67 H16
Kushum →, *Kazakhstan* .. 48 F10
Kuskokwim B., *U.S.A.* ... 100 C3
Kussharo-Ko, *Japan* 54 C12
Kustanay = Qostanay,
   Kazakhstan 50 D7
Kut, Ko, *Thailand* 65 G4
Kütahya, *Turkey* 39 B12
Kütahya □, *Turkey* 39 B11
Kutaisi, *Georgia* 49 J6
Kutaraja = Banda Aceh,
   Indonesia 62 C1
Kutch, Gulf of = Kachchh,
   Gulf of, *India* 68 H3
Kutch, Rann of =
   Kachchh, Rann of, *India* 68 H4
Kutina, *Croatia* 29 C13
Kutiyana, *India* 68 J4
Kutjevo, *Croatia* 42 E2
Kutkashen, *Azerbaijan* ... 49 K8
Kutná Hora, *Czech Rep.* . 26 B8
Kutno, *Poland* 45 F6
Kuttabul, *Australia* 94 C4
Kutu,
   Dem. Rep. of the Congo 84 E3
Kutum, *Sudan* 81 E1
Kúty, *Slovak Rep.* 27 C10
Kuujjuaq, *Canada* 101 C13
Kuŭp-tong, *N. Korea* ... 57 D14
Kuusamo, *Finland* 8 D23
Kuusankoski, *Finland* ... 9 F22
Kuvshinovo, *Russia* 46 D8
Kuwait = Al Kuwayt,
   Kuwait 70 D5
Kuwait ■, *Asia* 70 D5
Kuwana, *Japan* 55 G8
Kuybyshev = Samara,
   Russia 48 D10
Kuybyshev, *Russia* 50 D8
Kuybyshevo, *Ukraine* ... 47 J9
Kuybyshevskoye Vdkhr.,
   Russia 48 C9
Kuye He →, *China* 56 E6
Kūyeh, *Iran* 70 B5
Kūysanjaq, *Iraq* 70 B5
Kuyucak, *Turkey* 39 D10
Kuyumba, *Russia* 51 C10
Kuzey Anadolu Dağları,
   Turkey 72 B7
Kuzmin, *Serbia, Yug.* 42 E4
Kuznetsk, *Russia* 48 D8
Kvænangen, *Norway* 8 A19
Kværndrup, *Denmark* ... 11 J4
Kvaløy, *Norway* 8 B18
Kvänum, *Sweden* 11 F7
Kvareli = Qvareli, *Georgia* 49 K7
Kvarner, *Croatia* 29 D11
Kvarnerič, *Croatia* 29 D11
Kvicksund, *Sweden* 10 E10
Kvillsfors, *Sweden* 11 G9
Kvismare kanal, *Sweden* . 10 E9
Kvissleby, *Sweden* 10 B11
Kwabhaca, *S. Africa* 89 E4
Kwadacha →, *Canada* ... 104 B3
Kwakhanai, *Botswana* ... 88 C3
Kwakoegron, *Surinam* ... 125 B7
Kwale, *Kenya* 86 C4
Kwale, *Nigeria* 83 D6
Kwale □, *Kenya* 86 C4
KwaMashu, *S. Africa* 89 D5
Kwando →, *Africa* 88 B3
Kwangdaeri, *N. Korea* .. 57 D14
Kwangju, *S. Korea* 57 G14
Kwango →,
   Dem. Rep. of the Congo 77 G5

Kwangsi-Chuang =
   Guangxi Zhuangzu
   Zizhiqu □, *China* 58 F7
Kwangtung =
   Guangdong □, *China* .. 59 F9
Kwara □, *Nigeria* 83 D6
Kwataboahegan →,
   Canada 102 B3
Kwatisore, *Indonesia* 63 E8
KwaZulu Natal □,
   S. Africa 89 D5
Kweichow = Guizhou □,
   China 58 D6
Kwekwe, *Zimbabwe* 87 F2
Kwidzyn, *Poland* 44 E5
Kwimba □, *Tanzania* 86 C3
Kwinana New Town,
   Australia 93 F2
Kwisa →, *Poland* 45 G2
Kwoka, *Indonesia* 63 E8
Kyabra Cr. →, *Australia* . 95 D3
Kyabram, *Australia* 95 F4
Kyaikto, *Burma* 64 D1
Kyancutta, *Australia* 95 E2
Kyangin, *Burma* 67 K19
Kyaukpadaung, *Burma* ... 67 J19
Kyaukpyu, *Burma* 67 K18
Kyaukse, *Burma* 67 J20
Kybartai, *Lithuania* 44 D9
Kyburz, *U.S.A.* 116 G6
Kyenjojo, *Uganda* 86 B3
Kyjov, *Czech Rep.* 27 B10
Kyle Dam, *Zimbabwe* ... 87 G3
Kyle of Lochalsh, *U.K.* .. 14 D3
Kyll →, *Germany* 25 E7
Kyllburg, *Germany* 25 E7
Kymijoki →, *Finland* ... 9 F22
Kyneton, *Australia* 95 F3
Kynuna, *Australia* 94 C3
Kyō-ga-Saki, *Japan* 55 G7
Kyoga, L., *Uganda* 86 B3
Kyogle, *Australia* 95 D5
Kyongju, *S. Korea* 57 G15
Kyongpyaw, *Burma* 67 L19
Kyŏngsŏng, *N. Korea* ... 57 D15
Kyōto, *Japan* 55 G7
Kyōto □, *Japan* 55 G7
Kyparissovouno, *Cyprus* . 36 D12
Kyperounda, *Cyprus* 36 E11
Kyrenia, *Cyprus* 36 D12
Kyrgyzstan ■, *Asia* 50 E8
Kyritz, *Germany* 24 C8
Kyrkhult, *Sweden* 11 H8
Kyrönjoki →, *Finland* ... 8 E19
Kystatyam, *Russia* 51 C13
Kysucké Nové Mesto,
   Slovak Rep. 27 B11
Kythréa, *Cyprus* 36 D12
Kyunhla, *Burma* 67 H19
Kyuquot, *Canada* 104 C3
Kyurdamir = Kürdämir,
   Azerbaijan 49 K9
Kyūshū, *Japan* 55 H5
Kyūshū □, *Japan* 55 H5
Kyūshū-Sanchi, *Japan* ... 55 H5
Kyustendil, *Bulgaria* 40 D6
Kyusyur, *Russia* 51 B13
Kywong, *Australia* 95 E4
Kyyiv, *Ukraine* 47 G6
Kyyivske Vdskh., *Ukraine* 47 G6
Kyzyl, *Russia* 51 D10
Kyzyl Kum, *Uzbekistan* .. 50 E7
Kyzyl-Kyya, *Kyrgyzstan* .. 50 E8
Kzyl-Orda = Qyzylorda,
   Kazakhstan 50 E7

L

La Albuera, *Spain* 35 G4
La Alcarria, *Spain* 32 E2
La Almarcha, *Spain* 32 F2
La Almunia de Doña
   Godina, *Spain* 32 D3
La Asunción, *Venezuela* . 124 A6
La Banda, *Argentina* 126 B3
La Bañeza, *Spain* 34 C5
La Barca, *Mexico* 118 C4
La Barge, *U.S.A.* 114 E8
La Bastide-Puylaurent,
   France 20 D7
La Baule-Escoubiac, *France* 18 E4
La Belle, *U.S.A.* 109 M5
La Biche →, *Canada* 104 B4
La Bisbal d'Empordà,
   Spain 32 D8
La Bomba, *Mexico* 118 A1
La Bresse, *France* 19 D13
La Bureba, *Spain* 34 C7
La Calera, *Chile* 126 C1
La Campiña, *Spain* 35 H6
La Canal = Sa Canal,
   Spain 37 C7
La Cañiza = A Cañiza,
   Spain 34 C2
La Canourgue, *France* ... 20 D7
La Capelle, *France* 19 C10
La Carlota, *Argentina* ... 126 C3
La Carlota, *Phil.* 61 F5
La Carlota, *Spain* 35 H6
La Carolina, *Spain* 35 G7
La Cavalerie, *France* 20 D7
La Ceiba, *Honduras* 120 C2
La Chaise-Dieu, *France* .. 20 C7

La Chapelle d'Angillon,
   France 19 E9
La Chapelle-St-Luc, *France* 19 D11
La Chapelle-sur-Erdre,
   France 18 E5
La Charité-sur-Loire,
   France 19 E10
La Chartre-sur-le-Loir,
   France 18 E7
La Châtaigneraie, *France* . 20 B3
La Châtre, *France* 19 F9
La Chaux-de-Fonds, *Switz.* 25 H2
La Ciotat, *France* 21 E9
La Clayette, *France* 19 F11
La Cocha, *Argentina* 126 B2
La Concepción = Ri-Aba,
   Eq. Guin. 83 E6
La Concordia, *Mexico* ... 119 D6
La Conner, *U.S.A.* 114 B2
La Coruña = A Coruña,
   Spain 34 B2
La Coruña □, *Spain* 34 B2
La Côte-St-André, *France* . 21 C9
La Courtine-le-Trucq,
   France 20 C6
La Crau,
   Bouches-du-Rhône,
   France 21 E8
La Crau, *Var, France* 21 E10
La Crete, *Canada* 104 B5
La Crosse, *Kans., U.S.A.* . 112 F5
La Crosse, *Wis., U.S.A.* .. 112 D9
La Cruz, *Costa Rica* 120 D2
La Cruz, *Mexico* 118 C3
La Escondida, *Mexico* ... 118 C5
La Esmeralda, *Paraguay* . 126 A3
La Esperanza, *Cuba* 120 B3
La Esperanza, *Honduras* . 120 D2
La Estrada = A Estrada,
   Spain 34 C2
La Faouët, *France* 18 D3
La Fayette, *U.S.A.* 109 H3
La Fé, *Cuba* 120 B3
La Fère, *France* 19 C10
La Ferté-Bernard, *France* . 18 D7
La Ferté-Gaucher, *France* . 19 D10
La Ferté-Macé, *France* ... 18 D6
La Ferté-St-Aubin, *France* 19 E8
La Ferté-sous-Jouarre,
   France 19 D10
La Ferté-Vidame, *France* . 18 D7
La Flèche, *France* 18 E6
La Follette, *U.S.A.* 109 G3
La Fregeneda, *Spain* 34 E4
La Fuente de San Esteban,
   Spain 34 E4
La Gacilly, *France* 18 E4
La Gineta, *Spain* 33 F2
La Grand-Combe, *France* . 21 D8
La Grande, *U.S.A.* 114 D4
La Grande-Motte, *France* . 21 E8
La Grange, *Calif., U.S.A.* . 116 H6
La Grange, *Ga., U.S.A.* .. 109 J3
La Grange, *Ky., U.S.A.* .. 108 F3
La Grange, *Tex., U.S.A.* . 113 L6
La Grave, *France* 21 C10
La Guaira, *Venezuela* 124 A5
La Guardia = A Guarda,
   Spain 34 D2
La Gudiña = A Gudiña,
   Spain 34 C3
La Guerche-de-Bretagne,
   France 18 E5
La Guerche-sur-l'Aubois,
   France 19 F9
La Habana, *Cuba* 120 B3
La Harpe, *U.S.A.* 112 E9
La Haye-du-Puits, *France* . 18 C5
La Horra, *Spain* 34 D7
La Independencia, *Mexico* 119 D6
La Isabela, *Dom. Rep.* ... 121 C5
La Jara, *U.S.A.* 115 H11
La Jonquera, *Spain* 32 C7
La Junta, *U.S.A.* 113 F3
La Laguna, *Canary Is.* ... 37 F3
La Libertad, *Guatemala* .. 120 C1
La Libertad, *Mexico* 118 B2
La Ligua, *Chile* 126 C1
La Línea de la Concepción,
   Spain 35 J5
La Loche, *Canada* 105 B7
La Londe-les-Maures,
   France 21 E10
La Lora, *Spain* 34 C7
La Loupe, *France* 18 D8
La Louvière, *Belgium* 17 D4
La Machine, *France* 19 F10
La Maddalena, *Italy* 30 A2
La Malbaie, *Canada* 103 C5
La Mancha, *Spain* 33 F2
La Mariña, *Spain* 34 B3
La Mesa, *Calif., U.S.A.* .. 117 N9
La Mesa, *N. Mex., U.S.A.* 115 K10
La Mothe-Achard, *France* 18 F5
La Motte, *France* 21 D10
La Motte-Chalançon,
   France 21 D9
La Motte-Servolex, *France* 21 C9
La Moure, *U.S.A.* 112 B5
La Muela, *Spain* 32 D3
La Mure, *France* 21 D9
La Negra, *Chile* 126 A1
La Oliva, *Canary Is.* 37 F6
La Orotava, *Canary Is.* ... 37 F3
La Oroya, *Peru* 124
La Pacaudière, *France* ... 19 F10

La Palma, *Canary Is.* 37 F2
La Palma, *Panama* 120 E4
La Palma del Condado,
   Spain 35 H4
La Paloma, *Chile* 126 C1
La Pampa □, *Argentina* . 126 D2
La Paragua, *Venezuela* .. 124 B6
La Paz, *Entre Ríos,*
   Argentina 126 C4
La Paz, *San Luis,*
   Argentina 126 C2
La Paz, *Bolivia* 124 G5
La Paz, *Honduras* 120 D2
La Paz, *Mexico* 118 C2
La Paz, *Phil.* 61 D4
La Paz Centro, *Nic.* 120 D2
La Pedrera, *Colombia* ... 124 D5
La Perouse Str., *Asia* 54 B11
La Pesca, *Mexico* 119 C5
La Piedad, *Mexico* 118 C4
La Pine, *U.S.A.* 114 E3
La Plant, *U.S.A.* 112 C4
La Plata, *Argentina* 126 D4
La Pobla de Lillet, *Spain* . 32 C6
La Pola de Gordón, *Spain* 34 C5
La Porta, *France* 21 F13
La Porte, *U.S.A.* 108 E2
La Presanella, *Italy* 28 B7
La Puebla = Sa Pobla,
   Spain 32 F8
La Puebla de Cazalla,
   Spain 35 H5
La Puebla de los Infantes,
   Spain 35 H5
La Puebla de Montalbán,
   Spain 34 F6
La Puebla del Río, *Spain* . 35 H4
La Puerta de Segura, *Spain* 35 G8
La Purísima, *Mexico* 118 B2
La Push, *U.S.A.* 116 C2
La Quiaca, *Argentina* ... 126 A2
La Reine, *Canada* 102 C4
La Réole, *France* 20 D3
La Restinga, *Canary Is.* .. 37 G2
La Rioja, *Argentina* 126 B2
La Rioja □, *Argentina* ... 126 B2
La Rioja □, *Spain* 32 C2
La Robla, *Spain* 34 C5
La Roche-Bernard, *France* 18 E4
La Roche-Canillac, *France* 20 C5
La Roche-en-Ardenne,
   Belgium 17 D5
La Roche-sur-Foron,
   France 19 F13
La Roche-sur-Yon, *France* 18 F5
La Rochefoucauld, *France* 20 C4
La Rochelle, *France* 20 B2
La Roda, *Spain* 33 F2
La Roda de Andalucía,
   Spain 35 H6
La Romana, *Dom. Rep.* . 121 C6
La Ronge, *Canada* 105 B7
La Rumorosa, *Mexico* ... 117 N10
La Sabina = Sa Savina,
   Spain 37 C7
La Sagra, *Spain* 33 H2
La Salle, *U.S.A.* 112 E10
La Sanabria, *Spain* 34 C4
La Santa, *Canary Is.* 37 E6
La Sarre, *Canada* 102 C4
La Scie, *Canada* 103 C8
La Selva, *Spain* 32 C7
La Selva Beach, *U.S.A.* .. 116 J5
La Selva del Camp, *Spain* 32 D6
La Serena, *Chile* 126 B1
La Serena, *Spain* 35 G5
La Seu d'Urgell, *Spain* .. 32 C6
La Seyne-sur-Mer, *France* 21 E9
La Sila, *Italy* 31 C9
La Solana, *Spain* 35 G7
La Souterraine, *France* ... 19 F8
La Spézia, *Italy* 28 D6
La Suze-sur-Sarthe, *France* 18 E7
La Tagua, *Colombia* 124 C4
La Teste, *France* 20 D2
La Tortuga, *Venezuela* ... 121 D6
La Tour-du-Pin, *France* .. 21 C9
La Tranche-sur-Mer,
   France 18 F5
La Tremblade, *France* 20 C2
La Tuque, *Canada* 102 C5
La Unión, *Chile* 128 E2
La Unión, *El Salv.* 120 D2
La Unión, *Mexico* 118 D4
La Unión, *Spain* 33 H4
La Urbana, *Venezuela* ... 124 B5
La Vall d'Uixó, *Spain* ... 32 F4
La Vecilla de Curveño,
   Spain 34 C5
La Vega, *Dom. Rep.* 121 C5
La Vela, *Venezuela* 124 A5
La Veleta, *Spain* 35 H7
La Venta, *Mexico* 119 D6
La Venta, *Mexico* 118 C4
La Voulte-sur-Rhône,
   France 21 D8
Laa an der Thaya, *Austria* 27 C9
Laaber, Grosse →,
   Germany 25 G8
Laage, *Germany* 24 B8
Laba →, *Russia* 49 H4
Labason, *Phil.* 61 G5
Labastide-Murat, *France* . 20 D5
Labastide-Rouairoux,
   France 20 E6
Labbézenga, *Mali* 83 B5

Labe = Elbe →, *Europe* . 24 B4
Labé, *Guinea* 82 C2
Laberge, L., *Canada* 104 A1
Labin, *Croatia* 29 C11
Labinsk, *Russia* 49 H5
Labis, *Malaysia* 65 L4
Łabiszyn, *Poland* 45 F4
Labo, *Phil.* 61 D5
Laboe, *Germany* 24 A6
Laborec →, *Slovak Rep.* . 27 C14
Labouheyre, *France* 20 D3
Laboulaye, *Argentina* ... 126 C3
Labrador, *Canada* 103 B7
Labrador City, *Canada* .. 103 B6
Lábrea, *Brazil* 124 E6
Labrède, *France* 20 D3
Labruguière, *France* 20 E6
Labuan, *Malaysia* 62 C5
Labuan, Pulau, *Malaysia* . 62 C5
Labuha, *Indonesia* 63 E7
Labuhan, *Indonesia* 63 G11
Labuhanbajo, *Indonesia* . 63 F6
Labuk, Telok, *Malaysia* .. 62 C5
Labyrinth, L., *Australia* .. 95 E2
Labytnangi, *Russia* 50 C7
Laç, *Albania* 40 E3
Lac Bouchette, *Canada* .. 103 C5
Lac du Flambeau, *U.S.A.* . 112 B10
Lac Édouard, *Canada* ... 102 C5
Lac La Biche, *Canada* ... 104 C6
Lac la Martre = Wha Ti,
   Canada 100 B8
Lac-Mégantic, *Canada* .. 103 C5
Lac Seul, Res., *Canada* .. 102 B1
Lac Thien, *Vietnam* 64 F7
Lacanau, *France* 20 D2
Lacanau, Étang de, *France* 20 D2
Lacantúm →, *Mexico* ... 119 D6
Lacara →, *Spain* 35 G4
Lacaune, *France* 20 E6
Lacaune, Mts. de, *France* . 20 E6
Laccadive Is. =
   Lakshadweep Is.,
   Ind. Oc. 52 H11
Lacepede B., *Australia* ... 95 F2
Lacepede Is., *Australia* ... 92 C3
Lacerdónia, *Mozam.* 87 F4
Lacey, *U.S.A.* 116 C4
Lachhmangarh, *India* 68 F6
Lachi, *Pakistan* 68 C4
Lachine, *Canada* 102 C5
Lachlan →, *Australia* 95 E3
Lachute, *Canada* 102 C5
Lackawanna, *U.S.A.* 110 D6
Lacolle, *Canada* 111 A11
Lacombe, *Canada* 104 C6
Lacona, *U.S.A.* 111 C8
Láconi, *Italy* 30 C2
Laconia, *U.S.A.* 111 C13
Lacq, *France* 20 E3
Lacrosse, *U.S.A.* 114 C5
Ladakh Ra., *India* 69 C8
Lądek-Zdrój, *Poland* 45 H3
Ládhon →, *Greece* 38 D3
Ladik, *Turkey* 72 B6
Ladismith, *S. Africa* 88 E3
Ladíspoli, *Italy* 29 G9
Lādīz, *Iran* 71 D9
Ladnun, *India* 68 F6
Ladoga, L. = Ladozhskoye
   Ozero, *Russia* 46 B6
Ladozhskoye Ozero, *Russia* 46 B6
Lady Grey, *S. Africa* 88 E4
Ladybrand, *S. Africa* 88 D4
Ladysmith, *Canada* 104 D4
Ladysmith, *S. Africa* 89 D4
Ladysmith, *U.S.A.* 112 C9
Lae, *Papua N. G.* 96 H6
Laem Ngop, *Thailand* ... 65 F4
Laem Pho, *Thailand* 65 J3
Læsø, *Denmark* 11 G5
Læsø Rende, *Denmark* .. 11 G4
Lafayette, *Colo., U.S.A.* .. 112 F2
Lafayette, *Ind., U.S.A.* ... 108 E2
Lafayette, *La., U.S.A.* 113 K9
Lafayette, *Tenn., U.S.A.* . 109 G3
Laferte →, *Canada* 104 A5
Lafia, *Nigeria* 83 D6
Lafiagi, *Nigeria* 83 D6
Lafleche, *Canada* 105 D7
Lafon, *Sudan* 81 F3
Lagan, *Sweden* 11 H7
Lagan →, *Sweden* 11 H6
Lagan →, *U.K.* 15 B6
Lagarfljót →, *Iceland* 8 D6
Lage, *Germany* 24 D4
Lågen →, *Oppland,*
   Norway 9 F14
Lågen →, *Vestfold,*
   Norway 9 G14
Lägerdorf, *Germany* 24 B5
Laghouat, *Algeria* 78 B6
Lagnieu, *France* 21 C9
Lagny-sur-Marne, *France* . 19 D9
Lago, *Italy* 31 C9
Lagôa, *Portugal* 35 H2
Lagoaça, *Portugal* 34 D4
Lagodekhi, *Georgia* 49 K8
Lagónegro, *Italy* 31 B8
Lagonoy G., *Phil.* 61 E5
Lagos, *Nigeria* 83 D5
Lagos, *Portugal* 35 H2
Lagos de Moreno, *Mexico* 118 C4
Lagrange, *Australia* 92 C3
Lagrange B., *Australia* ... 92 C3
Laguardia, *Spain* 32 C2

Le Donjon

Laguépie, France 20 D5
Laguna, Brazil 127 B6
Laguna, U.S.A. 115 J10
Laguna Beach, U.S.A. 117 M9
Laguna de Duera, Spain 34 D6
Laguna Limpia, Argentina 126 B4
Laguna Madre, U.S.A. 119 B5
Lagunas, Chile 126 A2
Lagunas, Peru 124 E3
Lahad Datu, Malaysia 63 D5
Lahad Datu, Teluk, Malaysia 63 D5
Lahan Sai, Thailand 64 E4
Lahanam, Laos 64 D5
Laharpur, India 69 F9
Lahat, Indonesia 62 E2
Lahewa, Indonesia 62 D1
Lahiang Lahiang, Phil. 61 H4
Lāhījān, Iran 71 B6
Lahn →, Germany 25 E3
Lahnstein, Germany 25 E3
Laholm, Sweden 11 H7
Laholmsbukten, Sweden 11 H6
Lahontan Reservoir, U.S.A. 114 G4
Lahore, Pakistan 68 D6
Lahr, Germany 25 G3
Lahti, Finland 9 F21
Lahtis = Lahti, Finland 9 F21
Laï, Chad 79 G9
Lai Chau, Vietnam 64 A4
Lai'an, China 59 A12
Laibin, China 58 F7
Laidley, Australia 95 D5
Laifeng, China 58 C7
L'Aigle, France 18 D7
Laignes, France 19 E11
L'Aiguillon-sur-Mer, France 20 B2
Laikipia □, Kenya 86 B4
Laingsburg, S. Africa 88 E3
Lainio älv →, Sweden 8 C20
Lairg, U.K. 14 C4
Laishui, China 56 E8
Laissac, France 20 D6
Láives, Italy 29 B8
Laiwu, China 57 F9
Laixi, China 57 F11
Laiyang, China 57 F11
Laiyuan, China 56 E8
Laizhou Wan, China 57 F10
Laja →, Mexico 118 C4
Lajere, Nigeria 83 C7
Lajes, Brazil 127 B5
Lajkovac, Serbia, Yug. 40 B4
Lajosmizse, Hungary 42 C4
Lak Sao, Laos 64 C5
Lakaband, Pakistan 68 D3
Lake Alpine, U.S.A. 116 G7
Lake Andes, U.S.A. 112 D5
Lake Anse, U.S.A. 108 B1
Lake Arthur, U.S.A. 113 K8
Lake Cargelligo, Australia 95 E4
Lake Charles, U.S.A. 113 K8
Lake City, Colo., U.S.A. 115 G10
Lake City, Fla., U.S.A. 109 K4
Lake City, Iowa, U.S.A. 112 D7
Lake City, Mich., U.S.A. 108 C3
Lake City, Minn., U.S.A. 112 C8
Lake City, Pa., U.S.A. 110 D4
Lake City, S.C., U.S.A. 109 J6
Lake George, U.S.A. 111 C11
Lake Grace, Australia 93 F2
Lake Harbour = Kimmirut, Canada 101 B13
Lake Havasu City, U.S.A. 117 L12
Lake Hughes, U.S.A. 117 L8
Lake Isabella, U.S.A. 117 K8
Lake King, Australia 93 F2
Lake Lenore, Canada 105 C8
Lake Louise, Canada 104 C5
Lake Mead National Recreation Area, U.S.A. 117 K12
Lake Mills, U.S.A. 112 D8
Lake Nash, Australia 94 C2
Lake Providence, U.S.A. 113 J9
Lake River, Canada 102 B3
Lake Superior Prov. Park, Canada 102 C3
Lake Village, U.S.A. 113 J9
Lake Wales, U.S.A. 109 M5
Lake Worth, U.S.A. 109 M5
Lakefield, Canada 102 D4
Lakeland, Australia 94 B3
Lakeland, U.S.A. 109 M5
Lakemba, Fiji 91 D9
Lakeport, U.S.A. 116 F4
Lakes Entrance, Australia 95 F4
Lakeside, Ariz., U.S.A. 115 J9
Lakeside, Calif., U.S.A. 117 N10
Lakeside, Nebr., U.S.A. 112 D3
Lakeview, U.S.A. 114 E3
Lakewood, Colo., U.S.A. 112 F2
Lakewood, N.J., U.S.A. 111 F10
Lakewood, Ohio, U.S.A. 110 E3
Lakewood Center, U.S.A. 116 C4
Lakhaniá, Greece 36 D9
Lakhonpheng, Laos 64 E5
Lakhpat, India 68 H3
Läki, Azerbaijan 49 K8
Lakin, U.S.A. 113 G4
Lakitusaki →, Canada 102 B3
Lákkoi, Greece 36 D5
Lakonía □, Greece 38 E4
Lakonikós Kólpos, Greece 38 E4
Lakor, Indonesia 63 F7
Lakota, Ivory C. 82 D3
Lakota, U.S.A. 112 A5
Laksefjorden, Norway 8 A22
Lakselv, Norway 8 A21
Lakshadweep Is., Ind. Oc. 52 H11
Lakshmikantapur, India 69 H13
Lala Ghat, India 67 G18
Lala Musa, Pakistan 68 C5
Lalago, Tanzania 86 C3
Lalapanzi, Zimbabwe 87 F3
Lalapaşa, Turkey 41 E10
Lalbenque, France 20 D5
L'Albufera, Spain 33 F4
Lalganj, India 69 G11
Lalibela, Ethiopia 81 E4
Lalin, China 57 B14
Lalín, Spain 34 C2
Lalin He →, China 57 B13
Lalinde, France 20 D4
Lalitapur = Patan, Nepal 67 F14
Lalitpur, India 69 G8
Lam, Vietnam 64 B6
Lam Pao Res., Thailand 64 D4
Lama Kara, Togo 83 D5
Lamaing, Burma 67 M20
Lamar, Colo., U.S.A. 112 F3
Lamar, Mo., U.S.A. 113 G7
Lamas, Peru 124 E3
Lamastre, France 21 D8
Lambach, Austria 26 C6
Lamballe, France 18 D4
Lambaréné, Gabon 84 E2
Lambasa, Fiji 91 C8
Lambay I., Ireland 15 C5
Lambert, U.S.A. 112 B2
Lambert Glacier, Antarctica 5 D6
Lamberts Bay, S. Africa 88 E2
Lambesc, France 21 E9
Lambi Kyun, Burma 65 G2
Lámbia, Greece 38 D3
Lambro →, Italy 28 C6
Lame, Nigeria 83 C6
Lame Deer, U.S.A. 114 D10
Lamego, Portugal 34 D3
Lamèque, Canada 103 C7
Lameroo, Australia 95 F3
Lamesa, U.S.A. 113 J4
Lamía, Greece 38 C4
Lamitan, Phil. 61 H5
Lammermuir Hills, U.K. 14 F6
Lammhult, Sweden 11 G8
Lamon B., Phil. 61 D5
Lamont, Canada 104 C6
Lamont, U.S.A. 117 K8
Lamotte-Beuvron, France 19 E9
Lampa, Peru 124 G4
Lampang, Thailand 64 C2
Lampasas, U.S.A. 113 K5
Lampazos de Naranjo, Mexico 118 B4
Lampertheim, Germany 25 F4
Lampeter, U.K. 13 E3
Lampman, Canada 105 D8
Lamprechtshausen, Austria 26 D5
Lamprey, Canada 105 B10
Lampung □, Indonesia 62 F2
Lamu, Kenya 86 C5
Lamu □, Kenya 86 C5
Lamy, U.S.A. 115 J11
Lan Xian, China 56 E6
Lanai, U.S.A. 106 H16
Lanak La, India 69 B8
Lanak'o Shank'ou = Lanak La, India 69 B8
Lanao, L., Phil. 61 H6
Lanark, Canada 111 A8
Lanark, U.K. 14 F5
Lancang, China 58 F2
Lancang Jiang →, China 58 G3
Lancashire □, U.K. 12 D5
Lancaster, Canada 111 A10
Lancaster, U.K. 12 C5
Lancaster, Calif., U.S.A. 117 L8
Lancaster, Ky., U.S.A. 108 G3
Lancaster, N.H., U.S.A. 111 B13
Lancaster, N.Y., U.S.A. 110 D6
Lancaster, Pa., U.S.A. 111 F8
Lancaster, S.C., U.S.A. 109 H5
Lancaster, Wis., U.S.A. 112 D9
Lancaster Sd., Canada 4 B3
Lancer, Canada 105 C7
Lanchow = Lanzhou, China 56 F2
Lanciano, Italy 29 F11
Lancun, China 57 F11
Łańcut, Poland 45 H9
Landau, Bayern, Germany 25 G8
Landau, Rhld-Pfz., Germany 25 F4
Landeck, Austria 26 D3
Lander, U.S.A. 114 E9
Lander →, Australia 92 D5
Landerneau, France 18 D2
Landeryd, Sweden 11 G7
Landes, France 20 D2
Landes □, France 20 E3
Landete, Spain 32 F3
Landi Kotal, Pakistan 68 B4
Landivisiau, France 18 D2
Landor, Australia 93 E2
Landquart, Switz. 25 J5
Landrecies, France 19 B10
Land's End, U.K. 13 G2
Landsberg, Germany 25 G6
Landsborough Cr. →, Australia 94 C3
Landsbro, Sweden 11 G8
Landshut, Germany 25 G8
Landskrona, Sweden 11 J6
Landstuhl, Germany 25 F3
Landvetter, Sweden 11 G6
Lanesboro, U.S.A. 111 E9
Lanester, France 18 E3
Lanett, U.S.A. 109 J3
Lang Bay, Canada 104 D4
Lang Qua, Vietnam 64 A5
Lang Shan, China 56 D4
Lang Son, Vietnam 64 B6
Lang Suan, Thailand 65 H2
Långå, Denmark 11 H3
La'nga Co, China 67 D12
Långadhás, Greece 40 F7
Langádhia, Greece 38 D4
Långan →, Sweden 10 A8
Langar, Iran 71 C9
Langara I., Canada 104 C2
Långås, Sweden 11 H6
Langdai, China 58 D5
Langdon, U.S.A. 112 A5
Långe Jan = Ölands södra udde, Sweden 11 H10
Langeac, France 20 C7
Langeais, France 18 E7
Langeb Baraka →, Sudan 80 D4
Langeberg, S. Africa 88 E3
Langeberge, S. Africa 88 D3
Langeland, Denmark 11 K4
Langelands Bælt, Denmark 11 K4
Langen, Hessen, Germany 25 F4
Langen, Niedersachsen, Germany 24 B4
Langenburg, Canada 105 C8
Langeneß, Germany 24 A4
Langenlois, Austria 26 C8
Langeoog, Germany 24 B3
Langeskov, Denmark 11 J4
Länghem, Sweden 11 G7
Langhirano, Italy 28 D7
Langholm, U.K. 14 F5
Langjökull, Iceland 8 D3
Langkawi, Pulau, Malaysia 65 J2
Langklip, S. Africa 88 D3
Langkon, Malaysia 62 C5
Langlade, St- P. & M. 103 C8
Langlois, U.S.A. 114 E1
Langnau, Switz. 25 J3
Langogne, France 20 D7
Langon, France 20 D3
Langøya, Norway 8 B16
Langreo, Spain 34 B5
Langres, France 19 E12
Langres, Plateau de, France 19 E12
Langsa, Indonesia 62 D1
Långsele, Sweden 10 A11
Långshyttan, Sweden 10 D10
Langtry, U.S.A. 113 L4
Langu, Thailand 65 J2
Languedoc, France 20 E7
Languedoc-Roussillon □, France 20 E6
Langxi, China 59 B12
Langxiangzhen, China 56 E9
Langzhong, China 58 B5
Lanigan, Canada 105 C7
Lankao, China 56 G8
Länkäran, Azerbaijan 73 C13
Lanmeur, France 18 D3
Lannemezan, France 20 E4
Lannilis, France 18 D2
Lannion, France 18 D3
L'Annonciation, Canada 102 C5
Lanouaille, France 20 C5
Lanping, China 58 D2
Lansdale, U.S.A. 111 F9
Lansdowne, Australia 95 E5
Lansdowne, Canada 111 B8
Lansdowne House, Canada 102 B2
L'Anse, U.S.A. 102 C2
L'Anse au Loup, Canada 103 B8
Lansford, U.S.A. 111 F9
Lanshan, China 59 E9
Lansing, U.S.A. 108 D3
Lanslebourg-Mont-Cenis, France 21 C10
Lanta Yai, Ko, Thailand 65 J2
Lantian, China 56 G5
Lanus, Argentina 126 C4
Lanusei, Italy 30 C2
Lanuza, Phil. 61 G7
Lanxi, China 59 C12
Lanzarote, Canary Is. 37 F6
Lanzhou, China 56 F2
Lanzo Torinese, Italy 28 C4
Lao →, Italy 31 C8
Lao Bao, Laos 64 D6
Lao Cai, Vietnam 64 A4
Laoag, Phil. 61 B4
Laoang, Phil. 61 E6
Laoha He →, China 57 C11
Laois □, Ireland 15 D4
Laon, France 19 C10
Laona, U.S.A. 108 C1
Laos ■, Asia 64 D5
Lapa, Brazil 127 B6
Lapalisse, France 19 F10
Lapeer, U.S.A. 108 D4
Lapeyrade, France 20 D3
Lapithos, Cyprus 36 D12
Lapland = Lappland, Europe 8 B21
Laporte, U.S.A. 111 E8
Lapovo, Serbia, Yug. 40 B5
Lappeenranta, Finland 9 F23
Lappland, Europe 8 B21
Laprida, Argentina 126 D3
Lapseki, Turkey 72 B2
Laptev Sea, Russia 51 B13
Lapua, Finland 8 E20
Lăpuş →, Romania 43 C8
Lapuş, Munţii, Romania 43 C8
Lăpuşna, Moldova 43 D13
Łapy, Poland 45 F9
L'Aquila, Italy 29 F10
Lār, Āzarbājān-e Sharqī, Iran 70 B5
Lār, Fārs, Iran 71 E7
Larabanga, Ghana 82 D4
Laragne-Montéglin, France 21 D9
Laramie, U.S.A. 112 E2
Laramie Mts., U.S.A. 112 E2
Laranjeiras do Sul, Brazil 127 B5
Larantuka, Indonesia 63 F6
Larap, Phil. 61 D5
Larat, Indonesia 63 F8
L'Arbresle, France 21 C8
Lärbro, Sweden 11 G12
Larde, Mozam. 87 F4
Larder Lake, Canada 102 C4
Lardhos, Ákra = Líndhos, Ákra, Greece 36 C10
Lardhos, Órmos, Greece 36 C10
Laredo, Spain 34 B7
Laredo, U.S.A. 113 M5
Laredo Sd., Canada 104 C3
Largentière, France 21 D8
L'Argentière-la-Bessée, France 21 D10
Largo, U.S.A. 109 M4
Largs, U.K. 14 F4
Lari, Italy 28 E7
Lariang, Indonesia 63 E5
Larimore, U.S.A. 112 B6
Lārīn, Iran 71 C7
Larino, Italy 29 G11
Lárisa, Greece 38 B4
Lárisa □, Greece 38 B4
Larkana, Pakistan 68 F3
Larnaca, Cyprus 36 E12
Larnaca Bay, Cyprus 36 E12
Larne, U.K. 15 B6
Larned, U.S.A. 112 F5
Laroquebrou, France 20 D6
Larrimah, Australia 92 C5
Larsen Ice Shelf, Antarctica 5 C17
Laruns, France 20 F3
Larvik, Norway 9 G14
Larzac, Causse du, France 20 E7
Las Alpujarras, Spain 33 J1
Las Animas, U.S.A. 112 F3
Las Anod, Somali Rep. 74 F4
Las Arenas, Spain 34 B6
Las Brenãs, Argentina 126 B3
Las Cabezas de San Juan, Spain 35 J5
Las Cejas, Argentina 128 B4
Las Chimeneas, Mexico 117 N10
Las Cruces, U.S.A. 115 K10
Las Flores, Argentina 126 D4
Las Heras, Argentina 126 C2
Las Lajas, Argentina 128 D2
Las Lomitas, Argentina 126 A3
Las Marismas, Spain 35 H4
Las Minas, Spain 33 G3
Las Navas de la Concepción, Spain 35 H5
Las Navas del Marqués, Spain 34 E6
Las Palmas, Argentina 126 B4
Las Palmas, Canary Is. 37 F4
Las Palmas →, Mexico 117 N10
Las Pedroñas, Spain 33 F2
Las Piedras, Uruguay 127 C4
Las Pipinas, Argentina 126 D4
Las Plumas, Argentina 128 E3
Las Rosas, Argentina 126 C3
Las Rozas, Spain 34 E7
Las Tablas, Panama 120 E3
Las Termas, Argentina 126 B3
Las Truchas, Mexico 118 D4
Las Varillas, Argentina 126 C3
Las Vegas, N. Mex., U.S.A. 115 J11
Las Vegas, Nev., U.S.A. 117 J11
Lasarte, Spain 32 B2
Lascano, Uruguay 127 C5
Lashburn, Canada 105 C7
Lashio, Burma 67 H20
Lashkar, India 68 F8
Łasin, Poland 44 E6
Lasíthi, Greece 36 D7
Lasíthi □, Greece 36 D7
Lask, Poland 45 G6
Łaskarzew, Poland 45 G8
Laško, Slovenia 29 B12
Lassay-les-Châteaux, France 18 D6
Lassen Pk., U.S.A. 114 F3
Last Mountain L., Canada 105 C7
Lastchance Cr. →, U.S.A. 116 E5
Lastoursville, Gabon 84 E2
Lastovo, Croatia 29 F13
Lastovski Kanal, Croatia 29 F14
Lat Yao, Thailand 64 E2
Latacunga, Ecuador 124 D3
Latakia = Al Lādhiqīyah, Syria 70 C2
Latchford, Canada 102 C4
Laterza, Italy 31 B9
Latham, Australia 93 E2
Lathen, Germany 24 C3
Lathrop Wells, U.S.A. 117 J10
Latiano, Italy 31 B10
Latina, Italy 30 A5
Latisana, Italy 29 C10
Latium = Lazio □, Italy 29 F9
Laton, U.S.A. 116 J7
Latorytsya →, Slovak Rep. 27 C14
Latouche Treville, C., Australia 92 C3
Latrobe, Australia 94 G4
Latrobe, U.S.A. 110 F5
Latrónico, Italy 31 B9
Latvia ■, Europe 9 H20
Lau Group, Fiji 91 C9
Lauchhammer, Germany 24 D9
Lauda-Königshofen, Germany 25 F5
Lauenburg, Germany 24 B6
Lauf, Germany 25 F7
Laujar de Andarax, Spain 33 H2
Laukaa, Finland 9 E21
Launceston, Australia 94 G4
Launceston, U.K. 13 G3
Laune →, Ireland 15 D2
Launglon Bok, Burma 64 F1
Laupheim, Germany 25 G5
Laura, Australia 94 B3
Laureana di Borrello, Italy 31 D9
Laurel, Miss., U.S.A. 113 K10
Laurel, Mont., U.S.A. 114 D9
Laurencekirk, U.K. 14 E6
Laurens, U.S.A. 109 H4
Laurentian Plateau, Canada 103 B6
Laurentides, Parc Prov. des, Canada 103 C5
Lauria, Italy 31 B8
Laurie L., Canada 105 B8
Laurinburg, U.S.A. 109 H6
Laurium, U.S.A. 108 B1
Lausanne, Switz. 25 J2
Laut, Indonesia 65 K6
Laut Kecil, Kepulauan, Indonesia 62 E5
Lauterbach, Germany 24 E5
Lauterecken, Germany 25 F3
Lautoka, Fiji 91 C7
Lauzès, France 20 D5
Lauzon, Canada 103 C5
Lava Hot Springs, U.S.A. 114 E7
Lavagh More, Ireland 15 B3
Lavagna, Italy 28 D6
Laval, France 18 D6
Lavalle, Argentina 126 B2
Lávara, Greece 41 E10
Lavardac, France 20 D4
Lavaur, France 20 E5
Lavelanet, France 20 F5
Lavello, Italy 31 A8
Laverne, U.S.A. 113 G5
Laverton, Australia 93 E3
Lavis, Italy 28 B8
Lávkos, Greece 38 B5
Lavos, Portugal 34 E2
Lavradio, Portugal 35 G1
Lavras, Brazil 127 A7
Lavre, Portugal 35 G2
Lávrion, Greece 38 D6
Lávris, Greece 36 D6
Lavumisa, Swaziland 89 D5
Lawas, Malaysia 62 D5
Lawele, Indonesia 63 F6
Lawn Hill, Australia 94 B2
Lawng Pit, Burma 67 G20
Lawqah, Si. Arabia 70 D4
Lawra, Ghana 82 C4
Lawrence, N.Z. 91 L2
Lawrence, Kans., U.S.A. 112 F7
Lawrence, Mass., U.S.A. 111 D13
Lawrenceburg, Ind., U.S.A. 108 F3
Lawrenceburg, Tenn., U.S.A. 109 H2
Lawrenceville, U.S.A. 109 J4
Laws, U.S.A. 116 H8
Lawton, U.S.A. 113 H5
Lawu, Indonesia 63 G14
Laxå, Sweden 11 F8
Laxford, L., U.K. 14 C3
Laxou, France 19 D13
Lay →, France 20 B2
Laylān, Iraq 70 C5
Layon →, France 18 E6
Laysan I., Pac. Oc. 97 E11
Laytonville, U.S.A. 114 G2
Lazarevac, Serbia, Yug. 40 B4
Lazarevskoye, Russia 49 J4
Lazdijai, Lithuania 44 D10
Lazio □, Italy 29 F9
Lazo, Moldova 43 C13
Lazo, Russia 54 C6
Le Beausset, France 21 E9
Le Blanc, France 20 B5
Le Bleymard, France 20 D7
Le Bourgneuf-la-Fôret, France 18 D6
Le Bugue, France 20 D4
Le Canourgue = La Canourgue, France 20 D7
Le Cateau Cambrésis, France 19 B10
Le Caylar, France 20 E7
Le Chambon-Feugerolles, France 21 C8
Le Châtelet, France 19 F9
Le Chesne, France 19 C11
Le Cheylard, France 21 D8
Le Conquet, France 18 D2
Le Creusot, France 19 F11
Le Croisic, France 18 E4
Le Donjon, France 19 F10

Le Dorat, *France* 20 B5
Le François, *Martinique* .. 121 D7
Le Grand-Lucé, *France* ... 18 E7
Le Grand-Pressigny, *France* 18 F7
Le Grand-Quevilly, *France* 18 C8
Le Havre, *France* 18 C7
Le Lavandou, *France* 21 E10
Le Lion-d'Angers, *France* . 18 E6
Le Louroux-Béconnais,
   France 18 E6
Le Luc, *France* 21 E10
Le Lude, *France* 18 E7
Le Mans, *France* 18 E7
Le Mars, *U.S.A.* 112 D6
Le Mayet-de-Montagne,
   France 19 F10
Le Mêle-sur-Sarthe, *France* 18 D7
Le Monastier-sur-Gazeille,
   France 20 D7
Le Monêtier-les-Bains,
   France 21 D10
Le Mont-Dore, *France* ... 20 C6
Le Mont-St-Michel, *France* 18 D5
Le Moule, *Guadeloupe* ... 121 C7
Le Muy, *France* 21 E10
Le Palais, *France* 18 E3
Le Perthus, *France* 20 F6
Le Puy-en-Velay, *France* . 20 C7
Le Roy, *U.S.A.* 113 F7
Le Sueur, *U.S.A.* 112 C8
Le Teil, *France* 21 D8
Le Teilleul, *France* 18 D6
Le Theil, *France* 18 D7
Le Thillot, *France* 19 E13
Le Thuy, *Vietnam* 64 D6
Le Touquet-Paris-Plage,
   France 19 B8
Le Tréport, *France* 18 B8
Le Val-d'Ajol, *France* 19 E13
Le Verdon-sur-Mer, *France* 20 C2
Le Vigan, *France* 20 E7
Lea →, *U.K.* 13 F8
Leach, *Cambodia* 65 F4
Lead, *U.S.A.* 112 C3
Leader, *Canada* 105 C7
Leadville, *U.S.A.* 115 G10
Leaf →, *U.S.A.* 113 K10
Leakey, *U.S.A.* 113 L5
Leamington, *Canada* 102 D3
Leamington, *U.S.A.* 114 G7
Leamington Spa = Royal
   Leamington Spa, *U.K.* . 13 E6
Le'an, *China* 59 D10
Leandro Norte Alem,
   Argentina 127 B4
Leane, L., *Ireland* 15 D2
Learmonth, *Australia* 92 D1
Leask, *Canada* 105 C7
Leatherhead, *U.K.* 13 F7
Leavenworth, *Kans.*,
   U.S.A. 112 F7
Leavenworth, *Wash.*,
   U.S.A. 114 C3
Łeba, *Poland* 44 D4
Łeba →, *Poland* 44 D4
Lebach, *Germany* 25 F2
Lebak, *Phil.* 61 H6
Lebam, *U.S.A.* 116 D3
Lebane, *Serbia, Yug.* 40 D5
Lebanon, *Ind., U.S.A.* ... 108 E2
Lebanon, *Kans., U.S.A.* .. 112 F5
Lebanon, *Ky., U.S.A.* 108 G3
Lebanon, *Mo., U.S.A.* ... 113 G8
Lebanon, *Oreg., U.S.A.* .. 114 D2
Lebanon, *Pa., U.S.A.* ... 111 F8
Lebanon, *Tenn., U.S.A.* .. 109 G2
Lebanon ■, *Asia* 75 B5
Lebec, *U.S.A.* 117 L8
Lebedyan, *Russia* 47 F10
Lebedyn, *Ukraine* 47 G8
Lebomboberge, *S. Africa* . 89 C5
Lębork, *Poland* 44 D4
Lebrija, *Spain* 35 J4
Łebsko, Jezioro, *Poland* . 44 D4
Lebu, *Chile* 126 D1
Leca da Palmeira, *Portugal* 34 D2
Lecce, *Italy* 31 B11
Lecco, *Italy* 28 C6
Lecco, L. di, *Italy* 28 C6
Lécera, *Spain* 32 D4
Lech, *Austria* 26 D3
Lech →, *Germany* 25 G6
Lechang, *China* 59 E9
Lechtaler Alpen, *Austria* . 26 D3
Lectoure, *France* 20 E4
Łęczna, *Poland* 45 G9
Łęczyca, *Poland* 45 F6
Ledesma, *Spain* 34 D5
Ledong, *China* 64 C7
Leduc, *Canada* 104 C6
Lee, *U.S.A.* 111 D11
Lee →, *Ireland* 15 E3
Lee Vining, *U.S.A.* 116 H7
Leech L., *U.S.A.* 112 B7
Leedey, *U.S.A.* 113 H5
Leeds, *U.K.* 12 D6
Leeds, *U.S.A.* 109 J2
Leek, *Neths.* 17 A6
Leek, *U.K.* 12 D5
Leer, *Germany* 24 B3
Leesburg, *U.S.A.* 109 L5
Leesville, *U.S.A.* 113 K8
Leeton, *Australia* 95 E4
Leetonia, *U.S.A.* 110 F4
Leeu Gamka, *S. Africa* ... 88 E3
Leeuwarden, *Neths.* 17 A5
Leeuwin, C., *Australia* ... 93 F2

Leeward Is., *Atl. Oc.* 121 C7
Lefka, *Cyprus* 36 D11
Lefkoniko, *Cyprus* 36 D12
Lefors, *U.S.A.* 113 H4
Lefroy, L., *Australia* 93 F3
Łęg →, *Poland* 45 H8
Legal, *Canada* 104 C6
Leganés, *Spain* 34 E7
Legazpi, *Phil.* 61 E5
Legendre I., *Australia* 92 D2
Lège, *France* 20 D2
Leghorn = Livorno, *Italy* . 28 E7
Legionowo, *Poland* 45 F7
Legnago, *Italy* 29 C8
Legnano, *Italy* 28 C5
Legnica, *Poland* 45 G3
Legnica □, *Poland* 45 G3
Legrad, *Croatia* 29 B13
Legume, *Australia* 95 D5
Leh, *India* 69 B7
Lehi, *U.S.A.* 114 F8
Lehighton, *U.S.A.* 111 F9
Lehliu, *Romania* 43 F11
Lehrte, *Germany* 24 C5
Lehututu, *Botswana* 88 C3
Lei Shui →, *China* 59 D9
Leiah, *Pakistan* 68 D4
Leibnitz, *Austria* 26 E8
Leibo, *China* 58 C4
Leicester, *U.K.* 13 E6
Leicester City □, *U.K.* ... 13 E6
Leicestershire □, *U.K.* ... 13 E6
Leichhardt →, *Australia* .. 94 B2
Leichhardt Ra., *Australia* . 94 C4
Leiden, *Neths.* 17 B4
Leie →, *Belgium* 17 C3
Leifers = Láives, *Italy* ... 29 B8
Leimen, *Germany* 25 F4
Leine →, *Germany* 24 C5
Leinefelde, *Germany* 24 D6
Leinster, *Australia* 93 E3
Leinster □, *Ireland* 15 C4
Leinster, Mt., *Ireland* 15 D5
Leipalingis, *Lithuania* 44 D10
Leipzig, *Germany* 24 D8
Leiria, *Portugal* 34 F2
Leiria □, *Portugal* 34 F2
Leirvik, *Norway* 9 G11
Leisler, Mt., *Australia* 92 D4
Leith, *U.K.* 14 F5
Leith Hill, *U.K.* 13 F7
Leitha →, *Europe* 27 D10
Leitrim, *Ireland* 15 B3
Leitrim □, *Ireland* 15 B4
Leitza, *Spain* 32 B3
Leiyang, *China* 59 D9
Leizhou Bandao, *China* ... 60 D6
Leizhou Wan, *China* 59 G8
Lek →, *Neths.* 17 C4
Leka, *Norway* 8 D14
Lekáni, *Greece* 41 E8
Lekbibaj, *Albania* 40 D3
Lekeitio, *Spain* 32 B2
Lekhainá, *Greece* 38 D3
Leksand, *Sweden* 10 D9
Lékva Óros, *Greece* 36 D6
Leland, *U.S.A.* 113 J9
Leland Lakes, *Canada* ... 105 B6
Lelång, *Sweden* 10 E6
Leleque, *Argentina* 128 E2
Lelystad, *Neths.* 17 B5
Lem, *Denmark* 11 H2
Lema, *Nigeria* 83 C5
Léman, L., *Europe* 19 F13
Lemera,
   Dem. Rep. of the Congo 86 C2
Lemery, *Phil.* 61 E4
Lemhi Ra., *U.S.A.* 114 D7
Lemmer, *Neths.* 17 B5
Lemmon, *U.S.A.* 112 C3
Lemon Grove, *U.S.A.* 117 N9
Lemoore, *U.S.A.* 116 J7
Lempdes, *France* 20 C7
Lemvig, *Denmark* 11 H2
Lena →, *Russia* 51 B13
Lenart, *Slovenia* 29 B12
Lencloître, *France* 18 F7
Léndas, *Greece* 36 E6
Lendava, *Slovenia* 29 B13
Lendeh, *Iran* 71 D6
Lendinara, *Italy* 29 C8
Lengerich, *Germany* 24 C3
Lenggong, *Malaysia* 65 K3
Lenggries, *Germany* 25 H7
Lengua de Vaca, Pta.,
   Chile 126 C1
Lengyeltóti, *Hungary* 42 D2
Lenhovda, *Sweden* 11 G9
Lenina, Kanal →, *Russia* . 49 J7
Leninabad = Khudzhand,
   Tajikistan 50 E7
Leninakan = Gyumri,
   Armenia 49 K6
Leningrad = Sankt-
   Peterburg, *Russia* 46 C6
Lenino, *Ukraine* 47 K8
Leninogorsk, *Kazakstan* .. 50 D9
Leninsk, *Russia* 49 F7
Leninsk-Kuznetskiy, *Russia* 50 D9
Leninskoye, *Russia* 48 A8
Lenk, *Switz.* 25 J3
Lenkoran = Länkäran,
   Azerbaijan 73 C13
Lenmalu, *Indonesia* 63 E8
Lenne →, *Germany* 24 D3
Lennestadt, *Germany* 24 D4

Lennoxville, *Canada* 111 A13
Leno, *Italy* 28 C7
Lenoir, *U.S.A.* 109 H5
Lenoir City, *U.S.A.* 109 H3
Lenora, *U.S.A.* 112 F4
Lenore L., *Canada* 105 C8
Lenox, *U.S.A.* 111 D11
Lens, *France* 19 B9
Lensahn, *Germany* 24 A6
Lensk, *Russia* 51 C12
Lentekhi, *Georgia* 49 J6
Lenti, *Hungary* 42 D1
Lentini, *Italy* 31 E8
Lenwood, *U.S.A.* 117 L9
Lenzen, *Germany* 24 B7
Léo, *Burkina Faso* 82 C4
Leoben, *Austria* 26 D8
Leodhas = Lewis, *U.K.* ... 14 C2
Leola, *U.S.A.* 112 C5
Leominster, *U.K.* 13 E5
Leominster, *U.S.A.* 111 D13
León, *France* 20 E2
León, *Mexico* 118 C4
León, *Nic.* 120 D2
León, *Spain* 34 C5
Leon, *U.S.A.* 112 E8
León □, *Spain* 34 C5
León, Montes de, *Spain* .. 34 C4
Leonardtown, *U.S.A.* 108 F7
Leonberg, *Germany* 25 G5
Leonding, *Austria* 26 C7
Leonessa, *Italy* 29 F9
Leonforte, *Italy* 31 E7
Leongatha, *Australia* 95 F4
Leonídhion, *Greece* 38 D4
Leonora, *Australia* 93 E3
Léopold II, Lac = Mai-
   Ndombe, L.,
   Dem. Rep. of the Congo 84 E3
Leopoldina, *Brazil* 127 A7
Leopoldsburg, *Belgium* ... 17 C5
Léopoldville = Kinshasa,
   Dem. Rep. of the Congo 84 E3
Leoti, *U.S.A.* 112 F4
Leova, *Moldova* 43 D13
Leoville, *Canada* 105 C7
Lépa, L. do, *Angola* 88 B2
Lepe, *Spain* 35 H3
Lepel = Lyepyel, *Belarus* . 46 E5
Lepenoú, *Greece* 38 C3
Leping, *China* 59 C11
Lepontine, Alpi, *Italy* 28 B5
Leppävirta, *Finland* 9 E22
Lepsény, *Hungary* 42 D3
Lequeitio = Lekeitio, *Spain* 32 B2
Lercara Friddi, *Italy* 30 E6
Lerdo, *Mexico* 118 B4
Lere, *Nigeria* 83 D6
Léribe, *Lesotho* 89 D4
Lérici, *Italy* 28 D6
Lérida = Lleida, *Spain* ... 32 D5
Lérins, Îs. de, *France* 21 E11
Lerma, *Spain* 34 C7
Léros, *Greece* 39 D8
Lérouville, *France* 19 D12
Lerum, *Sweden* 11 G6
Lerwick, *U.K.* 14 A7
Les, *Romania* 42 D6
Les Abrets, *France* 21 C9
Les Andelys, *France* 18 C8
Les Borges Blanques, *Spain* 32 D5
Les Cayes, *Haiti* 121 C5
Les Essarts, *France* 18 F5
Les Étroits, *Canada* 103 C6
Les Herbiers, *France* 18 F5
Les Minquiers, Plateau des,
   Chan. Is. 18 D4
Les Pieux, *France* 18 C5
Les Ponts-de-Cé, *France* .. 18 E6
Les Riceys, *France* 19 E11
Les Sables-d'Olonne,
   France 20 B2
Les Vans, *France* 21 D8
Lesbos = Lésvos, *Greece* . 39 B8
L'Escala, *Spain* 32 C8
Leshan, *China* 58 C4
Lésina, *Italy* 29 G12
Lésina, L. di, *Italy* 29 G12
Lesjöfors, *Sweden* 10 E8
Lesko, *Poland* 45 J9
Leskovac, *Serbia, Yug.* ... 40 C5
Leskoviku, *Albania* 40 F4
Leslie, *U.S.A.* 113 H8
Leśna, *Poland* 45 G2
Lesneven, *France* 18 D2
Leśnica, *Poland* 45 H5
Leśnica, *Serbia, Yug.* 40 B3
Lesnoye, *Russia* 46 C9
Lesopilnoye, *Russia* 54 A7
Lesotho ■, *Africa* 89 D4
Lesozavodsk, *Russia* 54 B6
Lesparre-Médoc, *France* .. 20 C3
Lessay, *France* 18 C5
Lesse →, *Belgium* 17 D4
Lessebo, *Sweden* 11 H9
Lesser Antilles, *W. Indies* . 121 D7
Lesser Slave L., *Canada* .. 104 B5
Lesser Sunda Is., *Indonesia* 63 F6
Lessines, *Belgium* 17 D3
Lester, *U.S.A.* 116 C5
Lestock, *Canada* 105 C8
Lesuer I., *Australia* 92 B4
Lésvos, *Greece* 39 B8
Leszno, *Poland* 45 G3
Leszno □, *Poland* 45 G3
Liádhoi, *Greece* 39 E8
Lian Xian, *China* 59 E9

Létavértes, *Hungary* 42 C6
Letchworth, *U.K.* 13 F7
Letea, Ostrov, *Romania* .. 43 E14
Lethbridge, *Canada* 104 D6
Lethem, *Guyana* 124 C7
Leti, Kepulauan, *Indonesia* 63 F7
Leti Is. = Leti, Kepulauan,
   Indonesia 63 F7
Letiahau →, *Botswana* ... 88 C3
Leticia, *Colombia* 124 D5
Leting, *China* 57 E10
Letjiesbos, *S. Africa* 88 E3
Letlhakeng, *Botswana* 88 C3
Letpadan, *Burma* 67 L19
Letpan, *Burma* 67 K19
Letsôk-aw Kyun, *Burma* .. 65 G2
Letterkenny, *Ireland* 15 B4
Leu, *Romania* 43 F9
Leucadia, *U.S.A.* 117 M9
Leucate, *France* 20 F7
Leucate, Étang de, *France* 20 F7
Leuk, *Switz.* 25 J3
Leuşeni, *Moldova* 43 D13
Leuser, G., *Indonesia* 62 D1
Leutkirch, *Germany* 25 H6
Leuven, *Belgium* 17 D4
Leuze-en-Hainaut, *Belgium* 17 D3
Lev Tolstoy, *Russia* 46 F10
Levádhia, *Greece* 38 C4
Levan, *U.S.A.* 114 G8
Levanger, *Norway* 8 E14
Levani, *Albania* 40 F3
Levant, Î. du, *France* 21 E10
Lévanto, *Italy* 28 D6
Lévanzo, *Italy* 30 D5
Levelland, *U.S.A.* 113 J3
Leven, *U.K.* 14 E6
Leven, L., *U.K.* 14 E5
Leven, Toraka, *Madag.* ... 89 A8
Leveque C., *Australia* 92 C3
Leverano, *Italy* 31 B10
Leverkusen, *Germany* 24 D3
Levice, *Slovak Rep.* 27 C11
Lévico Terme, *Italy* 29 C8
Levie, *France* 21 G13
Levier, *France* 19 F13
Levin, *N.Z.* 91 J5
Lévis, *Canada* 103 C5
Levis, L., *Canada* 104 A5
Levítha, *Greece* 39 D8
Levka, *Bulgaria* 41 E10
Levkás, *Greece* 38 C2
Levkás □, *Greece* 38 C2
Levkímmi, *Greece* 36 B4
Levkímmi, Ákra, *Greece* .. 36 B4
Levkôsia = Nicosia, *Cyprus* 36 D12
Levoča, *Slovak Rep.* 27 B13
Levroux, *France* 19 F8
Levski, *Bulgaria* 41 C9
Levskigrad = Karlovo,
   Bulgaria 41 D8
Lewellen, *U.S.A.* 112 E3
Lewes, *U.K.* 13 G8
Lewes, *U.S.A.* 108 F8
Lewin Brzeski, *Poland* 45 H4
Lewis, *U.K.* 14 C2
Lewis →, *U.S.A.* 116 E4
Lewis, Butt of, *U.K.* 14 C2
Lewis Ra., *Australia* 92 D4
Lewis Range, *U.S.A.* 114 C7
Lewisburg, *Pa., U.S.A.* ... 110 F8
Lewisburg, *Tenn., U.S.A.* . 109 H2
Lewisporte, *Canada* 103 C8
Lewiston, *Idaho, U.S.A.* .. 114 C5
Lewiston, *Maine, U.S.A.* . 109 C11
Lewistown, *Mont., U.S.A.* 114 C9
Lewistown, *Pa., U.S.A.* .. 110 F7
Lexington, *Ill., U.S.A.* ... 112 E10
Lexington, *Ky., U.S.A.* ... 108 F3
Lexington, *Miss., U.S.A.* . 113 J9
Lexington, *Mo., U.S.A.* .. 112 F8
Lexington, *N.C., U.S.A.* .. 109 H5
Lexington, *Nebr., U.S.A.* . 112 E5
Lexington, *Ohio, U.S.A.* .. 110 F2
Lexington, *Oreg., U.S.A.* . 114 D4
Lexington, *Tenn., U.S.A.* . 109 H1
Lexington Park, *U.S.A.* ... 108 F7
Leyburn, *U.K.* 12 C6
Leye, *China* 58 E6
Leyland, *U.K.* 12 D5
Leyre →, *France* 20 D2
Leyte, *Phil.* 61 F6
Leyte Gulf, *Phil.* 61 F6
Leżajsk, *Poland* 45 H9
Lezay, *France* 20 B3
Lezha, *Albania* 40 E3
Lezhi, *China* 58 B5
Lézignan-Corbières, *France* 20 E6
Lezoux, *France* 20 C7
Lgov, *Russia* 47 G8
Lhasa, *China* 60 D4
Lhazê, *China* 60 D3
Lhokkruet, *Indonesia* 62 D1
Lhokseumawe, *Indonesia* . 62 C1
L'Hospitalet de Llobregat,
   Spain 32 D7
Lhuntsi Dzong, *India* 67 F17
Li, *Thailand* 64 D2
Li Shui →, *China* 59 C9
Li Xian, *Gansu, China* ... 56 G3
Li Xian, *Hebei, China* 56 E8
Li Xian, *Hunan, China* ... 59 C8
Li Xian, *Sichuan, China* .. 58 B4

Liancheng, *China* 59 E11
Lianga, *Phil.* 61 G7
Liangcheng,
   Nei Mongol Zizhiqu,
   China 56 D7
Liangcheng, *Shandong,*
   China 57 G10
Liangdang, *China* 56 H4
Lianghekou, *China* 58 C7
Liangping, *China* 58 B6
Lianhua, *China* 59 D9
Lianjiang, *Fujian, China* .. 59 D12
Lianjiang, *Guangdong,*
   China 59 G8
Lianping, *China* 59 E10
Lianshan, *China* 59 E9
Lianshanguan, *China* 57 D12
Lianshui, *China* 57 H10
Lianyuan, *China* 59 D8
Lianyungang, *China* 57 G10
Liao He →, *China* 57 D11
Liaocheng, *China* 56 F8
Liaodong Bandao, *China* . 57 E12
Liaodong Wan, *China* 57 D11
Liaoning □, *China* 57 D12
Liaoyang, *China* 57 D12
Liaoyuan, *China* 57 C13
Liaozhong, *China* 57 D12
Liapádhes, *Greece* 38 B1
Liard →, *Canada* 104 A4
Liari, *Pakistan* 68 G2
Libau = Liepāja, *Latvia* .. 9 H19
Libby, *U.S.A.* 114 B6
Libenge,
   Dem. Rep. of the Congo 84 D3
Liberal, *Kans., U.S.A.* 113 G4
Liberal, *Mo., U.S.A.* 113 G7
Liberec, *Czech Rep.* 26 A8
Liberia, *Costa Rica* 120 D2
Liberia ■, *W. Afr.* 82 D2
Liberty, *Mo., U.S.A.* 112 F7
Liberty, *Tex., U.S.A.* 113 K7
Libiąż, *Poland* 45 H6
Lîbîya, Sahrâ', *Africa* 79 C10
Libo, *China* 58 E6
Libobo, Tanjung, *Indonesia* 63 E7
Libode, *S. Africa* 89 E4
Libohava, *Albania* 40 F4
Libourne, *France* 20 D3
Libramont, *Belgium* 17 E5
Librazhdi, *Albania* 40 E4
Libreville, *Gabon* 84 D1
Libya ■, *N. Afr.* 79 C9
Libyan Desert = Lîbîya,
   Sahrâ', *Africa* 79 C10
Libyan Plateau = Ed-
   Déffa, *Egypt* 80 A2
Licantén, *Chile* 126 D1
Licata, *Italy* 30 E6
Lice, *Turkey* 73 C9
Licheng, *China* 56 F7
Lichfield, *U.K.* 13 E6
Lichinga, *Mozam.* 87 E4
Lichtenburg, *S. Africa* 88 D4
Lichtenfels, *Germany* 25 E7
Lichuan, *Hubei, China* ... 58 B7
Lichuan, *Jiangxi, China* .. 59 D11
Licosa, Punta, *Italy* 31 B7
Lida, *Belarus* 9 K21
Lida, *U.S.A.* 115 H5
Liden, *Sweden* 10 B10
Lidhoríkion, *Greece* 38 C4
Lidhult, *Sweden* 11 H7
Lidköping, *Sweden* 11 F7
Lido, *Italy* 29 C9
Lido, *Niger* 83 C5
Lido di Roma = Óstia,
   Italy 29 G9
Lidzbark, *Poland* 45 E6
Lidzbark Warmiński,
   Poland 44 D7
Liebenwalde, *Germany* ... 24 C9
Lieberose, *Germany* 24 D10
Liebig, Mt., *Australia* 92 D5
Liebling, *Romania* 42 E6
Liechtenstein ■, *Europe* .. 25 H5
Liège, *Belgium* 17 D5
Liège □, *Belgium* 17 D5
Liegnitz = Legnica, *Poland* 45 G3
Lienart,
   Dem. Rep. of the Congo 86 B2
Lienyünchiangshih =
   Lianyungang, *China* 57 G10
Lienz, *Austria* 26 E5
Liepāja, *Latvia* 9 H19
Liepāja □, *Latvia* 44 B8
Liepājas ezers, *Latvia* 44 B8
Lier, *Belgium* 17 C4
Liernais, *France* 19 E11
Liești, *Romania* 43 E12
Liévin, *France* 19 B9
Lièvre →, *Canada* 102 C4
Liezen, *Austria* 26 D7
Liffey →, *Ireland* 15 C5
Lifford, *Ireland* 15 B4
Liffré, *France* 18 D5
Lifudzin, *Russia* 54 B7
Lightning Ridge, *Australia* 95 D4
Lignano Sabbiadoro, *Italy* 29 C10
Ligny-en-Barrois, *France* .. 19 D12
Ligourión, *Greece* 38 D5
Ligueil, *France* 18 E7
Ligure □, *Italy* 28 D5
Ligurian Sea, *Medit. S.* .. 6 G7
Lihou Reefs and Cays,
   Australia 94 B5

Lihue, U.S.A. 106 H15
Lijiang, China 58 D3
Likasi,
  Dem. Rep. of the Congo 87 E2
Likenäs, Sweden 10 D8
Likhoslavl, Russia 46 D8
Likhovskoy, Russia 47 H11
Likoma I., Malawi 87 E3
Likumburu, Tanzania 87 D4
L'Île-Bouchard, France .. 18 E7
L'Île-Rousse, France 21 F12
Liling, China 59 D9
Lilla Edet, Sweden 11 F6
Lille, France 19 B10
Lille Bælt, Denmark 11 J3
Lillebonne, France 18 C7
Lillehammer, Norway 9 F14
Lillesand, Norway 9 G13
Lillhärdal, Sweden 10 C8
Lillian Point, Mt., Australia 93 E4
Lillo, Spain 34 F7
Lillooet →, Canada 104 D4
Lilongwe, Malawi 87 E3
Liloy, Phil. 63 C6
Lim →, Bos.-H. 40 C3
Lima, Indonesia 63 E7
Lima, Peru 124 F3
Lima, Mont., U.S.A. 114 D7
Lima, Ohio, U.S.A. 108 E3
Lima →, Portugal 34 D2
Limages, Canada 111 A9
Liman, Russia 49 H8
Limanowa, Poland 45 J7
Limassol, Cyprus 36 E12
Limavady, U.K. 15 A5
Limay →, Argentina 128 D3
Limay Mahuida, Argentina 126 D2
Limbach-Oberfrohna,
  Germany 24 E8
Limbang, Brunei 62 D5
Limbara, Mte., Italy 30 B2
Limbaži, Latvia 9 H21
Limbdi, India 68 H4
Limbe, Cameroon 83 E6
Limbri, Australia 95 E5
Limbunya, Australia 92 C4
Limburg, Germany 25 E4
Limburg □, Belgium 17 C5
Limburg □, Neths. 17 C5
Limedsforsen, Sweden ... 10 D7
Limeira, Brazil 127 A6
Limenária, Greece 41 F8
Limerick, Ireland 15 D3
Limerick □, Ireland 15 D3
Limestone, U.S.A. 110 D6
Limestone →, Canada 105 B10
Limfjorden, Denmark 11 H3
Limia = Lima →, Portugal 34 D2
Limín Khersonísou, Greece 39 F7
Limingen, Norway 8 D15
Limmared, Sweden 11 G7
Limmen Bight, Australia .. 94 A2
Limmen Bight →,
  Australia 94 B2
Límni, Greece 38 C5
Límnos, Greece 39 B7
Limoges, France 20 C5
Limón, Costa Rica 120 E3
Limon, U.S.A. 112 F3
Limone Piemonte, Italy ... 28 D4
Limousin, France 20 C5
Limousin, Plateaux du,
  France 20 C5
Limoux, France 20 E6
Limpopo →, Africa 89 D5
Limuru, Kenya 86 C4
Lin Xian, China 56 F6
Lin'an, China 59 B12
Linapacan I., Phil. 61 F3
Linapacan Str., Phil. 61 F3
Linares, Chile 126 D1
Linares, Mexico 119 C5
Linares, Spain 35 G7
Linares □, Chile 126 D1
Linaro, Capo, Italy 29 F8
Línas Mte., Italy 30 C1
Lincang, China 58 F3
Lincheng, China 56 F8
Linchuan, China 59 D11
Lincoln, Argentina 126 C3
Lincoln, N.Z. 91 K4
Lincoln, U.K. 12 D7
Lincoln, Calif., U.S.A. 116 G5
Lincoln, Ill., U.S.A. 112 E10
Lincoln, Kans., U.S.A. ... 112 F5
Lincoln, Maine, U.S.A. ... 103 C6
Lincoln, N.H., U.S.A. 111 B13
Lincoln, N. Mex., U.S.A. . 115 K11
Lincoln, Nebr., U.S.A. 112 E6
Lincoln Hav = Lincoln
  Sea, Arctic 4 A5
Lincoln Sea, Arctic 4 A5
Lincolnshire □, U.K. 12 D7
Lincolnshire Wolds, U.K. . 12 D7
Lincolnton, U.S.A. 109 H5
L'Incudine, France 21 G13
Lind, U.S.A. 114 C4
Linda, U.S.A. 116 F5
Lindau, Germany 25 H5
Linden, Guyana 124 B7
Linden, Calif., U.S.A. 116 G5
Linden, Tex., U.S.A. 113 J7
Lindenhurst, U.S.A. 111 F11
Lindesberg, Sweden 10 E9
Lindesnes, Norway 9 H12
Líndhos, Greece 36 C10
Líndhos, Ákra, Greece ... 36 C10

Lindi, Tanzania 87 D4
Lindi □, Tanzania 87 D4
Lindi →,
  Dem. Rep. of the Congo 86 B2
Lindö, Sweden 11 F10
Lindome, Sweden 11 G6
Lindoso, Portugal 34 D2
Lindow, Germany 24 C8
Lindsay, Canada 102 D4
Lindsay, Calif., U.S.A. ... 116 J7
Lindsay, Okla., U.S.A. 113 H6
Lindsborg, U.S.A. 112 F6
Lindsdal, Sweden 11 H10
Linfen, China 56 F6
Ling Xian, Hunan, China . 59 D9
Ling Xian, Shandong,
  China 56 F9
Lingao, China 64 C7
Lingayen, Phil. 63 A6
Lingayen G., Phil. 61 C4
Lingbi, China 57 H9
Lingbo, Sweden 10 C10
Lingchuan,
  Guangxi Zhuangzu,
  China 59 E8
Lingchuan, Shanxi, China . 56 G7
Lingen, Germany 24 C3
Lingga, Indonesia 62 E2
Lingga, Kepulauan,
  Indonesia 62 E2
Lingga Arch. = Lingga,
  Kepulauan, Indonesia .. 62 E2
Linghem, Sweden 11 F9
Lingle, U.S.A. 112 D2
Lingling, China 59 D8
Lingqiu, China 56 E8
Lingshan, China 58 F7
Lingshi, China 56 F6
Lingshou, China 56 E8
Lingshui, China 64 C8
Lingtai, China 56 G4
Linguère, Senegal 82 B1
Lingwu, China 56 E4
Lingyuan, China 57 D10
Lingyun, China 58 E6
Linhai, China 59 C13
Linhares, Brazil 125 G10
Linhe, China 56 D4
Linjiang, China 57 D14
Linköping, Sweden 11 F9
Linkou, China 57 B16
Linli, China 59 C8
Linnhe, L., U.K. 14 E3
Linqi, China 56 G7
Linqing, China 56 F8
Linqu, China 57 F10
Linru, China 56 G7
Lins, Brazil 127 A6
Linshui, China 58 B6
Lintao, China 56 G2
Linth →, Switz. 25 H5
Linthal, Switz. 25 J5
Lintlaw, Canada 105 C8
Linton, Canada 103 C5
Linton, Ind., U.S.A. 108 F2
Linton, N. Dak., U.S.A. ... 112 B4
Lintong, China 56 G5
Linville, Australia 95 D5
Linwood, Canada 110 C4
Linwu, China 59 E9
Linxi, China 57 C10
Linxia, China 60 C5
Linxiang, China 59 C9
Linyanti →, Africa 88 B4
Linyi, China 57 G10
Linz, Austria 26 C7
Linz, Germany 24 E3
Linzhenzhen, China 56 F5
Linzi, China 57 F10
Lion, G. du, France 20 E7
Lionárisso, Cyprus 36 D13
Lioni, Italy 31 B8
Lions, G. of = Lion, G.
  du, France 20 E7
Lion's Den, Zimbabwe ... 87 F3
Lion's Head, Canada 102 D3
Liozno = Lyozna, Belarus . 46 E6
Lipa, Phil. 61 E4
Lipali, Mozam. 87 F4
Lipany, Slovak Rep. 27 B13
Lípari, Italy 31 D7
Lípari, Is. = Eólie, Ís.,
  Italy 31 D7
Lipcani, Moldova 43 B11
Lipetsk, Russia 47 F10
Lipiany, Poland 45 E1
Liping, China 58 D7
Lipkany = Lipcani,
  Moldova 43 B11
Lipljan, Serbia, Yug. 40 D5
Lipník nad Bečvou,
  Czech Rep. 27 B10
Lipno, Poland 45 F6
Lipova, Romania 42 D6
Lipovcy Manzovka, Russia 54 B6
Lipovets, Ukraine 47 H5
Lippe →, Germany 24 D2
Lippstadt, Germany 24 D4
Lipscomb, U.S.A. 113 G4
Lipsk, Poland 44 E10
Lipsko, Poland 45 G8
Lipsói, Greece 39 D8
Liptovský Hrádok,
  Slovak Rep. 27 B12
Liptovský Mikuláš,
  Slovak Rep. 27 B12
Liptrap C., Australia 95 F4

Lipu, China 59 E8
Lira, Uganda 86 B3
Liri →, Italy 30 A6
Liria = Lliria, Spain 33 F4
Lisala,
  Dem. Rep. of the Congo 84 D4
Lisboa, Portugal 35 G1
Lisboa □, Portugal 35 F1
Lisbon = Lisboa, Portugal 35 G1
Lisbon, N. Dak., U.S.A. . 112 B6
Lisbon, N.H., U.S.A. 111 B13
Lisbon, Ohio, U.S.A. 110 F4
Lisburn, U.K. 15 B5
Liscannor B., Ireland 15 D2
Liscia →, Italy 30 A2
Lishe Jiang →, China 58 E3
Lishi, China 56 F6
Lishu, China 57 C13
Lishui, Jiangsu, China 59 B12
Lishui, Zhejiang, China ... 59 C12
Lisianski I., Pac. Oc. 96 E10
Lisichansk = Lysychansk,
  Ukraine 47 H10
Lisieux, France 18 C7
Liski, Russia 47 G10
L'Isle-Jourdain, Gers,
  France 20 E5
L'Isle-Jourdain, Vienne,
  France 20 B4
L'Isle-sur-la-Sorgue, France 21 E9
Lisle-sur-Tarn, France 20 E5
Lismore, Australia 95 D5
Lismore, Ireland 15 D4
Lista, Norway 9 G12
Lister, Mt., Antarctica ... 5 D11
Liston, Australia 95 D5
Listowel, Canada 102 D3
Listowel, Ireland 15 D2
Lit, Sweden 10 A8
Lit-et-Mixe, France 20 D2
Litang, Guangxi Zhuangzu,
  China 58 F7
Litang, Sichuan, China ... 58 B3
Litang Qu →, China 58 C3
Litani →, Lebanon 75 B4
Litchfield, Calif., U.S.A. .. 116 E6
Litchfield, Conn., U.S.A. . 111 E11
Litchfield, Ill., U.S.A. 112 F10
Litchfield, Minn., U.S.A. . 112 C7
Liteni, Romania 43 C11
Lithgow, Australia 95 E5
Líthinon, Ákra, Greece ... 36 E6
Lithuania ■, Europe 9 J20
Litija, Slovenia 29 B11
Litókhoron, Greece 40 F6
Litoměřice, Czech Rep. ... 26 A7
Litomyšl, Czech Rep. 27 B9
Litschau, Austria 26 C8
Little Abaco I., Bahamas . 120 A4
Little Barrier I., N.Z. 91 G5
Little Belt Mts., U.S.A. ... 114 C8
Little Blue →, U.S.A. 112 E6
Little Cadotte →, Canada 104 B5
Little Cayman, I.,
  Cayman Is. 120 C3
Little Churchill →, Canada 105 B9
Little Colorado →, U.S.A. 115 H8
Little Current, Canada 102 C3
Little Current →, Canada . 102 B3
Little Falls, Minn., U.S.A. 112 C7
Little Falls, N.Y., U.S.A. . 111 C10
Little Fork →, U.S.A. 112 A8
Little Grand Rapids,
  Canada 105 C9
Little Humboldt →,
  U.S.A. 114 F5
Little Inagua I., Bahamas . 121 B5
Little Karoo, S. Africa 88 E3
Little Lake, U.S.A. 117 K9
Little Laut Is. = Laut
  Kecil, Kepulauan,
  Indonesia 62 E5
Little Minch, U.K. 14 D2
Little Missouri →, U.S.A. 112 B3
Little Ouse →, U.K. 13 E9
Little Rann, India 68 H4
Little Red →, U.S.A. 113 H9
Little River, N.Z. 91 K4
Little Rock, U.S.A. 113 H8
Little Ruaha →, Tanzania 86 D4
Little Sable Pt., U.S.A. ... 108 D2
Little Sioux →, U.S.A. ... 112 E6
Little Smoky →, Canada . 104 C5
Little Snake →, U.S.A. ... 114 F9
Little Valley, U.S.A. 110 D6
Little Wabash →, U.S.A. . 108 G1
Littlefield, U.S.A. 113 J3
Littlefork, U.S.A. 112 A8
Littlehampton, U.K. 13 G7
Littleton, U.S.A. 111 B13
Litvinov, Czech Rep. 26 A6
Liu He →, China 57 D11
Liu Jiang →, China 58 F7
Liuba, China 56 H4
Liucheng, China 58 E7
Liugou, China 57 D10
Liuhe, China 57 C13
Liuheng Dao, China 59 C14
Liukang Tenggaja =
  Sabalana, Kepulauan,
  Indonesia 63 F5
Liuli, Tanzania 87 E3
Liuwa Plain, Zambia 85 G4
Liuyang, China 59 C9
Liuzhou, China 58 E7
Liuzhuang, China 57 H11
Livada, Romania 42 C8

Livadherón, Greece 40 F5
Livadhia, Cyprus 36 E12
Livádhion, Greece 38 A4
Livarot, France 18 D7
Live Oak, Calif., U.S.A. .. 116 F5
Live Oak, Fla., U.S.A. ... 109 K4
Liveras, Cyprus 36 D11
Liveringa, Australia 92 C3
Livermore, U.S.A. 116 H5
Livermore, Mt., U.S.A. ... 113 K2
Liverpool, Australia 95 E5
Liverpool, Canada 103 D7
Liverpool, U.K. 12 D4
Liverpool Bay, U.K. 12 D4
Liverpool Plains, Australia 95 E5
Liverpool Ra., Australia .. 95 E5
Livigno, Italy 28 B7
Livingston, Guatemala 120 C2
Livingston, U.K. 14 F5
Livingston, Calif., U.S.A. . 116 H6
Livingston, Mont., U.S.A. 114 D8
Livingston, Tex., U.S.A. .. 113 K7
Livingstone, Zambia 87 F2
Livingstone Mts., Tanzania 87 D3
Livingstonia, Malawi 87 E3
Livno, Bos.-H. 42 G2
Livny, Russia 47 F9
Livonia, U.S.A. 108 D4
Livorno, Italy 28 E7
Livramento, Brazil 127 C4
Livron-sur-Drôme, France 21 D8
Liwale, Tanzania 87 D4
Liwale □, Tanzania 87 D4
Lixi, China 58 D3
Lixoúrion, Greece 38 C2
Liyang, China 59 B12
Lizard I., Australia 94 A4
Lizard Pt., U.K. 13 H2
Lizzano, Italy 31 B10
Ljig, Serbia, Yug. 40 B4
Ljubija, Bos.-H. 29 D13
Ljubinje, Bos.-H. 40 D2
Ljubljana, Slovenia 29 B11
Ljubno, Slovenia 29 B11
Ljubovija, Serbia, Yug. ... 40 B3
Ljugarn, Sweden 11 G12
Ljung, Sweden 11 G7
Ljungan →, Sweden 10 B11
Ljungaverk, Sweden 10 B10
Ljungby, Sweden 9 H15
Ljungbyholm, Sweden 11 H10
Ljungdalen, Sweden 10 B6
Ljungsbro, Sweden 11 F9
Ljungskile, Sweden 11 F5
Ljusdal, Sweden 10 C10
Ljusfallshammar, Sweden . 11 F9
Ljusnan →, Sweden 10 C11
Ljusne, Sweden 10 C11
Ljutomer, Slovenia 29 B13
Llagostera, Spain 32 D7
Llancanelo, Salina,
  Argentina 126 D2
Llandeilo, U.K. 13 F4
Llandovery, U.K. 13 F4
Llandrindod Wells, U.K. .. 13 E4
Llandudno, U.K. 12 D4
Llanelli, U.K. 13 F3
Llanes, Spain 34 B6
Llangollen, U.K. 12 E4
Llanidloes, U.K. 13 E4
Llano, U.S.A. 113 K5
Llano →, U.S.A. 113 K5
Llano Estacado, U.S.A. .. 113 J3
Llanos, S. Amer. 122 C3
Llanquihue, L., Chile 128 E1
Llanwrtyd Wells, U.K. 13 E4
Llebeig, C. des, Spain ... 37 B9
Lleida, Spain 32 D5
Lleida □, Spain 32 C6
Llentrisca, C., Spain 37 C7
Llera, Mexico 119 C5
Llerena, Spain 35 G5
Lleyn Peninsula, U.K. 12 E3
Llico, Chile 126 C1
Lliria, Spain 33 F4
Llobregat →, Spain 32 D7
Llodio, Spain 32 B2
Lloret de Mar, Spain 32 D7
Lloyd B., Australia 94 A3
Lloyd L., Canada 105 B7
Lloydminster, Canada 105 C7
Llucena del Cid, Spain ... 32 E4
Llucmajor, Spain 37 B9
Llullaillaco, Volcán,
  S. Amer. 126 A2
Lo →, Vietnam 64 B5
Lo, U.S.A. 115 G8
Loa, U.S.A. 115 G8
Loa →, Chile 126 A1
Loano, Italy 28 D5
Lobatse, Botswana 88 D4
Löbau, Germany 24 D10
Lobenstein, Germany 24 E7
Lobería, Argentina 126 D4
Loberia, Argentina 126 D4
Lobito, Angola 85 G2
Lobos, Argentina 126 D4
Lobos, I. de, Canary Is. .. 37 F6
Lobos, I., Mexico 118 B2
Łobżenica, Poland 45 E4
Loc Binh, Vietnam 64 B6
Loc Ninh, Vietnam 65 G6
Locarno, Switz. 25 J4
Loch Baghasdail =
  Lochboisdale, U.K. 14 D1

Loch Garman = Wexford,
  Ireland 15 D5
Loch Nam Madadh =
  Lochmaddy, U.K. 14 D1
Lochaber, U.K. 14 E3
Locharbriggs, U.K. 14 F5
Lochboisdale, U.K. 14 D1
Lochem, Neths. 17 B6
Loches, France 18 E7
Lochgilphead, U.K. 14 E3
Lochinver, U.K. 14 C3
Lochmaddy, U.K. 14 D1
Lochnagar, Australia 94 C4
Lochnagar, U.K. 14 E5
Łochów, Poland 45 F8
Lochy, L., U.K. 14 E4
Lock, Australia 95 E2
Lock Haven, U.S.A. 110 E7
Lockeford, U.S.A. 116 G5
Lockeport, Canada 103 D6
Lockerbie, U.K. 14 F5
Lockhart, U.S.A. 113 L6
Lockhart, L., Australia ... 93 F2
Lockney, U.S.A. 113 H4
Lockport, U.S.A. 110 C6
Locminé, France 18 E4
Locri, Italy 31 D9
Locronan, France 18 D2
Lod, Israel 75 D3
Lodeinoye Pole, Russia ... 46 B7
Lodève, France 20 E7
Lodge Grass, U.S.A. 114 D10
Lodgepole, U.S.A. 112 E3
Lodgepole Cr. →, U.S.A. . 112 E2
Lodhran, Pakistan 68 E4
Lodi, Italy 28 C6
Lodi, U.S.A. 116 G5
Lodja,
  Dem. Rep. of the Congo 86 C1
Lodosa, Spain 32 C2
Lödöse, Sweden 11 F6
Lodwar, Kenya 86 B4
Łódź, Poland 45 G6
Łódź □, Poland 45 G6
Loei, Thailand 64 D3
Loengo,
  Dem. Rep. of the Congo 86 C2
Loeriesfontein, S. Africa .. 88 E2
Lofer, Austria 26 D5
Lofoten, Norway 8 B15
Lofsdalen, Sweden 10 B7
Lofsen →, Sweden 10 B7
Loftahammar, Sweden 11 G10
Logan, Kans., U.S.A. 112 F5
Logan, Ohio, U.S.A. 108 F4
Logan, Utah, U.S.A. 114 F8
Logan, W. Va., U.S.A. ... 108 G5
Logan, Mt., Canada 100 B5
Logan Pass, U.S.A. 104 D6
Logandale, U.S.A. 117 J12
Logansport, Ind., U.S.A. . 108 E2
Logansport, La., U.S.A. .. 113 K8
Logo, Sudan 81 F3
Logone →, Chad 79 F9
Logroño, Spain 32 C2
Logrosán, Spain 35 F5
Løgstør, Denmark 11 H3
Løgumkloster, Denmark .. 11 J2
Lohals, Denmark 11 J4
Lohardaga, India 69 H11
Lohja, Finland 9 F21
Löhne, Germany 24 C4
Lohr, Germany 25 F5
Loi-kaw, Burma 67 K20
Loimaa, Finland 9 F20
Loir →, France 18 E6
Loir-et-Cher □, France 18 E8
Loire □, France 21 C8
Loire →, France 18 E4
Loire-Atlantique □, France 18 E5
Loiret □, France 19 E9
Loitz, Germany 24 B9
Loja, Ecuador 124 D3
Loja, Spain 35 H6
Loji = Kawasi, Indonesia . 63 E7
Løjt Kirkeby, Denmark .. 11 J3
Loka, Sudan 81 G3
Lokandu,
  Dem. Rep. of the Congo 86 C2
Lokeren, Belgium 17 C3
Lokhvitsa, Ukraine 47 G7
Lokichokio, Kenya 86 B3
Lokitaung, Kenya 86 B4
Lokkan tekojärvi, Finland . 8 C22
Løkken, Denmark 11 G3
Loknya, Russia 46 D6
Lokoja, Nigeria 83 D6
Lokot, Russia 47 F8
Lol →, Sudan 81 F2
Lola, Guinea 82 D3
Lola, Mt., U.S.A. 116 F6
Lolibai, Gebel, Sudan 81 G3
Lolimi, Sudan 81 G3
Loliondo, Tanzania 86 C4
Lolland, Denmark 11 K5
Lollar, Germany 24 E4
Lolo, U.S.A. 114 C6
Lolodorf, Cameroon 83 E7
Lom, Bulgaria 40 C7
Lom →, Bulgaria 40 C7
Lom Kao, Thailand 64 D3
Lom Sak, Thailand 64 D3
Loma, U.S.A. 114 C8
Loma Linda, U.S.A. 117 L9
Lomami →,
  Dem. Rep. of the Congo 86 B1

Lomas de Zamóra,
  Argentina 126 C4
Lombadina, *Australia* 92 C3
Lombárdia □, *Italy* 28 C6
Lombardy = Lombárdia □,
  Italy 28 C6
Lomblen, *Indonesia* 63 F6
Lombok, *Indonesia* 62 F5
Lomé, *Togo* 83 D5
Lomela,
  Dem. Rep. of the Congo 84 E4
Lomela ➤,
  Dem. Rep. of the Congo 84 E4
Lometa, *U.S.A.* 113 K5
Łomianki, *Poland* 45 F7
Lomma, *Sweden* 11 J7
Lommel, *Belgium* 17 C5
Lomond, *Canada* 104 C6
Lomond, L., *U.K.* 14 E4
Lomphat, *Cambodia* 64 F6
Lompobatang, *Indonesia* .. 63 F5
Lompoc, *U.S.A.* 117 L6
Łomza, *Poland* 45 E9
Łomza □, *Poland* 45 E9
Loncoche, *Chile* 128 D2
Londa, *India* 66 M9
Londiani, *Kenya* 86 C4
Londinières, *France* 18 C8
London, *Canada* 102 D3
London, *U.K.* 13 F7
London, *Ky., U.S.A.* 108 G3
London, *Ohio, U.S.A.* 108 F4
London, Greater □, *U.K.* .. 13 F7
Londonderry, *U.K.* 15 B4
Londonderry □, *U.K.* 15 B4
Londonderry, C., *Australia* 92 B4
Londonderry, I., *Chile* ... 128 H2
Londres, *Argentina* 128 B3
Londrina, *Brazil* 127 A5
Lone Pine, *U.S.A.* 116 J8
Long Beach, *U.S.A.* 117 M8
Long Beach, *N.Y., U.S.A.* .. 111 F11
Long Beach, *Wash., U.S.A.* 116 D2
Long Branch, *U.S.A.* 111 F11
Long Creek, *U.S.A.* 114 D4
Long Eaton, *U.K.* 12 E6
Long I., *Australia* 94 C4
Long I., *Bahamas* 121 B4
Long I., *Ireland* 15 E2
Long I., *U.S.A.* 111 F11
Long Island Sd., *U.S.A.* .. 111 E12
Long L., *Canada* 102 C2
Long Lake, *U.S.A.* 111 C10
Long Pine, *U.S.A.* 112 D5
Long Point B., *Canada* ... 110 D4
Long Pt., *Nfld., Canada* .. 103 C8
Long Pt., *Ont., Canada* .. 110 D4
Long Range Mts., *Canada* 103 C8
Long Reef, *Australia* 92 B4
Long Str. = Longa, Proliv,
  Russia 4 C16
Long Thanh, *Vietnam* 65 G6
Long Xian, *China* 56 G4
Long Xuyen, *Vietnam* ... 65 G5
Longá, *Greece* 38 E3
Longa, Proliv, *Russia* 4 C16
Long'an, *China* 58 F6
Longarone, *Italy* 29 B9
Longbenton, *U.K.* 12 B6
Longchang, *China* 58 C5
Longchi, *China* 58 C4
Longchuan, *Guangdong,*
  China 59 E10
Longchuan, *Yunnan, China* 58 E1
Longde, *China* 56 G4
Longeau, *France* 19 E12
Longford, *Australia* 94 G4
Longford, *Ireland* 15 C4
Longford □, *Ireland* 15 C4
Longguan, *China* 56 D8
Longhua, *China* 57 D9
Longhui, *China* 59 D8
Longido, *Tanzania* 86 C4
Longiram, *Indonesia* 62 E5
Longkou, *Jiangxi, China* .. 59 D10
Longkou, *Shandong, China* 57 F11
Longlac, *Canada* 102 C2
Longli, *China* 58 D6
Longlin, *China* 58 E5
Longling, *China* 58 E2
Longmen, *China* 59 F10
Longming, *China* 58 F6
Longmont, *U.S.A.* 112 E2
Longnan, *China* 59 E10
Longnawan, *Indonesia* ... 62 D4
Longobucco, *Italy* 31 C9
Longquan, *China* 59 C12
Longreach, *Australia* 94 C3
Longshan, *China* 58 C7
Longsheng, *China* 59 E8
Longton, *Australia* 94 C4
Longué-Jumelles, *France* . 18 E6
Longueau, *France* 19 C9
Longueuil, *Canada* 111 A11
Longuyon, *France* 19 C12
Longvic, *France* 19 E12
Longview, *Canada* 104 C6
Longview, *Tex., U.S.A.* ... 113 J7
Longview, *Wash., U.S.A.* .. 116 D2
Longwy, *France* 19 C12
Longxi, *China* 56 G3
Longyou, *China* 59 C12
Longzhou, *China* 58 F6
Lonigo, *Italy* 29 C8
Löningen, *Germany* 24 C3
Lonja ➤, *Croatia* 29 C13

Lonoke, *U.S.A.* 113 H9
Lonquimay, *Chile* 128 D2
Lons-le-Saunier, *France* .. 19 F12
Lönsboda, *Sweden* 11 H8
Looe, *U.K.* 13 G3
Lookout, C., *Canada* 102 A3
Lookout, C., *U.S.A.* 109 H7
Loolmalasin, *Tanzania* .. 86 C4
Loon ➤, *Alta., Canada* .. 104 B5
Loon ➤, *Man., Canada* .. 105 B8
Loon Lake, *Canada* 105 C7
Loongana, *Australia* 93 F4
Loop Hd., *Ireland* 15 D2
Lop Buri, *Thailand* 64 E3
Lop Nor = Lop Nur, *China* 60 B4
Lop Nur, *China* 60 B4
Lopare, *Bos.-H.* 42 F3
Lopatin, *Russia* 49 J8
Lopatina, Gora, *Russia* .. 51 D15
Lopaye, *Sudan* 81 F3
Lopez, *Phil.* 61 E5
Lopez, C., *Gabon* 84 E1
Lopphavet, *Norway* 8 A19
Lora ➤, *Afghan.* 66 D4
Lora, Hamun-i-, *Pakistan* . 66 E4
Lora Cr. ➤, *Australia* ... 95 D2
Lora del Río, *Spain* 35 H5
Lorain, *U.S.A.* 110 E2
Loralai, *Pakistan* 68 D3
Lorca, *Spain* 33 H3
Lord Howe I., *Pac. Oc.* .. 96 L7
Lord Howe Ridge,
  Pac. Oc. 96 L8
Lordsburg, *U.S.A.* 115 K9
Loreto, *Brazil* 125 E9
Loreto, *Italy* 29 E10
Loreto, *Mexico* 118 B2
Lorgues, *France* 21 E10
Lorient, *France* 18 E3
Lőrinci, *Hungary* 42 C4
Lorn, *U.K.* 14 E3
Lorn, Firth of, *U.K.* 14 E3
Lorne, *Australia* 95 F3
Lorovouno, *Cyprus* 36 D11
Lörrach, *Germany* 25 H3
Lorraine □, *France* 19 D13
Lorrainville, *Canada* 102 C4
Los, *Sweden* 10 C9
Los, Îles de, *Guinea* 82 D2
Los Alamos, *Calif., U.S.A.* 117 L6
Los Alamos, *N. Mex.,*
  U.S.A. 115 J10
Los Altos, *U.S.A.* 116 H4
Los Andes, *Chile* 126 C1
Los Angeles, *Chile* 126 D1
Los Angeles, *U.S.A.* 117 M8
Los Angeles Aqueduct,
  U.S.A. 117 K9
Los Banos, *U.S.A.* 116 H6
Los Barrios, *Spain* 35 J5
Los Blancos, *Argentina* .. 126 A3
Los Corrales de Buelna,
  Spain 34 B6
Los Cristianos, *Canary Is.* 37 F3
Los Gallardos, *Spain* 33 H3
Los Gatos, *U.S.A.* 116 H5
Los Hermanos, *Venezuela* 121 D7
Los Islotes, *Canary Is.* ... 37 E6
Los Llanos de Aridane,
  Canary Is. 37 F2
Los Lunas, *U.S.A.* 115 J10
Los Mochis, *Mexico* 118 B3
Los Monegros, *Spain* ... 32 D4
Los Nietos, *Spain* 33 H4
Los Olivos, *U.S.A.* 117 L6
Los Palacios, *Cuba* 120 B3
Los Palacios y Villafranca,
  Spain 35 H5
Los Reyes, *Mexico* 118 D4
Los Roques, *Venezuela* .. 124 A5
Los Santos de Maimona,
  Spain 35 G4
Los Teques, *Venezuela* .. 124 A5
Los Testigos, *Venezuela* .. 124 A6
Los Vilos, *Chile* 126 C1
Los Yébenes, *Spain* 35 F7
Łosice, *Poland* 45 F9
Løsning, *Denmark* 11 J3
Lossiemouth, *U.K.* 14 D5
Lostwithiel, *U.K.* 13 G3
Lot □, *France* 20 D5
Lot ➤, *France* 20 D4
Lot-et-Garonne □, *France* 20 D4
Lota, *Chile* 126 D1
Loțfābād, *Iran* 71 B8
Lothair, *S. Africa* 89 D5
Lotorp, *Sweden* 11 F9
Lötschbergtunnel, *Switz.* .. 25 J3
Lotung, *Taiwan* 59 E13
Loubomo, *Congo* 84 E2
Loudéac, *France* 18 D4
Loudi, *China* 59 D8
Loudon, *U.S.A.* 109 H3
Loudonville, *U.S.A.* 110 F2
Loudun, *France* 18 E7
Loue ➤, *France* 19 E12
Louga, *Senegal* 82 B1
Loughborough, *U.K.* 12 E6
Loughrea, *Ireland* 15 C3
Loughros More B., *Ireland* 15 B3
Louhans, *France* 19 F12
Louis Trichardt, *S. Africa* . 89 C4
Louis XIV, Pte., *Canada* . 102 B4
Louisa, *U.S.A.* 108 F4
Louisbourg, *Canada* 103 C8
Louise I., *Canada* 104 C2

Louiseville, *Canada* 102 C5
Louisiade Arch.,
  Papua N. G. 96 J7
Louisiana □, *U.S.A.* 112 F9
Louisiana □, *U.S.A.* 113 K9
Louisville, *Ky., U.S.A.* ... 108 F3
Louisville, *Miss., U.S.A.* .. 113 J10
Loulay, *France* 20 B3
Loulé, *Portugal* 35 H3
Louny, *Czech Rep.* 26 A6
Loup ➤, *U.S.A.* 112 E5
Lourdes, *France* 20 E3
Lourdes-du-Blanc-Sablon,
  Canada 103 B8
Lourenço-Marques =
  Maputo, *Mozam.* 89 D5
Lourinhã, *Portugal* 35 F1
Lousã, *Portugal* 34 E2
Louth, *Australia* 95 E4
Louth, *Ireland* 15 C5
Louth, *U.K.* 12 D7
Louth □, *Ireland* 15 C5
Loutrá Aidhipsoú, *Greece* 38 C5
Loutráki, *Greece* 38 D4
Louvain = Leuven,
  Belgium 17 D4
Louviers, *France* 18 C8
Louwsburg, *S. Africa* 89 D5
Lovat ➤, *Russia* 46 C6
Lovćen, *Montenegro, Yug.* 40 D2
Love, *Canada* 105 C8
Lovech, *Bulgaria* 41 C8
Lovech □, *Bulgaria* 41 C8
Loveland, *U.S.A.* 112 E2
Lovell, *U.S.A.* 114 D9
Lovelock, *U.S.A.* 114 F4
Lóvere, *Italy* 28 C7
Lövestad, *Sweden* 11 J7
Loviisa, *Finland* 9 F22
Loving, *U.S.A.* 113 J2
Lovington, *U.S.A.* 113 J3
Lovisa = Loviisa, *Finland* . 9 F22
Lovosice, *Czech Rep.* 26 A7
Lovran, *Croatia* 29 C11
Lovrin, *Romania* 42 E5
Lövstabruk, *Sweden* 10 D11
Lövstabukten, *Sweden* .. 10 D11
Low Pt., *Australia* 93 F4
Low Tatra = Nízke Tatry,
  Slovak Rep. 27 C12
Lowa,
  Dem. Rep. of the Congo 86 C2
Lowa ➤,
  Dem. Rep. of the Congo 86 C2
Lowell, *U.S.A.* 111 D13
Lower Arrow L., *Canada* . 104 D5
Lower Austria =
  Niederösterreich □,
  Austria 26 C8
Lower California = Baja
  California, *Mexico* 118 A1
Lower Hutt, *N.Z.* 91 J5
Lower L., *U.S.A.* 114 F3
Lower Lake, *U.S.A.* 116 G4
Lower Post, *Canada* 104 B3
Lower Red L., *U.S.A.* 112 B7
Lower Saxony =
  Niedersachsen □,
  Germany 24 C4
Lower Tunguska =
  Tunguska,
  Nizhnyaya ➤, *Russia* .. 51 C9
Lowestoft, *U.K.* 13 E9
Łowicz, *Poland* 45 F6
Lowville, *U.S.A.* 111 C9
Loxton, *Australia* 95 E3
Loxton, *S. Africa* 88 E3
Loyalton, *U.S.A.* 116 F6
Loyalty Is. = Loyauté, Is.,
  N. Cal. 96 K8
Loyang = Luoyang, *China* 56 G7
Loyauté, Is., *N. Cal.* 96 K8
Loyev = Loyew, *Belarus* .. 47 G6
Loyew, *Belarus* 47 G6
Loyoro, *Uganda* 86 B3
Loz, *Slovenia* 29 C11
Lozère □, *France* 20 D7
Loznica, *Serbia, Yug.* ... 40 B3
Lozova, *Ukraine* 47 H9
Luachimo, *Angola* 84 F4
Lualaba ➤,
  Dem. Rep. of the Congo 86 B2
Luampa, *Zambia* 87 F1
Lu'an, *China* 59 B11
Luan Chau, *Vietnam* 64 B4
Luan He ➤, *China* 57 E10
Luan Xian, *China* 57 E10
Luancheng,
  Guangxi Zhuangzu,
  China 58 F7
Luancheng, *Hebei, China* . 56 F8
Luanco, *Spain* 34 B5
Luanda, *Angola* 84 F2
Luang, Thale, *Thailand* ... 65 J3
Luang Prabang, *Laos* 64 C4
Luangwa, *Zambia* 87 F3
Luangwa ➤, *Zambia* 87 E3
Luangwa Valley, *Zambia* . 87 E3
Luanne, *China* 57 D9
Luanping, *China* 57 D9
Luanshya, *Zambia* 87 E2
Luapula ➤, *Africa* 87 E2
Luarca, *Spain* 34 B4
Luashi,
  Dem. Rep. of the Congo 87 E1
Luau, *Angola* 84 G4

Lubaczów, *Poland* 45 H10
Lubań, *Poland* 45 G2
Lubana, Ozero = Lubānas
  Ezers, *Latvia* 9 H22
Lubānas Ezers, *Latvia* ... 9 H22
Lubang, *Phil.* 61 E4
Lubang Is., *Phil.* 63 B6
Lubartów, *Poland* 45 G9
Lubawa, *Poland* 44 E6
Lübbecke, *Germany* 24 C4
Lübben, *Germany* 24 D9
Lübbenau, *Germany* 24 D9
Lubbock, *U.S.A.* 113 J4
Lübeck, *Germany* 24 B6
Lübecker Bucht, *Germany* 24 A6
Lubefu,
  Dem. Rep. of the Congo 86 C1
Lubefu ➤,
  Dem. Rep. of the Congo 86 C1
Lubero = Luofu,
  Dem. Rep. of the Congo 86 C2
Lubersac, *France* 20 C5
Lubicon L., *Canada* 104 B5
Lubień Kujawski, *Poland* . 45 F6
Lubin, *Poland* 45 G3
Lublin, *Poland* 45 G9
Lublin □, *Poland* 45 G9
Lubliniec, *Poland* 45 H5
Lubnān, J., *Lebanon* 75 B4
Lubnān, Jabal, *Lebanon* .. 75 B4
Lubniewice, *Poland* 45 F2
Lubny, *Ukraine* 47 G7
Lubomierz, *Poland* 45 G2
Luboń, *Poland* 45 F3
Lubongola,
  Dem. Rep. of the Congo 86 C2
L'ubotín, *Slovak Rep.* ... 27 B13
Lubraniec, *Poland* 45 F5
Lubsko, *Poland* 45 G1
Lübtheen, *Germany* 24 B7
Lubuagan, *Phil.* 61 C4
Lubudi,
  Dem. Rep. of the Congo 87 D2
Lubuklinggau, *Indonesia* . 62 E2
Lubuksikaping, *Indonesia* . 62 D2
Lubumbashi,
  Dem. Rep. of the Congo 87 E2
Lubunda,
  Dem. Rep. of the Congo 86 D2
Lubungu, *Zambia* 87 E2
Lubutu,
  Dem. Rep. of the Congo 86 C2
Luc An Chau, *Vietnam* .. 64 A5
Luc-en-Diois, *France* 21 D9
Lucan, *Canada* 110 C3
Lucban, *Phil.* 61 D4
Lucca, *Italy* 28 E7
Luce ➤, *France* 18 D8
Luce Bay, *U.K.* 14 G4
Lucea, *Jamaica* 120 C4
Lucedale, *U.S.A.* 109 K1
Lucena, *Phil.* 61 E4
Lucena, *Spain* 35 H6
Lučenec, *Slovak Rep.* ... 27 C12
Lucera, *Italy* 31 A8
Lucerne = Luzern, *Switz.* . 25 H4
Lucerne, *U.S.A.* 116 F4
Lucerne Valley, *U.S.A.* ... 117 L10
Lucero, *Mexico* 118 A3
Luchena ➤, *Spain* 33 H3
Lucheng, *China* 56 F7
Lucheringo ➤, *Mozam.* .. 87 E4
Luchiang, *Taiwan* 59 E13
Lüchow, *Germany* 24 C7
Luchuan, *China* 59 F8
Luckau, *Germany* 24 D9
Luckenwalde, *Germany* .. 24 C9
Lucknow, *India* 69 F9
Luçon, *France* 20 B2
Lüda = Dalian, *China* 57 E11
Luda Kamchiya ➤,
  Bulgaria 41 C11
Ludbreg, *Croatia* 29 B13
Lüdenscheid, *Germany* .. 24 D3
Lüderitz, *Namibia* 88 D2
Ludewe □, *Tanzania* 87 E3
Ludhiana, *India* 68 D6
Ludian, *China* 58 D4
Luding Qiao, *China* 58 C4
Lüdinghausen, *Germany* . 24 D3
Ludington, *U.S.A.* 108 D2
Ludlow, *U.K.* 13 E5
Ludlow, *Calif., U.S.A.* ... 117 L10
Ludlow, *Vt., U.S.A.* 111 C12
Ludus, *Romania* 43 D9
Ludvika, *Sweden* 10 D9
Ludwigsburg, *Germany* .. 25 G5
Ludwigsfelde, *Germany* .. 24 C9
Ludwigshafen, *Germany* . 25 F4
Ludwigslust, *Germany* ... 24 B7
Ludza, *Latvia* 46 D4
Lueki,
  Dem. Rep. of the Congo 86 C2
Luena,
  Dem. Rep. of the Congo 87 D2
Luena, *Zambia* 87 E3
Lüeyang, *China* 56 H4
Lufeng, *Guangdong, China* 59 F10
Lufeng, *Yunnan, China* .. 58 E4
Lufira ➤,
  Dem. Rep. of the Congo 87 E1
Lufkin, *U.S.A.* 113 K7
Lufupa,
  Dem. Rep. of the Congo 87 E1
Luga, *Russia* 46 C5
Luga ➤, *Russia* 46 C5

Lugano, L. di, *Switz.* 28 C6
Lugansk = Luhansk,
  Ukraine 47 H10
Lugard's Falls, *Kenya* 86 C4
Lugela, *Mozam.* 87 F4
Lugenda ➤, *Mozam.* 87 E4
Lugh Ganana, *Somali Rep.* 74 G3
Lugnaquilla, *Ireland* 15 D5
Lugo, *Italy* 29 D8
Lugo, *Spain* 34 B3
Lugo □, *Spain* 34 C3
Lugoj, *Romania* 42 E6
Lugovoy, *Kazakstan* 50 E8
Luhe, *China* 59 A12
Luhe ➤, *Germany* 24 B6
Luhuo, *China* 58 B3
Luiana, *Angola* 88 B3
Luimneach = Limerick,
  Ireland 15 D3
Luing, *U.K.* 14 E3
Luino, *Italy* 28 C5
Luís Correia, *Brazil* 125 D10
Luitpold Coast, *Antarctica* 5 D1
Luiza,
  Dem. Rep. of the Congo 84 F4
Luizi,
  Dem. Rep. of the Congo 86 D2
Luján, *Argentina* 126 C4
Lujiang, *China* 59 B11
Lukanga Swamp, *Zambia* . 87 E2
Lukavac, *Bos.-H.* 42 F3
Lukenie ➤,
  Dem. Rep. of the Congo 84 E3
Lukhisaral, *India* 69 G12
Lůki, *Bulgaria* 41 E8
Lukolela,
  Dem. Rep. of the Congo 86 D1
Lukosi, *Zimbabwe* 87 F2
Lukovė, *Albania* 40 G3
Lukovit, *Bulgaria* 41 C8
Łuków, *Poland* 45 G9
Lukoyanov, *Russia* 48 C7
Lule älv ➤, *Sweden* 8 D19
Luleå, *Sweden* 8 D20
Lüleburgaz, *Turkey* 41 E11
Luliang, *China* 58 E4
Luling, *U.S.A.* 113 L6
Lulong, *China* 57 E10
Lulonga ➤,
  Dem. Rep. of the Congo 84 D3
Lulua ➤,
  Dem. Rep. of the Congo 84 E4
Luluabourg = Kananga,
  Dem. Rep. of the Congo 84 F4
Lumajang, *Indonesia* 63 H15
Lumbala N'guimbo, *Angola* 85 G4
Lumberton, *Miss., U.S.A.* . 113 K10
Lumberton, *N.C., U.S.A.* . 109 H6
Lumberton, *N. Mex.,*
  U.S.A. 115 H10
Lumbwa, *Kenya* 86 C4
Lumsden, *N.Z.* 91 L2
Lumut, *Malaysia* 65 K3
Lumut, Tanjung, *Indonesia* 62 E3
Luna, *Phil.* 61 C4
Lunan, *China* 58 E4
Lunavada, *India* 68 H5
Lunca, *Romania* 43 C10
Lunca Corbului, *Romania* . 43 F9
Lund, *Sweden* 11 J7
Lund, *U.S.A.* 114 G6
Lundazi, *Zambia* 87 E3
Lunderskov, *Denmark* ... 11 J3
Lundi ➤, *Zimbabwe* 87 G3
Lundu, *Malaysia* 62 D3
Lundy, *U.K.* 13 F3
Lune ➤, *U.K.* 12 C5
Lüneburg, *Germany* 24 B6
Lüneburg Heath =
  Lüneburger Heide,
  Germany 24 B6
Lüneburger Heide,
  Germany 24 B6
Lunel, *France* 21 E8
Lünen, *Germany* 24 D3
Lunenburg, *Canada* 103 D7
Lunéville, *France* 19 D13
Lunga ➤, *Zambia* 87 E2
Lungi Airport, *S. Leone* .. 82 D2
Lunglei, *India* 67 H18
Luni, *India* 68 G5
Luni ➤, *India* 68 G4
Luninets = Luninyets,
  Belarus 47 F4
Luning, *U.S.A.* 114 G4
Lunino, *Russia* 48 D7
Luninyets, *Belarus* 47 F4
Lunsemfwa ➤, *Zambia* .. 87 E3
Lunsemfwa Falls, *Zambia* . 87 E2
Luo He ➤, *China* 56 G6
Luocheng, *China* 58 E7
Luochuan, *China* 56 G5
Luoci, *China* 58 E4
Luodian, *China* 58 E6
Luoding, *China* 59 F8
Luofu,
  Dem. Rep. of the Congo 86 C2
Luohe, *China* 56 H8
Luojiang, *China* 58 B5
Luonan, *China* 56 G6
Luoning, *China* 56 G6
Luoshan, *China* 59 A10
Luotian, *China* 59 B10
Luoyang, *China* 56 G7
Luoyuan, *China* 59 D12
Luozigou, *China* 57 C16

Lupanshui, *China* 58 D5
Lupeni, *Romania* 43 E8
Lupilichi, *Mozam.* 87 E4
Łupków, *Poland* 45 J9
Lupoing, *China* 58 E5
Luquan, *China* 58 E4
Luque, *Paraguay* 126 B4
Lúras, *Italy* 30 B2
Luray, *U.S.A.* 108 F6
Lure, *France* 19 E13
Lurgan, *U.K.* 15 B5
Lusaka, *Zambia* 87 F2
Lusambo,
  Dem. Rep. of the Congo 86 C1
Lusangaye,
  Dem. Rep. of the Congo 86 C2
Luseland, *Canada* 105 C7
Lushan, *Henan, China* .. 56 H7
Lushan, *Sichuan, China* . 58 B4
Lushi, *China* 56 G6
Lushnja, *Albania* 40 F3
Lushoto, *Tanzania* 86 C4
Lushoto □, *Tanzania* .. 86 C4
Lushui, *China* 58 E2
Lüshun, *China* 57 E11
Lusignan, *France* 20 B4
Lusigny-sur-Barse, *France* 19 D11
Lusk, *U.S.A.* 112 D2
Lussac-les-Châteaux,
  France 20 B4
Lustenau, *Austria* 26 D2
Luta = Dalian, *China* .. 57 E11
Lutherstadt Wittenberg,
  Germany 24 D8
Luton, *U.K.* 13 F7
Luton □, *U.K.* 13 F7
Lutselke, *Canada* 105 A6
Lutsk, *Ukraine* 47 G3
Lützow Holmbukta,
  Antarctica 5 C4
Lutzputs, *S. Africa* ... 88 D3
Luverne, *U.S.A.* 112 D6
Luvua,
  Dem. Rep. of the Congo 87 D2
Luvua →,
  Dem. Rep. of the Congo 86 D2
Luwegu →, *Tanzania* ... 87 D4
Luwuk, *Indonesia* 63 E6
Luxembourg, *Lux.* 17 E6
Luxembourg □, *Belgium* . 17 E5
Luxembourg ■, *Europe* . 7 F7
Luxeuil-les-Bains, *France* 19 E13
Luxi, *Hunan, China* ... 59 C8
Luxi, *Yunnan, China* ... 58 E4
Luxi, *Yunnan, China* ... 58 E2
Luxor = El Uqsur, *Egypt* 80 B3
Luy-de-Béarn →, *France* 20 E3
Luy-de-France →, *France* 20 E3
Luyi, *China* 56 H8
Luz-St-Sauveur, *France* . 20 F4
Luzern, *Switz.* 25 H4
Luzern □, *Switz.* 25 H3
Luzhai, *China* 58 E7
Luzhou, *China* 58 C5
Luziânia, *Brazil* 125 G9
Luzon, *Phil.* 61 D4
Luzy, *France* 19 F10
Luzzi, *Italy* 31 C9
Lviv, *Ukraine* 47 H3
Lvov = Lviv, *Ukraine* .. 47 H3
Lwówek, *Poland* 45 F3
Lwówek Śląski, *Poland* . 45 G2
Lyakhavichy, *Belarus* .. 47 F4
Lyakhovskiye, Ostrova,
  Russia 51 B15
Lyaki = Läki, *Azerbaijan* 49 K8
Lyallpur = Faisalabad,
  Pakistan 68 D5
Lyaskovets, *Bulgaria* .. 41 C9
Lybster, *U.K.* 14 C5
Lycaonia, *Turkey* 72 D5
Lychen, *Germany* 24 B9
Lychkova, *Russia* 46 D7
Lycia, *Turkey* 39 E11
Lyckebyån →, *Sweden* .. 11 H9
Lycksele, *Sweden* 8 D18
Lycosura, *Greece* 38 D4
Lydda = Lod, *Israel* ... 75 D3
Lydenburg, *S. Africa* .. 89 D5
Lydia, *Turkey* 39 C10
Łydynia →, *Poland* 45 F7
Lyell, *N.Z.* 91 J4
Lyell I., *Canada* 104 C2
Lyepyel, *Belarus* 46 E5
Lygnern, *Sweden* 11 G6
Lyman, *U.S.A.* 114 F8
Lyme B., *U.K.* 13 G4
Lyme Regis, *U.K.* 13 G5
Lymington, *U.K.* 13 G6
Łyna →, *Poland* 9 J19
Lynchburg, *U.S.A.* 108 G6
Lynd →, *Australia* 94 B3
Lynd Ra., *Australia* ... 95 D4
Lynden, *Canada* 110 C4
Lynden, *U.S.A.* 116 B4
Lyndhurst, *Queens.,*
  Australia 94 B3
Lyndhurst, *S. Austral.,*
  Australia 95 E2
Lyndon →, *Australia* .. 93 D1
Lyndonville, *N.Y., U.S.A.* 110 C6
Lyndonville, *Vt., U.S.A.* 111 B12
Lyngen, *Norway* 8 B19
Lynher Reef, *Australia* . 92 C3
Lynn, *U.S.A.* 111 D14
Lynn Canal, *U.S.A.* ... 104 B1

Lynn Lake, *Canada* 105 B8
Lynnwood, *U.S.A.* 116 C4
Lynton, *U.K.* 13 F4
Lyntupy, *Belarus* 9 J22
Lynx L., *Canada* 105 A7
Lyon, *France* 21 C8
Lyonnais, *France* 21 C8
Lyons = Lyon, *France* .. 21 C8
Lyons, *Colo., U.S.A.* .. 112 E2
Lyons, *Ga., U.S.A.* ... 109 J4
Lyons, *Kans., U.S.A.* .. 112 F5
Lyons, *N.Y., U.S.A.* ... 110 C8
Lyozna, *Belarus* 46 E6
Lys = Leie →, *Belgium* . 17 C3
Lysá nad Labem,
  Czech Rep. 26 A7
Lysekil, *Sweden* 11 F5
Lyskovo, *Russia* 48 B7
Lystrup, *Denmark* 11 H4
Lysvik, *Sweden* 10 D7
Lysychansk, *Ukraine* .. 47 H10
Lytham St. Anne's, *U.K.* 12 D4
Lytle, *U.S.A.* 113 L5
Lyttelton, *N.Z.* 91 K4
Lytton, *Canada* 104 C4
Lyuban, *Russia* 46 C6
Lyubertsy, *Russia* 46 E9
Lyubim, *Russia* 46 C11
Lyubimets, *Bulgaria* .. 41 E10
Lyuboml, *Ukraine* 47 G3
Lyubotyn, *Ukraine* ... 47 H8
Lyubytino, *Russia* 46 C7
Lyudinovo, *Russia* 46 F8

M

Ma →, *Vietnam* 64 C5
Ma'adaba, *Jordan* 75 E4
Maamba, *Zambia* 88 B4
Ma'ān, *Jordan* 75 E4
Ma'ān □, *Jordan* 75 F5
Maanselkä, *Finland* ... 8 C23
Ma'anshan, *China* 59 B12
Maarianhamina, *Finland* 9 F18
Ma'arrat an Nu'mān, *Syria* 70 C3
Maas →, *Neths.* 17 C4
Maaseik, *Belgium* 17 C5
Maastricht, *Neths.* ... 17 D5
Maave, *Mozam.* 89 C5
Mabel L., *Canada* 104 C5
Mabenge,
  Dem. Rep. of the Congo 86 B1
Mabian, *China* 58 C4
Mablethorpe, *U.K.* ... 12 D8
Mably, *France* 19 F11
Maboma,
  Dem. Rep. of the Congo 86 B2
Mabrouk, *Mali* 83 B4
Mabton, *U.S.A.* 114 C3
Mac Bac, *Vietnam* 65 H6
Macachín, *Argentina* .. 126 D3
Macaé, *Brazil* 127 A7
Macael, *Spain* 33 H2
McAlester, *U.S.A.* 113 H7
McAllen, *U.S.A.* 113 M5
Macamic, *Canada* 102 C4
Macao = Macau ■, *Asia* 59 F9
Macão, *Portugal* 35 F3
Macapá, *Brazil* 125 C8
McArthur →, *Australia* 94 B2
McArthur, Port, *Australia* 94 B2
McArthur River, *Australia* 94 B2
Macau, *Brazil* 125 E11
Macau ■, *Asia* 59 F9
McBride, *Canada* 104 C4
McCall, *U.S.A.* 114 D5
McCamey, *U.S.A.* 113 K3
McCammon, *U.S.A.* 114 E7
McCauley I., *Canada* .. 104 C2
McCleary, *U.S.A.* 116 C3
Macclesfield, *U.K.* ... 12 D5
McClintock, *Canada* .. 105 B10
M'Clintock Chan., *Canada* 100 A9
McClintock Ra., *Australia* 92 C4
McCloud, *U.S.A.* 114 F2
McCluer I., *Australia* . 92 B5
McClure, *U.S.A.* 110 F7
McClure, L., *U.S.A.* .. 116 H6
M'Clure Str., *Canada* . 4 B2
McClusky, *U.S.A.* 112 B4
McComb, *U.S.A.* 113 K9
McConaughy, L., *U.S.A.* 112 E4
McCook, *U.S.A.* 112 E4
McCullough Mt., *U.S.A.* 117 K11
McCusker →, *Canada* .. 105 B7
McDame, *Canada* 104 B3
McDermitt, *U.S.A.* ... 114 F5
Macdonald, I., *Australia* 92 D4
McDonald Is., *Ind. Oc.* 3 G13
Macdonnell Ranges,
  Australia 92 D5
McDouall L., *Australia* 95 D1
MacDowell L., *Canada* 102 B1
Macduff, *U.K.* 14 D6
Maceda, *Spain* 34 C3
Macedonia ■, *Europe* .. 40 E5
Maceió, *Brazil* 125 E11
Maceira, *Portugal* ... 34 F2
Macenta, *Guinea* 82 D3
Macerata, *Italy* 29 E10
McFarland, *U.S.A.* ... 117 K7
McFarlane →, *Canada* .. 105 B7
Macfarlane, L., *Australia* 95 E2
McGehee, *U.S.A.* 113 J9

McGill, *U.S.A.* 114 G6
Macgillycuddy's Reeks,
  Ireland 15 E2
MacGregor, *Canada* ... 105 D9
McGregor, *U.S.A.* 112 D9
McGregor →, *Canada* .. 104 B4
McGregor Ra., *Australia* 95 D3
Mach, *Pakistan* 66 E5
Māch Kowr, *Iran* 71 E9
Machado = Jiparaná →,
  Brazil 124 E6
Machagai, *Argentina* .. 126 B3
Machakos, *Kenya* 86 C4
Machakos □, *Kenya* ... 86 C4
Machala, *Ecuador* 124 D3
Machanga, *Mozam.* 89 C6
Machattie, L., *Australia* 94 C2
Machault, *France* 19 C11
Machava, *Mozam.* 89 D5
Machece, *Mozam.* 87 F4
Machecoul, *France* ... 18 F5
Macheng, *China* 59 B10
Machero, *Spain* 35 F6
Machias, *U.S.A.* 103 D6
Machichi →, *Canada* .. 105 B10
Machico, *Madeira* 37 D3
Machilipatnam, *India* . 67 L12
Machiques, *Venezuela* . 124 A4
Machupicchu, *Peru* ... 124 F4
Machynlleth, *U.K.* ... 13 E4
Maciejowice, *Poland* .. 45 G8
McIlwraith Ra., *Australia* 94 A3
Măcin, *Romania* 43 E13
Macina, *Mali* 82 C4
McIntosh, *U.S.A.* 112 C4
McIntosh L., *Canada* . 105 B8
Macintosh Ra., *Australia* 93 E4
Macintyre →, *Australia* 95 D5
Macizo Galaico, *Spain* . 34 C3
Mackay, *Australia* ... 94 C4
Mackay, *U.S.A.* 114 E7
MacKay →, *Canada* ... 104 B6
Mackay, L., *Australia* . 92 D4
McKay Ra., *Australia* . 92 D3
McKeesport, *U.S.A.* .. 110 F5
McKenna, *U.S.A.* 116 C4
Mackenzie, *Canada* ... 104 B4
McKenzie, *U.S.A.* 109 G1
Mackenzie →, *Australia* 94 C4
Mackenzie →, *Canada* . 100 B6
McKenzie →, *U.S.A.* .. 114 D2
Mackenzie Bay, *Canada* 4 B1
Mackenzie City = Linden,
  Guyana 124 B7
Mackenzie Highway,
  Canada 104 B5
Mackenzie Mts., *Canada* 100 B7
Mackinaw City, *U.S.A.* 108 C3
McKinlay, *Australia* .. 94 C3
McKinlay →, *Australia* 94 C3
McKinley, Mt., *U.S.A.* . 4 C18
McKinley Sea, *Arctic* . 4 A7
McKinney, *U.S.A.* 113 J6
Mackinnon Road, *Kenya* 86 C4
Macksville, *Australia* . 95 E5
McLaughlin, *U.S.A.* .. 112 C4
Maclean, *Australia* ... 95 D5
McLean, *U.S.A.* 113 H4
McLeansboro, *U.S.A.* . 112 F10
Maclear, *S. Africa* ... 89 E4
Macleay →, *Australia* . 95 E5
McLennan, *Canada* 104 B5
MacLeod, B., *Canada* . 105 A7
McLeod, L., *Australia* 93 D1
MacLeod Lake, *Canada* 104 C4
McLoughlin, Mt., *U.S.A.* 114 E2
McLure, *Canada* 104 C4
McMechen, *U.S.A.* 110 G4
McMillan, L., *U.S.A.* . 113 J2
McMinnville, *Oreg., U.S.A.* 114 D2
McMinnville, *Tenn.,*
  U.S.A. 109 H3
McMorran, *Canada* 105 C7
McMurdo Sd., *Antarctica* 5 D11
McMurray = Fort
  McMurray, *Canada* ... 104 B6
McMurray, *U.S.A.* 116 B4
McNary, *U.S.A.* 115 J9
MacNutt, *Canada* 105 C8
Macodoene, *Mozam.* ... 89 C6
Macomb, *U.S.A.* 112 E9
Macomer, *Italy* 30 B1
Mâcon, *France* 19 F11
Macon, *Ga., U.S.A.* ... 109 J4
Macon, *Miss., U.S.A.* . 109 J1
Macon, *Mo., U.S.A.* .. 112 F8
Macossa, *Mozam.* 87 F3
Macoun L., *Canada* ... 105 B8
Macovane, *Mozam.* 89 C6
McPherson, *U.S.A.* ... 112 F6
McPherson Pk., *U.S.A.* 117 L7
McPherson Ra., *Australia* 95 D5
Macquarie Harbour,
  Australia 94 G4
Macquarie Is., *Pac. Oc.* 96 N7
MacRobertson Land,
  Antarctica 5 D6
Macroom, *Ireland* 15 E3
Macroy, *Australia* ... 92 D2
MacTier, *Canada* 110 A5
Macubela, *Mozam.* 87 F4
Macugnaga, *Italy* 28 C4
Macuiza, *Mozam.* 87 F3
Macusani, *Peru* 124 F4
Macuse, *Mozam.* 87 F4
Macuspana, *Mexico* ... 119 D6
Macusse, *Angola* 88 B3

McVille, *U.S.A.* 112 B5
Madadeni, *S. Africa* .. 89 D5
Madagali, *Nigeria* 83 C7
Madagascar ■, *Africa* . 89 C8
Madā'in Sālih, *Si. Arabia* 70 E3
Madama, *Niger* 79 D8
Madame I., *Canada* ... 103 C7
Madan, *Bulgaria* 41 E8
Madanapalle, *India* ... (not present)
Madaoua, *Niger* 83 C6
Madara, *Nigeria* 83 C7
Madaripur, *Bangla.* .. 67 H17
Madauk, *Burma* 67 L20
Madawaska, *Canada* ... 110 A7
Madawaska →, *Canada* . 102 C4
Madaya, *Burma* 67 H20
Madbar, *Sudan* 81 F3
Maddalena, *Italy* 30 A2
Maddaloni, *Italy* 31 A7
Madeira, *Atl. Oc.* ... 37 D3
Madeira →, *Brazil* ... 122 D5
Madeleine, Is. de la,
  Canada 103 C7
Maden, *Turkey* 73 C8
Madera, *Mexico* 118 B3
Madera, *U.S.A.* 116 J6
Madha, *India* 66 L9
Madhubani, *India* 69 F12
Madhya Pradesh □, *India* 68 J8
Madian, *China* 59 A11
Madidi →, *Bolivia* ... 124 F5
Madikeri, *India* 66 N9
Madill, *U.S.A.* 113 H6
Madimba,
  Dem. Rep. of the Congo 84 E3
Ma'din, *Syria* 70 C3
Madingou, *Congo* 84 E2
Madirovalo, *Madag.* .. 89 B8
Madison, *Calif., U.S.A.* 116 G5
Madison, *Fla., U.S.A.* . 109 K4
Madison, *Ind., U.S.A.* . 108 F3
Madison, *Nebr., U.S.A.* 112 E6
Madison, *Ohio, U.S.A.* 110 E3
Madison, *S. Dak., U.S.A.* 112 D6
Madison, *Wis., U.S.A.* 112 D10
Madison →, *U.S.A.* ... 114 D8
Madisonville, *Ky., U.S.A.* 108 G2
Madisonville, *Tex., U.S.A.* 113 K7
Madista, *Botswana* ... 88 C4
Madiun, *Indonesia* ... 63 G14
Madol, *Sudan* 81 F2
Madon →, *France* 19 D13
Madona, *Latvia* 9 H22
Madonie, *Italy* 30 E6
Madonna di Campíglio,
  Italy 28 B7
Madra Dağı, *Turkey* .. 39 B9
Madras = Chennai, *India* 66 N12
Madras = Tamil Nadu □,
  India 66 P10
Madras, *U.S.A.* 114 D3
Madre, L., *Mexico* ... 119 C5
Madre, Laguna, *U.S.A.* 113 M6
Madre, Sierra, *Phil.* . 61 C5
Madre de Dios →, *Bolivia* 122 E4
Madre de Dios, I., *Chile* 122 J3
Madre del Sur, Sierra,
  Mexico 119 D5
Madre Occidental, Sierra,
  Mexico 118 B3
Madre Oriental, Sierra,
  Mexico 118 C5
Madri, *India* 68 G5
Madrid, *Spain* 34 E7
Madrid □, *Spain* 34 E7
Madridejos, *Spain* ... 35 F7
Madrigal de las Altas
  Torres, *Spain* 34 D6
Madrona, Sierra, *Spain* 35 G6
Madroñera, *Spain* 35 F5
Madu, *Sudan* 81 E2
Madura, Selat, *Indonesia* 63 G15
Madura Motel, *Australia* 93 F4
Madurai, *India* 66 Q11
Madurantakam, *India* . 66 N11
Mae Chan, *Thailand* .. 64 B2
Mae Hong Son, *Thailand* 64 C2
Mae Khlong →, *Thailand* 64 F3
Mae Phrik, *Thailand* . 64 D2
Mae Ramat, *Thailand* . 64 D2
Mae Rim, *Thailand* ... 64 C2
Mae Sot, *Thailand* ... 64 D2
Mae Suai, *Thailand* .. 64 C2
Mae Tha, *Thailand* ... 64 C2
Maebashi, *Japan* 55 F9
Maella, *Spain* 32 D5
Maesteg, *U.K.* 13 F4
Maestra, Sierra, *Cuba* 120 B4
Maevatanana, *Madag.* . 89 B8
Mafeking = Mafikeng,
  S. Africa 88 D4
Mafeking, *Canada* 105 C8
Maféré, *Ivory C.* 82 D4
Mafeteng, *Lesotho* ... 88 D4
Maffra, *Australia* ... 95 F4
Mafia I., *Tanzania* .. 86 D4
Mafikeng, *S. Africa* .. 88 D4
Mafra, *Brazil* 127 B6
Mafra, *Portugal* 35 G1
Mafungabusi Plateau,
  Zimbabwe 87 F2
Magadan, *Russia* 51 D16
Magadi, *Kenya* 86 C4
Magadi, L., *Kenya* ... 86 C4
Magaliesburg, *S. Africa* 89 D4
Magallanes, Estrecho de,
  Chile 122 J3
Magalluf, *Spain* 33 F7

Magangué, *Colombia* .. 124 B4
Magaria, *Niger* 83 C6
Magburaka, *S. Leone* .. 82 D2
Magdalen Is. = Madeleine,
  Is. de la, *Canada* .. 103 C7
Magdalena, *Argentina* . 126 D4
Magdalena, *Bolivia* .. 124 F6
Magdalena, *Mexico* ... 118 A2
Magdalena, *U.S.A.* ... 115 J10
Magdalena →, *Colombia* 122 B3
Magdalena →, *Mexico* . 118 A2
Magdalena, B., *Mexico* 118 C2
Magdalena, Llano de la,
  Mexico 118 C2
Magdeburg, *Germany* .. 24 C7
Magdelaine Cays, *Australia* 94 B5
Magdub, *Sudan* 81 E2
Magee, *U.S.A.* 113 K10
Magelang, *Indonesia* .. 63 G14
Magellan's Str. =
  Magallanes, Estrecho de,
  Chile 122 J3
Magenta, *Italy* 28 C5
Magenta, L., *Australia* 93 F2
Magerøya, *Norway* 8 A21
Maggia →, *Switz.* 25 J4
Maggiorasca, Mte., *Italy* 28 D6
Maggiore, L., *Italy* .. 28 C5
Maghama, *Mauritania* . 82 B2
Magherafelt, *U.K.* ... 15 B5
Magione, *Italy* 29 E9
Magistralnyy, *Russia* . 51 D11
Maglaj, *Bos.-H.* 42 F3
Magliano in Toscana, *Italy* 29 F8
Máglie, *Italy* 31 B11
Magnac-Laval, *France* . 20 B5
Magnetic Pole (North) =
  North Magnetic Pole,
  Canada 4 B2
Magnetic Pole (South) =
  South Magnetic Pole,
  Antarctica 5 C9
Magnísia □, *Greece* .. 38 B5
Magnitogorsk, *Russia* . 50 D6
Magnolia, *Ark., U.S.A.* 113 J8
Magnolia, *Miss., U.S.A.* 113 K9
Magny-en-Vexin, *France* 19 C8
Magog, *Canada* 103 C5
Magoro, *Uganda* 86 B3
Magosa = Famagusta,
  Cyprus 36 D12
Magoye, *Zambia* 87 F2
Magpie L., *Canada* ... 103 B7
Magrath, *Canada* 104 D6
Magre →, *Spain* 33 F4
Magrur, Wadi →, *Sudan* 81 D2
Magu □, *Tanzania* 86 C3
Maguan, *China* 58 F5
Maguarinho, C., *Brazil* 125 D9
Magusa = Famagusta,
  Cyprus 36 D12
Maguse L., *Canada* ... 105 A9
Maguse Pt., *Canada* .. 105 A10
Magwe, *Burma* 67 J19
Maha Sarakham, *Thailand* 64 D4
Mahābād, *Iran* 70 B5
Mahabharat Lekh, *Nepal* 69 E10
Mahabo, *Madag.* 89 C7
Mahadeo Hills, *India* . 68 H8
Mahagi,
  Dem. Rep. of the Congo 86 B3
Mahajamba →, *Madag.* 89 B8
Mahajamba, Helodranon' i,
  Madag. 89 B8
Mahajan, *India* 68 E5
Mahajanga, *Madag.* .. 89 B8
Mahajanga □, *Madag.* 89 B8
Mahajilo →, *Madag.* .. 89 B8
Mahakam →, *Indonesia* 62 E5
Mahalapye, *Botswana* . 88 C4
Mahallāt, *Iran* 71 C6
Mahan, *Iran* 71 D8
Mahanadi →, *India* ... 67 J15
Mahananda →, *India* . 69 G12
Mahanoro, *Madag.* ... 89 B8
Mahanoy City, *U.S.A.* 111 F8
Maharashtra □, *India* . 66 J9
Mahari Mts., *Tanzania* 86 D3
Mahasham, W. →, *Egypt* 75 E3
Mahasolo, *Madag.* ... 89 B8
Mahattat ash Shīdīyah,
  Jordan 75 F4
Mahattat 'Unayzah, *Jordan* 75 E4
Mahaxay, *Laos* 64 D5
Mahbubnagar, *India* .. 66 L10
Mahdah, *Oman* 71 E7
Mahdia, *Tunisia* 79 A8
Mahe, *India* 69 C8
Mahenge, *Tanzania* ... 87 D4
Maheno, *N.Z.* 91 L3
Mahesana, *India* 68 H5
Mahia Pen., *N.Z.* 91 H6
Mahilyow, *Belarus* ... 46 F6
Mahmiya, *Sudan* 81 D3
Mahmud Kot, *Pakistan* 68 D4
Mahmudia, *Romania* .. 43 E14
Mahmudiye, *Turkey* ... 39 B12
Mahnomen, *U.S.A.* 112 B7
Maho, *Sri Lanka* 69 G8
Mahón = Maó, *Spain* .. 37 B11
Mahone Bay, *Canada* . 103 D7
Mahuta, *Nigeria* 83 C5
Mahya Daği, *Turkey* .. 41 E11
Mai-Ndombe □,
  Dem. Rep. of the Congo 84 E3
Mai-Sai, *Thailand* ... 64 B2

Maia, *Portugal* 34 D2
Maia, *Spain* 32 B3
Maials, *Spain* 32 D5
Maîche, *France* 19 E13
Maicurú →, *Brazil* 125 D8
Máida, *Italy* 31 D9
Maidan Khula, *Afghan.* 68 C3
Maidenhead, *U.K.* 13 F7
Maidi, *Yemen* 81 D5
Maidstone, *Canada* 105 C7
Maidstone, *U.K.* 13 F8
Maiduguri, *Nigeria* 83 C7
Măieruş, *Romania* 43 E10
Maignelay Montigny, *France* 19 C9
Maigo, *Phil.* 61 G5
Maigudo, *Ethiopia* 81 F4
Maijdi, *Bangla.* 67 H17
Maikala Ra., *India* 67 J12
Maillezais, *France* 20 B3
Mailsi, *Pakistan* 68 E5
Main →, *Germany* 25 F4
Main →, *U.K.* 15 B5
Main Centre, *Canada* 105 C7
Mainburg, *Germany* 25 G7
Maine, *France* 18 D6
Maine □, *U.S.A.* 103 C6
Maine →, *Ireland* 15 D2
Maine-et-Loire □, *France* 18 E6
Maïne-Soroa, *Niger* 83 C7
Maingkwan, *Burma* 67 F20
Mainit, L., *Phil.* 61 G6
Mainland, *Orkney, U.K.* 14 C5
Mainland, *Shet., U.K.* 14 A7
Mainpuri, *India* 69 F8
Maintal, *Germany* 25 E4
Maintenon, *France* 19 D8
Maintirano, *Madag.* 89 B7
Mainz, *Germany* 25 E4
Maipú, *Argentina* 126 D4
Maiquetía, *Venezuela* 124 A5
Máira →, *Italy* 28 D4
Mairabari, *India* 67 F18
Maisí, *Cuba* 121 B5
Maisi, Pta. de, *Cuba* 121 B5
Maitland, *N.S.W., Australia* 95 E5
Maitland, *S. Austral., Australia* 95 E2
Maitland →, *Canada* 110 C3
Maiyema, *Nigeria* 83 C5
Maiyuan, *China* 59 E11
Maiz, Is. del, *Nic.* 120 D3
Maizuru, *Japan* 55 G7
Majalengka, *Indonesia* 63 G13
Majene, *Indonesia* 63 E5
Majevica, *Bos.-H.* 42 F3
Maji, *Ethiopia* 81 F4
Majiang, *China* 58 D6
Major, *Canada* 105 C7
Majorca = Mallorca, *Spain* 37 B10
Maka, *Senegal* 82 C2
Makak, *Cameroon* 83 E7
Makale, *Indonesia* 63 E5
Makamba, *Burundi* 86 C2
Makarikari = Makgadikgadi Salt Pans, *Botswana* 88 C4
Makarovo, *Russia* 51 D11
Makarska, *Croatia* 29 E14
Makaryev, *Russia* 48 B6
Makasar = Ujung Pandang, *Indonesia* 63 F5
Makasar, Selat, *Indonesia* 63 E5
Makasar, Str. of = Makasar, Selat, *Indonesia* 63 E5
Makat, *Kazakstan* 50 E6
Makedonija = Macedonia ■, *Europe* 40 E5
Makena, *U.S.A.* 106 H16
Makeni, *S. Leone* 82 D2
Makeyevka = Makiyivka, *Ukraine* 47 H9
Makgadikgadi Salt Pans, *Botswana* 88 C4
Makhachkala, *Russia* 49 J8
Makharadze = Ozurgeti, *Georgia* 49 K5
Makhmūr, *Iraq* 70 C4
Makian, *Indonesia* 63 D7
Makindu, *Kenya* 86 C4
Makinsk, *Kazakstan* 50 D8
Makiyivka, *Ukraine* 47 H9
Makkah, *Si. Arabia* 80 C4
Makkovik, *Canada* 103 A8
Makó, *Hungary* 42 D5
Makokou, *Gabon* 84 D2
Makongo, *Dem. Rep. of the Congo* 86 B2
Makoro, *Dem. Rep. of the Congo* 86 B2
Maków Mazowiecki, *Poland* 45 F8
Maków Podhalański, *Poland* 45 J6
Makrá, *Greece* 39 E7
Makrai, *India* 66 H10
Makran Coast Range, *Pakistan* 66 G4
Makrana, *India* 68 F6
Mákri, *Greece* 41 F9
Makriyialos, *Greece* 36 D7
Mākū, *Iran* 70 B5
Makunda, *Botswana* 88 C3
Makurazaki, *Japan* 55 J5
Makurdi, *Nigeria* 83 D6
Makūyeh, *Iran* 71 D7
Makwassie, *S. Africa* 88 D4
Mal B., *Ireland* 15 D2
Mala, Pta., *Panama* 120 E3
Mala Belozërka, *Ukraine* 47 J8
Mala Kapela, *Croatia* 29 D12
Mała Panew →, *Poland* 45 H4
Mala Vyska, *Ukraine* 47 H6
Malabang, *Phil.* 61 H6
Malabar Coast, *India* 66 P9
Malabo = Rey Malabo, *Eq. Guin.* 83 E6
Malabon, *Phil.* 61 D4
Malacca, Str. of, *Indonesia* 65 L3
Malacky, *Slovak Rep.* 27 C10
Malad City, *U.S.A.* 114 E7
Maladeta, *Spain* 32 C5
Maladzyechna, *Belarus* 46 E4
Málaga, *Spain* 35 J6
Malaga, *U.S.A.* 113 J2
Málaga □, *Spain* 35 J6
Malagarasi, *Tanzania* 86 D3
Malagarasi →, *Tanzania* 86 D2
Malagón, *Spain* 35 F7
Malagón →, *Spain* 35 H3
Malahide, *Ireland* 15 C5
Malaimbandy, *Madag.* 89 C8
Malakâl, *Sudan* 81 F3
Malakand, *Pakistan* 68 B4
Malakoff, *U.S.A.* 113 J7
Malang, *Indonesia* 63 G15
Malangen, *Norway* 8 B18
Malanje, *Angola* 84 F3
Mälaren, *Sweden* 10 E11
Malargüe, *Argentina* 126 D2
Malartic, *Canada* 102 C4
Malaryta, *Belarus* 47 G3
Malatya, *Turkey* 73 C8
Malawi ■, *Africa* 87 E3
Malawi, L. = Nyasa, L., *Africa* 87 E3
Malay Pen., *Asia* 65 J3
Malaya Belozërka = Mala Belozërka, *Ukraine* 47 J8
Malaya Vishera, *Russia* 46 C7
Malaya Viska = Mala Vyska, *Ukraine* 47 H6
Malaybalay, *Phil.* 61 G6
Malāyer, *Iran* 71 C6
Malaysia ■, *Asia* 62 D4
Malazgirt, *Turkey* 73 C10
Malbon, *Australia* 94 C3
Malbooma, *Australia* 95 E1
Malbork, *Poland* 44 D6
Malcésine, *Italy* 28 C7
Malchin, *Germany* 24 B8
Malchow, *Germany* 24 B8
Malcolm, *Australia* 93 E3
Malcolm, Pt., *Australia* 93 F3
Malczyce, *Poland* 45 G3
Maldegem, *Belgium* 17 C3
Malden, *Mass., U.S.A.* 111 D13
Malden, *Mo., U.S.A.* 113 G10
Malden I., *Kiribati* 97 H12
Maldives ■, *Ind. Oc.* 52 J11
Maldonado, *Uruguay* 127 C5
Maldonado, Punta, *Mexico* 119 D5
Malè, *Italy* 28 B7
Malé Karpaty, *Slovak Rep.* 27 C10
Maléa, Ákra, *Greece* 38 E5
Malegaon, *India* 66 J9
Malei, *Mozam.* 87 F4
Malek Kandī, *Iran* 70 B5
Malela, *Dem. Rep. of the Congo* 86 C2
Malema, *Mozam.* 87 E4
Maléme, *Greece* 36 D5
Målerås, *Sweden* 11 H9
Malerkotla, *India* 68 D6
Máles, *Greece* 36 D7
Malesherbes, *France* 19 D9
Maleshevska Planina, *Europe* 40 E7
Malesína, *Greece* 38 C5
Malestroit, *France* 18 E4
Malfa, *Italy* 31 D7
Malgobek, *Russia* 49 J7
Malgomaj, *Sweden* 8 D17
Malgrat = Malgrat de Mar, *Spain* 32 D7
Malgrat de Mar, *Spain* 32 D7
Malha, *Sudan* 81 D2
Malheur →, *U.S.A.* 114 D5
Malheur L., *U.S.A.* 114 E4
Mali, *Guinea* 82 C2
Mali ■, *Africa* 82 B4
Mali →, *Burma* 67 G20
Mali Kanal, *Serbia, Yug.* 42 E4
Mali Kyun, *Burma* 64 F2
Malibu, *U.S.A.* 117 L8
Maliku, *Indonesia* 63 E6
Malili, *Indonesia* 63 E6
Målilla, *Sweden* 11 G9
Malimba, Mts., *Dem. Rep. of the Congo* 86 D2
Malin Hd., *Ireland* 15 A4
Malin Pen., *Ireland* 15 A4
Malindi, *Kenya* 86 C5
Malines = Mechelen, *Belgium* 17 C4
Malino, *Indonesia* 63 D6
Malinyi, *Tanzania* 87 D4
Malipo, *China* 58 F5
Maliqi, *Albania* 40 F4
Malita, *Phil.* 63 C7
Maljenik, *Serbia, Yug.* 40 C5
Malkara, *Turkey* 41 F10
Małkinia Górna, *Poland* 45 F9
Malko Tŭrnovo, *Bulgaria* 41 E11
Mallacoota, *Australia* 95 F4
Mallacoota Inlet, *Australia* 95 F4
Mallaig, *U.K.* 14 D3
Mallawan, *India* 69 F9
Mallawi, *Egypt* 80 B3
Mallemort, *France* 21 E9
Málles Venosta, *Italy* 28 B7
Mállia, *Greece* 36 D7
Mallión, Kólpos, *Greece* 36 D7
Mallorca, *Spain* 37 B10
Mallorytown, *Canada* 111 B9
Mallow, *Ireland* 15 D3
Malmbäck, *Sweden* 11 G8
Malmberget, *Sweden* 8 C19
Malmédy, *Belgium* 17 D6
Malmesbury, *S. Africa* 88 E2
Malmköping, *Sweden* 10 E10
Malmö, *Sweden* 11 J6
Malmöhus län □, *Sweden* 11 J7
Malmslätt, *Sweden* 11 F9
Malmyzh, *Russia* 48 B10
Malnaş, *Romania* 43 D10
Malo Konare, *Bulgaria* 41 D8
Maloarkhangelsk, *Russia* 47 F9
Malolos, *Phil.* 63 B6
Malombe L., *Malawi* 87 E4
Małomice, *Poland* 45 G2
Malomir, *Bulgaria* 41 D10
Malone, *U.S.A.* 111 B10
Malong, *China* 58 E4
Malorad, *Bulgaria* 40 C7
Måløy, *Norway* 9 F11
Maloyaroslovets, *Russia* 46 E9
Malpartida, *Spain* 35 F4
Malpaso, *Canary Is.* 37 G1
Malpelo, *Colombia* 124 C2
Malpica de Bergantiños, *Spain* 34 B2
Mals = Málles Venosta, *Italy* 28 B7
Malta, *Idaho, U.S.A.* 114 E7
Malta, *Mont., U.S.A.* 114 B10
Malta ■, *Europe* 36 D2
Maltahöhe, *Namibia* 88 C2
Maltepe, *Turkey* 41 F13
Malton, *Canada* 110 C5
Malton, *U.K.* 12 C7
Maluku, *Indonesia* 63 E7
Maluku □, *Indonesia* 63 E7
Maluku Sea = Molucca Sea, *Indonesia* 63 E6
Malumfashi, *Nigeria* 83 C6
Malung, *Sweden* 10 D7
Malungsfors, *Sweden* 10 D7
Malvan, *India* 66 L8
Malvern, *U.S.A.* 113 H8
Malvern Hills, *U.K.* 13 E5
Malvinas, Is. = Falkland Is. □, *Atl. Oc.* 128 G5
Malý Dunaj →, *Slovak Rep.* 27 D11
Malya, *Tanzania* 86 C3
Malyn, *Ukraine* 47 G5
Malyy Lyakhovskiy, Ostrov, *Russia* 51 B15
Mama, *Russia* 51 D12
Mamadysh, *Russia* 48 C10
Mamanguape, *Brazil* 125 E11
Mamasa, *Indonesia* 63 E5
Mambasa, *Dem. Rep. of the Congo* 86 B2
Mamberamo →, *Indonesia* 63 E9
Mambilima Falls, *Zambia* 87 E2
Mambirima, *Dem. Rep. of the Congo* 87 E2
Mambo, *Tanzania* 86 C4
Mambrui, *Kenya* 86 C5
Mamburao, *Phil.* 61 E4
Mameigwess L., *Canada* 102 B2
Mamers, *France* 18 D7
Mamfé, *Cameroon* 83 D6
Mammoth, *U.S.A.* 115 K8
Mamoré →, *Bolivia* 122 E4
Mamou, *Guinea* 82 C2
Mampatá, *Guinea-Biss.* 82 C2
Mampong, *Ghana* 83 D4
Mamry, Jezioro, *Poland* 44 D8
Mamuju, *Indonesia* 63 E5
Mamuras, *Albania* 40 E3
Man, *Ivory C.* 82 D3
Man, I. of, *U.K.* 12 C3
Man Na, *Burma* 67 H20
Mana →, *Fr. Guiana* 125 B8
Manaar, G. of = Mannar, G. of, *Asia* 66 Q11
Manacapuru, *Brazil* 124 D6
Manacor, *Spain* 37 B10
Manado, *Indonesia* 63 D6
Managua, *Nic.* 120 D2
Managua, L., *Nic.* 120 D2
Manakara, *Madag.* 89 C8
Manama = Al Manāmah, *Bahrain* 71 E6
Manambao →, *Madag.* 89 B7
Manambato, *Madag.* 89 A8
Manambolo →, *Madag.* 89 B7
Manambolosy, *Madag.* 89 B8
Mananara, *Madag.* 89 B8
Mananara →, *Madag.* 89 C8
Mananjary, *Madag.* 89 C8
Manantenina, *Madag.* 89 C8
Manaos = Manaus, *Brazil* 124 D7
Manapire →, *Venezuela* 124 B5
Manapouri, *N.Z.* 91 L1
Manapouri, L., *N.Z.* 91 L1
Manas, *China* 60 B3
Manas →, *India* 67 F17
Manaslu, *Nepal* 69 E11
Manasquan, *U.S.A.* 111 F10
Manassa, *U.S.A.* 115 H11
Manaung, *Burma* 67 K18
Manaus, *Brazil* 124 D7
Manavgat, *Turkey* 72 D4
Manawan L., *Canada* 105 B8
Manay, *Phil.* 61 H7
Manbij, *Syria* 70 B3
Mancelona, *U.S.A.* 108 C3
Mancha Real, *Spain* 35 H7
Manche □, *France* 18 C5
Manchester, *U.K.* 12 D5
Manchester, *Calif., U.S.A.* 116 G3
Manchester, *Conn., U.S.A.* 111 E12
Manchester, *Ga., U.S.A.* 109 J3
Manchester, *Iowa, U.S.A.* 112 D9
Manchester, *Ky., U.S.A.* 108 G4
Manchester, *N.H., U.S.A.* 111 D13
Manchester, *N.Y., U.S.A.* 110 D7
Manchester, *Vt., U.S.A.* 111 C11
Manchester L., *Canada* 105 A7
Manchuria = Dongbei, *China* 57 D13
Manchurian Plain, *China* 52 E16
Manciano, *Italy* 29 F8
Mancifa, *Ethiopia* 81 F5
Mand →, *Iran* 71 D7
Manda, *Chunya, Tanzania* 86 D3
Manda, *Ludewe, Tanzania* 87 E3
Mandabé, *Madag.* 89 C7
Mandaguari, *Brazil* 127 A5
Mandah, *Mongolia* 56 B5
Mandal, *Norway* 9 G12
Mandalay, *Burma* 67 J20
Mandale = Mandalay, *Burma* 67 J20
Mandalgovi, *Mongolia* 56 B4
Mandalī, *Iraq* 70 C5
Mandan, *U.S.A.* 112 B4
Mandaon, *Phil.* 61 E5
Mandar, Teluk, *Indonesia* 63 E5
Mándas, *Italy* 30 C2
Mandaue, *Phil.* 61 F5
Mandelieu-la-Napoule, *France* 21 E10
Mandera, *Kenya* 86 B5
Mandera □, *Kenya* 86 B5
Mandi, *India* 68 D7
Mandimba, *Mozam.* 87 E4
Mandioli, *Indonesia* 63 E7
Mandla, *India* 69 H9
Mandø, *Denmark* 11 J2
Mandoto, *Madag.* 89 B8
Mandoúdhion, *Greece* 38 C5
Mándra, *Greece* 38 C5
Mandra, *Pakistan* 68 C5
Mandrákhi, *Greece* 39 E9
Mandrare →, *Madag.* 89 D8
Mandritsara, *Madag.* 89 B8
Mandsaur, *India* 68 G6
Mandurah, *Australia* 93 F2
Mandúria, *Italy* 31 B10
Mandvi, *India* 68 H3
Mandya, *India* 66 N10
Mandzai, *Pakistan* 68 D2
Mané, *Burkina Faso* 83 C4
Maneh, *Iran* 71 B8
Manengouba, Mts., *Cameroon* 83 E6
Manérbio, *Italy* 28 C7
Maneroo, *Australia* 94 C3
Maneroo Cr. →, *Australia* 94 C3
Manfalût, *Egypt* 80 B3
Manfred, *Australia* 95 E3
Manfredónia, *Italy* 29 G12
Manfredónia, G. di, *Italy* 29 G13
Manga, *Burkina Faso* 83 C4
Manga, *Niger* 83 C7
Mangabeiras, Chapada das, *Brazil* 125 F9
Mangalia, *Romania* 43 G13
Mangalore, *India* 66 N9
Mangaweka, *N.Z.* 91 H5
Manggar, *Indonesia* 62 E3
Manggawitu, *Indonesia* 63 E8
Mangkalihat, Tanjung, *Indonesia* 63 D5
Mangla Dam, *Pakistan* 69 C5
Manglaur, *India* 68 E7
Mangnai, *China* 60 C4
Mango, *Togo* 83 C5
Mangoche, *Malawi* 87 E4
Mangoky →, *Madag.* 89 C7
Mangole, *Indonesia* 63 E7
Mangombe, *Dem. Rep. of the Congo* 86 C2
Mangonui, *N.Z.* 91 F4
Mangualde, *Portugal* 34 E3
Mangueira, L. da, *Brazil* 127 C5
Mangum, *U.S.A.* 113 H5
Mangyshlak Poluostrov, *Kazakstan* 50 E6
Manhattan, *U.S.A.* 112 F6
Manhiça, *Mozam.* 89 D5
Mania →, *Madag.* 89 B8
Maniago, *Italy* 29 B9
Manica, *Mozam.* 89 B5
Manica e Sofala □, *Mozam.* 89 B5
Manicaland □, *Zimbabwe* 87 F3
Manicoré, *Brazil* 124 E6
Manicouagan →, *Canada* 103 C6
Manīfah, *Si. Arabia* 71 E6
Manifold, *Australia* 94 C5
Manifold, C., *Australia* 94 C5
Maniganggo, *China* 58 B2
Manigotagan, *Canada* 105 C9
Manihiki, *Cook Is.* 97 J11
Manika, Plateau de la, *Dem. Rep. of the Congo* 87 E2
Manila, *Phil.* 61 D4
Manila, *U.S.A.* 114 F9
Manila B., *Phil.* 61 D4
Manilla, *Australia* 95 E5
Manimpé, *Mali* 82 C3
Maningrida, *Australia* 94 A1
Manipur □, *India* 67 G19
Manipur →, *Burma* 67 H19
Manisa, *Turkey* 39 C9
Manisa □, *Turkey* 39 C9
Manistee, *U.S.A.* 108 C2
Manistee →, *U.S.A.* 108 C2
Manistique, *U.S.A.* 108 C2
Manito L., *Canada* 105 C7
Manitoba □, *Canada* 105 B9
Manitoba, L., *Canada* 105 C9
Manitou, *Canada* 105 D9
Manitou I., *U.S.A.* 102 C2
Manitou Is., *U.S.A.* 108 C3
Manitou L., *Canada* 103 B6
Manitou Springs, *U.S.A.* 112 F2
Manitoulin I., *Canada* 102 C3
Manitowaning, *Canada* 102 C3
Manitowoc, *U.S.A.* 108 C2
Manizales, *Colombia* 124 B3
Manja, *Madag.* 89 C7
Manjacaze, *Mozam.* 89 C5
Manjakandriana, *Madag.* 89 B8
Manjhand, *Pakistan* 68 G3
Manjil, *Iran* 71 B6
Manjimup, *Australia* 93 F2
Manjra →, *India* 66 K10
Mankato, *Kans., U.S.A.* 112 F5
Mankato, *Minn., U.S.A.* 112 C8
Mankayane, *Swaziland* 89 D5
Mankono, *Ivory C.* 82 D3
Mankota, *Canada* 105 D7
Manlay, *Mongolia* 56 B4
Manlleu, *Spain* 32 C7
Manly, *Australia* 95 E5
Manmad, *India* 66 J9
Mann Ranges, *Australia* 93 E5
Manna, *Indonesia* 62 E2
Mannahill, *Australia* 95 E3
Mannar, *Sri Lanka* 66 Q11
Mannar, G. of, *Asia* 66 Q11
Mannar I., *Sri Lanka* 66 Q11
Mannheim, *Germany* 25 F4
Manning, *Canada* 104 B5
Manning, *Oreg., U.S.A.* 116 E3
Manning, *S.C., U.S.A.* 109 J5
Manning Prov. Park, *Canada* 104 D4
Mannington, *U.S.A.* 108 F5
Mannu →, *Italy* 30 C2
Mannu, C., *Italy* 30 B1
Mannum, *Australia* 95 E2
Mano, *S. Leone* 82 D2
Manokwari, *Indonesia* 63 E8
Manolás, *Greece* 38 C3
Manombo, *Madag.* 89 C7
Manono, *Dem. Rep. of the Congo* 86 D2
Manoppello, *Italy* 29 F11
Manosque, *France* 21 E9
Manouane, L., *Canada* 103 B5
Manpojin, *N. Korea* 57 D14
Manresa, *Spain* 32 D6
Mansa, *Gujarat, India* 68 H5
Mansa, *Punjab, India* 68 E6
Mansa, *Zambia* 87 E2
Månsåsen, *Sweden* 10 A8
Mansehra, *Pakistan* 68 B5
Mansel I., *Canada* 101 B12
Mansfield, *Australia* 95 F4
Mansfield, *U.K.* 12 D6
Mansfield, *La., U.S.A.* 113 J8
Mansfield, *Mass., U.S.A.* 111 D13
Mansfield, *Ohio, U.S.A.* 110 F2
Mansfield, *Pa., U.S.A.* 110 E7
Mansfield, *Wash., U.S.A.* 114 C4
Mansilla de las Mulas, *Spain* 34 C5
Mansle, *France* 20 C4
Mansoa, *Guinea-Biss.* 82 C1
Manson Creek, *Canada* 104 B4
Manta, *Ecuador* 124 D2
Mantalingajan, Mt., *Phil.* 61 G2
Mantare, *Tanzania* 86 C3
Manteca, *U.S.A.* 116 H5
Manteo, *U.S.A.* 109 H8
Mantes-la-Jolie, *France* 19 D8
Manthani, *India* 66 K11
Manti, *U.S.A.* 114 G8
Mantiqueira, Serra da, *Brazil* 127 A7
Manton, *U.S.A.* 108 C3
Mantorp, *Sweden* 11 F9
Mántova, *Italy* 28 C7
Mänttä, *Finland* 9 E21
Mantua = Mántova, *Italy* 28 C7
Manturovo, *Russia* 48 A7
Manu, *Peru* 124 F4
Manu →, *Peru* 124 F4
Manua Is., *Amer. Samoa* 91 B14
Manuae, *Cook Is.* 97 J12
Manuel Alves →, *Brazil* 125 F9
Manui, *Indonesia* 63 E6
Manuripi →, *Bolivia* 124 F5
Manville, *U.S.A.* 112 D2
Many, *U.S.A.* 113 K8
Manyara, L., *Tanzania* 86 C4
Manyas, *Turkey* 41 F11

Manych →, *Russia*	49	G5	
Manych-Gudilo, Ozero, *Russia*	49	G6	
Manyonga →, *Tanzania*	86	C3	
Manyoni, *Tanzania*	86	D3	
Manyoni □, *Tanzania*	86	D3	
Manzai, *Pakistan*	68	C4	
Manzala, Bahra el, *Egypt*	80	H7	
Manzanares, *Spain*	35	F7	
Manzaneda, *Spain*	34	C3	
Manzanillo, *Cuba*	120	B4	
Manzanillo, *Mexico*	118	D4	
Manzanillo, Pta., *Panama*	120	E4	
Manzano Mts., *U.S.A.*	115	J10	
Manẓarīyeh, *Iran*	71	C6	
Manzhouli, *China*	60	B6	
Manzini, *Swaziland*	89	D5	
Mao, *Chad*	79	F9	
Maó, *Spain*	37	B11	
Maoke, Pegunungan, *Indonesia*	63	E9	
Maolin, *China*	57	C12	
Maoming, *China*	59	G8	
Maowen, *China*	58	B4	
Maoxing, *China*	57	B13	
Mapam Yumco, *China*	60	C3	
Mapastepec, *Mexico*	119	D6	
Mapia, Kepulauan, *Indonesia*	63	D8	
Mapimí, *Mexico*	118	B4	
Mapimí, Bolsón de, *Mexico*	118	B4	
Maping, *China*	59	B9	
Mapinga, *Tanzania*	86	D4	
Mapinhane, *Mozam.*	89	C6	
Maple Creek, *Canada*	105	D7	
Maple Valley, *U.S.A.*	116	C4	
Mapleton, *U.S.A.*	114	D2	
Mapuera →, *Brazil*	124	D7	
Maputo, *Mozam.*	89	D5	
Maputo, B. de, *Mozam.*	89	D5	
Maqiaohe, *China*	57	B16	
Maqnā, *Si. Arabia*	70	D2	
Maqueda, *Spain*	34	E6	
Maquela do Zombo, *Angola*	84	F3	
Maquinchao, *Argentina*	128	E3	
Maquoketa, *U.S.A.*	112	D9	
Mar, Serra do, *Brazil*	127	B6	
Mar Chiquita, L., *Argentina*	126	C3	
Mar del Plata, *Argentina*	126	D4	
Mar Menor, *Spain*	33	H4	
Mara, *Tanzania*	86	C3	
Mara □, *Tanzania*	86	C3	
Maraã, *Brazil*	124	D5	
Marabá, *Brazil*	125	E9	
Maracá, I. de, *Brazil*	125	C8	
Maracaibo, *Venezuela*	124	A4	
Maracaibo, L. de, *Venezuela*	122	C3	
Maracaju, *Brazil*	127	A4	
Maracay, *Venezuela*	124	A5	
Maracena, *Spain*	35	H7	
Maradi, *Niger*	83	C6	
Maradun, *Nigeria*	83	C6	
Marägheh, *Iran*	70	B5	
Marāh, *Si. Arabia*	70	E5	
Marajó, I. de, *Brazil*	122	D6	
Marākand, *Iran*	70	B5	
Maralal, *Kenya*	86	B4	
Maralinga, *Australia*	93	F5	
Marama, *Australia*	95	F3	
Maramaraereğlisi, *Turkey*	41	F11	
Marampa, *S. Leone*	82	D2	
Maramureş □, *Romania*	43	C9	
Maran, *Malaysia*	65	L4	
Marana, *U.S.A.*	115	K8	
Maranboy, *Australia*	92	B5	
Maranchón, *Spain*	32	D2	
Marand, *Iran*	70	B5	
Marang, *Malaysia*	65	K4	
Maranguape, *Brazil*	125	D11	
Maranhão = São Luís, *Brazil*	125	D10	
Maranhão □, *Brazil*	125	E9	
Marano, L. di, *Italy*	29	C10	
Maranoa →, *Australia*	95	D4	
Marañón →, *Peru*	122	D3	
Marão, *Mozam.*	89	C5	
Maraş = Kahramanmaraş, *Turkey*	72	D7	
Mărăşeşti, *Romania*	43	E12	
Maratea, *Italy*	31	C8	
Marateca, *Portugal*	35	G2	
Marathasa □, *Cyprus*	36	E11	
Marathókambos, *Greece*	39	D8	
Marathon, *Australia*	94	C3	
Marathon, *Canada*	102	C2	
Marathón, *Greece*	38	C5	
Marathon, N.Y., *U.S.A.*	111	D8	
Marathon, Tex., *U.S.A.*	113	K3	
Marathóvouno, *Cyprus*	36	D12	
Maratua, *Indonesia*	63	D5	
Maravatío, *Mexico*	118	D4	
Marawi, City, *Phil.*	61	H6	
Marāwih, *U.A.E.*	71	E7	
Marbella, *Spain*	35	J6	
Marble Bar, *Australia*	92	D2	
Marble Falls, *U.S.A.*	113	K5	
Marblehead, *U.S.A.*	111	D14	
Marburg, *Germany*	24	E4	
Marcal →, *Hungary*	42	C2	
Marcali, *Hungary*	42	D2	
Marcaria, *Italy*	28	C7	
Mărcăuți, *Moldova*	43	B12	
March, *U.K.*	13	E8	
Marche, *France*	20	B5	
Marche □, *Italy*	29	E10	
Marche-en-Famenne, *Belgium*	17	D5	
Marchena, *Spain*	35	H5	
Marches = Marche □, *Italy*	29	E10	
Marciana Marina, *Italy*	28	F7	
Marcianise, *Italy*	31	A7	
Marcigny, *France*	19	F11	
Marcillat-en-Combraille, *France*	19	F9	
Marck, *France*	19	B8	
Marckolsheim, *France*	19	D14	
Marcos Juárez, *Argentina*	126	C3	
Mărculeşti, *Moldova*	43	C13	
Marcus I. = Minami-Tori-Shima, *Pac. Oc.*	96	E7	
Marcus Necker Ridge, *Pac. Oc.*	96	F9	
Marcy, Mt., *U.S.A.*	111	B11	
Mardan, *Pakistan*	68	B5	
Mardie, *Australia*	92	D2	
Mardin, *Turkey*	73	D9	
Mårdsjön, *Sweden*	10	A9	
Marécchia →, *Italy*	29	D9	
Maree, L., *U.K.*	14	D3	
Mareeba, *Australia*	94	B4	
Maremma, *Italy*	29	F8	
Maréna, *Mali*	82	C3	
Marengo, *U.S.A.*	112	E8	
Marennes, *France*	20	C2	
Marenyi, *Kenya*	86	C4	
Marerano, *Madag.*	89	C7	
Maréttimo, *Italy*	30	E5	
Mareuil, *France*	20	C4	
Marfa, *U.S.A.*	113	K2	
Marfa Pt., *Malta*	36	D1	
Marganets = Marhanets, *Ukraine*	47	J8	
Margaret →, *Australia*	92	C4	
Margaret Bay, *Canada*	104	C3	
Margaret L., *Canada*	104	B5	
Margaret River, *Australia*	92	F2	
Margarita, I. de, *Venezuela*	124	B4	
Margarítion, *Greece*	38	B2	
Margaritovo, *Russia*	54	C7	
Margate, *S. Africa*	89	E5	
Margate, *U.K.*	13	F9	
Margeride, Mts. de la, *France*	20	D7	
Margherita di Savóia, *Italy*	31	A9	
Marghita, *Romania*	42	C7	
Margonin, *Poland*	45	F4	
Margosatubig, *Phil.*	61	H5	
Marguerite, *Canada*	104	C4	
Marhanets, *Ukraine*	47	J8	
Mari El □, *Russia*	48	B8	
Mari Republic □ = Mari El □, *Russia*	48	B8	
María, Sa. de, *Spain*	33	H2	
María Elena, *Chile*	126	A2	
María Grande, *Argentina*	126	C4	
Maria I., N. Terr., *Australia*	94	A2	
Maria I., Tas., *Australia*	94	G4	
Maria van Diemen, C., *N.Z.*	91	F4	
Mariager, *Denmark*	11	H3	
Mariager Fjord, *Denmark*	11	H4	
Mariakani, *Kenya*	86	C4	
Marian L., *Canada*	104	A5	
Marianao, *Cuba*	120	B3	
Marianna, Ark., *U.S.A.*	113	H9	
Marianna, Fla., *U.S.A.*	109	K3	
Mariannelund, *Sweden*	11	G9	
Mariánské Lázně, *Czech Rep.*	26	B5	
Marias →, *U.S.A.*	114	C8	
Mariato, Punta, *Panama*	120	E3	
Mariazell, *Austria*	26	D8	
Maribo, *Denmark*	11	K5	
Maribor, *Slovenia*	29	B12	
Marico →, *Africa*	88	C4	
Maricopa, Ariz., *U.S.A.*	115	K7	
Maricopa, Calif., *U.S.A.*	117	K7	
Marîdî, *Sudan*	81	G2	
Maridi, Wadi →, *Sudan*	81	F2	
Marié →, *Brazil*	124	D5	
Marie Byrd Land, *Antarctica*	5	D14	
Marie-Galante, *Guadeloupe*	121	C7	
Mariecourt = Kangiqsujuaq, *Canada*	101	B12	
Mariefred, *Sweden*	10	E11	
Marieholm, *Sweden*	11	J7	
Marienbad = Mariánské Lázně, *Czech Rep.*	26	B5	
Marienberg, *Germany*	24	E9	
Mariental, *Namibia*	88	C2	
Marienville, *U.S.A.*	110	E5	
Mariestad, *Sweden*	11	F7	
Marietta, Ga., *U.S.A.*	109	J3	
Marietta, Ohio, *U.S.A.*	108	F5	
Marieville, *Canada*	111	A11	
Marignane, *France*	21	E9	
Marihatag, *Phil.*	61	G7	
Mariinsk, *Russia*	50	D9	
Mariinskiy Posad, *Russia*	48	B8	
Marijampolė, *Lithuania*	9	J20	
Marijampolė □, *Lithuania*	44	D10	
Marília, *Brazil*	127	A6	
Marillana, *Australia*	92	D2	
Marín, *Spain*	34	C2	
Marina, *U.S.A.*	116	J5	
Marina Plains, *Australia*	94	A3	
Marinduque, *Phil.*	61	E5	
Marine City, *U.S.A.*	108	D4	
Marineo, *Italy*	30	E6	
Marinette, *U.S.A.*	108	C2	
Maringá, *Brazil*	127	A5	
Marinha Grande, *Portugal*	34	F2	
Marino, *Italy*	29	G9	
Marion, Ala., *U.S.A.*	109	J2	
Marion, Ill., *U.S.A.*	113	G10	
Marion, Ind., *U.S.A.*	108	E3	
Marion, Iowa, *U.S.A.*	112	D9	
Marion, Kans., *U.S.A.*	112	F6	
Marion, Mich., *U.S.A.*	108	C3	
Marion, N.C., *U.S.A.*	109	H5	
Marion, Ohio, *U.S.A.*	108	E4	
Marion, S.C., *U.S.A.*	109	H6	
Marion, Va., *U.S.A.*	109	G5	
Marion, L., *U.S.A.*	109	J5	
Mariposa, *U.S.A.*	116	H7	
Mariscal Estigarribia, *Paraguay*	126	A3	
Maritime Alps = Maritimes, Alpes, *Europe*	21	D11	
Maritimes, Alpes, *Europe*	21	D11	
Maritsa = Évros →, *Bulgaria*	72	B2	
Maritsá, *Greece*	36	C10	
Mariupol, *Ukraine*	47	J9	
Marīvān, *Iran*	70	C5	
Markam, *China*	58	C2	
Markaryd, *Sweden*	11	H7	
Markazī □, *Iran*	71	C6	
Markdale, *Canada*	110	B4	
Marked Tree, *U.S.A.*	113	H9	
Markelsdorfer Huk, *Germany*	24	A7	
Market Drayton, *U.K.*	12	E5	
Market Harborough, *U.K.*	13	E7	
Market Rasen, *U.K.*	12	D7	
Markham, *Canada*	110	C5	
Markham, Mt., *Antarctica*	5	E11	
Markham L., *Canada*	105	A8	
Marki, *Poland*	45	F8	
Markkleeberg, *Germany*	24	D8	
Markleeville, *U.S.A.*	116	G7	
Markoupoulon, *Greece*	38	D5	
Markovac, *Serbia, Yug.*	40	B5	
Markovo, *Russia*	51	C17	
Markoye, *Burkina Faso*	83	C5	
Marks, *Russia*	48	E8	
Marksville, *U.S.A.*	113	K8	
Markt Schwaben, *Germany*	25	G7	
Marktoberdorf, *Germany*	25	H6	
Marktredwitz, *Germany*	25	E8	
Marl, *Germany*	24	D3	
Marla, *Australia*	95	D1	
Marlboro, *U.S.A.*	111	D13	
Marlborough, *Australia*	94	C4	
Marlborough, *U.K.*	13	F6	
Marlborough Downs, *U.K.*	13	F6	
Marle, *France*	19	C10	
Marlin, *U.S.A.*	113	K6	
Marlow, *Germany*	24	A8	
Marlow, *U.S.A.*	113	H6	
Marmagao, *India*	66	M8	
Marmande, *France*	20	D4	
Marmara, *Turkey*	41	F11	
Marmara, Sea of = Marmara Denizi, *Turkey*	41	F12	
Marmara Denizi, *Turkey*	41	F12	
Marmara Gölü, *Turkey*	39	C10	
Marmaris, *Turkey*	39	E10	
Marmaris Limanı, *Turkey*	39	E10	
Marmarth, *U.S.A.*	112	B3	
Marmion, Mt., *Australia*	93	E2	
Marmion L., *Canada*	102	C1	
Marmolada, Mte., *Italy*	29	B8	
Marmolejo, *Spain*	35	G6	
Marmora, *Canada*	102	D4	
Mármora, La, *Italy*	30	C2	
Marnay, *France*	19	E12	
Marne □, *France*	19	D11	
Marne →, *France*	19	D9	
Marneuli, *Georgia*	49	K7	
Maroala, *Madag.*	89	B8	
Maroantsetra, *Madag.*	89	B8	
Maromandia, *Madag.*	89	A8	
Marondera, *Zimbabwe*	87	F3	
Maroni →, *Fr. Guiana*	125	B8	
Marónia, *Greece*	41	F9	
Maronne →, *France*	20	C5	
Maroochydore, *Australia*	95	D5	
Maroona, *Australia*	95	F3	
Maros →, *Hungary*	42	D5	
Marosakoa, *Madag.*	89	B8	
Maróstica, *Italy*	29	C8	
Maroua, *Cameroon*	83	C7	
Marovoay, *Madag.*	89	B8	
Marquard, *S. Africa*	88	D4	
Marquesas Is. = Marquises, Is., *Pac. Oc.*	97	H14	
Marquette, *U.S.A.*	108	B2	
Marquise, *France*	19	B8	
Marquises, Is., *Pac. Oc.*	97	H14	
Marra, Gebel, *Sudan*	81	F2	
Marracuene, *Mozam.*	89	D5	
Marradi, *Italy*	29	D8	
Marrakech, *Morocco*	78	B4	
Marrawah, *Australia*	94	G3	
Marree, *Australia*	95	D2	
Marrilla, *Australia*	92	D1	
Marrimane, *Mozam.*	89	C5	
Marromeu, *Mozam.*	89	B6	
Marroquí, Punta, *Spain*	35	K5	
Marrowie Cr. →, *Australia*	95	E4	
Marrubane, *Mozam.*	87	F4	
Marrúbiu, *Italy*	30	C1	
Marrupa, *Mozam.*	87	E4	
Marsá Matrûh, *Egypt*	80	A2	
Marsabit, *Kenya*	86	B4	
Marsabit □, *Kenya*	86	B4	
Marsala, *Italy*	30	E5	
Marsalforn, *Malta*	36	C1	
Mârşani, *Romania*	43	F9	
Marsberg, *Germany*	24	D4	
Marsciano, *Italy*	29	F9	
Marsden, *Australia*	95	E4	
Marseillan, *France*	20	E7	
Marseille, *France*	21	E9	
Marseilles = Marseille, *France*	21	E9	
Marsh I., *U.S.A.*	113	L9	
Marsh L., *U.S.A.*	112	C7	
Marshall, *Liberia*	82	D2	
Marshall, Ark., *U.S.A.*	113	H8	
Marshall, Mich., *U.S.A.*	108	D3	
Marshall, Minn., *U.S.A.*	112	C7	
Marshall, Mo., *U.S.A.*	112	F8	
Marshall, Tex., *U.S.A.*	113	J7	
Marshall →, *Australia*	94	C2	
Marshall Is. ■, *Pac. Oc.*	96	G9	
Marshalltown, *U.S.A.*	112	D8	
Marshfield, Mo., *U.S.A.*	113	G8	
Marshfield, Wis., *U.S.A.*	112	C9	
Marshūn, *Iran*	71	B6	
Mársico Nuovo, *Italy*	31	B8	
Märsta, *Sweden*	10	E11	
Marstal, *Denmark*	11	K4	
Marstrand, *Sweden*	11	G5	
Mart, *U.S.A.*	113	K6	
Marta →, *Italy*	29	F8	
Martaban, *Burma*	67	L20	
Martaban, G. of, *Burma*	67	L20	
Martano, *Italy*	31	B11	
Martapura, Kalimantan, *Indonesia*	62	E4	
Martapura, Sumatera, *Indonesia*	62	E2	
Marte, *Nigeria*	83	C7	
Martel, *France*	20	D5	
Martelange, *Belgium*	17	E5	
Martellago, *Italy*	29	C9	
Martés, Sierra, *Spain*	33	F4	
Martfû, *Hungary*	42	C5	
Martha's Vineyard, *U.S.A.*	111	E14	
Martigné-Ferchaud, *France*	18	E5	
Martigny, *Switz.*	25	J3	
Martigues, *France*	21	E9	
Martin, *Slovak Rep.*	27	B11	
Martin, S. Dak., *U.S.A.*	112	D4	
Martin, Tenn., *U.S.A.*	113	G10	
Martín →, *Spain*	32	D4	
Martín L., *U.S.A.*	109	J3	
Martina Franca, *Italy*	31	B10	
Martinborough, *N.Z.*	91	J5	
Martinez, *U.S.A.*	116	G4	
Martinique ■, *W. Indies*	121	D7	
Martinique Passage, *W. Indies*	121	C7	
Martínon, *Greece*	38	C5	
Martinópolis, *Brazil*	127	A5	
Martins Ferry, *U.S.A.*	110	F4	
Martinsberg, *Austria*	26	C8	
Martinsburg, Pa., *U.S.A.*	110	F6	
Martinsburg, W. Va., *U.S.A.*	108	F7	
Martinsicuro, *Italy*	29	F10	
Martinsville, Ind., *U.S.A.*	108	F2	
Martinsville, Va., *U.S.A.*	109	G6	
Marton, *N.Z.*	91	J5	
Martorell, *Spain*	32	D6	
Martos, *Spain*	35	H7	
Martuni, *Armenia*	49	K7	
Maru, *Nigeria*	83	C6	
Marudi, *Malaysia*	62	D4	
Ma'ruf, *Afghan.*	66	D5	
Marugame, *Japan*	55	G6	
Marulan, *Australia*	95	E5	
Marunga, *Angola*	88	B3	
Marungu, Mts., *Dem. Rep. of the Congo*	86	D3	
Marvast, *Iran*	71	D7	
Marvejols, *France*	20	D7	
Marwar, *India*	68	G5	
Mary, *Turkmenistan*	50	F7	
Mary Frances L., *Canada*	105	A7	
Mary Kathleen, *Australia*	94	C2	
Maryborough = Port Laoise, *Ireland*	15	C4	
Maryborough, Queens., *Australia*	95	D5	
Maryborough, Vic., *Australia*	95	F3	
Maryfield, *Canada*	105	D8	
Maryland □, *U.S.A.*	108	F7	
Maryland Junction, *Zimbabwe*	87	F3	
Maryport, *U.K.*	12	C4	
Mary's Harbour, *Canada*	103	B8	
Marystown, *Canada*	103	C8	
Marysvale, *U.S.A.*	115	G7	
Marysville, *Canada*	104	D5	
Marysville, Calif., *U.S.A.*	116	F5	
Marysville, Kans., *U.S.A.*	112	F6	
Marysville, Mich., *U.S.A.*	110	D2	
Marysville, Ohio, *U.S.A.*	108	E4	
Marysville, Wash., *U.S.A.*	116	B4	
Maryvale, *Australia*	95	D5	
Maryville, *U.S.A.*	109	H4	
Marzūq, *Libya*	79	C8	
Masahunga, *Tanzania*	86	C3	
Masai Steppe, *Tanzania*	86	C4	
Masaka, *Uganda*	86	C3	
Masalembo, Kepulauan, *Indonesia*	62	F4	
Masalima, Kepulauan, *Indonesia*	62	F5	
Masallı, *Azerbaijan*	73	C13	
Masamba, *Indonesia*	63	E6	
Masan, *S. Korea*	57	G15	
Masasi, *Tanzania*	87	E4	
Masasi □, *Tanzania*	87	E4	
Masaya, *Nic.*	120	D2	
Masba, *Nigeria*	83	C7	
Masbate, *Phil.*	61	E5	
Máscali, *Italy*	31	E8	
Mascara, *Algeria*	78	A6	
Mascota, *Mexico*	118	C4	
Masela, *Indonesia*	63	F7	
Maseru, *Lesotho*	88	D4	
Mashaba, *Zimbabwe*	87	G3	
Mashābih, *Si. Arabia*	70	E3	
Mashan, *China*	58	F7	
Masherbrum, *Pakistan*	69	B7	
Mashhad, *Iran*	71	B8	
Mashi, *Nigeria*	83	C6	
Mashīz, *Iran*	71	D8	
Mashkel, Hamun-i-, *Pakistan*	66	E3	
Mashki Chāh, *Pakistan*	66	E3	
Mashonaland Central □, *Zimbabwe*	89	B5	
Mashonaland East □, *Zimbabwe*	89	B5	
Mashonaland West □, *Zimbabwe*	89	B4	
Mashtaga = Maştağa, *Azerbaijan*	49	K10	
Masindi, *Uganda*	86	B3	
Masindi Port, *Uganda*	86	B3	
Masisi, *Dem. Rep. of the Congo*	86	C2	
Masjed Soleyman, *Iran*	71	D6	
Mask, L., *Ireland*	15	C2	
Maslen Nos, *Bulgaria*	41	D11	
Maslinica, *Croatia*	29	E13	
Masnou = El Masnou, *Spain*	32	D7	
Masoala, Tanjon' i, *Madag.*	89	B9	
Masoarivo, *Madag.*	89	B7	
Masomeloka, *Madag.*	89	C8	
Mason, Nev., *U.S.A.*	116	G7	
Mason, Tex., *U.S.A.*	113	K5	
Mason City, *U.S.A.*	112	D8	
Maspalomas, *Canary Is.*	37	G4	
Maspalomas, Pta., *Canary Is.*	37	G4	
Masqat, *Oman*	74	C6	
Massa, *Italy*	28	D7	
Massa Maríttima, *Italy*	28	E7	
Massachusetts □, *U.S.A.*	111	D13	
Massachusetts B., *U.S.A.*	111	D14	
Massafra, *Italy*	31	B10	
Massakory, *Chad*	79	F9	
Massanella, *Spain*	37	B9	
Massangena, *Mozam.*	89	C5	
Massat, *France*	20	F5	
Massawa = Mitsiwa, *Eritrea*	81	D4	
Masséna, *U.S.A.*	111	B10	
Massénya, *Chad*	79	F9	
Masset, *Canada*	104	C2	
Masseube, *France*	20	E4	
Massiac, *France*	20	C7	
Massif Central, *France*	20	D7	
Massillon, *U.S.A.*	110	F3	
Massinga, *Mozam.*	89	C6	
Mässlingen, *Sweden*	10	B6	
Masson, *Canada*	111	A9	
Masson I., *Antarctica*	5	C7	
Maştağa, *Azerbaijan*	49	K10	
Mastanli = Momchilgrad, *Bulgaria*	41	E9	
Masterton, *N.Z.*	91	J5	
Mástikho, Ákra, *Greece*	39	C8	
Mastuj, *Pakistan*	69	A5	
Mastung, *Pakistan*	66	E5	
Mastūrah, *Si. Arabia*	80	C4	
Masty, *Belarus*	46	F3	
Masuda, *Japan*	55	G5	
Masvingo, *Zimbabwe*	87	G3	
Masvingo □, *Zimbabwe*	87	G3	
Maswa □, *Tanzania*	86	C3	
Maşyāf, *Syria*	70	C3	
Maszewo, *Poland*	44	E2	
Matabeleland North □, *Zimbabwe*	87	F2	
Matabeleland South □, *Zimbabwe*	87	G2	
Matachel →, *Spain*	35	G4	
Matachewan, *Canada*	102	C3	
Matad, *Mongolia*	60	B6	
Matadi, *Dem. Rep. of the Congo*	84	F2	
Matagalpa, *Nic.*	120	D2	
Matagami, *Canada*	102	C4	
Matagami, L., *Canada*	102	C4	
Matagorda, *U.S.A.*	113	L7	
Matagorda B., *U.S.A.*	113	L6	
Matagorda I., *U.S.A.*	113	L6	
Matak, *Indonesia*	65	L6	
Matakana, *Australia*	95	E4	
Matala, *Greece*	36	E6	
Matam, *Senegal*	82	B2	
Matameye, *Niger*	83	C6	
Matamoros, Campeche, *Mexico*	119	D6	
Matamoros, Coahuila, *Mexico*	118	B4	

Matamoros, *Puebla, Mexico* 119 D5
Matamoros, *Tamaulipas, Mexico* 119 B5
Ma'ṭan as Sarra, *Libya* 79 D10
Matandu →, *Tanzania* 87 D3
Matane, *Canada* 103 C6
Matang, *China* 58 F5
Matankari, *Niger* 83 C5
Matanzas, *Cuba* 120 B3
Matapan, C. = Taínaron, Ákra, *Greece* 38 E4
Matapédia, *Canada* 103 C6
Matara, *Sri Lanka* 66 S12
Mataram, *Indonesia* 62 F5
Matarani, *Peru* 124 G4
Mataranka, *Australia* 92 B5
Matarma, Râs, *Egypt* 75 E1
Mataró, *Spain* 32 D7
Matarraña →, *Spain* 32 D5
Mataruška Banja, *Serbia, Yug.* 40 C4
Matatiele, *S. Africa* 89 E4
Mataura, *N.Z.* 91 M2
Matehuala, *Mexico* 118 C4
Mateke Hills, *Zimbabwe* 87 G3
Matera, *Italy* 31 B9
Matese, Monti del, *Italy* 31 A7
Mátészalka, *Hungary* 42 C7
Matetsi, *Zimbabwe* 87 F2
Matfors, *Sweden* 10 B11
Matha, *France* 20 C4
Matheson Island, *Canada* 105 C9
Mathis, *U.S.A.* 113 L6
Mathráki, *Greece* 36 A3
Mathura, *India* 68 F7
Mati, *Phil.* 61 H7
Mati →, *Albania* 40 E3
Matías Romero, *Mexico* 119 D5
Matibane, *Mozam.* 87 E5
Matima, *Botswana* 88 C3
Matiri Ra., *N.Z.* 91 J4
Matlock, *U.K.* 12 D6
Matna, *Sudan* 81 E4
Mato Grosso □, *Brazil* 125 F8
Mato Grosso, Planalto do, *Brazil* 122 E5
Mato Grosso do Sul □, *Brazil* 125 G8
Matochkin Shar, *Russia* 50 B6
Matopo Hills, *Zimbabwe* 87 G2
Matopos, *Zimbabwe* 87 G2
Matosinhos, *Portugal* 34 D2
Matour, *France* 19 F11
Matsena, *Nigeria* 83 C7
Matsesta, *Russia* 49 J4
Matsu Tao, *Taiwan* 59 E13
Matsue, *Japan* 55 G6
Matsumae, *Japan* 54 D10
Matsumoto, *Japan* 55 F9
Matsusaka, *Japan* 55 G8
Matsuura, *Japan* 55 H4
Matsuyama, *Japan* 55 H6
Mattagami →, *Canada* 102 B3
Mattancheri, *India* 66 Q10
Mattawa, *Canada* 102 C4
Mattawamkeag, *U.S.A.* 103 C6
Matterhorn, *Switz.* 25 K3
Mattersburg, *Austria* 27 D9
Matthew Town, *Bahamas* 121 B5
Matthew's Ridge, *Guyana* 124 B6
Mattice, *Canada* 102 C3
Mattituck, *U.S.A.* 111 F12
Matuba, *Mozam.* 89 C5
Matucana, *Peru* 124 F3
Matun, *Afghan.* 68 C3
Maturín, *Venezuela* 124 B6
Matveyev Kurgan, *Russia* 47 J10
Matxitxako, C., *Spain* 32 B2
Mau, *India* 69 G10
Mau Escarpment, *Kenya* 86 C4
Mau Ranipur, *India* 69 G8
Maubeuge, *France* 19 B10
Maubourguet, *France* 20 E4
Maud, Pt., *Australia* 92 D1
Maude, *Australia* 95 E3
Maudin Sun, *Burma* 67 M19
Maués, *Brazil* 124 D7
Mauganj, *India* 67 G12
Maughold Hd., *U.K.* 12 C3
Mauguio, *France* 20 E7
Maui, *U.S.A.* 106 H16
Maulamyaing = Moulmein, *Burma* 67 L20
Maule □, *Chile* 126 D1
Mauléon-Licharre, *France* 20 E3
Maumee, *U.S.A.* 108 E4
Maumee →, *U.S.A.* 108 E4
Maumere, *Indonesia* 63 F6
Maumusson, Pertuis de, *France* 20 C2
Maun, *Botswana* 88 C3
Mauna Kea, *U.S.A.* 106 J17
Mauna Loa, *U.S.A.* 106 J17
Maungmagan Is., *Burma* 67 N20
Maungmagan Kyunzu, *Burma* 67 N20
Maupin, *U.S.A.* 114 D3
Maure-de-Bretagne, *France* 18 E5
Maurepas, L., *U.S.A.* 113 K9
Maures, *France* 21 E10
Mauriac, *France* 20 C6
Maurice, L., *Australia* 93 E5
Maurienne, *France* 21 C10
Mauritania ■, *Africa* 78 E3
Mauritius ■, *Ind. Oc.* 77 J9
Mauron, *France* 18 D4
Maurs, *France* 20 D6

Mauston, *U.S.A.* 112 D9
Mauterndorf, *Austria* 26 D6
Mauthen, *Austria* 26 E6
Mauvezin, *France* 20 E4
Mauzé-sur-le-Mignon, *France* 20 B3
Mavli, *India* 68 G5
Mavrova, *Albania* 40 F3
Mavuradonha Mts., *Zimbabwe* 87 F3
Mawa, *Dem. Rep. of the Congo* 86 B2
Mawana, *India* 68 E7
Mawand, *Pakistan* 68 E3
Mawk Mai, *Burma* 67 J20
Mawlaik, *Burma* 67 H19
Mawquq, *Si. Arabia* 70 E4
Mawson Coast, *Antarctica* 5 C6
Max, *U.S.A.* 112 B4
Maxcanú, *Mexico* 119 C6
Maxesibeni, *S. Africa* 89 E4
Maxhamish L., *Canada* 104 B4
Maxixe, *Mozam.* 89 C6
Maxville, *Canada* 111 A10
Maxwell, *U.S.A.* 116 F4
Maxwelton, *Australia* 94 C3
May Downs, *Australia* 94 C4
May Pen, *Jamaica* 120 C4
Maya →, *Russia* 51 D14
Maya Mts., *Belize* 119 D7
Mayaguana, *Bahamas* 121 B5
Mayagüez, *Puerto Rico* 121 C6
Mayahi, *Niger* 83 C6
Mayals = Maials, *Spain* 32 D5
Mayāmey, *Iran* 71 B7
Mayang, *China* 58 D7
Mayarí, *Cuba* 121 B4
Maybell, *U.S.A.* 114 F9
Maybole, *U.K.* 14 F4
Maychew, *Ethiopia* 81 E4
Maydān, *Iraq* 70 C5
Maydena, *Australia* 94 G4
Mayen, *Germany* 25 E3
Mayenne, *France* 18 D6
Mayenne □, *France* 18 D6
Mayenne →, *France* 18 E6
Mayer, *U.S.A.* 115 J7
Mayerthorpe, *Canada* 104 C5
Mayfield, *U.S.A.* 109 G1
Mayhill, *U.S.A.* 115 K11
Maykop, *Russia* 49 H5
Maymyo, *Burma* 64 A1
Maynard, *U.S.A.* 116 C4
Maynard Hills, *Australia* 93 E2
Mayne →, *Australia* 94 C3
Maynooth, *Ireland* 15 C5
Mayo, *Canada* 100 B6
Mayo □, *Ireland* 15 C2
Mayon Volcano, *Phil.* 61 E5
Mayor I., *N.Z.* 91 G6
Mayorga, *Spain* 34 C5
Mayotte □, *Mayotte* 77 H8
Mayraira Pt., *Phil.* 61 B4
Mayskiy, *Russia* 49 J7
Mayson L., *Canada* 105 B7
Maysville, *U.S.A.* 108 F4
Mayu, *Indonesia* 63 D7
Mayville, *N. Dak., U.S.A.* 112 B6
Mayville, *N.Y., U.S.A.* 110 D5
Mayya, *Russia* 51 C14
Mazabuka, *Zambia* 87 F2
Mazagán = El Jadida, *Morocco* 78 B4
Mazagão, *Brazil* 125 D8
Mazamet, *France* 20 E6
Mazán, *Peru* 124 D4
Māzandarān □, *Iran* 71 B7
Mazapil, *Mexico* 118 C4
Mazara del Vallo, *Italy* 30 E5
Mazarrón, *Spain* 33 H3
Mazarrón, G. de, *Spain* 33 H3
Mazaruni →, *Guyana* 124 B7
Mazatán, *Mexico* 118 B2
Mazatenango, *Guatemala* 120 D1
Mazatlán, *Mexico* 118 C3
Mažeikiai, *Lithuania* 9 H20
Māzhān, *Iran* 71 C8
Mazīnān, *Iran* 71 B8
Mazoe, *Mozam.* 87 F3
Mazoe →, *Mozam.* 87 F3
Mazowe, *Zimbabwe* 87 F3
Mazrûb, *Sudan* 81 E2
Mazu Dao, *China* 59 D12
Mazurian Lakes = Mazurski, Pojezierze, *Poland* 44 E7
Mazurski, Pojezierze, *Poland* 44 E7
Mazyr, *Belarus* 47 F5
Mbaba, *Senegal* 82 C1
Mbabane, *Swaziland* 89 D5
Mbagne, *Mauritania* 82 B2
M'bahiakro, *Ivory C.* 82 D4
Mbaïki, *C.A.R.* 84 D3
Mbala, *Zambia* 87 D3
Mbale, *Uganda* 86 B3
Mbalmayo, *Cameroon* 83 E7
Mbamba Bay, *Tanzania* 87 E3
Mbandaka, *Dem. Rep. of the Congo* 84 D3
Mbanga, *Cameroon* 83 E6
Mbanza Ngungu, *Dem. Rep. of the Congo* 84 F2
Mbarara, *Uganda* 86 C3
Mbashe →, *S. Africa* 89 E4
Mbatto, *Ivory C.* 82 D4

Mbenkuru →, *Tanzania* 87 D4
Mberengwa, *Zimbabwe* 87 G2
Mberengwa, Mt., *Zimbabwe* 87 G2
Mberubu, *Nigeria* 83 D6
Mbesuma, *Zambia* 87 E3
Mbeya, *Tanzania* 87 D3
Mbeya □, *Tanzania* 86 D3
Mbinga, *Tanzania* 87 E4
Mbinga □, *Tanzania* 87 E4
Mbini □, *Eq. Guin.* 84 D2
Mboki, *C.A.R.* 81 F2
Mboro, *Senegal* 82 B1
Mboune, *Senegal* 82 C2
Mbour, *Senegal* 82 C1
Mbout, *Mauritania* 82 B2
Mbozi □, *Tanzania* 87 D3
Mbuji-Mayi, *Dem. Rep. of the Congo* 86 D1
Mbulu, *Tanzania* 86 C4
Mbulu □, *Tanzania* 86 C4
Mburucuyá, *Argentina* 126 B4
Mchinja, *Tanzania* 87 D4
Mchinji, *Malawi* 87 E3
Mead, L., *U.S.A.* 117 J12
Meade, *U.S.A.* 113 G4
Meadow, *Australia* 93 E1
Meadow Lake, *Canada* 105 C7
Meadow Lake Prov. Park, *Canada* 105 C7
Meadow Valley Wash →, *U.S.A.* 117 J12
Meadville, *U.S.A.* 110 E4
Meaford, *Canada* 102 D3
Mealhada, *Portugal* 34 E2
Mealy Mts., *Canada* 103 B8
Meander River, *Canada* 104 B5
Meares, C., *U.S.A.* 114 D2
Mearim →, *Brazil* 125 D10
Meath □, *Ireland* 15 C5
Meath Park, *Canada* 105 C7
Meaulne, *France* 19 F9
Meaux, *France* 19 D9
Mebechi-Gawa →, *Japan* 54 D10
Mecanhelas, *Mozam.* 87 F4
Mecca = Makkah, *Si. Arabia* 80 C4
Mecca, *U.S.A.* 117 M10
Mechanicsburg, *U.S.A.* 110 F8
Mechanicville, *U.S.A.* 111 D11
Mechara, *Ethiopia* 81 F5
Mechelen, *Belgium* 17 C4
Mecheria, *Algeria* 78 B5
Mechernich, *Germany* 24 E2
Mechetinskaya, *Russia* 49 G5
Mecidiye, *Turkey* 41 F10
Mecitözü, *Turkey* 72 B6
Mecklenburg-Vorpommern □, *Germany* 24 B8
Mecklenburger Bucht, *Germany* 24 A7
Meconta, *Mozam.* 87 E4
Mecsek, *Hungary* 42 D3
Meda, *Australia* 92 C3
Meda, *Portugal* 34 E3
Medan, *Indonesia* 62 D1
Medanosa, Pta., *Argentina* 128 F3
Mede, *Italy* 28 C5
Médéa, *Algeria* 78 A6
Mededa, *Bos.-H.* 42 G4
Medellín, *Colombia* 124 B3
Medelpad, *Sweden* 10 B10
Medemblik, *Neths.* 17 B5
Mederdra, *Mauritania* 82 B1
Medford, *Mass., U.S.A.* 111 D13
Medford, *Oreg., U.S.A.* 114 E2
Medford, *Wis., U.S.A.* 112 C9
Medgidia, *Romania* 43 F13
Medi, *Sudan* 81 F3
Media Agua, *Argentina* 126 C2
Media Luna, *Argentina* 126 C2
Mediaş, *Romania* 43 D9
Medical Lake, *U.S.A.* 114 C5
Medicina, *Italy* 29 D8
Medicine Bow, *U.S.A.* 114 F10
Medicine Bow Pk., *U.S.A.* 114 F10
Medicine Bow Ra., *U.S.A.* 114 F10
Medicine Hat, *Canada* 105 D6
Medicine Lake, *U.S.A.* 112 A2
Medicine Lodge, *U.S.A.* 113 G5
Medina = Al Madīnah, *Si. Arabia* 70 E3
Medina, *N. Dak., U.S.A.* 112 B5
Medina, *N.Y., U.S.A.* 110 C6
Medina, *Ohio, U.S.A.* 110 E3
Medina →, *U.S.A.* 113 L5
Medina de Pomar, *Spain* 34 C7
Medina de Ríoseco, *Spain* 34 D5
Medina del Campo, *Spain* 34 D6
Medina L., *U.S.A.* 113 L5
Medina Sidonia, *Spain* 35 J5
Medinaceli, *Spain* 32 D2
Medinipur, *India* 69 H12
Mediterranean Sea, *Europe* 6 H7
Medley, *Canada* 105 C6
Médoc, *France* 20 C3
Medstead, *Canada* 105 C7
Medulin, *Croatia* 29 D10
Medveda, *Serbia, Yug.* 40 D5
Medvedev →, *Tver, Russia* 46 D9
Medveditsa →, *Volgograd, Russia* 48 F6
Medvedok, *Russia* 48 B10
Medvezhi, Ostrava, *Russia* 51 B17

Medvezhyegorsk, *Russia* 50 C4
Medway →, *U.K.* 13 F8
Medway Towns □, *U.K.* 13 F8
Medzev, *Slovak Rep.* 27 C13
Medzilaborce, *Slovak Rep.* 27 B14
Medžitlija, *Macedonia* 40 F5
Meeberrie, *Australia* 93 E2
Meekatharra, *Australia* 93 E2
Meeker, *U.S.A.* 114 F10
Meersburg, *Germany* 25 H5
Meerut, *India* 68 E7
Meeteetse, *U.S.A.* 114 D9
Mega, *Ethiopia* 81 G4
Megálo Khorío, *Greece* 39 E9
Megálo Petalí, *Greece* 38 D6
Megalópolis, *Greece* 38 D4
Meganísi, *Greece* 38 C2
Mégara, *Greece* 38 D5
Megdhova →, *Greece* 38 B3
Megève, *France* 21 C10
Meghalaya □, *India* 67 G17
Meghezez, *Ethiopia* 81 F4
Mégiscane, L., *Canada* 102 C4
Megiste, *Greece* 39 E11
Megra, *Russia* 46 B9
Mehadia, *Romania* 42 F7
Mehedeby, *Sweden* 10 D11
Mehedinţi □, *Romania* 42 F7
Meheisa, *Sudan* 80 D3
Mehndawal, *India* 69 F10
Mehr Jān, *Iran* 71 C7
Mehrān, *Iran* 70 C5
Mehrīz, *Iran* 71 D7
Mehun-sur-Yèvre, *France* 19 E9
Mei Jiang →, *China* 59 E11
Mei Xian, *Guangdong, China* 59 E11
Mei Xian, *Shaanxi, China* 56 G4
Meicheng, *China* 59 C12
Meichengzhen, *China* 59 C8
Meichuan, *China* 59 B10
Meiktila, *Burma* 67 J19
Meinerzhagen, *Germany* 24 D3
Meiningen, *Germany* 24 E6
Meira, Serra de, *Spain* 34 B3
Meiringen, *Switz.* 25 J4
Meishan, *China* 58 B4
Meissen, *Germany* 24 D9
Meissner, *Germany* 24 D5
Meitan, *China* 58 D6
Mejillones, *Chile* 126 A1
Meka, *Australia* 93 E2
Mekdela, *Ethiopia* 81 E4
Mekele, *Ethiopia* 81 E4
Mekhtar, *Pakistan* 66 D6
Meknès, *Morocco* 78 B4
Meko, *Nigeria* 83 D5
Mekong →, *Asia* 65 H6
Mekongga, *Indonesia* 63 E6
Mekvari = Kür →, *Azerbaijan* 73 C13
Mel, *Italy* 29 B9
Melagiri Hills, *India* 66 N10
Melaka, *Malaysia* 65 L4
Melalap, *Malaysia* 62 C5
Mélambes, *Greece* 36 D6
Melanesia, *Pac. Oc.* 96 H7
Melbourne, *Australia* 95 F4
Melbourne, *U.S.A.* 109 L5
Melchor Múzquiz, *Mexico* 118 B4
Melchor Ocampo, *Mexico* 118 C4
Méldola, *Italy* 29 D9
Meldorf, *Germany* 24 A5
Melegnano, *Italy* 28 C6
Melenci, *Serbia, Yug.* 42 E5
Melenki, *Russia* 48 C5
Mélèzes →, *Canada* 101 C12
Melfi, *Italy* 31 B8
Melfort, *Canada* 105 C8
Melfort, *Zimbabwe* 87 F3
Melgaço, *Portugal* 34 C2
Melgar de Fernamental, *Spain* 34 C6
Melhus, *Norway* 8 E14
Melide, *Spain* 34 C2
Meligalá, *Greece* 38 D3
Melilla, *N. Afr.* 78 A5
Melíli, *Italy* 31 E8
Melipilla, *Chile* 126 C1
Mélissa, Ákra, *Greece* 36 D6
Mélissa Óros, *Greece* 39 D8
Melita, *Canada* 105 D8
Mélito di Porto Salvo, *Italy* 31 E8
Melitopol, *Ukraine* 47 J8
Melk, *Austria* 26 C8
Mellan Fryken, *Sweden* 10 E7
Mellansel, *Sweden* 8 E18
Mellbystrand, *Sweden* 11 H6
Melle, *France* 20 B3
Melle, *Germany* 24 C4
Mellen, *U.S.A.* 112 B9
Mellerud, *Sweden* 11 F6
Mellette, *U.S.A.* 112 C5
Mellid = Melide, *Spain* 34 C2
Mellieha, *Malta* 36 D1
Mellit, *Sudan* 81 E2
Mellrichstadt, *Germany* 24 E6
Melnik, *Bulgaria* 40 E7
Mělník, *Czech Rep.* 26 A7
Melo, *Uruguay* 127 C5
Melolo, *Indonesia* 63 F6
Melouprey, *Cambodia* 64 F5
Melrose, *N.S.W., Australia* 95 E4
Melrose, *W. Austral., Australia* 93 E3
Melrose, *U.K.* 14 F6

Melrose, *U.S.A.* 113 H3
Melstone, *U.S.A.* 114 C10
Melsungen, *Germany* 24 D5
Melton Mowbray, *U.K.* 12 E7
Melun, *France* 19 D9
Melut, *Sudan* 81 E3
Melville, *Canada* 105 C8
Melville, C., *Australia* 94 A3
Melville, L., *Canada* 103 B8
Melville B., *Australia* 94 A2
Melville I., *Australia* 92 B5
Melville I., *Canada* 4 B2
Melville Pen., *Canada* 101 B11
Melvin →, *Ireland* 15 B3
Memaliaj, *Albania* 40 F3
Memba, *Mozam.* 87 E5
Memboro, *Indonesia* 63 F5
Membrilla, *Spain* 35 G7
Memel = Klaipėda, *Lithuania* 9 J19
Memel, *S. Africa* 89 D4
Memmingen, *Germany* 25 H6
Mempawah, *Indonesia* 62 D3
Memphis, *Tenn., U.S.A.* 113 H10
Memphis, *Tex., U.S.A.* 113 H4
Mena, *Ukraine* 47 G7
Mena, *U.S.A.* 113 H7
Mena →, *Ethiopia* 81 F5
Menai Strait, *U.K.* 12 D3
Ménaka, *Mali* 83 B5
Menan = Chao Phraya →, *Thailand* 64 F3
Menarandra →, *Madag.* 89 D7
Menard, *U.S.A.* 113 K5
Menasha, *U.S.A.* 108 C1
Mendawai →, *Indonesia* 62 E4
Mende, *France* 20 D7
Mendebo, *Ethiopia* 81 F4
Menden, *Germany* 24 D3
Menderes →, *Turkey* 39 C9
Mendez, *Mexico* 119 B5
Mendhar, *India* 69 C6
Mendi, *Ethiopia* 81 F4
Mendip Hills, *U.K.* 13 F5
Mendocino, *U.S.A.* 116 G2
Mendocino, C., *U.S.A.* 114 F1
Mendota, *Calif., U.S.A.* 116 J6
Mendota, *Ill., U.S.A.* 112 E10
Mendoza, *Argentina* 126 C2
Mendoza □, *Argentina* 126 C2
Mene Grande, *Venezuela* 124 B4
Menemen, *Turkey* 39 C9
Menen, *Belgium* 17 D3
Menfi, *Italy* 30 E5
Mengcheng, *China* 59 A11
Mengdingjie, *China* 58 F2
Mengeš, *Slovenia* 29 B11
Menggala, *Indonesia* 62 E3
Menghai, *China* 58 G3
Mengíbar, *Spain* 35 H7
Mengjin, *China* 56 G7
Mengla, *China* 58 G3
Menglian, *China* 58 F2
Mengshan, *China* 59 E8
Mengyin, *China* 57 G9
Mengzhe, *China* 58 F3
Mengzi, *China* 58 F4
Menihek L., *Canada* 103 B6
Menin = Menen, *Belgium* 17 D3
Menindee, *Australia* 95 E3
Menindee L., *Australia* 95 E3
Meningie, *Australia* 95 F2
Menlo Park, *U.S.A.* 116 H4
Menominee, *U.S.A.* 108 C2
Menominee →, *U.S.A.* 108 C2
Menomonie, *U.S.A.* 112 C9
Menongue, *Angola* 85 G3
Menorca, *Spain* 37 B11
Mentakab, *Malaysia* 65 L4
Mentawai, Kepulauan, *Indonesia* 62 E1
Menton, *France* 21 E11
Mentor, *U.S.A.* 110 E3
Menzies, *Australia* 93 E3
Me'ona, *Israel* 75 B4
Meoqui, *Mexico* 118 B3
Mepaco, *Mozam.* 87 F3
Meppel, *Neths.* 17 B6
Meppen, *Germany* 24 C3
Mequinenza, *Spain* 32 D5
Mequinenza, Embalse de, *Spain* 32 D5
Mer, *France* 18 E8
Merabéllou, Kólpos, *Greece* 36 D7
Meramangye, L., *Australia* 93 E5
Meran = Merano, *Italy* 29 B8
Merano, *Italy* 29 B8
Merate, *Italy* 28 C6
Merauke, *Indonesia* 63 F10
Merbein, *Australia* 95 E3
Merca, *Somali Rep.* 74 G3
Mercato Saraceno, *Italy* 29 E9
Merced, *U.S.A.* 116 H6
Merced Pk., *U.S.A.* 116 H7
Mercedes, *Buenos Aires, Argentina* 126 C4
Mercedes, *Corrientes, Argentina* 126 B4
Mercedes, *San Luis, Argentina* 126 C2
Mercedes, *Uruguay* 126 C4
Mercedes, *Chile* 126 B1
Mercer, *N.Z.* 91 G5
Mercer, *U.S.A.* 110 E4
Mercury, *U.S.A.* 117 J11

Mercy C., Canada 101 B13
Merdrignac, France 18 D4
Mere, U.K. 13 F5
Meredith, C., Falk. Is. . 128 G4
Meredith, L., U.S.A. 113 H4
Merefa, Ukraine 47 H9
Merei, Romania 43 E11
Merga = Nukheila, Sudan 80 D2
Mergui, Burma 64 F2
Mergui Arch. = Myeik
  Kyunzu, Burma 65 G1
Meriç, Turkey 41 E10
Meriç →, Turkey 41 F10
Mérida, Mexico 119 C7
Mérida, Spain 35 G4
Mérida, Venezuela 124 B4
Mérida, Cord. de,
  Venezuela 122 C3
Meriden, U.K. 13 E6
Meriden, U.S.A. 111 E12
Meridian, Calif., U.S.A. .. 116 F5
Meridian, Idaho, U.S.A. .. 114 E5
Meridian, Miss., U.S.A. .. 109 J1
Meridian, Tex., U.S.A. ... 113 K6
Mérignac, France 20 D3
Mering, Germany 25 G6
Meriruma, Brazil 125 C8
Merkel, U.S.A. 113 J5
Mermaid Reef, Australia . 92 C2
Merowe, Sudan 80 D3
Merredin, Australia 93 F2
Merrick, U.K. 14 F4
Merrickville, Canada ... 111 B9
Merrill, Oreg., U.S.A. ... 114 E3
Merrill, Wis., U.S.A. 112 C10
Merriman, U.S.A. 112 D4
Merritt, Canada 104 C4
Merriwa, Australia 95 E5
Merriwagga, Australia ... 95 E4
Merry I., Canada 102 A4
Merrygoen, Australia ... 95 E4
Merryville, U.S.A. 113 K8
Mersa Fatma, Eritrea ... 81 E5
Mersch, Lux. 17 E6
Merse →, Italy 29 E8
Mersea I., U.K. 13 F8
Merseburg, Germany ... 24 D7
Mersey →, U.K. 12 D4
Merseyside □, U.K. 12 D4
Mersin, Turkey 72 D6
Mersing, Malaysia 65 L4
Merta, India 68 F6
Merthyr Tydfil, U.K. ... 13 F4
Merthyr Tydfil □, U.K. .. 13 F4
Mértola, Portugal 35 H3
Mertzon, U.S.A. 113 K4
Méru, France 19 C9
Meru, Kenya 86 B4
Meru, Tanzania 86 C4
Meru □, Kenya 86 B4
Merville, France 19 B9
Méry-sur-Seine, France .. 19 D10
Merzifon, Turkey 72 B6
Merzig, Germany 25 F2
Mesa, U.S.A. 115 K8
Mesagne, Italy 31 B10
Mesanagrós, Greece 36 C9
Mesaoría □, Cyprus 36 D12
Mesarás, Kólpos, Greece . 36 D6
Meschede, Germany 24 D4
Mescit, Turkey 73 B9
Mesfinto, Ethiopia 81 E4
Mesgouez, L., Canada .. 102 B5
Meshchovsk, Russia 46 E8
Meshed = Mashhad, Iran . 71 B8
Meshoppen, U.S.A. 111 E8
Meshra er Req, Sudan .. 81 F2
Mesick, U.S.A. 108 C3
Mesilinka →, Canada ... 104 B4
Mesilla, U.S.A. 115 K10
Meslay-du-Maine, France . 18 E6
Mesocco, Switz. 25 J5
Mesolóngion, Greece 38 C3
Mesopotamia = Al Jazirah,
  Iraq 70 C5
Mesopotámon, Greece ... 38 B2
Mesoraca, Italy 31 C9
Mésou Volímais = Volímai,
  Greece 38 D2
Mesquite, U.S.A. 115 H6
Mess Cr. →, Canada ... 104 B2
Messac, France 18 E5
Messalo →, Mozam. 87 E4
Méssaména, Cameroon .. 83 E7
Messeue, Greece 38 D3
Messina, Italy 31 D8
Messina, S. Africa 89 C5
Messina, Str. di, Italy ... 31 D8
Messini, Greece 38 D4
Messíni, Greece 38 D3
Messiniakós Kólpos, Greece 38 E4
Messkirch, Germany ... 25 H5
Messonghi, Greece 36 B3
Mesta →, Bulgaria 40 E7
Mestá, Ákra, Greece 39 C7
Mestanza, Spain 35 G6
Mestre, Italy 29 C9
Mesudiye, Turkey 72 B7
Meta →, S. Amer. 122 C4
Metairie, U.S.A. 113 L9
Metalici, Munții, Romania 42 D7
Metaline Falls, U.S.A. .. 114 B5
Metallifere, Colline, Italy . 28 E8
Metán, Argentina 126 B3
Metangula, Mozam. 87 E3
Metauro →, Italy 29 E10
Metema, Ethiopia 81 E4

Metengobalame, Mozam. . 87 E3
Méthana, Greece 38 D5
Methóni, Greece 38 E3
Methven, N.Z. 91 K3
Methy L., Canada 105 B7
Metil, Mozam. 87 F4
Metkovets, Bulgaria 40 C7
Metković, Croatia 29 E14
Metlakatla, U.S.A. 104 B2
Metlika, Slovenia 29 C12
Metropolis, U.S.A. 113 G10
Métsovon, Greece 38 B3
Mettur Dam, India 66 P10
Metz, France 19 C13
Metzingen, Germany ... 25 G5
Meulaboh, Indonesia ... 62 D1
Meung-sur-Loire, France . 19 E8
Meureudu, Indonesia ... 62 C1
Meurthe →, France 19 D13
Meurthe-et-Moselle □,
  France 19 D13
Meuse □, France 19 C12
Meuse →, Europe 17 D5
Meuselwitz, Germany ... 24 D8
Mexia, U.S.A. 113 K6
Mexiana, I., Brazil 125 D9
Mexicali, Mexico 118 A1
Mexican Plateau, Mexico . 98 G9
México, Mexico 119 D5
Mexico, Maine, U.S.A. ... 111 B14
Mexico, Mo., U.S.A. 112 F9
México □, Mexico 118 D5
Mexico ■, Cent. Amer. .. 118 C4
Mexico, G. of, Cent. Amer. 119 C7
Meyenburg, Germany ... 24 B8
Meymac, France 20 C6
Meymaneh, Afghan. 66 B4
Meyrueis, France 20 D7
Meyssac, France 20 C5
Meyzieu, France 21 C8
Mezdra, Bulgaria 40 C7
Mèze, France 20 E7
Mezen, Russia 50 C5
Mezen →, Russia 50 C5
Mézenc, Mt., France ... 21 D8
Mezeş, Munții, Romania . 42 C8
Mezha →, Russia 46 E6
Mézidon-Canon, France .. 18 C6
Mézières-en-Brenne, France 20 B5
Mézilhac, France 21 D8
Mézin, France 20 D4
Mezöberény, Hungary .. 42 D6
Mezöfalva, Hungary 42 D3
Mezöhegyes, Hungary ... 42 D5
Mezökovácsháza, Hungary 42 D5
Mezökövesd, Hungary ... 42 C5
Mézos, France 20 D2
Mezötúr, Hungary 42 C5
Mezquital, Mexico 118 C4
Mezzolombardo, Italy ... 28 B8
Mgeta, Tanzania 87 D4
Mglin, Russia 47 F7
Mhlaba Hills, Zimbabwe . 87 F3
Mhow, India 68 H6
Miahuatlán, Mexico 119 D5
Miajadas, Spain 35 F5
Miallo, Australia 94 B4
Miami, Ariz., U.S.A. ... 115 K8
Miami, Fla., U.S.A. 109 N5
Miami, Tex., U.S.A. 113 H4
Miami →, U.S.A. 108 F3
Miami Beach, U.S.A. ... 109 N5
Mian Xian, China 56 H4
Mianchi, China 56 G6
Miandowāb, Iran 70 B5
Miandrivazo, Madag. ... 89 B8
Miāneh, Iran 70 B5
Mianning, China 58 C4
Mianwali, Pakistan 68 C4
Mianyang, Hubei, China . 59 B9
Mianyang, Sichuan, China 58 B5
Mianzhu, China 58 B5
Miaoli, Taiwan 59 E13
Miarinarivo, Madag. ... 89 B8
Miass, Russia 50 D7
Miasteczko Krajeńskie,
  Poland 45 E4
Miastko, Poland 44 E3
Micăsasa, Romania 43 D9
Michalovce, Slovak Rep. . 27 C14
Michigan □, U.S.A. 108 C3
Michigan, L., U.S.A. ... 108 D2
Michigan City, U.S.A. ... 108 E2
Michikamau L., Canada . 103 B7
Michipicoten, Canada ... 102 C3
Michipicoten I., Canada . 102 C2
Michoacan □, Mexico ... 118 D4
Michurin, Bulgaria 41 D11
Michurinsk, Russia 48 D5
Miclere, Australia 94 C4
Mico, Pta., Nic. 120 D3
Micronesia, Federated
  States of ■, Pac. Oc. .. 96 G7
Midai, Indonesia 65 L6
Midale, Canada 105 D8
Middelburg, Neths. 17 C3
Middelburg, Eastern Cape,
  S. Africa 88 E4
Middelburg, Mpumalanga,
  S. Africa 89 D4
Middelfart, Denmark ... 11 J3
Middelwit, S. Africa 88 C4
Middle Alkali L., U.S.A. . 114 F3
Middle Fork Feather →,
  U.S.A. 116 F5
Middle I., Australia 93 F3
Middle Loup →, U.S.A. . 112 E5

Middleboro, U.S.A. 111 E14
Middleburg, N.Y., U.S.A. . 111 D10
Middleburg, Pa., U.S.A. . 110 F7
Middlebury, U.S.A. 111 B11
Middleport, U.S.A. 108 F4
Middlesboro, U.S.A. 109 G4
Middlesbrough, U.K. ... 12 C6
Middlesbrough □, U.K. . 12 C6
Middlesex, Belize 120 C2
Middlesex, U.S.A. 111 F10
Middleton, Australia ... 94 C3
Middleton, Canada 103 D6
Middletown, U.K. 15 B5
Middletown, Calif., U.S.A. 116 G4
Middletown, Conn., U.S.A. 111 E12
Middletown, N.Y., U.S.A. . 111 E10
Middletown, Ohio, U.S.A. 108 F3
Middletown, Pa., U.S.A. . 111 F8
Midhurst, U.K. 13 G7
Midi, Canal du →, France 20 E5
Midi d'Ossau, Pic du,
  France 20 F3
Midi-Pyrénées □, France . 20 E5
Midland, Canada 102 D4
Midland, Calif., U.S.A. .. 117 M12
Midland, Mich., U.S.A. .. 108 D3
Midland, Pa., U.S.A. ... 110 F4
Midland, Tex., U.S.A. ... 113 K3
Midlands □, Zimbabwe . 87 F2
Midleton, Ireland 15 E3
Midlothian, U.S.A. 113 J6
Midlothian □, U.K. 14 F5
Midongy, Tangorombohitr'
  i, Madag. 89 C8
Midongy Atsimo, Madag. . 89 C8
Midou →, France 20 E3
Midouze →, France 20 E3
Midsayap, Phil. 61 H6
Midu, China 58 E3
Midway Is., Pac. Oc. ... 96 E10
Midway Wells, U.S.A. .. 117 N11
Midwest, U.S.A. 107 B9
Midwest, Wyo., U.S.A. .. 114 E10
Midwest City, U.S.A. ... 113 H6
Midyat, Turkey 73 D9
Midzör, Bulgaria 40 C6
Mie □, Japan 55 G8
Miechów, Poland 45 H7
Miedwie, Jezioro, Poland . 45 E1
Międzychód, Poland 45 F2
Międzylesie, Poland 45 H3
Międzyrzec Podlaski,
  Poland 45 G9
Międzyrzecz, Poland ... 45 F2
Międzyzdroje, Poland ... 44 E1
Miejska Górka, Poland .. 45 G3
Miélan, France 20 E4
Mielec, Poland 45 H8
Mienga, Angola 88 B2
Miercurea-Ciuc, Romania . 43 D10
Miercurea Sibiului,
  Romania 43 E8
Mieres, Spain 34 B5
Mieroszów, Poland 45 H3
Mieso, Ethiopia 81 F5
Mifflintown, U.S.A. 110 F7
Mifraz Ḥefa, Israel 75 C4
Migennes, France 19 E10
Migliarino, Italy 29 D8
Miguel Alemán, Presa,
  Mexico 119 D5
Miguelturra, Spain 35 G7
Mihăileni, Romania ... 43 C11
Mihăilești, Romania ... 43 F10
Mihailovca, Moldova ... 43 D13
Mihalgazi, Turkey 39 A12
Mihaliççık, Turkey 72 C4
Mihara, Japan 55 G6
Miheşu de Cîmpie,
  Romania 43 D9
Mijas, Spain 35 J6
Mikese, Tanzania 86 D4
Mikha-Tskhakaya =
  Senaki, Georgia 49 J6
Mikhailovka =
  Mykhaylivka, Ukraine . 47 J8
Mikhaylov, Russia 46 E10
Mikhaylovgrad = Montana,
  Bulgaria 40 C7
Mikhaylovka, Russia ... 48 E6
Mikhnevo, Russia 46 E9
Mikínai, Greece 38 D4
Mikkeli, Finland 9 F22
Mikkwa →, Canada ... 104 B6
Mikniya, Sudan 81 D3
Mikolajki, Poland 44 E8
Míkonos, Greece 39 D7
Mikrí Préspa, Límni,
  Greece 40 F5
Mikrón Dhérion, Greece . 41 E10
Mikulov, Czech Rep. ... 27 C9
Mikumi, Tanzania 86 D4
Milaca, U.S.A. 112 C8
Milagro, Ecuador 124 D3
Milagros, Phil. 61 E5
Milan = Milano, Italy .. 28 C6
Milan, Mo., U.S.A. 112 E8
Milan, Tenn., U.S.A. ... 109 H1
Milang, Australia 95 E2
Milange, Mozam. 87 F4
Milano, Italy 28 C6
Milâs, Turkey 39 D9
Mílatos, Greece 36 D7
Milazzo, Italy 31 D8

Milbank, U.S.A. 112 C6
Milden, Canada 105 C7
Mildenhall, U.K. 13 E8
Mildmay, Canada 110 B3
Mildura, Australia 95 E3
Mile, China 58 E4
Miléai, Greece 38 B5
Miles, Australia 95 D5
Miles, U.S.A. 113 K4
Miles City, U.S.A. 112 B2
Mileşti, Moldova 43 C13
Milestone, Canada 105 D8
Mileto, Italy 31 D9
Miletto, Mte., Italy 31 A7
Miletus, Turkey 39 D9
Mileura, Australia 93 E2
Milevsko, Czech Rep. ... 26 B7
Milford, Calif., U.S.A. .. 116 E6
Milford, Conn., U.S.A. .. 111 E11
Milford, Del., U.S.A. ... 108 F8
Milford, Mass., U.S.A. .. 111 D13
Milford, Pa., U.S.A. 111 E10
Milford, Utah, U.S.A. ... 115 G7
Milford Haven, U.K. ... 13 F2
Milford Sd., N.Z. 91 L1
Milgun, Australia 93 D2
Milḥ, Baḥr al, Iraq 70 C4
Milicz, Poland 45 G4
Miling, Australia 93 F2
Militello in Val di Catánia,
  Italy 31 E7
Milk →, U.S.A. 114 B10
Milk, Wadi el →, Sudan . 80 D3
Milk River, Canada 104 D6
Mill City, U.S.A. 114 D2
Mill I., Antarctica 5 C8
Mill Valley, U.S.A. 116 H4
Millárs →, Spain 32 F4
Millau, France 20 D7
Millbridge, Canada 110 B7
Millbrook, Canada 110 B6
Mille Lacs, L. des, Canada 102 C1
Mille Lacs L., U.S.A. ... 112 B8
Milledgeville, U.S.A. ... 109 J4
Millen, U.S.A. 109 J5
Miller, U.S.A. 112 C5
Millerovo, Russia 49 F5
Millersburg, Ohio, U.S.A. 110 F3
Millersburg, Pa., U.S.A. . 110 F8
Millerton, U.S.A. 111 E11
Millerton L., U.S.A. ... 116 J7
Millevaches, Plateau de,
  France 20 C6
Millicent, Australia 95 F3
Millinocket, U.S.A. 103 C6
Millmerran, Australia .. 95 D5
Millom, U.K. 12 C4
Mills L., Canada 104 A5
Millsboro, U.S.A. 110 G5
Milltown Malbay, Ireland . 15 D2
Millville, U.S.A. 108 F8
Millwood L., U.S.A. ... 113 J8
Milna, Croatia 29 E13
Milne →, Australia 94 C2
Milnor, U.S.A. 112 B6
Milo, Canada 104 C6
Mílos, Greece 38 E6
Miłosław, Poland 45 F4
Milot, Albania 40 E3
Milparinka P.O., Australia 95 D3
Miltenberg, Germany ... 25 F5
Milton, Canada 110 C5
Milton, N.Z. 91 M2
Milton, Calif., U.S.A. .. 116 G6
Milton, Fla., U.S.A. 109 K2
Milton, Pa., U.S.A. 110 F8
Milton-Freewater, U.S.A. 114 D4
Milton Keynes, U.K. ... 13 E7
Milton Keynes □, U.K. . 13 E7
Milverton, Canada 110 C4
Milwaukee, U.S.A. 108 D2
Milwaukee Deep, Atl. Oc. 121 C6
Milwaukie, U.S.A. 116 E4
Mim, Ghana 82 D4
Mimizan, France 20 D2
Mimoň, Czech Rep. 26 A7
Min Jiang →, Fujian,
  China 59 E12
Min Jiang →, Sichuan,
  China 58 C5
Min Xian, China 56 G3
Mina, U.S.A. 115 G4
Mina Pirquitas, Argentina 126 A2
Mīnā Su'ud, Si. Arabia . 71 D6
Mīnā'al Aḥmadī, Kuwait . 71 D6
Mīnāb, Iran 71 E8
Minago →, Canada ... 105 C9
Minaki, Canada 105 D10
Minamata, Japan 55 H5
Minami-Tori-Shima,
  Pac. Oc. 96 E7
Minas, Uruguay 127 C4
Minas, Sierra de las,
  Guatemala 120 C2
Minas Basin, Canada ... 103 C7
Minas de Rio Tinto =
  Minas de Riotinto, Spain 35 H4
Minas de Riotinto, Spain . 35 H4
Minas Gerais □, Brazil . 125 G9
Minatitlán, Mexico 119 D6
Minbu, Burma 67 J19
Mincio →, Italy 28 C7
Minčol, Slovak Rep. ... 27 B13
Mindanao, Phil. 61 H6
Mindanao Sea = Bohol
  Sea, Phil. 63 C6
Mindanao Trench, Pac. Oc. 61 F7

Mindel →, Germany 25 G6
Mindelheim, Germany .. 25 G6
Minden, Canada 110 B6
Minden, Germany 24 C4
Minden, La., U.S.A. 113 J8
Minden, Nev., U.S.A. ... 116 G7
Mindiptana, Indonesia .. 63 F10
Mindoro, Phil. 61 E4
Mindoro Str., Phil. 61 E4
Mine, Japan 55 G5
Minehead, U.K. 13 F4
Mineola, U.S.A. 113 J7
Mineral King, U.S.A. .. 116 J8
Mineral Wells, U.S.A. .. 113 J5
Mineralnyye Vody, Russia 49 H6
Minersville, Pa., U.S.A. . 111 F8
Minersville, Utah, U.S.A. 115 G7
Minerva, U.S.A. 110 F3
Minervino Murge, Italy . 31 A9
Minetto, U.S.A. 111 C8
Mingäçevir, Azerbaijan .. 49 K8
Mingäçevir Su Anbarı,
  Azerbaijan 49 K8
Mingan, Canada 103 B7
Mingechaur = Mingäçevir,
  Azerbaijan 49 K8
Mingechaurskoye Vdkhr. =
  Mingäçevir Su Anbarı,
  Azerbaijan 49 K8
Mingela, Australia 94 B4
Mingenew, Australia ... 93 E2
Mingera Cr. →, Australia 94 C2
Minggang, China 59 A10
Mingin, Burma 67 H19
Mingir, Moldova 43 D13
Minglanilla, Spain 33 F3
Minglun, China 58 E7
Mingorria, Spain 34 E6
Mingt'iehkaitafan =
  Mintaka Pass, Pakistan . 69 A6
Mingxi, China 59 D11
Mingyuegue, China 57 C15
Minho = Miño →, Spain . 34 D2
Minho, Portugal 34 D2
Minhou, China 59 E12
Miniçevo, Serbia, Yug. ... 42 G7
Minidoka, U.S.A. 114 E7
Minigwal, L., Australia . 93 E3
Minilya, Australia 93 D1
Minilya →, Australia ... 93 D1
Minipi, L., Canada 103 B7
Mink L., Canada 104 A5
Minna, Nigeria 83 D6
Minneapolis, Kans., U.S.A. 112 F6
Minneapolis, Minn., U.S.A. 112 C8
Minnedosa, Canada ... 105 C9
Minnesota □, U.S.A. ... 112 B8
Minnie Creek, Australia . 93 D2
Minnipa, Australia 95 E2
Minnitaki L., Canada .. 102 C1
Mino, Japan 55 G8
Miño, Spain 34 B2
Miño →, Spain 34 D2
Minoa, Greece 39 F7
Minorca = Menorca, Spain 37 B11
Minore, Australia 95 E4
Minot, U.S.A. 112 A4
Minqin, China 56 E2
Minqing, China 59 D12
Minsen, Germany 24 B3
Minsk, Belarus 46 F4
Mińsk Mazowiecki, Poland 45 F8
Mintaka Pass, Pakistan . 69 A6
Minton, Canada 105 D8
Minturn, U.S.A. 114 G10
Minturno, Italy 30 A6
Minūf, Egypt 80 H7
Minusinsk, Russia 51 D10
Minutang, India 67 E20
Minya el Qamh, Egypt .. 80 H7
Mionica, Serbia, Yug. ... 40 B4
Mionica, Bos.-H. 42 F3
Mir, Niger 83 C7
Mīr Kūh, Iran 71 E8
Mīr Shahdād, Iran 71 E8
Mira, Italy 29 C9
Mira, Portugal 34 E2
Mira →, Portugal 35 H2
Mira por vos Cay, Bahamas 121 B5
Mirabella Eclano, Italy . 31 A7
Miraj, India 66 L9
Miram Shah, Pakistan . 68 C4
Miramar, Argentina ... 126 D4
Miramar, Mozam. 89 C6
Miramas, France 21 E8
Mirambeau, France 20 C3
Miramichi B., Canada .. 103 C7
Miramont-de-Guyenne,
  France 20 D4
Miranda, Brazil 125 H7
Miranda →, Brazil 124 G7
Miranda de Ebro, Spain . 32 C2
Miranda do Corvo, Spain . 34 E2
Miranda do Douro,
  Portugal 34 D4
Mirande, France 20 E4
Mirandela, Portugal ... 34 D3
Mirando City, U.S.A. ... 113 M5
Mirándola, Italy 28 D8
Mirandópolis, Brazil ... 127 A5
Mirango, Malawi 87 E3
Mirani, Australia 94 C4
Mirano, Italy 29 C9
Miras, Albania 40 F4
Mirassol, Brazil 127 A6
Mirbāṭ, Oman 74 D5
Mirear, Egypt 80 C4

Mirebeau, Côte-d'Or, France 19 E12
Mirebeau, Vienne, France . 18 F7
Mirecourt, France 19 D13
Mirgorod = Myrhorod, Ukraine 47 H7
Miri, Malaysia 62 D4
Miriam Vale, Australia .. 94 C5
Miribel, France 19 G11
Mirim, L., S. Amer. 127 C5
Mirnyy, Russia 51 C12
Miroč, Serbia, Yug. 40 B6
Mirond L., Canada 105 B8
Mirosławiec, Poland 44 E3
Mirpur, Pakistan 69 C5
Mirpur Bibiwari, Pakistan 68 E2
Mirpur Khas, Pakistan ... 68 G3
Mirpur Sakro, Pakistan ... 68 G2
Mirria, Niger 83 C6
Mirror, Canada 104 C6
Mirsk, Poland 45 H2
Miryang, S. Korea 57 G15
Mirzapur, India 69 G10
Mirzapur-cum-Vindhyachal = Mirzapur, India 69 G10
Misantla, Mexico 119 D5
Misawa, Japan 54 D10
Miscou I., Canada 103 C7
Mish'āb, Ra'as al, Si. Arabia 71 D6
Mishan, China 60 B8
Mishawaka, U.S.A. 108 E2
Mishbih, Gebel, Egypt ... 80 C3
Mishima, Japan 55 G9
Misión, Mexico 117 N10
Misiones □, Argentina ... 127 B5
Misiones □, Paraguay ... 126 B4
Miskah, Si. Arabia 70 E4
Miskitos, Cayos, Nic. 120 D3
Miskolc, Hungary 42 B5
Misoke, Dem. Rep. of the Congo 86 C2
Misool, Indonesia 63 E8
Misrātah, Libya 79 B9
Missanabie, Canada 102 C3
Missinaibi →, Canada ... 102 B3
Missinaibi L., Canada ... 102 C3
Mission, S. Dak., U.S.A. . 112 D4
Mission, Tex., U.S.A. ... 113 M5
Mission City, Canada 104 D4
Mission Viejo, U.S.A. ... 117 M9
Missisa L., Canada 102 B2
Mississagi →, Canada ... 102 C3
Mississippi □, U.S.A. ... 113 J10
Mississippi →, U.S.A. ... 113 L10
Mississippi L., Canada ... 111 A8
Mississippi River Delta, U.S.A. 113 L9
Mississippi Sd., U.S.A. ... 113 K10
Missoula, U.S.A. 114 C7
Missouri □, U.S.A. 112 F8
Missouri →, U.S.A. 112 F9
Missouri Valley, U.S.A. .. 112 E7
Mist, U.S.A. 116 E3
Mistake B., Canada 105 A10
Mistassini →, Canada ... 103 C5
Mistassini L., Canada ... 102 B5
Mistastin L., Canada 103 A7
Mistatim, Canada 105 C8
Mistelbach, Austria 27 C9
Misterbianco, Italy 31 E8
Mistretta, Italy 31 E7
Misty L., Canada 105 B8
Misurata = Misrātah, Libya 79 B9
Mît Ghamr, Egypt 80 H7
Mitatib, Sudan 81 D4
Mitchell, Australia 95 D4
Mitchell, Canada 110 C3
Mitchell, Ind., U.S.A. ... 108 F2
Mitchell, Nebr., U.S.A. .. 112 E3
Mitchell, Oreg., U.S.A. .. 114 D3
Mitchell, S. Dak., U.S.A. . 112 D6
Mitchell →, Australia 94 B3
Mitchell, Mt., U.S.A. 109 H4
Mitchell Ranges, Australia 94 A2
Mitchelstown, Ireland ... 15 D3
Mitha Tiwana, Pakistan . 68 C5
Míthimna, Greece 39 B8
Mitilíni, Greece 39 B8
Mitilinoí, Greece 39 D8
Mito, Japan 55 F10
Mitrofanovka, Russia 47 H10
Mitrovica = Kosovska Mitrovica, Serbia, Yug. . 40 D4
Mitsinjo, Madag. 89 B8
Mitsiwa, Eritrea 81 D4
Mitsiwa Channel, Eritrea . 81 D5
Mitsukaidō, Japan 55 F9
Mittagong, Australia 95 E5
Mittelberg, Austria 26 D3
Mittelfranken □, Germany 25 F6
Mittellandkanal →, Germany 24 C4
Mittenwalde, Germany .. 24 C9
Mittersill, Austria 26 D5
Mitterteich, Germany ... 25 F8
Mittweida, Germany 24 E8
Mitú, Colombia 124 C4
Mitumba, Tanzania 86 D3
Mitumba, Mts., Dem. Rep. of the Congo 86 D2
Mitwaba, Dem. Rep. of the Congo 87 D2
Mityana, Uganda 86 B3
Mixteco →, Mexico 119 D5

Miyagi □, Japan 54 E10
Miyâh, W. el →, Egypt .. 80 C3
Miyah, W. el →, Syria .. 70 C3
Miyake-Jima, Japan 55 G9
Miyako, Japan 54 E10
Miyako-Jima, Japan 55 M2
Miyako-Rettō, Japan ... 55 M2
Miyakonojō, Japan 55 J5
Miyanoura-Dake, Japan . 55 J5
Miyazaki, Japan 55 J5
Miyazaki □, Japan 55 H5
Miyazu, Japan 55 G7
Miyet, Bahr el = Dead Sea, Asia 75 D4
Miyi, China 58 D4
Miyoshi, Japan 55 G6
Miyun, China 56 D9
Miyun Shuiku, China 57 D9
Mizdah, Libya 79 B8
Mizen Hd., Cork, Ireland . 15 E2
Mizen Hd., Wick., Ireland 15 D5
Mizhi, China 56 F6
Mizil, Romania 43 F11
Mizoram □, India 67 H18
Mizpe Ramon, Israel 75 E3
Mizusawa, Japan 54 E10
Mjällby, Sweden 11 H8
Mjöbäck, Sweden 11 G6
Mjölby, Sweden 11 F9
Mjörn, Sweden 11 G6
Mjøsa, Norway 9 F14
Mkata, Tanzania 86 D4
Mkokotoni, Tanzania ... 86 D4
Mkomazi, Tanzania 86 C4
Mkomazi →, S. Africa .. 89 E5
Mkulwe, Tanzania 87 D3
Mkumbi, Ras, Tanzania . 86 D4
Mkushi, Zambia 87 E2
Mkushi River, Zambia ... 87 E2
Mkuze, S. Africa 89 D5
Mladá Boleslav, Czech Rep. 26 A7
Mladenovac, Serbia, Yug. . 40 B4
Mlala Hills, Tanzania 86 D3
Mlange = Mulanje, Malawi 87 F4
Mlava →, Serbia, Yug. .. 40 B5
Mława, Poland 45 E7
Mlinište, Bos.-H. 29 D13
Mljet, Croatia 29 F14
Mljetski Kanal, Croatia .. 29 F14
Młynary, Poland 44 D6
Mmabatho, S. Africa 88 D4
Mme, Cameroon 83 D7
Mnichovo Hradiště, Czech Rep. 26 A7
Mo i Rana, Norway 8 C16
Moa, Indonesia 63 F7
Moa →, S. Leone 82 D2
Moab, U.S.A. 115 G9
Moala, Fiji 91 D8
Moalie Park, Australia ... 95 D3
Moate, Ireland 15 C4
Moba, Dem. Rep. of the Congo 86 D2
Mobārakābād, Iran 71 D7
Mobārakīyeh, Iran 71 C6
Mobaye, C.A.R. 84 D4
Mobayi, Dem. Rep. of the Congo 84 D4
Moberly, U.S.A. 112 F8
Moberly →, Canada 104 B4
Mobile, U.S.A. 109 K1
Mobile B., U.S.A. 109 K2
Mobridge, U.S.A. 112 C4
Mobutu Sese Seko, L. = Albert L., Africa 86 B3
Moc Chau, Vietnam 64 B5
Moc Hoa, Vietnam 65 G5
Mocabe Kasari, Dem. Rep. of the Congo 87 D2
Moçambique, Mozam. ... 87 F5
Moçâmedes = Namibe, Angola 85 H2
Mochudi, Botswana 88 C4
Mocimboa da Praia, Mozam. 87 E5
Mociu, Romania 43 D9
Möckeln, Sweden 11 H8
Mockfjärd, Sweden 10 D8
Moclips, U.S.A. 116 C2
Mocoa, Colombia 124 C3
Mococa, Brazil 127 A6
Mocorito, Mexico 118 B3
Moctezuma, Mexico 118 B3
Moctezuma →, Mexico . 119 C5
Mocuba, Mozam. 87 F4
Mocúzari, Presa, Mexico . 118 B3
Modane, France 21 C10
Modasa, India 68 H5
Modder →, S. Africa 88 D3
Modderrivier, S. Africa .. 88 D3
Módena, Italy 28 D7
Modena, U.S.A. 115 H7
Modesto, U.S.A. 116 H6
Módica, Italy 31 F7
Mödling, Austria 27 C9
Modo, Sudan 81 F3
Modra, Slovak Rep. 27 C10
Modriča, Bos.-H. 42 F3
Moe, Australia 95 F4
Moebase, Mozam. 87 F4
Moëlan-sur-Mer, France . 18 E3
Moengo, Surinam 125 B8
Moffat, U.K. 14 F5
Moga, India 68 D6
Mogadishu = Muqdisho, Somali Rep. 74 G4

Mogador = Essaouira, Morocco 78 B4
Mogadouro, Portugal ... 34 D4
Mogalakwena →, S. Africa 89 C4
Mogami →, Japan 54 E10
Mogán, Canary Is. 37 G4
Mogaung, Burma 67 G20
Mogente = Moixent, Spain 33 G4
Mogho, Ethiopia 81 G5
Mogi das Cruzes, Brazil . 127 A6
Mogi-Guaçu →, Brazil .. 127 A6
Mogi-Mirim, Brazil 127 A6
Mogielnica, Poland 45 G7
Mogilev = Mahilyow, Belarus 46 F6
Mogilev-Podolskiy = Mohyliv-Podilskyy, Ukraine 47 H4
Mogilno, Poland 45 F4
Mogincual, Mozam. 87 F5
Mogliano Véneto, Italy .. 29 C9
Mogocha, Russia 51 D12
Mogok, Burma 67 H20
Mógoro, Italy 30 C1
Moguer, Spain 35 H4
Mogumber, Australia ... 93 F2
Mohács, Hungary 42 E3
Mohales Hoek, Lesotho . 88 E4
Mohall, U.S.A. 112 A4
Mohammadābād, Iran .. 71 B8
Mohave, L., U.S.A. 117 K12
Moheda, Sweden 11 G8
Mohawk →, U.S.A. 111 D11
Möhne →, Germany 24 D3
Mohoro, Tanzania 86 D4
Mohyliv-Podilskyy, Ukraine 47 H4
Moia, Sudan 81 F2
Moidart, L., U.K. 14 E3
Moineşti, Romania 43 D11
Moirans, France 21 C9
Moirans-en-Montagne, France 19 F12
Moíres, Greece 36 D6
Moisaküla, Estonia 9 G21
Moisie, Canada 103 B6
Moisie →, Canada 103 B6
Moissac, France 20 D5
Moita, Portugal 35 G2
Moixent, Spain 33 G4
Mojácar, Spain 33 H3
Mojados, Spain 34 D6
Mojave, U.S.A. 117 K8
Mojave Desert, U.S.A. .. 117 L10
Mojiang, China 58 F3
Mojkovac, Montenegro, Yug. 40 D3
Mojo, Bolivia 126 A2
Mojo, Ethiopia 81 F4
Mojokerto, Indonesia ... 63 G15
Mokai, N.Z. 91 H5
Mokambo, Dem. Rep. of the Congo 87 E2
Mokameh, India 69 G11
Mokelumne →, U.S.A. . 116 G5
Mokelumne Hill, U.S.A. . 116 G6
Mokhós, Greece 36 D7
Mokhotlong, Lesotho ... 89 D4
Möklinta, Sweden 10 D10
Mokokchung, India 67 F19
Mokpo, S. Korea 57 G14
Mokra Gora, Serbia, Yug. 40 D4
Mokronog, Slovenia 29 C12
Moksha →, Russia 48 C6
Mokshan, Russia 48 D7
Mol, Belgium 17 C5
Mola di Bari, Italy 31 A10
Mola, Croatia 29 D11
Moláoi, Greece 38 E4
Molara, Italy 30 B2
Molat, Croatia 29 D11
Molchanovo, Russia 50 D9
Mold, U.K. 12 D4
Moldavia = Moldova ■, Europe 43 C13
Moldavia, Romania 43 D12
Molde, Norway 8 E12
Moldova ■, Europe 43 C13
Moldova Nouă, Romania . 42 F6
Moldoveana, Vf., Romania 43 E9
Moldoviţa, Romania 43 C10
Mole →, U.K. 13 F7
Molepolole, Botswana .. 88 C4
Molfetta, Italy 31 A9
Molina de Aragón, Spain . 32 E3
Molina de Segura, Spain . 33 G3
Moline, U.S.A. 112 E9
Molinella, Italy 29 D8
Molinos, Argentina 126 B2
Moliro, Dem. Rep. of the Congo 86 D3
Moliterno, Italy 31 B8
Molkom, Sweden 10 E7
Mollahat, Bangla. 69 H13
Mölle, Sweden 11 H6
Molledo, Spain 34 B6
Mollendo, Peru 124 D3
Mollerin, L., Australia ... 93 F2
Mollerussa, Spain 32 D5
Mollina, Spain 35 H6
Mölln, Germany 24 B6
Mölltorp, Sweden 11 F8
Mölnlycke, Sweden 11 G6
Molochansk, Ukraine ... 47 J8
Molochnoye, Ozero, Ukraine 47 J8

Molodechno = Maladzyechna, Belarus . 46 E4
Molokai, U.S.A. 106 H16
Molong, Australia 95 E4
Molopo →, Africa 88 D3
Mólos, Greece 38 C4
Molotov = Perm, Russia . 50 D6
Molsheim, France 19 D14
Molson L., Canada 105 C9
Molteno, S. Africa 88 E4
Molu, Indonesia 63 F8
Molucca Sea, Indonesia . 63 E6
Moluccas = Maluku, Indonesia 63 E7
Moma, Dem. Rep. of the Congo 86 C1
Moma, Mozam. 87 F4
Mombasa, Kenya 86 C4
Mombetsu, Japan 54 B11
Mombuey, Spain 34 C4
Momchilgrad, Bulgaria .. 41 E9
Momi, Dem. Rep. of the Congo 86 C2
Mompós, Colombia 124 B4
Møn, Denmark 11 K6
Mona, Canal de la, W. Indies 121 C6
Mona, Isla, Puerto Rico . 121 C6
Mona, Pta., Costa Rica .. 120 E3
Monaco ■, Europe 21 E11
Monadhliath Mts., U.K. . 14 D4
Monaghan, Ireland 15 B5
Monaghan □, Ireland ... 15 B5
Monahans, U.S.A. 113 K3
Monapo, Mozam. 87 E5
Monar, L., U.K. 14 D3
Monarch Mt., Canada .. 104 C3
Monasterevin, Ireland .. 15 C4
Monastir = Bitola, Macedonia 40 E5
Moncada, Phil. 61 D4
Moncalieri, Italy 28 D4
Moncalvo, Italy 28 C5
Moncão, Portugal 34 C2
Moncarapacho, Portugal . 35 H3
Moncayo, Sierra del, Spain 32 D3
Mönchengladbach, Germany 24 D2
Monchique, Portugal ... 35 H2
Monclova, Mexico 118 B4
Moncontour, France ... 18 D4
Moncton, Canada 103 C7
Mondariz, Spain 34 C2
Mondego →, Portugal .. 34 E2
Mondego, C., Portugal .. 34 E2
Mondeodo, Indonesia .. 63 E6
Mondeville, France 18 C6
Mondolfo, Italy 29 E10
Mondoñedo, Spain 34 B3
Mondoví, Italy 28 D4
Mondovi, U.S.A. 112 C9
Mondragon, Phil. 61 E6
Mondragone, Italy 30 A6
Mondrain I., Australia .. 93 F3
Monduli □, Tanzania ... 86 C4
Monemvasía, Greece ... 38 E5
Monessen, U.S.A. 110 F5
Monesterio, Spain 35 G4
Monestier-de-Clermont, France 21 D9
Monett, U.S.A. 113 G8
Moneymore, U.K. 15 B5
Monflanquin, France ... 20 D4
Monforte, Portugal 35 F3
Monforte de Lemos, Spain 34 C3
Mong Hsu, Burma 67 J21
Mong Kung, Burma 67 J20
Mong Nai, Burma 67 J20
Mong Pawk, Burma 67 H21
Mong Ton, Burma 67 J21
Mong Wa, Burma 67 J22
Mong Yai, Burma 67 H21
Mongalla, Sudan 81 F3
Mongers, L., Australia .. 93 E2
Monghyr = Munger, India 69 G12
Mongibello = Etna, Italy . 31 E7
Mongo, Chad 79 F9
Mongolia ■, Asia 60 B5
Mongonu, Nigeria 83 C7
Mongu, Zambia 85 H4
Môngua, Angola 88 B2
Monifieth, U.K. 14 E6
Monistrol-sur-Loire, France 21 C8
Monkey Bay, Malawi ... 87 E4
Monkey River, Belize ... 119 D7
Mońki, Poland 44 E9
Monkira, Australia 94 C3
Monkoto, Dem. Rep. of the Congo 84 E4
Monmouth, U.K. 13 F5
Monmouth, U.S.A. 112 E9
Monmouthshire □, U.K. . 13 F5
Mono L., U.S.A. 116 H7
Monolith, U.S.A. 117 K8
Monólithos, Greece 36 C9
Monongahela, U.S.A. .. 110 F5
Monópoli, Italy 31 B10
Monor, Hungary 42 C4
Monóvar, Spain 33 G4
Monreal del Campo, Spain 32 E3
Monreale, Italy 30 D6
Monroe, La., U.S.A. 113 J8
Monroe, Mich., U.S.A. .. 108 E4
Monroe, N.C., U.S.A. ... 109 H5

Monroe, N.Y., U.S.A. ... 111 E10
Monroe, Utah, U.S.A. ... 115 G7
Monroe, Wash., U.S.A. .. 116 C5
Monroe, Wis., U.S.A. ... 112 D10
Monroe City, U.S.A. 112 F9
Monroeville, Ala., U.S.A. 109 K2
Monroeville, Pa., U.S.A. . 110 F5
Monrovia, Liberia 82 D2
Mons, Belgium 17 D3
Møns Klint, Denmark ... 11 K6
Monsaraz, Portugal 35 G3
Monse, Indonesia 63 E6
Monségur, France 20 D4
Monsélice, Italy 29 C8
Mönsterås, Sweden 11 G10
Mont Cenis, Col du, France 21 C10
Mont-de-Marsan, France . 20 E3
Mont-Joli, Canada 103 C6
Mont-Laurier, Canada .. 102 C4
Mont-roig del Camp, Spain 32 D5
Mont-St-Michel, Le = Le Mont-St-Michel, France . 18 D5
Mont Tremblant Prov. Park, Canada 102 C5
Montabaur, Germany ... 24 E3
Montagnac, France 20 E7
Montagnana, Italy 29 C8
Montagu, S. Africa 88 E3
Montagu I., Antarctica .. 5 B1
Montague, Canada 103 C7
Montague, U.S.A. 114 F2
Montague, I., Mexico ... 118 A2
Montague Ra., Australia . 93 E2
Montague Sd., Australia . 92 B4
Montaigu, France 18 F5
Montalbán, Spain 32 E4
Montalbo, Spain 32 F2
Montalegre, Portugal ... 34 D3
Montalto, Italy 31 D8
Montalto di Castro, Italy . 29 F8
Montalto Uffugo, Italy .. 31 C9
Montalvo, U.S.A. 117 L7
Montamarta, Spain 34 D5
Montana, Bulgaria 40 C7
Montana, Peru 124 E4
Montana □, Bulgaria ... 40 C7
Montana □, U.S.A. 114 C9
Montaña Clara, I., Canary Is. 37 E6
Montánchez, Spain 35 F4
Montargil, Portugal 35 F2
Montargis, France 19 E9
Montauban, France 20 D5
Montauk, U.S.A. 111 E13
Montauk Pt., U.S.A. ... 111 E13
Montbard, France 19 E11
Montbarrey, France 19 E12
Montbéliard, France ... 19 E13
Montblanc, Spain 32 D6
Montbrison, France 21 C8
Montcalm, Pic de, France . 20 F5
Montceau-les-Mines, France 19 F11
Montcenis, France 21 B8
Montclair, U.S.A. 111 F10
Montcornet, France 19 C11
Montcuq, France 20 D5
Montdidier, France 19 C9
Monte Albán, Mexico ... 119 D5
Monte Alegre, Brazil ... 125 D8
Monte Azul, Brazil 125 G10
Monte Bello Is., Australia 92 D2
Monte-Carlo, Monaco .. 21 E11
Monte Caseros, Argentina 126 C4
Monte Comán, Argentina 126 C2
Monte Cristi, Dom. Rep. . 121 C5
Monte Lindo →, Paraguay 126 A4
Monte Quemado, Argentina 126 B3
Monte Redondo, Portugal 34 F2
Monte Rio, U.S.A. 116 G4
Monte San Giovanni Campano, Italy 30 A6
Monte San Savino, Italy . 29 E8
Monte Sant' Ángelo, Italy 29 G12
Monte Santu, C. di, Italy . 30 B2
Monte Vista, U.S.A. ... 115 H10
Monteagudo, Argentina . 127 B5
Montealegre del Castillo, Spain 33 G3
Montebello, Canada 102 C5
Montebello Iónico, Italy . 31 E8
Montebelluna, Italy 29 C9
Montebourg, France ... 18 C5
Montecastrilli, Italy 29 F9
Montecatini Terme, Italy . 28 E7
Montecito, U.S.A. 117 L7
Montecristo, Italy 28 F7
Montefalco, Italy 29 F9
Montefiascone, Italy ... 29 F9
Montefrío, Spain 35 H7
Montegiórgio, Italy 29 E10
Montego Bay, Jamaica .. 120 C4
Montehermoso, Spain .. 34 E4
Montejicar, Spain 35 H7
Montejinnie, Australia .. 92 C5
Montélimar, France 21 D8
Montella, Italy 31 B8
Montellano, Spain 35 J5
Montello, U.S.A. 112 D10
Montemor-o-Novo, Portugal 35 G2
Montemor-o-Velho, Portugal 34 E2
Montemorelos, Mexico .. 119 B5
Montendre, France 20 C3
Montenegro, Brazil 127 B5

Montenegro □, *Yugoslavia* 40 D3
Montenero di Bisáccia,
  Italy 29 G11
Montepuez, *Mozam.* 87 E4
Montepuez →, *Mozam.* ... 87 E5
Montepulciano, *Italy* 29 E8
Montereale, *Italy* 29 F10
Montereau-Faut-Yonne,
  France 19 D9
Monterey, *U.S.A.* 116 J5
Monterey B., *U.S.A.* 116 J5
Montería, *Colombia* 124 B3
Monteros, *Argentina* 126 B2
Monterotondo, *Italy* 29 F9
Monterrey, *Mexico* 118 B4
Montes Claros, *Brazil* ... 125 G10
Montesano, *U.S.A.* 116 D3
Montesano sulla
  Marcellana, *Italy* 31 B8
Montesárchio, *Italy* 31 A7
Montescaglioso, *Italy* 31 B9
Montesilvano, *Italy* 29 F11
Montevarchi, *Italy* 29 E8
Montevideo, *Uruguay* 127 C4
Montevideo, *U.S.A.* 112 C7
Montezuma, *U.S.A.* 112 E8
Montfaucon, *France* 18 E5
Montfaucon-d'Argonne,
  France 19 C12
Montfaucon-en-Velay,
  France 21 C8
Montfort, *France* 18 D5
Montfort-le-Gesnois,
  France 18 D7
Montgenèvre, *France* 21 D10
Montgomery = Sahiwal,
  Pakistan 68 D5
Montgomery, *U.K.* 13 E4
Montgomery, *Ala., U.S.A.* 109 J2
Montgomery, *W. Va.,*
  U.S.A. 108 F5
Montguyon, *France* 20 C3
Monthermé, *France* 19 C11
Monthey, *Switz.* 25 J2
Monthois, *France* 19 C11
Monti, *Italy* 30 B2
Monticelli d'Ongina, *Italy* . 28 C6
Monticello, *Ark., U.S.A.* . 113 J9
Monticello, *Fla., U.S.A.* .. 109 K4
Monticello, *Ind., U.S.A.* .. 108 E2
Monticello, *Iowa, U.S.A.* .. 112 D9
Monticello, *Ky., U.S.A.* .. 109 G3
Monticello, *Minn., U.S.A.* . 112 C8
Monticello, *Miss., U.S.A.* . 113 K9
Monticello, *N.Y., U.S.A.* . 111 E10
Monticello, *Utah, U.S.A.* . 115 H9
Montichiari, *Italy* 28 C7
Montier-en-Der, *France* .. 19 D11
Montignac, *France* 20 C5
Montigny-les-Metz, *France* 19 C13
Montigny-sur-Aube, *France* 19 E11
Montijo, *Portugal* 35 G2
Montijo, *Spain* 35 G4
Montilla, *Spain* 35 H6
Montivilliers, *France* 18 C7
Montluçon, *France* 19 F9
Montmagny, *Canada* 103 C5
Montmarault, *France* 19 F9
Montmartre, *Canada* 105 C8
Montmédy, *France* 19 C12
Montmélian, *France* 21 C10
Montmirail, *France* 19 D10
Montmoreau-St-Cybard,
  France 20 C4
Montmorency, *Canada* ... 103 C5
Montmorillon, *France* ... 20 B4
Montmort-Lucy, *France* .. 19 D10
Monto, *Australia* 94 C5
Montoire-sur-le-Loir,
  France 18 E7
Montório al Vomano, *Italy* 29 F10
Montoro, *Spain* 35 G6
Montour Falls, *U.S.A.* ... 110 D8
Montpelier, *Idaho, U.S.A.* 114 E8
Montpelier, *Ohio, U.S.A.* . 108 E3
Montpelier, *Vt., U.S.A.* .. 111 B12
Montpellier, *France* 20 E7
Montpezat-de-Quercy,
  France 20 D5
Montpon-Ménestérol,
  France 20 D4
Montréal, *Canada* 102 C5
Montréal, *Aude, France* .. 20 E6
Montréal, *Gers, France* ... 20 E4
Montreal L., *Canada* 105 C7
Montreal Lake, *Canada* .. 105 C7
Montredon-Labessonnié,
  France 20 E6
Montrésor, *France* 18 E8
Montret, *France* 19 F12
Montreuil, *Pas-de-Calais,*
  France 19 B8
Montreuil, *Seine-St-Denis,*
  France 19 D9
Montreuil-Bellay, *France* . 18 E6
Montreux, *Switz.* 25 J2
Montrevel-en-Bresse,
  France 19 F12
Montrichard, *France* 18 E8
Montrose, *U.K.* 14 E6
Montrose, *Colo., U.S.A.* . 115 G10
Montrose, *Pa., U.S.A.* ... 111 E9
Monts, Pte. des, *Canada* . 103 C6
Montsalvy, *France* 20 D6
Montsant, Serra de, *Spain* 32 D6
Montsauche-les-Settons,
  France 19 E11

Montsech, Serra del, *Spain* 32 C5
Montserrat, *Spain* 32 D6
Montserrat ■, *W. Indies* .. 121 C7
Montuenga, *Spain* 34 D6
Montuiri, *Spain* 37 B9
Monywa, *Burma* 67 H19
Monza, *Italy* 28 C6
Monze, *Zambia* 87 F2
Monze, C., *Pakistan* 68 G2
Monzón, *Spain* 32 D5
Mooi River →, *S. Africa* .. 89 D4
Moolawatana, *Australia* .. 95 D2
Mooliabeenee, *Australia* .. 93 F2
Mooloogool, *Australia* 93 E2
Moomin Cr. →, *Australia* 95 D4
Moonah →, *Australia* 94 C2
Moonbeam, *Canada* 102 C3
Moonda, L., *Australia* 94 D3
Moonie, *Australia* 95 D5
Moonie →, *Australia* 95 D4
Moonta, *Australia* 95 E2
Moora, *Australia* 93 F2
Mooraberree, *Australia* .. 94 D3
Moorarie, *Australia* 93 E2
Moorcroft, *U.S.A.* 112 C2
Moore →, *Australia* 93 F2
Moore, L., *Australia* 93 E2
Moore Reefs, *Australia* .. 94 B4
Moorefield, *U.S.A.* 108 F6
Moores Res., *U.S.A.* 111 B13
Mooresville, *U.S.A.* 109 H5
Moorfoot Hills, *U.K.* 14 F5
Moorhead, *U.S.A.* 112 B6
Moormerland, *Germany* .. 24 B3
Mooroopna, *Australia* ... 95 F4
Moorpark, *U.S.A.* 117 L8
Moorreesburg, *S. Africa* .. 88 E2
Moosburg, *Germany* 25 G7
Moose →, *Canada* 102 B3
Moose Factory, *Canada* .. 102 B3
Moose I., *Canada* 105 C9
Moose Jaw, *Canada* 105 C7
Moose Jaw →, *Canada* .. 105 C7
Moose Lake, *Canada* 105 C8
Moose Lake, *U.S.A.* 112 B8
Moose Mountain Cr. →,
  Canada 105 D8
Moose Mountain Prov.
  Park, *Canada* 105 D8
Moose River, *Canada* 102 B3
Moosehead L., *U.S.A.* ... 103 C6
Moosomin, *Canada* 105 C8
Moosonee, *Canada* 102 B3
Moosup, *U.S.A.* 111 E13
Mopeia Velha, *Mozam.* .. 87 F4
Mopipi, *Botswana* 88 C3
Mopoi, *C.A.R.* 86 A2
Mopti, *Mali* 82 C4
Moqatta, *Sudan* 81 E4
Moquegua, *Peru* 124 G4
Mór, *Hungary* 42 C3
Móra, *Portugal* 35 G2
Mora, *Spain* 35 F7
Mora, *Sweden* 10 C8
Mora, *Minn., U.S.A.* 112 C8
Mora, *N. Mex., U.S.A.* ... 115 J11
Mora de Ebro = Mòra
  d'Ebre, *Spain* 32 D5
Mora de Rubielos, *Spain* . 32 E4
Mòra d'Ebre, *Spain* 32 D5
Mòra la Nova. *Spain* 32 D5
Morača →,
  Montenegro, Yug. 40 D3
Moradabad, *India* 69 E8
Morafenobe, *Madag.* 89 B7
Morąg, *Poland* 44 E6
Moral de Calatrava, *Spain* 35 G7
Moraleja, *Spain* 34 E4
Moramanga, *Madag.* 89 B8
Moran, *Kans., U.S.A.* 113 G7
Moran, *Wyo., U.S.A.* 114 E8
Moranbah, *Australia* 94 C4
Morano Cálabro, *Italy* ... 31 C9
Morant Cays, *Jamaica* ... 120 C4
Morant Pt., *Jamaica* 120 C4
Morar, L., *U.K.* 14 E3
Moratalla, *Spain* 33 G3
Moratuwa, *Sri Lanka* 66 R11
Morava →, *Slovak Rep.* .. 27 C3
Moravia, *U.S.A.* 112 E8
Moravian Hts. =
  Českomoravská
  Vrchovina, *Czech Rep.* .. 26 B8
Moravica →, *Serbia, Yug.* 40 C4
Moraviţa, *Romania* 42 E6
Moravská Třebová,
  Czech Rep. 27 B9
Moravské Budějovice,
  Czech Rep. 26 B8
Morawa, *Australia* 93 E2
Morawhanna, *Guyana* ... 124 B7
Moray □, *U.K.* 14 D5
Moray Firth, *U.K.* 14 D5
Morbach, *Germany* 25 F3
Morbegno, *Italy* 28 B6
Morbi, *India* 68 H4
Morbihan □, *France* 18 E4
Mörbylånga, *Sweden* 11 H10
Morcenx, *France* 20 D3
Morcone, *Italy* 31 A7
Mordelles, *France* 18 D5
Morden, *Canada* 105 D9
Mordoğan, *Turkey* 39 C8
Mordovian Republic □ =
  Mordvinia □, *Russia* ... 48 C7
Mordovo, *Russia* 48 D5
Mordvinia □, *Russia* 48 C7

Mordy, *Poland* 45 F9
Morea, *Australia* 95 F3
Morea, *Greece* 6 H10
Moreau →, *U.S.A.* 112 C4
Morecambe, *U.K.* 12 C5
Morecambe B., *U.K.* 12 C5
Moree, *Australia* 95 D4
Morehead, *U.S.A.* 108 F4
Morehead City, *U.S.A.* .. 109 H7
Morelia, *Mexico* 118 D4
Morella, *Australia* 94 C3
Morella, *Spain* 32 E4
Morelos, *Mexico* 118 B3
Morelos □, *Mexico* 119 D5
Morena, Sierra, *Spain* ... 35 G7
Morenci, *U.S.A.* 115 K9
Moreni, *Romania* 43 F10
Moreno Valley, *U.S.A.* ... 117 M10
Moresby I., *Canada* 104 C2
Morestel, *France* 21 C9
Moreton, *Australia* 94 A3
Moreton I., *Australia* 95 D5
Moreuil, *France* 19 C9
Morey, *Spain* 37 B10
Morez, *France* 19 F13
Morgan, *Australia* 95 E2
Morgan, *U.S.A.* 114 F8
Morgan City, *U.S.A.* 113 L9
Morgan Hill, *U.S.A.* 116 H5
Morganfield, *U.S.A.* 108 G2
Morganton, *U.S.A.* 109 H5
Morgantown, *U.S.A.* 108 F6
Morgenzon, *S. Africa* 89 D4
Morghak, *Iran* 71 D8
Morgongåva, *Sweden* 10 E10
Morhange, *France* 19 D13
Mori, *Italy* 28 C7
Morice L., *Canada* 104 C3
Moriki, *Nigeria* 83 C6
Morinville, *Canada* 104 C6
Morioka, *Japan* 54 E10
Moris, *Mexico* 118 B3
Morlaàs, *France* 20 E3
Morlaix, *France* 18 D3
Mörlunda, *Sweden* 11 G9
Mormanno, *Italy* 31 C8
Mormant, *France* 19 D9
Mornington, *Vic., Australia* 95 F4
Mornington, *W. Austral.,*
  Australia 92 C4
Mornington, I., *Chile* 128 F1
Mornington I., *Australia* .. 94 B2
Mórnos →, *Greece* 38 C3
Moro, *Sudan* 81 E3
Moro G., *Phil.* 61 H5
Morocco ■, *N. Afr.* 78 B4
Morogoro, *Tanzania* 86 D4
Morogoro □, *Tanzania* ... 86 D4
Moroleón, *Mexico* 118 C4
Morombe, *Madag.* 89 C7
Moron, *Argentina* 126 C4
Morón, *Cuba* 120 B4
Morón de Almazán, *Spain* 32 D2
Morón de la Frontera,
  Spain 35 H5
Morona →, *Peru* 124 D3
Morondava, *Madag.* 89 C7
Morondo, *Ivory C.* 82 D3
Morongo Valley, *U.S.A.* .. 117 L10
Moronou, *Ivory C.* 82 D4
Morotai, *Indonesia* 63 D7
Moroto, *Uganda* 86 B3
Moroto Summit, *Kenya* .. 86 B3
Morozov, *Bulgaria* 41 D9
Morozovsk, *Russia* 49 F5
Morpeth, *U.K.* 12 B6
Morphou, *Cyprus* 36 D11
Morphou Bay, *Cyprus* ... 36 D11
Morrilton, *U.S.A.* 113 H8
Morrinhos, *Brazil* 125 G9
Morrinsville, *N.Z.* 91 G5
Morris, *Canada* 105 D9
Morris, *Ill., U.S.A.* 108 E1
Morris, *Minn., U.S.A.* ... 112 C7
Morris, Mt., *Australia* ... 93 E5
Morrisburg, *Canada* 102 D4
Morrison, *U.S.A.* 112 E1
Morristown, *Ariz., U.S.A.* 115 K7
Morristown, *N.J., U.S.A.* . 111 F10
Morristown, *S. Dak.,*
  U.S.A. 112 C4
Morristown, *Tenn., U.S.A.* 109 G4
Morro, Pta., *Chile* 126 B1
Morro Bay, *U.S.A.* 116 K6
Morro del Jable, *Canary Is.* 37 F5
Morro Jable, Pta. de,
  Canary Is. 37 F5
Morrosquillo, G. de,
  Colombia 120 E4
Mörrum, *Sweden* 11 H8
Morrumbene, *Mozam.* ... 89 C6
Mörrumsån →, *Sweden* .. 11 H8
Mors, *Denmark* 11 H2
Morshansk, *Russia* 48 D5
Mörsil, *Sweden* 10 A7
Mortagne →, *France* 19 D13
Mortagne-au-Perche,
  France 18 D7
Mortagne-sur-Gironde,
  France 20 C3
Mortagne-sur-Sèvre, *France* 18 F6
Mortain, *France* 18 D6
Mortara, *Italy* 28 C5
Morteau, *France* 19 E13
Morteros, *Argentina* 126 C3

Mortlake, *Australia* 95 F3
Morton, *Tex., U.S.A.* 113 J3
Morton, *Wash., U.S.A.* ... 116 D4
Morundah, *Australia* 95 E4
Moruya, *Australia* 95 F5
Morvan, *France* 19 E11
Morven, *Australia* 95 D4
Morvern, *U.K.* 14 E3
Morwell, *Australia* 95 F4
Moryń, *Poland* 45 F1
Mosalsk, *Russia* 46 E8
Mosbach, *Germany* 25 F5
Mošćenice, *Croatia* 29 C11
Mosciano Sant' Angelo,
  Italy 29 F10
Moscos Is. = Maungmagan
  Is., *Burma* 67 N20
Moscow = Moskva, *Russia* 46 E9
Moscow, *U.S.A.* 114 C5
Mosel →, *Europe* 19 B14
Moselle = Mosel →,
  Europe 19 B14
Moselle □, *France* 19 D13
Moses Lake, *U.S.A.* 114 C4
Mosgiel, *N.Z.* 91 L3
Moshi, *Tanzania* 86 C4
Moshi □, *Tanzania* 86 C4
Moshupa, *Botswana* 88 C4
Mosina, *Poland* 45 F3
Mosjøen, *Norway* 8 D15
Moskenesøya, *Norway* ... 8 C15
Moskenstraumen, *Norway* 8 C15
Moskva, *Russia* 46 E9
Moskva →, *Russia* 46 E10
Moslavačka Gora, *Croatia* 29 C13
Mosomane, *Botswana* ... 88 C4
Moson-magyaróvár,
  Hungary 42 C2
Mošorin, *Serbia, Yug.* ... 42 E5
Mospino, *Ukraine* 47 J9
Mosquera, *Colombia* 124 C3
Mosquero, *U.S.A.* 113 H3
Mosqueruela, *Spain* 32 E4
Mosquitia, *Honduras* 120 C3
Mosquitos, G. de los,
  Panama 120 E3
Moss, *Norway* 9 G14
Moss Vale, *Australia* 95 E5
Mossbank, *Canada* 105 D7
Mossburn, *N.Z.* 91 L2
Mosselbaai, *S. Africa* 88 E3
Mossendjo, *Congo* 84 E2
Mossgiel, *Australia* 95 E3
Mossingen, *Germany* 25 G5
Mossman, *Australia* 94 B4
Mossoró, *Brazil* 125 E11
Mossuril, *Mozam.* 87 E5
Mossy →, *Canada* 105 C8
Most, *Czech Rep.* 26 A6
Mosta, *Malta* 36 D1
Moşţafāābād, *Iran* 71 C7
Mostaganem, *Algeria* 78 A6
Mostar, *Bos.-H.* 42 G2
Mostardas, *Brazil* 127 C5
Mostiska = Mostyska,
  Ukraine 47 H2
Móstoles, *Spain* 34 E7
Mosty = Masty, *Belarus* .. 46 F3
Mostyska, *Ukraine* 47 H2
Mosul = Al Mawşil, *Iraq* . 70 B4
Mosulpo, *S. Korea* 57 H14
Mota del Cuervo, *Spain* .. 33 F2
Mota del Marqués, *Spain* 34 D5
Motagua →, *Guatemala* . 120 C2
Motala, *Sweden* 11 F9
Motçala, *Romania* 43 C11
Motherwell, *U.K.* 14 F5
Motihari, *India* 69 F11
Motilla del Palancar, *Spain* 33 F3
Motnik, *Slovenia* 29 B11
Motovun, *Croatia* 29 C10
Motozintla de Mendoza,
  Mexico 119 D6
Motril, *Spain* 35 J7
Motru, *Romania* 42 F7
Motru →, *Romania* 43 F8
Mott, *U.S.A.* 112 B3
Móttola, *Italy* 31 B10
Motueka, *N.Z.* 91 J4
Motueka →, *N.Z.* 91 J4
Motul, *Mexico* 119 C7
Mouchalagane →, *Canada* 103 B6
Moúdhros, *Greece* 39 B7
Mouding, *China* 58 E3
Moudjeria, *Mauritania* ... 82 B2
Moudon, *Switz.* 25 J2
Mouila, *Gabon* 84 E2
Moulamein, *Australia* ... 95 F3
Mouliana, *Greece* 36 D7
Moulins, *France* 19 F10
Moulmein, *Burma* 67 L20
Moulton, *U.S.A.* 113 L6
Moultrie, *U.S.A.* 109 K4
Mound City, *Mo., U.S.A.* 112 E7
Mound City, *S. Dak.,*
  U.S.A. 112 C4
Moúnda, Ákra, *Greece* .. 38 C2
Moundou, *Chad* 79 G9
Moundsville, *U.S.A.* 110 G4
Moung, *Cambodia* 64 F4
Mount Airy, *U.S.A.* 109 G5
Mount Albert, *Canada* ... 110 B5
Mount Amherst, *Australia* 92 C4
Mount Angel, *U.S.A.* 114 D2
Mount Augustus, *Australia* 92 D2

Mount Barker, *S. Austral.,*
  Australia 95 F2
Mount Barker, *W. Austral.,*
  Australia 93 F2
Mount Carmel, *U.S.A.* ... 108 F2
Mount Clemens, *U.S.A.* . 102 D3
Mount Coolon, *Australia* . 94 C4
Mount Darwin, *Zimbabwe* 87 F3
Mount Desert I., *U.S.A.* .. 103 D6
Mount Dora, *U.S.A.* 109 L5
Mount Douglas, *Australia* 94 C4
Mount Eba, *Australia* 95 E2
Mount Edgecumbe, *U.S.A.* 104 B1
Mount Elizabeth, *Australia* 92 C4
Mount Fletcher, *S. Africa* . 89 E4
Mount Forest, *Canada* ... 102 D3
Mount Gambier, *Australia* 95 F3
Mount Garnet, *Australia* . 94 B4
Mount Hope, *N.S.W.,*
  Australia 95 E4
Mount Hope, *S. Austral.,*
  Australia 95 E2
Mount Hope, *U.S.A.* 108 G5
Mount Horeb, *U.S.A.* ... 112 D10
Mount Howitt, *Australia* . 95 D3
Mount Isa, *Australia* 94 C2
Mount Keith, *Australia* ... 93 E3
Mount Laguna, *U.S.A.* ... 117 N10
Mount Larcom, *Australia* . 94 C5
Mount Lofty Ra., *Australia* 95 E2
Mount Magnet, *Australia* . 93 E2
Mount Margaret, *Australia* 95 D3
Mount Maunganui, *N.Z.* . 91 G6
Mount Molloy, *Australia* . 94 B4
Mount Monger, *Australia* . 93 F3
Mount Morgan, *Australia* . 94 C5
Mount Morris, *U.S.A.* ... 110 D7
Mount Mulligan, *Australia* 94 B3
Mount Narryer, *Australia* . 93 E2
Mount Oxide Mine,
  Australia 94 B2
Mount Pearl, *Canada* 103 C9
Mount Perry, *Australia* ... 95 D5
Mount Phillips, *Australia* . 92 D2
Mount Pleasant, *Iowa,*
  U.S.A. 112 E9
Mount Pleasant, *Mich.,*
  U.S.A. 108 D3
Mount Pleasant, *Pa.,*
  U.S.A. 110 F5
Mount Pleasant, *S.C.,*
  U.S.A. 109 J6
Mount Pleasant, *Tenn.,*
  U.S.A. 109 H2
Mount Pleasant, *Tex.,*
  U.S.A. 113 J7
Mount Pleasant, *Utah,*
  U.S.A. 114 G8
Mount Pocono, *U.S.A.* .. 111 E9
Mount Rainier National
  Park, *Canada* 116 D5
Mount Revelstoke Nat.
  Park, *Canada* 104 C5
Mount Robson Prov. Park,
  Canada 104 C5
Mount Sandiman, *Australia* 93 D2
Mount Shasta, *U.S.A.* ... 114 F2
Mount Signal, *U.S.A.* 117 N11
Mount Sterling, *Ill., U.S.A.* 112 F9
Mount Sterling, *Ky.,*
  U.S.A. 108 F4
Mount Surprise, *Australia* . 94 B3
Mount Union, *U.S.A.* 110 F7
Mount Vernon, *Australia* . 92 D2
Mount Vernon, *Ind.,*
  U.S.A. 112 F10
Mount Vernon, *N.Y.,*
  U.S.A. 111 F11
Mount Vernon, *Ohio,*
  U.S.A. 110 F2
Mount Vernon, *Wash.,*
  U.S.A. 116 B4
Mountain Ash, *U.K.* 13 F4
Mountain Center, *U.S.A.* . 117 M10
Mountain City, *Nev.,*
  U.S.A. 114 F6
Mountain City, *Tenn.,*
  U.S.A. 109 G5
Mountain Grove, *U.S.A.* . 113 G8
Mountain Home, *Ark.,*
  U.S.A. 113 G8
Mountain Home, *Idaho,*
  U.S.A. 114 E6
Mountain Iron, *U.S.A.* ... 112 B8
Mountain Park, *Canada* .. 104 C5
Mountain Pass, *U.S.A.* ... 117 K11
Mountain View, *Ark.,*
  U.S.A. 113 H8
Mountain View, *Calif.,*
  U.S.A. 116 H4
Mountainair, *U.S.A.* 115 J10
Mountmellick, *Ireland* ... 15 C4
Mountrath, *Ireland* 15 D4
Moura, *Australia* 94 C4
Moura, *Brazil* 124 D6
Moura, *Portugal* 35 G3
Mourão, *Portugal* 35 G3
Mourdi, Dépression du,
  Chad 79 E10
Mourdiah, *Mali* 82 C3
Mourenx-Ville-Nouvelle,
  France 20 E3
Mouri, *Ghana* 83 D4
Mourilyan, *Australia* 94 B4
Mourmelon-le-Grand,
  France 19 C11
Mourne →, *U.K.* 15 B4

Mourne Mts., *U.K.* 15 B5
Mourniaí, *Greece* 36 D6
Mournies = Mourniaí, *Greece* 36 D6
Mouscron, *Belgium* 17 D3
Moussoro, *Chad* 79 F9
Mouthe, *France* 19 F13
Moutier, *Switz.* 25 H3
Moûtiers, *France* 21 C10
Moutohara, *N.Z.* 91 H6
Moutong, *Indonesia* 63 D6
Mouy, *France* 19 C9
Mouzáki, *Greece* 38 B3
Mouzon, *France* 19 C12
Movas, *Mexico* 118 B3
Moville, *Ireland* 15 A4
Moy →, *Ireland* 15 B2
Moyale, *Kenya* 81 G4
Moyamba, *S. Leone* 82 D2
Moyen Atlas, *Morocco* ... 78 B4
Moyo, *Indonesia* 62 F5
Moyobamba, *Peru* 124 E3
Moyyero →, *Russia* 51 C11
Moyynty, *Kazakstan* 50 E8
Mozambique = Moçambique, *Mozam.* .. 87 F5
Mozambique ■, *Africa* .. 87 F4
Mozambique Chan., *Africa* 89 B7
Mozdok, *Russia* 49 J7
Mozdūrān, *Iran* 71 B9
Mozhaysk, *Russia* 46 E9
Mozhga, *Russia* 48 B11
Mozhnābād, *Iran* 71 C9
Mozirje, *Slovenia* 29 B11
Mozyr = Mazyr, *Belarus* . 47 F5
Mpanda, *Tanzania* 86 D3
Mpanda □, *Tanzania* 86 D3
Mpésoba, *Mali* 82 C3
Mpika, *Zambia* 87 E3
Mpulungu, *Zambia* 87 D3
Mpumalanga, *S. Africa* .. 89 D5
Mpumalanga □, *S. Africa* 89 B5
Mpwapwa, *Tanzania* 86 D4
Mpwapwa □, *Tanzania* .. 86 D4
Mqinvartsveri = Kazbek, *Russia* 49 J7
Mrągowo, *Poland* 44 E8
Mramor, *Serbia, Yug.* ... 40 C5
Mrkonjić Grad, *Bos.-H.* .. 42 F2
Mrkopalj, *Croatia* 29 C11
Mrocza, *Poland* 45 E4
Msambansovu, *Zimbabwe* 87 F3
Msoro, *Zambia* 87 E3
Msta →, *Russia* 46 C6
Mstislavl = Mstsislaw, *Belarus* 46 E6
Mstsislaw, *Belarus* 46 E6
Mszana Dolna, *Poland* .. 45 J7
Mszczonów, *Poland* 45 G7
Mtama, *Tanzania* 87 E4
Mtilikwe →, *Zimbabwe* . 87 G3
Mtsensk, *Russia* 46 F9
Mtskheta, *Georgia* 49 K7
Mtubatuba, *S. Africa* ... 89 D5
Mtwara-Mikindani, *Tanzania* 87 E5
Mu Gia, Deo, *Vietnam* .. 64 D5
Mu Us Shamo, *China* ... 56 E5
Muang Chiang Rai, *Thailand* 64 C2
Muang Khong, *Laos* 64 E5
Muang Lamphun, *Thailand* 64 C2
Muang Pak Beng, *Laos* .. 64 C3
Muar, *Malaysia* 65 L4
Muarabungo, *Indonesia* . 62 E2
Muaraenim, *Indonesia* .. 62 E2
Muarajuloi, *Indonesia* .. 62 E4
Muarakaman, *Indonesia* . 62 E5
Muaratebo, *Indonesia* .. 62 E2
Muaratembesi, *Indonesia* 62 E2
Muaratewe, *Indonesia* .. 62 E4
Mubarakpur, *India* 69 F10
Mubarraz = Al Mubarraz, *Si. Arabia* 71 E6
Mubende, *Uganda* 86 B3
Mubi, *Nigeria* 83 C7
Mubur, Pulau, *Indonesia* 65 L6
Mucajaí →, *Brazil* 124 C6
Muchachos, Roque de los, *Canary Is.* 37 F2
Mücheln, *Germany* 24 D7
Muchinga Mts., *Zambia* . 87 E3
Muchkapskiy, *Russia* 48 E6
Muck, *U.K.* 14 E2
Muckadilla, *Australia* ... 95 D4
Mucur, *Turkey* 72 C6
Mucuri, *Brazil* 125 G11
Mucusso, *Angola* 88 B3
Muda, *Canary Is.* 37 F6
Mudan Jiang →, *China* .. 57 A15
Mudanjiang, *China* 57 B15
Mudanya, *Turkey* 41 F12
Muddy Cr. →, *U.S.A.* ... 115 H8
Mudgee, *Australia* 95 E4
Mudjatik →, *Canada* ... 105 B7
Mudurnu, *Turkey* 72 B4
Muecate, *Mozam.* 87 E4
Mueda, *Mozam.* 87 E4
Mueller Ra., *Australia* .. 92 C4
Muende, *Mozam.* 87 E3
Muerto, Mar, *Mexico* ... 119 D6
Mufindi □, *Tanzania* 87 D4
Mufu Shan, *China* 59 C10
Mufulira, *Zambia* 87 E2
Mufumbiro Range, *Africa* 86 C2
Mugardos, *Spain* 34 B2
Muge →, *Portugal* 35 F2

Múggia, *Italy* 29 C10
Mughayrā', *Si. Arabia* ... 70 D3
Mugi, *Japan* 55 H7
Mugia = Muxía, *Spain* .. 34 B1
Mugila, Mts., *Dem. Rep. of the Congo* 86 D2
Muğla, *Turkey* 39 D10
Muğla □, *Turkey* 39 D10
Müglizh, *Bulgaria* 41 D9
Mugu, *Nepal* 69 E10
Muhammad, Râs, *Egypt* . 80 B3
Muhammad Qol, *Sudan* . 80 C4
Muhammadabad, *India* .. 69 F10
Muhesi →, *Tanzania* 86 D4
Muheza □, *Tanzania* 86 D4
Mühlacker, *Germany* 25 G4
Mühldorf, *Germany* 25 G8
Mühlhausen, *Germany* ... 24 D6
Mühlig Hofmann fjell, *Antarctica* 5 D3
Mühlviertel, *Austria* 26 C7
Muhos, *Finland* 8 D22
Muhu, *Estonia* 9 G20
Muhutwe, *Tanzania* 86 C3
Muikamachi, *Japan* 55 F9
Muine Bheag, *Ireland* .. 15 D5
Muir, L., *Australia* 93 F2
Mukacheve, *Ukraine* 47 H2
Mukachevo = Mukacheve, *Ukraine* 47 H2
Mukah, *Malaysia* 62 D4
Mukawwa, Geziret, *Egypt* 80 C4
Mukdahan, *Thailand* 64 D5
Mukden = Shenyang, *China* 57 D12
Mukhtolovo, *Russia* 48 C6
Mukhtuya = Lensk, *Russia* 51 C12
Mukinbudin, *Australia* .. 93 F2
Mukishi, *Dem. Rep. of the Congo* 87 D1
Mukomuko, *Indonesia* .. 62 E2
Mukomwenze, *Dem. Rep. of the Congo* 86 D2
Muktsar, *India* 68 D6
Mukur, *Afghan.* 68 C2
Mukutawa →, *Canada* .. 105 C9
Mukwela, *Zambia* 87 F2
Mula, *Spain* 33 G3
Mulange, *Dem. Rep. of the Congo* 86 C2
Mulanje, *Malawi* 87 F4
Mulchén, *Chile* 126 D1
Mulde →, *Germany* 24 D8
Mule Creek, *U.S.A.* 112 D2
Muleba, *Tanzania* 86 C3
Muleba □, *Tanzania* 86 C3
Muleshoe, *U.S.A.* 113 H3
Mulgathing, *Australia* .. 95 E1
Mulgrave, *Canada* 103 C7
Mulhacén, *Spain* 35 H7
Mülheim, *Germany* 24 D2
Mulhouse, *France* 19 E14
Muli, *China* 58 D3
Muling, *China* 57 B16
Mull, *U.K.* 14 E3
Mull, Sound of, *U.K.* ... 14 E3
Mullaittivu, *Sri Lanka* .. 66 Q12
Mullen, *U.S.A.* 112 D4
Mullengudgery, *Australia* 95 E4
Mullens, *U.S.A.* 108 G5
Muller, Pegunungan, *Indonesia* 62 D4
Mullet Pen., *Ireland* ... 15 B1
Mullewa, *Australia* 93 E2
Müllheim, *Germany* 25 H3
Mulligan →, *Australia* .. 94 D2
Mullin, *U.S.A.* 113 K5
Mullingar, *Ireland* 15 C4
Mullins, *U.S.A.* 109 H6
Mullsjö, *Sweden* 11 G7
Mullumbimby, *Australia* . 95 D5
Mulobezi, *Zambia* 87 F2
Mulroy B., *Ireland* 15 A4
Multan, *Pakistan* 68 D4
Mulumbe, Mts., *Dem. Rep. of the Congo* 87 D2
Mulungushi Dam, *Zambia* 87 E2
Mulvane, *U.S.A.* 113 G6
Mulwad, *Sudan* 80 D3
Mulwala, *Australia* 95 F4
Mumbai, *India* 66 K8
Mumbwa, *Zambia* 87 F2
Mumra, *Russia* 49 H8
Mun →, *Thailand* 64 E5
Muna, *Indonesia* 63 F6
Munamagi, *Estonia* 9 H22
Münchberg, *Germany* ... 25 E7
Müncheberg, *Germany* .. 24 C10
München, *Germany* 25 G7
Munchen-Gladbach = Mönchengladbach, *Germany* 24 D2
Muncho Lake, *Canada* .. 104 B3
Munchŏn, *N. Korea* 57 E14
Muncie, *U.S.A.* 108 E3
Muncoonie, L., *Australia* 94 D2
Mundare, *Canada* 104 C6
Munday, *U.S.A.* 113 J5
Münden, *Germany* 24 D5
Mundiwindi, *Australia* .. 92 D3
Mundo →, *Spain* 33 G2
Mundo Novo, *Brazil* 125 F10
Mundra, *India* 68 H3
Mundrabilla, *Australia* .. 93 F4
Munera, *Spain* 33 F2
Mungallala, *Australia* ... 95 D4

Mungallala Cr. →, *Australia* 95 D4
Mungana, *Australia* 94 B3
Mungaoli, *India* 68 G8
Mungari, *Mozam.* 87 F3
Mungbere, *Dem. Rep. of the Congo* 86 B2
Munger, *India* 69 G12
Mungindi, *Australia* 95 D4
Munich = München, *Germany* 25 G7
Munising, *U.S.A.* 108 B2
Munka-Ljungby, *Sweden* . 11 H6
Munkedal, *Sweden* 11 F5
Munkfors, *Sweden* 10 E7
Munku-Sardyk, *Russia* .. 51 D11
Münnerstadt, *Germany* .. 25 E6
Muñoz Gamero, Pen., *Chile* 128 G2
Munroe L., *Canada* 105 B9
Munsan, *S. Korea* 57 F14
Munster, *France* 19 D14
Munster, *Niedersachsen, Germany* 24 C6
Münster, *Nordrhein-Westfalen, Germany* 24 D3
Munster □, *Ireland* 15 D3
Muntadgin, *Australia* ... 93 F2
Muntele Mare, Vf., *Romania* 43 D8
Muntok, *Indonesia* 62 E3
Munyama, *Zambia* 87 F2
Munzur Dağları, *Turkey* . 73 C8
Muong Beng, *Laos* 64 B3
Muong Boum, *Vietnam* . 64 A4
Muong Et, *Laos* 64 B5
Muong Hai, *Laos* 64 B3
Muong Hiem, *Laos* 64 B4
Muong Houn, *Laos* 64 B3
Muong Hung, *Vietnam* . 64 B4
Muong Kau, *Laos* 64 E5
Muong Khao, *Laos* 64 C4
Muong Khoua, *Laos* 64 B4
Muong Liep, *Laos* 64 C3
Muong May, *Laos* 64 E6
Muong Ngeun, *Laos* 64 B3
Muong Ngoi, *Laos* 64 B4
Muong Nhie, *Vietnam* .. 64 A4
Muong Nong, *Laos* 64 D6
Muong Ou Tay, *Laos* ... 64 A3
Muong Oua, *Laos* 64 C3
Muong Peun, *Laos* 64 B4
Muong Phalane, *Laos* ... 64 D5
Muong Phieng, *Laos* ... 64 C3
Muong Phine, *Laos* 64 D6
Muong Sai, *Laos* 64 B3
Muong Saiapoun, *Laos* . 64 C3
Muong Sen, *Vietnam* ... 64 C5
Muong Sing, *Laos* 64 B3
Muong Son, *Laos* 64 B4
Muong Soui, *Laos* 64 C4
Muong Va, *Laos* 64 B4
Muong Xia, *Vietnam* ... 64 B5
Muonio, *Finland* 8 C20
Muonionjoki →, *Finland* 8 C20
Muping, *China* 57 F11
Muqaddam, Wadi →, *Sudan* 80 D3
Muqdisho, *Somali Rep.* . 74 G4
Mur →, *Austria* 27 E9
Mur-de-Bretagne, *France* 18 D4
Muradiye, Manisa, *Turkey* 39 C9
Muradiye, Van, *Turkey* .. 73 C10
Murakami, *Japan* 54 E9
Murallón, Cerro, *Chile* .. 128 F2
Muranda, *Rwanda* 86 C2
Murang'a, *Kenya* 86 C4
Murashi, *Russia* 50 D5
Murat, *France* 20 C6
Murat →, *Turkey* 73 C9
Murat Dağı, *Turkey* 39 C11
Muratlı, *Turkey* 41 E11
Murato, *France* 21 F13
Murau, *Austria* 26 D7
Muravera, *Italy* 30 C2
Murayama, *Japan* 54 E10
Murban, *U.A.E.* 71 F7
Murça, *Portugal* 34 D3
Murchison →, *Australia* 93 E1
Murchison, Mt., *Antarctica* 5 D11
Murchison Falls, *Uganda* 86 B3
Murchison House, *Australia* 93 E1
Murchison Ra., *Australia* 94 C1
Murchison Rapids, *Malawi* 87 F3
Murcia, *Spain* 33 G3
Murcia □, *Spain* 33 H3
Murdo, *U.S.A.* 112 D4
Murdoch Pt., *Australia* . 94 A3
Mürefte, *Turkey* 41 F11
Mureş →, *Romania* 42 D5
Mureşul = Mureş →, *Romania* 42 D5
Muret, *France* 20 E5
Murfreesboro, *U.S.A.* ... 109 H2
Murgab = Murghob, *Tajikistan* 50 F8
Murgeni, *Romania* 43 D13
Murghob, *Tajikistan* 50 F8
Murgon, *Australia* 95 D5
Murgoo, *Australia* 93 E2
Muria, *Indonesia* 63 G14
Muriaé, *Brazil* 127 A7
Murias de Paredes, *Spain* 34 C4
Muriel Mine, *Zimbabwe* . 87 F3

Müritz, *Germany* 24 B8
Murka, *Kenya* 86 C4
Murmansk, *Russia* 50 C4
Murnau, *Germany* 25 H7
Muro, *France* 21 F12
Muro, *Spain* 37 B10
Muro, C. de, *France* 21 G12
Muro de Alcoy, *Spain* .. 33 G4
Muro Lucano, *Italy* 31 B8
Murom, *Russia* 48 C6
Muroran, *Japan* 54 C10
Muros, *Spain* 34 C1
Muros y de Noya, Ría de, *Spain* 34 C1
Muroto, *Japan* 55 H7
Muroto-Misaki, *Japan* .. 55 H7
Murowana Goślina, *Poland* 45 F3
Murphy, *U.S.A.* 114 E5
Murphys, *U.S.A.* 116 G6
Murphysboro, *U.S.A.* ... 113 G10
Murrat, *Sudan* 80 D2
Murray, Ky., *U.S.A.* 109 G1
Murray, Utah, *U.S.A.* ... 114 F8
Murray →, *Australia* ... 95 F2
Murray →, *Canada* 104 B4
Murray, L., *U.S.A.* 109 H5
Murray Bridge, *Australia* 95 F2
Murray Downs, *Australia* 94 C1
Murray Harbour, *Canada* 103 C7
Murraysburg, *S. Africa* . 88 E3
Murree, *Pakistan* 68 C5
Murrieta, *U.S.A.* 117 M9
Murrin Murrin, *Australia* 93 E3
Murrumbidgee →, *Australia* 95 E3
Murrumburrah, *Australia* 95 E4
Murrurundi, *Australia* .. 95 E5
Murshid, *Sudan* 80 C3
Murshidabad, *India* 69 G13
Murska Sobota, *Slovenia* 29 B13
Murtle L., *Canada* 104 C5
Murtoa, *Australia* 95 F3
Murtosa, *Portugal* 34 E2
Murungu, *Tanzania* 86 C3
Murwara, *India* 69 H9
Murwillumbah, *Australia* 95 D5
Mürz →, *Austria* 26 D8
Mürzzuschlag, *Austria* .. 26 D8
Muş, *Turkey* 73 C9
Mûsa, Gebel, *Egypt* 80 J8
Musa Khel, *Pakistan* ... 68 D3
Mûsá Qal'eh, *Afghan.* .. 66 C4
Musafargarh, *Pakistan* .. 66 D7
Musala, *Bulgaria* 40 D7
Musala, *Indonesia* 62 D1
Musan, *N. Korea* 57 C15
Musangu, *Dem. Rep. of the Congo* 87 E1
Musasa, *Tanzania* 86 C3
Musay'īd, *Qatar* 71 E6
Muscat = Masqat, *Oman* 74 C6
Muscat & Oman = Oman ■, *Asia* 74 C6
Muscatine, *U.S.A.* 112 E9
Musgrave, *Australia* 94 A3
Musgrave Ranges, *Australia* 93 E5
Mushie, *Dem. Rep. of the Congo* 84 E3
Mushin, *Nigeria* 83 D5
Musi →, *Indonesia* 62 E2
Muskeg →, *Canada* 104 A4
Muskegon, *U.S.A.* 108 D2
Muskegon →, *U.S.A.* .. 108 D2
Muskegon Heights, *U.S.A.* 108 D2
Muskogee, *U.S.A.* 113 H7
Muskwa →, *Canada* ... 104 B4
Muslīmiyah, *Syria* 70 B3
Musmar, *Sudan* 80 D4
Musofu, *Zambia* 87 E2
Musoma, *Tanzania* 86 C3
Musoma □, *Tanzania* ... 86 C3
Musquaro, L., *Canada* .. 103 B7
Musquodoboit Harbour, *Canada* 103 C7
Musselburgh, *U.K.* 14 F5
Musselshell →, *U.S.A.* . 114 C10
Mussidan, *France* 20 C4
Mussomeli, *Italy* 30 E6
Mussoorie, *India* 68 D8
Mussuco, *Angola* 88 B2
Mustafakemalpaşa, *Turkey* 41 F12
Mustang, *Nepal* 69 E10
Musters, L., *Argentina* .. 128 F3
Musudan, *N. Korea* 57 D15
Muswellbrook, *Australia* 95 E5
Muszyna, *Poland* 45 J7
Mût, *Egypt* 80 B2
Mut, *Turkey* 72 D5
Mutanda, *Mozam.* 89 C5
Mutanda, *Zambia* 87 E2
Mutare, *Zimbabwe* 87 F3
Muting, *Indonesia* 63 F10
Mutoray, *Russia* 51 C11
Mutshatsha, *Dem. Rep. of the Congo* 87 E1
Mutsu, *Japan* 54 D10
Mutsu-Wan, *Japan* 54 D10
Muttaburra, *Australia* .. 94 C3
Muttalip, *Turkey* 39 B12
Mutton I., *Ireland* 15 D2
Mutuáli, *Mozam.* 87 E4
Muweilih, *Egypt* 75 E3
Muxía, *Spain* 34 B1
Muy Muy, *Nic.* 120 D2
Muyinga, *Burundi* 86 C3
Muynak, *Uzbekistan* 50 E6

Muzaffarabad, *Pakistan* . 69 B5
Muzaffargarh, *Pakistan* . 68 D4
Muzaffarnagar, *India* ... 68 E7
Muzaffarpur, *India* 69 F11
Muzhi, *Russia* 50 C7
Muzillac, *France* 18 E4
Muzon, C., *U.S.A.* 104 C2
Muztag, *China* 60 C3
Mvôlô, *Sudan* 81 F2
Mvuma, *Zimbabwe* 87 F3
Mvurwi, *Zimbabwe* 87 F3
Mwadui, *Tanzania* 86 C3
Mwambo, *Tanzania* 87 E5
Mwandi, *Zambia* 87 F1
Mwanza, *Dem. Rep. of the Congo* 86 D2
Mwanza, *Tanzania* 86 C3
Mwanza, *Zambia* 87 F1
Mwanza □, *Tanzania* ... 86 C3
Mwaya, *Tanzania* 87 D3
Mweelrea, *Ireland* 15 C2
Mweka, *Dem. Rep. of the Congo* 84 E4
Mwenezi, *Zimbabwe* 87 G3
Mwenezi →, *Mozam.* ... 87 G3
Mwenga, *Dem. Rep. of the Congo* 86 C2
Mweru, L., *Zambia* 87 D2
Mweza Range, *Zimbabwe* 87 G3
Mwilambwe, *Dem. Rep. of the Congo* 86 D2
Mwimbi, *Tanzania* 87 D3
Mwinilunga, *Zambia* 87 E1
My Tho, *Vietnam* 65 G6
Myajlar, *India* 68 F4
Myanaung, *Burma* 67 K19
Myanmar = Burma ■, *Asia* 67 J20
Myaungmya, *Burma* 67 L19
Myeik Kyunzu, *Burma* .. 65 G1
Myerstown, *U.S.A.* 111 F8
Myingyan, *Burma* 67 J19
Myitkyina, *Burma* 67 G20
Myjava, *Slovak Rep.* ... 27 C10
Mykhaylivka, *Ukraine* .. 47 J8
Mykines, *Færoe Is.* 8 E9
Mykolayiv, *Ukraine* 47 J7
Mymensingh, *Bangla.* .. 67 G17
Mynydd Du, *U.K.* 13 F4
Mýrdalsjökull, *Iceland* .. 8 E4
Myrhorod, *Ukraine* 47 H7
Myroodah, *Australia* ... 92 C3
Myrtle Beach, *U.S.A.* ... 109 J6
Myrtle Creek, *U.S.A.* ... 114 E2
Myrtle Point, *U.S.A.* ... 114 E1
Myrtou, *Cyprus* 36 D12
Mysia, *Turkey* 41 G11
Myślenice, *Poland* 45 J6
Myślibórz, *Poland* 45 F1
Mysłowice, *Poland* 45 H6
Mysore = Karnataka □, *India* 66 N10
Mysore, *India* 66 N10
Mystic, *U.S.A.* 111 E13
Myszków, *Poland* 45 H6
Myszyniec, *Poland* 44 E8
Mytishchi, *Russia* 46 E9
Myton, *U.S.A.* 114 F8
Mývatn, *Iceland* 8 D5
Mže →, *Czech Rep.* 26 B6
Mzimba, *Malawi* 87 E3
Mzimkulu →, *S. Africa* 89 E5
Mzimvubu →, *S. Africa* 89 E4
Mzuzu, *Malawi* 87 E3

N

N' Dioum, *Senegal* 82 B2
Na Hearadh = Harris, *U.K.* 14 D2
Na Noi, *Thailand* 64 C3
Na Phao, *Laos* 64 D5
Na Sam, *Vietnam* 64 A6
Na San, *Vietnam* 64 B5
Naab →, *Germany* 25 F8
Na'am, *Sudan* 81 F2
Naantali, *Finland* 9 F19
Naas, *Ireland* 15 C5
Nababiep, *S. Africa* 88 D2
Nabadwip = Navadwip, *India* 69 H13
Nabari, *Japan* 55 G8
Nabawa, *Australia* 93 E1
Nabberu, L., *Australia* .. 93 E3
Nabburg, *Germany* 25 F8
Naberezhnyye Chelny, *Russia* 48 C11
Nabeul, *Tunisia* 79 A8
Nabha, *India* 68 D7
Nabīd, *Iran* 71 D8
Nabire, *Indonesia* 63 E9
Nabisar, *Pakistan* 68 G3
Nabisipi →, *Canada* ... 103 B7
Nabiswera, *Uganda* 86 B3
Nablus = Nābulus, *West Bank* 75 C4
Naboomspruit, *S. Africa* 89 C4
Nabua, *Phil.* 61 E5
Nābulus, *West Bank* 75 C4
Nacala, *Mozam.* 87 E5
Nacala-Velha, *Mozam.* .. 87 E5
Nacaome, *Honduras* 120 D2
Nacaroa, *Mozam.* 87 E4
Naches, *U.S.A.* 114 C3
Naches →, *U.S.A.* 116 D6

Nachingwea, *Tanzania* ... 87 E4
Nachingwea □, *Tanzania* . 87 E4
Nachna, *India* 68 F4
Náchod, *Czech Rep.* 26 A9
Nacimiento Reservoir,
  U.S.A. 116 K6
Nackara, *Australia* 95 E2
Naco, *Mexico* 118 A3
Naco, *U.S.A.* 115 L9
Nacogdoches, *U.S.A.* 113 K7
Nácori Chico, *Mexico* ... 118 B3
Nacozari, *Mexico* 118 A3
Nadi, *Sudan* 80 D3
Nadiad, *India* 68 H5
Nădlac, *Romania* 42 D5
Nadur, *Malta* 36 C1
Nadūshan, *Iran* 71 C7
Nadvirna, *Ukraine* 47 H3
Nadvornaya = Nadvirna,
  Ukraine 47 H3
Nadym, *Russia* 50 C8
Nadym →, *Russia* 50 C8
Nærbø, *Norway* 9 G11
Næstved, *Denmark* 11 J5
Nafada, *Nigeria* 83 C7
Naftshahr, *Iran* 70 C5
Nafud Desert = An Nafūd,
  Si. Arabia 70 D4
Nag Hammâdi, *Egypt* ... 80 B3
Naga, *Phil.* 61 E5
Nagagami →, *Canada* .. 102 C3
Nagahama, *Japan* 55 G8
Nagai, *Japan* 54 E10
Nagaland □, *India* 67 G19
Nagano, *Japan* 55 F9
Nagano □, *Japan* 55 F9
Nagaoka, *Japan* 55 F9
Nagappattinam, *India* .. 66 P11
Nagar Parkar, *Pakistan* . 68 G4
Nagasaki, *Japan* 55 H4
Nagasaki □, *Japan* 55 H4
Nagato, *Japan* 55 G5
Nagaur, *India* 68 F5
Nagercoil, *India* 66 Q10
Nagina, *India* 69 E8
Nagîneh, *Iran* 71 C8
Nagir, *Pakistan* 69 A6
Naglarby, *Sweden* 10 D9
Nagold, *Germany* 25 G4
Nagold →, *Germany* ... 25 G4
Nagoorin, *Australia* 94 C5
Nagorno-Karabakh,
  Azerbaijan 73 C12
Nagornyy, *Russia* 51 D13
Nagoya, *Japan* 55 G8
Nagpur, *India* 66 J11
Nagua, *Dom. Rep.* 121 C6
Nagyatád, *Hungary* 42 D2
Nagyecsed, *Hungary* ... 42 C7
Nagykálló, *Hungary* ... 42 C6
Nagykanizsa, *Hungary* . 42 D2
Nagykáta, *Hungary* 42 C4
Nagykőrös, *Hungary* ... 42 C4
Naha, *Japan* 55 L3
Nahanni Butte, *Canada* . 104 A4
Nahanni Nat. Park, *Canada* 104 A4
Nahariyya, *Israel* 70 C2
Nahāvand, *Iran* 71 C6
Nahe →, *Germany* 25 F3
Nahîya, W. →, *Egypt* .. 80 J7
Nahlin, *Canada* 104 B2
Naicá, *Mexico* 118 B3
Naicam, *Canada* 105 C8
Naila, *Germany* 25 E7
Nain, *Canada* 103 A7
Nā'īn, *Iran* 71 C7
Naini Tal, *India* 69 E8
Nainpur, *India* 66 H12
Naintré, *France* 18 F7
Naipu, *Romania* 43 F10
Nairn, *U.K.* 14 D5
Nairobi, *Kenya* 86 C4
Naissaar, *Estonia* 9 G21
Naivasha, *Kenya* 86 C4
Naivasha, L., *Kenya* ... 86 C4
Najac, *France* 20 D5
Najafābād, *Iran* 71 C6
Nájera, *Spain* 32 C2
Najerilla →, *Spain* 32 C2
Najibabad, *India* 68 E8
Najin, *N. Korea* 57 C16
Najmah, *Si. Arabia* ... 71 E6
Naju, *S. Korea* 57 G14
Nakadōri-Shima, *Japan* . 55 H4
Nakalagba,
  Dem. Rep. of the Congo 86 B2
Nakaminato, *Japan* 55 F10
Nakamura, *Japan* 55 H6
Nakano, *Japan* 55 F9
Nakano-Shima, *Japan* .. 55 K4
Nakashibetsu, *Japan* ... 54 C12
Nakfa, *Eritrea* 81 D4
Nakhichevan = Naxçıvan,
  Azerbaijan 73 C11
Nakhichevan Republic □ =
  Naxçıvan □, *Azerbaijan* 50 F5
Nakhl, *Egypt* 75 F2
Nakhl-e Taqī, *Iran* 71 E7
Nakhodka, *Russia* 54 C6
Nakhon Nayok, *Thailand* . 64 E3
Nakhon Pathom, *Thailand* 64 F3
Nakhon Phanom, *Thailand* 64 D5
Nakhon Ratchasima,
  Thailand 64 E4
Nakhon Sawan, *Thailand* . 64 E3
Nakhon Si Thammarat,
  Thailand 65 H3

Nakhon Thai, *Thailand* ... 64 D3
Nakina, *B.C., Canada* 104 B2
Nakina, *Ont., Canada* 102 B2
Nakło nad Noteią, *Poland* 45 E4
Nakodar, *India* 68 D6
Nakskov, *Denmark* 11 K5
Naktong →, *S. Korea* ... 57 G15
Nakuru, *Kenya* 86 C4
Nakuru □, *Kenya* 86 C4
Nakuru, L., *Kenya* 86 C4
Nakusp, *Canada* 104 C5
Nal →, *Pakistan* 68 G1
Nalchik, *Russia* 49 J6
Nałęczów, *Poland* 45 G9
Nalerigu, *Ghana* 83 C4
Nalgonda, *India* 66 L11
Nalhati, *India* 69 G12
Nallamalai Hills, *India* .. 66 M11
Nallhan, *Turkey* 72 B4
Nalón →, *Spain* 34 B4
Nam Can, *Vietnam* 65 H5
Nam Co, *China* 60 C4
Nam Dinh, *Vietnam* 64 B6
Nam Du, Hon, *Vietnam* .. 65 H5
Nam Ngum Dam, *Laos* .. 64 C4
Nam-Phan = Cochin
  China, *Vietnam* 65 G6
Nam Phong, *Thailand* ... 64 D4
Nam Tha, *Laos* 64 B3
Nam Tok, *Thailand* 64 E2
Namacunde, *Angola* 88 B2
Namacurra, *Mozam.* 89 B6
Namak, Daryācheh-ye, *Iran* 71 C7
Namak, Kavir-e, *Iran* 71 C8
Namaland, *Namibia* 88 C2
Namangan, *Uzbekistan* .. 50 E8
Namapa, *Mozam.* 87 E4
Namaqualand, *S. Africa* .. 88 E2
Namasagali, *Uganda* 86 B3
Namber, *Indonesia* 63 E8
Nambour, *Australia* 95 D5
Nambucca Heads, *Australia* 95 E5
Namche Bazar, *Nepal* ... 69 F12
Namchonjŏm, *N. Korea* .. 57 E14
Namecunda, *Mozam.* ... 87 E4
Nameponda, *Mozam.* ... 87 F4
Náměšt' nad Oslavou,
  Czech Rep. 27 B9
Námestovo, *Slovak Rep.* . 27 B12
Nametil, *Mozam.* 87 F4
Namew L., *Canada* 105 C8
Namib Desert =
  Namibwoestyn, *Namibia* 88 C2
Namibe, *Angola* 85 H2
Namibe □, *Angola* 88 B1
Namibia ■, *Africa* 88 C2
Namibwoestyn, *Namibia* . 88 C2
Namīn, *Iran* 73 C13
Namlea, *Indonesia* 63 E7
Namoi →, *Australia* 95 E4
Nampa, *U.S.A.* 114 E5
Nampo, *N. Korea* 57 E13
Nampō-Shotō, *Japan* ... 55 J10
Nampula, *Mozam.* 87 F4
Namrole, *Indonesia* 63 E7
Namse Shankou, *China* .. 67 E13
Namsen →, *Norway* 8 D14
Namsos, *Norway* 8 D14
Namtsy, *Russia* 51 C13
Namtu, *Burma* 67 H20
Namtumbo, *Tanzania* ... 87 E4
Namu, *Canada* 104 C3
Namur, *Belgium* 17 D4
Namur □, *Belgium* 17 D4
Namutoni, *Namibia* 88 B2
Namwala, *Zambia* 87 F2
Namwŏn, *S. Korea* 57 G14
Namysłów, *Poland* 45 G4
Nan, *Thailand* 64 C3
Nan →, *Thailand* 64 E3
Nan Xian, *China* 59 C9
Nana, *Romania* 43 F11
Nanaimo, *Canada* 104 D4
Nanam, *N. Korea* 57 D15
Nanan, *China* 59 E12
Nanango, *Australia* 95 D5
Nan'ao, *China* 59 F11
Nanao, *Japan* 55 F8
Nanbu, *China* 58 B6
Nanchang, *China* 59 C10
Nancheng, *China* 59 D11
Nanching = Nanjing, *China* 59 A12
Nanchong, *China* 58 B6
Nanchuan, *China* 58 C6
Nancy, *France* 19 D13
Nanda Devi, *India* 69 D8
Nandan, *China* 58 E6
Nandan, *Japan* 55 G7
Nanded, *India* 66 K10
Nandewar Ra., *Australia* . 95 E5
Nandi, *Fiji* 91 C7
Nandi □, *Kenya* 86 B4
Nandurbar, *India* 66 J9
Nandyal, *India* 66 M11
Nanfeng, *Guangdong,*
  China 59 F8
Nanfeng, *Jiangxi, China* . 59 D11
Nanga, *Australia* 93 E1
Nanga-Eboko, *Cameroon* . 83 E7
Nanga Parbat, *Pakistan* . 69 B6
Nangade, *Mozam.* 87 E4
Nangapinoh, *Indonesia* . 62 E4
Nangarhár □, *Afghan.* .. 66 B7
Nangatayap, *Indonesia* . 62 E4
Nangeya Mts., *Uganda* .. 86 B3
Nangis, *France* 19 D10
Nangong, *China* 56 F8

Nanhua, *China* 58 E3
Nanhuang, *China* 57 F11
Nanhui, *China* 59 B13
Nanji Shan, *China* 59 D13
Nanjian, *China* 58 E3
Nanjiang, *China* 58 A6
Nanjing, *Fujian, China* ... 59 E11
Nanjing, *Jiangsu, China* .. 59 A12
Nanjirinji, *Tanzania* 87 D4
Nankana Sahib, *Pakistan* . 68 D5
Nankang, *China* 59 E10
Nanking = Nanjing, *China* 59 A12
Nankoku, *Japan* 55 H6
Nanling, *China* 59 B12
Nanning, *China* 58 F7
Nannup, *Australia* 93 F2
Nanpan Jiang →, *China* .. 58 E6
Nanpara, *India* 69 F9
Nanpi, *China* 56 E9
Nanping, *Fujian, China* .. 59 D12
Nanping, *Henan, China* .. 59 C9
Nanri Dao, *China* 59 E12
Nanripe, *Mozam.* 87 E4
Nansei-Shotō = Ryūkyū-
  rettō, *Japan* 55 M3
Nansen Sd., *Canada* 4 A3
Nansio, *Tanzania* 86 C3
Nant, *France* 20 D7
Nanterre, *France* 19 D9
Nantes, *France* 18 E5
Nantiat, *France* 20 B5
Nanticoke, *U.S.A.* 111 E8
Nanton, *Canada* 104 C6
Nantong, *China* 59 A13
Nantua, *France* 19 F12
Nantucket I., *U.S.A.* ... 98 E12
Nantwich, *U.K.* 12 D5
Nanuque, *Brazil* 125 G10
Nanusa, Kepulauan,
  Indonesia 63 D7
Nanutarra, *Australia* 92 D2
Nanxiong, *China* 59 E10
Nanyang, *China* 56 H7
Nanyi Hu, *China* 59 B12
Nanyuan, *China* 56 E9
Nanyuki, *Kenya* 86 B4
Nanzhang, *China* 59 B8
Nao, C. de la, *Spain* 33 G5
Naococane L., *Canada* .. 103 B5
Naoetsu, *Japan* 55 F9
Náousa, *Imathía, Greece* . 40 F6
Náousa, *Kikládhes, Greece* 39 D7
Naozhou Dao, *China* 59 G8
Napa, *U.S.A.* 116 G4
Napa →, *U.S.A.* 116 G4
Napanee, *Canada* 102 D4
Napanoch, *U.S.A.* 111 E10
Nape, *Laos* 64 C5
Nape Pass = Keo Neua,
  Deo, *Vietnam* 64 C5
Napier, *N.Z.* 91 H6
Napier Broome B.,
  Australia 92 B4
Napier Downs, *Australia* . 92 C3
Napier Pen., *Australia* ... 95 A2
Naples = Nápoli, *Italy* .. 31 B7
Naples, *U.S.A.* 109 M5
Napo, *China* 58 F5
Napo →, *U.S.A.* 122 D3
Napoleon, *N. Dak., U.S.A.* 112 B5
Napoleon, *Ohio, U.S.A.* . 108 E3
Nápoli, *Italy* 31 B7
Nápoli, G. di, *Italy* 31 B7
Napopo,
  Dem. Rep. of the Congo 86 B2
Nappa Merrie, *Australia* . 95 D3
Naqâda, *Egypt* 80 B3
Naqadeh, *Iran* 73 D11
Naqqāsh, *Iran* 71 C6
Nara, *Japan* 55 G7
Nara, *Mali* 82 B3
Nara □, *Japan* 55 G8
Nara Canal, *Pakistan* ... 68 G3
Nara Visa, *U.S.A.* 113 H3
Naracoorte, *Australia* ... 95 F3
Naradhan, *Australia* 95 E4
Narasapur, *India* 67 L12
Narathiwat, *Thailand* ... 65 J3
Narayanganj, *Bangla.* ... 67 H17
Narayanpet, *India* 66 L10
Narbonne, *France* 20 E7
Narcea →, *Spain* 34 B4
Nardīn, *Iran* 71 B7
Nardò, *Italy* 31 B11
Narembeen, *Australia* .. 93 F2
Nares Str., *Arctic* 98 A13
Naretha, *Australia* 93 F3
Narew →, *Poland* 45 F7
Nari →, *Pakistan* 68 F2
Narin, *Afghan.* 66 A6
Narindra, Helodranon' i,
  Madag. 89 A8
Narita, *Japan* 55 G10
Närke, *Sweden* 10 E8
Narmada →, *India* 68 J5
Narman, *Turkey* 73 B9
Narmland, *Sweden* 9 F15
Narnaul, *India* 68 E7
Narni, *Italy* 29 F9
Naro, *Ghana* 82 C4
Naro Fominsk, *Russia* .. 46 E9
Narodnaya, *Russia* 6 B17
Narok, *Kenya* 86 C4
Narok □, *Kenya* 86 C4
Narón, *Spain* 34 B2
Narooma, *Australia* 95 F5

Narowal, *Pakistan* 68 C6
Narrabri, *Australia* 95 E4
Narran →, *Australia* 95 D4
Narrandera, *Australia* ... 95 E4
Narraway →, *Canada* ... 104 B5
Narrogin, *Australia* 93 F2
Narromine, *Australia* ... 95 E4
Narsimhapur, *India* 69 H8
Nartes, L. e, *Albania* 40 F3
Nartkala, *Russia* 49 J6
Naruto, *Japan* 55 G7
Narva, *Estonia* 46 C5
Narva →, *Russia* 9 G22
Narvik, *Norway* 8 B17
Narvskoye Vdkhr., *Russia* 46 C5
Narwana, *India* 68 E7
Naryilco, *Australia* 95 D3
Narym, *Russia* 50 D9
Naryn, *Kyrgyzstan* 50 E8
Nasa, *Norway* 8 C16
Nasarawa, *Nigeria* 83 D6
Năsăud, *Romania* 43 C9
Naseby, *N.Z.* 91 L3
Naselle, *U.S.A.* 116 D3
Naser, Buheirat en, *Egypt* 80 C3
Nashua, *Iowa, U.S.A.* .. 112 D8
Nashua, *Mont., U.S.A.* . 114 B10
Nashua, *N.H., U.S.A.* .. 111 D13
Nashville, *Ark., U.S.A.* . 113 J8
Nashville, *Ga., U.S.A.* . 109 K4
Nashville, *Tenn., U.S.A.* 109 G2
Našice, *Croatia* 42 E3
Nasielsk, *Poland* 45 F7
Nasik, *India* 66 K8
Nasipit, *Phil.* 61 G6
Nasirabad, *India* 68 F6
Naskaupi →, *Canada* ... 103 B7
Naso, *Italy* 31 D7
Nass →, *Canada* 104 C3
Nassau, *Bahamas* 120 A4
Nassau, *U.S.A.* 111 D11
Nassau, B., *Chile* 128 H3
Nasser, L. = Naser,
  Buheirat en, *Egypt* 80 C3
Nasser City = Kôm Ombo,
  Egypt 80 C3
Nassian, *Ivory C.* 82 D4
Nässjö, *Sweden* 11 G8
Nasugbu, *Phil.* 61 D4
Näsum, *Sweden* 11 H8
Näsviken, *Sweden* 10 C10
Nat Kyizin, *Burma* 67 M20
Nata, *Botswana* 88 C4
Natal, *Brazil* 125 E11
Natal, *Canada* 104 D6
Natal, *Indonesia* 62 D1
Natalinci, *Serbia, Yug.* . 42 F5
Naṭanz, *Iran* 71 C6
Natashquan, *Canada* ... 103 B7
Natashquan →, *Canada* . 103 B7
Natchez, *U.S.A.* 113 K9
Natchitoches, *U.S.A.* ... 113 K8
Nathalia, *Australia* 95 F4
Nathdwara, *India* 68 G5
Nati, Pta., *Spain* 37 A10
Natimuk, *Australia* 95 F3
Nation →, *Canada* 104 B4
National City, *U.S.A.* ... 117 N9
Natitingou, *Benin* 83 C5
Natividad, I., *Mexico* ... 118 B1
Natoma, *U.S.A.* 112 F5
Natron, L., *Tanzania* 86 C4
Natrona Heights, *U.S.A.* 110 F5
Natrûn, W. el →, *Egypt* . 80 H7
Nättraby, *Sweden* 11 H9
Natuna Besar, Kepulauan,
  Indonesia 65 L7
Natuna Is. = Natuna
  Besar, Kepulauan,
  Indonesia 65 L7
Natuna Selatan,
  Kepulauan, *Indonesia* . 65 L7
Natural Bridge, *U.S.A.* .. 111 B9
Naturaliste, C., *Australia* 94 G4
Nau Qala, *Afghan.* 68 B3
Naubinway, *U.S.A.* 102 C2
Naucelle, *France* 20 D6
Nauders, *Austria* 26 E3
Nauen, *Germany* 24 C8
Naugatuck, *U.S.A.* 111 E11
Naujoji Akmenė, *Lithuania* 44 B9
Naumburg, *Germany* ... 24 D7
Nā'ūr at Tunayb, *Jordan* . 75 D4
Nauru ■, *Pac. Oc.* 96 H8
Naushahra = Nowshera,
  Pakistan 66 C8
Nauta, *Peru* 124 D4
Nautanwa, *India* 67 F13
Nautla, *Mexico* 119 C5
Nava, *Mexico* 118 B4
Nava del Rey, *Spain* 34 D5
Nava, *Mexico* 118 B4
Navadwip, *India* 69 H13
Navahermosa, *Spain* ... 35 F6
Navahrudak, *Belarus* ... 46 F3
Navajo Reservoir, *U.S.A.* 115 H10
Navalcarnero, *Spain* ... 34 E6
Navalmoral de la Mata,
  Spain 34 F5
Navalvillar de Pela, *Spain* 35 F5
Navan = An Uaimh,
  Ireland 15 C5
Navapolatsk, *Belarus* ... 46 E5
Navarino, *Chile* 128 H3
Navarra □, *Spain* 32 C3

Navarre, *U.S.A.* 110 F3
Navarro →, *U.S.A.* 116 F3
Navas de San Juan, *Spain* . 35 G7
Navasota, *U.S.A.* 113 K6
Navassa, *W. Indies* 121 C5
Nävekvarn, *Sweden* 11 F10
Naver →, *U.K.* 14 C4
Navia, *Spain* 34 B4
Navia →, *Spain* 34 B4
Navia de Suarna, *Spain* .. 34 C3
Navidad, *Chile* 126 C1
Navlya, *Russia* 47 F8
Năvodari, *Romania* 43 F13
Navoi = Nawoiy,
  Uzbekistan 50 E7
Navojoa, *Mexico* 118 B3
Navolato, *Mexico* 118 C3
Návpaktos, *Greece* 38 C3
Návplion, *Greece* 38 D4
Navrongo, *Ghana* 83 C4
Navsari, *India* 66 J8
Nawa Kot, *Pakistan* 68 E4
Nawabganj, *Ut. P., India* . 69 F9
Nawabganj, *Ut. P., India* . 69 E8
Nawabshah, *Pakistan* ... 68 F3
Nawada, *India* 69 G11
Nawakot, *Nepal* 69 F11
Nawalgarh, *India* 68 F6
Nawanshahr, *India* 69 C6
Nawi, *Sudan* 80 D3
Nawoiy, *Uzbekistan* 50 E7
Naxçıvan, *Azerbaijan* ... 73 C11
Naxçıvan □, *Azerbaijan* . 50 F5
Náxos, *Greece* 39 D7
Nay, *France* 20 E3
Nāy Band, *Iran* 71 E7
Nayakhan, *Russia* 51 C16
Nayarit □, *Mexico* 118 C4
Nayé, *Senegal* 82 C2
Nayong, *China* 58 D5
Nayoro, *Japan* 54 B11
Nayyāl, W. →, *Si. Arabia* 70 D3
Nazaré, *Brazil* 125 F11
Nazaré, *Portugal* 35 F1
Nazareth = Naẕerat, *Israel* 75 C4
Nazas, *Mexico* 118 B4
Nazas →, *Mexico* 118 B4
Nazca, *Peru* 124 F4
Naze, The, *U.K.* 13 F9
Naẕerat, *Israel* 75 C4
Nazık, *Iran* 70 B5
Nazilli, *Turkey* 39 D10
Nazir Hat, *Bangla.* 67 H17
Nazko, *Canada* 104 C4
Nazko →, *Canada* 104 C4
Nazret, *Ethiopia* 81 F4
Nchanga, *Zambia* 87 E2
Ncheu, *Malawi* 87 E3
Ndala, *Tanzania* 86 C3
Ndalatando, *Angola* ... 84 F2
Ndali, *Benin* 83 D5
Ndareda, *Tanzania* 86 C4
Ndélé, *C.A.R.* 84 C4
Ndjamena, *Chad* 79 F8
Ndola, *Zambia* 87 E2
Ndoto Mts., *Kenya* 86 B4
Nduguti, *Tanzania* 86 C3
Néa Alikarnassós, *Greece* 39 F7
Néa Ankhíalos, *Greece* . 38 B4
Néa Epídhavros, *Greece* . 38 D5
Néa Flippiás, *Greece* ... 38 B3
Néa Ionía, *Greece* 38 B4
Néa Kallikrátia, *Greece* . 40 F7
Néa Mákri, *Greece* 38 C5
Néa Moudhaniá, *Greece* . 40 F7
Néa Péramos, *Attikí,*
  Greece 38 C5
Néa Péramos, *Kaválla,*
  Greece 41 F8
Néa Víssi, *Greece* 41 E10
Néa Zíkhna, *Greece* 40 E7
Neagh, Lough, *U.K.* 15 B5
Neah Bay, *U.S.A.* 116 B2
Neale, L., *Australia* 92 D5
Neamţ □, *Romania* 43 C11
Neápolis, *Kozáni, Greece* 40 F5
Neápolis, *Kríti, Greece* .. 36 D7
Neápolis, *Lakonía, Greece* 38 E5
Near Is., *U.S.A.* 100 C1
Neath, *U.K.* 13 F4
Neath Port Talbot □, *U.K.* 13 F4
Nebbou, *Burkina Faso* .. 83 C4
Nebine Cr. →, *Australia* . 95 D4
Nebitdag, *Turkmenistan* . 50 F6
Nebolchy, *Russia* 46 C7
Nebraska □, *U.S.A.* 112 E5
Nebraska City, *U.S.A.* .. 112 E7
Nébrodi, Monti, *Italy* ... 31 E7
Necedah, *U.S.A.* 112 C9
Nechako →, *Canada* ... 104 C4
Neches →, *U.S.A.* 113 L8
Neckar →, *Germany* ... 25 F4
Necochea, *Argentina* ... 126 D4
Neda, *Spain* 34 B2
Nédha →, *Greece* 38 D3
Nedelino, *Bulgaria* 41 E9
Nedelišće, *Croatia* 29 B13
Needles, *U.S.A.* 117 L12
Needles, The, *U.K.* 13 G6
Neembucú □, *Paraguay* . 126 B4
Neemuch = Nimach, *India* 68 G6
Neenah, *U.S.A.* 108 C1
Neepawa, *Canada* 105 C9
Neftçala, *Azerbaijan* ... 73 C13
Neftegorsk, *Russia* 49 H4
Neftekumsk, *Russia* ... 49 H7
Nefyn, *U.K.* 12 E3

Negapatam =
  Nagappattinam, India .. 66 P11
Negaunee, U.S.A. 108 B2
Negele, Ethiopia 81 F4
Negev Desert = Hanegev,
  Israel 75 E4
Negoiul, Vf., Romania .. 43 E9
Negombo, Sri Lanka 66 R11
Negotin, Serbia, Yug. ... 40 B6
Negotino, Macedonia ... 40 E6
Negra, Peña, Spain 34 C4
Negra, Pta., Peru 122 D2
Negrais, C. = Maudin Sun,
  Burma 67 M19
Negreşti, Romania 43 D12
Negreşti-Oaş, Romania .. 43 C8
Negro →, Argentina 122 H4
Negro →, Brazil 122 D4
Negro →, Uruguay 127 C4
Negros, Phil. 61 G5
Negru Vodă, Romania .. 43 G13
Nehalem →, U.S.A. 116 E3
Nehāvand, Iran 71 C6
Nehbandān, Iran 71 D9
Nehoiu, Romania 43 E11
Nei Monggol Zizhiqu □,
  China 56 D7
Neidpath, Canada 105 C7
Neihart, U.S.A. 114 C8
Neijiang, China 58 C5
Neilton, U.S.A. 114 C2
Neiqiu, China 56 F8
Neiva, Colombia 124 C3
Neixiang, China 56 H6
Nejanilini L., Canada ... 105 B9
Nejo, Ethiopia 81 F4
Nekā, Iran 71 B7
Nekemte, Ethiopia 81 F4
Nekheb, Egypt 80 B3
Neksø, Denmark 11 J9
Nelas, Portugal 34 E3
Nelia, Australia 94 C3
Nelidovo, Russia 46 D7
Neligh, U.S.A. 112 D5
Nelkan, Russia 51 D14
Nellore, India 66 M11
Nelson, Canada 104 D5
Nelson, N.Z. 91 J4
Nelson, U.K. 12 D5
Nelson, U.S.A. 115 J7
Nelson →, Canada 105 C9
Nelson, C., Australia ... 95 F3
Nelson, Estrecho, Chile . 128 G2
Nelson Forks, Canada ... 104 B4
Nelson House, Canada ... 105 B9
Nelson L., Canada 105 B8
Nelspoort, S. Africa 88 E3
Nelspruit, S. Africa 89 D5
Néma, Mauritania 82 B3
Neman, Russia 9 J20
Neman →, Lithuania ... 9 J20
Neméa, Greece 38 D4
Nemeiben L., Canada ... 105 B7
Nemërçkës, Mal, Albania . 40 F4
Nemira, Vf., Romania .. 43 D11
Nemours, France 19 D9
Nemšová, Slovak Rep. .. 27 C11
Nemunas = Neman →,
  Lithuania 9 J20
Nemuro, Japan 54 C12
Nemuro-Kaikyō, Japan .. 54 C12
Nen Jiang →, China ... 57 B13
Nenagh, Ireland 15 D3
Nenasi, Malaysia 65 L4
Nene →, U.K. 13 E8
Nénita, Greece 39 C8
Nenjiang, China 60 B7
Neno, Malawi 87 F3
Neodesha, U.S.A. 113 G7
Neokhórion,
  Aitolía kai Akarnanía,
  Greece 38 C3
Neokhórion, Árta, Greece 38 B2
Néon Karlovásion, Greece 39 D8
Néon Petrítsi, Greece ... 40 E7
Neosho, U.S.A. 113 G7
Neosho →, U.S.A. 113 H7
Nepal ■, Asia 69 F11
Nepalganj, Nepal 69 E9
Nephi, U.S.A. 114 G8
Nephin, Ireland 15 B2
Nepi, Italy 29 F9
Nepomuk, Czech Rep. .. 26 B6
Neptune, U.S.A. 111 F10
Nera →, Italy 29 F9
Nera →, Romania 42 F6
Nérac, France 20 D4
Neratovice, Czech Rep. .. 26 A7
Nerchinsk, Russia 51 D12
Nereju, Romania 43 E11
Nerekhta, Russia 46 D11
Néret L., Canada 103 B5
Neretvanski Kanal, Croatia 29 E14
Neringa, Lithuania 9 J19
Nerja, Spain 35 J7
Nerl →, Russia 46 D11
Nerpio, Spain 33 G2
Nerva, Spain 35 H4
Nervi, Italy 28 D6
Nesebŭr, Bulgaria 41 D11
Ness, L., U.K. 14 D4
Nesterov, Poland 47 G2
Nestórion, Greece 40 F5
Néstos →, Greece 41 E8
Nesvady, Slovak Rep. .. 27 D11
Nesvizh = Nyasvizh,
  Belarus 47 F4

Netanya, Israel 75 C3
Nete →, Belgium 17 C4
Netherdale, Australia 94 C4
Netherlands ■, Europe .. 17 C5
Netherlands Antilles ■,
  W. Indies 124 A5
Neto →, Italy 31 C10
Nettancourt, France 19 D11
Nettetal, Germany 24 D2
Nettilling L., Canada 101 B12
Nettuno, Italy 30 A5
Netzahualcoyotl, Presa,
  Mexico 119 D6
Neu-Isenburg, Germany . 25 E4
Neu-Ulm, Germany 25 G6
Neubrandenburg, Germany 24 B9
Neubukow, Germany ... 24 A7
Neuburg, Germany 25 G7
Neuchâtel, Switz. 25 J2
Neuchâtel □, Switz. 25 J2
Neuchâtel, Lac de, Switz. . 25 J2
Neudau, Austria 26 D9
Neuenhagen, Germany . 24 C9
Neuenhaus, Germany .. 24 C2
Neuf-Brisach, France 19 D14
Neufahrn, Bayern,
  Germany 25 G8
Neufahrn, Bayern,
  Germany 25 G7
Neufchâteau, Belgium .. 17 E5
Neufchâteau, France 19 D12
Neufchâtel-en-Bray, France 18 C8
Neufchâtel-sur-Aisne,
  France 19 C11
Neuhaus, Germany 24 B6
Neuillé-Pont-Pierre, France 18 E7
Neuilly-St-Front, France .. 19 C10
Neukalen, Germany 24 B8
Neumarkt, Germany ... 25 F7
Neumünster, Germany .. 24 A5
Neung-sur-Beuvron, France 19 E8
Neunkirchen, Austria 26 D9
Neunkirchen, Germany .. 25 F3
Neuquén, Argentina 128 D3
Neuquén □, Argentina .. 126 D2
Neuruppin, Germany ... 24 C8
Neusäss, Germany 25 G6
Neuse →, U.S.A. 109 H7
Neusiedl, Austria 27 D9
Neusiedler See, Austria .. 27 D9
Neuss, Germany 24 D2
Neussargues-Moissac,
  France 20 C7
Neustadt, Bayern, Germany 25 F8
Neustadt, Bayern, Germany 25 G7
Neustadt, Bayern, Germany 25 F6
Neustadt, Bayern, Germany 25 E7
Neustadt, Brandenburg,
  Germany 24 C8
Neustadt, Hessen, Germany 24 E5
Neustadt, Niedersachsen,
  Germany 24 C5
Neustadt, Rhld.-Pfz.,
  Germany 25 F4
Neustadt, Sachsen,
  Germany 24 D10
Neustadt,
  Schleswig-Holstein,
  Germany 24 A6
Neustadt, Thüringen,
  Germany 24 E7
Neustrelitz, Germany ... 24 B9
Neuvic, France 20 C6
Neuville-sur-Saône, France 21 C8
Neuvy-le-Roi, France 18 E7
Neuvy-St-Sépulchre, France 19 F8
Neuvy-sur-Barangeon,
  France 19 E9
Neuwerk, Germany 24 B4
Neuwied, Germany 24 E3
Neva →, Russia 46 C6
Nevada, U.S.A. 113 G7
Nevada □, U.S.A. 114 G5
Nevada, Sierra, Spain ... 35 H7
Nevada, Sierra, U.S.A. .. 114 G3
Nevada City, U.S.A. 116 F6
Nevado, Cerro, Argentina 126 D2
Nevel, Russia 46 D5
Nevers, France 19 F10
Nevertire, Australia 95 E4
Nevesinje, Bos.-H. 40 C2
Neville, Canada 105 D7
Nevinnomyssk, Russia .. 49 H6
Nevis, W. Indies 121 C7
Nevrokop = Gotse
  Delchev, Bulgaria 40 E7
Nevşehir, Turkey 72 C6
New Albany, Ind., U.S.A. 108 F3
New Albany, Miss., U.S.A. 113 H10
New Albany, Pa., U.S.A. . 111 E8
New Amsterdam, Guyana 124 B7
New Angledool, Australia 95 D4
New Bedford, U.S.A. ... 111 E14
New Bern, U.S.A. 109 H7
New Bethlehem, U.S.A. . 110 F5
New Bloomfield, U.S.A. . 110 F7
New Boston, U.S.A. 113 J7
New Braunfels, U.S.A. .. 113 L5
New Brighton, N.Z. 91 K4
New Brighton, U.S.A. ... 110 F4
New Britain, Papua N. G. 96 H7
New Britain, U.S.A. 111 E12
New Brunswick, U.S.A. .. 111 F10
New Brunswick □, Canada 103 C6
New Bussa, Nigeria 83 D5
New Caledonia ■, Pac. Oc. 96 K8
New Castle, Ind., U.S.A. . 108 F3

New Castle, Pa., U.S.A. .. 110 F4
New City, U.S.A. 111 E11
New Cumberland, U.S.A. . 110 F4
New Cuyama, U.S.A. ... 117 L7
New Delhi, India 68 E7
New Denver, Canada ... 104 D5
New Don Pedro Reservoir,
  U.S.A. 116 H6
New England, U.S.A. ... 112 B3
New England Ra.,
  Australia 95 E5
New Forest, U.K. 13 G6
New Galloway, U.K. 14 F4
New Glasgow, Canada .. 103 C7
New Guinea, Oceania ... 96 H5
New Hamburg, Canada .. 110 C4
New Hampshire □, U.S.A. 111 C13
New Hampton, U.S.A. .. 112 D8
New Hanover, S. Africa . 89 D5
New Haven, Conn., U.S.A. 111 E12
New Haven, Mich., U.S.A. 110 D2
New Hazelton, Canada .. 104 B3
New Hebrides =
  Vanuatu ■, Pac. Oc. ... 96 J8
New Iberia, U.S.A. 113 K9
New Ireland, Papua N. G. 96 H7
New Jersey □, U.S.A. ... 111 F10
New Kensington, U.S.A. . 110 F5
New Lexington, U.S.A. .. 108 F4
New Liskeard, Canada .. 102 C4
New London, Conn.,
  U.S.A. 111 E12
New London, Minn.,
  U.S.A. 112 C7
New London, Ohio, U.S.A. 110 E2
New London, Wis., U.S.A. 112 C10
New Madrid, U.S.A. 113 G10
New Meadows, U.S.A. .. 114 D5
New Melones L., U.S.A. . 116 H6
New Mexico □, U.S.A. .. 115 J10
New Milford, Conn.,
  U.S.A. 111 E11
New Milford, Pa., U.S.A. 111 E9
New Norcia, Australia ... 93 F2
New Norfolk, Australia .. 94 G4
New Orleans, U.S.A. 113 L9
New Philadelphia, U.S.A. 110 F3
New Plymouth, N.Z. 91 H5
New Plymouth, U.S.A. .. 114 E5
New Providence, Bahamas 120 A4
New Quay, U.K. 13 E3
New Radnor, U.K. 13 E4
New Richmond, U.S.A. .. 112 C8
New Roads, U.S.A. 113 K9
New Rochelle, U.S.A. ... 111 F11
New Rockford, U.S.A. ... 112 B5
New Romney, U.K. 13 G8
New Ross, Ireland 15 D5
New Salem, U.S.A. 112 B4
New Scone, U.K. 14 E5
New Siberian I. = Novaya
  Sibir, Ostrov, Russia ... 51 B16
New Siberian Is. =
  Novosibirskiye Ostrova,
  Russia 51 B15
New Smyrna Beach, U.S.A. 109 L5
New South Wales □,
  Australia 95 E4
New Springs, Australia .. 93 E3
New Town, U.S.A. 112 B3
New Tredegar, U.K. 13 F4
New Ulm, U.S.A. 112 C7
New Waterford, Canada . 103 C7
New Westminster, Canada 104 D4
New York □, U.S.A. 111 D9
New York City, U.S.A. .. 111 F11
New Zealand ■, Oceania 91 J6
Newala, Tanzania 87 E4
Newala □, Tanzania 87 E4
Newark, Del., U.S.A. ... 108 F8
Newark, N.J., U.S.A. ... 111 F10
Newark, N.Y., U.S.A. ... 110 C7
Newark, Ohio, U.S.A. ... 110 F2
Newark-on-Trent, U.K. .. 12 D7
Newaygo, U.S.A. 108 D3
Newberg, U.S.A. 114 D2
Newberry, Mich., U.S.A. . 108 B3
Newberry, S.C., U.S.A. .. 109 H5
Newberry Springs, U.S.A. 117 L10
Newbridge = Droichead
  Nua, Ireland 15 C5
Newbrook, Canada 104 C6
Newburgh, U.S.A. 111 E10
Newbury, U.K. 13 F6
Newbury, U.S.A. 111 B12
Newburyport, U.S.A. ... 111 D14
Newcastle, Australia 95 E5
Newcastle, Canada 103 C6
Newcastle, S. Africa 89 D4
Newcastle, U.K. 15 B6
Newcastle, Calif., U.S.A. . 116 G5
Newcastle, Wyo., U.S.A. 112 D2
Newcastle Emlyn, U.K. .. 13 E3
Newcastle Ra., Australia . 92 C5
Newcastle-under-Lyme,
  U.K. 12 D5
Newcastle-upon-Tyne, U.K. 12 C6
Newcastle Waters, Australia 94 B1
Newcastle West, Ireland . 15 D2
Newdegate, Australia ... 93 F2
Newell, U.S.A. 112 C3
Newfoundland, Canada .. 103 B8
Newfoundland I., N. Amer. 98 E14
Newhalem, U.S.A. 104 B4
Newhall, U.S.A. 117 L8
Newhaven, U.K. 13 G8
Newkirk, U.S.A. 113 G6

Newlyn, U.K. 13 G2
Newman, Australia 92 D2
Newman, U.S.A. 116 H5
Newmarket, Canada ... 110 B5
Newmarket, Ireland 15 D2
Newmarket, U.K. 13 E8
Newmarket, U.S.A. 111 C14
Newnan, U.S.A. 109 J3
Newport, Ireland 15 C2
Newport, I. of W., U.K. . 13 G6
Newport, Newp., U.K. .. 13 F5
Newport, Ark., U.S.A. .. 113 H9
Newport, Ky., U.S.A. ... 108 F3
Newport, N.H., U.S.A. .. 111 C12
Newport, Oreg., U.S.A. . 114 D1
Newport, Pa., U.S.A. ... 110 F7
Newport, R.I., U.S.A. ... 111 E13
Newport, Tenn., U.S.A. . 109 H4
Newport, Vt., U.S.A. ... 111 B12
Newport □, U.K. 13 F4
Newport Beach, U.S.A. . 117 M9
Newport News, U.S.A. .. 108 G7
Newport Pagnell, U.K. .. 13 E7
Newquay, U.K. 13 G2
Newry, U.K. 15 B5
Newton, Iowa, U.S.A. .. 112 E8
Newton, Mass., U.S.A. .. 111 D13
Newton, Miss., U.S.A. .. 113 J10
Newton, N.C., U.S.A. ... 109 H5
Newton, N.J., U.S.A. ... 111 E10
Newton, Tex., U.S.A. ... 113 K8
Newton Abbot, U.K. 13 G4
Newton Aycliffe, U.K. ... 12 C6
Newton Boyd, Australia . 95 D5
Newton Stewart, U.K. ... 14 G4
Newtonmore, U.K. 14 D4
Newtown, U.K. 13 E4
Newtownabbey, U.K. ... 15 B6
Newtownards, U.K. 15 B6
Newtownbarry = Bunclody,
  Ireland 15 D5
Newtownstewart, U.K. .. 15 B4
Newville, U.S.A. 110 F7
Nexon, France 20 C5
Neya, Russia 48 A6
Neyrīz, Iran 71 D7
Neyshābūr, Iran 71 B8
Nezhin = Nizhyn, Ukraine 47 G6
Nezperce, U.S.A. 114 C5
Ngabang, Indonesia 62 D3
Ngabordamlu, Tanjung,
  Indonesia 63 F8
Ngambé, Cameroon 83 D7
Ngami Depression,
  Botswana 88 C3
Ngamo, Zimbabwe 87 F2
Nganglong Kangri, China 67 C12
Ngao, Thailand 64 C2
Ngaoundéré, Cameroon . 84 C2
Ngapara, N.Z. 91 L3
Ngara, Tanzania 86 C3
Ngara □, Tanzania 86 C3
Ngawi, Indonesia 63 G14
Nghia Lo, Vietnam 64 B5
Ngoma, Malawi 87 E3
Ngomahura, Zimbabwe . 87 G3
Ngomba, Tanzania 87 D3
Ngop, Sudan 81 F3
Ngoring Hu, China 60 C4
Ngorkou, Mali 82 B4
Ngorongoro, Tanzania .. 86 C4
Ngozi, Burundi 86 C2
Ngudu, Tanzania 86 C3
Nguigmi, Niger 79 F8
Ngukurr, Australia 94 A1
Ngunga, Tanzania 86 C3
Nguru, Nigeria 83 C7
Nguru Mts., Tanzania .. 86 D4
Nguyen Binh, Vietnam .. 64 A5
Nha Trang, Vietnam 65 F7
Nhacoongo, Mozam. ... 89 C6
Nhamaabué, Mozam. ... 87 F4
Nhamundá →, Brazil .. 125 D7
Nhangutazi, L., Mozam. . 89 C5
Nhill, Australia 95 F3
Nho Quan, Vietnam 64 B5
Nhulunbuy, Australia ... 94 A2
Nia-nia,
  Dem. Rep. of the Congo 86 B2
Niafounké, Mali 82 B4
Niagara, U.S.A. 108 C2
Niagara Falls, Canada .. 102 D4
Niagara Falls, U.S.A. ... 110 C6
Niagara-on-the-Lake,
  Canada 110 C5
Niah, Malaysia 62 D4
Niamey, Niger 83 C5
Nianforando, Guinea ... 82 D2
Niangara,
  Dem. Rep. of the Congo 86 B2
Nias, Indonesia 62 D1
Niassa □, Mozam. 87 E4
Nibe, Denmark 11 H3
Nicaragua ■, Cent. Amer. 120 D2
Nicaragua, L. de, Nic. ... 120 D2
Nicastro, Italy 31 D9
Nice, France 21 E11
Niceville, U.S.A. 109 K2
Nichinan, Japan 55 J5
Nicholás, Canal, W. Indies 120 B3
Nicholasville, U.S.A. ... 108 G3
Nichols, U.S.A. 111 D8
Nicholson, Australia ... 92 C4
Nicholson, U.S.A. 111 E9
Nicholson →, Australia . 94 B2
Nicholson Ra., Australia . 93 E2

Nicobar Is., Ind. Oc. 52 J13
Nicola, Canada 104 C4
Nicolet, Canada 102 C5
Nicolls Town, Bahamas . 120 A4
Nicopolis, Greece 38 B2
Nicosia, Cyprus 36 D12
Nicosia, Italy 31 E7
Nicótera, Italy 31 D8
Nicoya, Costa Rica 120 D2
Nicoya, G. de, Costa Rica 120 E3
Nicoya, Pen. de, Costa Rica 120 E2
Nidd →, U.K. 12 D6
Nidda, Germany 25 E5
Nidda →, Germany ... 25 E4
Nidwalden □, Switz. ... 25 J4
Nidzica, Poland 45 E7
Niebüll, Germany 24 A4
Nied →, Germany 19 C13
Niederaula, Germany .. 24 E5
Niederbayern □, Germany 25 G8
Niederbronn-les-Bains,
  France 19 D14
Niedere Tauern, Austria . 26 D7
Niederlausitz, Germany . 24 D9
Niedersachsen □, Germany 24 C4
Niederrkoop, S. Africa .. 88 D3
Niellé, Ivory C. 82 C3
Niemba,
  Dem. Rep. of the Congo 86 D2
Niemen = Neman →,
  Lithuania 9 J20
Niemodlin, Poland 45 H4
Nienburg, Poland 24 C5
Niepołomice, Poland ... 45 H7
Niers →, Germany 24 D1
Niesky, Germany 24 D10
Nieszawa, Poland 45 F5
Nieu Bethesda, S. Africa . 88 E3
Nieuw Amsterdam,
  Surinam 125 B7
Nieuw Nickerie, Surinam 125 B7
Nieuwoudtville, S. Africa . 88 E2
Nieuwpoort, Belgium .. 17 C2
Nieves, Pico de las,
  Canary Is. 37 G4
Nièvre □, France 19 E10
Niğde, Turkey 72 D6
Nigel, S. Africa 89 D4
Niger ■, W. Afr. 83 B7
Niger →, W. Afr. 83 D6
Nigeria ■, W. Afr. 83 D6
Nightcaps, N.Z. 91 L2
Nigríta, Greece 40 F7
Nihtaur, India 69 E8
Nii-Jima, Japan 55 G9
Niigata, Japan 54 F9
Niigata □, Japan 54 F9
Niihama, Japan 55 H6
Niihau, U.S.A. 106 H14
Niimi, Japan 55 G6
Niitsu, Japan 54 F9
Níjar, Spain 33 J2
Nijil, Jordan 75 E4
Nijkerk, Neths. 17 B5
Nijmegen, Neths. 17 C5
Nijverdal, Neths. 17 B6
Nīk Pey, Iran 71 B6
Nike, Nigeria 83 D6
Nikiniki, Indonesia 63 F6
Nikísiani, Greece 41 F8
Nikítas, Greece 40 F7
Nikki, Benin 83 D5
Nikkō, Japan 55 F9
Nikolayev = Mykolayiv,
  Ukraine 47 J7
Nikolayevsk, Russia 48 E7
Nikolayevsk-na-Amur,
  Russia 51 D15
Nikolsk, Russia 48 D8
Nikolskoye, Russia 51 D17
Nikopol, Bulgaria 41 C8
Nikopol, Ukraine 47 J8
Niksar, Turkey 72 B7
Nīkshahr, Iran 71 E9
Nikšić, Montenegro, Yug. 40 D2
Nîl, Nahr en →, Africa . 80 H7
Nîl el Abyad →, Sudan . 81 D3
Nîl el Azraq →, Sudan . 81 D3
Niland, U.S.A. 117 M11
Nile = Nîl, Nahr en →,
  Africa 80 H7
Nile Delta, Egypt 80 H7
Niles, U.S.A. 110 E4
Nilüfer →, Turkey 41 F12
Nimach, India 68 G6
Nimbahera, India 68 G6
Nîmes, France 21 E8
Nimfaíon, Ákra = Pínnes,
  Ákra, Greece 41 F8
Nimmitabel, Australia .. 95 F4
Nimule, Sudan 81 G3
Nin, Croatia 29 D12
Ninawá, Iraq 70 B4
Nindigully, Australia ... 95 D4
Ninemile, U.S.A. 104 B2
Nineveh = Ninawá, Iraq . 70 B4
Ning Xian, China 56 G4
Ning'an, China 57 B15
Ningbo, China 59 C13
Ningcheng, China 57 D10
Ningde, China 59 D12
Ningdu, China 59 D10
Ninggang, China 59 D9
Ningguo, China 59 B12

Novi Vinodolski

Ninghai, *China* 59 C13
Ninghua, *China* 59 D11
Ningjin, *China* 56 F8
Ningjing Shan, *China* 58 C2
Ninglang, *China* 58 D3
Ningling, *China* 56 G8
Ningming, *China* 58 F6
Ningnan, *China* 58 D4
Ningpo = Ningbo, *China* 59 C13
Ningqiang, *China* 56 H4
Ningshan, *China* 56 H5
Ningsia Hui A.R. = Ningxia Huizu Zizhiqu □, *China* 56 F4
Ningwu, *China* 56 E7
Ningxia Huizu Zizhiqu □, *China* 56 F4
Ningxiang, *China* 59 C9
Ningyang, *China* 56 G9
Ningyuan, *China* 59 E8
Ninh Binh, *Vietnam* 64 B5
Ninh Giang, *Vietnam* 64 B6
Ninh Hoa, *Vietnam* 64 F7
Ninh Ma, *Vietnam* 64 F7
Ninove, *Belgium* 17 D4
Nioaque, *Brazil* 127 A4
Niobrara, *U.S.A.* 112 D6
Niobrara →, *U.S.A.* 112 D6
Niono, *Mali* 82 C3
Nioro du Rip, *Senegal* 82 C1
Nioro du Sahel, *Mali* 82 B3
Niort, *France* 20 B3
Nipawin, *Canada* 105 C8
Nipawin Prov. Park, *Canada* 105 C8
Nipfjället, *Sweden* 10 C6
Nipigon, *Canada* 102 C2
Nipigon, L., *Canada* 102 C2
Nipin →, *Canada* 105 B7
Nipishish L., *Canada* 103 B7
Nipissing L., *Canada* 102 C4
Nipomo, *U.S.A.* 117 K6
Nipton, *U.S.A.* 117 K11
Niquelândia, *Brazil* 125 F9
Nīr, *Iran* 70 B5
Nirasaki, *Japan* 55 G9
Nirmal, *India* 66 K11
Nirmali, *India* 69 F12
Niš, *Serbia, Yug.* 40 C5
Nisa, *Portugal* 35 F3
Nişāb, *Si. Arabia* 70 D5
Nişāb, *Yemen* 74 E4
Nišava →, *Serbia, Yug.* 40 C5
Niscemi, *Italy* 31 E7
Nishinomiya, *Japan* 55 G7
Nishino'omote, *Japan* 55 J5
Nishiwaki, *Japan* 55 G7
Nísíros, *Greece* 39 E9
Niška Banja, *Serbia, Yug.* 40 C6
Niskibi →, *Canada* 102 A2
Nisko, *Poland* 45 H9
Nisporeni, *Moldova* 43 C13
Nisqually →, *U.S.A.* 116 C4
Nissáki, *Greece* 36 A3
Nissan →, *Sweden* 11 H6
Nissum Bredning, *Denmark* 11 H2
Nissum Fjord, *Denmark* 11 H2
Nistru = Dnister →, *Europe* 47 J6
Nisutlin →, *Canada* 104 A2
Nitchequon, *Canada* 103 B5
Niterói, *Brazil* 127 A7
Nith →, *U.K.* 14 F5
Nitra, *Slovak Rep.* 27 C11
Nitra →, *Slovak Rep.* 27 D11
Nitriansky □, *Slovak Rep.* 27 C11
Nittenau, *Germany* 25 F8
Niuafo'ou, *Tonga* 91 B11
Niue, *Cook Is.* 97 J11
Niulan Jiang →, *China* 58 D4
Niut, *Indonesia* 62 D4
Niutou Shan, *China* 59 C13
Niuzhuang, *China* 57 D12
Nivala, *Finland* 8 E21
Nivelles, *Belgium* 17 D4
Nivernais, *France* 19 E10
Nixon, *U.S.A.* 113 L6
Nizamabad, *India* 66 K11
Nizamghat, *India* 67 E19
Nizhne Kolymsk, *Russia* 51 C17
Nizhnegorskiy = Nyzhnohirskyy, *Ukraine* 47 K8
Nizhnekamsk, *Russia* 48 C10
Nizhneudinsk, *Russia* 51 D10
Nizhnevartovsk, *Russia* 50 C8
Nizhniy Chir, *Russia* 49 F6
Nizhniy Lomov, *Russia* 48 D6
Nizhniy Novgorod, *Russia* 48 B7
Nizhniy Tagil, *Russia* 50 D6
Nizhyn, *Ukraine* 47 G6
Nizina Mazowiecka, *Poland* 45 F8
Nizip, *Turkey* 72 D7
Nízké Tatry, *Slovak Rep.* 27 C12
Nízký Jeseník, *Czech Rep.* 27 B10
Nizza Monferrato, *Italy* 28 D5
Njakwa, *Malawi* 87 E3
Njanji, *Zambia* 87 E3
Njegoš, *Montenegro, Yug.* 40 D2
Njinjo, *Tanzania* 87 D4
Njombe, *Tanzania* 87 D3
Njombe □, *Tanzania* 87 D3
Njombe →, *Tanzania* 86 D4
Njurundabommen, *Sweden* 10 B11
Nkambe, *Cameroon* 83 D7
Nkana, *Zambia* 87 E2
Nkawkaw, *Ghana* 83 D4
Nkayi, *Zimbabwe* 87 F2
Nkhotakota, *Malawi* 87 E3
Nkongsamba, *Cameroon* 83 E6
Nkurenkuru, *Namibia* 88 B2
Nkwanta, *Ghana* 82 D4
Nmai →, *Burma* 67 G20
Noakhali = Maijdi, *Bangla.* 67 H17
Nobel, *Canada* 110 A4
Nobeoka, *Japan* 55 H5
Noblejas, *Spain* 34 F7
Noblesville, *U.S.A.* 108 E3
Noce →, *Italy* 28 B8
Nocera Inferiore, *Italy* 31 B7
Nocera Umbra, *Italy* 29 E9
Noci, *Italy* 31 B10
Nockatunga, *Australia* 95 D3
Nocona, *U.S.A.* 113 J6
Nocrich, *Romania* 43 E9
Noda, *Japan* 55 G9
Noel, *U.S.A.* 113 G7
Nogales, *Mexico* 118 A2
Nogales, *U.S.A.* 115 L8
Nogaro, *France* 20 E3
Nogat →, *Poland* 44 D6
Nōgata, *Japan* 55 H5
Nogent, *France* 19 D12
Nogent-le-Rotrou, *France* 18 D7
Nogent-sur-Seine, *France* 19 D10
Noggerup, *Australia* 93 F2
Noginsk, *Moskva, Russia* 46 E10
Noginsk, *Tunguska, Russia* 51 C10
Nogoa →, *Australia* 94 C4
Nogoyá, *Argentina* 126 C4
Nógrád □, *Hungary* 42 C4
Noguera Pallaresa →, *Spain* 32 D5
Noguera Ribagorzana →, *Spain* 32 D5
Nohar, *India* 68 E6
Nohfelden, *Germany* 25 F3
Noia, *Spain* 34 C2
Noire, Montagne, *France* 20 E6
Noire, Mt., *France* 18 D3
Noirétable, *France* 20 C7
Noirmoutier, Î. de, *France* 18 F4
Noirmoutier-en-l'Île, *France* 18 F4
Nojane, *Botswana* 88 C3
Nojima-Zaki, *Japan* 55 G9
Nok Kundi, *Pakistan* 66 E3
Nokaneng, *Botswana* 88 B3
Nokia, *Finland* 9 F20
Nokomis, *Canada* 105 C8
Nokomis L., *Canada* 105 B8
Nol, *Sweden* 11 G6
Nola, *C.A.R.* 84 D3
Nola, *Italy* 31 B7
Nolay, *France* 19 F11
Noli, C. di, *Italy* 28 D5
Nolinsk, *Russia* 48 B9
Noma Omuramba →, *Namibia* 88 B3
Noman L., *Canada* 105 A7
Nombre de Dios, *Panama* 120 E4
Nome, *U.S.A.* 100 B3
Nomo-Zaki, *Japan* 55 H4
Nonacho L., *Canada* 105 A7
Nonancourt, *France* 18 D8
Nonda, *Australia* 94 C3
None, *Italy* 28 D4
Nong Chang, *Thailand* 64 E2
Nong Het, *Laos* 64 C4
Nong Khai, *Thailand* 64 D4
Nong'an, *China* 57 B13
Nongoma, *S. Africa* 89 D5
Nonoava, *Mexico* 118 B3
Nonthaburi, *Thailand* 64 F3
Nontron, *France* 20 C4
Nonza, *France* 21 F13
Noonamah, *Australia* 92 B5
Noonan, *U.S.A.* 112 A3
Noondoo, *Australia* 95 D4
Noonkanbah, *Australia* 92 C3
Noord Brabant □, *Neths.* 17 C5
Noord Holland □, *Neths.* 17 B4
Noordbeveland, *Neths.* 17 C3
Noordoostpolder, *Neths.* 17 B5
Noordwijk, *Neths.* 17 B4
Nootka, *Canada* 104 D3
Nootka I., *Canada* 104 D3
Nora, *Eritrea* 81 D5
Nora, *Sweden* 10 E9
Noranda = Rouyn-Noranda, *Canada* 102 C4
Norberg, *Sweden* 10 D9
Nórcia, *Italy* 29 F10
Norco, *U.S.A.* 117 M9
Nord □, *France* 19 B10
Nord-Ostsee-Kanal, *Germany* 24 A5
Nord-Pas-de-Calais □, *France* 19 B9
Nordaustlandet, *Svalbard* 4 B9
Nordborg, *Denmark* 11 J3
Nordby, *Denmark* 11 J2
Norddeich, *Germany* 24 B3
Nordegg, *Canada* 104 C5
Norden, *Germany* 24 B3
Nordenham, *Germany* 24 B4
Norderney, *Germany* 24 B3
Norderstedt, *Germany* 24 B6
Nordfjord, *Norway* 9 F11
Nordfriesische Inseln, *Germany* 24 A4
Nordhausen, *Germany* 24 D6
Nordhorn, *Germany* 24 C3
Norðoyar, *Færoe Is.* 8 E9
Nordingrå, *Sweden* 10 B12
Nordjyllands Amtskommune □, *Denmark* 11 G4
Nordkapp, *Norway* 8 A21
Nordkapp, *Svalbard* 4 A9
Nordkinn = Kinnarodden, *Norway* 6 A11
Nordkinn-halvøya, *Norway* 8 A22
Nördlingen, *Germany* 25 G6
Nordrhein-Westfalen □, *Germany* 24 D3
Nordstrand, *Germany* 24 A4
Nordvik, *Russia* 51 B12
Nore →, *Ireland* 15 D4
Norembega, *Canada* 102 C3
Norfolk, *Nebr., U.S.A.* 112 D6
Norfolk, *Va., U.S.A.* 108 G7
Norfolk □, *U.K.* 13 E8
Norfolk I., *Pac. Oc.* 96 K8
Norfork Res., *U.S.A.* 113 G8
Norilsk, *Russia* 51 C9
Norley, *Australia* 95 D3
Norma, Mt., *Australia* 94 C3
Normal, *U.S.A.* 112 E10
Norman, *U.S.A.* 113 H6
Norman →, *Australia* 94 B3
Norman Wells, *Canada* 100 B7
Normanby →, *Australia* 94 A3
Normandin, *Canada* 102 C5
Normanhurst, Mt., *Australia* 93 E3
Normanton, *Australia* 94 B3
Norquay, *Canada* 105 C8
Norquinco, *Argentina* 128 E2
Norra Dellen, *Sweden* 10 C10
Norra Ulvön, *Sweden* 10 A12
Norrahammar, *Sweden* 11 G8
Norrbotten □, *Sweden* 8 C19
Nørre Åby, *Denmark* 11 J3
Nørre Alslev, *Denmark* 11 K5
Nørresundby, *Denmark* 11 G3
Norrhult, *Sweden* 11 G9
Norris, *U.S.A.* 114 D8
Norristown, *U.S.A.* 111 F9
Norrköping, *Sweden* 11 F10
Norrland, *Sweden* 9 E16
Norrsundet, *Sweden* 10 D11
Norrtälje, *Sweden* 10 E12
Norseman, *Australia* 93 F3
Norsk, *Russia* 51 D14
Norte, Pta. del, *Canary Is.* 37 G2
Norte, Serra do, *Brazil* 124
North Adams, *U.S.A.* 111 D11
North Ayrshire □, *U.K.* 14 F4
North Battleford, *Canada* 105 C7
North Bay, *Canada* 102 C4
North Belcher Is., *Canada* 102 A4
North Bend, *Canada* 104 D4
North Bend, *Oreg., U.S.A.* 114 E1
North Bend, *Pa., U.S.A.* 110 E7
North Bend, *Wash., U.S.A.* 116 C5
North Berwick, *U.K.* 14 E6
North Berwick, *U.S.A.* 111 C14
North C., *Canada* 103 C7
North C., *N.Z.* 91 F4
North Canadian →, *U.S.A.* 113 H7
North Cape = Nordkapp, *Norway* 8 A21
North Cape = Nordkapp, *Svalbard* 4 A9
North Caribou L., *Canada* 102 B1
North Carolina □, *U.S.A.* 109 H6
North Channel, *Canada* 102 C3
North Channel, *U.K.* 14 F3
North Charleston, *U.S.A.* 109 J6
North Chicago, *U.S.A.* 108 D2
North Dakota □, *U.S.A.* 112 B5
North Dandalup, *Australia* 93 F2
North Downs, *U.K.* 13 F8
North East, *U.S.A.* 110 D5
North East Frontier Agency = Arunachal Pradesh □, *India* 67 F19
North East Lincolnshire □, *U.K.* 12 D7
North East Providence Chan., *W. Indies* 120 A4
North Eastern □, *Kenya* 86 B5
North Esk →, *U.K.* 14 E6
North European Plain, *Europe* 6 E10
North Foreland, *U.K.* 13 F9
North Fork, *U.S.A.* 116 H7
North Fork American →, *U.S.A.* 116 G5
North Fork Feather →, *U.S.A.* 116 F5
North Frisian Is. = Nordfriesische Inseln, *Germany* 24 A4
North Henik L., *Canada* 105 A9
North Highlands, *U.S.A.* 116 G5
North Horr, *Kenya* 86 B4
North I., *Kenya* 86 B4
North I., *N.Z.* 91 H5
North Kingsville, *U.S.A.* 110 E4
North Knife →, *Canada* 105 B10
North Koel →, *India* 69 G10
North Korea ■, *Asia* 57 E14
North Lakhimpur, *India* 67 F19
North Lanarkshire □, *U.K.* 14 F5
North Las Vegas, *U.S.A.* 117 J11
North Lincolnshire □, *U.K.* 12 D7
North Little Rock, *U.S.A.* 113 H8
North Loup →, *U.S.A.* 112 E5
North Magnetic Pole, *Canada* 4 B2
North Minch, *U.K.* 14 C3
North Nahanni →, *Canada* 104 A4
North Olmsted, *U.S.A.* 110 E3
North Ossetia □, *Russia* 49 J7
North Pagai, I. = Pagai Utara, Pulau, *Indonesia* 62 E2
North Palisade, *U.S.A.* 116 H8
North Platte, *U.S.A.* 112 E4
North Platte →, *U.S.A.* 112 E4
North Pole, *Arctic* 4 A
North Portal, *Canada* 105 D8
North Powder, *U.S.A.* 114 D5
North Pt., *Canada* 103 C7
North Rhine Westphalia □ = Nordrhein-Westfalen □, *Germany* 24 D3
North Ronaldsay, *U.K.* 14 B6
North Saskatchewan →, *Canada* 105 C7
North Sea, *Europe* 6 D6
North Somerset □, *U.K.* 13 F5
North Sporades = Vóriai Sporádhes, *Greece* 38 B5
North Sydney, *Canada* 103 C7
North Taranaki Bight, *N.Z.* 91 H5
North Thompson →, *Canada* 104 C4
North Tonawanda, *U.S.A.* 110 C6
North Troy, *U.S.A.* 111 B12
North Truchas Pk., *U.S.A.* 115 J11
North Twin I., *Canada* 102 B4
North Tyne →, *U.K.* 12 B5
North Uist, *U.K.* 14 D1
North Vancouver, *Canada* 104 D4
North Vernon, *U.S.A.* 108 F3
North Wabasca L., *Canada* 104 B6
North Walsham, *U.K.* 12 E9
North-West □, *S. Africa* 88 D4
North West C., *Australia* 92 D1
North West Christmas I. Ridge, *Pac. Oc.* 97 G11
North West Frontier □, *Pakistan* 68 C4
North West Highlands, *U.K.* 14 D4
North West Providence Channel, *W. Indies* 120 A4
North West River, *Canada* 103 B7
North Western □, *Zambia* 87 E2
North York Moors, *U.K.* 12 C7
North Yorkshire □, *U.K.* 12 C6
Northallerton, *U.K.* 12 C6
Northam, *S. Africa* 88 C4
Northampton, *Australia* 93 E1
Northampton, *U.K.* 13 E7
Northampton, *Mass., U.S.A.* 111 D12
Northampton, *Pa., U.S.A.* 111 F9
Northampton Downs, *Australia* 94 C4
Northamptonshire □, *U.K.* 13 E7
Northbridge, *U.S.A.* 111 D13
Northcliffe, *Australia* 93 F2
Northeim, *Germany* 24 D6
Northern □, *Malawi* 87 E3
Northern □, *Uganda* 86 B3
Northern □, *Zambia* 87 E3
Northern Cape □, *S. Africa* 88 D3
Northern Circars, *India* 67 L13
Northern Indian L., *Canada* 105 B9
Northern Ireland □, *U.K.* 15 B5
Northern Light, L., *Canada* 102 C1
Northern Marianas ■, *Pac. Oc.* 96 F6
Northern Province □, *S. Leone* 82 D2
Northern Territory □, *Australia* 92 D5
Northern Transvaal □, *S. Africa* 89 C4
Northfield, *U.S.A.* 112 C8
Northland □, *N.Z.* 91 F4
Northome, *U.S.A.* 112 B7
Northport, *Ala., U.S.A.* 109 J2
Northport, *Mich., U.S.A.* 108 C3
Northport, *Wash., U.S.A.* 114 B5
Northumberland □, *U.K.* 12 B6
Northumberland, C., *Australia* 95 F3
Northumberland Is., *Australia* 94 C4
Northumberland Str., *Canada* 103 C7
Northwest Territories □, *Canada* 100 B9
Northwood, *Iowa, U.S.A.* 112 D8
Northwood, *N. Dak., U.S.A.* 112 B6
Norton, *U.S.A.* 112 F5
Norton, *Zimbabwe* 87 F3
Norton Sd., *U.S.A.* 100 B3
Nortorf, *Germany* 24 A5
Norwalk, *Calif., U.S.A.* 117 M8
Norwalk, *Conn., U.S.A.* 111 E11
Norwalk, *Ohio, U.S.A.* 110 E2
Norway, *U.S.A.* 108 C2
Norway ■, *Europe* 8 E14
Norway House, *Canada* 105 C9
Norwegian Sea, *Atl. Oc.* 4 C8
Norwich, *Canada* 110 D4
Norwich, *U.K.* 13 E9
Norwich, *Conn., U.S.A.* 111 E12
Norwich, *N.Y., U.S.A.* 111 D9
Norwood, *Canada* 110 B7
Noshiro, *Japan* 54 D10
Nosivka, *Ukraine* 47 G6
Nosovka = Nosivka, *Ukraine* 47 G6
Noss Hd., *U.K.* 14 C5
Nossebro, *Sweden* 11 F6
Nossob →, *S. Africa* 88 D3
Nosy Be, *Madag.* 85 G9
Nosy Boraha, *Madag.* 89 B8
Nosy Varika, *Madag.* 89 C8
Noteć →, *Poland* 45 F2
Notigi Dam, *Canada* 105 B9
Notikewin →, *Canada* 104 B5
Notios Evvoïkos Kólpos, *Greece* 38 C5
Noto, *Italy* 31 F8
Noto, G. di, *Italy* 31 F8
Notodden, *Norway* 9 G13
Notre-Dame, *Canada* 103 C7
Notre Dame B., *Canada* 103 C8
Notre Dame de Koartac = Quaqtaq, *Canada* 101 B13
Notre Dame d'Ivugivic = Ivujivik, *Canada* 101 B12
Notsé, *Togo* 83 D5
Nottaway →, *Canada* 102 B4
Nottingham, *U.K.* 12 E6
Nottingham, City of □, *U.K.* 12 E6
Nottinghamshire □, *U.K.* 12 D6
Nottoway →, *U.S.A.* 108 G7
Notwane →, *Botswana* 88 C4
Nouâdhibou, *Mauritania* 78 D2
Nouâdhibou, Ras, *Mauritania* 78 D2
Nouakchott, *Mauritania* 82 B1
Nouméa, *N. Cal.* 96 K8
Noupoort, *S. Africa* 88 E3
Nouveau Comptoir = Wemindji, *Canada* 102 B4
Nouvelle-Calédonie = New Caledonia ■, *Pac. Oc.* 96 K8
Nouzonville, *France* 19 C11
Nová Baňa, *Slovak Rep.* 27 C11
Nová Bystřice, *Czech Rep.* 26 B8
Nova Casa Nova, *Brazil* 125 E10
Nova Esperança, *Brazil* 127 A5
Nova Friburgo, *Brazil* 127 A7
Nova Gaia = Cambundi-Catembo, *Angola* 84 G3
Nova Gorica, *Slovenia* 29 C10
Nova Gradiška, *Croatia* 42 E2
Nova Iguaçu, *Brazil* 127 A7
Nova Iorque, *Brazil* 125 E10
Nova Kakhovka, *Ukraine* 47 J7
Nova Lamego, *Guinea-Biss.* 82 C2
Nova Lima, *Brazil* 127 A7
Nova Lisboa = Huambo, *Angola* 85 G3
Nova Lusitânia, *Mozam.* 87 F3
Nova Mambone, *Mozam.* 89 C6
Nova Odesa, *Ukraine* 47 J6
Nová Paka, *Czech Rep.* 26 A8
Nova Pavova, *Serbia, Yug.* 42 F5
Nova Scotia □, *Canada* 103 C7
Nova Siri, *Italy* 31 B9
Nova Sofala, *Mozam.* 89 C5
Nova Varoš, *Serbia, Yug.* 40 C3
Nova Venécia, *Brazil* 125 G10
Nova Zagora, *Bulgaria* 41 D10
Novaci, *Macedonia* 40 E5
Novaci, *Romania* 43 E8
Novaféltria, *Italy* 29 E9
Novaleksandrovskaya = Novoaleksandrovsk, *Russia* 49 H5
Novannenskiy = Novoannenskiy, *Russia* 48 E6
Novara, *Italy* 28 C5
Novato, *U.S.A.* 116 G4
Novaya Kakhovka = Nova Kakhovka, *Ukraine* 47 J7
Novaya Kazanka, *Kazakstan* 49 F9
Novaya Ladoga, *Russia* 46 B7
Novaya Lyalya, *Russia* 50 D7
Novaya Sibir, Ostrov, *Russia* 51 B16
Novaya Zemlya, *Russia* 50 B6
Nové Město, *Slovak Rep.* 27 C10
Nové Město na Moravě, *Czech Rep.* 26 B9
Nové Město nad Metují, *Czech Rep.* 27 A9
Nové Zámky, *Slovak Rep.* 27 C11
Novelda, *Spain* 33 G4
Novellara, *Italy* 28 D7
Noventa Vicentina, *Italy* 29 C8
Novgorod, *Russia* 46 C6
Novgorod-Severskiy = Novhorod-Siverskyy, *Ukraine* 47 G7
Novhorod-Siverskyy, *Ukraine* 47 G7
Novi Bečej, *Serbia, Yug.* 42 E5
Novi Iskar, *Bulgaria* 40 D7
Novi Kneževac, *Serbia, Yug.* 42 D5
Novi Lígure, *Italy* 28 D5
Novi Pazar, *Bulgaria* 41 C11
Novi Pazar, *Serbia, Yug.* 40 C4
Novi Sad, *Serbia, Yug.* 42 E4
Novi Slankamen, *Serbia, Yug.* 42 E5
Novi Travnik, *Bos.-H.* 42 F2
Novi Vinodolski, *Croatia* 29 C11

Novigrad, Istra, Croatia .. 29 C10
Novigrad, Zadar, Croatia .. 29 D12
Novigradsko More, Croatia . 29 D12
Nôvo Hamburgo, Brazil .. 127 B5
Novo Mesto, Slovenia 29 C12
Novo Miloševo,
  Serbia, Yug. 42 E5
Novo Remanso, Brazil ... 125 E10
Novoaleksandrovsk, Russia 49 H5
Novoannenskiy, Russia ... 48 E6
Novoataysk, Russia 50 D9
Novoazovsk, Ukraine 47 J10
Novocheboksarsk, Russia .. 48 B8
Novocherkassk, Russia ... 49 G5
Novodevichye, Russia 48 D9
Novogrudok =
  Navahrudak, Belarus .. 46 F3
Novohrad-Volynskyy,
  Ukraine 47 G4
Novokachalinsk, Russia ... 54 B6
Novokazalinsk =
  Zhangaqazaly, Kazakstan 50 E7
Novokhopersk, Russia 48 E5
Novokuybyshevsk, Russia .. 48 D9
Novokuznetsk, Russia 50 D9
Novomirgorod, Ukraine ... 47 H6
Novomoskovsk, Russia 46 E10
Novomoskovsk, Ukraine ... 47 H8
Novopolotsk =
  Navapolatsk, Belarus .. 46 E5
Novorossiysk, Russia 47 K9
Novorybnoye, Russia 51 B11
Novorzhev, Russia 46 D5
Novosej, Albania 40 E4
Novoselytsya, Ukraine 47 H4
Novoshakhtinsk, Russia ... 47 J10
Novosibirsk, Russia 50 D9
Novosibirskiye Ostrova,
  Russia 51 B15
Novosil, Russia 47 F9
Novosokolniki, Russia 46 D6
Novotitarovskaya, Russia .. 49 H4
Novotroitsk, Russia 50 D6
Novoukrayinka, Ukraine ... 47 H6
Novouljanovsk, Russia 48 C9
Novouzensk, Russia 48 E9
Novovolynsk, Ukraine 47 G3
Novovoronezhskiy, Russia . 47 G10
Novozybkov, Russia 47 F6
Novska, Croatia 29 C14
Nový Bor, Czech Rep. ... 26 A7
Novy Bug = Novyy Buh,
  Ukraine 47 J7
Nový Bydžov, Czech Rep. . 26 A8
Nowy Dwór Mazowiecki,
  Poland 45 F7
Nový Jičín, Czech Rep. ... 27 B11
Novyy Afon, Georgia 49 J5
Novyy Buh, Ukraine 47 J7
Novyy Oskol, Russia 47 G9
Novyy Port, Russia 50 C8
Now Shahr, Iran 71 B6
Nowa Deba, Poland 45 H8
Nowa Ruda, Poland 45 H3
Nowa Sarzyna, Poland 45 H9
Nowa Sól, Poland 45 G2
Nowbarān, Iran 71 C6
Nowe, Poland 44 E5
Nowe Miasteczko, Poland . 45 G2
Nowe Miasto, Poland 45 G7
Nowe Miasto Lubawskie,
  Poland 44 E6
Nowe Skalmierzyce, Poland 45 G4
Nowe Warpno, Poland ... 44 E1
Nowghāb, Iran 71 C8
Nowgong, India 67 F18
Nowogard, Poland 44 E2
Nowogród, Poland 45 E8
Nowogród Bobrzanski,
  Poland 45 G2
Nowogrodziec, Poland 45 G2
Nowra, Australia 95 E5
Nowshera, Pakistan 66 C8
Nowy Dwór Gdański,
  Poland 44 D6
Nowy Sącz, Poland 45 J7
Nowy Sącz □, Poland ... 45 J7
Nowy Staw, Poland 44 D6
Nowy Targ, Poland 45 J7
Nowy Tomyśl, Poland 45 F3
Nowy Wiśnicz, Poland ... 45 J7
Noxen, U.S.A. 111 E8
Noxon, U.S.A. 114 C6
Noyant, France 18 E7
Noyers, France 19 E10
Noyes I., U.S.A. 104 B2
Noyon, France 19 C9
Noyon, Mongolia 56 C2
Nozay, France 18 E5
Nsanje, Malawi 87 F4
Nsawam, Ghana 83 D4
Nsomba, Zambia 87 E2
Nsukka, Nigeria 83 D6
Nu Jiang →, China 58 C1
Nu Shan, China 58 E2
Nuba Mts. = Nubah,
  Jibalan, Sudan 81 E3
Nubah, Jibalan, Sudan ... 81 E3
Nubia, Africa 76 D7
Nubian Desert = Nûbîya,
  Es Saḥrâ en, Sudan 80 C3
Nûbîya, Es Saḥrâ en,
  Sudan 80 C3
Nuble □, Chile 126 D1
Nubledo, Spain 34 B5
Nuboai, Indonesia 63 E9
Nubra →, India 69 B7

Nucet, Romania 42 D7
Nueces →, U.S.A. 113 M6
Nueltin L., Canada 105 A9
Nueva Asunción □,
  Paraguay 126 A3
Nueva Carteya, Spain 35 H6
Nueva Gerona, Cuba 120 B3
Nueva Palmira, Uruguay . 126 C4
Nueva Rosita, Mexico ... 118 B4
Nueva San Salvador,
  El Salv. 120 D2
Nueva Tabarca, Spain 33 G4
Nuéve de Julio, Argentina . 126 D3
Nuevitas, Cuba 120 B4
Nuevo, G., Argentina ... 128 E4
Nuevo Guerrero, Mexico . 119 B5
Nuevo Laredo, Mexico ... 119 B5
Nuevo León □, Mexico .. 118 C5
Nuevo Rocafuerte, Ecuador 124 D3
Nugget Pt., N.Z. 91 M2
Nugrus, Gebel, Egypt 80 C3
Nuhaka, N.Z. 91 H6
Nuits-St-Georges, France . 19 E11
Nukey Bluff, Australia ... 95 E2
Nukheila, Sudan 80 D2
Nukhuyb, Iraq 73 F10
Nuku'alofa, Tonga 91 E12
Nukus, Uzbekistan 50 E6
Nules, Spain 32 F4
Nullagine →, Australia .. 92 D3
Nullarbor, Australia 93 F5
Nullarbor Plain, Australia . 93 F4
Numalla, L., Australia 95 D3
Numan, Nigeria 83 D7
Numata, Japan 55 F9
Numatinna →, Sudan 81 F2
Numazu, Japan 55 G9
Numbulwar, Australia 94 A2
Numfoor, Indonesia 63 E8
Numurkah, Australia 95 F4
Nunaksaluk I., Canada ... 103 A7
Nunavut □, Canada 101 B11
Nungo, Mozam. 87 E4
Nungwe, Tanzania 86 C3
Nunivak I., U.S.A. 100 C3
Nunkun, India 69 C7
Núoro, Italy 30 B2
Nure →, Italy 28 C6
Nuremberg = Nürnberg,
  Germany 25 F7
Nuri, Mexico 118 B3
Nurina, Australia 93 F4
Nuriootpa, Australia 95 E2
Nurlat, Russia 48 C10
Nurmes, Finland 8 E23
Nürnberg, Germany 25 F7
Nurra, La, Italy 30 B1
Nurran, L. = Terewah, L.,
  Australia 95 D4
Nurrari Lakes, Australia .. 93 E5
Nurri, Italy 30 C2
Nürtingen, Germany 25 G5
Nurzec →, Poland 45 F9
Nus, Italy 28 C4
Nusa Barung, Indonesia .. 63 H15
Nusa Kambangan,
  Indonesia 63 G13
Nusa Tenggara Barat □,
  Indonesia 62 F5
Nusa Tenggara Timur □,
  Indonesia 63 F6
Nusaybin, Turkey 73 D9
Nushki, Pakistan 68 E2
Nutwood Downs, Australia 94 B1
Nuuk, Greenland 4 C5
Nuwakot, Nepal 69 E10
Nuweiba', Egypt 80 B3
Nuweveldberge, S. Africa . 88 E3
Nuyts, C., Australia 93 F5
Nuyts Arch., Australia ... 95 E1
Nxau-Nxau, Botswana ... 88 B3
Nyaake, Liberia 82 E3
Nyack, U.S.A. 111 E11
Nyah West, Australia ... 95 F3
Nyahanga, Tanzania 86 C3
Nyahua, Tanzania 86 D3
Nyahururu, Kenya 86 B4
Nyainqentanglha Shan,
  China 60 C4
Nyakanazi, Tanzania 86 C3
Nyakrom, Ghana 83 D4
Nyâlâ, Sudan 81 E1
Nyamandhlovu, Zimbabwe 87 F2
Nyambiti, Tanzania 86 C3
Nyamwaga, Tanzania ... 86 C3
Nyandekwa, Tanzania ... 86 C3
Nyanding →, Sudan 81 F3
Nyandoma, Russia 46 B11
Nyangana, Namibia 88 B3
Nyanguge, Tanzania 86 C3
Nyankpala, Ghana 83 D4
Nyanza, Rwanda 86 C2
Nyanza □, Kenya 86 C3
Nyanza-Lac, Burundi ... 86 C2
Nyarling →, Canada ... 104 A6
Nyasa, L. = Africa 87 E3
Nyasvizh, Belarus 47 F4
Nyazura, Zimbabwe 87 F3
Nyazwidzi →, Zimbabwe . 87 G3
Nyborg, Denmark 11 J4
Nybro, Sweden 11 H9
Nyda, Russia 50 C8
Nyeri, Kenya 86 C4
Nyerol, Sudan 81 F3
Nyhammar, Sweden 10 D8
Nyíel, Sudan 81 F3

Nyinahin, Ghana 82 D4
Nyíradony, Hungary 42 C6
Nyírbátor, Hungary 42 C7
Nyíregyháza, Hungary ... 42 C6
Nykøbing, Storstrøm,
  Denmark 11 K5
Nykøbing, Vestsjælland,
  Denmark 11 J5
Nykøbing, Viborg,
  Denmark 11 H2
Nyköping, Sweden 11 F11
Nykroppa, Sweden 10 E8
Nykvarn, Sweden 10 E11
Nyland, Sweden 10 A11
Nylstroom, S. Africa 89 C4
Nymagee, Australia 95 E4
Nymburk, Czech Rep. ... 26 A8
Nynäshamn, Sweden ... 11 F11
Nyngan, Australia 95 E4
Nyoman = Neman →,
  Lithuania 9 J20
Nyon, Switz. 25 J2
Nyong →, Cameroon ... 83 E6
Nyons, France 21 D9
Nyou, Burkina Faso 83 C4
Nýrsko, Czech Rep. 26 B6
Nysa, Poland 45 H4
Nysa →, Europe 24 C10
Nysa Kłodzka →, Poland 45 H4
Nysäter, Sweden 10 E6
Nyssa, U.S.A. 114 E5
Nysted, Denmark 11 K5
Nyunzu,
  Dem. Rep. of the Congo 86 D2
Nyurba, Russia 51 C12
Nyzhnohirskyy, Ukraine . 47 K8
Nzega, Tanzania 86 C3
Nzega □, Tanzania 86 C3
N'zérékoré, Guinea 82 D3
Nzeto, Angola 84 F2
Nzilo, Chutes de,
  Dem. Rep. of the Congo 87 E2
Nzubuka, Tanzania 86 C3

O

O Barco, Spain 34 C4
O Carballiño, Spain 34 C2
O Corgo, Spain 34 C3
O Pino, Spain 34 C2
O Porriño, Spain 34 C2
Ō-Shima, Nagasaki, Japan 55 G4
Ō-Shima, Shizuoka, Japan 55 G9
Oa, Mull of, U.K. 14 F2
Oacoma, U.S.A. 112 D5
Oahe, L., U.S.A. 112 C4
Oahe Dam, U.S.A. 112 C4
Oahu, U.S.A. 106 H16
Oak Creek, U.S.A. 114 F10
Oak Harbor, U.S.A. 116 B4
Oak Hill, U.S.A. 108 G5
Oak Park, U.S.A. 108 E2
Oak Ridge, U.S.A. 109 G3
Oak View, U.S.A. 117 L7
Oakan-Dake, Japan 54 C12
Oakbank, Australia 95 E3
Oakdale, Calif., U.S.A. .. 116 H6
Oakdale, La., U.S.A. ... 113 K8
Oakes, U.S.A. 112 B5
Oakesdale, U.S.A. 114 C5
Oakey, Australia 95 D5
Oakham, U.K. 13 E7
Oakhurst, U.S.A. 116 H7
Oakland, Calif., U.S.A. .. 116 H4
Oakland, Oreg., U.S.A. . 114 E2
Oakland City, U.S.A. ... 108 F2
Oakley, Idaho, U.S.A. .. 114 E7
Oakley, Kans., U.S.A. .. 112 F4
Oakover →, Australia .. 92 D3
Oakridge, U.S.A. 114 E2
Oakville, U.S.A. 116 D3
Oamaru, N.Z. 91 L3
Oancea, Romania 43 E12
Oasis, Calif., U.S.A. ... 117 M10
Oasis, Nev., U.S.A. 116 H9
Oates Land, Antarctica .. 5 C11
Oatman, U.S.A. 117 K12
Oaxaca, Mexico 119 D5
Oaxaca □, Mexico 119 D5
Ob →, Russia 50 C7
Oba, Canada 102 C3
Obala, Cameroon 83 E7
Obama, Japan 55 G7
Oban, U.K. 14 E3
Obbia, Somali Rep. 74 F4
Obed, Canada 104 C5
Obera, Argentina 127 B4
Oberammergau, Germany 25 H7
Oberasbach, Germany .. 25 F6
Oberbayern □, Germany . 25 G7
Oberdrauburg, Austria .. 26 E5
Oberfranken □, Germany 25 E7
Oberhausen, Germany .. 24 D2
Oberkirch, Germany 25 G4
Oberlin, Kans., U.S.A. .. 112 F4
Oberlin, La., U.S.A. 113 K8
Oberlin, Ohio, U.S.A. .. 110 E2
Obernai, France 19 D14
Oberndorf, Germany ... 25 G4
Oberon, Australia 95 E4
Oberösterreich □, Austria 26 C7
Oberpfalz □, Germany .. 25 F8

Oberpfälzer Wald,
  Germany 25 F8
Oberstdorf, Germany ... 25 H6
Oberursel, Germany 25 E4
Oberwart, Austria 27 D9
Obi, Kepulauan, Indonesia 63 E7
Obi Is. = Obi, Kepulauan,
  Indonesia 63 E7
Obiaruku, Nigeria 83 D6
Óbidos, Brazil 125 D7
Óbidos, Portugal 35 F1
Obihiro, Japan 54 C11
Obilatu, Indonesia 63 E7
Obilnoye, Russia 49 G7
Obing, Germany 25 G8
Objat, France 20 C5
Obluchye, Russia 51 E14
Obninsk, Russia 46 E9
Obo, C.A.R. 86 A2
Obo, Ethiopia 81 G4
Oboa, Mt., Uganda 86 B3
Obock, Djibouti 81 E5
Oborniki, Poland 45 F3
Oborniki Śląskie, Poland . 45 G3
Oboyan, Russia 47 G9
Obozerskaya =
  Obozerskiy, Russia ... 50 C5
Obozerskiy, Russia 50 C5
Obrenovac, Serbia, Yug. . 40 B4
Obrovac, Croatia 29 D12
Obruk, Turkey 72 C5
Observatory Inlet, Canada 104 B3
Obshchi Syrt, Russia 6 E16
Obskaya Guba, Russia .. 50 C8
Obuasi, Ghana 83 D4
Obubra, Nigeria 83 D6
Obwalden □, Switz. 25 J4
Obzor, Bulgaria 41 D11
Ocala, U.S.A. 109 L4
Ocampo, Mexico 118 B3
Ocaña, Spain 34 F7
Ocanomowoc, U.S.A. ... 112 D10
Ocate, U.S.A. 113 G2
Occidental, Cordillera,
  Colombia 122 C3
Ocean City, N.J., U.S.A. . 108 F8
Ocean City, Wash., U.S.A. 116 C2
Ocean I. = Banaba,
  Kiribati 96 H8
Ocean Park, U.S.A. 116 D2
Oceano, U.S.A. 117 K6
Oceanport, U.S.A. 111 F10
Oceanside, U.S.A. 117 M9
Ochagavía, Spain 32 C3
Ochakiv, Ukraine 47 J6
Ochamchira, Georgia ... 49 J5
Ochil Hills, U.K. 14 E5
Ochre River, Canada ... 105 C9
Ochsenfurt, Germany ... 25 F6
Ochsenhausen, Germany . 25 G5
Ocilla, U.S.A. 109 K4
Ocmulgee →, U.S.A. .. 109 K4
Ocna Mureş, Romania .. 43 D8
Ocna Sibiului, Romania . 43 E9
Ocnele Mari, Romania .. 43 E9
Ocniţa, Moldova 43 B12
Oconee →, U.S.A. 109 K4
Oconto, U.S.A. 108 C2
Oconto Falls, U.S.A. ... 108 C1
Ocosingo, Mexico 119 D6
Ocotal, Nic. 120 D2
Ocotlán, Mexico 118 C4
Ocreza →, Portugal ... 35 F3
Ócsa, Hungary 42 C4
Octave, U.S.A. 115 J7
Octeville, France 18 C5
Oda, Ghana 83 D4
Ōda, Japan 55 G6
Oda, J., Sudan 80 C4
Ódáðahraun, Iceland ... 8 D5
Ödåkra, Sweden 11 H6
Odate, Japan 54 D10
Odawara, Japan 55 G9
Odda, Norway 9 F12
Odder, Denmark 11 J4
Odei →, Canada 105 B9
Odemira, Portugal 35 H2
Ödemiş, Turkey 39 C9
Odendaalsrus, S. Africa . 88 D4
Odensbacken, Sweden .. 10 E9
Odense, Denmark 11 J4
Odenwald, Germany ... 25 F5
Oder →, Europe 24 B10
Oder-Havel Kanal,
  Germany 24 C10
Oderzo, Italy 29 C9
Odesa, Ukraine 47 J6
Ödeshög, Sweden 11 F8
Odessa = Odesa, Ukraine 47 J6
Odessa, Canada 111 B8
Odessa, Tex., U.S.A. ... 113 K3
Odessa, Wash., U.S.A. .. 114 C4
Odiakwe, Botswana 88 C4
Odiel →, Spain 35 H4
Odienné, Ivory C. 82 D3
Odintsovo, Russia 46 E9
Odiongan, Phil. 61 E4
Odobeşti, Romania 43 E12
Odolanów, Poland 45 G4
O'Donnell, U.S.A. 113 J4
Odorheiu Secuiesc,
  Romania 43 D10
Odoyevo, Russia 46 F9
Odra = Oder →, Europe 24 B10
Odra →, Spain 34 C6

Odžaci, Serbia, Yug. 42 E4
Odžak, Bos.-H. 42 E3
Odzi, Zimbabwe 89 B5
Odzi →, Zimbabwe 87 F3
Oebisfelde, Germany ... 24 C6
Oeiras, Brazil 125 E10
Oeiras, Portugal 35 G1
Oelrichs, U.S.A. 112 D3
Oelsnitz, Germany 25 E8
Oelwein, U.S.A. 112 D9
Oenpelli, Australia 92 B5
Oetz, Austria 26 D3
Of, Turkey 73 B9
Ofanto →, Italy 31 A9
Offa, Nigeria 83 D5
Offaly □, Ireland 15 C4
Offenbach, Germany ... 25 E4
Offenburg, Germany ... 25 G3
Offida, Italy 29 F10
Ofidhousa, Greece 39 E8
Ofotfjorden, Norway ... 8 B17
Ōfunato, Japan 54 E10
Oga, Japan 54 E9
Oga-Hantō, Japan 54 E9
Ogahalla, Canada 102 B2
Ōgaki, Japan 55 G8
Ogallala, U.S.A. 112 E4
Ogasawara Gunto,
  Pac. Oc. 96 E6
Ogbomosho, Nigeria ... 83 D5
Ogden, Iowa, U.S.A. ... 112 D8
Ogden, Utah, U.S.A. ... 114 F7
Ogdensburg, U.S.A. 111 B9
Ogeechee →, U.S.A. .. 109 K5
Ogilby, U.S.A. 117 N12
Oglio →, Italy 28 C7
Ogmore, Australia 94 C4
Ognon →, France 19 E12
Ogoja, Nigeria 83 D6
Ogoki →, Canada 102 B2
Ogoki L., Canada 102 B2
Ogoki Res., Canada 102 B2
Ogooué →, Gabon 84 E1
Ogosta →, Bulgaria ... 40 C7
Ogowe = Ogooué →,
  Gabon 84 E1
Ogr = Sharafa, Sudan .. 81 E2
Ograźden, Macedonia .. 40 E6
Ogre, Latvia 9 H21
Ogrein, Sudan 80 D3
Ogulin, Croatia 29 C12
Ogun □, Nigeria 83 D5
Oguta, Nigeria 83 D6
Ogwashi-Uku, Nigeria .. 83 D6
Ohai, N.Z. 91 L2
Ohakune, N.Z. 91 H5
Ohata, Japan 54 D10
Ohau, L., N.Z. 91 L2
Ohio □, U.S.A. 108 E3
Ohio →, U.S.A. 108 G1
Ohře →, Czech Rep. .. 26 A7
Ohre →, Germany 24 C7
Ohrid, Macedonia 40 E4
Ohridsko Jezero,
  Macedonia 40 E4
Öhringen, Germany 25 F5
Oiapoque, Brazil 125
Oikou, China 57 E9
Oil City, U.S.A. 110 E5
Oildale, U.S.A. 117 K7
Oinousa, Greece 39 C8
Oise □, France 19 C9
Oise →, France 19 C9
Ōita, Japan 55 H5
Ōita □, Japan 55 H5
Oiticica, Brazil 125 E10
Ojai, U.S.A. 117 L7
Ojinaga, Mexico 118 B4
Ojiya, Japan 55 F9
Ojos del Salado, Cerro,
  Argentina 126 B2
Oka →, Russia 48 B7
Okaba, Indonesia 63 F9
Okahandja, Namibia ... 88 C2
Okahukura, N.Z. 91 H5
Okanagan L., Canada ... 104 D5
Okanogan, U.S.A. 114 B4
Okanogan →, U.S.A. .. 114 B4
Okany, Hungary 42 D6
Okaputa, Namibia 88 C2
Okara, Pakistan 68 D5
Okarito, N.Z. 91 K3
Okaukuejo, Namibia ... 88 B2
Okavango Swamps,
  Botswana 88 B3
Okaya, Japan 55 F9
Okayama, Japan 55 G6
Okayama □, Japan 55 G6
Okazaki, Japan 55 G8
Oke-Iho, Nigeria 83 D5
Okeechobee, U.S.A. ... 109 M5
Okeechobee, L., U.S.A. . 109 M5
Okefenokee Swamp,
  U.S.A. 109 K4
Okehampton, U.K. 13 G4
Okene, Nigeria 83 D6
Oker →, Germany 24 C6
Okha, Russia 51 D15
Ókhi Óros, Greece 38 C6
Okhotsk, Russia 51 D15
Okhotsk, Sea of, Asia .. 51 D15
Okhotskiy Perevoz, Russia 51 C14
Okhtyrka, Ukraine 47 G8
Oki-Shotō, Japan 55 F6
Okiep, S. Africa 88 D2
Okigwi, Nigeria 83 D6

Okija, *Nigeria* 83 D6
Okinawa □, *Japan* 55 L4
Okinawa-Guntō, *Japan* ... 55 L4
Okinawa-Jima, *Japan* .. 55 L4
Okino-erabu-Shima, *Japan* 55 L4
Okitipupa, *Nigeria* 83 D5
Oklahoma □, *U.S.A.* 113 H6
Oklahoma City, *U.S.A.* .. 113 H6
Okmulgee, *U.S.A.* 113 H7
Oknitsa = Ocnița, *Moldova* 43 B12
Okolo, *Uganda* 86 B3
Okolona, *U.S.A.* 113 J10
Okonek, *Poland* 44 E3
Okrika, *Nigeria* 83 E6
Oksibil, *Indonesia* 63 E10
Oktabrsk = Oktyabrsk,
  Kazakstan 50 E6
Oktyabrsk, *Kazakstan* 50 E6
Oktyabrsk, *Russia* 48 D9
Oktyabrskiy = Aktsyabrski,
  Belarus 47 F5
Oktyabrskiy, *Russia* 49 G5
Oktyabrskoy Revolyutsii,
  Ostrov, *Russia* 51 B10
Oktyabrskoye =
  Zhovtneve, *Ukraine* 47 J7
Okulovka, *Russia* 46 C7
Okuru, *N.Z.* 91 K2
Okushiri-Tō, *Japan* 54 C9
Okuta, *Nigeria* 83 D5
Okwa →, *Botswana* 88 C3
Ola, *U.S.A.* 113 H8
Ólafsfjörður, *Iceland* 8 C4
Ólafsvík, *Iceland* 8 D2
Olaine, *Latvia* 44 B10
Olancha, *U.S.A.* 117 J8
Olancha Pk., *U.S.A.* 117 J8
Olanchito, *Honduras* 120 C2
Öland, *Sweden* 11 H10
Ölands norra udde, *Sweden* 11 G11
Ölands södra udde, *Sweden* 11 H10
Olargues, *France* 20 E6
Olary, *Australia* 95 E3
Olascoaga, *Argentina* ... 126 D3
Olathe, *U.S.A.* 112 F7
Olavarría, *Argentina* 126 D3
Oława, *Poland* 45 H4
Olbernhau, *Germany* ... 24 E9
Ólbia, *Italy* 30 B2
Ólbia, G. di, *Italy* 30 B2
Olching, *Germany* 25 G7
Old Bahama Chan. =
  Bahama, Canal Viejo de,
  W. Indies 120 B4
Old Baldy Pk. = San
  Antonio, Mt., *U.S.A.* .. 117 L9
Old Cork, *Australia* 94 C3
Old Crow, *Canada* 100 B6
Old Dale, *U.S.A.* 117 L11
Old Dongola, *Sudan* 80 D3
Old Forge, *N.Y., U.S.A.* . 111 C10
Old Forge, *Pa., U.S.A.* .. 111 E9
Old Fort →, *Canada* 105 B6
Old Shinyanga, *Tanzania* . 86 C3
Old Speck Mt., *U.S.A.* .. 111 B14
Old Town, *U.S.A.* 103 D6
Old Wives L., *Canada* ... 105 C7
Oldbury, *U.K.* 13 F5
Oldcastle, *Ireland* 15 C4
Oldeani, *Tanzania* 86 C4
Oldenburg, *Niedersachsen,*
  Germany 24 B4
Oldenburg,
  Schleswig-Holstein,
  Germany 24 A6
Oldenzaal, *Neths.* 17 B6
Oldham, *U.K.* 12 D5
Oldman →, *Canada* 104 D6
Oldmeldrum, *U.K.* 14 D6
Olds, *Canada* 104 C6
Olean, *U.S.A.* 110 D6
Olecko, *Poland* 44 D9
Oléggio, *Italy* 28 C5
Oleiros, *Portugal* 34 F3
Oleiros, *Spain* 34 B2
Olekma →, *Russia* 51 C13
Olekminsk, *Russia* 51 C13
Oleksandriya, *Kirovohrad,*
  Ukraine 47 H7
Oleksandriya, *Rivne,*
  Ukraine 47 G4
Oleksandrovka, *Ukraine* . 47 H7
Olema, *U.S.A.* 116 G4
Olenek, *Russia* 51 C12
Olenek →, *Russia* 51 B13
Olenino, *Russia* 46 D7
Oléron, Î. d', *France* 20 C2
Oleśnica, *Poland* 45 G4
Olesno, *Poland* 45 H5
Olevsk, *Ukraine* 47 G4
Olga, *Russia* 51 E14
Olga, L., *Canada* 102 C4
Olga, Mt., *Australia* 93 E5
Ølgod, *Denmark* 11 J2
Olhão, *Portugal* 35 H3
Olib, *Croatia* 29 D11
Oliena, *Italy* 30 B2
Oliete, *Spain* 32 D4
Olifants →, *Africa* 89 C5
Olifantshoek, *S. Africa* .. 88 D3
Ólimbos, *Greece* 39 F9
Ólimbos, Óros, *Greece* .. 40 F6
Olímpia, *Brazil* 127 A6
Olinda, *Brazil* 125 E12
Olite, *Spain* 32 C3
Oliva, *Argentina* 126 C3
Oliva, *Spain* 33 G4

Oliva, Punta del, *Spain* ... 34 B5
Oliva de la Frontera, *Spain* 35 G4
Olivares, *Spain* 32 F2
Olivehurst, *U.S.A.* 116 F5
Oliveira de Azeméis,
  Portugal 34 E2
Oliveira do Douro,
  Portugal 34 D2
Olivenza, *Spain* 35 G3
Oliver, *Canada* 104 D5
Oliver L., *Canada* 105 B8
Olivet, *France* 19 E8
Olkhovka, *Russia* 48 F7
Olkusz, *Poland* 45 H6
Ollagüe, *Chile* 126 A2
Olmedo, *Spain* 34 D6
Olmeto, *France* 21 G12
Olney, *Ill., U.S.A.* 108 F1
Olney, *Tex., U.S.A.* 113 J5
Olofström, *Sweden* 11 H8
Oloma, *Cameroon* 83 E7
Olomane →, *Canada* ... 103 B7
Olomouc, *Czech Rep.* ... 27 B10
Olonets, *Russia* 46 B7
Olongapo, *Phil.* 61 D4
Olonne-sur-Mer, *France* . 20 B2
Oloron, Gave d' →,
  France 20 E2
Oloron-Ste-Marie, *France* . 20 E3
Olot, *Spain* 32 C7
Olovo, *Bos.-H.* 42 F3
Olovyannaya, *Russia* ... 51 D12
Oløy →, *Russia* 51 C16
Olsberg, *Germany* 24 D4
Olshammar, *Sweden* 11 F8
Olshanka, *Ukraine* 47 H6
Olshany, *Ukraine* 47 G8
Olsztyn, *Poland* 44 E7
Olsztyn □, *Poland* 44 E7
Olsztynek, *Poland* 44 E7
Olt □, *Romania* 43 F9
Olt →, *Romania* 43 G9
Olten, *Switz.* 25 H3
Oltenița, *Romania* 43 F11
Olton, *U.S.A.* 113 H3
Oltu, *Turkey* 73 B9
Olula del Río, *Spain* 33 H2
Olur, *Turkey* 73 B10
Olutanga, *Phil.* 61 H5
Olvega, *Spain* 32 D2
Olvera, *Spain* 35 J5
Olymbos, *Cyprus* 36 D12
Olympia, *Greece* 38 D3
Olympia, *U.S.A.* 116 D4
Olympic Mts., *U.S.A.* ... 116 C3
Olympic Nat. Park, *U.S.A.* 116 C3
Olympus, *Cyprus* 36 E11
Olympus, Mt. = Ólimbos,
  Óros, *Greece* 40 F6
Olympus, Mt. = Uludağ,
  Turkey 41 F13
Olympus, Mt., *U.S.A.* ... 116 C3
Olyphant, *U.S.A.* 111 E9
Om →, *Russia* 50 D8
Om Hajer, *Eritrea* 81 E4
Om Koi, *Thailand* 64 D2
Ōma, *Japan* 54 D10
Ōmachi, *Japan* 55 F8
Omae-Zaki, *Japan* 55 G9
Ōmagari, *Japan* 54 E10
Omagh, *U.K.* 15 B4
Omagh □, *U.K.* 15 B4
Omaha, *U.S.A.* 112 E7
Omak, *U.S.A.* 114 B4
Omalos, *Greece* 36 D5
Oman ■, *Asia* 74 C6
Oman, G. of, *Asia* 71 E8
Omaruru, *Namibia* 88 C2
Omaruru →, *Namibia* ... 88 C1
Omate, *Peru* 124 G4
Ombai, Selat, *Indonesia* . 63 F6
Omboué, *Gabon* 84 E1
Ombrone →, *Italy* 28 F8
Omdurmân, *Sudan* 81 D3
Omegna, *Italy* 28 C5
Omeonga,
  Dem. Rep. of the Congo 86 C1
Ometepe, I. de, *Nic.* 120 D2
Ometepec, *Mexico* 119 D5
Omineca →, *Canada* 104 B4
Omiš, *Croatia* 29 E13
Omišalj, *Croatia* 29 C11
Omitara, *Namibia* 88 C2
Ōmiya, *Japan* 55 G9
Omme Å →, *Denmark* .. 11 J2
Ommen, *Neths.* 17 B6
Ömnögovĭ □, *Mongolia* . 56 C3
Omo →, *Ethiopia* 81 F4
Omodeo, L., *Italy* 30 B1
Omodhos, *Cyprus* 36 E11
Omolon →, *Russia* 51 C16
Omono-Gawa →, *Japan* . 54 E10
Omsk, *Russia* 50 D8
Omsukchan, *Russia* 51 C16
Ōmu, *Japan* 54 B11
Omul, Vf., *Romania* 43 E10
Omulew →, *Poland* 45 E8
Ōmura, *Japan* 55 H4
Omuramba Omatako →,
  Namibia 85 H4
Omurtag, *Bulgaria* 41 C10
Ōmuta, *Japan* 55 H5
Oña, *Spain* 34 C7
Onaga, *U.S.A.* 112 F6
Onalaska, *U.S.A.* 112 D9
Onamia, *U.S.A.* 112 B8

Onancock, *U.S.A.* 108 G8
Onang, *Indonesia* 63 E5
Onaping L., *Canada* 102 C3
Oñati, *Spain* 32 B2
Onavas, *Mexico* 118 B3
Onawa, *U.S.A.* 112 D6
Onaway, *U.S.A.* 108 C3
Oncócua, *Angola* 88 B1
Onda, *Spain* 32 F4
Ondaejin, *N. Korea* 57 D15
Ondangua, *Namibia* 88 B2
Ondarroa, *Spain* 32 B2
Ondava →, *Slovak Rep.* . 27 C14
Ondjiva, *Angola* 88 B2
Ondo, *Nigeria* 83 D5
Ondo □, *Nigeria* 83 D6
Öndörhaan, *Mongolia* ... 60 B6
Öndörshil, *Mongolia* 56 B5
Öndverðarnes, *Iceland* .. 8 D1
Onega, *Russia* 50 C4
Onega →, *Russia* 6 C13
Onega, L. = Onezhskoye
  Ozero, *Russia* 46 B8
Onehunga, *N.Z.* 91 G5
Oneida, *U.S.A.* 111 C9
Oneida L., *U.S.A.* 111 C9
O'Neill, *U.S.A.* 112 D5
Onekotan, Ostrov, *Russia* 51 E16
Onema,
  Dem. Rep. of the Congo 86 C1
Oneonta, *Ala., U.S.A.* ... 109 J2
Oneonta, *N.Y., U.S.A.* .. 111 D9
Oneşti, *Romania* 43 D11
Onezhskoye Ozero, *Russia* 46 B8
Ongarue, *N.Z.* 91 H5
Ongerup, *Australia* 93 F2
Ongjin, *N. Korea* 57 F13
Ongkharak, *Thailand* ... 64 E3
Ongniud Qi, *China* 57 C10
Ongoka,
  Dem. Rep. of the Congo 86 C2
Ongole, *India* 66 M12
Ongon, *Mongolia* 56 B7
Oni, *Georgia* 49 J6
Onida, *U.S.A.* 112 C4
Onilahy →, *Madag.* 89 C7
Onitsha, *Nigeria* 83 D6
Onoda, *Japan* 55 G5
Onpyŏng-ni, *S. Korea* ... 57 H14
Ons, I. de, *Spain* 34 C2
Onslow, *Australia* 92 D2
Onslow B., *U.S.A.* 109 H7
Ontake-San, *Japan* 55 G8
Ontario, *Calif., U.S.A.* .. 117 L9
Ontario, *Oreg., U.S.A.* .. 114 D5
Ontario □, *Canada* 102 B3
Ontario, L., *U.S.A.* 102 D4
Ontinyent, *Spain* 33 G4
Ontonagon, *U.S.A.* 112 B10
Ontur, *Spain* 33 G3
Onyx, *U.S.A.* 117 K8
Oodnadatta, *Australia* ... 95 D2
Ooldea, *Australia* 93 F5
Oombulgurri, *Australia* .. 92 C4
Oona River, *Canada* 104 C2
Oorindi, *Australia* 94 C3
Oost-Vlaanderen □,
  Belgium 17 C3
Oostende, *Belgium* 17 C2
Oosterhout, *Neths.* 17 C4
Oosterschelde, *Neths.* ... 17 C4
Oosterwolde, *Neths.* 17 B6
Ootacamund =
  Udagamandalam, *India* . 66 P10
Ootsa L., *Canada* 104 C3
Opaka, *Bulgaria* 41 C10
Opala,
  Dem. Rep. of the Congo 86 C1
Opalenica, *Poland* 45 F3
Opan, *Bulgaria* 41 D9
Opanake, *Sri Lanka* 66 R12
Opasatika, *Canada* 102 C3
Opasquia, *Canada* 105 C10
Opatija, *Croatia* 29 C11
Opatów, *Poland* 45 H8
Opava, *Czech Rep.* 27 B10
Opelousas, *U.S.A.* 113 K8
Opémisca, L., *Canada* ... 102 C5
Opheim, *U.S.A.* 114 B10
Ophthalmia Ra., *Australia* 92 D2
Opi, *Nigeria* 83 D6
Opinaca →, *Canada* 102 B4
Opinaca L., *Canada* 102 B4
Opiskotish, L., *Canada* .. 103 B6
Opobo, *Nigeria* 83 E6
Opochka, *Russia* 46 D5
Opoczno, *Poland* 45 G7
Opole, *Poland* 45 H4
Opole □, *Poland* 45 H4
Opole Lubelskie, *Poland* . 45 G8
Oporto = Porto, *Portugal* 34 D2
Opotiki, *N.Z.* 91 M1
Opp, *U.S.A.* 109 K2
Oppdal, *Norway* 9 E13
Óppido Mamertina, *Italy* . 31 D8
Oprişor, *Romania* 42 F8
Oprtalj, *Croatia* 29 C10
Opua, *N.Z.* 91 F5
Opunake, *N.Z.* 91 H4
Opuzen, *Croatia* 29 E14
Ora, *Cyprus* 36 E12
Ora Banda, *Australia* 93 F3
Oracle, *U.S.A.* 115 K8
Oradea, *Romania* 42 C6
Öræfajökull, *Iceland* 8 D5
Orahovac, *Serbia, Yug.* .. 40 D4

Orahovica, *Croatia* 42 E2
Orai, *India* 69 G8
Oraison, *France* 21 E9
Oral = Zhayyq →,
  Kazakstan 50 E6
Oral, *Kazakstan* 48 E10
Oran, *Algeria* 78 A5
Oran, *Argentina* 126 A3
Orange, *Australia* 95 E4
Orange, *France* 21 D8
Orange, *Calif., U.S.A.* ... 117 M9
Orange, *Mass., U.S.A.* .. 111 D12
Orange, *Tex., U.S.A.* 113 K8
Orange, *Va., U.S.A.* 108 F6
Orange →, *S. Africa* 88 D2
Orange, C., *Brazil* 122 C5
Orange Cove, *U.S.A.* 116 J7
Orange Free State □ =
  Free State □, *S. Africa* . 88 D4
Orange Grove, *U.S.A.* ... 113 M6
Orange Walk, *Belize* 119 D7
Orangeburg, *U.S.A.* 109 J5
Orangeville, *Canada* 102 D3
Orani, *Phil.* 61 D4
Oranienburg, *Germany* .. 24 C9
Oranje = Orange →,
  S. Africa 88 D2
Oranje Vrystaat □ = Free
  State □, *S. Africa* 88 D4
Oranjemund, *Namibia* ... 88 D2
Oranjerivier, *S. Africa* ... 88 D3
Oras, *Phil.* 61 E6
Orašje, *Bos.-H.* 42 E3
Orăştie, *Romania* 43 E8
Oraşul Stalin = Braşov,
  Romania 43 E10
Orava →, *Slovak Rep.* ... 27 B12
Orava, Vodná nádrž,
  Slovak Rep. 27 B12
Oravița, *Romania* 42 E6
Orb →, *France* 20 E7
Orba →, *Italy* 28 D5
Ørbæk, *Denmark* 11 J4
Orbe, *Switz.* 25 J2
Orbec, *France* 18 C7
Orbetello, *Italy* 29 F8
Órbigo →, *Spain* 34 C5
Orbost, *Australia* 95 F4
Örbyhus, *Sweden* 10 D11
Orce, *Spain* 33 H2
Orce →, *Spain* 33 H2
Orchies, *France* 19 B10
Orchila, I., *Venezuela* ... 124 A5
Órcia →, *Italy* 29 F8
Orco →, *Italy* 28 C4
Orcutt, *U.S.A.* 117 L6
Ord, *Australia* 92 C4
Ord, Mt., *Australia* 92 C4
Ordenes = Ordes, *Spain* . 34 B2
Orderville, *U.S.A.* 115 H7
Ordes, *Spain* 34 B2
Ording = St-Peter-Ording,
  Germany 24 A4
Ordos = Mu Us Shamo,
  China 56 E5
Ordu, *Turkey* 72 B7
Ordubad, *Azerbaijan* 73 C12
Orduña, Álava, *Spain* 32 C2
Orduña, Granada, *Spain* . 35 H7
Ordway, *U.S.A.* 112 F3
Ordzhonikidze =
  Vladikavkaz, *Russia* ... 49 J7
Ordzhonikidze, *Ukraine* . 47 J8
Ore,
  Dem. Rep. of the Congo 86 B2
Ore Mts. = Erzgebirge,
  Germany 24 E9
Orebić, *Croatia* 29 F14
Örebro, *Sweden* 10 E9
Örebro län □, *Sweden* .. 10 E8
Oregon, *U.S.A.* 112 D10
Oregon □, *U.S.A.* 114 E3
Oregon City, *U.S.A.* 116 E4
Öregrund, *Sweden* 10 D12
Öregrundsgrepen, *Sweden* 10 D12
Orekhov = Orikhiv,
  Ukraine 47 J8
Orekhovo-Zuyevo, *Russia* 46 E10
Orel, *Russia* 47 F9
Orel →, *Ukraine* 47 H8
Orellana, *Spain* 35 F5
Orellana, Canal de, *Spain* 35 F5
Orellana, Embalse de,
  Spain 35 F5
Orem, *U.S.A.* 114 F8
Ören, *Turkey* 39 D9
Orenburg, *Russia* 50 D6
Örencik, *Turkey* 39 B11
Orense = Ourense, *Spain* . 34 C3
Orense □, *Spain* 34 C3
Orepuki, *N.Z.* 91 M1
Orestiás, *Greece* 41 E10
Øresund, *Europe* 11 J6
Orford Ness, *U.K.* 13 E9
Organ̄ = Organyà, *Spain* 32 C6
Organos, Pta. de los,
  Canary Is. 37 F2
Organyà, *Spain* 32 C6
Orgaz, *Spain* 35 F7
Orgeyev = Orhei, *Moldova* 43 C13
Orhaneli, *Turkey* 41 G12
Orhaneli →, *Turkey* 41 G12
Orhangazi, *Turkey* 41 F13
Orhei, *Moldova* 43 C13
Orhon Gol →, *Mongolia* . 60 A5
Óri, *Italy* 31 B10
Orient, *Australia* 95 D3

Oriental, Cordillera,
  Colombia 122 C3
Oriente, *Argentina* 126 D3
Orihuela, *Spain* 33 G4
Orihuela del Tremedal,
  Spain 32 E3
Orikhiv, *Ukraine* 47 J8
Oriku, *Albania* 40 F3
Orinoco →, *Venezuela* .. 122 C4
Orissa □, *India* 67 K14
Orissaare, *Estonia* 9 G20
Oristano, *Italy* 30 C1
Oristano, G. di, *Italy* 30 C1
Orizaba, *Mexico* 119 D5
Orizare, *Bulgaria* 41 D11
Orjen, *Bos.-H.* 40 D2
Orjiva, *Spain* 35 J7
Orkanger, *Norway* 8 E13
Örkelljunga, *Sweden* 11 H7
Örken, *Sweden* 11 G9
Örkény, *Hungary* 42 C4
Orkla →, *Norway* 8 E13
Orkney, *S. Africa* 88 D4
Orkney □, *U.K.* 14 B5
Orkney Is., *U.K.* 14 B6
Orland, *U.S.A.* 116 F4
Orlando, *U.S.A.* 109 L5
Orlando, C. d', *Italy* 31 D7
Orléanais, *France* 19 E9
Orléans, *France* 19 E8
Orleans, *U.S.A.* 111 B12
Orléans, Î. d', *Canada* ... 103 C5
Orlice →, *Czech Rep.* ... 27 A8
Orlov, *Slovak Rep.* 27 B13
Orlov Gay, *Russia* 48 E9
Orlová, *Czech Rep.* 27 B11
Orlovat, *Serbia, Yug.* 42 E5
Ormara, *Pakistan* 66 G4
Ormea, *Italy* 28 D4
Órmília, *Greece* 40 F7
Ormoc, *Phil.* 61 F6
Ormond, *N.Z.* 91 H6
Ormond Beach, *U.S.A.* .. 109 L5
Ormož, *Slovenia* 29 B13
Ormskirk, *U.K.* 12 D5
Ormstown, *Canada* 111 A11
Ornans, *France* 19 E13
Orne □, *France* 18 D7
Orne →, *France* 18 C6
Orneta, *Poland* 44 D7
Ornö, *Sweden* 10 E12
Örnsköldsvik, *Sweden* ... 10 A12
Oro, *N. Korea* 57 D14
Oro →, *Mexico* 118 B3
Oro Grande, *U.S.A.* 117 L9
Orobie, Alpi, *Italy* 28 B6
Orocué, *Colombia* 124 C4
Orodo, *Nigeria* 83 D6
Orogrande, *U.S.A.* 115 K10
Orol Dengizi = Aral Sea,
  Asia 50 E7
Oromocto, *Canada* 103 C6
Oron, *Nigeria* 83 E6
Orono, *Canada* 110 C6
Oronsay, *U.K.* 14 E2
Oropesa, *Spain* 34 F5
Oroquieta, *Phil.* 61 G5
Orosei, *Italy* 30 B2
Orosei, G. di, *Italy* 30 B2
Orosháza, *Hungary* 42 D5
Orotukan, *Russia* 51 C16
Oroszlány, *Hungary* 42 C3
Oroville, *Calif., U.S.A.* .. 116 F5
Oroville, *Wash., U.S.A.* .. 114 B4
Oroville, L., *U.S.A.* 116 F5
Orrefors, *Sweden* 11 H9
Orroroo, *Australia* 95 E2
Orrviken, *Sweden* 10 A8
Orrville, *U.S.A.* 110 F3
Orsa, *Sweden* 10 C8
Orsara di Púglia, *Italy* ... 31 A8
Orsasjön, *Sweden* 10 C8
Orsha, *Belarus* 46 E6
Örsjö, *Sweden* 11 H9
Orsk, *Russia* 50 D6
Orşova, *Romania* 42 F7
Ørsted, *Denmark* 11 H4
Örsundsbro, *Sweden* 10 E11
Orta, L. d', *Italy* 28 C5
Orta Nova, *Italy* 31 A8
Ortaca, *Turkey* 39 E10
Ortakent, *Turkey* 39 D9
Ortaklar, *Turkey* 39 D9
Ortaköy, *Çorum, Turkey* . 72 B6
Ortaköy, *Niğde, Turkey* . 72 C6
Orte, *Italy* 29 F9
Ortegal, C., *Spain* 34 B3
Orthez, *France* 20 E3
Ortigueira, *Spain* 34 B3
Orting, *U.S.A.* 116 C4
Ortisei, *Italy* 29 B8
Ortles, *Italy* 28 B7
Ortón →, *Bolivia* 124 C4
Ortona, *Italy* 29 F11
Orūmīyeh, *Iran* 70 B5
Orūmīyeh, Daryācheh-ye,
  Iran 70 B5
Orune, *Italy* 30 B2
Oruro, *Bolivia* 124 G5
Orust, *Sweden* 11 F5
Oruzgān □, *Afghan.* 66 C5
Orvault, *France* 18 E5
Orvieto, *Italy* 29 F9
Orwell, *U.S.A.* 110 E4
Orwell →, *U.K.* 13 F9
Oryakhovo, *Bulgaria* 40 C7
Orzinuovi, *Italy* 28 C6

Orzyc →, Poland 45 F8
Orzysz, Poland 44 E8
Osa →, Poland 44 E5
Osa, Pen. de, Costa Rica . 120 E3
Osage, Iowa, U.S.A. 112 D8
Osage, Wyo., U.S.A. 112 D2
Osage →, U.S.A. 112 F9
Osage City, U.S.A. 112 F7
Ōsaka, Japan 55 G7
Osan, S. Korea 57 F14
Osawatomie, U.S.A. 112 F7
Osborne, U.S.A. 112 F5
Osby, Sweden 11 H7
Osceola, Ark., U.S.A. ... 113 H10
Osceola, Iowa, U.S.A. ... 112 E8
Oschatz, Germany 24 D9
Oschersleben, Germany . 24 C7
Óschiri, Italy 30 B2
Oscoda, U.S.A. 110 B1
Osečina, Serbia, Yug. ... 40 B3
Ösel = Saaremaa, Estonia 9 G20
Osery, Russia 46 E10
Osh, Kyrgyzstan 50 E8
Oshawa, Canada 102 D4
Oshkosh, Nebr., U.S.A. . 112 E3
Oshkosh, Wis., U.S.A. .. 112 C10
Oshmyany = Ashmyany,
  Belarus 9 J21
Oshnovīyeh, Iran 70 B5
Oshogbo, Nigeria 83 D5
Oshtorīnān, Iran 71 C6
Oshwe,
  Dem. Rep. of the Congo 84 E3
Osieczna, Poland 45 G3
Osijek, Croatia 42 E3
Ósilo, Italy 30 B1
Ósimo, Italy 29 E10
Osintorf, Belarus 46 E6
Osipenko = Berdyansk,
  Ukraine 47 J9
Osipovichi = Asipovichy,
  Belarus 46 F5
Osizweni, S. Africa 89 D5
Oskaloosa, U.S.A. 112 E8
Oskarshamn, Sweden ... 11 G10
Oskarström, Sweden ... 11 H6
Oskélanéo, Canada 102 C4
Öskemen, Kazakstan ... 50 E9
Oskol →, Ukraine 47 H9
Oslo, Norway 9 G14
Oslob, Phil. 61 G5
Oslofjorden, Norway ... 9 G14
Osmanabad, India 66 K10
Osmancık, Turkey 72 B6
Osmaniye, Turkey 72 D7
Osmanlı, Turkey 41 E10
Ösmo, Sweden 10 F11
Osnabrück, Germany ... 24 C4
Ošno Lubuskie, Poland .. 45 F1
Osoblaha, Czech Rep. ... 27 A10
Osogovska Planina,
  Macedonia 40 D6
Osor, Italy 29 D11
Osório, Brazil 127 B5
Osorno, Chile 128 E2
Osorno, Spain 34 C6
Osoyoos, Canada 104 D5
Osøyro, Norway 9 F11
Ospika →, Canada 104 B4
Osprey Reef, Australia .. 94 A4
Oss, Neths. 17 C5
Ossa, Mt., Australia 94 G4
Óssa, Óros, Greece 38 B4
Ossa de Montiel, Spain .. 33 G2
Ossabaw I., U.S.A. 109 K5
Osse →, France 20 D4
Ossi, Italy 30 B1
Ossining, U.S.A. 111 E11
Ossipee, U.S.A. 111 C13
Ossokmanuan L., Canada 103 B7
Ossora, Russia 51 D17
Ostashkov, Russia 46 D7
Östavall, Sweden 10 B9
Oste →, Germany 24 B5
Ostend = Oostende,
  Belgium 17 C2
Oster, Ukraine 47 G6
Osterburg, Germany ... 24 C7
Osterburken, Germany . 25 F5
Österbybruk, Sweden ... 10 D11
Österbymo, Sweden 11 G9
Österdalälven, Sweden .. 10 C7
Østerdalen, Norway 9 F14
Österfärnebo, Sweden .. 10 D10
Österforse, Sweden 10 A11
Östergötlands län □,
  Sweden 11 F9
Osterholz-Scharmbeck,
  Germany 24 B4
Østerild, Denmark 11 G2
Osterode, Germany 24 D6
Östersund, Sweden 10 A8
Östervåla, Sweden 10 D11
Ostfriesische Inseln,
  Germany 24 B3
Ostfriesland, Germany .. 24 B3
Østhammar, Sweden ... 10 D12
Ostiglia, Italy 29 C8
Óstia, Lido di, Italy 29 G9
Östmark, Sweden 10 D6
Östra Husby, Sweden ... 11 F10
Ostrava, Czech Rep. 27 B11
Ostróda, Poland 44 E6
Ostrogozhsk, Russia ... 47 G10
Ostroh, Ukraine 47 G4
Ostrołęka, Poland 45 E8
Ostrołęka □, Poland ... 45 F8

Ostrov, Bulgaria 41 C8
Ostrov, Czech Rep. 26 A5
Ostrov, Romania 43 F12
Ostrov, Russia 46 D5
Ostrów Lubelski, Poland . 45 G9
Ostrów Mazowiecka,
  Poland 45 F8
Ostrów Wielkopolski,
  Poland 45 G4
Ostrowiec-Świętokrzyski,
  Poland 45 H8
Ostrožac, Bos.-H. 42 G2
Ostrzeszów, Poland 45 G4
Ostseebad Kühlungsborn,
  Germany 24 A7
Osttirol □, Austria 26 E5
Ostuni, Italy 31 B10
Osům →, Bulgaria 41 C8
Osumi →, Albania 40 F4
Ōsumi-Kaikyō, Japan ... 55 J5
Ōsumi-Shotō, Japan ... 55 J5
Osun □, Nigeria 83 D5
Osuna, Spain 35 H5
Oswego, U.S.A. 111 C8
Oswestry, U.K. 12 E4
Oświęcim, Poland 45 H6
Otaci, Moldova 43 B12
Otago □, N.Z. 91 L2
Otago Harbour, N.Z. ... 91 L3
Ōtake, Japan 55 G6
Otaki, N.Z. 91 J5
Otaru, Japan 54 C10
Otaru-Wan = Ishikari-
  Wan, Japan 54 C10
Otava →, Czech Rep. ... 26 B7
Otavalo, Ecuador 124 C3
Otavi, Namibia 88 B2
Otchinjau, Angola 88 B1
Otelec, Romania 42 E5
Oțelu Roșu, Romania .. 42 E7
Otero de Rey = Outeiro de
  Rei, Spain 34 B3
Othello, U.S.A. 114 C4
Othonoí, Greece 38 B1
Óthris, Óros, Greece ... 38 B4
Otira Gorge, N.Z. 91 K3
Otis, U.S.A. 112 E3
Otjiwarongo, Namibia .. 88 C2
Otmuchów, Poland 45 H4
Otočac, Croatia 29 D12
Otoineppu, Japan 54 B11
Otok, Croatia 29 E13
Otorohanga, N.Z. 91 H5
Otoskwin →, Canada .. 102 B2
Otosquen, Canada 105 C8
Otra →, Norway 9 G13
Otradnyy, Russia 48 D10
Otranto, Italy 31 B11
Otranto, C. d', Italy ... 31 B11
Otranto, Str. of, Italy .. 31 B11
Otrokovice, Czech Rep. . 27 B10
Otse, S. Africa 88 D4
Ōtsu, Japan 55 G7
Ōtsuki, Japan 55 G9
Ottawa = Outaouais →,
  Canada 102 C5
Ottawa, Canada 102 C4
Ottawa, Ill., U.S.A. 112 E10
Ottawa, Kans., U.S.A. .. 112 F7
Ottawa Is., Canada 101 C11
Ottélé, Cameroon 83 E7
Ottensheim, Austria ... 26 C7
Otter L., Canada 105 B8
Otter Rapids, Ont., Canada 102 B3
Otter Rapids, Sask.,
  Canada 105 B8
Otterndorf, Germany ... 24 B4
Otterup, Denmark 11 J4
Otterville, Canada 110 D4
Ottery St. Mary, U.K. .. 13 G4
Otto Beit Bridge,
  Zimbabwe 87 F2
Ottosdal, S. Africa 88 D4
Ottumwa, U.S.A. 112 E8
Otu, Nigeria 83 D5
Otukpa, Nigeria 83 D6
Oturkpo, Nigeria 83 D6
Otway, Chile 128 G2
Otway, C., Australia ... 95 F3
Otwock, Poland 45 F8
Ötztaler Ache →, Austria 26 D3
Ötztaler Alpen, Austria .. 26 E3
Ou →, Laos 64 B4
Ou Neua, Laos 64 A3
Ou-Sammyaku, Japan .. 54 E10
Ouachita →, U.S.A. ... 113 K9
Ouachita, L., U.S.A. ... 113 H8
Ouachita Mts., U.S.A. .. 113 H7
Ouagadougou,
  Burkina Faso 83 C4
Ouahigouya, Burkina Faso 82 C4
Ouahran = Oran, Algeria . 78 A5
Oualâta, Mauritania ... 82 B3
Ouallene, Algeria 78 D6
Ouarane, Mauritania ... 82 B2
Ouargla, Algeria 78 B7
Ouarzazate, Morocco .. 78 B4
Ouatagouna, Mali 83 B5
Oubangi →,
  Dem. Rep. of the Congo 84 E3
Ouche →, France 19 E12
Ouddorp, Neths. 17 C3
Oude Rijn →, Neths. .. 17 B4
Oudenaarde, Belgium .. 17 D3
Oudon →, France 18 E6
Oudtshoorn, S. Africa .. 88 E3
Ouellé, Ivory C. 82 D4
Ouessa, Burkina Faso .. 82 C4

Ouessant, Î. d', France ... 18 D1
Ouesso, Congo 84 D3
Ouest, Pte., Canada 103 C7
Ouezzane, Morocco 78 B4
Oughterard, Ireland 15 C2
Ouidah, Benin 83 D5
Ouistreham, France 18 C6
Oujda, Morocco 78 B5
Ould Yenjé, Mauritania .. 82 B2
Oulainen, Finland 8 D21
Oullins, France 21 C8
Oulu, Finland 8 D21
Oulujärvi, Finland 8 D22
Oulujoki →, Finland ... 8 D21
Oulx, Italy 28 C3
Oum Chalouba, Chad .. 79 E10
Oum Hadjer, Chad 79 F9
Oumé, Ivory C. 82 D3
Ounasjoki →, Finland .. 8 C21
Ounguati, Namibia 88 C2
Ounianga Sérir, Chad .. 79 E10
Our →, Lux. 17 E6
Ouranópolis, Greece ... 40 F7
Ouray, U.S.A. 115 G10
Ourcq →, France 19 C10
Ourense, Spain 34 C3
Ouricuri, Brazil 125 E10
Ourinhos, Brazil 127 A6
Ourique, Portugal 35 H2
Ouro Fino, Brazil 127 A6
Ouro Prêto, Brazil 127 A7
Ouro Sogui, Senegal ... 82 B2
Oursi, Burkina Faso ... 83 C4
Ourthe →, Belgium ... 17 D5
Ouse, Australia 94 G4
Ouse →, E. Susx., U.K. . 13 G8
Ouse →, N. Yorks., U.K. 12 D7
Oust, France 20 F5
Oust →, France 18 E4
Outaouais →, Canada .. 102 C5
Outardes →, Canada .. 103 C6
Outeiro de Rei, Spain .. 34 B3
Outer Hebrides, U.K. ... 14 D1
Outer I., Canada 103 B8
Outes = Serra de Outes,
  Spain 34 C2
Outjo, Namibia 88 C2
Outlook, Canada 105 C7
Outlook, U.S.A. 112 A2
Outokumpu, Finland ... 8 E23
Outreau, France 19 B8
Ouvèze →, France 21 E8
Ouyen, Australia 95 F3
Ouzouer-le-Marché, France 19 E8
Ovada, Italy 28 D5
Ovalau, Fiji 91 C8
Ovalle, Chile 126 C1
Ovamboland, Namibia .. 88 B2
Ovar, Portugal 34 E2
Overath, Germany 24 E3
Overflakkee, Neths. ... 17 C4
Overijssel □, Neths. ... 17 B6
Overland Park, U.S.A. .. 112 F7
Overton, U.S.A. 117 J12
Övertorneå, Sweden ... 8 C20
Överum, Sweden 11 F10
Ovid, U.S.A. 112 E3
Ovidiopol, Ukraine 47 J6
Ovidiu, Romania 43 F13
Oviedo, Spain 34 B5
Oviksfjällen, Sweden ... 10 A7
Oviši, Latvia 9 H19
Övör Hangay □, Mongolia 56 B2
Ovoro, Nigeria 83 D6
Øvre Årdal, Norway ... 9 F12
Øvre Fryken, Sweden .. 10 E7
Ovruch, Ukraine 47 G5
Owaka, N.Z. 91 M2
Owambo = Ovamboland,
  Namibia 88 B2
Owase, Japan 55 G8
Owatonna, U.S.A. 112 C8
Owbeh, Afghan. 66 B3
Owego, U.S.A. 111 D8
Owen Falls Dam, Uganda 86 B3
Owen Sound, Canada .. 102 D3
Owens →, U.S.A. 116 J9
Owens L., U.S.A. 117 J9
Owensboro, U.S.A. ... 108 G1
Owensville, U.S.A. ... 112 F9
Owerri, Nigeria 83 D6
Owl →, Canada 105 B10
Owo, Nigeria 83 D6
Owosso, U.S.A. 108 D3
Owyhee, U.S.A. 114 F5
Owyhee →, U.S.A. 114 E5
Owyhee, L., U.S.A. ... 114 E5
Ox Mts. = Slieve Gamph,
  Ireland 15 B3
Öxarfjörður, Iceland ... 8 C5
Oxelösund, Sweden ... 11 F11
Oxford, N.Z. 91 K4
Oxford, U.K. 13 F6
Oxford, Miss., U.S.A. .. 113 H10
Oxford, N.C., U.S.A. ... 109 G6
Oxford, Ohio, U.S.A. .. 108 F3
Oxfordshire □, U.K. ... 13 F6
Oxía, Greece 38 C3
Oxie, Sweden 11 J7
Oxílithos, Greece 38 C6
Oxley, Australia 95 E3
Oxnard, U.S.A. 117 L7
Oxsjövålen, Sweden ... 10 B7
Oxus = Amudarya →,
  Uzbekistan 50 E6
Oya, Malaysia 62 D4

Oyama, Japan 55 F9
Oyem, Gabon 84 D2
Oyen, Canada 105 C6
Oykel →, U.K. 14 D4
Oyo, Nigeria 83 D5
Oyo □, Nigeria 83 D5
Oyonnax, France 19 F12
Oyster Bay, U.S.A. 111 F11
Ōyūbari, Japan 54 C11
Özalp, Turkey 73 C10
Ozamiz, Phil. 61 G5
Ozark, Ala., U.S.A. ... 109 K3
Ozark, Ark., U.S.A. ... 113 H8
Ozark, Mo., U.S.A. ... 113 G8
Ozark Plateau, U.S.A. .. 113 G9
Ozarks, L. of the, U.S.A. 112 F8
Ożarów, Poland 45 H8
Özd, Hungary 42 B5
Ozernoye, Russia 48 E10
Ozette L., U.S.A. 116 B2
Ozieri, Italy 30 B2
Ozimek, Poland 45 H5
Ozinki, Russia 48 E9
Ozona, U.S.A. 113 K4
Ozorków, Poland 45 G6
Ozren, Bos.-H. 42 G3
Ozuluama, Mexico 119 C5
Ozun, Romania 43 E10
Ozurgeti, Georgia 49 K5

P

Pa, Burkina Faso 82 C4
Pa-an, Burma 67 L20
Pa Mong Dam, Thailand . 64 D4
Paamiut = Frederikshåb,
  Greenland 4 C5
Paar →, Germany 25 G7
Paarl, S. Africa 88 E2
Paauilo, U.S.A. 106 H17
Pab Hills, Pakistan ... 68 F2
Pabbay, U.K. 14 D1
Pabianice, Poland 45 G6
Pabna, Bangla. 67 G16
Pabo, Uganda 86 B3
Pacaja →, Brazil 125 D8
Pacaraima, Sierra,
  Venezuela 122 C4
Pacasmayo, Peru 124 E3
Paceco, Italy 30 E5
Pachhar, India 68 G7
Pachino, Italy 31 F8
Pachitea →, Peru 124 E4
Pachpadra, India 66 G8
Pachuca, Mexico 119 C5
Pacific, Canada 104 C3
Pacific-Antarctic Ridge,
  Pac. Oc. 97 M16
Pacific Grove, U.S.A. .. 116 J5
Pacific Ocean, Pac. Oc. . 97 G14
Pacifica, U.S.A. 116 H4
Pacitan, Indonesia 63 H14
Packwood, U.S.A. 116 D5
Pacov, Czech Rep. 26 B8
Pacy-sur-Eure, France . 18 C8
Padaido, Kepulauan,
  Indonesia 63 E9
Padang, Indonesia 62 E2
Padang Endau, Malaysia . 65 L4
Padangpanjang, Indonesia 62 E2
Padangsidempuan,
  Indonesia 62 D1
Padborg, Denmark 11 K3
Paddockwood, Canada . 105 C7
Paderborn, Germany .. 24 D4
Padeş, Vf., Romania ... 42 E7
Padina, Romania 43 F12
Pádova, Italy 29 C8
Padra, India 68 H5
Padrauna, India 69 F10
Padre I., U.S.A. 113 M6
Padrón, Spain 34 C2
Padstow, U.K. 13 G3
Padua = Pádova, Italy . 29 C8
Paducah, Ky., U.S.A. .. 108 G1
Paducah, Tex., U.S.A. .. 113 H4
Padul, Spain 35 H7
Paengnyong-do, S. Korea 57 F13
Paeroa, N.Z. 91 G5
Paesana, Italy 28 D4
Pafúri, Mozam. 89 C5
Pag, Croatia 29 D12
Paga, Ghana 83 C4
Pagadian, Phil. 61 H5
Pagai Selatan, Pulau,
  Indonesia 62 E2
Pagai Utara, Pulau,
  Indonesia 62 E2
Pagalu = Annobón,
  Atl. Oc. 77 G4
Pagastikós Kólpos, Greece 38 B5
Pagatan, Indonesia ... 62 E5
Page, Ariz., U.S.A. ... 115 H8
Page, N. Dak., U.S.A. .. 112 B6
Pagėgiai, Lithuania ... 44 C10
Pago Pago, Amer. Samoa 91 B13
Pagosa Springs, U.S.A. . 115 H10
Pagwa River, Canada .. 102 B2
Pahala, U.S.A. 106 J17
Pahang □, Malaysia ... 65 L4
Pahiatua, N.Z. 91 J5
Pahokee, U.S.A. 109 M5
Pahrump, U.S.A. 117 J11

Pahute Mesa, U.S.A. ... 116 H10
Pai, Thailand 64 C2
Paia, U.S.A. 106 H16
Paicines, U.S.A. 116 J5
Paide, Estonia 9 G21
Paignton, U.K. 13 G4
Paiho, Taiwan 59 F13
Päijänne, Finland 9 F21
Pailin, Cambodia 64 F4
Paimpol, France 18 D3
Painan, Indonesia ... 62 E2
Painesville, U.S.A. ... 110 E3
Paint Hills = Wemindji,
  Canada 102 B4
Paint L., Canada 105 B9
Paint Rock, U.S.A. 113 K5
Painted Desert, U.S.A. . 115 J8
Paintsville, U.S.A. ... 108 G4
País Vasco □, Spain .. 32 C2
Paisley, Canada 110 B3
Paisley, U.K. 14 F4
Paisley, U.S.A. 114 E3
Paita, Peru 124 E2
Paiva →, Portugal ... 34 D2
Paizhou, China 59 B9
Pajares, Spain 34 B5
Pajares, Puerto de, Spain . 34 C5
Pajęczno, Poland 45 G5
Pak Lay, Laos 64 C3
Pak Phanang, Thailand . 65 H3
Pak Sane, Laos 64 C4
Pak Song, Laos 64 E6
Pak Suong, Laos 64 C4
Pákhnes, Greece 36 D6
Pakistan ■, Asia 68 E4
Pakkading, Laos 64 C4
Pakokku, Burma 67 J19
Pakość, Poland 45 F5
Pakpattan, Pakistan .. 68 D5
Pakrac, Croatia 42 E2
Pakruojis, Lithuania .. 44 C10
Paks, Hungary 42 D3
Paktīā □, Afghan. 66 C6
Pakwach, Uganda 86 B3
Pakxe, Laos 64 E5
Pala, Chad 79 G9
Pala,
  Dem. Rep. of the Congo 86 D2
Pala, U.S.A. 117 M9
Palabek, Uganda 86 B3
Palacios, U.S.A. 113 L6
Palafrugell, Spain ... 32 D8
Palagiano, Italy 31 B10
Palagonía, Italy 31 E7
Palagruža, Croatia ... 29 F13
Palaiokastron, Greece . 36 D8
Palaiokhóra, Greece .. 36 D5
Pálairos, Greece 38 C2
Palaiseau, France 19 D9
Palam, India 66 K10
Palamás, Greece 38 B4
Palamòs, Spain 32 D8
Palampur, India 68 C7
Palamut, Turkey 39 C9
Palana, Australia 94 F4
Palana, Russia 51 D16
Palanan, Phil. 61 C5
Palanan Pt., Phil. ... 61 C5
Palandri, Pakistan ... 69 C5
Palanga, Lithuania ... 9 J19
Palangkaraya, Indonesia 62 E4
Palani Hills, India ... 66 P10
Palanpur, India 68 G5
Palapye, Botswana ... 88 C4
Palas, Pakistan 69 B5
Palas de Rei, Spain .. 34 C3
Palatka, Russia 51 C16
Palatka, U.S.A. 109 L5
Palau, Italy 30 A2
Palau ■, Pac. Oc. 96 G5
Palauk, Burma 64 F2
Palawan, Phil. 61 G3
Palayankottai, India .. 66 Q10
Palazzo, Pte., France . 21 F12
Palazzo San Gervásio, Italy 31 B8
Palazzolo Acréide, Italy . 31 E7
Paldiski, Estonia 9 G21
Pale, Bos.-H. 42 G3
Paleleh, Indonesia ... 63 D6
Palembang, Indonesia . 62 E2
Palena →, Chile 128 E2
Palencia, Spain 34 C6
Palencia □, Spain ... 34 C6
Paleokastrítsa, Greece . 36 A3
Paleometokho, Cyprus . 36 D12
Palermo, Italy 30 D6
Palermo, U.S.A. 114 G3
Palestina, Chile 128 A3
Palestine, Asia 75 D4
Palestine, U.S.A. 113 K7
Palestrina, Italy 29 G9
Paletwa, Burma 67 J18
Palghat, India 66 P10
Palgrave, Mt., Australia . 92 D2
Pali, India 68 G5
Palinuro, Italy 31 B8
Palinuro, C., Italy ... 31 B8
Paliouríon, Ákra, Greece 40 G7
Palisade, U.S.A. 112 E4
Paliseul, Belgium ... 17 E5
Palitana, India 68 J4
Palizada, Mexico 119 D6
Palk Bay, Asia 66 Q11
Palk Strait, Asia 66 Q11
Palla Road = Dinokwe,
  Botswana 88 C4
Pallanza = Verbánia, Italy 28 C5

Pallasovka, Russia 48 E8
Pallës, Bishti i, Albania ... 40 E3
Pallisa, Uganda 86 B3
Pallu, India 68 E6
Palm Bay, U.S.A. 109 L5
Palm Beach, U.S.A. 109 M6
Palm Desert, U.S.A. 117 M10
Palm Is., Australia 94 B4
Palm Springs, U.S.A. ... 117 M10
Palma, Mozam. 87 E5
Palma, B. de, Spain 37 B9
Palma de Mallorca, Spain . 37 B9
Palma del Río, Spain 35 H5
Palma di Montechiaro, Italy 30 E6
Palma Soriano, Cuba 120 B4
Palmares, Brazil 125 E11
Palmarola, Italy 30 B5
Palmas, Brazil 127 B5
Palmas, C., Liberia 82 E3
Pálmas, G. di, Italy 30 D1
Palmdale, U.S.A. 117 L8
Palmeira dos Índios, Brazil 125 E11
Palmela, Portugal 35 G2
Palmer, U.S.A. 100 B5
Palmer →, Australia 94 B3
Palmer Arch., Antarctica . 5 C17
Palmer Lake, U.S.A. 112 F2
Palmer Land, Antarctica . 5 D18
Palmerston, Canada 110 C4
Palmerston, N.Z. 91 L3
Palmerston North, N.Z. .. 91 J5
Palmerton, U.S.A. 111 F9
Palmetto, U.S.A. 109 M4
Palmi, Italy 31 D8
Palmira, Argentina 126 C2
Palmira, Colombia 124 C3
Palmyra = Tudmur, Syria 70 C3
Palmyra, Mo., U.S.A. ... 112 F9
Palmyra, N.Y., U.S.A. .. 110 C7
Palmyra Is., Pac. Oc. ... 97 G11
Palo Alto, U.S.A. 116 H4
Palo Verde, U.S.A. 117 M12
Palompon, Phil. 61 F6
Palopo, Indonesia 63 E6
Palos, C. de, Spain 33 H4
Palos de la Frontera, Spain 35 H4
Palos Verdes, U.S.A. 117 M8
Palos Verdes, Pt., U.S.A. . 117 M8
Palouse, U.S.A. 114 C5
Palparara, Australia 94 C3
Pålsboda, Sweden 10 E9
Palu, Indonesia 63 E5
Palu, Turkey 73 C9
Paluzza, Italy 29 B10
Palwal, India 68 E7
Pama, Burkina Faso 83 C5
Pamanukan, Indonesia .. 63 G12
Pamiers, France 20 E5
Pamir, Tajikistan 50 F8
Pamlico →, U.S.A. 109 H7
Pamlico Sd., U.S.A. 109 H8
Pampa, U.S.A. 113 H4
Pampa de las Salinas, Argentina 126 C2
Pampanua, Indonesia 63 E6
Pampas, Argentina 126 D3
Pampas, Peru 124 F4
Pamphylia, Turkey 72 D4
Pamplona, Colombia 124 B4
Pamplona, Spain 32 C3
Pampoenpoort, S. Africa . 88 E3
Pamukçu, Turkey 39 B9
Pamukkale, Turkey 39 D11
Pan Xian, China 58 E5
Pana, U.S.A. 112 F10
Panabo, Phil. 61 H6
Panaca, U.S.A. 115 H6
Panagyurishte, Bulgaria . 41 D8
Panaitan, Indonesia 63 G11
Panamá, Panama 120 E4
Panama ■, Cent. Amer. .. 120 E4
Panamá, G. de, Panama .. 120 E4
Panama Canal, Panama .. 120 E4
Panama City, U.S.A. 109 K3
Panamint Range, U.S.A. . 117 J9
Panamint Springs, U.S.A. . 117 J9
Panão, Peru 124 E3
Panaon I., Phil. 61 F6
Panare, Thailand 65 J3
Panarea, Italy 31 D8
Panaro →, Italy 29 D8
Panay, Phil. 61 F5
Panay, G., Phil. 61 F5
Pancake Range, U.S.A. .. 115 G6
Pančevo, Serbia, Yug. .. 42 F5
Panciu, Romania 43 E12
Pancorbo, Desfiladero, Spain 34 C7
Pâncota, Romania 42 D6
Pandan, Antique, Phil. .. 61 F5
Pandan, Catanduanes, Phil. 61 D6
Pandegelang, Indonesia .. 63 G12
Pandharpur, India 66 L9
Pando, Uruguay 127 C4
Pando, L. = Hope, L., Australia 95 D2
Pandokrátor, Greece 36 A3
Pandora, Costa Rica 120 E3
Pandrup, Denmark 11 G3
Panevėžys, Lithuania 9 J21
Panfilov, Kazakstan 50 E9
Panfilovo, Russia 48 E6
Pang-Long, Burma 67 H21
Pang-Yang, Burma 67 H21
Panga, Dem. Rep. of the Congo 86 B2

Pangaíon Óros, Greece ... 41 F8
Pangalanes, Canal des, Madag. 89 C8
Pangani, Tanzania 86 D4
Pangani □, Tanzania 86 D4
Pangani →, Tanzania 86 D4
Pangfou = Bengbu, China 57 H9
Pangil, Dem. Rep. of the Congo 86 C2
Pangkah, Tanjung, Indonesia 63 G15
Pangkajene, Indonesia ... 63 E5
Pangkalanbrandan, Indonesia 62 D1
Pangkalanbuun, Indonesia 62 E4
Pangkalpinang, Indonesia . 62 E3
Pangnirtung, Canada 101 B13
Panguitch, U.S.A. 115 H7
Pangutaran Group, Phil. .. 61 H4
Panhandle, U.S.A. 113 H4
Pani Mines, India 68 H5
Pania-Mutombo, Dem. Rep. of the Congo 86 D1
Panipat, India 68 E7
Panjal Range, India 68 C7
Panjgur, Pakistan 66 F4
Panjim = Panaji, India ... 66 M8
Panjinad Barrage, Pakistan 68 E7
Panjwai, Afghan. 68 D1
Pankshin, Nigeria 83 D6
Panmunjŏm, N. Korea ... 57 F14
Panna, India 69 G9
Panna Hills, India 69 G9
Pano Lefkara, Cyprus ... 36 E12
Pano Panayia, Cyprus ... 36 E11
Panorama, Brazil 127 A5
Pánormon, Greece 36 D6
Panshan, China 57 D12
Panshi, China 57 C14
Pantanal, Brazil 124 H7
Pantar, Indonesia 63 F6
Pante Macassar, Indonesia 63 F6
Pantelleria, Italy 30 F4
Pantón, Spain 34 C3
Pánuco, Mexico 119 C5
Panyam, Nigeria 83 D6
Panyu, China 59 F9
Páola, Italy 31 C9
Paola, Malta 36 D2
Paola, U.S.A. 112 F7
Paonia, U.S.A. 115 G10
Paoting = Baoding, China 56 E8
Paot'ou = Baotou, China . 56 D6
Paoua, C.A.R. 84 C3
Pápa, Hungary 42 C2
Papa Stour, U.K. 14 A7
Papa Westray, U.K. 14 B6
Papagayo →, Mexico 119 D5
Papagayo, G. de, Costa Rica 120 D2
Papakura, N.Z. 91 G5
Papantla, Mexico 119 C5
Papar, Malaysia 62 C5
Pápas, Ákra, Greece 38 C3
Papenburg, Germany 24 B3
Paphlagonia, Turkey 72 B5
Paphos, Cyprus 36 E11
Papien Chiang = Da →, Vietnam 64 B5
Papigochic →, Mexico ... 118 B3
Paposo, Chile 126 B1
Papoutsa, Cyprus 36 E12
Papua New Guinea ■, Oceania 96 H6
Papudo, Chile 126 C1
Papuk, Croatia 42 E2
Papun, Burma 67 K20
Papunya, Australia 92 D5
Pará = Belém, Brazil 125 D9
Pará □, Brazil 125 D8
Paraburdoo, Australia ... 92 D2
Paracale, Phil. 61 D5
Paracatu, Brazil 125 G9
Paracel Is., S. China Sea . 62 A4
Parachilna, Australia 95 E2
Parachinar, Pakistan 68 C4
Paracín, Serbia, Yug. 40 C5
Paradas, Spain 35 H5
Paradela, Spain 34 C3
Paradhísi, Greece 36 C10
Paradip, India 67 J15
Paradise, Calif., U.S.A. .. 116 F5
Paradise, Mont., U.S.A. .. 114 C6
Paradise, Nev., U.S.A. .. 117 J11
Paradise →, Canada 103 B8
Paradise Valley, U.S.A. .. 114 F5
Parado, Indonesia 63 F5
Paragould, U.S.A. 113 G9
Paragua →, Venezuela .. 124 B6
Paraguaçu →, Brazil 125 F11
Paraguaçu Paulista, Brazil 127 A5
Paraguaná, Pen. de, Venezuela 124 A5
Paraguarí, Paraguay 126 B4
Paraguarí □, Paraguay ... 126 B4
Paraguay ■, S. Amer. 126 A4
Paraguay →, Paraguay ... 126 B4
Paraíba = João Pessoa, Brazil 125 E12
Paraíba □, Brazil 125 E11
Paraíba do Sul →, Brazil . 127 A7
Parainen, Finland 9 F20
Paraíso, Mexico 119 D6
Parak, Iran 71 E7
Parakhino Paddubye, Russia 46 C7
Parakou, Benin 83 D5

Paralimni, Cyprus 36 D12
Parálion-Astrous, Greece . 38 D4
Paramaribo, Surinam 125 B7
Paramithiá, Greece 38 B2
Paramushir, Ostrov, Russia 51 D16
Paran →, Israel 75 E4
Paraná, Argentina 126 C3
Paranã, Brazil 125 F9
Paraná □, Brazil 127 A5
Paraná →, Argentina 126 C4
Paranaguá, Brazil 127 B6
Paranaíba, Brazil 125 G8
Paranaíba →, Brazil 125 H8
Paranapanema →, Brazil . 127 A5
Paranapiacaba, Serra do, Brazil 127 A6
Paranavaí, Brazil 127 A5
Parang, Jolo, Phil. 61 J4
Parang, Mindanao, Phil. .. 63 C6
Parângul Mare, Vf., Romania 43 E8
Parapóla, Greece 38 E5
Paraspóri, Ákra, Greece .. 39 F9
Paratoo, Australia 95 E2
Parattah, Australia 94 G4
Paray-le-Monial, France .. 19 F11
Parbati →, India 68 G7
Parbhani, India 66 K10
Parchim, Germany 24 B7
Parczew, Poland 45 G9
Pardes Hanna-Karkur, Israel 75 C3
Pardilla, Spain 34 D7
Pardo →, Bahia, Brazil . 125 G11
Pardo →, Mato Grosso, Brazil 127 A5
Pardubice, Czech Rep. .. 26 A8
Pare, Indonesia 63 G15
Pare □, Tanzania 86 C4
Pare Mts., Tanzania 86 C4
Parecis, Serra dos, Brazil . 124 F7
Paredes de Nava, Spain .. 34 C6
Pareh, Iran 70 B5
Paren, Russia 51 C17
Parent, Canada 102 C5
Parent, L., Canada 102 C4
Parentis-en-Born, France . 20 D2
Parepare, Indonesia 63 E5
Parfino, Russia 46 D6
Párga, Greece 38 B2
Pargo, Pta. do, Madeira .. 37 D2
Pariaguán, Venezuela 124 B6
Paricutín, Cerro, Mexico . 118 D4
Parigi, Indonesia 63 E6
Parika, Guyana 124 B7
Parikkala, Finland 46 B5
Parima, Serra, Brazil 124 C6
Parinari, Peru 124 D4
Pariñas, Pta., S. Amer. ... 122 D2
Parincea, Romania 43 D12
Parintins, Brazil 125 D7
Pariparit Kyun, Burma ... 67 M18
Paris, Canada 102 D3
Paris, France 19 D9
Paris, Idaho, U.S.A. 114 E8
Paris, Ky., U.S.A. 108 F3
Paris, Tenn., U.S.A. 109 G1
Paris, Tex., U.S.A. 113 J7
Paris, Ville de □, France .. 19 D9
Parish, U.S.A. 111 C8
Park, U.S.A. 116 B4
Park City, U.S.A. 114 F8
Park Falls, U.S.A. 112 C9
Park Range, U.S.A. 114 G10
Park Rapids, U.S.A. 112 B7
Park River, U.S.A. 112 A6
Park Rynie, S. Africa 89 E5
Parkā Bandar, Iran 71 E8
Parkano, Finland 9 E20
Parker, Ariz., U.S.A. 117 L12
Parker, S. Dak., U.S.A. .. 112 D6
Parker Dam, U.S.A. 117 L12
Parkersburg, U.S.A. 108 F5
Parkerview, Canada 105 C8
Parkes, Australia 95 E4
Parkfield, U.S.A. 116 K6
Parkland, U.S.A. 116 C4
Parkside, Canada 105 C7
Parkston, U.S.A. 112 D6
Parksville, Canada 104 D4
Parla, Spain 34 E7
Pârlița, Moldova 43 C12
Parma, Italy 28 D7
Parma, Idaho, U.S.A. 114 E5
Parma, Ohio, U.S.A. 110 E3
Parma →, Italy 28 D7
Parnaguá, Brazil 125 F10
Parnaíba, Brazil 125 D10
Parnaíba →, Brazil 122 D6
Parnassós, Greece 38 C4
Párnis, Greece 38 C5
Párnon Óros, Greece 38 D4
Pärnu, Estonia 9 G21
Paroo →, Australia 95 E3
Páros, Greece 39 D7
Parowan, U.S.A. 115 H7
Parpaillon, France 21 D10
Parral, Chile 126 D1
Parramatta, Australia 95 E5
Parras, Mexico 118 B4
Parrett →, U.K. 13 F4
Parris I., U.S.A. 109 J5
Parrsboro, Canada 103 C7
Parry Is., Canada 4 B2
Parry Sound, Canada 102 C4
Parsberg, Germany 25 F7
Parsęta →, Poland 44 D2

Parshall, U.S.A. 112 B3
Parsnip →, Canada 104 B4
Parsons, U.S.A. 113 G7
Parsons Ra., Australia ... 94 A2
Partanna, Italy 30 E5
Parthenay, France 18 F6
Partinico, Italy 30 D6
Partizánske, Slovak Rep. . 27 C11
Paru →, Brazil 125 D8
Parvān □, Afghan. 66 B6
Parvatipuram, India 67 K13
Parys, S. Africa 88 D4
Pas, Pta. des, Spain 37 C7
Pas-de-Calais □, France . 19 B9
Pasada, Spain 34 B5
Pasadena, Calif., U.S.A. .. 117 L8
Pasadena, Tex., U.S.A. .. 113 L7
Pasaje →, Argentina 126 B3
Paşalimanı, Turkey 41 F11
Pasay, Phil. 61 D4
Pascagoula, U.S.A. 113 K10
Pascagoula →, U.S.A. ... 113 K10
Paşcani, Romania 43 C11
Pasco, U.S.A. 114 C4
Pasco, Cerro de, Peru ... 124 F3
Pascua, I. de, Pac. Oc. ... 97 K17
Pasewalk, Germany 24 B9
Pasfield L., Canada 105 B7
Pasha →, Russia 46 B7
Pashiwari, Pakistan 69 B6
Pashmakli = Smolyan, Bulgaria 41 E8
Pasinler, Turkey 73 C9
Pasir Mas, Malaysia 65 J4
Pasirian, Indonesia 63 H15
Pasirkuning, Indonesia .. 62 E2
Påskallavik, Sweden 11 G10
Pasküh, Iran 71 E9
Pasłęk, Poland 44 D6
Pasłęka →, Poland 44 D6
Pasley, C., Australia 93 F3
Pašman, Croatia 29 E12
Pasni, Pakistan 66 G3
Paso Cantinela, Mexico .. 117 N11
Paso de Indios, Argentina . 128 E3
Paso de los Libres, Argentina 126 B4
Paso de los Toros, Uruguay 126 C4
Paso Robles, U.S.A. 115 J3
Paspébiac, Canada 103 C6
Pasrur, Pakistan 68 C6
Passage West, Ireland ... 15 E3
Passaic, U.S.A. 111 F10
Passau, Germany 25 G9
Passero, C., Italy 31 F8
Passo Fundo, Brazil 127 B5
Passos, Brazil 125 H9
Passow, Germany 24 B10
Passy, France 21 C10
Pastavy, Belarus 9 J22
Pasto, Colombia 124 C3
Pastrana, Spain 32 E2
Pasuruan, Indonesia 63 G15
Pasym, Poland 44 E7
Pásztó, Hungary 42 C4
Patagonia, Argentina 122 H4
Patagonia, U.S.A. 115 L8
Patambar, Iran 71 D9
Patan, India 66 H8
Patan, Maharashtra, India 68 H5
Patan, Nepal 67 F14
Patani, Indonesia 63 D7
Pătârlagele, Romania 43 E11
Pataudi, India 68 E7
Patchewollock, Australia . 95 F3
Patchogue, U.S.A. 111 F11
Patea, N.Z. 91 H5
Paternion, Austria 26 E6
Paternò, Italy 31 E7
Pateros, U.S.A. 114 B4
Paterson, U.S.A. 111 F10
Paterson Ra., Australia ... 92 D3
Pathankot, India 68 C6
Pathfinder Reservoir, U.S.A. 114 E10
Pathiu, Thailand 65 G2
Pathum Thani, Thailand . 64 E3
Pati, Indonesia 63 G14
Patía →, Colombia 124 C3
Patiala, India 68 D7
Patine Kouka, Senegal ... 82 C2
Patitírion, Greece 38 B5
Patkai Bum, India 67 F19
Pátmos, Greece 39 D8
Patna, India 69 G11
Patnos, Turkey 73 C10
Pato Branco, Brazil 128 B6
Patonga, Uganda 86 B3
Patos, Brazil 125 E11
Patos, L. dos, Brazil 127 C5
Patos de Minas, Brazil ... 125 G9
Patosi, Albania 40 F3
Patquía, Argentina 126 C2
Pátrai, Greece 38 C3
Pátraikós Kólpos, Greece . 38 C3
Patras = Pátrai, Greece .. 38 C3
Patrocínio, Brazil 125 G9
Patta, Kenya 86 C5
Pattada, Italy 30 B2
Pattani, Thailand 65 J3
Patten, U.S.A. 103 C6
Patterson, Calif., U.S.A. . 116 H5

Patterson, La., U.S.A. ... 113 L9
Patterson, Mt., U.S.A. ... 116 G7
Patti, India 68 D6
Patti, Italy 31 D7
Pattoki, Pakistan 68 D5
Patton, U.S.A. 110 F6
Patuakhali, Bangla. 67 H17
Patuca →, Honduras 120 C3
Patuca, Punta, Honduras . 120 C3
Pătulele, Romania 42 F7
Pátzcuaro, Mexico 118 D4
Pau, France 20 E3
Pau, Gave de →, France . 20 E2
Pauillac, France 20 C3
Pauk, Burma 67 J19
Paul I., Canada 103 A7
Paulhan, France 20 E7
Paulis = Isiro, Dem. Rep. of the Congo 86 B2
Paulistana, Brazil 125 E10
Paullina, U.S.A. 112 D7
Paulo Afonso, Brazil 125 E11
Paulpietersburg, S. Africa . 89 D5
Pauls Valley, U.S.A. 113 H6
Pauma Valley, U.S.A. ... 117 M10
Păveh, Iran 70 C5
Pavelets, Russia 46 F10
Pavia, Italy 28 C6
Pavilly, France 18 C7
Pāvilosta, Latvia 9 H19
Pavlikeni, Bulgaria 41 C9
Pavlodar, Kazakstan 50 D8
Pavlograd = Pavlohrad, Ukraine 47 H8
Pavlohrad, Ukraine 47 H8
Pavlovo, Russia 48 C6
Pavlovsk, Russia 48 E6
Pavlovskaya, Russia 49 G4
Pavlovskiy-Posad, Russia . 46 E10
Pavullo nel Frignano, Italy 28 D7
Pawhuska, U.S.A. 113 G6
Pawling, U.S.A. 111 E11
Pawnee, U.S.A. 113 G6
Pawnee City, U.S.A. 112 E6
Pawtucket, U.S.A. 111 E13
Paximádhia, Greece 36 E6
Paxoí, Greece 38 B2
Paxton, Ill., U.S.A. 108 E1
Paxton, Nebr., U.S.A. .. 112 E4
Payakumbuh, Indonesia . 62 E2
Payerne, Switz. 25 J2
Payette, U.S.A. 114 D5
Paymogo, Spain 35 H3
Payne Bay = Kangirsuk, Canada 101 C13
Paynes Find, Australia ... 93 E2
Paynesville, Liberia 82 D2
Paynesville, U.S.A. 112 C7
Pays de la Loire □, France 18 E6
Paysandú, Uruguay 126 C4
Payson, Ariz., U.S.A. ... 115 J8
Payson, Utah, U.S.A. ... 114 F8
Paz →, Guatemala 120 D1
Paz, B. la, Mexico 118 C2
Pāzanān, Iran 71 D6
Pazar, Turkey 73 B9
Pazarcık, Turkey 72 D7
Pazardzhik, Bulgaria 41 D8
Pazarköy, Turkey 39 B9
Pazarlar, Turkey 39 C11
Pazaryeri, Turkey 39 B11
Pazaryolu, Turkey 73 B9
Pazin, Croatia 29 C10
Pčinja →, Macedonia 40 E5
Pe Ell, U.S.A. 116 D3
Peabody, U.S.A. 111 D14
Peace →, Canada 104 B6
Peace Point, Canada 104 B6
Peace River, Canada 104 B5
Peach Springs, U.S.A. ... 115 J7
Peak, The = Kinder Scout, U.K. 12 D6
Peak Downs, Australia ... 94 C4
Peak Downs Mine, Australia 94 C4
Peak Hill, N.S.W., Australia 95 E4
Peak Hill, W. Austral., Australia 93 E2
Peak Ra., Australia 94 C4
Peake, Australia 95 F2
Peake Cr. →, Australia .. 95 D2
Peal de Becerro, Spain .. 35 H7
Peale, Mt., U.S.A. 115 G9
Pearblossom, U.S.A. 117 L9
Pearl →, U.S.A. 113 K10
Pearl City, U.S.A. 106 H16
Pearl River, U.S.A. 113 L5
Pearsall, U.S.A. 113 L5
Pearse I., Canada 104 C2
Peary Land, Greenland ... 4 A6
Pease →, U.S.A. 113 H5
Pebane, Mozam. 87 F4
Pebas, Peru 124 D4
Pebble Beach, U.S.A. ... 116 J5
Peć, Serbia, Yug. 40 D4
Péccioli, Italy 28 E7
Pechea, Romania 43 E12
Pechenga, Russia 50 C4
Pechenizhyn, Ukraine ... 47 H3
Pechiguera, Pta., Canary Is. 37 F6
Pechnezhskoye Vdkhr., Ukraine 47 G9
Pechora, Russia 50 C6
Pechorskaya Guba, Russia 50 C6
Pecica, Romania 42 D6
Pecka, Serbia, Yug. 40 B3

Pécora, C., *Italy* 30 C1
Pečory, *Russia* 9 H22
Pecos, *U.S.A.* 113 K3
Pecos →, *U.S.A.* 113 L3
Pécs, *Hungary* 42 D3
Pedder, L., *Australia* .. 94 G4
Peddie, *S. Africa* 89 E4
Pédernales, *Dom. Rep.* . 121 C5
Pedieos →, *Cyprus* 36 D12
Pedirka, *Australia* 95 D2
Pedra Azul, *Brazil* 125 G10
Pedreguer, *Spain* 33 G5
Pedreiras, *Brazil* 125 D10
Pedro Afonso, *Brazil* .. 125 E9
Pedro Cays, *Jamaica* ... 120 C4
Pedro de Valdivia, *Chile* . 126 A2
Pedro Juan Caballero,
  Paraguay 127 A4
Pedro Muñoz, *Spain* ... 35 F8
Pedrógão Grande, *Portugal* 34 F2
Peebinga, *Australia* 95 E3
Peebles, *U.K.* 14 F5
Peekskill, *U.S.A.* 111 E11
Peel, *U.K.* 12 C3
Peel →, *Australia* 95 E5
Peel →, *Canada* 100 B6
Peene →, *Germany* 24 A9
Peera Peera Poolanna L.,
  Australia 95 D2
Peers, *Canada* 104 C5
Pegasus Bay, *N.Z.* 91 K4
Peggau, *Austria* 26 D8
Pegnitz, *Germany* 25 F7
Pegnitz →, *Germany* ... 25 F6
Pego, *Spain* 33 G4
Pegu, *Burma* 67 L20
Pegu Yoma, *Burma* 67 K20
Pehčevo, *Macedonia* ... 40 E6
Pehlivanköy, *Turkey* ... 41 E10
Pehuajó, *Argentina* 126 D3
Pei Xian, *China* 56 G9
Peichiang, *Taiwan* 59 F13
Peine, *Chile* 126 A2
Peine, *Germany* 24 C6
Peip'ing = Beijing, *China* . 56 E9
Peipus, L. = Chudskoye,
  Oz., *Russia* 9 G22
Peissenberg, *Germany* ... 25 H7
Peitz, *Germany* 24 D10
Peixe, *Brazil* 125 F9
Peixe →, *Brazil* 125 H8
Pek →, *Serbia, Yug.* ... 40 B5
Pekalongan, *Indonesia* .. 63 G13
Pekan, *Malaysia* 65 L4
Pekanbaru, *Indonesia* .. 62 D2
Pekin, *U.S.A.* 112 E10
Peking = Beijing, *China* . 56 E9
Pelabuhan Kelang,
  Malaysia 65 L3
Pelabuhan Ratu, Teluk,
  Indonesia 63 G12
Pelabuhanratu, *Indonesia* . 63 G12
Pélagos, *Greece* 38 B6
Pelaihari, *Indonesia* ... 62 E4
Pelat, Mt., *France* 21 D10
Pełczyce, *Poland* 45 E2
Peleaga, Vf., *Romania* .. 42 E7
Pelée, Mt., *Martinique* . 121 D7
Pelee, Pt., *Canada* 102 D3
Pelee I., *Canada* 102 D3
Pelekech, *Kenya* 86 B4
Peleng, *Indonesia* 63 E6
Pelham, *U.S.A.* 109 K3
Pelhřimov, *Czech Rep.* ... 26 B8
Pelican L., *Canada* 105 C8
Pelican Narrows, *Canada* . 105 B8
Pelican Rapids, *Canada* . 105 C8
Pelješac, *Croatia* 29 F14
Pelkosenniemi, *Finland* . 8 C22
Pella, *Greece* 40 F6
Pella, *S. Africa* 88 D2
Pella, *U.S.A.* 112 E8
Pélla □, *Greece* 40 F6
Pello, *Finland* 8 C21
Pellworm, *Germany* 24 A4
Pelly →, *Canada* 100 B6
Pelly Bay, *Canada* 101 B11
Peloponnese =
  Pelopónnisos □, *Greece* 38 D4
Pelopónnisos □, *Greece* . 38 D4
Peloritani, Monti, *Italy* . 31 D8
Pelorus Sd., *N.Z.* 91 J4
Pelotas, *Brazil* 127 C5
Pelovo, *Bulgaria* 41 C8
Pelplin, *Poland* 44 E5
Pelvoux, Massif du, *France* 21 D10
Pemalang, *Indonesia* ... 63 G13
Pematangsiantar, *Indonesia* 62 D1
Pemba, *Mozam.* 87 E5
Pemba, *Zambia* 87 F2
Pemba Channel, *Tanzania* 86 D4
Pemba I., *Tanzania* 86 D4
Pemberton, *Australia* .. 93 F2
Pemberton, *Canada* 104 C4
Pembina, *U.S.A.* 112 A6
Pembina →, *U.S.A.* 105 D9
Pembine, *U.S.A.* 108 C2
Pembroke, *Canada* 102 C4
Pembroke, *U.K.* 13 F3
Pembroke, *U.S.A.* 109 J5
Pembrokeshire □, *U.K.* . 13 F3
Pen-y-Ghent, *U.K.* 12 C5
Peña, Sierra de la, *Spain* . 32 C4
Peña de Francia, Sierra de
  la, *Spain* 34 E4
Penafiel, *Portugal* 34 D2
Peñafiel, *Spain* 34 D6

Peñaflor, *Spain* 35 H5
Peñalara, *Spain* 34 E7
Penamacôr, *Portugal* ... 34 E3
Penang = Pinang, *Malaysia* 65 K3
Penápolis, *Brazil* 127 A6
Peñaranda de Bracamonte,
  Spain 34 E5
Peñarroya, *Spain* 32 E4
Peñarroya-Pueblonuevo,
  Spain 35 G5
Penarth, *U.K.* 13 F4
Peñas, C. de, *Spain* 34 B5
Penas, G. de, *Chile* 122 H3
Peñas de San Pedro, *Spain* 33 G3
Peñas del Chache,
  Canary Is. 37 E6
Peñausende, *Spain* 34 D5
Pench'i = Benxi, *China* . 57 D12
Pend Oreille →, *U.S.A.* . 114 B5
Pend Oreille L., *U.S.A.* . 114 C5
Pendálofon, *Greece* 40 F5
Pendembu, *S. Leone* ... 82 D2
Pender B., *Australia* ... 92 C3
Pendik, *Turkey* 41 F13
Pendleton, *Calif., U.S.A.* 117 M9
Pendleton, *Oreg., U.S.A.* 114 D4
Penedo, *Brazil* 125 F11
Penetanguishene, *Canada* 102 D4
Peng Xian, *China* 58 B4
Pengalengan, *Indonesia* . 63 G12
Penge, *Kasai Or.,*
  Dem. Rep. of the Congo 86 D1
Penge, *Kivu,*
  Dem. Rep. of the Congo 86 C2
Penglai, *China* 57 F11
Pengshui, *China* 58 C7
Penguin, *Australia* 94 G4
Pengxi, *China* 58 B5
Pengze, *China* 59 C11
Penhalonga, *Zimbabwe* . 87 F3
Peniche, *Portugal* 35 F1
Penicuik, *U.K.* 14 F5
Penida, *Indonesia* 62 F5
Peninnes, Alpes =
  Pennine, Alpi, *Alps* .. 25 J3
Peninsular Malaysia □,
  Malaysia 65 L4
Peñíscola, *Spain* 32 E5
Penitente, Serra dos, *Brazil* 125 E9
Penkridge, *U.K.* 12 E5
Penmarch, *France* 18 E2
Penmarch, Pte. de, *France* 18 E2
Penn Hills, *U.S.A.* 110 F5
Penn Yan, *U.S.A.* 110 D7
Penna, Punta della, *Italy* . 29 F11
Pennant, *Canada* 105 C7
Penne, *France* 19 F10
Penner →, *India* 66 M12
Pennine, Alpi, *Alps* 25 J3
Pennines, *U.K.* 12 C5
Pennington, *U.S.A.* 116 F5
Pennino, Mte., *Italy* ... 29 E9
Pennsylvania □, *U.S.A.* . 108 E7
Penny, *Canada* 104 C4
Peno, *Russia* 46 D7
Penola, *Australia* 95 F3
Penong, *Australia* 93 F5
Penonomé, *Panama* 120 E3
Penrith, *Australia* 95 E5
Penrith, *U.K.* 12 C5
Penryn, *U.K.* 13 G2
Pensacola, *U.S.A.* 109 K2
Pensacola Mts., *Antarctica* 5 E1
Pense, *Canada* 105 C8
Penshurst, *Australia* ... 95 F3
Penticton, *Canada* 104 D5
Pentland, *Australia* 94 C4
Pentland Firth, *U.K.* ... 14 C5
Pentland Hills, *U.K.* ... 14 F5
Penylan L., *Canada* 105 A7
Penza, *Russia* 48 D7
Penzance, *U.K.* 13 G2
Penzberg, *Germany* 25 H7
Penzhino, *Russia* 51 C17
Penzhinskaya Guba, *Russia* 51 C17
Penzlin, *Germany* 24 B9
Peoria, *Ariz., U.S.A.* ... 115 K7
Peoria, *Ill., U.S.A.* 112 E10
Peqini, *Albania* 40 E3
Pera Hd., *Australia* 94 A3
Perabumulih, *Indonesia* . 62 E2
Perak →, *Malaysia* 65 K3
Perakhóra, *Greece* 38 C4
Perales de Alfambra, *Spain* 32 E4
Perales del Puerto, *Spain* . 34 E4
Pérama, *Kérkira, Greece* . 36 A3
Pérama, *Kríti, Greece* ... 36 D6
Peräpohjola, *Finland* ... 8 C22
Perast, *Montenegro, Yug.* 40 D2
Percé, *Canada* 103 C7
Perche, *France* 18 D8
Perchtoldsdorf, *Austria* . 27 C9
Percival Lakes, *Australia* 92 D4
Percy, *France* 18 D5
Percy Is., *Australia* 94 C5
Perdido, Mte., *Spain* ... 32 C5
Perdu, Mt. = Perdido,
  Mte., *Spain* 32 C5
Pereira, *Colombia* 124 C3
Perekerten, *Australia* .. 95 E3
Perelazovskiy, *Russia* .. 49 F6
Perenjori, *Australia* ... 93 E2
Peresecina, *Moldova* ... 43 C13
Pereslavl-Zalesskiy, *Russia* 46 D10
Peretu, *Romania* 43 F10
Pereyaslav-Khmelnytskyy,
  Ukraine 47 G6

Pérez, I., *Mexico* 119 C7
Perg, *Austria* 26 C7
Pergamino, *Argentina* ... 126 C3
Pergau →, *Malaysia* ... 65 K3
Pérgine Valsugana, *Italy* . 29 B8
Pérgola, *Italy* 29 E9
Perham, *U.S.A.* 112 B7
Periam, *Romania* 42 D5
Péribonca →, *Canada* .. 103 C5
Péribonca, L., *Canada* .. 103 B5
Perico, *Argentina* 126 A2
Pericos, *Mexico* 118 B3
Périers, *France* 18 C5
Périgord, *France* 20 D4
Périgueux, *France* 20 C4
Perijá, Sierra de, *Colombia* 124 B4
Peristéra, *Greece* 38 B5
Peristerona →, *Cyprus* . 36 D12
Perito Moreno, *Argentina* 128 F2
Perivol = Dragovishtitsa,
  Bulgaria 40 D6
Perković, *Croatia* 29 E13
Perlas, Arch. de las,
  Panama 120 E4
Perlas, Punta de, *Nic.* ... 120 D3
Perleberg, *Germany* 24 B7
Perlez, *Serbia, Yug.* ... 42 E5
Perm, *Russia* 50 D6
Përmeti, *Albania* 40 F4
Pernambuco = Recife,
  Brazil 125 E12
Pernambuco □, *Brazil* ... 125 E11
Pernatty Lagoon, *Australia* 95 E2
Pernik, *Bulgaria* 40 D7
Peron, C., *Australia* ... 93 E1
Peron Is., *Australia* ... 92 B5
Peron Pen., *Australia* .. 93 E1
Péronne, *France* 19 C9
Perosa Argentina, *Italy* . 28 D4
Perow, *Canada* 104 C3
Perpendicular Pt., *Australia* 95 E5
Perpignan, *France* 20 F6
Perris, *U.S.A.* 117 M9
Perros-Guirec, *France* .. 18 D3
Perry, *Fla., U.S.A.* 109 K4
Perry, *Ga., U.S.A.* 109 J4
Perry, *Iowa, U.S.A.* ... 112 E7
Perry, *Maine, U.S.A.* ... 109 C12
Perry, *Okla., U.S.A.* ... 113 G6
Perryton, *U.S.A.* 113 G4
Perryville, *U.S.A.* 113 G10
Persan, *France* 19 C9
Persberg, *Sweden* 10 E8
Perşembe, *Turkey* 72 B7
Pershotravensk, *Ukraine* 47 G4
Persia = Iran ■, *Asia* .. 71 C7
Persian Gulf = Gulf, The,
  Asia 71 E6
Perstorp, *Sweden* 11 H7
Pertek, *Turkey* 73 C8
Perth, *Australia* 93 F2
Perth, *Canada* 102 D4
Perth, *U.K.* 14 E5
Perth & Kinross □, *U.K.* . 14 E5
Perth Amboy, *U.S.A.* .. 111 F10
Pertuis, *France* 21 E9
Pertusato, C., *France* .. 21 G13
Peru, *Ill., U.S.A.* 112 E10
Peru, *Ind., U.S.A.* 108 E2
Peru ■, *S. Amer.* 124 D4
Peru-Chile Trench,
  Pac. Oc. 124 G3
Perúgia, *Italy* 29 E9
Perušić, *Croatia* 29 D12
Pervomaysk, *Russia* ... 48 C6
Pervomaysk, *Ukraine* .. 47 H6
Pervouralsk, *Russia* ... 50 D6
Pésaro, *Italy* 29 E9
Pescara, *Italy* 29 F11
Pescara →, *Italy* 29 F11
Peschanokopskoye, *Russia* 49 G5
Péscia, *Italy* 28 E7
Pescina, *Italy* 29 F10
Peshawar, *Pakistan* ... 68 B4
Peshkopi, *Albania* 40 E4
Peshtera, *Bulgaria* 41 D8
Peshtigo, *U.S.A.* 108 C2
Peski, *Russia* 48 E6
Pêso da Régua, *Portugal* 34 D3
Pesqueira, *Brazil* 125 E11
Pessac, *France* 20 D3
Pest □, *Hungary* 42 C4
Pestovo, *Russia* 46 C9
Pestravka, *Russia* 48 D9
Péta, *Greece* 38 B3
Petah Tiqwa, *Israel* ... 75 C3
Petalídhion, *Greece* ... 38 E3
Petaling Jaya, *Malaysia* . 65 L3
Petaloudhes, *Greece* ... 36 C10
Petaluma, *U.S.A.* 116 G4
Pétange, *Lux.* 17 E5
Petatlán, *Mexico* 118 D4
Petauke, *Zambia* 87 E3
Petawawa, *Canada* 102 C4
Petén Itzá, L., *Guatemala* 120 C2
Peter I.s Øy, *Antarctica* . 5 C16
Peter Pond L., *Canada* . 105 B7
Peterbell, *Canada* 102 C3
Peterborough, *Australia* . 95 E2
Peterborough, *Canada* .. 110 B6
Peterborough, *U.K.* 13 E7
Peterborough, *U.S.A.* .. 111 D13
Peterborough □, *U.K.* .. 13 E7
Peterculter, *U.K.* 14 D6
Peterhead, *U.K.* 14 D7
Peterlee, *U.K.* 12 C6

Petermann Bjerg,
  Greenland 98 B17
Petersburg, *Alaska, U.S.A.* 104 B2
Petersburg, *Ind., U.S.A.* 108 F2
Petersburg, *Va., U.S.A.* 108 G7
Petersburg, *W. Va., U.S.A.* 108 F6
Petersfield, *U.K.* 13 F7
Petershagen, *Germany* .. 24 C4
Petford, *Australia* 94 B3
Petília Policastro, *Italy* .. 31 C9
Petit Bois I., *U.S.A.* ... 109 K1
Petit-Cap, *Canada* 103 C7
Petit Goâve, *Haiti* 121 C5
Petit Lac Manicouagan,
  Canada 103 B6
Petit Saint Bernard, Col
  du, *Italy* 21 C10
Petitcodiac, *Canada* ... 103 C6
Petite Baleine →, *Canada* 102 A4
Petite Saguenay, *Canada* . 103 C5
Petitsikapau, L., *Canada* . 103 B6
Petlad, *India* 68 H5
Peto, *Mexico* 119 C7
Petone, *N.Z.* 91 J5
Petoskey, *U.S.A.* 108 C3
Petra, *Jordan* 75 E4
Petra, *Spain* 37 B10
Petra, Ostrova, *Russia* .. 4 B13
Petra Velikogo, Zaliv,
  Russia 54 C6
Petrel = Petrer, *Spain* .. 33 G4
Petrella, Monte, *Italy* ... 30 A6
Petrer, *Spain* 33 G4
Petreto-Bicchisano, *France* 21 G12
Petrich, *Bulgaria* 40 E7
Petrijanec, *Croatia* 29 B13
Petrikov = Pyetrikaw,
  Belarus 47 F5
Petrila, *Romania* 43 E8
Petrinja, *Croatia* 29 C13
Petrodvorets, *Russia* ... 46 C5
Petrograd = Sankt-
  Peterburg = *Russia* ... 46 C6
Petrolândia, *Brazil* 125 E11
Petrolia, *Canada* 102 D3
Petrolina, *Brazil* 125 E10
Petropavl, *Kazakstan* .. 50 D7
Petropavlovsk = Petropavl,
  Kazakstan 50 D7
Petropavlovsk-
  Kamchatskiy, *Russia* ... 51 D16
Petropavlovskiy =
  Akhtubinsk, *Russia* ... 49 F8
Petrópolis, *Brazil* 127 A7
Petroşani, *Romania* 43 E8
Petrova Gora, *Croatia* .. 29 C12
Petrovac, *Montenegro, Yug.* 40 D2
Petrovac, *Serbia, Yug.* . 40 B5
Petrovaradin, *Serbia, Yug.* 42 E4
Petrovsk, *Russia* 48 D7
Petrovsk-Zabaykalskiy,
  Russia 51 D11
Petrovskaya, *Russia* ... 47 K9
Petrovskoye = Svetlograd,
  Russia 49 H6
Petrozavodsk, *Russia* .. 46 B8
Petrus Steyn, *S. Africa* . 89 D4
Petrusburg, *S. Africa* .. 88 D4
Petzeck, *Austria* 26 E5
Peumo, *Chile* 126 C1
Peureulak, *Indonesia* .. 62 D1
Pevek, *Russia* 51 C18
Peveragno, *Italy* 28 D4
Peyrehorade, *France* ... 20 E2
Peyruis, *France* 21 D9
Pézenas, *France* 20 E7
Pezinok, *Slovak Rep.* ... 27 C10
Pfaffenhofen, *Germany* . 25 G7
Pfarrkirchen, *Germany* . 25 G8
Pfeffenhausen, *Germany* 25 G7
Pforzheim, *Germany* ... 25 G4
Pfullendorf, *Germany* .. 25 H5
Pfungstadt, *Germany* .. 25 F4
Phagwara, *India* 66 D9
Phaistós, *Greece* 36 D6
Phala, *Botswana* 88 C4
Phalera = Phulera, *India* . 68 F6
Phalodi, *India* 68 F5
Phalsbourg, *France* 19 D14
Phan, *Thailand* 64 C2
Phan Rang, *Vietnam* ... 65 G7
Phan Ri = Hoa Da,
  Vietnam 65 G7
Phan Thiêt, *Vietnam* ... 65 G7
Phanae, *Greece* 39 C7
Phanat Nikhom, *Thailand* 64 F3
Phangan, Ko, *Thailand* . 65 H3
Phangnga, *Thailand* ... 65 H2
Phanh Bho Ho Chi Minh,
  Vietnam 65 G6
Phanom Sarakham,
  Thailand 64 F3
Pharenda, *India* 69 F10
Phatthalung, *Thailand* . 65 J3
Phayao, *Thailand* 64 C2
Phelps, *N.Y., U.S.A.* ... 110 D7
Phelps, *Wis., U.S.A.* ... 112 B10
Phelps L., *Canada* 105 B8
Phenix City, *U.S.A.* ... 109 J3
Phet Buri, *Thailand* ... 64 F2
Phetchabun, *Thailand* .. 64 D3
Phetchabun, Thiu Khao,
  Thailand 64 E3
Phetchaburi = Phet Buri,
  Thailand 64 F2
Phi Phi, Ko, *Thailand* .. 65 J2
Phiafay, *Laos* 64 E6

Phibun Mangsahan,
  Thailand 64 E5
Phichai, *Thailand* 64 D3
Phichit, *Thailand* 64 D3
Philadelphia, *Miss., U.S.A.* 113 J10
Philadelphia, *N.Y., U.S.A.* 111 B9
Philadelphia, *Pa., U.S.A.* 111 G9
Philip, *U.S.A.* 112 C4
Philippeville, *Belgium* .. 17 D4
Philippi, *Greece* 41 E8
Philippi L., *Australia* .. 94 C2
Philippines ■, *Asia* 61 F5
Philippolis, *S. Africa* ... 88 E4
Philippopolis = Plovdiv,
  Bulgaria 41 D8
Philipsburg, *Mont., U.S.A.* 114 C7
Philipsburg, *Pa., U.S.A.* 110 F6
Philipstown = Daingean,
  Ireland 15 C4
Philipstown, *S. Africa* .. 88 E3
Phillip I., *Australia* 95 F4
Phillips, *Tex., U.S.A.* .. 113 H4
Phillips, *Wis., U.S.A.* .. 112 C9
Phillipsburg, *Kans., U.S.A.* 112 F5
Phillipsburg, *N.J., U.S.A.* 111 F9
Phillott, *Australia* 95 D4
Philmont, *U.S.A.* 111 D11
Philomath, *U.S.A.* 114 D2
Phimai, *Thailand* 64 E4
Phitsanulok, *Thailand* . 64 D3
Phnom Penh, *Cambodia* 65 G5
Phnom Penh = Phnom
  Penh, *Cambodia* 65 G5
Phoenix, *Ariz., U.S.A.* . 115 K7
Phoenix, *N.Y., U.S.A.* . 111 C8
Phoenix Is., *Kiribati* ... 96 H10
Phoenixville, *U.S.A.* ... 111 F9
Phon, *Thailand* 64 E4
Phon Tiou, *Laos* 64 D5
Phong →, *Thailand* ... 64 D4
Phong Saly, *Laos* 64 B4
Phong Tho, *Vietnam* ... 64 A4
Phonhong, *Laos* 64 C4
Phonum, *Thailand* 65 H2
Phosphate Hill, *Australia* 94 C2
Photharam, *Thailand* .. 64 F2
Phra Nakhon Si Ayutthaya,
  Thailand 64 E3
Phra Thong, Ko, *Thailand* 65 H2
Phrae, *Thailand* 64 C3
Phrom Phiram, *Thailand* 64 D3
Phrygia, *Turkey* 72 C4
Phu Dien, *Vietnam* 64 C5
Phu Loi, *Laos* 64 B4
Phu Ly, *Vietnam* 64 B5
Phu Quoc, Dao, *Vietnam* 65 G4
Phu Tho, *Vietnam* 64 B5
Phuket, *Thailand* 65 J2
Phuket, Ko, *Thailand* .. 65 J2
Phulera, *India* 68 F6
Phun Phin, *Thailand* .. 65 H2
Piacenza, *Italy* 28 C6
Pialba, *Australia* 95 D5
Pian Cr. →, *Australia* . 95 E4
Piana, *France* 21 F12
Pianella, *Italy* 29 F11
Pianosa, *Puglia, Italy* .. 29 F12
Pianosa, *Toscana, Italy* . 28 F7
Piapot, *Canada* 105 D7
Pias, *Portugal* 35 G3
Piaseczno, *Poland* 45 F8
Piaski, *Poland* 45 G9
Piastów, *Poland* 45 F7
Piatra, *Romania* 43 G10
Piatra Neamţ, *Romania* . 43 D11
Piatra Olt, *Romania* ... 43 F9
Piauí □, *Brazil* 125 E10
Piauí →, *Brazil* 125 E10
Piave →, *Italy* 29 C9
Piazza Armerina, *Italy* . 31 E7
Pibor →, *Sudan* 81 F3
Pibor Post, *Sudan* 81 F3
Picardie, *France* 19 C10
Picardie, Plaine de, *France* 19 C9
Picardy = Picardie, *France* 19 C10
Picayune, *U.S.A.* 113 K10
Picerno, *Italy* 31 B8
Pichilemu, *Chile* 126 C1
Pickerel L., *Canada* ... 102 C1
Pickering, *U.K.* 12 C7
Pickering, Vale of, *U.K.* . 12 C7
Pickle Lake, *Canada* ... 102 B1
Pico Truncado, *Argentina* 128 F3
Picos, *Brazil* 125 E10
Picton, *Australia* 95 E5
Picton, *Canada* 102 D4
Picton, *N.Z.* 91 J5
Pictou, *Canada* 103 C7
Picture Butte, *Canada* .. 104 D6
Picún Leufú, *Argentina* . 128 D3
Pidurutalagala, *Sri Lanka* 66 R12
Piechowice, *Poland* ... 45 H2
Piedmont = Piemonte □,
  Italy 28 D5
Piedmont, *U.S.A.* 109 J3
Piedmont Plateau, *U.S.A.* 109 J5
Piedmonte Matese, *Italy* . 31 A7
Piedra →, *Spain* 32 D3
Piedrabuena, *Spain* ... 35 G6
Piedrahita, *Spain* 34 E5
Piedralaves, *Spain* 34 E6
Piedras Blancas, *Spain* . 34 B5
Piedras Negras, *Mexico* . 118 B4
Piekary Śląskie, *Poland* . 45 H5
Pieksämäki, *Finland* ... 9 E22
Piemonte □, *Italy* 28 D5

Pieniężno, Poland	44	D7
Pieńsk, Poland	45	G2
Pierce, U.S.A.	114	C6
Piercefield, U.S.A.	111	B10
Piería □, Greece	40	F6
Pierre, U.S.A.	112	C4
Pierre-Buffière, France	20	C5
Pierre-de-Bresse, France	19	F12
Pierrefontaine-les-Varans, France	19	E13
Pierrefort, France	20	D6
Pierrelatte, France	21	D8
Pieštany, Slovak Rep.	27	C10
Piesting →, Austria	27	C9
Pieszyce, Poland	45	H3
Piet Retief, S. Africa	89	D5
Pietarsaari, Finland	8	E20
Pietermaritzburg, S. Africa	89	D5
Pietersburg, S. Africa	89	C4
Pietragalla, Italy	31	B8
Pietrasanta, Italy	28	E7
Pietroşiţa, Romania	43	E10
Pietrosul, Vf., Maramureş, Romania	43	C9
Pietrosul, Vf., Suceava, Romania	43	C10
Pieve di Cadore, Italy	29	B9
Pieve di Teco, Italy	28	D4
Pievepélago, Italy	28	D7
Pigadhítsa, Greece	40	G5
Pigeon, U.S.A.	108	D4
Piggott, U.S.A.	113	G9
Pigna, Italy	28	E4
Pigüe, Argentina	126	D3
Pihani, India	69	F9
Pihlajavesi, Finland	9	F23
Pikalevo, Russia	46	C8
Pikes Peak, U.S.A.	112	F2
Piketberg, S. Africa	88	E2
Pikeville, U.S.A.	108	G4
Pikou, China	57	E12
Pikwitonei, Canada	105	B9
Piła, Poland	45	E3
Pila, Spain	33	G3
Piła □, Poland	45	E3
Pilaía, Greece	40	F6
Pilani, India	68	E6
Pilar, Paraguay	126	B4
Pilar de la Horadada, Spain	33	H4
Pilawa, Poland	45	G8
Pilaya →, Bolivia	124	H6
Pilcomayo →, Paraguay	126	B4
Pilcomayo →, Paraguay	126	B4
Pilgrimstad, Sweden	10	B9
Pili, Greece	39	E9
Pilibhit, India	69	E8
Pilica →, Poland	45	G8
Pilion, Greece	38	B5
Pilis, Hungary	42	C4
Pilisvörösvár, Hungary	42	C3
Pilkhawa, India	68	E7
Pílos, Greece	38	E3
Pilot Mound, Canada	105	D9
Pilot Point, U.S.A.	113	J6
Pilot Rock, U.S.A.	114	D4
Pilsen = Plzeň, Czech Rep.	26	B6
Pilštanj, Slovenia	29	B12
Piltene, Latvia	44	A8
Pilzno, Poland	45	J8
Pima, U.S.A.	115	K9
Pimba, Australia	95	E2
Pimenta Bueno, Brazil	124	F6
Pimentel, Peru	124	E3
Pina de Ebro, Spain	32	D4
Pinamalayan, Phil.	61	E4
Pinang, Malaysia	65	K3
Pinar, C. des, Spain	37	B10
Pinar del Río, Cuba	120	B3
Pınarbaşı, Çanakkale, Turkey	39	B8
Pınarbaşı, Kayseri, Turkey	72	C7
Pınarhisar, Turkey	41	E11
Pincehely, Hungary	42	D3
Pinchang, China	58	B6
Pincher Creek, Canada	104	D6
Pinchi L., Canada	104	C4
Pinckneyville, U.S.A.	112	F10
Pińczów, Poland	45	H7
Pind Dadan Khan, Pakistan	68	C5
Pindar, Australia	93	E2
Pindi Gheb, Pakistan	68	C5
Pindiga, Nigeria	83	D7
Pindos Óros, Greece	38	B3
Pindus Mts. = Pindos Óros, Greece	38	B3
Pine, U.S.A.	115	J8
Pine →, Canada	105	B7
Pine →, Canada	103	C9
Pine Bluff, U.S.A.	113	H9
Pine City, U.S.A.	112	C8
Pine Falls, Canada	105	C9
Pine Flat L., U.S.A.	116	J7
Pine Pass, Canada	104	C4
Pine Point, Canada	104	A6
Pine Ridge, U.S.A.	112	D3
Pine River, Canada	105	C8
Pine River, U.S.A.	112	B7
Pine Valley, U.S.A.	117	N10
Pinecrest, U.S.A.	116	G6
Pineda de Mar, Spain	32	D7
Pinedale, U.S.A.	116	J7
Pinega →, Russia	50	C5
Pinehill, Australia	94	C4
Pinerolo, Italy	28	D4
Pineto, Italy	29	F11
Pinetop, U.S.A.	115	J9
Pinetown, S. Africa	89	D5
Pinetree, U.S.A.	114	E11
Pineville, Ky., U.S.A.	109	G4
Pineville, La., U.S.A.	113	K8
Piney, France	19	D11
Ping →, Thailand	64	E3
Pingaring, Australia	93	F2
Pingba, China	58	D6
Pingchuan, China	58	D3
Pingding, China	56	F7
Pingdingshan, China	56	H7
Pingdong, Taiwan	59	F13
Pingdu, China	57	F10
Pingelly, Australia	93	F2
Pingguo, China	58	F6
Pinghe, China	59	E11
Pinghu, China	59	B13
Pingjiang, China	59	C9
Pingle, China	59	E8
Pingli, China	58	A7
Pingliang, China	56	G4
Pinglu, China	56	E7
Pingluo, China	56	E4
Pingnan, Fujian, China	59	D12
Pingnan, Guangxi Zhuangzu, China	59	F8
Pingquan, China	57	D10
Pingrup, Australia	93	F2
Pingtan, China	59	E12
Pingtang, China	58	E6
P'ingtung, Taiwan	59	F13
Pingwu, China	56	H3
Pingxiang, Guangxi Zhuangzu, China	58	F6
Pingxiang, Jiangxi, China	59	D9
Pingyao, China	56	F7
Pingyi, China	57	G9
Pingyin, China	56	F9
Pingyuan, Guangdong, China	59	E10
Pingyuan, Shandong, China	56	F9
Pingyuanjie, China	58	F4
Pinhal, Brazil	127	A6
Pinhal Novo, Portugal	35	G2
Pinheiro, Brazil	125	D9
Pinhel, Portugal	34	E3
Pini, Indonesia	62	D1
Piniós →, Ilía, Greece	38	D3
Piniós →, Tríkkala, Greece	38	B4
Pinjarra, Australia	93	F2
Pink →, Canada	105	B8
Pinkafeld, Austria	27	D9
Pinnacles, Australia	93	E3
Pinnacles, U.S.A.	116	J5
Pinnaroo, Australia	95	F3
Pinneberg, Germany	24	B5
Pínnes, Ákra, Greece	41	F8
Pinon Hills, U.S.A.	117	L9
Pinos, Mexico	118	C4
Pinos, Mt., U.S.A.	117	L7
Pinos Pt., U.S.A.	115	H4
Pinos Puente, Spain	35	H7
Pinotepa Nacional, Mexico	119	D5
Pinrang, Indonesia	63	E5
Pinsk, Belarus	47	F4
Pintados, Chile	124	H5
Pintumba, Australia	93	F5
Pinyang, China	59	D13
Pinyug, Russia	50	C5
Pioche, U.S.A.	115	H6
Piombino, Italy	28	F7
Piombino, Canale di, Italy	28	F7
Pioner, Ostrov, Russia	51	B10
Pionki, Poland	45	G8
Piorini, L., Brazil	124	D6
Piotrków Trybunalski, Poland	45	G6
Piotrków Trybunalski □, Poland	45	G6
Piove di Sacco, Italy	29	C9
Pīp, Iran	71	E9
Pipar, India	68	F5
Piparia, India	68	H8
Pipéri, Greece	38	B6
Pipestone, U.S.A.	112	D6
Pipestone →, Canada	102	B2
Pipestone Cr. →, Canada	105	D8
Pipmuacan, Rés., Canada	103	C5
Pippingarra, Australia	92	D2
Pipriac, France	18	E5
Piqua, U.S.A.	108	E3
Piquiri →, Brazil	127	A5
Pīr Sohrāb, Iran	71	E9
Piracicaba, Brazil	127	A6
Piracuruca, Brazil	125	D10
Piræus = Piraiévs, Greece	38	D5
Piraiévs, Greece	38	D5
Pirajuí, Brazil	127	A6
Piran, Slovenia	29	C10
Pirané, Argentina	126	B4
Pirano = Piran, Slovenia	29	C10
Pirapora, Brazil	125	G10
Pirdop, Bulgaria	41	D8
Pírgos, Ilía, Greece	38	D3
Pírgos, Kríti, Greece	39	F7
Pirgovo, Bulgaria	41	C9
Piribebuy, Paraguay	126	B4
Pirin Planina, Bulgaria	40	E7
Pirineos = Pyrénées, Europe	20	F4
Piripiri, Brazil	125	D10
Pirmasens, Germany	25	F3
Pirna, Germany	24	E9
Pirot, Serbia, Yug.	40	C6
Piru, Indonesia	63	E7
Piru, U.S.A.	117	L8
Piryatin = Pyryatyn, Ukraine	47	G7
Piryí, Greece	39	C7
Pisa, Italy	28	E7
Pisa →, Poland	45	E8
Pisagne, Italy	28	C7
Pisagua, Chile	124	G4
Pisarovina, Croatia	29	C12
Pisco, Peru	124	F3
Piscu, Romania	43	E12
Písek, Czech Rep.	26	B7
Pishan, China	60	C2
Pishin Lora →, Pakistan	68	E1
Pisidia, Turkey	72	D4
Pising, Indonesia	63	F6
Pismo Beach, U.S.A.	117	K6
Pissis, Cerro, Argentina	126	B2
Pissos, France	20	D3
Pissouri, Cyprus	36	E11
Pisticci, Italy	31	B9
Pistóia, Italy	28	E7
Pistol B., Canada	105	A10
Pisuerga →, Spain	34	D6
Pisz, Poland	44	E8
Pitarpunga, L., Australia	95	E3
Pitcairn I., Pac. Oc.	97	K14
Pite älv →, Sweden	8	D19
Piteå, Sweden	8	D19
Piterka, Russia	48	E8
Piteşti, Romania	43	F9
Pithapuram, India	67	L13
Pithara, Australia	93	F2
Píthion, Greece	41	E10
Pithiviers, France	19	D9
Pitigliano, Italy	29	F8
Pitkyaranta, Russia	46	B6
Pitlochry, U.K.	14	E5
Pitsilía □, Cyprus	36	E12
Pitt I., Canada	104	C3
Pittsburg, Kans., U.S.A.	113	G7
Pittsburg, Tex., U.S.A.	113	J7
Pittsburgh, U.S.A.	110	F5
Pittsfield, Ill., U.S.A.	112	F9
Pittsfield, Mass., U.S.A.	111	D11
Pittsfield, N.H., U.S.A.	111	C13
Pittston, U.S.A.	111	E9
Pittsworth, Australia	95	D5
Pituri →, Australia	94	C2
Piura, Peru	124	E2
Piva →, Montenegro, Yug.	40	C2
Piwniczna, Poland	45	J7
Pixley, U.S.A.	116	K7
Piyai, Greece	38	B3
Pizarra, Spain	35	J6
Pizzo, Italy	31	D9
Placentia, Canada	103	C9
Placentia B., Canada	103	C9
Placer, Phil.	61	F5
Placerville, U.S.A.	116	G6
Placetas, Cuba	120	B4
Plačkovica, Macedonia	40	E6
Plain Dealing, U.S.A.	113	J8
Plainfield, U.S.A.	111	F10
Plains, Kans., U.S.A.	113	G4
Plains, Mont., U.S.A.	114	C6
Plains, Tex., U.S.A.	113	J3
Plainview, Nebr., U.S.A.	112	D6
Plainview, Tex., U.S.A.	113	H4
Plainville, U.S.A.	112	F5
Plainwell, U.S.A.	108	D3
Plaisance, France	20	E4
Pláka, Greece	39	B7
Pláka, Ákra, Greece	36	D8
Plakenska Planina, Macedonia	40	E5
Planá, Czech Rep.	26	B5
Plana Cays, Bahamas	121	B5
Planada, U.S.A.	116	H6
Plancoët, France	18	D4
Plandište, Serbia, Yug.	42	E6
Plankinton, U.S.A.	112	D5
Plano, U.S.A.	113	J6
Plant City, U.S.A.	109	M4
Plaquemine, U.S.A.	113	K9
Plasencia, Spain	34	E4
Plaški, Croatia	29	C12
Plaster City, U.S.A.	117	N11
Plaster Rock, Canada	103	C6
Plastun, Russia	54	B8
Plasy, Czech Rep.	26	B6
Plata, Río de la, S. Amer.	126	C4
Plátani →, Italy	30	E6
Plátanos, Greece	36	D5
Plateau □, Nigeria	83	D6
Plateau du Coteau du Missouri, U.S.A.	112	B4
Platí, Ákra, Greece	41	F8
Platte, U.S.A.	112	D5
Platte →, Mo., U.S.A.	112	F7
Platte →, Nebr., U.S.A.	98	E10
Platteville, U.S.A.	112	E2
Plattling, Germany	25	G8
Plattsburgh, U.S.A.	111	B11
Plattsmouth, U.S.A.	112	E7
Plau, Germany	24	B8
Plauen, Germany	24	E8
Plauer See, Germany	24	B8
Plav, Montenegro, Yug.	40	D3
Plavinas, Latvia	9	H21
Plavnica, Montenegro, Yug.	40	D3
Plavno, Croatia	29	D13
Plavsk, Russia	46	F9
Playa Blanca, Canary Is.	37	F6
Playa Blanca Sur, Canary Is.	37	F6
Playa de las Americas, Canary Is.	37	F3
Playa de Mogán, Canary Is.	37	G4
Playa del Inglés, Canary Is.	37	G4
Playa Esmerelda, Canary Is.	37	F5
Playgreen L., Canada	105	C9
Pleasant Bay, Canada	103	C7
Pleasant Hill, Calif., U.S.A.	116	H4
Pleasant Hill, Mo., U.S.A.	112	F7
Pleasanton, U.S.A.	113	L5
Pleasantville, U.S.A.	108	F8
Pléaux, France	20	C6
Plei Ku, Vietnam	64	F7
Pleiße →, Germany	24	D8
Plélan-le-Grand, France	18	E4
Pléneuf-Val-André, France	18	D4
Plenița, Romania	43	F8
Plenty →, Australia	94	C2
Plenty, B. of, N.Z.	91	G6
Plentywood, U.S.A.	112	A2
Plérin, France	18	D4
Plessisville, Canada	103	C5
Plestin-les-Grèves, France	18	D3
Pleternica, Croatia	42	E2
Pleszew, Poland	45	G4
Pletipi L., Canada	103	B5
Pleven, Bulgaria	41	C8
Plevlja, Montenegro, Yug.	40	C3
Plješevica, Croatia	29	D12
Ploaghe, Italy	30	B1
Plo'ana, Slovak Rep.	27	C12
Pločno, Croatia	29	E14
Płock, Poland	45	F6
Płock □, Poland	45	F6
Plöckenpass, Italy	29	B9
Plöckenstein, Germany	25	G9
Ploemeur, France	18	E3
Ploërmel, France	18	E4
Ploiești, Romania	43	F11
Plomárion, Greece	39	C8
Plombières-les-Bains, France	19	E13
Plomin, Croatia	29	C11
Plön, Germany	24	A6
Plonge, Lac la, Canada	105	B7
Płońsk, Poland	45	F7
Plopeni, Romania	43	E10
Plopiș, Munții, Romania	42	C7
Płoty, Poland	44	E2
Plouaret, France	18	D3
Plouay, France	18	E3
Ploučnice →, Czech Rep.	26	A7
Ploudalmézeau, France	18	D2
Plouescat, France	18	D2
Plougasnou, France	18	D3
Plougastel-Daoulas, France	18	D2
Plouguerneau, France	18	D2
Plouha, France	18	D4
Plouhinec, France	18	E2
Plovdiv, Bulgaria	41	D8
Plovdiv □, Bulgaria	41	D8
Plum, U.S.A.	110	F5
Plum I., U.S.A.	111	E12
Plumas, U.S.A.	116	F7
Plummer, U.S.A.	114	C5
Plumtree, Zimbabwe	87	G2
Plunge, Lithuania	9	J19
Pluvigner, France	18	E3
Plymouth, Calif., U.S.A.	116	G6
Plymouth, U.K.	13	G3
Plymouth, Ind., U.S.A.	108	E2
Plymouth, Mass., U.S.A.	111	E14
Plymouth, N.C., U.S.A.	109	H7
Plymouth, N.H., U.S.A.	111	C13
Plymouth, Pa., U.S.A.	111	E9
Plymouth, Wis., U.S.A.	108	D2
Plynlimon = Pumlumon Fawr, U.K.	13	E4
Plyusa, Russia	46	C5
Plyusa →, Russia	46	C5
Plyussa = Plyusa →, Russia	46	C5
Plzeň, Czech Rep.	26	B6
Pniewy, Poland	45	F3
Pô, Burkina Faso	83	C4
Po →, Italy	29	D9
Po, Foci del, Italy	29	D9
Po Hai = Bo Hai, China	57	E10
Pobé, Benin	83	D5
Pobeda, Russia	51	C15
Pobedy, Pik, Kyrgyzstan	50	E8
Pobiedziska, Poland	45	F4
Pobla de Segur, Spain	32	C5
Pobladura del Valle, Spain	34	C5
Pobra de Trives, Spain	34	C3
Pocahontas, Ark., U.S.A.	113	G9
Pocahontas, Iowa, U.S.A.	112	D7
Pocatello, U.S.A.	114	E7
Počátky, Czech Rep.	26	B8
Pochep, Russia	47	F7
Pochinki, Russia	48	C7
Pochinok, Russia	46	E7
Pöchlarn, Austria	26	C8
Pochutla, Mexico	119	D5
Pocito Casas, Mexico	118	B2
Pocking, Germany	25	G8
Pocomoke City, U.S.A.	108	F8
Poços de Caldas, Brazil	127	A6
Podberezye, Czech Rep.	26	A6
Poděbrady, Czech Rep.	26	A8
Podensac, France	20	D3
Podenzano, Italy	28	D6
Podgorač, Croatia	42	E3
Podgorica, Montenegro, Yug.	40	D3
Podgorie, Albania	40	F4
Podilska Vysochyna, Ukraine	47	H4
Podkova, Bulgaria	41	E9
Podlapača, Croatia	29	D12
Podoleni, Romania	43	D11
Podolínec, Slovak Rep.	27	B13
Podolsk, Russia	46	E9
Podor, Senegal	82	B1
Podporozhy, Russia	46	B8
Podu Iloaiei, Romania	43	C12
Podu Turcului, Romania	43	D12
Podujevo, Serbia, Yug.	40	D5
Poel, Germany	24	B6
Pofadder, S. Africa	88	D2
Pogamasing, Canada	102	C3
Poggiardo, Italy	31	B11
Poggibonsi, Italy	28	E8
Póggio Mirteto, Italy	29	F9
Pogoanele, Romania	43	F12
Pogorzela, Poland	45	G4
Pogradeci, Albania	40	F4
Pogranitšnyi, Russia	54	B5
Poh, Indonesia	63	E6
Pohang, S. Korea	57	F15
Pohjanmaa, Finland	8	E20
Pohnpei, Pac. Oc.	96	G7
Pohorelá, Slovak Rep.	27	C13
Pohořelice, Czech Rep.	27	C9
Pohorje, Slovenia	29	B12
Poiana Mare, Romania	42	G8
Poiana Ruscăi, Munții, Romania	42	E7
Poiana Stampei, Romania	43	C10
Poinsett, C., Antarctica	5	C8
Point Edward, Canada	102	D3
Point Pedro, Sri Lanka	66	Q12
Point Pleasant, N.J., U.S.A.	111	F10
Point Pleasant, W. Va., U.S.A.	108	F4
Pointe-à-la Hache, U.S.A.	113	L10
Pointe-à-Pitre, Guadeloupe	121	C7
Pointe-Noire, Congo	84	E2
Poio, Spain	34	C2
Poirino, Italy	28	D4
Poisonbush Ra., Australia	92	D3
Poitiers, France	18	F7
Poitou, France	20	B3
Poitou-Charentes □, France	20	B4
Poix-de-Picardie, France	19	C8
Poix-Terron, France	19	C11
Pojoaque Valley, U.S.A.	115	J11
Pokaran, India	66	F7
Pokataroo, Australia	95	D4
Pokhara, Nepal	69	E10
Pokhvistnevo, Russia	48	D11
Poko, Dem. Rep. of the Congo	86	B2
Poko, Sudan	81	F3
Pokrov, Russia	46	E10
Pokrovsk = Engels, Russia	48	E8
Pokrovsk, Russia	51	C13
Pokrovskoye, Russia	47	J10
Pola = Pula, Croatia	29	D10
Pola, Russia	46	D7
Pola de Allande, Spain	34	B4
Pola de Lena, Spain	34	B5
Pola de Siero, Spain	34	B5
Pola de Somiedo, Spain	34	B4
Polacca, U.S.A.	115	J8
Polan, Iran	71	E9
Poland ■, Europe	45	G3
Polanica-Zdrój, Poland	45	H3
Połaniec, Poland	45	H8
Polanów, Poland	44	D3
Polatlı, Turkey	72	C5
Polatsk, Belarus	46	E5
Polcura, Chile	126	D1
Połczyn-Zdrój, Poland	44	E3
Polessk, Russia	9	J19
Polesye = Pripet Marshes, Europe	47	F5
Polgár, Hungary	42	C6
Pŏlgyo-ri, S. Korea	57	G14
Poliaigos, Greece	38	E6
Policastro, G. di, Italy	31	C8
Police, Poland	44	E1
Polička, Czech Rep.	27	B9
Policoro, Italy	31	B9
Polignano a Mare, Italy	31	A9
Poligny, France	19	F12
Políkhnitos, Greece	39	B8
Polillo Is., Phil.	61	D5
Polillo Strait, Phil.	61	D5
Polis, Cyprus	36	D11
Polístena, Italy	31	D9
Políyiros, Greece	40	F7
Polk, U.S.A.	110	E5
Polkowice, Poland	45	G3
Polla, Italy	31	B8
Pollachi, India	66	P10
Pollença, Spain	37	B10
Pollença, B. de, Spain	37	B10
Póllica, Italy	31	B8
Pollino, Mte., Italy	31	C9
Polna, Russia	46	C5
Polnovat, Russia	50	C7
Pology, Ukraine	47	J9
Polonnoye = Polonne, Ukraine	47	G4
Polski Trůmbesh, Bulgaria	41	C9
Polsko Kosovo, Bulgaria	41	C9
Polson, U.S.A.	114	C6

Poltár

Poltár, *Slovak Rep.* 27 C12
Poltava, *Ukraine* 47 H8
Põltsamaa, *Estonia* 9 G21
Polunochnoye, *Russia* 50 C7
Põlva, *Estonia* 9 G22
Polynesia, *Pac. Oc.* 97 J11
Polynésie française = French Polynesia ■, *Pac. Oc.* 97 K13
Pomarance, *Italy* 28 E7
Pomaro, *Mexico* 118 D4
Pombal, *Portugal* 34 F2
Pómbia, *Greece* 36 E6
Pomeroy, *Ohio, U.S.A.* 108 F4
Pomeroy, *Wash., U.S.A.* 114 C5
Pomézia, *Italy* 30 A5
Pomichna, *Ukraine* 47 H6
Pomona, *U.S.A.* 117 L9
Pomorie, *Bulgaria* 41 D11
Pomorskie, Pojezierze, *Poland* 44 E3
Pomos, *Cyprus* 36 D11
Pomos, C., *Cyprus* 36 D11
Pompano Beach, *U.S.A.* 109 M5
Pompei, *Italy* 31 B7
Pompey, *France* 19 D13
Pompeys Pillar, *U.S.A.* 114 D10
Ponape = Pohnpei, *Pac. Oc.* 96 G7
Ponask, L., *Canada* 102 B1
Ponass L., *Canada* 105 C8
Ponca, *U.S.A.* 112 D6
Ponca City, *U.S.A.* 113 G6
Ponce, *Puerto Rico* 121 C6
Ponchatoula, *U.S.A.* 113 K9
Poncheville, L., *Canada* 102 B4
Pond, *U.S.A.* 117 K7
Pond Inlet, *Canada* 101 A12
Pondicherry, *India* 66 P11
Ponds, I. of, *Canada* 103 B8
Ponferrada, *Spain* 34 C4
Pongo, Wadi →, *Sudan* 81 F2
Poniatowa, *Poland* 45 G9
Poniec, *Poland* 45 G3
Ponikva, *Slovenia* 29 B12
Ponnani, *India* 66 P9
Ponnyadaung, *Burma* 67 J19
Ponoka, *Canada* 104 C6
Ponorogo, *Indonesia* 63 G14
Pons = Ponts, *Spain* 32 D6
Pons, *France* 20 C3
Ponsul →, *Portugal* 34 F3
Pont-à-Mousson, *France* 19 D13
Pont-Audemer, *France* 18 C7
Pont-Aven, *France* 18 E3
Pont Canavese, *Italy* 28 C4
Pont-d'Ain, *France* 19 F12
Pont-de-Roide, *France* 19 E13
Pont-de-Salars, *France* 20 D6
Pont-de-Vaux, *France* 19 F11
Pont-de-Veyle, *France* 19 F11
Pont-du-Château, *France* 19 G10
Pont-l'Abbé, *France* 18 E2
Pont-l'Évêque, *France* 18 C7
Pont-St-Esprit, *France* 21 D8
Pont-St-Martin, *Italy* 28 C4
Pont-Ste-Maxence, *France* 19 C9
Pont-sur-Yonne, *France* 19 D10
Ponta do Sol, *Madeira* 37 D2
Ponta Grossa, *Brazil* 127 B5
Ponta Pora, *Brazil* 127 A4
Pontacq, *France* 20 E3
Pontailler-sur-Saône, *France* 19 E12
Pontarlier, *France* 19 F13
Pontassieve, *Italy* 29 E8
Pontaumur, *France* 20 C6
Pontcharra, *France* 21 C10
Pontchartrain L., *U.S.A.* 113 K10
Pontchâteau, *France* 18 E4
Ponte da Barca, *Portugal* 34 D2
Ponte de Sor, *Portugal* 35 F2
Ponte dell'Ólio, *Italy* 28 D6
Ponte di Legno, *Italy* 28 B7
Ponte do Lima, *Portugal* 34 D2
Ponte do Pungué, *Mozam.* 87 F3
Ponte-Leccia, *France* 21 F13
Ponte nelle Alpi, *Italy* 29 B9
Ponte Nova, *Brazil* 127 A7
Ponteareas, *Spain* 34 C2
Pontebba, *Italy* 29 B10
Ponteceso, *Spain* 34 B2
Pontecorvo, *Italy* 30 A6
Pontedeume, *Spain* 34 B2
Ponteix, *Canada* 105 D7
Pontevedra, *Spain* 34 C2
Pontevedra □, *Spain* 34 C2
Pontevedra, R. de →, *Spain* 34 C2
Pontevico, *Italy* 28 C7
Pontiac, *Ill., U.S.A.* 112 E10
Pontiac, *Mich., U.S.A.* 108 D4
Pontian Kecil, *Malaysia* 65 M4
Pontianak, *Indonesia* 62 E3
Pontine Is. = Ponziane, Ísole, *Italy* 30 B5
Pontine Mts. = Kuzey Anadolu Dağları, *Turkey* 72 B7
Pontínia, *Italy* 30 A6
Pontivy, *France* 18 D4
Pontoise, *France* 19 C9
Ponton →, *Canada* 104 B5
Pontorson, *France* 18 D5
Pontrémoli, *Italy* 28 D6
Pontrieux, *France* 18 D3
Ponts, *Spain* 32 D6
Pontypool, *Canada* 110 B6
Pontypool, *U.K.* 13 F4
Ponza, *Italy* 30 B5
Ponziane, Ísole, *Italy* 30 B5
Poochera, *Australia* 95 E1
Poole, *U.K.* 13 G6
Poole □, *U.K.* 13 G6
Pooley I., *Canada* 104 C3
Poona = Pune, *India* 66 K8
Pooncarie, *Australia* 95 E3
Poopelloe L., *Australia* 95 E3
Poopó, L. de, *Bolivia* 122 E4
Popanyinning, *Australia* 93 F2
Popayán, *Colombia* 124 C3
Poperinge, *Belgium* 17 D2
Popilta, L., *Australia* 95 E3
Popina, *Bulgaria* 41 B10
Popio L., *Australia* 95 E3
Poplar, *U.S.A.* 112 A2
Poplar →, *Man., Canada* 105 C9
Poplar →, *N.W.T., Canada* 104 A4
Poplar Bluff, *U.S.A.* 113 G9
Poplarville, *U.S.A.* 113 K10
Popocatépetl, Volcán, *Mexico* 119 D5
Popokabaka, *Dem. Rep. of the Congo* 84 F3
Pópoli, *Italy* 29 F10
Popovača, *Croatia* 29 C13
Popovo, *Bulgaria* 41 C10
Poppberg, *Germany* 25 F7
Poppi, *Italy* 29 E8
Poprad, *Slovak Rep.* 27 B13
Poprad →, *Slovak Rep.* 27 B13
Porali →, *Pakistan* 68 G2
Porbandar, *India* 68 J3
Porcher I., *Canada* 104 C2
Porcuna, *Spain* 35 H6
Porcupine →, *Canada* 105 B8
Porcupine →, *U.S.A.* 100 B5
Pordenone, *Italy* 29 C9
Pordim, *Bulgaria* 41 C8
Poreč, *Croatia* 29 C10
Poretskoye, *Russia* 48 C8
Pori, *Finland* 9 F19
Porí, *Greece* 38 F5
Porkhov, *Russia* 46 D5
Porlamar, *Venezuela* 124 A6
Porlezza, *Italy* 28 B6
Porma →, *Spain* 34 C5
Pornic, *France* 18 E4
Poronaysk, *Russia* 51 E15
Póros, *Greece* 38 D5
Poroshiri-Dake, *Japan* 54 C11
Poroszló, *Hungary* 42 C5
Poroto Mts., *Tanzania* 87 D3
Porpoise B., *Antarctica* 5 C9
Porquerolles, Î. de, *France* 21 F10
Porrentruy, *Switz.* 25 H3
Porreres, *Spain* 37 B10
Porsangen, *Norway* 8 A21
Porsgrunn, *Norway* 9 G13
Port Adelaide, *Australia* 95 E2
Port Alberni, *Canada* 104 D4
Port Alfred, *Canada* 103 C5
Port Alfred, *S. Africa* 88 E4
Port Alice, *Canada* 104 C3
Port Allegany, *U.S.A.* 110 E6
Port Allen, *U.S.A.* 113 K9
Port Alma, *Australia* 94 C5
Port Angeles, *U.S.A.* 116 B3
Port Antonio, *Jamaica* 120 C4
Port Aransas, *U.S.A.* 113 M6
Port Arthur = Lüshun, *China* 57 E11
Port Arthur, *Australia* 94 G4
Port Arthur, *U.S.A.* 113 L8
Port au Port B., *Canada* 103 C8
Port-au-Prince, *Haiti* 121 C5
Port Augusta, *Australia* 95 E2
Port Augusta West, *Australia* 95 E2
Port Austin, *U.S.A.* 102 D3
Port Bell, *Uganda* 86 B3
Port Bergé Vaovao, *Madag.* 89 B8
Port Blandford, *Canada* 103 C9
Port Bouët, *Ivory C.* 82 D4
Port Bradshaw, *Australia* 94 A2
Port Broughton, *Australia* 95 E2
Port Burwell, *Canada* 102 D3
Port Canning, *India* 69 H13
Port-Cartier, *Canada* 103 B6
Port Chalmers, *N.Z.* 91 L3
Port Chester, *U.S.A.* 111 F11
Port Clements, *Canada* 104 C2
Port Clinton, *U.S.A.* 108 E4
Port Colborne, *Canada* 102 D4
Port Coquitlam, *Canada* 104 D4
Port Credit, *Canada* 110 C5
Port Curtis, *Australia* 94 C5
Port d'Alcúdia, *Spain* 37 B10
Port Dalhousie, *Canada* 110 C5
Port Darwin, *Australia* 92 B5
Port Darwin, *Falk. Is.* 128 G5
Port Davey, *Australia* 94 G4
Port-de-Bouc, *France* 21 E8
Port-de-Paix, *Haiti* 121 C5
Port de Pollença, *Spain* 37 B10
Port de Sóller, *Spain* 37 B9
Port Dickson, *Malaysia* 65 L3
Port Douglas, *Australia* 94 B4
Port Dover, *Canada* 110 D4
Port Edward, *Canada* 104 C2
Port Elgin, *Canada* 102 D3
Port Elizabeth, *S. Africa* 88 E4
Port Ellen, *U.K.* 14 F2
Port-en-Bessin, *France* 18 C6
Port Erin, *U.K.* 12 C3
Port Essington, *Australia* 92 B5
Port Etienne = Nouâdhibou, *Mauritania* 78 D2
Port Fairy, *Australia* 95 F3
Port Fouâd = Bûr Fuad, *Egypt* 80 H8
Port Gamble, *U.S.A.* 116 C4
Port-Gentil, *Gabon* 84 E1
Port Gibson, *U.S.A.* 113 K9
Port Glasgow, *U.K.* 14 F4
Port Harcourt, *Nigeria* 83 E6
Port Hardy, *Canada* 104 C3
Port Harrison = Inukjuak, *Canada* 101 C12
Port Hawkesbury, *Canada* 103 C7
Port Hedland, *Australia* 92 D2
Port Henry, *U.S.A.* 111 B11
Port Hood, *Canada* 103 C7
Port Hope, *Canada* 102 D4
Port Hueneme, *U.S.A.* 117 L7
Port Huron, *U.S.A.* 108 D4
Port Iliç, *Azerbaijan* 73 C13
Port Isabel, *U.S.A.* 113 M6
Port Jefferson, *U.S.A.* 111 F11
Port Jervis, *U.S.A.* 111 E10
Port-Joinville, *France* 18 F4
Port Katon, *Russia* 47 J10
Port Kelang = Pelabuhan Kelang, *Malaysia* 65 L3
Port Kembla, *Australia* 95 E5
Port Kenny, *Australia* 95 E1
Port-la-Nouvelle, *France* 20 E7
Port Lairge = Waterford, *Ireland* 15 D4
Port Laoise, *Ireland* 15 C4
Port Lavaca, *U.S.A.* 113 L6
Port Lincoln, *Australia* 95 E2
Port Loko, *S. Leone* 82 D2
Port Louis, *France* 18 E3
Port Lyautey = Kenitra, *Morocco* 78 B4
Port MacDonnell, *Australia* 95 F3
Port Macquarie, *Australia* 95 E5
Port Maria, *Jamaica* 120 C4
Port Mellon, *Canada* 104 D4
Port-Menier, *Canada* 103 C7
Port Morant, *Jamaica* 120 C4
Port Moresby, *Papua N. G.* 96 H6
Port Mouton, *Canada* 103 D7
Port Musgrave, *Australia* 94 A3
Port-Navalo, *France* 18 E4
Port Nelson, *Canada* 105 B10
Port Nolloth, *S. Africa* 88 D2
Port Nouveau-Québec = Kangiqsualujjuaq, *Canada* 101 C13
Port O'Connor, *U.S.A.* 113 L6
Port of Spain, *Trin. & Tob.* 121 D7
Port Orchard, *U.S.A.* 116 C4
Port Orford, *U.S.A.* 114 E1
Port Pegasus, *N.Z.* 91 M1
Port Perry, *Canada* 102 D4
Port Phillip B., *Australia* 95 F3
Port Pirie, *Australia* 95 E2
Port Radium = Echo Bay, *Canada* 100 B8
Port Renfrew, *Canada* 104 D4
Port Roper, *Australia* 94 A2
Port Rowan, *Canada* 102 D3
Port Safaga = Bûr Safâga, *Egypt* 80 B3
Port Said = Bûr Sa'îd, *Egypt* 80 H8
Port St. Joe, *U.S.A.* 109 L3
Port St. Johns, *S. Africa* 89 E4
Port-St-Louis-du-Rhône, *France* 21 E8
Port-Ste-Marie, *France* 20 D4
Port Sanilac, *U.S.A.* 102 D3
Port Saunders, *Canada* 103 B8
Port Severn, *Canada* 110 B5
Port Shepstone, *S. Africa* 89 E5
Port Simpson, *Canada* 104 C2
Port Stanley = Stanley, *Falk. Is.* 128 G5
Port Stanley, *Canada* 102 D3
Port Sudan = Bûr Sûdân, *Sudan* 80 D4
Port-sur-Saône, *France* 19 E13
Port Talbot, *U.K.* 13 F4
Port Taufiq = Bûr Taufiq, *Egypt* 80 J8
Port Townsend, *U.S.A.* 116 B4
Port-Vendres, *France* 20 F7
Port Wakefield, *Australia* 95 E2
Port Washington, *U.S.A.* 108 D2
Port Weld = Kuala Sepetang, *Malaysia* 65 K3
Portadown, *U.K.* 15 B5
Portaferry, *U.K.* 15 B6
Portage, *U.S.A.* 112 D10
Portage La Prairie, *Canada* 105 D9
Portageville, *U.S.A.* 113 G10
Portalegre, *Portugal* 35 F3
Portalegre □, *Portugal* 35 F3
Portales, *U.S.A.* 113 H3
Portarlington, *Ireland* 15 C4
Portbou, *Spain* 32 C8
Portel, *Portugal* 35 G3
Porter L., *N.W.T., Canada* 105 A7
Porter L., *Sask., Canada* 105 B7
Porterville, *S. Africa* 88 E2
Porterville, *U.S.A.* 116 J8
Portes-lès-Valence, *France* 21 D8
Porthcawl, *U.K.* 13 F4
Porthill, *U.S.A.* 114 B5
Porthmadog, *U.K.* 12 E3
Portile de Fier, *Europe* 42 F7
Portimão, *Portugal* 35 H2
Portishead, *U.K.* 13 F5
Portiţei, Gura, *Romania* 43 F14
Portknockie, *U.K.* 14 D6
Portland, *N.S.W., Australia* 95 E5
Portland, *Vic., Australia* 95 F3
Portland, *Canada* 111 B8
Portland, *Conn., U.S.A.* 111 E12
Portland, *Maine, U.S.A.* 103 D5
Portland, *Mich., U.S.A.* 108 D3
Portland, *Oreg., U.S.A.* 116 E4
Portland, I. of, *U.K.* 13 G5
Portland B., *Australia* 95 F3
Portland Bill, *U.K.* 13 G5
Portlands Roads, *Australia* 94 A3
Portmadoc = Porthmadog, *U.K.* 12 E3
Portneuf, *Canada* 103 C5
Porto, *France* 21 F12
Porto, *Portugal* 34 D2
Porto □, *Portugal* 34 D2
Porto, G. de, *France* 21 F12
Pôrto Alegre, *Brazil* 127 C5
Porto Amboim = Gunza, *Angola* 84 G2
Porto Azzurro, *Italy* 28 F7
Porto Cristo, *Spain* 37 B10
Pôrto de Móz, *Brazil* 125 D8
Porto Empédocle, *Italy* 30 E6
Pôrto Esperança, *Brazil* 124 G7
Pôrto Franco, *Brazil* 125 E9
Porto Lágos, *Greece* 41 E9
Porto Mendes, *Brazil* 127 A5
Porto Moniz, *Madeira* 37 D2
Pôrto Murtinho, *Brazil* 124 H7
Pôrto Nacional, *Brazil* 125 F9
Porto-Novo, *Benin* 83 D5
Porto Petro, *Spain* 37 B10
Porto San Giórgio, *Italy* 29 E10
Porto Sant' Elpídio, *Italy* 29 E10
Porto Santo, *Madeira* 78 B2
Porto Santo Stéfano, *Italy* 28 F8
Pôrto São José, *Brazil* 127 A5
Pôrto Seguro, *Brazil* 125 G11
Porto Tolle, *Italy* 29 D9
Porto Tórres, *Italy* 30 B1
Pôrto União, *Brazil* 127 B5
Pôrto Válter, *Brazil* 124 E4
Porto-Vecchio, *France* 21 G13
Pôrto Velho, *Brazil* 124 E6
Portobelo, *Panama* 120 E4
Portoferráio, *Italy* 28 F7
Portogruaro, *Italy* 29 C9
Portola, *U.S.A.* 116 F6
Portomaggiore, *Italy* 29 D8
Portoscuso, *Italy* 30 C1
Portovénere, *Italy* 28 D6
Portoviejo, *Ecuador* 124 D2
Portpatrick, *U.K.* 14 G3
Portree, *U.K.* 14 D2
Portrush, *U.K.* 15 A5
Portsmouth, *Domin.* 121 C7
Portsmouth, *U.K.* 13 G6
Portsmouth, *N.H., U.S.A.* 111 C14
Portsmouth, *Ohio, U.S.A.* 108 F4
Portsmouth, *R.I., U.S.A.* 111 E13
Portsmouth, *Va., U.S.A.* 108 G7
Portsmouth □, *U.K.* 13 G6
Portsoy, *U.K.* 14 D6
Portstewart, *U.K.* 15 A5
Porttipahtan tekojärvi, *Finland* 8 B22
Portugal ■, *Europe* 34 F3
Portugalete, *Spain* 32 B1
Portumna, *Ireland* 15 C3
Portville, *U.S.A.* 110 D6
Porvenir, *Chile* 128 G2
Porvoo, *Finland* 9 F21
Porzuna, *Spain* 35 F6
Posadas, *Italy* 30 B2
Posada →, *Italy* 30 B2
Posadas, *Argentina* 127 B4
Posadas, *Spain* 35 H5
Poschiavo, *Switz.* 25 J6
Posets, *Spain* 32 C5
Poshan = Boshan, *China* 57 F9
Posht-e-Badam, *Iran* 71 C7
Posídhion, Ákra, *Greece* 40 G7
Posidium, *Greece* 39 F9
Poso, *Indonesia* 63 E6
Posong, *S. Korea* 57 G14
Posse, *Brazil* 125 F9
Possession I., *Antarctica* 5 D11
Pössneck, *Germany* 24 E7
Post, *U.S.A.* 113 J4
Post Falls, *U.S.A.* 114 C5
Postavy = Pastavy, *Belarus* 9 J22
Postmasburg, *S. Africa* 88 D3
Postojna, *Slovenia* 29 C11
Poston, *U.S.A.* 117 M12
Potamós, *Andikíthira, Greece* 38 F5
Potamós, *Kíthira, Greece* 38 E4
Potchefstroom, *S. Africa* 88 D4
Potcoava, *Romania* 43 F9
Poteau, *U.S.A.* 113 H7
Poteet, *U.S.A.* 113 L5
Potenza, *Italy* 31 B8
Potenza →, *Italy* 29 E10
Potenza Picena, *Italy* 29 E10
Poteriteri, L., *N.Z.* 91 M1
Potgietersrus, *S. Africa* 89 C4
Poti, *Georgia* 49 J5
Potiskum, *Nigeria* 83 C7
Potlogi, *Romania* 43 F10
Potomac →, *U.S.A.* 108 G7
Potosí, *Bolivia* 124 G5
Potosi Mt., *U.S.A.* 117 K11
Pototan, *Phil.* 61 F5
Potrerillos, *Chile* 126 B2
Potsdam, *Germany* 24 C9
Potsdam, *U.S.A.* 111 B10
Pottenstein, *Germany* 25 F7
Potter, *U.S.A.* 112 E3
Pottery Hill = Abû Ballas, *Egypt* 80 C2
Pottstown, *U.S.A.* 111 F9
Pottsville, *U.S.A.* 111 F8
Pottuvil, *Sri Lanka* 66 R12
P'otzu, *Taiwan* 59 F13
Pouancé, *France* 18 E5
Pouce Coupé, *Canada* 104 B4
Poughkeepsie, *U.S.A.* 111 E11
Pouilly-sur-Loire, *France* 19 E9
Poulaphouca Res., *Ireland* 15 C5
Poulsbo, *U.S.A.* 116 C4
Poulton-le-Fylde, *U.K.* 12 D5
Pouso Alegre, *Brazil* 127 A6
Pouthisat, *Cambodia* 64 F4
Pouzauges, *France* 18 F6
Pova de Sta. Iria, *Portugal* 35 G1
Považská Bystrica, *Slovak Rep.* 27 B11
Poverty B., *N.Z.* 91 H7
Povlen, *Serbia, Yug.* 40 B3
Póvoa de Lanhosa, *Portugal* 34 D2
Póvoa de Varzim, *Portugal* 34 D2
Povorino, *Russia* 48 E6
Powassan, *Canada* 102 C4
Poway, *U.S.A.* 117 N9
Powder →, *U.S.A.* 112 B2
Powder River, *U.S.A.* 114 E10
Powell, *U.S.A.* 114 D9
Powell, L., *U.S.A.* 115 H8
Powell River, *Canada* 104 D4
Powers, *Mich., U.S.A.* 108 C2
Powers, *Oreg., U.S.A.* 114 E1
Powers Lake, *U.S.A.* 112 A3
Powys □, *U.K.* 13 E4
Poyang Hu, *China* 59 C11
Poyarkovo, *Russia* 51 E13
Poysdorf, *Austria* 27 C9
Poza de la Sal, *Spain* 34 C7
Poza Rica, *Mexico* 119 C5
Pozanti, *Turkey* 72 D6
Požarevac, *Serbia, Yug.* 40 B5
Pozazal, Puerto, *Spain* 34 C6
Požega, *Croatia* 42 E2
Požega, *Serbia, Yug.* 40 C4
Poznań, *Poland* 45 F3
Poznań □, *Poland* 45 F3
Pozo, *U.S.A.* 117 K6
Pozo Alcón, *Spain* 35 H8
Pozo Almonte, *Chile* 124 H5
Pozo Colorado, *Paraguay* 126 A4
Pozo del Dátil, *Mexico* 118 B2
Pozoblanco, *Spain* 35 G6
Pozzallo, *Italy* 31 F7
Pozzomaggiore, *Italy* 30 B1
Pozzuoli, *Italy* 31 B7
Pra →, *Ghana* 83 D4
Prabuty, *Poland* 44 E6
Prača, *Bos.-H.* 42 G3
Prachatice, *Czech Rep.* 26 B6
Prachin Buri, *Thailand* 64 F3
Prachuap Khiri Khan, *Thailand* 65 G2
Pradelles, *France* 20 D7
Prades, *France* 20 F6
Prado, *Brazil* 125 G11
Prado del Rey, *Spain* 35 J5
Præstø, *Denmark* 11 J6
Pragersko, *Slovenia* 29 B12
Prague = Praha, *Czech Rep.* 26 A7
Praha, *Czech Rep.* 26 A7
Prahecq, *France* 20 B3
Prahova □, *Romania* 43 E10
Prahova →, *Romania* 43 F10
Prahovo, *Serbia, Yug.* 40 B6
Praia, *C. Verde Is.* 77 E1
Práia a Mare, *Italy* 31 C8
Praid, *Romania* 43 D10
Prainha, *Amazonas, Brazil* 124 E6
Prainha, *Pará, Brazil* 125 D8
Prairie, *Australia* 94 C3
Prairie →, *U.S.A.* 113 H5
Prairie City, *U.S.A.* 114 D4
Prairie du Chien, *U.S.A.* 112 D9
Pramánda, *Greece* 38 B3
Pran Buri, *Thailand* 64 F2
Prang, *Ghana* 83 D4
Prapat, *Indonesia* 62 D1
Prasonísi, Ákra, *Greece* 36 D9
Prästmon, *Sweden* 10 A11
Praszka, *Poland* 45 G5
Prata, *Brazil* 125 G9
Pratapgarh, *India* 68 G6
Prato, *Italy* 28 E8
Prátola Peligna, *Italy* 29 F10
Prats-de-Mollo-la-Preste, *France* 20 F6
Pratt, *U.S.A.* 113 G5
Prattville, *U.S.A.* 109 J2
Pravdinsk, *Russia* 48 B6
Pravets, *Bulgaria* 40 D7
Pravia, *Spain* 34 B4
Praya, *Indonesia* 62 F5
Pré-en-Pail, *France* 18 D6
Precordillera, *Argentina* 126 C2

Predáppio, *Italy* 29 D8
Predazzo, *Italy* 29 B8
Predeal, *Romania* 43 E10
Predejane, *Serbia, Yug.* .. 40 D6
Preeceville, *Canada* ... 105 C8
Preetz, *Germany* 24 A6
Pregrada, *Croatia* 29 B12
Preiļi, *Latvia* 9 H22
Preko, *Croatia* 29 D12
Prelate, *Canada* 105 C7
Prelog, *Croatia* 29 B13
Prémery, *France* 19 E10
Premià de Mar, *Spain* ... 32 D7
Premier, *Canada* 104 B3
Premont, *U.S.A.* 113 M5
Premuda, *Croatia* 29 D11
Prenjasi, *Albania* 40 E4
Prentice, *U.S.A.* 112 C9
Prenzlau, *Germany* 24 B9
Preobrazheniye, *Russia* .. 54 C6
Preparis North Channel,
 Ind. Oc. 67 M18
Preparis South Channel,
 Ind. Oc. 67 M18
Přerov, *Czech Rep.* 27 B10
Prescott, *Canada* 102 D4
Prescott, *Ariz., U.S.A.* . 115 J7
Prescott, *Ark., U.S.A.* .. 113 J8
Preservation Inlet, *N.Z.* .. 91 M1
Preševo, *Serbia, Yug.* ... 40 D5
Presho, *U.S.A.* 112 D4
Presicce, *Italy* 31 C11
Presidencia de la Plaza,
 Argentina 126 B4
Presidencia Roque Saenz
 Peña, *Argentina* 126 B3
Presidente Epitácio, *Brazil* 125 H8
Presidente Hayes □,
 Paraguay 126 A4
Presidente Prudente, *Brazil* 127 A5
Presidio, *Mexico* 118 B4
Presidio, *U.S.A.* 113 L2
Preslav, *Bulgaria* 41 C10
Preslavska Planina,
 Bulgaria 41 C10
Prešov, *Slovak Rep.* 27 B14
Prešovský □, *Slovak Rep.* 27 B13
Prespa, *Bulgaria* 41 E8
Prespa, L. = Prespansko
 Jezero, *Macedonia* 40 F5
Prespansko Jezero,
 Macedonia 40 F5
Presque Isle, *U.S.A.* ... 103 C6
Prestatyn, *U.K.* 12 D4
Prestea, *Ghana* 82 D4
Presteigne, *U.K.* 13 E5
Přeštice, *Czech Rep.* ... 26 B6
Preston, *Canada* 110 C4
Preston, *U.K.* 12 D5
Preston, *Idaho, U.S.A.* .. 114 E8
Preston, *Minn., U.S.A.* .. 112 D8
Preston, *Nev., U.S.A.* ... 114 G6
Preston, C., *Australia* .. 92 D2
Prestwick, *U.K.* 14 F4
Pretoria, *S. Africa* 89 D4
Preuilly-sur-Claise, *France* 18 F7
Préveza, *Greece* 38 C2
Préveza □, *Greece* 38 B2
Prey Veng, *Cambodia* ... 65 G5
Priazovskoye, *Ukraine* .. 47 J8
Pribilof Is., *U.S.A.* 4 D17
Priboj, *Serbia, Yug.* 40 C3
Příbram, *Czech Rep.* ... 26 B7
Price, *U.S.A.* 114 G8
Price I., *Canada* 104 C3
Prichard, *U.S.A.* 109 K1
Priego, *Spain* 32 E2
Priego de Córdoba, *Spain* .. 35 H6
Priekule, *Latvia* 9 H19
Prien, *Germany* 25 H8
Prienai, *Lithuania* 44 D10
Prieska, *S. Africa* 88 D3
Priest →, *U.S.A.* 114 B5
Priest L., *U.S.A.* 114 B5
Priest Valley, *U.S.A.* ... 116 J6
Priestly, *Canada* 104 C3
Prievidza, *Slovak Rep.* .. 27 C11
Prignitz, *Germany* 24 B7
Prijedor, *Bos.-H.* 29 D13
Prijepolje, *Serbia, Yug.* .. 40 C3
Prikaspiyskaya
 Nizmennost = Caspian
 Depression, *Eurasia* ... 49 G9
Prikubanskaya Nizmennost,
 Russia 47 K10
Prilep, *Macedonia* 40 E5
Priluki = Pryluky, *Ukraine* 47 G7
Prime Seal I., *Australia* .. 94 G4
Primorsk, *Russia* 46 B5
Primorsko, *Bulgaria* 41 D11
Primorsko-Akhtarsk, *Russia* 47 J10
Primorskoye, *Ukraine* .. 47 J9
Primrose L., *Canada* ... 105 C7
Prince Albert, *Canada* .. 105 C7
Prince Albert, *S. Africa* . 88 E3
Prince Albert Mts.,
 Antarctica 5 D11
Prince Albert Nat. Park,
 Canada 105 C7
Prince Albert Pen., *Canada* 100 A8
Prince Albert Sd., *Canada* 100 A8
Prince Alfred, C., *Canada* . 4 B1
Prince Charles I., *Canada* . 101 B12
Prince Charles Mts.,
 Antarctica 5 D6
Prince Edward I. □,
 Canada 103 C7

Prince Edward Is., *Ind. Oc.* . 3 G11
Prince George, *Canada* ... 104 C4
Prince of Wales, C., *U.S.A.* 98 C3
Prince of Wales I.,
 Australia 94 A3
Prince of Wales I., *Canada* . 4 B3
Prince of Wales I., *U.S.A.* 104 B2
Prince Patrick I., *Canada* . 4 B2
Prince Regent Inlet,
 Canada 4 B3
Prince Rupert, *Canada* ... 104 C2
Princess Charlotte B.,
 Australia 94 A3
Princess May Ranges,
 Australia 92 C4
Princess Royal I., *Canada* 104 C3
Princeton, *Canada* 104 D4
Princeton, *Calif., U.S.A.* 116 F4
Princeton, *Ill., U.S.A.* .. 112 E10
Princeton, *Ind., U.S.A.* .. 108 F2
Princeton, *Ky., U.S.A.* .. 108 G2
Princeton, *Mo., U.S.A.* .. 112 E8
Princeton, *N.J., U.S.A.* .. 111 F10
Princeton, *W. Va., U.S.A.* 108 G5
Principe, I. de, *Atl. Oc.* .. 76 F4
Principe Chan., *Canada* . 104 C3
Principe da Beira, *Brazil* . 124 F6
Prineville, *U.S.A.* 114 D3
Prins Harald Kyst,
 Antarctica 5 D4
Prinsesse Astrid Kyst,
 Antarctica 5 D3
Prinsesse Ragnhild Kyst,
 Antarctica 5 D4
Prinzapolca, *Nic.* 120 D3
Prior, C., *Spain* 34 B2
Priozersk, *Russia* 46 B6
Pripet → = Prypyat →,
 Europe 47 G6
Pripet Marshes, *Europe* .. 47 F5
Pripyat Marshes = Pripet
 Marshes, *Europe* 47 F5
Pripyats = Prypyat →,
 Europe 47 G6
Prislop, Pasul, *Romania* . 43 C9
Pristen, *Russia* 47 G9
Priština, *Serbia, Yug.* ... 40 D5
Pritzwalk, *Germany* 24 B8
Privas, *France* 21 D8
Priverno, *Italy* 30 A6
Privolzhsk, *Russia* 48 B5
Privolzhskaya
 Vozvyshennost, *Russia* . 48 E7
Privolzhskiy, *Russia* 48 E8
Privolzhye, *Russia* 48 D9
Priyutnoye, *Russia* 49 G6
Prizren, *Serbia, Yug.* 40 D4
Prizzi, *Italy* 30 E6
Prnjavor, *Bos.-H.* 42 F2
Probolinggo, *Indonesia* .. 63 G15
Prochowice, *Poland* 45 G3
Proddatur, *India* 66 M11
Prodhromos, *Cyprus* ... 36 E11
Profítis Ilías, *Greece* 36 C9
Profondeville, *Belgium* .. 17 D4
Progreso, *Mexico* 119 C7
Prokhladnyy, *Russia* 49 J7
Prokletije, *Albania* 40 D3
Prokopyevsk, *Russia* 50 D9
Prokuplje, *Serbia, Yug.* .. 40 C5
Proletarsk, *Russia* 49 G5
Prome = Pyè, *Burma* ... 67 K19
Prophet →, *Canada* ... 104 B4
Propriá, *Brazil* 125 F11
Propriano, *France* 21 G12
Proserpine, *Australia* ... 94 C4
Prosna →, *Poland* 45 F4
Prosser, *U.S.A.* 114 C4
Prostějov, *Czech Rep.* .. 27 B10
Prostki, *Poland* 44 E9
Proston, *Australia* 95 D5
Proszowice, *Poland* 45 H7
Protection, *U.S.A.* 113 G5
Próti, *Greece* 38 D3
Provadiya, *Bulgaria* 41 C11
Provence, *France* 21 E9
Provence-Alpes-Côte
 d'Azur □, *France* 21 D10
Providence, *Ky., U.S.A.* . 108 G2
Providence, *R.I., U.S.A.* 111 E13
Providence Bay, *Canada* . 102 C3
Providence Mts., *U.S.A.* 115 J6
Providencia, I. de,
 Colombia 120 D3
Providenciya, *Russia* ... 51 C19
Provins, *France* 19 D10
Provo, *U.S.A.* 114 F8
Provost, *Canada* 105 C6
Prozor, *Bos.-H.* 42 G2
Prud'homme, *Canada* .. 105 C7
Prudnik, *Poland* 45 H4
Prüm, *Germany* 25 E2
Prundu, *Romania* 43 F11
Pruszcz Gdański, *Poland* . 44 D5
Pruszków, *Poland* 45 F7
Prut →, *Romania* 43 E13
Pružany, *Belarus* 47 F3
Prvič, *Croatia* 29 D11
Prydz B., *Antarctica* 5 C6
Pryluky, *Ukraine* 47 G7
Pryor, *U.S.A.* 113 G7
Prypyat →, *Europe* 47 G6
Przasnysz, *Poland* 45 E7
Przedbórz, *Poland* 45 G6
Przedecz, *Poland* 45 F5
Przemków, *Poland* 45 G2

Przemyśl, *Poland* 45 J9
Przemyśl □, *Poland* 45 J9
Przeworsk, *Poland* 45 H9
Przewóz, *Poland* 45 G1
Przhevalsk, *Kyrgyzstan* . 50 E8
Przysucha, *Poland* 45 G7
Psará, *Greece* 39 C7
Psakhná, *Greece* 38 C5
Psathoúra, *Greece* 38 B6
Psel →, *Ukraine* 47 H7
Pserimos, *Greece* 39 E9
Psíra, *Greece* 36 D7
Pskov, *Russia* 46 D5
Pskovskoye, Ozero, *Russia* 9 H22
Psunj, *Croatia* 42 E2
Pteleón, *Greece* 38 B4
Ptich = Ptsich →, *Belarus* 47 F5
Ptolemaís, *Greece* 40 F5
Ptsich →, *Belarus* 47 F5
Ptuj, *Slovenia* 29 B12
Ptujska Gora, *Slovenia* .. 29 B12
Pu Xian, *China* 56 F6
Pua, *Thailand* 64 C3
Puán, *Argentina* 126 D3
Pu'an, *China* 58 E5
Puan, *S. Korea* 57 G14
Pubei, *China* 58 F7
Pucallpa, *Peru* 124 E4
Pucheng, *China* 59 D12
Pucheni, *Romania* 43 E10
Puchheim, *Germany* 25 G7
Púchov, *Slovak Rep.* ... 27 B11
Pucioasa, *Romania* 43 E10
Pučišća, *Croatia* 29 E13
Puck, *Poland* 44 D5
Pucka, Zatoka, *Poland* .. 44 D5
Puçol, *Spain* 33 F4
Pudasjärvi, *Finland* 8 D22
Puding, *China* 58 D5
Pudozh, *Russia* 46 B9
Pudukkottai, *India* 66 P11
Puebla, *Mexico* 119 D5
Puebla □, *Mexico* 119 D5
Puebla de Alcocer, *Spain* . 35 G5
Puebla de Don Fadrique,
 Spain 33 H2
Puebla de Don Rodrigo,
 Spain 35 F6
Puebla de Guzmán, *Spain* 35 H3
Puebla de la Calzada, *Spain* 35 G4
Puebla de Sanabria, *Spain* 34 C4
Puebla de Trives = Pobra
 de Trives, *Spain* 34 C3
Pueblo, *U.S.A.* 112 F2
Pueblo Hundido, *Chile* . 126 B1
Puelches, *Argentina* ... 126 D2
Puelén, *Argentina* 126 D2
Puente Alto, *Chile* 126 C1
Puente-Genil, *Spain* 35 H6
Puente la Reina, *Spain* .. 32 C3
Puenteareas = Ponteareas,
 Spain 34 C2
Puentedeume =
 Pontedeume, *Spain* ... 34 B2
Puentes de Garcia
 Rodriguez = As Pontes
 de García Rodríquez,
 Spain 34 B3
Pu'er, *China* 58 F3
Puerco →, *U.S.A.* 115 J10
Puerto, *Canary Is.* 37 F2
Puerto Aisén, *Chile* 128 F2
Puerto Ángel, *Mexico* .. 119 D5
Puerto Arista, *Mexico* .. 119 D6
Puerto Armuelles, *Panama* 120 E3
Puerto Ayacucho,
 Venezuela 124 B5
Puerto Barrios, *Guatemala* 120 C2
Puerto Bermejo, *Argentina* 126 B4
Puerto Bermúdez, *Peru* . 124 F4
Puerto Bolívar, *Ecuador* . 124 D2
Puerto Cabello, *Venezuela* 124 A5
Puerto Cabezas, *Nic.* ... 120 D3
Puerto Cabo Gracias á
 Dios, *Nic.* 120 D3
Puerto Carreño, *Colombia* 124 B5
Puerto Castilla, *Honduras* 120 C2
Puerto Chicama, *Peru* .. 124 E3
Puerto Coig, *Argentina* .. 128 G3
Puerto Cortés, *Costa Rica* 120 E3
Puerto Cortés, *Honduras* 120 C2
Puerto Cumarebo,
 Venezuela 124 A5
Puerto de Alcudia = Port
 d'Alcúdia, *Spain* 37 B10
Puerto de Andraitx, *Spain* 37 B9
Puerto de Cabrera, *Spain* . 37 B9
Puerto de Gran Tarajal,
 Canary Is. 37 F5
Puerto de la Cruz,
 Canary Is. 37 F3
Puerto de Mazarrón, *Spain* 33 H3
Puerto de Pozo Negro,
 Canary Is. 37 F6
Puerto de Sóller = Port de
 Sóller, *Spain* 37 B9
Puerto de Somosierra,
 Spain 34 D7
Puerto del Carmen,
 Canary Is. 37 F6
Puerto del Rosario,
 Canary Is. 37 F6
Puerto Deseado, *Argentina* 128 F3
Puerto Heath, *Bolivia* .. 124 F5
Puerto Inírida, *Colombia* 124 C5
Puerto Juárez, *Mexico* .. 119 C7
Puerto La Cruz, *Venezuela* 124 A6

Puerto Leguízamo,
 Colombia 124 D4
Puerto Limón, *Colombia* . 124 C4
Puerto Lobos, *Argentina* . 128 E3
Puerto Lumbreras, *Spain* . 33 H3
Puerto Madryn, *Argentina* 128 E3
Puerto Maldonado, *Peru* . 124 F5
Puerto Manotí, *Cuba* ... 120 B4
Puerto Mazarrón = Puerto
 de Mazarrón, *Spain* .. 33 H3
Puerto Montt, *Chile* 128 E2
Puerto Morelos, *Mexico* . 119 C7
Puerto Natales, *Chile* ... 128 G2
Puerto Padre, *Cuba* 120 B4
Puerto Páez, *Venezuela* . 124 B5
Puerto Peñasco, *Mexico* . 118 A2
Puerto Pinasco, *Paraguay* 126 A4
Puerto Plata, *Dom. Rep.* . 121 C5
Puerto Pollensa = Port de
 Pollença, *Spain* 37 B10
Puerto Princesa, *Phil.* ... 61 G3
Puerto Quepos, *Costa Rica* 120 E3
Puerto Real, *Spain* 35 J4
Puerto Rico, *Canary Is.* .. 37 G4
Puerto Rico ■, *W. Indies* . 121 C6
Puerto Rico Trench,
 Atl. Oc. 121 C6
Puerto San Julián,
 Argentina 128 F3
Puerto Sastre, *Paraguay* .. 126 A4
Puerto Serrano, *Spain* ... 35 J5
Puerto Suárez, *Bolivia* .. 124 G7
Puerto Vallarta, *Mexico* . 118 C3
Puerto Wilches, *Colombia* 124 B4
Puertollano, *Spain* 35 G6
Pueyrredón, L., *Argentina* 128 F2
Puffin I., *Ireland* 15 E1
Pugachev, *Russia* 48 D9
Puge, *China* 58 D4
Puge, *Tanzania* 86 C3
Puget Sound, *U.S.A.* ... 114 C2
Puget-Théniers, *France* . 21 E10
Púglia □, *Italy* 31 A9
Pugŏdong, *N. Korea* ... 57 C16
Pugu, *Tanzania* 86 D4
Pūgūnzī, *Iran* 71 E8
Pui, *Romania* 42 E8
Puiești, *Romania* 43 D12
Puig Major, *Spain* 37 B9
Puigcerdà, *Spain* 32 C6
Puigmal, *Spain* 32 C7
Puigpunyent, *Spain* 37 B9
Puisaye, Collines de la,
 France 19 E10
Puiseaux, *France* 19 D9
Pujols, *France* 20 D3
Pujon □, *N. Korea* 57 D14
Puka, *Albania* 40 D3
Pukaki L., *N.Z.* 91 L3
Pukapuka, *Cook Is.* 97 J11
Pukatawagan, *Canada* . 105 B8
Pukchin, *N. Korea* 57 D13
Pukch'ŏng, *N. Korea* .. 57 D15
Pukekohe, *N.Z.* 91 G5
Pukou, *China* 59 A12
Pula, *Croatia* 29 D10
Pula, *Italy* 30 C1
Pulacayo, *Bolivia* 124 H5
Pulaski, *N.Y., U.S.A.* .. 111 C8
Pulaski, *Tenn., U.S.A.* .. 109 H2
Pulaski, *Va., U.S.A.* ... 108 G5
Puławy, *Poland* 45 G8
Pulga, *U.S.A.* 116 F5
Pulicat, L., *India* 66 N12
Pullman, *U.S.A.* 114 C5
Pulog, *Phil.* 61 C4
Pułtusk, *Poland* 45 F8
Pülümür, *Turkey* 73 C8
Pumlumon Fawr, *U.K.* . 13 E4
Puná, I., *Ecuador* 124 D2
Punakha, *Bhutan* 67 F16
Punasar, *India* 68 F5
Punata, *Bolivia* 124 G5
Punch, *India* 69 C6
Pungsan, *N. Korea* 57 D15
Pungue, Ponte de, *Mozam.* 87 F3
Puning, *China* 59 F11
Punjab □, *India* 68 D7
Punjab □, *Pakistan* 68 E6
Puno, *Peru* 124 G4
Punta Alta, *Argentina* .. 128 D4
Punta Arenas, *Chile* ... 128 G2
Punta de Díaz, *Chile* ... 126 B1
Punta Gorda, *Belize* ... 119 D7
Punta Gorda, *U.S.A.* ... 109 M5
Punta Prieta, *Mexico* ... 118 B2
Punta Prima, *Spain* 37 B11
Punta Umbría, *Spain* ... 35 H4
Puntabie, *Australia* 95 E1
Puntarenas, *Costa Rica* . 120 E3
Punto Fijo, *Venezuela* .. 124 A4
Punxsatawney, *U.S.A.* .. 110 F6
Puqi, *China* 59 C9
Puquio, *Peru* 124 F4
Pur →, *Russia* 50 C8
Purace, Vol., *Colombia* . 124 C3
Puralia = Puruliya, *India* . 69 H12
Purbeck, Isle of, *U.K.* .. 13 G6
Purcell, *U.S.A.* 113 H6
Puri, *India* 67 K14
Purmerend, *Neths.* 17 B4
Purnia, *India* 69 G12
Pursat = Pouthisat,
 Cambodia 64 F4
Purukcahu, *Indonesia* .. 62 E4

Puruliya, *India* 69 H12
Purus →, *Brazil* 122 D4
Puruvesi, *Finland* 46 B5
Půrvomay, *Bulgaria* 41 D9
Purwakarta, *Indonesia* . 63 G12
Purwodadi, *Indonesia* .. 63 G14
Purwokerto, *Indonesia* . 63 G13
Puryŏng, *N. Korea* 57 C15
Pusan, *S. Korea* 57 G15
Pushkin, *Russia* 46 C6
Pushkino, *Moskva, Russia* 46 D9
Pushkino, *Saratov, Russia* 48 E8
Püspökladány, *Hungary* . 42 C6
Pustoshka, *Russia* 46 D5
Puszczykowo, *Poland* ... 45 F3
Putahow L., *Canada* ... 105 B8
Putao, *Burma* 67 F20
Putaruru, *N.Z.* 91 H5
Putbus, *Germany* 24 A9
Putein Myit →, *Burma* . 67 M19
Putian, *China* 59 E12
Putignano, *Italy* 31 B10
Puting, Tanjung, *Indonesia* 62 E4
Putlitz, *Germany* 24 B8
Putna, *Romania* 43 C10
Putna →, *Romania* 43 E12
Putnam, *U.S.A.* 111 E13
Putnok, *Hungary* 42 B5
Putorana, Gory, *Russia* . 51 C10
Puttalam, *Sri Lanka* ... 66 Q11
Puttgarden, *Germany* ... 24 A7
Putumayo →, *S. Amer.* . 122 D4
Putuo, *China* 59 C14
Putussibau, *Indonesia* .. 62 D4
Puy-de-Dôme, *France* .. 20 C6
Puy-de-Dôme □, *France* . 20 C7
Puy-l'Évêque, *France* .. 20 D5
Puyallup, *U.S.A.* 116 C4
Puyang, *China* 56 G8
Puylaurens, *France* 20 E6
Pũzeh Rĩg, *Iran* 71 E8
Pwani □, *Tanzania* 86 D4
Pweto,
 Dem. Rep. of the Congo 87 D2
Pwllheli, *U.K.* 12 E3
Pyana →, *Russia* 48 C8
Pyapon, *Burma* 67 L19
Pyasina →, *Russia* 51 B9
Pyatigorsk, *Russia* 49 H6
Pyatykhatky, *Ukraine* .. 47 H7
Pydna, *Greece* 40 F6
Pyè, *Burma* 67 K19
Pyetrikaw, *Belarus* 47 F5
Pyhäjoki, *Finland* 8 D21
Pyinmana, *Burma* 67 K20
Pyla, C., *Cyprus* 36 E12
Pyŏktong, *N. Korea* ... 57 D13
Pyŏnggang, *N. Korea* .. 57 E14
Pyŏngtaek, *S. Korea* ... 57 F14
P'yŏngyang, *N. Korea* .. 57 E13
Pyote, *U.S.A.* 113 K3
Pyramid L., *U.S.A.* 114 G4
Pyramid Pk., *U.S.A.* ... 117 J10
Pyramids, *Egypt* 80 J7
Pyrénées, *Europe* 20 F4
Pyrénées-Atlantiques □,
 France 20 E3
Pyrénées-Orientales □,
 France 20 F6
Pyryatyn, *Ukraine* 47 G7
Pyrzyce, *Poland* 45 E1
Pyskowice, *Poland* 45 H5
Pytalovo, *Russia* 46 D4
Pyu, *Burma* 67 K20
Pyzdry, *Poland* 45 F4

Q

Qaanaaq = Thule,
 Greenland 4 B4
Qabirri →, *Azerbaijan* ... 49 K8
Qachasnek, *S. Africa* ... 89 E4
Qa'el Jafr, *Jordan* 75 E5
Qa'emābād, *Iran* 71 D9
Qā'emshahr, *Iran* 71 B7
Qagan Nur, *China* 56 C8
Qahar Youyi Zhongqi,
 China 56 D7
Qahremānshahr =
 Bākhtarān, *Iran* 70 C5
Qaidam Pendi, *China* ... 60 C4
Qajarīyeh, *Iran* 71 D6
Qala, Ras il, *Malta* 36 C1
Qala-i-Jadid, *Afghan.* .. 68 D2
Qala Yangi, *Afghan.* 68 B2
Qal'at al Akḩḑar,
 Si. Arabia 70 E3
Qal'at Dīzah, *Iraq* 73 D11
Qal'eh Darreh, *Iran* 70 B5
Qal'eh Shaharak, *Afghan.* 66 B4
Qalyūb, *Egypt* 80 H7
Qamdo, *China* 58 B1
Qamruddin Karez, *Pakistan* 68 D3
Qandahār, *Afghan.* 66 D4
Qandahār □, *Afghan.* ... 66 D4
Qapān, *Iran* 71 B7
Qapshaghay, *Kazakstan* . 50 E8
Qaqortoq = Julianehåb,
 Greenland 4 C5
Qâra, *Egypt* 80 B2
Qara Qash →, *India* ... 69 B8
Qarabutaq, *Kazakstan* .. 50 E7

Qaraçala, *Azerbaijan* 49 L9
Qaraghandy, *Kazakstan* .. 50 E8
Qārah, *Si. Arabia* 70 D4
Qarataū, *Kazakstan* 50 E8
Qardud, *Sudan* 81 E2
Qareh →, *Iran* 70 B5
Qareh Tekān, *Iran* 71 B6
Qarqan, *China* 60 C3
Qarqan He →, *China* 60 C3
Qarqaraly, *Kazakstan* 50 E8
Qarrasa, *Sudan* 81 E3
Qarshi, *Uzbekistan* 50 F7
Qartabā, *Lebanon* 75 A4
Qaryat al Gharab, *Iraq* ... 70 D5
Qaryat al 'Ulyā, *Si. Arabia* 70 E5
Qasr 'Amra, *Jordan* 70 D3
Qaṣr-e Qand, *Iran* 71 E9
Qasr Farâfra, *Egypt* 80 B2
Qatanā, *Syria* 75 B5
Qatar ■, *Asia* 71 E6
Qatlīsh, *Iran* 71 B8
Qattâra, *Egypt* 80 A2
Qattâra, Munkhafed el, *Egypt* 80 B2
Qattâra Depression = Qattâra, Munkhafed el, *Egypt* 80 B2
Qawām al Ḥamzah, *Iraq* .. 70 D5
Qāyen, *Iran* 71 C8
Qazaqstan = Kazakstan ■, *Asia* 50 E8
Qazimämmäd, *Azerbaijan* . 49 K9
Qazvin, *Iran* 71 B6
Qena, *Egypt* 80 B3
Qena, W. →, *Egypt* 80 B3
Qeqertarsuaq = Disko, *Greenland* 4 C5
Qeqertarsuaq = Godhavn, *Greenland* 4 C5
Qeshlāq, *Iran* 70 C5
Qeshm, *Iran* 71 E8
Qezi'ot, *Israel* 75 E3
Qi Xian, *China* 56 G8
Qian Gorlos, *China* 57 B13
Qian Xian, *China* 56 G5
Qiancheng, *China* 58 D7
Qianjiang, *Guangxi Zhuangzu, China* 58 F7
Qianjiang, *Hubei, China* .. 59 B9
Qianjiang, *Sichuan, China* 58 C7
Qianshan, *China* 59 B11
Qianwei, *China* 58 C4
Qianxi, *China* 58 D6
Qianyang, *China* 59 D8
Qianyang, *Shaanxi, China* 56 G4
Qianyang, *Zhejiang, China* 59 B12
Qiaojia, *China* 58 D4
Qibā', *Si. Arabia* 70 E5
Qichun, *China* 59 B10
Qidong, *Hunan, China* ... 59 D9
Qidong, *Jiangsu, China* .. 59 B13
Qijiang, *China* 58 C6
Qila Safed, *Pakistan* 66 E2
Qila Saifullāh, *Pakistan* .. 68 D3
Qilian Shan, *China* 60 C4
Qimen, *China* 59 C11
Qin He →, *China* 56 G7
Qin Jiang →, *China* 59 D10
Qin Ling = Qinling Shandi, *China* 56 H5
Qin'an, *China* 56 G3
Qing Xian, *China* 56 E9
Qingcheng, *China* 57 F9
Qingdao, *China* 57 F11
Qingfeng, *China* 56 G8
Qinghai □, *China* 60 C4
Qinghai Hu, *China* 60 C5
Qinghecheng, *China* 57 D13
Qinghemen, *China* 57 D11
Qingjian, *China* 56 F6
Qingjiang, *Jiangsu, China* 57 H10
Qingjiang, *Jiangxi, China* . 59 C10
Qingliu, *China* 59 D11
Qinglong, *China* 58 E5
Qingping, *China* 58 D6
Qingpu, *China* 59 B13
Qingshui, *China* 56 G4
Qingshuihe, *China* 56 E6
Qingtian, *China* 59 C13
Qingtongxia Shuiku, *China* 56 F3
Qingxi, *China* 58 D7
Qingxu, *China* 56 F7
Qingyang, *Anhui, China* .. 59 B11
Qingyang, *Gansu, China* .. 56 F4
Qingyi Jiang →, *China* ... 58 C4
Qingyuan, *Guangdong, China* 59 F9
Qingyuan, *Liaoning, China* 57 C13
Qingyuan, *Zhejiang, China* 59 D12
Qingyun, *China* 57 F9
Qingzhen, *China* 58 D6
Qinhuangdao, *China* 57 E10
Qinling Shandi, *China* 56 H5
Qinshui, *China* 56 G7
Qinyang, *China* 56 G7
Qinyuan, *China* 56 F7
Qinzhou, *China* 64 C8
Qionghai, *China* 64 C8
Qionglai, *China* 58 B4
Qionglai Shan, *China* 58 B4
Qiongzhou Haixia, *China* . 64 B8
Qiqihar, *China* 60 B7
Qiraîya, W. →, *Egypt* 75 E3
Qiryat Ata, *Israel* 75 C4
Qiryat Gat, *Israel* 75 D3
Qiryat Mal'akhi, *Israel* ... 75 D3

Qiryat Shemona, *Israel* ... 75 B4
Qiryat Yam, *Israel* 75 C4
Qishan, *China* 56 G4
Qitai, *China* 60 B3
Qiubei, *China* 58 E5
Qiyang, *China* 59 D8
Qızılağac Körfäzi, *Azerbaijan* 73 C13
Qojūr, *Iran* 70 B5
Qom, *Iran* 71 C6
Qomsheh, *Iran* 71 D6
Qorveh, *Iran* 73 E12
Qostanay, *Kazakstan* 50 D7
Qotūr, *Iran* 73 C11
Qu Jiang →, *China* 58 B6
Qu Xian, *Sichuan, China* . 58 B6
Qu Xian, *Zhejiang, China* 59 C12
Quairading, *Australia* 93 F2
Quakenbrück, *Germany* .. 24 C3
Quakertown, *U.S.A.* 111 F9
Qualeup, *Australia* 93 F2
Quambatook, *Australia* ... 95 F3
Quambone, *Australia* 95 E4
Quamby, *Australia* 94 C3
Quan Long = Ca Mau, *Vietnam* 65 H5
Quanah, *U.S.A.* 113 H5
Quandialla, *Australia* 95 E4
Quang Ngai, *Vietnam* 64 E7
Quang Tri, *Vietnam* 64 D6
Quang Yen, *Vietnam* 64 B6
Quannan, *China* 59 E10
Quanzhou, *Fujian, China* . 59 E12
Quanzhou, *Guangxi Zhuangzu, China* 59 E8
Quaqtaq, *Canada* 101 B13
Quaraí, *Brazil* 126 C4
Quarré-les-Tombes, *France* 19 E11
Quarteira, *Portugal* 35 H2
Quartu Sant'Élena, *Italy* .. 30 C2
Quartzsite, *U.S.A.* 117 M12
Quatsino, *Canada* 104 C3
Quatsino Sd., *Canada* ... 104 C3
Quba, *Azerbaijan* 49 K9
Qūchān, *Iran* 71 B8
Queanbeyan, *Australia* ... 95 F4
Québec, *Canada* 103 C5
Québec □, *Canada* 103 C6
Quedlinburg, *Germany* .. 24 D7
Queen Alexandra Ra., *Antarctica* 5 E11
Queen Charlotte, *Canada* . 104 C2
Queen Charlotte Is., *Canada* 104 C2
Queen Charlotte Sd., *Canada* 104 C3
Queen Elizabeth Is., *Canada* 98 B10
Queen Elizabeth Nat. Park, *Uganda* 86 C3
Queen Mary Land, *Antarctica* 5 D7
Queen Maud G., *Canada* . 100 B9
Queen Maud Land, *Antarctica* 5 D3
Queen Maud Mts., *Antarctica* 5 E13
Queens Chan., *Australia* .. 92 C4
Queenscliff, *Australia* 95 F3
Queensland □, *Australia* . 94 C3
Queenstown, *Australia* ... 94 G4
Queenstown, *N.Z.* 91 L2
Queenstown, *S. Africa* ... 88 E4
Queets, *U.S.A.* 116 C2
Queguay Grande →, *Uruguay* 126 C4
Queimadas, *Brazil* 125 F11
Quelimane, *Mozam.* 87 F4
Quellón, *Chile* 128 E2
Quelpart = Cheju Do, *S. Korea* 57 H14
Queluz, *Portugal* 35 G1
Quemado, *N. Mex., U.S.A.* 115 J9
Quemado, *Tex., U.S.A.* .. 113 L4
Quemoy = Chinmen, *Taiwan* 59 E13
Quemú-Quemú, *Argentina* 126 D3
Quequén, *Argentina* 126 D4
Querétaro, *Mexico* 118 C4
Querétaro □, *Mexico* 118 C5
Querfurt, *Germany* 24 D7
Quérigut, *France* 20 F6
Querqueville, *France* 18 C5
Quesada, *Spain* 35 H7
Queshan, *China* 56 H8
Quesnel, *Canada* 104 C4
Quesnel →, *Canada* 104 C4
Quesnel L., *Canada* 104 C4
Questa, *U.S.A.* 115 H11
Questembert, *France* 18 E4
Quetico Prov. Park, *Canada* 102 C1
Quetta, *Pakistan* 68 D2
Quezaltenango, *Guatemala* 120 D1
Quezon City, *Phil.* 61 D4
Qufār, *Si. Arabia* 70 E4
Qui Nhon, *Vietnam* 64 F7
Quibaxe, *Angola* 84 F2
Quibdo, *Colombia* 124 B3
Quiberon, *France* 18 E3
Quiberon, Presqu'île de, *France* 18 E3
Quick, *Canada* 104 C3
Quickborn, *Germany* 24 B5

Quiet L., *Canada* 104 A2
Quiindy, *Paraguay* 126 B4
Quila, *Mexico* 118 C3
Quilán, C., *Chile* 128 E2
Quilcene, *U.S.A.* 116 C4
Quilimarí, *Chile* 126 C1
Quilino, *Argentina* 126 C3
Quillabamba, *Peru* 124 F4
Quillagua, *Chile* 126 A2
Quillaicillo, *Chile* 126 C1
Quillan, *France* 20 F6
Quillota, *Chile* 126 C1
Quilmes, *Argentina* 126 C4
Quilon, *India* 66 Q10
Quilpie, *Australia* 95 D3
Quilpué, *Chile* 126 C1
Quilua, *Mozam.* 87 F4
Quimilí, *Argentina* 126 B3
Quimper, *France* 18 E2
Quimperlé, *France* 18 E3
Quinault →, *U.S.A.* 116 C2
Quincy, *Calif., U.S.A.* ... 116 F6
Quincy, *Fla., U.S.A.* 109 K3
Quincy, *Ill., U.S.A.* 112 F9
Quincy, *Mass., U.S.A.* ... 111 D14
Quincy, *Wash., U.S.A.* .. 114 C4
Quines, *Argentina* 126 C2
Quinga, *Mozam.* 87 F5
Quingey, *France* 19 E12
Quintana de la Serena, *Spain* 35 G5
Quintana Roo □, *Mexico* . 119 D7
Quintanar de la Orden, *Spain* 35 F7
Quintanar de la Sierra, *Spain* 32 D2
Quintanar del Rey, *Spain* . 33 F3
Quintero, *Chile* 126 C1
Quintin, *France* 18 D4
Quinto, *Spain* 32 D4
Quinyambie, *Australia* ... 95 E3
Quípar →, *Spain* 33 G3
Quirihue, *Chile* 126 D1
Quirindi, *Australia* 95 E5
Quirinópolis, *Brazil* 125 G8
Quiroga, *Spain* 34 C3
Quissac, *France* 21 E8
Quissanga, *Mozam.* 87 E5
Quitilipi, *Argentina* 126 B3
Quitman, *Ga., U.S.A.* ... 109 K4
Quitman, *Miss., U.S.A.* .. 109 J1
Quitman, *Tex., U.S.A.* ... 113 J7
Quito, *Ecuador* 124 D3
Quixadá, *Brazil* 125 D11
Quixaxe, *Mozam.* 87 F5
Qujing, *China* 58 E4
Qul'ân, Jazâ'ir, *Egypt* ... 80 C4
Qumbu, *S. Africa* 89 E4
Quneitra, *Syria* 75 B4
Qünghirot, *Uzbekistan* .. 50 E6
Quoin I., *Australia* 92 B4
Quoin Pt., *S. Africa* 88 E2
Quondong, *Australia* 95 E3
Quorn, *Australia* 95 E2
Qüqon, *Uzbekistan* 50 E8
Qurein, *Sudan* 81 E3
Qurnat as Sawdā', *Lebanon* 75 A5
Qûs, *Egypt* 80 B3
Qusar, *Azerbaijan* 49 K9
Qusaybah, *Iraq* 70 C4
Quseir, *Egypt* 80 B3
Qūshchī, *Iran* 70 B5
Quthing, *Lesotho* 89 E4
Qūṭīābād, *Iran* 71 C6
Quwo, *China* 56 G6
Quyang, *China* 56 E8
Quynh Nhai, *Vietnam* ... 64 B4
Quzi, *China* 56 F4
Qvareli, *Georgia* 49 K7
Qytet Stalin = Kuçovë, *Albania* 40 F3
Qyzylorda, *Kazakstan* 50 E7

R

Ra, Ko, *Thailand* 65 H2
Raab, *Austria* 26 C6
Raahe, *Finland* 8 D21
Raalte, *Neths.* 17 B6
Raasay, *U.K.* 14 D2
Raasay, Sd. of, *U.K.* 14 D2
Rab, *Croatia* 29 D11
Raba, *Indonesia* 63 F5
Rába →, *Hungary* 42 C2
Raba →, *Poland* 45 H7
Rabaçal →, *Portugal* ... 34 D3
Rabah, *Nigeria* 83 C6
Rabai, *Kenya* 86 C4
Rabastens, *France* 20 E5
Rabastens-de-Bigorre, *France* 20 E4
Rabat, *Malta* 36 D1
Rabat, *Morocco* 78 B4
Rabaul, *Papua N. G.* 96 H7
Rabbit →, *Canada* 104 B3
Rabbit Lake, *Canada* 105 C7
Rabbitskin →, *Canada* .. 104 A4
Rabka, *Poland* 45 J6
Rābor, *Iran* 71 D8
Râbniţa, *Moldova* 43 C14
Rača, *Serbia, Yug.* 40 B4
Răcăciuni, *Romania* 43 D11
Răcăşdia, *Romania* 42 F6
Racconigi, *Italy* 28 D4

Race, C., *Canada* 103 C9
Rach Gia, *Vietnam* 65 G5
Raciąż, *Poland* 45 F7
Racibórz, *Poland* 45 H5
Racine, *U.S.A.* 108 D2
Rackerby, *U.S.A.* 116 F5
Radama, Nosy, *Madag.* .. 89 A8
Radama, Saikanosy, *Madag.* 89 A8
Radan, *Serbia, Yug.* 40 D5
Rădăuți, *Romania* 43 C10
Rădăuți-Prut, *Romania* .. 43 B11
Radbuza →, *Czech Rep.* . 26 B6
Radebeul, *Germany* 24 D9
Radeburg, *Germany* 24 D9
Radeče, *Slovenia* 29 B12
Radekhiv, *Ukraine* 47 G3
Radekhov = Radekhiv, *Ukraine* 47 G3
Radenthein, *Austria* 26 E6
Radew →, *Poland* 44 D2
Radford, *U.S.A.* 108 G5
Radhanpur, *India* 68 H4
Radika →, *Macedonia* .. 40 E4
Radisson, *Canada* 105 C7
Radium Hot Springs, *Canada* 104 C5
Radlje ob Dravi, *Slovenia* . 29 B12
Radnevo, *Bulgaria* 41 D9
Radnice, *Czech Rep.* 26 B6
Radnor Forest, *U.K.* 13 E4
Radolfzell, *Germany* 25 H4
Radom, *Poland* 45 G8
Radom □, *Poland* 45 G8
Radomir, *Bulgaria* 40 D7
Radomka →, *Poland* ... 45 G8
Radomsko, *Poland* 45 G6
Radomyśl, *Ukraine* 47 G5
Radomyśl Wielki, *Poland* . 45 H8
Radoszyce, *Poland* 45 G7
Radoviš, *Macedonia* 40 E6
Radovljica, *Slovenia* ... 29 B11
Radstadt, *Austria* 26 D6
Radstock, C., *Australia* .. 95 E1
Răducăneni, *Romania* ... 43 D12
Raduša, *Serbia, Yug.* ... 40 D5
Radviliškis, *Lithuania* .. 9 J20
Radville, *Canada* 105 D8
Radymno, *Poland* 45 J9
Radzanów, *Poland* 45 F7
Radziejów, *Poland* 45 F5
Radzyń Chełmiński, *Poland* 45 E5
Radzyń Podlaski, *Poland* . 45 G9
Rae, *Canada* 104 A5
Rae Bareli, *India* 69 F9
Rae Isthmus, *Canada* ... 101 B11
Raeren, *Germany* 17 D6
Raeside, L., *Australia* ... 93 E3
Raetihi, *N.Z.* 91 H5
Rafaela, *Argentina* 126 C3
Rafah, *Gaza Strip* 75 D3
Rafai, *C.A.R.* 86 B1
Raffadali, *Italy* 30 E6
Rafḥā, *Si. Arabia* 70 D4
Rafsanjān, *Iran* 71 D8
Raft Pt., *Australia* 92 C3
Ragachow, *Belarus* 47 F6
Ragag, *Sudan* 81 E1
Ragama, *Sri Lanka* 66 R11
Ragged, Mt., *Australia* .. 93 F3
Raglan, *Australia* 94 C5
Raglan, *N.Z.* 91 G5
Ragusa, *Italy* 31 F7
Raha, *Indonesia* 63 E6
Rahad, Nahr ed →, *Sudan* 81 E3
Rahaeng = Tak, *Thailand* 64 D2
Rahden, *Germany* 24 C4
Raheita, *Eritrea* 81 E5
Raḥīmah, *Si. Arabia* 71 E6
Rahimyar Khan, *Pakistan* . 68 E4
Rāhjerd, *Iran* 71 C6
Raichur, *India* 66 L10
Raiganj, *India* 69 G13
Raigarh, *India* 67 J13
Raijua, *Indonesia* 63 F6
Railton, *Australia* 94 G4
Rainbow Lake, *Canada* .. 104 B5
Rainier, *U.S.A.* 116 D4
Rainier, Mt., *U.S.A.* 116 D5
Rainy L., *Canada* 105 D10
Rainy River, *Canada* 105 D10
Raippaluoto, *Finland* ... 8 E19
Raipur, *India* 67 J12
Raisio, *Finland* 9 F20
Raj Nandgaon, *India* ... 67 J12
Raja, Ujung, *Indonesia* . 62 D1
Raja Ampat, Kepulauan, *Indonesia* 63 E8
Rajahmundry, *India* 67 L12
Rajang →, *Malaysia* 62 D4
Rajapalaiyam, *India* 66 Q10
Rajasthan □, *India* 68 F5
Rajasthan Canal, *India* .. 68 F5
Rajauri, *India* 69 C6
Rajgarh, *Mad. P., India* . 68 G7
Rajgarh, *Raj., India* 68 E6
Rajgród, *Poland* 44 E9
Rajkot, *India* 68 H4
Rajmahal Hills, *India* ... 69 G12
Rajpipla, *India* 66 J8
Rajpura, *India* 68 D7
Rajshahi, *India* 69 G13
Rajshahi □, *Bangla.* 69 G13

Rakata, Pulau, *Indonesia* . 62 F3
Rakhiv, *Ukraine* 47 H3
Rakhni, *Pakistan* 68 D3
Rakitnoye, *Russia* 54 B7
Rakitovo, *Bulgaria* 41 E8
Rakoniewice, *Poland* ... 45 F3
Rakops, *Botswana* 88 C3
Rakovica, *Croatia* 29 D12
Rakovník, *Czech Rep.* ... 26 A6
Rakovski, *Bulgaria* 41 D8
Rakvere, *Estonia* 9 G22
Raleigh, *U.S.A.* 109 H6
Raleigh B., *U.S.A.* 109 H7
Ralja, *Serbia, Yug.* 40 B4
Ralls, *U.S.A.* 113 J4
Ram →, *Canada* 104 A4
Rām Allāh, *West Bank* ... 75 D4
Ram Hd., *Australia* 95 F4
Rama, *Nic.* 120 D3
Ramacca, *Italy* 31 E7
Ramales de la Victoria, *Spain* 34 B7
Raman, *Thailand* 65 J3
Ramanathapuram, *India* . 66 Q11
Ramanetaka, B. de, *Madag.* 89 A8
Ramat Gan, *Israel* 75 C3
Ramatlhabama, *S. Africa* . 88 D4
Ramban, *India* 69 C6
Rambervillers, *France* .. 19 D13
Rambipuji, *Indonesia* ... 63 H15
Rambouillet, *France* 19 D8
Ramea, *Canada* 103 C8
Ramechhap, *Nepal* 69 F12
Ramenskoye, *Russia* ... 46 E10
Ramgarh, *Bihar, India* .. 69 H11
Ramgarh, *Raj., India* ... 68 F6
Ramgarh, *Raj., India* ... 68 F4
Rāmhormoz, *Iran* 71 D6
Ramīān, *Iran* 71 B7
Ramingining, *Australia* . 94 A2
Ramla, *Israel* 75 D3
Ramlu, *Eritrea* 81 E5
Râmna →, *Romania* ... 43 E12
Ramnad = Ramanathapuram, *India* 66 Q11
Ramnagar, *India* 69 C6
Ramnäs, *Sweden* 10 E10
Râmnicu Sărat, *Romania* . 43 E12
Râmnicu Vâlcea, *Romania* 43 E9
Ramon, *Russia* 47 G10
Ramona, *U.S.A.* 117 M10
Ramonville-St-Agne, *France* 20 E5
Ramore, *Canada* 102 C3
Ramotswa, *Botswana* .. 88 C4
Rampur, *H.P., India* 68 D7
Rampur, *Mad. P., India* . 68 H5
Rampur, *Ut. P., India* ... 69 E8
Rampur Hat, *India* 69 G12
Rampura, *India* 68 G6
Ramree I. = Ramree Kyun, *Burma* 67 K19
Ramree Kyun, *Burma* ... 67 K19
Rāmsar, *Iran* 71 B6
Ramsey, *Canada* 102 C3
Ramsey, *U.K.* 12 C3
Ramsgate, *U.K.* 13 F9
Ramsjö, *Sweden* 10 B9
Ramstein, *Germany* 25 F3
Ramtek, *India* 66 J11
Ramvik, *Sweden* 10 B11
Ranaghat, *India* 69 H13
Ranahu, *Pakistan* 68 G3
Ranau, *Malaysia* 62 C5
Rancagua, *Chile* 126 C1
Rance →, *France* 18 D5
Rancheria →, *Canada* .. 104 A3
Ranchester, *U.S.A.* 114 D10
Ranchi, *India* 69 H11
Rancho Cucamonga, *U.S.A.* 117 L9
Randalstown, *U.K.* 15 B5
Randan, *France* 19 F10
Randazzo, *Italy* 31 E7
Randers, *Denmark* 11 H4
Randers Fjord, *Denmark* . 11 H4
Randfontein, *S. Africa* .. 89 D4
Randle, *U.S.A.* 116 D5
Randolph, *Mass., U.S.A.* . 111 D13
Randolph, *N.Y., U.S.A.* . 110 D6
Randolph, *Utah, U.S.A.* . 114 F8
Randolph, *Vt., U.S.A.* ... 111 C12
Råne älv →, *Sweden* ... 8 D20
Rangae, *Thailand* 65 J3
Rangaunu B., *N.Z.* 91 F4
Rangely, *U.S.A.* 114 F9
Ranger, *U.S.A.* 113 J5
Rangia, *India* 67 F17
Rangiora, *N.Z.* 91 K4
Rangitaiki →, *N.Z.* 91 G6
Rangitata →, *N.Z.* 91 K3
Rangkasbitung, *Indonesia* 63 G12
Rangon →, *Burma* 67 L20
Rangoon, *Burma* 67 L20
Rangpur, *Bangla.* 67 G16
Rangsit, *Thailand* 64 F3
Ranibennur, *India* 66 M9
Raniganj, *India* 69 H12
Ranikhet, *India* 69 E8
Raniwara, *India* 66 G8
Rāniyah, *Iraq* 70 B5
Ranken →, *Australia* ... 94 C2
Rankin, *U.S.A.* 113 K4
Rankin Inlet, *Canada* ... 100 B10
Rankins Springs, *Australia* 95 E4
Rankweil, *Austria* 26 D2

Rannoch, L., *U.K.* 14 E4
Rannoch Moor, *U.K.* 14 E4
Ranobe, Helodranon' i,
  Madag. 89 C7
Ranohira, *Madag.* 89 C8
Ranomafana, *Toamasina,*
  Madag. 89 B8
Ranomafana, *Toliara,*
  Madag. 89 C8
Ranong, *Thailand* 65 H2
Rānsa, *Iran* 71 C6
Ransiki, *Indonesia* 63 E8
Rantauprapat, *Indonesia* .. 62 D1
Rantemario, *Indonesia* 63 E5
Rantoul, *U.S.A.* 108 E1
Ranum, *Denmark* 11 H3
Raoᴜ l'Étape, *France* 19 D13
Raoyang, *China* 56 E8
Rapa, *Pac. Oc.* 97 K13
Rapallo, *Italy* 28 D6
Rāpch, *Iran* 71 E8
Rapid →, *Canada* 104 B3
Rapid City, *U.S.A.* 112 D3
Rapid River, *U.S.A.* 108 C2
Rapides des Joachims,
  Canada 102 C4
Rapla, *Estonia* 9 G21
Rapu Rapu I., *Phil.* 61 E6
Rarotonga, *Cook Is.* 97 K12
Ra's al 'Ayn, *Syria* 70 B4
Ra's al Khaymah, *U.A.E.* . 71 E8
Ra's an Naqb, *Jordan* 75 F4
Ras Dashen, *Ethiopia* 81 E4
Râs Ghârib, *Egypt* 80 J8
Ras Mallap, *Egypt* 80 J8
Râs Timirist, *Mauritania* .. 82 B1
Rasca, Pta. de la,
  Canary Is. 37 G3
Răşcani, *Moldova* 43 C12
Raseiniai, *Lithuania* 9 J20
Rashad, *Sudan* 81 E3
Rashîd, *Egypt* 80 H7
Rashîd, Masabb, *Egypt* ... 80 H7
Rasht, *Iran* 71 B6
Rasi Salai, *Thailand* 64 E5
Raška, *Serbia, Yug.* 40 C4
Râsnov, *Romania* 43 E10
Rason L., *Australia* 93 E3
Raşova, *Romania* 43 F12
Rasovo, *Bulgaria* 40 C7
Rasra, *India* 69 G10
Rasskazovo, *Russia* 48 D5
Rast, *Romania* 43 G8
Rastatt, *Germany* 25 G4
Rastede, *Germany* 24 B4
Răstoliţa, *Romania* 43 D9
Raszków, *Poland* 45 G4
Rat Buri, *Thailand* 64 F2
Rat Islands, *U.S.A.* 100 C1
Rat River, *Canada* 104 A6
Ratangarh, *India* 68 E6
Rätansbyn, *Sweden* 10 B8
Raţāwī, *Iraq* 70 D5
Rath, *India* 69 G8
Rath Luirc, *Ireland* 15 D3
Rathdrum, *Ireland* 15 D5
Rathenow, *Germany* 24 C8
Rathkeale, *Ireland* 15 D3
Rathlin I., *U.K.* 15 A5
Rathmelton, *Ireland* 15 A4
Ratibor = Racibórz,
  Poland 45 H5
Rätikon, *Austria* 26 D2
Ratingen, *Germany* 24 D2
Ratlam, *India* 68 H6
Ratnagiri, *India* 66 L8
Raton, *U.S.A.* 113 G2
Rattaphum, *Thailand* 65 J3
Ratten, *Austria* 26 D8
Rattray Hd., *U.K.* 14 D7
Rättvik, *Sweden* 10 D9
Ratz, Mt., *Canada* 104 B2
Ratzeburg, *Germany* 24 B6
Raub, *Malaysia* 65 L3
Rauch, *Argentina* 126 D4
Raufarhöfn, *Iceland* 8 C6
Raufoss, *Norway* 9 F14
Raukumara Ra., *N.Z.* 91 H6
Rauma, *Finland* 9 F19
Raurkela, *India* 69 H11
Rausu-Dake, *Japan* 54 B12
Răut →, *Moldova* 43 C14
Rava-Ruska, *Poland* 47 G2
Rava Russkaya = Rava-
  Ruska, *Poland* 47 G2
Ravänsar, *Iran* 70 C5
Ravanusa, *Italy* 30 E6
Rāvar, *Iran* 71 D8
Ravena, *U.S.A.* 111 D11
Ravenna, *Italy* 29 D9
Ravenna, *Nebr., U.S.A.* .. 112 E5
Ravenna, *Ohio, U.S.A.* ... 110 E3
Ravensburg, *Germany* 25 E5
Ravenshoe, *Australia* 94 B4
Ravensthorpe, *Australia* .. 93 F3
Ravenswood, *Australia* ... 94 C4
Ravenswood, *U.S.A.* 108 F5
Ravi →, *Pakistan* 68 D4
Ravna Gora, *Croatia* 29 C11
Ravna Reka, *Serbia, Yug.* . 40 B5
Ravne na Koroškem,
  Slovenia 29 B11
Rawa Mazowiecka, *Poland* . 45 G7
Rawāndūz, *Iraq* 70 B5
Rawang, *Malaysia* 65 L3
Rawdon, *Canada* 102 C5

Rawene, *N.Z.* 91 F4
Rawicz, *Poland* 45 G3
Rawka →, *Poland* 45 F7
Rawlinna, *Australia* 93 F4
Rawlins, *U.S.A.* 114 F10
Rawlinson Ra., *Australia* .. 93 D4
Rawson, *Argentina* 128 E3
Ray, *U.S.A.* 112 A3
Ray, C., *Canada* 103 C8
Rayadurg, *India* 66 M10
Rayagada, *India* 67 K13
Raychikhinsk, *Russia* 51 E13
Rāyen, *Iran* 71 D8
Rayleigh, *U.K.* 13 F8
Raymond, *Canada* 104 D6
Raymond, *Calif., U.S.A.* .. 116 H7
Raymond, *Wash., U.S.A.* . 116 D3
Raymondville, *U.S.A.* 113 M6
Raymore, *Canada* 105 C8
Rayne, *U.S.A.* 113 K8
Rayón, *Mexico* 118 B2
Rayong, *Thailand* 64 F3
Rayville, *U.S.A.* 113 J9
Raz, Pte. du, *France* 18 D2
Razan, *Iran* 71 C6
Ražana, *Serbia, Yug.* 40 B3
Ražanj, *Serbia, Yug.* 40 C5
Razdelna, *Bulgaria* 41 C11
Razdel'naya = Rozdilna,
  Ukraine 47 J6
Razdolnoye, *Russia* 54 C5
Razdolnoye, *Ukraine* 47 K7
Razeh, *Iran* 71 C6
Razgrad, *Bulgaria* 41 C10
Razim, Lacul, *Romania* .. 43 F14
Razlog, *Bulgaria* 40 E7
Razmak, *Pakistan* 68 C3
Ré, Î. de, *France* 20 B2
Reading, *U.K.* 13 F7
Reading, *U.S.A.* 111 F9
Reading □, *U.K.* 13 F7
Realicó, *Argentina* 126 D3
Réalmont, *France* 20 E6
Ream, *Cambodia* 65 G4
Reata, *Mexico* 118 B4
Rebais, *France* 19 D10
Rebecca, L., *Australia* ... 93 F3
Rebi, *Indonesia* 63 F8
Rebiana, *Libya* 79 D10
Rebun-Tō, *Japan* 54 B10
Recanati, *Italy* 29 E10
Recaş, *Romania* 42 E6
Recco, *Italy* 28 D6
Recherche, Arch. of the,
  Australia 93 F3
Rechytsa, *Belarus* 47 F6
Recife, *Brazil* 125 E12
Recklinghausen, *Germany* . 24 D3
Reconquista, *Argentina* .. 126 B4
Recreo, *Argentina* 126 B2
Recz, *Poland* 44 E2
Red →, *La., U.S.A.* 113 K9
Red →, *N. Dak., U.S.A.* . 112 A6
Red Bank, *U.S.A.* 111 F10
Red Bay, *Canada* 103 B8
Red Bluff, *U.S.A.* 114 F2
Red Bluff L., *U.S.A.* 113 K3
Red Cliffs, *Australia* 95 E3
Red Cloud, *U.S.A.* 112 E5
Red Deer, *Canada* 104 C6
Red Deer →, *Alta.,*
  Canada 105 C7
Red Deer →, *Man.,*
  Canada 105 C8
Red Deer L., *Canada* 105 C8
Red Indian L., *Canada* ... 103 C8
Red Lake, *Canada* 105 C10
Red Lake Falls, *U.S.A.* .. 112 B6
Red Lodge, *U.S.A.* 114 D9
Red Mountain, *U.S.A.* ... 117 K9
Red Oak, *U.S.A.* 112 E7
Red Rock, *Canada* 102 C2
Red Rock, L., *U.S.A.* 112 E8
Red Rocks Pt., *Australia* . 93 F4
Red Sea, *Asia* 74 C2
Red Slate Mt., *U.S.A.* ... 116 H8
Red Sucker L., *Canada* ... 105 C10
Red Tower Pass = Turnu
  Roşu, P., *Romania* ... 43 E9
Red Wing, *U.S.A.* 112 C8
Reda, *Poland* 44 D5
Redange, *Lux.* 17 E5
Redcar, *U.K.* 12 C6
Redcar & Cleveland □,
  U.K. 12 C7
Redcliff, *Canada* 105 C6
Redcliffe, *Australia* 95 D5
Redcliffe, Mt., *Australia* .. 93 E3
Reddersburg, *S. Africa* ... 88 D4
Redding, *U.S.A.* 114 F2
Redditch, *U.K.* 13 E6
Redfield, *U.S.A.* 112 C5
Redkino, *Russia* 46 D9
Redknife →, *Canada* 104 A5
Redlands, *U.S.A.* 117 M9
Redmond, *Australia* 93 F2
Redmond, *Oreg., U.S.A.* . 114 D3
Redmond, *Wash., U.S.A.* . 116 C4
Redon, *France* 18 E4
Redonda, *Antigua* 121 C7
Redondela, *Spain* 34 C2
Redondo, *Portugal* 35 G3
Redondo Beach, *U.S.A.* .. 117 M8
Redrock Pt., *Canada* 104 A5
Redruth, *U.K.* 13 G2
Redvers, *Canada* 105 D8

Redwater, *Canada* 104 C6
Redwood, *U.S.A.* 111 B9
Redwood City, *U.S.A.* ... 116 H4
Redwood Falls, *U.S.A.* ... 112 C7
Ree, L., *Ireland* 15 C3
Reed, L., *Canada* 105 C8
Reed City, *U.S.A.* 108 D3
Reeder, *U.S.A.* 112 B3
Reedley, *U.S.A.* 116 J7
Reedsburg, *U.S.A.* 112 D9
Reedsport, *U.S.A.* 114 E1
Reefton, *N.Z.* 91 K3
Rees, *Germany* 24 D2
Refahiye, *Turkey* 73 C8
Reftele, *Sweden* 11 G7
Refugio, *U.S.A.* 113 L6
Rega →, *Poland* 44 D2
Regalbuto, *Italy* 31 E7
Regen, *Germany* 25 G9
Regen →, *Germany* 25 F8
Regensburg, *Germany* 25 F8
Regenstauf, *Germany* 25 F8
Reggello, *Italy* 29 E8
Réggio di Calábria, *Italy* .. 31 D8
Réggio nell'Emília, *Italy* .. 28 D7
Reghin, *Romania* 43 D9
Regina, *Canada* 105 C8
Registro, *Brazil* 127 A6
Reguengos de Monsaraz,
  Portugal 35 G3
Rehar →, *India* 69 H10
Rehoboth, *Namibia* 88 C2
Rehovot, *Israel* 75 D3
Reichenbach, *Germany* ... 24 E8
Reid, *Australia* 93 F4
Reid River, *Australia* 94 B4
Reidsville, *U.S.A.* 109 G6
Reigate, *U.K.* 13 F7
Reillo, *Spain* 32 F3
Reims, *France* 19 C11
Reina Adelaida, Arch.,
  Chile 128 G2
Reinbeck, *U.S.A.* 112 D8
Reinbek, *Germany* 24 B6
Reindeer →, *Canada* 105 B8
Reindeer I., *Canada* 105 C9
Reindeer L., *Canada* 105 B8
Reinga, C., *N.Z.* 91 F4
Reinosa, *Spain* 34 B6
Reitz, *S. Africa* 89 D4
Reivilo, *S. Africa* 88 D3
Rejmyre, *Sweden* 11 F9
Rejowiec Fabryczny,
  Poland 45 G10
Reka →, *Slovenia* 29 C11
Rekovac, *Serbia, Yug.* ... 40 C5
Reliance, *Canada* 105 A7
Rémalard, *France* 18 D7
Remarkable, Mt., *Australia* 95 E2
Rembang, *Indonesia* 63 G14
Remedios, *Panama* 120 E3
Remeshk, *Iran* 71 E8
Remetea, *Romania* 43 D10
Remich, *Lux.* 17 E6
Remiremont, *France* 19 D13
Remo, *Ethiopia* 81 F5
Remontnoye, *Russia* 49 G6
Remoulins, *France* 21 E8
Remscheid, *Germany* 24 D3
Ren Xian, *China* 56 F8
Rende, *Italy* 31 C9
Rendína, *Greece* 38 B3
Rendsburg, *Germany* 24 A5
Renfrew, *Canada* 102 C4
Renfrewshire □, *U.K.* 14 F4
Rengat, *Indonesia* 62 E2
Rengo, *Chile* 126 C1
Renhua, *China* 59 E9
Renhuai, *China* 58 D6
Reni, *Ukraine* 47 K5
Renk, *Sudan* 81 E3
Renmark, *Australia* 95 E3
Rennell Sd., *Canada* 104 C2
Renner Springs T.O.,
  Australia 94 B1
Rennes, *France* 18 D5
Reno, *U.S.A.* 116 F7
Reno →, *Italy* 29 D9
Renovo, *U.S.A.* 110 E7
Renqiu, *China* 56 E9
Rens, *Denmark* 11 K3
Rensselaer, *Ind., U.S.A.* .. 108 E2
Rensselaer, *N.Y., U.S.A.* . 111 D11
Rentería, *Spain* 32 B3
Renton, *U.S.A.* 116 C4
Réo, *Burkina Faso* 82 C4
Reocín, *Spain* 34 B6
Reotipur, *India* 69 G10
Répcelak, *Hungary* 42 C2
Republic, *Mich., U.S.A.* .. 108 B2
Republic, *Wash., U.S.A.* . 114 B4
Republican →, *U.S.A.* ... 112 F6
Republican City, *U.S.A.* .. 112 E5
Repulse Bay, *Canada* 101 B11
Requena, *Peru* 124 E4
Requena, *Spain* 33 F3
Réquista, *France* 20 D6
Resadiye = Datça, *Turkey* 39 E9
Reşadiye, *Turkey* 72 B7
Reşadiye Yarımadası,
  Turkey 39 E9
Resavica, *Serbia, Yug.* ... 40 B5
Resen, *Macedonia* 40 E5
Reserve, *Canada* 105 C8
Reserve, *U.S.A.* 115 K9
Resht = Rasht, *Iran* 71 B6
Resistencia, *Argentina* ... 126 B4

Reşiţa, *Romania* 42 E6
Resko, *Poland* 44 E2
Resolution I., *Canada* 101 B13
Resolution I., *N.Z.* 91 L1
Ressano Garcia, *Mozam.* . 89 D5
Reston, *Canada* 105 D8
Reszel, *Poland* 44 D8
Retalhuleu, *Guatemala* ... 120 D1
Retenue, L. de,
  Dem. Rep. of the Congo 87 E2
Retezat, Munţii, *Romania* . 42 E8
Retford, *U.K.* 12 D7
Rethel, *France* 19 C11
Rethem, *Germany* 24 C5
Réthímnon, *Greece* 36 D6
Réthímnon □, *Greece* 36 D6
Retiche, Alpi, *Switz.* 25 J6
Retiers, *France* 18 E5
Retortillo, *Spain* 34 E4
Retournac, *France* 21 C8
Rétság, *Hungary* 42 C4
Réunion ■, *Ind. Oc.* 77 J9
Reus, *Spain* 32 D6
Reuterstadt Stavenhagen,
  Germany 24 B8
Reutlingen, *Germany* 25 G5
Reutte, *Austria* 26 D3
Reval = Tallinn, *Estonia* .. 9 G21
Revel, *France* 20 E6
Revelganj, *India* 69 G11
Revelstoke, *Canada* 104 C5
Reventazón, *Peru* 124 E2
Revigny-sur-Ornain, *France* 19 D11
Revilla Gigedo, Is.,
  Pac. Oc. 97 F16
Revillagigedo I., *U.S.A.* .. 104 B2
Revin, *France* 19 C11
Revúca, *Slovak Rep.* 27 C13
Revuè →, *Mozam.* 87 F3
Rewa, *India* 69 G9
Rewari, *India* 68 E7
Rexburg, *U.S.A.* 114 E8
Rey, *Iran* 71 C6
Rey, I. del, *Panama* 120 E4
Rey, Rio del →, *Nigeria* . 83 E6
Rey Malabo, *Eq. Guin.* .. 83 E6
Reyðarfjörður, *Iceland* ... 8 D6
Reyes, Pt., *U.S.A.* 116 H3
Reyhanlı, *Turkey* 72 D7
Reykjahlíð, *Iceland* 8 D5
Reykjanes, *Iceland* 8 E2
Reykjavík, *Iceland* 8 D3
Reynolds, *Canada* 105 D9
Reynolds Ra., *Australia* .. 92 D5
Reynoldsville, *U.S.A.* 110 E6
Reynosa, *Mexico* 119 B5
Rēzekne, *Latvia* 9 H22
Rezina, *Moldova* 43 C13
Rezovo, *Bulgaria* 41 D12
Rezvān, *Iran* 71 E8
Rgotina, *Serbia, Yug.* 40 B6
Rhamnus, *Greece* 38 C6
Rhayader, *U.K.* 13 E4
Rheda-Wiedenbrück,
  Germany 24 D4
Rhede, *Germany* 24 D2
Rhein, *Canada* 105 C8
Rhein →, *Europe* 17 C6
Rhein-Main-Donau-Kanal,
  Germany 25 F7
Rheinbach, *Germany* 24 E2
Rheine, *Germany* 24 C3
Rheinfelden, *Germany* 25 H3
Rheinhessen-Pfalz □,
  Germany 25 F3
Rheinland-Pfalz □,
  Germany 25 E2
Rheinsberg, *Germany* 24 B8
Rhin = Rhein →, *Europe* . 17 C6
Rhine = Rhein →, *Europe* 17 C6
Rhineland-Palatinate □ =
  Rheinland-Pfalz □,
  Germany 25 E2
Rhinelander, *U.S.A.* 112 C10
Rhinns Pt., *U.K.* 14 F2
Rhino Camp, *Uganda* 86 B3
Rho, *Italy* 28 C6
Rhode Island □, *U.S.A.* .. 111 E13
Rhodes = Ródhos, *Greece* 36 C10
Rhodesia = Zimbabwe ■,
  Africa 87 F3
Rhodope Mts. = Rhodopi
  Planina, *Bulgaria* 41 E8
Rhodopi Planina, *Bulgaria* 41 E8
Rhön = Rhön, *Germany* . 24 E5
Rhön, *Germany* 24 E5
Rhondda, *U.K.* 13 F4
Rhondda Cynon Taff □,
  U.K. 13 F4
Rhône □, *France* 21 C8
Rhône →, *France* 21 E8
Rhône-Alpes □, *France* .. 21 C9
Rhum, *U.K.* 14 E2
Rhyl, *U.K.* 12 D4
Ri-Aba, *Eq. Guin.* 83 E6
Riachão, *Brazil* 125 E9
Riaño, *Spain* 34 C5
Rians, *France* 21 E9
Riansáres →, *Spain* 35 F7
Riasi, *India* 69 C6
Riau □, *Indonesia* 62 E2
Riau, Kepulauan, *Indonesia* 62 D2
Riau Arch. = Riau,
  Kepulauan, *Indonesia* . 62 D2
Riaza, *Spain* 34 D7
Riaza →, *Spain* 34 D7
Riba de Saelices, *Spain* .. 32 E2

Riba-Roja de Turia, *Spain* 33 F4
Ribadavia, *Spain* 34 C2
Ribadeo, *Spain* 34 B3
Ribadesella, *Spain* 34 B5
Ribas = Ribes de Freser,
  Spain 32 C7
Ribas do Rio Pardo, *Brazil* 125 H8
Ribble →, *U.K.* 12 D5
Ribe, *Denmark* 11 J2
Ribe Amtskommune □,
  Denmark 11 J2
Ribeauvillé, *France* 19 D14
Ribécourt-Dreslincourt,
  France 19 C9
Ribeira = Santa Uxía,
  Spain 34 C2
Ribeira Brava, *Madeira* ... 37 D2
Ribeirão Prêto, *Brazil* 127 A6
Ribemont, *France* 19 C10
Ribera, *Italy* 30 E6
Ribérac, *France* 20 C4
Riberalta, *Bolivia* 124 F5
Ribes de Freser, *Spain* ... 32 C7
Ribnica, *Slovenia* 29 C11
Ribnitz-Damgarten,
  Germany 24 A8
Ričany, *Czech Rep.* 26 B7
Riccarton, *N.Z.* 91 K4
Ríccia, *Italy* 31 A7
Riccione, *Italy* 29 E9
Rice, *U.S.A.* 117 L12
Rice L., *Canada* 110 B6
Rice Lake, *U.S.A.* 112 C9
Rich Hill, *U.S.A.* 113 F7
Richards Bay, *S. Africa* .. 89 D5
Richards L., *Canada* 105 B7
Richardson →, *Canada* .. 105 B6
Richardson Springs, *U.S.A.* 116 F5
Richardton, *U.S.A.* 112 B3
Riche, C., *Australia* 93 F2
Richelieu, *France* 18 E7
Richey, *U.S.A.* 112 B2
Richfield, *Idaho, U.S.A.* .. 114 E6
Richfield, *Utah, U.S.A.* ... 115 G8
Richford, *U.S.A.* 111 B12
Richibucto, *Canada* 103 C7
Richland, *Ga., U.S.A.* 109 J3
Richland, *Oreg., U.S.A.* .. 114 D5
Richland, *Wash., U.S.A.* . 114 C4
Richland Center, *U.S.A.* .. 112 D9
Richlands, *U.S.A.* 108 G5
Richmond, *N.S.W.,*
  Australia 95 E5
Richmond, *Queens.,*
  Australia 94 C3
Richmond, *N.Z.* 91 J4
Richmond, *U.K.* 12 C6
Richmond, *Calif., U.S.A.* . 116 H4
Richmond, *Ind., U.S.A.* .. 108 F3
Richmond, *Ky., U.S.A.* ... 108 G3
Richmond, *Mich., U.S.A.* . 110 D2
Richmond, *Mo., U.S.A.* .. 112 F8
Richmond, *Tex., U.S.A.* .. 113 L7
Richmond, *Utah, U.S.A.* . 114 F8
Richmond, *Va., U.S.A.* ... 108 G7
Richmond Ra., *Australia* .. 95 D5
Richton, *U.S.A.* 109 K1
Richwood, *U.S.A.* 108 F5
Ricla, *Spain* 32 D3
Ridder = Leninogorsk,
  Kazakstan 50 D9
Ridgecrest, *U.S.A.* 117 K9
Ridgedale, *Canada* 105 C8
Ridgefield, *U.S.A.* 116 E4
Ridgeland, *U.S.A.* 109 J5
Ridgelands, *Australia* 94 C5
Ridgetown, *Canada* 102 D3
Ridgewood, *U.S.A.* 111 F10
Ridgway, *U.S.A.* 110 E6
Riding Mountain Nat.
  Park, *Canada* 105 C9
Ridley, Mt., *Australia* 93 F3
Ried, *Austria* 26 C6
Riedlingen, *Germany* 25 G5
Riedstadt, *Germany* 25 F4
Rienza →, *Italy* 29 B8
Riesa, *Germany* 24 D9
Riesi, *Italy* 31 E7
Riet →, *S. Africa* 88 D3
Rietavas, *Lithuania* 44 C8
Rieti, *Italy* 29 F9
Rieupeyroux, *France* 20 D6
Riez, *France* 21 E10
Riffe L., *U.S.A.* 116 D4
Rifle, *U.S.A.* 114 G10
Rift Valley □, *Kenya* 86 B4
Rīga, *Latvia* 9 H21
Riga, G. of, *Latvia* 9 H20
Rīgān, *Iran* 71 D8
Rīgas Jūras Līcis = Riga,
  G. of, *Latvia* 9 H20
Rigaud, *Canada* 111 A10
Rigby, *U.S.A.* 114 E8
Rīgestān □, *Afghan.* 66 D4
Riggins, *U.S.A.* 114 D5
Rignac, *France* 20 D6
Rigolet, *Canada* 103 B8
Riihimäki, *Finland* 9 F21
Riiser-Larsen-halvøya,
  Antarctica 5 C4
Rijau, *Nigeria* 83 C6
Rijeka, *Croatia* 29 C11
Rijeka Crnojevića,
  Montenegro, Yug. 40 D3
Rijssen, *Neths.* 17 B6
Rike, *Ethiopia* 81 E4
Rikuzentakada, *Japan* 54 E10

Rila, *Bulgaria* 40 D7
Rila Planina, *Bulgaria* 40 D7
Riley, *U.S.A.* 114 E4
Rima →, *Nigeria* 83 C6
Rimah, Wadi ar →,
Si. Arabia 70 E4
Rimavská Sobota,
Slovak Rep. 27 C13
Rimbey, *Canada* 104 C6
Rimbo, *Sweden* 10 E12
Rimforsa, *Sweden* 11 F9
Rimi, *Nigeria* 83 C6
Rímini, *Italy* 29 D9
Rimouski, *Canada* 103 C6
Rimrock, *U.S.A.* 116 D5
Rinca, *Indonesia* 63 F5
Rincón de la Victoria,
Spain 35 J6
Rincón de Romos, *Mexico* 118 C4
Rinconada, *Argentina* ... 126 A2
Ringarum, *Sweden* 11 F10
Ringe, *Denmark* 11 J4
Ringim, *Nigeria* 83 C6
Ringkøbing, *Denmark* 11 H2
Ringkøbing
Amtskommune □,
Denmark 11 H2
Ringkøbing Fjord,
Denmark 11 H2
Ringling, *U.S.A.* 114 C8
Ringsjön, *Sweden* 11 J7
Ringsted, *Denmark* 11 J5
Ringvassøy, *Norway* 8 B18
Riní, *Greece* 39 D7
Rinjani, *Indonesia* 62 F5
Rinteln, *Germany* 24 C5
Río, Punta del, *Spain* ... 33 J2
Rio Branco, *Brazil* 124 E5
Río Branco, *Uruguay* 127 C5
Rio Brilhante, *Brazil* 127 A5
Rio Claro, *Brazil* 127 A6
Rio Claro, *Trin. & Tob.* .. 121 D7
Río Colorado, *Argentina* . 128 D4
Río Cuarto, *Argentina* ... 126 C3
Rio das Pedras, *Mozam.* .. 89 C6
Rio de Janeiro, *Brazil* ... 127 A7
Rio de Janeiro □, *Brazil* . 127 A7
Rio do Sul, *Brazil* 127 B6
Río Gallegos, *Argentina* . 128 G3
Río Grande, *Argentina* .. 128 G3
Rio Grande, *Brazil* 127 C5
Río Grande, *Mexico* 118 C4
Río Grande, *Nic.* 120 D3
Rio Grande →, *U.S.A.* ... 113 N6
Rio Grande City, *U.S.A.* . 113 M5
Río Grande del Norte →,
N. Amer. 107 E7
Rio Grande do Norte □,
Brazil 125 E11
Rio Grande do Sul □,
Brazil 127 C5
Río Hato, *Panama* 120 E3
Río Lagartos, *Mexico* 119 C7
Río Largo, *Brazil* 125 E11
Rio Maior, *Portugal* 35 F2
Rio Marina, *Italy* 28 F7
Río Mulatos, *Bolivia* 124 G5
Río Muni = Mbini □,
Eq. Guin. 84 D2
Rio Negro, *Brazil* 127 B6
Rio Pardo, *Brazil* 127 C5
Río Segundo, *Argentina* . 126 C3
Río Tercero, *Argentina* .. 126 C3
Rio Tinto, *Portugal* 34 D2
Rio Verde, *Brazil* 125 G8
Río Verde, *Mexico* 119 C5
Rio Vista, *U.S.A.* 116 G5
Ríobamba, *Ecuador* 124 D3
Ríohacha, *Colombia* 124 A4
Riom, *France* 20 C7
Riom-ès-Montagnes, *France* 20 C6
Rion-des-Landes, *France* . 20 E3
Rionero in Vúlture, *Italy* . 31 B8
Rioni →, *Georgia* 49 J5
Ríos, *Spain* 34 D3
Ríosucio, *Colombia* 124 B3
Riou L., *Canada* 105 B7
Rioz, *France* 19 E13
Ripatransone, *Italy* 29 F10
Ripley, *Canada* 110 B3
Ripley, *Calif., U.S.A.* ... 117 M12
Ripley, *N.Y., U.S.A.* 110 D5
Ripley, *Tenn., U.S.A.* ... 113 H10
Ripoll, *Spain* 32 C7
Ripon, *U.K.* 12 C6
Ripon, *Calif., U.S.A.* 116 H5
Ripon, *Wis., U.S.A.* 108 D1
Riposto, *Italy* 31 E8
Risalpur, *Pakistan* 68 B4
Risan, *Montenegro, Yug.* . 40 D2
Riscle, *France* 20 E3
Rishā', W. ar →,
Si. Arabia 70 E5
Rishiri-Tō, *Japan* 54 B10
Rishon le Ziyyon, *Israel* . 75 D3
Risle →, *France* 18 C7
Rison, *U.S.A.* 113 J8
Risør, *Norway* 9 G13
Riti, *Nigeria* 83 D6
Rittman, *U.S.A.* 110 F3
Ritzville, *U.S.A.* 114 C4
Riva del Garda, *Italy* 28 C7
Riva Lígure, *Italy* 28 E4
Rivadavia, *Buenos Aires,*
Argentina 126 D3
Rivadavia, *Mendoza,*
Argentina 126 C2

Rivadavia, *Salta, Argentina* 126 A3
Rivadavia, *Chile* 126 B1
Rivarolo Canavese, *Italy* . 28 C4
Rivas, *Nic.* 120 D2
Rive-de-Gier, *France* 21 C8
River Cess, *Liberia* 82 D3
Rivera, *Argentina* 128 D4
Rivera, *Uruguay* 127 C4
Riverdale, *U.S.A.* 116 J7
Riverhead, *U.S.A.* 111 F12
Riverhurst, *Canada* 105 C7
Riverina, *Australia* 93 E3
Rivers, *Canada* 105 C8
Rivers □, *Nigeria* 83 E6
Rivers, L. of the, *Canada* . 105 D7
Rivers Inlet, *Canada* 104 C3
Riversdale, *S. Africa* 88 E3
Riverside, *Calif., U.S.A.* . 117 M9
Riverside, *Wyo., U.S.A.* .. 114 F10
Riversleigh, *Australia* 94 B2
Riverton, *Australia* 95 E2
Riverton, *Canada* 105 C9
Riverton, *N.Z.* 91 M2
Riverton, *U.S.A.* 114 E9
Riverton Heights, *U.S.A.* . 116 C4
Rives, *France* 21 C9
Rivesaltes, *France* 20 F6
Riviera di Levante, *Italy* . 28 D6
Riviera di Ponente, *Italy* . 28 D5
Rivière-à-Pierre, *Canada* . 103 C5
Rivière-au-Renard, *Canada* 103 C7
Rivière-du-Loup, *Canada* . 103 C6
Rivière-Pentecôte, *Canada* 103 C6
Rivière-Pilote, *Martinique* 121 D7
Rivne, *Ukraine* 47 G4
Rívoli, *Italy* 28 C4
Rivoli B., *Australia* 95 F3
Rixheim, *France* 19 E14
Riyadh = Ar Riyāḍ,
Si. Arabia 70 E5
Rize, *Turkey* 73 B9
Rizhao, *China* 57 G10
Rizokarpaso, *Cyprus* 36 D13
Rizzuto, C., *Italy* 31 D10
Rjukan, *Norway* 9 G13
Ro, *Greece* 39 E11
Roa, *Spain* 34 D7
Road Town, *Virgin Is.* ... 121 C7
Roanne, *France* 19 F11
Roanoke, *Ala., U.S.A.* ... 109 J3
Roanoke, *Va., U.S.A.* ... 108 G6
Roanoke →, *U.S.A.* 109 H7
Roanoke I., *U.S.A.* 109 H8
Roanoke Rapids, *U.S.A.* . 109 G7
Roatán, *Honduras* 120 C2
Robbins I., *Australia* 94 G4
Róbbio, *Italy* 28 C5
Robe →, *Australia* 92 D2
Röbel, *Germany* 24 B8
Robert Lee, *U.S.A.* 113 K4
Roberts, *U.S.A.* 114 E7
Robertsganj, *India* 69 G10
Robertson, *S. Africa* 88 E2
Robertson I., *Antarctica* . 5 C18
Robertson Ra., *Australia* . 92 D3
Robertsport, *Liberia* 82 D2
Robertstown, *Australia* .. 95 E2
Roberval, *Canada* 103 C5
Robeson Chan., *Greenland* 4 A4
Robinson →, *Australia* ... 94 B2
Robinson Ra., *Australia* .. 93 E2
Robinson River, *Australia* 94 B2
Robinvale, *Australia* 95 E3
Robledo, *Spain* 33 G2
Roblin, *Canada* 105 C8
Roboré, *Bolivia* 124 G7
Robson, Mt., *Canada* 104 C5
Robstown, *U.S.A.* 113 M6
Roca, C. da, *Portugal* 35 G1
Roca Partida, I., *Mexico* . 118 D2
Rocamadour, *France* 20 D5
Rocas, I., *Brazil* 125 D12
Rocca San Casciano, *Italy* 29 D8
Roccadáspide, *Italy* 31 B8
Roccastrada, *Italy* 29 F8
Roccella Iónica, *Italy* 31 D9
Rocha, *Uruguay* 127 C5
Rochdale, *U.K.* 12 D5
Rochechouart, *France* ... 20 C4
Rochefort, *Belgium* 17 D5
Rochefort, *France* 20 C3
Rochefort-en-Terre, *France* 18 E4
Rochelle, *U.S.A.* 112 E10
Rocher River, *Canada* ... 104 A6
Rocheservière, *France* ... 18 F5
Rochester, *Canada* 104 C6
Rochester, *U.K.* 13 F8
Rochester, *Ind., U.S.A.* .. 108 E2
Rochester, *Minn., U.S.A.* 112 C8
Rochester, *N.H., U.S.A.* . 111 C14
Rochester, *N.Y., U.S.A.* . 110 C7
Rociu, *Romania* 43 F10
Rock →, *Canada* 104 A3
Rock Hill, *U.S.A.* 109 H5
Rock Island, *U.S.A.* 112 E9
Rock Rapids, *U.S.A.* 112 D6
Rock River, *U.S.A.* 114 F11
Rock Sound, *Bahamas* ... 120 B4
Rock Springs, *Mont.,*
U.S.A. 114 C10
Rock Springs, *Wyo.,*
U.S.A. 114 F9
Rock Valley, *U.S.A.* 112 D6
Rockall, *Atl. Oc.* 6 D3
Rockdale, *Tex., U.S.A.* ... 113 K6
Rockdale, *Wash., U.S.A.* . 116 C5

Rockefeller Plateau,
Antarctica 5 E14
Rockford, *U.S.A.* 112 D10
Rockglen, *Canada* 105 D7
Rockhampton, *Australia* . 94 C5
Rockhampton Downs,
Australia 94 B2
Rockingham, *Australia* ... 93 F2
Rockingham B., *Australia* 94 B4
Rocklake, *U.S.A.* 112 A5
Rockland, *Canada* 111 A9
Rockland, *Idaho, U.S.A.* . 114 E7
Rockland, *Maine, U.S.A.* . 103 D6
Rockland, *Mich., U.S.A.* . 112 B10
Rocklin, *U.S.A.* 116 G5
Rockmart, *U.S.A.* 108 H3
Rockport, *Mo., U.S.A.* .. 112 E7
Rockport, *Tex., U.S.A.* .. 113 L6
Rocksprings, *U.S.A.* 113 K4
Rockville, *Conn., U.S.A.* . 111 E12
Rockville, *Md., U.S.A.* ... 108 F7
Rockwall, *U.S.A.* 113 J6
Rockwell City, *U.S.A.* ... 112 D7
Rockwood, *U.S.A.* 109 H3
Rocky Ford, *U.S.A.* 112 F3
Rocky Gully, *Australia* ... 93 F2
Rocky Lane, *Canada* 104 B5
Rocky Mount, *U.S.A.* ... 109 H7
Rocky Mountain House,
Canada 104 C6
Rocky Mts., *N. Amer.* ... 104 C4
Rockyford, *Canada* 104 C6
Rocroi, *France* 19 C11
Rod, *Pakistan* 66 E3
Rødby, *Denmark* 11 K5
Rødbyhavn, *Denmark* ... 11 K5
Roddickton, *Canada* 103 B8
Rødding, *Denmark* 11 J3
Rødekro, *Denmark* 11 J3
Rodenkirchen, *Germany* . 24 B4
Roderick I., *Canada* 104 C3
Rodez, *France* 20 D6
Rodholívas, *Greece* 40 F7
Rodhópi □, *Greece* 41 E9
Rodhopoú, *Greece* 36 D5
Ródhos, *Greece* 36 C10
Rodi Gargánico, *Italy* 29 G12
Rodna, *Romania* 43 C9
Rodnei, Munţii, *Romania* . 43 C9
Rodney, *Canada* 110 D3
Rodney, C., *N.Z.* 91 G5
Rodniki, *Russia* 48 B5
Rodonit, Kepi i, *Albania* . 40 E3
Rodriguez, *Ind. Oc.* 3 E13
Roe →, *U.K.* 15 A5
Roebling, *U.S.A.* 111 F10
Roebourne, *Australia* 92 D2
Roebuck B., *Australia* ... 92 C3
Roebuck Plains, *Australia* 92 C3
Roermond, *Neths.* 17 C6
Roes Welcome Sd., *Canada* 101 B11
Roeselare, *Belgium* 17 D3
Rogachev = Ragachow,
Belarus 47 F6
Rogačica, *Serbia, Yug.* ... 40 B3
Rogagua, L., *Bolivia* 124 F5
Rogaška Slatina, *Slovenia* 29 B12
Rogatec, *Slovenia* 29 B12
Rogatica, *Bos.-H.* 42 G4
Rogatyn, *Ukraine* 47 H3
Rogdhia, *Greece* 36 D7
Rogers, *U.S.A.* 113 G7
Rogers City, *U.S.A.* 108 C4
Rogerson, *U.S.A.* 114 E6
Rogersville, *U.S.A.* 109 G4
Roggan River, *Canada* ... 102 B4
Roggeveldberge, *S. Africa* 88 E3
Roggiano Gravina, *Italy* .. 31 C9
Rogliano, *France* 21 F13
Rogliano, *Italy* 31 C9
Rogoaguado, L., *Bolivia* . 124 F5
Rogoźno, *Poland* 45 F3
Rogue →, *U.S.A.* 114 E1
Rohan, *France* 18 D4
Róhda, *Greece* 36 A3
Rohnert Park, *U.S.A.* 116 G4
Rohri, *Pakistan* 68 F3
Rohri Canal, *Pakistan* ... 68 F3
Rohtak, *India* 68 E7
Roi Et, *Thailand* 64 D4
Roja, *Latvia* 9 H20
Rojas, *Argentina* 126 C3
Rojişte, *Romania* 43 F8
Rojo, C., *Mexico* 119 C5
Rokan →, *Indonesia* 62 D2
Rokeby, *Australia* 94 A3
Rokiškis, *Lithuania* 9 J21
Rokitno, *Russia* 47 G8
Rokycany, *Czech Rep.* ... 26 B6
Rolândia, *Brazil* 127 A5
Rolette, *U.S.A.* 112 A5
Rolla, *Kans., U.S.A.* 113 G4
Rolla, *N. Dak., U.S.A.* ... 112 A5
Rolleston, *Australia* 94 C4
Rollingstone, *Australia* .. 94 B4
Rom, *Sudan* 81 F3
Roma, *Australia* 95 D4
Roma, *Italy* 29 G9
Roma, *Sweden* 11 G12
Roman, *Bulgaria* 40 C7
Roman, *Romania* 43 D11
Roman-Kosh, Gora,
Ukraine 47 K8
Romanche →, *France* ... 21 C9
Romang, *Indonesia* 63 F7

Români, *Egypt* 75 E1
Romania ■, *Europe* 43 D10
Romanija, *Bos.-H.* 42 G3
Romano, Cayo, *Cuba* ... 120 B4
Romanovka =
Basarabeasca, *Moldova* . 43 D13
Romans-sur-Isère, *France* 21 C9
Romanshorn, *Switz.* 25 H5
Romblon, *Phil.* 61 E5
Rome = Roma, *Italy* 29 G9
Rome, *Ga., U.S.A.* 109 H3
Rome, *N.Y., U.S.A.* 111 C9
Rometta, *Italy* 31 D8
Romilly-sur-Seine, *France* 19 D10
Romney, *U.S.A.* 108 F6
Romney Marsh, *U.K.* 13 F8
Romny, *Ukraine* 47 G7
Rømø, *Denmark* 11 J2
Romodan, *Ukraine* 47 G7
Romodanovo, *Russia* 48 C7
Romont, *Switz.* 25 J2
Romorantin-Lanthenay,
France 19 E8
Romsdalen, *Norway* 9 E12
Romsey, *U.K.* 13 G6
Ron, *Vietnam* 64 D6
Rona, *U.K.* 14 D3
Ronan, *U.S.A.* 114 C6
Roncador, Cayos,
Caribbean 120 D3
Roncador, Serra do, *Brazil* 125 F8
Ronceverte, *U.S.A.* 108 G5
Ronciglione, *Italy* 29 F9
Ronco →, *Italy* 29 D9
Ronda, *Spain* 35 J5
Ronda, Serranía de, *Spain* 35 J5
Rondane, *Norway* 9 F13
Rondônia □, *Brazil* 124 F6
Rondonópolis, *Brazil* 125 G8
Rong Jiang →, *China* ... 58 E7
Rong Xian,
Guangxi Zhuangzu,
China 59 F8
Rong Xian, *Sichuan, China* 58 C5
Rong'an, *China* 58 E7
Rongcheng, *China* 58 E7
Ronge, L. la, *Canada* 105 B7
Rongjiang, *China* 58 E7
Rongshui, *China* 58 E7
Rønne, *Denmark* 11 J8
Ronne Ice Shelf, *Antarctica* 5 D18
Ronneby, *Sweden* 11 H9
Ronnebyån →, *Sweden* .. 11 H9
Rönnöskär, *Sweden* 11 F9
Ronsard, C., *Australia* ... 93 D1
Ronse, *Belgium* 17 D3
Roodepoort, *S. Africa* ... 89 D4
Roof Butte, *U.S.A.* 115 H9
Roorkee, *India* 68 E7
Roosendaal, *Neths.* 17 C4
Roosevelt, *Minn., U.S.A.* 112 A7
Roosevelt, *Utah, U.S.A.* . 114 F8
Roosevelt →, *Brazil* 122 D4
Roosevelt, Mt., *Canada* .. 104 B3
Roosevelt I., *Antarctica* .. 5 D12
Roosevelt Res., *U.S.A.* ... 115 K8
Ropczyce, *Poland* 45 H8
Roper →, *Australia* 94 A2
Ropesville, *U.S.A.* 113 J3
Roque Pérez, *Argentina* . 126 D4
Roquefort, *France* 20 D3
Roquemaure, *France* 21 D8
Roquetas de Mar, *Spain* . 33 J2
Roquetes, *Spain* 32 E5
Roquevaire, *France* 21 E9
Roraima □, *Brazil* 124 C6
Roraima, Mt., *Venezuela* . 122 C4
Rorketon, *Canada* 105 C9
Røros, *Norway* 9 E14
Rorschach, *Switz.* 25 H5
Rosa, *Zambia* 87 D3
Rosa, Monte, *Italy* 28 C4
Rosal de la Frontera, *Spain* 35 H3
Rosalia, *U.S.A.* 114 C5
Rosamond, *U.S.A.* 117 L8
Rosans, *France* 21 D9
Rosário, *Brazil* 125 D10
Rosario,
Baja Calif.,
Mexico 118 B1
Rosario, *Sinaloa, Mexico* 118 C3
Rosario, *Paraguay* 126 A4
Rosario de la Frontera,
Argentina 126 B3
Rosario de Lerma,
Argentina 126 A2
Rosario del Tala, *Argentina* 126 C4
Rosário do Sul, *Brazil* ... 127 C5
Rosarito, *Mexico* 117 N9
Rosarno, *Italy* 31 D8
Rosas = Roses, *Spain* ... 32 C8
Roscoe, *U.S.A.* 112 C5
Roscoff, *France* 18 D3
Roscommon, *Ireland* 15 C3
Roscommon, *U.S.A.* 108 C3
Roscommon □, *Ireland* .. 15 C3
Roscrea, *Ireland* 15 D4
Rose →, *Australia* 94 A2
Rose Blanche, *Canada* ... 103 C8
Rose Harbour, *Canada* .. 104 C2
Rose Pt., *Canada* 104 C2
Rose Valley, *Canada* 105 C8
Roseau, *Domin.* 121 C7
Roseau, *U.S.A.* 112 A7
Rosebery, *Australia* 94 G4
Rosebud, *U.S.A.* 113 K6

Roseburg, *U.S.A.* 114 E2
Rosedale, *Australia* 94 C5
Rosedale, *U.S.A.* 113 J9
Roseland, *U.S.A.* 116 G4
Rosemary, *Canada* 104 C6
Rosenberg, *U.S.A.* 113 L7
Rosendaël, *France* 19 A9
Rosenheim, *Germany* ... 25 H8
Roses, *Spain* 32 C8
Roses, G. de, *Spain* 32 C8
Roseto degli Abruzzi, *Italy* 29 F11
Rosetown, *Canada* 105 C7
Rosetta = Rashîd, *Egypt* . 80 H7
Roseville, *U.S.A.* 116 G5
Rosewood, *N. Terr.,*
Australia 92 C4
Rosewood, *Queens.,*
Australia 95 D5
Roshkhvār, *Iran* 71 C8
Rosières-en-Santerre,
France 19 C9
Rosignano Maríttimo, *Italy* 28 E7
Rosignol, *Guyana* 124 B7
Roşiori de Vede, *Romania* 43 F10
Rositsa, *Bulgaria* 41 C11
Rositsa →, *Bulgaria* 41 C9
Roskilde, *Denmark* 11 J6
Roskilde Amtskommune □,
Denmark 11 J6
Roskovec, *Albania* 40 F3
Roslavl, *Russia* 46 F7
Roslyn, *Australia* 95 E4
Rosmaninhal, *Portugal* .. 34 F3
Rosmead, *S. Africa* 88 E4
Røsnæs, *Denmark* 11 J4
Rosolini, *Italy* 31 F7
Rosporden, *France* 18 E3
Ross, *Australia* 94 G4
Ross, *N.Z.* 91 K3
Ross I., *Antarctica* 5 D11
Ross Ice Shelf, *Antarctica* 5 E12
Ross L., *U.S.A.* 114 B3
Ross-on-Wye, *U.K.* 13 F5
Ross Sea, *Antarctica* 5 D11
Rossall Pt., *U.K.* 12 D4
Rossan Pt., *Ireland* 15 B3
Rossano, *Italy* 31 C9
Rossburn, *Canada* 105 C8
Rosseau, *Canada* 110 A5
Rosses, The, *Ireland* 15 A3
Rossignol, L., *Canada* ... 102 B5
Rossignol Res., *Canada* .. 103 D6
Rossland, *Canada* 104 D5
Rosslare, *Ireland* 15 D5
Rosslau, *Germany* 24 D8
Rosso, *Mauritania* 82 B1
Rosso, C., *France* 21 F12
Rossosh, *Russia* 47 G10
Rossport, *Canada* 102 C2
Røssvatnet, *Norway* 8 D16
Rossville, *Australia* 94 B4
Røst, *Norway* 8 C15
Rosthern, *Canada* 105 C7
Rostock, *Germany* 24 A8
Rostov, *Don, Russia* 47 J10
Rostov, *Yaroslavl, Russia* . 46 D10
Rostrenen, *France* 18 D3
Roswell, *Ga., U.S.A.* 109 H3
Roswell, *N. Mex., U.S.A.* 113 J2
Rota, *Spain* 35 J4
Rotan, *U.S.A.* 113 J4
Rotenburg, *Hessen,*
Germany 24 E5
Rotenburg, *Niedersachsen,*
Germany 24 B5
Roth, *Germany* 25 F7
Rothaargebirge, *Germany* 24 D4
Rothenburg ob der Tauber,
Germany 25 F6
Rother →, *U.K.* 13 G8
Rotherham, *U.K.* 12 D6
Rothes, *U.K.* 14 D5
Rothesay, *Canada* 103 C6
Rothesay, *U.K.* 14 F3
Roti, *Indonesia* 63 F6
Rotja, Pta., *Spain* 33 G6
Roto, *Australia* 95 E4
Rotoroa, L., *N.Z.* 91 J4
Rotorua, *N.Z.* 91 H6
Rotorua, L., *N.Z.* 91 H6
Rott →, *Germany* 25 G9
Rottenburg, *Germany* ... 25 G8
Rottenmann, *Austria* 26 D7
Rotterdam, *Neths.* 17 C4
Rottne, *Sweden* 11 G8
Rottnest I., *Australia* 93 F2
Rottumeroog, *Neths.* 17 A6
Rottweil, *Germany* 25 G4
Rotuma, *Fiji* 96 J9
Roubaix, *France* 19 B10
Roudnice nad Labem,
Czech Rep. 26 A7
Rouen, *France* 18 C8
Rouergue, *France* 20 D5
Rouillac, *France* 20 C3
Rouleau, *Canada* 105 C8
Round Mountain, *U.S.A.* 114 G5
Round Mt., *Australia* 95 E5
Roundup, *U.S.A.* 114 C9
Rousay, *U.K.* 14 B5
Rouses Point, *U.S.A.* ... 111 B11
Roussillon, *Isère, France* . 21 C8
Roussillon, *Pyrénées-Or.,*
France 20 F6
Rouxville, *S. Africa* 88 E4
Rouyn-Noranda, *Canada* . 102 C4
Rovaniemi, *Finland* 8 C21

Rovato, *Italy* ... 28 C7
Rovenki, *Ukraine* ... 47 H10
Rovereto, *Italy* ... 28 C8
Rovigo, *Italy* ... 29 C8
Rovinj, *Croatia* ... 29 C10
Rovno = Rivne, *Ukraine* ... 47 G4
Rovnoye, *Russia* ... 48 E8
Rovuma = Ruvuma →, *Tanzania* ... 87 E5
Row'ān, *Iran* ... 71 C6
Rowena, *Australia* ... 95 D4
Rowley Shoals, *Australia* ... 92 C2
Roxa, *Guinea-Biss.* ... 82 C1
Roxas, *Capiz, Phil.* ... 61 F5
Roxas, *Isabela, Phil.* ... 61 C4
Roxas, *Mindoro, Phil.* ... 61 E4
Roxboro, *U.S.A.* ... 109 G6
Roxborough Downs, *Australia* ... 94 C2
Roxburgh, *N.Z.* ... 91 L2
Roxen, *Sweden* ... 11 F9
Roy, *Mont., U.S.A.* ... 114 C9
Roy, *N. Mex., U.S.A.* ... 113 H2
Roy Hill, *Australia* ... 92 D2
Royal Canal, *Ireland* ... 15 C4
Royal Leamington Spa, *U.K.* ... 13 E6
Royal Tunbridge Wells, *U.K.* ... 13 F8
Royan, *France* ... 20 C2
Roye, *France* ... 19 C9
Royston, *U.K.* ... 13 E7
Rožaj, *Montenegro, Yug.* ... 40 D4
Rózan, *Poland* ... 45 F8
Rozay-en-Brie, *France* ... 19 D9
Rozdilna, *Ukraine* ... 47 J6
Rozhyshche, *Ukraine* ... 47 G3
Rožmitál pod Třemšínem, *Czech Rep.* ... 26 B6
Rožňava, *Slovak Rep.* ... 27 C13
Rozogi, *Poland* ... 44 E8
Rozoy-sur-Serre, *France* ... 19 C11
Rozzano, *Italy* ... 28 C6
Rrësheni, *Albania* ... 40 E3
Rrogozhino, *Albania* ... 40 E3
Rtanj, *Serbia, Yug.* ... 40 C5
Rtishchevo, *Russia* ... 48 D6
Rúa = A Rúa, *Spain* ... 34 C3
Ruacaná, *Angola* ... 88 B1
Ruahine Ra., *N.Z.* ... 91 H6
Ruapehu, *N.Z.* ... 91 H5
Ruapuke I., *N.Z.* ... 91 M2
Ruaq, W. →, *Egypt* ... 75 F2
Rub' al Khālī, *Si. Arabia* ... 74 D4
Rubeho Mts., *Tanzania* ... 86 D4
Rubezhnoye = Rubizhne, *Ukraine* ... 47 H10
Rubh a' Mhail, *U.K.* ... 14 F2
Rubha Hunish, *U.K.* ... 14 D2
Rubha Robhanais = Lewis, Butt of, *U.K.* ... 14 C2
Rubi, *Spain* ... 32 D7
Rubicon →, *U.S.A.* ... 116 G5
Rubicone →, *Italy* ... 29 D9
Rubik, *Albania* ... 40 E3
Rubino, *Ivory C.* ... 82 D4
Rubio, *Venezuela* ... 124 B4
Rubizhne, *Ukraine* ... 47 H10
Rubtsovsk, *Russia* ... 50 D9
Ruby L., *U.S.A.* ... 114 F6
Ruby Mts., *U.S.A.* ... 114 F6
Rucheng, *China* ... 59 E9
Ruciane-Nida, *Poland* ... 44 E8
Rūd Sar, *Iran* ... 71 B6
Ruda, *Sweden* ... 11 G10
Ruda Śląska, *Poland* ... 45 H5
Rudall, *Australia* ... 95 E2
Rudall →, *Australia* ... 92 D3
Rüdersdorf, *Germany* ... 24 C9
Rudewa, *Tanzania* ... 87 E3
Rudkøbing, *Denmark* ... 11 K4
Rudna, *Poland* ... 45 G3
Rudnik, *Bulgaria* ... 41 D11
Rudnik, *Poland* ... 45 H9
Rudnik, *Serbia, Yug.* ... 40 B4
Rudnya, *Russia* ... 46 E6
Rudnyy, *Kazakhstan* ... 50 D7
Rudo, *Bos.-H.* ... 42 G4
Rudolfa, Ostrov, *Russia* ... 50 A6
Rudolstadt, *Germany* ... 24 E7
Rudong, *China* ... 59 A13
Rudozem, *Bulgaria* ... 41 E8
Rudyard, *U.S.A.* ... 108 B3
Rue, *France* ... 19 B8
Rufa'a, *Sudan* ... 81 E3
Rufiji □, *Tanzania* ... 86 D4
Rufiji →, *Tanzania* ... 86 D4
Rufino, *Argentina* ... 126 C3
Rufisque, *Senegal* ... 82 C1
Rufunsa, *Zambia* ... 87 F2
Rugao, *China* ... 59 A13
Rugby, *U.K.* ... 13 E6
Rugby, *U.S.A.* ... 112 A5
Rügen, *Germany* ... 24 A9
Rugles, *France* ... 18 D7
Ruhengeri, *Rwanda* ... 86 C2
Ruhla, *Germany* ... 24 E6
Ruhland, *Germany* ... 24 D9
Ruhnu, *Estonia* ... 9 H20
Ruhr →, *Germany* ... 24 D2
Ruhuhu →, *Tanzania* ... 87 E3
Rui'an, *China* ... 59 D13
Ruichang, *China* ... 59 C10
Ruidosa, *U.S.A.* ... 113 L2
Ruidoso, *U.S.A.* ... 115 K11
Ruili, *China* ... 58 E1
Ruivo, Pico, *Madeira* ... 37 D3

Ruj, *Bulgaria* ... 40 D6
Rujen, *Macedonia* ... 40 D6
Rum Tal'at al Jamā'ah, *Jordan* ... 75 E4
Ruk, *Pakistan* ... 68 F3
Rukwa □, *Tanzania* ... 86 D3
Rukwa, L., *Tanzania* ... 86 D3
Rulhieres, C., *Australia* ... 92 B4
Rum = Rhum, *U.K.* ... 14 E2
Rum Cay, *Bahamas* ... 121 B5
Rum Jungle, *Australia* ... 92 B5
Ruma, *Serbia, Yug.* ... 42 E4
Rumāḥ, *Si. Arabia* ... 70 E5
Rumania = Romania ■, *Europe* ... 43 D10
Rumaylah, *Iraq* ... 70 D5
Rumbalara, *Australia* ... 94 D1
Rumbêk, *Sudan* ... 81 F2
Rumburk, *Czech Rep.* ... 26 A7
Rumford, *U.S.A.* ... 111 B14
Rumia, *Poland* ... 44 D5
Rumilly, *France* ... 21 C9
Rumoi, *Japan* ... 54 C10
Rumonge, *Burundi* ... 86 C2
Rumsey, *Canada* ... 104 C6
Rumula, *Australia* ... 94 B4
Rumuruti, *Kenya* ... 86 B4
Runan, *China* ... 56 H8
Runanga, *N.Z.* ... 91 K3
Runaway, C., *N.Z.* ... 91 G6
Runcorn, *U.K.* ... 12 D5
Rungwa, *Tanzania* ... 86 D3
Rungwa →, *Tanzania* ... 86 D3
Rungwe, *Tanzania* ... 87 D3
Rungwe □, *Tanzania* ... 87 D3
Runka, *Nigeria* ... 83 C6
Runn, *Sweden* ... 10 D9
Runton Ra., *Australia* ... 92 D3
Ruokolahti, *Finland* ... 46 B5
Ruoqiang, *China* ... 60 C3
Rupa, *India* ... 67 F18
Rupar, *India* ... 68 D7
Rupat, *Indonesia* ... 62 D2
Rupea, *Romania* ... 43 D10
Rupert →, *Canada* ... 102 B4
Rupert House = Waskaganish, *Canada* ... 102 B4
Rur →, *Germany* ... 24 D1
Rurrenabaque, *Bolivia* ... 124 F5
Rus →, *Spain* ... 33 F2
Rusambo, *Zimbabwe* ... 87 F3
Rusape, *Zimbabwe* ... 87 F3
Ruschuk = Ruse, *Bulgaria* ... 41 C9
Ruse, *Bulgaria* ... 41 C9
Ruse □, *Bulgaria* ... 41 C10
Ruşeţu, *Romania* ... 43 F12
Rush, *Ireland* ... 15 C5
Rushan, *China* ... 57 F11
Rushden, *U.K.* ... 13 E7
Rushford, *U.S.A.* ... 112 D9
Rushville, *Ill., U.S.A.* ... 112 E9
Rushville, *Ind., U.S.A.* ... 108 F3
Rushville, *Nebr., U.S.A.* ... 112 D3
Rushworth, *Australia* ... 95 F4
Russas, *Brazil* ... 125 D11
Russell, *Canada* ... 105 C8
Russell, *U.S.A.* ... 112 F5
Russell L., *Man., Canada* ... 105 B8
Russell L., *N.W.T., Canada* ... 104 A5
Russellkonda, *India* ... 67 K14
Russellville, *Ala., U.S.A.* ... 109 H2
Russellville, *Ark., U.S.A.* ... 113 H8
Russellville, *Ky., U.S.A.* ... 109 G2
Rüsselsheim, *Germany* ... 25 F4
Russi, *Italy* ... 29 D9
Russia ■, *Eurasia* ... 51 C11
Russian →, *U.S.A.* ... 116 G3
Russkoye Ustie, *Russia* ... 4 B15
Rust, *Austria* ... 27 D9
Rustam, *Pakistan* ... 68 B5
Rustam Shahr, *Pakistan* ... 68 F2
Rustavi, *Georgia* ... 49 K7
Rustenburg, *S. Africa* ... 88 D4
Ruston, *U.S.A.* ... 113 J8
Rutana, *Burundi* ... 86 C3
Rute, *Spain* ... 35 H6
Ruteng, *Indonesia* ... 63 F6
Ruth, *Mich., U.S.A.* ... 110 C2
Ruth, *Nev., U.S.A.* ... 114 G6
Rutherford, *U.S.A.* ... 116 G4
Rutland, *U.K.* ... 13 E7
Rutland Plains, *Australia* ... 94 B3
Rutland Water, *U.K.* ... 13 E7
Rutledge →, *Canada* ... 105 A6
Rutledge L., *Canada* ... 105 A6
Rutqa, W. →, *Syria* ... 73 E9
Rutshuru, *Dem. Rep. of the Congo* ... 86 C2
Ruvo di Púglia, *Italy* ... 31 A9
Ruvu, *Tanzania* ... 86 D4
Ruvuma □, *Tanzania* ... 87 E4
Ruvuma →, *Tanzania* ... 87 E5
Ruwais, *U.A.E.* ... 71 E7
Ruwenzori, *Africa* ... 86 B2
Ruyigi, *Burundi* ... 86 C3
Ruyuan, *China* ... 59 E9
Ruzayevka, *Russia* ... 48 C7
Růžheve Konare, *Bulgaria* ... 41 D8
Ružomberok, *Slovak Rep.* ... 27 B12
Rwanda ■, *Africa* ... 86 C3
Ryakhovo, *Bulgaria* ... 41 C10
Ryan, L., *U.K.* ... 14 G3
Ryazan, *Russia* ... 46 E10
Ryazhsk, *Russia* ... 46 F11

Rybache = Rybachye, *Kazakstan* ... 50 E9
Rybachye = Ysyk-Köl, *Kyrgyzstan* ... 52 E11
Rybachye, *Kazakstan* ... 50 E9
Rybinsk, *Russia* ... 46 C10
Rybinskoye Vdkhr., *Russia* ... 46 C10
Rybnik, *Poland* ... 45 H5
Rybnitsa = Râbnița, *Moldova* ... 43 C14
Rybnoye, *Russia* ... 46 E10
Rychnov nad Kněžnou, *Czech Rep.* ... 27 A9
Rychwał, *Poland* ... 45 F5
Ryd, *Sweden* ... 11 H8
Rydaholm, *Sweden* ... 11 H8
Ryde, *U.K.* ... 13 G6
Ryderwood, *U.S.A.* ... 116 D3
Rydzyna, *Poland* ... 45 G3
Rye, *U.K.* ... 13 G8
Rye →, *U.K.* ... 12 C7
Rye Bay, *U.K.* ... 13 G8
Rye Patch Reservoir, *U.S.A.* ... 114 F4
Ryegate, *U.S.A.* ... 114 C9
Ryki, *Poland* ... 45 G8
Rylsk, *Russia* ... 47 G8
Rylstone, *Australia* ... 95 E4
Rymanów, *Poland* ... 45 J8
Ryn, *Poland* ... 44 E8
Ryn Peski, *Kazakstan* ... 49 G9
Ryōthu, *Japan* ... 54 E9
Rypin, *Poland* ... 45 E6
Ryssby, *Sweden* ... 11 H8
Ryūgasaki, *Japan* ... 55 G10
Ryūkyū Is. = Ryūkyū-rettō, *Japan* ... 55 M3
Ryūkyū-rettō, *Japan* ... 55 M3
Rzepin, *Poland* ... 45 F1
Rzeszów, *Poland* ... 45 H8
Rzeszów □, *Poland* ... 45 J8
Rzhev, *Russia* ... 46 D8

S

Sa, *Thailand* ... 64 C3
Sa Canal, *Spain* ... 37 C7
Sa Conillera, *Spain* ... 37 C7
Sa Dec, *Vietnam* ... 65 G5
Sa Dragonera, , *Spain* ... 37 B9
Sa Mesquida, *Spain* ... 37 B11
Sa Pobla, *Spain* ... 32 F8
Sa Savina, *Spain* ... 37 C7
Sa'ādatābād, *Fārs, Iran* ... 71 D7
Sa'ādatābād, *Kermān, Iran* ... 71 D7
Saale →, *Germany* ... 24 D7
Saaler Bodden, *Germany* ... 24 A8
Saalfeld, *Germany* ... 24 E7
Saalfelden, *Austria* ... 26 D5
Saane →, *Switz.* ... 25 H3
Saar →, *Europe* ... 17 E6
Saarbrücken, *Germany* ... 25 F2
Saarburg, *Germany* ... 25 F2
Saaremaa, *Estonia* ... 9 G20
Saarijärvi, *Finland* ... 9 E21
Saariselkä, *Finland* ... 8 B23
Saarland □, *Germany* ... 25 F2
Saarlouis, *Germany* ... 25 F2
Sab 'Abar, *Syria* ... 70 C3
Saba, *W. Indies* ... 121 C7
Šabac, *Serbia, Yug.* ... 40 B3
Sabadell, *Spain* ... 32 D7
Sabah □, *Malaysia* ... 62 C5
Sabak Bernam, *Malaysia* ... 65 L3
Sabalān, Kūhhā-ye, *Iran* ... 73 C12
Sabalana, Kepulauan, *Indonesia* ... 63 F5
Sábana de la Mar, *Dom. Rep.* ... 121 C6
Sábanalarga, *Colombia* ... 124 A4
Sabang, *Indonesia* ... 62 C1
Săbăoani, *Romania* ... 43 C11
Sabará, *Brazil* ... 125 G10
Sabattis, *U.S.A.* ... 111 B10
Sabáudia, *Italy* ... 30 A6
Saberania, *Indonesia* ... 63 E9
Sabhah, *Libya* ... 79 C8
Sabie, *S. Africa* ... 89 D5
Sabinal, *Mexico* ... 118 A3
Sabinal, *U.S.A.* ... 113 L5
Sabiñánigo, *Spain* ... 32 C4
Sabinar, Punta del, *Spain* ... 33 J2
Sabinas, *Mexico* ... 118 B4
Sabinas →, *Mexico* ... 118 B4
Sabinas Hidalgo, *Mexico* ... 118 B4
Sabine →, *U.S.A.* ... 113 L8
Sabine L., *U.S.A.* ... 113 L8
Sabine Pass, *U.S.A.* ... 113 L8
Sabinov, *Slovak Rep.* ... 27 B14
Sabirabad, *Azerbaijan* ... 49 K9
Sabkhet el Bardawîl, *Egypt* ... 75 D2
Sablayan, *Phil.* ... 61 E4
Sable, C., *Canada* ... 103 D6
Sable, C., *U.S.A.* ... 107 E10
Sable I., *Canada* ... 103 D8
Sablé-sur-Sarthe, *France* ... 18 E6
Sabor →, *Portugal* ... 34 D3
Sabou, *Burkina Faso* ... 82 C4
Sabres, *France* ... 20 D3
Sabrina Coast, *Antarctica* ... 5 C9
Sabugal, *Portugal* ... 34 E3
Sabulubbek, *Indonesia* ... 62 E1
Sabuncu, *Turkey* ... 39 B12
Sabzevār, *Iran* ... 71 B8

Sabzvārān, *Iran* ... 71 D8
Sac City, *U.S.A.* ... 112 D7
Sacedón, *Spain* ... 32 E2
Săcele, *Romania* ... 43 E10
Sachigo →, *Canada* ... 102 A2
Sachigo, L., *Canada* ... 102 B1
Sachkhere, *Georgia* ... 49 J6
Sachsen □, *Germany* ... 24 E9
Sachsen-Anhalt □, *Germany* ... 24 D7
Sacile, *Italy* ... 29 C9
Sackets Harbor, *U.S.A.* ... 111 C8
Saco, *Maine, U.S.A.* ... 109 D10
Saco, *Mont., U.S.A.* ... 114 B10
Sacramento, *U.S.A.* ... 116 G5
Sacramento →, *U.S.A.* ... 116 G5
Sacramento Mts., *U.S.A.* ... 115 K11
Sacramento Valley, *U.S.A.* ... 116 G5
Sacratif, C., *Spain* ... 35 J7
Sada, *Spain* ... 34 B2
Sádaba, *Spain* ... 32 C3
Sadani, *Tanzania* ... 86 D4
Sadao, *Thailand* ... 65 J3
Sadd el Aali, *Egypt* ... 80 C3
Saddle Mt., *U.S.A.* ... 116 E3
Sade, *Nigeria* ... 83 C7
Sadimi, *Dem. Rep. of the Congo* ... 87 D1
Sa'dīyah, Hawr as, *Iraq* ... 73 F12
Sado, *Japan* ... 54 F9
Sado →, *Portugal* ... 35 G2
Sadon, *Burma* ... 67 G20
Sadon, *Russia* ... 49 J6
Sæby, *Denmark* ... 11 G4
Saegertown, *U.S.A.* ... 110 E4
Saelices, *Spain* ... 32 F2
Safaalan, *Turkey* ... 41 E12
Safaga, *Egypt* ... 80 B3
Şafānīya, *Si. Arabia* ... 70 E3
Şafīābād, *Iran* ... 71 B8
Safīd Kūh, *Afghan.* ... 66 B3
Safonovo, *Russia* ... 46 E7
Safranbolu, *Turkey* ... 72 B5
Safwān, *Iraq* ... 70 D5
Sag Harbor, *U.S.A.* ... 111 F12
Saga, *Japan* ... 55 H5
Saga □, *Japan* ... 55 H5
Sagae, *Japan* ... 54 E10
Sagala, *Mali* ... 82 C3
Sagar, *India* ... 66 M9
Sagara, L., *Tanzania* ... 86 D3
Sagay, *Phil.* ... 61 F5
Sagil, *Mongolia* ... 60 A4
Saginaw, *U.S.A.* ... 108 D4
Saginaw B., *U.S.A.* ... 108 D4
Sagleipie, *Liberia* ... 82 D3
Saglouc = Salluit, *Canada* ... 101 B12
Sagŏ-ri, *S. Korea* ... 57 G14
Sagone, *France* ... 21 F12
Sagone, G. de, *France* ... 21 F12
Sagres, *Portugal* ... 35 J2
Sagua la Grande, *Cuba* ... 120 B3
Saguache, *U.S.A.* ... 115 G10
Saguenay →, *Canada* ... 103 C5
Sagunt = Sagunto, *Spain* ... 32 F4
Sagunto, *Spain* ... 32 F4
Sahaba, *Sudan* ... 80 D3
Sahagún, *Spain* ... 34 C5
Saham al Jawlān, *Syria* ... 75 C4
Sahand, Kūh-e, *Iran* ... 70 B5
Sahara, *Africa* ... 78 D6
Saharan Atlas = Saharien, Atlas, *Algeria* ... 78 B6
Saharanpur, *India* ... 68 E7
Saharien, Atlas, *Algeria* ... 78 B6
Sahasinaka, *Madag.* ... 89 C8
Sahaswan, *India* ... 69 E8
Sahel, Canal du, *Mali* ... 82 C3
Sahibganj, *India* ... 69 G12
Şāḥiliyah, *Iran* ... 70 C4
Sahiwal, *Pakistan* ... 68 D5
Şahneh, *Iran* ... 70 C5
Sahtaneh →, *Canada* ... 104 B4
Sahuaripa, *Mexico* ... 118 B3
Sahuarita, *U.S.A.* ... 115 L8
Sahuayo, *Mexico* ... 118 C4
Şāhy, *Slovak Rep.* ... 27 C11
Sai Buri, *Thailand* ... 65 J3
Sa'id Bundas, *Sudan* ... 79 G10
Sa'īdābād, *Kermān, Iran* ... 71 D7
Sa'īdābād, *Semnān, Iran* ... 71 B7
Sa'īdīyeh, *Iran* ... 71 B6
Saidpur, *Bangla.* ... 67 G16
Saidu, *Pakistan* ... 69 B5
Saignes, *France* ... 20 C6
Saigon = Phanh Bho Ho Chi Minh, *Vietnam* ... 65 G6
Saijō, *Japan* ... 55 H6
Saikhoa Ghat, *India* ... 67 F19
Saiki, *Japan* ... 55 H5
Saillans, *France* ... 21 D9
Sailolof, *Indonesia* ... 63 E8
Saimaa, *Finland* ... 9 F23
Saimbeyli, *Turkey* ... 72 D7
Şa'in Dezh, *Iran* ... 70 B5
St. Abb's Head, *U.K.* ... 14 F6
St-Affrique, *France* ... 20 E6
St-Agrève, *France* ... 21 C8
St-Aignan, *France* ... 18 E8

St. Alban's, *Canada* ... 103 C8
St. Albans, *Vt., U.S.A.* ... 111 B11
St. Albans, *W. Va., U.S.A.* ... 108 F5
St. Alban's Head, *U.K.* ... 13 G5
St. Albert, *Canada* ... 104 C6
St-Amand-en-Puisaye, *France* ... 19 E10
St-Amand-les-Eaux, *France* ... 19 B10
St-Amand-Montrond, *France* ... 19 F9
St-Amarin, *France* ... 19 E14
St-Amour, *France* ... 19 F12
St-André-de-Cubzac, *France* ... 20 D3
St-André-les-Alpes, *France* ... 21 E10
St. Andrew's, *Canada* ... 103 C8
St. Andrews, *U.K.* ... 14 E6
St-Anicet, *Canada* ... 111 A10
St. Ann B., *Canada* ... 103 C7
St. Ann's Bay, *Jamaica* ... 120 C4
St. Anthony, *Canada* ... 103 B8
St. Anthony, *U.S.A.* ... 114 E8
St-Antonin-Noble-Val, *France* ... 20 D5
St. Arnaud, *Australia* ... 95 F3
St. Arthur, *Canada* ... 103 C6
St-Astier, *France* ... 20 C4
St-Aubin-du-Cormier, *France* ... 18 D5
St-Augustin-Saguenay, *Canada* ... 103 B8
St. Augustine, *U.S.A.* ... 109 L5
St-Aulaye, *France* ... 20 C4
St. Austell, *U.K.* ... 13 G3
St-Avold, *France* ... 19 C13
St-Barthélemy, *W. Indies* ... 121 C7
St-Béat, *France* ... 20 F4
St. Bees Hd., *U.K.* ... 12 C4
St-Benoît-du-Sault, *France* ... 20 B5
St. Boniface, *Canada* ... 105 D9
St-Bonnet, *France* ... 21 D10
St-Brévin-les-Pins, *France* ... 18 E4
St-Brice-en-Coglès, *France* ... 18 D5
St. Bride's, *Canada* ... 103 C9
St. Brides B., *U.K.* ... 13 F2
St-Brieuc, *France* ... 18 D4
St-Calais, *France* ... 18 E7
St-Cast-le-Guildo, *France* ... 18 D4
St. Catharines, *Canada* ... 102 D4
St. Catherines I., *U.S.A.* ... 109 K5
St. Catherine's Pt., *U.K.* ... 13 G6
St-Céré, *France* ... 20 D5
St-Cergue, *Switz.* ... 25 J2
St-Cernin, *France* ... 20 C6
St-Chamond, *France* ... 21 C8
St. Charles, *Ill., U.S.A.* ... 108 E1
St. Charles, *Mo., U.S.A.* ... 112 F9
St-Chély-d'Apcher, *France* ... 20 D7
St-Chinian, *France* ... 20 E6
St. Christopher = St. Kitts, *W. Indies* ... 121 C7
St. Christopher-Nevis ■ = St. Kitts & Nevis ■, *W. Indies* ... 121 C7
St-Ciers-sur-Gironde, *France* ... 20 C3
St. Clair, *Mich., U.S.A.* ... 110 D2
St. Clair, *Pa., U.S.A.* ... 111 F8
St. Clair, L., *Canada* ... 102 D3
St. Clairsville, *U.S.A.* ... 110 F4
St-Claud, *France* ... 20 C4
St. Claude, *Canada* ... 105 D9
St-Claude, *France* ... 19 F12
St. Cloud, *Fla., U.S.A.* ... 109 L5
St. Cloud, *Minn., U.S.A.* ... 112 C7
St-Coeur de Marie, *Canada* ... 103 C5
St. Cricq, C., *Australia* ... 93 E1
St. Croix, *Virgin Is.* ... 121 C7
St. Croix →, *U.S.A.* ... 112 C8
St. Croix Falls, *U.S.A.* ... 112 C8
St-Cyprien, *France* ... 20 F7
St-Cyr-sur-Mer, *France* ... 21 E9
St. David's, *Canada* ... 103 C8
St. David's, *U.K.* ... 13 F2
St. David's Head, *U.K.* ... 13 F2
St-Denis, *France* ... 19 D9
St-Dié, *France* ... 19 D13
St-Dizier, *France* ... 19 D11
St-Égrève, *France* ... 21 C9
St. Elias, Mt., *U.S.A.* ... 100 B5
St. Elias Mts., *Canada* ... 104 A1
St-Éloy-les-Mines, *France* ... 19 F9
St-Émilion, *France* ... 20 D3
St-Étienne-de-Tinée, *France* ... 21 D10
St-Étienne-du-Rouvray, *France* ... 18 C8
St. Eugène, *Canada* ... 111 A10
St. Eustatius, *W. Indies* ... 121 C7
St-Fargeau, *France* ... 19 E10
St-Félicien, *Canada* ... 102 C5
St-Florent, *France* ... 21 F13
St-Florent, G. de, *France* ... 21 F13
St-Florent-sur-Cher, *France* ... 19 F9
St-Florentin, *France* ... 19 E10
St-Flour, *France* ... 20 C7
St. Francis, *U.S.A.* ... 112 F4
St. Francis →, *U.S.A.* ... 113 H9
St. Francis, C., *S. Africa* ... 88 E3
St. Francisville, *U.S.A.* ... 113 K9
St-François, L., *Canada* ... 111 A10
St-Fulgent, *France* ... 18 F5
St-Gabriel-de-Brandon, *Canada* ... 102 C5
St. Gallen = Sankt Gallen, *Switz.* ... 25 H5

St-Galmier, France 19 G11
St-Gaudens, France 20 E4
St-Gaultier, France 18 F8
St-Gengoux-le-National, France 19 F11
St-Geniez-d'Olt, France .. 20 D6
St. George, Australia 95 D4
St. George, Canada 103 C6
St. George, S.C., U.S.A. .. 109 J5
St. George, Utah, U.S.A. .. 115 H7
St. George, C., Canada .. 103 C8
St. George, C., U.S.A. ... 109 L3
St. George Ra., Australia . 92 C4
St. George's, Canada 103 C8
St-Georges, Canada 103 C5
St. George's, Grenada ... 121 D7
St. George's B., Canada .. 103 C8
St. Georges Basin, Australia 92 C4
St. George's Channel, Europe 15 E6
St. Georges Hd., Australia . 95 F5
St-Georges-lès-Baillargeaux, France ... 20 B4
St-Germain-de-Calberte, France 20 D7
St-Germain-en-Laye, France 19 D9
St-Germain-Lembron, France 20 C7
St-Gervais-d'Auvergne, France 19 F9
St-Gervais-les-Bains, France 21 C10
St-Gildas, Pte. de, France . 18 E4
St-Gilles, France 21 E8
St-Girons, Ariège, France . 20 F5
St-Girons, Landes, France . 20 E2
St. Gotthard P. = San Gottardo, P. del, Switz. . 25 J4
St. Helena, U.S.A. 114 G2
St. Helena ■, Atl. Oc. ... 77 H3
St. Helena, Mt., U.S.A. .. 116 G4
St. Helena B., S. Africa .. 88 E2
St. Helens, Australia 94 G4
St. Helens, U.K. 12 D5
St. Helens, U.S.A. 116 E4
St. Helens, Mt., U.S.A. .. 116 D4
St. Helier, U.K. 13 H5
St-Herblain, France 18 E5
St-Hilaire-du-Harcouët, France 18 D5
St-Hippolyte, France 19 E13
St-Hippolyte-du-Fort, France 20 D7
St-Honoré-les-Bains, France 19 F10
St-Hubert, Belgium 17 D5
St-Hyacinthe, Canada ... 102 C5
St. Ignace, U.S.A. 108 C3
St. Ignace I., Canada ... 102 C2
St. Ignatius, U.S.A. 114 C6
St-Imier, Switz. 25 H2
St. Ives, U.K. 13 G2
St-James, France 18 D5
St. James, U.S.A. 112 D7
St-Jean, Canada 102 C5
St-Jean →, Canada 103 B7
St-Jean, L., Canada 103 C5
St. Jean Baptiste, Canada . 105 D9
St-Jean-d'Angély, France . 20 C3
St-Jean-de-Braye, France . 19 E8
St-Jean-de-Luz, France .. 20 E2
St-Jean-de-Maurienne, France 21 C10
St-Jean-de-Monts, France . 18 F4
St-Jean-du-Gard, France .. 20 D7
St-Jean-en-Royans, France 21 C9
St-Jean-Pied-de-Port, France 20 E2
St-Jean-Port-Joli, Canada . 103 C5
St-Jérôme, Qué., Canada . 102 C5
St-Jérôme, Qué., Canada . 103 C5
St. John, Canada 103 C6
St. John, Kans., U.S.A. .. 113 G5
St. John, N. Dak., U.S.A. 112 A5
St. John →, U.S.A. 103 C6
St. John, C., Canada 103 C8
St. John's, Antigua 121 C7
St. John's, Canada 103 C9
St. Johns, Ariz., U.S.A. .. 115 J9
St. Johns, Mich., U.S.A. . 108 D3
St. Johns →, U.S.A. 109 K5
St. John's Pt., Ireland ... 15 B3
St. Johnsbury, U.S.A. 111 B12
St. Johnsville, U.S.A. 111 D10
St. Joseph, La., U.S.A. ... 113 K9
St. Joseph, Mich., U.S.A. . 108 D2
St. Joseph, Mo., U.S.A. .. 112 F7
St. Joseph →, U.S.A. 108 D2
St. Joseph, I., Canada ... 102 C3
St. Joseph, L., Canada ... 102 B1
St-Jovite, Canada 102 C5
St-Juéry, France 20 E6
St-Julien-Chapteuil, France 21 C8
St-Julien-de-Vouvantes, France 18 E5
St-Julien-en-Genevois, France 19 F13
St-Junien, France 20 C4
St-Just-en-Chaussée, France 19 C9
St-Just-en-Chevalet, France 20 C7
St. Kilda, N.Z. 91 L3
St. Kitts, U.S.A. 121 C7
St. Kitts & Nevis ■, W. Indies 121 C7
St. Laurent, Canada 105 C9
St-Laurent-de-la-Salanque, France 20 F6

St-Laurent-du-Pont, France 21 C9
St-Laurent-en-Grandvaux, France 19 F12
St-Laurent-et-Benon, France 20 C3
St. Lawrence, Australia ... 94 C4
St. Lawrence, Canada ... 103 C8
St. Lawrence →, Canada . 103 C6
St. Lawrence, Gulf of, Canada 103 C7
St. Lawrence I., U.S.A. ... 100 B3
St. Leonard, Canada 103 C6
St-Léonard-de-Noblat, France 20 C5
St. Lewis →, Canada 103 B8
St-Lô, France 18 C5
St-Louis, France 19 E14
St. Louis, Senegal 82 B1
St. Louis, Mich., U.S.A. . 108 D3
St. Louis, Mo., U.S.A. ... 112 F9
St. Louis →, U.S.A. 112 B8
St-Loup-sur-Semouse, France 19 E13
St. Lucia ■, W. Indies ... 121 D7
St. Lucia, L., S. Africa ... 89 D5
St. Lucia Channel, W. Indies 121 D7
St. Lunaire-Griquet, Canada 103 B8
St. Maarten, W. Indies ... 121 C7
St. Magnus B., U.K. 14 A7
St-Maixent-l'École, France 20 B3
St-Malo, France 18 D4
St-Malo, G. de, France .. 18 D4
St-Mandrier-sur-Mer, France 21 E9
St-Marc, Haiti 121 C5
St-Marcellin, France 21 C9
St-Marcouf, Îs., France .. 18 C5
St. Maries, U.S.A. 114 C5
St. Martin, W. Indies 121 C7
St. Martin, L., Canada ... 105 C9
St-Martin-de-Crau, France 21 E8
St-Martin-de-Ré, France .. 20 B2
St-Martin-d'Hères, France 21 C9
St-Martin-Vésubie, France 21 D11
St. Martins, Canada 103 C6
St. Martinville, U.S.A. ... 113 K9
St-Martory, France 20 E4
St. Mary Pk., Australia .. 95 E2
St. Marys, Australia 94 G4
St. Marys, Canada 110 C3
St. Mary's, Corn., U.K. .. 13 H1
St. Mary's, Orkney, U.K. . 14 C6
St. Marys, U.S.A. 110 E6
St. Mary's, C., Canada ... 103 C9
St. Mary's B., Canada ... 103 C9
St. Marys Bay, Canada .. 103 D6
St-Mathieu, Pte., France .. 18 D2
St. Matthews, I. = Zadetkyi Kyun, Burma . 65 H2
St-Maurice →, Canada .. 102 C5
St-Maximin-la-Ste-Baume, France 21 E9
St-Médard-en-Jalles, France 20 D3
St-Méen-le-Grand, France 18 D4
St-Mihiel, France 19 D12
St. Moritz, Switz. 25 J5
St-Nazaire, France 18 E4
St. Neots, U.K. 13 E7
St-Nicolas-de-Port, France 19 D13
St-Niklaas, Belgium 17 C4
St-Omer, France 19 B9
St-Pacome, Canada 103 C6
St-Palais-sur-Mer, France . 20 C2
St-Pamphile, Canada 103 C6
St-Pardoux-la-Rivière, France 20 C4
St. Pascal, Canada 103 C6
St. Paul, Canada 104 C6
St-Paul, France 21 D10
St. Paul, Minn., U.S.A. .. 112 C8
St. Paul, Nebr., U.S.A. .. 112 E5
St. Paul, I., Ind. Oc. 3 F13
St-Paul-de-Fenouillet, France 20 F6
St. Paul I., Canada 103 C7
St-Paul-lès-Dax, France ... 20 E2
St-Péray, France 21 D8
St. Peter, U.S.A. 112 C8
St. Peter-Ording, Germany 24 A4
St. Peter Port, U.K. 13 H5
St. Peters, N.S., Canada . 103 C7
St. Peters, P.E.I., Canada . 103 C7
St. Petersburg = Sankt-Peterburg, Russia 46 C6
St. Petersburg, U.S.A. ... 109 M4
St-Philbert-de-Grand-Lieu, France 18 E5
St-Pierre, St- P. & M. 103 C8
St-Pierre, L., Canada 102 C5
St-Pierre-d'Oléron, France 20 C2
St-Pierre-en-Port, France . 18 C7
St-Pierre et Miquelon □, St- P. & M. 103 C8
St-Pierre-le-Moûtier, France 19 F10
St-Pierre-sur-Dives, France 18 C6
St-Pol-de-Léon, France ... 18 D2
St-Pol-sur-Mer, France .. 19 A9
St-Pol-sur-Ternoise, France 19 B9
St-Pons, France 20 E6
St-Pourçain-sur-Sioule, France 19 F10
St-Priest, France 21 C8
St-Quay-Portrieux, France 18 D4
St-Quentin, France 19 C10

St-Rambert-d'Albon, France 21 C8
St-Raphaël, France 21 E10
St. Regis, U.S.A. 114 C6
St-Renan, France 18 D2
St-Saëns, France 18 C8
St-Savin, France 20 B4
St-Savinien, France 20 C3
St. Sebastien, Tanjon' i, Madag. 89 A8
St-Seine-l'Abbaye, France 19 E11
St-Sernin-sur-Rance, France 20 E6
St-Sever, France 20 E3
St-Siméon, Canada 103 C6
St. Stephen, Canada 103 C6
St-Sulpice, France 20 E5
St-Sulpice-Laurière, France 20 B5
St-Sulpice-les-Feuilles, France 20 B5
St-Syprien = St-Cyprien, France 20 F7
St-Thégonnec, France 18 D3
St. Thomas, Canada 102 D3
St. Thomas I., Virgin Is. . 121 C7
St-Tite, Canada 102 C5
St-Tropez, France 21 E10
St. Troud = St. Truiden, Belgium 17 D5
St. Truiden, Belgium 17 D5
St-Vaast-la-Hougue, France 18 C5
St-Valery-en-Caux, France 18 C7
St-Valéry-sur-Somme, France 19 B8
St-Vallier, France 19 F11
St-Vallier-de-Thiey, France 21 E10
St-Varent, France 18 F6
St-Vaury, France 20 B5
St. Vincent, Italy 28 C4
St. Vincent, W. Indies ... 121 D7
St. Vincent, G., Australia . 95 F2
St. Vincent & the Grenadines ■, W. Indies 121 D7
St-Vincent-de-Tyrosse, France 20 E2
St. Vincent Passage, W. Indies 121 D7
St-Vith, Belgium 17 D6
St-Vivien-de-Médoc, France 20 C2
St-Yrieix-la-Perche, France 20 C5
Ste-Adresse, France 18 C7
Ste-Agathe-des-Monts, Canada 102 C5
Ste-Anne de Beaupré, Canada 103 C5
Ste-Anne-des-Monts, Canada 103 C6
Ste-Croix, Switz. 25 J2
Ste-Enimie, France 20 D7
Ste-Foy-la-Grande, France 20 D4
Ste. Genevieve, U.S.A. .. 112 G9
Ste-Hermine, France 20 B2
Ste-Livrade-sur-Lot, France 20 D4
Ste-Marguerite →, Canada 103 B6
Ste-Marie, Martinique ... 121 D7
Ste-Marie-aux-Mines, France 19 D14
Ste-Marie de la Madeleine, Canada 103 C5
Ste-Maure-de-Touraine, France 18 E7
Ste-Maxime, France 21 E10
Ste-Menehould, France .. 19 C11
Ste-Mère-Église, France .. 18 C5
Ste-Rose, Guadeloupe ... 121 C7
Ste. Rose du Lac, Canada 105 C9
Ste-Savine, France 19 D11
Ste-Sigolène, France 21 C8
Saintes, France 20 C3
Saintes, I. des, Guadeloupe 121 C7
Stes-Maries-de-la-Mer, France 21 E8
Saintfield, U.K. 15 B6
Saintonge, France 20 C3
Saipan, Pac. Oc. 96 F6
Sairang, India 67 H18
Sairecábur, Cerro, Bolivia 126 A2
Saitama □, Japan 55 F9
Saiti, Moldova 43 D14
Sajama, Bolivia 124 G5
Sajan, Serbia, Yug. 42 E5
Sajó →, Hungary 42 D6
Sajószentpéter, Hungary . 42 B5
Sajum, India 69 C8
Sak →, S. Africa 88 E3
Sakai, Japan 55 G7
Sakaide, Japan 55 G6
Sakaiminato, Japan 55 G6
Sakākah, Si. Arabia 70 D4
Sakakawea, L., U.S.A. .. 112 B4
Sakami, L., Canada 102 B4
Sakania, Dem. Rep. of the Congo 87 E2
Sakarya = Adapazarı, Turkey 72 B4
Sakarya →, Turkey 72 B4
Sakashima-Guntō, Japan . 55 M2
Sakata, Japan 54 E9
Sakchu, N. Korea 57 D13
Sakeny →, Madag. 89 C8
Sakété, Benin 83 D5
Sakha □, Russia 51 C14
Sakhalin, Russia 51 D15
Sakhalinskiy Zaliv, Russia 51 D15
Şakiai, Lithuania 9 J20
Sakon Nakhon, Thailand . 64 D5
Sakrand, Pakistan 68 F3

Sakrivier, S. Africa 88 E3
Sakskøbing, Denmark ... 11 K5
Sakuma, Japan 55 G8
Sakurai, Japan 55 G7
Saky, Ukraine 47 K7
Sal →, Russia 49 G5
Šaľa, Slovak Rep. 27 C10
Sala, Sweden 10 E10
Sala Consilina, Italy 31 B8
Sala-y-Gómez, Pac. Oc. . 97 K17
Salaberry-de-Valleyfield, Canada 102 C5
Saladas, Argentina 126 B4
Saladillo, Argentina 126 D4
Salado →, Buenos Aires, Argentina 126 D4
Salado →, La Pampa, Argentina 128 D3
Salado →, Santa Fe, Argentina 126 C3
Salado →, Mexico 118 B5
Salaga, Ghana 83 D4
Salala, Liberia 82 D2
Salala, Sudan 80 C4
Salālah, Oman 74 D5
Salamanca, Chile 126 C1
Salamanca, Spain 34 E5
Salamanca, U.S.A. 110 D6
Salamanca □, Spain 34 E5
Salāmatābād, Iran 70 C5
Salamis, Cyprus 36 D12
Salamís, Greece 38 D5
Salar de Atacama, Chile . 126 A2
Salar de Uyuni, Bolivia . 124 H5
Sălard, Romania 42 C7
Salas, Spain 34 B4
Salas de los Infantes, Spain 34 C7
Salatiga, Indonesia 63 G14
Salaverry, Peru 124 E3
Salawati, Indonesia 63 E8
Salayar, Indonesia 63 F6
Salazar →, Spain 32 C3
Salbris, France 19 E9
Salcia, Romania 43 G9
Sălciua, Romania 43 D8
Salcombe, U.K. 13 G4
Saldaña, Spain 34 C6
Saldanha, S. Africa 88 E2
Saldanha B., S. Africa .. 88 E2
Saldus, Latvia 9 H20
Saldus □, Latvia 44 B9
Sale, Australia 95 F4
Sale, Italy 28 D5
Salé, Morocco 78 B4
Sale, U.K. 12 D5
Salekhard, Russia 50 C7
Salem, India 66 P11
Salem, Ind., U.S.A. 108 F2
Salem, Mass., U.S.A. ... 111 D14
Salem, Mo., U.S.A. 113 G9
Salem, N.J., U.S.A. 108 F8
Salem, Ohio, U.S.A. ... 110 F4
Salem, Oreg., U.S.A. ... 114 D2
Salem, S. Dak., U.S.A. .. 112 D6
Salem, Va., U.S.A. 108 G5
Salemi, Italy 30 E5
Sälen, Sweden 10 C7
Salernes, France 21 E10
Salerno, Italy 31 B7
Salerno, G. di, Italy 31 B7
Salford, U.K. 12 D5
Salgir →, Ukraine 47 K8
Salgótarján, Hungary ... 42 B4
Salgueiro, Brazil 125 E11
Salida, U.S.A. 106 C5
Salies-de-Béarn, France . 20 E3
Salihli, Turkey 72 C3
Salihorsk, Belarus 47 F4
Salima, Malawi 85 G6
Salina, Italy 31 D7
Salina, Kans., U.S.A. ... 112 F6
Salina Cruz, Mexico 119 D5
Salinas, Brazil 125 G10
Salinas, Chile 126 A2
Salinas, Ecuador 124 D2
Salinas, U.S.A. 116 J5
Salinas →, Guatemala .. 119 D6
Salinas →, U.S.A. 116 J5
Salinas, B. de, Nic. 120 D2
Salinas, Pampa de las, Argentina 126 C2
Salinas Ambargasta, Argentina 126 B3
Salinas de Hidalgo, Mexico 118 C4
Salinas Grandes, Argentina 126 C3
Saline →, Ark., U.S.A. .. 113 J8
Saline →, Kans., U.S.A. . 112 F6
Salines, Spain 37 B10
Salines, C. de, Spain ... 37 B10
Salinópolis, Brazil 125 D9
Salins-les-Bains, France . 19 F12
Salir, Portugal 35 H2
Salisbury = Harare, Zimbabwe 87 F3
Salisbury, Australia 95 E2
Salisbury, U.K. 13 F6
Salisbury, Md., U.S.A. .. 108 F8
Salisbury, N.C., U.S.A. . 109 H5
Salisbury Plain, U.K. ... 13 F6

Sallent, Spain 32 D6
Salles, France 20 D3
Salles-Curan, France 20 D6
Salling, Denmark 11 H2
Sallisaw, U.S.A. 113 H7
Sallom Junction, Sudan .. 80 D4
Salluit, Canada 101 B12
Salmās, Iran 70 B5
Salmerón, Spain 32 E2
Salmo, Canada 104 D5
Salmon, U.S.A. 114 D7
Salmon →, Canada 104 C4
Salmon →, U.S.A. 114 D5
Salmon Arm, Canada ... 104 C5
Salmon Falls, U.S.A. ... 114 E6
Salmon Gums, Australia . 93 F3
Salmon Res., Canada ... 103 C8
Salmon River Mts., U.S.A. 114 D6
Salo, Finland 9 F20
Salò, Italy 28 C7
Salobreña, Spain 35 J7
Salome, U.S.A. 117 M13
Salon-de-Provence, France 21 E9
Salonica = Thessaloníki, Greece 40 F6
Salonta, Romania 42 D6
Salor →, Spain 35 F3
Salou, Spain 32 D6
Salou, C. de, Spain 32 D6
Salpausselkä, Finland ... 9 F22
Salsacate, Argentina 126 C2
Salses, France 20 F6
Salsk, Russia 49 G5
Salso →, Italy 30 E6
Salsomaggiore Terme, Italy 28 D6
Salt →, Canada 104 B6
Salt →, U.S.A. 115 K7
Salt Creek, Australia ... 95 F2
Salt Fork Arkansas →, U.S.A. 113 G6
Salt Lake City, U.S.A. .. 114 F8
Salt Range, Pakistan ... 68 C5
Salta, Argentina 126 A2
Salta □, Argentina 126 A2
Saltash, U.K. 13 G3
Saltburn by the Sea, U.K. 12 C7
Saltcoats, U.K. 14 F4
Saltee Is., Ireland 15 D5
Saltfjellet, Norway 8 C16
Saltfjorden, Norway 8 C16
Saltholm, Denmark 11 J6
Saltillo, Mexico 118 B4
Salto, Argentina 126 C3
Salto, Uruguay 126 C4
Salto del Guaíra, Paraguay 128 A6
Salton City, U.S.A. 117 M11
Salton Sea, U.S.A. 117 M11
Saltpond, Ghana 83 D4
Saltsjöbaden, Sweden ... 10 E12
Saltville, U.S.A. 108 G5
Saluda →, U.S.A. 109 J5
Salûm, Egypt 80 A2
Salûm, Khâlig el, Egypt . 80 A2
Salur, India 67 K13
Saluzzo, Italy 28 D4
Salvador, Brazil 125 F11
Salvador, Canada 105 C7
Salvador, L., U.S.A. ... 113 L9
Salvaterra de Magos, Portugal 35 F2
Sálvora, I. de, Spain ... 34 C2
Salween →, Burma 67 L20
Salyan, Azerbaijan 73 C13
Salyersville, U.S.A. 108 G4
Salza →, Austria 26 D7
Salzach →, Austria 26 C5
Salzburg, Austria 26 D6
Salzburg □, Austria 26 D6
Salzgitter, Germany 24 C6
Salzkotten, Germany ... 24 D4
Salzwedel, Germany ... 24 C7
Sam Neua, Laos 64 B5
Sam Ngao, Thailand ... 64 D2
Sam Rayburn Reservoir, U.S.A. 113 K7
Sam Son, Vietnam 64 C5
Sam Teu, Laos 64 C5
Sama de Langreo = Langreo, Spain 34 B5
Samagaltay, Russia 51 D10
Samales Group, Phil. ... 61 J5
Samālūt, Egypt 80 J7
Samana, India 68 D7
Samana Cay, Bahamas . 121 B5
Samandağı, Turkey 72 D6
Samandıra, Turkey 41 F13
Samangwa, Dem. Rep. of the Congo 86 C1
Samani, Japan 54 C11
Samanli Dağları, Turkey . 41 F13
Samar, Phil. 61 B7
Samara, Russia 48 D10
Samara →, Russia 48 D10
Samara, Ukraine 47 H8
Samaria = Shōmrōn, West Bank 75 C4
Samariá, Greece 36 D5
Samarinda, Indonesia ... 62 E5
Samarkand = Samarqand, Uzbekistan 50 F7
Samarqand, Uzbekistan . 50 F7
Samarra, Iraq 70 C4
Samastipur, India 69 G11
Şamaxı, Azerbaijan 49 K9

Samba,
  Dem. Rep. of the Congo 86 C2
Samba, *India* 69 C6
Sambalpur, *India* 67 J14
Sambar, Tanjung, *Indonesia* 62 E4
Sambava, *Madag.* 89 A9
Sambhal, *India* 69 E8
Sambhar, *India* 68 F6
Sambiase, *Italy* 31 D9
Sambir, *Ukraine* 47 H2
Sambor, *Cambodia* 64 F6
Sambuca di Sicília, *Italy* .. 30 E6
Samburu □, *Kenya* 86 B4
Samch'ŏk, *S. Korea* 57 F15
Samchonpo, *S. Korea* 57 G15
Same, *Tanzania* 86 C4
Samer, *France* 19 B8
Samfya, *Zambia* 87 E2
Sámi, *Greece* 38 C2
Şämkir, *Azerbaijan* 49 K8
Şamlı, *Turkey* 39 B9
Samnah, *Si. Arabia* 70 E3
Samo Alto, *Chile* 126 C1
Samobor, *Croatia* 29 C12
Samoëns, *France* 19 F13
Samokov, *Bulgaria* 40 D7
Samoorombón, B.,
  Argentina 126 D4
Šamorín, *Slovak Rep.* 27 C10
Samorogouan,
  Burkina Faso 82 C4
Sámos, *Greece* 39 D8
Samoš, *Serbia, Yug.* 42 E5
Samos, *Spain* 34 C3
Sámos □, *Greece* 39 D8
Samothráki = Mathráki,
  Greece 36 A3
Samothráki, *Greece* 41 F9
Samoylovka, *Russia* 48 E6
Sampa, *Ghana* 82 D4
Sampacho, *Argentina* 126 C3
Sampang, *Indonesia* 63 G15
Samper de Calanda, *Spain* 32 D4
Sampéyre, *Italy* 28 D4
Sampit, *Indonesia* 62 E4
Sampit, Teluk, *Indonesia* . 62 E4
Samrong, *Cambodia* 64 E4
Samrong, *Thailand* 64 E3
Samsø, *Denmark* 11 J4
Samsø Bælt, *Denmark* ... 11 J4
Samsun, *Turkey* 72 B7
Samtredia, *Georgia* 49 J6
Samui, Ko, *Thailand* 65 H3
Samur →, *Russia* 49 K9
Samurskiy Khrebet, *Russia* 49 K8
Samusole,
  Dem. Rep. of the Congo 87 E1
Samut Prakan, *Thailand* .. 64 F3
Samwari, *Pakistan* 68 E2
San, *Mali* 82 C4
San →, *Cambodia* 64 F5
San →, *Poland* 45 H8
San Adrián, *Spain* 32 C3
San Adrián, C. de, *Spain* . 34 B2
San Agustín, C., *Phil.* ... 61 H7
San Agustín de Valle Fértil,
  Argentina 126 C2
San Ambrosio, *Pac. Oc.* .. 122 F3
San Andreas, *U.S.A.* 116 G6
San Andrés, I. de,
  Caribbean 120 D3
San Andrés del Rabanedo,
  Spain 34 C5
San Andres Mts., *U.S.A.* . 115 K10
San Andrés Tuxtla, *Mexico* 119 D5
San Angelo, *U.S.A.* 113 K4
San Anselmo, *U.S.A.* 116 H4
San Antonio, *Belize* 119 D7
San Antonio, *Chile* 126 C1
San Antonio, *Phil.* 61 D4
San Antonio, *N. Mex.,*
  U.S.A. 115 K10
San Antonio, *Tex., U.S.A.* 113 L5
San Antonio →, *U.S.A.* .. 113 L6
San Antonio, C., *Argentina* 126 D4
San Antonio, C., *Cuba* ... 120 B3
San Antonio, C. de, *Spain* 33 G5
San Antonio, Mt., *U.S.A.* 117 L9
San Antonio de los Baños,
  Cuba 120 B3
San Antonio de los Cobres,
  Argentina 126 A2
San Antonio Oeste,
  Argentina 128 E4
San Arcángelo, *Italy* 31 B9
San Ardo, *U.S.A.* 116 J6
San Augustín, *Canary Is.* . 37 G4
San Augustine, *U.S.A.* ... 113 K7
San Bartolomé, *Canary Is.* 37 F6
San Bartolomé de Tirajana,
  Canary Is. 37 G4
San Bartolomeo in Galdo,
  Italy 31 A8
San Benedetto del Tronto,
  Italy 29 F10
San Benedetto Po, *Italy* .. 28 C7
San Benedicto, I., *Mexico* 118 D2
San Benito, *U.S.A.* 113 M6
San Benito →, *U.S.A.* ... 116 J5
San Benito Mt., *U.S.A.* .. 116 J6
San Bernardo, *U.S.A.* ... 117 L9
San Bernardino Mts.,
  U.S.A. 117 L10
San Bernardino Str., *Phil.* 61 E6
San Bernardo, *Chile* 126 C1

San Bernardo. I. de,
  Colombia 124 B3
San Blas, *Mexico* 118 B3
San Blas, Arch. de,
  Panama 120 E4
San Blas, C., *U.S.A.* 109 L3
San Bonifacio, *Italy* 29 C8
San Borja, *Bolivia* 124 F5
San Buenaventura, *Mexico* 118 B4
San Carlos = Butuku-Luba,
  Eq. Guin. 83 E6
San Carlos = Sant Carles,
  Spain 37 B8
San Carlos, *Argentina* ... 126 C2
San Carlos, *Chile* 126 D1
San Carlos, *Mexico* 118 B4
San Carlos, *Nic.* 120 D3
San Carlos, *Negros, Phil.* . 61 F5
San Carlos, *Pangasinan,*
  Phil. 61 D4
San Carlos, *Uruguay* 127 C5
San Carlos, *U.S.A.* 115 K8
San Carlos, *Cojedes,*
  Venezuela 124 B5
San Carlos, *Cojedes,*
  Venezuela 124 B5
San Carlos de Bariloche,
  Argentina 128 E2
San Carlos de Bolívar,
  Argentina 128 D4
San Carlos de la Rápita =
  Sant Carles de la Ràpita,
  Spain 32 E5
San Carlos del Zulia,
  Venezuela 124 B4
San Carlos L., *U.S.A.* ... 115 K8
San Cataldo, *Italy* 30 E6
San Celoni = Sant Celoni,
  Spain 32 D7
San Clemente, *Chile* 126 D1
San Clemente, *Spain* 33 F2
San Clemente I., *U.S.A.* . 117 N8
San Clemente I., *U.S.A.* . 117 N8
San Cristóbal = Es Migjorn
  Gran, *Spain* 37 B11
San Cristóbal, *Argentina* . 126 C3
San Cristóbal, *Dom. Rep.* 121 C5
San Cristóbal, *Mexico* ... 119 D6
San Cristóbal, *Venezuela* 124 B4
San Damiano d'Asti, *Italy* 28 D5
San Daniele del Friuli, *Italy* 29 B10
San Diego, *Calif., U.S.A.* 117 N9
San Diego, *Tex., U.S.A.* . 113 M5
San Diego, C., *Argentina* . 128 G3
San Diego de la Unión,
  Mexico 118 C4
San Dimitri, Ras, *Malta* . 36 C1
San Donà di Piave, *Italy* . 29 C9
San Estanislao, *Paraguay* 126 A4
San Esteban de Gormaz,
  Spain 32 D1
San Felice Circeo, *Italy* .. 30 A6
San Felice sul Panaro, *Italy* 29 D8
San Felipe, *Chile* 126 C1
San Felipe, *Mexico* 118 A2
San Felipe, *Venezuela* ... 124 A5
San Félix, *Pac. Oc.* 122 F2
San Fernando = Sant
  Ferran, *Spain* 37 C7
San Fernando, *Chile* 126 C1
San Fernando, *Mexico* .. 118 B1
San Fernando, *La Union,*
  Phil. 61 C4
San Fernando, *Pampanga,*
  Phil. 61 D4
San Fernando, *Spain* 35 J4
San Fernando,
  Trin. & Tob. 121 D7
San Fernando, *U.S.A.* ... 117 L8
San Fernando →, *Mexico* 118 C5
San Fernando de Apure,
  Venezuela 124 B5
San Fernando de Atabapo,
  Venezuela 124 C5
San Fernando di Púglia,
  Italy 31 A9
San Francisco, *Argentina* . 126 C3
San Francisco, *U.S.A.* ... 116 H4
San Francisco →, *U.S.A.* 115 K9
San Francisco, Paso de,
  S. Amer. 126 B2
San Francisco de Macorís,
  Dom. Rep. 121 C5
San Francisco del Monte de
  Oro, *Argentina* 126 C2
San Francisco del Oro,
  Mexico 118 B3
San Francisco Javier = Sant
  Francesc de Formentera,
  Spain 37 C7
San Francisco Solano, Pta.,
  Colombia 124 B2
San Fratello, *Italy* 31 D7
San Gavino Monreale, *Italy* 30 C1
San Gimignano, *Italy* ... 28 E8
San Giórgio di Nogaro,
  Italy 29 C10
San Giórgio Iónico, *Italy* . 31 B10
San Giovanni Bianco, *Italy* 28 C6
San Giovanni in Fiore, *Italy* 31 C9
San Giovanni in Persiceto,
  Italy 29 D8
San Giovanni Rotondo,
  Italy 29 G12
San Giovanni Valdarno,
  Italy 29 E8

San Giuliano Terme, *Italy* 28 E7
San Gorgonio Mt., *U.S.A.* 117 L10
San Gottardo, P. del,
  Switz. 25 J4
San Gregorio, *Uruguay* .. 127 C4
San Gregorio, *U.S.A.* 116 H4
San Guiseppe Jato, *Italy* . 30 E6
San Ignacio, *Belize* 119 D7
San Ignacio, *Bolivia* 124 G6
San Ignacio, *Mexico* 118 B2
San Ignacio, *Paraguay* ... 126 B4
San Ignacio, L., *Mexico* . 118 B2
San Ildefonso, C., *Phil.* .. 61 D5
San Isidro, *Argentina* ... 126 C4
San Jacinto, *U.S.A.* 117 M10
San Jaime = Sant Jaume,
  Spain 37 B11
San Javier, *Misiones,*
  Argentina 127 B4
San Javier, *Santa Fe,*
  Argentina 126 C4
San Javier, *Bolivia* 124 G6
San Javier, *Chile* 126 D1
San Javier, *Spain* 33 H4
San Jeronimo Taviche,
  Mexico 119 D5
San Joaquin, *U.S.A.* 116 J6
San Joaquin →, *U.S.A.* . 116 G5
San Joaquin Valley, *U.S.A.* 116 J6
San Jordi = Sant Jordi,
  Spain 37 B9
San Jorge, *Argentina* 126 C3
San Jorge, *Spain* 37 C7
San Jorge, B. de, *Mexico* . 118 A2
San Jorge, G., *Argentina* . 128 F3
San Jorge, G. of, *Argentina* 122 H4
San José = San Josep,
  Spain 37 C7
San José, *Costa Rica* 120 E3
San José, *Guatemala* 120 D1
San José, *Mexico* 118 C2
San Jose, *Luzon, Phil.* ... 61 D4
San Jose, *Mindoro, Phil.* . 61 E4
San Jose, *U.S.A.* 116 H5
San Jose →, *U.S.A.* 115 J10
San José de Chiquitos,
  Bolivia 124 G6
San José de Feliciano,
  Argentina 126 C4
San José de Jáchal,
  Argentina 126 C2
San José de Mayo, *Uruguay* 126 C4
San José del Cabo, *Mexico* 118 C3
San José del Guaviare,
  Colombia 124 C4
San Josep, *Spain* 37 C7
San Juan, *Argentina* 126 C2
San Juan, *Mexico* 118 C4
San Juan, *Phil.* 61 G7
San Juan, *Puerto Rico* ... 121 C6
San Juan □, *Argentina* .. 126 C2
San Juan →, *Argentina* . 126 C2
San Juan →, *Nic.* 120 D3
San Juan →, *U.S.A.* 115 H8
San Juan Bautista = Sant
  Joan Baptista, *Spain* ... 37 B8
San Juan Bautista,
  Paraguay 126 B4
San Juan Bautista, *U.S.A.* 116 J5
San Juan Bautista Valle
  Nacional, *Mexico* 119 D5
San Juan Capistrano,
  U.S.A. 117 M9
San Juan Cr. →, *U.S.A.* . 116 J5
San Juan de Alicante,
  Spain 33 G4
San Juan de Guadalupe,
  Mexico 118 C4
San Juan de los Morros,
  Venezuela 124 B5
San Juan del Norte, *Nic.* . 120 D3
San Juan del Norte, B. de,
  Nic. 120 D3
San Juan del Río, *Mexico* 119 C5
San Juan del Sur, *Nic.* ... 120 D2
San Juan Mts., *U.S.A.* .. 115 H10
San Just, Sierra de, *Spain* 32 E4
San Justo, *Argentina* 126 C3
San Kamphaeng, *Thailand* 64 C2
San Lázaro, C., *Mexico* .. 118 C2
San Lázaro, Sa., *Mexico* . 118 C3
San Leandro, *U.S.A.* 116 H4
San Leonardo de Yagüe,
  Spain 32 D1
San Lorenzo = Sant
  Llorenç des Cardassar,
  Spain 37 B10
San Lorenzo, *Argentina* . 126 C3
San Lorenzo, *Ecuador* ... 124 C3
San Lorenzo, *Paraguay* .. 126 B4
San Lorenzo →, *Mexico* 118 C3
San Lorenzo, I., *Mexico* . 118 B2
San Lorenzo, Mt.,
  Argentina 128 F2
San Lorenzo de la Parrilla,
  Spain 32 F2
San Lorenzo de Morunys =
  Sant Llorenç de
  Morunys, *Spain* 32 C6
San Ramón de la Nueva
  Orán, *Argentina* 126 A3
San Remo, *Italy* 28 E4
San Roque, *Argentina* ... 126 B4
San Roque, *Spain* 35 J5
San Rosendo, *Chile* 126 D1
San Saba, *U.S.A.* 113 K5
San Salvador, *Bahamas* .. 121 B5

San Lúcido, *Italy* 31 C9
San Luis, *Argentina* 126 C2
San Luis, *Cuba* 120 B3
San Luis, *Guatemala* 120 C2
San Luis, I., *Mexico* 118 B2
San Luis, Sierra de,
  Argentina 126 C2
San Luis de la Paz, *Mexico* 118 C4
San Luis Obispo, *U.S.A.* . 117 K6
San Luis Potosí, *Mexico* . 118 C4
San Luis Potosí □, *Mexico* 118 C4
San Luis Reservoir, *U.S.A.* 116 H5
San Luis Río Colorado,
  Mexico 118 A2
San Marco, C., *Italy* 30 C1
San Marco Argentano, *Italy* 31 C9
San Marco in Lámis, *Italy* 29 G12
San Marcos, *Guatemala* . 120 D1
San Marcos, *Mexico* 118 B2
San Marcos, *U.S.A.* 113 L6
San Marino, *San Marino* . 29 E9
San Marino ■, *Europe* .. 29 E9
San Martín, *Argentina* .. 126 C2
San Martín →, *Bolivia* .. 124 F6
San Martín, L., *Argentina* 128 F2
San Martín de la Vega,
  Spain 34 E7
San Martin de los Andes,
  Argentina 128 E2
San Martín de
  Valdeiglesias, *Spain* ... 34 E6
San Mateo = Sant Mateu,
  Baleares, Spain 37 B7
San Mateo = Sant Mateu,
  Valencia, Spain 32 E5
San Mateo, *Phil.* 61 C4
San Mateo, *U.S.A.* 116 H4
San Matías, *Bolivia* 124 G7
San Matías, G., *Argentina* 122 H4
San Miguel = Sant Miquel,
  Spain 37 B7
San Miguel, *El Salv.* 120 D2
San Miguel, *Panama* 120 E4
San Miguel, *U.S.A.* 116 K6
San Miguel →, *Bolivia* .. 124 F6
San Miguel de Tucumán,
  Argentina 126 B2
San Miguel del Monte,
  Argentina 126 D4
San Miguel I., *U.S.A.* ... 117 L6
San Miniato, *Italy* 28 E7
San Narciso, *Phil.* 61 D4
San Nicolás, *Canary Is.* .. 37 G4
San Nicolas, *Phil.* 61 B4
San Nicolás de los Arroyas,
  Argentina 126 C3
San Nicolas I., *U.S.A.* ... 117 M7
San Onofre, *U.S.A.* 117 M9
San Pablo, *Bolivia* 126 A2
San Pablo, *Phil.* 61 D4
San Páolo di Civitate, *Italy* 29 G12
San Pedro, *Buenos Aires,*
  Argentina 127 B5
San Pedro, *Jujuy, Argentina* 126 A3
San Pedro, *Ivory C.* 82 E3
San Pedro, *Mexico* 118 C2
San Pedro □, *Paraguay* .. 126 A4
San Pedro →, *Chihuahua,*
  Mexico 118 B3
San Pedro →, *Michoacan,*
  Mexico 118 D4
San Pedro →, *Nayarit,*
  Mexico 118 C3
San Pedro →, *U.S.A.* ... 115 K8
San Pedro, Pta., *Chile* ... 126 B1
San Pedro, Sierra de, *Spain* 35 F4
San Pedro Channel, *U.S.A.* 117 M8
San Pedro de Atacama,
  Chile 126 A2
San Pedro de Jujuy,
  Argentina 126 A3
San Pedro de las Colonias,
  Mexico 118 B4
San Pedro de Macorís,
  Dom. Rep. 121 C6
San Pedro del Norte, *Nic.* 120 D3
San Pedro del Paraná,
  Paraguay 126 B4
San Pedro del Pinatar,
  Spain 33 H4
San Pedro Mártir, Sierra,
  Mexico 118 A1
San Pedro Mixtepec,
  Mexico 119 D5
San Pedro Ocampo =
  Melchor Ocampo,
  Mexico 118 C4
San Pedro Sula, *Honduras* 120 C2
San Pietro, *Italy* 30 C1
San Pietro Vernótico, *Italy* 31 B11
San Quintín, *Mexico* 118 A1
San Rafael, *Argentina* ... 126 C2
San Rafael, *Calif., U.S.A.* 116 H4
San Rafael, *N. Mex.,*
  U.S.A. 115 J10
San Rafael Mt., *U.S.A.* .. 117 L7
San Rafael Mts., *U.S.A.* . 117 L7

San Salvador, *El Salv.* ... 120 D2
San Salvador, *Spain* 37 B10
San Salvador de Jujuy,
  Argentina 126 A3
San Salvador I., *Bahamas* . 121 B5
San Salvo, *Italy* 29 F11
San Sebastián = Donostia-
  San Sebastián, *Spain* .. 32 B3
San Sebastián, *Argentina* . 128 G3
San Sebastian de la
  Gomera, *Canary Is.* ... 37 F2
San Serra = Son Serra,
  Spain 37 B10
San Severino Marche, *Italy* 29 E10
San Severo, *Italy* 29 G12
San Simeon, *U.S.A.* 116 K5
San Simon, *U.S.A.* 115 K9
San Stéfano di Cadore,
  Italy 29 B9
San Stino di Livenza, *Italy* 29 C9
San Telmo = Sant Telm,
  Spain 37 B9
San Telmo, *Mexico* 118 A1
San Tiburcio, *Mexico* ... 118 C4
San Valentin, Mte., *Chile* 122 H3
San Vicente, *Phil.* 61 B5
San Vicente de Alcántara,
  Spain 35 F3
San Vicente de la
  Barquera, *Spain* 34 B6
San Vicente del Raspeig,
  Spain 33 G4
San Vincenzo, *Italy* 28 E7
San Vito, *Italy* 30 C2
San Vito, C., *Italy* 30 D5
San Vito al Tagliamento,
  Italy 29 C9
San Vito Chietino, *Italy* . 29 F11
San Vito dei Normanni,
  Italy 31 B10
San Ygnacio, *U.S.A.* 113 M5
Sana', *Yemen* 74 D3
Sana →, *Bos.-H.* 29 C13
Sanaba, *Burkina Faso* ... 82 C4
Şanāfir, *Si. Arabia* 80 B3
Sanaga →, *Cameroon* ... 83 E6
Sanaloa, Presa, *Mexico* .. 118 C3
Sanana, *Indonesia* 63 E7
Sanand, *India* 68 H5
Sanandaj, *Iran* 70 C5
Sanandita, *Bolivia* 126 A3
Sanary-sur-Mer, *France* . 21 E9
Sanawad, *India* 68 H7
Sancellas = Sencelles,
  Spain 37 B9
Sancergues, *France* 19 E8
Sancerre, *France* 19 E9
Sancerrois, Collines du,
  France 19 E9
Sancha He →, *China* ... 58 D6
Sanchahe, *China* 57 B14
Sánchez, *Dom. Rep.* 121 C6
Sanchor, *India* 68 G4
Sancoins, *France* 19 E9
Sancti Spíritus, *Cuba* ... 120 B4
Sancy, Puy de, *France* ... 20 C6
Sand →, *S. Africa* 89 C5
Sand Springs, *U.S.A.* ... 113 G6
Sanda, *Japan* 55 G7
Sandakan, *Malaysia* 62 C5
Sandan = Sambor,
  Cambodia 64 F6
Sandanski, *Bulgaria* 40 E7
Sandaré, *Mali* 82 C2
Sandared, *Sweden* 11 G6
Sandarne, *Sweden* 10 C11
Sanday, *U.K.* 14 B6
Sandefjord, *Norway* 9 G14
Sanders, *U.S.A.* 115 J9
Sanderson, *U.S.A.* 113 K3
Sandfly L., *Canada* 105 B7
Sandgate, *Australia* 95 D5
Sandhammaren, C., *Sweden* 11 J8
Sandía, *Peru* 124 F5
Sandıklı, *Turkey* 39 C12
Sandnes, *Norway* 9 G11
Sandnessjøen, *Norway* .. 8 C15
Sandoa,
  Dem. Rep. of the Congo 84 F4
Sandomierz, *Poland* 45 H8
Sândominic, *Romania* ... 43 D10
Sandover →, *Australia* .. 94 C2
Sandoway, *Burma* 67 K19
Sandoy, *Færoe Is.* 8 F9
Sandpoint, *U.S.A.* 114 B5
Sandray, *U.K.* 14 E1
Sandringham, *U.K.* 12 E8
Sandspit, *Canada* 104 C2
Sandstone, *Australia* 93 E2
Sandu, *China* 58 E6
Sandusky, *Mich., U.S.A.* 102 D3
Sandusky, Ohio, *U.S.A.* . 110 E2
Sandvig, *Sweden* 11 J8
Sandviken, *Sweden* 10 D10
Sandwich, C., *Australia* .. 94 B4
Sandwich B., *Canada* ... 103 B8
Sandwich B., *Namibia* .. 88 C1
Sandwip Chan., *Bangla.* . 67 H17
Sandy, *Nev., U.S.A.* 117 K11
Sandy, *Oreg., U.S.A.* ... 116 E4
Sandy, *Utah, U.S.A.* 114 F8
Sandy Bight, *Australia* ... 93 F3
Sandy, C., *Queens.,*
  Australia 94 C5
Sandy, C., *Tas., Australia* 94 G3
Sandy Cay, *Bahamas* 121 B4
Sandy Cr. →, *U.S.A.* ... 114 F9

Name	Page	Grid
Sandy L., *Canada*	102	B1
Sandy Lake, *Canada*	102	B1
Sandy Narrows, *Canada*	105	B8
Sanford, *Fla., U.S.A.*	109	L5
Sanford, *Maine, U.S.A.*	111	C14
Sanford, *N.C., U.S.A.*	109	H6
Sanford →, *Australia*	93	E2
Sanford, Mt., *U.S.A.*	100	B5
Sang-i-Masha, *Afghan.*	68	C2
Sanga, *Mozam.*	87	E4
Sanga →, *Congo*	84	E3
Sangamner, *India*	66	K9
Sangar, *Afghan.*	68	C1
Sangar, *Russia*	51	C13
Sangar Sarai, *Afghan.*	68	B4
Sangatte, *France*	19	B8
Sangay, *Ecuador*	124	D3
Sange, *Dem. Rep. of the Congo*	86	D2
Sangeang, *Indonesia*	63	F5
Sângeorz-Băi, *Romania*	43	C9
Sanger, *U.S.A.*	116	J7
Sângera, *Moldova*	43	D13
Sangerhausen, *Germany*	24	D7
Sanggan He →, *China*	56	E9
Sanggau, *Indonesia*	62	D4
Sangihe, Kepulauan, *Indonesia*	63	D7
Sangihe, Pulau, *Indonesia*	63	D7
Sangju, *S. Korea*	57	F15
Sangkapura, *Indonesia*	62	F4
Sangkhla, *Thailand*	64	E2
Sangli, *India*	66	L9
Sangmélima, *Cameroon*	83	E7
Sangre de Cristo Mts., *U.S.A.*	113	G2
Sangro →, *Italy*	29	F11
Sangudo, *Canada*	104	C6
Sangue →, *Brazil*	124	F7
Sangüesa, *Spain*	32	C3
Sanguinaires, Îs., *France*	21	G12
Sangzhi, *China*	59	C8
Sanhala, *Ivory C.*	82	C3
Sanje, *Uganda*	86	C3
Sanjiang, *China*	58	E7
Sanjo, *Japan*	54	F9
Sankt Andrä, *Austria*	26	E7
Sankt Augustin, *Germany*	24	E3
Sankt Blasien, *Germany*	25	H4
Sankt Gallen, *Switz.*	25	H5
Sankt Gallen □, *Switz.*	25	H5
Sankt Goar, *Germany*	25	E3
Sankt Ingbert, *Germany*	25	F3
Sankt Johann im Pongau, *Austria*	26	D6
Sankt Johann in Tirol, *Austria*	26	D5
Sankt-Peterburg, *Russia*	46	C6
Sankt Pölten, *Austria*	26	C8
Sankt Ulrich = Ortisei, *Italy*	29	B8
Sankt Valentin, *Austria*	26	C7
Sankt Veit an der Glan, *Austria*	26	E7
Sankt Wendel, *Germany*	25	F3
Sankt Wolfgang, *Austria*	26	D6
Sankuru →, *Dem. Rep. of the Congo*	84	E4
Sanliurfa, *Turkey*	73	D8
Sanlúcar de Barrameda, *Spain*	35	J4
Sanluri, *Italy*	30	C1
Sânmartin, *Romania*	43	D10
Sanmenxia, *China*	56	G6
Sanming, *China*	59	D11
Sannaspos, *S. Africa*	88	D4
Sannicandro Gargánico, *Italy*	29	G12
Sânnicolau Mare, *Romania*	42	D5
Sannieshof, *S. Africa*	88	D4
Sannīn, J., *Lebanon*	75	B4
Sanok, *Poland*	45	J9
Sanquhar, *U.K.*	14	F5
Sansanding Dam, *Mali*	82	C3
Sansepolcro, *Italy*	29	E9
Sansha, *China*	59	D13
Sanshui, *China*	59	F9
Sanski Most, *Bos.-H.*	29	D13
Sansui, *China*	58	D7
Sant Antoni Abat, *Spain*	37	C7
Sant Boi de Llobregat, *Spain*	32	D7
Sant Carles, *Spain*	37	B8
Sant Carles de la Ràpita, *Spain*	32	E5
Sant Celoni, *Spain*	32	D7
Sant Feliu de Guíxols, *Spain*	32	D8
Sant Feliu de Llobregat, *Spain*	32	D7
Sant Ferran, *Spain*	37	C7
Sant Francesc de Formentera, *Spain*	37	C7
Sant Jaume, *Spain*	37	B11
Sant Joan Baptista, *Spain*	37	B8
Sant Jordi, *Spain*	37	B9
Sant Jordi, G. de, *Spain*	32	E6
Sant Llorenç de Morunys, *Spain*	32	C6
Sant Llorenç des Cardassar, *Spain*	37	B10
Sant Mateu, *Baleares, Spain*	37	B7
Sant Mateu, *Valencia, Spain*	32	E5
Sant Miquel, *Spain*	37	B7
Sant Telm, *Spain*	37	B9
Sant' Ágata Militello, *Italy*	31	D7
Santa Agnés, *Spain*	37	B7
Santa Ana, *Bolivia*	124	F5
Santa Ana, *El Salv.*	120	D2
Santa Ana, *Mexico*	118	A2
Santa Ana, *U.S.A.*	117	M9
Sant' Ángelo Lodigiano, *Italy*	28	C6
Sant' Antíoco, *Italy*	30	C1
Santa Bárbara, *Honduras*	120	D2
Santa Bárbara, *Mexico*	118	B3
Santa Barbara, *Spain*	32	E5
Santa Barbara, *U.S.A.*	117	L7
Santa Bárbara, Mt., *Spain*	33	H2
Santa Barbara Channel, *U.S.A.*	117	L7
Santa Barbara I., *U.S.A.*	117	M7
Santa Catalina, *Mexico*	118	B2
Santa Catalina, Gulf of, *U.S.A.*	117	N9
Santa Catalina I., *U.S.A.*	117	M8
Santa Catarina □, *Brazil*	127	B6
Santa Catarina, I. de, *Brazil*	127	B6
Santa Caterina di Pittinuri, *Italy*	30	B1
Santa Caterina Villarmosa, *Italy*	31	E7
Santa Cecília, *Brazil*	127	B5
Santa Clara, *Cuba*	120	B4
Santa Clara, *Calif., U.S.A.*	116	H5
Santa Clara, *Utah, U.S.A.*	115	H7
Santa Clara de Olimar, *Uruguay*	127	C5
Santa Clotilde, *Peru*	124	D4
Santa Coloma de Farners, *Spain*	32	D7
Santa Coloma de Gramenet, *Spain*	32	D7
Santa Comba, *Spain*	34	B2
Santa Croce Camerina, *Italy*	31	F7
Santa Croce di Magliano, *Italy*	29	G11
Santa Cruz, *Argentina*	128	G3
Santa Cruz, *Bolivia*	124	G6
Santa Cruz, *Chile*	126	C1
Santa Cruz, *Costa Rica*	120	D2
Santa Cruz, *Madeira*	37	D3
Santa Cruz, *Phil.*	61	D4
Santa Cruz, *U.S.A.*	116	J4
Santa Cruz →, *Argentina*	128	G3
Santa Cruz de la Palma, *Canary Is.*	37	F2
Santa Cruz de Mudela, *Spain*	35	G7
Santa Cruz de Tenerife, *Canary Is.*	37	F3
Santa Cruz del Norte, *Cuba*	120	B3
Santa Cruz del Retamar, *Spain*	34	E6
Santa Cruz del Sur, *Cuba*	120	B4
Santa Cruz do Rio Pardo, *Brazil*	127	A6
Santa Cruz do Sul, *Brazil*	127	B5
Santa Cruz I., *U.S.A.*	117	M7
Santa Cruz Is., *Solomon Is.*	96	J8
Santa Domingo, Cay, *Bahamas*	120	B4
Sant' Egídio alla Vibrata, *Italy*	29	F10
Santa Elena, *Argentina*	126	C4
Santa Elena, C., *Costa Rica*	120	D2
Sant' Eufémia, G. di, *Italy*	31	D9
Santa Eugenia, Pta., *Mexico*	118	B1
Santa Eulària des Riu, *Spain*	37	C8
Santa Fe, *Argentina*	126	C3
Santa Fe, *Spain*	35	H7
Santa Fe, *U.S.A.*	115	J11
Santa Fé □, *Argentina*	126	C3
Santa Fé do Sul, *Brazil*	125	H8
Santa Filomena, *Brazil*	125	E9
Santa Fiora, *Italy*	29	F8
Santa Gertrudis, *Spain*	37	C7
Santa Giustina, *Italy*	29	B9
Santa Inês, *Brazil*	125	F11
Santa Inés, *Spain*	35	G5
Santa Inés, I., *Chile*	122	J3
Santa Isabel = Rey Malabo, *Eq. Guin.*	83	E6
Santa Isabel, *Argentina*	126	D2
Santa Isabel, Pico, *Eq. Guin.*	83	E6
Santa Isabel do Morro, *Brazil*	125	F8
Santa Lucía, *Corrientes, Argentina*	126	B4
Santa Lucía, *San Juan, Argentina*	126	C2
Santa Lucía, *Spain*	33	H4
Santa Lucia, *Uruguay*	126	C4
Santa Lucia Range, *U.S.A.*	116	K5
Santa Magdalena, I., *Mexico*	118	C2
Santa Margarita, *Argentina*	126	D3
Santa Margarita, *Mexico*	118	C2
Santa Margarita, *Spain*	37	B10
Santa Margarita, *U.S.A.*	116	K6
Santa Margarita →, *U.S.A.*	117	M9
Santa Margherita, *Italy*	30	D1
Santa Margherita Ligure, *Italy*	28	D6
Santa María, *Argentina*	126	B2
Santa Maria, *Brazil*	127	B5
Santa Maria, *Phil.*	61	C4
Santa Maria, *U.S.A.*	117	L6
Santa María →, *Mexico*	118	A3
Santa María, *Colombia*	124	A4
Santa Maria, C. de, *Portugal*	35	J3
Santa Maria Cápua Vétere, *Italy*	31	A7
Santa Maria da Feira, *Portugal*	34	E2
Santa Maria da Vitória, *Brazil*	125	F10
Santa Maria del Camí, *Spain*	37	B9
Santa Maria di Léuca, C., *Italy*	31	C11
Santa María la Real de Nieva, *Spain*	34	D6
Santa Marinella, *Italy*	29	F8
Santa Marta, *Colombia*	124	A4
Santa Marta, Sierra Nevada de, *Colombia*	122	B3
Santa Marta de Tormes, *Spain*	34	E5
Santa Marta Grande, C., *Brazil*	127	B6
Santa Marta Ortigueira, Ría de, *Spain*	34	B3
Santa Monica, *U.S.A.*	117	M8
Santa Olalla, *Huelva, Spain*	35	H4
Santa Olalla, *Toledo, Spain*	34	E6
Santa Pola, *Spain*	33	G4
Santa Ponsa, *Spain*	37	B9
Santa Rita, *U.S.A.*	115	K10
Santa Rosa, *La Pampa, Argentina*	126	D3
Santa Rosa, *San Luis, Argentina*	126	C2
Santa Rosa, *Brazil*	127	B5
Santa Rosa, *Calif., U.S.A.*	116	G4
Santa Rosa, *N. Mex., U.S.A.*	113	H2
Santa Rosa de Copán, *Honduras*	120	D2
Santa Rosa de Río Primero, *Argentina*	126	C3
Santa Rosa del Sara, *Bolivia*	124	G6
Santa Rosa I., *Calif., U.S.A.*	117	M6
Santa Rosa I., *Fla., U.S.A.*	109	K2
Santa Rosa Range, *U.S.A.*	114	F5
Santa Rosalía, *Mexico*	118	B2
Santa Sylvina, *Argentina*	126	B3
Santa Tecla = Nueva San Salvador, *El Salv.*	120	D2
Santa Teresa, *Argentina*	126	C3
Santa Teresa, *Mexico*	119	B5
Santa Teresa di Riva, *Italy*	31	E8
Santa Teresa Gallura, *Italy*	30	A2
Santa Uxía, *Spain*	34	C2
Santa Vitória do Palmar, *Brazil*	127	C5
Santa Ynez, *U.S.A.*	117	L6
Santa Ynez Mts., *U.S.A.*	117	L6
Santa Ysabel, *U.S.A.*	117	M10
Santadi, *Italy*	30	C1
Santaella, *Spain*	35	H6
Santai, *China*	58	B5
Santana, *Madeira*	37	D3
Sântana, *Romania*	42	D6
Santana, Coxilha de, *Brazil*	127	C4
Santana do Livramento, *Brazil*	127	C4
Santander, *Spain*	34	B7
Santander Jiménez, *Mexico*	119	C5
Santanyí, *Spain*	37	B10
Santaquin, *U.S.A.*	114	G8
Santarcángelo di Romagna, *Italy*	29	D9
Santarém, *Brazil*	125	D8
Santarém, *Portugal*	35	F2
Santarém □, *Portugal*	35	F2
Santaren Channel, *W. Indies*	120	B4
Santee, *U.S.A.*	117	N10
Santéramo in Colle, *Italy*	31	B9
Santerno →, *Italy*	29	D8
Santhià, *Italy*	28	C5
Santiago, *Brazil*	127	B5
Santiago, *Chile*	126	C1
Santiago, *Panama*	120	E3
Santiago, *Phil.*	61	C4
Santiago □, *Chile*	126	C1
Santiago →, *Mexico*	98	G9
Santiago →, *Peru*	124	D3
Santiago, Punta de, *Eq. Guin.*	83	E6
Santiago de Compostela, *Spain*	34	C2
Santiago de Cuba, *Cuba*	120	C4
Santiago de los Cabelleros, *Dom. Rep.*	121	C5
Santiago del Estero, *Argentina*	126	B3
Santiago del Estero □, *Argentina*	126	B3
Santiago del Teide, *Canary Is.*	37	F3
Santiago do Cacém, *Portugal*	35	G2
Santiago Ixcuintla, *Mexico*	118	C3
Santiago Papasquiaro, *Mexico*	118	C3
Santiaguillo, L. de, *Mexico*	118	C4
Santillana, *Spain*	34	B6
Santisteban del Puerto, *Spain*	35	G7
Santo Amaro, *Brazil*	125	F11
Santo Anastácio, *Brazil*	127	A5
Santo André, *Brazil*	127	A6
Santo Ângelo, *Brazil*	127	B5
Santo Antônio do Içá, *Brazil*	124	D5
Santo Domingo, *Dom. Rep.*	121	C6
Santo Domingo, *Baja Calif., Mexico*	118	A1
Santo Domingo, *Baja Calif. S., Mexico*	118	B2
Santo Domingo, *Nic.*	120	D3
Santo Domingo de la Calzada, *Spain*	32	C2
Santo Domingo de los Colorados, *Ecuador*	124	D3
Santo Stéfano di Camastro, *Italy*	31	D7
Santo Tirso, *Portugal*	34	D2
Santo Tomás, *Mexico*	118	A1
Santo Tomás, *Peru*	124	F4
Santo Tomé, *Argentina*	127	B4
Santo Tomé de Guayana = Ciudad Guayana, *Venezuela*	124	B6
Santomera, *Spain*	33	G3
Santoña, *Spain*	34	B7
Santoríni = Thíra, *Greece*	39	E7
Santos, *Brazil*	127	A6
Santos, Sierra de los, *Spain*	35	G5
Santos Dumont, *Brazil*	127	A7
Sanxenxo, *Spain*	34	C2
Sanyuan, *China*	56	G5
São Anastácio, *Brazil*	127	A5
São Bartolomeu de Messines, *Portugal*	35	H2
São Bernardo do Campo, *Brazil*	127	A6
São Borja, *Brazil*	127	B4
São Brás de Alportel, *Portugal*	35	H3
São Carlos, *Brazil*	127	A6
São Cristóvão, *Brazil*	125	F11
São Domingos, *Brazil*	125	F9
São Francisco, *Brazil*	125	G10
São Francisco →, *Brazil*	122	E7
São Francisco do Sul, *Brazil*	127	B6
São Gabriel, *Brazil*	127	C5
São Gonçalo, *Brazil*	127	A7
Sao Hill, *Tanzania*	87	D4
São João da Boa Vista, *Brazil*	127	A6
São João da Madeira, *Portugal*	34	E2
São João da Pesqueira, *Portugal*	34	D3
São João del Rei, *Brazil*	127	A7
São João do Araguaia, *Brazil*	125	E9
São João do Piauí, *Brazil*	125	E10
São Jorge, Pta. de, *Madeira*	37	D3
São José do Rio Prêto, *Brazil*	127	A6
São José dos Campos, *Brazil*	127	A6
São Leopoldo, *Brazil*	127	B5
São Lourenço, *Brazil*	127	A6
São Lourenço →, *Brazil*	125	G7
São Lourenço, Pta. de, *Madeira*	37	D3
São Luís, *Brazil*	125	D10
São Luís Gonzaga, *Brazil*	127	B5
São Marcos →, *Brazil*	125	G9
São Marcos, B. de, *Brazil*	125	D10
São Martinho da Cortiça, *Portugal*	34	E2
São Mateus, *Brazil*	125	G11
São Paulo, *Brazil*	127	A6
São Paulo □, *Brazil*	127	A6
São Paulo, I., *Atl. Oc.*	2	D8
São Paulo de Olivença, *Brazil*	124	D5
São Pedro do Sul, *Portugal*	34	E2
São Roque, *Madeira*	37	D3
São Roque, C. de, *Brazil*	122	D7
São Sebastião, I. de, *Brazil*	127	A6
São Sebastião do Paraíso, *Brazil*	127	A6
São Teotónio, *Portugal*	35	H2
São Tomé, *Atl. Oc.*	76	F4
São Tomé, C. de, *Brazil*	127	A7
São Tomé & Príncipe ■, *Africa*	77	F4
São Vicente, *Brazil*	127	A6
São Vicente, *Madeira*	37	D2
São Vicente, C. de, *Portugal*	35	H1
Saona →, *Dom. Rep.*	121	C6
Saône →, *France*	19	G11
Saône-et-Loire □, *France*	19	F11
Saonek, *Indonesia*	63	E8
Sápai, *Greece*	41	E9
Sapanca, *Turkey*	72	B4
Saparua, *Indonesia*	63	E7
Sapele, *Nigeria*	83	D6
Sapelo I., *U.S.A.*	109	K5
Saphane, *Turkey*	39	B11
Sapiéntza, *Greece*	38	E3
Sapone, *Burkina Faso*	83	C4
Saposoa, *Peru*	124	E3
Sapozhok, *Russia*	48	D5
Sappho, *U.S.A.*	116	B2
Sapporo, *Japan*	54	C10
Sapri, *Italy*	31	B8
Sapulpa, *U.S.A.*	113	H7
Saqqez, *Iran*	70	B5
Sar Dasht, *Iran*	71	C6
Sar Gachīneh, *Iran*	71	D6
Sar Planina, *Macedonia*	40	E4
Sara, *Burkina Faso*	82	C4
Sara,	61	F5
Sara Buri = Saraburi, *Thailand*	64	E3
Sárāb, *Iran*	70	B5
Sarabadi, *Iraq*	70	C5
Saraburi, *Thailand*	64	E3
Sarada →, *India*	67	F12
Saragossa = Zaragoza, *Spain*	32	D4
Saraguro, *Ecuador*	124	D3
Saraiu, *Romania*	43	F13
Sarajevo, *Bos.-H.*	42	G3
Saran, Gunung, *Indonesia*	62	E4
Saranac Lake, *U.S.A.*	111	B10
Saranda, *Tanzania*	86	D3
Sarandë, *Albania*	40	G3
Sarandí del Yi, *Uruguay*	127	C4
Sarandí Grande, *Uruguay*	126	C4
Sarangani B., *Phil.*	61	J6
Sarangani Is., *Phil.*	61	J6
Sarangarh, *India*	67	J13
Saransk, *Russia*	48	C7
Sarapul, *Russia*	50	D6
Sarasota, *U.S.A.*	109	M4
Saratoga, *Calif., U.S.A.*	116	H4
Saratoga, *Wyo., U.S.A.*	114	F10
Saratoga Springs, *U.S.A.*	111	C11
Saratov, *Russia*	48	E7
Saravane, *Laos*	64	E6
Sarawak □, *Malaysia*	62	D4
Saray, *Tekirdağ, Turkey*	41	E11
Saray, *Van, Turkey*	73	C11
Saraya, *Senegal*	82	C2
Saraycık, *Turkey*	39	B11
Sarayköy, *Turkey*	39	D10
Saraylar, *Turkey*	41	F11
Sarayönü, *Turkey*	72	C5
Sarbāz, *Iran*	71	E9
Sarbīsheh, *Iran*	71	C8
Sárbogárd, *Hungary*	42	D3
Sarca →, *Italy*	28	C7
Sarcelles, *France*	19	D9
Sarda → = Sarada →, *India*	67	F12
Sardarshahr, *India*	68	E6
Sardegna □, *Italy*	30	B1
Sardhana, *India*	68	E7
Sardina, Pta., *Canary Is.*	37	F4
Sardinia = Sardegna □, *Italy*	30	B1
Sardis, *Turkey*	39	C10
Sārdūīyeh = Dar Mazār, *Iran*	71	D8
S'Arenal, *Spain*	37	B9
Sarentino, *Italy*	29	B8
Saréyamou, *Mali*	82	B4
Sargent, *U.S.A.*	112	E5
Sargodha, *Pakistan*	68	C5
Sarh, *Chad*	79	G9
Sārī, *Iran*	71	B7
Sari d'Orcino, *France*	21	F12
Sária, *Greece*	39	F9
Sarıbeyler, *Turkey*	39	B9
Sarıgöl, *Turkey*	72	C3
Sarıkamış, *Turkey*	73	B10
Sarıkaya, *Turkey*	72	C6
Sarikei, *Malaysia*	62	D4
Sarıköy, *Turkey*	41	F11
Sarina, *Australia*	94	C4
Sariñena, *Spain*	32	D4
Sarita, *U.S.A.*	113	M6
Sariwon, *N. Korea*	57	E13
Sariyar Baraji, *Turkey*	72	B4
Sariyer, *Turkey*	41	E13
Sark, *U.K.*	13	H5
Sarkad, *Hungary*	42	D6
Şarkışla, *Turkey*	72	C7
Şarköy, *Turkey*	41	F11
Sarlat-la-Canéda, *France*	20	D5
Sarles, *U.S.A.*	112	A5
Sărmăşag, *Romania*	42	C7
Sărmaşu, *Romania*	43	D9
Sarmi, *Indonesia*	63	E9
Sarmiento, *Argentina*	128	F3
Särna, *Sweden*	10	C7
Sarnano, *Italy*	29	E10
Sarnen, *Switz.*	25	J4
Sarnia, *Canada*	102	D3
Sarno, *Italy*	31	B7
Sarnthein = Sarentino, *Italy*	29	B8
Särö, *Sweden*	11	G5
Sarolangun, *Indonesia*	62	E2
Saronno, *Italy*	28	C6
Saronikós Kólpos, *Greece*	38	D5
Saros Körfezi, *Turkey*	41	F10
Sárospatak, *Hungary*	42	B6
Sarpsborg, *Norway*	9	G14
Sarracín, *Spain*	34	C7
Sarralbe, *France*	19	D14
Sarre = Saar →, *Europe*	17	E6
Sarre, *Italy*	28	C4
Sarre-Union, *France*	19	D14
Sarrebourg, *France*	19	D14
Sarreguemines, *France*	19	C14

Sarria, *Spain* 34 C3
Sarrión, *Spain* 32 E4
Sarro, *Mali* 82 C3
Sarstedt, *Germany* 24 C5
Sartène, *France* 21 G12
Sarthe □, *France* 18 D7
Sarthe →, *France* 18 E6
Sartilly, *France* 18 D5
Saruhanlı, *Turkey* 39 C9
Sărulești, *Romania* 43 F11
Sárvár, *Hungary* 42 C1
Sarvestān, *Iran* 71 D7
Särvfjället, *Sweden* 10 B7
Sárviz →, *Hungary* 42 D3
Sary-Tash, *Kyrgyzstan* ... 50 F8
Sarych, Mys, *Ukraine* 47 K7
Saryshagan, *Kazakstan* ... 50 E8
Sarzana, *Italy* 28 D6
Sarzeau, *France* 18 E4
Sasaram, *India* 69 G11
Sasebo, *Japan* 55 H4
Saser, *India* 69 B7
Saskatchewan □, *Canada* . 105 C7
Saskatchewan →, *Canada* . 105 C8
Saskatoon, *Canada* 105 C7
Saskylakh, *Russia* 51 B12
Sasolburg, S. *Africa* 89 D4
Sasovo, *Russia* 48 C5
Sassandra, *Ivory C.* ... 82 B4
Sassandra →, *Ivory C.* ... 82 E3
Sássari, *Italy* 30 B1
Sassnitz, *Germany* 24 A9
Sasso Marconi, *Italy* 29 D8
Sassocorvaro, *Italy* 29 E9
Sassoferrato, *Italy* 29 E9
Sasstown, *Liberia* 82 E3
Sassuolo, *Italy* 28 D7
Sástago, *Spain* 32 D4
Sasumua Dam, *Kenya* 86 C4
Sasyk, Ozero, *Ukraine* 47 K5
Sata-Misaki, *Japan* 55 J5
Satadougou, *Mali* 82 C2
Satakunta, *Finland* 9 F20
Satanta, *U.S.A.* 113 G4
Satara, *India* 66 L8
Sātenäs, *Sweden* 11 F6
Säter, *Sweden* 10 D9
Satilla →, *U.S.A.* 109 K5
Satmala Hills, *India* 66 J9
Satna, *India* 69 G9
Šator, *Bos.-H.* 29 D13
Sátoraljaújhely, *Hungary* . 42 B6
Satpura Ra., *India* 68 J7
Satrup, *Germany* 24 A5
Satsuma-Shotō, *Japan* ... 55 K5
Sattahip, *Thailand* 64 F3
Satu Mare, *Romania* 42 C7
Satu Mare □, *Romania* ... 42 C8
Satui, *Indonesia* 62 E5
Satun, *Thailand* 65 J3
Saturnina →, *Brazil* 124 F7
Sauce, *Argentina* 126 C4
Sauceda, *Mexico* 118 B4
Saucillo, *Mexico* 118 B3
Sauda, *Norway* 9 G12
Sauðarkrókur, *Iceland* ... 8 D4
Saudi Arabia ■, *Asia* 74 B3
Saugeen →, *Canada* 110 B3
Saugerties, *U.S.A.* 111 D11
Saugues, *France* 20 D7
Saujon, *France* 20 C3
Sauk Centre, *U.S.A.* 112 C7
Sauk Rapids, *U.S.A.* 112 C7
Saulgau, *Germany* 25 G5
Saulieu, *France* 19 E11
Sault, *France* 21 D9
Sault Ste. Marie, *Canada* . 102 C3
Sault Ste. Marie, *U.S.A.* . 108 B3
Saumlaki, *Indonesia* 63 F8
Saumur, *France* 18 E6
Saunders C., *N.Z.* 91 L3
Saunders I., *Antarctica* .. 5 B1
Saunders Point, *Australia* . 93 E4
Sauri, *Nigeria* 83 C6
Saurimo, *Angola* 84 F4
Sausalito, *U.S.A.* 116 H4
Sauveterre-de-Béarn,
    France 20 E3
Sauzé-Vaussais, *France* .. 20 B4
Savá, *Honduras* 120 C2
Sava, *Italy* 31 B10
Sava →, *Serbia, Yug.* ... 42 F5
Savage, *U.S.A.* 112 B2
Savage I. = Niue, *Cook Is.* 97 J11
Savai'i, *W. Samoa* 91 A12
Savalou, *Benin* 83 D5
Savane, *Mozam.* 87 F4
Savanna, *U.S.A.* 112 D9
Savanna-la-Mar, *Jamaica* . 120 C4
Savannah, Ga., *U.S.A.* ... 109 J5
Savannah, Mo., *U.S.A.* .. 112 F7
Savannah, Tenn., *U.S.A.* . 109 H1
Savannah →, *U.S.A.* 109 J5
Savannakhet, *Laos* 64 D5
Savant L., *Canada* 102 B1
Savant Lake, *Canada* 102 B1
Savanur, *India* 66 M9
Săvârșin, *Romania* 42 D7
Savaştepe, *Turkey* 39 B9
Savé, *Benin* 83 D5
Save →, *France* 20 E5
Save →, *Mozam.* 89 C5
Săveh, *Iran* 71 C6
Savelugu, *Ghana* 83 D4
Savenay, *France* 18 E5
Săveni, *Romania* 43 C11

Saverdun, *France* 20 E5
Saverne, *France* 19 D14
Savigliano, *Italy* 28 D4
Savigny-sur-Braye, *France* 18 E7
Sávio →, *Italy* 29 D9
Šavrik, *Montenegro, Yug.* 40 D3
Savo, *Finland* 8 E22
Savoie □, *France* 21 C10
Savona, *Italy* 28 D5
Savonlinna, *Finland* 46 B5
Şavşat, *Turkey* 73 B10
Sävsjö, *Sweden* 11 G8
Sawahlunto, *Indonesia* .. 62 E2
Sawai, *Indonesia* 63 E7
Sawai Madhopur, *India* .. 68 G7
Sawang Daen Din,
    Thailand 64 D4
Sawankhalok, *Thailand* .. 64 D2
Sawara, *Japan* 55 G10
Sawatch Mts., *U.S.A.* .. 115 G10
Sawel Mt., *U.K.* 15 B4
Sawi, *Thailand* 65 G2
Sawmills, *Zimbabwe* 87 F2
Sawu, *Indonesia* 63 F6
Sawu Sea, *Indonesia* 63 F6
Saxby →, *Australia* 94 B3
Saxmundham, *U.K.* 13 E9
Saxony, Lower =
    Niedersachsen □,
    Germany 24 C4
Saxton, *U.S.A.* 110 F6
Şay, *Niger* 83 C5
Saya, *Nigeria* 83 D5
Sayabec, *Canada* 103 C6
Sayaboury, *Laos* 64 C3
Sayán, *Peru* 124 F3
Sayan, Vostochnyy, *Russia* 51 D10
Sayan, Zapadnyy, *Russia* . 51 D10
Saydā, *Lebanon* 75 B4
Sayhan-Ovoo, *Mongolia* .. 56 B2
Sayhandulaan, *Mongolia* . 56 B5
Sayḩūt, *Yemen* 74 D5
Saykhin, *Kazakstan* 49 F8
Saynshand, *Mongolia* ... 56 B6
Sayre, Okla., *U.S.A.* 113 H5
Sayre, Pa., *U.S.A.* 111 E8
Sayula, *Mexico* 118 D4
Sazanit, *Albania* 40 F3
Sázava →, *Czech Rep.* ... 26 B7
Sazin, *Pakistan* 69 B5
Sazlika →, *Bulgaria* 41 E9
Scaër, *France* 18 D3
Scafell Pike, *U.K.* 12 C4
Scalea, *Italy* 31 C8
Scalloway, *U.K.* 14 A7
Scalpay, *U.K.* 14 D3
Scandia, *Canada* 104 C6
Scandiano, *Italy* 28 D7
Scandicci, *Italy* 29 E8
Scandinavia, *Europe* 6 C8
Scansano, *Italy* 29 F8
Scapa Flow, *U.K.* 14 C5
Scappoose, *U.S.A.* 116 E4
Scarámia, Capo, *Italy* ... 31 F7
Scarba, *U.K.* 14 E3
Scarborough, *Trin. & Tob.* 121 D7
Scarborough, *U.K.* 12 C7
Scariff I., *Ireland* 15 E1
Scarp, *U.K.* 14 C1
Scebeli, Wabi →,
    Somali Rep. 81 G5
Šćedro, *Croatia* 29 E13
Scenic, *U.S.A.* 112 D3
Schaal See, *Germany* 24 B6
Schaffhausen, *Switz.* ... 25 H4
Schagen, *Neths.* 17 B4
Schärding, *Austria* 26 C6
Scharhörn, *Germany* 24 B4
Scheessel, *Germany* 24 B5
Schefferville, *Canada* ... 103 B6
Scheibbs, *Austria* 26 C8
Schelde →, *Neths.* 17 C4
Schell Creek Ra., *U.S.A.* . 114 G6
Schenectady, *U.S.A.* ... 111 D11
Scherfede, *Germany* 24 D5
Schesslitz, *Germany* 25 F7
Schiedam, *Neths.* 17 C4
Schiermonnikoog, *Neths.* . 17 A6
Schiltigheim, *France* 19 D14
Schio, *Italy* 29 C8
Schladming, *Austria* 26 D6
Schlanders = Silandro, *Italy* 28 B8
Schlei →, *Germany* 24 A5
Schleiden, *Germany* 24 E2
Schleiz, *Germany* 24 E7
Schleswig, *Germany* 24 A5
Schleswig-Holstein □,
    Germany 24 A5
Schlüchtern, *Germany* ... 25 E5
Schmalkalden, *Germany* . 24 E6
Schmölln, *Germany* 24 E8
Schneeberg, *Austria* 26 D8
Schneeberg, *Germany* ... 24 E8
Schneverdingen, *Germany* 24 B5
Schofield, *U.S.A.* 112 C10
Scholls, *U.S.A.* 116 E4
Schönberg,
    Mecklenburg-Vorpommern,
    Germany 24 B6
Schönberg,
    Schleswig-Holstein,
    Germany 24 A6
Schönebeck, *Germany* ... 24 C7
Schongau, *Germany* 25 H6
Schöningen, *Germany* ... 24 C6
Schopfheim, *Germany* ... 25 H3

Schorndorf, *Germany* 25 G5
Schortens, *Germany* 24 B3
Schouten I., *Australia* ... 94 G4
Schouten Is. = Supiori,
    Indonesia 63 E9
Schouwen, *Neths.* 17 C3
Schramberg, *Germany* ... 25 G4
Schrankogel, *Austria* 26 D4
Schreiber, *Canada* 102 C2
Schrems, *Austria* 26 C8
Schrobenhausen, *Germany* 25 G7
Schruns, *Austria* 26 D2
Schuler, *Canada* 105 C6
Schumacher, *Canada* 102 C3
Schurz, *U.S.A.* 114 G4
Schuyler, *U.S.A.* 112 E6
Schuylkill Haven, *U.S.A.* . 111 F8
Schwabach, *Germany* ... 25 F7
Schwaben □, *Germany* ... 25 G6
Schwäbisch Gmünd,
    Germany 25 G5
Schwäbisch Hall, *Germany* 25 F5
Schwäbische Alb, *Germany* 25 G5
Schwabmünchen, *Germany* 25 G6
Schwalmstadt, *Germany* . 24 E5
Schwandorf, *Germany* ... 25 F8
Schwaner, Pegunungan,
    Indonesia 62 E4
Schwanewede, *Germany* . 24 B4
Schwarmstedt, *Germany* . 24 C5
Schwarze Elster →,
    Germany 24 D8
Schwarzenberg, *Germany* . 24 E8
Schwarzwald, *Germany* .. 25 G4
Schwaz, *Austria* 26 D4
Schwechat, *Austria* 27 C9
Schwedt, *Germany* 24 B10
Schweinfurt, *Germany* ... 25 E6
Schweizer-Reneke,
    S. *Africa* 88 D4
Schwenningen = Villingen-
    Schwenningen, *Germany* 25 G4
Schwerin, *Germany* 24 B7
Schweriner See, *Germany* . 24 B7
Schwetzingen, *Germany* . 25 F4
Schwyz, *Switz.* 25 H4
Schwyz □, *Switz.* 25 H4
Sciacca, *Italy* 30 E6
Scicli, *Italy* 31 F7
Scilla, *Italy* 31 D8
Scilly, Isles of, *U.K.* 13 H1
Ścinawa, *Poland* 45 G3
Scione, *Greece* 40 G7
Scioto →, *U.S.A.* 108 F4
Scobey, *U.S.A.* 112 A2
Scone, *Australia* 95 E5
Scordia, *Italy* 31 E7
Scoresbysund, *Greenland* . 4 B6
Scornicești, *Romania* ... 43 F9
Scotia, Calif., *U.S.A.* ... 114 F1
Scotia, N.Y., *U.S.A.* 111 D11
Scotia Sea, *Antarctica* ... 5 B18
Scotland, *U.S.A.* 112 D6
Scotland □, *U.K.* 14 E5
Scotland Neck, *U.S.A.* ... 109 G7
Scott, C., *Australia* 92 B4
Scott City, *U.S.A.* 112 F4
Scott Glacier, *Antarctica* . 5 C8
Scott I., *Antarctica* 5 C11
Scott Is., *Canada* 104 C3
Scott L., *Canada* 105 B7
Scott Reef, *Australia* 92 B3
Scottburgh, S. *Africa* ... 89 E5
Scottdale, *U.S.A.* 110 F5
Scottish Borders □, *U.K.* . 14 F6
Scottsbluff, *U.S.A.* 112 E3
Scottsboro, *U.S.A.* 109 H3
Scottsburg, *U.S.A.* 108 F3
Scottsdale, *Australia* 94 G4
Scottsdale, *U.S.A.* 115 K7
Scottsville, Ky., *U.S.A.* .. 109 G2
Scottsville, N.Y., *U.S.A.* . 110 C7
Scottville, *U.S.A.* 108 D2
Scranton, *U.S.A.* 111 E9
Scugog, L., *Canada* 110 B6
Sculeni, *Moldova* 43 C12
Scunthorpe, *U.K.* 12 D7
Scuol, *Switz.* 25 J6
Scutari = Üsküdar, *Turkey* 41 F13
Seabrook, L., *Australia* .. 93 F2
Seaford, *U.K.* 13 G8
Seaford, *U.S.A.* 108 F8
Seaforth, *Canada* 102 D3
Seaforth, L., *U.K.* 14 D2
Seagraves, *U.S.A.* 113 J3
Seaham, *U.K.* 12 C6
Seal →, *Canada* 105 B10
Seal Cove, *Canada* 103 C8
Seal L., *Canada* 103 B7
Sealy, *U.S.A.* 113 L6
Searchlight, *U.S.A.* 117 K12
Searcy, *U.S.A.* 113 H9
Searles L., *U.S.A.* 117 K9
Seascale, *U.K.* 12 C4
Seaside, Calif., *U.S.A.* .. 116 J5
Seaside, Oreg., *U.S.A.* .. 116 E3
Seaspray, *Australia* 95 F4
Seattle, *U.S.A.* 116 C4
Seaview Ra., *Australia* ... 94 B4
Sebastián Vizcaíno, B.,
    Mexico 118 B2

Sebeş, *Romania* 43 E8
Sebeşului, Munţii, *Romania* 43 E8
Sebewaing, *U.S.A.* 108 D4
Sebezh, *Russia* 46 D5
Sebha = Sabhah, *Libya* .. 79 C8
Sébi, *Mali* 82 B4
Şebinkarahisar, *Turkey* .. 73 B8
Sebiş, *Romania* 42 D7
Sebkhet Te-n-Dghâmcha,
    Mauritania 82 B1
Sebnitz, *Germany* 24 E10
Sebring, Fla., *U.S.A.* 109 M5
Sebring, Ohio, *U.S.A.* ... 110 F3
Sebringville, *Canada* 110 C3
Sebta = Ceuta, N. *Afr.* .. 78 A4
Sebuku, *Indonesia* 62 E5
Sebuku, Teluk, *Malaysia* . 62 D5
Sečanj, *Serbia, Yug.* 42 E5
Secchia →, *Italy* 28 C8
Sechelt, *Canada* 104 D4
Sechura, Desierto de, *Peru* 124 E2
Seclin, *France* 19 B10
Secondigny, *France* 18 F6
Sečovce, *Slovak Rep.* ... 27 C14
Secretary I., *N.Z.* 91 L1
Secunderabad, *India* 66 L11
Sedalia, *U.S.A.* 112 F8
Sedan, *Australia* 95 E2
Sedan, *France* 19 C11
Sedan, *U.S.A.* 113 G6
Sedano, *Spain* 34 C7
Seddon, *N.Z.* 91 J5
Seddonville, *N.Z.* 91 J4
Sedeh, Fārs, *Iran* 71 D7
Sedeh, Khorāsān, *Iran* ... 71 C8
Séderon, *France* 21 D9
Sederot, *Israel* 75 D3
Sedgewick, *Canada* 104 C6
Sédhiou, *Senegal* 82 C1
Sedico, *Italy* 29 B9
Sedley, *Canada* 105 C8
Sedova, Pik, *Russia* 50 B6
Sedro Woolley, *U.S.A.* .. 116 B4
Šeduva, *Lithuania* 44 C10
Sędziejów, *Poland* 45 H7
Sędziszów Małopolski,
    Poland 45 H8
Seebad Ahlbeck, *Germany* 24 B10
Seefeld in Tirol, *Austria* . 26 D4
Seehausen, *Germany* 24 C7
Seeheim, *Namibia* 88 D2
Seeheim-Jugenheim,
    Germany 25 F4
Seekoei →, S. *Africa* ... 88 E4
Seelow, *Germany* 24 C10
Seesen, *Germany* 24 D6
Seevetal, *Germany* 24 B6
Sefadu, S. *Leone* 82 D2
Seferihisar, *Turkey* 39 C8
Séfeto, *Mali* 82 C3
Sefwi Bekwai, *Ghana* 82 D4
Segamat, *Malaysia* 65 L4
Şegarcea, *Romania* 43 F8
Segbwema, S. *Leone* 82 D2
Seget, *Indonesia* 63 E8
Segezha, *Russia* 48 B5
Seginen-Auxois, *France*. 19 E11
Ségou, *Mali* 82 C3
Segovia = Coco →,
    Cent. Amer. 120 D3
Segovia, *Spain* 34 E6
Segovia □, *Spain* 34 E6
Segré, *France* 18 E6
Segre →, *Spain* 32 D5
Séguéla, *Ivory C.* 82 D3
Seguin, *U.S.A.* 113 L6
Segundo →, *Argentina* .. 126 C3
Segura →, *Spain* 33 G4
Segura, Sierra de, *Spain* . 33 G2
Seh Qal'eh, *Iran* 71 C8
Sehithwa, *Botswana* 88 C3
Sehore, *India* 68 H7
Sehwan, *Pakistan* 68 F2
Şeica Mare, *Romania* ... 43 D9
Seil, *U.K.* 14 E3
Seiland, *Norway* 8 A20
Seilhac, *France* 20 C5
Seiling, *U.S.A.* 113 G5
Seille →, Moselle, *France* 19 C13
Seille →, Saône-et-Loire,
    France 19 F11
Sein, Î. de, *France* 18 D2
Seinäjoki, *Finland* 9 E20
Seine →, *France* 18 C7
Seine-et-Marne □, *France* 19 D10
Seine-Maritime □, *France* 18 C7
Seine-St-Denis □, *France* . 19 D9
Seini, *Romania* 43 C8
Seistan, *Iran* 71 D9
Seistan, Daryācheh-ye, *Iran* 66 D2
Sejerø, *Denmark* 11 J5
Sejerø Bugt, *Denmark* ... 11 J5
Sejny, *Poland* 44 D10
Seka, *Ethiopia* 81 F4
Sekayu, *Indonesia* 62 E2
Seke, *Tanzania* 86 C3
Sekenke, *Tanzania* 86 C3
Seki, *Turkey* 39 E11
Sekondi-Takoradi, *Ghana* . 82 E4
Seksna, *Russia* 46 C10
Sekuma, *Botswana* 88 C3
Selah, *U.S.A.* 114 C3

Selama, *Malaysia* 65 K3
Selárgius, *Italy* 30 C2
Selaru, *Indonesia* 63 F8
Selb, *Germany* 25 E8
Selby, *U.K.* 12 D6
Selby, *U.S.A.* 112 C4
Selca, *Croatia* 29 E13
Selçuk, *Turkey* 39 D9
Selden, *U.S.A.* 112 F4
Sele →, *Italy* 31 B7
Selebi-Pikwe, *Botswana* . 89 C4
Selemdzha →, *Russia* ... 51 D13
Selendi, Manisa, *Turkey* . 39 C10
Selendi, Manisa, *Turkey* . 39 C9
Selenga = Selenge
    Mörön →, *Asia* 60 A5
Selenge Mörön →, *Asia* . 60 A5
Selenica, *Albania* 40 F3
Selenter See, *Germany* .. 24 A6
Sélestat, *France* 19 D14
Seletan, Tanjung, *Indonesia* 62 E4
Selevac, *Serbia, Yug.* ... 40 B4
Selfridge, *U.S.A.* 112 B4
Sélibabi, *Mauritania* 82 B2
Seliger, Ozero, *Russia* ... 46 D7
Seligman, *U.S.A.* 115 J7
Selim, *Turkey* 73 B10
Selîma, El Wâhât el, *Sudan* 80 C2
Selimiye, *Turkey* 39 D9
Selinda Spillway, *Botswana* 88 B3
Selinoús, *Greece* 38 D3
Selizharovo, *Russia* 46 D7
Selkirk, *Canada* 105 C9
Selkirk, *U.K.* 14 F6
Selkirk I., *Canada* 105 C9
Selkirk Mts., *Canada* ... 104 C5
Selliá, *Greece* 36 D6
Sellières, *France* 19 F12
Sells, *U.S.A.* 115 L8
Sellye, *Hungary* 42 E2
Selma, Ala., *U.S.A.* 109 J2
Selma, Calif., *U.S.A.* ... 116 J7
Selma, N.C., *U.S.A.* 109 H6
Selmer, *U.S.A.* 109 H1
Selongey, *France* 19 E12
Selowandoma Falls,
    Zimbabwe 87 G3
Selpele, *Indonesia* 63 E8
Selsey Bill, *U.K.* 13 G7
Seltso, *Russia* 46 F8
Seltz, *France* 19 D15
Selu, *Indonesia* 63 F8
Sélune →, *France* 18 D5
Selva = La Selva del
    Camp, *Spain* 32 D6
Selva, *Argentina* 126 B3
Selvas, *Brazil* 122 D4
Selwyn, *Australia* 94 C3
Selwyn L., *Canada* 105 B8
Selwyn Ra., *Australia* ... 94 C3
Semani →, *Albania* 40 F3
Semarang, *Indonesia* ... 63 G14
Sembabule, *Uganda* 86 C3
Şemdinli, *Turkey* 73 D11
Sémé, *Senegal* 82 B2
Semeih, *Sudan* 81 E3
Semenov, *Russia* 48 B7
Semenovka, Chernihiv,
    Ukraine 47 F7
Semenovka, Kremenchuk,
    Ukraine 47 H7
Semeru, *Indonesia* 63 H15
Semey, *Kazakstan* 50 D9
Semikarakorskiy, *Russia* . 49 G5
Semiluki, *Russia* 47 G10
Seminoe Reservoir, *U.S.A.* 114 F10
Seminole, Okla., *U.S.A.* . 113 H6
Seminole, Tex., *U.S.A.* .. 113 J3
Semipalatinsk = Semey,
    Kazakstan 50 D9
Semirara Is., *Phil.* 61 F4
Semitau, *Indonesia* 62 D4
Semiyarka, *Kazakstan* ... 50 D8
Semiyarskoye = Semiyarka,
    Kazakstan 50 D8
Semmering P., *Austria* .. 26 D8
Semnān, *Iran* 71 C7
Semnān □, *Iran* 71 C7
Semporna, *Malaysia* 63 D5
Semuda, *Indonesia* 62 E4
Semur-en-Auxois, *France* 19 E11
Senā, *Iran* 71 D6
Sena, *Mozam.* 87 F3
Sena Madureira, *Brazil* .. 124 E5
Senador Pompeu, *Brazil* . 125 E11
Senaki, *Georgia* 49 J6
Senanga, *Zambia* 88 B3
Senatobia, *U.S.A.* 113 H10
Sencelles, *Spain* 37 B9
Sendafa, *Ethiopia* 81 F4
Sendai, Kagoshima, *Japan* 55 J5
Sendai, Miyagi, *Japan* ... 54 E10
Sendai-Wan, *Japan* 54 E10
Senden, Bayern, *Germany* 25 G6
Senden,
    Nordrhein-Westfalen,
    Germany 24 D3
Senec, *Slovak Rep.* 27 C10
Seneca, S.C., *U.S.A.* ... 109 H4
Seneca Falls, *U.S.A.* 111 D8
Seneca L., *U.S.A.* 110 D8
Senegal ■, W. *Afr.* 82 C2
Senegal →, W. *Afr.* 82 B1
Senegambia, *Africa* 76 E2
Senekal, S. *Africa* 89 D4

Senftenberg, Germany 24 D10
Senga Hill, Zambia 87 D3
Senge Khambab =
  Indus →, Pakistan 68 G2
Sengerema □, Tanzania .. 86 C3
Sengiley, Russia 48 D9
Sengua →, Zimbabwe 87 F2
Senhor-do-Bonfim, Brazil . 125 F10
Senica, Slovak Rep. 27 C10
Senigállia, Italy 29 E10
Senio →, Italy 29 D9
Senirkent, Turkey 39 C12
Senise, Italy 31 B9
Senj, Croatia 29 D11
Senja, Norway 8 B17
Senlis, France 19 C9
Senmonorom, Cambodia .. 64 F6
Sennâr, Sudan 81 E3
Senneterre, Canada 102 C4
Senniquelle, Liberia 82 D3
Senno, Belarus 46 E5
Sénnori, Italy 30 B1
Seno, Laos 64 D5
Senonches, France 18 D8
Senorbì, Italy 30 C2
Senožeče, Slovenia 29 C11
Sens, France 19 D10
Senta, Serbia, Yug. 42 E5
Sentani, Indonesia 63 E10
Sentery,
  Dem. Rep. of the Congo 86 D2
Sentinel, U.S.A. 115 K7
Šentjur, Slovenia 29 B12
Senya Beraku, Ghana 83 D4
Seo de Urgel = La Seu
  d'Urgell, Spain 32 C6
Seohara, India 69 E8
Seoni, India 69 H8
Seoul = Sŏul, S. Korea .. 57 F14
Separation Point, Canada . 103 B6
Sepīdān, Iran 71 D7
Sepo-ri, N. Korea 57 E14
Sępólno Krajeńskie, Poland 44 E4
Sepone, Laos 64 D6
Sępopol, Poland 44 D8
Sept-Îles, Canada 103 B6
Septemvri, Bulgaria 41 D8
Sepúlveda, Spain 34 D7
Sequeros, Spain 34 E4
Sequim, U.S.A. 116 B3
Sequoia National Park,
  U.S.A. 116 J8
Serafimovich, Russia 48 F6
Seraing, Belgium 17 D5
Seraja, Indonesia 65 L7
Serakhis →, Cyprus 36 D11
Seram, Indonesia 63 E7
Seram Sea, Indonesia 63 E7
Serang, Indonesia 63 G12
Serasan, Indonesia 65 L7
Seravezza, Italy 28 E7
Şerbettar, Turkey 41 E10
Serbia □, Yugoslavia 40 C5
Şercaia, Romania 43 E10
Serdo, Ethiopia 81 E5
Serdobsk, Russia 48 D7
Sered', Slovak Rep. 27 C10
Seredka, Russia 46 C5
Şereflikoçhisar, Turkey .. 72 C5
Seregno, Italy 28 C6
Seremban, Malaysia 65 L3
Serengeti □, Tanzania 86 C3
Serengeti Plain, Tanzania . 86 C4
Serenje, Zambia 87 E3
Sereth = Siret →,
  Romania 43 E12
Sergach, Russia 48 C7
Sergen, Turkey 41 E11
Sergipe □, Brazil 125 F11
Sergiyev Posad, Russia .. 46 D10
Seria, Brunei 62 D4
Serian, Malaysia 62 D4
Seriate, Italy 28 C6
Seribu, Kepulauan,
  Indonesia 62 F3
Sérifontaine, France 19 C8
Sérifos, Greece 38 D6
Sérignan, France 20 E7
Serik, Turkey 72 D4
Seringapatam Reef,
  Australia 92 B3
Serinhisar, Turkey 39 D11
Sermaize-les-Bains, France 19 D11
Sermata, Indonesia 63 F7
Sérmide, Italy 29 D8
Sernovodsk, Russia 48 D10
Sernur, Russia 48 B9
Serock, Poland 44 E8
Serón, Spain 33 H2
Seròs, Spain 32 D5
Serov, Russia 50 D7
Serowe, Botswana 88 C4
Serpa, Portugal 35 H3
Serpeddí, Punta, Italy .. 30 C2
Serpentara, Italy 30 C2
Serpentine, Australia 93 F2
Serpentine Lakes, Australia 93 E4
Serpis →, Spain 33 G4
Serpukhov, Russia 46 E9
Serra do Outes, Spain 34 C2
Serra do Navio, Brazil .. 125 C8
Serra San Bruno, Italy 31 D9
Serradilla, Spain 34 F4
Sérrai, Greece 40 E7
Sérrai □, Greece 40 E7
Serramanna, Italy 30 C1

Serravalle Scrívia, Italy ... 28 D5
Serre-Ponçon, L. de,
  France 21 D10
Serres, France 21 D9
Serrezuela, Argentina 126 C2
Serrinha, Brazil 125 F11
Sersale, Italy 31 C9
Sertã, Portugal 34 F2
Sertanópolis, Brazil 127 A5
Sêrtar, China 58 A3
Serua, Indonesia 63 F8
Serui, Indonesia 63 E9
Serule, Botswana 88 C4
Sérvia, Greece 40 F6
Serzedelo, Portugal 34 D2
Sese Is., Uganda 86 C3
Sesepe, Indonesia 63 E7
Sesfontein, Namibia 88 B1
Sesheke, Zambia 88 B3
Sésia →, Italy 28 C5
Sesimbra, Portugal 35 G1
S'Espalmador, Spain 37 C7
S'Espardell, Spain 37 C7
Sessa Aurunca, Italy 30 A6
S'Estanyol, Spain 37 B9
Sestao, Spain 32 B2
Sesto Calende, Italy 28 C5
Sesto San Giovanni, Italy . 28 C6
Sestri Levante, Italy 28 D6
Sestriere, Italy 28 D3
Sestroretsk, Russia 46 B6
Sestrunj, Croatia 29 D11
Sestu, Italy 30 C2
Setana, Japan 54 C9
Sète, France 20 E7
Sete Lagôas, Brazil 125 G10
Sétif, Algeria 78 A7
Seto, Japan 55 G8
Setonaikai, Japan 55 G6
Settat, Morocco 78 B4
Séttimo Torinese, Italy .. 28 C4
Setting L., Canada 105 C9
Settle, U.K. 12 C5
Settlement Pt., Bahamas . 109 M6
Setúbal, Portugal 35 G2
Setúbal □, Portugal 35 G2
Setúbal, B. de, Portugal . 35 G2
Seugne →, France 20 C3
Seurre, France 19 F12
Sevan, Armenia 49 K7
Sevan, Ozero = Sevana
  Lich, Armenia 49 K7
Sevana Lich, Armenia 49 K7
Sevastopol, Ukraine 47 K7
Seven Emu, Australia 94 B2
Seven Sisters, Canada 104 C3
Sever →, Spain 35 F3
Severn →, Canada 102 A2
Severn →, U.K. 13 F5
Severn L., Canada 102 B1
Severnaya Zemlya, Russia 51 B11
Severo-Kurilsk, Russia .. 51 D16
Severo-Yeniseyskiy, Russia 51 C10
Severočeský □, Czech Rep. 26 A7
Severodonetsk =
  Syeverodonetsk, Ukraine 47 H10
Severodvinsk, Russia 50 C4
Severomoravský □,
  Czech Rep. 27 B10
Sevier, U.S.A. 115 G7
Sevier →, U.S.A. 115 G7
Sevier L., U.S.A. 114 G7
Sevilla, Spain 35 H5
Sevilla □, Spain 35 H5
Seville = Sevilla, Spain .. 35 H5
Sevlievo, Bulgaria 41 C9
Sevnica, Slovenia 29 B12
Sèvre-Nantaise →, France 18 E5
Sèvre-Niortaise →, France 20 B3
Sevsk, Russia 47 F8
Seward, Alaska, U.S.A. .. 100 B5
Seward, Nebr., U.S.A. .. 112 E6
Seward Peninsula, U.S.A. 100 B3
Sewell, Chile 126 C1
Sewer, Indonesia 63 F8
Sewickley, U.S.A. 110 F4
Sexsmith, Canada 104 B5
Seychelles ■, Ind. Oc. .. 52 K9
Seyðisfjörður, Iceland ... 8 D6
Seydişehir, Turkey 72 D4
Seydvān, Iran 70 B5
Seyhan →, Turkey 72 D6
Seyhan Barajı, Turkey .. 72 D6
Seyitgazi, Turkey 39 B12
Seyitömer, Turkey 39 B11
Seym →, Ukraine 47 G7
Seymen, Turkey 41 E11
Seymour, Australia 95 F4
Seymour, S. Africa 89 E4
Seymour, Conn., U.S.A. . 111 E11
Seymour, Ind., U.S.A. .. 108 F3
Seymour, Tex., U.S.A. .. 113 J5
Seymour, Wis., U.S.A. .. 108 C1
Seyne, France 21 D10
Seyssel, France 21 C9
Sezze, Italy 30 A6
Sfântu Gheorghe, Covasna,
  Romania 43 E10
Sfântu Gheorghe, Tulcea,
  Romania 43 F14
Sfântu Gheorghe,
  Brațul →, Romania .. 43 F14
Sfax, Tunisia 79 B8

Sha Xi →, China 59 D12
Sha Xian, China 59 D11
Shaanxi □, China 56 G5
Shaba =
  Dem. Rep. of the Congo 86 D2
Shabla, Bulgaria 41 C12
Shabunda,
  Dem. Rep. of the Congo 86 C2
Shache, China 60 C2
Shackleton Ice Shelf,
  Antarctica 5 C8
Shackleton Inlet, Antarctica 5 E11
Shādegān, Iran 71 D6
Shadi, China 59 D10
Shadi, India 69 C7
Shadrinsk, Russia 50 D7
Shaffa, Nigeria 83 C7
Shafter, Calif., U.S.A. .. 117 K7
Shafter, Tex., U.S.A. .. 113 L2
Shaftesbury, U.K. 13 F5
Shagamu, Nigeria 83 D5
Shagram, Pakistan 69 A5
Shah Bunder, Pakistan .. 68 G2
Shahabad, Punjab, India . 68 D7
Shahabad, Raj., India .. 68 G7
Shahabad, Ut. P., India . 69 F8
Shahadpur, Pakistan 68 G3
Shahba, Syria 75 C5
Shahdād, Iran 71 D8
Shahdadkot, Pakistan .. 68 F2
Shahe, China 56 F8
Shahganj, India 69 F10
Shahgarh, India 68 F6
Shahjahanpur, India 69 F8
Shahpur, India 68 H7
Shahpur, Pakistan 68 E3
Shahpura, India 69 H9
Shahr-e Kord, Iran 71 C6
Shāhrakht, Iran 71 C9
Shahrig, Pakistan 68 D2
Shahukou, China 56 D7
Shaikhabad, Afghan. 68 B3
Shajapur, India 68 H7
Shakargarh, Pakistan .. 68 C6
Shakawe, Botswana 88 B3
Shaker Heights, U.S.A. . 110 E3
Shakhty, Russia 49 G5
Shakhunya, Russia 48 B8
Shaki, Nigeria 83 D5
Shala, L., Ethiopia 81 F4
Shali, Russia 49 J7
Shallow Lake, Canada .. 110 B3
Shalqar, Kazakstan 50 E6
Shalskiy, Russia 46 B8
Shaluli Shan, China 58 B2
Shām, Iran 71 E8
Shamâl Dârfûr □, Sudan 81 E2
Shamâl Kordofân □, Sudan 81 E3
Shamattawa, Canada 105 B10
Shamattawa →, Canada . 102 A2
Shambe, Sudan 81 F3
Shambu, Ethiopia 81 F4
Shamīl, Iran 71 E8
Shamkhor = Şämkir,
  Azerbaijan 49 K8
Shāmkūh, Iran 71 C8
Shamli, India 68 E7
Shamo = Gobi, Asia 56 C6
Shamo, L., Ethiopia 81 F4
Shamokin, U.S.A. 111 F8
Shamrock, U.S.A. 113 H4
Shamva, Zimbabwe 87 F3
Shan □, Burma 67 J21
Shan Xian, China 56 G9
Shanan →, Ethiopia 81 F5
Shanchengzhen, China .. 57 C13
Shāndak, Iran 71 D9
Shandon, U.S.A. 116 K6
Shandong □, China 57 G10
Shandong Bandao, China . 57 F11
Shang Xian, China 56 H5
Shangalowe,
  Dem. Rep. of the Congo 87 E2
Shangani →, Zimbabwe .. 87 F2
Shangbancheng, China .. 57 D10
Shangcai, China 59 A10
Shangcheng, China 59 B10
Shangchuan Dao, China . 59 G9
Shangdu, China 56 D7
Shanggao, China 59 C10
Shanghai, China 59 B13
Shanghang, China 59 E11
Shanghe, China 57 F9
Shangjin, China 59 A8
Shanglin, China 58 F7
Shangnan, China 56 H6
Shangqiu, China 56 G8
Shangrao, China 59 C11
Shangshui, China 56 H8
Shangsi, China 58 F6
Shangyou, China 59 E10
Shangzhi, China 57 B14
Shanhetun, China 57 B14
Shani, Nigeria 83 C7
Shaniko, U.S.A. 114 D3
Shannon, N.Z. 91 J5
Shannon →, Ireland 15 D2
Shannon, Mouth of the,
  Ireland 15 D2
Shannon Airport, Ireland . 15 D3
Shansi = Shanxi □,
  China 56 F7
Shantar, Ostrov Bolshoy,
  Russia 51 D14
Shantipur, India 69 H13
Shantou, China 59 F11
Shantung = Shandong □,
  China 57 G10

Shanxi □, China 56 F7
Shanyang, China 56 H5
Shanyin, China 56 E7
Shaoguan, China 59 E9
Shaowu, China 59 D11
Shaoxing, China 59 C13
Shaoyang, Hunan, China . 59 D8
Shaoyang, Hunan, China . 59 D8
Shap, U.K. 12 C5
Shapinsay, U.K. 14 B6
Shaqra', Si. Arabia 70 E5
Shaqrā', Yemen 74 E4
Sharafa, Sudan 81 E2
Sharafkhāneh, Iran 73 C11
Sharbot Lake, Canada ... 111 B8
Shari, Japan 54 C12
Sharjah = Ash Shāriqah,
  U.A.E. 71 E7
Shark B., Australia 93 E1
Sharm el Sheikh, Egypt .. 80 B3
Sharon, Mass., U.S.A. .. 111 D13
Sharon, Pa., U.S.A. 110 E4
Sharon Springs, U.S.A. .. 112 F4
Sharp Pt., Australia 94 A3
Sharpe L., Canada 105 C10
Sharpsville, U.S.A. 110 E4
Sharq el Istiwa'iya □,
  Sudan 81 G3
Sharya, Russia 48 A7
Shasha, Ethiopia 81 F4
Shashemene, Ethiopia .. 81 F4
Shashi, Botswana 89 C4
Shashi, China 59 B9
Shashi →, Africa 87 G2
Shasta, Mt., U.S.A. 114 F2
Shasta L., U.S.A. 114 F2
Shatsk, Russia 48 C5
Shatt al'Arab →, Iraq .. 71 D6
Shattuck, U.S.A. 113 G5
Shatura, Russia 46 E10
Shaumyani = Shulaveri,
  Georgia 49 K7
Shaunavon, Canada 105 D7
Shaver L., U.S.A. 116 H7
Shaw →, Australia 92 D2
Shaw I., Australia 94 C4
Shawan, China 60 B3
Shawanaga, Canada 110 A4
Shawano, U.S.A. 108 C1
Shawinigan, Canada 102 C5
Shawnee, U.S.A. 113 H6
Shaybārā, Si. Arabia .. 70 E3
Shayib el Banat, Gebel,
  Egypt 80 B3
Shaykh Sa'īd, Iraq 70 C5
Shchekino, Russia 46 E9
Shcherbakov = Rybinsk,
  Russia 46 C10
Shchigry, Russia 47 G9
Shchors, Ukraine 47 G6
Shchuchinsk, Kazakstan . 50 D8
She Xian, Anhui, China . 59 C12
She Xian, Hebei, China .. 56 F7
Shebekino, Russia 47 G9
Shebele = Scebeli,
  Wabi →, Somali Rep. . 81 G5
Sheboygan, U.S.A. 108 D2
Shediac, Canada 103 C7
Sheelin, L., Ireland 15 C4
Sheep Haven, Ireland .. 15 A4
Sheerness, U.K. 13 F8
Sheet Harbour, Canada . 103 D7
Sheffield, U.K. 12 D6
Sheffield, Ala., U.S.A. .. 109 H2
Sheffield, Mass., U.S.A. . 111 D11
Sheffield, Pa., U.S.A. .. 110 E5
Sheffield, Tex., U.S.A. .. 113 K4
Sheho, Canada 105 C8
Shehojele, Ethiopia 81 E4
Shehong, China 58 B5
Sheikhpura, India 69 G11
Shek Hasan, Ethiopia .. 81 E4
Shekhupura, Pakistan .. 68 D5
Sheki = Şaki, Azerbaijan . 49 K8
Shelburne, N.S., Canada . 103 D6
Shelburne, Ont., Canada . 102 D3
Shelburne, B., Australia .. 94 A3
Shelburne Falls, U.S.A. . 111 D12
Shelby, Mich., U.S.A. .. 108 D2
Shelby, Mont., U.S.A. .. 114 B8
Shelby, N.C., U.S.A. 109 H5
Shelby, Ohio, U.S.A. 110 F2
Shelbyville, Ill., U.S.A. .. 112 F10
Shelbyville, Ind., U.S.A. . 108 F3
Shelbyville, Tenn., U.S.A. 109 H2
Sheldon, U.S.A. 112 D7
Sheldrake, Canada 103 B7
Shelikhova, Zaliv, Russia . 51 D16
Shell Lake, Canada 105 C7
Shell Lakes, Australia .. 93 E4
Shellbrook, Canada 105 C7
Shellharbour, Australia .. 95 E5
Shelon →, Russia 46 C6
Shelton, Conn., U.S.A. .. 111 E11
Shelton, Wash., U.S.A. .. 116 C3
Shemakha = Şamaxi,
  Azerbaijan 49 K9
Shen Xian, China 56 F8
Shenandoah, Iowa, U.S.A. 112 E7
Shenandoah, Pa., U.S.A. . 111 F8
Shenandoah, Va., U.S.A. . 108 F6
Shenchi, China 56 E7
Shendam, Nigeria 83 D6
Shendî, Sudan 81 D3

Sheng Xian, China 59 C13
Shengfang, China 56 E9
Shēngjergji, Albania 40 E4
Shēngjin, Albania 40 E3
Shenjingzi, China 57 B13
Shenmēria, Albania 40 D4
Shenmu, China 56 E6
Shennongjia, China 59 B8
Shenqiu, China 56 H8
Shenqiucheng, China 56 H8
Shensi = Shaanxi □, China 56 G5
Shenyang, China 57 D12
Shenzhen, China 59 F10
Sheopur Kalan, India .. 66 G10
Shepetivka, Ukraine 47 G4
Shepparton, Australia .. 95 F4
Sheppey, I. of, U.K. 13 F8
Shepton Mallet, U.K. .. 13 F5
Sheqi, China 56 H7
Sher Qila, Pakistan 69 A6
Sherborne, U.K. 13 G5
Sherbro I., S. Leone 82 D2
Sherbrooke, Canada 103 C5
Shereik, Sudan 80 D3
Sheridan, Ark., U.S.A. .. 113 H8
Sheridan, Wyo., U.S.A. .. 114 D10
Sheringham, U.K. 12 E9
Sherkin I., Ireland 15 E2
Sherkot, India 69 E8
Sherman, U.S.A. 113 J6
Sherridon, Canada 105 B8
Sherwood, N. Dak., U.S.A. 112 A4
Sherwood, Tex., U.S.A. .. 113 K4
Sherwood Forest, U.K. .. 12 D6
Sheslay, Canada 104 B2
Sheslay →, Canada 104 B2
Shethanei L., Canada .. 105 B9
Shetland □, U.K. 14 A7
Shetland Is., U.K. 14 A7
Shewa □, Ethiopia 81 F4
Shewa Gimira, Ethiopia . 81 F4
Sheyenne, U.S.A. 112 B5
Sheyenne →, U.S.A. 112 B6
Shibām, Yemen 74 D4
Shibata, Japan 54 F9
Shibecha, Japan 54 C12
Shibetsu, Japan 54 B11
Shibîn el Kôm, Egypt .. 80 H7
Shibîn el Qanâtir, Egypt . 80 H7
Shibing, China 58 D7
Shibogama L., Canada .. 102 B2
Shibushi, Japan 55 J5
Shicheng, China 59 D11
Shickshock Mts. = Chic-
  Chocs, Mts., Canada .. 103 C6
Shidao, China 57 F12
Shidian, China 58 E2
Shido, Japan 55 G7
Shiel, L., U.K. 14 E3
Shiga □, Japan 55 G8
Shigu, China 58 D2
Shiguaigou, China 56 D6
Shihchiachuangi =
  Shijiazhuang, China .. 56 E8
Shijaku, Albania 40 E3
Shijiazhuang, China 56 E8
Shijiu Hu, China 59 B12
Shikarpur, India 68 E8
Shikarpur, Pakistan 68 F3
Shikoku □, Japan 55 H6
Shikoku-Sanchi, Japan .. 55 H6
Shiliguri, India 67 F16
Shilka, Russia 51 D12
Shilka →, Russia 51 D13
Shillelagh, Ireland 15 D5
Shillong, India 67 G17
Shilo, West Bank 75 C4
Shilong, China 59 F9
Shilou, China 56 F6
Shilovo, Russia 48 C5
Shimabara, Japan 55 H5
Shimada, Japan 55 G9
Shimane □, Japan 55 G6
Shimanovsk, Russia 51 D13
Shimenjie, China 59 C11
Shimian, China 58 C4
Shimizu, Japan 55 G9
Shimodate, Japan 55 F9
Shimoga, India 66 N9
Shimoni, Kenya 86 C4
Shimonoseki, Japan 55 H5
Shimpuru Rapids, Angola 88 B2
Shimsk, Russia 46 C6
Shin, L., U.K. 14 C4
Shin-Tone →, Japan 55 G10
Shinan, China 58 F7
Shinano →, Japan 55 F9
Shīndand, Afghan. 66 C3
Shingleton, U.S.A. 102 C2
Shingū, Japan 55 H7
Shinjō, Japan 54 E10
Shinkafe, Nigeria 83 C6
Shinshār, Syria 75 A5
Shinyanga, Tanzania 86 C3
Shinyanga □, Tanzania .. 86 C3
Shiogama, Japan 54 E10
Shiojiri, Japan 55 F8
Ship I., U.S.A. 113 K10
Shipchenski Prokhod,
  Bulgaria 41 D9
Shiping, China 58 F4
Shipki La, India 66 D11
Shippegan, Canada 103 C7
Shippensburg, U.S.A. .. 110 F7

Shiprock, U.S.A. 115 H9
Shiqian, China 58 D7
Shiqma, N. →, Israel ... 75 D3
Shiquan, China 56 H5
Shīr Kūh, Iran 71 D7
Shirakawa, Fukushima, Japan 55 F10
Shirakawa, Gifu, Japan ... 55 F8
Shirane-San, Gumma, Japan 55 F9
Shirane-San, Yamanashi, Japan 55 G9
Shiraoi, Japan 54 C10
Shīrāz, Iran 71 D7
Shirbin, Egypt 80 H7
Shire →, Africa 87 F4
Shiretoko-Misaki, Japan .. 54 B12
Shirinab →, Pakistan ... 68 D2
Shiriya-Zaki, Japan 54 D10
Shiroishi, Japan 54 F10
Shīrvān, Iran 71 B8
Shirwa, L. = Chilwa, L., Malawi 87 F4
Shishou, China 59 C9
Shitai, China 59 B11
Shivpuri, India 68 G7
Shixian, China 57 C15
Shixing, China 59 E10
Shiyan, China 59 A8
Shiyata, Egypt 80 B2
Shizhu, China 58 C7
Shizong, China 58 E5
Shizuishan, China 56 E4
Shizuoka, Japan 55 G9
Shizuoka □, Japan 55 G9
Shklov = Shklow, Belarus 46 E6
Shklow, Belarus 46 E6
Shkoder = Shkodra, Albania 40 D3
Shkodra, Albania 40 D3
Shkumbini →, Albania ... 40 E3
Shmidta, Ostrov, Russia .. 51 A10
Shō-Gawa →, Japan ... 55 F8
Shoal Lake, Canada ... 105 C8
Shōdo-Shima, Japan ... 55 G7
Sholapur = Solapur, India 66 L9
Shologontsy, Russia ... 51 C12
Shōmrōn, West Bank 75 C4
Shoreham by Sea, U.K. .. 13 G7
Shoshone, Calif., U.S.A. . 117 K10
Shoshone, Idaho, U.S.A. . 114 E6
Shoshone L., U.S.A. 114 D8
Shoshone Mts., U.S.A. .. 114 G5
Shoshong, Botswana ... 88 C4
Shoshoni, U.S.A. 114 E9
Shostka, Ukraine 47 G7
Shou Xian, China 59 A11
Shouchang, China 59 C12
Shouguang, China 57 F10
Shouning, China 59 D12
Shouyang, China 56 F7
Show Low, U.S.A. 115 J9
Shpola, Ukraine 47 H6
Shreveport, U.S.A. 113 J8
Shrewsbury, U.K. 13 E5
Shrirampur, India 69 H13
Shropshire □, U.K. 13 E5
Shu, Kazakstan 50 E8
Shu →, Kazakstan 52 E10
Shuangbai, China 58 E3
Shuangcheng, China ... 57 B14
Shuangfeng, China 59 D9
Shuanggou, China 57 G9
Shuangjiang, China .. 58 F2
Shuangliao, China ... 57 C12
Shuangshanzi, China .. 57 D10
Shuangyang, China ... 57 C13
Shuangyashan, China .. 60 B8
Shucheng, China 59 B11
Shugozero, Russia 46 C8
Shuguri Falls, Tanzania .. 87 D4
Shuiji, China 59 D12
Shuiye, China 56 F8
Shujalpur, India 68 H7
Shukpa Kunzang, India .. 69 B8
Shulan, China 57 B14
Shulaveri, Georgia 49 K7
Shule, China 60 C2
Shumagin Is., U.S.A. .. 100 C4
Shumen, Bulgaria 41 C10
Shumerlya, Russia 48 C8
Shumikha, Russia 50 D7
Shunchang, China 59 D11
Shunde, China 59 F9
Shungay, Kazakstan ... 49 F8
Shuo Xian, China 56 E7
Shūr →, Iran 71 D7
Shūr Āb, Iran 71 C6
Shūr Gaz, Iran 71 D8
Shūrāb, Iran 71 C8
Shūrjestān, Iran 71 D7
Shurugwi, Zimbabwe .. 87 F3
Shūsf, Iran 71 D9
Shūsh, Iran 73 F13
Shūshtar, Iran 71 D6
Shuswap L., Canada .. 104 C5
Shuya, Russia 48 B5
Shuyang, China 57 G10
Shūzū, Iran 71 D7
Shwebo, Burma 67 H19
Shwegu, Burma 67 G20
Shweli →, Burma 67 H20
Shymkent, Kazakstan .. 50 E7
Shyok, India 69 B8
Shyok →, Pakistan ... 69 B6

Si Chen, Thailand 65 H2
Si Kiang = Xi Jiang →, China 59 F9
Si-ngan = Xi'an, China .. 56 G5
Si Prachan, Thailand 64 E3
Si Racha, Thailand 64 F3
Si Xian, China 57 H9
Siahan Range, Pakistan .. 66 F4
Siaksriindrapura, Indonesia 62 D2
Sialkot, Pakistan 68 C6
Siam = Thailand ■, Asia . 64 E4
Sianów, Poland 44 D3
Siantan, Indonesia 62 D3
Sīāreh, Iran 71 D9
Siargao, Phil. 61 G7
Siar., Pakistan 69 B7
Siasi, Phil. 63 C6
Siasi I., Phil. 61 J4
Siau, Indonesia 63 D7
Šiauliai, Lithuania 9 J20
Šiauliai □, Lithuania ... 44 C10
Siaya □, Kenya 86 C3
Siazan = Siyäzän, Azerbaijan 49 K9
Sibâi, Gebel el, Egypt .. 80 B3
Sibayi, L., S. Africa 89 D5
Šibenik, Croatia 29 E12
Siberia, Russia 4 D13
Siberut, Indonesia 62 E1
Sibi, Pakistan 68 E2
Sibil = Oksibil, Indonesia . 63 E10
Sibiti, Congo 84 E2
Sibiu, Romania 43 E9
Sibiu □, Romania 43 E9
Sibley, Iowa, U.S.A. .. 112 D7
Sibley, La., U.S.A. ... 113 J8
Sibolga, Indonesia ... 62 D1
Sibsagar, India 67 F19
Sibu, Malaysia 62 D4
Sibuco, Phil. 61 H5
Sibuguey B., Phil. 61 H5
Sibut, C.A.R. 84 C3
Sibutu, Phil. 63 D5
Sibutu Group, Phil. ... 61 J3
Sibutu Passage, E. Indies . 63 D6
Sibuyan, Phil. 61 E5
Sibuyan Sea, Phil. ... 61 E5
Sic, Romania 43 D8
Sicamous, Canada ... 104 C5
Sichuan □, China ... 58 B5
Sicilia, Italy 31 E7
Sicily = Sicilia, Italy ... 31 E7
Sicuani, Peru 124 F4
Šid, Serbia, Yug. 42 E4
Sidamo □, Ethiopia ... 81 G4
Sidaouet, Niger 83 B6
Sidári, Greece 36 A3
Siddhapur, India 68 H5
Siddipet, India 66 K11
Sidensjö, Sweden ... 10 A12
Sidéradougou, Burkina Faso 82 C4
Siderno, Italy 31 D9
Sídheros, Ákra, Greece .. 36 D8
Sidhirókastron, Greece .. 40 E7
Sîdi Abd el Rahmân, Egypt 80 H6
Sîdi Barrâni, Egypt ... 80 A2
Sidi-bel-Abbès, Algeria ... 78 A5
Sidi Haneish, Egypt ... 80 A2
Sidi Omar, Egypt 80 A1
Sidlaw Hills, U.K. 14 E5
Sidley, Mt., Antarctica .. 5 D14
Sidmouth, U.K. 13 G4
Sidmouth, C., Australia .. 94 A3
Sidney, Canada 104 D4
Sidney, Mont., U.S.A. .. 112 B2
Sidney, N.Y., U.S.A. .. 111 D9
Sidney, Nebr., U.S.A. .. 112 E3
Sidney, Ohio, U.S.A. .. 108 E3
Sidoarjo, Indonesia ... 63 G15
Sidon = Saydā, Lebanon 75 B4
Sidra, G. of = Surt, Khalīj, Libya 79 B9
Siedlce, Poland 45 F9
Siedlce □, Poland 45 F9
Sieg →, Germany 24 E3
Siegburg, Germany ... 24 E3
Siegen, Germany 24 E4
Siem Pang, Cambodia .. 64 E6
Siem Reap = Siemreab, Cambodia 64 F4
Siemiatycze, Poland ... 45 F9
Siemreab, Cambodia ... 64 F4
Siena, Italy 29 E8
Sieniawa, Poland 45 H9
Sieradz, Poland 45 G5
Sieradz □, Poland 45 G5
Sieraków, Poland 45 F3
Sierck-les-Bains, France .. 19 C13
Sierning, Austria 26 C7
Sierpc, Poland 45 F6
Sierra Blanca, U.S.A. ... 115 L11
Sierra Blanca Peak, U.S.A. 115 K11
Sierra City, U.S.A. 116 F6
Sierra Colorada, Argentina 128 E3
Sierra de Yeguas, Spain .. 35 H6
Sierra Gorda, Chile ... 126 A2
Sierra Leone ■, W. Afr. .. 82 D2
Sierra Madre, Mexico .. 119 D6
Sierra Mojada, Mexico .. 118 B4
Sierraville, U.S.A. 116 F6
Sierre, Switz. 25 J3
Sífnos, Greece 38 E6
Sifton, Canada 105 C8
Sifton Pass, Canada .. 104 B3

Sigean, France 20 E6
Sighetu-Marmației, Romania 43 C8
Sighișoara, Romania ... 43 D9
Sigli, Indonesia 62 C1
Siglufjörður, Iceland ... 8 C4
Sigmaringen, Germany .. 25 G5
Signa, Italy 28 E8
Signakhi = Tsnori, Georgia 49 K7
Signal, U.S.A. 117 L13
Signal Pk., U.S.A. 117 M12
Signy-l'Abbaye, France .. 19 C11
Sigsig, Ecuador 124 D3
Sigüenza, Spain 32 D2
Siguiri, Guinea 82 C3
Sigulda, Latvia 9 H21
Sigurd, U.S.A. 115 G8
Sihanoukville = Kampong Saom, Cambodia ... 65 G4
Sihui, China 59 F9
Siikajoki →, Finland ... 8 D21
Siilinjärvi, Finland 8 E22
Siirt, Turkey 73 D9
Sijarira Ra., Zimbabwe .. 87 F2
Sikao, Thailand 65 J2
Sikar, India 68 F6
Sikasso, Mali 82 C3
Sikeston, U.S.A. 113 G10
Sikhote Alin, Khrebet, Russia 54 B8
Sikhote Alin Ra. = Sikhote Alin, Khrebet, Russia .. 54 B8
Sikiá, Greece 40 F7
Síkinos, Greece 39 E7
Sikkani Chief →, Canada 104 B4
Sikkim □, India 67 F16
Siklós, Hungary 42 E3
Sikotu-Ko, Japan 54 C10
Sil →, Spain 34 C3
Silacayoapan, Mexico .. 119 D5
Šilalė, Lithuania 44 C9
Silandro, Italy 28 B7
Silay, Phil. 61 F5
Silba, Croatia 29 D11
Silchar, India 67 G18
Silcox, Canada 105 B10
Sile, Turkey 41 E13
Siler City, U.S.A. 109 H6
Silgarhi Doti, Nepal ... 69 E9
Silghat, India 67 F18
Silifke, Turkey 72 D5
Siliguri = Shiliguri, India . 67 F16
Siling Co, China 60 C3
Silistea Nouă, Romania .. 43 F10
Silistra, Bulgaria 41 B11
Silivri, Turkey 41 E12
Siljan, Sweden 10 D8
Siljansnäs, Sweden ... 10 D8
Silkeborg, Denmark ... 11 H3
Silla, Spain 33 F4
Sillajhuay, Cordillera, Chile 124 G5
Sillamäe, Estonia 9 G22
Sillé-le-Guillaume, France 18 D6
Silleda, Spain 34 C2
Silloth, U.K. 12 C4
Sílo, Greece 41 E9
Siloam Springs, U.S.A. .. 113 G7
Silopi, Turkey 73 D10
Silsbee, U.S.A. 113 K7
Šilutė, Lithuania 9 J19
Silva Porto = Kuito, Angola 85 G3
Silvan, Turkey 73 C9
Silver City, N. Mex., U.S.A. 115 K9
Silver City, Nev., U.S.A. . 114 G4
Silver Cr. →, U.S.A. ... 114 E4
Silver Creek, U.S.A. ... 110 D5
Silver L., Calif., U.S.A. .. 116 G6
Silver L., Calif., U.S.A. .. 117 K10
Silver Lake, U.S.A. 114 E3
Silver Streams, S. Africa .. 88 D3
Silverdalen, Sweden ... 11 G9
Silverton, Colo., U.S.A. .. 115 H10
Silverton, Tex., U.S.A. .. 113 H4
Silves, Portugal 35 H2
Silvi Marina, Italy 29 F11
Silvies →, U.S.A. 114 E4
Silvretthorn, Switz. ... 28 B7
Silwa Bahari, Egypt ... 80 C3
Silz, Austria 26 D3
Simanggang = Bandar Sri Aman, Malaysia ... 62 D4
Simao, China 58 F3
Simard, L., Canada ... 102 C4
Şīmareh →, Iran 73 F12
Simav, Turkey 39 B10
Simav →, Turkey 41 F12
Simav Dağları, Turkey .. 39 B10
Simba, Tanzania 86 C4
Simbach, Germany ... 25 G9
Simbirsk, Russia 48 C9
Simbo, Tanzania 86 C2
Simcoe, Canada 102 D3
Simcoe, L., Canada ... 102 D4
Simenovgrad, Bulgaria .. 41 D9
Simeria, Romania 42 E8
Simeto →, Italy 31 E7
Simeulue, Indonesia ... 62 D1
Simferopol, Ukraine ... 47 K8
Sími, Greece 39 E9
Simi Valley, U.S.A. ... 117 L8
Simikot, Nepal 69 E9
Simitli, Bulgaria 40 E7
Simla, India 68 D7
Simlångsdalen, Sweden .. 11 H7

Şimleu-Silvaniei, Romania 42 C7
Simmern, Germany ... 25 F3
Simmie, Canada 105 D7
Simmler, U.S.A. 117 K7
Simnas, Lithuania 44 D10
Simojoki →, Finland ... 8 D21
Simojovel, Mexico ... 119 D6
Simonette →, Canada .. 104 B5
Simonstown, S. Africa .. 88 E2
Simontornya, Hungary ... 42 D3
Simplon P., Switz. 25 J4
Simplontunnel, Switz. .. 25 J4
Simpson Desert, Australia 94 D2
Simpungdong, N. Korea . 57 D15
Simrishamn, Sweden ... 11 J8
Simushir, Ostrov, Russia .. 51 E16
Sinabang, Indonesia ... 62 D1
Sinadogo, Somali Rep. .. 74 F4
Sinai = Es Sînâ', Egypt .. 80 J8
Sinai, Mt. = Mûsa, Gebel, Egypt 80 J8
Sinai Peninsula, Egypt ... 75 F3
Sinaia, Romania 43 E10
Sinaloa □, Mexico 118 C3
Sinaloa de Leyva, Mexico . 118 B3
Sinalunga, Italy 29 E8
Sinan, China 58 D7
Sînandrei, Romania ... 42 E6
Sinarádhes, Greece ... 36 A3
Sincan, Turkey 72 B5
Sincanlı, Turkey 39 C12
Sincelejo, Colombia ... 124 B3
Sinchang, N. Korea ... 57 D15
Sinchang-ni, N. Korea .. 57 E14
Sinclair, U.S.A. 114 F10
Sinclair Mills, Canada .. 104 C4
Sinclair's B., U.K. 14 C5
Sincorá, Serra do, Brazil . 125 F10
Sind, Pakistan 68 G3
Sind □, Pakistan 68 G3
Sind →, India 69 B6
Sind Sagar Doab, Pakistan 68 D4
Sindal, Denmark 11 G4
Sindangan, Phil. 61 G5
Sindangbarang, Indonesia . 63 G12
Sinde, Zambia 87 F2
Sindelfingen, Germany .. 25 G4
Sindirgi, Turkey 39 B10
Sinegorskiy, Russia ... 49 G5
Sinelki, Turkey 41 E12
Sinelnikovo = Synelnykove, Ukraine .. 47 H8
Sines, Portugal 35 H2
Sines, C. de, Portugal ... 35 H2
Sineu, Spain 37 B10
Sinfra, Ivory C. 82 D3
Sing Buri, Thailand ... 64 E3
Singa, Sudan 81 E3
Singapore ■, Asia 65 M4
Singapore, Straits of, Asia 65 M5
Singaraja, Indonesia ... 62 F5
Singen, Germany 25 H4
Singida, Tanzania 86 C3
Singida □, Tanzania ... 86 D3
Singitikós Kólpos, Greece . 40 F7
Singkaling Hkamti, Burma 67 G19
Singkang, Indonesia ... 63 E6
Singkawang, Indonesia .. 62 D3
Singkep, Indonesia ... 62 E2
Singleton, Australia ... 95 E5
Singleton, Mt., N. Terr., Australia 92 D5
Singleton, Mt., W. Austral., Australia 93 E2
Singö, Sweden 10 D12
Singoli, India 68 G6
Singora = Songkhla, Thailand 65 J3
Singosan, N. Korea ... 57 E14
Sinhung, N. Korea ... 57 D14
Sinií □, Egypt 75 F3
Siniátsikon, Óros, Greece . 40 F5
Siniscóla, Italy 30 B2
Sinj, Croatia 29 E13
Sinjai, Indonesia 63 F6
Sinjajevina, Montenegro, Yug. .. 40 D3
Sinjār, Iraq 70 B4
Sinkat, Sudan 80 D4
Sinkiang Uighur = Xinjiang Uygur Zizhiqu □, China 60 B3
Sinmak, N. Korea 57 E14
Sinnamary, Fr. Guiana .. 125 B8
Sinni →, Italy 31 B9
Sinnuris, Egypt 80 J7
Sinoie, Lacul, Romania .. 43 F13
Sinop, Turkey 72 A6
Sinpo, N. Korea 57 E15
Sinsheim, Germany ... 25 F4
Sinsk, Russia 51 C13
Sint Eustatius, I., Neth. Ant. 121 C7
Sint Maarten, I., W. Indies 121 C7
Sintang, Indonesia ... 62 D4
Sinton, U.S.A. 113 L6
Sintra, Portugal 35 G1
Sinŭiju, N. Korea 57 D13
Sinyukha →, Ukraine .. 47 H6
Sinzig, Germany 24 E3
Sió →, Hungary 42 D3
Siocon, Phil. 61 H5
Siófok, Hungary 42 D3
Sioma, Zambia 88 B3
Sion, Switz. 25 J3
Sion Mills, U.K. 15 B4
Sioux City, U.S.A. ... 112 D6

Sioux Falls, U.S.A. 112 D6
Sioux Lookout, Canada .. 102 B1
Sipalay, Phil. 61 G5
Šipan, Croatia 40 D1
Siping, China 57 C13
Sipiwesk L., Canada ... 105 B9
Šipovo, Bos.-H. 42 F2
Sipura, Indonesia 62 E1
Siquia →, Nic. 120 D3
Siquijor, Phil. 61 G5
Siquirres, Costa Rica ... 120 D3
Sir Edward Pellew Group, Australia 94 B2
Sir Graham Moore Is., Australia 92 B4
Sira →, Norway 9 G12
Siracusa, Italy 31 E8
Sirajganj, Bangla. ... 69 G13
Sirakoro, Mali 82 C3
Şiran, Turkey 73 B8
Sirasso, Ivory C. 82 D3
Sīrdān, Iran 71 B6
Sirdaryo = Syrdarya →, Kazakstan 50 E7
Sirer, Spain 37 C7
Siret, Romania 43 C11
Siret →, Romania ... 43 E12
Şiria, Romania 42 D6
Sirino, Mte., Italy 31 B8
Sírna, Greece 39 E8
Şırnak, Turkey 73 D10
Sirohi, India 68 G5
Sironj, India 68 G7
Síros, Greece 38 D6
Sirretta Pk., U.S.A. .. 117 K8
Sirsa, India 68 E6
Siruela, Spain 35 G5
Sisak, Croatia 29 C13
Sisaket, Thailand 64 E5
Sisante, Spain 33 F2
Sisargas, Is., Spain .. 34 B2
Sishen, S. Africa 88 D3
Sishui, Henan, China .. 56 G7
Sishui, Shandong, China . 57 G9
Sisipuk L., Canada ... 105 B8
Sisophon, Cambodia ... 64 F4
Sisseton, U.S.A. 112 C6
Sissonne, France 19 C10
Sīstān va Balūchestān □, Iran 71 E9
Sisteron, France 21 D9
Sisters, U.S.A. 114 D3
Sitamarhi, India 69 F11
Sitapur, India 69 F9
Siteki, Swaziland 89 D5
Sitges, Spain 32 D6
Sithoniá, Greece 40 F7
Sitía, Greece 36 D8
Sitka, U.S.A. 100 C6
Sitoti, Botswana 88 C3
Sitra, Egypt 80 B2
Sittang Myit →, Burma . 67 L20
Sittard, Neths. 17 C5
Sittensen, Germany ... 24 B5
Sittingbourne, U.K. ... 13 F8
Sittona, Eritrea 81 E4
Sittwe, Burma 67 J18
Siuna, Nic. 120 D3
Siuri, India 69 H12
Siutghiol, Lacul, Romania 43 F13
Sivana, India 68 E8
Sīvand, Iran 71 D7
Sivas, Turkey 72 C7
Sivasli, Turkey 39 C11
Siverek, Turkey 73 D8
Sivrihisar, Turkey ... 72 C4
Sîwa, El Wâhât es, Egypt . 80 B2
Siwa Oasis, Egypt ... 76 D6
Siwalik Range, Nepal .. 69 F10
Siwan, India 69 F11
Sixmilebridge, Ireland .. 15 D3
Siyäl, Jazā'ir, Egypt .. 80 C4
Siyäzän, Azerbaijan ... 49 K9
Siziwang Qi, China ... 56 D6
Sjælland, Denmark ... 11 J5
Sjællands Odde, Denmark 11 J5
Sjenica, Serbia, Yug. .. 40 C3
Sjöbo, Sweden 11 J7
Sjötofta, Sweden ... 11 G7
Sjötorp, Sweden 11 F8
Sjumen = Shumen, Bulgaria 41 C10
Sjuntorp, Sweden ... 11 F6
Skadarsko Jezero, Montenegro, Yug. ... 40 D3
Skadovsk, Ukraine ... 47 J7
Skælskør, Denmark ... 11 J5
Skærbæk, Denmark ... 11 J2
Skaftafell, Iceland ... 8 D5
Skagafjörður, Iceland .. 8 D4
Skagastølstindane, Norway 9 F12
Skagaströnd, Iceland .. 8 D3
Skagen, Denmark ... 11 G4
Skagern, Sweden 11 F8
Skagerrak, Denmark .. 11 G2
Skagit →, U.S.A. 116 B4
Skagway, U.S.A. 104 B1
Skala-Podilska, Ukraine .. 47 H4
Skala Podolskaya = Skala-Podilska, Ukraine .. 47 H4
Skalat, Ukraine 47 H3
Skalbmierz, Poland ... 45 H7
Skälderviken, Sweden .. 11 H6
Skalica, Slovak Rep. .. 27 C10
Skallingen, Denmark .. 11 J2

207

Skalni Dol = Kamenyak, Bulgaria ... 41 C10
Skanderborg, Denmark ... 11 H3
Skåne, Sweden ... 11 J7
Skänninge, Sweden ... 11 F9
Skanör med Falsterbo, Sweden ... 11 J6
Skantzoúra, Greece ... 38 B6
Skara, Sweden ... 11 F7
Skaraborgs län □, Sweden ... 11 F7
Skärblacka, Sweden ... 11 F9
Skåre, Sweden ... 10 E7
Skardu, Pakistan ... 69 B6
Skärhamn, Sweden ... 11 G5
Skarszewy, Poland ... 44 D5
Skaryszew, Poland ... 45 G8
Skarżysko-Kamienna, Poland ... 45 G7
Skattkärr, Sweden ... 10 E7
Skattungbyn, Sweden ... 10 C8
Skawina, Poland ... 45 J6
Skebobruk, Sweden ... 10 E12
Skeena →, Canada ... 104 C2
Skeena Mts., Canada ... 104 B3
Skegness, U.K. ... 12 D8
Skeldon, Guyana ... 124 B7
Skellefte älv →, Sweden ... 8 D19
Skellefteå, Sweden ... 8 D19
Skelleftehamn, Sweden ... 8 D19
Skender Vakuf, Bos.-H. ... 42 F2
Skerries, The, U.K. ... 12 D3
Skhíza, Greece ... 38 E3
Skhoinoúsa, Greece ... 39 E7
Ski, Norway ... 9 G14
Skíathos, Greece ... 38 B5
Skibbereen, Ireland ... 15 E2
Skiddaw, U.K. ... 12 C4
Skídhra, Greece ... 40 F6
Skien, Norway ... 9 G13
Skierniewice, Poland ... 45 G7
Skierniewice □, Poland ... 45 G7
Skikda, Algeria ... 78 A7
Skillingaryd, Sweden ... 11 G8
Skillinge, Sweden ... 11 J8
Skilloura, Cyprus ... 36 D12
Skinári, Ákra, Greece ... 38 D2
Skinnskatteberg, Sweden ... 10 E9
Skipton, Australia ... 95 F3
Skipton, U.K. ... 12 D5
Skirmish Pt., Australia ... 94 A1
Skiropoúla, Greece ... 38 C6
Skíros, Greece ... 38 C6
Skivarp, Sweden ... 11 J7
Skive, Denmark ... 11 H3
Skjálfandafljót →, Iceland ... 8 D5
Skjálfandi, Iceland ... 8 C5
Skjern, Denmark ... 11 J2
Skoczów, Poland ... 45 J5
Škofja Loka, Slovenia ... 29 B11
Skoghall, Sweden ... 10 E7
Skogstorp, Sweden ... 10 E10
Skoki, Poland ... 45 F4
Skole, Ukraine ... 47 H2
Skópelos, Greece ... 38 B5
Skopí, Greece ... 36 D8
Skopin, Russia ... 46 F10
Skopje, Macedonia ... 40 D5
Skórcz, Poland ... 44 E5
Skørping, Denmark ... 11 H3
Skövde, Sweden ... 11 F7
Skovorodino, Russia ... 51 D13
Skowhegan, U.S.A. ... 103 D6
Skownan, Canada ... 105 C9
Skradin, Croatia ... 29 E12
Skrea, Sweden ... 11 H6
Skrunda, Latvia ... 44 B9
Skrwa →, Poland ... 45 F6
Skull, Ireland ... 15 E2
Skultorp, Sweden ... 11 F7
Skultuna, Sweden ... 10 E10
Skunk →, U.S.A. ... 112 E9
Skuodas, Lithuania ... 9 H19
Skurup, Sweden ... 11 J7
Skutskär, Sweden ... 10 D11
Skvyra, Ukraine ... 47 H5
Skwierzyna, Poland ... 45 F2
Skye, U.K. ... 14 D2
Skykomish, U.S.A. ... 114 C3
Skyttorp, Sweden ... 10 D11
Slættaratindur, Færoe Is. ... 8 E9
Slagelse, Denmark ... 11 J5
Slamet, Indonesia ... 63 G13
Slaney →, Ireland ... 15 D5
Slănic, Romania ... 43 E10
Slano, Croatia ... 40 D1
Slantsy, Russia ... 46 C5
Slaný, Czech Rep. ... 26 A7
Slätbaken, Sweden ... 11 F10
Slate Is., Canada ... 102 C2
Slatina, Croatia ... 42 E2
Slatina, Romania ... 43 F9
Slatina Timiş, Romania ... 42 E7
Slaton, U.S.A. ... 113 J4
Slave →, Canada ... 104 A6
Slave Coast, W. Afr. ... 83 D5
Slave Lake, Canada ... 104 B6
Slave Pt., Canada ... 104 A5
Slavgorod, Russia ... 50 D8
Slavinja, Serbia, Yug. ... 40 C6
Slavkov u Brna, Czech Rep. ... 27 B9
Slavonija, Europe ... 42 E2
Slavonski Brod, Croatia ... 42 E3
Slavuta, Ukraine ... 47 G4
Slavyanka, Russia ... 54 C5
Slavyanovo, Bulgaria ... 41 C8

Slavyansk = Slovyansk, Ukraine ... 47 H9
Slavyansk-na-Kubani, Russia ... 47 K10
Sława, Poland ... 45 G3
Sławharad, Belarus ... 46 F6
Sławno, Poland ... 44 D3
Sławoborze, Poland ... 44 E2
Sleaford, U.K. ... 12 D7
Sleaford B., Australia ... 95 E2
Sleat, Sd. of, U.K. ... 14 D3
Sleeper Is., Canada ... 101 C11
Sleepy Eye, U.S.A. ... 112 C7
Slemon L., Canada ... 104 A5
Ślesin, Poland ... 45 F5
Slidell, U.S.A. ... 113 K10
Sliema, Malta ... 36 D2
Slieve Aughty, Ireland ... 15 C3
Slieve Bloom, Ireland ... 15 C4
Slieve Donard, U.K. ... 15 B6
Slieve Gamph, Ireland ... 15 B3
Slieve Gullion, U.K. ... 15 B5
Slieve Mish, Ireland ... 15 D2
Slievenamon, Ireland ... 15 D4
Sligeach = Sligo, Ireland ... 15 B3
Sligo, Ireland ... 15 B3
Sligo □, Ireland ... 15 B3
Sligo B., Ireland ... 15 B3
Slite, Sweden ... 11 G12
Sliven, Bulgaria ... 41 D10
Slivnitsa, Bulgaria ... 40 D7
Sljeme, Croatia ... 29 C12
Sloan, U.S.A. ... 117 K11
Sloansville, U.S.A. ... 111 D10
Slobozia, Moldova ... 43 D14
Slobozia, Argeş, Romania ... 43 F10
Slobozia, Ialomiţa, Romania ... 43 F12
Slocan, Canada ... 104 D5
Słomniki, Poland ... 45 H7
Slonim, Belarus ... 47 F3
Slough, U.K. ... 13 F7
Slough □, U.K. ... 13 F7
Sloughhouse, U.S.A. ... 116 G5
Slovak Rep. ■, Europe ... 27 C13
Slovakia = Slovak Rep. ■, Europe ... 27 C13
Slovakian Ore Mts. = Slovenské Rudohorie, Slovak Rep. ... 27 C12
Slovenia ■, Europe ... 29 C11
Slovenija = Slovenia ■, Europe ... 29 C11
Slovenj Gradec, Slovenia ... 29 B12
Slovenska Bistrica, Slovenia ... 29 B12
Slovenske Konjice, Slovenia ... 29 B12
Slovenské Rudohorie, Slovak Rep. ... 27 C12
Slovyansk, Ukraine ... 47 H9
Słubice, Poland ... 45 F1
Sluch →, Ukraine ... 47 G4
Sluis, Neths. ... 17 C3
Słunchev Bryag, Bulgaria ... 41 D11
Slunj, Croatia ... 29 C12
Słupca, Poland ... 45 F4
Słupia →, Poland ... 44 D3
Słupsk, Poland ... 44 D4
Słupsk □, Poland ... 44 D4
Slurry, S. Africa ... 88 D4
Slutsk, Belarus ... 47 F4
Slyne Hd., Ireland ... 15 C1
Slyudyanka, Russia ... 51 D11
Småland, Sweden ... 11 G9
Smålandsfarvandet, Denmark ... 11 J5
Smålandsstenar, Sweden ... 11 G7
Smalltree L., Canada ... 105 A8
Smallwood Res., Canada ... 103 B7
Smara, Morocco ... 78 B4
Smarhon, Belarus ... 46 E4
Smarje, Slovenia ... 29 B12
Smartt Syndicate Dam, S. Africa ... 88 E3
Smartville, U.S.A. ... 116 F5
Smeaton, Canada ... 105 C8
Smedby, Sweden ... 11 H10
Smederevo, Serbia, Yug. ... 40 B4
Smederevska Palanka, Serbia, Yug. ... 40 B4
Smedjebacken, Sweden ... 10 D9
Smela = Smila, Ukraine ... 47 H6
Smerwick Harbour, Ireland ... 15 D1
Smethport, U.S.A. ... 110 E6
Smidovich, Russia ... 51 E14
Śmigiel, Poland ... 45 F3
Smila, Ukraine ... 47 H6
Smiley, Canada ... 105 C7
Smilyan, Bulgaria ... 41 E8
Smith, Canada ... 104 B6
Smith →, Canada ... 104 B3
Smith Center, U.S.A. ... 112 F5
Smith Sund, Greenland ... 4 B4
Smithburne →, Australia ... 94 B3
Smithers, Canada ... 104 C3
Smithfield, S. Africa ... 89 E4
Smithfield, N.C., U.S.A. ... 109 H6
Smithfield, Utah, U.S.A. ... 114 F8
Smiths Falls, Canada ... 102 D4
Smithton, Australia ... 94 G4
Smithtown, Australia ... 95 E5
Smithville, Canada ... 110 C5
Smithville, U.S.A. ... 113 K6
Smoky →, Canada ... 104 B5
Smoky Bay, Australia ... 95 E1
Smoky Falls, Canada ... 102 B3
Smoky Hill →, U.S.A. ... 112 F6

Smoky Lake, Canada ... 104 C6
Smøla, Norway ... 8 E13
Smolensk, Russia ... 46 E7
Smolikas, Óros, Greece ... 40 F4
Smolník, Slovak Rep. ... 27 C13
Smolyan, Bulgaria ... 41 E8
Smooth Rock Falls, Canada ... 102 C3
Smoothstone L., Canada ... 105 C7
Smorgon = Smarhon, Belarus ... 46 E4
Smulţi, Romania ... 43 E12
Smyadovo, Bulgaria ... 41 C11
Smygehamn, Sweden ... 11 J7
Smyrna = Izmir, Turkey ... 39 C9
Snæfell, Iceland ... 8 D6
Snaefell, U.K. ... 12 C3
Snæfellsjökull, Iceland ... 8 D2
Snake →, U.S.A. ... 114 C4
Snake I., Australia ... 95 F4
Snake L., Canada ... 105 B7
Snake Range, U.S.A. ... 114 G6
Snake River Plain, U.S.A. ... 114 E7
Snasahögarna, Sweden ... 10 A6
Snåsavatnet, Norway ... 8 D14
Snedsted, Denmark ... 11 H2
Sneek, Neths. ... 17 A5
Sneeuberge, S. Africa ... 88 E3
Snejbjerg, Denmark ... 11 H2
Snelling, U.S.A. ... 116 H6
Snezhnoye, Ukraine ... 47 J10
Snežnik, Slovenia ... 29 C11
Śniadowo, Poland ... 45 E8
Sniardwy, Jezioro, Poland ... 45 E8
Śnieżka, Europe ... 26 A8
Snigirevka = Snihurivka, Ukraine ... 47 J7
Snihurivka, Ukraine ... 47 J7
Snina, Slovak Rep. ... 27 C15
Snizort, L., U.K. ... 14 D2
Snøhetta, Norway ... 9 E13
Snohomish, U.S.A. ... 116 C4
Snoul, Cambodia ... 65 F6
Snow Hill, U.S.A. ... 108 F8
Snow Lake, Canada ... 105 C8
Snow Mt., U.S.A. ... 116 F4
Snowbird L., Canada ... 105 A8
Snowdon, U.K. ... 12 D3
Snowdrift →, Canada ... 105 A6
Snowflake, U.S.A. ... 115 J8
Snowshoe Pk., U.S.A. ... 114 B6
Snowtown, Australia ... 95 E2
Snowville, U.S.A. ... 114 F7
Snowy →, Australia ... 95 F4
Snowy Mts., Australia ... 95 F4
Snug Corner, Bahamas ... 121 B5
Snyatyn, Ukraine ... 47 H3
Snyder, Okla., U.S.A. ... 113 H5
Snyder, Tex., U.S.A. ... 113 J4
Soahanina, Madag. ... 89 B7
Soalala, Madag. ... 89 B8
Soan →, Pakistan ... 68 C4
Soanierana-Ivongo, Madag. ... 89 B8
Soap Lake, U.S.A. ... 114 C4
Şoarş, Romania ... 43 E9
Sobat, Nahr →, Sudan ... 81 F3
Soběslav, Czech Rep. ... 26 B7
Sobhapur, India ... 68 H8
Sobinka, Russia ... 46 E11
Sobótka, Poland ... 45 H3
Sobra, Croatia ... 29 F14
Sobradinho, Reprêsa de, Brazil ... 125 E10
Sobral, Brazil ... 125 D10
Sobrance, Slovak Rep. ... 27 C15
Sobreira Formosa, Portugal ... 34 F3
Soc Giang, Vietnam ... 64 A6
Soc Trang, Vietnam ... 65 H5
Soch'e = Shache, China ... 60 C2
Sochi, Russia ... 49 J4
Société, Is. de la, Pac. Oc. ... 97 J12
Society Is. = Société, Is. de la, Pac. Oc. ... 97 J12
Socompa, Portezuelo de, Chile ... 126 A2
Socorro, U.S.A. ... 115 J10
Socorro, I., Mexico ... 118 D2
Socotra, Ind. Oc. ... 74 E5
Socovos, Spain ... 33 G3
Socuéllamos, Spain ... 33 F2
Soda L., U.S.A. ... 115 J5
Soda Plains, India ... 69 B8
Soda Springs, U.S.A. ... 114 E8
Sodankylä, Finland ... 8 C22
Soderala, Sweden ... 10 C10
Söderbärke, Sweden ... 10 D9
Söderfors, Sweden ... 10 D11
Söderhamn, Sweden ... 10 C11
Söderköping, Sweden ... 11 F10
Södermanland, Sweden ... 9 G17
Södermanlands län □, Sweden ... 10 E10
Södertälje, Sweden ... 10 E11
Sodiri, Sudan ... 81 E2
Sodo, Ethiopia ... 81 F4
Södra Dellen, Sweden ... 10 C10
Södra Finnskoga, Sweden ... 10 D6
Södra Sandby, Sweden ... 11 J7
Södra Ulvön, Sweden ... 10 B12
Södra Vi, Sweden ... 11 G9
Sodražica, Slovenia ... 29 C11
Sodus, U.S.A. ... 110 C7
Soekmekaar, S. Africa ... 89 C4
Soest, Germany ... 24 D4
Soest, Neths. ... 17 B5

Sofádhes, Greece ... 38 B4
Sofara, Mali ... 82 C4
Sofia = Sofiya, Bulgaria ... 40 D7
Sofia →, Madag. ... 89 B8
Sofievka, Ukraine ... 47 H7
Sofikón, Greece ... 38 D5
Sofiya, Bulgaria ... 40 D7
Sofiya □, Bulgaria ... 40 D7
Sōfu-Gan, Japan ... 55 K10
Sogakofe, Ghana ... 83 D5
Sogamoso, Colombia ... 124 B4
Sogār, Iran ... 71 E8
Sögel, Germany ... 24 C3
Sogndalsfjøra, Norway ... 9 F12
Søgne, Norway ... 9 G12
Sognefjorden, Norway ... 9 F11
Söğüt, Bilecik, Turkey ... 39 A12
Söğüt, Burdur, Turkey ... 39 D11
Söğüt Dağı, Turkey ... 39 D11
Söğütköy, Turkey ... 39 E10
Sōgwi-po, S. Korea ... 57 H14
Soh, Iran ... 71 C6
Sohâg, Egypt ... 80 B3
Sohori, N. Korea ... 57 D15
Soignies, Belgium ... 17 D4
Soira, Eritrea ... 81 E4
Soissons, France ... 19 C10
Sōja, Japan ... 55 G6
Sojat, India ... 68 G5
Sok →, Russia ... 48 D10
Sokal, Ukraine ... 47 G3
Söke, Turkey ... 39 D9
Sokelo, Dem. Rep. of the Congo ... 87 D1
Sokhós, Greece ... 40 F7
Sokhumi, Georgia ... 49 J5
Soko Banja, Serbia, Yug. ... 40 C5
Sokodé, Togo ... 83 D5
Sokol, Russia ... 46 C11
Sokolac, Bos.-H. ... 42 G3
Sokółka, Poland ... 44 E10
Sokolo, Mali ... 82 C3
Sokolov, Czech Rep. ... 26 A5
Sokołów Małopolski, Poland ... 45 H9
Sokołów Podlaski, Poland ... 45 F9
Sokoły, Poland ... 45 F9
Sokoto, Nigeria ... 83 C6
Sokoto □, Nigeria ... 83 C6
Sokoto →, Nigeria ... 83 C5
Sol Iletsk, Russia ... 50 D6
Sola →, Poland ... 45 H6
Solai, Kenya ... 86 B4
Solano, Phil. ... 61 C4
Solapur, India ... 66 L9
Solca, Romania ... 43 C10
Solda Gölü, Turkey ... 39 D11
Soldáneşti, Moldova ... 43 C13
Soldàtna, U.S.A. ... 100 B4
Soléa □, Cyprus ... 36 D12
Solec Kujawski, Poland ... 45 E5
Soledad, Colombia ... 124 A4
Soledad, U.S.A. ... 116 J5
Soledad, Venezuela ... 124 B6
Solent, The, U.K. ... 13 G6
Solenzara, France ... 21 G13
Solesmes, France ... 19 B10
Solfonn, Norway ... 9 F12
Solhan, Turkey ... 73 C9
Soligorsk = Salihorsk, Belarus ... 47 F4
Solihull, U.K. ... 13 E6
Solikamsk, Russia ... 50 D6
Solila, Madag. ... 89 C8
Solimões = Amazonas →, S. Amer. ... 122 D5
Solin, Croatia ... 29 E13
Solingen, Germany ... 24 D3
Sollebrunn, Sweden ... 11 F6
Solleftea, Sweden ... 10 A11
Sollentuna, Sweden ... 10 E11
Sóller, Spain ... 37 B9
Sollerön, Sweden ... 10 D8
Solling, Germany ... 24 D5
Solnechnogorsk, Russia ... 46 D9
Solofra, Italy ... 31 B7
Sologne, France ... 19 E8
Solok, Indonesia ... 62 E2
Solola, Guatemala ... 120 D1
Solomon, N. Fork →, U.S.A. ... 112 F5
Solomon, S. Fork →, U.S.A. ... 112 F5
Solomon Is. ■, Pac. Oc. ... 96 H7
Solon, China ... 60 B7
Solon Springs, U.S.A. ... 112 B9
Solor, Indonesia ... 63 F6
Solotcha, Russia ... 46 E10
Solothurn, Switz. ... 25 H3
Solothurn □, Switz. ... 25 H3
Solsona, Spain ... 32 C6
Solt, Hungary ... 42 D4
Šolta, Croatia ... 29 E13
Solţānābād, Khorāsān, Iran ... 71 C8
Solţānābād, Khorāsān, Iran ... 71 B8
Solţānābād, Markazī, Iran ... 71 C6
Soltau, Germany ... 24 C5
Soltsy, Russia ... 46 C6
Solunska Glava, Macedonia ... 40 E5
Solvang, U.S.A. ... 117 L6
Solvay, U.S.A. ... 111 C8
Sölvesborg, Sweden ... 11 H8
Solway Firth, U.K. ... 12 C4
Solwezi, Zambia ... 87 E2
Sōma, Japan ... 54 F10
Soma, Turkey ... 39 B9
Somali Pen., Africa ... 76 F8
Somali Rep. ■, Africa ... 74 F4

Somalia = Somali Rep. ■, Africa ... 74 F4
Sombernon, France ... 19 E11
Sombor, Serbia, Yug. ... 42 E4
Sombra, Canada ... 110 D2
Sombrerete, Mexico ... 118 C4
Sombrero, Anguilla ... 121 C7
Şomcuta Mare, Romania ... 43 C8
Somers, U.S.A. ... 114 B6
Somerset, Canada ... 105 D9
Somerset, Colo., U.S.A. ... 115 G10
Somerset, Ky., U.S.A. ... 108 G3
Somerset, Mass., U.S.A. ... 111 E13
Somerset, Pa., U.S.A. ... 110 F5
Somerset □, U.K. ... 13 F5
Somerset East, S. Africa ... 88 E4
Somerset I., Canada ... 4 B3
Somerset West, S. Africa ... 88 E2
Somerton, U.S.A. ... 115 K6
Somerville, U.S.A. ... 111 F10
Someş →, Romania ... 42 C7
Someşul Mare →, Romania ... 43 C8
Sommariva, Australia ... 95 D4
Somme □, France ... 19 C9
Somme →, France ... 19 B8
Somme, B. de la, France ... 18 B8
Sommen, Jönköping, Sweden ... 11 F8
Sommen, Östergötland, Sweden ... 11 F9
Sommepy-Tahure, France ... 19 C11
Sömmerda, Germany ... 24 D7
Sommesous, France ... 19 D11
Sommières, France ... 21 E8
Somogy □, Hungary ... 42 D2
Somogyszob, Hungary ... 42 D2
Somoto, Nic. ... 120 D2
Sompolno, Poland ... 45 F5
Somport, Puerto de, Spain ... 32 C4
Son Ha, Vietnam ... 64 E7
Son Hoa, Vietnam ... 64 F7
Son La, Vietnam ... 64 B4
Son Serra, Spain ... 37 B10
Son Servera, Spain ... 32 F8
Son Tay, Vietnam ... 64 B5
Soná, Panama ... 120 E3
Sonamarg, India ... 69 B6
Sonamukhi, India ... 69 H12
Sonchŏn, N. Korea ... 57 E13
Sondags →, S. Africa ... 88 E4
Sóndalo, Italy ... 28 B7
Sondar, India ... 69 C6
Sønder Felding, Denmark ... 11 J2
Sønder Omme, Denmark ... 11 J2
Sønderborg, Denmark ... 11 K3
Sønderjyllands Amtskommune □, Denmark ... 11 J3
Sondershausen, Germany ... 24 D6
Sóndrio, Italy ... 28 B6
Sone, Mozam. ... 87 F3
Sonepur, India ... 67 J13
Song, Thailand ... 64 C3
Song Cau, Vietnam ... 64 F7
Song Xian, China ... 56 G7
Songchŏn, N. Korea ... 57 E14
Songea, Tanzania ... 87 E4
Songea □, Tanzania ... 87 E4
Songeons, France ... 19 C8
Songhua Hu, China ... 57 C14
Songhua Jiang →, China ... 60 B8
Songjiang, China ... 59 B13
Songjin, N. Korea ... 57 D15
Songjŏng-ni, S. Korea ... 57 G14
Songkan, China ... 58 C6
Songkhla, Thailand ... 65 J3
Songming, China ... 58 E4
Songnim, N. Korea ... 57 E13
Songpan, China ... 58 A4
Songtao, China ... 58 C7
Songwe, Dem. Rep. of the Congo ... 86 C2
Songwe →, Africa ... 87 D3
Songxi, China ... 59 D12
Songzi, China ... 59 B8
Sonid Youqi, China ... 56 C7
Sonipat, India ... 68 E7
Sonkovo, Russia ... 46 D9
Sonmiani, Pakistan ... 68 G2
Sonnino, Italy ... 30 A6
Sono →, Brazil ... 125 E9
Sonora, Calif., U.S.A. ... 116 H6
Sonora, Tex., U.S.A. ... 113 K4
Sonora □, Mexico ... 118 B2
Sonora →, Mexico ... 118 B2
Sonora Desert, U.S.A. ... 117 L12
Sonoyta, Mexico ... 118 A2
Sonqor, Iran ... 73 E12
Sŏnsan, S. Korea ... 57 F15
Sonseca, Spain ... 35 F7
Sonsonate, El Salv. ... 120 D2
Sonstorp, Sweden ... 11 F9
Sonthofen, Germany ... 25 H6
Soochow = Suzhou, China ... 59 B13
Sop Hao, Laos ... 64 B5
Sop Prap, Thailand ... 64 D2
Sopelana, Spain ... 32 B2
Sopi, Indonesia ... 63 D7
Sopo, Nahr →, Sudan ... 81 F2
Sopot, Bulgaria ... 41 D8
Sopot, Poland ... 44 D5
Sopot, Serbia, Yug. ... 40 B4
Sopotnica, Macedonia ... 40 E5
Sopron, Hungary ... 42 C1
Sop's Arm, Canada ... 103 C8

Sopur, India ... 69 B6
Sør-Rondane, Antarctica . 5 D4
Sora, Italy ... 29 G10
Sorah, Pakistan ... 68 F3
Söråker, Sweden ... 10 B11
Sorano, Italy ... 29 F8
Sorbas, Spain ... 33 H2
Sörbygden, Sweden ... 10 B10
Sore, France ... 20 D3
Sorel, Canada ... 102 C5
Soresina, Italy ... 28 C6
Sörforsa, Sweden ... 10 C10
Sórgono, Italy ... 30 B2
Sorgues, France ... 21 D8
Sorgun, Turkey ... 72 C6
Soria, Spain ... 32 D2
Soria □, Spain ... 32 D2
Soriano, Uruguay ... 126 C4
Soriano nel Cimino, Italy . 29 F9
Sorkh, Kuh-e, Iran ... 71 C8
Sorø, Denmark ... 11 J5
Soro, Guinea ... 82 C3
Soroca, Moldova ... 43 B13
Sorocaba, Brazil ... 127 A6
Soroki = Soroca, Moldova . 43 B13
Soron, India ... 69 F8
Sorong, Indonesia ... 63 E8
Soroní, Greece ... 36 C10
Soroti, Uganda ... 86 B3
Sørøya, Norway ... 8 A20
Sørøysundet, Norway ... 8 A20
Sorraia →, Portugal ... 35 G2
Sorrento, Australia ... 95 F3
Sorrento, Italy ... 31 B7
Sorsele, Sweden ... 8 D17
Sörsjön, Sweden ... 10 C7
Sorso, Italy ... 30 B1
Sorsogon, Phil. ... 61 E6
Sortavala, Russia ... 46 B6
Sortino, Italy ... 31 E8
Sortland, Norway ... 8 B16
Sorvizhi, Russia ... 48 B9
Sos = Sos del Rey
Católico, Spain ... 32 C3
Sos del Rey Católico, Spain 32 C3
Sŏsan, S. Korea ... 57 F14
Soscumica, L., Canada ... 102 B4
Sösdala, Sweden ... 11 H7
Sosna →, Russia ... 47 F10
Sosnovka, Kirov, Russia .. 48 B10
Sosnovka, Tambov, Russia . 48 D5
Sosnovyy Bor, Russia 46 C5
Sosnowiec, Poland ... 45 H6
Sospel, France ... 21 E11
Šoštanj, Slovenia ... 29 B12
Sŏsura, N. Korea ... 57 C16
Sotkamo, Finland ... 8 D23
Soto del Barco, Spain ... 34 B4
Soto la Marina →, Mexico 119 C5
Soto y Amío, Spain ... 34 C5
Sotrondio, Spain ... 34 B5
Sotuta, Mexico ... 119 C7
Souanké, Congo ... 84 D2
Soúdha, Greece ... 36 D6
Soúdhas, Kólpos, Greece .. 36 D6
Souflíon, Greece ... 41 E10
Souillac, France ... 20 D5
Souilly, France ... 19 C12
Soukhouma, Laos ... 64 E5
Sŏul, S. Korea ... 57 F14
Soulac-sur-Mer, France ... 20 C2
Soultz-sous-Forêts, France 19 D14
Sound, The, = Øresund,
Europe ... 11 J6
Sound, The, U.K. ... 13 G3
Soúnion, Ákra, Greece ... 38 D6
Sources, Mt. aux, Lesotho 89 D4
Soure, Brazil ... 125 D9
Soure, Portugal ... 34 E2
Souris, Man., Canada ... 105 D8
Souris, P.E.I., Canada ... 103 C7
Souris →, Canada ... 112 A5
Soúrpi, Greece ... 38 B4
Sousa, Brazil ... 125 E11
Sousel, Portugal ... 35 G3
Sousse, Tunisia ... 79 A8
Soustons, France ... 20 E2
South Africa ■, Africa ... 88 E3
South Atlantic Ocean ... 122 H7
South Aulatsivik I., Canada 103 A7
South Australia □,
Australia ... 95 E2
South Ayrshire □, U.K. ... 14 F4
South Baldy, U.S.A. ... 115 J10
South Bend, Ind., U.S.A. . 108 E2
South Bend, Wash., U.S.A. 116 D3
South Boston, U.S.A. ... 109 G6
South Branch, Canada ... 103 C8
South Brook, Canada ... 103 C8
South Carolina □, U.S.A. 109 J5
South Charleston, U.S.A. . 108 F5
South China Sea, Asia ... 62 C4
South Dakota □, U.S.A. .. 112 C5
South Downs, U.K. ... 13 G7
South East C., Australia .. 94 G4
South East Is., Australia . 93 F3
South Esk →, U.K. ... 14 E6
South Foreland, U.K. ... 13 F9
South Fork →, U.S.A. ... 114 C7
South Fork, American →,
U.S.A. ... 116 G5
South Fork, Feather →,
U.S.A. ... 116 F5
South Georgia, Antarctica 5 B1
South Gloucestershire □,
U.K. ... 13 F5

South Haven, U.S.A. ... 108 D2
South Henik, L., Canada . 105 A9
South Honshu Ridge,
Pac. Oc. ... 96 E6
South Horr, Kenya ... 86 B4
South I., Kenya ... 86 B4
South I., N.Z. ... 91 L3
South Invercargill, N.Z. .. 91 M2
South Knife →, Canada .. 105 B10
South Korea ■, Asia ... 57 G15
South Lake Tahoe, U.S.A. 116 G6
South Lanarkshire □, U.K. 14 F5
South Loup →, U.S.A. ... 112 E5
South Magnetic Pole,
Antarctica ... 5 C9
South Milwaukee, U.S.A. . 108 D2
South Molton, U.K. ... 13 F4
South Nahanni →, Canada 104 A4
South Natuna Is. = Natuna
Selatan, Kepulauan,
Indonesia ... 65 L7
South Negril Pt., Jamaica . 120 C4
South Orkney Is.,
Antarctica ... 5 C18
South Ossetia □, Georgia . 49 J7
South Pagai, I. = Pagai
Selatan, Pulau, Indonesia 62 E2
South Pass, U.S.A. ... 114 E9
South Pittsburg, U.S.A. ... 109 H3
South Platte →, U.S.A. .. 112 E4
South Pole, Antarctica ... 5 E
South Porcupine, Canada . 102 C3
South River, Canada ... 102 C4
South River, U.S.A. ... 111 F10
South Ronaldsay, U.K. ... 14 C6
South Sandwich Is.,
Antarctica ... 5 B1
South Saskatchewan →,
Canada ... 105 C7
South Seal →, Canada ... 105 B9
South Shetland Is.,
Antarctica ... 5 C18
South Shields, U.K. ... 12 C6
South Sioux City, U.S.A. . 112 D6
South Taranaki Bight, N.Z. 91 H5
South Thompson →,
Canada ... 104 C4
South Twin I., Canada ... 102 B4
South Tyne →, U.K. ... 12 C5
South Uist, U.K. ... 14 D1
South West Africa =
Namibia ■, Africa ... 88 C2
South West C., Australia . 94 G4
South Yorkshire □, U.K. . 12 D6
Southampton, Canada ... 102 D3
Southampton, U.K. ... 13 G6
Southampton, U.S.A. ... 111 F12
Southampton □, U.K. ... 13 G6
Southampton I., Canada .. 4 C3
Southbridge, N.Z. ... 91 K4
Southbridge, U.S.A. ... 111 D12
Southend, Canada ... 105 B8
Southend-on-Sea, U.K. ... 13 F8
Southend-on-Sea □, U.K. . 13 F8
Southern □, Malawi ... 87 F4
Southern □, S. Leone ... 82 D2
Southern □, Uganda ... 86 C3
Southern □, Zambia ... 87 F2
Southern Alps, N.Z. ... 91 K3
Southern Cross, Australia . 93 F2
Southern Hills, Australia . 93 F3
Southern Indian L., Canada 105 B9
Southern Ocean, Antarctica 5 C6
Southern Pines, U.S.A. ... 109 H6
Southern Uplands, U.K. .. 14 F5
Southington, U.S.A. ... 111 E12
Southold, U.S.A. ... 111 E12
Southport, Australia ... 95 D5
Southport, U.K. ... 12 D4
Southport, U.S.A. ... 109 J6
Southwest C., N.Z. ... 91 M1
Southwold, U.K. ... 13 E9
Soutpansberg, S. Africa .. 89 C4
Souvigny, France ... 19 F10
Sovata, Romania ... 43 D10
Soverato, Italy ... 31 D9
Sovetsk, Kaliningd., Russia 9 J19
Sovetsk, Kirov, Russia ... 48 B9
Sovetskaya Gavan =
Vanino, Russia ... 51 E15
Sovicille, Italy ... 29 E8
Soweto, S. Africa ... 89 D4
Sŏya-Kaikyŏ = La Perouse
Str., Asia ... 54 B11
Sŏya-Misaki, Japan ... 54 B10
Soyaux, France ... 20 C4
Sozh →, Belarus ... 47 F6
Sozopol, Bulgaria ... 41 D11
Spa, Belgium ... 17 D5
Spain ■, Europe ... 7 H5
Spalding, Australia ... 95 E2
Spalding, U.K. ... 12 E7
Spalding, U.S.A. ... 112 E5
Spangler, U.S.A. ... 110 F6
Spaniard's Bay, Canada .. 103 C9
Spanish, Canada ... 102 C3
Spanish Fork, U.S.A. ... 114 F8
Spanish Town, Jamaica ... 120 C4
Sparks, U.S.A. ... 116 F7
Sparreholm, Sweden ... 10 E10
Sparta = Spárti, Greece ... 38 D4
Sparta, Ga., U.S.A. ... 109 J4
Sparta, Wis., U.S.A. ... 112 D9
Spartanburg, U.S.A. ... 109 H5
Spartansburg, U.S.A. ... 110 E5
Spárti, Greece ... 38 D4

Spartivento, C., Calabria,
Italy ... 31 E9
Spartivento, C., Sard., Italy 30 D1
Spas-Demensk, Russia ... 46 E7
Spas-Klepiki, Russia ... 46 E11
Spassk Dalniy, Russia ... 54 B6
Spassk-Ryazanskiy, Russia 46 E11
Spátha, Ákra, Greece ... 36 D5
Spatsizi →, Canada ... 104 B3
Spean →, U.K. ... 14 E4
Spearfish, U.S.A. ... 112 C3
Spearman, U.S.A. ... 113 G4
Speers, Canada ... 105 C7
Speia, Moldova ... 43 D14
Speightstown, Barbados .. 121 D8
Speke Gulf, Tanzania ... 86 C3
Spello, Italy ... 29 F9
Spencer, Idaho, U.S.A. ... 114 D7
Spencer, Iowa, U.S.A. ... 112 D7
Spencer, N.Y., U.S.A. ... 111 D8
Spencer, Nebr., U.S.A. ... 112 D5
Spencer, W. Va., U.S.A. .. 108 F5
Spencer, C., Australia ... 95 F2
Spencer B., Namibia ... 88 D1
Spencer G., Australia ... 95 E2
Spencerville, Canada ... 111 B9
Spences Bridge, Canada .. 104 C4
Spennymoor, U.K. ... 12 C6
Spenser Mts., N.Z. ... 91 K4
Spentrup, Denmark ... 11 H4
Sperkhiós →, Greece ... 38 C4
Sperrin Mts., U.K. ... 15 B5
Spessart, Germany ... 25 F5
Spétsai, Greece ... 38 D5
Spey →, U.K. ... 14 D5
Speyer, Germany ... 25 F4
Spezzano Albanese, Italy . 31 C9
Spiekeroog, Germany ... 24 A4
Spiez, Switz. ... 25 J3
Spíli, Greece ... 36 D6
Spilimbergo, Italy ... 29 B9
Spin Baldak = Qala-i-
Jadid, Afghan. ... 68 D2
Spinalónga, Greece ... 36 D7
Spinazzola, Italy ... 31 B9
Spineni, Romania ... 43 F9
Spirit Lake, Idaho, U.S.A. 114 C5
Spirit Lake, Wash., U.S.A. 116 D4
Spirit River, Canada ... 104 B5
Spiritwood, Canada ... 105 C7
Spišská Nová Ves,
Slovak Rep. ... 27 C13
Spišské Podhradie,
Slovak Rep. ... 27 B13
Spital, Austria ... 26 D7
Spithead, U.K. ... 13 G6
Spittal an der Drau, Austria 26 E6
Spitzbergen = Svalbard,
Arctic ... 4 B8
Spjelkavik, Norway ... 9 E12
Split, Croatia ... 29 E13
Split L., Canada ... 105 B9
Splitski Kanal, Croatia ... 29 E13
Splügenpass, Switz. ... 25 J5
Spofford, U.S.A. ... 113 L4
Spokane, U.S.A. ... 114 C5
Spoleto, Italy ... 29 F9
Spooner, U.S.A. ... 112 C9
Sporyy Navolok, Mys,
Russia ... 50 B7
Spragge, Canada ... 102 C3
Sprague, U.S.A. ... 114 C5
Sprague River, U.S.A. ... 114 E3
Spratly Is., S. China Sea . 62 C4
Spray, U.S.A. ... 114 D4
Spreča →, Bos.-H. ... 42 F3
Spree →, Germany ... 24 C9
Spreewald, Germany ... 24 D9
Spremberg, Germany ... 24 D10
Sprengisandur, Iceland ... 8 D5
Spring City, U.S.A. ... 114 G8
Spring Mts., U.S.A. ... 115 H6
Spring Valley, Calif.,
U.S.A. ... 117 N10
Spring Valley, Minn.,
U.S.A. ... 112 D8
Springbok, S. Africa ... 88 D2
Springdale, Canada ... 103 C8
Springdale, Ark., U.S.A. . 113 G7
Springdale, Wash., U.S.A. 114 B5
Springe, Germany ... 24 C5
Springer, U.S.A. ... 113 G2
Springerville, U.S.A. ... 115 J9
Springfield, Canada ... 110 D4
Springfield, N.Z. ... 91 K3
Springfield, Colo., U.S.A. 113 G3
Springfield, Ill., U.S.A. .. 112 F10
Springfield, Mass., U.S.A. 111 D12
Springfield, Mo., U.S.A. .. 113 G8
Springfield, Ohio, U.S.A. . 108 F4
Springfield, Oreg., U.S.A. 114 D2
Springfield, Tenn., U.S.A. 109 G2
Springfield, Vt., U.S.A. ... 111 C12
Springfontein, S. Africa .. 88 E4
Springhill, Canada ... 103 C7
Springhouse, Canada ... 104 C4
Springhurst, Australia ... 95 F4
Springs, S. Africa ... 89 D4
Springsure, Australia ... 94 C4
Springvale, Queens.,
Australia ... 94 C3
Springvale, W. Austral.,
Australia ... 92 C4
Springvale, U.S.A. ... 111 C14
Springville, Calif., U.S.A. 116 J8

Springville, N.Y., U.S.A. . 110 D6
Springville, Utah, U.S.A. . 114 F8
Springwater, Canada ... 105 C7
Spruce-Creek, U.S.A. ... 110 F6
Spur, U.S.A. ... 113 J4
Spurn Hd., U.K. ... 12 D8
Spuž, Montenegro, Yug. ... 40 D3
Spuzzum, Canada ... 104 D4
Squam L., U.S.A. ... 111 C13
Squamish, Canada ... 104 D4
Square Islands, Canada ... 103 B8
Squillace, G. di, Italy ... 31 D9
Squinzano, Italy ... 31 B11
Squires, Mt., Australia ... 93 E4
Srbac, Bos.-H. ... 42 E2
Srbija = Serbia □,
Yugoslavia ... 40 C5
Srbobran, Serbia, Yug. ... 42 E4
Sre Ambel, Cambodia ... 65 G4
Sre Khtum, Cambodia ... 65 F6
Sre Umbell = Sre Ambel,
Cambodia ... 65 G4
Srebrenica, Bos.-H. ... 42 F4
Sredinny Ra. = Sredinnyy
Khrebet, Russia ... 51 D17
Sredinnyy Khrebet, Russia 51 D17
Središče, Slovenia ... 29 B13
Sredna Gora, Bulgaria ... 41 D8
Srednekolymsk, Russia ... 51 C16
Sredni Rodopi, Bulgaria .. 41 E8
Srednogorie, Bulgaria ... 41 D8
Śrem, Poland ... 45 F4
Sremska Mitrovica,
Serbia, Yug. ... 42 F4
Sremski Karlovci,
Serbia, Yug. ... 42 E4
Srepok →, Cambodia ... 64 F6
Sretensk, Russia ... 51 D12
Sri Lanka ■, Asia ... 66 R12
Srikakulam, India ... 67 K13
Srinagar, India ... 69 B6
Środa Śląska, Poland ... 45 G3
Środa Wielkopolski, Poland 45 F4
Srpska Crnja, Serbia, Yug. 42 E5
Srpski Itebej, Serbia, Yug. 42 E5
Staaten →, Australia ... 94 B3
Staberhuk, Germany ... 24 A7
Stade, Germany ... 24 B5
Stadskanaal, Neths. ... 17 A6
Stadtallendorf, Germany .. 24 E5
Stadthagen, Germany ... 24 C5
Stadtlohn, Germany ... 24 D2
Stadtroda, Germany ... 24 E7
Staffa, U.K. ... 14 E2
Staffanstorp, Sweden ... 11 J7
Stafford, U.K. ... 12 E5
Stafford, U.S.A. ... 113 G5
Stafford Springs, U.S.A. . 111 E12
Staffordshire □, U.K. ... 12 E5
Stagnone, Italy ... 30 E5
Staines, U.K. ... 13 F7
Stainz, Austria ... 26 E8
Stakhanov, Ukraine ... 47 H10
Stalać, Serbia, Yug. ... 40 C5
Stalingrad = Volgograd,
Russia ... 49 F7
Staliniri = Tskhinvali,
Georgia ... 49 J7
Stalino = Donetsk, Ukraine 47 J9
Stalinogorsk =
Novomoskovsk, Russia . 46 E10
Stalis, Greece ... 36 D7
Stallarholmen, Sweden ... 10 E11
Ställdalen, Sweden ... 10 E8
Stalowa Wola, Poland ... 45 H9
Stalybridge, U.K. ... 12 D5
Stamford, Australia ... 94 C3
Stamford, U.K. ... 13 E7
Stamford, Conn., U.S.A. . 111 E11
Stamford, Tex., U.S.A. ... 113 J5
Stamps, U.S.A. ... 113 J8
Stanberry, U.S.A. ... 112 E7
Stančevo = Kalipetrovo,
Bulgaria ... 41 B11
Standerton, S. Africa ... 89 D4
Standish, U.S.A. ... 108 D4
Stanford, U.S.A. ... 114 C8
Stånga, Sweden ... 11 G12
Stanger, S. Africa ... 89 D5
Stanišić, Serbia, Yug. ... 42 E4
Stanislaus →, U.S.A. ... 116 H5
Stanislav = Ivano-
Frankivsk, Ukraine ... 47 H3
Stanisławów, Poland ... 45 F8
Stanley, Australia ... 94 G4
Stanley, N.B., Canada ... 103 C6
Stanley, Sask., Canada ... 105 B8
Stanley, Falk. Is. ... 128 G5
Stanley, U.K. ... 12 C6
Stanley, Idaho, U.S.A. ... 114 D6
Stanley, N. Dak., U.S.A. . 112 A3
Stanley, N.Y., U.S.A. ... 110 D7
Stanley, Wis., U.S.A. ... 112 C9
Stanovoy Khrebet, Russia . 51 D14
Stanovoy Ra. = Stanovoy
Khrebet, Russia ... 51 D14
Stansmore Ra., Australia . 92 D4
Stanthorpe, Australia ... 95 D5
Stanton, U.S.A. ... 113 J4
Stanwood, U.S.A. ... 116 B4
Staples, U.S.A. ... 112 B7
Stapleton, U.S.A. ... 112 E4
Stąporków, Poland ... 45 G7
Star City, Canada ... 105 C8
Stará L'ubovňa,
Slovak Rep. ... 27 B13

Stara Moravica,
Serbia, Yug. ... 42 E4
Stara Pazova, Serbia, Yug. 42 F5
Stara Planina, Bulgaria ... 40 C7
Stará Turá, Slovak Rep. .. 27 C10
Stara Zagora, Bulgaria ... 41 D9
Starachowice, Poland ... 45 G8
Starachiojd, Romania ... 43 E11
Stargard Szczeciński,
Poland ... 44 E2
Stari Bar,
Montenegro, Yug. ... 40 D3
Stari Trg, Slovenia ... 29 C12
Staritsa, Russia ... 46 D8
Starke, U.S.A. ... 109 L4
Starkville, Colo., U.S.A. . 113 G2
Starkville, Miss., U.S.A. .. 109 J1
Starnberg, Germany ... 25 H7
Starnberger See, Germany 25 H7
Starobilsk, Ukraine ... 47 H10
Starodub, Russia ... 47 F7
Starogard Gdański, Poland 44 E5
Starokonstantinov =
Starokonstyantyniv,
Ukraine ... 47 H4
Starokonstyantyniv,
Ukraine ... 47 H4
Starominskaya, Russia ... 47 J10
Staroshcherbinovskaya,
Russia ... 47 J10
Start Pt., U.K. ... 13 G4
Stary Sącz, Poland ... 45 J7
Staryy Biryuzyak, Russia . 49 H8
Staryy Chartoriysk, Ukraine 47 G3
Staryy Krym, Ukraine ... 47 K8
Staryy Oskol, Russia ... 47 G9
Stassfurt, Germany ... 24 D7
Staszów, Poland ... 45 H8
State College, U.S.A. ... 110 F7
Stateline, U.S.A. ... 116 G7
Staten, I. = Estados, I. de
Los, Argentina ... 122 J4
Staten I., U.S.A. ... 111 F10
Statesboro, U.S.A. ... 109 J5
Statesville, U.S.A. ... 109 H5
Stauffer, U.S.A. ... 117 L7
Staunton, Ill., U.S.A. ... 112 F10
Staunton, Va., U.S.A. ... 108 F6
Stavanger, Norway ... 9 G11
Staveley, N.Z. ... 91 K3
Stavelot, Belgium ... 17 D5
Stavern, Norway ... 9 G14
Stavoren, Neths. ... 17 B5
Stavropol, Russia ... 49 H6
Stavros, Cyprus ... 36 D11
Stavrós, Greece ... 36 D6
Stavros, Ákra, Greece ... 36 D6
Stavroúpolis, Greece ... 41 E8
Stawell, Australia ... 95 F3
Stawell →, Australia ... 94 C3
Stawiski, Poland ... 44 E9
Stawiszyn, Poland ... 45 G5
Stayner, Canada ... 110 B4
Steamboat Springs, U.S.A. 114 F10
Stebleva, Albania ... 40 E4
Steele, U.S.A. ... 112 B5
Steelton, U.S.A. ... 110 F8
Steelville, U.S.A. ... 113 G9
Steen River, Canada ... 104 B5
Steenkool = Bintuni,
Indonesia ... 63 E8
Steenwijk, Neths. ... 17 B6
Steep Pt., Australia ... 93 E1
Steep Rock, Canada ... 105 C9
Ştefan Vodă, Moldova ... 43 D14
Ştefăneşti, Romania ... 43 C12
Stefanie L. = Chew Bahir,
Ethiopia ... 81 G4
Stefansson Bay, Antarctica 5 C5
Stege, Denmark ... 11 K6
Ştei, Romania ... 42 D7
Steiermark □, Austria ... 26 D8
Steigerwald, Germany ... 25 F6
Steilacoom, U.S.A. ... 116 C4
Steinbach, Canada ... 105 D9
Steinfurt, Germany ... 24 C3
Steinheim, Germany ... 24 D5
Steinhuder Meer, Germany 24 C5
Steinkjer, Norway ... 8 D14
Steinkopf, S. Africa ... 88 D2
Stellarton, Canada ... 103 C7
Stellenbosch, S. Africa ... 88 E2
Stelvio, Paso dello, Italy .. 28 B7
Stenay, France ... 19 C12
Stendal, Germany ... 24 C7
Stende, Latvia ... 44 A9
Stenhamra, Sweden ... 10 E11
Stenstorp, Sweden ... 11 F7
Stenungsund, Sweden ... 11 F5
Steornabhaigh =
Stornoway, U.K. ... 14 C2
Stepanakert = Xankändi,
Azerbaijan ... 73 C12
Stepanavan, Armenia ... 49 K7
Stephen, U.S.A. ... 112 A6
Stephens Creek, Australia 95 E3
Stephens I., Canada ... 104 C2
Stephenville, Canada ... 103 C8
Stephenville, U.S.A. ... 113 J5
Stepnica, Poland ... 44 E1
Stepnoi = Elista, Russia .. 49 G7
Steppe, Asia ... 52 D9
Stereá Ellas □, Greece ... 38 C4
Sterkstroom, S. Africa 88 E4

Sterling

Sterling, *Colo., U.S.A.* 112 E3
Sterling, *Ill., U.S.A.* 112 E10
Sterling, *Kans., U.S.A.* 112 F5
Sterling City, *U.S.A.* 113 K4
Sterling Run, *U.S.A.* 110 E6
Sterlitamak, *Russia* 50 D6
Sternberg, *Germany* 24 B7
Šternberk, *Czech Rep.* 27 B10
Stérnes, *Greece* 36 D6
Sterzing = Vipiteno, *Italy* 29 B8
Stettin = Szczecin, *Poland* 44 E1
Stettiner Haff, *Germany* 24 B10
Stettler, *Canada* 104 C6
Steubenville, *U.S.A.* 110 F4
Stevenage, *U.K.* 13 F7
Stevens Point, *U.S.A.* 112 C10
Stevenson, *U.S.A.* 116 E5
Stevenson L., *Canada* 105 C9
Stevns Klint, *Denmark* 11 J6
Stewart, *Canada* 104 B3
Stewart, *U.S.A.* 116 F7
Stewart, C., *Australia* 94 A1
Stewart, I., *Chile* 128 G2
Stewart I., *N.Z.* 91 M1
Stewarts Point, *U.S.A.* 116 G3
Stewiacke, *Canada* 103 C7
Steynsburg, *S. Africa* 88 E4
Steyr, *Austria* 26 C7
Steyr →, *Austria* 26 C7
Steytlerville, *S. Africa* 88 E3
Stia, *Italy* 29 E8
Stigler, *U.S.A.* 113 H7
Stigliano, *Italy* 31 B9
Stigtomta, *Sweden* 11 F10
Stikine →, *Canada* 104 B2
Stilfontein, *S. Africa* 88 D4
Stilís, *Greece* 38 C4
Stillwater, *N.Z.* 91 K3
Stillwater, *Minn., U.S.A.* 112 C8
Stillwater, *N.Y., U.S.A.* 111 D11
Stillwater, *Okla., U.S.A.* 113 G6
Stillwater Range, *U.S.A.* 114 G4
Stilo, Pta., *Italy* 31 D9
Stilwell, *U.S.A.* 113 H7
Štip, *Macedonia* 40 E6
Stíra, *Greece* 38 C6
Stirling, *Australia* 94 B3
Stirling, *Canada* 104 D6
Stirling, *U.K.* 14 E5
Stirling □, *U.K.* 14 E4
Stirling Ra., *Australia* 93 F2
Stittsville, *Canada* 111 A9
Stjernøya, *Norway* 8 A20
Stjørdalshalsen, *Norway* 8 E14
Stockach, *Germany* 25 H5
Stockaryd, *Sweden* 11 G8
Stockerau, *Austria* 27 C9
Stockett, *U.S.A.* 114 C8
Stockholm, *Sweden* 10 E12
Stockholms län □, *Sweden* 10 E12
Stockport, *U.K.* 12 D5
Stocksbridge, *U.K.* 12 D6
Stockton, *Calif., U.S.A.* 116 H5
Stockton, *Kans., U.S.A.* 112 F5
Stockton, *Mo., U.S.A.* 113 G8
Stockton-on-Tees, *U.K.* 12 C6
Stockton-on-Tees □, *U.K.* 12 C6
Stoczek Łukowski, *Poland* 45 G8
Stöde, *Sweden* 10 B10
Stoeng Treng, *Cambodia* 64 F5
Stoer, Pt. of, *U.K.* 14 C3
Stogovo, *Macedonia* 40 E4
Stoholm, *Denmark* 11 H3
Stoke-on-Trent, *U.K.* 12 D5
Stoke-on-Trent □, *U.K.* 12 D5
Stokes Bay, *Canada* 102 D3
Stokes Pt., *Australia* 94 G3
Stokes Ra., *Australia* 92 C5
Stokksnes, *Iceland* 8 D6
Stokmarknes, *Norway* 8 B16
Stolac, *Bos.-H.* 40 C1
Stolberg, *Germany* 24 E2
Stolbovoy, Ostrov, *Russia* 51 D17
Stolbtsy = Stowbtsy, *Belarus* 46 F4
Stolin, *Belarus* 47 G4
Stöllet, *Sweden* 10 D7
Stolnici, *Romania* 43 F9
Stomíon, *Greece* 36 D5
Ston, *Croatia* 29 F14
Stone, *U.K.* 12 E5
Stonehaven, *U.K.* 14 E6
Stonehenge, *Australia* 94 C3
Stonehenge, *U.K.* 13 F6
Stonewall, *Canada* 105 C9
Stony L., *Man., Canada* 105 B9
Stony L., *Ont., Canada* 110 B6
Stony Rapids, *Canada* 105 B7
Stony Tunguska = Tunguska, Podkamennaya →, *Russia* 51 C10
Stonyford, *U.S.A.* 116 F4
Stopnica, *Poland* 45 H7
Storå, *Sweden* 10 E9
Storå →, *Denmark* 11 H2
Stora Gla, *Sweden* 10 E6
Stora Le, *Sweden* 10 E5
Stora Lulevatten, *Sweden* 8 C18
Storavan, *Sweden* 8 D18
Stord, *Norway* 9 G11
Store Bælt, *Denmark* 11 J4
Store Creek, *Australia* 95 E4
Store Heddinge, *Denmark* 11 J6
Storebro, *Sweden* 11 G9
Storfors, *Sweden* 10 E8
Storlien, *Sweden* 10 A6
Storm B., *Australia* 94 G4
Storm Lake, *U.S.A.* 112 D7
Stormberge, *S. Africa* 88 E4
Stormsrivier, *S. Africa* 88 E3
Stornoway, *U.K.* 14 C2
Storo, *Italy* 28 C7
Storozhinets = Storozhynets, *Ukraine* 47 H3
Storozhynets, *Ukraine* 47 H3
Storsjön, *Gävleborg, Sweden* 10 D10
Storsjön, *Jämtland, Sweden* 10 B7
Storsjön, *Jämtland, Sweden* 10 A8
Storstrøms Amtskommune □, *Denmark* 11 J5
Storuman, *Sweden* 8 D17
Storuman, sjö, *Sweden* 8 D17
Storvätteshågna, *Sweden* 10 B6
Storvik, *Sweden* 10 D10
Storvreta, *Sweden* 10 E11
Stoughton, *Canada* 105 D8
Stour →, *Dorset, U.K.* 13 G6
Stour →, *Kent, U.K.* 13 F9
Stour →, *Suffolk, U.K.* 13 F9
Stourbridge, *U.K.* 13 E5
Stout, L., *Canada* 105 C10
Stove Pipe Wells Village, *U.S.A.* 117 J9
Støvring, *Denmark* 11 H3
Stowbtsy, *Belarus* 46 F4
Stowmarket, *U.K.* 13 E9
Strabane, *U.K.* 15 B4
Stracin, *Macedonia* 40 D6
Stradella, *Italy* 28 C6
Strahan, *Australia* 94 G4
Strajitsa, *Bulgaria* 41 C9
Strakonice, *Czech Rep.* 26 B6
Straldzha, *Bulgaria* 41 D10
Stralsund, *Germany* 24 A9
Strand, *S. Africa* 88 E2
Stranda, *Møre og Romsdal, Norway* 9 E12
Stranda, *Nord-Trøndelag, Norway* 8 E14
Strandby, *Denmark* 11 G4
Strangford L., *U.K.* 15 B6
Strängnäs, *Sweden* 10 E11
Strangsville, *U.S.A.* 110 E3
Stranraer, *U.K.* 14 G3
Strasbourg, *Canada* 105 C8
Strasbourg, *France* 19 D14
Strasburg, *Germany* 24 B9
Strasburg, *U.S.A.* 112 B4
Strășeni, *Moldova* 43 C13
Stråssa, *Sweden* 10 E9
Stratford, *Canada* 102 D3
Stratford, *N.Z.* 91 H5
Stratford, *Calif., U.S.A.* 116 J7
Stratford, *Conn., U.S.A.* 111 E11
Stratford, *Tex., U.S.A.* 113 G3
Stratford-upon-Avon, *U.K.* 13 E6
Strath Spey, *U.K.* 14 D5
Strathalbyn, *Australia* 95 F2
Strathaven, *U.K.* 14 F4
Strathcona Prov. Park, *Canada* 104 D3
Strathmore, *Australia* 94 B3
Strathmore, *Canada* 104 C6
Strathmore, *U.K.* 14 E5
Strathmore, *U.S.A.* 116 J7
Strathnaver, *Canada* 104 C4
Strathpeffer, *U.K.* 14 D4
Strathroy, *Canada* 102 D3
Strathy Pt., *U.K.* 14 C4
Stratton, *U.S.A.* 112 F3
Straubing, *Germany* 25 G8
Straumnes, *Iceland* 8 C2
Strausberg, *Germany* 24 C9
Strawberry Reservoir, *U.S.A.* 114 F8
Strawn, *U.S.A.* 113 J5
Strážnice, *Czech Rep.* 27 C10
Streaky B., *Australia* 95 E1
Streaky Bay, *Australia* 95 E1
Streator, *U.S.A.* 112 E10
Středočeský □, *Czech Rep.* 26 B7
Streeter, *U.S.A.* 112 B5
Streetsville, *Canada* 110 C5
Strehaia, *Romania* 43 F8
Strelcha, *Bulgaria* 41 D8
Strelka, *Russia* 51 D10
Streng →, *Cambodia* 64 F4
Stresa, *Italy* 28 C5
Streymoy, *Færoe Is.* 8 E9
Strezhevoy, *Russia* 50 C8
Stříbro, *Czech Rep.* 26 A6
Strimón →, *Greece* 40 F7
Strimonikós Kólpos, *Greece* 40 F7
Strofádhes, *Greece* 38 D3
Stroma, *U.K.* 14 C5
Strómboli, *Italy* 31 D8
Stromeferry, *U.K.* 14 D3
Stromness, *U.K.* 14 C5
Strömsbruk, *Sweden* 10 C11
Stromsburg, *U.S.A.* 112 E6
Strömsnäsbruk, *Sweden* 11 H7
Strömstad, *Sweden* 11 F5
Strömsund, *Sweden* 8 E16
Strongilí, *Greece* 39 E11
Stróngoli, *Italy* 31 C10
Stronie Śląskie, *Poland* 45 H3
Stronsay, *U.K.* 14 B6
Stropkov, *Slovak Rep.* 27 B14
Stroud, *U.K.* 13 F5
Stroud Road, *Australia* 95 E5
Stroudsburg, *U.S.A.* 111 F9
Stroumbi, *Cyprus* 36 E11
Struer, *Denmark* 11 H2
Struga, *Macedonia* 40 E4
Strugi Krasnyye, *Russia* 46 C5
Strumica, *Macedonia* 40 E6
Strumica →, *Europe* 40 E7
Struthers, *Canada* 102 C2
Struthers, *U.S.A.* 110 E4
Stryama, *Bulgaria* 41 D8
Stryker, *U.S.A.* 114 B6
Stryków, *Poland* 45 G6
Stryy, *Ukraine* 47 H2
Strzegom, *Poland* 45 H3
Strzelce Krajeńskie, *Poland* 45 F2
Strzelce Opolskie, *Poland* 45 H5
Strzelecki Cr. →, *Australia* 95 D2
Strzelin, *Poland* 45 H4
Strzelno, *Poland* 45 F5
Strzybnica, *Poland* 45 H5
Strzyżów, *Poland* 45 J8
Stuart, *Fla., U.S.A.* 109 M5
Stuart, *Nebr., U.S.A.* 112 D5
Stuart →, *Canada* 104 C4
Stuart Bluff Ra., *Australia* 92 D5
Stuart L., *Canada* 104 C4
Stuart Ra., *Australia* 95 D1
Stubbekøbing, *Denmark* 11 K6
Stuben, *Austria* 26 D3
Studen Kladenets, Yazovir, *Bulgaria* 41 E9
Studenka, *Czech Rep.* 27 B11
Stugun, *Sweden* 10 A9
Stuhr, *Germany* 24 B4
Stull, L., *Canada* 102 B1
Stung Treng = Stoeng Treng, *Cambodia* 64 F5
Stupart →, *Canada* 105 B10
Stupava, *Slovak Rep.* 27 C10
Stupino, *Russia* 46 E10
Sturgeon B., *Canada* 105 C9
Sturgeon Bay, *U.S.A.* 108 C2
Sturgeon Falls, *Canada* 102 C4
Sturgeon L., *Alta., Canada* 104 B5
Sturgeon L., *Ont., Canada* 102 C1
Sturgeon L., *Ont., Canada* 110 B6
Sturgis, *Mich., U.S.A.* 108 E3
Sturgis, *S. Dak., U.S.A.* 112 C3
Sturkö, *Sweden* 11 H9
Štúrovo, *Slovak Rep.* 27 D11
Sturt Cr. →, *Australia* 92 C4
Sturt Creek, *Australia* 92 C4
Stutterheim, *S. Africa* 88 E4
Stuttgart, *Germany* 25 G5
Stuttgart, *U.S.A.* 113 H9
Stuyvesant, *U.S.A.* 111 D11
Stykkishólmur, *Iceland* 8 D2
Styria = Steiermark □, *Austria* 26 D8
Styrsö, *Sweden* 11 G5
Su Xian, *China* 56 H9
Suakin, *Sudan* 80 D4
Suan, *N. Korea* 57 E14
Suaqui, *Mexico* 118 B3
Subang, *Indonesia* 63 G12
Subansiri →, *India* 67 F18
Subayhah, *Si. Arabia* 70 D3
Subcetate, *Romania* 42 E8
Subi, *Indonesia* 65 L7
Subiaco, *Italy* 29 G10
Subotica, *Serbia, Yug.* 42 D4
Success, *Canada* 105 C7
Suceava, *Romania* 43 C11
Suceava □, *Romania* 43 C10
Suceava →, *Romania* 43 C11
Sucha-Beskidzka, *Poland* 45 J6
Suchań, *Poland* 45 E2
Suchan, *Russia* 54 C6
Suchedniów, *Poland* 45 G7
Suchitoto, *El Salv.* 120 D2
Suchou = Suzhou, *China* 59 B13
Süchow = Xuzhou, *China* 57 G9
Suchowola, *Poland* 44 E10
Suck →, *Ireland* 15 C3
Sucre, *Bolivia* 124 G5
Sućuraj, *Croatia* 29 E14
Sucuriú →, *Brazil* 125 H8
Sud, Pte., *Canada* 103 C7
Sud-Ouest, Pte. du, *Canada* 103 C7
Suda →, *Russia* 46 C9
Sudak, *Ukraine* 47 K8
Sudan, *U.S.A.* 113 H3
Sudan ■, *Africa* 81 E3
Sudbury, *Canada* 102 C3
Sudbury, *U.K.* 13 E8
Sûdd, *Sudan* 81 F3
Süderbrarup, *Germany* 24 A5
Süderlügum, *Germany* 24 A4
Süderoogsand, *Germany* 24 A4
Sudeten Mts. = Sudety, *Europe* 27 A9
Sudety, *Europe* 27 A9
Suðuroy, *Færoe Is.* 8 F9
Sudi, *Tanzania* 87 E4
Sudirman, Pegunungan, *Indonesia* 63 E9
Sudiți, *Romania* 43 F12
Sudogda, *Russia* 48 C5
Sudr, *Egypt* 80 J8
Sudzha, *Russia* 47 G8
Sueca, *Spain* 33 F4
Süedinenie, *Bulgaria* 41 D8
Suez = El Suweis, *Egypt* 80 J8
Suez, G. of = Suweis, Khalîg el, *Egypt* 80 J8
Suez Canal = Suweis, Qanâ es, *Egypt* 80 H8
Suffield, *Canada* 105 C6
Suffolk, *U.S.A.* 108 G7
Suffolk □, *U.K.* 13 E9
Şugag, *Romania* 43 E8
Sugar City, *U.S.A.* 112 F3
Suğla Gölü, *Turkey* 72 D5
Sugluk = Salluit, *Canada* 101 B12
Suhaia, Lacul, *Romania* 43 G10
Şuḥār, *Oman* 71 E8
Sühbaatar, *Mongolia* 60 A5
Sühbaatar □, *Mongolia* 56 B8
Suhl, *Germany* 24 E6
Şuhut, *Turkey* 39 C12
Sui Xian, *Henan, China* 56 G8
Sui Xian, *Henan, China* 59 B9
Šuica, *Bos.-H.* 42 G2
Suichang, *China* 59 C12
Suichuan, *China* 59 D10
Suide, *China* 56 F6
Suifenhe, *China* 57 B16
Suihua, *China* 60 B7
Suijiang, *China* 58 C4
Suining, *Hunan, China* 59 D8
Suining, *Jiangsu, China* 57 H9
Suining, *Sichuan, China* 58 B5
Suiping, *China* 56 H7
Suippes, *France* 19 C11
Suir →, *Ireland* 15 D4
Suixi, *China* 59 G8
Suiyang, *Guizhou, China* 58 D6
Suiyang, *Heilongjiang, China* 57 B16
Suizhong, *China* 57 D11
Sujangarh, *India* 68 F6
Sukabumi, *Indonesia* 63 G12
Sukadana, *Indonesia* 62 E4
Sukagawa, *Japan* 55 F10
Sukaraja, *Indonesia* 62 E4
Sukarnapura = Jayapura, *Indonesia* 63 E10
Sukchŏn, *N. Korea* 57 E13
Sukhindol, *Bulgaria* 41 C9
Sukhinichi, *Russia* 46 E8
Sukhona →, *Russia* 50 D4
Sukhothai, *Thailand* 64 D2
Sukhumi = Sokhumi, *Georgia* 49 J5
Sukkur, *Pakistan* 68 F3
Sukkur Barrage, *Pakistan* 68 F3
Sukovo, *Serbia, Yug.* 40 C6
Sukumo, *Japan* 55 H6
Sukunka →, *Canada* 104 B4
Sula →, *Ukraine* 47 H7
Sula, Kepulauan, *Indonesia* 63 E7
Sulaco →, *Honduras* 120 C2
Sulaiman Range, *Pakistan* 68 D3
Sulak →, *Russia* 49 J8
Sūlār, *Iran* 71 D6
Sulawesi □, *Indonesia* 63 E6
Sulawesi Sea = Celebes Sea, *Indonesia* 63 D6
Sulechów, *Poland* 45 F2
Sulęcin, *Poland* 45 F2
Sulejów, *Poland* 45 G6
Sulejówek, *Poland* 45 F8
Süleymanlı, *Turkey* 39 C9
Sulima, *S. Leone* 82 D2
Sulina, *Romania* 43 E14
Sulina, Bratul →, *Romania* 43 E14
Sulingen, *Germany* 24 C4
Sulița, *Romania* 43 C11
Sulitjelma, *Norway* 8 C17
Sułkowice, *Poland* 45 J6
Sullana, *Peru* 124 D2
Süller, *Turkey* 39 C11
Sullivan, *Ill., U.S.A.* 112 F10
Sullivan, *Ind., U.S.A.* 108 F2
Sullivan, *Mo., U.S.A.* 112 F9
Sullivan Bay, *Canada* 104 C3
Sullivan I. = Lambi Kyun, *Burma* 65 G2
Sully-sur-Loire, *France* 19 E9
Sulmierzyce, *Poland* 45 G4
Sulmona, *Italy* 29 F10
Süloğlu, *Turkey* 41 E10
Sulphur, *La., U.S.A.* 113 K8
Sulphur, *Okla., U.S.A.* 113 H6
Sulphur Pt., *Canada* 104 A6
Sulphur Springs, *U.S.A.* 113 J7
Sulphur Springs Draw →, *U.S.A.* 113 J4
Sultan, *Canada* 102 C3
Sultan, *U.S.A.* 116 C5
Sultan Dağları, *Turkey* 72 C4
Sultanhisar, *Turkey* 39 D10
Sultaniça, *Turkey* 41 F10
Sultaniye, *Turkey* 41 F12
Sultanpur, *India* 69 F10
Sulu Arch., *Phil.* 61 J4
Sulu Sea, *E. Indies* 61 H4
Sülüklü, *Turkey* 72 C5
Sululta, *Ethiopia* 81 F4
Suluova, *Turkey* 72 B6
Suluq, *Libya* 79 B10
Sulzbach, *Germany* 25 F3
Sulzbach-Rosenberg, *Germany* 25 F7
Sulzberger Ice Shelf, *Antarctica* 5 D10
Sumalata, *Indonesia* 63 D6
Sumampa, *Argentina* 126 B3
Sumatera □, *Indonesia* 62 D2
Sumatra = Sumatera □, *Indonesia* 62 D2
Sumatra, *U.S.A.* 114 C10
Sumba, *Indonesia* 63 F5
Sumba, Selat, *Indonesia* 63 F5
Sumbawa, *Indonesia* 62 F5
Sumbawa Besar, *Indonesia* 62 F5
Sumbawanga □, *Tanzania* 86 D3
Sumbe, *Angola* 84 G2
Sumburgh Hd., *U.K.* 14 B7
Sumdo, *India* 69 B8
Sumedang, *Indonesia* 63 G12
Sümeg, *Hungary* 42 D2
Šumen = Shumen, *Bulgaria* 41 C10
Sumenep, *Indonesia* 63 G15
Sumgait = Sumqayıt, *Azerbaijan* 49 K9
Summer L., *U.S.A.* 114 E3
Summerland, *Canada* 104 D5
Summerside, *Canada* 103 C7
Summerville, *Ga., U.S.A.* 109 H3
Summerville, *S.C., U.S.A.* 109 J5
Summit Lake, *Canada* 104 C4
Summit Peak, *U.S.A.* 115 H10
Sumner, *Iowa, U.S.A.* 112 D8
Sumner, *Wash., U.S.A.* 116 C4
Šumoto, *Japan* 55 G7
Šumperk, *Czech Rep.* 27 B9
Sumqayıt, *Azerbaijan* 49 K9
Sumter, *U.S.A.* 109 J5
Sumy, *Ukraine* 47 G8
Sun City, *Ariz., U.S.A.* 115 K7
Sun City, *Calif., U.S.A.* 117 M9
Sunagawa, *Japan* 54 C10
Sunan, *N. Korea* 57 E13
Sunart, L., *U.K.* 14 E3
Sunburst, *U.S.A.* 114 B8
Sunbury, *Australia* 95 F3
Sunbury, *U.S.A.* 111 F8
Sunchales, *Argentina* 126 C3
Suncho Corral, *Argentina* 126 B3
Sunchon, *S. Korea* 57 G14
Suncook, *U.S.A.* 111 C13
Sunda, Selat, *Indonesia* 62 F3
Sunda Is., *Indonesia* 96 H2
Sunda Str. = Sunda, Selat, *Indonesia* 62 F3
Sundance, *U.S.A.* 112 C2
Sundarbans, The, *Asia* 67 J16
Sundargarh, *India* 67 H14
Sundays = Sondags →, *S. Africa* 88 E4
Sunderland, *Canada* 110 B5
Sunderland, *U.K.* 12 C6
Sundre, *Canada* 104 C6
Sundridge, *Canada* 102 C4
Sunds, *Denmark* 11 H3
Sundsvall, *Sweden* 10 B11
Sundsvallsbukten, *Sweden* 10 B11
Sung Hei, *Vietnam* 65 G6
Sungai Kolok, *Thailand* 65 J3
Sungai Lembing, *Malaysia* 65 L4
Sungai Petani, *Malaysia* 65 K3
Sungaigerong, *Indonesia* 62 E2
Sungailiat, *Indonesia* 62 E3
Sungaipenuh, *Indonesia* 62 E2
Sungari = Songhua Jiang →, *China* 60 B8
Sunghua Chiang = Songhua Jiang →, *China* 60 B8
Sungikai, *Sudan* 81 E2
Sungurlu, *Turkey* 72 B6
Sunja, *Croatia* 29 C13
Sunnansjö, *Sweden* 10 D8
Sunndalsøra, *Norway* 9 E13
Sunne, *Sweden* 10 E7
Sunnemo, *Sweden* 10 E7
Sunnyside, *Utah, U.S.A.* 114 G8
Sunnyside, *Wash., U.S.A.* 114 C3
Sunnyvale, *U.S.A.* 116 H4
Sunray, *U.S.A.* 113 G4
Suntar, *Russia* 51 C12
Sunyani, *Ghana* 82 D4
Suomenselkä, *Finland* 8 E21
Suomussalmi, *Finland* 8 D23
Suoyarvi, *Russia* 46 A7
Supai, *U.S.A.* 115 H7
Supaul, *India* 69 F12
Superior, *Ariz., U.S.A.* 115 K8
Superior, *Mont., U.S.A.* 114 C6
Superior, *Nebr., U.S.A.* 112 E5
Superior, *Wis., U.S.A.* 112 B8
Superior, L., *U.S.A.* 102 C2
Supetar, *Croatia* 29 E13
Suphan Buri, *Thailand* 64 E3
Suphan Dağı, *Turkey* 73 C10
Supiori, *Indonesia* 63 E9
Supraśl, *Poland* 45 E10
Supraśl →, *Poland* 45 E9
Supung Shuiku, *China* 57 D13
Sūq Suwayq, *Si. Arabia* 70 E3
Suqian, *China* 57 H10
Sūr, *Lebanon* 75 B4
Sur, Pt., *U.S.A.* 116 J5
Sura →, *Russia* 48 C8
Surab, *Pakistan* 68 E2
Surabaja = Surabaya, *Indonesia* 63 G15
Surabaya, *Indonesia* 63 G15
Surahammar, *Sweden* 10 E10
Suraia, *Romania* 43 E12
Surakarta, *Indonesia* 63 G14
Surakhany, *Azerbaijan* 49 K10
Šurany, *Slovak Rep.* 27 C11
Surat, *Australia* 95 D4
Surat, *India* 66 J8
Surat Thani, *Thailand* 65 H2
Suratgarh, *India* 68 E5

Suraż, Poland 45 F9
Surazh, Belarus 46 E6
Surazh, Russia 47 F7
Surduc, Romania 43 C8
Surduc Pasul, Romania .. 43 E8
Surdulica, Serbia, Yug. .. 40 D6
Surendranagar, India 68 H4
Surf, U.S.A. 117 L6
Surgères, France 20 B3
Surgut, Russia 50 C8
Sùria, Spain 32 D6
Suriapet, India 66 L11
Surigao, Phil. 61 G6
Surigao Strait, Phil. 61 F6
Surin, Thailand 64 E4
Surin Nua, Ko, Thailand . 65 H1
Surinam ■, S. Amer. 125 C7
Suriname = Surinam ■,
   S. Amer. 125 C7
Suriname →, Surinam .. 125 B7
Sürmaq, Iran 71 D7
Sürmene, Turkey 73 B9
Surovikino, Russia 49 F6
Surprise L., Canada 104 B2
Surrey □, U.K. 13 F7
Sursee, Switz. 25 H4
Sursk, Russia 48 D7
Surskoye, Russia 48 C8
Surt, Libya 79 B9
Surt, Khalīj, Libya 79 B9
Surte, Sweden 11 G6
Surtsey, Iceland 8 E3
Sürüç, Turkey 73 D8
Suruga-Wan, Japan 55 G9
Susa, Italy 28 C4
Suså →, Denmark 11 J5
Sušac, Croatia 29 F13
Susak, Croatia 29 D11
Susaki, Japan 55 H6
Süsangerd, Iran 71 D6
Susanville, U.S.A. 114 F3
Susch, Switz. 25 J6
Suşehri, Turkey 73 B8
Sušice, Czech Rep. 26 B6
Susleni, Moldova 43 C13
Susong, China 59 B11
Susquehanna →, U.S.A. . 111 G8
Susquehanna Depot,
   U.S.A. 111 E9
Susques, Argentina 126 A2
Sussex, Canada 103 C6
Sussex, U.S.A. 111 E10
Sussex, E. □, U.K. 13 G8
Sussex, W. □, U.K. 13 G7
Sustut →, Canada 104 B3
Susuman, Russia 51 C15
Susunu, Indonesia 63 E8
Susurluk, Turkey 39 B10
Susuz, Turkey 73 B10
Susz, Poland 44 E6
Sütçüler, Turkey 72 D4
Suteşti, Romania 43 E12
Sutherland, S. Africa 88 E3
Sutherland, U.S.A. 112 E4
Sutherland Falls, N.Z. ... 91 L1
Sutherlin, U.S.A. 114 E2
Sutlej →, Pakistan 68 E4
Sutter, U.S.A. 116 F5
Sutter Creek, U.S.A. 116 G6
Sutton, Canada 111 A12
Sutton, U.S.A. 112 E6
Sutton □, Canada 102 A3
Sutton →, Canada 102 A3
Sutton Coldfield, U.K. ... 13 E6
Sutton in Ashfield, U.K. .. 12 D6
Suttor →, Australia 94 C4
Suttsu, Japan 54 C10
Suva, Fiji 91 D8
Suva Gora, Macedonia ... 40 E5
Suva Planina, Serbia, Yug. 40 C6
Suva Reka, Serbia, Yug. .. 40 D4
Suvorov, Russia 46 E9
Suvorov Is. = Suwarrow
   Is., Cook Is. 97 J11
Suvorovo, Bulgaria 41 C11
Suwałki, Poland 44 D9
Suwałki □, Poland 44 E9
Suwannaphum, Thailand . 64 E4
Suwannee →, U.S.A. ... 109 L4
Suwanose-Jima, Japan ... 55 K4
Suwarrow Is., Cook Is. .. 97 J11
Suwayq aş Şuqban, Iraq . 70 D5
Suweis, Khalîg el, Egypt . 80 J8
Suweis, Qanâ es, Egypt .. 80 H8
Suwŏn, S. Korea 57 F14
Suzdal, Russia 46 D11
Suzhou, China 59 B13
Suzu, Japan 55 F8
Suzu-Misaki, Japan 55 F8
Suzuka, Japan 55 G8
Suzzara, Italy 28 D7
Svalbard, Arctic 4 B8
Svalöv, Sweden 11 J7
Svängsta, Sweden 11 H3
Svanskog, Sweden 10 E6
Svappavaara, Sweden ... 8 C19
Svärdsjö, Sweden 10 D9
Svartå, Sweden 10 E8
Svartisen, Norway 8 C15
Svartvik, Sweden 10 B11
Svatove, Ukraine 47 H10
Svatovo = Svatove,
   Ukraine 47 H10
Svay Chek, Cambodia ... 64 F4
Svay Rieng, Cambodia .. 65 G5
Svealand □, Sweden 10 D9

Svedala, Sweden 11 J7
Sveg, Sweden 10 B8
Svendborg, Denmark 11 J4
Sven'junga, Sweden 11 G7
Svenstavik, Sweden 10 B8
Svenstrup, Denmark 11 H3
Sverdlovsk =
   Yekaterinburg, Russia . 50 D7
Sverdlovsk, Ukraine 47 H10
Sverdrup Is., Canada ... 4 B3
Svetac, Croatia 29 E12
Sveti Nikola, Prokhad,
   Europe 40 C6
Sveti Nikole, Macedonia .. 40 E5
Sveti Rok, Croatia 29 D12
Svetlaya, Russia 54 A9
Svetlogorsk =
   Svyetlahorsk, Belarus . 47 F5
Svetlograd, Russia 49 H6
Svetlovodsk = Svitlovodsk,
   Ukraine 47 H7
Svidník, Slovak Rep. 27 B14
Svilaja Planina, Croatia .. 29 E13
Svilajnac, Serbia, Yug. ... 40 B5
Svilengrad, Bulgaria 41 E10
Svir →, Russia 46 B7
Sviritsa, Russia 46 B7
Svishtov, Bulgaria 41 C9
Svislach, Belarus 47 F3
Svitava →, Czech Rep. .. 27 B9
Svitavy, Czech Rep. 27 B9
Svitlovodsk, Ukraine 47 H7
Svobodnyy, Russia 51 D13
Svoge, Bulgaria 40 D7
Svolvær, Norway 8 B16
Svratka →, Czech Rep. .. 27 B9
Svrljig, Serbia, Yug. 40 C6
Svyetlahorsk, Belarus ... 47 F5
Swabian Alps =
   Schwäbische Alb,
   Germany 25 G5
Swainsboro, U.S.A. 109 J4
Swakopmund, Namibia .. 88 C1
Swale →, U.K. 12 C6
Swan Hill, Australia 95 F3
Swan Hills, Canada 104 C5
Swan Is., W. Indies 120 C3
Swan L., Canada 105 C8
Swan River, Canada 105 C8
Swanage, U.K. 13 G6
Swansea, Australia 95 E5
Swansea, U.K. 13 F4
Swansea □, U.K. 13 F3
Swar →, Pakistan 69 B5
Swartberge, S. Africa ... 88 E3
Swartmodder, S. Africa .. 88 D3
Swartruggens, S. Africa .. 88 D4
Swarzędz, Poland 45 F4
Swastika, Canada 102 C3
Swatow = Shantou, China 59 F11
Swaziland ■, Africa 89 D5
Sweden ■, Europe 9 G16
Swedru, Ghana 83 D4
Sweet Home, U.S.A. ... 114 D2
Sweetwater, Nev., U.S.A. 116 G7
Sweetwater, Tex., U.S.A. 113 J4
Sweetwater →, U.S.A. . 114 E10
Swellendam, S. Africa .. 88 E3
Swider →, Poland 45 F8
Świdnica, Poland 45 H3
Świdnik, Poland 45 G9
Świdwin, Poland 44 E2
Świebodzice, Poland 45 H3
Świebodzin, Poland 45 F2
Świecie, Poland 44 E5
Świerzawa, Poland 45 G2
Świętokrzyskie, Góry,
   Poland 45 H7
Swift Current, Canada .. 105 C7
Swiftcurrent →, Canada . 105 C7
Swilly, L., Ireland 15 A4
Swindle, I., Canada 104 C3
Swindon, U.K. 13 F6
Swindon □, U.K. 13 F6
Swinemünde =
   Świnoujście, Poland .. 44 E1
Swinford, Ireland 15 C3
Świnoujście, Poland 44 E1
Switzerland ■, Europe .. 25 J4
Swords, Ireland 15 C5
Syasstroy, Russia 46 B7
Sychevka, Russia 46 E8
Syców, Poland 45 G4
Sydney, Australia 95 E5
Sydney, Canada 103 C7
Sydney Mines, Canada .. 103 C7
Sydprøven, Greenland .. 4 C5
Sydra, G. of = Surt,
   Khalīj, Libya 79 B9
Syeverodonetsk, Ukraine 47 H10
Syke, Germany 24 C4
Syktyvkar, Russia 50 C6
Sylacauga, U.S.A. 109 J2
Sylarna, Sweden 8 E15
Sylhet, Bangla. 67 G17
Sylt, Germany 24 A4
Sylvan Lake, Canada ... 104 C6
Sylvania, U.S.A. 109 J5
Sylvester, U.S.A. 109 K4
Sym, Russia 50 C9
Symón, Mexico 118 C4
Synelnykove, Ukraine ... 47 H8
Synnott Ra., Australia .. 92 C4
Syracuse, Kans., U.S.A. . 113 G4
Syracuse, N.Y., U.S.A. . 111 C8
Syrdarya →, Kazakhstan . 50 E7

Syria ■, Asia 70 C3
Syrian Desert = Ash Shām,
   Bādiyat, Asia 52 F7
Sysslebäck, Sweden 10 D6
Syzran, Russia 48 D9
Szabolcs-Szatmár-Bereg □,
   Hungary 42 B6
Szadek, Poland 45 G5
Szamocin, Poland 45 E4
Szamos →, Hungary ... 42 B7
Szamotuły, Poland 45 F3
Száraz →, Hungary 42 D6
Szarvas, Hungary 42 D5
Százhalombatta, Hungary . 42 C3
Szczawnica, Poland 45 J7
Szczebrzeszyn, Poland .. 45 H9
Szczecin, Poland 44 E1
Szczecin □, Poland 44 E1
Szczecinek, Poland 44 E3
Szczeciński, Zalew =
   Stettiner Haff, Germany 24 B10
Szczekociny, Poland 45 H6
Szczucin, Poland 45 H8
Szczuczyn, Poland 44 E9
Szczyrk, Poland 45 J6
Szczytna, Poland 45 H3
Szczytno, Poland 44 E7
Szechwan = Sichuan □,
   China 58 B5
Szécsény, Hungary 42 B4
Szeged, Hungary 42 D5
Szeghalom, Hungary ... 42 C6
Székesfehérvár, Hungary . 42 C3
Szekszárd, Hungary 42 D3
Szendrő, Hungary 42 B5
Szentendre, Hungary ... 42 C4
Szentes, Hungary 42 D5
Szentgotthárd, Hungary . 42 D1
Szentlőrinc, Hungary ... 42 D3
Szerencs, Hungary 42 B6
Szigetszentmiklós, Hungary 42 C4
Szigetvár, Hungary 42 D2
Szikszó, Hungary 42 B5
Szklarska Poreba, Poland . 45 H2
Szkwa →, Poland 45 E8
Szlichtyngowa, Poland .. 45 G3
Szob, Hungary 42 C3
Szolnok, Hungary 42 C5
Szombathely, Hungary .. 42 C1
Szprotawa, Poland 45 G2
Sztum, Poland 44 E6
Sztutowo, Poland 44 D6
Szubin, Poland 45 E4
Szydłowiec, Poland 45 G7
Szypliszki, Poland 44 D10

T

Ta Khli Khok, Thailand .. 64 E3
Ta Lai, Vietnam 65 G6
Tab, Hungary 42 D3
Tabacal, Argentina 126 A3
Tabaco, Phil. 61 E5
Tabagné, Ivory C. 82 D4
Ţabah, Si. Arabia 70 E4
Ţabas, Khorāsān, Iran .. 71 C9
Ţabas, Khorāsān, Iran .. 71 C8
Tabasará, Serranía de,
   Panama 120 E3
Tabasco □, Mexico 119 D6
Tabatinga, Serra da, Brazil 125 F10
Tabāzīn, Iran 71 D8
Taber, Canada 104 D6
Taberg, Sweden 11 G8
Tablas, Phil. 61 E5
Tablas Strait, Phil. 61 E4
Table B. = Tafelbaai,
   S. Africa 88 E2
Table B., Canada 103 B8
Table Mt., S. Africa 88 E2
Tableland, Australia 92 C4
Tabletop, Mt., Australia . 94 C4
Tábor, Czech Rep. 26 B7
Tabora, Tanzania 86 D3
Tabora □, Tanzania 86 D3
Tabou, Ivory C. 82 E4
Tabrīz, Iran 70 B5
Tabuaeran, Pac. Oc. ... 97 G12
Tabuelan, Phil. 61 F5
Tabuenca, Spain 32 D3
Tabūk, Si. Arabia 70 D3
Tāby, Sweden 10 E12
Tacámbaro de Codallos,
   Mexico 118 D4
Tacheng, China 60 B3
Tachia, Taiwan 59 E13
Tach'ing Shan = Daqing
   Shan, China 56 D6
Tachov, Czech Rep. 26 B5
Tácina →, Italy 31 D9
Tacloban, Phil. 61 F6
Tacna, Peru 124 G4
Tacoma, U.S.A. 116 C4
Tacuarembó, Uruguay .. 127 C4
Tademaït, Plateau du,
   Algeria 78 C6
Tadjoura, Djibouti 81 E5
Tadjoura, Golfe de,
   Djibouti 81 E5
Tadmor, N.Z. 91 J4
Tadoule L., Canada 105 B9
Tadoussac, Canada 103 C6
Tadzhikistan =
   Tajikistan ■, Asia 50 F8

Taechŏn-ni, S. Korea 57 F14
Taegu, S. Korea 57 G15
Taegwan, N. Korea 57 D13
Taejŏn, S. Korea 57 F14
Tafalla, Spain 32 C3
Tafar, Sudan 81 F2
Tafelbaai, S. Africa 88 E2
Tafermaar, Indonesia ... 63 F8
Tafí Viejo, Argentina ... 126 B2
Tafīhān, Iran 71 D7
Tafiré, Ivory C. 82 D3
Taft, Iran 71 D7
Taft, Phil. 61 F6
Taft, Calif., U.S.A. 117 K7
Taft, Tex., U.S.A. 113 M6
Taga Dzong, Bhutan ... 67 F16
Taganrog, Russia 47 J10
Taganrogskiy Zaliv, Russia 47 J10
Tagânt, Mauritania 82 B2
Tagatay, Phil. 61 D4
Tagbilaran, Phil. 61 G5
Tagish, Canada 104 A2
Tagish L., Canada 104 A2
Tagliacozzo, Italy 29 F10
Tagliamento →, Italy ... 29 C10
Táglio di Po, Italy 29 D9
Tago, Phil. 61 G7
Tagomago, Spain 37 B8
Taguatinga, Brazil 125 F10
Tagudin, Phil. 61 C4
Tagum, Phil. 61 H6
Tagus = Tejo →, Europe 35 F2
Tahakopa, N.Z. 91 M2
Tahan, Gunong, Malaysia 65 K4
Tahat, Algeria 78 D7
Tāherī, Iran 71 E7
Tahiti, Pac. Oc. 97 J13
Tahoe, L., U.S.A. 116 G6
Tahoe City, U.S.A. 116 F6
Taholah, U.S.A. 116 C2
Tahoua, Niger 83 C6
Tahta, Egypt 80 B3
Tahtaköprü, Turkey 41 G13
Tahtalı Dağları, Turkey .. 72 C7
Tahulandang, Indonesia . 63 D7
Tahuna, Indonesia 63 D7
Taï, Ivory C. 82 D3
Tai Hu, China 60 C7
Tai Shan, China 57 F9
Tai Xian, China 59 A13
Tai'an, China 57 F9
Taibei = T'aipei, Taiwan . 59 E13
Taibique, Canary Is. ... 37 G2
Taibus Qi, China 56 D8
T'aichung, Taiwan 59 E13
Taieri →, N.Z. 91 M3
Taigu, China 56 F7
Taihang Shan, China ... 56 G7
Taihape, N.Z. 91 H5
Taihe, Anhui, China ... 56 H8
Taihe, Jiangxi, China ... 59 D10
Taihu, China 59 B11
Taijiang, China 58 D7
Taikang, China 56 G8
Tailem Bend, Australia . 95 F2
Tailfingen, Germany ... 25 G5
Taimyr Peninsula =
   Taymyr, Poluostrov,
   Russia 51 B11
Tain, U.K. 14 D4
T'ainan, Taiwan 59 F13
Taínaron, Ákra, Greece .. 38 E4
Taining, China 59 D11
T'aipei, Taiwan 59 E13
Taiping, China 59 B12
Taiping, Malaysia 65 K3
Taipingzhen, China 56 H6
Tairbeart = Tarbert, U.K. 14 D2
Taishan, China 59 F9
Taishun, China 59 D12
Taita □, Kenya 86 C4
Taita Hills, Kenya 86 C4
Taitao, Pen. de, Chile .. 122 H3
T'aitung, Taiwan 59 F13
Taivalkoski, Finland ... 8 D23
Taiwan ■, Asia 59 F13
Taixing, China 59 A13
Taiyetos Óros, Greece ... 38 D4
Taiyiba, Israel 75 C4
Taiyuan, China 56 F7
Taizhong = T'aichung,
   Taiwan 59 E13
Taizhou, China 59 A13
Taizhou Liedao, China .. 59 C13
Ta'izz, Yemen 74 E3
Tājābād, Iran 71 D7
Tajikistan ■, Asia 50 F8
Tajima, Japan 55 F9
Tajo = Tejo →, Europe . 35 F2
Tajrīsh, Iran 71 C6
Tak, Thailand 64 D2
Takāb, Iran 70 B5
Takachiho, Japan 55 H5
Takada, Japan 55 F9
Takahagi, Japan 55 F10
Takaka, N.Z. 91 J4
Takamatsu, Japan 55 G7
Takaoka, Japan 55 F8
Takapuna, N.Z. 91 G5
Takasaki, Japan 55 F9
Takatsuki, Japan 55 G7
Takaungu, Kenya 86 C4
Takayama, Japan 55 F8
Take-Shima, Japan 55 J5
Takefu, Japan 55 G8

Takengon, Indonesia 62 D1
Takeo, Japan 55 H5
Tåkern, Sweden 11 F8
Tākestān, Iran 71 C6
Taketa, Japan 55 H5
Takev, Cambodia 65 G5
Takh, India 69 C7
Takikawa, Japan 54 C10
Takla L., Canada 104 B3
Takla Landing, Canada . 104 B3
Takla Makan =
   Taklamakan Shamo,
   China 52 F12
Taklamakan Shamo, China 52 F12
Taku →, Canada 104 B2
Takum, Nigeria 83 D6
Tal Halāl, Iran 71 D7
Tala, Uruguay 127 C4
Talachyn, Belarus 46 E5
Talacogan, Phil. 61 G6
Talagante, Chile 126 C1
Talak, Niger 83 B6
Talamanca, Cordillera de,
   Cent. Amer. 120 E3
Talant, France 19 E11
Talara, Peru 124 D2
Talas, Kyrgyzstan 50 E8
Talas, Turkey 72 C6
Talâta, Egypt 75 E1
Talata Mafara, Nigeria ... 83 C6
Talaud, Kepulauan,
   Indonesia 63 D7
Talaud Is. = Talaud,
   Kepulauan, Indonesia . 63 D7
Talavera de la Reina, Spain 34 F6
Talavera la Real, Spain .. 35 G4
Talawana, Australia 92 D3
Talayan, Phil. 61 H6
Talayuela, Spain 34 F5
Talbert, Sillon de, France . 18 D3
Talbot, C., Australia ... 92 B4
Talbragar →, Australia . 95 E4
Talca, Chile 126 D1
Talca □, Chile 126 D1
Talcahuano, Chile 126 D1
Talcher, India 67 J14
Talcho, Niger 83 C5
Taldy Kurgan =
   Taldyqorghan, Kazakstan 50 E8
Taldyqorghan, Kazakstan . 50 E8
Tālesh, Iran 71 B6
Tālesh, Kūhhā-ye, Iran ... 71 B6
Talguharai, Sudan 80 D4
Tali Post, Sudan 81 F3
Talibon, Phil. 61 F6
Talibong, Ko, Thailand . 65 J2
Talihina, U.S.A. 113 H7
Talisayan, Phil. 61 G6
Taliwang, Indonesia ... 62 F5
Tall 'Afar, Iraq 70 B4
Tall Kalakh, Syria 75 A5
Talla, Egypt 80 J7
Talladega, U.S.A. 109 J2
Tallahassee, U.S.A. 109 K3
Tallangatta, Australia .. 95 F4
Tallard, France 21 D10
Tallarook, Australia ... 95 F4
Tällberg, Sweden 10 D9
Tallering Pk., Australia . 93 E2
Tallinn, Estonia 9 G21
Tallulah, U.S.A. 113 J9
Tălmaciu, Romania 43 E9
Talmont-St-Hilaire, France 20 B2
Talne, Ukraine 47 H6
Talnoye = Talne, Ukraine 47 H6
Talodi, Sudan 81 E3
Talovaya, Russia 48 F5
Taloyoak, Canada 100 B10
Talpa de Allende, Mexico 118 C4
Talsi, Latvia 44 A9
Taltal, Chile 126 B1
Taltson →, Canada 104 A6
Talwood, Australia 95 D4
Talyawalka Cr. →,
   Australia 95 E3
Tam Chau, Vietnam ... 65 G5
Tam Ky, Vietnam 64 E7
Tam Quan, Vietnam ... 64 E7
Tama, U.S.A. 112 E8
Tamale, Australia 93 E1
Tamale, Ghana 83 D4
Taman, Russia 47 K9
Tamano, Japan 55 G6
Tamanrasset, Algeria ... 78 D7
Tamaqua, U.S.A. 111 F9
Tamar →, U.K. 13 G3
Tamarang, Australia ... 95 E5
Tamarinda, Spain 37 B10
Tamarite de Litera, Spain 32 D5
Tamashima, Japan 55 G6
Tamási, Hungary 42 D3
Tamaské, Niger 83 C6
Tamaulipas □, Mexico . 119 C5
Tamaulipas, Sierra de,
   Mexico 119 C5
Tamazula, Mexico 118 C3
Tamazunchale, Mexico . 119 C5
Tamba, Guinea 82 C2
Tambacounda, Senegal . 82 C2
Tambelan, Kepulauan,
   Indonesia 62 D3
Tambellup, Australia ... 93 F2
Tambo, Australia 94 C4
Tambo de Mora, Peru .. 124 F3
Tambohorano, Madag. .. 89 B7

Tambora

Tambora, *Indonesia* 62 F5
Tambov, *Russia* 48 D5
Tambre →, *Spain* 34 C2
Tambuku, *Indonesia* 63 G15
Tamburâ, *Sudan* 81 F2
Tâmchekket, *Mauritania* 82 B2
Tâmega →, *Portugal* 34 D2
Tamenglong, *India* 67 G18
Tamiahua, L. de, *Mexico* 119 C5
Tamil Nadu □, *India* 66 P10
Tamis →, *Serbia, Yug.* 42 F5
Tamluk, *India* 69 H12
Tammerfors = Tampere, *Finland* 9 F20
Tammisaari, *Finland* 9 F20
Tämnaren, *Sweden* 10 D11
Tamo Abu, Pegunungan, *Malaysia* 62 D5
Tampa, *U.S.A.* 109 M4
Tampa B., *U.S.A.* 109 M4
Tampere, *Finland* 9 F20
Tampico, *Mexico* 119 C5
Tampin, *Malaysia* 65 L4
Tamsagbulag, *Mongolia* 60 B6
Tamsweg, *Austria* 26 D6
Tamu, *Burma* 67 G19
Tamuja →, *Spain* 35 F4
Tamworth, *Australia* 95 E5
Tamworth, *U.K.* 13 E6
Tamyang, *S. Korea* 57 G14
Tan An, *Vietnam* 65 G6
Tana →, *Kenya* 86 C5
Tana →, *Norway* 8 A23
Tana, L., *Ethiopia* 81 E4
Tana River, *Kenya* 86 C4
Tanabe, *Japan* 55 H7
Tanafjorden, *Norway* 8 A23
Tanaga, Pta., *Canary Is.* 37 G1
Tanahbala, *Indonesia* 62 E1
Tanahgrogot, *Indonesia* 62 E5
Tanahjampea, *Indonesia* 63 F6
Tanahmasa, *Indonesia* 62 E1
Tanahmerah, *Indonesia* 63 F10
Tanakura, *Japan* 55 F10
Tanami, *Australia* 92 C4
Tanami Desert, *Australia* 92 C5
Tanana →, *U.S.A.* 100 B4
Tananarive = Antananarivo, *Madag.* 89 B8
Tánaro →, *Italy* 28 D5
Tanbar, *Australia* 94 D3
Tancheng, *China* 57 G10
Tanchŏn, *N. Korea* 57 D15
Tanda, *Ut. P., India* 69 F10
Tanda, *Ut. P., India* 69 E8
Tanda, *Ivory C.* 82 D4
Tandag, *Phil.* 61 G7
Tandaia, *Tanzania* 87 D3
Tăndărei, *Romania* 43 F12
Tandaué, *Angola* 88 B2
Tandil, *Argentina* 126 D4
Tandil, Sa. del, *Argentina* 126 D4
Tandlianwala, *Pakistan* 68 D5
Tando Adam, *Pakistan* 68 G3
Tandou L., *Australia* 95 E3
Tandragee, *U.K.* 15 B5
Tandsjöborg, *Sweden* 10 C8
Tane-ga-Shima, *Japan* 55 J5
Taneatua, *N.Z.* 91 H6
Tanen Tong Dan, *Burma* 67 L21
Tanew →, *Poland* 45 H9
Tanezrouft, *Algeria* 78 D6
Tang, Koh, *Cambodia* 65 G4
Tang Krasang, *Cambodia* 64 F5
Tanga, *Tanzania* 86 D4
Tanga □, *Tanzania* 86 D4
Tanganyika, L., *Africa* 86 D3
Tanger = Tangier, *Morocco* 78 A4
Tangerang, *Indonesia* 63 G12
Tangerhütte, *Germany* 24 C7
Tangermünde, *Germany* 24 C7
Tanggu, *China* 57 E9
Tanggula Shan, *China* 60 C4
Tanghe, *China* 56 H7
Tangier, *Morocco* 78 A4
Tangorin P.O., *Australia* 94 C3
Tangshan, *China* 57 E10
Tangtou, *China* 57 G10
Tanguiéta, *Benin* 83 C5
Tangxi, *China* 59 C12
Tangyan He →, *China* 58 C7
Tanimbar, Kepulauan, *Indonesia* 63 F8
Tanimbar Is. = Tanimbar, Kepulauan, *Indonesia* 63 F8
Taninthari, *Burma* 65 F2
Tanjay, *Phil.* 61 G5
Tanjong Malim, *Malaysia* 65 L3
Tanjore = Thanjavur, *India* 66 P11
Tanjung, *Indonesia* 62 E5
Tanjungbalai, *Indonesia* 62 D1
Tanjungbatu, *Indonesia* 62 D5
Tanjungkarang Telukbetung, *Indonesia* 62 F3
Tanjungpandan, *Indonesia* 62 E3
Tanjungpinang, *Indonesia* 62 D2
Tanjungredeb, *Indonesia* 62 D5
Tanjungselor, *Indonesia* 62 D5
Tank, *Pakistan* 68 C4
Tännäs, *Sweden* 10 B6
Tannis Bugt, *Denmark* 11 G4
Tannu-Ola, *Russia* 51 D10
Tano →, *Ghana* 82 D4
Tanon Str., *Phil.* 61 F5
Tanout, *Niger* 83 C6
Tanshui, *Taiwan* 59 E13
Tanta, *Egypt* 80 H7
Tantoyuca, *Mexico* 119 C5
Tantung = Dandong, *China* 57 D13
Tanumshede, *Sweden* 11 F5
Tanunda, *Australia* 95 E2
Tanus, *France* 20 D6
Tanzania ■, *Africa* 86 D3
Tanzilla →, *Canada* 104 B2
Tao, Ko, *Thailand* 65 G2
Tao'an, *China* 57 B12
Tao'er He →, *China* 57 B13
Taohua Dao, *China* 59 C14
Taolanaro, *Madag.* 89 D8
Taole, *China* 56 E4
Taormina, *Italy* 31 E8
Taos, *U.S.A.* 115 H11
Taoudenni, *Mali* 78 D5
Taoyuan, *China* 59 C8
T'aoyüan, *Taiwan* 59 E13
Tapa, *Estonia* 9 G21
Tapa Shan = Daba Shan, *China* 58 B7
Tapachula, *Mexico* 119 E6
Tapah, *Malaysia* 65 K3
Tapajós →, *Brazil* 122 D5
Tapaktuan, *Indonesia* 62 D1
Tapanahoni →, *Surinam* 125 C8
Tapanui, *N.Z.* 91 L2
Tapauá →, *Brazil* 124 E6
Tapeta, *Liberia* 82 D3
Taphan Hin, *Thailand* 64 D3
Tapi →, *India* 66 J8
Tapia de Casariego, *Spain* 34 B4
Tapirapecó, Serra, *Venezuela* 124 C6
Tapolca, *Hungary* 42 D2
Tappahannock, *U.S.A.* 108 G7
Tapuaenuku, Mt., *N.Z.* 91 K4
Tapul Group, *Phil.* 61 J4
Tapurucuará, *Brazil* 124 D5
Taqīābād, *Iran* 71 C8
Ţaqţaq, *Iraq* 70 C5
Taquara, *Brazil* 127 B5
Taquari →, *Brazil* 124 G7
Tara, *Australia* 95 D5
Tara, *Canada* 110 B3
Tara, *Russia* 50 D8
Tara, *Zambia* 87 F2
Tara →, *Montenegro, Yug.* 40 C2
Taraba □, *Nigeria* 83 D7
Tarabagatay, Khrebet, *Kazakstan* 50 E9
Tarābulus, *Lebanon* 75 A4
Tarābulus, *Libya* 79 B8
Taraclia, *Moldova* 43 D14
Taraclia, *Moldova* 43 E13
Tarajalejo, *Canary Is.* 37 F5
Tarakan, *Indonesia* 62 D5
Tarakit, Mt., *Kenya* 86 B4
Taralga, *Australia* 95 E4
Tarama-Jima, *Japan* 55 M2
Taran, Mys, *Russia* 9 J18
Taranagar, *India* 68 E6
Taranaki □, *N.Z.* 91 H5
Tarancón, *Spain* 32 E1
Taranga, *India* 68 H5
Taranga Hill, *India* 68 H5
Taransay, *U.K.* 14 D1
Táranto, *Italy* 31 B10
Táranto, G. di, *Italy* 31 B10
Tarapacá, *Colombia* 124 D5
Tarapacá □, *Chile* 126 A2
Tarapoto, *Peru* 124 E3
Tarare, *France* 21 C8
Tararua Ra., *N.Z.* 91 J5
Tarascon, *France* 21 E8
Tarascon-sur-Ariège, *France* 20 F5
Tarashcha, *Ukraine* 47 H6
Tarauacá, *Brazil* 124 E4
Tarauacá →, *Brazil* 124 E5
Taravo →, *France* 21 G12
Tarawera, *N.Z.* 91 H6
Tarawera L., *N.Z.* 91 H6
Tarazona, *Spain* 32 D3
Tarazona de la Mancha, *Spain* 33 F3
Tarbat Ness, *U.K.* 14 D5
Tarbela Dam, *Pakistan* 68 B5
Tarbert, *Arg. & Bute, U.K.* 14 F3
Tarbert, *W. Isles, U.K.* 14 D2
Tarbes, *France* 20 E4
Tarboro, *U.S.A.* 109 H7
Tarbrax, *Australia* 94 C3
Tărcău, Munţii, *Romania* 43 D11
Tarcento, *Italy* 29 B10
Tarcoola, *Australia* 95 E1
Tarcoon, *Australia* 95 E4
Tardets-Sorholus, *France* 20 E3
Tardoire →, *France* 20 C4
Taree, *Australia* 95 E5
Tarfa, W. el →, *Egypt* 80 J7
Tarfaya, *Morocco* 78 C3
Târgovişte, *Romania* 43 F10
Târgu Bujor, *Romania* 43 E12
Târgu Cărbuneşti, *Romania* 43 F8
Târgu Frumos, *Romania* 43 C12
Târgu-Jiu, *Romania* 43 E8
Târgu Lăpuş, *Romania* 43 C8
Târgu Mureş, *Romania* 43 D9
Târgu Neamţ, *Romania* 43 C11
Târgu Ocna, *Romania* 43 D11
Târgu Secuiesc, *Romania* 43 E11
Târguşor, *Romania* 43 F13
Tărhăus, Vf., *Romania* 43 D11
Tarifa, *Spain* 35 J5
Tarija, *Bolivia* 126 A3
Tarija □, *Bolivia* 126 A3
Tariku →, *Indonesia* 63 E9
Tarim Basin = Tarim Pendi, *China* 60 C3
Tarim He →, *China* 60 C3
Tarim Pendi, *China* 60 C3
Tarime □, *Tanzania* 86 C3
Taritatu →, *Indonesia* 63 E9
Tarka →, *S. Africa* 88 E4
Tarkastad, *S. Africa* 88 E4
Tarkhankut, Mys, *Ukraine* 47 K7
Tarko Sale, *Russia* 50 C8
Tarkwa, *Ghana* 82 D4
Tarlac, *Phil.* 61 D4
Tarlton Downs, *Australia* 94 C2
Tarm, *Denmark* 11 J2
Tarma, *Peru* 124 F3
Tarn □, *France* 20 E6
Tarn →, *France* 20 D5
Tarn-et-Garonne □, *France* 20 D5
Tarna →, *Hungary* 42 C4
Târnava Mare →, *Romania* 43 D8
Târnava Mică →, *Romania* 43 D8
Târnăveni, *Romania* 43 D9
Tarnica, *Poland* 45 J9
Tarnobrzeg, *Poland* 45 H8
Tarnobrzeg □, *Poland* 45 H8
Tarnogród, *Poland* 45 H9
Tarnos, *France* 20 E2
Târnova, *Moldova* 43 B12
Târnova, *Romania* 42 E6
Tarnów, *Poland* 45 H8
Tarnów □, *Poland* 45 J7
Tarnowskie Góry, *Poland* 45 H5
Tärnsjö, *Sweden* 10 D10
Táro →, *Italy* 28 C7
Taroom, *Australia* 95 D4
Taroudannt, *Morocco* 78 B4
Tarp, *Germany* 24 A5
Tarpon Springs, *U.S.A.* 109 L4
Tarquínia, *Italy* 29 F8
Tarragona, *Spain* 32 D6
Tarragona □, *Spain* 32 D6
Tarrasa = Terrassa, *Spain* 32 D7
Tàrrega, *Spain* 32 D6
Tarrytown, *U.S.A.* 111 E11
Tårs, *Denmark* 11 G4
Tarshiha = Me'ona, *Israel* 75 B4
Tarso Emissi, *Chad* 79 D9
Tarsus, *Turkey* 72 D6
Tartagal, *Argentina* 126 A3
Tärtär, *Azerbaijan* 49 K8
Tärtär →, *Azerbaijan* 49 K8
Tartas, *France* 20 E3
Tartu, *Estonia* 9 G22
Ţarţūs, *Syria* 70 C2
Tarumizu, *Japan* 55 J5
Tarussa, *Russia* 46 E9
Tarutao, Ko, *Thailand* 65 J2
Tarutung, *Indonesia* 62 D1
Tarvísio, *Italy* 29 B10
Taschereau, *Canada* 102 C4
Taseko →, *Canada* 104 C4
Tash-Kömür, *Kyrgyzstan* 50 E8
Tash-Kumyr = Tash-Kömür, *Kyrgyzstan* 50 E8
Tashauz = Dashhowuz, *Turkmenistan* 50 E6
Tashi Chho Dzong = Thimphu, *Bhutan* 67 F16
Tashkent = Toshkent, *Uzbekistan* 50 E7
Tashtagol, *Russia* 50 D9
Tasikmalaya, *Indonesia* 63 G13
Tåsinge, *Denmark* 11 J4
Tåsjön, *Sweden* 8 D16
Taskan, *Russia* 51 C16
Taşköprü, *Turkey* 72 B6
Taşlâc, *Moldova* 43 C14
Tasman B., *N.Z.* 91 J4
Tasman Mts., *N.Z.* 91 J4
Tasman Pen., *Australia* 94 G4
Tasman Sea, *Pac. Oc.* 96 L8
Tasmania □, *Australia* 94 G4
Tăşnad, *Romania* 42 C7
Tassili n'Ajjer, *Algeria* 76 D4
Tasu Sd., *Canada* 104 C2
Tata, *Hungary* 42 C3
Tatabánya, *Hungary* 42 C3
Tatar Republic □ = Tatarstan □, *Russia* 48 C10
Tatarbunary, *Ukraine* 47 K5
Tatarsk, *Russia* 50 D8
Tatarstan □, *Russia* 48 C10
Tateyama, *Japan* 55 G9
Tathlina L., *Canada* 104 A5
Tathra, *Australia* 95 F4
Tatinnai L., *Canada* 105 A9
Tatlısu, *Turkey* 41 F11
Tatnam, C., *Canada* 105 B10
Tatra = Tatry, *Slovak Rep.* 27 B13
Tatry, *Slovak Rep.* 27 B13
Tatsuno, *Japan* 55 G7
Tatta, *Pakistan* 68 G2
Tatuí, *Brazil* 127 A6
Tatum, *U.S.A.* 113 J3
Tat'ung = Datong, *China* 56 D7
Tatvan, *Turkey* 73 C10
Taubaté, *Brazil* 127 A6
Tauberbischofsheim, *Germany* 25 F5
Taucha, *Germany* 24 D8
Tauern-tunnel, *Austria* 26 D6
Taufikia, *Sudan* 81 F3
Taulé, *France* 18 D3
Taumarunui, *N.Z.* 91 H5
Taumaturgo, *Brazil* 124 E4
Taung, *S. Africa* 88 D3
Taungdwingyi, *Burma* 67 J19
Taunggyi, *Burma* 67 J20
Taungup, *Burma* 67 K19
Taungup Pass, *Burma* 67 K19
Taungup Taunggya, *Burma* 67 K18
Taunsa Barrage, *Pakistan* 68 D4
Taunton, *U.K.* 13 F4
Taunton, *U.S.A.* 111 E13
Taunus, *Germany* 25 E4
Taupo, *N.Z.* 91 H6
Taupo, L., *N.Z.* 91 H5
Tauragė, *Lithuania* 9 J20
Tauragė □, *Lithuania* 44 C9
Tauranga, *N.Z.* 91 G6
Tauranga Harb., *N.Z.* 91 G6
Taurianova, *Italy* 31 D9
Taurus Mts. = Toros Dağları, *Turkey* 72 D5
Tauste, *Spain* 32 D3
Tauz = Tovuz, *Azerbaijan* 49 K7
Tavas, *Turkey* 39 D11
Tavda, *Russia* 50 D7
Tavda →, *Russia* 50 D7
Tavernes de la Valldigna, *Spain* 33 F4
Taveta, *Tanzania* 86 C4
Taveuni, *Fiji* 91 C9
Taviano, *Italy* 31 C11
Tavignano →, *France* 21 F13
Tavira, *Portugal* 35 H3
Tavistock, *Canada* 110 C4
Tavistock, *U.K.* 13 G3
Tavolara, *Italy* 30 B2
Távora →, *Portugal* 34 D3
Tavoy = Dawei, *Burma* 64 E2
Tavşanlı, *Turkey* 39 B11
Taw →, *U.K.* 13 F3
Tawas City, *U.S.A.* 108 C4
Tawau, *Malaysia* 62 D5
Tawitawi, *Phil.* 61 J4
Taxila, *Pakistan* 68 C5
Tay →, *U.K.* 14 E5
Tay, Firth of, *U.K.* 14 E5
Tay, L., *Australia* 93 F3
Tay, L., *U.K.* 14 E4
Tay Ninh, *Vietnam* 65 G6
Tayabamba, *Peru* 124 E3
Tayabas Bay, *Phil.* 61 E4
Taylakova, *Russia* 50 D8
Taylakovy = Taylakova, *Russia* 50 D8
Taylor, *Canada* 104 B4
Taylor, *Nebr., U.S.A.* 112 E5
Taylor, *Pa., U.S.A.* 111 E9
Taylor, *Tex., U.S.A.* 113 K6
Taylor, Mt., *U.S.A.* 115 J10
Taylorville, *U.S.A.* 112 F10
Taymā, *Si. Arabia* 70 E3
Taymyr, Oz., *Russia* 51 B11
Taymyr, Poluostrov, *Russia* 51 B11
Tayport, *U.K.* 14 E6
Tayshet, *Russia* 51 D10
Taytay, *Phil.* 61 F3
Taz →, *Russia* 50 C8
Taza, *Morocco* 78 B5
Tāzah Khurmātū, *Iraq* 70 C5
Tazawa-Ko, *Japan* 54 E10
Tazin L., *Canada* 105 B7
Tazovskiy, *Russia* 50 C8
Tbilisi, *Georgia* 49 K7
Tchad = Chad ■, *Africa* 79 F8
Tchad, L., *Chad* 79 F8
Tchaourou, *Benin* 83 D5
Tch'eng-tou = Chengdu, *China* 58 B5
Tchentlo L., *Canada* 104 B4
Tchibanga, *Gabon* 84 E2
Tchien, *Liberia* 82 D3
Tchin Tabaraden, *Niger* 83 B6
Tch'ong-k'ing = Chongqing, *China* 58 C6
Tczew, *Poland* 44 D5
Te Anau, L., *N.Z.* 91 L1
Te Aroha, *N.Z.* 91 G5
Te Awamutu, *N.Z.* 91 H5
Te Kuiti, *N.Z.* 91 H5
Te Puke, *N.Z.* 91 G6
Te Waewae B., *N.Z.* 91 M1
Tea Tree, *Australia* 94 C1
Teaca, *Romania* 43 D9
Teague, *U.S.A.* 113 K6
Teano, *Italy* 31 A7
Teapa, *Mexico* 119 D6
Teba, *Spain* 35 J6
Tebakang, *Malaysia* 62 D4
Teberda, *Russia* 49 J5
Tébessa, *Algeria* 78 A7
Tebicuary →, *Paraguay* 126 B4
Tebingtinggi, *Indonesia* 62 D1
Tebulos, *Georgia* 49 J7
Tecate, *Mexico* 117 N10
Tecer Dağları, *Turkey* 72 C7
Tech →, *France* 20 F7
Techiman, *Ghana* 82 D4
Techirghiol, *Romania* 43 F13
Tecka, *Argentina* 128 E2
Tecomán, *Mexico* 118 D4
Tecopa, *U.S.A.* 117 K10
Tecoripa, *Mexico* 118 B3
Tecuala, *Mexico* 118 C3
Tecuci, *Romania* 43 E12
Tecumseh, *U.S.A.* 108 D4
Tedzhen = Tejen, *Turkmenistan* 50 F7
Tees →, *U.K.* 12 C6
Tees B., *U.K.* 12 C6
Teeswater, *Canada* 110 C3
Tefé, *Brazil* 124 D6
Tefenni, *Turkey* 39 D11
Tegal, *Indonesia* 63 G13
Tegernsee, *Germany* 25 H7
Teggiano, *Italy* 31 B8
Teghra, *India* 69 G11
Tegid, L. = Bala, L., *U.K.* 12 E4
Tegina, *Nigeria* 83 C6
Tegucigalpa, *Honduras* 120 D2
Tehachapi, *U.S.A.* 117 K8
Tehachapi Mts., *U.S.A.* 117 L8
Tehamiyam, *Sudan* 80 D4
Tehilla, *Sudan* 80 D4
Téhini, *Ivory C.* 82 D4
Tehoru, *Indonesia* 63 E7
Tehrān, *Iran* 71 C6
Tehuacán, *Mexico* 119 D5
Tehuantepec, *Mexico* 119 D5
Tehuantepec, G. de, *Mexico* 119 D5
Tehuantepec, Istmo de, *Mexico* 119 D6
Teide, *Canary Is.* 37 F3
Teifi →, *U.K.* 13 E3
Teign →, *U.K.* 13 G4
Teignmouth, *U.K.* 13 G4
Teiuş, *Romania* 43 D8
Teixeira Pinto, *Guinea-Biss.* 82 C1
Tejen, *Turkmenistan* 50 F7
Tejo →, *Europe* 35 F2
Tejon Pass, *U.S.A.* 117 L8
Tekamah, *U.S.A.* 112 E6
Tekapo, L., *N.Z.* 91 K3
Tekax, *Mexico* 119 C7
Teke, *Turkey* 41 E13
Tekeli, *Kazakstan* 50 E8
Tekeze →, *Ethiopia* 81 E4
Tekija, *Serbia, Yug.* 40 B6
Tekirdağ, *Turkey* 41 F11
Tekirdağ □, *Turkey* 41 E11
Tekirova, *Turkey* 39 E12
Tekkali, *India* 67 K14
Tekke, *Turkey* 72 B7
Tekman, *Turkey* 73 C9
Tekoa, *U.S.A.* 114 C5
Tel Aviv-Yafo, *Israel* 75 C3
Tel Lakhish, *Israel* 75 D3
Tel Megiddo, *Israel* 75 C4
Tela, *Honduras* 120 C2
Telanaipura = Jambi, *Indonesia* 62 E2
Telavi, *Georgia* 49 J7
Telč, *Czech Rep.* 26 B8
Telciu, *Romania* 43 C9
Telde, *Canary Is.* 37 G4
Telegraph Creek, *Canada* 104 B2
Telekhany = Tsyelyakhany, *Belarus* 47 F3
Telemark, *Norway* 9 G12
Telén, *Argentina* 126 D2
Teleneşti, *Moldova* 43 C13
Teleng, *Iran* 71 E9
Teleño, *Spain* 34 C4
Teleorman □, *Romania* 43 G10
Teleorman →, *Romania* 43 G10
Teles Pires →, *Brazil* 122 D5
Telescope Pk., *U.S.A.* 117 J9
Teletaye, *Mali* 83 B5
Telford, *U.K.* 13 E5
Telford and Wrekin □, *U.K.* 12 E5
Telfs, *Austria* 26 D4
Télimélé, *Guinea* 82 C2
Telkwa, *Canada* 104 C3
Tell City, *U.S.A.* 108 G2
Tellicherry, *India* 66 P9
Telluride, *U.S.A.* 115 H10
Teloloapán, *Mexico* 119 D5
Telpos Iz, *Russia* 6 C17
Telsen, *Argentina* 128 E3
Telšiai, *Lithuania* 9 H20
Telšiai □, *Lithuania* 44 C9
Teltow, *Germany* 24 C9
Teluk Anson = Teluk Intan, *Malaysia* 65 K3
Teluk Betung = Tanjungkarang Telukbetung, *Indonesia* 62 F3
Teluk Intan, *Malaysia* 65 K3
Telukbutun, *Indonesia* 65 K7
Telukdalem, *Indonesia* 62 D1
Tema, *Ghana* 83 D5
Temapache, *Mexico* 119 C5
Temax, *Mexico* 119 C7
Temba, *S. Africa* 89 D4
Tembe, *Dem. Rep. of the Congo* 86 C2
Tembleque, *Spain* 34 F7
Temblor Range, *U.S.A.* 117 K7
Teme →, *U.K.* 13 E5
Temecula, *U.S.A.* 117 M9
Temerloh, *Malaysia* 62 D2
Temir, *Kazakstan* 50 E6
Temirtau, *Kazakstan* 50 D8
Temirtau, *Russia* 50 D9
Témiscaming, *Canada* 102 C4
Temma, *Australia* 94 G3
Temnikov, *Russia* 48 C6
Temo →, *Italy* 30 B1

Temora, Australia 95 E4
Temosachic, Mexico 118 B3
Tempe, U.S.A. 115 K8
Tempe Downs, Australia 92 D5
Témpio Pausánia, Italy 30 B2
Tempiute, U.S.A. 116 H11
Temple, U.S.A. 113 K6
Temple B., Australia 94 A3
Templemore, Ireland 15 D4
Templeton, U.S.A. 116 K6
Templeton →, Australia 94 C2
Templin, Germany 24 B9
Tempoal, Mexico 119 C5
Temryuk, Russia 47 K9
Temska →, Serbia, Yug. 40 C6
Temuco, Chile 128 D2
Temuka, N.Z. 91 L3
Tenabo, Mexico 119 C6
Tenaha, U.S.A. 113 K7
Tenali, India 66 L12
Tenancingo, Mexico 119 D5
Tenango, Mexico 119 D5
Tenasserim = Tanintharī, Burma 65 F2
Tenasserim □, Burma 64 F2
Tenby, U.K. 13 F3
Tenda, Colle di, France 21 D11
Tendaho, Ethiopia 81 E5
Tende, France 21 D11
Tendelti, Sudan 81 E3
Tendrovskaya Kosa, Ukraine 47 J6
Teneida, Egypt 80 B2
Ténéré, Niger 83 B7
Tenerife, Canary Is. 37 F3
Tenerife, Pico, Canary Is. 37 G1
Teng Xian, Guangxi Zhuangzu, China 59 F8
Teng Xian, Shandong, China 57 G9
Tengah □, Indonesia 63 E6
Tengah, Kepulauan, Indonesia 62 F5
Tengchong, China 58 E2
Tengchowfu = Penglai, China 57 F11
Tenggara □, Indonesia 63 E6
Tenggarong, Indonesia 62 E5
Tenggol, Pulau, Malaysia 65 K4
Tengiz, Ozero, Kazakstan 50 D7
Tenhult, Sweden 11 G8
Tenino, U.S.A. 116 D4
Tenkasi, India 66 Q10
Tenke, Shaba, Dem. Rep. of the Congo 87 E2
Tenke, Shaba, Dem. Rep. of the Congo 87 E2
Tenkodogo, Burkina Faso 83 C4
Tenna →, Italy 29 E10
Tennant Creek, Australia 94 B1
Tennessee □, U.S.A. 109 H2
Tennessee →, U.S.A. 108 G1
Tennille, U.S.A. 109 J4
Teno, Pta. de, Canary Is. 37 F3
Tenom, Malaysia 62 C5
Tenosique, Mexico 119 D6
Tenryū-Gawa →, Japan 55 G8
Tent L., Canada 105 A7
Tenterden, U.K. 13 F8
Tenterfield, Australia 95 D5
Teo, Spain 34 C2
Teófilo Otoni, Brazil 125 G10
Teotihuacán, Mexico 119 D5
Tepa, Indonesia 63 F7
Tepalcatepec →, Mexico 118 D4
Tepecik, Bursa, Turkey 41 F12
Tepecik, Kütahya, Turkey 39 B11
Tepehuanes, Mexico 118 B3
Tepelena, Albania 40 F4
Tepetongo, Mexico 118 C4
Tepic, Mexico 118 C4
Teplá, Czech Rep. 26 B5
Teplice, Czech Rep. 26 A6
Tepoca, C., Mexico 118 A2
Tequila, Mexico 118 C4
Ter →, Spain 32 C8
Ter Apel, Neths. 17 B7
Téra, Niger 83 C5
Tera →, Spain 34 D5
Teraina, Kiribati 97 G11
Téramo, Italy 29 F10
Terang, Australia 95 F3
Tercan, Turkey 73 C9
Tercero →, Argentina 126 C3
Terebovlya, Ukraine 47 H3
Teregova, Romania 42 E7
Terek →, Russia 49 J8
Tereshka →, Russia 48 E8
Teresina, Brazil 125 E10
Terespol, Poland 45 F10
Terewah, L., Australia 95 D4
Terges →, Portugal 35 H3
Tergnier, France 19 C10
Teridgerie Cr. →, Australia 95 E4
Terlizzi, Italy 31 A9
Terme, Turkey 72 B7
Termez = Termiz, Uzbekistan 50 F7
Términi Imerese, Italy 30 E6
Términos, L. de, Mexico 119 D6
Termiz, Uzbekistan 50 F7
Térmoli, Italy 29 F12
Ternate, Indonesia 63 D7
Terneuzen, Neths. 17 C3
Terney, Russia 54 B8
Terni, Italy 29 F9
Ternitz, Austria 26 D9
Ternopil, Ukraine 47 H3
Ternopol = Ternopil, Ukraine 47 H3
Terowie, N.S.W., Australia 95 E4
Terowie, S. Austral., Australia 95 E2
Terpní, Greece 40 F7
Terra Bella, U.S.A. 117 K7
Terrace, Canada 104 C3
Terrace Bay, Canada 102 C2
Terracina, Italy 30 A6
Terralba, Italy 30 C1
Terranova = Ólbia, Italy 30 B2
Terrasini, Italy 30 D6
Terrassa, Spain 32 D7
Terrasson-la-Villedieu, France 20 C5
Terre Haute, U.S.A. 108 F2
Terrebonne B., U.S.A. 113 L9
Terrell, U.S.A. 113 J6
Terrenceville, Canada 103 C9
Terrick Terrick, Australia 94 C4
Terry, U.S.A. 112 B2
Terschelling, Neths. 17 A5
Tersko-Kumskiy Kanal →, Russia 49 H7
Tertenía, Italy 30 C2
Terter → = Tärtär →, Azerbaijan 49 K8
Teruel, Spain 32 E3
Teruel □, Spain 32 E4
Tervel, Bulgaria 41 C11
Tervola, Finland 8 C21
Teryaweyna L., Australia 95 E3
Tešanj, Bos.-H. 42 F3
Teseney, Eritrea 81 D4
Tesha →, Russia 48 C6
Teshio, Japan 54 B10
Teshio-Gawa →, Japan 54 B10
Tešica, Serbia, Yug. 40 C5
Tesiyn Gol →, Mongolia 60 A4
Teslić, Bos.-H. 42 F2
Teslin, Canada 104 A2
Teslin →, Canada 104 A2
Teslin L., Canada 104 A2
Tessalit, Mali 83 A5
Tessaoua, Niger 83 C6
Tessin, Germany 24 A8
Tessit, Mali 83 B5
Test →, U.K. 13 G6
Testa del Gargano, Italy 29 G13
Tét, Hungary 42 C2
Têt →, France 20 F7
Tetachuck L., Canada 104 C3
Tetas, Pta., Chile 126 A1
Tete, Mozam. 87 F3
Tete □, Mozam. 87 F3
Teterev →, Ukraine 47 G6
Teterow, Germany 24 B8
Teteven, Bulgaria 41 D8
Tethul →, Canada 104 A6
Tetiyev, Ukraine 47 H5
Teton →, U.S.A. 114 C8
Tétouan, Morocco 78 A4
Tetovo, Macedonia 40 D4
Tetyukhe Pristan, Russia 54 B7
Tetyushi, Russia 48 C9
Teuco →, Argentina 126 B3
Teulada, Italy 30 D1
Teulon, Canada 105 C9
Teun, Indonesia 63 F7
Teutoburger Wald, Germany 24 C4
Tevere →, Italy 29 G9
Teverya, Israel 75 C4
Teviot →, U.K. 14 F6
Tewantin, Australia 95 D5
Tewkesbury, U.K. 13 F5
Texada I., Canada 104 D4
Texarkana, Ark., U.S.A. 113 J8
Texarkana, Tex., U.S.A. 113 J7
Texas, Australia 95 D5
Texas □, U.S.A. 113 K5
Texas City, U.S.A. 113 L7
Texel, Neths. 17 A4
Texhoma, U.S.A. 113 G4
Texline, U.S.A. 113 G3
Texoma, L., U.S.A. 113 J6
Teykovo, Russia 46 D11
Teza →, Russia 48 B5
Tezin, Afghan. 68 B3
Teziutlán, Mexico 119 D5
Tezpur, India 67 F18
Tezzeron L., Canada 104 C4
Tha-anne →, Canada 105 A10
Tha Deua, Laos 64 D4
Tha Deua, Laos 64 C3
Tha Pla, Thailand 64 D3
Tha Rua, Thailand 64 E3
Tha Sala, Thailand 65 H2
Tha Song Yang, Thailand 64 D1
Thaba Putsoa, Lesotho 89 D4
Thabana Ntlenyana, Lesotho 89 D4
Thabazimbi, S. Africa 89 C4
Thai Binh, Vietnam 64 B6
Thai Muang, Thailand 65 H2
Thai Nguyen, Vietnam 64 B5
Thailand ■, Asia 64 E4
Thailand, G. of, Asia 65 G3
Thakhek, Laos 64 D5
Thal, Pakistan 68 C4
Thal Desert, Pakistan 68 D4
Thala La, Burma 67 E20
Thalabarivat, Cambodia 64 F5
Thallon, Australia 95 D4
Thalwil, Switz. 25 H4
Thames, N.Z. 91 G5
Thames →, Canada 102 D3
Thames →, U.K. 13 F8
Thames →, U.S.A. 111 E12
Thames Estuary, U.K. 13 F8
Thamesford, Canada 110 C4
Thamesville, Canada 110 D3
Than Uyen, Vietnam 64 B4
Thane, India 66 K8
Thanesar, India 68 D7
Thanet, I. of, U.K. 13 F9
Thangoo, Australia 92 C3
Thangool, Australia 94 C5
Thanh Hoa, Vietnam 64 C5
Thanh Hung, Vietnam 65 H5
Thanh Pho Ho Chi Minh = Phanh Bho Ho Chi Minh, Vietnam 65 G6
Thanh Thuy, Vietnam 64 A5
Thanjavur, India 66 P11
Thann, France 19 E14
Thaon-les-Vosges, France 19 D13
Thap Sakae, Thailand 65 G2
Thap Than, Thailand 64 E2
Thar Desert, India 68 F5
Tharad, India 68 G4
Thargomindah, Australia 95 D3
Tharrawaddy, Burma 67 L19
Tharthār, Mileh, Iraq 70 C4
Tharthār, W. ath →, Iraq 70 C4
Thasopoúla, Greece 41 F8
Thásos, Greece 41 F8
That Khe, Vietnam 64 A6
Thatcher, Ariz., U.S.A. 115 K9
Thatcher, Colo., U.S.A. 113 G2
Thaton, Burma 67 L20
Thau, Bassin de, France 20 E7
Thaungdut, Burma 67 G19
Thayer, U.S.A. 113 G9
Thayetmyo, Burma 67 K19
Thazi, Burma 67 J20
The Alberga →, Australia 95 D2
The Bight, Bahamas 121 B4
The Coorong, Australia 95 F2
The Dalles, U.S.A. 114 D3
The English Company's Is., Australia 94 A2
The Frome →, Australia 95 D2
The Grampians, Australia 95 F3
The Great Divide = Great Dividing Ra., Australia 94 C4
The Hague = 's-Gravenhage, Neths. 17 B4
The Hamilton →, Australia 95 D2
The Macumba →, Australia 95 D2
The Neales →, Australia 95 D2
The Officer →, Australia 93 E5
The Pas, Canada 105 C8
The Range, Zimbabwe 87 F3
The Rock, Australia 95 F4
The Salt L., Australia 95 E3
The Stevenson →, Australia 95 D2
The Warburton →, Australia 95 D2
Thebes = Thívai, Greece 38 C5
Thebes, Egypt 80 B3
Thedford, Canada 110 C3
Thedford, U.S.A. 112 E4
Theebine, Australia 95 D5
Thekulthili L., Canada 105 A7
Thelon →, Canada 105 A8
Thénezay, France 18 F6
Thenon, France 20 C5
Theodore, Australia 94 C5
Thepha, Thailand 65 J3
Thérain →, France 19 C9
Theresa, U.S.A. 111 B9
Thermaïkós Kólpos, Greece 40 F6
Thermí, Greece 39 B8
Thermopolis, U.S.A. 114 E9
Thermopylae P., Greece 38 C4
Thesprotía □, Greece 38 B2
Thessalía □, Greece 38 B4
Thessalon, Canada 102 C3
Thessaloníki, Greece 40 F6
Thessaloníki □, Greece 40 F7
Thessaloniki, Gulf of = Thermaïkós Kólpos, Greece 40 F6
Thessaly = Thessalía □, Greece 38 B4
Thetford, U.K. 13 E8
Thetford Mines, Canada 103 C5
Theun →, Laos 64 C5
Theunissen, S. Africa 88 D4
Thevenard, Australia 95 E1
Thiámis →, Greece 38 B2
Thiberville, France 18 C7
Thibodaux, U.S.A. 113 L9
Thicket Portage, Canada 105 B9
Thief River Falls, U.S.A. 112 A6
Thiel Mts., Antarctica 5 E16
Thiene, Italy 29 C8
Thiérache, France 19 C10
Thiers, France 20 C7
Thiès, Senegal 82 C1
Thiesi, Italy 30 B1
Thiet, Sudan 81 F2
Thika, Kenya 86 C4
Thikombia, Fiji 91 B9
Thille-Boubacar, Senegal 82 B1
Thimphu, Bhutan 67 F16
þingvallavatn, Iceland 8 D3
Thionville, France 19 C13
Thíra, Greece 39 E7
Thirasía, Greece 39 E7
Thirsk, U.K. 12 C6
Thisted, Denmark 11 H2
Thistle I., Australia 95 F2
Thívai, Greece 38 C5
Thiviers, France 20 C4
Thizy, France 19 F11
þjórsá →, Iceland 8 E3
Thlewiaza →, Man., Canada 105 B8
Thlewiaza →, N.W.T., Canada 105 A10
Thmar Puok, Cambodia 64 F4
Tho Vinh, Vietnam 64 C5
Thoa →, Canada 105 A7
Thoen, Thailand 64 D2
Thoeng, Thailand 64 C3
Tholdi, Pakistan 69 B7
Thomas, Okla., U.S.A. 113 H5
Thomas, W. Va., U.S.A. 108 F6
Thomas, L., Australia 95 D2
Thomaston, U.S.A. 109 J3
Thomasville, Ala., U.S.A. 109 K2
Thomasville, Ga., U.S.A. 109 K4
Thomasville, N.C., U.S.A. 109 H5
Thompson, Canada 105 B9
Thompson, U.S.A. 115 G9
Thompson →, Canada 104 C4
Thompson →, U.S.A. 112 F8
Thompson Falls, U.S.A. 114 C6
Thompson Landing, Canada 105 A6
Thompson Pk., U.S.A. 114 F2
Thomson's Falls = Nyahururu, Kenya 86 B4
Thônes, France 21 C10
Thonon-les-Bains, France 19 F13
Thorez, Ukraine 47 H10
þórisvatn, Iceland 8 D4
Thornaby on Tees, U.K. 12 C6
Thornbury, Canada 110 B4
Thorne, U.K. 12 D7
Thorold, Canada 110 C5
þórshöfn, Iceland 8 C6
Thouarcé, France 18 E6
Thouars, France 18 F6
Thouet →, France 18 E6
Thouin, C., Australia 92 D2
Thousand Oaks, U.S.A. 117 L8
Thrace, Turkey 41 F10
Thrakikón Pélagos, Greece 41 F8
Three Forks, U.S.A. 114 D8
Three Hills, Canada 104 C6
Three Hummock I., Australia 94 G3
Three Lakes, U.S.A. 112 C10
Three Points, C., Ghana 82 E4
Three Rivers, Australia 93 E2
Three Rivers, Calif., U.S.A. 116 J8
Three Rivers, Tex., U.S.A. 113 L5
Three Sisters, U.S.A. 114 D3
Throssell, L., Australia 93 E3
Throssell Ra., Australia 92 D3
Thuan Hoa, Vietnam 65 H5
Thubun Lakes, Canada 105 A6
Thueyts, France 21 D8
Thuin, Belgium 17 D4
Thuir, France 20 F6
Thule, Greenland 4 B4
Thun, Switz. 25 J3
Thundelarra, Australia 93 E2
Thunder B., U.S.A. 110 B1
Thunder Bay, Canada 102 C2
Thunersee, Switz. 25 J3
Thung Song, Thailand 65 H2
Thunkar, Bhutan 67 F17
Thuong Tra, Vietnam 64 D6
Thur →, Switz. 25 H5
Thurgau □, Switz. 25 H5
Thüringen □, Germany 24 D6
Thüringer Wald, Germany 24 E6
Thurles, Ireland 15 D4
Thurloo Downs, Australia 95 D3
Thurn P., Austria 26 D5
Thurrock □, U.K. 13 F8
Thursday I., Australia 94 A3
Thurso, Canada 102 C4
Thurso, U.K. 14 C5
Thurso →, U.K. 14 C5
Thurston I., Antarctica 5 D16
Thury-Harcourt, France 18 D6
Thutade L., Canada 104 B3
Thy, Denmark 11 H2
Thyborøn, Denmark 11 H2
Thylungra, Australia 95 D3
Thyolo, Malawi 87 F4
Thysville = Mbanza Ngungu, Dem. Rep. of the Congo 84 F2
Ti-n-Barraouene, O. →, Africa 83 B5
Tia, Australia 95 E5
Tian Shan, Asia 60 B3
Tianchang, China 59 A12
Tiandong, China 58 F6
Tian'e, China 58 E6
Tianhe, China 58 E7
Tianjin, China 57 E9
Tiankoura, Burkina Faso 82 C4
Tianlin, China 58 E6
Tianmen, China 59 B9
Tianquan, China 58 B4
Tianshui, China 56 G3
Tiantai, China 59 C13
Tianyang, China 58 F6
Tianzhen, China 56 D8
Tianzhu, China 58 D7
Tianzhuangtai, China 57 D12
Tiaret, Algeria 78 A6
Tiassalé, Ivory C. 82 D4
Tibagi, Brazil 127 A5
Tibagi →, Brazil 127 A5
Tibati, Cameroon 83 D7
Tiber = Tevere →, Italy 29 G9
Tiber Reservoir, U.S.A. 114 B8
Tiberias = Teverya, Israel 75 C4
Tiberias, L. = Yam Kinneret, Israel 75 C4
Tibesti, Chad 79 D9
Tibet = Xizang Zizhiqu □, China 60 C3
Tibet, Plateau of, Asia 52 F12
Tibiao, Phil. 61 F5
Tibiri, Niger 83 C6
Ţibleş, Vf., Romania 43 C9
Ţibleşului, Munţii, Romania 43 C9
Tibnī, Syria 70 C3
Tibooburra, Australia 95 D3
Tibro, Sweden 11 F8
Tiburón, Mexico 118 B2
Ticao I., Phil. 61 E5
Tîchît, Mauritania 82 B3
Ticho, Ethiopia 81 F4
Ticino □, Switz. 25 J4
Ticino →, Italy 25 K5
Ticleni, Romania 43 F8
Ticonderoga, U.S.A. 111 C11
Ticul, Mexico 119 C7
Tidaholm, Sweden 11 F7
Tidan, Sweden 11 F8
Tiddim, Burma 67 H18
Tidjikja, Mauritania 82 B2
Tidore, Indonesia 63 D7
Tiébissou, Ivory C. 82 D3
Tiel, Neths. 17 C5
Tiel, Senegal 82 C1
Tieling, China 57 C12
Tielt, Belgium 17 C3
Tien Shan = Tian Shan, Asia 60 B3
Tien-tsin = Tianjin, China 57 E9
Tien Yen, Vietnam 64 B6
T'ienching = Tianjin, China 57 E9
Tienen, Belgium 17 D4
Tiénigbé, Ivory C. 82 D3
Tientsin = Tianjin, China 57 E9
Tierp, Sweden 10 D11
Tierra Amarilla, Chile 126 B1
Tierra Amarilla, U.S.A. 115 H10
Tierra Colorada, Mexico 119 D5
Tierra de Barros, Spain 35 G4
Tierra de Campos, Spain 34 C6
Tierra del Fuego, I. Gr. de, Argentina 122 J4
Tiétar →, Spain 34 F4
Tieté →, Brazil 127 A5
Tieyon, Australia 95 D1
Tiffin, U.S.A. 108 E4
Tiflis = Tbilisi, Georgia 49 K7
Tifton, U.S.A. 109 K4
Tifu, Indonesia 63 E7
Tighina, Moldova 43 D14
Tigil, Russia 51 D16
Tignish, Canada 103 C7
Tigray □, Ethiopia 81 E4
Tigre →, Peru 124 D4
Tigre →, Venezuela 124 B6
Tigris = Dijlah, Nahr →, Asia 70 D5
Tigveni, Romania 43 E9
Tigyaing, Burma 67 H20
Tîh, Gebel el, Egypt 80 J8
Tijuana, Mexico 117 N9
Tikal, Guatemala 120 C2
Tikamgarh, India 69 G8
Tikhoretsk, Russia 49 H5
Tikhvin, Russia 46 C7
Tiko, Cameroon 83 E6
Tikrīt, Iraq 70 C4
Tiksi, Russia 51 B13
Tilamuta, Indonesia 63 D6
Tilburg, Neths. 17 C5
Tilbury, Canada 102 D3
Tilbury, U.K. 13 F8
Tilcara, Argentina 126 A2
Tilden, Nebr., U.S.A. 112 D6
Tilden, Tex., U.S.A. 113 L5
Tilemses, Niger 83 B5
Tilemsi, Vallée du, Mali 83 B5
Tilhar, India 69 F8
Tilichiki, Russia 51 C17
Tílissos, Greece 36 D7
Till →, U.K. 12 B5
Tillabéri, Niger 83 C5
Tillamook, U.S.A. 114 D2
Tillberga, Sweden 10 E10
Tillia, Niger 83 B5
Tillsonburg, Canada 102 D3
Tillyeria □, Cyprus 36 D11
Tílos, Greece 39 E9
Tilpa, Australia 95 E3
Tilsit = Sovetsk, Russia 9 J19
Tilt →, U.K. 14 E5
Tilton, U.S.A. 111 C13
Tim, Denmark 11 H2

Timagami L., *Canada* 102 C3
Timaru, *N.Z.* 91 L3
Timashevo, *Russia* 48 D10
Timashevsk, *Russia* 49 H4
Timau, *Kenya* 86 B4
Timbákion, *Greece* 36 D6
Timbedgha, *Mauritania* ... 82 B3
Timber Lake, *U.S.A.* 112 C4
Timber Mt., *U.S.A.* 116 H10
Timboon, *Australia* 95 F3
Timbuktu = Tombouctou,
Mali 82 B4
Timétrine Montanges, *Mali* 83 B4
Timfi Óros, *Greece* 38 B2
Timfristós, Óros, *Greece* .. 38 C3
Timi, *Cyprus* 36 E11
Timia, *Niger* 83 B6
Timimoun, *Algeria* 78 C6
Timiş = Tamis →,
Serbia, Yug. 42 F5
Timiş □, *Romania* 42 E6
Timişoara, *Romania* 42 E6
Timmersdala, *Sweden* 11 F7
Timmins, *Canada* 102 C3
Timok →, *Serbia, Yug.* .. 40 B6
Timor, *Indonesia* 63 F7
Timor Sea, *Ind. Oc.* 92 B4
Timor Timur □, *Indonesia* 63 F7
Timrå, *Sweden* 10 B11
Tin Gornai, *Mali* 83 B4
Tin Mt., *U.S.A.* 116 J9
Tina, Khalîg el, *Egypt* ... 80 H8
Tinaca Pt., *Phil.* 61 J6
Tinajo, *Canary Is.* 37 E6
Tinca, *Romania* 42 D6
Tindouf, *Algeria* 78 C4
Tinée →, *France* 21 E11
Tineo, *Spain* 34 B4
Ting Jiang →, *China* 59 E11
Tinggi, Pulau, *Malaysia* ... 65 L5
Tinglev, *Denmark* 11 K3
Tingo Maria, *Peru* 124 E3
Tingsryd, *Sweden* 11 H9
Tingstäde, *Sweden* 11 G12
Tinh Bien, *Vietnam* 65 G5
Tinkurrin, *Australia* 93 F2
Tinnevelly = Tirunelveli,
India 66 Q10
Tinogasta, *Argentina* 126 B2
Tínos, *Greece* 39 D7
Tiñoso, C., *Spain* 33 H3
Tintina, *Argentina* 126 B3
Tintinara, *Australia* 95 F3
Tinto →, *Spain* 35 H4
Tioga, *U.S.A.* 110 E7
Tioman, Pulau, *Malaysia* .. 65 L5
Tione di Trento, *Italy* 28 B7
Tionesta, *U.S.A.* 110 E5
Tior, *Sudan* 81 F3
Tipongpani, *India* 67 F19
Tipperary, *Ireland* 15 D3
Tipperary □, *Ireland* 15 D4
Tipton, *Calif., U.S.A.* ... 116 J7
Tipton, *Ind., U.S.A.* 108 E2
Tipton, *Iowa, U.S.A.* ... 112 E9
Tipton Mt., *U.S.A.* 117 K12
Tiptonville, *U.S.A.* 113 G10
Tīrān, *Iran* 71 C6
Tīrān, *Si. Arabia* 80 B3
Tirana, *Albania* 40 E3
Tiranë = Tirana, *Albania* . 40 E3
Tirano, *Italy* 28 B7
Tiraspol, *Moldova* 43 D14
Tirdout, *Mali* 83 B4
Tire, *Turkey* 39 C9
Tirebolu, *Turkey* 73 B8
Tiree, *U.K.* 14 E2
Tiree, Passage of, *U.K.* .. 14 E2
Tîrgovişte = Târgovişte,
Romania 43 F10
Tîrgu-Jiu = Târgu-Jiu,
Romania 43 E8
Tîrgu Mureş = Târgu
Mureş, *Romania* 43 D9
Tirich Mir, *Pakistan* 66 A7
Tiriolo, *Italy* 31 D9
Tírnavos, *Greece* 38 B4
Tirodi, *India* 66 J11
Tirol □, *Austria* 26 D3
Tirso →, *Italy* 30 C1
Tirstrup, *Denmark* 11 H4
Tiruchchirappalli, *India* .. 66 P11
Tirunelveli, *India* 66 Q10
Tirupati, *India* 66 N11
Tiruppur, *India* 66 P10
Tiruvannamalai, *India* ... 66 N11
Tisa →, *Serbia, Yug.* 42 E5
Tisdale, *Canada* 105 C8
Tishomingo, *U.S.A.* 113 H6
Tisjön, *Sweden* 10 D7
Tisnaren, *Sweden* 11 F9
Tišnov, *Czech Rep.* 27 B9
Tisovec, *Slovak Rep.* 27 C12
Tisza = Tisa →,
Serbia, Yug. 42 E5
Tiszaföldvár, *Hungary* ... 42 D5
Tiszafüred, *Hungary* 42 C6
Tiszalök, *Hungary* 42 B6
Tiszavasvári, *Hungary* ... 42 C6
Tit-Ary, *Russia* 51 B13
Titaguas, *Spain* 32 F3
Titel, *Serbia, Yug.* 42 E5
Tithwal, *Pakistan* 69 B5
Titicaca, L., *S. Amer.* 122 E4
Titisee, *Germany* 25 H4

Titiwa, *Nigeria* 83 C7
Tito, *Italy* 31 B8
Titograd = Podgorica,
Montenegro, Yug. 40 D3
Titova Korenica, *Croatia* . 29 D12
Titu, *Romania* 43 F10
Titule,
Dem. Rep. of the Congo 86 B2
Titusville, *Fla., U.S.A.* ... 109 L5
Titusville, *Pa., U.S.A.* ... 110 E5
Tivaouane, *Senegal* 82 C1
Tivat, *Montenegro, Yug.* .. 40 D2
Tiverton, *U.K.* 13 G4
Tívoli, *Italy* 29 G9
Tiyo, *Eritrea* 81 E5
Tizi-Ouzou, *Algeria* 78 A6
Tizimín, *Mexico* 119 C7
Tjæreborg, *Denmark* 11 J2
Tjällmo, *Sweden* 11 F9
Tjeggelvas, *Sweden* 8 C17
Tjirebon = Cirebon,
Indonesia 63 G13
Tjörn, *Sweden* 11 F5
Tkibuli = Tqibuli, *Georgia* 49 J6
Tkvarcheli = Tqvarcheli,
Georgia 49 J5
Tlacotalpan, *Mexico* 119 D5
Tlahualilo, *Mexico* 118 B4
Tlaquepaque, *Mexico* 118 C4
Tlaxcala, *Mexico* 119 D5
Tlaxcala □, *Mexico* 119 D5
Tlaxiaco, *Mexico* 119 D5
Tlell, *Canada* 104 C2
Tlemcen, *Algeria* 78 B5
Tłuszcz, *Poland* 45 F8
Tlyarata, *Russia* 49 J8
To Bong, *Vietnam* 64 F7
Toad →, *Canada* 104 B4
Toamasina, *Madag.* 89 B8
Toamasina □, *Madag.* ... 89 B8
Toay, *Argentina* 126 D3
Toba, *Japan* 55 G8
Toba, Danau, *Indonesia* .. 62 D1
Toba Kakar, *Pakistan* 68 D3
Toba Tek Singh, *Pakistan* . 68 D5
Tobago, *W. Indies* 121 D7
Tobarra, *Spain* 33 G3
Tobelo, *Indonesia* 63 D7
Tobermorey, *Australia* ... 94 C2
Tobermory, *Canada* 102 C3
Tobermory, *U.K.* 14 E2
Tobin, *U.S.A.* 116 F5
Tobin, L., *Australia* 92 D4
Tobin L., *Canada* 105 C8
Toboali, *Indonesia* 62 E3
Tobol →, *Russia* 50 D7
Toboli, *Indonesia* 63 E6
Tobolsk, *Russia* 50 D7
Tobruk = Tubruq, *Libya* . 79 B10
Tobyhanna, *U.S.A.* 111 E9
Tobyl = Tobol →, *Russia* 50 D7
Tocantinópolis, *Brazil* ... 125 E9
Tocantins □, *Brazil* 125 F9
Tocantins →, *Brazil* 122 D6
Toccoa, *U.S.A.* 109 H4
Toce →, *Italy* 28 C5
Tochigi, *Japan* 55 F9
Tochigi □, *Japan* 55 F9
Tocina, *Spain* 35 H5
Töcksfors, *Sweden* 10 E5
Tocopilla, *Chile* 126 A1
Tocumwal, *Australia* 95 F4
Tocuyo →, *Venezuela* ... 124 A5
Todd →, *Australia* 94 C2
Todeli, *Indonesia* 63 E6
Todenyang, *Kenya* 86 B4
Todi, *Italy* 29 F9
Todos os Santos, B. de,
Brazil 125 F11
Todos Santos, *Mexico* ... 118 C2
Todtnau, *Germany* 25 H3
Toe Hd., *U.K.* 14 D1
Toecé, *Burkina Faso* 83 C4
Tofield, *Canada* 104 C6
Tofino, *Canada* 104 D3
Tofua, *Tonga* 91 D11
Tōgane, *Japan* 55 G10
Togba, *Mauritania* 82 B2
Togian, Kepulauan,
Indonesia 63 E6
Togliatti, *Russia* 48 D9
Togo ■, *W. Afr.* 83 D5
Togtoh, *China* 56 D6
Tohma →, *Turkey* 72 C7
Tōhoku □, *Japan* 54 E10
Toinya, *Sudan* 81 F2
Tojikiston = Tajikistan ■,
Asia 50 F8
Tojo, *Indonesia* 63 E6
Tōjō, *Japan* 55 G6
Tokachi-Dake, *Japan* ... 54 C11
Tokachi-Gawa →, *Japan* . 54 C11
Tokaj, *Hungary* 42 B6
Tokala, *Indonesia* 63 E6
Tōkamachi, *Japan* 55 F9
Tokanui, *N.Z.* 91 M2
Tokar, *Sudan* 80 D4
Tokara-Rettō, *Japan* 55 K4
Tokarahi, *N.Z.* 91 L3
Tokashiki-Shima, *Japan* .. 55 L3
Tokat, *Turkey* 72 B7
Tŏkchŏn, *N. Korea* 57 E14
Tokeland, *U.S.A.* 116 D3
Tokelau Is., *Pac. Oc.* 96 H10
Tokmak, *Kyrgyzstan* 50 E8

Tokmak, *Ukraine* 47 J8
Toko Ra., *Australia* 94 C2
Tokoro-Gawa →, *Japan* . 54 B12
Tokuno-Shima, *Japan* ... 55 L4
Tokushima, *Japan* 55 G7
Tokushima □, *Japan* 55 H7
Tokuyama, *Japan* 55 G5
Tōkyō, *Japan* 55 G9
Tolaga Bay, *N.Z.* 91 H7
Tolbukhin = Dobrich,
Bulgaria 41 C11
Toledo, *Spain* 34 F6
Toledo, *Ohio, U.S.A.* ... 108 E4
Toledo, *Oreg., U.S.A.* ... 114 D2
Toledo, *Wash., U.S.A.* .. 114 C2
Toledo, Montes de, *Spain* 35 F6
Tolentino, *Italy* 29 E10
Tolfa, *Italy* 29 F8
Toliara, *Madag.* 89 C7
Toliara □, *Madag.* 89 C8
Tolima, *Colombia* 124 C3
Tolitoli, *Indonesia* 63 D6
Tolkmicko, *Poland* 44 D6
Tollarp, *Sweden* 11 J7
Tollensee, *Germany* 24 B9
Tollhouse, *U.S.A.* 116 H7
Tolmachevo, *Russia* 46 C5
Tolmezzo, *Italy* 29 B10
Tolmin, *Slovenia* 29 B10
Tolna, *Hungary* 42 D3
Tolna □, *Hungary* 42 D3
Tolo, Teluk, *Indonesia* .. 63 E6
Tolochin = Talachyn,
Belarus 46 E5
Tolosa, *Spain* 32 B2
Tolox, *Spain* 35 J6
Toluca, *Mexico* 119 D5
Tom Burke, *S. Africa* ... 89 C4
Tom Price, *Australia* 92 D2
Tomah, *U.S.A.* 112 D9
Tomahawk, *U.S.A.* 112 C10
Tomai, *Moldova* 43 D13
Tomakomai, *Japan* 54 C10
Tomales, *U.S.A.* 116 G4
Tomales B., *U.S.A.* 116 G3
Tomar, *Portugal* 35 F2
Tómaros, Óros, *Greece* .. 38 B2
Tomarza, *Turkey* 72 C6
Tomaszów Lubelski,
Poland 45 H10
Tomaszów Mazowiecki,
Poland 45 G7
Tomatlán, *Mexico* 118 D3
Tombador, Serra do, *Brazil* 124 F7
Tombé, *Sudan* 81 F3
Tombigbee →, *U.S.A.* .. 109 K2
Tombouctou, *Mali* 82 B4
Tombstone, *U.S.A.* 115 L8
Tombua, *Angola* 88 B1
Tomé, *Chile* 126 D1
Tomelilla, *Sweden* 11 J7
Tomelloso, *Spain* 35 F7
Tomingley, *Australia* 95 E4
Tomini, *Indonesia* 63 D6
Tomini, Teluk, *Indonesia* . 63 E6
Tominian, *Mali* 82 C4
Tomiño, *Spain* 34 D2
Tomintoul, *U.K.* 14 D5
Tomislavgrad, *Bos.-H.* .. 42 G2
Tomkinson Ranges,
Australia 93 E4
Tommot, *Russia* 51 D13
Tomnop Ta Suos,
Cambodia 65 G5
Tomo →, *Colombia* 124 B5
Toms Place, *U.S.A.* 116 H8
Toms River, *U.S.A.* 111 G10
Tomsk, *Russia* 50 D9
Tomtabacken, *Sweden* .. 11 G8
Tona, *Spain* 32 D7
Tonalá, *Mexico* 119 D6
Tonale, Passo del, *Italy* .. 28 B7
Tonalea, *U.S.A.* 115 H8
Tonantins, *Brazil* 124 D5
Tonasket, *U.S.A.* 114 B4
Tonawanda, *U.S.A.* 110 D6
Tonbridge, *U.K.* 13 F8
Tondano, *Indonesia* 63 D6
Tondela, *Portugal* 34 E2
Tønder, *Denmark* 11 K2
Tondi Kiwindi, *Niger* ... 83 C5
Tondibi, *Mali* 83 B4
Tonekābon, *Iran* 71 B6
Tong Xian, *China* 56 E9
Tonga ■, *Pac. Oc.* 91 D11
Tonga Trench, *Pac. Oc.* . 96 J10
Tongaat, *S. Africa* 89 D5
Tong'an, *China* 59 E12
Tongareva, *Cook Is.* 97 H12
Tongatapu, *Tonga* 91 E12
Tongbai, *China* 59 A9
Tongcheng, *Anhui, China* . 59 B11
Tongcheng, *Hubei, China* . 59 C9
Tongchŏn-ni, *N. Korea* .. 57 E14
Tongchuan, *China* 56 G5
Tongdao, *China* 58 D7
Tongeren, *Belgium* 17 D5
Tonggu, *China* 59 C10
Tongguan, *China* 56 G6
Tonghai, *China* 58 E4
Tonghua, *China* 57 D13
Tongjiang, *Heilongjiang,*
China 60 B8
Tongjiang, *Sichuan, China* 58 B6
Tongjosŏn Man, *N. Korea* 57 E15
Tongking, G. of = Tonkin,
G. of, *Asia* 64 C7

Tongliang, *China* 58 C6
Tongliao, *China* 57 C12
Tongling, *China* 59 B11
Tonglu, *China* 59 C12
Tongnae, *S. Korea* 57 G15
Tongnan, *China* 58 B5
Tongobory, *Madag.* 89 C7
Tongoy, *Chile* 126 C1
Tongren, *China* 58 D7
Tongres = Tongeren,
Belgium 17 D5
Tongsa Dzong, *Bhutan* .. 67 F17
Tongue, *U.K.* 14 C4
Tongue →, *U.S.A.* 112 B2
Tongwei, *China* 56 G3
Tongxin, *China* 56 F3
Tongyang, *N. Korea* 57 E14
Tongyu, *China* 57 B12
Tongzi, *China* 58 C6
Tonj, *Sudan* 81 F2
Tonk, *India* 68 F6
Tonkawa, *U.S.A.* 113 G6
Tonkin = Bac Phan,
Vietnam 64 B5
Tonkin, G. of, *Asia* 64 C7
Tonle Sap, *Cambodia* ... 64 F5
Tonnay-Charente, *France* . 20 C3
Tonneins, *France* 20 D4
Tonnerre, *France* 19 E10
Tönning, *Germany* 24 A4
Tono, *Japan* 54 E10
Tonopah, *U.S.A.* 115 G5
Tonosí, *Panama* 120 E3
Tønsberg, *Norway* 9 G14
Tonya, *Turkey* 73 B8
Toobanna, *Australia* 94 B4
Toodyay, *Australia* 93 F2
Tooele, *U.S.A.* 114 F7
Toompine, *Australia* 95 D3
Toonpan, *Australia* 94 B4
Toora, *Australia* 95 F4
Toora-Khem, *Russia* 51 D10
Toowoomba, *Australia* .. 95 D5
Topalu, *Romania* 43 F13
Topaz, *U.S.A.* 116 G7
Topeka, *U.S.A.* 112 F7
Topl'a →, *Slovak Rep.* .. 27 C14
Topley, *Canada* 104 C3
Toplica →, *Serbia, Yug.* . 40 C5
Topliţa, *Romania* 43 D10
Topocalma, Pta., *Chile* .. 126 C1
Topock, *U.S.A.* 117 L12
Topola, *Serbia, Yug.* 40 B4
Topolčani, *Macedonia* ... 40 E5
Topol'čany, *Slovak Rep.* . 27 C11
Topolnitsa →, *Bulgaria* .. 41 D8
Topolobampo, *Mexico* .. 118 B3
Topoloveni, *Romania* ... 43 F10
Topolovgrad, *Bulgaria* .. 41 D10
Topolváțu Mare, *Romania* 42 E6
Toppenish, *U.S.A.* 114 C3
Topraisar, *Romania* 43 F13
Topusko, *Croatia* 29 C12
Torà, *Spain* 32 D6
Tora Kit, *Sudan* 81 E3
Toraka Vestale, *Madag.* . 89 B7
Torata, *Peru* 124 G4
Torbalı, *Turkey* 39 C9
Torbay, *Canada* 103 C9
Torbay □, *U.K.* 13 G4
Torbjörntorp, *Sweden* ... 11 F7
Tordesillas, *Spain* 34 D6
Torekov, *Sweden* 11 H6
Torellò, *Spain* 32 C7
Toreno, *Spain* 34 C4
Torfaen □, *U.K.* 13 F4
Torgau, *Germany* 24 D8
Torgelow, *Germany* 24 B10
Torhamn, *Sweden* 11 H9
Torhout, *Belgium* 17 C3
Tori, *Ethiopia* 81 F3
Tori-Shima, *Japan* 55 J10
Torigni-sur-Vire, *France* . 18 C6
Torija, *Spain* 32 E1
Torin, *Mexico* 118 B2
Torino, *Italy* 28 C4
Torit, *Sudan* 81 G3
Torkamān, *Iran* 73 D12
Torkovichi, *Russia* 46 C6
Tormac, *Romania* 42 E6
Tormes →, *Spain* 34 D4
Tornado Mt., *Canada* ... 104 D6
Tornal'a, *Slovak Rep.* ... 27 C13
Torne älv →, *Sweden* ... 8 D21
Torneå = Tornio, *Finland* 8 D21
Torneträsk, *Sweden* 8 B18
Tornio, *Finland* 8 D21
Tornionjoki →, *Finland* . 8 D21
Tornquist, *Argentina* ... 126 D3
Toro, *Baleares, Spain* ... 37 B11
Toro, *Zamora, Spain* 34 D5
Torö, *Sweden* 11 F11
Toro, Cerro del, *Chile* ... 126 B2
Toro Pk., *U.S.A.* 117 M10
Törökszentmiklós, *Hungary* 42 C5
Toroníios Kólpos, *Greece* . 40 F7
Toronto, *Canada* 102 D4
Toronto, *U.S.A.* 110 F4
Toropets, *Russia* 46 D6
Tororo, *Uganda* 86 B3
Torquay, *Canada* 105 D8
Torquay, *U.K.* 13 G4
Torquemada, *Spain* 34 C6
Torrance, *U.S.A.* 117 M8
Torrão, *Portugal* 35 G2

Torre Annunziata, *Italy* .. 31 B7
Torre de Moncorvo,
Portugal 34 D3
Torre del Campo, *Spain* . 35 H7
Torre del Greco, *Italy* ... 31 B7
Torre del Mar, *Spain* ... 35 J6
Torre-Pacheco, *Spain* ... 33 H4
Torre Péllice, *Italy* 28 D4
Torreblanca, *Spain* 32 E5
Torrecampo, *Spain* 35 G6
Torrecilla en Cameros,
Spain 32 C2
Torredembarra, *Spain* ... 32 D6
Torredonjimeno, *Spain* .. 35 H7
Torrejón de Ardoz, *Spain* . 34 E7
Torrejoncillo, *Spain* 34 F4
Torrelaguna, *Spain* 34 E7
Torrelavega, *Spain* 34 B6
Torremaggiore, *Italy* 29 G12
Torremolinos, *Spain* 35 J6
Torrens, L., *Australia* ... 95 E2
Torrens Cr. →, *Australia* . 94 C4
Torrens Creek, *Australia* . 94 C4
Torrent, *Spain* 33 F4
Torrenueva, *Spain* 35 G7
Torreón, *Mexico* 118 B4
Torreperogil, *Spain* 35 G7
Torres, *Mexico* 118 B2
Torres Novas, *Portugal* .. 35 F2
Torres Strait, *Australia* .. 96 H6
Torres Vedras, *Portugal* . 35 F1
Torrevieja, *Spain* 33 H4
Torrey, *U.S.A.* 115 G8
Torridge →, *U.K.* 13 G3
Torridon, L., *U.K.* 14 D3
Torrijos, *Spain* 34 F6
Tørring, *Denmark* 11 J3
Torrington, *Conn., U.S.A.* 111 E11
Torrington, *Wyo., U.S.A.* 112 D2
Torroella de Montgrì, *Spain* 32 C8
Torrox, *Spain* 35 J7
Torsås, *Sweden* 11 H9
Torsby, *Sweden* 10 D6
Torshälla, *Sweden* 10 E10
Tórshavn, *Færoe Is.* 8 E9
Torslanda, *Sweden* 11 G5
Torsö, *Sweden* 11 F7
Tortola, *Virgin Is.* 121 C7
Tórtoles de Esgueva, *Spain* 34 D6
Tortolì, *Italy* 30 C2
Tortona, *Italy* 28 D5
Tortorici, *Italy* 31 D7
Tortosa, *Spain* 32 E5
Tortosa, C., *Spain* 32 E5
Tortosendo, *Portugal* ... 34 E3
Tortue, I. de la, *Haiti* ... 121 B5
Tortum, *Turkey* 73 B9
Torūd, *Iran* 71 C7
Torul, *Turkey* 73 B8
Toruń, *Poland* 45 E5
Toruń □, *Poland* 45 E5
Tory I., *Ireland* 15 A3
Torysa →, *Slovak Rep.* .. 27 C14
Torzhok, *Russia* 46 D8
Torzym, *Poland* 45 F2
Tosa, *Japan* 55 H6
Tosa-Shimizu, *Japan* ... 55 H6
Tosa-Wan, *Japan* 55 H6
Toscana □, *Italy* 28 E8
Toscano, Arcipelago, *Italy* 28 F7
Toshkent, *Uzbekistan* ... 50 E7
Tosno, *Russia* 46 C6
Tossa de Mar, *Spain* ... 32 D7
Tösse, *Sweden* 11 F6
Tostado, *Argentina* 126 B3
Tostedt, *Germany* 24 B5
Tostón, Pta. de, *Canary Is.* 37 F5
Tosu, *Japan* 55 H5
Tosya, *Turkey* 72 B6
Toszek, *Poland* 45 H5
Totana, *Spain* 33 H3
Totebo, *Sweden* 11 G10
Toteng, *Botswana* 88 C3
Tôtes, *France* 18 C8
Tótkomlós, *Hungary* ... 42 D5
Totma, *Russia* 50 D5
Totnes, *U.K.* 13 G4
Totonicapán, *Guatemala* 120 D1
Totten Glacier, *Antarctica* 5 C8
Tottenham, *Australia* ... 95 E4
Tottenham, *Canada* 110 B5
Tottori, *Japan* 55 G7
Tottori □, *Japan* 55 G7
Touba, *Ivory C.* 82 D3
Toubkal, Djebel, *Morocco* 78 B4
Toucy, *France* 19 E10
Tougan, *Burkina Faso* .. 82 C4
Touggourt, *Algeria* 78 B7
Tougué, *Guinea* 82 C2
Toul, *France* 19 D12
Toulepleu, *Ivory C.* 82 D3
Toulon, *France* 21 E9
Toulouse, *France* 20 E5
Toummo, *Niger* 79 D8
Toumodi, *Ivory C.* 82 D3
Tounan, *Taiwan* 59 F13
Toungoo, *Burma* 67 K20
Touques →, *France* ... 18 C7
Touraine, *France* 18 E7
Tourane = Da Nang,
Vietnam 64 D7
Tourcoing, *France* 19 B10
Touriñán, C., *Spain* 34 B1
Tournai, *Belgium* 17 D3
Tournan-en-Brie, *France* .. 19 D9

Tournay, France 20 E4
Tournon-St-Martin, France 18 F7
Tournon-sur-Rhône, France 21 C8
Tournus, France 19 F11
Tours, France 18 E7
Touwsrivier, S. Africa 88 E3
Tovarkovskiy, Russia 46 F10
Tovuz, Azerbaijan 49 K7
Towada, Japan 54 D10
Towada-Ko, Japan 54 D10
Towamba, Australia 95 F4
Towanda, U.S.A. 111 E8
Towang, India 67 F17
Tower, U.S.A. 112 B8
Towerhill Cr. →, Australia 94 C3
Towner, U.S.A. 112 A4
Townsend, U.S.A. 114 C8
Townshend I., Australia 94 C5
Townsville, Australia 94 B4
Towson, U.S.A. 108 F7
Toya-Ko, Japan 54 C10
Toyah, U.S.A. 113 K3
Toyahvale, U.S.A. 113 K3
Toyama, Japan 55 F8
Toyama □, Japan 55 F8
Toyama-Wan, Japan 55 F8
Toyohashi, Japan 55 G8
Toyokawa, Japan 55 G8
Toyonaka, Japan 55 G7
Toyooka, Japan 55 G7
Toyota, Japan 55 G8
Tozeur, Tunisia 78 B7
Tqibuli, Georgia 49 J6
Tqvarcheli, Georgia 49 J5
Trá Li = Tralee, Ireland 15 D2
Tra On, Vietnam 65 H5
Trabancos →, Spain 34 D5
Traben-Trarbach, Germany 25 F3
Trabzon, Turkey 73 B8
Tracadie, Canada 103 C7
Tracy, Calif., U.S.A. 116 H5
Tracy, Minn., U.S.A. 112 C7
Tradate, Italy 28 C5
Trafalgar, C., Spain 35 J4
Traian, Brăila, Romania 43 E12
Traian, Tulcea, Romania 43 E13
Trail, Canada 104 D5
Trainor L., Canada 104 A4
Trákhonas, Cyprus 36 D12
Tralee, Ireland 15 D2
Tralee B., Ireland 15 D2
Tramore, Ireland 15 D4
Tramore B., Ireland 15 D4
Tran Ninh, Cao Nguyen, Laos 64 C4
Tranås, Sweden 11 F8
Tranbjerg, Denmark 11 H4
Trancas, Argentina 126 B2
Trancoso, Portugal 34 E3
Tranebjerg, Denmark 11 J4
Tranemo, Sweden 11 G7
Trang, Thailand 65 J2
Trangahy, Madag. 89 B7
Trangan, Indonesia 63 F8
Trangie, Australia 95 E4
Trångsviken, Sweden 10 A7
Trani, Italy 31 A9
Tranoroa, Madag. 89 C8
Tranqueras, Uruguay 127 C4
Trans Nzoia □, Kenya 86 B4
Transantarctic Mts., Antarctica 5 E12
Transcona, Canada 105 D9
Transilvania, Romania 43 D9
Transilvanian Alps = Carpaţii Meridionali, Romania 43 E9
Transtrand, Sweden 10 C7
Transtrandsfjällen, Sweden 10 C6
Transylvania = Transilvania, Romania 43 D9
Trápani, Italy 30 D5
Trapper Pk., U.S.A. 114 D6
Traralgon, Australia 95 F4
Trarza, Mauritania 82 B2
Trasacco, Italy 29 G10
Trăscău, Munţii, Romania 43 D8
Trasimeno, L., Italy 29 E9
Träslövsläge, Sweden 11 G6
Trasvase Tajo-Segura, Canal de, Spain 32 E2
Trat, Thailand 65 F4
Traun, Austria 26 C7
Traunreut, Germany 25 H8
Traunsee, Austria 26 D6
Traunstein, Germany 25 H8
Traveller's L., Australia 95 E3
Travemünde, Germany 24 B6
Travers, Mt., N.Z. 91 K4
Traverse City, U.S.A. 108 C3
Travnik, Bos.-H. 42 F2
Trayning, Australia 93 F2
Trbovlje, Slovenia 29 B12
Trébbia →, Italy 28 C6
Trebel →, Germany 24 B9
Trébeurden, France 18 D3
Třebíč, Czech Rep. 26 B8
Trebinje, Bos.-H. 40 D2
Trebisacce, Italy 31 C9
Trebišnjica →, Bos.-H. 40 D2
Trebišov, Slovak Rep. 27 C14
Trebižat →, Bos.-H. 29 E14
Trebnje, Slovenia 29 C12
Třeboň, Czech Rep. 26 B7
Trebujena, Spain 35 J4
Trecate, Italy 28 C5

Trece Martires, Phil. 61 D4
Tregaron, U.K. 13 E4
Tregnago, Italy 29 C8
Tregrosse Is., Australia 94 B5
Tréguier, France 18 D3
Trégunc, France 18 E3
Treherne, Canada 105 D9
Tréia, Italy 29 E10
Treignac, France 20 C5
Treinta y Tres, Uruguay 127 C5
Treis-karden, Germany 25 E3
Treklyano, Bulgaria 40 D6
Trélazé, France 18 E6
Trelew, Argentina 128 E3
Trélissac, France 20 C4
Trelleborg, Sweden 11 J7
Tremadog Bay, U.K. 12 E3
Tremiti, Italy 29 F12
Tremonton, U.S.A. 114 F7
Tremp, Spain 32 C5
Trenche →, Canada 102 C5
Trenčiansky □, Slovak Rep. 27 C11
Trenčín, Slovak Rep. 27 C11
Trenggalek, Indonesia 63 H14
Trenque Lauquen, Argentina 126 D3
Trent →, U.K. 12 D7
Trentino-Alto Adige □, Italy 29 B8
Trento, Italy 28 B8
Trenton, Canada 102 D4
Trenton, Mo., U.S.A. 112 E8
Trenton, N.J., U.S.A. 111 F10
Trenton, Nebr., U.S.A. 112 E4
Trenton, Tenn., U.S.A. 113 H10
Trepassey, Canada 103 C9
Trepuzzi, Italy 31 B11
Tres Arroyos, Argentina 126 D3
Três Corações, Brazil 127 A6
Três Lagoas, Brazil 125 H8
Tres Marías, Mexico 118 C3
Tres Montes, C., Chile 128 F1
Tres Pinos, U.S.A. 116 J5
Três Pontas, Brazil 127 A6
Tres Puentes, Chile 126 B1
Tres Puntas, C., Argentina 128 F3
Três Rios, Brazil 127 A7
Tres Valles, Mexico 119 D5
Tresco, U.K. 13 H1
Treska →, Macedonia 40 E5
Treskavica, Bos.-H. 42 G3
Trespaderne, Spain 34 C7
Trets, France 21 E9
Treuchtlingen, Germany 25 G6
Treuenbrietzen, Germany 24 C8
Trevi, Italy 29 F9
Treviglio, Italy 28 C6
Trevínca, Peña, Spain 34 C4
Treviso, Italy 29 C9
Trévoux, France 21 C8
Trgovište, Serbia, Yug. 40 D6
Triabunna, Australia 94 G4
Triánda, Greece 36 C10
Triaucourt-en-Argonne, France 19 D12
Tribsees, Germany 24 A8
Tribulation, C., Australia 94 B4
Tribune, U.S.A. 112 F4
Tricárico, Italy 31 B9
Tricase, Italy 31 C11
Trichinopoly = Tiruchchirappalli, India 66 P11
Trichur, India 66 P10
Trida, Australia 95 E4
Trier, Germany 25 F2
Trieste, Italy 29 C10
Trieste, G. di, Italy 29 C10
Trieux →, France 18 D3
Triggiano, Italy 31 A9
Triglav, Slovenia 29 B10
Trigno →, Italy 29 F11
Trigueros, Spain 35 H4
Tríkeri, Greece 38 B5
Trikhonis, Límni, Greece 38 C3
Tríkkala, Greece 38 B3
Tríkkala □, Greece 38 B3
Trikomo, Cyprus 36 D12
Trikora, Puncak, Indonesia 63 E9
Trilj, Croatia 29 E13
Trillo, Spain 32 E2
Trim, Ireland 15 C5
Trincomalee, Sri Lanka 66 Q12
Trindade, Brazil 125 G9
Trindade, I., Atl. Oc. 2 F8
Trinidad, Bolivia 124 F6
Trinidad, Bolivia 124 F6
Trinidad, Cuba 120 B4
Trinidad, Uruguay 126 C4
Trinidad, U.S.A. 113 G2
Trinidad, W. Indies 121 D7
Trinidad →, Mexico 119 D5
Trinidad & Tobago ■, W. Indies 121 D7
Trinitápoli, Italy 31 A9
Trinity, Canada 103 C9
Trinity →, Calif., U.S.A. 114 F2
Trinity →, Tex., U.S.A. 113 L7
Trinity B., Canada 103 C9
Trinity Range, U.S.A. 114 F4

Tripoli = Tarābulus, Lebanon 75 A4
Tripoli = Tarābulus, Libya 79 B8
Trípolis, Greece 38 D4
Tripolitania, Libya 76 C5
Tripp, U.S.A. 112 D6
Tripura □, India 67 H18
Tripylos, Cyprus 36 E11
Trischen, Germany 24 A4
Tristan da Cunha, Atl. Oc. 77 K2
Trivandrum, India 66 Q10
Trivento, Italy 29 G11
Trnava, Slovak Rep. 27 C10
Trnavský □, Slovak Rep. 27 C10
Troarn, France 18 C6
Trochu, Canada 104 C6
Trodely I., Canada 102 B4
Troezen, Greece 38 D5
Trogir, Croatia 29 E13
Troglav, Croatia 29 E13
Tróia, Italy 31 A8
Troilus, L., Canada 102 B5
Troina, Italy 31 E7
Trois-Pistoles, Canada 103 C6
Trois-Rivières, Canada 102 C5
Troisdorf, Germany 24 E3
Troitsk, Russia 50 D7
Troitsko Pechorsk, Russia 50 C6
Trölladyngja, Iceland 8 D5
Trollhättan, Sweden 11 F6
Trollheimen, Norway 8 E13
Trombetas →, Brazil 125 D7
Tromsø, Norway 8 B18
Trona, U.S.A. 117 K9
Tronador, Argentina 128 E2
Trøndelag, Norway 8 D14
Trondheim, Norway 8 E14
Trondheimsfjorden, Norway 8 E14
Trönninge, Sweden 11 H6
Tronto →, Italy 29 F10
Troodos, Cyprus 36 E11
Troon, U.K. 14 F4
Tropea, Italy 31 D8
Tropic, U.S.A. 115 H7
Tropoja, Albania 40 D4
Trosa, Sweden 11 F11
Trostan, U.K. 15 A5
Trostberg, Germany 25 G8
Trostyanets, Ukraine 47 G8
Troup, U.S.A. 113 J7
Trout →, Canada 104 A5
Trout L., N.W.T., Canada 104 A4
Trout L., Ont., Canada 105 C10
Trout Lake, Mich., U.S.A. 102 C2
Trout Lake, Wash., U.S.A. 116 E5
Trout River, Canada 103 C8
Trouville-sur-Mer, France 18 C7
Trowbridge, U.K. 13 F5
Troy, Turkey 39 B8
Troy, Ala., U.S.A. 109 K3
Troy, Idaho, U.S.A. 114 C5
Troy, Kans., U.S.A. 112 F7
Troy, Mo., U.S.A. 112 F9
Troy, Mont., U.S.A. 114 B6
Troy, N.Y., U.S.A. 111 D11
Troy, Ohio, U.S.A. 108 E3
Troyan, Bulgaria 41 D8
Troyes, France 19 D11
Trpanj, Croatia 29 E14
Trstenik, Serbia, Yug. 40 C5
Trubchevsk, Russia 47 F7
Trucial States = United Arab Emirates ■, Asia 71 F7
Truckee, U.S.A. 116 F6
Trudfront, Russia 49 H8
Trudovoye, Russia 54 C6
Trujillo, Honduras 120 C2
Trujillo, Peru 124 E3
Trujillo, Spain 35 F5
Trujillo, U.S.A. 113 H2
Trujillo, Venezuela 124 B4
Truk, Pac. Oc. 96 G7
Trumann, U.S.A. 113 H9
Trumbull, Mt., U.S.A. 115 H7
Trǔn, Bulgaria 40 D6
Trun, France 18 D7
Trundle, Australia 95 E4
Trung-Phan = Annam, Vietnam 64 E7
Truro, Canada 103 C7
Truro, U.K. 13 G2
Truskavets, Ukraine 47 H2
Truslove, Australia 93 F3
Trǔstenik, Bulgaria 41 C8
Trustrup, Denmark 11 H4
Truth or Consequences, U.S.A. 115 K10
Trutnov, Czech Rep. 26 A8
Truyère →, France 20 D6
Tryavna, Bulgaria 41 D9
Tryon, U.S.A. 109 H4
Tryonville, U.S.A. 110 E5
Trzcianka, Poland 45 E3
Trzciel, Poland 45 F2
Trzcińsko Zdrój, Poland 45 F1
Trzebiatów, Poland 44 D2
Trzebiez, Poland 44 E1
Trzebnica, Poland 45 G4
Trzemeszno, Poland 45 F4
Tržič, Slovenia 29 B11

Tsarevo = Michurin, Bulgaria 41 D11
Tsarevo, Bulgaria 41 D9
Tsaritsáni, Greece 38 B4
Tsau, Botswana 88 C3
Tsebrykove, Ukraine 47 J6
Tselinograd = Aqmola, Kazakstan 50 D8
Tsetserleg, Mongolia 60 B5
Tshabong, Botswana 88 D3
Tshane, Botswana 88 C3
Tshela, Dem. Rep. of the Congo 84 E2
Tshesebe, Botswana 89 C4
Tshibeke, Dem. Rep. of the Congo 86 C2
Tshibinda, Dem. Rep. of the Congo 86 C2
Tshikapa, Dem. Rep. of the Congo 84 F4
Tshilenge, Dem. Rep. of the Congo 86 D1
Tshinsenda, Dem. Rep. of the Congo 87 E2
Tshofa, Dem. Rep. of the Congo 86 D2
Tshwane, Botswana 88 C3
Tsigara, Botswana 88 C4
Tsihombe, Madag. 89 D8
Tsimlyansk, Russia 49 G6
Tsimlyansk Res. = Tsimlyanskoye Vdkhr., Russia 49 F6
Tsimlyanskoye Vdkhr., Russia 49 F6
Tsinan = Jinan, China 56 F9
Tsineng, S. Africa 88 D3
Tsínga, Greece 41 E8
Tsinghai = Qinghai □, China 60 C4
Tsingtao = Qingdao, China 57 F11
Tsinjomitondraka, Madag. 89 B8
Tsiroanomandidy, Madag. 89 B8
Tsiteli-Tsqaro, Georgia 49 K8
Tsivilsk, Russia 48 C8
Tsivory, Madag. 89 C8
Tskhinvali, Georgia 49 J7
Tsna →, Russia 48 C6
Tsnori, Georgia 49 K7
Tso Moriri, L., India 69 C8
Tsodilo Hill, Botswana 88 B3
Tsogttsetsiy, Mongolia 56 C3
Tsolo, S. Africa 89 E4
Tsomo, S. Africa 89 E4
Tsu, Japan 55 G8
Tsu L., Canada 104 A6
Tsuchiura, Japan 55 F10
Tsugaru-Kaikyō, Japan 54 D10
Tsumeb, Namibia 88 B2
Tsumis, Namibia 88 C2
Tsuruga, Japan 55 G8
Tsurugi-San, Japan 55 H7
Tsuruoka, Japan 54 E9
Tsushima, Gifu, Japan 55 G8
Tsushima, Nagasaki, Japan 55 G4
Tsvetkovo, Ukraine 47 H6
Tsyelyakhany, Belarus 47 F3
Tua →, Portugal 34 D3
Tual, Indonesia 63 F8
Tuam, Ireland 15 C3
Tuamotu Arch. = Tuamotu Is., Pac. Oc. 97 J13
Tuamotu Is., Pac. Oc. 97 J13
Tuamotu Ridge, Pac. Oc. 97 K14
Tuanfeng, China 59 B10
Tuanxi, China 58 D6
Tuao, Phil. 61 C4
Tuapse, Russia 49 H4
Tuatapere, N.Z. 91 M1
Tuba City, U.S.A. 115 H8
Tuban, Indonesia 63 G15
Tubarão, Brazil 127 B6
Tūbās, West Bank 75 C4
Tübingen, Germany 25 G5
Tubruq, Libya 79 B10
Tubuai Is., Pac. Oc. 97 K13
Tuc Trung, Vietnam 65 G6
Tucacas, Venezuela 124 A5
Tuchodi →, Canada 104 B4
Tuchola, Poland 44 E4
Tuchów, Poland 45 J8
Tucson, U.S.A. 115 K8
Tucumán □, Argentina 126 B2
Tucumcari, U.S.A. 113 H3
Tucupita, Venezuela 124 B6
Tucuruí, Brazil 125 D9
Tucuruí, Reprêsa de, Brazil 125 D9
Tuczno, Poland 45 E3
Tudela, Spain 32 C3
Tudmur, Syria 70 C3
Tudor, L., Canada 103 A6
Tudora, Romania 43 C11
Tuella →, Portugal 34 D3
Tuen, Australia 95 D4
Tugela →, S. Africa 89 D5
Tuguegarao, Phil. 61 C4
Tugur, Russia 51 D14
Tui, Spain 34 C2
Tuineje, Canary Is. 37 F5
Tukangbesi, Kepulauan, Indonesia 63 F6
Tukarak I., Canada 102 A4
Tukayyid, Iraq 70 D5
Tūkh, Egypt 80 H7
Tukobo, Ghana 82 D4

Tuktoyaktuk, Canada 100 B6
Tukums, Latvia 9 H20
Tukums □, Latvia 44 B10
Tukuyu, Tanzania 87 D3
Tula, Hidalgo, Mexico 119 C5
Tula, Tamaulipas, Mexico 119 C5
Tula, Nigeria 83 D7
Tula, Russia 46 E9
Tulancingo, Mexico 119 C5
Tulare, Serbia, Yug. 40 D5
Tulare, U.S.A. 116 J7
Tulare Lake Bed, U.S.A. 116 K7
Tularosa, U.S.A. 115 K10
Tulbagh, S. Africa 88 E2
Tulcán, Ecuador 124 C3
Tulcea, Romania 43 E13
Tulcea □, Romania 43 E13
Tulchyn, Ukraine 47 H5
Tūleh, Iran 71 C7
Tulemalu L., Canada 105 A9
Tulgheş, Romania 43 D10
Tuli, Zimbabwe 87 G2
Tulia, U.S.A. 113 H4
Tuliszków, Poland 45 F5
Tulita, Canada 100 B7
Tulkarm, West Bank 75 C4
Tulla, Ireland 15 D3
Tullahoma, U.S.A. 109 H2
Tullamore, Australia 95 E4
Tullamore, Ireland 15 C4
Tulle, France 20 C5
Tullibigeal, Australia 95 E4
Tulln, Austria 26 C9
Tullow, Ireland 15 D5
Tullus, Sudan 81 E1
Tully, Australia 94 B4
Tulmur, Australia 94 C3
Tulnici, Romania 43 E11
Tulovo, Bulgaria 41 D9
Tulsa, U.S.A. 113 G7
Tulsequah, Canada 104 B2
Tulu Milki, Ethiopia 81 F4
Tulu Welel, Ethiopia 81 F3
Tulua, Colombia 124 C3
Tulucești, Romania 43 E13
Tulun, Russia 51 D11
Tulungagung, Indonesia 63 H14
Tuma →, Nic. 120 D3
Tumaco, Colombia 124 C3
Tumatumari, Guyana 124 B7
Tumba, Sweden 10 E11
Tumba, L., Dem. Rep. of the Congo 84 E3
Tumbarumba, Australia 95 F4
Túmbaya, Argentina 126 A2
Tumbes, Peru 124 D2
Tumbwe, Dem. Rep. of the Congo 87 E2
Tumby Bay, Australia 95 E2
Tümd Youqi, China 56 D6
Tumen, China 57 C15
Tumen Jiang →, China 57 C16
Tumeremo, Venezuela 124 B6
Tumkur, India 66 N10
Tump, Pakistan 66 F3
Tumpat, Malaysia 65 J4
Tumu, Ghana 82 C4
Tumucumaque, Serra, Brazil 122 C5
Tumut, Australia 95 F4
Tumwater, U.S.A. 114 C2
Tunadal, Sweden 10 B11
Tunas de Zaza, Cuba 120 B4
Tunbridge Wells = Royal Tunbridge Wells, U.K. 13 F8
Tunçbilek, Turkey 39 B11
Tunceli, Turkey 73 C8
Tuncurry, Australia 95 E5
Tunduru, Tanzania 87 E4
Tunduru □, Tanzania 87 E4
Tundzha →, Bulgaria 41 E10
Tunga Pass, India 67 E19
Tungabhadra →, India 66 M11
Tungaru, Sudan 81 E3
Tungla, Nic. 120 D3
Tungshih, Taiwan 59 E13
Tungsten, Canada 104 A3
Tunguska, Nizhnyaya →, Russia 51 C9
Tunguska, Podkamennaya →, Russia 51 C10
Tunica, U.S.A. 113 H9
Tunis, Tunisia 79 A8
Tunisia ■, Africa 79 A7
Tunja, Colombia 124 B4
Tunkhannock, U.S.A. 111 E9
Tunliu, China 56 F7
Tunnsjøen, Norway 8 D15
Tunø, Denmark 11 J4
Tunungayualok I., Canada 103 A7
Tunuyán, Argentina 126 C2
Tunuyán →, Argentina 126 C2
Tunxi, China 59 C12
Tuo Jiang →, China 58 C5
Tuolumne, U.S.A. 116 H6
Tuolumne →, U.S.A. 116 H5
Tūp Āghāj, Iran 70 B5
Tupã, Brazil 127 A5
Tupelo, U.S.A. 109 H1
Tupik, Russia 46 E7
Tupinambaranas, Brazil 124 D7
Tupiza, Bolivia 126 A2
Tupižnica, Serbia, Yug. 40 C6
Tupman, U.S.A. 117 K7

Tupper

Tupper, *Canada* 104 B4
Tupper Lake, *U.S.A.* 111 B10
Tupungato, Cerro, *S. Amer.* 126 C2
Tuquan, *China* 57 B11
Túquerres, *Colombia* 124 C3
Tura, *Russia* 51 C11
Turabah, *Si. Arabia* 70 D4
Tūrān, *Iran* 71 C8
Turan, *Russia* 51 D10
Turayf, *Si. Arabia* 70 D3
Turbacz, *Poland* 45 J7
Turbe, *Bos.-H.* 42 F2
Turčianske Teplice, *Slovak Rep.* 27 C11
Turcoaia, *Romania* 43 E13
Turda, *Romania* 43 D8
Turek, *Poland* 45 F5
Turen, *Venezuela* 124 B5
Turfan = Turpan, *China* 60 B3
Turfan Depression = Turpan Hami, *China* 60 B3
Tŭrgovishte, *Bulgaria* 41 C10
Turgut, *Turkey* 39 D10
Turgutlu, *Turkey* 39 C9
Turhal, *Turkey* 72 B7
Turia →, *Spain* 33 F4
Turiaçu, *Brazil* 125 D9
Turiaçu →, *Brazil* 125 D9
Turiec →, *Slovak Rep.* 27 B11
Turin = Torino, *Italy* 28 C4
Turin, *Canada* 104 D6
Turkana □, *Kenya* 86 B4
Turkana, L., *Africa* 86 B4
Türkeli, *Turkey* 41 F11
Turkestan = Türkistan, *Kazakstan* 50 E7
Túrkeve, *Hungary* 42 C5
Turkey ■, *Eurasia* 72 C7
Turkey Creek, *Australia* 92 C4
Turki, *Russia* 48 D6
Türkistan, *Kazakstan* 50 E7
Türkmenbashi, *Turkmenistan* 50 F6
Turkmenistan ■, *Asia* 50 F6
Türkmenli, *Turkey* 39 B8
Türkoğlu, *Turkey* 72 D7
Turks & Caicos Is. ■, *W. Indies* 121 B5
Turks Island Passage, *W. Indies* 121 B5
Turku, *Finland* 9 F20
Turkwel →, *Kenya* 86 B4
Turlock, *U.S.A.* 116 H6
Turnagain →, *Canada* 104 B3
Turnagain, C., *N.Z.* 91 J6
Turneffe Is., *Belize* 119 D7
Turner, *Australia* 92 C4
Turner, *U.S.A.* 114 B9
Turner Pt., *Australia* 94 A1
Turner Valley, *Canada* 104 C6
Turners Falls, *U.S.A.* 111 D12
Turnhout, *Belgium* 17 C4
Türnitz, *Austria* 26 D8
Turnor L., *Canada* 105 B7
Turnov, *Czech Rep.* 26 A8
Tŭrnovo = Veliko Tŭrnovo, *Bulgaria* 41 C9
Turnu Măgurele, *Romania* 43 G9
Turnu Roşu, P., *Romania* 43 E9
Turobin, *Poland* 45 H9
Turon, *U.S.A.* 113 G5
Turpan, *China* 60 B3
Turpan Hami, *China* 60 B3
Turrës, Kalaja e, *Albania* 40 E3
Turriff, *U.K.* 14 D6
Tursāq, *Iraq* 70 C5
Tursi, *Italy* 31 B9
Turtle Head I., *Australia* 94 A3
Turtle L., *Canada* 105 C7
Turtle Lake, *N. Dak., U.S.A.* 112 B4
Turtle Lake, *Wis., U.S.A.* 112 C8
Turtleford, *Canada* 105 C7
Turukhansk, *Russia* 51 C9
Turzovka, *Slovak Rep.* 27 B11
Tuscaloosa, *U.S.A.* 109 J2
Tuscánia, *Italy* 29 F8
Tuscany = Toscana □, *Italy* 28 E8
Tuscola, *Ill., U.S.A.* 108 F1
Tuscola, *Tex., U.S.A.* 113 J5
Tuscumbia, *U.S.A.* 109 H2
Tuskegee, *U.S.A.* 109 J3
Tustin, *U.S.A.* 117 M9
Tuszyn, *Poland* 45 G6
Tutak, *Turkey* 73 C10
Tutayev, *Russia* 46 D10
Tuticorin, *India* 66 Q11
Tutin, *Serbia, Yug.* 40 D4
Tutóia, *Brazil* 125 D10
Tutong, *Brunei* 62 D4
Tutova →, *Romania* 43 D12
Tutrakan, *Bulgaria* 41 B10
Tutshi L., *Canada* 104 B2
Tuttle, *U.S.A.* 112 B5
Tuttlingen, *Germany* 25 H4
Tutuala, *Indonesia* 63 F7
Tutuila, *Amer. Samoa* 91 B13
Tututepec, *Mexico* 119 D5
Tuva □, *Russia* 51 D10
Tuvalu ■, *Pac. Oc.* 96 H9
Tuxer Alpen, *Austria* 26 D4
Tuxpan, *Mexico* 119 C5
Tuxtla Gutiérrez, *Mexico* 119 D6
Tuy = Tui, *Spain* 34 C2
Tuy An, *Vietnam* 64 F7
Tuy Duc, *Vietnam* 65 F6
Tuy Hoa, *Vietnam* 64 F7
Tuy Phong, *Vietnam* 65 G7
Tuya L., *Canada* 104 B2
Tuyen Hoa, *Vietnam* 64 D6
Tuyen Quang, *Vietnam* 64 B5
Tūysarkān, *Iran* 71 C6
Tuz Gölü, *Turkey* 72 C5
Ţūz Khurmātū, *Iraq* 70 C5
Tuzi, *Montenegro, Yug.* 40 D3
Tuzla, *Bos.-H.* 42 F3
Tuzlov →, *Russia* 47 J10
Tuzluca, *Turkey* 73 B10
Tvååker, *Sweden* 11 G6
Tvardiţa, *Moldova* 43 D13
Tver, *Russia* 46 D8
Tvrdošin, *Slovak Rep.* 27 B12
Tvrdošovce, *Slovak Rep.* 27 C11
Tvŭrditsa, *Bulgaria* 41 D9
Twain, *U.S.A.* 116 E5
Twain Harte, *U.S.A.* 116 G6
Twardogóra, *Poland* 45 G4
Tweed, *Canada* 110 B7
Tweed →, *U.K.* 14 F6
Tweed Heads, *Australia* 95 D5
Tweedsmuir Prov. Park, *Canada* 104 C3
Twentynine Palms, *U.S.A.* 117 L10
Twillingate, *Canada* 103 C9
Twin Bridges, *U.S.A.* 114 D7
Twin Falls, *U.S.A.* 114 E6
Twin Valley, *U.S.A.* 112 B6
Twisp, *U.S.A.* 114 B3
Twistringen, *Germany* 24 C4
Two Harbors, *U.S.A.* 112 B9
Two Hills, *Canada* 104 C6
Two Rivers, *U.S.A.* 108 C2
Twofold B., *Australia* 95 F4
Tyachiv, *Ukraine* 47 H2
Tychy, *Poland* 45 H5
Tyczyn, *Poland* 45 J9
Tykocin, *Poland* 45 E9
Tyler, *U.S.A.* 107 D7
Tyler, *Minn., U.S.A.* 112 C6
Tyler, *Tex., U.S.A.* 113 J7
Tyligul →, *Ukraine* 47 J6
Týn nad Vltavou, *Czech Rep.* 26 B7
Tynda, *Russia* 51 D13
Tyne →, *U.K.* 12 C6
Tyne & Wear □, *U.K.* 12 B6
Týnec nad Sázavou, *Czech Rep.* 26 B7
Tynemouth, *U.K.* 12 B6
Tyre = Sūr, *Lebanon* 75 B4
Tyrifjorden, *Norway* 9 F14
Tyringe, *Sweden* 11 H7
Tyrnyauz, *Russia* 49 J6
Tyrol = Tirol □, *Austria* 26 D3
Tyrone, *U.S.A.* 110 F6
Tyrone □, *U.K.* 15 B4
Tyrrell →, *Australia* 95 F3
Tyrrell, L., *Australia* 95 F3
Tyrrell Arm, *Canada* 105 A9
Tyrrell L., *Canada* 105 A7
Tyrrhenian Sea, *Medit. S.* 6 G8
Tysfjorden, *Norway* 8 B17
Tystberga, *Sweden* 11 F11
Tytuvėnai, *Lithuania* 44 C10
Tyub Karagan, Mys, *Kazakstan* 49 H10
Tyuleni, Ostrova, *Kazakstan* 49 H10
Tyuleniy, *Russia* 49 H8
Tyuleniy, Mys, *Azerbaijan* 49 K10
Tyumen, *Russia* 50 D7
Tywi →, *U.K.* 13 F3
Tywyn, *U.K.* 13 E3
Tzaneen, *S. Africa* 89 C5
Tzermiádhes, *Greece* 36 D7
Tzoumérka, Óros, *Greece* 38 B3
Tzukong = Zigong, *China* 58 C5

U

U Taphao, *Thailand* 64 F3
U.S.A. = United States of America ■, *N. Amer.* 106 C7
Uanda, *Australia* 94 C3
Uasin □, *Kenya* 86 B4
Uatumã →, *Brazil* 124 D7
Uaupés, *Brazil* 124 D5
Uaupés →, *Brazil* 124 C5
Uaxactún, *Guatemala* 120 C2
Ub, *Serbia, Yug.* 40 B4
Ubá, *Brazil* 127 A7
Ubaitaba, *Brazil* 125 F11
Ubangi = Oubangi →, *Dem. Rep. of the Congo* 84 E3
Ubauro, *Pakistan* 68 E3
Ubaye →, *France* 21 D10
Ubayyiḑ, W. al →, *Iraq* 73 F10
Ube, *Japan* 55 H5
Úbeda, *Spain* 35 G7
Uberaba, *Brazil* 125 G9
Uberlândia, *Brazil* 125 G9
Überlingen, *Germany* 25 H5
Ubiaja, *Nigeria* 83 D6
Ubolratna Res., *Thailand* 64 D4
Ubombo, *S. Africa* 89 D5
Ubon Ratchathani, *Thailand* 64 E5
Ubondo, *Dem. Rep. of the Congo* 86 C2
Ubort →, *Belarus* 47 F5
Ubrique, *Spain* 35 J5
Ubundu, *Dem. Rep. of the Congo* 86 C2
Ucayali →, *Peru* 122 D3
Uchi Lake, *Canada* 105 C10
Uchiura-Wan, *Japan* 54 C10
Uchte, *Germany* 24 C4
Uchur →, *Russia* 51 D14
Uckermark, *Germany* 24 B9
Ucluelet, *Canada* 104 D3
Uda →, *Russia* 51 D14
Udagamandalam, *India* 66 P10
Udaipur, *India* 68 G5
Udaipur Garhi, *Nepal* 69 F12
Udbina, *Croatia* 29 D12
Uddeholm, *Sweden* 10 D7
Uddevalla, *Sweden* 11 F5
Uddjaur, *Sweden* 8 D17
Uden, *Neths.* 17 C5
Udgir, *India* 66 K10
Udhampur, *India* 69 C6
Udi, *Nigeria* 83 D6
Údine, *Italy* 29 B10
Udmurtia □, *Russia* 50 D6
Udon Thani, *Thailand* 64 D4
Udupi, *India* 66 N9
Udvoy Balkan, *Bulgaria* 41 D10
Udzungwa Range, *Tanzania* 87 D4
Ueckermünde, *Germany* 24 B10
Ueda, *Japan* 55 F9
Uedineniya, Os., *Russia* 4 B12
Uele →, *Dem. Rep. of the Congo* 84 D4
Uelen, *Russia* 51 C19
Uelzen, *Germany* 24 C6
Uetersen, *Germany* 24 B5
Uetze, *Germany* 24 C6
Ufa, *Russia* 50 D6
Uffenheim, *Germany* 25 F6
Ugab →, *Namibia* 88 C1
Ugalla →, *Tanzania* 86 D3
Uganda ■, *Africa* 86 B3
Ugento, *Italy* 31 C11
Ugep, *Nigeria* 83 D6
Ugie, *S. Africa* 89 E4
Ugíjar, *Spain* 35 J7
Ugine, *France* 21 C10
Uglegorsk, *Russia* 51 E15
Uglich, *Russia* 46 D10
Ugljan, *Croatia* 29 D12
Ugljane, *Croatia* 29 E13
Ugra →, *Russia* 46 E9
Ugŭrchin, *Bulgaria* 41 C8
Uh →, *Slovak Rep.* 27 C15
Uherské Hradiště, *Czech Rep.* 27 B10
Uherský Brod, *Czech Rep.* 27 B10
Úhlava →, *Czech Rep.* 26 B6
Uhrichsville, *U.S.A.* 110 F3
Uibhist a Deas = South Uist, *U.K.* 14 D1
Uibhist a Tuath = North Uist, *U.K.* 14 D1
Uig, *U.K.* 14 D2
Uíge, *Angola* 84 F2
Uijŏngbu, *S. Korea* 57 F14
Ŭiju, *N. Korea* 57 D13
Uinta Mts., *U.S.A.* 114 F8
Uitenhage, *S. Africa* 88 E4
Uithuizen, *Neths.* 17 A6
Ujazd, *Poland* 45 H5
Újfehértó, *Hungary* 42 C6
Ujhani, *India* 69 F8
Uji-guntō, *Japan* 55 J4
Ujjain, *India* 68 H6
Ujście, *Poland* 45 E3
Újszász, *Hungary* 42 C5
Ujung Pandang, *Indonesia* 63 F5
Uka, *Russia* 51 D17
Ukara I., *Tanzania* 86 C3
Uke-Shima, *Japan* 55 K4
Ukerewe □, *Tanzania* 86 C3
Ukerewe I., *Tanzania* 86 C3
Ukholovo, *Russia* 48 D5
Ukhrul, *India* 67 G19
Ukhta, *Russia* 50 C6
Ukiah, *U.S.A.* 116 F3
Ukki Fort, *India* 69 C7
Ukmergė, *Lithuania* 9 J21
Ukraine ■, *Europe* 47 H7
Ukwi, *Botswana* 88 C3
Ulaanbaatar, *Mongolia* 60 B5
Ulaangom, *Mongolia* 60 A4
Ulamba, *Dem. Rep. of the Congo* 87 D1
Ulan Bator = Ulaanbaatar, *Mongolia* 60 B5
Ulan Erge, *Russia* 49 G7
Ulan Khol, *Russia* 49 H8
Ulan Ude, *Russia* 51 D11
Ulanga □, *Tanzania* 87 D4
Ulanów, *Poland* 45 H9
Ulaş, *Sivas, Turkey* 72 C7
Ulaş, *Tekirdağ, Turkey* 41 E11
Ulaya, *Morogoro, Tanzania* 86 D4
Ulaya, *Tabora, Tanzania* 86 C3
Ulcinj, *Montenegro, Yug.* 40 E3
Ulco, *S. Africa* 88 D3
Ulefoss, *Norway* 9 G13
Ulëza, *Albania* 40 E3
Ulfborg, *Denmark* 11 H2
Ulhasnagar, *India* 66 K8
Uljma, *Serbia, Yug.* 42 E6
Ulla →, *Spain* 34 C2
Ulladulla, *Australia* 95 F5
Ullapool, *U.K.* 14 D3
Ullared, *Sweden* 11 G6
Ulldecona, *Spain* 32 E5
Ullswater, *U.K.* 12 C5
Ullung-do, *S. Korea* 57 F16
Ulm, *Germany* 25 G5
Ulmarra, *Australia* 95 D5
Ulmeni, *Buzău, Romania* 43 E11
Ulmeni, *Maramureş, Romania* 43 C8
Ulonguè, *Mozam.* 87 E3
Ulricehamn, *Sweden* 11 G7
Ulrika, *Sweden* 11 F9
Ulsan, *S. Korea* 57 G15
Ulsta, *U.K.* 14 A7
Ulster □, *U.K.* 15 B5
Ulstrem, *Bulgaria* 41 D10
Ulubaria, *India* 69 H13
Ulubat Gölü, *Turkey* 41 F12
Ulubey, *Turkey* 39 C11
Uluborlu, *Turkey* 39 C12
Uluçinar, *Turkey* 72 D6
Uludağ, *Turkey* 41 F13
Uludere, *Turkey* 73 D10
Uluguru Mts., *Tanzania* 86 D4
Ulukışla, *Turkey* 72 D6
Ulungur He →, *China* 60 B3
Uluru = Ayers Rock, *Australia* 93 E5
Ulutau, *Kazakstan* 50 E7
Ulva, *U.K.* 14 E2
Ulverston, *U.K.* 12 C4
Ulverstone, *Australia* 94 G4
Ulya, *Russia* 51 D15
Ulyanovsk = Simbirsk, *Russia* 48 C9
Ulyasutay, *Mongolia* 60 B4
Ulysses, *U.S.A.* 113 G4
Umag, *Croatia* 29 C10
Umala, *Bolivia* 124 G5
Uman, *Ukraine* 47 H6
Umaria, *India* 67 H12
Umarkot, *Pakistan* 66 G6
Umatilla, *U.S.A.* 114 D4
Umbértide, *Italy* 29 E9
Umbrella Mts., *N.Z.* 91 L2
Umbria □, *Italy* 29 F9
Ume älv →, *Sweden* 8 E19
Umeå, *Sweden* 8 E19
Umera, *Indonesia* 63 E7
Umfuli →, *Zimbabwe* 87 F2
Umgusa, *Zimbabwe* 87 F2
Umka, *Serbia, Yug.* 40 B4
Umkomaas, *S. Africa* 89 E5
Umm ad Daraj, J., *Jordan* 75 C4
Umm al Qaywayn, *U.A.E.* 71 E7
Umm al Qittayn, *Jordan* 75 C5
Umm Arda, *Sudan* 81 D3
Umm Bāb, *Qatar* 71 E6
Umm Bel, *Sudan* 81 E2
Umm Dubban, *Sudan* 81 D3
Umm el Fahm, *Israel* 75 C4
Umm Koweika, *Sudan* 81 E3
Umm Lajj, *Si. Arabia* 70 E3
Umm Merwa, *Sudan* 80 D3
Umm Ruwaba, *Sudan* 81 E3
Umm Sidr, *Sudan* 81 E2
Umnak I., *U.S.A.* 100 C3
Umniati →, *Zimbabwe* 87 F2
Umpqua →, *U.S.A.* 114 E1
Umreth, *India* 68 H5
Umtata, *S. Africa* 89 E4
Umuahia, *Nigeria* 83 D6
Umuarama, *Brazil* 127 A5
Umurbey, *Turkey* 41 F10
Umvukwe Ra., *Zimbabwe* 87 F3
Umzimvubu = Port St. Johns, *S. Africa* 89 E4
Umzingwane →, *Zimbabwe* 87 G2
Umzinto, *S. Africa* 89 E5
Una, *India* 68 J4
Una →, *Bos.-H.* 29 D13
Unac →, *Bos.-H.* 29 D13
Unadilla, *U.S.A.* 111 D9
Unalaska, *U.S.A.* 100 C3
'Unayzah, *Si. Arabia* 70 E4
'Unāzah, J., *Asia* 73 F8
Uncastillo, *Spain* 32 C3
Uncía, *Bolivia* 124 G5
Uncompahgre Peak, *U.S.A.* 115 G10
Unden, *Sweden* 11 F8
Underbool, *Australia* 95 F3
Undersaker, *Sweden* 10 A7
Unecha, *Russia* 47 F7
Ungarie, *Australia* 95 E4
Ungarra, *Australia* 95 E2
Ungava, Pén. d', *Canada* 101 C12
Ungava B., *Canada* 101 C13
Ungeny = Ungheni, *Moldova* 43 C12
Unggi, *N. Korea* 57 C16
Ungheni, *Moldova* 43 C12
Ungwatiri, *Sudan* 81 D4
Uni, *Russia* 48 B10
União da Vitória, *Brazil* 127 B5
Uničov, *Czech Rep.* 27 B10
Uniejów, *Poland* 45 G5
Unije, *Croatia* 29 D11
Unimak I., *U.S.A.* 100 C3
Union, *Miss., U.S.A.* 113 J10
Union, *Mo., U.S.A.* 112 F9
Union, *S.C., U.S.A.* 109 H5
Union, Mt., *U.S.A.* 115 J7
Union City, *Calif., U.S.A.* 116 H4
Union City, *N.J., U.S.A.* 111 F10
Union City, *Pa., U.S.A.* 110 E5
Union City, *Tenn., U.S.A.* 113 G10
Union Gap, *U.S.A.* 114 C3
Union Springs, *U.S.A.* 109 J3
Uniondale, *S. Africa* 88 E3
Uniontown, *U.S.A.* 108 F6
Unionville, *U.S.A.* 112 E8
Unirea, *Romania* 43 F12
United Arab Emirates ■, *Asia* 71 F7
United Kingdom ■, *Europe* 7 E5
United States of America ■, *N. Amer.* 106 C7
Unity, *Canada* 105 C7
Universales, Mtes., *Spain* 32 E3
Unjha, *India* 68 H5
Unna, *Germany* 24 D3
Unnao, *India* 69 F9
Uno, Ilha, *Guinea-Biss.* 82 C1
Unst, *U.K.* 14 A8
Unstrut →, *Germany* 24 D7
Unterfranken □, *Germany* 25 F5
Unterschleissheim, *Germany* 25 G7
Unuk →, *Canada* 104 B2
Ünye, *Turkey* 72 B7
Unzha, *Russia* 48 A7
Unzha →, *Russia* 48 B6
Uozu, *Japan* 55 F8
Upata, *Venezuela* 124 B6
Upemba, L., *Dem. Rep. of the Congo* 87 D2
Upernavik, *Greenland* 4 B5
Upington, *S. Africa* 88 D3
Upleta, *India* 68 J4
Upolu, *W. Samoa* 91 A13
Upper Alkali Lake, *U.S.A.* 114 F3
Upper Arrow L., *Canada* 104 C5
Upper Austria = Oberösterreich □, *Austria* 26 C7
Upper Foster L., *Canada* 105 B7
Upper Hutt, *N.Z.* 91 J5
Upper Klamath L., *U.S.A.* 114 E3
Upper Lake, *U.S.A.* 116 F4
Upper Musquodoboit, *Canada* 103 C7
Upper Red L., *U.S.A.* 112 A7
Upper Sandusky, *U.S.A.* 108 E4
Upper Volta = Burkina Faso ■, *Africa* 82 C4
Upphärad, *Sweden* 11 F6
Uppland, *Sweden* 10 E11
Upplands-Väsby, *Sweden* 10 E11
Uppsala, *Sweden* 10 E11
Uppsala län □, *Sweden* 10 D11
Upshi, *India* 69 C7
Upstart, C., *Australia* 94 B4
Upton, *U.S.A.* 112 C2
Ur, *Iraq* 70 D5
Uracara, *Brazil* 124 D7
Urad Qianqi, *China* 56 D5
Urakawa, *Japan* 54 C11
Ural = Zhayyq →, *Kazakstan* 50 E6
Ural, *Australia* 95 E4
Ural Mts. = Uralskie Gory, *Eurasia* 50 D6
Uralla, *Australia* 95 E5
Uralsk = Oral, *Kazakstan* 48 E10
Uralskie Gory, *Eurasia* 50 D6
Urambo, *Tanzania* 86 D3
Urambo □, *Tanzania* 86 D3
Urandangi, *Australia* 94 C2
Uranium City, *Canada* 105 B7
Uranquinty, *Australia* 95 F4
Uraricoera →, *Brazil* 124 C6
Urawa, *Japan* 55 G9
Uray, *Russia* 50 C7
'Uray'irah, *Si. Arabia* 71 E6
Urbana, *Ill., U.S.A.* 108 E1
Urbana, *Ohio, U.S.A.* 108 E4
Urbánia, *Italy* 29 E9
Urbel →, *Spain* 34 C7
Urbino, *Italy* 29 E9
Urbión, Picos de, *Spain* 32 C2
Urcos, *Peru* 124 F4
Urdinarrain, *Argentina* 126 C4
Urdos, *France* 20 F3
Urdzhar, *Kazakstan* 50 E9
Ure →, *U.K.* 12 C6
Uren, *Russia* 48 B7
Ures, *Mexico* 118 B2
Urfa = Sanliurfa, *Turkey* 73 D8
Urganch, *Uzbekistan* 50 E7
Urgench = Urganch, *Uzbekistan* 50 E7
Uri, *India* 69 B6
Uri □, *Switz.* 25 J4
Uribia, *Colombia* 124 A4
Uricani, *Romania* 42 E8
Uriondo, *Bolivia* 126 A3
Urique, *Mexico* 118 B3
Urique →, *Mexico* 118 B3
Urk, *Neths.* 17 B5
Urla, *Turkey* 39 C8
Urlaţi, *Romania* 43 F11
Urmia = Orūmīyeh, *Iran* 70 B5
Urmia, L. = Orūmīyeh, Daryācheh-ye, *Iran* 70 B5
Uroševac, *Serbia, Yug.* 40 D5
Urshult, *Sweden* 11 H8
Uruaçu, *Brazil* 125 F9
Uruapan, *Mexico* 118 D4

Urubamba →, Peru 124 F4
Uruçuí, Brazil 125 E10
Uruguai →, Brazil 127 B5
Uruguaiana, Brazil 126 B4
Uruguay ■, S. Amer. 126 C4
Uruguay →, S. Amer. ... 126 C4
Urumchi = Ürümqi, China 60 B3
Ürümqi, China 60 B3
Urup →, Russia 49 H5
Urup, Ostrov, Russia 51 E16
Uryupinsk, Russia 48 E5
Urzhum, Russia 48 B9
Urziceni, Romania 43 F11
Uşak, Turkey 39 C11
Uşak □, Turkey 39 C11
Usakos, Namibia 88 C2
Ušće, Serbia, Yug. 40 C4
Usedom, Germany 24 B10
'Usfān, Si. Arabia 80 C4
Ush-Tobe, Kazakstan 50 E8
Ushakova, Ostrov, Russia . 4 A12
Ushant = Ouessant, Î. d',
  France 18 D1
Ushashi, Tanzania 86 C3
Ushat, Sudan 81 F2
Ushibuka, Japan 55 H5
Ushuaia, Argentina 128 G3
Ushumun, Russia 51 D13
Usk →, U.K. 13 F5
Üsküdar, Turkey 41 F13
Uslar, Germany 24 D5
Usman, Russia 47 F10
Usoke, Tanzania 86 D3
Usolye Sibirskoye, Russia . 51 D11
Usoro, Nigeria 83 D6
Uspallata, P. de, Argentina 126 C2
Uspenskiy, Kazakstan 50 E8
Ussel, France 20 C6
Usson-du-Poitou, France . 20 B4
Ussuri →, Asia 54 A7
Ussuriysk, Russia 54 C5
Ussurka, Russia 54 B6
Ust-Aldan = Batamay,
  Russia 51 C13
Ust Amginskoye =
  Khandyga, Russia 51 C14
Ust-Bolsheretsk, Russia . 51 D16
Ust Buzulukskaya, Russia . 48 E6
Ust Chaun, Russia 51 C18
Ust-Donetskiy, Russia ... 49 G5
Ust Ilimpeya = Yukta,
  Russia 51 C11
Ust-Ilimsk, Russia 51 D11
Ust Ishim, Russia 50 D8
Ust-Kamchatsk, Russia .. 51 D17
Ust-Kamenogorsk =
  Öskemen, Kazakstan ... 50 E9
Ust Khayryuzovo, Russia . 51 D16
Ust-Kut, Russia 51 D11
Ust Kuyga, Russia 51 B14
Ust-Labinsk, Russia 49 H4
Ust Luga, Russia 46 C5
Ust Maya, Russia 51 C14
Ust-Mil, Russia 51 D14
Ust-Nera, Russia 51 C15
Ust-Nyukzha, Russia 51 D13
Ust Olenek, Russia 51 B12
Ust-Omchug, Russia 51 C15
Ust Port, Russia 50 C9
Ust Tsilma, Russia 50 C6
Ust Urt = Ustyurt Plateau,
  Asia 50 E6
Ustaritz, France 20 E2
Uster, Switz. 25 H4
Ústí nad Labem,
  Czech Rep. 26 A7
Ústí nad Orlicí, Czech Rep. 27 B9
Ústica, Italy 30 D6
Ustinov = Izhevsk, Russia 50 D6
Ustka, Poland 44 D3
Ustroń, Poland 45 J5
Ustrzyki Dolne, Poland .. 45 J9
Ustyurt Plateau, Asia 50 E6
Ustyuzhna, Russia 46 C9
Usu, China 60 B3
Usuki, Japan 55 H5
Usulután, El Salv. 120 D2
Usumacinta →, Mexico . 119 D6
Usumbura = Bujumbura,
  Burundi 86 C2
Usure, Tanzania 86 C3
Uta, Indonesia 63 E9
Utah □, U.S.A. 114 G8
Utah L., U.S.A. 114 F8
Utansjö, Sweden 10 B11
Ute Creek →, U.S.A. ... 113 H3
Utebo, Spain 32 D3
Utena, Lithuania 9 J21
Utete, Tanzania 86 D4
Uthai Thani, Thailand ... 64 E3
Uthal, Pakistan 68 G2
Utiariti, Brazil 124 F7
Utica, N.Y., U.S.A. 111 C9
Utica, Ohio, U.S.A. 110 F2
Utiel, Spain 33 F3
Utik L., Canada 105 B9
Utikuma L., Canada 104 B5
Utö, Sweden 10 F12
Utrecht, Neths. 17 B5
Utrecht, S. Africa 89 D5
Utrecht □, Neths. 17 B5
Utrera, Spain 35 H5
Utsjoki, Finland 8 B22
Utsunomiya, Japan 55 F9
Uttar Pradesh □, India .. 69 F9

Uttaradit, Thailand 64 D3
Uttoxeter, U.K. 12 E6
Uummannarsuaq = Farvel,
  Kap, Greenland 4 D5
Uusikaarlepyy, Finland .. 8 E20
Uusikaupunki, Finland ... 9 F19
Uva, Russia 48 B11
Uvac →, Serbia, Yug. ... 40 C3
Uvalde, U.S.A. 113 L5
Uvarovo, Russia 48 E6
Uvat, Russia 50 D7
Uvinza, Tanzania 86 D3
Uvira,
  Dem. Rep. of the Congo 86 C2
Uvs Nuur, Mongolia 60 A4
Uwajima, Japan 55 H6
Uweinat, Jebel, Sudan ... 80 C1
Uxbridge, Canada 110 B5
Uxin Qi, China 56 E5
Uxmal, Mexico 119 C7
Uyo, Nigeria 83 D6
Üyüklü Tepe, Turkey 39 D9
Uyûn Mûsa, Egypt 75 F1
Uyuni, Bolivia 124 H5
Uzbekistan ■, Asia 50 E7
Uzen, Bolshoi →,
  Kazakstan 49 F9
Uzen, Mal →, Kazakstan 49 F9
Uzerche, France 20 C5
Uzès, France 21 D8
Uzh →, Ukraine 47 G6
Uzhgorod = Uzhhorod,
  Ukraine 47 H2
Uzhhorod, Ukraine 47 H2
Užice, Serbia, Yug. 40 C3
Uzlovaya, Russia 46 F10
Üzümlü, Turkey 39 E11
Uzunköprü, Turkey 41 E10
Uzunkuyu, Turkey 39 C8

V

Vaal →, S. Africa 88 D3
Vaal Dam, S. Africa 89 D4
Vaalwater, S. Africa 89 C4
Vaasa, Finland 8 E19
Vabre, France 20 E6
Vác, Hungary 42 C4
Vacaria, Brazil 127 B5
Vacaville, U.S.A. 116 G5
Vaccarès, Étang de, France 21 E8
Vach →= Vakh →,
  Russia 50 C8
Vache, Î. à, Haiti 121 C5
Väckelsång, Sweden 11 H8
Väddö, Sweden 10 D12
Väderstad, Sweden 11 F8
Vadnagar, India 68 H5
Vado Lígure, Italy 28 D5
Vadodara, India 68 H5
Vadsø, Norway 8 A23
Vadstena, Sweden 11 F8
Vaduz, Liech. 25 H5
Værøy, Norway 8 C15
Vágar, Færoe Is. 8 E9
Vaggeryd, Sweden 11 G8
Vagney, France 19 D13
Vagnhärad, Sweden 11 F11
Vagos, Portugal 34 E2
Vågsfjorden, Norway ... 8 B17
Váh →, Slovak Rep. ... 27 D11
Vahsel B., Antarctica ... 5 D1
Vaï, Greece 36 D8
Vaigach, Russia 50 B6
Vaiges, France 18 D6
Vaihingen, Germany ... 25 G4
Vailly-sur-Aisne, France . 19 C10
Vaison-la-Romaine, France 21 D9
Vakarel, Bulgaria 40 D7
Vakfıkebir, Turkey 73 B8
Vakh →, Russia 50 C8
Vakhtan, Russia 48 B8
Vál, Hungary 42 C3
Val-de-Marne □, France . 19 D9
Val-d'Isère, France 21 C10
Val-d'Oise □, France ... 19 C9
Val-d'Or, Canada 102 C4
Val Marie, Canada 105 D7
Valaam, Russia 46 B6
Valadares, Portugal 34 D2
Valahia, Romania 43 F9
Valais □, Switz. 25 J3
Valais, Alpes du, Switz. . 25 J3
Valandovo, Macedonia .. 40 E6
Valašské Meziříčí,
  Czech Rep. 27 B10
Valáxa, Greece 38 C6
Valbo, Sweden 10 E7
Valbondione, Italy 28 B7
Vâlcani, Romania 42 D5
Vâlcea □, Romania 43 F9
Valcheta, Argentina ... 128 E3
Valdagno, Italy 29 C8
Valdahon, France 19 E13
Valday, Russia 46 D7
Valdayskaya
  Vozvyshennost, Russia . 46 D7
Valdeazogues →, Spain . 35 G6
Valdecañas, Embalse de,
  Spain 34 F5
Valdemarsvik, Sweden ... 11 F10

Valdemoro, Spain 34 E7
Valdepeñas, Spain 35 G7
Valderaduey →, Spain .. 34 D5
Valdérice, Italy 30 D5
Valderrobres, Spain 32 E5
Valdés, Pen., Argentina . 122 H4
Valdez, U.S.A. 100 B5
Valdivia, Chile 128 D2
Valdobbiádene, Italy 29 C8
Valdosta, U.S.A. 109 K4
Valdoviño, Spain 34 B2
Vale, Georgia 49 K6
Vale, U.S.A. 114 E5
Vale of Glamorgan □,
  U.K. 13 F4
Valea lui Mihai, Romania . 42 C7
Valea Mărului, Romania .. 43 E12
Valença, Brazil 125 F11
Valença, Portugal 34 C2
Valença do Piauí, Brazil .. 125 E10
Valençay, France 19 E8
Valence = Valence d'Agen,
  France 20 D4
Valence, France 21 D8
Valence d'Agen, France .. 20 D4
Valencia, Spain 33 F4
Valencia, Venezuela 124 A5
Valencia □, Spain 33 F4
Valencia, G. de, Spain ... 33 F5
Valencia de Alcántara,
  Spain 35 F3
Valencia de Don Juan,
  Spain 34 C5
Valencia I., Ireland 15 E1
Valenciennes, France ... 19 B10
Văleni, Romania 43 D12
Vălenii de Munte, Romania 43 E11
Valensole, France 21 E9
Valentigney, France 19 E13
Valentim, Sa. do, Brazil .. 125 E10
Valentin, Russia 54 C7
Valentine, Nebr., U.S.A. . 112 D4
Valentine, Tex., U.S.A. .. 113 K2
Valenza, Italy 28 C5
Valera, Venezuela 124 B4
Valga, Estonia 9 H22
Valguarnera Caropepe,
  Italy 31 E7
Valier, U.S.A. 114 B7
Valinco, G. de, France .. 21 G12
Valjevo, Serbia, Yug. ... 40 B3
Valka, Latvia 9 H21
Valkeakoski, Finland ... 9 F20
Valkenswaard, Neths. .. 17 C5
Vall de Uxó = La Vall
  d'Uixó, Spain 32 F4
Valla, Sweden 10 E10
Valladolid, Mexico 119 C7
Valladolid, Spain 34 D6
Valladolid □, Spain 34 D6
Vallata, Italy 31 A8
Valldemossa, Spain 37 B9
Valle d'Aosta □, Italy ... 28 C4
Valle de Arán, Spain ... 32 C5
Valle de la Pascua,
  Venezuela 124 B5
Valle de las Palmas, Mexico 117 N10
Valle de Santiago, Mexico 118 C4
Valle de Suchil, Mexico . 118 C4
Valle de Zaragoza, Mexico 118 B3
Valle Fértil, Sierra del,
  Argentina 126 C2
Valle Hermoso, Mexico . 119 B5
Valledupar, Colombia ... 124 A4
Vallehermoso, Canary Is. . 37 F2
Vallejo, U.S.A. 116 G4
Vallenar, Chile 126 B1
Vallentuna, Sweden 10 E12
Valleraugue, France 20 D7
Vallet, France 18 E5
Valletta, Malta 36 D2
Valley Center, U.S.A. ... 117 M9
Valley City, U.S.A. 112 B6
Valley Falls, U.S.A. 114 E3
Valley Springs, U.S.A. .. 116 G6
Valley Wells, U.S.A. 117 K11
Valleyview, Canada 104 B5
Valli di Comácchio, Italy . 29 D9
Vallimanca, Arroyo,
  Argentina 126 D4
Vallo della Lucánia, Italy . 31 B8
Vallon-Pont-d'Arc, France 21 D8
Vallorbe, Switz. 25 J2
Valls, Spain 32 D6
Valmiera, Latvia 9 H21
Valnera, Spain 34 B7
Valognes, France 18 C5
Valona = Vlóra, Albania . 40 F3
Valongo, Portugal 34 D2
Valozhyn, Belarus 46 E4
Valpaços, Portugal 34 D3
Valparaíso, Chile 126 C1
Valparaíso, Mexico 118 C4
Valparaiso, U.S.A. 108 E2
Valparaíso □, Chile 126 C1
Valpovo, Croatia 42 E3
Valréas, France 21 D9
Vals, Switz. 25 J5
Vals →, S. Africa 88 D4
Vals, Tanjung, Indonesia . 63 F9
Vals-les-Bains, France .. 21 D8
Valsad, India 66 J8

Valtellina, Italy 28 B6
Valuyki, Russia 47 G10
Valverde, Canary Is. 37 G2
Valverde del Camino,
  Spain 35 H4
Valverde del Fresno, Spain 34 E4
Vama, Romania 43 C10
Vamdrup, Denmark 11 J3
Våmhus, Sweden 10 C8
Vammala, Finland 9 F20
Vámos, Greece 36 D6
Van, Turkey 73 C10
Van, L. = Van Gölü,
  Turkey 73 C10
Van Alstyne, U.S.A. 113 J6
Van Blommestein Meer,
  Surinam 125 C7
Van Bruyssel, Canada ... 103 C5
Van Buren, Canada 103 C6
Van Buren, Ark., U.S.A. . 113 H7
Van Buren, Maine, U.S.A. 109 B11
Van Buren, Mo., U.S.A. . 113 G9
Van Canh, Vietnam 64 F7
Van Diemen, C., N. Terr.,
  Australia 92 B5
Van Diemen, C., Queens.,
  Australia 94 B2
Van Diemen G., Australia 92 B5
Van Gölü, Turkey 73 C10
Van Horn, U.S.A. 113 K2
Van Ninh, Vietnam 64 F7
Van Rees, Pegunungan,
  Indonesia 63 E9
Van Tassell, U.S.A. 112 D2
Van Wert, U.S.A. 108 E3
Van Yen, Vietnam 64 B5
Vanadzor, Armenia 49 K7
Vanavara, Russia 51 C11
Vancouver, Canada 104 D4
Vancouver, U.S.A. 116 E4
Vancouver, C., Australia . 93 G2
Vancouver I., Canada ... 104 D3
Vandalia, Ill., U.S.A. ... 112 F10
Vandalia, Mo., U.S.A. .. 112 F9
Vandenburg, U.S.A. 117 L6
Vanderbijlpark, S. Africa . 89 D4
Vandergrift, U.S.A. 110 F5
Vanderhoof, Canada ... 104 C4
Vanderkloof Dam,
  S. Africa 88 E3
Vanderlin I., Australia ... 94 B2
Vandyke, Australia 94 C4
Vänern, Sweden 11 F7
Vänersborg, Sweden ... 11 F6
Vang Vieng, Laos 64 C4
Vanga, Kenya 86 C4
Vangaindrano, Madag. .. 89 C8
Vanguard, Canada 105 D7
Vanier, Canada 102 C4
Vanino, Russia 51 E15
Vânju Mare, Romania .. 42 F7
Vankleek Hill, Canada .. 102 C5
Vanna, Norway 8 A18
Vännäs, Sweden 8 E18
Vannes, France 18 E4
Vanoise, France 21 C10
Vanrhynsdorp, S. Africa . 88 E2
Vanrook, Australia 94 B3
Vansbro, Sweden 10 D8
Vansittart B., Australia .. 92 B4
Vantaa, Finland 9 F21
Vanthli, India 68 J4
Vanua Levu, Fiji 91 C8
Vanua Balavu, Fiji 91 C9
Vanuatu ■, Pac. Oc. ... 96 J8
Vanwyksvlei, S. Africa .. 88 E3
Vanzylsrus, S. Africa ... 88 D3
Vapnyarka, Ukraine 47 H5
Var □, France 21 E10
Var →, France 21 E11
Vara, Sweden 11 F6
Varades, France 18 E5
Varáita →, Italy 28 D4
Varallo, Italy 28 C5
Varanasi, India 69 G10
Varanger-halvøya, Norway 8 A23
Varangerfjorden, Norway . 8 A23
Varano, Lago di, Italy ... 29 G12
Varaždin, Croatia 29 B13
Varazze, Italy 28 D5
Varberg, Sweden 11 G6
Vardar = Axiós →, Greece 40 F6
Varde, Denmark 11 J2
Varde Å →, Denmark .. 11 J2
Vardø, Norway 8 A24
Varel, Germany 24 B4
Varella, Mui, Vietnam .. 64 F7
Vårena, Lithuania 9 J21
Varennes-sur-Allier, France 19 F10
Varennes-Vauzelles, France 19 E10
Vareš, Bos.-H. 42 F3
Varese, Italy 28 C5
Vårfurile, Romania 42 D7
Vårgårda, Sweden 11 F6
Varginha, Brazil 127 A6
Vargón, Sweden 11 F6
Variadero, U.S.A. 113 H2
Varillas, Chile 126 A1
Varkaus, Finland 9 E22
Varkens, Finland 9 E22
Värmdölandet, Sweden .. 10 E12
Värmeln, Sweden 10 E6
Värmlands Bro, Sweden . 10 E7
Värmlands län □, Sweden 10 E6
Varna, Bulgaria 41 C11
Varna □, Bulgaria 41 C11

Värnamo, Sweden 11 G8
Varnsdorf, Czech Rep. .. 26 A7
Várpalota, Hungary 42 C3
Vars, Canada 111 A9
Vars, France 21 D10
Varto, Turkey 73 C9
Varvarin, Serbia, Yug. .. 40 C5
Varzaneh, Iran 71 C7
Varzi, Italy 28 D6
Varzo, Italy 28 B5
Varzy, France 19 E10
Vas □, Hungary 42 C1
Vasa Barris →, Brazil .. 125 F11
Vásárosnamény, Hungary . 42 B7
Vascão →, Portugal 35 H3
Vașcău, Romania 42 D7
Vascongadas = País
  Vasco □, Spain 32 C2
Vasht = Khāsh, Iran ... 66 E2
Vasilevichi, Belarus ... 47 F5
Vasilikón, Greece 38 C5
Vasilkov = Vasylkiv,
  Ukraine 47 G6
Vaslui, Romania 43 D12
Vaslui □, Romania 43 D12
Väsman, Sweden 10 D9
Vassar, Canada 105 D9
Vassar, U.S.A. 108 D4
Västerås, Sweden 10 E10
Västerbotten, Sweden .. 8 D18
Västerdalälven →, Sweden 10 D8
Västergötland, Sweden .. 11 F7
Västerhaninge, Sweden . 10 E12
Västervik, Sweden 11 G10
Västmanland, Sweden .. 9 G16
Västmanlands län □,
  Sweden 10 E10
Vasto, Italy 29 F11
Vasvár, Hungary 42 C1
Vasylkiv, Ukraine 47 G6
Vatan, France 19 E8
Vatersay, U.K. 14 E1
Váthia, Greece 38 E4
Vatican City ■, Europe . 29 G9
Vaticano, C., Italy 31 D8
Vatili, Cyprus 36 D12
Vatin, Serbia, Yug. 42 F6
Vatnajökull, Iceland ... 8 D5
Vatoa, Fiji 91 D9
Vatólakkos, Greece ... 36 D5
Vatoloha, Madag. 89 B8
Vatomandry, Madag. .. 89 B8
Vatra-Dornei, Romania . 43 C10
Vättern, Sweden 11 F8
Vaucluse □, France ... 21 E9
Vaucouleurs, France .. 19 D12
Vaud □, Switz. 25 J2
Vaughn, Mont., U.S.A. . 114 C8
Vaughn, N. Mex., U.S.A. 115 J11
Vaupés = Uaupés →,
  Brazil 124 C5
Vaupes □, Colombia ... 124 C4
Vauvert, France 21 E8
Vauxhall, Canada 104 C6
Vava'u, Tonga 91 D12
Vavoua, Ivory C. 82 D3
Vawkavysk, Belarus ... 47 F3
Vaxholm, Sweden 10 E12
Växjö, Sweden 11 H8
Våxtorp, Sweden 11 H7
Vaygach, Ostrov, Russia . 50 C7
Váyia, Greece 36 C10
Váyia, Ákra, Greece .. 36 C10
Vechelde, Germany ... 24 C6
Vechta, Germany 24 C4
Vechte →, Neths. 17 B6
Vedea →, Romania ... 43 G10
Vedia, Argentina 126 C3
Vedum, Sweden 11 F7
Veendam, Neths. 17 A6
Veenendaal, Neths. .. 17 B5
Vefsna →, Norway ... 8 D15
Vega, Norway 8 D14
Vega, U.S.A. 113 H3
Vegadeo, Spain 34 B3
Vegorrítis, Límni, Greece 40 F5
Vegreville, Canada ... 104 C6
Veinge, Sweden 11 H7
Veisiejai, Lithuania .. 44 D10
Vejbystrand, Sweden . 11 H6
Vejen, Denmark 11 J3
Vejer de la Frontera, Spain 35 J5
Vejle, Denmark 11 J3
Vejle Amtskommune □,
  Denmark 11 J3
Vejle Fjord, Denmark .. 11 J3
Vela Luka, Croatia ... 29 F13
Velas, C., Costa Rica .. 120 D2
Velasco, Sierra de,
  Argentina 126 B2
Velay, Mts. du, France . 20 D7
Velddrif, S. Africa ... 88 E2
Velddrif, S. Africa ... 88 E2
Velbert, Germany 24 D3
Velddrif, S. Africa ... 88 E2
Velebit Planina, Croatia . 29 D11
Velebitski Kanal, Croatia . 29 D11
Veleka →, Bulgaria ... 41 D11
Velenje, Slovenia ... 29 B12
Veles, Macedonia 40 E5
Velestíno, Greece 38 B4
Vélez-Málaga, Spain .. 35 J6
Vélez Rubio, Spain ... 33 H2
Velhas →, Brazil 125 G10

Velika, *Croatia* 42 E2
Velika Gorica, *Croatia* ... 29 C13
Velika Kapela, *Croatia* ... 29 C12
Velika Kladuša, *Bos.-H.* .. 29 C12
Velika Morava →,
  Serbia, Yug. 40 B5
Velika Plana, *Serbia, Yug.* 40 B5
Velikaya →, *Russia* 46 D5
Velikaya Kema, *Russia* ... 54 B8
Velikaya Lepetikha,
  Ukraine 47 J7
Veliké Kapušany,
  Slovak Rep. 27 C15
Velike Lašče, *Slovenia* ... 29 C11
Veliki Jastrebac,
  Serbia, Yug. 40 C5
Veliki Kanal, *Serbia, Yug.* 42 E4
Veliki Popović,
  Serbia, Yug. 40 B5
Velikiye Luki, *Russia* 46 D6
Veliko Gradište,
  Serbia, Yug. 40 B5
Veliko Tŭrnovo, *Bulgaria* . 41 C9
Velikonda Range, *India* .. 66 M11
Velingrad, *Bulgaria* 40 D7
Velino, Mte., *Italy* 29 F10
Velizh, *Russia* 46 E6
Velké Karlovice,
  Czech Rep. 27 B11
Velké Meziříčí, *Czech Rep.* 26 B9
Vel'ký Javorník,
  Slovak Rep. 27 B11
Vel'ký Krtíš, *Slovak Rep.* . 27 C12
Vel'ký Meder, *Slovak Rep.* 27 D10
Vel'ký Tribeč, *Slovak Rep.* 27 C11
Velletri, *Italy* 30 A5
Vellinge, *Sweden* 11 J6
Vellmar, *Germany* 24 D5
Vellore, *India* 66 N11
Velsk, *Russia* 46 B11
Velten, *Germany* 24 C9
Velva, *U.S.A.* 112 A4
Velvendós, *Greece* 40 F6
Vemb, *Denmark* 11 H2
Vemdalen, *Sweden* 10 B7
Ven, *Sweden* 11 J6
Venaco, *France* 21 F13
Venado Tuerto, *Argentina* 126 C3
Venafro, *Italy* 31 A7
Venarey-les-Laumes,
  France 19 E11
Venaría, *Italy* 28 C4
Venčane, *Serbia, Yug.* 40 B4
Vence, *France* 21 E11
Vendas Novas, *Portugal* .. 35 G2
Vendée □, *France* 18 F5
Vendée →, *France* 18 F5
Vendéen, Bocage, *France* . 20 B2
Vendeuvre-sur-Barse,
  France 19 D11
Vendôme, *France* 18 E8
Vendrell = El Vendrell,
  Spain 32 D6
Vendsyssel, *Denmark* 11 G4
Venelles, *France* 21 E9
Véneta, L., *Italy* 29 C9
Véneto □, *Italy* 29 C9
Venev, *Russia* 46 E10
Venézia, *Italy* 29 C9
Venézia, G. di, *Italy* 29 C10
Venezuela ■, *S. Amer.* ... 124 B5
Venezuela, G. de,
  Venezuela 122 B3
Vengurla, *India* 66 M8
Venice = Venézia, *Italy* .. 29 C9
Vénissieux, *France* 21 C8
Venjansjön, *Sweden* 10 D8
Venkatapuram, *India* 67 K12
Venlo, *Neths.* 17 C6
Vennesla, *Norway* 9 G12
Venosa, *Italy* 31 B8
Venray, *Neths.* 17 C6
Venta, *Lithuania* 44 B9
Venta →, *Latvia* 44 A8
Venta de Baños, *Spain* ... 34 D6
Venta de Cardeña =
  Cardeña, *Spain* 35 G6
Ventana, Punta de la,
  Mexico 118 C3
Ventana, Sa. de la,
  Argentina 126 D3
Ventersburg, *S. Africa* ... 88 D4
Venterstad, *S. Africa* 88 E4
Ventimíglia, *Italy* 28 E4
Ventnor, *U.K.* 13 G6
Ventotene, *Italy* 30 B6
Ventoux, Mt., *France* 21 D9
Ventspils, *Latvia* 9 H19
Ventspils □, *Latvia* 44 A8
Ventuarí →, *Venezuela* .. 124 C5
Ventucopa, *U.S.A.* 117 L7
Ventura, *U.S.A.* 117 L7
Venus B., *Australia* 95 F4
Vera, *Argentina* 126 B3
Vera, *Spain* 33 H3
Veracruz, *Mexico* 119 D5
Veracruz □, *Mexico* 119 D5
Veraval, *India* 68 J4
Verbánia, *Italy* 28 C5
Verbicaro, *Italy* 31 C8
Verbier, *Switz.* 25 J3
Vercelli, *Italy* 28 C5
Verchovcevo, *Ukraine* 47 H8
Verdalsøra, *Norway* 8 E14
Verde →, *Argentina* 128 E3

Verde →, *Goiás, Brazil* .. 125 G8
Verde →,
  Mato Grosso do Sul,
  Brazil 125 H8
Verde →, *Chihuahua,*
  Mexico 118 B3
Verde →, *Oaxaca, Mexico* 119 D5
Verde →, *Veracruz,*
  Mexico 118 C4
Verde →, *Paraguay* 126 A4
Verde, Cay, *Bahamas* ... 120 B4
Verde Island Pass, *Phil.* .. 61 E4
Verden, *Germany* 24 C5
Verdhikoúsa, *Greece* 38 B3
Verdi, *U.S.A.* 116 F7
Verdigre, *U.S.A.* 112 D6
Verdon →, *France* 21 E9
Verdun, *France* 19 C12
Verdun-sur-le-Doubs,
  France 19 F12
Vereeniging, *S. Africa* ... 89 D4
Vérendrye, Parc Prov. de
  la, *Canada* 102 C4
Verga, C., *Guinea* 82 C2
Vergato, *Italy* 28 D8
Vergemont, *Australia* 94 C3
Vergemont Cr. →,
  Australia 94 C3
Vergennes, *U.S.A.* 111 B11
Vergt, *France* 20 C4
Verín, *Spain* 34 D3
Verkhnedvinsk =
  Vyerkhnyadzvinsk,
  Belarus 46 E4
Verkhnevilyuysk, *Russia* .. 51 C13
Verkhniy Baskunchak,
  Russia 49 F8
Verkhovye, *Russia* 47 F9
Verkhoyansk, *Russia* 51 C14
Verkhoyansk Ra. =
  Verkhoyanskiy Khrebet,
  Russia 51 C13
Verkhoyanskiy Khrebet,
  Russia 51 C13
Verlo, *Canada* 105 C7
Vermenton, *France* 19 E10
Vermilion, *Canada* 105 C6
Vermilion →, *Alta.,*
  Canada 105 C6
Vermilion →, *Qué.,*
  Canada 102 C5
Vermilion, B., *U.S.A.* 113 L9
Vermilion Bay, *Canada* ... 105 D10
Vermilion Chutes, *Canada* 104 B6
Vermilion L., *U.S.A.* 112 B8
Vermillion, *U.S.A.* 112 D6
Vermont □, *U.S.A.* 111 C12
Vermosh, *Albania* 40 D3
Vernal, *U.S.A.* 114 F9
Vernalis, *U.S.A.* 116 H5
Vernazza, *Italy* 28 D6
Verner, *Canada* 102 C3
Verneuil-sur-Avre, *France* 18 D7
Verneukpan, *S. Africa* ... 88 E3
Vernier, *Switz.* 25 J2
Vérnio, *Italy* 28 D8
Vernon, *Canada* 104 C5
Vernon, *France* 18 C8
Vernon, *U.S.A.* 113 H5
Vernonia, *U.S.A.* 116 E3
Vernouillet, *France* 18 D8
Vero Beach, *U.S.A.* 109 M5
Véroia, *Greece* 40 F6
Véroli, *Italy* 29 G10
Verona, *Italy* 28 C7
Verrès, *Italy* 28 C4
Versailles, *France* 19 D9
Versmold, *Germany* 24 C4
Vert, C., *Senegal* 82 C1
Vertou, *France* 18 E5
Vertus, *France* 19 D11
Verulam, *S. Africa* 89 D5
Verviers, *Belgium* 17 D5
Vervins, *France* 19 C10
Veržej, *Slovenia* 29 B13
Verzy, *France* 19 C11
Vescovato, *France* 21 F13
Veselí nad Lužnicí,
  Czech Rep. 26 B7
Veselie, *Bulgaria* 41 D11
Veselovskoye Vdkhr.,
  Russia 49 G5
Veshenskaya, *Russia* 48 F5
Vesle →, *France* 19 C10
Vesoul, *France* 19 E13
Vessigebro, *Sweden* 11 H6
Vesterålen, *Norway* 8 B16
Vestfjorden, *Norway* 8 C15
Vestmannaeyjar, *Iceland* . 8 E3
Vestsjællands
  Amtskommune □,
  Denmark 11 J5
Vestspitsbergen, *Svalbard* . 4 B8
Vestvågøy, *Norway* 8 B15
Vesúvio, *Italy* 31 B7
Vesuvius, Mt. = Vesúvio,
  Italy 31 B7
Vesyegonsk, *Russia* 46 C9
Veszprém, *Hungary* 42 C2
Veszprém □, *Hungary* 42 C2
Vésztő, *Hungary* 42 D6
Vetlanda, *Sweden* 11 G9
Vetluga, *Russia* 48 B8
Vetlugu →, *Russia* 48 B8
Vetluzhskiy, *Kostroma,*
  Russia 48 A7

Vetluzhskiy,
  Nizhniy Novgorod,
  Russia 48 B7
Vetovo, *Bulgaria* 41 C10
Vetralla, *Italy* 29 F9
Vetren, *Bulgaria* 41 D8
Vettore, Mte., *Italy* 29 F10
Veurne, *Belgium* 17 C2
Vevey, *Switz.* 25 J2
Vévi, *Greece* 40 F5
Veynes, *France* 21 D9
Veys, *Iran* 71 D6
Vézelay, *France* 19 E10
Vézelise, *France* 19 D13
Vézère →, *France* 20 D4
Vezhen, *Bulgaria* 41 D8
Vezirköprü, *Turkey* 72 B6
Vi Thanh, *Vietnam* 65 H5
Viacha, *Bolivia* 124 G5
Viadana, *Italy* 28 D7
Viamão, *Brazil* 127 C5
Viana, *Brazil* 125 D10
Viana, *Spain* 32 C2
Viana do Alentejo,
  Portugal 35 G3
Viana do Bolo, *Spain* 34 C3
Viana do Castelo, *Portugal* 34 D2
Viana do Castelo □,
  Portugal 34 D2
Vianden, *Lux.* 17 E6
Vianópolis, *Brazil* 125 G9
Viar →, *Spain* 35 H5
Viaréggio, *Italy* 28 E7
Viaur →, *France* 20 D5
Vibank, *Canada* 105 C8
Vibble, *Sweden* 11 G12
Vibo Valéntia, *Italy* 31 D9
Viborg, *Denmark* 11 H3
Vigsø Bugt, *Denmark* 11 G2
Viborg Amtskommune □,
  Denmark 11 H3
Vibraye, *France* 18 D7
Vic, *Spain* 32 D7
Vic, Étang de, *France* 20 E7
Vic-en-Bigorre, *France* ... 20 E4
Vic-Fézensac, *France* 20 E4
Vic-le-Comte, *France* 19 G10
Vic-sur-Cère, *France* 20 D6
Vícar, *Spain* 33 J2
Vicenza, *Italy* 29 C8
Vich = Vic, *Spain* 32 D7
Vichada →, *Colombia* 124 C5
Vichuga, *Russia* 48 B5
Vichy, *France* 19 F10
Vicksburg, *Ariz., U.S.A.* . 117 M13
Vicksburg, *Mich., U.S.A.* . 108 D3
Vicksburg, *Miss., U.S.A.* . 113 J9
Vico, *France* 21 F12
Vico, L. di, *Italy* 29 F9
Vico del Gargano, *Italy* ... 29 G12
Vicovu de Sus, *Romania* .. 43 C10
Victor, *India* 68 J4
Victor, *Colo., U.S.A.* 112 F2
Victor, *N.Y., U.S.A.* 110 D7
Victor Harbor, *Australia* .. 95 F2
Victoria = Labuan,
  Malaysia 62 C5
Victoria, *Argentina* 126 C3
Victoria, *Canada* 104 D4
Victoria, *Chile* 128 D2
Victoria, *Guinea* 82 C2
Victoria, *Malta* 36 C1
Victoria, *Phil.* 61 D4
Victoria, *Romania* 43 E9
Victoria, *Kans., U.S.A.* ... 112 F5
Victoria, *Tex., U.S.A.* 113 L6
Victoria □, *Australia* 95 F3
Victoria →, *Australia* 92 C4
Victoria, Grand L., *Canada* 102 C4
Victoria, L., *Africa* 86 C3
Victoria, L., *Australia* 95 E3
Victoria Beach, *Canada* .. 105 C9
Victoria de Durango =
  Durango, *Mexico* 118 C4
Victoria de las Tunas, *Cuba* 120 B4
Victoria Falls, *Zimbabwe* . 87 F2
Victoria Harbour, *Canada* 102 D4
Victoria I., *Canada* 100 A8
Victoria Ld., *Antarctica* .. 5 D11
Victoria Nile →, *Uganda* . 86 B3
Victoria Res., *Canada* 103 C8
Victoria River Downs,
  Australia 92 C5
Victoria Taungdeik, *Burma* 67 J18
Victoria West, *S. Africa* .. 88 E3
Victorias, *Phil.* 61 F5
Victoriaville, *Canada* 103 C5
Victorica, *Argentina* 126 D2
Victorville, *U.S.A.* 117 L9
Vicuña, *Chile* 126 C1
Vicuña Mackenna,
  Argentina 126 C3
Vidal, *U.S.A.* 117 L12
Vidal Junction, *U.S.A.* ... 117 L12
Vidalia, *U.S.A.* 109 J4
Vidauban, *France* 21 E10
Videbæk, *Denmark* 11 H2
Videle, *Romania* 43 F10
Vídho, *Greece* 36 A3
Vidigueira, *Portugal* 35 G3
Vidin, *Bulgaria* 40 C6
Vidio, C., *Spain* 34 B4
Vidisha, *India* 68 H7
Vidra, *Romania* 43 E11
Viduša, *Bos.-H.* 40 D2

Vidzy, *Belarus* 9 J22
Viechtach, *Germany* 25 F8
Viedma, *Argentina* 128 E4
Viedma, L., *Argentina* ... 128 F2
Vieira do Minho, *Portugal* 34 D2
Vielha, *Spain* 32 C5
Viella = Vielha, *Spain* 32 C5
Vielsalm, *Belgium* 17 D5
Vienenburg, *Germany* 24 D6
Vieng Pou Kha, *Laos* 64 B3
Vienna = Wien, *Austria* ... 27 C9
Vienna, *U.S.A.* 113 G10
Vienne, *France* 21 C8
Vienne □, *France* 20 B4
Vienne →, *France* 18 E7
Vientiane, *Laos* 64 D4
Vientos, Paso de los,
  Caribbean 121 C5
Viernheim, *Germany* 25 F4
Viersen, *Germany* 24 D2
Vierwaldstättersee, *Switz.* . 25 J4
Vierzon, *France* 19 E9
Vieste, *Italy* 29 G13
Vietnam ■, *Asia* 64 C6
Vieux-Boucau-les-Bains,
  France 20 E2
Vif, *France* 21 C9
Vigan, *Phil.* 61 C4
Vigévano, *Italy* 28 C5
Vigia, *Brazil* 125 D9
Vigía Chico, *Mexico* 119 D7
Víglas, Ákra, *Greece* 36 D9
Vignemale, *France* 20 F3
Vigneulles-lès-Hattonchâtel,
  France 19 D12
Vignola, *Italy* 28 D8
Vigo, *Spain* 34 C2
Vigo, Ría de, *Spain* 34 C2
Vihiers, *France* 18 E6
Vijayawada, *India* 67 L12
Vík, *Iceland* 8 E4
Vika, *Sweden* 10 D9
Vikarbyn, *Sweden* 10 D9
Vikeke, *Indonesia* 63 F7
Viken, *Malmöhus, Sweden* 11 H6
Viken, *Skaraborg, Sweden* 11 F8
Viking, *Canada* 104 C6
Vikmanshyttan, *Sweden* .. 10 D9
Vikna, *Norway* 8 D14
Vila da Maganja, *Mozam.* 87 F4
Vila de João Belo = Xai-
  Xai, *Mozam.* 89 D5
Vila de Rei, *Portugal* 34 F2
Vila do Bispo, *Portugal* ... 35 H2
Vila do Chibuto, *Mozam.* . 89 C5
Vila do Conde, *Portugal* .. 34 D2
Vila Franca de Xira,
  Portugal 35 G2
Vila Gamito, *Mozam.* 87 E3
Vila Gomes da Costa,
  Mozam. 89 C5
Vila Machado, *Mozam.* ... 87 F3
Vila Mouzinho, *Mozam.* .. 87 E3
Vila Nova de Famalicão,
  Portugal 34 D2
Vila Nova de Fos Côa,
  Portugal 34 D3
Vila Nova de Foscôa =
  Vila Nova de Fos Côa,
  Portugal 34 D3
Vila Nova de Gaia,
  Portugal 34 D2
Vila Nova de Ourém,
  Portugal 34 F2
Vila Pouca de Aguiar,
  Portugal 34 D3
Vila Real, *Portugal* 34 D3
Vila Real □, *Portugal* 34 D3
Vila-real de los Infantes,
  Spain 32 F4
Vila Real de Santo
  António, *Portugal* 35 H3
Vila Vasco da Gama,
  Mozam. 87 E3
Vila Velha, *Brazil* 127 A7
Vila Viçosa, *Portugal* 35 G3
Vilafranca del Maestrat,
  Spain 32 E4
Vilafranca del Penedès,
  Spain 32 D6
Vilagarcía de Arousa, *Spain* 34 C2
Vilaine →, *France* 18 E4
Vilanandro, Tanjona,
  Madag. 89 B7
Vilanculos, *Mozam.* 89 C6
Vilanova de Castelló, *Spain* 33 F4
Vilanova i la Geltrú, *Spain* 32 D6
Vilar Formoso, *Portugal* ... 34 E4
Vilaseca, *Spain* 32 D6
Vilaseca-Salou = Vilaseca,
  Spain 32 D6
Vilhelmina, *Sweden* 8 D17
Vilhena, *Brazil* 124 F6
Viliga, *Russia* 51 C16
Viliya →, *Lithuania* 9 J21
Viljandi, *Estonia* 9 G21
Vilkaviškis, *Lithuania* 44 D10
Vilkija, *Lithuania* 44 C10
Vilkitskogo, Proliv, *Russia* 51 B11
Vilkovo = Vylkove,
  Ukraine 47 K5

Villa Abecia, *Bolivia* 126 A2
Villa Ahumada, *Mexico* .. 118 A3
Villa Ana, *Argentina* 126 B4
Villa Ángela, *Argentina* .. 126 B3
Villa Bella, *Bolivia* 124 F5
Villa Bens = Tarfaya,
  Morocco 78 C3
Villa Cañás, *Argentina* ... 126 C3
Villa Cisneros = Dakhla,
  W. Sahara 78 D2
Villa Colón, *Argentina* ... 126 C2
Villa Constitución,
  Argentina 126 C3
Villa de María, *Argentina* . 126 B3
Villa del Rio, *Spain* 35 H6
Villa Dolores, *Argentina* .. 126 C2
Villa Frontera, *Mexico* ... 118 B4
Villa Guillermina,
  Argentina 126 B4
Villa Hayes, *Paraguay* ... 126 B4
Villa Iris, *Argentina* 126 D3
Villa Juárez, *Mexico* 118 B4
Villa María, *Argentina* ... 126 C3
Villa Mazán, *Argentina* ... 126 B2
Villa Minozzo, *Italy* 28 D7
Villa Montes, *Bolivia* 126 A3
Villa Ocampo, *Argentina* .. 126 B4
Villa Ocampo, *Mexico* ... 118 B3
Villa Ojo de Agua,
  Argentina 126 B3
Villa San Giovanni, *Italy* . 31 D8
Villa San José, *Argentina* . 126 C4
Villa San Martín, *Argentina* 126 B3
Villa Santina, *Italy* 29 B9
Villa Unión, *Mexico* 118 C3
Villablino, *Spain* 34 C4
Villacarlos, *Spain* 37 B11
Villacarriedo, *Spain* 34 B7
Villacarrillo, *Spain* 35 G7
Villacastín, *Spain* 34 E6
Villach, *Austria* 26 E6
Villacidro, *Italy* 30 C1
Villada, *Spain* 34 C6
Villadiego, *Spain* 34 C6
Villadóssola, *Italy* 28 B5
Villafeliche, *Spain* 32 D3
Villafranca, *Spain* 32 C3
Villafranca de los Barros,
  Spain 35 G4
Villafranca de los
  Caballeros, *Baleares,*
  Spain 37 B10
Villafranca de los
  Caballeros, *Toledo, Spain* 35 F7
Villafranca del Cid =
  Vilafranca del Maestrat,
  Spain 32 E4
Villafranca del Panadés =
  Vilafranca del Penedès,
  Spain 32 D6
Villafranca di Verona, *Italy* 28 C7
Villafranca Tirrena, *Italy* . 31 D8
Villagrán, *Mexico* 119 C5
Villaguay, *Argentina* 126 C4
Villaharta, *Spain* 35 G6
Villahermosa, *Mexico* 119 D6
Villahermosa, *Spain* 33 G2
Villaines-la-Juhel, *France* . 18 D6
Villajoyosa, *Spain* 33 G4
Villalba, *Spain* 34 B3
Villalba de Guardo, *Spain* 34 C6
Villalón de Campos, *Spain* 34 C5
Villalpando, *Spain* 34 D5
Villaluenga, *Spain* 34 E7
Villamanán, *Spain* 34 C5
Villamartín, *Spain* 35 J5
Villamayor de Santiago,
  Spain 32 F2
Villablard, *France* 20 C4
Villanova Monteleone, *Italy* 30 B1
Villanueva, *U.S.A.* 115 J11
Villanueva de Castellón =
  Vilanova de Castelló,
  Spain 33 F4
Villanueva de Córdoba,
  Spain 35 G6
Villanueva de la Fuente,
  Spain 33 G2
Villanueva de la Serena,
  Spain 35 G5
Villanueva de la Sierra,
  Spain 34 E4
Villanueva de los
  Castillejos, *Spain* 35 H3
Villanueva de los Infantes,
  Spain 35 G7
Villanueva del Arzobispo,
  Spain 33 G2
Villanueva del Fresno,
  Spain 35 G3
Villaputzu, *Italy* 30 C2
Villaquilambre, *Spain* 34 C5
Villar del Arzobispo, *Spain* 32 F4
Villar del Rey, *Spain* 35 F4
Villard-de-Lans, *France* ... 21 C9
Villarramiel, *Spain* 34 C6
Villarreal = Vila-real de los
  Infantes, *Spain* 32 F4
Villarrica, *Chile* 128 D2
Villarrica, *Paraguay* 126 B4
Villarrobledo, *Spain* 33 F2
Villarroya de la Sierra,
  Spain 32 D3

Waingapu

Villarrubia de los Ojos, *Spain* 35 F7
Villars-les-Dombes, *France* 19 F12
Villasayas, *Spain* 32 D2
Villaseca de los Gamitos = Villaseco de los Gamitos, *Spain* 34 D4
Villaseco de los Gamitos, *Spain* 34 D4
Villasimíus, *Italy* 30 C2
Villastar, *Spain* 32 E3
Villatobas, *Spain* 34 F7
Villavicencio, *Argentina* 126 C2
Villavicencio, *Colombia* 124 C4
Villaviciosa, *Spain* 34 B5
Villazón, *Bolivia* 126 A2
Ville-Marie, *Canada* 102 C4
Ville Platte, *U.S.A.* 113 K8
Villedieu-les-Poêles, *France* 18 D5
Villefort, *France* 20 D7
Villefranche-de-Lauragais, *France* 20 E5
Villefranche-de-Rouergue, *France* 20 D6
Villefranche-du-Périgord, *France* 20 D5
Villefranche-sur-Saône, *France* 21 C8
Villel, *Spain* 32 E3
Villemur-sur-Tarn, *France* 20 E5
Villena, *Spain* 33 G4
Villenauxe-la-Grande, *France* 19 D10
Villenave-d'Ornon, *France* 20 D3
Villeneuve-d'Ascq, *France* 19 B10
Villeneuve-l'Archevêque, *France* 19 D10
Villeneuve-lès-Avignon, *France* 21 E8
Villeneuve-sur-Allier, *France* 19 F10
Villeneuve-sur-Lot, *France* 20 D4
Villeneuve-sur-Yonne, *France* 19 D10
Villeréal, *France* 20 D4
Villers-Bocage, *France* 18 C6
Villers-Cotterêts, *France* 19 C10
Villers-sur-Mer, *France* 18 C6
Villersexel, *France* 19 E13
Villerupt, *France* 19 C12
Villeurbanne, *France* 21 C8
Villiers, *S. Africa* 89 D4
Villingen-Schwenningen, *Germany* 25 G4
Villisca, *U.S.A.* 112 E7
Vilna, *Canada* 104 C6
Vilnius, *Lithuania* 9 J21
Vils, *Austria* 26 D3
Vils →, *Bayern, Germany* 25 G9
Vils →, *Bayern, Germany* 25 F7
Vilsbiburg, *Germany* 25 G8
Vilshofen, *Germany* 25 G9
Vilusi, *Montenegro, Yug.* 40 D2
Vilvoorde, *Belgium* 17 D4
Vilyuy →, *Russia* 51 C13
Vilyuysk, *Russia* 51 C13
Vimianzo, *Spain* 34 B1
Vimioso, *Portugal* 34 D4
Vimmerby, *Sweden* 11 G9
Vimoutiers, *France* 18 D7
Vimperk, *Czech Rep.* 26 B6
Viña del Mar, *Chile* 126 C1
Vinarós, *Spain* 32 E5
Vincennes, *U.S.A.* 108 F2
Vincent, *U.S.A.* 117 L8
Vinchina, *Argentina* 126 B2
Vindelälven →, *Sweden* 8 E18
Vindeln, *Sweden* 8 D18
Vinderup, *Denmark* 11 H2
Vindhya Ra., *India* 68 H7
Vineland, *U.S.A.* 108 F8
Vineuil, *France* 18
Vinga, *Romania* 42 D6
Vingåker, *Sweden* 10 E9
Vinh, *Vietnam* 64 C5
Vinh Linh, *Vietnam* 64 D6
Vinh Long, *Vietnam* 65 G5
Vinh Yen, *Vietnam* 64 B5
Vinhais, *Portugal* 34 D3
Vinica, *Croatia* 29 B13
Vinica, *Macedonia* 40 E6
Vinica, *Slovenia* 29 C12
Vinita, *U.S.A.* 113 G7
Vinkovci, *Croatia* 42 E3
Vinnitsa = Vinnytsya, *Ukraine* 47 H5
Vinnytsya, *Ukraine* 47 H5
Vinslöv, *Sweden* 11 H7
Vintjärn, *Sweden* 10 D10
Vinton, *Calif., U.S.A.* 116 F6
Vinton, *Iowa, U.S.A.* 112 D8
Vinton, *La., U.S.A.* 113 K8
Vinţu de Jos, *Romania* 43 D8
Viöl, *Germany* 24 A5
Vipava, *Slovenia* 29 C10
Vipiteno, *Italy* 29 B8
Vir, *Croatia* 29 D12
Virac, *Phil.* 61 E6
Virachei, *Cambodia* 64 F6
Virago Sd., *Canada* 104 C2
Viramgam, *India* 68 H5
Viranşehir, *Turkey* 73 D8
Virbalis, *Lithuania* 44 D9
Virden, *Canada* 105 D8
Vire, *France* 18 D6
Vire →, *France* 18 C5
Vírgenes, C., *Argentina* 128 G3
Virgin →, *Canada* 105 B7
Virgin →, *U.S.A.* 115 H6
Virgin Gorda, *Virgin Is.* 121 C7
Virgin Is. (British) ■, *W. Indies* 121 C7
Virgin Is. (U.S.) ■, *W. Indies* 121 C7
Virginia, *S. Africa* 88 D4
Virginia, *U.S.A.* 112 B8
Virginia □, *U.S.A.* 108 G7
Virginia Beach, *U.S.A.* 108 G8
Virginia City, *Mont., U.S.A.* 114 D8
Virginia City, *Nev., U.S.A.* 116 F7
Virginia Falls, *Canada* 104 A3
Virginiatown, *Canada* 102 C4
Virje, *Croatia* 29 B13
Viroqua, *U.S.A.* 112 D9
Virovitica, *Croatia* 42 E2
Virpazar, *Montenegro, Yug.* 40 D3
Virserum, *Sweden* 11 G9
Virton, *Belgium* 17 E5
Virudunagar, *India* 66 Q10
Vis, *Croatia* 29 E13
Visalia, *U.S.A.* 116 J7
Visayan Sea, *Phil.* 61 F5
Visby, *Sweden* 11 G12
Viscount Melville Sd., *Canada* 4 B2
Visé, *Belgium* 17 D5
Višegrad, *Bos.-H.* 42 G4
Viseu, *Brazil* 125 D9
Viseu, *Portugal* 34 E3
Viseu □, *Portugal* 34 E3
Vişeu de Sus, *Romania* 43 C9
Vishakhapatnam, *India* 67 L13
Vişina, *Romania* 43 G9
Vişineşti, *Moldova* 43 D13
Visingsö, *Sweden* 11 F8
Viskafors, *Sweden* 11 G6
Viskan →, *Sweden* 11 G6
Viški Kanal, *Croatia* 29 E13
Vislanda, *Sweden* 11 H8
Visnagar, *India* 68 H5
Višnja Gora, *Slovenia* 29 C11
Viso, Mte., *Italy* 28 D4
Viso del Marqués, *Spain* 35 G7
Visoko, *Bos.-H.* 42 G3
Visokoi I., *Antarctica* 5 B1
Visp, *Switz.* 25 J3
Vissefjärda, *Sweden* 11 H9
Visselhövede, *Germany* 24 C5
Vissenbjerg, *Denmark* 11 J4
Vista, *U.S.A.* 117 M9
Vistonikos, Ormos = Vistonís, Límni, *Greece* 41 E9
Vistonís, Límni, *Greece* 41 E9
Vistula = Wisła →, *Poland* 44 D5
Vit →, *Bulgaria* 41 C8
Vitanje, *Slovenia* 29 B12
Vitebsk = Vitsyebsk, *Belarus* 46 E6
Viterbo, *Italy* 29 F9
Vitez, *Bos.-H.* 42 F2
Viti Levu, *Fiji* 91 C7
Vitigudino, *Spain* 34 D4
Vitim, *Russia* 51 D12
Vitim →, *Russia* 51 D12
Vitina, *Bos.-H.* 29 E14
Vitína, *Greece* 38 D4
Vítkov, *Czech Rep.* 27 B10
Vitória, *Brazil* 125 H10
Vitória da Conquista, *Brazil* 125 F10
Vitória de São Antão, *Brazil* 125 E11
Vitoria-Gasteiz, *Spain* 32 C2
Vitré, *France* 18 D5
Vitry-le-François, *France* 19 D11
Vitry-sur-Seine, *France* 19 D9
Vitsand, *Sweden* 10 D7
Vitsi, Óros, *Greece* 40 F5
Vitsyebsk, *Belarus* 46 E6
Vittaryd, *Sweden* 11 H7
Vitteaux, *France* 19 E11
Vittel, *France* 19 D12
Vittória, *Italy* 31 F7
Vittório Véneto, *Italy* 29 C9
Vittsjö, *Sweden* 11 H7
Viveiro, *Spain* 34 B3
Viviers, *France* 21 D8
Vivonne, *France* 20 B4
Vizcaíno, Desierto de, *Mexico* 118 B2
Vizcaíno, Sierra, *Mexico* 118 B2
Vizcaya □, *Spain* 32 B2
Vize, *Turkey* 41 E11
Vizianagaram, *India* 67 K13
Vizille, *France* 21 C9
Viziñada, *Croatia* 29 C10
Viziru, *Romania* 43 E12
Vizzini, *Italy* 31 E7
Vjosa →, *Albania* 40 F3
Vlaardingen, *Neths.* 17 C4
Vlădeasa, Vf., *Romania* 42 D7
Vladičin Han, *Serbia, Yug.* 40 D6
Vladikavkaz, *Russia* 49 J7
Vladimir, *Russia* 46 D11
Vladimir Volynskiy = Volodymyr-Volynskyy, *Ukraine* 47 G3
Vladimirci, *Serbia, Yug.* 40 B3
Vladimirovac, *Serbia, Yug.* 42 E5
Vladimirovka, *Russia* 49 F8
Vladimirovo, *Bulgaria* 40 C7
Vladimorvka, *Kazakstan* 48 E10
Vladislavovka, *Ukraine* 47 K8
Vladivostok, *Russia* 54 C5
Vlăhiţa, *Romania* 43 D10
Vlakhiótis, *Greece* 38 E4
Vlasenica, *Bos.-H.* 42 F3
Vlašić, *Bos.-H.* 42 F2
Vlašim, *Czech Rep.* 26 B7
Vlasinsko Jezero, *Serbia, Yug.* 40 D6
Vlasotince, *Serbia, Yug.* 40 D6
Vlieland, *Neths.* 17 A4
Vlissingen, *Neths.* 17 C3
Vlóra, *Albania* 40 F3
Vlorës, Gjiri i, *Albania* 40 F3
Vltava →, *Czech Rep.* 26 A7
Vo Dat, *Vietnam* 65 G6
Vobarno, *Italy* 28 C7
Voćin, *Croatia* 42 E2
Vöcklabruck, *Austria* 26 C6
Vodice, *Croatia* 29 E12
Vodňany, *Czech Rep.* 26 B7
Vodnjan, *Croatia* 29 D10
Voe, *U.K.* 14 A7
Vogelkop = Doberai, Jazirah, *Indonesia* 63 E8
Vogelsberg, *Germany* 24 E5
Voghera, *Italy* 28 D6
Vohibinany, *Madag.* 89 B8
Vohimarina = Iharana, *Madag.* 89 A9
Vohimena, Tanjon' i, *Madag.* 89 D8
Vohipeno, *Madag.* 89 C8
Voi, *Kenya* 86 C4
Void-Vacon, *France* 19 D12
Voineşti, *Iaşi, Romania* 43 C12
Voineşti, *Prahova, Romania* 43 E10
Voíotía □, *Greece* 38 C5
Voiron, *France* 21 C9
Voisey B., *Canada* 103 A7
Voitsberg, *Austria* 26 D8
Vojens, *Denmark* 11 J3
Vojmsjön, *Sweden* 8 D17
Vojnić, *Croatia* 29 C12
Vojnik, *Italy* 29 B12
Vojvodina □, *Serbia, Yug.* 42 E5
Vokhtoga, *Russia* 46 C11
Volary, *Czech Rep.* 26 C6
Volborg, *U.S.A.* 112 C2
Volcano Is. = Kazan-Rettō, *Pac. Oc.* 96 E6
Volchansk = Vovchansk, *Ukraine* 47 G9
Volchya →, *Ukraine* 47 H8
Volda, *Norway* 9 E12
Volga, *Russia* 46 C10
Volga →, *Russia* 49 G9
Volga Hts. = Privolzhskaya Vozvyshennost, *Russia* 48 E7
Volgo-Baltiyskiy Kanal, *Russia* 46 B9
Volgo-Donskoy Kanal, *Russia* 49 F7
Volgodonsk, *Russia* 49 G6
Volgograd, *Russia* 49 F7
Volgogradskoye Vdkhr., *Russia* 48 E8
Volgorechensk, *Russia* 48 B5
Volímai, *Greece* 38 D2
Volintiri, *Moldova* 43 D14
Volissós, *Greece* 39 C7
Volkach, *Germany* 25 F6
Völkermarkt, *Austria* 26 E7
Volkhov, *Russia* 46 C7
Volkhov →, *Russia* 46 B7
Völklingen, *Germany* 25 F2
Volkovysk = Vawkavysk, *Belarus* 47 F3
Volksrust, *S. Africa* 89 D4
Volnansk, *Ukraine* 47 H8
Volnovakha, *Ukraine* 47 J9
Volochanka, *Russia* 51 B10
Volodarsk, *Russia* 48 B6
Volodymyr-Volynskyy, *Ukraine* 47 G3
Vologda, *Russia* 46 C10
Volokolamsk, *Russia* 46 D8
Volokonovka, *Russia* 47 G9
Vólos, *Greece* 38 B4
Volosovo, *Russia* 46 C5
Volovets, *Ukraine* 47 H2
Volovo, *Russia* 46 F10
Volozhin = Valozhyn, *Belarus* 46 E4
Volsk, *Russia* 48 D8
Volta →, *Ghana* 83 D5
Volta, L., *Ghana* 83 D5
Volta Blanche = White Volta →, *Ghana* 83 D4
Volta Redonda, *Brazil* 127 A7
Voltaire, C., *Australia* 92 B4
Volterra, *Italy* 28 E7
Voltri, *Italy* 28 D5
Volturno →, *Italy* 30 A6
Vólvi, L., *Greece* 40 F7
Volvo, *Australia* 95 E3
Volyně, *Czech Rep.* 26 B6
Volzhsk, *Russia* 48 C9
Volzhskiy, *Russia* 49 F7
Vondrozo, *Madag.* 89 C8
Vónitsa, *Greece* 38 C2
Vopnafjörður, *Iceland* 8 D6
Vorarlberg □, *Austria* 26 D2
Vóras Óros, *Greece* 40 F5
Vorbasse, *Denmark* 11 J3
Vorchdorf, *Austria* 26 C6
Vorderrhein →, *Switz.* 25 J5
Vordingborg, *Denmark* 11 J5
Vorë, *Albania* 40 E3
Voreppe, *France* 21 C9
Vóriai Sporádhes, *Greece* 38 B5
Vórios Aiyaíon □, *Greece* 39 C7
Vórios Evvoïkos Kólpos, *Greece* 38 C5
Vorkuta, *Russia* 50 C7
Vormsi, *Estonia* 9 G20
Vorona →, *Russia* 48 E6
Voronezh, *Russia* 47 G10
Voronezh, *Ukraine* 47 G7
Voronezh →, *Russia* 47 G10
Vorontsovo-Aleksandrovskoye = Zelenokumsk, *Russia* 49 H6
Voroshilovgrad = Luhansk, *Ukraine* 47 H10
Voroshilovsk = Alchevsk, *Ukraine* 47 H10
Vórroi, *Greece* 38 F6
Vorskla →, *Ukraine* 47 H8
Võrts Järv, *Estonia* 9 G22
Vöru, *Estonia* 9 H22
Vosges, *France* 19 D14
Vosges □, *France* 19 D13
Voskopoja, *Albania* 40 F4
Voskresensk, *Russia* 46 E10
Voskresenskoye, *Russia* 48 B7
Voss, *Norway* 9 F12
Vostok I., *Kiribati* 97 J12
Votice, *Czech Rep.* 26 B7
Vouga →, *Portugal* 34 E2
Vouillé, *France* 18 F7
Voúxa, Ákra, *Greece* 36 D5
Vouzela, *Portugal* 34 E2
Vouziers, *France* 19 C11
Vovchansk, *Ukraine* 47 G9
Vozhe Ozero, *Russia* 46 B10
Vozhega, *Russia* 46 B11
Voznesensk, *Ukraine* 47 J6
Voznesenye, *Russia* 46 B8
Vrå, *Denmark* 11 G3
Vráble, *Slovak Rep.* 27 C11
Vraćevšnica, *Serbia, Yug.* 40 B4
Vrakhnéïka, *Greece* 38 C3
Vrancea □, *Romania* 43 E11
Vrancei, Munţii, *Romania* 43 E11
Vrangelya, Ostrov, *Russia* 51 B19
Vranica, *Bos.-H.* 42 G2
Vranje, *Serbia, Yug.* 40 D5
Vranjska Banja, *Serbia, Yug.* 40 D6
Vranov nad Topl'ou, *Slovak Rep.* 27 C14
Vransko, *Slovenia* 29 B11
Vransko Jezero, *Croatia* 29 E12
Vrapčište, *Macedonia* 40 E4
Vratsa, *Bulgaria* 40 C7
Vrbas, *Serbia, Yug.* 42 E4
Vrbas →, *Bos.-H.* 42 E2
Vrbnik, *Croatia* 29 C11
Vrbovec, *Croatia* 29 C13
Vrbovsko, *Croatia* 29 C12
Vrchlabí, *Czech Rep.* 26 A8
Vrede, *S. Africa* 89 D4
Vredefort, *S. Africa* 88 D4
Vreden, *Germany* 24 C2
Vredenburg, *S. Africa* 88 E2
Vredendal, *S. Africa* 88 E2
Vretstorp, *Sweden* 10 E8
Vrgorac, *Croatia* 29 E14
Vrhnika, *Slovenia* 29 C11
Vridi, *Ivory C.* 82 D4
Vrigstad, *Sweden* 11 G8
Vrindavan, *India* 68 F7
Vríses, *Greece* 36 D6
Vrnograč, *Bos.-H.* 29 C12
Vrondádhes, *Greece* 39 C8
Vrpolje, *Croatia* 42 E3
Vršac, *Serbia, Yug.* 42 E6
Vrsacki Kanal, *Serbia, Yug.* 42 E5
Vrútky, *Slovak Rep.* 27 B11
Vryburg, *S. Africa* 88 D3
Vryheid, *S. Africa* 89 D5
Vsetín, *Czech Rep.* 27 B11
Vu Liet, *Vietnam* 64 C5
Vŭcha →, *Bulgaria* 41 D8
Vučitrn, *Serbia, Yug.* 40 D4
Vukovar, *Croatia* 42 E3
Vulcan, *Canada* 104 C6
Vulcan, *Romania* 43 E8
Vulcan, *U.S.A.* 108 C2
Vulcaneşti, *Moldova* 43 E13
Vulcano, *Italy* 31 D7
Vŭlchedruma, *Bulgaria* 40 C7
Vulkaneshty = Vulcaneşti, *Moldova* 43 E13
Vunduzi →, *Mozam.* 87 F3
Vung Tau, *Vietnam* 65 G6
Vŭrbitsa, *Bulgaria* 41 D10
Vurshets, *Bulgaria* 40 C7
Vutcani, *Romania* 43 D12
Vyartsilya, *Russia* 46 A6
Vyatka = Kirov, *Russia* 50 D5
Vyatka →, *Russia* 48 C10
Vyatskiye Polyany, *Russia* 48 B10
Vyazemskiy, *Russia* 51 E14
Vyazma, *Russia* 46 E8
Vyazniki, *Russia* 48 B6
Vyborg, *Russia* 46 B5
Vychegda →, *Russia* 50 C5
Východné Beskydy, *Europe* 27 B15
Východočeský □, *Czech Rep.* 26 E8
Vyerkhnyadzvinsk, *Belarus* 46 E4
Vyksa, *Russia* 48 C6
Vylkove, *Ukraine* 47 K5
Vynohradiv, *Ukraine* 47 H2
Vyrnwy, L., *U.K.* 12 E4
Vyshniy Volochek, *Russia* 46 D8
Vyškov, *Czech Rep.* 27 B9
Vysoké Mýto, *Czech Rep.* 27 B9
Vysokovsk, *Russia* 46 D9
Vyšší Brod, *Czech Rep.* 26 C7
Vytegra, *Russia* 46 B9

W

W.A.C. Bennett Dam, *Canada* 104 B4
Wa, *Ghana* 82 C4
Waal →, *Neths.* 17 C5
Waalwijk, *Neths.* 17 C5
Wabakimi L., *Canada* 102 B2
Wabana, *Canada* 103 C9
Wabasca, *Canada* 104 B6
Wabash, *U.S.A.* 108 E3
Wabash →, *U.S.A.* 108 G1
Wabeno, *U.S.A.* 108 C1
Wabi →, *Ethiopia* 81 F5
Wabigoon L., *Canada* 105 D10
Wabowden, *Canada* 105 C9
Wąbrzeźno, *Poland* 45 E5
Wabu Hu, *China* 59 A11
Wabuk Pt., *Canada* 102 A2
Wabush, *Canada* 103 B6
Wabuska, *U.S.A.* 114 G4
Wąchock, *Poland* 45 G8
Wächtersbach, *Germany* 25 E5
Waco, *U.S.A.* 113 K6
Waconichi, L., *Canada* 102 B5
Wad, *Pakistan* 68 F2
Wad Ban Naqa, *Sudan* 81 D3
Wad Banda, *Sudan* 81 E2
Wad el Haddad, *Sudan* 81 E3
Wad en Nau, *Sudan* 81 E3
Wad Hamid, *Sudan* 81 D3
Wâd Medanî, *Sudan* 81 E3
Wadai, *Africa* 76 E5
Wadayama, *Japan* 55 G7
Waddeneilanden, *Neths.* 17 A5
Waddenzee, *Neths.* 17 A5
Wadderin Hill, *Australia* 93 F2
Waddington, *U.S.A.* 111 B9
Waddington, Mt., *Canada* 104 C3
Waddy Pt., *Australia* 95 C5
Wadebridge, *U.K.* 13 G3
Wadena, *Canada* 105 C8
Wadena, *U.S.A.* 112 B7
Wädenswil, *Switz.* 25 H4
Wadern, *Germany* 25 F2
Wadesboro, *U.S.A.* 109 H5
Wadhams, *Canada* 104 C3
Wādī as Sīr, *Jordan* 75 D4
Wadi Gemâl, *Egypt* 80 C4
Wadi Halfa, *Sudan* 80 C3
Wadian, *China* 59 A9
Wadlew, *Poland* 45 G6
Wadowice, *Poland* 45 J6
Wadsworth, *U.S.A.* 114 G4
Waegwan, *S. Korea* 57 G15
Wafrah, *Si. Arabia* 70 D5
Wageningen, *Neths.* 17 C5
Wager B., *Canada* 101 B11
Wagga Wagga, *Australia* 95 F4
Waghete, *Indonesia* 63 E9
Wagin, *Australia* 93 F2
Wagon Mound, *U.S.A.* 113 G2
Wagoner, *U.S.A.* 113 H7
Wagrowiec, *Poland* 45 F4
Wah, *Pakistan* 68 C5
Wahai, *Indonesia* 63 E7
Wahiawa, *U.S.A.* 106 H15
Wâḥid, *Egypt* 75 E1
Wahnai, *Afghan.* 68 C1
Wahoo, *U.S.A.* 112 E6
Wahpeton, *U.S.A.* 112 B6
Wai, Koh, *Cambodia* 65 H4
Waiau →, *N.Z.* 91 K4
Waibeem, *Indonesia* 63 E8
Waiblingen, *Germany* 25 G5
Waidhofen an der Thaya, *Austria* 26 C8
Waidhofen an der Ybbs, *Austria* 26 D7
Waigeo, *Indonesia* 63 E8
Waihi, *N.Z.* 91 G5
Waihou →, *N.Z.* 91 G5
Waika, *Dem. Rep. of the Congo* 86 C2
Waikabubak, *Indonesia* 63 F5
Waikari, *N.Z.* 91 K4
Waikato →, *N.Z.* 91 G5
Waikerie, *Australia* 95 E3
Waikokopu, *N.Z.* 91 H6
Waikouaiti, *N.Z.* 91 L3
Waimakariri →, *N.Z.* 91 K4
Waimate, *N.Z.* 91 L3
Wainganga →, *India* 66 K11
Waingapu, *Indonesia* 63 F6

Waini →, *Guyana* 124 B7
Wainwright, *Canada* 105 C6
Waiouru, *N.Z.* 91 H5
Waipara, *N.Z.* 91 K4
Waipawa, *N.Z.* 91 H6
Waipiro, *N.Z.* 91 H7
Waipu, *N.Z.* 91 F5
Waipukurau, *N.Z.* 91 J6
Wairakei, *N.Z.* 91 H6
Wairarapa, L., *N.Z.* 91 J5
Wairoa, *N.Z.* 91 H6
Waitaki →, *N.Z.* 91 L3
Waitara, *N.Z.* 91 H5
Waitsburg, *U.S.A.* 114 C5
Waiuku, *N.Z.* 91 G5
Wajima, *Japan* 55 F8
Wajir, *Kenya* 86 B5
Wajir □, *Kenya* 86 B5
Wakasa, *Japan* 55 G7
Wakasa-Wan, *Japan* 55 G7
Wakatipu, L., *N.Z.* 91 L2
Wakaw, *Canada* 105 C7
Wakayama, *Japan* 55 G7
Wakayama-ken □, *Japan* . 55 H7
Wake Forest, *U.S.A.* 109 H6
Wake I., *Pac. Oc.* 96 F8
Wakefield, *N.Z.* 91 J4
Wakefield, *U.K.* 12 D6
Wakefield, *Mass., U.S.A.* . 111 D13
Wakefield, *Mich., U.S.A.* . 112 B10
Wakema, *Burma* 67 L19
Wakkanai, *Japan* 54 B10
Wakkerstroom, *S. Africa* . 89 D5
Wakool, *Australia* 95 F3
Wakool →, *Australia* 95 F3
Wakre, *Indonesia* 63 E8
Wakuach L., *Canada* 103 A6
Walamba, *Zambia* 87 E2
Wałbrzych, *Poland* 45 H4
Walbury Hill, *U.K.* 13 F6
Walcha, *Australia* 95 E5
Walcheren, *Neths.* 17 C3
Walcott, *U.S.A.* 114 F10
Wałcz, *Poland* 45 E3
Waldbröl, *Germany* 24 E3
Waldburg Ra., *Australia* . 92 D2
Waldeck, *Germany* 24 D5
Walden, *Colo., U.S.A.* ... 114 F10
Walden, *N.Y., U.S.A.* ... 111 E10
Waldkirch, *Germany* 25 G3
Waldkirchen, *Germany* .. 25 G5
Waldkraiburg, *Germany* . 25 G8
Waldport, *U.S.A.* 114 D1
Waldron, *U.S.A.* 113 H7
Waldviertel, *Austria* 26 C8
Walembele, *Ghana* 82 C4
Walensee, *Switz.* 25 H5
Wales □, *U.K.* 13 E3
Walewale, *Ghana* 83 C4
Walgett, *Australia* 95 E4
Walgreen Coast, *Antarctica* 5 D15
Walhalla, *Australia* 95 F4
Walhalla, *U.S.A.* 105 D9
Walker, *U.S.A.* 112 B7
Walker L., *Man., Canada* 105 C9
Walker L., *Qué., Canada* . 103 B6
Walker L., *U.S.A.* 114 G4
Walkerston, *Australia* ... 94 C4
Walkerton, *Canada* 110 B3
Wall, *U.S.A.* 112 D3
Walla Walla, *U.S.A.* 114 C4
Wallabadah, *Australia* ... 94 B3
Wallace, *Idaho, U.S.A.* .. 114 C6
Wallace, *N.C., U.S.A.* ... 109 H7
Wallace, *Nebr., U.S.A.* .. 112 E4
Wallaceburg, *Canada* 102 D3
Wallachia = Valahia,
  Romania 43 F9
Wallal, *Australia* 95 D4
Wallal Downs, *Australia* . 92 C3
Wallambin, L., *Australia* . 93 F2
Wallaroo, *Australia* 95 E2
Walldürn, *Germany* 25 F5
Wallenhorst, *Germany* ... 24 C4
Wallerawang, *Australia* .. 95 E5
Wallhallow, *Australia* ... 94 B2
Wallingford, *U.S.A.* 111 E12
Wallis & Futuna, Is.,
  Pac. Oc. 96 J10
Wallowa, *U.S.A.* 114 D5
Wallowa Mts., *U.S.A.* ... 114 D5
Walls, *U.K.* 14 A7
Wallsend, *Australia* 95 E5
Wallula, *U.S.A.* 114 C4
Wallumbilla, *Australia* .. 95 D4
Walmsley, L., *Canada* ... 105 A7
Walney, I. of, *U.K.* 12 C4
Walnut Creek, *U.S.A.* ... 116 H4
Walnut Ridge, *U.S.A.* ... 113 G9
Wals, *Austria* 26 D5
Walsall, *U.K.* 13 E6
Walsenburg, *U.S.A.* 113 G2
Walsh, *U.S.A.* 113 G3
Walsh →, *Australia* 94 B3
Walsh P.O., *Australia* ... 94 B3
Walsrode, *Germany* 24 C5
Walterboro, *U.S.A.* 109 J5
Walters, *U.S.A.* 113 H5
Waltershausen, *Germany* . 24 E6
Waltham, *U.S.A.* 111 D13
Waltham Station, *Canada* . 102 C4
Waltman, *U.S.A.* 114 E10
Walton, *U.S.A.* 111 D9
Walton-on-the-Naze, *U.K.* . 13 F9
Walvis Bay, *Namibia* 88 C1

Walvisbaai = Walvis Bay,
  Namibia 88 C1
Wamba,
  Dem. Rep. of the Congo 86 B2
Wamba, *Kenya* 86 B4
Wamego, *U.S.A.* 112 F6
Wamena, *Indonesia* 63 E9
Wamulan, *Indonesia* 63 E7
Wan Xian, *China* 56 E8
Wana, *Pakistan* 68 C3
Wanaaring, *Australia* ... 95 D3
Wanaka, *N.Z.* 91 L2
Wanaka L., *N.Z.* 91 L2
Wan'an, *China* 59 D10
Wanapitei L., *Canada* ... 102 C3
Wanbi, *Australia* 95 E3
Wandarrie, *Australia* 93 E2
Wandel Sea = McKinley
  Sea, *Arctic* 4 A7
Wanderer, *Zimbabwe* 87 F3
Wandoan, *Australia* 95 D4
Wanfu, *China* 57 D12
Wang →, *Thailand* 64 D2
Wang Kai, *Sudan* 81 F2
Wang Noi, *Thailand* 64 E3
Wang Saphung, *Thailand* . 64 D3
Wang Thong, *Thailand* .. 64 D3
Wanga,
  Dem. Rep. of the Congo 86 B2
Wangal, *Indonesia* 63 F8
Wanganella, *Australia* ... 95 F3
Wanganui, *N.Z.* 91 H5
Wangaratta, *Australia* ... 95 F4
Wangary, *Australia* 95 E2
Wangcang, *China* 58 A6
Wangdu, *China* 56 E8
Wangen, *Germany* 25 H5
Wangerooge, *Germany* ... 24 B3
Wangi, *Kenya* 86 C5
Wangiwangi, *Indonesia* .. 63 F6
Wangjiang, *China* 59 B11
Wangmo, *China* 58 E6
Wangqing, *China* 57 C15
Wankaner, *India* 68 H4
Wanless, *Canada* 105 C8
Wannian, *China* 59 C11
Wanning, *Taiwan* 64 C8
Wanon Niwat, *Thailand* . 64 D4
Wanquan, *China* 56 D8
Wanrong, *China* 56 G6
Wanshan, *China* 58 D7
Wanshengchang, *China* .. 58 C6
Wantage, *U.K.* 13 F6
Wanxian, *China* 58 B7
Wanyuan, *China* 58 A4
Wanzai, *China* 59 C10
Wapakoneta, *U.S.A.* 108 E3
Wapato, *U.S.A.* 114 C3
Wapawekka L., *Canada* .. 105 C8
Wapikopa L., *Canada* ... 102 B2
Wappingers Falls, *U.S.A.* . 111 E11
Wapsipinicon →, *U.S.A.* . 112 E9
Warangal, *India* 66 L11
Waratah, *Australia* 94 G4
Waratah B., *Australia* ... 95 F4
Warburg, *Germany* 24 D5
Warburton, *Vic., Australia* 95 F4
Warburton, *W. Austral.,*
  Australia 93 E4
Warburton Ra., *Australia* . 93 E4
Ward, *N.Z.* 91 J5
Ward →, *Australia* 95 D4
Ward Cove, *U.S.A.* 104 B2
Ward Mt., *U.S.A.* 116 H8
Warden, *S. Africa* 89 D4
Wardha, *India* 66 J11
Wardha →, *India* 66 K11
Wardlow, *Canada* 104 C6
Ware, *Canada* 104 B3
Ware, *U.S.A.* 111 D12
Waregem, *Belgium* 17 D3
Wareham, *U.S.A.* 111 E14
Waremme, *Belgium* 17 D5
Waren, *Germany* 24 B8
Warendorf, *Germany* 24 D4
Warialda, *Australia* 95 D5
Wariap, *Indonesia* 63 E8
Warin Chamrap, *Thailand* 64 E5
Warka, *Poland* 45 G8
Warkopi, *Indonesia* 63 E8
Warm Springs, *U.S.A.* .. 115 G5
Warman, *Canada* 105 C7
Warmbad, *Namibia* 88 D2
Warmbad, *S. Africa* 89 C4
Warminster, *U.K.* 13 F5
Warnambool Downs,
  Australia 94 C3
Warnemünde, *Germany* .. 24 A8
Warner, *Canada* 104 D6
Warner Mts., *U.S.A.* 114 F3
Warner Robins, *U.S.A.* .. 109 J4
Warnow →, *Germany* ... 24 A8
Waroona, *Australia* 93 F2
Warracknabeal, *Australia* . 95 F3
Warragul, *Australia* 95 F4
Warrawagine, *Australia* .. 92 D3
Warrego →, *Australia* ... 95 E4
Warrego Ra., *Australia* .. 94 C4
Warren, *Australia* 95 E4
Warren, *Ark., U.S.A.* ... 113 J8
Warren, *Mich., U.S.A.* .. 108 D4
Warren, *Minn., U.S.A.* .. 112 A6
Warren, *Ohio, U.S.A.* ... 110 E4
Warren, *Pa., U.S.A.* 110 E5
Warrenpoint, *U.K.* 15 B5
Warrensburg, *U.S.A.* 112 F8

Warrenton, *S. Africa* 88 D3
Warrenton, *U.S.A.* 116 D3
Warrenville, *Australia* ... 95 D4
Warri, *Nigeria* 83 D6
Warrina, *Australia* 95 D2
Warrington, *U.K.* 12 D5
Warrington, *U.S.A.* 109 K2
Warrington □, *U.K.* 12 D5
Warrnambool, *Australia* . 95 F3
Warroad, *U.S.A.* 112 A7
Warsa, *Indonesia* 63 E9
Warsaw = Warszawa,
  Poland 45 F8
Warsaw, *Ind., U.S.A.* ... 108 E3
Warsaw, *N.Y., U.S.A.* ... 110 D6
Warsaw, *Ohio, U.S.A.* ... 110 F3
Warstein, *Germany* 24 D4
Warszawa, *Poland* 45 F8
Warszawa □, *Poland* 45 F7
Warta, *Poland* 45 G5
Warta →, *Poland* 45 F1
Warthe = Warta →,
  Poland 45 F1
Waru, *Indonesia* 63 E8
Warwick, *Australia* 95 D5
Warwick, *U.K.* 13 E6
Warwick, *U.S.A.* 111 E13
Warwickshire □, *U.K.* ... 13 E6
Wasaga Beach, *Canada* .. 110 B4
Wasatch Ra., *U.S.A.* 114 F8
Wasbank, *S. Africa* 89 D5
Wasco, *Calif., U.S.A.* ... 117 K7
Wasco, *Oreg., U.S.A.* ... 114 D3
Waseca, *U.S.A.* 112 C8
Wasekamio L., *Canada* .. 105 B7
Wash, The, *U.K.* 12 E8
Washago, *Canada* 110 B5
Washburn, *N. Dak.,*
  U.S.A. 112 B4
Washburn, *Wis., U.S.A.* . 112 B9
Washim, *India* 66 J10
Washington, *U.K.* 12 C6
Washington, *D.C., U.S.A.* 108 F7
Washington, *Ga., U.S.A.* 109 J4
Washington, *Ind., U.S.A.* 108 F2
Washington, *Iowa, U.S.A.* 112 E9
Washington, *Mo., U.S.A.* 112 F9
Washington, *N.C., U.S.A.* 109 H7
Washington, *N.J., U.S.A.* 111 F10
Washington, *Pa., U.S.A.* . 110 F4
Washington, *Utah, U.S.A.* 115 H7
Washington □, *U.S.A.* .. 114 C3
Washington, *Mt., U.S.A.* . 111 B13
Washington I., *U.S.A.* ... 108 C2
Washougal, *U.S.A.* 116 E4
Wasian, *Indonesia* 63 E8
Wasilków, *Poland* 45 E10
Wasior, *Indonesia* 63 E8
Waskaganish, *Canada* ... 102 B4
Waskaiowaka, L., *Canada* 105 B9
Waskesiu Lake, *Canada* . 105 C7
Wasserburg, *Germany* ... 25 G8
Wasserkuppe, *Germany* . 24 E5
Wassy, *France* 19 D11
Waswanipi, *Canada* 102 C4
Waswanipi, L., *Canada* .. 102 C4
Watampone, *Indonesia* .. 63 E6
Water Park Pt., *Australia* . 94 C5
Water Valley, *U.S.A.* ... 113 H10
Waterberge, *S. Africa* ... 89 C4
Waterbury, *Conn., U.S.A.* 111 E11
Waterbury, *Vt., U.S.A.* .. 111 B12
Waterbury L., *Canada* ... 105 B8
Waterdown, *Canada* 110 C5
Waterford, *Canada* 110 D4
Waterford, *Ireland* 15 D4
Waterford, *U.S.A.* 116 H6
Waterford □, *Ireland* ... 15 D4
Waterford Harbour, *Ireland* 15 D5
Waterhen L., *Man.,*
  Canada 105 C9
Waterhen L., *Sask.,*
  Canada 105 C7
Waterloo, *Belgium* 17 D4
Waterloo, *Ont., Canada* . 102 D3
Waterloo, *Qué., Canada* . 111 A12
Waterloo, *S. Leone* 82 D2
Waterloo, *Ill., U.S.A.* ... 112 F9
Waterloo, *Iowa, U.S.A.* . 112 D8
Waterloo, *N.Y., U.S.A.* . 110 D8
Watersmeet, *U.S.A.* 112 B10
Waterton-Glacier
  International Peace Park,
  U.S.A. 114 B7
Watertown, *Conn., U.S.A.* 111 E11
Watertown, *N.Y., U.S.A.* 111 C9
Watertown, *S. Dak.,*
  U.S.A. 112 C6
Watertown, *Wis., U.S.A.* . 112 D10
Waterval-Boven, *S. Africa* 89 D5
Waterville, *Canada* 111 A13
Waterville, *Maine, U.S.A.* 103 D6
Waterville, *N.Y., U.S.A.* . 111 D9
Waterville, *Pa., U.S.A.* .. 110 E7
Waterville, *Wash., U.S.A.* 114 C3
Watervliet, *U.S.A.* 111 D11
Wates, *Indonesia* 63 G14
Watford, *Canada* 110 D3
Watford, *U.K.* 13 F7
Watford City, *U.S.A.* ... 112 B3
Watham, *Canada* 105 B8
Watheroo, *Australia* 93 F2
Wating, *China* 56 G4
Watkins Glen, *U.S.A.* ... 110 D8
Watling I. = San Salvador,
  Bahamas 121 B5

Watonga, *U.S.A.* 113 H5
Watrous, *Canada* 105 C7
Watrous, *U.S.A.* 113 H2
Watsa,
  Dem. Rep. of the Congo 86 B2
Watseka, *U.S.A.* 108 E2
Watson, *Australia* 93 F5
Watson, *Canada* 105 C8
Watson Lake, *Canada* ... 104 A3
Watsonville, *U.S.A.* 116 J5
Wattiwarriganna Cr. →,
  Australia 95 D2
Wattwil, *Switz.* 25 H5
Watuata = Batuata,
  Indonesia 63 F6
Watubela, Kepulauan,
  Indonesia 63 E8
Watubela Is. = Watubela,
  Kepulauan, *Indonesia* . 63 E8
Wau, *Sudan* 77 F6
Waubamik, *Canada* 110 A4
Waubay, *U.S.A.* 112 C6
Waubra, *Australia* 95 F3
Wauchope, *Australia* 95 E5
Wauchula, *U.S.A.* 109 M5
Waugh, *Canada* 105 D9
Waukarlycarly, L.,
  Australia 92 D3
Waukegan, *U.S.A.* 108 D2
Waukesha, *U.S.A.* 108 D1
Waukon, *U.S.A.* 112 D9
Wauneta, *U.S.A.* 112 E4
Waupaca, *U.S.A.* 112 C10
Waupun, *U.S.A.* 112 D10
Waurika, *U.S.A.* 113 H6
Wausau, *U.S.A.* 112 C10
Wautoma, *U.S.A.* 112 C10
Wauwatosa, *U.S.A.* 108 D2
Wave Hill, *Australia* 92 C5
Waveney →, *U.K.* 13 E9
Waverley, *N.Z.* 91 H5
Waverly, *Iowa, U.S.A.* .. 112 D8
Waverly, *N.Y., U.S.A.* .. 111 E8
Wavre, *Belgium* 17 D4
Wâw, *Sudan* 81 F2
Wāw al Kabīr, *Libya* 79 C9
Wawa, *Canada* 102 C3
Wawa, *Nigeria* 83 D5
Wawa, *Sudan* 80 C3
Wawanesa, *Canada* 105 D9
Wawona, *U.S.A.* 116 H7
Waxahachie, *U.S.A.* 113 J6
Way, L., *Australia* 93 E3
Wayatinah, *Australia* ... 94 G4
Waycross, *U.S.A.* 109 K4
Wayi, *Sudan* 81 F3
Wayne, *Nebr., U.S.A.* ... 112 D6
Wayne, *W. Va., U.S.A.* .. 108 F4
Waynesboro, *Ga., U.S.A.* 109 J4
Waynesboro, *Miss., U.S.A.* 109 K1
Waynesboro, *Pa., U.S.A.* . 108 F7
Waynesboro, *Va., U.S.A.* 108 F6
Waynesburg, *U.S.A.* 108 F5
Waynesville, *U.S.A.* 109 H4
Waynoka, *U.S.A.* 113 G5
Wazirabad, *Pakistan* 68 C6
Wda →, *Poland* 44 E5
We, *Indonesia* 62 C1
Weald, The, *U.K.* 13 F8
Wear →, *U.K.* 12 C6
Weatherford, *Okla.,*
  U.S.A. 113 H5
Weatherford, *Tex., U.S.A.* 113 J6
Weaverville, *U.S.A.* 114 F2
Webb City, *U.S.A.* 113 G7
Webo = Nyaake, *Liberia* . 82 E3
Webster, *Mass., U.S.A.* . 111 D13
Webster, *N.Y., U.S.A.* .. 110 C7
Webster, *S. Dak., U.S.A.* 112 C6
Webster, *Wis., U.S.A.* .. 112 C8
Webster City, *U.S.A.* ... 112 D8
Webster Green, *U.S.A.* . 112 F9
Webster Springs, *U.S.A.* 108 F5
Weda, *Indonesia* 63 D7
Weda, Teluk, *Indonesia* . 63 D7
Weddell I., *Falk. Is.* 128 G4
Weddell Sea, *Antarctica* . 5 D1
Wedderburn, *Australia* .. 95 F3
Wedel, *Germany* 24 B5
Wedemark, *Germany* ... 24 C5
Wedgeport, *Canada* 103 D6
Wedza, *Zimbabwe* 87 F3
Wee Waa, *Australia* 95 E4
Weed, *U.S.A.* 114 F2
Weed Heights, *U.S.A.* .. 116 G7
Weedsport, *U.S.A.* 111 C8
Weedville, *U.S.A.* 110 E6
Weemelah, *Australia* 95 D4
Weenen, *S. Africa* 89 D5
Weener, *Germany* 24 B3
Weert, *Neths.* 17 C5
Węgierska-Górka, *Poland* 45 J6
Węgliniec, *Poland* 45 G2
Węgorzewo, *Poland* 44 D8
Węgorzyno, *Poland* 44 E2
Węgrów, *Poland* 45 F9
Wei He →, *Hebei, China* 56 F8
Wei He →, *Shaanxi, China* 56 G6
Weichang, *China* 57 D9
Weichuan, *China* 56 G7
Weida, *Germany* 24 E8
Weiden, *Germany* 25 F8
Weifang, *China* 57 F10
Weihai, *China* 57 F12
Weil, *Germany* 25 H3
Weilburg, *Germany* 24 E4

Weilheim, *Germany* 25 H7
Weimar, *Germany* 24 E7
Weinan, *China* 56 G5
Weingarten, *Germany* ... 25 H5
Weinheim, *Germany* 25 F4
Weining, *China* 58 D5
Weipa, *Australia* 94 A3
Weir →, *Australia* 95 D4
Weir →, *Canada* 105 B10
Weir River, *Canada* 105 B10
Weirton, *U.S.A.* 110 F4
Weiser, *U.S.A.* 114 D5
Weishan, *Shandong, China* 57 G9
Weishan, *Yunnan, China* . 58 E3
Weissenburg, *Germany* .. 25 F6
Weissenfels, *Germany* ... 24 D7
Weisswasser, *Germany* .. 24 D10
Wéitra, *Austria* 26 C7
Weixi, *China* 58 D2
Weixin, *China* 58 D5
Weiyuan, *China* 56 G3
Weiz, *Austria* 26 D8
Weizhou Dao, *China* 58 G7
Wejherowo, *Poland* 44 D5
Wekusko L., *Canada* 105 C9
Welbourn Hill, *Australia* . 95 D1
Welch, *U.S.A.* 108 G5
Weldya, *Ethiopia* 81 E4
Welega □, *Ethiopia* 81 F3
Welkite, *Ethiopia* 81 F4
Welkom, *S. Africa* 88 D4
Welland, *Canada* 102 D4
Welland →, *U.K.* 13 E7
Wellesley Is., *Australia* .. 94 B2
Wellingborough, *U.K.* ... 13 E7
Wellington, *Australia* ... 95 E4
Wellington, *Canada* 102 D4
Wellington, *N.Z.* 91 J5
Wellington, *S. Africa* 88 E2
Wellington, *Somst., U.K.* . 13 G4
Wellington,
  Telford & Wrekin, U.K. . 13 E5
Wellington, *Colo., U.S.A.* 112 E2
Wellington, *Kans., U.S.A.* 113 G6
Wellington, *Nev., U.S.A.* 116 G7
Wellington, *Ohio, U.S.A.* 110 E2
Wellington, *Tex., U.S.A.* 113 H4
Wellington, I., *Chile* 122 H3
Wellington, L., *Australia* . 95 F4
Wells, *U.K.* 13 F5
Wells, *Maine, U.S.A.* ... 111 C14
Wells, *Minn., U.S.A.* ... 112 D8
Wells, *Nev., U.S.A.* 114 F6
Wells, L., *Australia* 93 E3
Wells Gray Prov. Park,
  Canada 104 C4
Wells-next-the-Sea, *U.K.* . 12 E8
Wells River, *U.S.A.* 111 B12
Wellsboro, *U.S.A.* 110 E7
Wellsburg, *U.S.A.* 110 F4
Wellsville, *Mo., U.S.A.* .. 112 F9
Wellsville, *N.Y., U.S.A.* . 110 D7
Wellsville, *Ohio, U.S.A.* . 110 F4
Wellsville, *Utah, U.S.A.* . 114 F8
Wellton, *U.S.A.* 115 K6
Welmel, Wabi →, *Ethiopia* 81 F5
Welo □, *Ethiopia* 81 E4
Wels, *Austria* 26 C7
Welshpool, *U.K.* 13 E4
Welwyn Garden City, *U.K.* 13 F7
Wem, *U.K.* 12 E5
Wembere →, *Tanzania* .. 86 C3
Wemindji, *Canada* 102 B4
Wen Xian, *Gansu, China* . 56 H3
Wen Xian, *Henan, China* . 56 G7
Wenatchee, *U.S.A.* 114 C3
Wenchang, *China* 58 D6
Wencheng, *China* 59 D13
Wenchi, *Ghana* 82 D4
Wenchow = Wenzhou,
  China 59 D13
Wenchuan, *China* 58 B4
Wendell, *U.S.A.* 114 E6
Wenden, *U.S.A.* 117 M13
Wendeng, *China* 57 F12
Wendesi, *Indonesia* 63 E8
Wendo, *Ethiopia* 81 F4
Wendover, *U.S.A.* 114 F6
Weng'an, *China* 58 D6
Wengcheng, *China* 59 E9
Wengyuan, *China* 59 E10
Wenjiang, *China* 58 B4
Wenling, *China* 59 C13
Wenlock →, *Australia* .. 94 A3
Wenshan, *China* 58 F5
Wenshang, *China* 56 G9
Wenshui, *Guizhou, China* 58 C6
Wenshui, *Shanxi, China* . 56 F7
Wensleydale, *U.K.* 12 C6
Wensu, *China* 60 B3
Wensum →, *U.K.* 12 E8
Wentworth, *Australia* ... 95 E3
Wenut, *Indonesia* 63 E8
Wenxi, *China* 56 G6
Wenzhou, *China* 59 D13
Weott, *U.S.A.* 114 F2
Wepener, *S. Africa* 88 D4
Werda, *Botswana* 88 D3
Werdau, *Germany* 24 E8
Werder, *Germany* 24 C8
Werder, *Ethiopia* 81 F5
Wereilu, *Ethiopia* 81 E4
Weri, *Indonesia* 63 E8
Werneck, *Germany* 25 F6
Wernigerode, *Germany* . 24 D6
Werra →, *Germany* 24 D5

Werribee, Australia 95 F3
Werrimull, Australia 95 E3
Werris Creek, Australia .. 95 E5
Wertach →, Germany 25 G6
Wertheim, Germany 25 F5
Wertingen, Germany 25 G6
Wesel, Germany 24 D2
Weser →, Germany 24 B4
Weser-Ems □, Germany .. 24 C3
Weserbergland, Germany . 24 C5
Wesiri, Indonesia 63 F7
Wesley Vale, U.S.A. 115 J10
Wesleyville, Canada 103 C9
Wesleyville, U.S.A. 110 D4
Wessel, C., Australia 94 A2
Wessel Is., Australia 94 A2
Wesselburen, Germany ... 24 A4
Wessington, U.S.A. 112 C5
Wessington Springs, U.S.A. 112 C5
West, U.S.A. 113 K6
West Allis, U.S.A. 108 D1
West B., U.S.A. 113 L10
West Baines →, Australia . 92 C4
West Bank □, Asia 75 C4
West Bend, U.S.A. 108 D1
West Bengal □, India 69 H13
West Berkshire □, U.K. .. 13 F6
West Beskids = Západné
   Beskydy, Europe 27 B12
West Branch, U.S.A. 108 C3
West Bromwich, U.K. 13 E6
West Burra, U.K. 14 A7
West Cape Howe, Australia 93 G2
West Chazy, U.S.A. 111 B11
West Chester, U.S.A. 108 F8
West Columbia, U.S.A. ... 113 L7
West Covina, U.S.A. 117 L9
West Des Moines, U.S.A. . 112 E8
West Dunbartonshire □,
   U.K. 14 F4
West End, Bahamas 120 A4
West Falkland, Falk. Is. .. 122 J4
West Fjord = Vestfjorden,
   Norway 8 C15
West Frankfort, U.S.A. ... 112 G10
West Hartford, U.S.A. 111 E12
West Haven, U.S.A. 111 E12
West Helena, U.S.A. 113 H8
West Ice Shelf, Antarctica . 5 C7
West Indies, Cent. Amer. .. 121 D7
West Lorne, Canada 110 D3
West Lothian □, U.K. 14 F5
West Lunga →, Zambia .. 87 E1
West Memphis, U.S.A. ... 113 H9
West Midlands □, U.K. ... 13 E6
West Mifflin, U.S.A. 110 F5
West Monroe, U.S.A. 113 J8
West Newton, U.S.A. 110 F5
West Nicholson, Zimbabwe 87 G2
West Palm Beach, U.S.A. . 109 M5
West Plains, U.S.A. 113 G9
West Point, Ga., U.S.A. .. 109 J3
West Point, Miss., U.S.A. . 109 J1
West Point, Nebr., U.S.A. . 112 E6
West Point, Va., U.S.A. .. 108 G7
West Pokot □, Kenya ... 86 B4
West Pt. = Ouest, Pte.,
   Canada 103 C7
West Pt., Australia 95 F2
West Road →, Canada ... 104 C4
West Rutland, U.S.A. 111 C11
West Schelde =
   Westerschelde →, Neths. 17 C3
West Seneca, U.S.A. 110 D6
West Siberian Plain, Russia 52 C11
West Sussex □, U.K. 13 G7
West-Terschelling, Neths. .. 17 A5
West Valley City, U.S.A. .. 114 F8
West Virginia □, U.S.A. . 108 F5
West-Vlaanderen □,
   Belgium 17 D2
West Walker →, U.S.A. .. 116 G7
West Wyalong, Australia . 95 E4
West Yellowstone, U.S.A. . 114 D8
West Yorkshire □, U.K. .. 12 D6
Westall Pt., Australia 95 E1
Westbrook, Maine, U.S.A. 109 D10
Westbrook, Texas, U.S.A. . 113 J4
Westbury, Australia 94 G4
Westby, U.S.A. 112 A2
Westend, U.S.A. 117 K9
Westerland, Germany ... 9 J13
Western □, Kenya 86 B3
Western □, Uganda 86 B3
Western □, Zambia 87 F1
Western Australia □,
   Australia 93 E2
Western Cape □, S. Africa 88 E3
Western Dvina =
   Daugava →, Latvia ... 9 H21
Western Ghats, India ... 66 N9
Western Isles □, U.K. ... 14 D1
Western Sahara ■, Africa 78 D3
Western Samoa ■,
   Pac. Oc. 91 B13
Westernport, U.S.A. 108 F6
Westerschelde →, Neths. .. 17 C3
Westerstede, Germany ... 24 B3
Westerwald, Germany 24 E3
Westfield, Mass., U.S.A. . 111 D12
Westfield, N.Y., U.S.A. .. 110 D5
Westfield, Pa., U.S.A. 110 E7
Westhill, U.K. 14 D6
Westhope, U.S.A. 112 A4
Westland Bight, N.Z. 91 K3
Westlock, Canada 104 C6

Westmeath □, Ireland ... 15 C4
Westminster, U.S.A. 108 F7
Westmorland, U.S.A. 115 K6
Weston, Oreg., U.S.A. ... 114 D4
Weston, W. Va., U.S.A. .. 108 F5
Weston I., Canada 102 B4
Weston-super-Mare, U.K. . 13 F5
Westport, Canada 111 B8
Westport, Ireland 15 C2
Westport, N.Z. 91 J3
Westport, Oreg., U.S.A. .. 116 D3
Westport, Wash., U.S.A. . 114 C1
Westray, Canada 105 C8
Westray, U.K. 14 B5
Westree, Canada 102 C3
Westville, Calif., U.S.A. .. 116 F6
Westville, Ill., U.S.A. 108 E2
Westville, Okla., U.S.A. .. 113 H7
Westwood, U.S.A. 114 F3
Wetar, Indonesia 63 F7
Wetaskiwin, Canada 104 C6
Wetherby, U.K. 12 D6
Wethersfield, U.S.A. 111 E12
Wetteren, Belgium 17 D3
Wetzlar, Germany 24 E4
Wewoka, U.S.A. 113 H6
Wexford, Ireland 15 D5
Wexford □, Ireland 15 D5
Wexford Harbour, Ireland . 15 D5
Weyburn, Canada 105 D8
Weyburn L., Canada 104 A5
Weyer Markt, Austria 26 D7
Weyhe, Germany 24 C4
Weyib →, Ethiopia 81 F5
Weymouth, Canada 103 D6
Weymouth, U.K. 13 G5
Weymouth, U.S.A. 111 D14
Weymouth, C., Australia . 94 A3
Wha Ti, Canada 100 B8
Whakatane, N.Z. 91 G6
Whale →, Canada 103 A6
Whale Cove, Canada 105 A10
Whales, B. of, Antarctica . 5 D12
Whalsay, U.K. 14 A8
Whangamomona, N.Z. ... 91 H5
Whangarei, N.Z. 91 F5
Whangarei Harb., N.Z. .. 91 F5
Wharfe →, U.K. 12 D6
Wharfedale, U.K. 12 C5
Wharton, N.J., U.S.A. ... 111 F10
Wharton, Pa., U.S.A. 110 E6
Wharton, Tex., U.S.A. ... 113 L6
Wheatland, Calif., U.S.A. 116 F5
Wheatland, Wyo., U.S.A. 112 D2
Wheatley, Canada 110 D2
Wheaton, U.S.A. 112 C6
Wheelbarrow Pk., U.S.A. 116 H10
Wheeler, Oreg., U.S.A. .. 114 D2
Wheeler, Tex., U.S.A. ... 113 H4
Wheeler →, Canada 105 B7
Wheeler Pk., N. Mex.,
   U.S.A. 115 H11
Wheeler Pk., Nev., U.S.A. 115 G6
Wheeler Ridge, U.S.A. ... 117 L8
Wheeling, U.S.A. 110 F4
Whernside, U.K. 12 C5
Whidbey I., U.S.A. 104 D4
Whiskey Gap, Canada ... 104 D6
Whiskey Jack L., Canada 105 B8
Whistleduck Cr. →,
   Australia 94 C2
Whitby, Canada 110 C6
Whitby, U.K. 12 C7
White →, Ark., U.S.A. .. 113 J9
White →, Ind., U.S.A. .. 108 F2
White →, S. Dak., U.S.A. 112 D5
White →, Wash., U.S.A. 114 F9
White →, Wash., U.S.A. 116 C4
White, L., Australia 92 D4
White B., Canada 103 C8
White Bear Res., Canada . 103 C8
White Bird, U.S.A. 114 D5
White Butte, U.S.A. 112 B3
White City, U.S.A. 112 F6
White Cliffs, Australia ... 95 E3
White Deer, U.S.A. 113 H4
White Hall, U.S.A. 112 F9
White Haven, U.S.A. 111 E9
White Horse, Vale of, U.K. 13 F6
White I., N.Z. 91 G6
White L., Canada 111 A8
White L., U.S.A. 113 L8
White Mts., Calif., U.S.A. 116 H8
White Mts., N.H., U.S.A. 111 B13
White Nile = Nîl el
   Abyad →, Sudan 81 D3
White Nile Dam =
   Khazzân Jabal el Awlîya,
   Sudan 81 D3
White Otter L., Canada . 102 C1
White Pass, Canada 104 B1
White Pass, U.S.A. 116 D5
White Plains, U.S.A. 111 E11
White River, Canada 102 C2
White River, S. Africa ... 89 D5
White River, U.S.A. 112 D4
White Russia = Belarus ■,
   Europe 46 F4
White Sea = Beloye More,
   Russia 50 C4
White Sulphur Springs,
   Mont., U.S.A. 114 C8
White Sulphur Springs,
   W. Va., U.S.A. 108 G5
White Swan, U.S.A. 116 D6
White Volta →, Ghana .. 83 D4

Whitecliffs, N.Z. 91 K3
Whitecourt, Canada 104 C5
Whiteface, U.S.A. 113 J3
Whitefield, U.S.A. 111 B13
Whitefish, U.S.A. 114 B6
Whitefish L., Canada 105 A7
Whitefish Point, U.S.A. .. 108 B3
Whitegull, L., Canada ... 103 A7
Whitehall, Mich., U.S.A. . 108 D2
Whitehall, Mont., U.S.A. . 114 D7
Whitehall, N.Y., U.S.A. .. 111 C11
Whitehall, Wis., U.S.A. .. 112 C9
Whitehaven, U.K. 12 C4
Whitehorse, Canada 104 A1
Whitemark, Australia 94 G4
Whitemouth, Canada 105 D9
Whiteplains, Liberia 82 D2
Whitesboro, N.Y., U.S.A. 111 C9
Whitesboro, Tex., U.S.A. . 113 J6
Whiteshell Prov. Park,
   Canada 105 D9
Whitetail, U.S.A. 112 A2
Whiteville, U.S.A. 109 H6
Whitewater, U.S.A. 108 D1
Whitewater Baldy, U.S.A. 115 K9
Whitewater L., Canada .. 102 B2
Whitewood, Australia ... 94 C3
Whitewood, Canada 105 C8
Whitfield, Australia 95 F4
Whithorn, U.K. 14 G4
Whitianga, N.Z. 91 G5
Whitman, U.S.A. 111 D14
Whitmire, U.S.A. 109 H5
Whitney, Canada 102 C4
Whitney, Mt., U.S.A. 116 J8
Whitney Point, U.S.A. ... 111 D9
Whitstable, U.K. 13 F9
Whitsunday I., Australia . 94 C4
Whittier, U.S.A. 117 M8
Whittlesea, Australia 95 F4
Whitwell, U.S.A. 109 H3
Wholdaia L., Canada ... 105 A8
Whyalla, Australia 95 E2
Whyjonta, Australia 95 D3
Wiarton, Canada 102 D3
Wiawso, Ghana 82 D4
Wiay, U.K. 14 D1
Wibaux, U.S.A. 112 B2
Wichian Buri, Thailand .. 64 E3
Wichita, U.S.A. 113 G6
Wichita Falls, U.S.A. 113 J5
Wick, U.K. 14 C5
Wickenburg, U.S.A. 115 K7
Wickepin, Australia 93 F2
Wickham, C., Australia .. 94 F3
Wickliffe, U.S.A. 110 E3
Wicklow, Ireland 15 D5
Wicklow □, Ireland 15 D5
Wicklow Hd., Ireland 15 D6
Wicklow Mts., Ireland ... 15 C5
Widawa, Poland 45 G5
Widawka →, Poland 45 G5
Widgiemooltha, Australia . 93 F3
Widnes, U.K. 12 D5
Więcbork, Poland 45 E4
Wiehl, Germany 24 E3
Wiek, Germany 24 A9
Wielbark, Poland 44 E7
Wieleń, Poland 45 F3
Wielichowo, Poland 45 F3
Wieliczka, Poland 45 J7
Wieluń, Poland 45 G5
Wien, Austria 27 C9
Wiener Neustadt, Austria . 27 D9
Wieprz →, Poland 45 G8
Wieprza →, Poland 45 D3
Wieruszów, Poland 45 G5
Wiesbaden, Germany ... 25 E4
Wiesental, Germany 25 F4
Wiesloch, Germany 25 F4
Wiesmoor, Germany 24 B3
Wieżyca, Poland 44 D5
Wigan, U.K. 12 D5
Wiggins, Colo., U.S.A. .. 112 E2
Wiggins, Miss., U.S.A. ... 113 K10
Wight, I. of □, U.K. 13 G6
Wigry, Jezioro, Poland ... 44 D10
Wigston, U.K. 13 E6
Wigton, U.K. 12 C4
Wigtown, U.K. 14 G4
Wigtown B., U.K. 14 G4
Wil, Switz. 25 H5
Wilamowice, Poland 45 J6
Wilber, U.S.A. 112 E6
Wilberforce, Canada 110 A6
Wilberforce, C., Australia . 94 A2
Wilburton, U.S.A. 113 H7
Wilcannia, Australia 95 E3
Wilcox, U.S.A. 110 E6
Wildbad, Germany 25 G4
Wildeshausen, Germany . 24 C4
Wildon, Austria 26 E8
Wildrose, Calif., U.S.A. .. 117 J9
Wildrose, N. Dak., U.S.A. 112 A3
Wildspitze, Austria 26 E3
Wildwood, U.S.A. 108 F8
Wilga →, Poland 45 G8
Wilge →, S. Africa 89 D4
Wilhelm II Coast,
   Antarctica 5 C7
Wilhelmsburg, Austria ... 26 C8
Wilhelmshaven, Germany . 24 B4
Wilhelmstal, Namibia ... 88 C2
Wilkes-Barre, U.S.A. 111 E9
Wilkesboro, U.S.A. 109 G5

Wilkie, Canada 105 C7
Wilkinsburg, U.S.A. 110 F5
Wilkinson Lakes, Australia 93 E5
Willamina, U.S.A. 114 D2
Willandra Billabong
   Creek →, Australia ... 95 E4
Willapa B., U.S.A. 114 C2
Willapa Hills, U.S.A. 116 D3
Willard, N. Mex., U.S.A. . 115 J10
Willard, Utah, U.S.A. ... 114 F7
Willcox, U.S.A. 115 K9
Willemstad, Neth. Ant. .. 121 D6
Willeroo, Australia 92 C5
William →, Canada 105 B7
William Creek, Australia . 95 D2
Williambury, Australia .. 93 D2
Williams, Australia 93 F2
Williams, Ariz., U.S.A. .. 115 J7
Williams, Calif., U.S.A. .. 116 F4
Williams Lake, Canada ... 104 C4
Williamsburg, Ky., U.S.A. 109 G3
Williamsburg, Pa., U.S.A. 110 F6
Williamsburg, Va., U.S.A. 108 G7
Williamson, N.Y., U.S.A. 110 C7
Williamson, W. Va.,
   U.S.A. 108 G4
Williamsport, U.S.A. 110 E7
Williamston, U.S.A. 109 H7
Williamstown, Australia . 95 F3
Williamstown, Mass.,
   U.S.A. 111 D11
Williamstown, N.Y.,
   U.S.A. 111 C9
Williamsville, U.S.A. 113 G9
Willimantic, U.S.A. 111 E12
Willis Group, Australia .. 94 B5
Williston, S. Africa 88 E3
Williston, Fla., U.S.A. ... 109 L4
Williston, N. Dak., U.S.A. 112 A3
Williston L., Canada 104 B4
Willits, U.S.A. 114 G2
Willmar, U.S.A. 112 C7
Willoughby, U.S.A. 110 E3
Willow Bunch, Canada .. 105 D7
Willow L., Canada 104 A5
Willow Lake, U.S.A. 112 C6
Willow Springs, U.S.A. .. 113 G9
Willow Wall, The, China . 57 C12
Willowlake →, Canada .. 104 A4
Willowmore, S. Africa ... 88 E3
Willows, Australia 94 C4
Willows, U.S.A. 116 F4
Willowvale = Gatyana,
   S. Africa 89 E4
Wills, L., Australia 92 D4
Wills Cr. →, Australia ... 94 C3
Wills Point, U.S.A. 113 J7
Wilmette, U.S.A. 108 D2
Wilmington, Australia ... 95 E2
Wilmington, Del., U.S.A. 108 F8
Wilmington, Ill., U.S.A. . 108 E1
Wilmington, N.C., U.S.A. 109 H7
Wilmington, Ohio, U.S.A. 108 F4
Wilmslow, U.K. 12 D5
Wilpena Cr. →, Australia 95 E2
Wilsall, U.S.A. 114 D8
Wilson, U.S.A. 109 H7
Wilson →, Queens.,
   Australia 95 D3
Wilson →, W. Austral.,
   Australia 92 C4
Wilson Bluff, Australia .. 93 F4
Wilsons Promontory,
   Australia 95 F4
Wilster, Germany 24 B5
Wilton, U.S.A. 112 B4
Wilton →, Australia 94 A1
Wiltshire □, U.K. 13 F6
Wiltz, Lux. 17 E5
Wiluna, Australia 93 E3
Wimborne Minster, U.K. . 13 G6
Wimereux, France 19 B8
Wimmera →, Australia .. 95 F3
Winam G., Kenya 86 C3
Winburg, S. Africa 88 D4
Winchendon, U.S.A. 111 D12
Winchester, U.K. 13 F6
Winchester, Conn., U.S.A. 111 E11
Winchester, Idaho, U.S.A. 114 C5
Winchester, Ind., U.S.A. 108 E3
Winchester, Ky., U.S.A. . 108 G3
Winchester, N.H., U.S.A. 111 D12
Winchester, Nev., U.S.A. 117 J11
Winchester, Tenn., U.S.A. 109 H2
Winchester, Va., U.S.A. . 108 F6
Wind →, U.S.A. 114 E9
Wind River Range, U.S.A. 114 E9
Windau = Ventspils, Latvia 9 H19
Windber, U.S.A. 110 F6
Windermere, U.K. 12 C5
Windfall, Canada 104 C5
Windflower L., Canada .. 104 A5
Windhoek, Namibia 88 C2
Windischgarsten, Austria . 26 D7
Windom, U.S.A. 112 D7
Windorah, Australia 94 D3
Window Rock, U.S.A. ... 115 J9
Windrush →, U.K. 13 F6
Windsor, Australia 95 E5
Windsor, N.S., Canada .. 103 D7
Windsor, Nfld., Canada .. 103 C8
Windsor, Ont., Canada .. 102 D3
Windsor, U.K. 13 F7
Windsor, Colo., U.S.A. .. 112 E2
Windsor, Conn., U.S.A. .. 111 E12

Windsor, Mo., U.S.A. 112 F8
Windsor, N.Y., U.S.A. ... 111 D9
Windsor, Vt., U.S.A. 111 C12
Windsor & Maidenhead □,
   U.K. 13 F7
Windsorton, S. Africa ... 88 D3
Windward Is., W. Indies . 121 D7
Windward Passage =
   Vientos, Paso de los,
   Caribbean 121 C5
Windy L., Canada 105 A8
Winefred L., Canada 105 B6
Winejok, Sudan 81 F2
Winfield, U.S.A. 113 G6
Wingate Mts., Australia .. 92 B5
Wingen, Australia 95 E5
Wingham, Australia 95 E5
Wingham, Canada 102 D3
Winifred, U.S.A. 114 C9
Winisk, Canada 102 A2
Winisk →, Canada 102 A2
Winisk L., Canada 102 B2
Wink, U.S.A. 113 K3
Winkler, Canada 105 D9
Winklern, Austria 26 E5
Winlock, U.S.A. 116 D4
Winneba, Ghana 83 D4
Winnebago, U.S.A. 112 D7
Winnebago, L., U.S.A. .. 108 D1
Winnecke Cr. →, Australia 92 C5
Winnemucca, U.S.A. 114 F5
Winnemucca L., U.S.A. . 114 F4
Winner, U.S.A. 112 D5
Winnett, U.S.A. 114 C9
Winnfield, U.S.A. 113 K8
Winnibigoshish, L., U.S.A. 112 B7
Winning, Australia 92 D1
Winnipeg, Canada 105 D9
Winnipeg →, Canada ... 105 C9
Winnipeg, L., Canada ... 105 C9
Winnipeg Beach, Canada . 105 C9
Winnipegosis, Canada ... 105 C9
Winnipegosis L., Canada . 105 C9
Winnipesaukee, L., U.S.A. 111 C13
Winnsboro, La., U.S.A. .. 113 J9
Winnsboro, S.C., U.S.A. 109 H5
Winnsboro, Tex., U.S.A. . 113 J7
Winokapau, L., Canada .. 103 B7
Winona, Minn., U.S.A. .. 112 C9
Winona, Miss., U.S.A. ... 113 J10
Winooski, U.S.A. 111 B11
Winschoten, Neths. 17 A7
Winsen, Germany 24 B6
Winsford, U.K. 12 D5
Winslow, Ariz., U.S.A. .. 115 J8
Winslow, Wash., U.S.A. . 116 C4
Winsted, U.S.A. 111 E11
Winston-Salem, U.S.A. .. 109 G5
Winter Garden, U.S.A. .. 109 L5
Winter Haven, U.S.A. ... 109 M5
Winter Park, U.S.A. 109 L5
Winterberg, Germany ... 24 D4
Winterhaven, U.S.A. 117 N12
Winters, Calif., U.S.A. ... 116 G5
Winters, Tex., U.S.A. 113 K5
Winterset, U.S.A. 112 E8
Wintersville, U.S.A. 110 F4
Winterswijk, Neths. 17 C6
Winterthur, Switz. 25 H4
Winthrop, Minn., U.S.A. 112 C7
Winthrop, Wash., U.S.A. 114 B3
Winton, Australia 94 C3
Winton, N.Z. 91 M2
Winton, U.S.A. 109 G7
Wipper →, Germany ... 24 D7
Wirrulla, Australia 95 E1
Wisbech, U.K. 13 E8
Wisconsin □, U.S.A. 112 C10
Wisconsin →, U.S.A. ... 112 D9
Wisconsin Dells, U.S.A. . 112 D10
Wisconsin Rapids, U.S.A. 112 C10
Wisdom, U.S.A. 114 D7
Wishaw, U.K. 14 F5
Wishek, U.S.A. 112 B5
Wisła, Poland 45 J5
Wisła →, Poland 44 D5
Wisłok →, Poland 45 H9
Wisłoka →, Poland 45 H8
Wismar, Germany 24 B7
Wisner, U.S.A. 112 E6
Wissant, France 19 B8
Wissembourg, France ... 19 C14
Wisznice, Poland 45 G10
Witbank, S. Africa 89 D4
Witdraai, S. Africa 88 D3
Witham, U.K. 13 F8
Witham →, U.K. 12 E7
Withernsea, U.K. 12 D8
Witkowo, Poland 45 F4
Witney, U.K. 13 F6
Witnica, Poland 45 F1
Witnossob →, Namibia . 88 D3
Wittdün, Germany 24 A4
Witten, Germany 24 D3
Wittenberge, Germany .. 24 B7
Wittenburg, Germany ... 24 B7
Wittenheim, France 19 E14
Wittenoom, Australia ... 92 D2
Wittingen, Germany 24 C6
Wittlich, Germany 25 F2
Wittmund, Germany 24 B3
Wittow, Germany 24 A9
Wittstock, Germany 24 B8
Witzenhausen, Germany . 24 D5
Wkra →, Poland 45 F7
Władysławowo, Poland ... 44 D5

Wleń, *Poland* 45 G2
Wlingi, *Indonesia* 63 H15
Włocławek, *Poland* 45 F6
Włocławek □, *Poland* 45 F6
Włodawa, *Poland* 45 G10
Włoszczowa, *Poland* 45 H6
Woburn, *U.S.A.* 111 D13
Wodian, *China* 56 H7
Wodonga, *Australia* 95 F4
Wodzisław Śląski, *Poland* 45 H5
Wœrth, *France* 19 D14
Woinbogoin, *China* 58 A2
Woippy, *France* 19 C13
Wojcieszów, *Poland* 45 H2
Wokam, *Indonesia* 63 F8
Woking, *U.K.* 13 F7
Wokingham □, *U.K.* 13 F7
Wolbrom, *Poland* 45 H6
Wołczyn, *Poland* 45 G5
Woldegk, *Germany* 24 B9
Wolf →, *Canada* 104 A2
Wolf Creek, *U.S.A.* 114 C7
Wolf L., *Canada* 104 A2
Wolf Point, *U.S.A.* 112 A2
Wolfe I., *Canada* 102 D4
Wolfen, *Germany* 24 D8
Wolfenbüttel, *Germany* 24 C6
Wolfratshausen, *Germany* 25 H7
Wolfsberg, *Austria* 26 E7
Wolfsburg, *Germany* 24 C6
Wolgast, *Germany* 24 A9
Wolhusen, *Switz.* 25 H4
Wolin, *Poland* 44 E1
Wollaston, Is., *Chile* 128 H3
Wollaston L., *Canada* 105 B8
Wollaston Pen., *Canada* 100 B8
Wollogorang, *Australia* 94 B2
Wollongong, *Australia* 95 E5
Wolmaransstad, *S. Africa* 88 D4
Wolmirstedt, *Germany* 24 C7
Wołomin, *Poland* 45 F8
Wołów, *Poland* 45 G3
Wolseley, *Australia* 95 F3
Wolseley, *Canada* 105 C8
Wolseley, *S. Africa* 88 E2
Wolstenholme, C., *Canada* 98 C12
Wolsztyn, *Poland* 45 F3
Wolvega, *Neths.* 17 B6
Wolverhampton, *U.K.* 13 E5
Wonarah, *Australia* 94 B2
Wondai, *Australia* 95 D5
Wongalarroo L., *Australia* 95 E3
Wongan Hills, *Australia* 93 F2
Wongawol, *Australia* 93 E3
Wŏnju, *S. Korea* 57 F14
Wonosari, *Indonesia* 63 G14
Wŏnsan, *N. Korea* 57 E14
Wonthaggi, *Australia* 95 F4
Woocalla, *Australia* 95 E2
Wood Buffalo Nat. Park, *Canada* 104 B6
Wood Is., *Australia* 92 C3
Wood L., *Canada* 105 B8
Wood Lake, *U.S.A.* 112 D4
Woodah I., *Australia* 94 A2
Woodanilling, *Australia* 93 F2
Woodbridge, *Canada* 110 C5
Woodbridge, *U.K.* 13 E9
Woodburn, *Australia* 95 D5
Woodenbong, *Australia* 95 D5
Woodend, *Australia* 95 F3
Woodfords, *U.S.A.* 116 G7
Woodgreen, *Australia* 94 C1
Woodlake, *U.S.A.* 116 J7
Woodland, *U.S.A.* 116 G5
Woodlands, *Australia* 92 D2
Woodpecker, *Canada* 104 C4
Woodridge, *Canada* 105 D9
Woodroffe, Mt., *Australia* 93 E5
Woodruff, *Ariz., U.S.A.* 115 J8
Woodruff, *Utah, U.S.A.* 114 F8
Woods, L., *Australia* 94 B1
Woods, L., *Canada* 103 B6
Woods, L. of the, *Canada* 105 D10
Woodstock, *Queens., Australia* 94 B4
Woodstock, *W. Austral., Australia* 92 D2
Woodstock, *N.B., Canada* 103 C6
Woodstock, *Ont., Canada* 102 D3
Woodstock, *U.K.* 13 F6
Woodstock, *Ill., U.S.A.* 112 D10
Woodstock, *Vt., U.S.A.* 111 C12
Woodsville, *U.S.A.* 111 B13
Woodville, *N.Z.* 91 J5
Woodville, *U.S.A.* 113 K7
Woodward, *U.S.A.* 113 G5
Woody, *U.S.A.* 117 K8
Woolamai, C., *Australia* 95 F4
Wooler, *U.K.* 12 B5
Woolgoolga, *Australia* 95 E5
Woombye, *Australia* 95 D5
Woomera, *Australia* 95 E2
Woonsocket, *R.I., U.S.A.* 111 E13
Woonsocket, *S. Dak., U.S.A.* 112 C5
Wooramel, *Australia* 93 E1
Wooramel →, *Australia* 93 E1
Wooroloo, *Australia* 93 F2
Wooster, *U.S.A.* 110 F3
Worcester, *S. Africa* 88 E2
Worcester, *U.K.* 13 E5
Worcester, *Mass., U.S.A.* 111 D13
Worcester, *N.Y., U.S.A.* 111 D10
Worcestershire □, *U.K.* 13 E5
Wörgl, *Austria* 26 D5
Workington, *U.K.* 12 C4
Worksop, *U.K.* 12 D6
Workum, *Neths.* 17 B5
Worland, *U.S.A.* 114 D10
Wormhout, *France* 19 B9
Worms, *Germany* 25 F4
Wörth, *Germany* 25 F8
Wortham, *U.S.A.* 113 K6
Wörther See, *Austria* 26 E7
Worthing, *U.K.* 13 G7
Worthington, *U.S.A.* 112 D7
Wosi, *Indonesia* 63 E7
Wou-han = Wuhan, *China* 59 B10
Wousi = Wuxi, *China* 59 B13
Wowoni, *Indonesia* 63 E6
Woy Woy, *Australia* 95 E5
Wrangel I. = Vrangelya, Ostrov, *Russia* 51 B19
Wrangell, *U.S.A.* 100 C6
Wrangell I., *U.S.A.* 104 B2
Wrangell Mts., *U.S.A.* 100 B5
Wrath, C., *U.K.* 14 C3
Wray, *U.S.A.* 112 E3
Wrekin, The, *U.K.* 13 E5
Wrens, *U.S.A.* 109 J4
Wrexham, *U.K.* 12 D4
Wrexham □, *U.K.* 12 D5
Wriezen, *Germany* 24 C10
Wright, *Canada* 104 C4
Wright, *Phil.* 61 F6
Wrightson Mt., *U.S.A.* 115 L8
Wrightwood, *U.S.A.* 117 L9
Wrigley, *Canada* 100 B7
Wrocław, *Poland* 45 G4
Wrocław □, *Poland* 45 G4
Wronki, *Poland* 45 F3
Września, *Poland* 45 F4
Wschowa, *Poland* 45 G3
Wu Jiang →, *China* 58 C6
Wu'an, *China* 56 F8
Wubin, *Australia* 93 F2
Wubu, *China* 56 F6
Wuchang, *China* 57 B14
Wucheng, *China* 56 F9
Wuchuan, *Guangdong, China* 59 G8
Wuchuan, *Guizhou, China* 58 C7
Wuchuan, *Nei Mongol Zizhiqu, China* 56 D6
Wudi, *China* 57 F9
Wuding, *China* 58 E4
Wuding He →, *China* 56 F6
Wudu, *China* 56 H3
Wufeng, *China* 59 B8
Wugang, *China* 59 D8
Wugong Shan, *China* 59 D10
Wuhan, *China* 59 B10
Wuhe, *China* 57 H9
Wuhsi = Wuxi, *China* 59 B13
Wuhu, *China* 59 B12
Wujiang, *China* 59 B13
Wukari, *Nigeria* 83 D6
Wulajie, *China* 57 B14
Wulanbulang, *China* 56 D6
Wulehe, *Ghana* 83 D5
Wulian, *China* 57 G10
Wuliang Shan, *China* 58 E3
Wuliaru, *Indonesia* 63 F8
Wulumuchi = Ürümqi, *China* 60 B3
Wum, *Cameroon* 83 D7
Wuming, *China* 58 F7
Wuning, *China* 59 C10
Wunnummin L., *Canada* 102 B2
Wunsiedel, *Germany* 25 E8
Wunstorf, *Germany* 24 C5
Wuntho, *Burma* 67 H19
Wuping, *China* 59 E11
Wuppertal, *Germany* 24 D3
Wuppertal, *S. Africa* 88 E2
Wuqing, *China* 57 E9
Wurung, *Australia* 94 B3
Würzburg, *Germany* 25 F5
Wurzen, *Germany* 24 D8
Wushan, *Gansu, China* 56 G3
Wushan, *Sichuan, China* 58 B7
Wusuli Jiang = Ussuri →, *Asia* 54 A7
Wutach →, *Germany* 25 H4
Wutai, *China* 56 E7
Wuting = Huimin, *China* 57 F9
Wutong, *China* 59 E8
Wutonghaolai, *China* 57 C11
Wutongqiao, *China* 58 C4
Wuwei, *Anhui, China* 59 B11
Wuwei, *Gansu, China* 60 C5
Wuxi, *Jiangsu, China* 59 B13
Wuxi, *Sichuan, China* 58 B7
Wuxiang, *China* 56 F7
Wuxing, *China* 59 B13
Wuxuan, *China* 58 F7
Wuyang, *China* 56 H7
Wuyi, *Hebei, China* 56 F8
Wuyi, *Zhejiang, China* 59 C12
Wuyi Shan, *China* 59 D11
Wuyo, *Nigeria* 83 C7
Wuyuan, *Jiangxi, China* 59 C11
Wuyuan, *Nei Mongol Zizhiqu, China* 56 D5
Wuzhai, *China* 56 E6
Wuzhi Shan, *China* 60 E5
Wuzhong, *China* 56 E4
Wuzhou, *China* 59 F8
Wyaaba Cr. →, *Australia* 94 B3
Wyalkatchem, *Australia* 93 F2
Wyalusing, *U.S.A.* 111 E8
Wyandotte, *U.S.A.* 108 D4
Wyandra, *Australia* 95 D4
Wyangala Res., *Australia* 95 E4
Wyara, L., *Australia* 95 D3
Wycheproof, *Australia* 95 F3
Wye →, *U.K.* 13 F5
Wyemandoo, *Australia* 93 E2
Wyk, *Germany* 24 A4
Wymondham, *U.K.* 13 E9
Wymore, *U.S.A.* 112 E6
Wynbring, *Australia* 95 E1
Wyndham, *Australia* 92 C4
Wyndham, *N.Z.* 91 M2
Wyndmere, *U.S.A.* 112 B6
Wynne, *U.S.A.* 113 H9
Wynnum, *Australia* 95 D5
Wynyard, *Australia* 94 G4
Wynyard, *Canada* 105 C8
Wyola, L., *Australia* 93 E5
Wyoming □, *U.S.A.* 114 E10
Wyong, *Australia* 95 E5
Wyrzysk, *Poland* 45 E4
Wyśmierzyce, *Poland* 45 G7
Wysoka, *Poland* 45 E4
Wysokie, *Poland* 45 H9
Wysokie Mazowieckie, *Poland* 45 F9
Wyszków, *Poland* 45 F8
Wyszogród, *Poland* 45 F7
Wytheville, *U.S.A.* 108 G5
Wyżyna Małopolska, *Poland* 45 H7

X

Xaçmaz, *Azerbaijan* 49 K9
Xai-Xai, *Mozam.* 89 D5
Xainza, *China* 60 C3
Xangongo, *Angola* 88 B2
Xankändi, *Azerbaijan* 73 C12
Xanlar, *Azerbaijan* 49 K8
Xanten, *Germany* 24 D2
Xánthi, *Greece* 41 E8
Xánthi □, *Greece* 41 E8
Xanthos, *Turkey* 39 E11
Xapuri, *Brazil* 124 F5
Xar Moron He →, *China* 57 C11
Xarrë, *Albania* 40 G4
Xátiva, *Spain* 33 G4
Xau, L., *Botswana* 88 C3
Xavantina, *Brazil* 127 A5
Xenia, *U.S.A.* 108 F4
Xeropotamos →, *Cyprus* 36 E11
Xertigny, *France* 19 D13
Xhora, *S. Africa* 89 E4
Xhumo, *Botswana* 88 C3
Xi Jiang →, *China* 59 F9
Xi Xian, *Henan, China* 59 A10
Xi Xian, *Shanxi, China* 56 F6
Xia Xian, *China* 56 G6
Xiachengzi, *China* 57 B16
Xiachuan Dao, *China* 59 G9
Xiaguan, *China* 58 E3
Xiajiang, *China* 59 D10
Xiajin, *China* 56 F9
Xiamen, *China* 59 E12
Xi'an, *China* 56 G5
Xian Xian, *China* 56 E9
Xianfeng, *China* 58 C7
Xiang Jiang →, *China* 59 C9
Xiangcheng, *Henan, China* 56 H8
Xiangcheng, *Henan, China* 56 H7
Xiangcheng, *Sichuan, China* 58 C2
Xiangdu, *China* 58 F6
Xiangfan, *China* 59 A9
Xianghuang Qi, *China* 56 C7
Xiangning, *China* 56 G6
Xiangquan, *China* 56 F7
Xiangshan, *China* 59 C13
Xiangshui, *China* 57 G10
Xiangtan, *China* 59 D9
Xiangxiang, *China* 59 D9
Xiangyin, *China* 59 C9
Xiangyun, *China* 58 E3
Xiangzhou, *China* 58 F7
Xianju, *China* 59 C13
Xianning, *China* 59 C10
Xianshui He →, *China* 58 B3
Xianyang, *China* 56 G5
Xianyou, *China* 59 E12
Xiao Hinggan Ling, *China* 60 B7
Xiao Xian, *China* 56 G9
Xiaofeng, *China* 59 B12
Xiaogan, *China* 59 B9
Xiaojin, *China* 58 B4
Xiaolan, *China* 59 F9
Xiaoshan, *China* 59 B13
Xiaoyi, *China* 56 F6
Xiapu, *China* 59 D12
Xiawa, *China* 57 C11
Xiayi, *China* 56 G9
Xichang, *China* 58 D4
Xichong, *China* 58 B5
Xichuan, *China* 56 H6
Xiemahe, *China* 59 B8
Xieng Khouang, *Laos* 64 C4
Xifei He →, *China* 56 H9
Xifeng, *Guizhou, China* 58 D6
Xifeng, *Liaoning, China* 57 C13
Xifengzhen, *China* 56 G4
Xigazê, *China* 60 D3
Xihe, *China* 56 G3
Xihua, *China* 56 H8
Xilagani, *Greece* 41 F9
Xiliao He →, *China* 57 C12
Xilin, *China* 58 E5
Xilókastron, *Greece* 38 C4
Xin Jiang →, *China* 59 C11
Xin Xian, *China* 56 E7
Xinavane, *Mozam.* 89 D5
Xinbin, *China* 57 D13
Xincai, *China* 59 A10
Xinchang, *China* 59 C13
Xincheng, *Guangxi Zhuangzu, China* 58 E7
Xincheng, *Jiangxi, China* 59 D10
Xinfeng, *Guangdong, China* 59 E10
Xinfeng, *Jiangxi, China* 59 D11
Xinfeng, *Jiangxi, China* 59 E10
Xing Xian, *China* 56 E6
Xing'an, *Guangxi Zhuangzu, China* 59 E8
Xingan, *Jiangxi, China* 59 D10
Xingcheng, *China* 57 D11
Xingguo, *China* 59 D10
Xinghe, *China* 56 D7
Xinghua, *China* 57 H10
Xinghua Wan, *China* 59 E12
Xinglong, *China* 57 D9
Xingning, *China* 59 E10
Xingping, *China* 56 G5
Xingren, *China* 58 E5
Xingshan, *China* 59 B8
Xingtai, *China* 56 F8
Xingu →, *Brazil* 122 D5
Xingyang, *China* 56 G7
Xinhe, *China* 56 F8
Xinhua, *China* 59 D8
Xinhuang, *China* 58 D7
Xinhui, *China* 59 F9
Xining, *China* 60 C5
Xinjiang, *China* 56 G6
Xinjiang Uygur Zizhiqu □, *China* 60 B3
Xinjie, *China* 58 D3
Xinjin, *Liaoning, China* 57 E11
Xinjin, *Sichuan, China* 58 B4
Xinkai He →, *China* 57 C12
Xinle, *China* 56 E8
Xinlitun, *China* 57 D12
Xinlong, *China* 58 B3
Xinmin, *China* 57 D12
Xinning, *China* 59 D8
Xinping, *China* 58 E3
Xinshao, *China* 59 D8
Xintai, *China* 57 G9
Xintian, *China* 59 E9
Xinxiang, *China* 56 G7
Xinxing, *China* 59 F9
Xinyang, *China* 59 A10
Xinye, *China* 59 A9
Xinyi, *China* 59 F8
Xinyu, *China* 59 D10
Xinzhan, *China* 57 C14
Xinzheng, *China* 56 G7
Xinzhou, *China* 59 B10
Xinzo de Limia, *Spain* 34 C3
Xiong Xian, *China* 56 E9
Xiongyuecheng, *China* 57 D12
Xiping, *Henan, China* 56 H8
Xiping, *Henan, China* 56 H6
Xiping, *Zhejiang, China* 59 C12
Xique-Xique, *Brazil* 125 F10
Xisha Qundao = Paracel Is., *S. China Sea* 62 A4
Xishui, *China* 59 B10
Xituozhen, *China* 58 B7
Xiuning, *China* 59 C12
Xiuren, *China* 59 E8
Xiushan, *China* 58 C7
Xiushui, *China* 59 C10
Xiuwen, *China* 58 D6
Xiuyan, *China* 57 D12
Xixabangma Feng, *China* 67 E14
Xixia, *China* 56 H6
Xixiang, *China* 56 H4
Xiyang, *China* 56 F7
Xizang Zizhiqu □, *China* 60 C3
Xlendi, *Malta* 36 C1
Xu Jiang →, *China* 59 D11
Xuan Loc, *Vietnam* 65 G6
Xuancheng, *China* 59 B12
Xuan'en, *China* 58 C7
Xuanhan, *China* 58 B6
Xuanhua, *China* 56 D8
Xuchang, *China* 56 G7
Xudat, *Azerbaijan* 49 K9
Xuefeng Shan, *China* 59 D8
Xuejiaping, *China* 59 B8
Xun Jiang →, *China* 59 F8
Xun Xian, *China* 56 G8
Xundian, *China* 58 E4
Xunwu, *China* 59 E10
Xunyang, *China* 56 H5
Xunyi, *China* 56 G5
Xupu, *China* 59 D8
Xúquer →, *Spain* 33 F4
Xushui, *China* 56 E8
Xuwen, *China* 59 G8
Xuyen Moc, *Vietnam* 65 G6
Xuyong, *China* 58 C5
Xuzhou, *China* 57 G9
Xylophagou, *Cyprus* 36 E12

Y

Ya Xian, *China* 64 C7
Yaamba, *Australia* 94 C5
Ya'an, *China* 58 C4
Yaapeet, *Australia* 95 F3
Yabassi, *Cameroon* 83 E6
Yabelo, *Ethiopia* 81 G4
Yablanitsa, *Bulgaria* 41 C8
Yablonovy Ra. = Yablonovyy Khrebet, *Russia* 51 D12
Yablonovyy Khrebet, *Russia* 51 D12
Yabrai Shan, *China* 56 E2
Yabrūd, *Syria* 75 B5
Yacheng, *China* 64 C7
Yacuiba, *Bolivia* 126 A3
Yacuma →, *Bolivia* 124 F5
Yadgir, *India* 66 L10
Yadkin →, *U.S.A.* 109 H5
Yadrin, *Russia* 48 C8
Yagaba, *Ghana* 83 C4
Yağcılar, *Turkey* 39 B10
Yagodnoye, *Russia* 51 C15
Yahila, *Dem. Rep. of the Congo* 86 B1
Yahk, *Canada* 104 D5
Yahotyn, *Ukraine* 47 G6
Yahuma, *Dem. Rep. of the Congo* 84 D4
Yahyalı, *Turkey* 72 C6
Yaita, *Japan* 55 F9
Yaiza, *Canary Is.* 37 F6
Yajiang, *China* 58 B3
Yajua, *Nigeria* 83 C7
Yakima, *U.S.A.* 114 C3
Yakima →, *U.S.A.* 114 C3
Yako, *Burkina Faso* 82 C4
Yakoruda, *Bulgaria* 40 D7
Yakovlevka, *Russia* 54 B6
Yaku-Shima, *Japan* 55 J5
Yakutat, *U.S.A.* 100 C6
Yakutia = Sakha □, *Russia* 51 C14
Yakutsk, *Russia* 51 C13
Yala, *Thailand* 65 J3
Yalbalgo, *Australia* 93 E1
Yalboroo, *Australia* 94 C4
Yale, *U.S.A.* 110 C2
Yalgoo, *Australia* 93 E2
Yalinga, *C.A.R.* 84 C4
Yalkubul, Punta, *Mexico* 119 C7
Yalleroi, *Australia* 94 C4
Yalobusha →, *U.S.A.* 113 J9
Yalong Jiang →, *China* 58 D3
Yalova, *Turkey* 41 F13
Yalta, *Ukraine* 47 K8
Yalu Jiang →, *China* 57 E13
Yalvaç, *Turkey* 72 C4
Yam Ha Melah = Dead Sea, *Asia* 75 D4
Yam Kinneret, *Israel* 75 C4
Yamada, *Japan* 55 H5
Yamagata, *Japan* 54 E10
Yamagata □, *Japan* 54 E10
Yamaguchi, *Japan* 55 G5
Yamaguchi □, *Japan* 55 G5
Yamal, Poluostrov, *Russia* 50 B8
Yamal Pen. = Yamal, Poluostrov, *Russia* 50 B8
Yamanashi □, *Japan* 55 G9
Yamba, *N.S.W., Australia* 95 D5
Yamba, *S. Austral., Australia* 95 E3
Yambah, *Australia* 94 C1
Yambarran Ra., *Australia* 92 C5
Yâmbiô, *Sudan* 81 G2
Yambol, *Bulgaria* 41 D10
Yamdena, *Indonesia* 63 F8
Yame, *Japan* 55 H5
Yamethin, *Burma* 67 J20
Yamil, *Nigeria* 83 C6
Yamma-Yamma, L., *Australia* 95 D3
Yamoussoukro, *Ivory C.* 82 D3
Yampa →, *U.S.A.* 114 F9
Yampi Sd., *Australia* 92 C3
Yampil, *Moldova* 47 H5
Yampol = Yampil, *Moldova* 47 H5
Yamrat, *Nigeria* 83 C6
Yamrukchal = Botev, *Bulgaria* 41 D8
Yamuna →, *India* 69 G9
Yamzho Yumco, *China* 60 D4
Yan, *Nigeria* 83 C7
Yana →, *Russia* 51 B14
Yanac, *Australia* 95 F3
Yanagawa, *Japan* 55 H5
Yanai, *Japan* 55 H6
Yan'an, *China* 56 F5
Yanbian, *China* 58 D3
Yanbu 'al Baḩr, *Si. Arabia* 70 F3
Yancannia, *Australia* 95 E3
Yanchang, *China* 56 F6
Yancheng, *Henan, China* 56 H8
Yancheng, *Jiangsu, China* 57 H11
Yanchi, *China* 56 F4
Yanchuan, *China* 56 F6
Yanco Cr. →, *Australia* 95 F4
Yandal, *Australia* 93 E3
Yandanooka, *Australia* 93 E2
Yandaran, *Australia* 94 C5
Yandoon, *Burma* 67 L19
Yanfeng, *China* 58 E3

Žabljak

Yanfolila, Mali 82 C3
Yang Xian, China 56 H4
Yangambi, Dem. Rep. of the Congo 86 B1
Yangbi, China 58 E2
Yangcheng, China 56 G7
Yangch'ü = Taiyuan, China 56 F7
Yangchun, China 59 F8
Yanggao, China 56 D7
Yanggu, China 56 F8
Yangjiang, China 59 G8
Yangliuqing, China 57 E9
Yangon = Rangoon, Burma 67 L20
Yangping, China 59 B8
Yangpingguan, China 56 H4
Yangquan, China 56 F7
Yangshan, China 59 E9
Yangshuo, China 59 E8
Yangtse = Chang Jiang →, China 59 B13
Yangtze Kiang = Chang Jiang →, China 59 B13
Yangxin, China 59 C10
Yangyang, S. Korea 57 E15
Yangyuan, China 56 D8
Yangzhou, China 59 A12
Yanhe, China 58 C7
Yanji, China 57 C15
Yanjin, China 58 C5
Yanjing, China 58 C2
Yankton, U.S.A. 112 D6
Yanna, Australia 95 D4
Yanonge, Dem. Rep. of the Congo 86 B1
Yanqi, China 60 B3
Yanqing, China 56 D8
Yanshan, Hebei, China 57 E9
Yanshan, Jiangxi, China 59 C11
Yanshan, Yunnan, China 58 F5
Yanshou, China 57 B15
Yantabulla, Australia 95 D4
Yantai, China 57 F11
Yanting, China 58 B5
Yantra →, Bulgaria 41 C9
Yanwa, China 58 D2
Yanyuan, China 58 D3
Yanzhou, China 56 G9
Yao Xian, China 56 G5
Yao Yai, Ko, Thailand 65 J2
Yao'an, China 58 E3
Yaodu, China 58 A5
Yaoundé, Cameroon 83 E7
Yaowan, China 57 G10
Yap I., Pac. Oc. 96 G5
Yapen, Indonesia 63 E9
Yapen, Selat, Indonesia 63 E9
Yappar →, Australia 94 B3
Yaqui →, Mexico 118 B2
Yar-Sale, Russia 50 C8
Yaraka, Australia 94 C3
Yaransk, Russia 48 B8
Yarbasan, Turkey 39 C10
Yardea P.O., Australia 95 E2
Yardımcı Burnu, Turkey 39 E12
Yare →, U.K. 13 E9
Yaremcha, Ukraine 47 H3
Yarensk, Russia 50 C5
Yarí →, Colombia 124 D4
Yarkand = Shache, China 60 C2
Yarker, Canada 111 B8
Yarkhun →, Pakistan 69 A5
Yarmouth, Canada 103 D6
Yarmūk →, Syria 75 C4
Yaroslavl, Russia 46 D10
Yarqa, W. →, Egypt 75 F2
Yarra Yarra Lakes, Australia 93 E2
Yarraden, Australia 94 A3
Yarraloola, Australia 92 D2
Yarram, Australia 95 F4
Yarraman, Australia 95 D5
Yarranvale, Australia 95 D4
Yarras, Australia 95 E5
Yarrowmere, Australia 94 C4
Yartsevo, Sib., Russia 51 C10
Yartsevo, Smolensk, Russia 46 E7
Yarumal, Colombia 124 B3
Yasawa Group, Fiji 91 C7
Yaselda, Belarus 47 F4
Yashi, Nigeria 83 C6
Yashkul, Russia 49 G7
Yasin, Pakistan 69 A5
Yasinovataya, Ukraine 47 H9
Yasinski, L., Canada 102 B4
Yasinya, Ukraine 47 H3
Yasothon, Thailand 64 E5
Yass, Australia 95 E4
Yatağan, Turkey 39 D10
Yates Center, U.S.A. 113 G7
Yathkyed L., Canada 105 A9
Yatsushiro, Japan 55 H5
Yatta Plateau, Kenya 86 C4
Yavari →, Peru 124 D4
Yavatmal, India 66 J11
Yavne, Israel 75 D3
Yavoriv, Ukraine 47 H2
Yavorov = Yavoriv, Ukraine 47 H2
Yavuzeli, Turkey 72 D7
Yawatahama, Japan 55 H6
Yawri B., S. Leone 82 D2
Yaxi, China 58 D6
Yayama-Rettō, Japan 55 M1
Yazd, Iran 71 D7
Yazd □, Iran 71 D7
Yazıköy, Turkey 39 E9
Yazoo →, U.S.A. 113 J9
Yazoo City, U.S.A. 113 J9
Ybbs, Austria 26 C8
Yding Skovhøj, Denmark 11 J3
Ye Xian, Henan, China 56 H7
Ye Xian, Shandong, China 57 F10
Yealering, Australia 93 F2
Yebyu, Burma 67 M21
Yechŏn, S. Korea 57 F15
Yecla, Spain 33 G3
Yécora, Mexico 118 B3
Yedintsy = Edineţ, Moldova 43 B12
Yeeda, Australia 92 C3
Yeelanna, Australia 95 E2
Yefremov, Russia 46 F10
Yeghegnadzor, Armenia 73 C11
Yegorlyk →, Russia 49 G5
Yegorlykskaya, Russia 49 G5
Yegoryevsk, Russia 46 E10
Yegros, Paraguay 126 B4
Yehuda, Midbar, Israel 75 D4
Yei, Sudan 81 G3
Yei, Nahr →, Sudan 81 F3
Yejmiadzin, Armenia 49 K7
Yekaterinburg, Russia 50 D7
Yekaterinodar = Krasnodar, Russia 49 H4
Yelabuga, Russia 48 C11
Yelan, Russia 48 E6
Yelarbon, Australia 95 D5
Yelatma, Russia 48 C5
Yelets, Russia 47 F10
Yélimané, Mali 82 B2
Yelizavetgrad = Kirovohrad, Ukraine 47 H7
Yell, U.K. 14 A7
Yell Sd., U.K. 14 A7
Yellow Sea, China 57 G12
Yellowhead Pass, Canada 104 C5
Yellowknife, Canada 104 A6
Yellowknife →, Canada 104 A6
Yellowstone →, U.S.A. 112 B3
Yellowstone L., U.S.A. 114 D8
Yellowstone National Park, U.S.A. 114 D9
Yellowtail Res., U.S.A. 114 D9
Yelnya, Russia 46 E7
Yelsk, Belarus 47 G5
Yelvertoft, Australia 94 C2
Yelwa, Nigeria 83 C5
Yemen ■, Asia 74 E3
Yen Bai, Vietnam 64 B5
Yenakiyeve, Ukraine 47 H10
Yenakiyevo = Yenakiyeve, Ukraine 47 H10
Yenangyaung, Burma 67 J19
Yenbo = Yanbu 'al Baḩr, Si. Arabia 70 F3
Yenda, Australia 95 E4
Yendéré, Ivory C. 82 C4
Yendi, Ghana 83 D4
Yenice, Ankara, Turkey 72 C5
Yenice, Aydın, Turkey 39 D10
Yenice, Çanakkale, Turkey 39 B9
Yenice, Edirne, Turkey 41 F10
Yenice →, Turkey 72 D6
Yenifoça, Turkey 39 C8
Yenihisar, Turkey 39 D9
Yeniköy, Bursa, Turkey 41 F13
Yeniköy, Çanakkale, Turkey 39 B8
Yeniköy, Kütahya, Turkey 39 C11
Yenipazar, Turkey 39 D10
Yenisaía, Greece 41 E8
Yenişehir, Turkey 41 F13
Yenisey →, Russia 50 B9
Yeniseysk, Russia 51 D10
Yeniseyskiy Zaliv, Russia 50 B9
Yennádhi, Greece 36 C9
Yenne, France 21 C9
Yenotayevka, Russia 49 G8
Yenyuka, Russia 51 D13
Yeo →, U.K. 13 G5
Yeo, L., Australia 93 E3
Yeola, India 66 J9
Yeoryioúpolis, Greece 36 D6
Yeovil, U.K. 13 G5
Yepes, Spain 34 F7
Yeppoon, Australia 94 C5
Yeráki, Greece 38 D4
Yerbent, Turkmenistan 50 F6
Yerbogachen, Russia 51 C11
Yerevan, Armenia 49 K7
Yerilla, Australia 93 E3
Yerkesik, Turkey 39 D10
Yerköy, Turkey 72 C6
Yermak, Kazakstan 50 D8
Yermo, U.S.A. 117 L10
Yerólakkos, Cyprus 36 D12
Yeropol, Russia 51 C17
Yeropótamos →, Greece 36 D6
Yeroskipos, Cyprus 36 E11
Yershov, Russia 48 E9
Yerushalayim = Jerusalem, Israel 75 D4
Yerville, France 18 C7
Yes Tor, U.K. 13 G4
Yesan, S. Korea 57 F14
Yeşilhisar, Turkey 72 C6
Yeşilırmak →, Turkey 72 B7
Yeşilkent, Turkey 72 D7
Yeşilköy, Turkey 41 F12
Yeşilova, Turkey 39 D11
Yeşilyurt, Manisa, Turkey 39 C10
Yeşilyurt, Muğla, Turkey 39 D10
Yesnogorsk, Russia 46 E9
Yeso, U.S.A. 113 H2
Yessentuki, Russia 49 H6
Yessey, Russia 51 C11
Yeste, Spain 33 G2
Yeu, Î. d', France 18 F4
Yevlakh = Yevlax, Azerbaijan 49 K8
Yevlax, Azerbaijan 49 K8
Yevpatoriya, Ukraine 47 K7
Yeya →, Russia 47 J10
Yeysk, Russia 47 J10
Yezd = Yazd, Iran 71 D7
Yezerishche, Belarus 46 E5
Yhati, Paraguay 126 B4
Yhú, Paraguay 127 B4
Yi →, Uruguay 126 C4
Yi 'Allaq, G., Egypt 75 E2
Yi He →, China 57 G10
Yi Xian, Anhui, China 59 C11
Yi Xian, Hebei, China 56 E8
Yi Xian, Liaoning, China 57 D11
Yialí, Greece 39 E9
Yialiás →, Cyprus 36 D12
Yi'allaq, G., Egypt 80 H8
Yialousa, Cyprus 36 D13
Yiáltra, Greece 38 C4
Yianisádhes, Greece 36 D8
Yiannitsa, Greece 40 F6
Yibin, China 58 C5
Yichang, China 59 B8
Yicheng, Henan, China 59 B9
Yicheng, Shanxi, China 56 G6
Yichuan, China 56 F6
Yichun, Heilongjiang, China 60 B7
Yichun, Jiangxi, China 59 D10
Yidu, Hubei, China 59 B8
Yidu, Shandong, China 57 F10
Yidun, China 58 B2
Yihuang, China 59 D11
Yijun, China 56 G5
Yıldız Dağları, Turkey 41 E11
Yıldızeli, Turkey 72 C7
Yiliang, Yunnan, China 58 D5
Yiliang, Yunnan, China 58 E4
Yilong, China 58 B6
Yimen, China 58 E4
Yimianpo, China 57 B15
Yinchuan, China 56 E4
Yindarlgooda, L., Australia 93 F3
Ying He →, China 56 H9
Ying Xian, China 56 E7
Yingcheng, China 59 B9
Yingde, China 59 E9
Yingjiang, China 58 E1
Yingjing, China 58 C4
Yingkou, China 57 D12
Yingshan, Henan, China 59 B9
Yingshan, Hubei, China 59 B10
Yingshan, Sichuan, China 58 B6
Yingshang, China 59 A11
Yingtan, China 60 D6
Yining, China 60 B3
Yinjiang, China 58 C7
Yinmabin, Burma 67 H19
Yinnietharra, Australia 92 D2
Yiofiros →, Greece 36 D7
Yioúra, Nótios Aiyaíon, Greece 38 D6
Yioúra, Thessalía, Greece 38 B6
Yipinglang, China 58 E3
Yirga Alem, Ethiopia 81 F4
Yishan, China 58 E7
Yishui, China 57 G10
Yíthion, Greece 38 E4
Yitiaoshan, China 56 F3
Yitong, China 57 C13
Yiwu, China 59 C13
Yixing, China 59 B12
Yiyang, Henan, China 56 G7
Yiyang, Hunan, China 59 C9
Yiyang, Jiangxi, China 59 C11
Yizhang, China 59 E9
Yizheng, China 59 A12
Yli-Kitka, Finland 8 C23
Ylitornio, Finland 8 C20
Ylivieska, Finland 8 D21
Yngaren, Sweden 11 F10
Yoakum, U.S.A. 113 L6
Yobe □, Nigeria 83 C7
Yog Pt., Phil. 63 B6
Yogan, Togo 83 D5
Yoğuntaş, Turkey 41 E11
Yogyakarta, Indonesia 63 G14
Yoho Nat. Park, Canada 104 C5
Yojoa, L. de, Honduras 120 D2
Yŏju, S. Korea 57 F14
Yokadouma, Cameroon 84 D2
Yokkaichi, Japan 55 G8
Yoko, Cameroon 83 D7
Yokohama, Japan 55 G9
Yokosuka, Japan 55 G9
Yokote, Japan 54 E10
Yola, Nigeria 83 D7
Yolaina, Cordillera de, Nic. 120 D3
Yonago, Japan 55 G6
Yonaguni-Jima, Japan 55 M1
Yŏnan, N. Korea 57 F14
Yonezawa, Japan 54 F10
Yong Peng, Malaysia 65 M4
Yong Sata, Thailand 65 J2
Yongamp'o, N. Korea 57 E13
Yong'an, China 59 E11
Yongcheng, China 56 H9
Yŏngchŏn, S. Korea 57 G15
Yongchuan, China 58 C5
Yongchun, China 59 E12
Yongdeng, China 56 F2
Yongding, China 59 E11
Yŏngdŏk, S. Korea 57 F15
Yŏngdŭngpo, S. Korea 57 F14
Yongfeng, China 59 D10
Yongfu, China 58 E7
Yonghe, China 56 F6
Yŏnghŭng, N. Korea 57 E14
Yongji, China 56 G6
Yŏngju, S. Korea 57 F15
Yongkang, Yunnan, China 58 E2
Yongkang, Zhejiang, China 59 C13
Yongnian, China 56 F8
Yongning, Guangxi Zhuangzu, China 58 F7
Yongning, Ningxia Huizu, China 56 E4
Yongping, China 58 E2
Yongqing, China 56 E9
Yongren, China 58 D3
Yongshan, China 58 C4
Yongsheng, China 58 D3
Yongshun, China 58 C7
Yongtai, China 59 E12
Yŏngwŏl, S. Korea 57 F15
Yongxin, China 59 D10
Yongxing, China 59 D9
Yongxiu, China 59 C10
Yonibana, S. Leone 82 D2
Yonkers, U.S.A. 111 F11
Yonne □, France 19 E10
Yonne →, France 19 D9
York, Australia 93 F2
York, U.K. 12 D6
York, Ala., U.S.A. 109 J1
York, Nebr., U.S.A. 112 E6
York, Pa., U.S.A. 108 F7
York, C., Australia 94 A3
York, City of □, U.K. 12 D6
York, Kap, Greenland 4 B4
York, Vale of, U.K. 12 C6
York Sd., Australia 92 C4
Yorke Pen., Australia 95 E2
Yorkshire Wolds, U.K. 12 C7
Yorkton, Canada 105 C8
Yorktown, U.S.A. 113 L6
Yorkville, U.S.A. 116 G3
Yornup, Australia 93 F2
Yoro, Honduras 120 C2
Yoron-Jima, Japan 55 L4
Yos Sudarso, Pulau = Dolak, Pulau, Indonesia 63 F9
Yosemite National Park, U.S.A. 116 H7
Yosemite Village, U.S.A. 116 H7
Yoshkar Ola, Russia 48 B8
Yŏsu, S. Korea 57 G14
Yotvata, Israel 75 F4
You Xian, China 59 D9
Youbou, Canada 104 D4
Youghal, Ireland 15 E4
Youghal B., Ireland 15 E4
Youkounkoun, Guinea 82 C2
Young, Australia 95 E4
Young, Canada 105 C7
Young, Uruguay 126 C4
Younghusband, L., Australia 95 E2
Younghusband Pen., Australia 95 F2
Youngstown, Canada 105 C6
Youngstown, N.Y., U.S.A. 110 C5
Youngstown, Ohio, U.S.A. 110 E4
Youngsville, U.S.A. 110 E5
Youxi, China 59 D12
Youyang, China 58 C7
Youyu, China 56 D7
Yowerabbie, Australia 93 E2
Yozgat, Turkey 72 C6
Ypané →, Paraguay 126 A4
Yport, France 18 C7
Ypres = Ieper, Belgium 17 D2
Ypsilanti, U.S.A. 108 D4
Yreka, U.S.A. 114 F2
Ysleta, U.S.A. 115 L10
Yssingeaux, France 21 C8
Ystad, Sweden 11 J7
Ysyk-Köl, Kyrgyzstan 52 E11
Ysyk-Köl, Ozero, Kyrgyzstan 50 E8
Ythan →, U.K. 14 D7
Ytterhogdal, Sweden 10 B8
Ytyk Kyuyel, Russia 51 C14
Yu Jiang →, China 60 D6
Yu Xian, Hebei, China 56 E8
Yu Xian, Henan, China 56 G7
Yu Xian, Shanxi, China 56 E7
Yuan Jiang →, Hunan, China 59 C8
Yuan Jiang →, Yunnan, China 58 F4
Yuan'an, China 59 B8
Yuanjiang, Hunan, China 59 C9
Yuanjiang, Yunnan, China 58 F4
Yüanli, Taiwan 59 E13
Yüanlin, Taiwan 59 F13
Yuanlin, Taiwan 59 F13
Yuanling, China 59 C8
Yuanmou, China 58 E3
Yuanqu, China 56 G6
Yuanyang, Henan, China 56 G7
Yuanyang, Yunnan, China 58 F4
Yuba →, U.S.A. 116 F5
Yuba City, U.S.A. 116 F5
Yūbari, Japan 54 C10
Yūbetsu, Japan 54 B11
Yucatán □, Mexico 119 C7
Yucatán, Canal de, Caribbean 120 B2
Yucatán, Península de, Mexico 98 H11
Yucatán Basin, Cent. Amer. 98 H11
Yucatan Str. = Yucatán, Canal de, Caribbean 120 B2
Yucca, U.S.A. 117 L12
Yucca Valley, U.S.A. 117 L10
Yucheng, China 56 F9
Yuci, China 56 F7
Yudu, China 59 E10
Yuendumu, Australia 92 D5
Yueqing, China 59 C13
Yueqing Wan, China 59 C13
Yuexi, Anhui, China 59 B11
Yuexi, Sichuan, China 58 C4
Yueyang, China 59 C9
Yugan, China 59 C11
Yugoslavia ■, Europe 40 C4
Yuhuan, China 59 C13
Yujiang, China 59 C11
Yukhnov, Russia 46 E8
Yukon →, U.S.A. 100 B3
Yukon Territory □, Canada 100 B6
Yüksekova, Turkey 73 D11
Yukta, Russia 51 C11
Yukuhashi, Japan 55 H5
Yule →, Australia 92 D2
Yuli, Nigeria 83 D7
Yulin, Guangxi Zhuangzu, China 59 F8
Yulin, Shaanxi, China 56 E5
Yulin, Shensi, China 64 C7
Yuma, Ariz., U.S.A. 117 N12
Yuma, Colo., U.S.A. 112 E3
Yuma, B. de, Dom. Rep. 121 C6
Yumbe, Uganda 86 B3
Yumbi, Dem. Rep. of the Congo 86 C2
Yumen, China 60 C4
Yumurtalık, Turkey 72 D6
Yun Ho →, China 57 E9
Yun Xian, Hubei, China 59 A8
Yun Xian, Yunnan, China 58 E3
Yunak, Turkey 72 C4
Yunan, China 59 F8
Yuncheng, Henan, China 56 G8
Yuncheng, Shanxi, China 56 G6
Yundamindra, Australia 93 E3
Yunfu, China 59 F9
Yungas, Bolivia 124 G5
Yungay, Chile 126 D1
Yunhe, China 59 C12
Yunlin, Taiwan 59 F13
Yunling, China 58 D2
Yunlong, China 58 E2
Yunmeng, China 59 B9
Yunnan □, China 58 E4
Yunquera de Henares, Spain 32 E1
Yunt Dağı, Turkey 39 C9
Yunta, Australia 95 E2
Yunxi, China 56 H6
Yunxiao, China 59 F11
Yunyang, China 58 B7
Yuping, China 58 D7
Yupyongdong, N. Korea 57 D15
Yuqing, China 58 D6
Yurga, Russia 50 D9
Yurimaguas, Peru 124 E3
Yuryev-Polskiy, Russia 46 D10
Yuryevets, Russia 48 B6
Yuryung Kaya, Russia 51 B12
Yuscarán, Honduras 120 D2
Yushanzhen, China 58 C7
Yushe, China 56 F7
Yushu, Jilin, China 57 B14
Yushu, Qinghai, China 60 C4
Yusufeli, Turkey 73 B9
Yutai, China 56 G9
Yutian, China 57 E9
Yuxarı Qarabağ = Nagorno-Karabakh, Azerbaijan 73 C12
Yuxi, China 58 E4
Yuyao, China 59 B13
Yuzawa, Japan 54 E10
Yuzha, Russia 48 B6
Yuzhno-Sakhalinsk, Russia 51 E15
Yvelines □, France 19 D8
Yverdon, Switz. 25 J2
Yvetot, France 18 C7
Yzeure, France 19 F10

Z

Zaanstad, Neths. 17 B4
Zāb al Kabīr →, Iraq 70 C4
Zāb aş Şagīr →, Iraq 70 C4
Žabalj, Serbia, Yug. 42 E5
Žabari, Serbia, Yug. 40 B5
Zabarjad, Egypt 80 C4
Zabaykalsk, Russia 51 E12
Zabki, Poland 45 F8
Ząbkowice Śląskie, Poland 45 H3
Žabljak, Montenegro, Yug. 40 C3

Zabłudów

Zabłudów, *Poland* 45 F9
Ząbno, *Poland* 45 H7
Zābol, *Iran* 71 D9
Zāboli, *Iran* 71 E9
Zabré, *Burkina Faso* 83 C4
Zábřeh, *Czech Rep.* 27 B9
Zabrze, *Poland* 45 H5
Zacapa, *Guatemala* 120 D2
Zacapu, *Mexico* 118 D4
Zacatecas, *Mexico* 118 C4
Zacatecas □, *Mexico* 118 C4
Zacatecoluca, *El Salv.* 120 D2
Zacoalco, *Mexico* 118 C4
Zacualtipán, *Mexico* 119 C5
Zadar, *Croatia* 29 D12
Zadawa, *Nigeria* 83 C7
Zadetkyi Kyun, *Burma* 65 H2
Zadonsk, *Russia* 47 F10
Zafarqand, *Iran* 71 C7
Zafora, *Greece* 39 E8
Zafra, *Spain* 35 G4
Żagań, *Poland* 45 G2
Žagarė, *Lithuania* 44 B10
Zagazig, *Egypt* 80 H7
Zāgheh, *Iran* 71 C6
Zaglivérion, *Greece* 40 F7
Zagnanado, *Benin* 83 D5
Zagorá, *Greece* 38 B5
Zagorje, *Slovenia* 29 B11
Zagórów, *Poland* 45 F4
Zagorsk = Sergiyev Posad, *Russia* 46 D10
Zagórz, *Poland* 45 J9
Zagreb, *Croatia* 29 C12
Zāgros, Kūhhā-ye, *Iran* 71 C6
Zagros Mts. = Zāgros, Kūhhā-ye, *Iran* 71 C6
Žagubica, *Serbia, Yug.* 40 B5
Zaguinaso, *Ivory C.* 82 C3
Zagyva →, *Hungary* 42 C5
Zāhedān, *Fārs, Iran* 71 D7
Zāhedān, *Sīstān va Balūchestān, Iran* 71 D9
Zahlah, *Lebanon* 75 B4
Zahna, *Germany* 24 D8
Záhony, *Hungary* 42 B7
Zainsk, *Russia* 48 C11
Zaïre = Congo, Dem. Rep. of the ■, *Africa* 84 E4
Zaïre → = Congo →, *Africa* 84 F2
Zaječar, *Serbia, Yug.* 40 C6
Zakamensk, *Russia* 51 D11
Zakataly = Zaqatala, *Azerbaijan* 49 K8
Zakháro, *Greece* 38 D3
Zakhodnaya Dzvina = Daugava →, *Latvia* 9 H21
Zākhū, *Iraq* 70 B4
Zákinthos, *Greece* 38 D2
Zákinthos □, *Greece* 38 D2
Zakopane, *Poland* 45 J6
Zakroczym, *Poland* 45 F7
Zákros, *Greece* 36 D8
Zala □, *Hungary* 42 D1
Zala →, *Hungary* 42 D2
Zalaegerszeg, *Hungary* 42 D1
Zalakomár, *Hungary* 42 D2
Zalalövő, *Hungary* 42 D1
Zalamea de la Serena, *Spain* 35 G5
Zalamea la Real, *Spain* 35 H4
Zalău, *Romania* 42 C8
Žalec, *Slovenia* 29 B12
Zaleshchiki = Zalishchyky, *Ukraine* 47 H3
Zalew Wiślany, *Poland* 44 D6
Zalewo, *Poland* 44 E6
Zalingei, *Sudan* 79 F10
Zalishchyky, *Ukraine* 47 H3
Zambeke, *Dem. Rep. of the Congo* 86 B2
Zambeze →, *Africa* 87 F4
Zambezi = Zambeze →, *Africa* 87 F4
Zambezi, *Zambia* 85 G4
Zambezia □, *Mozam.* 87 F4
Zambia ■, *Africa* 87 F2
Zamboanga, *Phil.* 61 H5
Zamboanguita, *Phil.* 61 G5
Zambrów, *Poland* 45 F9
Zametchino, *Russia* 48 D6
Zamora, *Mexico* 118 D4
Zamora, *Spain* 34 D5
Zamora □, *Spain* 34 D5
Zamość, *Poland* 45 H10
Zamość □, *Poland* 45 H10
Zan, *Ghana* 83 D4
Záncara →, *Spain* 33 F1
Zandvoort, *Neths.* 17 B4
Zanesville, *U.S.A.* 110 G2
Zangābād, *Iran* 70 B5
Zangue →, *Mozam.* 87 F4
Zanjān, *Iran* 71 B6
Zanjān □, *Iran* 71 B6
Zannone, *Italy* 30 B6
Zante = Zákinthos, *Greece* 38 D2
Zanthus, *Australia* 93 F3
Zanzibar, *Tanzania* 86 D4
Zaouiet El-Kala = Bordj Omar Driss, *Algeria* 78 C7
Zaouiet Reggane, *Algeria* 78 C6
Zaoyang, *China* 59 A9
Zaozhuang, *China* 57 G9
Zap Suyu = Zāb al Kabīr →, *Iraq* 70 C4
Zapadna Morava →, *Serbia, Yug.* 40 C5
Zapadnaya Dvina, *Russia* 46 D7
Zapadnaya Dvina → = Daugava →, *Latvia* 9 H21
Západné Beskydy, *Europe* 27 B12
Zapadni Rodopi, *Bulgaria* 40 E7
Západočeský □, *Czech Rep.* 26 B6
Zapala, *Argentina* 128 D2
Zapaleri, Cerro, *Bolivia* 126 A2
Zapata, *U.S.A.* 113 M5
Zapatón →, *Spain* 35 F4
Zaporizhzhya, *Ukraine* 47 J8
Zaporozhye = Zaporizhzhya, *Ukraine* 47 J8
Zaqatala, *Azerbaijan* 49 K8
Zara, *Turkey* 72 C7
Zaragoza, *Coahuila, Mexico* 118 B4
Zaragoza, *Nuevo León, Mexico* 119 C5
Zaragoza, *Spain* 32 D4
Zaragoza □, *Spain* 32 D4
Zarand, *Kermān, Iran* 71 D8
Zarand, *Markazī, Iran* 71 C6
Zărandului, Munţii, *Romania* 42 D7
Zaranj, *Afghan.* 66 D2
Zarasai, *Lithuania* 9 J22
Zarate, *Argentina* 126 C4
Zarautz, *Spain* 32 B2
Zaraysk, *Russia* 46 E10
Zāreh, *Iran* 71 C6
Zarembo I., *U.S.A.* 104 B2
Zaria, *Nigeria* 83 C6
Żarki, *Poland* 45 H6
Zárkon, *Greece* 38 B4
Zarneh, *Iran* 70 C5
Zărneşti, *Romania* 43 E10
Zarós, *Greece* 36 D6
Żarów, *Poland* 45 H3
Zarqā', Nahr az →, *Jordan* 75 C4
Zarrīn, *Iran* 71 C7
Zaruma, *Ecuador* 124 D3
Żary, *Poland* 45 G2
Zarza de Granadilla, *Spain* 34 E4
Zarzis, *Tunisia* 79 B8
Zas, *Spain* 34 B2
Zaskar →, *India* 69 B7
Zaskar Mts., *India* 69 C7
Zastron, *S. Africa* 88 E4
Žatec, *Czech Rep.* 26 A6
Zaterechnyy, *Russia* 49 H7
Zator, *Poland* 45 J6
Zavala, *Bos.-H.* 40 D1
Zavāreh, *Iran* 71 C7
Zavetnoye, *Russia* 49 G6
Zavidovići, *Bos.-H.* 42 F3
Zavitinsk, *Russia* 51 D13
Zavodovski, I., *Antarctica* 5 B1
Zavolzhsk, *Russia* 48 B6
Zavolzhye, *Russia* 48 B6
Zawadzkie, *Poland* 45 H5
Zawichost, *Poland* 45 H8
Zawidów, *Poland* 45 G2
Zawiercie, *Poland* 45 H6
Zāwiyat al Bayḍā = Al Bayḍā, *Libya* 79 B10
Zâwyet Shammas, *Egypt* 80 A2
Zâwyet Um el Rakham, *Egypt* 80 A2
Zâwyet Ungeîla, *Egypt* 80 A2
Zāyā, *Iraq* 70 C5
Zaysan, *Kazakstan* 50 E9
Zaysan, Oz., *Kazakstan* 50 E9
Zayü, *China* 58 C1
Zázrivá, *Slovak Rep.* 27 B12
Zbarazh, *Ukraine* 47 H3
Zbąszyń, *Poland* 45 F2
Zbąszynek, *Poland* 45 F2
Zblewo, *Poland* 44 E5
Žďár nad Sázavov, *Czech Rep.* 26 B8
Zdolbuniv, *Ukraine* 47 G4
Ždrelo, *Serbia, Yug.* 40 B5
Zduńska Wola, *Poland* 45 G5
Zduny, *Poland* 45 G4
Zeballos, *Canada* 104 D3
Zebediela, *S. Africa* 89 C4
Zeebrugge, *Belgium* 17 C3
Zeehan, *Australia* 94 G4
Zeeland □, *Neths.* 17 C3
Zeerust, *S. Africa* 88 D4
Zefat, *Israel* 75 C4
Zege, *Ethiopia* 81 E4
Zégoua, *Mali* 82 C3
Zehdenick, *Germany* 24 C9
Zeil, Mt., *Australia* 92 D5
Zeila, *Somali Rep.* 74 E3
Zeist, *Neths.* 17 B5
Zeitz, *Germany* 24 D8
Żelechów, *Poland* 45 G8
Zelengora, *Bos.-H.* 40 C2
Zelenodolsk, *Russia* 48 C9
Zelenogorsk, *Russia* 46 B5
Zelenograd, *Russia* 46 D9
Zelenogradsk, *Russia* 9 J19
Zelenokumsk, *Russia* 49 H6
Železná Ruda, *Czech Rep.* 26 B6
Železnik, *Serbia, Yug.* 40 B4
Želiezovce, *Slovak Rep.* 27 C11
Zelina, *Croatia* 29 C13
Zell, *Baden-W., Germany* 25 H3
Zell, *Rhld-Pfz., Germany* 25 E3
Zell am See, *Austria* 26 D5
Zella-Mehlis, *Germany* 24 E6
Zelów, *Poland* 45 G6
Zeltweg, *Austria* 26 D7
Zémio, *C.A.R.* 86 A2
Zempléni-hegység, *Hungary* 42 B6
Zemplínska šírava, *Slovak Rep.* 27 C15
Zemun, *Serbia, Yug.* 40 B4
Zengbe, *Cameroon* 83 D7
Zengcheng, *China* 59 F9
Zenica, *Bos.-H.* 42 F2
Žepče, *Bos.-H.* 42 F3
Zeraf, Bahr ez →, *Sudan* 81 F3
Zerbst, *Germany* 24 D8
Żerków, *Poland* 45 F4
Zermatt, *Switz.* 25 J3
Zernez, *Switz.* 25 J6
Zernograd, *Russia* 49 G5
Zerqani, *Albania* 40 E4
Zestaponi, *Georgia* 49 J6
Zetel, *Germany* 24 B3
Zeulenroda, *Germany* 24 E7
Zeven, *Germany* 24 B5
Zevenaar, *Neths.* 17 C6
Zévio, *Italy* 28 C8
Zeya, *Russia* 51 D13
Zeya →, *Russia* 51 D13
Zeytinbaği, *Turkey* 41 F12
Zeytindağ, *Turkey* 39 C9
Zghartā, *Lebanon* 75 A4
Zgierz, *Poland* 45 G6
Zgorzelec, *Poland* 45 G2
Zguriţa, *Moldova* 43 B13
Zhabinka, *Belarus* 47 F3
Zhailma, *Kazakstan* 50 D7
Zhambyl, *Kazakstan* 50 E8
Zhangaly, *Kazakstan* 49 G10
Zhangaqazaly, *Kazakstan* 50 E7
Zhangbei, *China* 56 D8
Zhangguangcai Ling, *China* 57 B15
Zhangjiakou, *China* 56 D8
Zhangping, *China* 59 E11
Zhangpu, *China* 59 E11
Zhangwu, *China* 57 C12
Zhangye, *China* 60 C5
Zhangzhou, *China* 59 E11
Zhanhua, *China* 57 F10
Zhanjiang, *China* 59 G8
Zhannetty, Ostrov, *Russia* 51 B16
Zhanyi, *China* 58 E4
Zhanyu, *China* 57 B12
Zhao Xian, *China* 56 F8
Zhao'an, *China* 59 F11
Zhaocheng, *China* 56 F6
Zhaojue, *China* 58 C4
Zhaoping, *China* 59 E8
Zhaoqing, *China* 59 F9
Zhaotong, *China* 58 D4
Zhaoyuan, *Heilongjiang, China* 57 B13
Zhaoyuan, *Shandong, China* 57 F11
Zharkovskiy, *Russia* 46 E7
Zhashkiv, *Ukraine* 47 H6
Zhashui, *China* 56 H5
Zhayyq →, *Kazakstan* 50 E6
Zhdanov = Mariupol, *Ukraine* 47 J9
Zhecheng, *China* 56 G8
Zhegao, *China* 59 B11
Zhejiang □, *China* 59 C13
Zheleznogorsk, *Russia* 47 F8
Zheleznogorsk-Ilimskiy, *Russia* 51 D11
Zheltyye Vody = Zhovti Vody, *Ukraine* 47 H7
Zhen'an, *China* 56 H5
Zhenfeng, *China* 58 E5
Zheng'an, *China* 58 C6
Zhengding, *China* 56 E8
Zhenghe, *China* 59 D12
Zhengyang, *China* 59 A10
Zhengyangguan, *China* 59 A11
Zhengzhou, *China* 56 G7
Zhenhai, *China* 59 C13
Zhenjiang, *China* 59 A12
Zhenlai, *China* 57 B12
Zhenning, *China* 58 D5
Zhenping, *Henan, China* 56 H7
Zhenping, *Shaanxi, China* 58 B7
Zhenxiong, *China* 58 D5
Zhenyuan, *Gansu, China* 56 G4
Zhenyuan, *Guizhou, China* 58 D7
Zherdevka, *Russia* 48 E5
Zherong, *China* 59 D12
Zhetiqara, *Kazakstan* 50 D7
Zhezqazghan, *Kazakstan* 50 E7
Zhidan, *China* 56 F5
Zhigansk, *Russia* 51 C13
Zhigulevsk, *Russia* 48 D9
Zhijiang, *Hubei, China* 59 B8
Zhijiang, *Hunan, China* 58 D7
Zhijin, *China* 58 D5
Zhilinda, *Russia* 51 C12
Zhirnovsk, *Russia* 48 E7
Zhitomir = Zhytomyr, *Ukraine* 47 G5
Zhizdra, *Russia* 46 F8
Zhlobin, *Belarus* 47 F6
Zhmerinka = Zhmerynka, *Ukraine* 47 H5
Zhmerynka, *Ukraine* 47 H5
Zhob, *Pakistan* 68 D3
Zhodino = Zhodzina, *Belarus* 46 E5
Zhodzina, *Belarus* 46 E5
Zhokhova, Ostrov, *Russia* 51 B16
Zhong Xian, *China* 58 B7
Zhongdian, *China* 58 D2
Zhongdong, *China* 58 F6
Zhongdu, *China* 58 E7
Zhongning, *China* 56 F3
Zhongshan, *Guangdong, China* 59 F9
Zhongshan, *Guangxi Zhuangzu, China* 59 E8
Zhongtiao Shan, *China* 56 G6
Zhongwei, *China* 56 F3
Zhongxiang, *China* 59 B9
Zhongyang, *China* 56 F6
Zhoucun, *China* 57 F9
Zhouning, *China* 59 D12
Zhoushan Dao, *China* 59 C14
Zhouzhi, *China* 56 G5
Zhovti Vody, *Ukraine* 47 H7
Zhovtneve, *Ukraine* 47 J7
Zhovtnevoye = Zhovtneve, *Ukraine* 47 J7
Zhuanghe, *China* 57 E12
Zhucheng, *China* 57 G10
Zhugqu, *China* 56 H3
Zhuhai, *China* 59 F9
Zhuji, *China* 59 C13
Zhukovka, *Russia* 46 F7
Zhumadian, *China* 56 H8
Zhuo Xian, *China* 56 E8
Zhuolu, *China* 56 D8
Zhuozi, *China* 56 D7
Zhushan, *China* 59 A8
Zhuxi, *China* 58 A7
Zhuzhou, *China* 59 D9
Zhytomyr, *Ukraine* 47 G5
Zi Shui →, *China* 59 C9
Žiar nad Hronom, *Slovak Rep.* 27 C11
Zīārān, *Iran* 71 B6
Ziarat, *Pakistan* 68 D2
Zibo, *China* 57 F10
Zichang, *China* 56 F5
Zidarovo, *Bulgaria* 41 D11
Ziębice, *Poland* 45 H4
Zielona Góra, *Poland* 45 G2
Zielona Góra □, *Poland* 45 G2
Zierikzee, *Neths.* 17 C3
Ziesar, *Germany* 24 C8
Zifta, *Egypt* 80 H7
Zigey, *Chad* 79 F9
Zigong, *China* 58 C5
Zigui, *China* 59 B8
Ziguinchor, *Senegal* 82 C1
Zihuatanejo, *Mexico* 118 D4
Zijin, *China* 59 F10
Zile, *Turkey* 72 B6
Žilina, *Slovak Rep.* 27 B11
Žilinský □, *Slovak Rep.* 27 B12
Zillah, *Libya* 79 C9
Zillertaler Alpen, *Austria* 26 D4
Zima, *Russia* 51 D11
Zimapán, *Mexico* 119 C5
Zimba, *Zambia* 87 F2
Zimbabwe, *Zimbabwe* 87 G3
Zimbabwe ■, *Africa* 87 F3
Zimnicea, *Romania* 43 G10
Zimovniki, *Russia* 49 G6
Zinder, *Niger* 83 C6
Zinga, *Tanzania* 87 D4
Zingst, *Germany* 24 A8
Ziniaré, *Burkina Faso* 83 C4
Zinnowitz, *Germany* 24 A9
Zion National Park, *U.S.A.* 115 H7
Zirbitzkogel, *Austria* 26 D7
Zirc, *Hungary* 42 C2
Žiri, *Slovenia* 29 B11
Žirje, *Croatia* 29 E12
Zirl, *Austria* 26 D4
Zirndorf, *Germany* 25 F6
Ziros, *Greece* 36 D8
Zisterdorf, *Austria* 27 C9
Zitácuaro, *Mexico* 118 D4
Žitava →, *Slovak Rep.* 27 C11
Žitište, *Serbia, Yug.* 42 E5
Zítsa, *Greece* 38 B2
Zittau, *Germany* 24 E10
Zitundo, *Mozam.* 89 D5
Živinice, *Bos.-H.* 42 F3
Ziway, L., *Ethiopia* 81 F4
Zixi, *China* 59 D11
Zixing, *China* 59 E9
Ziyang, *Shaanxi, China* 56 H5
Ziyang, *Sichuan, China* 58 B5
Ziyun, *China* 58 E6
Zizhixian, *China* 58 E8
Zizhong, *China* 58 C5
Zlarin, *Croatia* 29 E12
Zlatar, *Croatia* 29 B13
Zlatar, *Serbia, Yug.* 40 C3
Zlataritsa, *Bulgaria* 41 C9
Zlaté Moravce, *Slovak Rep.* 27 C11
Zlatibor, *Serbia, Yug.* 40 C3
Zlatitsa, *Bulgaria* 41 D8
Zlatna, *Romania* 43 D8
Zlatna Panega, *Bulgaria* 41 C8
Zlatni Pyasŭtsi, *Bulgaria* 41 C12
Zlatograd, *Bulgaria* 41 E9
Zlatoust, *Russia* 50 D6
Zletovo, *Macedonia* 40 E6
Zlín, *Czech Rep.* 27 B10
Złocieniec, *Poland* 44 E3
Złoczew, *Poland* 45 G5
Zlot, *Serbia, Yug.* 40 B5
Złotoryja, *Poland* 45 G2
Złotów, *Poland* 44 E4
Zmeinogorsk, *Kazakstan* 50 D9
Żmigród, *Poland* 45 G3
Zmiyev, *Ukraine* 47 H9
Znamenka = Znamyanka, *Ukraine* 47 H7
Znamyanka, *Ukraine* 47 H7
Żnin, *Poland* 45 F4
Znojmo, *Czech Rep.* 26 C9
Zobeyrī, *Iran* 70 C5
Zobia, *Dem. Rep. of the Congo* 86 B2
Zoetermeer, *Neths.* 17 B4
Zogang, *China* 58 C1
Zogno, *Italy* 28 C6
Zogqên, *China* 58 A2
Zolochiv, *Ukraine* 47 H3
Zolotonosha, *Ukraine* 47 H7
Zomba, *Malawi* 87 F4
Zongo, *Dem. Rep. of the Congo* 84 D3
Zonguldak, *Turkey* 72 B4
Zonqor Pt., *Malta* 36 D2
Zonza, *France* 21 G13
Zorgo, *Burkina Faso* 83 C4
Zorita, *Spain* 35 F5
Zorleni, *Romania* 43 D12
Zornitsa, *Bulgaria* 41 D10
Zorritos, *Peru* 124 D2
Żory, *Poland* 45 H5
Zorzor, *Liberia* 82 D3
Zossen, *Germany* 24 C9
Zou Xiang, *China* 56 G9
Zouar, *Chad* 79 D9
Zouérate = Zouîrât, *Mauritania* 78 D3
Zouîrât, *Mauritania* 78 D3
Zoushan Dao, *China* 59 B14
Zoutkamp, *Neths.* 17 A6
Zrenjanin, *Serbia, Yug.* 42 E5
Zuarungu, *Ghana* 83 C4
Zuba, *Nigeria* 83 D6
Zubayr, *Yemen* 81 D5
Zubtsov, *Russia* 46 D8
Zuénoula, *Ivory C.* 82 D3
Zuera, *Spain* 32 D4
Zufār, *Oman* 74 D5
Zug □, *Switz.* 25 H4
Zugdidi, *Georgia* 49 J5
Zugersee, *Switz.* 25 H4
Zugspitze, *Germany* 25 H6
Zuid-Holland □, *Neths.* 17 C4
Zuidbeveland, *Neths.* 17 C3
Zuidhorn, *Neths.* 17 A6
Zújar, *Spain* 35 H8
Zújar →, *Spain* 35 F5
Żukowo, *Poland* 44 D5
Zula, *Eritrea* 81 D4
Zülpich, *Germany* 24 E2
Zumaia, *Spain* 32 B2
Zumárraga, *Spain* 32 B2
Zumbo, *Mozam.* 87 F3
Zummo, *Nigeria* 83 D7
Zumpango, *Mexico* 119 D5
Zungeru, *Nigeria* 83 D6
Zunhua, *China* 57 D9
Zuni, *U.S.A.* 115 J9
Zunyi, *China* 58 D6
Zuoquan, *China* 56 F7
Zuozhou, *China* 58 F6
Županja, *Croatia* 42 E3
Žur, *Serbia, Yug.* 40 D4
Zurbātīyah, *Iraq* 70 C5
Zürich, *Switz.* 25 H4
Zürich □, *Switz.* 25 H4
Zürichsee, *Switz.* 25 H4
Żuromin, *Poland* 45 E6
Zuru, *Nigeria* 83 C6
Žut, *Croatia* 29 E12
Zutphen, *Neths.* 17 B6
Zuwārah, *Libya* 79 B8
Zūzan, *Iran* 71 C8
Žužemberk, *Slovenia* 29 C11
Zvenigorodka = Zvenyhorodka, *Ukraine* 47 H6
Zvenyhorodka, *Ukraine* 47 H6
Zverinogolovskoye, *Russia* 50 D7
Zvezdets, *Bulgaria* 41 D11
Zvishavane, *Zimbabwe* 87 G3
Zvolen, *Slovak Rep.* 27 C12
Zvonce, *Serbia, Yug.* 40 D6
Zvornik, *Bos.-H.* 42 F4
Zwedru = Tchien, *Liberia* 82 D3
Zweibrücken, *Germany* 25 F3
Zwenkau, *Germany* 24 D8
Zwettl, *Austria* 26 C8
Zwickau, *Germany* 24 E8
Zwierzyniec, *Poland* 45 H9
Zwiesel, *Germany* 25 F9
Zwoleń, *Poland* 45 G8
Zwolle, *Neths.* 17 B6
Zwolle, *U.S.A.* 113 K8
Żychlin, *Poland* 45 F6
Zymoetz →, *Canada* 104 C3
Żyrardów, *Poland* 45 F7
Zyryan, *Kazakstan* 50 E9
Zyryanka, *Russia* 51 C16
Zyryanovsk = Zyryan, *Kazakstan* 50 E9
Żywiec, *Poland* 45 J6
Zyyi, *Cyprus* 36 E12

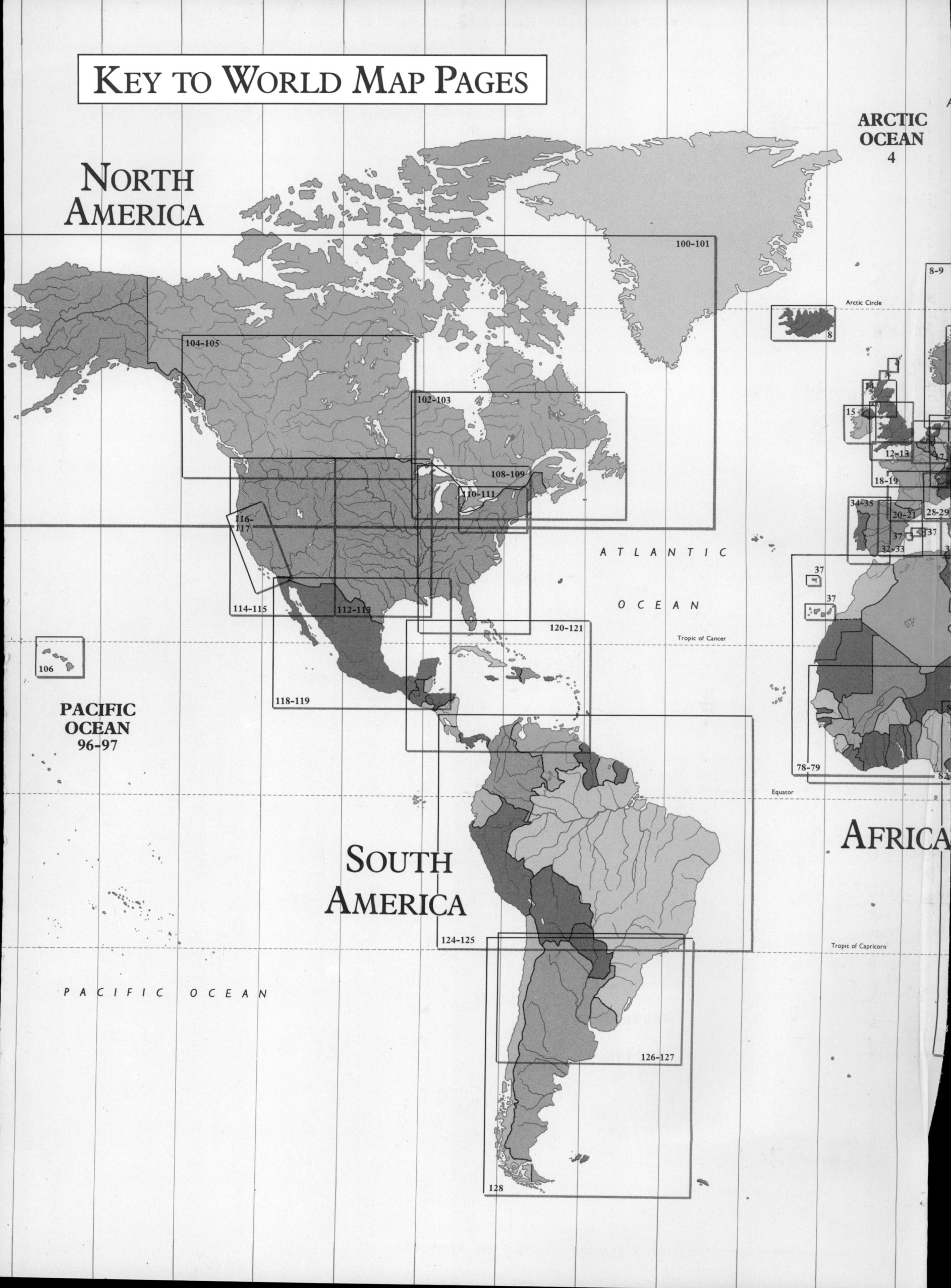

KEY TO WORLD MAP PAGES

NORTH AMERICA

ARCTIC OCEAN
4

AFRICA

SOUTH AMERICA

PACIFIC OCEAN
96-97

ATLANTIC

OCEAN

PACIFIC OCEAN

Arctic Circle

Tropic of Cancer

Equator

Tropic of Capricorn

8

8-9

15

12-13

18-19

34-35

20-21

28-29

37

32-33

37

37

78-79

82

100-101

104-105

102-103

108-109

110-111

116-117

114-115

112-113

118-119

120-121

106

124-125

126-127

128